CHOICES

Edited by Carolyn Sherwood Flemming & Donna Schatt

JOHN GORDON BURKE PUBLISHER, INC.

To Art with love and ABCs,
and to R1 with love
　　　—Carolyn Sherwood Flemming

To the "Guys" for never giving up
　　　—Donna Schatt

Choices: A Core Collection for Young Reluctant Readers is published by John Gordon Burke Publisher, Inc., P. O. Box 1492, Evanston, Illinois 60204-1492. ISSN 0735-6358. Portions of Choices may be photocopied for the purpose of educational and scientific advancement and the improvement of library service for library users.

Introduction

A third grader who does not read will likely become a tenth grader and later an adult who does not read. Even with the wonders of electronic media we cannot afford non-reading laborers, businessmen, government workers, and parents. And yet, unless we take positive steps to reinforce the skills and the desirability of reading we will be faced with just that. In a 1977 *School Library Journal* article, Barbara Bates challenged writers, publishers, editors, and librarians to provide books for "reluctant older readers" in the hope that "we may yet turn them into enthusiastic readers."[1] Since then, literally hundreds of high interest–low reading level books (hi/lo) have been written, and several bibliographies of such materials have been compiled. Because we are convinced that Bates's concern for the reluctant reader is just as valid for younger children as for older students, we set out to provide teachers, librarians, reading specialists, and parents with a tool to use while working with reluctant second through sixth grade readers.

"Reluctant reader" is a term that deserves some clarification. Judith Goldberger, who writes a column for *Booklist*, observed in 1978, "I have always thought of reluctant readers . . . as a minority group. But the more schools I visit, the more teachers, librarians, parents, and students to whom I listen, the less that 'minority' concept seems to ring true . . . . The reluctant reader . . . is the rule rather than the exception."[2] One reason why reluctant readers seem so plentiful is that there are two groups of students who fall into that category. Most people assume that the term "reluctant reader" refers only to those children who read below their own grade level and thus find reading a chore they would prefer to avoid. Occasionally someone such as Jerry Johns[3] will remind us of the second group: students who read at or even above their grade level but who find little or no satisfaction in reading. Although it is our primary purpose to supply a list of books for the first group of students, there are many titles included in this bibliography that are also useful for the second. Whenever such a title appears, it has been given the special subject heading "GROUP 2" and gathered together with other such titles in the subject index.

In compiling this bibliography we purposely chose to concentrate on general literature rather than hi/lo materials. As is true of most formula-written materials, hi/lo stories often seem stylistically stilted, artificial in plot, and lacking in depth and characterization. Why feed reluctant readers such a bland diet especially when you might arouse their interest by providing some spice? Library and bookstore collections contain many books that can and should be used for the latter purpose, but without some searching those titles are not readily apparent. After a good deal of investigation, during which we made no attempt to gather every available book from general literature, we have put together a basic collection of titles for use with young reluctant readers.

PROCEDURE

Of the more than 5,000 books considered, approximately 360 met all our criteria for inclusion in this bibliography. We started by gathering the 4,000 or so titles suggested as additional reading by 13 basal reading series. (A list of the series can be found in Appendix I). Well over 1,000 additional titles came from searching our own extensive collection at the University of Chicago Laboratory School elementary school library (which houses more than 25,000 volumes) and recent issues of review journals. About 50 percent of those original 5,000 + titles proved to be out of print and could be immediately discarded. Several hundred more could not be located at our library, Chicago Public Library, or the library maintained by the *Bulletin of the Center for Children's Books*. Upon examination, another 1,000 titles were eliminated because they were obviously too difficult for children whose reading levels were below their grade levels or because of an overly juvenile format, a highly unattractive physical appearance, excessively small print, narrow margins, or extreme length.

Approximately 1,400 titles remained to be tested for readability levels. Some of the titles still under consideration had already been tested and assigned reading levels in either *Elementary School Library Collection*[4] and/or Gale Sypher Jacob's *Independent Reading Grades One Through Three*.[5] After performing our own tests and seeing that our results were consistent with theirs, we decided not to retest those titles that appeared in either or both sources. Unless there was a discrepancy between the two sources (in which case we performed our own test) we have used their

---

1. Bates, Barbara S. "Identifying High Interest/Low Reading Level Books." *School Library Journal*, November 1977, p. 21.
2. Goldberger, Judith. "The Rule of the Reluctant Reader." *Booklist*, October 15, 1978, p. 382.
3. Johns, Jerry L. "Motivating Reluctant Readers." *Journal of Research and Development in Education*, vol. 11, no. 3 (1978), p. 69.
4. *The Elementary School Library Collection; Twelfth Edition.* Bro-Dart Foundation, 1979.
5. Jacob, Gale Sypher. *Independent Reading Grades One Through Three.* Bro-Dart Publishing Company, 1975.

test results. For the remaining 900 or more titles we applied the Spache and/or Dale-Chall readability formulas to at least three passages in each book to determine its reading level.

We decided to use the Spache readability formula for books below fourth grade reading level and the Dale-Chall formula for materials past third grade. It is true that both formulas are more difficult and time consuming to apply than other formulas available, but they are highly compatible and are also considered the most reliable.[6] Both the Spache and (to a somewhat lesser extent) the Dale-Chall formula produce reading levels specific to the grade and month within that grade. But, because there is an error factor built into any formula that tests only samples rather than an entire book, the readability level of a book should always be interpreted as approximate. We have, therefore, rounded off the test scores for each book to the nearest half year.

After testing, about 700 titles still appeared to be worth serious consideration. The other 700 either had very inconsistent reading levels or were too difficult for their intended readers. After reading them, we eliminated still another 340 books because they were either too slow-moving, too complex, too abstract, or too unfamiliar. The remaining 360 titles are what constitute the substance of our monograph.

ORGANIZATION AND USE

For each listing we have included full bibliographic data, except for the price. With a few purposely chosen exceptions, we have attempted to insure that each book listed in our bibliography was still in print, and thus easily available.

The bibliography consists of detailed book descriptions and a subject index. Armed with knowledge of a child's reading level, the child's interests, and grade level, the adult user of this bibliography should be able to find several books for any reluctant reader from second through sixth grade.

The book descriptions include numerous subject headings, an indication of the book's reading level, the grade level of the children to whom the book will most likely appeal (interest level), plot summary and/or description, evaluative notes about the book's use and bibliographic information.

The subject index is divided so that the user may start a search for titles by using either a child's grade level (interest level), reading level, or general interests. When the user turns to the "INTEREST LEVEL" (grade level) index, one will find within each range of grade levels a list of book titles of varying degrees of reading difficulty that are likely to appeal to that age child. This is particularly useful to teachers wishing to put together a collection of books other than basal readers to cover the range of children's abilities within their own classrooms. For working with groups of children at a particular reading level, the user will find the "READING LEVEL" index a helpful place to start. Placed together, the user will find *all* the books at any reading level from 1.1 to 5.1. From the appropriate reading level listings, the teacher can tailor reading suggestions to match the level of skill of any child. In addition, each of the 360 titles included in this bibliography has been assigned a number of subject headings. Using *Sears List of Subject Headings*[7] as our guide, we chose the subject headings both to describe the book's contents and to coincide with potential readers' interests. Thus, for example, when looking for books for a reluctant reader who appreciates nothing but mysteries and frogs, the user should check the subject index under "MYSTERY AND DETECTIVE STORIES" and under "FROGS" to find possible book titles and authors. We have tried to make the interest index as detailed and self-explanatory as possible. To facilitate use of the subject index, each listing includes full bibliographic information, as well as the complete annotation. Further subject headings that may be used to suggest additional book titles may also be found with each annotation.

The most significant factor in the search for books for reluctant readers is the child's interests. "Children's interests are the most important single influence upon their attitude toward reading. . . . Books that are high in interest may be reacted to as appropriate in difficulty even though actually two or more grade levels above the pupil's reading level. At the same time, books are often rated by children as too hard even though below pupil's reading levels, when interest is low."[8] Reading levels are, after all, only measures of the level of proficiency a person needs in order to read the words. They do not measure complexity of understanding or style. And, because it is usually based on only three sample passages, a book's tested reading level is not an absolutely accurate measure of even that. Despite efforts to choose representative test passages, the scores will vary some with the selection of alternate samples.

Even the creators of readability formulas admit that their formulas are only estimates and not precise measures. Spache acknowledges that his formula has a probable error of 3.3 months, and

6. Cramer, Eugene H. "A Quick Guide to Readability Formulas." *Curriculum Review*, December 1978, pp. 416-417.

7. Westby, Barbara M. *Sears List of Subject Headings; Eleventh Edition.* H.W. Wilson, 1977.

8. Spache, George D. *Good Reading for Poor Readers.* Garrard, 1978, pp. 6-7.

the Fry Formula's estimated error is one year. Keep in mind too the final test score is an average for the book and does not reflect the variability within the book. In a 1978 *Reading Teacher* article, Timothy C. Standal closed by saying, "Readability formulas are best thought of as guides or general indicators of a possible range of materials suited to any given child. They are not absolute. If they are regarded as general indicators, they can be quite useful. . .the various formulas cannot take interest and previous experience into consideration. But the teacher can—and should."[9]

It is important to be creative in using children's interests to match them with a book. A child's known interest, if approached imaginatively, may provide the adult user of this bibliography with many more subject headings to search than expected. For example, a child who likes jokes and riddles might be persuaded, after reading a riddle book, to try a book about magic or optical illusions. From there it is a logical step to books about scientific experiments, nature study, and animals. In another direction, the child might enjoy books about secret codes, spy stories, war, and then history. Not every attempt at creativity will end in success, but the more numerous and varied the approaches to finding something a reluctant reader will want to read, the greater the likelihood of success.

Some children's interests are harder to pinpoint than others. For those children we have included two special subject headings. The first is for children who say they want something about "kids and sort of everyday things." What they are usually looking for is a light, slightly humorous, non-judgmental story about growing up, making friends and getting along with families. For them we have included the subject heading "EVERYDAY STORIES". There, among other places, you will find Judy Blume, Ellen Conford, Constance Greene, and other authors.

Even more difficult is finding a book for the child who will not admit having any interests or having enjoyed any book. Those children need a book that will appeal to practically everyone—an almost guaranteed success. We have gathered the books that fit such a description under the subject heading "BEST SELLERS".

Simply finding a book that will appeal to a child's interests does not guarantee that the child will read it. Reluctant readers need to be encouraged to think that a book is truly worth the effort it will take to read it. After finding a book calculated to appeal to the child, the best way to provide that encouragement is to read the book and to speak of it enthusiastically from one's own experience. Because we realize that this is often impossible, we have included book descriptions so detailed and narrative that, if necessary, the adult user can rely solely upon this bibliography to introduce a book to a potential reader.

Reading part or all of a book aloud is another excellent way of illustrating both the joys of reading in general, and the enjoyment that can be had from reading a particular book. Children who don't read freely do not have to miss the benefits of a good story if it is read to them. Many of those children may ask to read the book on their own after hearing it read aloud or may need only a brief introductory reading to be convinced that the book is worthwhile. Time after time professional journals speak of the importance of reading aloud in developing a child's appreciation of reading. Books that can be read aloud are by no means limited to those listed here, but we have included a list of good choices in the subject index under the subject heading, appropriately, "READ ALOUD".

Obviously our primary intent is to present reluctant readers with materials to enjoy as they become better readers and with reasons to want to read, but the bibliography has other uses as well. Children who are unsure of their reading ability and who need further self-confidence may be able to find it by reading several carefully selected books listed here. The bibliography can also be used to suggest manageable report and project sources for below grade level readers. As we mentioned earlier, it can be used to select books for reading groups or to build collections of materials for the classroom. We certainly hope it will inspire users to look in new places for reluctant reader materials and to approach general literature collections with some new ideas. The bibliography we have compiled is meant to be a beginning, both for adult users and the children they are trying to help.

It is our intention to publish a revised edition of this bibliography every three years. We feel that a new edition of this book every three years will enable us to cover the publication of significant new children's literature, and also delete on a timely basis the material that is out of print. On this time schedule, we feel that *Choices: A Core Collection for Young Reluctant Readers* can become a ready reference for librarians, teachers, and parents.

---

9. Standal, Timothy C. "Readability Formulas: What's Out, What's In?" *The Reading Teacher*, March 1978, p. 646.

RECOMMENDED ADDITIONAL READING

1. White, Marian E., et al. *High Interest-Easy Reading for Junior and Senior High School Students.* National Council of Teachers of English, 1979.

2. Williams, Helen Elizabeth. *The High/Low Consensus.* Bro-Dart Publishing Company, 1980.

3. LeBretto, Ellen V. *High/Low Handbook: Books, Materials, and Services for the Teenage Problem Reader.* Bowker, 1981.

4. *The High/Low Report.* The High/Low Report, 20 Waterside Plaza, New York, New York 10010 (Monthly Review Journal).

5. Graves, Michael F., et al. *Easy Reading: Book Series and Periodicals for Less Able Readers.* International Reading Association, Inc., 1979.

AUTHORS

ABISCH, Roz. Mixed bag of magic tricks; illus by Boche Kaplan.   Walker & Co. 1973, 64 pp.

The definition of magic is broadened here to include optical illusions, puzzles, age and date guessing formulae, as well as slight of hand and prearranged tricks. There are 25 "feats of magic" here, with especially good tips on performance, practice, costumes, and props. Although tricks in *Science Puzzles, It's Magic?, Funny Magic,* and *Magic Secrets* are showier, this is a more solid introduction to the subject. The Knot Magic Trick receives its best explanation here. See *It's Magic?* and *Science Puzzles* for others. Bonus: The book looks like a manual and not like a reader, therefore it should be useful even with sixth graders. It is now available in paperback version only; published by Grosset and Dunlap (Activity Books).

Interest Level: 2-6. Reading Level: 2.2. Further Search Topics: Magic, Optical Illusions, Puzzles.

ADLER, Irving and Adler, Ruth.
Your eyes.   John Day 1962, 48 pp.

Getting a young reader past this book's unattractive appearance may be difficult. Everything about the book's physical appearance screams "old." Some of the information and lack of information conveys the same message (e.g. no mention of contact lenses). For basic material about eyes and sight however, there is much here that is accessible and interesting to readers in grades two to six. Includes pronunciation guide, glossary, and detailed table of contents. No index. The Reason Why Series

Interest Level: 2-6. Reading Level: 3.1. Further Search Topics: Vision, Physically Handicapped, Group 2.

ADLER, Ruth, jt. auth., see Adler, Irving.

ADOFF, Arnold. Malcolm X; illus by John Wilson. Har-Row 1970, 41 pp.

This is a simple, intellectually honest biography of a very controversial man. Taught a strong sense of self-respect by his father, Malcolm X could not accept the second-class status that white society tried to impose upon him. Instead he turned away from whites and all they stood for. He hated high school, the detention home he lived in after his father's death, and his mother's placement in a state hospital. He didn't feel comfortable until he moved to Harlem. There he found friends, but he also found crime. While he was in prison, Malcolm X began to read of great, black societies and people. His brother told him about the Nation of Islam, the Black Muslims, and Elijah Muhammad, the leader of the religion. He began corresponding with Mr. Muhammad. Shortly after he was released from prison, Malcolm X met Elijah Muhammad and eventually became a minister of the religion. There was even talk that he would be Elijah Muhammad's successor. But, as the years went on, Malcolm X began to think that black Christians as well as Muslims should be united in the fight for black rights. Despite threats against his life Malcolm X formed the Organization of Afro-American Unity. Both blacks and whites were angry with him. The threats continued until his house was firebombed; and, only a week later, at a public meeting, Malcolm X was assassinated.

An excellent overview of a complex man. The book may well prompt readers to learn more about the man and his beliefs. At the very least it will expose readers, in an interesting manner, to someone they should know. The book shares the same semi-picture book format of the others in Harper and Row/Crowell's biography series, therefore it will need a careful introduction to potential readers.

Interest Level: 3-5. Reading Level: 3.1. Further Search Topics: Blacks-Biography, Civil Rights, Biography, Crime, Religion, Assassinations, Prejudice, Poverty, Foster Homes.

ADRIAN, Mary. The fireball mystery illus by Reisie Lonette.   Hastings 1977, 118 pp.

While stargazing one night, Tim and Vicky and their friend Joey saw a meteor fall onto their private island. Before they were able to find it the children realized that someone else was trying to steal the meteorite from them. As much astronomy as mystery here. Beyond fourth grade, the reader may begin to find the astronomy lesson heavy-handed and the mystery light.

Interest Level: 2-4. Reading Level: 3.1. Further Search Topics: Mystery and Detective Stories, Astronomy, Flying Saucers-Fiction, Outer Space-Fiction, Group 2.

AESOP. Aesop's Fables; retold by Ann Terry White; illus by Helen Siegl.   Random 1964, 77 pp.

An attractive, appealing-looking collection of forty of Aesop's fables. Children without a background in folklore are not likely to read these short tales without encouragement. Where there is such encouragement, or a curricular need, this is an excellent source. The use of many proper nouns in the text means the book tests artificially low at 2.2. It is probably more appropriate to consider it 3.1.

Interest Level: 2-6. Reading Level: 3.1. Further Search Topics: Fables, Folklore, Group 2.

ALEXANDER, Sue. Small plays for you and a friend; illus by Olivia H. Cole.   Seabury 1974, 48 pp.

Five very short and very simple plays for two actors that will be of more interest to the players than the audience. However, because the reading level is low, and because children's love of acting is strong and their tolerance of weak plot is high, this can be used through grade three. A companion volume *Small Plays for Special Days* presents seven more short plays for two characters.

Interest Level: 1-3. Reading Level: 2.1. Further Search Topics: Acting, Drama, Group 2.

ALLEN, Gertrude. Everyday turtles, toads and their kin.   HM 1970, 48 pp.

Straight-forward, short, chapter discussions of turtles, lizards, snakes, salamanders, toads, frogs and tree toads. Black and white drawings done by the author amplify the text. The major part of the book is simple enough to be understood at second grade, but should still be interesting to fourth and fifth graders. A few terms may need explanation: i.e., venomous, prey. The chapters on the turtle, lizard, frog and tree frog are the easiest. No index, but still useful for reports.

Interest Level: 2-5. Reading Level: 2.2. Further Search Topics: Turtles, Reptiles, Lizards, Toads, Frogs, Snakes, Salamanders.

ALLEN, Linda. Lionel and the spy next door; illus by Margot Apple.   Morrow 1980, 94 pp.

No one in Lionel's family understood why he wanted to be a spy; but then, he couldn't understand why they were anthropologists and motorcycle freaks. Even though he wasn't supposed to do any more spying (especially while his parents were away) Lionel couldn't resist watching the man who moved into Miss Bannister's house, next-door. Mark Shakespeare was his name. His name was suspicious enough, but his actions firmly convinced Lionel that Mark was a spy.

Lionel's attempts to trail Shakespeare only succeeded in angering others in the neighborhood. He interrupted a bird watcher and irritated a woman walking a large dog. She was already angry with Lionel's grandfather for disturbing the quiet neighborhood with his motorcycles. The closer Lionel got to finding proof that Mark was a spy, the friendlier Mark became. Mark even gave Lionel the old clock which Lionel and Miss Bannister had carefully wound each week until the old woman's death. When Lionel's grandfather finally convinced Lionel that Mark should be left alone, Mark enlisted Lionel's help in a project that left Lionel wondering again. Much to Lionel's surprise, he learned that the papers and secret documents he and Mark had burned had all belonged to Miss Bannister, Mark's great-aunt. Forty years earlier she, not Mark, had been a spy. Lionel had been wrong about who it was, but right about a spy living next-door.

Here we find a slightly anti-climactic ending to an otherwise enjoyable book. A grandfather who rides with motorcycle gangs and the intrigue of spying should be of interest to many readers. Readers may need a little help with the few British phrases that dot the book, but otherwise, the book has an impressively consistent reading level.

Interest Level: 4-6. Reading Level: 3.1. Further Search Topics: Spies-Fiction, Family-Fiction, Mystery and Detective Stories, Individualists-Fiction, Motorcycles-Fiction, Occupations-Fiction.

AMES, Gerald, jt. auth., see Wyler, Rose.

AMON, Aline. Talking hands: Indian sign language. Doubleday 1968, 80 pp.

If you can ignore the author's patronizing tone and air of self-satisfaction, this is a book with great appeal. Children love ways of communicating privately, be it Pig Latin, codes and ciphers, or just whispering. This book appeals to that love by clearly, though unattractively, demonstrating over 200 words in American Indian sign language. By the time the young reader finishes the book, he/she will not only have had the fun of learning another method of communication, but will have learned a few simple generalities about North American Indians. The index is detailed enough that any word can be quickly checked. The book is useful for history, social studies, or language arts units, as well as for fun.

Interest Level: 2-6. Reading Level: 2.2. Further Search Topics: Indians of North America-Sign Language, Communication, Nonverbal Communication, Ethnic Groups.

ANDERSON, C. S. The blind Connemara. Macmillan 1971, 80 pp.

Rhonda, not wealthy enough to own a horse of her own, was given a beautiful Connemara pony. Unfortunately, it had begun to go blind. A blind pony is usually put away, but Rhonda loved this pony too much to let that happen. Against all odds, Rhonda not only taught Pony to trot, canter, and even jump with confidence, but went on to win a ribbon at an important horse show. Though sentimental and predictable, this book is an almost insured success with lovers of horses and champions of the underdog. Be alert to the occasional descriptive passage that is both longer and more difficult than the rest of the text.

Interest Level: 4-6. Reading Level: 3.2. Further Search Topics: Vision-Fiction, Physically Handicapped-Fiction, Horses-Fiction.

ANGELL, Judie. Dear Lola; or how to build your own family.   Bradbury 1980, 166 pp.

Arthur (age 18), James (13), Annie and Al-Willie (twins, age 10), Edmund (9), and Ben (5) wanted to run away from the orphanage and find a place where they could be a real family. After waiting months, their chance arrived one night. They escaped in a van and began living on the road. It was weeks before they found a house in which they thought they could live. They didn't want trouble with local authorities, so most of the children enrolled in school and pretended to be living with their widowed grandfather. Only James (who never left his room) and Arthur stayed home. Arthur was the anonymous author of a nationally syndicated newspaper advice column. It was with the income from his "Dear Lola" column that Arthur was able to support the "family." When the townspeople eventually began to wonder about the "strange" behavior of the children, they investigated and found no adult in charge of the household. Arthur went to court to be appointed the childrens' guardian, but the judge ruled against him. Rather than be sent to foster homes again, Arthur and the children raced from the courtroom. The book ends as the family is once more together and on their own. An unusual cast of characters in a surprisingly warm and humorous book.

Interest Level: 4-6. Reading Level 3.1. Further Search Topics: Loners-Fiction, Runaways-Fiction, Orphans-Fiction, Survival-Fiction, Family Problems-Fiction, Family-Fiction, Read Aloud, Foster Homes-Fiction, Individualists-Fiction, Humorous Fiction.

ARKHURST, Joyce. The adventures of Spider; West African folktales; illus by Jerry Pinkney.   Little 1964, 58 pp.

A delightful collection of six West African folktales about Spider. Spider is mischievous, greedy, lazy and clever. He loves to eat and he hates to work. Four of the stories tell of Spider's ill-fated attempts to get food without having to work for it ("How Spider Got a Thin Waist," "How Spider Got a Bald Head," "How Spider Helped a Fisherman," and "Why Spiders Live in Dark Corners"). One story tells of his greed ("How the World Got Wisdom"), and only one story is complimentary ("Why Spider Lives in Ceilings"). All are short, gentle, humorous, and adapt well to dramatization or retelling.

Interest Level: 2-6. Reading Level 3.1. Further Search Topics: Humorous Fiction, Spiders-Fiction, Folklore, Tricksters-Fiction, Africa-Folklore, Group 2, Read Aloud, Creation-Fiction, Drama.

AVI. No more magic.   Pantheon 1975, 138 pp.

Avi has woven a mixture of mystery and magic to produce an excellent story. Chris' belief in magic is bolstered when his new bicycle disappears on Halloween night. Chris, his best friend Eddie, and a new friend, Muffin, eventually decide that strange Mr. Bullen, the junk dealer, has magical powers. In order to keep his powers a secret, Mr. Bullen had to steal back the magical bike he sold Chris. With plenty of intriguing complications along the way, the three children attempt to prove their theory correct but only prove themselves wrong. The age of the protagonists (fourth grade) is touched on so lightly and the plot is interesting enough that even sixth grade readers should find the book enjoyable.

Interest Level: 3-6. Reading Level: 4.2. Further Search Topics: Divorce and Separation-Fiction, Mystery and Detective Stories, Magic-Fiction, Halloween-Fiction, Witches-Fiction, Group 2, Read Aloud, Bicycles and Bicycling–Fiction.

AYLESWORTH, Thomas G. Movie monsters. Lippincott 1975, 79 pp.

If you are looking for an example of fine writing, you won't find it here. What you will find is a collection of monster movie photographs and facts. This is a wealth of trivia about eleven famous monsters (including King Kong, Godzilla, the Fly, Frankenstein's monster, the Mummy, Dracula, Wolf Man and others), their films, sequels, historic backgrounds, identifying characteristics, and more. There is an extensive index, a list of monster movies and their credits, and even brief information about famous monster actors. The book is not great literature, but it is interesting and fun.

Interest Level: 1-6. Reading Level 3.1. Further Search Topics: Acting, Motion Pictures, Monsters, Horror-Fiction, Group 2, Best Sellers.

BAKER, Betty. The pig war; illus by Robert Lopshire.   Har-Row 1969, 64 pp.

A brief, fictionalized account of an 1859 land squabble between the United States and Britain. The incident, which took place in what is now the state of Washington, became known as the Pig War. Frightened British pigs destroyed the American farmers' gardens. When the farmers shot one of the pigs, the war began. Simply told and humorously illustrated. Should appeal to history or military fans. Early reader format.

Interest Level: 2-4. Reading Level: 2.1. Further Search Topics: United States-History-War-Fiction, Great Britain-History-Fiction, War-Fiction, Washington (state)-Fiction, Historical Fiction, Pigs-Fiction.

BALES, Carol Ann. Chinatown Sunday; the story of Lillian Der.   Contemp Bks. 1973, 32 pp.

A short, personal visit with a fifth grade Chinese-American girl who lives in a Chicago suburb. The author transcribed taped interviews with Lillian Der to produce a first-person description of Lillian's daily life. The uniquely Chinese-American features of Lillian's life are casually intertwined with experiences common to most American children. Month-old parties, the celebration of Chinese New Year, lucky money, old-age birthday parties, Girl Scout meetings, homework, and being a tomboy are all important to Lillian. Not only is this an interesting portrait of Lillian, but it can be a useful part of a multi-ethnic unit or an introduction to autobiography. The book's usefulness is further extended by its introduction to Chinese immigration and by the glossary, which explains terms such as "abacus," "Chinese calendar," and "sea cucumber." The author saves the over-sized book from looking like a picture book by using photographs instead of drawings, thus she makes the book comfortable even for a sixth grade reader.

Interest Level: 3-6. Reading Level: 3.1. Further Search Topics: Ethnic Groups, Chinese-Americans, Biography, Chicago, Immigration and Emigration.

BAYLOR, Byrd. And it is still that way: legends told by Arizona Indian children.   Scribner 1976, 85 pp.

Byrd Baylor has collected and written notes for forty-one short American Indian legends from seven Arizona tribes whose school children were asked to write down or illustrate their favorite legend. The result is a collection that reflects the concerns, the history, religion, humor and pride of the children and their ancestors. This excellent collection is not only interesting reading, but it also fits well into social studies and language arts units.

Interest Level: 2-6. Reading Level: 3.1. Further Search Topics: Legends, Arizona-Fiction, Navajo Indians, Hopi Indians, Papago Indians, Pima Indians, Apache Indians, Quechan Indians, Cocopah Indians, Indians of North America-Legends, Mythology, Group 2.

BAYLOR, Byrd. Sometimes I dance mountains; illus by Ken Longtemps and Bill Sears.   Scribner 1973, 42 pp.

The author feels strongly that dance is a creative personal statement. That feeling becomes very clear in this combination of photographs and drawings. The photographs record a young girl's dance interpretation of the author's prose. The background drawings enlarge upon the poetic mood of the sparse text. For the dance enthusiast.

Interest Level: 2-6. Reading Level: 2.2. Further Search Topics: Dancing.

BEAME, Rona. Ladder company 108.   Messner 1973, 63 pp.

The reader of this book will literally live through several days with a New York City fire company. The author's "Dragnet"-like writing style, her use of photographs, and actual people, all make the firefighters' experiences very real. It is an exciting, engrossing and satisfying book. The heavily-used jargon will be quickly understood, thus should pose no real obstacle to most readers.

Interest Level 2-6. Reading Level: 3.1. Further Search Topics: Firefighters, Occupations, City Life, New York City, Group 2, Best Sellers.

BENCHLEY, Nathaniel. Sam the Minutemen; illus by Arnold Lobel.   Har-Row 1969, 62 pp.

A good but limited book. It is a simple, personalized account of the beginning of the Revolutionary War as seen by the young son of a Minuteman. The book is a fairly exciting, uncomplicated and enjoyable story. Its limitations rest in its format (it's designed as a reader), the apparent young age of the main character, and the fact that it is told as a story. Its usefulness extends no further than grade three. An I Can Read History Book

Interest Level: 1-3. Reading Level: 2.2. Further Search Topics: United States-History-War-Fiction, Historical Fiction, War-Fiction, Group 2, Courage-Fiction.

BENCHLEY, Nathaniel. Small Wolf; illus by Joan Sandin.   Har-Row 1972, 64 pp.

A straight-forward telling of white man's purchase of Manhattan and the resulting displacement of the Indians. The text is simple. The tone is sympathetic to the plight of the Indians. The reader is neither lectured nor patronized, but the early-reader format will prevent using the book comfortably beyond fourth grade. An I Can Read History Book.

Interest Level: 1-4. Reading Level 2.2. Further Search Topics: Historical Fiction, New York City-Fiction, United States-History-Fiction, Indians of North America-Fiction, Group 2.

BENDICK, Jeanne. The first book of airplanes. Watts 1975, revised edition, 65 pp.

It will take a determined reader to get much technical information from this overview of airplanes. The first sections (thrust, lift gravity, drag, and parts of a plane) promise simple, understandable explanations of complicated topics. The next portion of the book fails to live up to that promise. The descriptions of airplane engines will be intelligible only to the reader who already knows how an engine works. The history of flight is little more than an outline. The two-page chapter on air maps and distances will do more to confuse than instruct most readers. On the other hand, the information about airports, control towers, and types and uses of aircrafts is better. The book is well-indexed and includes a four-page glossary. It is perhaps best used as a general introduction to airplanes (skip the three areas mentioned above). For technical information about flight, look elsewhere. Print size is adequate but spacing between lines could have been more generous.

Interest Level: 4-6. Reading Level: 3.2. Further Search Topics: Airports, Engines, Flight, Airplanes.

BENNETT, Jay. The pigeon.   Methuen 1980, 147 pp.

Despite a low testing score, this is not a truly easy book to read. The author assumes his readers are fairly sophisticated and worldly, thus he does not explain the meaning of the Iron Cross symbol or the word Aryan. The book's language varies from simple to difficult, making the reading level inconsistent (2.1 - 4.1). The setting is dark and forbidding; an underground world of fugitives and terrorists. And yet, the book will be popular with many readers in sixth grade; it will be even more popular with older readers. The tension in this story of a teenage boy, blamed for the murder of his ex-girlfriend, is almost palpable. Brian's flight from the police and his desire to find Donna's murderer take him directly into the midst of a ring of terrorists, for whom life has no meaning. In Brian's attempt to prove his innocence, two more lives are lost, but hundreds more are saved as Brian discovers and stops a bomb threat. The author has used riveting action, short, clipped sentences, and terse dialogue to create a very successful, highly suspenseful book. Print size is only moderate.

Interest Level: 6 . Reading Level: 3.2. Further Search Topics: Mystery and Detective Stories, Terrorism-Fiction, Murder-Fiction, Best Sellers, Crime-Fiction, Courage-Fiction, Survival-Fiction, Runaways-Fiction.

BERENDS, Polly Berrien. The case of the elevator duck; illus by James K. Washburn.   Random 1973, 54 pp.

Although it would be stretching the meaning of the word to call this a mystery, it is a story of an 11-year-old detective. Albert tells his own story in a clipped style that resembles adult detective novels. One morning Albert found a duck abandoned in the apartment house elevator. He was determined to find the owner of the duck and return it. He had to be very careful as he searched because pets were absolutely forbidden in the housing projects. Anyone who saw him with the duck might report him. Albert and his parents had waited too long to get into the projects to be kicked out because of a duck. When Albert finally found the duck's owner (a young, sad child named Julio), Julio's sister forced Albert to take the duck back. Still angry at Julio's sister, Albert took the duck to the project's day care center, where the teacher agreed to formally adopt the duck. Albert stayed at the center long enough to see Julio's happy surprise when he arrived and found the duck. Its appealing characters, the tension created by the writing style, and the book's humor make this a delightful story.

Interest Level: 2-5. Reading Level 2.2. Further Search Topics: Humorous Fiction, City Life-Fiction, Housing Projects-Fiction, Detectives-Fiction, Pets-Fiction, Ducks-Fiction, Read Aloud.

BERENSTAIN, Jan, jt. auth., see Berenstain, Stan.

BERENSTAIN, Stan and Berenstain, Jan. Bears in the night.   Random 1971, 30 pp.

This is for the very beginning reader. Only 24 words plus illustrations are used to tell the story of a bedtime adventure for seven small bears. Bravely they sneak out of the house, through the woods, and up Spook Hill. Frightened by an owl's hoot, they run back over the same route until they are safely back in bed again.

Interest Level: K-2. Reading Level: 1.1. Further Search Topics: Bears-Fiction, Group 2, Courage-Fiction, Humorous Fiction.

BERENSTAIN, Stan and Berenstain, Jan. The bike lesson.   Beginner 1964, 61 pp.

This story of a bumbling father trying to teach his eager son how to ride a bike is pure silliness. Much of the action is shown in the humorous illustrations. The rhymed text adds dialogue and description. Good fun.

Interest Level: K-3. Reading Level: 1.2. Further Search Topics: Humorous Fiction, Bicycles and Bicycling-Fiction, Stories in Rhyme, Group 2.

BERGER, Melvin. Time after time; illus by Richard Cuffari.   Coward 1975, 45 pp.

The book begins with a description of inner clocks, proceeds into measurement of time, the seasons, and finally demonstrates the making of a simple clock. The explanations are simple but interesting. One point logically follows from another. It is a solid, serviceable tool limited only somewhat by the fact that it looks like a cross between a picture book and a reader. A brief index is included.

Interest Level: 1-4. Reading Level: 2.2. Further Search Topics: Time, Clocks and Watches, Seasons, Group 2.

BERNSTEIN, Margery and Kobrin, Janet. Coyote goes hunting for fire; illus by Ed Heffernan.   Scribner 1974, 40 pp.

A delightful story that can be read for fun or used as part of a unit on North American Indians. A long time ago when there was no fire, all the animals but Coyote banded together to find it. The animals left Coyote behind because he was always spoiling their plans. Coyote saw them leave, chased after them and once more tried to direct everything, but only ended up losing fire. Cartoon-like illustrations add to the humor of the story. This book should make a simple, but effective play.

Interest Level: 1-4. Reading Level 2.1. Further Search Topics: Animals-Fiction, Legends, Mythology, Fire-Fiction, Indians of North America-Legends, Coyotes-Fiction, Group 2, Creation-Fiction, Drama.

BERNSTEIN, Margery and Kobrin, Janet. The first morning; illus by Enid Warner Romanek. Scribner 1976, 44 pp.

Spider, Mouse, and Fly volunteered to ask the king of the sky for light to take back to earth because the animals on earth were tired of living in darkness. The king didn't want to give away any light and so he set what he thought was an impossible task for the three animals. They were able to outwit the king three times and finally return to earth with a box Mouse was sure contained light. When they opened the box all they found was a rooster. Poor Mouse was ashamed at having been so badly tricked. But then Rooster crowed up the first morning and has done so ever since. A competent retelling of an African myth, nicely complemented by bold illustrations. Good candidate for dramatization.

Interest Level: 1-3. Reading Level: 2.1. Further Search Topics: Animals-Fiction, Group 2, Mythology, Light-Fiction, Drama, Time-Fiction, Calendars-Fiction, Creation-Fiction, Africa-Folklore.

BLEGVAD, Lenore. The great hamster hunt; illus by Erik Blegvad.   HarBraceJ 1969, 32 pp.

Nicholas wanted a hamster; but, because his mother didn't like them, he couldn't have one. She did, however, agree to let Nicholas take care of his friend Tony's hamster for a week. It was a good and happy week for Nicholas until the evening before Tony was to return for his hamster. Nicholas accidentally broke the glass front of Harvey's cage and temporarily replaced it with cardboard. By morning Harvey had chewed through the cardbroad and was gone. Nicholas and his family searched all day but couldn't find Harvey. They finally bought another hamster and waited for Tony to arrive. As evening came Nicholas realized that hamsters are nocturnal and began to look for Harvey once more. This time Harvey was awake and active. The happy result was that Harvey was found and the new hampster became Nicholas' own pet. A simple, satisfying story even to fourth grade readers.

Interest Level: 1-4. Reading Level: 2.2. Further Search Topics: Pets-Fiction, Hamsters-Fiction, Group 2, Everyday Stories.

BLUME, Judy. Are you there God? It's me, Margaret.   Bradbury 1970, 149 pp.

Sixth grade was a year of growth for Margaret and her friends. They all wondered when they would start growing breasts and when they would begin menstruating. Each was kissed for the first time. It was also a year in which Margaret tried to decide whether to be Jewish or Christian and ended up neither. She simply remained friends with God, just as she was when the year began. The book is a reassuring, very open, and humorous treatment of the pains and promise of maturation. It is exceptionally popular with older elementary school readers, so the book's slightly small print and narrow lines should not impede an interested reader's progress.

Interest Level: 4-6. Reading Level: 3.2. Further Search Topics: School Stories, Family-Fiction, Children-Growth-Fiction, Religion-Fiction, Humorous Fiction, Love-Fiction, Best Sellers, Grandparents-Fiction, Everyday Stories.

BLUME, Judy. Blubber.   Bradbury 1974, 153 pp.

Jill, like all the other fifth graders in her class, did exactly as Wendy directed her. When Wendy nicknamed one of the class members Blubber and launched a campaign against her, Jill joined right in. It wasn't until the tables were turned and Jill became Wendy's next victim that Jill realized how much it hurt to be the target of such nastiness. It was only then that Jill could stand up to Wendy. Wendy's meanness is extreme and her classmates, without exception, actively follow her lead, yet all adult characters in the book are blind to what happens. Despite those drawbacks, the book deals with a problem very real to children and thus it has guaranteed audience appeal.

Interest Level: 4-6. Reading Level: 3.1. School Stories, Bullies-Fiction, Weight-Fiction, Loners-Fiction, Gangs-Fiction, Read Aloud, Cruelty-Fiction, Best Sellers, Troublemakers-Fiction, Friendship-Fiction.

BLUME, Judy. Deenie.   Bradbury 1973, 159 pp.

Deenie's mother wanted Deenie to be a model. Deenie didn't know what she wanted until she learned that she had scoliosis (curvature of the spine) and would have to wear a brace for four years. Then she knew she only wanted to be normal. She was repulsed by deformities of any kind. She couldn't stand the idea of a brace. Her mother's attitude made Deenie's adjustment even more difficult. It was her father, her doctor, her sister, and a new friend with excema who finally helped Deenie accept her brace and the idea of physical differences. Subplots include Deenie's budding romance with an eighth grade boy, her strained relationship with her mother, and her growing awareness of sex (masturbation and intercourse). Print and line spacing are similar to *Are You There God? It's Me, Margaret.*

Interest Level: 5-6. Reading Level: 3.1. Further Search Topics: Models, Fashion-Fiction, Beauty-Fiction, Scoliosis-Fiction, Physically Handicapped-Fiction, Children-Growth-Fiction, Sex-Fiction, Love-Fiction, Family Problems-Fiction, Illness-Fiction, Adolescence-Fiction.

BLUME, Judy. Freckle juice; illus by Sonia O. Lisker.   Four Winds 1971, 40 pp.

A very funny story that should appeal to almost everyone. Andrew wanted freckles so that the dirt on his skin wouldn't show as much and he wouldn't have to wash as often. As luck would have it, Sharon, the most obnoxious girl in class, had a freckle juice recipe that she was willing to sell for 50 cents. Even after drinking the brew of grape juice, vinegar, mustard, olive oil, and more, Andrew didn't see any freckles, but, he certainly was sick. Although the protagonists are younger, this book will hold even a fifth grade reader's interest.

Interest Level: 2-5. Reading Level 3.1. Further Search Topics: Humorous Fiction, Group 2, Read Aloud, Everyday Stories, Beauty-Fiction, School Stories, Magic-Fiction, Best Sellers.

BLUME, Judy. It's not the end of the world.   Bradbury 1972, 169 pp.

This is a one theme book (as are many of Judy Blume's titles). It is the story of 11-year-old Karen's attempt to prevent her parents' divorce and then to accept it. In this first-person story she tells of her disappointment, anger, fear, and lack of understanding. She describes her parents' fights and her brother's and sister's reactions, too. It is a book with an obvious and mostly reassuring message to its readers, but it is not just for readers whose families may be in similar situations. It is also a book that will be enjoyed by any Judy Blume enthusiast.

Interest Level: 4-6. Reading Level: 3.1. Further Search Topics: Divorce and Separation-Fiction, Family Problems-Fiction, Everyday Stories.

BLUME, Judy. Otherwise known as Sheila the great.   Dutton 1972, 128 pp.

Sheila first appears in *Tales of a Fourth Grade Nothing* as Peter Thatcher's neighbor. Sheila was a bundle of fears. She was afraid of dogs, thunderstorms, spiders, horses, putting her face in water, and strange noises at night. The summer she and her family rented a house in Tarrytown, New York, she confronted each one of her fears, even mastered one (putting her face in the water) and learned how to swim. That gave her the self-confidence to face a dog without running away. Sheila's progress was aided by her friend Mouse's steadfast belief that a person should always be honest about herself. Sheila's problems are treated realistically and with dignity, yet humorously. Reading level varies greatly from 1.2 - 4.1, therefore, the book is *most* suitable to grades four through six.

Interest Level: 3-6. Reading Level: 3.1. Further Search Topics: Humorous Fiction, Courage-Fiction, Camp-Fiction, Group 2, Vacation-Fiction, Swimming-Fiction, Brothers and Sisters-Fiction, Friendship-Fiction, Everyday Stories.

BLUME, Judy. Superfudge.   Dutton 1980, 166 pp.

On Fudge's first day in school his older brother Peter had to rescue him from the top of the kindergarten storage cabinets. Later in the school year Fudge's eagerness to join a school guest speaker on stage almost spelled disaster. Then when Fudge unexpectedly disappeared one day everyone, including Peter, thought he had drowned. In addition to Peter's problems with Fudge, Peter had to cope with a baby sister, moving to Princeton, New Jersey, a new job for his mother, and his father's attempts to write a book. Although the book is a sequel and is best enjoyed as such, it can be read alone. It is not as amusing or well-written as it's predecessor, *Tales of a Fourth Grade Nothing*, but will still be popular with young readers.

Interest Level: 3-6. Reading Level 3.1. Further Search Topics: Brothers and Sisters-Fiction, Moving, Household-Fiction, Infants-Fiction, Working Parents-Fiction, School Stories, Family-Fiction, Best Sellers, Humorous Fiction, Everyday Stories.

BLUME, Judy. Tales of a fourth grade nothing; illus by Roy Doty.   Dutton 1972, 120 pp.

Another humorous Blume book that can be counted on to appeal to third and fourth grade readers. If fifth and sixth graders can ignore the title's reference to fourth grade, they too will love it. The story is an exaggeration of a common theme—an older child whose life is in continual turmoil because of a somewhat spoiled younger sibling. Peter's problems with three-year-old Fudge become worse with each chapter until the final disaster when Fudge swallows Peter's pet turtle. Each approximately 15-page chapter is a complete, very funny episode.

Interest Level: 3-6. Reading Level 3.1. Further Search Topics: Humorous Fiction, Turtles-Fiction, Brothers and Sisters-Fiction, Pets-Fiction, Family-Fiction, Read Aloud, Best Sellers, Everyday Stories, Troublemakers-Fiction.

BLUME, Judy. Tiger eyes.   Bradbury 1981, 206 pp.

Davey's father's death was a shock that for awhile separated Davey from her mother. They occupied the same space, but Davey felt herself unable to communicate with her mother or with her aunt and uncle with whom they were living. The horror of the night her father was shot in a robbery attempt was too great for Davey to confront. It was too much for Davey's mother too, and so instead of growing closer, they draw apart. They let Davey's aunt and uncle direct their lives for almost a year before each was able to accept Mr. Wexler's death. During that time Davey's closest, most helpful friend was a loner named only Wolf. With him Davey lost enough fear and hatred that she was finally able to begin to talk about her father.

The setting (New Mexico) is much more important than in most of Blume's stories, the book's reading level is considerably more difficult, and the plot is about experiences more unique than usual. It will not fail to draw crowds of older readers however, for in most other respects the book follows Blume's successful formula.

Interest Level: 6+. Reading Level 5.1. Further Search Topics: Death-Fiction, Moving, Household-Fiction, Love-Fiction, Single Parent Family-Fiction, Family Problems-Fiction.

BONHAM, Frank. The mystery of the fat cat; illus by Alvin Smith.   Dutton 1968, 160 pp.

Although noticeably dated at times, this is still an exciting story of an inner city neighborhood. Buddy, Little Pie, Rich, and Cool were among the many who used the local Boys' Club as their hangout. It was a place to stay out of trouble and off the streets, but it was also a haven for rats. The rats were big and brazen; so brazen that one attacked Buddy in the swimming pool. The club needed a new building desperately. The money was there; they just weren't able to use it. Fifteen years earlier an eccentric old woman willed the Boys' Club over $600,000, but stated that the money was first to be used to support her cat until it died. A caretaker, a lawyer, and a veterinarian all benefited as long as the cat lived. Buddy and his friends took on the job of discovering if the cat really was alive or if the Boys' Club was being cheated out of half a million dollars. It was a job that nearly killed them before they set things right. Plenty of action, some violence, a cast of street-smart characters, realistic trouble with the police, as well as a slight mystery almost insure the book's success with older readers. Moderate sized print. Line spacing somewhat narrow.

Interest Level: 6+ Reading Level: 5.1. Further Search Topics: Humorous Fiction, Cats-Fiction, Gangs-Fiction, City Life-Fiction, Mystery and Detective Stories, Poverty-Fiction, Friendship-Fiction, Juvenile Delinquency-Fiction, Crime-Fiction, Best Sellers.

BONSALL, Crosby. And I mean it, Stanley.   Har-Row 1974, 32 pp.

A little girl builds "the very best thing I ever made," but all the while calls to Stanley to tell him not to look and to stay on the other side of the fence. Stanley pays attention only long enough for the "thing" to be completed - then crashes through the fence and bounds into the "thing." He draws no anger from the little girl, though, for Stanley is an enormous, loveable mutt. Told as much through pictures as words, this very easy reader will draw smiles from most first and second graders - especially dog lovers. An Early I Can Read Book.

Interest Level: 1-2. Reading Level: 1.2. Further Search Topics: Dogs-Fiction, Humorous Fiction, Best Sellers.

BONSALL, Crosby. The day I had to play with my sister.   Har-Row 1972, 32 pp.

A very easy reader, only slightly less universally appealing and humorous than *And I Mean It, Stanley*. This time a little boy tries very hard to teach his younger sister to play hide-and-seek. He is totally unsuccessful and thoroughly frustrated. Again the story is told as much with pictures as with words. Useful through second grade. Reader format. An Early I Can Read Book.

Interest Level: 1-2. Reading Level: 1.1. Further Search Topics: Humorous Fiction, Games-Fiction, Brothers and Sisters-Fiction, Everyday Stories.

BRANLEY, Franklyn M. Eclipse: darkness in daytime; illus by Donald Crews.   Har-Row 1973, 33 pp.

The subject is so well-explained and the book is so physically attractive, it's a shame that some older readers will be put off by this title's picture book appearance. Aside from an occasional jarring, condescending note, this is a fine introduction to an interesting subject. Use comfortably with third and fourth graders. Recommend to fifth graders with caution. No index or table of contents. Lets-Read-and-Find-Out-Science-Book series.

Interest Level: 2-4. Reading Level: 2.2. Further Search Topics: Sun, Astronomy, Eclipses, Moon.

BRANLEY, Franklyn M. High sounds, low sounds; illus by Paul Galdone.   Har-Row 1967, 35 pp.

A no-nonsense, informative, thorough introduction to sound, sound waves, and hearing. Includes a couple of simple, illustrative experiments. Useful through third and fourth grade with no problems. The picture book format and opening and closing questions to the reader may turn away fifth and sixth grade users. Worth trying anyway. No index or table of contents. Let's-Read-and-Find-Out-Science-Book series.

Interest Level: 2-4. Reading Level: 2.2. Further Search Topics: Sound, Experiments, Scientific.

BRANLEY, Franklyn M. Oxygen keeps you alive; illus by Don Madden.   Har-Row 1971, 33 pp.

A well-explained, beginning treatment of the functions, importance, and uses of oxygen. The explanation is not limited to humans, but extends to plants and animals as well. Although the book can be stretched to use with fifth graders, its picture book format and sometimes condescending tone indicate it is most easily used through fourth grade. No index or table to contents. Let's-Read-and-Find-Out-Science-Book series.

Interest Level: 2-4. Reading Level: 2.2. Further Search Topics: Air, Respiration, Scuba Diving, Astronauts.

BRANLEY, Franklyn M. Roots are food finders; illus by Joseph Low.   Har-Row 1975, 33 pp.

It really is a shame that the picture book format of this and other *Let's-Read-and-Find-Out-Science-Books* will prevent older children from using them. There is much good information here that is thoroughly and logically explained without patronizing the reader. Functions and types of roots are described. Experiments to show root growth, root hairs, and absorption are given. A very useful book through third grade and possibly fourth grade. Beyond fourth grade children will certainly balk at the book's "babyish" appearance. Let's-Read-and-Find-Out-Science-Book series:

Interest Level: 1-4. Reading Level: 2.2. Further Search Topics: Nature Study, Botany, Group 2, Experiments, Scientific.

BRENNER, Barbara. Baltimore Orioles; illus by J. Winslow Higginbottom.   Har-Row 1974, 62 pp.

An impressive combination of very easy, as well as interesting and informative reading. Within the barest skeleton of a story the author gives a great deal of information about young Baltimore Orioles and the mating and hatching cycle of the older birds. Unfortunately its easy reader format will discourage use beyond third grade. Use freely until that point. Science I Can Read Book series.

Interest Level: 1-3. Reading Level 1.2. Further Search Topics: Birds, Nature Study.

BRYANT, Bernice. George Gershwin: young composer; illus by Nathan Goldstein.   Bobbs 1965, 200 pp.

Even when George Gershwin was very young he loved music, showed signs of musical talent, and longed to play the piano. However, any boy who played the piano in George's neighborhood was called a sissy and George didn't like being teased in that

way. When he was no longer able to keep his music lessons a secret, he stopped them for fear of the teasing. But each time George quit playing the piano, he always went back to it, even when his parents pressured him not to waste his time at the piano. A young teacher told George that he would never be a musician. One of George's teachers actually taught him to play poorly, instead of well. In time, however, George learned to play well and to compose his own music. Then came the hard work of determining his own style. Gradually, more and more people heard and appreciated his American jazz, until George Gershwin's music was heard all around the world.

Another adequate entry in the *Childhood of Famous Americans* series. Includes the usual glossary, bibliography, time line, and follow-up questions. It is most likely to appeal to the reader already interested in music. Childhood of Famous Americans series.

Interest Level: 3-6. Reading Level: 3.1. Further Search Topics: Biography, Composers, Immigration and Emigration-Biography, Jazz Music, Bullies, Music-Biography, Pianists,

BUCKLEY, Peter. I am from Puerto Rico.   S ËAN S 1971, 127 pp.

Federico Ramirez had enjoyed his two years in New York City and didn't like the idea of moving back to Puerto Rico. When he arrived, he had no friends, no T.V., and nothing to do. Then Neri taught Federico the local games, showed him the sights and introduced him to Narcisco, a special fisherman. Narcisco took Federico through the wonders of the coral reefs. He taught him how to dive and fish. Within several months Federico was thoroughly at home in the water and loved Puerto Rico.

There is so much information about Puerto Rico and marine life that the book is never dry. Federico tells his own story as a series of fascinating experiences (meeting up with a shark, playing pinball, scuba diving at night, keeping a large turtle as a pet, etc.). There are abundant black and white photographs. An excellent choice for research (no index) or recreational reading. The print size is slightly on the small side, but the space between lines is good. Recently out of print, but worth looking for.

Interest Level: 5-6. Reading Level: 5.1. Further Search Topics: Puerto Rico, Fishing, Moving, Household-Fiction, Marine Biology, Scuba Diving, Ethnic Groups.

BULLA, Clyde Robert . Dexter; illus by Glo Coalson. Har-Row 1973, 69 pp.

This is not as simple a story as it first appears. Dave, 12 years old and lonely, had hoped his new neighbors would be friends. But, the Arvin family kept very much to themselves until Dave accidentally discovered Alex, the Arvin's son, doing tricks on a trapeze in the barn. Because Dave kept the secret and shared Alex's love for Dexter, his circus pony, the boys soon became friends. Then in one horrible night, the Arvins were forced to leave the town and Dexter was so badly hurt he was believed to be dead. A week later Dave found Dexter alive, but crippled for life and so frightened that no one could get near him. The horse surprised everyone and managed to live through a very harsh winter as well as the townspeople's determination to kill him. When Alex and his father returned, almost a year later, they found Dexter and took the old and feeble horse back to a ranch with them. The story is told with sympathy, with an understanding of how it feels to be lonely, and with tension and suspense. It's appeal should last from third through sixth grade. Print size is smaller than Bulla's usual.

Interest Level: 3-6. Reading Level: 3.1. Further Search Topics: Survival-Fiction, Acrobats and Acrobatics-Fiction, Horses-Fiction, Read Aloud, Circus-Fiction, Loneliness-Fiction, Friendship-Fiction.

BULLA, Clyde Robert. The ghost of windy hill; illus by Don Bolognese. Har-Row 168, 84 pp.

If the reader doesn't expect a high adventure ghost story, he or she will not be disappointed by this low-keyed tale of a family who goes to live in a house that is supposedly haunted. Mr. Giddings asked the Carver family to move into his country home while he and his wife stayed in Boston. His intent was that the Carvers should either prove to his wife that the house was not haunted or drive the ghost out. The Carvers found no ghosts—at first—only an interesting group of neighbors. There was shy Miss Miggie who drifted around in a long, white dress and wore a flower-covered hat. Bruno was the gruff beggar boy who couldn't walk and had no friends but a goat, until the Carver children came along. Near the end of their stay Lorna Carver mentioned that because they had seen no ghosts the family would soon leave and the Giddings would return. Strange occurrences began almost immediately after Lorna's statement and ended only when the Carvers caught Bruno trying to convince them that he was the ghost. Lorna and Jamie were his only friends, so he had risked his guardians wrath and given up the pretense of being lame to trick the Carvers into staying. All ends well as Bruno's cruel guardian is run off, the Carvers take responsibility for Bruno's care, and Mrs. Giddings admits she made up the ghost story because she hated living in the country and had wanted to return to the city. Another serviceable book in the very successful Bulla style.

Interest Level: 2-5. Reading Level: 2.1. Further Search Topics: Ghosts-Fiction, Brothers and Sisters-Fiction, Orphans-Fiction, Country Life-Fiction, Courage-Fiction, Challenges-Fiction, Friendship-Fiction.

BULLA, Clyde Robert. Ghost town treasure; illus by Don Freeman. Har-Row 1957, 87 pp.

A very simple story whose title is somewhat misleading. Instead of a mystery or an exciting story of buried treasure, Bulla has written a very pleasant story of a family whose fortunes are reversed by the accidental discovery of a nearby cave. Young Ty Jackson and his family were the last people living in Gold Rock, California. Everyone else had moved out when the new highway had bypassed the town. The Jacksons had been able to stay on only because some of the nearby ranchers had continued to buy food and supplies from the Jacksons' store. Just as they, too, were preparing to move out, Ty's pen pals wrote that they were coming to visit the town. Their grandfather had died there, years earlier, during his search for gold. When Paul and Nora arrived, they brought with them their grandfather's diary. The last entry in the journal seemed to indicate that their grandfather had found gold in an isolated cave in the nearby canyon. After a long search, the children discovered the cave, but no gold. Ty's disappointment changed to joy when tourists started arriving to see the new natural attraction. Once again his parents could sell their groceries, the hotel could be reopened and Gold Rock would flourish.

Interest Level: 2-5. Reading Level: 2.2. Further Search Topics: Treasure-Fiction, Family Problems-Fiction, West-Fiction, California-Fiction, Family-Fiction, Pen Pals-Fiction.

BULLA, Clyde Robert. Indian hill; illus by James J. Spanfeller. T Y Crowell 1963, 74 pp.

A very low-key story of a Navajo family who moved from the reservation to a city because they could no longer support themselves on the reservation. The move was necessary, but it was not appreciated by young Kee and his mother. They hated their ugly apartment and the crowded city, and wanted to go home. When an excuse to return to the reservation arose, Kee and his mother left the city. However, by the time Kee's father arrived to tell them he had been wrong to force them to move, Kee and his mother had realized they never gave their new home a chance. They were ready to try again. No excitement here, only an understanding look at the difficulties of moving.

Interest Level: 2-5. Reading Level: 2.1. Further Search Topics: Indians of North America-Fiction, Navajo Indians-Fiction, City Life-Fiction, Moving, Household-Fiction.

BULLA, Clyde Robert. John Billington, friend of Squanto; illus by Peter Burchard. Har-Row 1956, 88 pp.

This historical novel about the Mayflower voyage and the Pilgrims' first year at Plymouth centers on young John Billington. John was considered the troublemaker of the children. His problems are woven around the events of the year, including the Pilgrims' first meetings with the Wampanoag Indians. It was finally John, however, who was responsible for bringing peace between the Pilgrims and the Wampanoag tribe who lived further down Cape Cod. The book is not as exciting or convincing as Bulla's books are generally. It also contains a few minor historical inaccuracies; yet it remains useful as both an introduction to American history and historical fiction.

Interest Level: 2-5. Reading Level: 2.1. Further Search Topics: Pilgrims-Fiction, Historical Fiction, United States-History-Fiction, Thanksgiving-Fiction, Troublemakers-Fiction, Indians of North America-Fiction.

BULLA, Clyde Robert. A lion to guard us; illus by Michele Chessare. Har-Row 1981, 117 pp.

Bulla's writing isn't quite as successful here as elsewhere. This story of three London children's attempt to go to their father in Jamestown, Virginia, has danger, adventure, daring and promise. It also has too many characters to allow the reader to get to know any of them well. There are also too many very short chapters to allow plot development (23 chapters and 117 pages). The short sentences help to keep the reading level low, but a glossary would have been useful to fully explain the many unfamiliar terms.

Despite its problems, the book is still useful. The story is based on the 1609 voyage of the Sea Adventure. Blown far off course and badly damaged by a storm, the ship landed at Bermuda rather than Jamestown. The survivors were unable to sail again for over nine months. When they reached Jamestown, they found that few people had survived the very harsh year.

The three Freebold children are the focus of this story. When their mother died they left London to find their father in the New World. Having no money of their own, they were lucky to find a doctor friend to pay their ship's passage and to go with them. Halfway across the ocean, the doctor was swept overboard and drowned. From that time until they found their father barely alive, the children were on their own, even though they were still with the ship's passengers.

Although not the best of Bulla, this is still serviceable as a piece of historical fiction (hard to get children to read), or as a choice for the lover of survival and/or sea stories.

Interest Level: 3-5. Reading Level: 2.1. Further Search Topics: United States-History-Fiction, Historical Fiction, Courage-Fiction, Survival-Fiction, Shipwrecks-Fiction, Voyages and Travels-Fiction, Seafaring Life-Fiction.

BULLA, Clyde Robert. Marco Moonlight; illus by Julia Noonan.   T Y Crowell 1976, 104 pp.

No one could explain Marco's strange, recurring dream. The dream seemed to be about a brother, but Marco had no brother. He had no family but his wealthy grandparents with whom he lived. Marco loved his grandparents very much, but he couldn't help wondering about his own past. He knew only what he and his grandparents could figure out from a few clues. His mother had run away to marry and for three years Marco's grandparents had heard nothing. Then, suddenly, they received a note that she was dying, had parted from her husband, and needed them. By the time they arrived, she was dead and two-year-old Marco could tell them no more. About the time of his thirteenth birthday Marco made friends with a strange man named Flint, who later became the gardener on Marco's grandparents' estate. Rather than live in the room provided for him with the other servants, Flint chose a bleak and isolated beach cottage. Being very careful that no one should suspect, Flint locked Marco into the cottage and forced Marco to change clothes with Matt, who was Marco's long-lost identical twin. Flint and Matt planned that Matt would steal all the money he could from the estate before killing Marco and fleeing. But when Matt began to realize how nice his grandparents were, how much he liked Marco, and how evil Flint was, he decided to thwart Flint's plan. In Matt and Marco's desperate attempt to flee from Flint, Flint was accidentally killed, leaving Marco free to return home and Matt free to find a way to feel he also had the right to claim his heritage before joining Marco.

The tense and dramatic plot immediately involves the reader and the short, fast-paced chapters sustain interest to the end of the book. Readers should also appreciate the small, paperback-size format. A good choice.

Interest Level: 3-6. Reading Level: 2.1. Further Search Topics: Dreams-Fiction, Mystery and Detective Stories, Kidnapping-Fiction, Twins-Fiction, Orphans-Fiction, Grandparents-Fiction, Best Sellers, Brothers and Sisters-Fiction, Jealousy-Fiction, Courage-Fiction.

BULLA, Clyde Robert. My friend the monster; illus by Michele Chessare.   Har-Row 1980, 75 pp.

Even though Hal was plain and not very clever, his disappointed parents knew that he was still a prince; thus he had to be raised as one. Hal didn't like his lonely, dull life until a new world was accidentally opened to him. A servant's child gave him an old book of monsters and told him that the monsters still lived under the distant mountains. Hal finally made a trip to the mountains, spent a day exploring, and by chance met Humbert, a young monster curious about the world. But, Hal's cruel cousin Archer captured Humbert and put him in a cage. Hal's daring rescue

attempt almost resulted in disaster for both Humbert and Hal.

This is another example of Bulla's forte; a book with an action-filled plot, short chapters, large print, wide spaces between the lines, and a low reading level. A book about monsters has almost guaranteed appeal through third grade. Although the book is useful beyond third grade, readers in fourth and fifth grade may be more sensitive to Hal's apparent youth and the fantastic elements of the story.

Interest Level: 1-3. Reading Level: 2.1. Further Search Topics: Fantasy, Monsters-Fiction, Royalty-Fiction, Group 2, Read Aloud, Best Sellers.

BULLA, Clyde Robert. Open the door and see all the people; illus by Wendy Watson.   T Y Crowell 1972, 69 pp.

A slight story that makes up for its lack of excitement with warmth. When Joann, Teeney and Mama were burned out of their house in the country, they decided it was time to move to the city. With the help of a friend, Mama was quickly able to find a job and an apartment. Only Teeney was noticeably unhappy. She missed her doll and resented anyone else who had one. Then the girls learned about the Toy House, a place to borrow or adopt toys. Both girls found dolls they wanted to adopt. Just before the end of the six week trial period Tenney lost her doll and almost lost her chance to adopt it. After the doll was found and repaired, the people at the Toy House realized how much she wanted the doll and let Teeney keep it.

Because of the ages of the characters, (six and eight), and the subject matter, the book's appeal is doubtful beyond third grade. Print size slightly smaller than usual for Bulla.

Interest Level: 1-3. Reading Level: 2.1. Further Search Topics: Dolls-Fiction, Brothers and Sisters-Fiction, Moving, Household-Fiction, Family-Fiction, Group 2.

BULLA, Clyde Robert. Pirate's promise; illus by Peter Burchard.   Har-Row 1958, 87 pp.

After their mother and father died, Tom and Dinah Pippin had nowhere to go but to their Uncle John's house. Uncle John had no place for them, so he sold Tom into bondage but kept Dinah to help his wife with housework. Tom was to be taken by ship to America where the ship's captain would sell him to the highest bidder. After several years, Tom would be free. But, Tom couldn't accept the idea of one person being another's property, so he spoke out at every opportunity. Tom spoke up to the seaman who dragged him aboard ship, to the captain, to the others who had been bonded, even to the pirate captain who captured their ship. Captain Land was so impressed by Tom's bravery that although he set everyone else he had captured adrift on a small boat, he kept Tom with him. He and Tom became good friends. He never asked Tom to become a pirate and Tom never did. Instead, they enjoyed each other's company. When the pirate ship needed work, they stopped at a safe island where Tom met and impressed Captain Red, a fierce enemy of Captain Land. Captain Red's insistence that Tom join his pirate ship led to another clash between the enemies. Although he was ill, Captain Land fought a duel with Captain Red and lost. Land's last requests were that Benjy, a freed slave who loved him, take all his gold, and that Tom go to Charlestown, South Carolina to find Land's family. Benjy led their flight from Captain Red and arranged a way for Tom to sail to Charlestown before putting Tom on his own. When Tom reached Charlestown he found

Land's parents were so angry with Land that at first they didn't even want to hear about him. But, eventually, they not only asked all about their son, but also asked Tom if he and Dinah would like to live with them as their family.

There is enough excitement, danger, and warmth here to satisfy almost any arm-chair adventurer. Usual format of short, episodic chapters.

Interest Level: 3-6. Reading Level 2.1. Further Search Topics: Pirates-Fiction, Seafaring Life-Fiction, Orphans-Fiction, Slavery-Fiction, Brothers and Sisters-Fiction, Best Sellers, Courage-Fiction.

BULLA, Clyde Robert. Riding the pony express; illus by Grace Paull.   Har-Row 1948, 95 pp.

Although somewhat marred by the stereotyped speech of a young Indian boy, this is otherwise an exciting piece of historical fiction set in the 1860s. Dick was sent from New York City to join his father in St. Joseph, Missouri, only to find his father had moved to Nebraska to become a pony express rider. When Dick finally found his father, after a long stagecoach ride, he thought his father didn't want him. Dick stayed at the way station and helped with the chores because he didn't know what else to do. Then one day the house was burned, his father was shot, and the horses were almost stolen. There was no one around who could carry the mail, except Dick. Despite a wolf pack at his heels, Dick rode to the next way station. On his way home he realized his father really did want him and he no longer wanted to leave his father. Chapters are short with separate episodes that tie them together. A few simple songs appear between the chapters.

Interest Level: 2-5. Reading Level: 2.1. Further Search Topics: Horses-Fiction, West-Fiction, United States-History-Fiction, Historical Fiction, Voyages and Travels-Fiction, Courage-Fiction, Frontier and Pioneer Life-Fiction.

BULLA, Clyde Robert. Shoeshine girl; illus by Leigh Grant.   Har-Row 1975, 84 pp.

A well-written, realistic story of 10-year-old Sarah who was sent to spend the summer with her Aunt Claudia. Sarah's parents felt that Sarah put too much importance on money and so insisted that Aunt Claudia give her no allowance for the summer. Sure that Aunt Claudia would call her bluff, Sarah threatened to get a job. Instead, Aunt Claudia thought it was a good idea. Sarah's experience as a shoeshine girl forced her to grow, to learn to like working, and finally to take responsibility for the stand when her boss was hit by a car. Told with quiet humor. For the reader who enjoys Judy Blume's books.

Interest Level: 2-5. Reading Level: 2.2. Further Search Topics: Children-Growth-Fiction, Family Problems-Fiction, Vacation-Fiction, Occupations-Fiction, Everyday Stories.

BULLA, Clyde Robert. The sugar pear tree; illus by Taro Yashima.   T Y Crowell 1960, 54 pp.

Lonnie lived with his mother and his grandfather in a house owned by the state. A new highway was to be built that would force the family to move, but Gramp refused to acknowledge that the state could force them out of their home. He chased away every state representative who came to warn the family that they should move. Lonnie's mother had always been at work when the representatives came and so knew nothing about the warnings until she came home to find their belongings on the sidewalk and their house on wheels. The only person they could turn to was

their friend Nick. Nick owned a nursery in town and a small house with a large yard in the country. He had become a friend of Lonnie's when he gave Lonnie first prize in a school essay contest on the topic of "favorite trees." Lonnie's prize had been a sugar pear tree, his favorite. Nick had next become Lonnie's mother's friend. Nick arranged for them to stay in the greenhouse at his country place. The longer they stayed, the better friends Nick and Lonnie's mother became. Gramp was the only person who didn't adjust to the move. He stopped speaking the moment he was carried out of his old home. In a final and successful attempt to make Gramp happy, Nick bought the old house and had it moved out to his country lot.

The idea of a state government being able to force a family to move may need some explaining. The story's warmth and very consistent early second grade reading level make this a particularly useful book with quiet readers.

Interest Level: 2-4. Reading Level: 2.1. Further Search Topics: Trees-Fiction, Moving, Household-Fiction, Family Problems-Fiction, Grandparents-Fiction, Poverty-Fiction.

BULLA, Clyde Robert. The sword in the tree; illus by Paul Galdone.   Har-Row 1956, 113 pp.

Shan didn't like or trust his Uncle Lionel, who had suddenly appeared at the castle gates after being away many years. Just as suddenly, Shan's father disappeared or died. Shan and his mother soon realized that Lionel wanted to take over the castle, even if it meant killing them. To save themselves, Shan and his mother fled. After walking many miles, they found a poor goat herder and his family who gave them a place to live. Sometime later Shan decided to travel to see King Arthur and ask for help in reclaiming the castle from Lionel. It wasn't until Shan was able to prove the castle was his, and Lionel lost a duel to one of Arthur's knights, that Shan was given back his home. Deep in the castle dungeon Shan found his father, still alive but imprisoned by Lionel.

This book, with its short chapters, short sentences, and steadily progressing plot should interest even the most reluctant reader from grade two through six.

Interest Level: 2-6. Reading Level: 2.2. Further Search Topics: Knights and Knighthood-Fiction, Survival-Fiction, Royalty-Fiction, Best Sellers, Courage-Fiction.

BULLA, Clyde Robert. Viking adventure; illus by Douglas Gorsline.   T Y Crowell 1963, 117 pp.

An exciting story of a young Norwegian boy named Sigurd. Sigurd realized his dream when he finally set sail on a Viking ship in search of Wineland (Vinland). Leif Eriksson had told of his North American findings over 100 years earlier. Sigurd and his father's friend Grom, the captain of the ship, were sure they could find that land again. Their determination finally brought Grom's death at the hands of the ship's owner, Sigurd's near death, and the destruction of the ship.

This book, too, is true to Bulla's style of short chapters, short sentences, much action and high appeal. Although it is a little higher reading level than many of Bulla's others, it is still a good choice. Recently out of print, but worth a search.

Interest Level: 2-6. Reading Level: 3.1. Further Search Topics: Norway-Fiction, Historical Fiction, Seafaring Life-Fiction, Voyages and Travels-Fiction, Shipwrecks-Fiction, Explorers-Fiction, Vikings-Fiction, Courage-Fiction, Best Sellers, Group 2.

BULLA, Clyde Robert. White bird; illus by Leonard Weisgard.   T Y Crowell 1966, 79 pp.

This book is meant for a special reader. It will not appeal to the reader who wants only action and excitement from a book. It is a story of complex human relationships and differing definitions of love. John Thomas lost his parents in a river accident when he was just a baby. His cradle had been pulled from the river and he had been raised by reclusive Luke Vail. Luke placed no trust in the world or in people outside his tiny valley home and so forbade John Thomas to have anything to do with either one. Luke didn't allow John Thomas a pet either because he thought that John Thomas would only be hurt when he no longer had the animal. Despite Luke's argument, when he found an injured white crow, John Thomas kept it and tended it until the crow was stolen by three strangers as Luke stood by. Angry at Luke as much as at the strangers, John Thomas ran away to search for the bird, but found that it had been shot. Far from being fruitless, however, John Thomas's trip out of the valley gave him an entirely different view of people than the one Luke had shown him. Upon a friend's encouragement, John Thomas returned to Luke to share that view.

Subtle and unusual, this book needs a mature, sensitive reader and/or discussion in order to be fully appreciated.

Interest Level: 4-6. Reading Level 2.1. Further Search Topics: Pets-Fiction, Orphans-Fiction, Runaways-Fiction, Birds-Fiction, Love-Fiction, Loners-Fiction, Courage-Fiction.

BUNTING, Eve. The skate patrol; illus by Don Madden.   Albert Whitman 1980, 40 pp.

The book is funny, clever, undemanding and short. The combination of those qualities plus its slight mystery and its consistent reading level make this a very appealing and useful book for young readers. The plot is simple: in the hopes that their neighbors would be so grateful that they would allow the boys to roller skate in the neighborhood again, two friends decided to capture a local thief. James and Milton even knew who the thief was. He was the "mysterious man" who sat in the park. They only had to capture him in the act of stealing to prove that they were correct. They watched him continuously and trailed him as he followed old ladies. Then came the day that they heard Mrs. Grump scream that her purse had been snatched. The boys sped after the "mysterious man" on their skates. They caught him and knocked him down. To their surprise he declared that he was an undercover policeman and they were letting the real thief get away. Off they went again. This time they caught the right person and were rewarded just the way that they had hoped: Mrs. Crump (not Grump) promised that the boys would be allowed to roller skate any time they wished. A light and lively entertainment.

Interest Level: 2-4. Reading Level: 2.2. Further Search Topics: Mystery and Detective Stories, Humorous Fiction, Spies-Fiction, Roller Skating-Fiction, Crime-Fiction, Best Sellers.

BURCH, Robert. Queenie Peavy; illus by Jerry Lazare.   Viking Pr. 1966, 159 pp.

Queenie was always in trouble. She could be mean, really mean, but, she was also bright, talented, independent and resilient. Queenie blamed her problems on the fact that people teased her because her father was in jail and because she was poor. She thought that she had to defend herself against the world. Queenie was proud of her poor reputation until she accidentally-on-purpose caused a classmate to break his leg. Then, when her father returned home and wasn't the person she'd hoped he'd be, Queenie realized that only she could make her life better. Being the strong person she was, she set out to do just that.

Queenie is a wonderfully alive and sympathetic character, one well worth introducing to older readers despite the book's reading level. Print somewhat small. Line spacing average width.

Interest Level: 5-6. Reading Level: 5.1. Further Search Topics: Family Problems-Fiction, Crime-Fiction, Loners-Fiction, Poverty-Fiction, Humorous Fiction, Bullies-Fiction, Troublemakers-Fiction, Academic Problems-Fiction, Read Aloud.

BURCHARD, Marshall. Sports hero: Bill Walton. Putnam 1978, 94 pp.

Burchard's series of *Sports Hero* biographies is better than many other sports biography series. Although heavy emphasis is placed on the subject's playing time, each person's life is capsulized from childhood to just before the book's publication date. Marshall and Sue Burchard (with whom he has collaborated and who writes an almost identical series called *Sports Stars*) treat each figure favorably and with enthusiasm. But, contrary to many children's writers, particularly sports biographers, these writers at least touch on those personal foibles that make players human (i.e. Joe Namath's tendency to break training is briefly described). Each book is abundantly illustrated with photographs, avoids patronizing the reader and is consistently interesting. Each is reliable, very useful and can be depended on to appeal to the sports enthusiast. Problems arise, however, with inconsistent and/or artificially inflated reading levels. The reading level of a title may vary from 2.2 to 4.2. The same passage tested on both a Spache and a Dale-Chall scale may show a similar two-year spread. The problem seems to be with jargon. Most sports jargon does not appear on either Spache's or Chall's list of familiar words and thus raises a book's reading level. But, the words may well be known to the reader (or quickly recognized after one introduction and so not truly unfamiliar). Keep in mind, therefore, that the true sports fan will often be able to read a title that tests well above his/her actual reading level.

Bill Walton's career is covered only through the end of the 1976-1977 season when the Portland Trailblazers won the NBA title. The reading level of this title is one of the most inconsistent of the series (from 2.2 to 4.2).

Interest Level: 2-6. Reading Level: 3.2. Further Search Topics: Biography, Walton, Bill, Basketball-Biography, Group 2.

BURCHARD, Marshall and Burchard, Sue. Sports hero: Billie Jean King.   Putnam 1975, 95 pp.

Winner of every major women's tennis title and a very important person to women's professional sports. Consistent reading level. Book includes glossary of tennis terms. See entry under *Sports Hero: Bill Walton* Sports Hero series.

Interest Level: 3-6. Reading Level: 3.2. Further Search Topics: Biography, King, Billie Jean, Tennis-Biography, Women-Biography.

BURCHARD, Marshall. Sports hero: Dr. J.   Putnam 1976, 89 pp.

Julius Erving can jump higher and stay in the air longer than almost any other basketball player. He can also move around the court with the most agile of players. All in all he is a very exciting player to watch. This book includes his college and pro records (through 1975). See *Sports Hero: Bill Walton* for more information. Sports Hero series.

Interest Level: 3-6. Reading Level: 4.1. Further Search Topics: Biography, Blacks-Biography, Basketball-Biography, Erving, Julius, Group 2.

BURCHARD, Marshall. Sports hero: Fran Tarkenton.   Putnam 1977, 95 pp.

From a strict religious background where athletics were not encouraged, Fran went on to set every NFL passing record possible See *Sports Hero: Bill Walton.* Sports Hero series.

Interest Level: 3-6. Reading Level: 3.2. Further Search Topics: Biography, Tarkenton, Fran, Football-Biography, Religion-Biography.

BURCHARD, Marshall. Sports hero: Fred Lynn. Putnam 1976, 95 pp.

Fred Lynn was baseball's first rookie to be named Most Valuable Player. Consistent reading level. See *Sports Hero: Bill Walton.* Sports Hero series.

Interest Level: 2-6. Reading Level: 3.2. Further Search Topics: Biography, Lynn, Fred, Baseball-Biography, Group 2.

BURCHARD, Marshall and Burchard, Sue.
Sports hero: Henry Aaron.   Putnam 1974, 96 pp.
Baseball's homerun king. See entry under *Sports Hero: Bill Walton* for more information. Sports Hero series.

Interest Level: 2-6. Reading Level: 3.1. Further Search Topics: Biography, Aaron, Henry, Baseball-Biography, Blacks-Biography.

BURCHARD, Marshall. Sports hero: Joe Morgan. Putnam 1978, 93 pp.

Joe Morgan has been described as one of baseball's most complete players. He could field, hit, run and steal bases with the best. See *Sports Hero: Bill Walton* for more details about the book. Sports Hero series.

Interest Level: 2-6. Reading Level: 3.2. Further Search Topics: Biography, Morgan, Joe, Baseball-Biography, Blacks-Biography, Group 2.

BURCHARD, Marshall and Burchard, Sue.
Sports hero: Joe Namath.   Putnam 1971, 95 pp.
One of football's best and flashiest quarterbacks. See *Sports Hero: Bill Walton* entry. Sports Hero series.

Interest Level: 2-6. Reading Level: 2.2. Further Search Topics: Biography, Namath, Joe, Football-Biography.

BURCHARD, Marshall and Burchard, Sue.
Sports hero: Johnny Bench.   Putnam 1973, 95 pp.
The youngest baseball player to receive the National League's Most Valuable Player award. See *Sports Hero: Bill Walton* for information about the book. Sports Hero series.

Interest Level: 2-6. Reading Level: 3.1. Further Search Topics: Biography, Bench, Johnny, Baseball-Biography, Group 2.

BURCHARD, Marshall and Burchard, Sue.
Sports hero: Larry Csonka.   Putnam 1975, 95 pp.
Larry Csonka was almost the stereotype of a football player; big, fearless and driving. For more information about the books in the series see *Sports Hero: Bill Walton.* Sports Hero series.

Interest Level: 2-6. Reading Level: 3.1. Further Search Topics: Biography, Csonka, Larry, Football-Biography, Group 2.

BURCHARD, Marshall. Sports hero: Mario Andretti. Putnam 1977, 90 pp.

Auto racing's all-around superstar. See *Sports Hero: Bill Walton* for details about the series. Sports Hero series.

Interest Level: 3-6. Reading Level: 3.2. Further Search Topics: Biography, Andretti, Mario, Auto Racing-Biography.

BURCHARD, Marshall. Sports hero: Muhammad Ali. Putnam 1975, 95 pp.

The man who brought a quick tongue as well as fast feet and flying fists to the sport of boxing. Entry for *Sports Hero: Bill Walton* gives series notes. Ring record included here. Sports Hero series.

Interest Level: 3-6. Reading Level: 4.1. Further Search Topics: Boxing-Biography, Blacks-Biography, Ali, Muhammad, Group 2.

BURCHARD, Marshall and Burchard, Sue.
Sports Hero: O.J. Simpson.   Putnam 1975, 95 pp.
O.J. Simpson, who now flies through airports, still holds at least three NFL records, including most yards gained in a single season. See *Sports Hero: Bill Walton* for series information. Sports Hero series.

Interest Level: 2-6. Reading Level: 3.2. Further Search Topics: Biography, Simpson, O.J., Football-Biography, Blacks-Biography, Group 2.

BURCHARD, Marshall. Sports hero: Reggie Jackson.   Putnam 1975, 93 pp.

Reggie Jackson was one of the big reasons why the Oakland A's won baseball's World Series three years in a row. *Sports Hero: Bill Walton* gives more information about the books in the series. Sports Hero series.

Interest Level: 2-6. Reading Level: 3.2. Further Search Topics: Biography, Jackson, Reggie, Baseball-Biography, Blacks-Biography, Group 2.

BURCHARD, Marshall. Sports hero: Rick Barry. Putnam 1977, 95 pp.

Rick Barry, now a color commentator for televised basketball games, was once one of the best forwards in basketball. Details about the series with *Sports Hero: Bill Walton* entry. Sports Hero series.

Interest Level: 2-6. Reading Level: 3.1. Further Search Topics: Biography, Barry, Rick, Basketball-Biography, Group 2.

BURCHARD, Marshall. Sports hero: Ron Guidry. Putnam 1981, 95 pp.

The Cajun, left-handed pitcher who led the Yankees to two World Championships. See *Sports Hero: Bill Walton* for series details. Sports Hero series.

Interest Level: 3-6. Reading Level: 3.2. Further Search Topics: Baseball-Biography, Biography, Guidry, Ron.

BURCHARD, Marshall. Sports hero: Terry Bradshaw.   Putnam 1980, 95 pp.

Once labeled a "dumb hick," Terry Bradshaw went on to prove he was a talented and thinking quarterback, good enough to be named NFL Player of the Year. He is also a deeply religious man. Reading level of this title varies from 3.1 to 4.1. For more details about the series, see *Sports Hero: Bill Walton.* Sports Hero series.

Interest Level: 3-6. Reading Level: 3.2. Further Search Topics: Biography, Bradshaw, Terry, Football-Biography, Religion-Biography.

BURCHARD, Sue, jt. auth., see Burchard, Marshall.

BURCHARD, Susan H. Sports star: Dorothy Hamill. HarBraceJ 1978, 63 pp.

Although written by Susan Burchard, this and most of the following listings are true to Marshall Burchard's *Sports Hero* format. For more explanation see *Sports Hero: Bill Walton*.

Dorothy Hamill was the darling of ice skating in 1976 and is now a top professional figure skater. This makes her rise to stardom sound romantic and glamorous. Skating jargon pushes the reading level from 3.1 to 3.2. Sports Star series.

Interest Level: 2-6. Reading Level: 3.2. Further Search Topics: Hamill, Dorothy, Ice Skating-Biography, Women-Biography, Biography, Group 2.

BURCHARD, Susan H. Sports star: Earl Campbell. HarBraceJ 1980, 63 pp.

The Houston Oiler's star running back, probably the best in football, has only been out of college a few years. He should have a long career ahead of him. *Sports Star: Elvin Hayes* includes series notes. Sports Star series.

Interest Level: 3-6. Reading Level: 3.1. Further Search Topics: Football-Biography, Blacks-Biography, Campbell, Earl, Biography.

BURCHARD, Susan H. Sports star: Elvin Hayes. HarBraceJ 1980, 63 pp.

Only this and three other Sue Burchard titles listed here differ much from the format described for the *Sports Hero* series (see *Sports Hero: Bill Walton*). It appears that in 1979 Ms. Burchard's books took on a slick new look. The covers began to sport color photos rather than black and white. The print size became noticeably smaller, although still of adequate size. More emphasis was placed on the players early life and background, in an apparent attempt to make him or her understandable as an individual rather than just as a star. A short career summary was added at the end of each book. All-in-all, the new, flashier approach should make the books more appealing than ever to older students.

Elvin Hayes came from a very poor family who lived in a town where blacks were badly treated. He went on to become one of the best college basketball players of his time. His deep religious convictions helped him through some rough times in his early years as a pro. Now he is happy, not just when he wins, but when he knows he has played his best. Sports Star series.

Interest Level: 3-6. Reading Level: 3.1. Further Search Topics: Biography, Hayes, Elvin, Basketball-Biography, Blacks-Biography, Religion-Biography.

BURCHARD, Susan H. Sports star: Franco Harris. HarBraceJ 1976, 64 pp.

Franco is the talented son of a black Army man and his Italian wife. He became a hero to thousands of Pittsburgh Steeler fans, who called themselves Franco's Italian Army. See *Sports Hero: Bill Walton*, by Marshall Burchard for series details. Sports Star series.

Interest Level: 2-6. Reading Level: 3.1. Further Search Topics: Biography, Group 2, Harris, Franco, Football-Biography, Blacks-Biography.

BURCHARD, Susan H. Sports star: Jim "Catfish" Hunter. HarBraceJ 1976, 64 pp.

The pitcher who, because of contract violations by his club's owner, became the first free agent in baseball. See Marshall Burchard's *Sports Hero: Bill Walton* for information about the series. Sports Star series.

Interest Level: 2-6. Reading Level: 3.1. Further Search Topics: Biography, Baseball-Biography, Hunter, Jim "Catfish", Group 2.

BURCHARD, Susan H. Sports star: John McEnroe. HarBraceJ 1979, 63 pp.

In 1977, feisty John McEnroe became the youngest semi-finalist ever to play at Wimbledon. Both before and since then, he has been noted almost as often for his temper as his talent. The level of difficulty of this book varies from 3.1 to 4.1. See *Sports Star: Elvin Hayes* for more details about the book. Sports Star series.

Interest Level: 3-6. Reading Level: 3.2. Further Search Topics: Biography, Tennis-Biography, McEnroe, John.

BURCHARD, Susan H. Sports star: Mark "The Bird" Fidrych. HarBraceJ 1977, 64 pp.

Although his major league career was short, it was also notable. Mark Fidrych's way of concentrating on his pitching was by talking to the baseball. Entry for *Sports Hero: Bill Walton*, by Marshall Burchard, provides more information about the book. Sports Star series.

Interest Level: 2-6. Reading Level: 2.2. Further Search Topics: Biography, Baseball-Biography, Fidrych, Mark "The Bird."

BURCHARD, Susan H. Sports star: "Mean" Joe Greene. HarBraceJ 1976, 64 pp.

"Mean" Joe Greene's nickname is appropriate. He is big, "mean" on the playing field, and likes to win. He usually does. More details about the book under *Sports Hero: Bill Walton*, by Marshall Burchard. Sports Star series.

Interest Level: 2-6. Reading Level: 3.2. Further Search Topics: Biography, Football-Biography, Greene, "Mean" Joe, Blacks-Biography, Group 2.

BURCHARD, Susan H. Sports star: Pele. HarBrace J 1976, 64 pp.

At age 35, when many people thought he might be "past his prime," Pele proved he could still play superior soccer. More details about the series in *Sports Hero: Bill Walton* entry, by Marshall Burchard. Sports Star series.

Interest Level: 2-6. Reading Level: 3.1. Further Search Topics: Biography, Soccer-Biography, Pele, Group 2.

BURCHARD, Susan H. Sports star: Tommy John. HarBraceJ 1981, 63 pp.

Tommy John's elbow injury was severe enough that no one thought he would be able to pitch again. He proved that the skeptics were wrong. For series notes see *Sports Star: Elvin Hayes*. Sports Star series.

Interest Level: 3-6. Reading Level: 4.1. Further Search Topics: Baseball-Biography, John, Tommy, Biography, Group 2, Physically Handicapped.

BURCHARD, Susan H. Sports star: Tony Dorsett. HarBraceJ 1978, 64 pp.

One year after he set the college rushing record and won the Heisman Trophy, Tony Dorsett was named the NFL's Rookie of the Year and found himself playing in the Super Bowl. Reading level of this title varies from 2.2 to 3.2. For more information about the series see the entry for Marshall Burchard's *Sports Hero: Bill Walton*. Sports Star series.

Interest Level: 2-6. Reading Level: 3.2. Further Search Topics: Biography, Football-Biography, Dorsett, Tony, Blacks-Biography, Group 2.

BURCHARD, Susan H. Sports star: Walt Frazier. HarBraceJ 1975, 64 pp.

Walt Frazier earned his nickname Clyde (from *Bonnie and Clyde*) because of his style both on and off the basketball court. He could steal the ball from almost anyone on the court and he enjoyed high living and fancy dressing off the court. Entry for *Sports Hero: Bill Walton* gives more information about the series. Sports Star series.

Interest Level: 2-6. Reading Level: 3.1. Further Search Topics: Biography, Basketball-Biography, Frazier, Walt, Blacks-Biography.

BUTTERWORTH, William E. Next stop, Earth; illus by Paul Frame.   Walker 1978, 80 pp.

After two years on a desolate planet, 12-year-old Charley and his family were anticipating their return to Earth. But when Charley was awakened from sleep by a spaceship robot, he learned that an asteroid disturbance had caused several key systems on the ship to malfunction. Of 24 passengers on board the spaceship, only 10 were still alive and only Charley and his sister were able to be awakened. It was up to Charley to pilot the ship to its landing on Earth. The controls were all in an adjacent room which a faulty robot kept Charley from entering. Without someone at the controls the ship would burn up when re-entering Earth's atmosphere. By tricking the robot and commanding the ship's main computer, Charley was able to get to the control panel just in time to wake his father, help with reentry and save the ship.

Though the story tends to be heavy with conversations between Charley and various computers and robots, it is also that dialogue that helps maintain suspense. It is a story for the confirmed science fiction fan, not for the inductee.

Interest Level: 3-6. Reading Level: 2.2. Further Search Topics: Science Fiction, Outer Space-Fiction, Voyages and Travels-Fiction, Robots-Fiction, Computers-Fiction.

BYARS, Betsy. After the goat man; illus by Ronald Himler.   Viking Pr. 1974, 126 pp.

Harold was fat and over-sensitive. Ada was serious and independent. Figgy was lonely, poor and in need of help. Figgy and his grandfather, the Goat Man, had been forced to move from their cabin to make room for a highway. The Goat Man had returned to the cabin with a shotgun, vowing to defend his right to live there. Figgy knew he had to persuade his grandfather to leave or someone would be hurt. But, in the children's hurry to reach the Goat Man, it was Figgy who was hurt and Harold who rescued both Figgy and the Goat Man. Harold grew up that day. He stopped dreaming about the way he wanted things to be and faced life realistically for the first time.

The book is very much a character study. Realistic characters are treated with sympathy and dignity and given a chance to grow. Introspective readers will understand and enjoy the book more than those looking for adventure. Print size is fairly large, but lines are separated by only average width.

Interest Level: 4-6. Reading Level: 3.2. Further Search Topics: Loneliness-Fiction, Weight-Fiction, Moving, Household-Fiction, Courage-Fiction, Grandparents-Fiction, Orphans-Fiction.

BYARS, Betsy. The Cybil war; illus by Gail Owens. Viking Pr. 1981, 126 pp.

Simon and Tony both had a crush on Cybil, but according to Tony, Cybil liked Tony better than she liked Simon. Simon was unhappily willing to accept Tony's word even though he knew Tony was a chronic liar. After all, Cybil had been the one to talk their teacher out of giving the lead in the class play about nutrition to Simon. Consequently Simon was being forced to impersonate a jar of peanut butter. In an elaborate attempt to win Cybil's affection Tony began telling Cybil lies about Simon and then set up a double date with Cybil and Harriet. On their walk home, Simon learned from Harriet that Cybil had only agreed to the date because Simon was going along. Happy at last, Simon realized he wanted no more lies and tricks; that he wanted to be truthful with Cybil and with himself. In the name of truth, he was even willing to accept the fact that his father, who had deserted the family, would not be returning.

A good story with just enough humor and romance to make it widely appealing as either a shared book (read aloud) or a personal pick. Print is fairly small.

Interest Level: 5-6. Reading Level: 4.2. Further Search Topics: Humorous Fiction, Love-Fiction, School Stories, Honesty-Fiction, Friendship-Fiction, Single Parent Family-Fiction, Read Aloud, Everyday Stories, Adolescence-Fiction.

BYARS, Betsy. The house of wings; illus by Daniel Schwarts.   Viking Pr. 1972, 142 pp.

Sammy was the youngest of eight children. His parents were tired of raising children when Sammy was born, so they almost let Sammy raise himself. That meant that he grew up to be independent. It didn't mean it was any easier for Sammy to accept being left behind unexpectedly with his strange grandfather when his parents moved to Detroit. His reaction when his grandfather told him that his parents had gone was to deny it and to run away. He ran until he could run no more. When he stopped running, the old man stopped chasing him and they found a wild but blind crane in desperate need of help. Helping the crane heal and find the desire to live again taught Sammy and his grandfather respect and, most of all, love for each other.

The parallels between Sammy and the crane are strong but subtle. The story is a compelling one, but may need a brief introductory note to alleviate confusion in the first two chapters.

Interest Level: 5-6. Reading Level: 4.2. Further Search Topics: Grandparents-Fiction, Birds-Fiction, Family Problems-Fiction, Poverty-Fiction, Physically Handicapped-Fiction, Runaways-Fiction.

BYARS, Betsy. Trouble River; illus by Rocco Negri. Viking Pr. 1969, 158 pp.

A gripping adventure story of survival. After being attacked by an Indian in the middle of the night, Dewey and his grandmother rushed to Trouble River to board a small raft which Dewey had just finished making. They thought they would only need to navigate a few miles down the river to safety at a neighbor's home, but found instead that the neighbor's cabin had been burned down. For almost 40 miles they fought against the unknown river, wolves and rapids.

This is a book that should satisfy many reluctant readers. It's frequent dialogue, fast action and high interest are only occasionally marred by an overly long sentence.

Interest Level: 3-6. Reading Level: 3.1. Further Search Topics: Courage-Fiction, Frontier and Pioneer Life-Fiction, Survival-Fiction, Grandparents-Fiction, Voyages and Travels-Fiction, Best Sellers, Read Aloud.

BYARS, Betsy. The 18th emergency; illus by Robert Grossman.   Viking Pr. 1973, 126 pp.

When your best friend knows how to escape from the world's 17 worst emergencies and you're faced with the eighteenth, you're in trouble. That was the spot in which Mouse found himself one day. He had drawn an arrow towards a large picture of the Neanderthal man and written Marv Hammerman's name. Hammerman had seen him do it and was out to kill, maim, or at least beat up Mouse. Mouse finally ran out of ways to avoid Hammerman and had to face the fight. When it was over and he was once again able to stand up, Mouse realized he felt better for having allowed Hammerman to regain his honor and for having taken responsibility for his own actions.

A funny, fast-moving look at real feelings of fear, honor and responsibility. Very popular. Print is dark and of good size but lines could have been spaced farther apart.

Interest Level: 4-6. Reading Level: 3.2. Further Search Topics: Bullies-Fiction, Humorous Fiction, Courage-Fiction, Best Sellers, Challenges-Fiction, Read Aloud.

CERF, Bennett. Bennett Cerf's book of animal riddles; illus by Roy McKie.   Beginner 1964, 62 pp.

A slightly more difficult selection of riddles than the following listing. The riddles are longer and less familiar, but still very useful. See *Bennett Cerf's Book of Riddles* for more explanation. Reader format.

Interest Level: 1-3. Reading Level: 2.1. Further Search Topics: Riddles, Wit and Humor, Group 2.

CERF, Bennett. Bennett Cerf's book of riddles; illus by Roy McKie.   Beginner 1960, 64 pp.

Simple, well-known riddles that are always popular with children. The riddle is introduced on one page and answered on the reverse side of the page. Silly drawings illustrate each riddle and answer. Because each riddle and answer stands alone, even the most problematic of readers can have the satisfaction of completing a unit in a short time. That satisfaction, plus the universal appeal of humor make this book and the preceding listing useful through grade four, despite the book's reader format.

Interest Level: 1-4. Reading Level: 2.1. Further Search Topics: Riddles, Wit and Humor, Group 2.

CHAIKIN, Miriam. Finders weepers; illus Richard Egielski.   Har-Row 1980, 120 pp.

The children most likely to read this are those who have enjoyed *I Should Worry, I Should Care*. On her way home from school one day, Molly found a ring. Rather than try to find its owner, she made up excuses to keep the ring. Molly knew it was a sin to keep something that belonged to someone else, she even knew who *did* own the ring. When she finally decided to return it, the ring had become stuck on Molly's finger and wouldn't come off. With Yom Kippur just a few days away, Molly became convinced that all the unpleasant things happening around her were punishments for her sin. She finally had to have the ring cut off her finger. After she prayed for forgiveness life immediately went back to normal.

There's enough guilt here to satisfy even the most demanding reader. There is also the same solid family group that appeared in the first book. But this book probably lacks enough excitement and/or empathy to

interest a reader new to Molly and her family. Print is dark but spacing between lines could have been wider.

Interest Level: 3-5. Reading Level: 3.1. Further Search Topics: Family-Fiction, Jews-Fiction, Honesty-Fiction, Holidays-Fiction, Religion-Fiction.

CHAIKIN, Miriam. I should worry, I should care; illus by Richard Egielski.   Har-Row 1979, 103 pp.

A warm, well-written story about life in a Jewish family in Brooklyn just before World War II. This is the story of young Molly's adjustment to moving, to leaving old friends, to making and losing new friends (one by death) and to the small happenings that make up her life. In the background, but always there, is Hitler's ever-increasing threat to the world.

A comfortable, truthful look at a close-knit family. Also useful for its picture of the times and the place. An occasional Yiddish expression may slow the reader but adds to the book's authenticity. Print is slightly lighter and smaller than *Finders Weepers*.

Interest Level: 3-5. Reading Level: 2.2. Further Search Topics: Moving, Household-Fiction, Friendship-Fiction, City Life-Fiction, Jews-Fiction, Family-Fiction.

CHARLIP, Remy and Miller, Mary Beth. Handtalk; an ABC of finger spelling and sign language; photos by George Ancona.   Schol. Bk. Serv. 1974, 42 pp.

This is not a book to be read and put away. It is a challenge to learn finger spelling (forming words letter by letter with the fingers) and signing (forming whole words or ideas by making a picture using one or both hands). It is a challenge that appeals to almost any child, reader and non-reader. One letter of the manual alphabet is shown at the top of each page. At the bottom of the page is a series of pictures that spell out a word which begins with the letter for that page. In the center of the page a model signs that same word. Only the first few words are explained, although there are hints for some of the more difficult words. The rest must be deciphered by the reader. In addition, the book includes over 25 more signs and a sentence about a very ugly vampire. The entire manual alphabet is also shown on a quick-reference, double page spread. The book provides an enjoyable and successful experience with language, especially if two or more children work with the book together. Although its picture book format would ordinarily turn older children away, interest in the book remains high through sixth grade. Because there are so few words that a child needs to read to enjoy this book, its reading level is an estimate.

Interest Level: 2-6. Reading Level: 2.1. Further Search Topics: Nonverbal Communication, Physically Handicapped, Communication.

CHAROSH, Mannis. Mathematical games for one or two; illus by Lois Ehlert.   T Y Crowell 1975, 33 pp.

It will take a very special reader to appreciate this book, one who is excited by math puzzles and games and who is also willing to overlook the book's picture book format. Starting with a very simple, one-player game, the book progresses through six types of games, each progressively more taxing mentally. Each type of game is introduced by a very simple example that is thoroughly explained. For the up-and-coming Einstein.

Interest Level: 3-4. Reading Level: 2.2. Further Search Topics: Mathematics, Puzzles, Games.

CHENERY, Janet. Wolfie; illus by Marc Simont. Har-Row 1969, 64 pp.

This slight but satisfying story is the vehicle for much information about spiders. Harry caught a wolf spider. To keep his sister Polly out of the way, Harry and his friend George told her she could see the spider only after she caught 100 flies to feed it. In the meantime, they took the spider to the nature center where they were treated to a fascinating lesson about insects and spiders (especially wolf spiders). It's too bad that the book's cartoon style illustrations prevent this book from being very useful beyond grade three.

Interest Level: 1-3. Reading Level: 2.1. Further Search Topics: Spiders, Pets, Nature Study, Group 2.

CHEW, Ruth. Earthstar magic. Hastings 1979, 128 pp.

This is one of a series of similar stories by Ruth Chew. Each story involves two children and an old woman they usually suspect is a witch. As their suspicions become convictions they also find that, contrary to their expectation, the witch is very nice and often in need of help.

The children in this tale are brother and sister. Ben and Elizabeth first saw and then didn't see Trudy as she searched for a magical mushroom called an earthstar. Accidentally thrown together again, Ben and Elizabeth took a liking to Trudy, especially when she explained that she had been thrown out of her coven because she was so inept. In fact, she wasn't even able to control the earthstar. The earthstar manages to get all three in and out of adventures (including becoming tiny, flying and almost being eaten) before they learn to control its power. As the story ends, Trudy, finally respected by the other witches, flies off with a promise that Ben and Elizabeth will see her again.

Very lightweight but also very popular with young lovers of witch stories. There seems to be just the right amount of adventure to make up for the very benign witch.

Interest Level: 2-5. Reading Level: 2.2. Further Search Topics: Witches-Fiction, Magic-Fiction, Fantasy, Vacation-Fiction, Brothers and Sisters-Fiction, Transformations-Fiction.

CHEW, Ruth. No such thing as a witch. Hastings 1971, 112 pp.

Despite the fact that their mother said there was no such thing as a witch, Tad and Nora were convinced that their neighbor Maggie Brown was indeed a witch. And they were right! Maggie Brown knew how to make a special kind of fudge that could make anyone into an animal-lover, enable people to talk with animals, or actually transform someone into an animal. All you had to do was to eat one, two, or three pieces of fudge respectively. But Maggie's overzealous love of animals and her disenchantment with housework eventually attracted the attention of her neighbors and the city health department. Only Tad and Nora's frantic efforts to help her saved Maggie from losing all of her animal friends.

A fairly detailed plot, the fascination of being able to change size and appearance and the intrigue involved in fooling the adults around Maggie make this one of Chew's best books.

Interest Level: 2-5. Reading Level: 2.2. Further Search Topics: Individualists-Fiction, Witches-Fiction, Animals-Fiction, Fantasy, Magic-Fiction, Brothers and Sisters-Fiction, Transformations-Fiction.

CHEW, Ruth. What the witch left. Hastings 1973, 128 pp.

One afternoon Katy and Louise decided to search through the locked drawer of an old dresser. Inside they found strange-looking gloves, an old robe, boots, a mirror and a tin box. The girls quickly learned that each item was magical. With the gloves on, the girls could draw, play piano, weave or write. They thought their new talents were wonderful until they each wrote identical school compositions. When she wore the robe for the school play, Louise found out that it made people invisible. The boots, which travelled 21 miles with each step, took the girls to Mexico, but made them late for lunch at home. The mirror showed them anything they wanted to see, and the box "found" everything that was lost. A very light story for children who don't need high adventure but like a mixture of humor and magic.

Interest Level: 3-5. Reading Level: 3.1. Further Search Topics: Magic-Fiction, Mexico-Fiction, Witches-Fiction, Fantasy, Humorous Fiction.

CHEW, Ruth. The wishing tree. Hastings 1980, 142 pp.

Peggy and Brian's discovery of a talking cat, a bird with a beautiful song, and a strange and frightening tree led them to a shopping bag lady, a giant named Fred, a gold key and a magical tablecloth. In a rather complicated series of events, the children and the cat finally succeeded in retrieving the tablecloth from Annie (the old woman to whom Puss had loaned it) and giving it back to Fred, who needed it to help satisfy his gigantic appetite. In addition, they returned Fred to normal human size, rescued Annie from a fall on the ice, introduced the two characters and encouraged them to live together in Fred's castle.

Complicated enough already, the story's lengthy adventure that leads up to the discovery of the key (climbing into the magical tree and swimming in a pond) makes the plot even more complex. If a reader doesn't expect more than benign fantasy and fun this is an adequate choice.

Interest Level: 2-5. Reading Level: 2.2. Further Search Topics: Magic-Fiction, Fantasy, Brothers and Sisters-Fiction, Giants-Fiction, Cats-Fiction.

CHEW, Ruth. Witch's broom. Dodd 1977, 128 pp.

Amy's mother was the one who found the blue broom, but Amy and her friend Jean were the ones who learned it was magical. One night the broom flew Amy into a mountain cave where a coven of witches was meeting. It even forced Amy to answer the roll call for someone named Beryl. But it wasn't until it took both Amy and Jean back to the cave that they discovered the broom's connection to the strange bluejay that had been following them. The bluejay was really Beryl, a young and headstrong witch who had turned herself into the bluejay and then couldn't turn herself back. With the girls' unwitting help, Beryl found the charm to turn herself back into a witch and flew off on a scrawny old broom, leaving the blue broom for Amy and Jean.

What youngster wouldn't want a flying broomstick and the misadventures that go with owning one? Wish fulfillment can never be overrated as an appeal of Ruth Chew's books.

Interest Level: 2-5. Reading Level: 3.1. Further Search Topics: Witches-Fiction, Magic-Fiction, Fantasy, Birds-Fiction, Group 2, Transformations-Fiction.

CHEW, Ruth. The witch's garden.   Hastings 1978, 112 pp.

Although its elements seem to promise an exciting adventure story, this is a disappointing book. The witch who moved into the dark, old home next door to Josh and Susan, was trying to improve her overgrown garden when Susan and Josh offered to help. The children accidentally splashed themselves with the witch's newest brew and found they suddenly became very tiny inhabitants of a dense and threatening jungle (the garden). After they regained their normal size, they dug into other areas of the garden. One hole they dug opened into an underground tunnel that they found was inhabited by a fire-breathing dragon. When the dragon cornered Mrs. Muldoon, Susan and Josh ran out of the tunnel, found the brew and splashed it onto the dragon. The dragon shrank away, Mrs. Muldoon was safe and the tunnel closed over.

Because there is little more suspense than in this description, the book fails to live up to its promise. In addition, the children's first sudden size change is just subtle enough to be confusing. Despite its problems the book is popular with Ruth Chew fans and therefore useful.

Interest Level: 2-5. Reading Level: 2.2. Further Search Topics: Witches-Fiction, Brothers and Sisters-Fiction, Magic-Fiction, Fantasy, Dragons-Fiction, Transformations-Fiction.

CHEW, Ruth. The would-be witch.   Hastings 1976, 112 pp.

Robin and her brother Andy took a liking to the clumsy white cat they saw in Zelda's Antique Shop. The cat apparently liked them, too, for it followed them home. Not having enough money to offer to buy Pearl from Zelda, the children tried to polish up an old pair of silver birds to trade for the cat. The polish turned out to be magical and made the birds real. When they tried the polish on a broom in Zelda's store, the broom began to fly. Upon discovering that Zelda wanted to be a witch but had failed the coven entrance exam, Rob helped her learn to fly and told her of the witches' meeting place that she and Andy had discovered. But the 12 witches who had been turned into cats were wicked enough to want to use Zelda to regain their human form and turn *her* into a cat. In attempting to prevent such a fate, Rob, Andy and Zelda set fire to the abandoned building being used as a meeting place. The 12 witches were rescued from the fire but charged with arson, which meant probable jail sentences for all of them. Zelda, finally a happy and capable witch, gave Pearl to Rob and Andy to thank them for their help.

A better-crafted story than many of the others, this also has a more evil cast of characters to provide additional interest.

Interest Level: 2-5. Reading Level: 2.2. Further Search Topics: Witches-Fiction, Brothers and Sisters-Fiction, Magic-Fiction, Fantasy, Transformations-Fiction, Cats-Fiction.

CHRISTOPHER, Matt. Devil pony; illus by Lorence Bjorkland.   Little 1977, 103 pp.

This book is a bit of a change from the usual Matt Christopher story line. There is no sports interest here; instead there is a good suspense story about a boy, his cousin and a horse. Stu had watched the black Morgan named Midnight being born and had fallen in love with him. A year later he returned to his aunt and uncle's ranch to claim the horse, as he had been promised he could, but strange things began to happen around him. His cousin Wilbur warned him that he had probably annoyed the ranch poltergeist by

deciding to take Midnight away. The bizarre occurrences escalated until Stu was almost tempted to leave Midnight at the ranch. Then Stu discovered Wilbur had been orchestrating everything that had happened because he had wanted to keep the horse himself. Although Stu decided to take Midnight home as he had planned, their new honesty led Stu to believe that he and Wilbur could be friends after all. A surprisingly good story with strong reader appeal.

Interest Level: 3-6. Reading Level: 3.1. Further Search Topics: Horses-Fiction, Supernatural-Fiction, Ghosts-Fiction, Jealousy-Fiction, Relatives-Fiction.

CHRISTOPHER, Matt. Face-off; illus by Harvey Kidder.   Little 1972, 131 pp.

Christopher sticks strictly to the sports story formula here. The characters seem to have no time or thoughts for anything but sports. They epitomize the macho image, and once their problems with sports are solved everything in life seems to fall into place. But, for the young sports enthusiast who doesn't really like to read, this formula of much sports action and very little else is successful.

Scott had never played hockey but he was an extremely fast skater. When Del and Skinny asked him to join their hockey team and to be one of the Three Icekateers, Scott was thrilled. But Scott's performance was less than inspiring and Del's patience with his failures was short. The two almost came to blows when Scott discovered that he was puck-shy and would duck every time someone took a shot near him. Their coach's advice to both of them helped clear up Scott's problem and Del's impatience. All ends happily as Scott played well and he and Del became friends once more.

Interest Level: 3-6. Reading Level: 3.1. Further Search Topics: Hockey-Fiction, Ice Skating-Fiction, Courage-Fiction, Friendship-Fiction.

CHRISTOPHER, Matt. Football fugitive; illus by Larry Johnson.   Little 1976, 119 pp.

Larry had been writing to the great football player Yancey Roote for about two years when his letters suddenly went unanswered. Because his relationship with his father was cool and distant, Larry's friendship with Yancey had meant a great deal to him. Shortly after Larry learned that Yancey was in legal trouble, Yancey showed up in town to ask Larry's father, a famous lawyer, to defend him in court. The court case and Yancey helped to bring Larry and his father closer together and to provide each one with new respect for the other. Lots of football action plus a realistic and somewhat common problem (though an unrealistic solution) make this a useful selection.

Interest Level: 3-6. Reading Level: 3.1. Further Search Topics: Football-Fiction, Lawyers-Fiction, Family Problems-Fiction.

CHRISTOPHER, Matt. No arm in left field; illus by Byron Goto.   Little 1974, 131 pp.

Matt Christopher's books are just the thing for sports junkies. The play-by-play accounts of several sports events (here it is baseball games) are loosely tied together by secondary plot developments. Usually the plot revolves around the main character's successful attempt to overcome a difficulty of some sort.

Terry was a good baseball player so, when he was invited to join a local team shortly after he moved to Pennsylvania, he was very pleased. Almost immediately, he learned that a teammate was not at all happy about playing with Terry. Terry was black and his teammate, Tony, was very prejudiced. Terry had dealt with people like Tony before, so he was able to ignore most, but not all, of Tony's unkind comments and actions. But the day finally came when Tony realized that to play well as a team, they had to work together instead of against each other.

Interest Level: 3-6. Reading Level: 3.2. Further Search Topics: Prejudice-Fiction, Baseball-Fiction, Friendship-Fiction, Challenges-Fiction.

CHRISTOPHER, Matt. Wild pitch.   Little 1980, 137 pp.

This is one of Christopher's better written books but it is also one that will find a smaller audience than usual. Here he has drawn interesting characters of flesh and bone rather than his normal stereotypes. The sports action is still detailed, but it is no longer the core around which a purely skeletal plot is stretched. Christopher has produced an intriguing story line here.

Eddie was a good strong pitcher who sometimes threw wild pitches. One of his wild pitches hit Phyl Monahan, the only girl playing in his league. It was well known that Eddie didn't like the idea of girls playing in the same league as the boys, so people accused him of purposely hitting Phyl. Eddie knew he hadn't meant to hit her, but he still felt very guilty that his pitch had put her into the hospital. He went to the hospital many times before he was finally able to see Phyl and apologize. When he did, he found that she was very likeable and reasonable. When she confessed that she wasn't sure she wanted to play baseball again, Eddie decided he owed it to her to help her regain her confidence. As they worked together each one gained respect for the other until theirs became a very solid friendship. The test for both was when Phyl had to hit against Eddie again.

For many baseball fans there may be too much plot here and not enough baseball. Because the problem of how to control wild pitches is never addressed, other readers may also find the book disappointing. But, for those baseball fans who are open to more than box scores and replays, this is a good story.

Interest Level: 6+. Reading Level: 4.2. Further Search Topics: Baseball-Fiction, Sex Role-Fiction, Friendship-Fiction, Courage-Fiction.

CHRISTOPHER, Matt. The year mom won the pennant; illus by Foster Caddell.   Little 1968, 147 pp.

When no one's father had the time to coach the Thunderballs it began to look like the team would be disbanded. They just didn't seem to be able to work together without a coach. Then Nick Vassey's mother volunteered to coach for the season. After all, she knew baseball as well as anyone else and had watched her husband coach for several years. Nick wasn't at all pleased, but had to accept the idea when his teammates voted to make his mother their coach. Nick's embarrassment was almost as great as the rival coach's skepticism, but before the season was over Nick was proud of his mother. She coached the team to first place and forced even the rival coach to admit she was a good coach. Much baseball action. See note about (*No Arm In Left Field*).

Interest Level: 2-6. Reading Level: 3.1. Further Search Topics: Group 2, Baseball-Fiction, Friendship-Fiction, Prejudice-Fiction, Sex Role-Fiction, Women-Fiction.

CIARDI, John. I met a man; illus by Robert Osborn. HM 1961, 74 pp.

Ciardi's poems are pure fun. About half are riddle poems (poems that describe something without naming it until the end) and the rest are humorous descriptions or nonsense poems. There is a problem, however, with the riddle poems: they are somewhat more difficult to read than the other poems, but of interest to younger rather than older readers. For that reason pages 1-21 (primarily nonsense verse) can be recommended for grades one through five. The remainder of the book, although enjoyable to the very young, needs to be read to them or needs a strong young reader.

Interest Level: 1-5. Reading Level: 2.2. Further Search Topics: Wit and Humor, Poetry, Riddles, Group 2.

CLARK, Margaret Goff. Barney and the UFO; illus by Ted Lewin.   Dodd 1979, 159 pp.

Barney felt a strange prickly sensation several times before he discovered that it was caused by Tibbo, a Gark from the planet Ornam. Tibbo had selected Barney as a friend who would accompany him back to Ornam. Barney was to learn the peaceful ways of Gark and then return to Earth to help persuade the world to accept the aliens. At first the idea of visiting Ornam appealed to Barney because he liked Tibbo and felt very lonely and unsure of his adoptive family's love. Those were the very reasons that Tibbo had chosen Barney: he wanted someone without strong ties to Earth and Barney's only tie when he was first contacted by Tibbo was his little brother Scott. As the time to go grew closer, Barney found a new and strong friendship with Dave, a science whiz-kid, and great love for his new parents. Tibbo, however, was determined to hold Barney to his promise. Only a last minute confrontation between Tibbo and Barney, David, Scott and Mr. and Mrs. Crandall prevented Tibbo from succeeding. But even as Tibbo left, he and Barney acknowledged their new friendship and agreed to keep in touch.

Because of its fairly slow beginning, readers must be well-introduced to this book. If they can be persuaded to be patient while the author sets the stage for about 18 pages they will be rewarded with a decent, if somewhat wordy, story of friendship, UFO's, space travel and family affection.

Interest Level: 3-6. Reading Level: 3.2. Further Search Topics: Science Fiction, Flying Saucers-Fiction, Kidnapping-Fiction, Foster Homes-Fiction, Family-Fiction, Adoption-Fiction, Aliens-Fiction, Loneliness-Fiction, Orphans-Fiction.

CLARK, Margaret Goff. Barney in space; illus by Ted Lewin.   Dodd 1981, 155 pp.

This is a sequel to *Barney and the UFO*, but it stands by itself quite well. It's title is a misnomer, however, for it isn't until the last third of the book that Barney goes into space. In the previous book Barney made friends with Tibbo, a Gark from the planet Ornam. In this book Tibbo tries to save Barney from an evil Gark named Rokell. Because Barney knew about Garks, Rokell was afraid Barney would betray them and turn humans against Garks. To prevent that from happening, Rokell was determined to kidnap Barney. Tibbo was too far from Earth to do more than warn Barney of Rokell's intentions and tell him not to be alone at any time. Barney's friends Dick and Kara tried to protect Barney but only succeeded in endangering their own lives. When Kara was almost killed by Rokell, Barney decided to face Rokell alone and try to defeat him, but Rokell's powers were too strong for Barney. Against their wills both Barney and David were taken aboard a spaceship. They discovered later, to their relief, that the spaceship belonged to a friend of Tibbo's who was commanding the ship from the moon. Barney and Dick were to be taken to the moon for safety until Rokell could be controlled. Rokell didn't give up easily. He attacked the ship twice before he captured it and set it down on a remote portion of the moon. Only Barney's quick thinking stopped Rokell permanently and saved both Barney and Dick.

The preliminary sequences are more suspenseful and exciting than the space travel; however, the book will not disappoint young science fiction fans.

Interest Level: 4-6. Reading Level: 4.2. Further Search Topics: Science Fiction, Flying Saucers-Fiction, Outer Space-Fiction, Orphans-Fiction, Kidnapping-Fiction, Aliens-Fiction, Adoption-Fiction.

CLEARY, Beverly. Henry and Beezus; illus by Louis Darling.   Morrow 1952, 192 pp.

When Henry's dog Ribsy stole the meat from a neighbor's barbecue, a friend rode after Ribsy on his bike and saved the meat. Henry was so embarrassed and jealous that he boasted about an even nicer bike that he was going to get. At first Henry thought he'd be able to earn money to buy a bike in a very short time (he found 49 boxes of bubble gum that he could sell). When that scheme fell through, Henry tried taking over a friend's paper route, but Ribsy kept retrieving the newspapers Henry delivered. Eventually Henry decided to buy a used bike at the police department auction. Beezus, who made a bid for Henry, ended up buying him a beaten-up girl's bike that was hardly worth fixing. The money finally appeared when Henry least expected it; he won $50.00 worth of work at a beauty salon.

Although all seven chapters continue the same story, Chapters 1, 2, 3 and 7, can each stand alone. Henry is definitely old-fashioned, but children still enjoy his humorous escapades and empathize with his desire for a bicycle. The revised paperback cover makes the book's physical appearance less dated. Reading level is somewhat inconsistent: from 2.2 to 3.2.

Interest Level: 2-5. Reading Level: 3.1. Further Search Topics: Humorous Fiction, Occupations-Fiction, Everyday Stories, Bicycles and Bicycling-Fiction, Read Aloud, Group 2.

CLEARY, Beverly. Henry Huggins; illus by Louis Darling.   Morrow 1950, 155 pp.

Henry Huggins is over 30 years old now, so if he occasionally seems a little old-fashioned, it is not surprising. What is surprising is how well he has withstood the years. His antics are innocent, but humorous and realistic. The book's six chapters are six separate stories that follow the same cast of characters through an entire year.

In the first chapter, Henry finds a stray dog (Ribsy) whom he must then transport home on a bus. Ribsy was too large and too frisky not to get into trouble, so before Henry finally gets him home, they have been kicked off of three buses and have ridden in a police car. The second chapter describes what happens when Henry buys two guppies and ends up with millions. In the third chapter Henry accidentally throws his friend's football into the back seat of a speeding car and tries to earn the money to replace it by catching and selling 1,331 night crawlers. The fourth chapter involves Henry's attempts to get out of playing the lead in a school Christmas play. His last minute rescue comes in the form of a can of green paint that spills all over him. It is Ribsy's turn to change colors in Chapter 5. Henry tries to cover Ribsy's dirt spots with talcolm powder for a dog show, but only succeeds in turning Ribsy pink. And in Chapter 6, Ribsy's original owner finally finds him and wants him back, but Ribsy chooses to stay with Henry. Only the occasional extra

cute expression and Henry's age (third grade) keep this from being enjoyed beyond fourth grade.

Interest Level: 1-4. Reading Level: 2.2. Further Search Topics: Humorous Fiction, Everyday Stories, Read Aloud Pets-Fiction, Dogs-Fiction, Group 2.

CLEARY, Beverly. Otis Spofford; illus by Louis Darling.   Morrow 1953, 191 pp.

Here are six separate humorous adventures that link together, but can be read separately and out of order. Otis' favorite activity was "stirring up a little excitement," but his definition of excitement usually meant trouble. The school fiesta turned into a disaster when Otis decided to rechoreograph the bullfight and make the bull win. His attempt to liven up the reading lesson about Indians meant he almost scalped a classmate. However, a wild day at the skating pond finally gave everyone a chance to take revenge for all the things Otis had done to them. The remaining three chapters (2, 3 and 4) are slightly less exciting, but useful if a reader has enjoyed the others. There is much humor in Otis' antics and his tendency to act on every thought that comes to mind is one many readers can appreciate.

Interest Level: 2-6. Reading Level: 5.1. Further Search Topics: Troublemakers-Fiction, Group 2, Read Aloud, Everyday Stories, Humorous Fiction, School Stories.

CLIFFORD, Eth. The dastardly murder of Dirty Pete; illus by George Hughes.   HM 1981, 120 pp.

Although this is a sequel to *Help, I'm a Prisoner in the Library*, it does not depend on the previous title, and in fact, is likely to be the more successful introduction to Mary Rose and Jo-Beth Onetree. Given the choice, most young readers will take a mystery set in a ghost town over a mystery set in a library.

Mary Rose, Jo-Beth and their father were on their way across country when they became lost. As night grew closer, the only place they could find to stay was an old hotel in the ghost town where Sorehead Jones had allegedly killed Dirty Pete. It was Sorehead's ghost who was supposed to haunt the town, and indeed there was someone or something who was in the town with the Onetrees. To their surprise, that someone turned out to be Sourdough Sam, an aging actor who had become senile and spent his days acting out all the parts in the Dirty Pete story. The town was only a movie set and the story was only a movie script. The Onetrees discovered the truth bit by bit after a frightening venture into an abandoned gold mine, a harrowing night in the haunted hotel and a jail sentence for Mr. Onetree.

Beware of the rare, very difficult descriptive passage that may cause trouble for some readers.

Interest Level: 2-5. Reading Level: 3.1. Further Search Topics: Mystery and Detective Stories, West-Fiction, Brothers and Sisters-Fiction, Motion Pictures-Fiction, Ghosts-Fiction, Treasure-Fiction, Group 2, Acting-Fiction, Aging-Fiction, Mental Illness-Fiction.

CLIFFORD, Eth. Help, I'm a prisoner in the library; illus by George Hughes.   HM 1979, 103 pp.

When their car stopped, Mary Rose and Jo-Beth were left alone in a strange city while their father went to find some gas. Jo-Beth needed to use the bathroom, so the sisters headed for the closest public building they could see, the library. No one saw them go in, so no one knew that they were locked inside when the librarian secured the building for the night. With the lights out and a blizzard outside, the library was a very spooky place. The girls tried calling the police, but the police wouldn't take them seriously. Then they heard groans and eerie moans from the second floor. Gathering all their courage, the girls went to investigate, only to discover the librarian lying hurt and unconscious. Their ingenuity and imagination helped the sisters through the difficult hours before they were all rescued.

Don't read it too carefully or the book's implausibilities will become very evident. Most young readers, however, will enjoy this story for its suspense, spooky atmosphere and adventurous girls, and they will ignore its weaknesses.

Interest Level: 2-5. Reading Level: 3.1. Further Search Topics: Disasters-Fiction, Snow-Fiction, Brothers and Sisters-Fiction, Libraries-Fiction, Survival-Fiction, Courage-Fiction, Group 2.

CLYMER, Eleanor. Chipmunk in the forest; illus by Ingrid Fetz.   Atheneum 1965, 56 pp.

A simple story of an Indian boy who learned the meaning of the word "courage". Chipmunk had never admitted to anyone that he was afraid of the forest. But when his uncle tried to teach him to hunt, Chipmunk was too frightened to be quiet, and thus he scared away all the animals. He returned to the village in disgrace to do "women's work." One of his jobs was to watch Little Brother. When Little Brother disappeared, Chipmunk went in search of him. It began to snow as Chipmunk went farther and farther into the forest, but even though he was frightened, Chipmunk kept on looking. By the time he found Little Brother, the snow had covered their tracks. Chipmunk had to use all that he had learned from his uncle to get them safely home. When he arrived back at the village, Chipmunk had finally proven that he was brave.

Interest Level: 2-4. Reading Level: 2.1. Further Search Topics: Indians of North America-Fiction, Courage-Fiction, Snow-Fiction, Hunting-Fiction, Survival-Fiction.

CLYMER, Eleanor. Luke was there; illus by Diane de Groat.   HR & W 1973, 74 pp.

Julius' father, uncle and finally his step-father had all walked out on him. Even his mother had left him, although she hadn't wanted to go. When his mother had been taken to the hospital, Julius and his younger brother Danny were sent to a children's home. Julius felt alone and cheated until he met a young, black, social worker named Luke. Luke liked and respected Julius and helped Julius learn to feel the same way about himself. When Luke, too, left Julius, Julius was so angry at the world that he stole food and then money. Afraid to go back to the children's home because he thought he'd be caught and punished, Julius ran away. It wasn't until he found an abandoned child, about Danny's age, who needed care, that Julius returned to the home. Luke was there when he arrived, just when Julius needed him most. Luke listened to Julius' unhappy feelings, arranged for him to see his mother and helped him begin to accept the fact that life is not always fair.

Julius tells his own story in a realistic, straight-forward book that will touch most readers. Only the lack of quotation marks and inadequate spacing between the lines may slow the reader.

Interest Level: 3-6. Reading Level: 2.2. Further Search Topics: Runaways-Fiction, Orphans-Fiction, Juvenile Delinquency-Fiction, Divorce and Separation-Fiction, Friendship-Fiction, Courage-Fiction, Survival-Fiction, Loneliness-Fiction, Best Sellers, Read Aloud.

CLYMER, Eleanor. Me and the Eggman; illus by David K. Stone.   Dutton 1972, 57 pp.

As Donald's life became more and more miserable and as his chores and responsibilities around his small, overcrowded, urban apartment increased, he began to look for a way to escape. Thinking that if he could just get to the country, life would be better, Donald sneaked into a truck owned by a farmer who delivered eggs to the city. Not surprisingly the farmer, a sharp speaking, independent old man, was not at all happy to find Donald. Reluctantly, the Eggman, as the farmer was called, agreed to let Donald stay a week and help to work his rundown farm. The week stretched into a summer in which Donald learned to face and accept reality, to love the Eggman and to like himself.

This book is a surprisingly consistent success with reluctant readers, especially boys. Watch for the lack of quotation marks around the dialogue and the somewhat small print.

Interest Level: 3-6. Reading Level: 3.2. Further Search Topics: Family Problems-Fiction, Poverty-Fiction, Vacation-Fiction, Runaways-Fiction, Farm Life-Fiction, Best Sellers.

CLYMER, Eleanor. Santiago's silver mine; illus by Ingrid Fetz.   Atheneum 1973, 74 pp.

Although somewhat complicated by a large number of background incidents, especially early in the book, the story is both interesting and informative. Santiago and his friend Andreas wanted to be rich. The year's harvest had been very poor, so there was little food to eat. Both of their fathers had gone to Mexico City to find jobs and their mothers worked for very few pesos near home. Andreas wanted to search the old mine in the hills outside of town for silver, but the mining company had left a guard named Jose to prevent people from getting into the mines. While up on a hill, tending a cow, Andreas found an old piece of pottery and a back entrance to the mine. As they started to enter the mine, Andreas and Santiago found a basket full of old pottery pieces that Jose had apparently dug from the hill. Not knowing what the pottery pieces were, the boys took them to the local school teacher who identified them as ancient archeological treasures that by law belonged to the government. As soon as he realized others had found out that he had been selling the pottery, Jose disappeared. Shortly afterwards, the government paved the road through town and opened the hill as an official archaeological site. The extra jobs meant that the boys' fathers could once again find work at home. Although they hadn't become exactly rich, Santiago and Andreas had certainly found treasure.

Local flavor abounds, along with some history. Useful for Social Studies units. Print size fairly small, but spaces between lines are good sized. Recently out-of-print, but still worth looking for.

Interest Level: 3-5. Reading Level: 3.1. Further Search Topics: Archaeology-Fiction, Poverty-Fiction, Mexico-Fiction, Country Life-Fiction, Treasure-Fiction, Miners-Fiction.

COERR, Eleanor. Sadako and the thousand paper cranes; illus by Ronand Himler.   Putnam 1977, 64 pp.

This is a beautiful and very sad story of a young girl who was only two years old when the atomic bomb was dropped on Hiroshima. Ten years later she contracted leukemia and died a slow, painful death. A fast and enthusiastic runner, she had been full of life and energy before her illness. Soon after she became sick Sadako's best friend folded a paper crane for her and reminded her of an old story: If someone folded

1000 paper cranes, the gods would give that person good health again. Sadako was able to fold only 644 before she died. After her death her classmates made 356 more in order that she could be buried with all 1000 paper cranes. About three years later, a statue, erected in Peace Park in Hiroshima, was dedicated to Sadako and to a hope for world peace.

Because of the theme and its straight-forward handling, this book needs a fairly mature reader.

Interest Level: 4-6. Reading Level: 3.1. Further Search Topics: Japan-Fiction, Historical Fiction, World War II-Fiction, Death-Fiction, Illness-Fiction, War-Fiction, Running-Fiction, Origami-Fiction, Read Aloud.

COHEN, Barbara. The carp in the bathtub; illus by Joan Halpern.　Lothrop 1972, 48 pp.

Leah and Harry couldn't face the prospect of seeing Joe, their pet carp, made into gefilte fish, even for such a special occasion as the Seder on the first night of Passover. The large, friendly carp had lived in the family's bathtub for over a week. It even swam right over to Leah and Harry to be fed everytime they went into the bathroom. At a time when most children in New York didn't have pets, Joe was as close to being a pet as possible. So, Leah and Harry hid Joe in a neighbor's apartment until their father discovered what they had done. When Joe's destiny was fulfilled, the children had to face a difficult fact of life. A week later, however, their despair became delight, when their father brought home a pet cat.

A short, warm and satisfying story.

Interest Level: 2-5. Reading Level: 3.1. Further Search Topics: Group 2, Jews-Fiction, Religion-Fiction, Pets-Fiction, Passover-Fiction, Family-Fiction, Holidays-Fiction, Read Aloud, Brothers and Sisters-Fiction.

COHEN, Barbara. Thank you, Jackie Robinson; illus by Richard Cuffari.　Lothrop 1974, 125 pp.

This story is not for everyone, but for the right reader it is perfect. The book is a catalog of baseball facts, thus it is likely to appeal primarily to baseball fans. But it is not the typical story of a child overcoming a problem through practice and perserverance, as are most sports books. This is a sensitive story of a fatherless boy whose life centered around the New York Dodgers.

Sam could repeat the starting line-up and details of any game the Dodgers had played within the last three years; however, no one cared. In fact, most people were bored when Sam began reciting. Only Davey, the old, black cook at the inn where Sam and his family lived, took any interest. Davey was as much a fan as Sam. They began spending hours together talking and then watching baseball as Davey and his daughter took Sam to the games with them. It was Sam and Davey's dream to catch a fly ball and have it autograped by all the Dodgers, especially Jackie Robinson, the first black major league player. When Davey had a severe heart attack, Sam gathered all his courage to make that dream come true. He bought a baseball, took the subway to a game, and argued with the ushers until he was finally able to get Jackie Robinson's and the team's autographs. Just a few days before Davey died Sam took the baseball to the hospital and gave it to Davey. Sam's feelings about Davey's death are real and painful. He felt sorry for himself, lonely, angry, sad and confused. But a remark by his mother and one more Jackie Robinson hit helped Sam accept Davey's death.

Because the story is told as a first-person flashback set in the late 1940s, it may need a little introduction. It also alludes to racial problems and practices that young readers may not understand without explanation (i.e., why Davey had some hesitation about taking a white child with him to the ballpark or on a trip).

Interest Level: 4-6. Reading Level: 4.2. Further Search Topics: Baseball-Fiction, Blacks-Fiction, Aging-Fiction, Single Parent Family-Fiction, Friendship-Fiction, Death-Fiction, Robinson, Jackie.

COHEN, Daniel. Creatures from UFOs.　Dodd 1978, 112 pp.

A series of reports about close encounters of the third kind. The author offers both sides of each story, then allows the reader to draw his or her own conclusions. Stories will intrigue even those readers not already interested in UFOs. Index. Photographs. A natural. Parts can even be read aloud.

Interest Level: 3-6. Reading Level: 3.1. Further Search Topics: Best Sellers, Flying Saucers.

COLE, Joanna. Dinosaur story; illus by Mort Kunstler.　Morrow 1974, unp (30 pp).

A general introduction to eight dinosaurs: Brontosaurus, Allosaurus, Stegosaurus, Ornitholestes, Protoceratops, Triceratops, Tyrannosaurus rex and Duckbills. Although not a wealth of information, there is more than enough interesting material here to attract a young dinosaur enthusiast. Because of the short sentences, the text is somewhat plodding. The subject matter's great appeal and the appropriately fierce-looking illustrations, however, make up for that problem.

Interest Level: 1-3. Reading Level: 2.1. Further Search Topics: Group 2, Dinosaurs, Prehistory.

COLE, Joanna. My puppy is born; photos by Jerome Wexler.　Morrow 1973, unp (38 pp).

This is an unadorned description of a dachshund puppy's birth and first eight weeks of growth. The black and white photographs are large, sometimes graphic, and most often charming. The text is direct, carefully worded, concise and interesting. It is only the intrusion of an obviously young narrator that keeps this excellent book from being useful beyond third grade.

Interest Level: 1-3. Reading Level: 2.1. Further Search Topics: Group 2, Infants, Dogs, Pets, Birth.

CONE, Molly. The amazing memory of Harvey Bean; illus by Robert MacLean.　HM 1980, 83 pp.

It had been a long time since Harvey had been happy. His memory was so bad that he was always in trouble at school. And now that his parents were separating, he had trouble at home, too. Because he thought that neither one of his parents wanted him he told each one that he was going to stay with the other and instead decided to spend the summer alone. A few hours after he left home, Harry ran into Mr. and Mrs. Katz and before he completely realized it, he was living with them.

Mr. Katz couldn't stand to see anything go to waste. He collected the usable food thrown out behind grocery stores, old furniture, tools, windows and more. Mrs. Katz, whose memory was just as bad as Harvey's, loved to cook, so she could always find a way to use the food. Everything else bulged from the house and garage into the driveway and yard. Harvey spent a happy summer learning to scavenge, eating well, learning not to worry about what others thought of him and even improving his memory. When his parents finally found him, Harvey realized that they really did want him, even if they were separated. He decided to live with his mother on weekdays, his father on weekends, and the Katzs during the summers.

The plot problems that are obvious to adult readers are ones that most young readers will be able to ignore (i.e. neither parent checks on Harvey for over two months). Young readers will enjoy the humor and realism of Harvey's pain, happiness and eventual feeling of self-confidence and triumph. The ten short chapters, good-sized print and adequate space between the lines help lower the book's reading level to late fourth grade.

Interest Level: 3-6. Reading Level: 5.1. Further Search Topics: Loners-Fiction, Vacation-Fiction, Divorce and Separation-Fiction, Humorous Fiction, Group 2, Memory-Fiction, Runaways-Fiction, Academic Problems-Fiction, Individualists-Fiction.

CONE, Molly. Leonard Bernstein; illus by Robert Galster.   Har-Row 1970, 33 pp.

This is a bare bones outline that will appeal to music enthusiasts but will not attract anyone else. The reader catches very little of Bernstein's personality, but *is* awed by an impressive list of his accomplishments. The few attempts made to recreate the real person may have to be explained (i.e., references to Bernstein forgetting to get his hair cut because he was so busy). Picture book format of the hardback may deter some readers. Now published in paperback edition only. Crowell Biography series.

Interest Level: 2-4. Reading Level: 2.2. Further Search Topics: Music-Biography, Biography, Conductors, Composers, Pianists, Group 2.

CONFORD, Ellen. And this is Laura.   Little 1977, 179 pp.

As a member of a family of high-achievers, Laura was convinced that she was unloved and worthless because she had no talents. Then, suddenly Laura discovered she had very special psychic powers; powers she began to exploit. At first it was fun to give readings after school each day. Gradually, however, as Laura foresaw her friend hurt and her brother missing, she realized that having ESP was also a frightening responsibility. Finally, her ESP became the vehicle that made it possible for Laura to tell her parents her true feelings and to understand that they loved her for herself, not for her achievements.

The author treats a common concern with sensitivity and humor. An especially good choice for Judy Blume lovers. Print somewhat small.

Interest Level: 4-6. Reading Level: 4.2. Further Search Topics: Occult-Fiction, Courage-Fiction, Extra Sensory Perception-Fiction, Family-Fiction, Humorous Fiction, Everyday Stories, Talent-Fiction.

CONFORD, Ellen. The luck of Pokey Bloom; illus by Bernice Loewenstein.   Little 1975, 135 pp.

Pokey Bloom's passion was entering contests. She entered every contest she heard of and always thought she would win. Unfortunately, she never won anything. She even went so far as to practice concentrating three times each day on winning every contest she had entered. Someone who had been interviewed on the radio had *guaranteed* she would win that way. She didn't! It only made more trouble for her at school and at home. Pokey had enough trouble getting along with her older brother and didn't need any more problems at home.

There isn't much plot or direction to this story, but it does have some amusing moments. It is an extra book for the reader who enjoys Judy Blume-type books and wants another story about "regular kids."

Interest Level: 4-6. Reading Level: 3.1. Further Search Topics: Family-Fiction, Contests-Fiction, Brothers and Sisters-Fiction, Humorous Fiction, Everyday Stories.

CONFORD, Ellen. The revenge of the incredible Dr. Rancid and his youthful assistant, Jeffrey.   Little 1980, 119 pp.

There were two people Jeff hated and feared: Dewey Belasco, the sixth grade bully and Lana McCabe, Dewey's female counterpart. Only in his imagination could Jeff stand up to them. In the stories Jeff wrote in a notebook, he and his friend Dr. Rancid were superheroes who rid the world of such scum as Lana and Dewey. In real life, Jeff ran from bullies rather than face them; even if it meant that an eight-year-old boy and a girl Jeff's age were left to stand up to Dewey by themselves. Although the way Jeff took care of an injured child soon had most everyone thinking of Jeff as a hero, he saw that, too, as an indication of his failings at first. Finally, something inside Jeff snapped and he answered Dewey back when Dewey insulted him. Before long Jeff found himself flat on his back with a bloody nose and so many pains he couldn't count them. But, he had finally faced Dewey and showed Dewey that he was no longer afraid. Jeff felt good.

Similar to *The 18th Emergency* but a higher reading level. The notebook stories will appeal to fans of superheroes, but because they are stories within a story, they may also cause difficulties. Spacing between lines is somewhat narrow.

Interest Level: 5-6. Reading Level: 4.2. Further Search Topics: Courage-Fiction, Bullies-Fiction, Writing-Fiction, School Stories, Superheroes-Fiction, Humorous Fiction.

CONKLIN, Gladys. Little apes; illus by Joseph Cellini.   Holiday 1970, unp (32pp).

An informative as well as interesting look at gorillas, chimpanzees, orangutans and gibbons. Their habits and behavior patterns are described by following a young one of each species through a full day in its natural surroundings. The text is simple without being condescending and the illustrations are so life-like that they almost walk off the pages. An excellent treatment of a popular subject makes this a very useful book.

Interest Level: 2-5. Reading Level: 2.2. Further Search Topics: Apes, Gorillas, Nature Study, Infants, Group 2.

COOMBS, Charles. Be a winner in baseball.   Morrow 1973, 127 pp.

A solid, though chauvanistic discussion of baseball basics. After a very short summary of baseball's history, the author spends a chapter emphasizing the importance of practice and physical training. From there he goes on to cover techniques of pitching, catching, hitting, running bases, playing the infield and playing the outfield. Directions are clear and often well-illustrated. There is great emphasis placed on playing correctly to avoid injury and on out-smarting the opponent. The book concludes with a reminder that the game is, above all, meant to be fun.

Although the book's reading level tests at 5.2, the jargon that influences the tests will be familiar to most baseball fans. For enthusiasts, therefore, the reading level is probably 4.2 to 5.1. Includes glossary and index.

Interest Level: 4-6. Reading Level: 5.1. Further Search Topics: Baseball.

CORBETT, Scott. The lemonade trick; illus by Paul Galdone.   Little 1960, 103 pp.

This is the first book in a series of quite enjoyable stories (most of which are, unfortunately, too difficult to recommend here). Kerby was given an odd chemistry set by a strange old woman whom he helped one day. When he used the set to put together a brew, Kerby found himself completely under its spell. The sweet-smelling liquid he had concocted forced him to be good, so good that his parents began to worry about him. Luckily the spell wore off in a short time. But, Kerby kept experimenting with it: on himself, on his dog, on his friend, on his enemy and finally in desperation, on the entire boy's choir at church.

A succession of innocently humorous incidents are woven together into a satisfying story. Print size is on the small side.

Interest Level: 3-6. Reading Level: 3.1. Further Search Topics: Humorous Fiction, Bullies-Fiction, Magic-Fiction, Magicians-Fiction, Chemistry-Fiction, Read Aloud.

CURTIS, Philip. The invasion of the Brain Sharpeners; illus by Tony Ross.   Knopf 1979, 117 pp.

This book is one of a number of books published by Albert Knopf under the series title Capers. They are meant to be (and with few exceptions are) light, easy-to-read fiction, published simultaneously in hardcover and paperback editions. Each book is about 120 pages long with chapter length varying from 9 to 14 pages. Print is plenty large and spacing between lines is always adequate. Plots are built around an idea of guaranteed appeal, descriptive passages are kept to a minimum and action (often suspenseful) abounds. This should, on the whole, be a very useful series. Some entries (i.e., *Man From the Sky* and *Who Stole the Wizard of Oz*, both by Avi) are either too difficult or too obscure to be widely appealing, but they are by far the exceptions to the rule.

Invasion of the Brain Sharpeners is the catchy science fiction story of Michael's successful, but risky, attempt to rid his fifth grade classroom of the overpowering influence of the Brain Sharpeners. The Brain Sharpeners came from another galaxy to search for humans to help them colonize their Planet Five. Humans were so lacking in brain power that the Brain Sharpeners' plan was to periodically expose each child to brain-developing rays, then put them through intensive courses of study guided by their also-exposed teacher. When the children had all learned enough to be beneficial to the Brain Sharpeners, they were to be taken from Earth to Planet Five. Michael was the only one to see the danger they were in and to attempt to stop the plot. He managed to chase the aliens away and to prevent his classmates and teacher from receiving their second dose of rays, but in doing so, he sent the principal to the spaceship. Michael's classmates were thus saved, but his principal was never heard from again. Capers series.

Interest Level: 3-6. Reading Level: 3.1. Further Search Topics: Science Fiction, Flying Saucers-Fiction, Aliens-Fiction, School Stories, Kidnapping-Fiction, Best Sellers, Academic Problems-Fiction, Brainwashing-Fiction.

DANZIGER, Paula. The cat ate my gymsuit. Delacorte 1974, 147 pp.

Another book for fans of Judy Blume. Marcy was shy and insecure, unhappy at school and unhappy at home. She was self-conscious about being heavy and sure she would never have a date. Only Ms. Finney (a new teacher), her English class and Smedley (a communications group) meant anything to Marcy. When Ms. Finney was fired because of her refusal to recite the pledge of allegiance and her unorthodox teaching methods, Marcy began to organize a protest movement. Marcy's commitment brought more problems at school and at home, but eventually resulted in Ms. Finney's vindication and Marcy's and her mother's growth and understanding.

Don't expect much depth of characterization. Most of the characters are flat and stereotypical, but the book will have great appeal in spite of its faults, for Marcy's insecurities are ones with which many young readers can identify.

Interest Level: 5-6. Reading Level: 5.1. Further Search Topics: School Stories, Everyday Stories, Family Problems-Fiction, Challenges-Fiction, Weight-Fiction, Courage-Fiction, Individualists-Fiction, Sex Role-Fiction.

DANZIGER, Paula. The pistachio prescription. Delacorte 1978 154 pp.

Just as Cassie entered her freshman year in high school, the old stand-by that had helped her deal with all her problems (eating pistachio nuts) began to fail. To be sure, she did get through the class elections and was elected president. She met and started dating Bernie. She gained self-confidence. She even managed to stand up to a particularly mean teacher. But, eating pistachios didn't help at all at home where Cassie really needed them. She could hardly stand to be in the same room with her older sister. She hated the importance her mother placed on looking right and dressing well. Most of all, she hated the way her parents were constantly fighting. The only person with whom she was really confortable was her brother. But, before the year was over, Cassie's parents decided to get a divorce, she and her sister became friends and Cassie learned to accept her family.

Another Judy Blume-style author, but Danziger's portraits of adults tend to be even more one-dimensional and exaggerated than Blume's. Very popular anyway.

Interest Level: 6+ Reading Level: 5.1. Further Search Topics: Divorce and Separation-Fiction, Family Problems-Fiction, Beauty-Fiction, School Stories, Adolescence-Fiction, Love-Fiction, Brothers and Sisters-Fiction, Everyday Stories.

DANZIGER, Paula. There's a bat in bunk five. Delacorte 1980, 150 pp.

Although this is a sequel to *The Cat Ate My Gymsuit*, it can be read alone. Marcy accepted an offer to become a junior counselor at an arts camp run by her ex-English teacher Ms. Finney and Ms. Finney's husband. After a nervous beginning, Marcy found herself enjoying the other counselors and the campers, but most of all, her first romance. Marcy's only difficulty was dealing with Ginger, a very troubled 10-year-old in Marcy's cabin. Marcy couldn't seem to get through to Ginger. When Ginger ran away, Marcy was forced to consider whether she should have spent more time with the campers and not quite so much time with Ted.

Marcy is a normal teenager whose problems, questions and activities are appealing to many teen and pre-teen readers. The characters who surround Marcy here are less stereotyped and flat than those in The Cat Ate My Gymsuit. Even Marcy's parents are more human. The author's light touch is just right for Marcy's story.

Interest Level: 5-6. Reading Level: 3.2. Further Search Topics: Humorous Fiction, Camp-Fiction, Everyday Stories, Love-Fiction, Vacation-Fiction, Occupations-Fiction, Adolescence-Fiction.

DAVIDSON, Carson. Fast-talking dolphin; illus by Sylvia Stone.   Dodd 1978, 127 pp.

After a rather slow start, this story develops into a well-paced adventure-fantasy with touches of warmth and humor. Eric wasn't just surprised when he found a dolphin in the 10-foot fish pond, he was astonished. Not only had there never been a dolphin there before, but this dolphin spoke in poetry. His name was Wallingford Ullingham Lowell III; Wallingford for short. He was elegant, proud and cultured; but as Eric soon found out, he was very impractical. He didn't seem to realize that he needed salt water and more fish than those in the pond in order to live. It was Eric who figured out a way to keep salt flowing into the pond and a supply of fresh fish. He also kept Wallingford's presence a secret, just as Wallingford requested. The day that Wallingford was discovered was the day that Eric had to break his promise. In order to find out who else had found out about Wallingford, Eric talked with his brother. Together they scouted the town before they realized that Herbert Benson was the only other person who had seen Wallingford.

Herbert reluctantly admitted that he had told his father about the dolphin. Eric knew enough about Mr. Benson to realize that he was just crazy enough to want to harm the dolphin. Eric and his brother gathered all the local children together to shield Wallingford from Mr. Benson. Even Herbert dared to defy his father for the first time. As Mr. Benson struggled with Eric and his brother, he fell, hit his head and rolled into the pond. Wallingford dove to save him, but his leg was caught between two rocks. With the others' help, Wallingford, Eric and his brother Karl were able to save Mr. Benson from drowning.

A few days later Eric, with new-found skills, spontaneously recited a poem about friendship to Wallingford. Wallingford answered with a rare compliment and for the first time used Eric's name (a show of respect). They were such true friends that when Wallingford was helicopter-lifted out of the pond and taken back to his research project, Eric couldn't understand why his father didn't tell him of Wallingford's departure. Eventually he realized that his father had been right; he would rather remember Wallingford swimming in the pond than in a helicopter's sling. Also, Wallingford would have been embarrassed to be seen making so undignified a departure. Wallingford's final message to Eric was a note that Eric found scratched in the dirt thanking him for the salt and the fish and saying that they would one day meet again.

Don't take the plot too seriously or peruse it too carefully for it won't stand up to scrutiny. This is merely a pleasant story with enough humor, action and originality to intrigue many readers. The book's major drawback is the poetry Wallingford spouts: the poetic form and somewhat difficult language will throw some readers. On the other hand, the book could be very useful in a classroom unit about poetry.

Interest Level: 3-5. Reading Level: 3.1. Further Search Topics: Poetry, Dolphins-Fiction, Pets-Fiction, Fantasy, Friendship-Fiction, Humorous Fiction.

DAVIDSON, Margaret. Nine true dolphin stories: illus by Roger Wilson.   Hastings 1974, 67 pp.

Nine short stories about dolphins preceded by a brief description of their physical characteristics, their habits and their behavior. Each story is true, although some are more anecdotes than stories. Most are amusing; all are interesting. Satisfying to the dolphin enthusiast from grades two through five.

Interest Level: 2-5. Reading Level: 3.1. Further Search Topics: Dolphins, Group 2.

DOBRIN, Arnold. Jillions of gerbils.   Lothrop 1973, 64 pp.

Right after his family moved into a big and very old house, David's gerbil disappeared. Before long, the replacement gerbil disappeared also. The house was very old and did have strange creakings. Could there also have been secret hiding places for ghosts, maybe? Determined to find out, David searched the entire house until he really did find a secret room. And in that room he found his two gerbils with their new family — the beginnings of David's millions and billions and jillions of gerbils.

A comfortable, somewhat old-fashioned book that is neatly divided into six short chapters. It includes a page of facts about gerbils at the end. A good choice to follow the very easy readers; it is easy, but not "too babyish."

Interest Level: 1-4. Reading Level: 2.1. Further Search Topics: Gerbils-Fiction, Pets-Fiction, Group 2, Humorous Fiction.

DOLAN, Edward F., Jr. Let's make magic; photos by Jay Irving.   Doubleday 1981, 96 pp.

With playing cards, coins, paper, a few commonly available odds and ends and some practice, the reader can perform most of the tricks in this book. The book is not a step-by-step description of how to put together a magic show (as some of the other titles are), but is more like a casual chat with a friend who wants to teach you to perform a few tricks. Some are simply optical illusions; some are brain teasers that involve mathematical calculations; some are card tricks; and others are much more traditional magic tricks.

Very little is said about how to use conversation as audience distraction or how to link the tricks together into a show. Instead, it is the kind of book that allows the reader to pick and choose any tricks he or she may want to learn without feeling pressured to do more than entertain a friend or two for a few moments. The tricks, with the possible exception of the mathematical brain teasers, are all easily manageable by third through sixth grade readers and yet are impressive to their peers. The use of photographs, rather than cartoon illustrations, helps to make the book a probable success, especially with older readers who like to entertain, enjoy the spotlight, or are interested in magic.

Interest Level: 3-6. Reading Level: 3.1. Further Search Topics: Magic, Optical illusions, Best Sellers.

DOLCH, Edward W, Dolch, Marguerite P. and Jackson, Beulah F.

Andersen stories; illus by Carmen Mowry.   Garrard 1956, 165 pp.

The best way to be introduced to Andersen's fairy tales is to hear them told or read aloud. Because they are beautifully written literary tales they suffer tremendously when the language is simplified enough so that the stories can be included in a reader. Furthermore, episodes have been cut out of some tales ("Big Klaus and Little Klaus") and others have been divided into chapters ("The Ugly Duckling"). But, where there is a need for such an easy version of Hans Christian Andersen, this selection will do. The 18 chapters tell only 11 stories. Most of the included stories are familiar ("The Emperor's New Clothes,"

"The Little Mermaid," "Thumbelina" etc.); all are enjoyable. Illustrations, however, are unattractive and uninspiring. One further caution: the reading level jumps from 2.1 to 3.2. Dolch Pleasure Reading Book series.

Interest Level: 2-5. Reading Level: 3.1. Further Search Topics: Folklore, Fantasy, Group 2, Fairy Tales, Andersen, Hans Christian.

DOLCH, Edward W and Dolch, Marguerite P.
Circus stories; illus by Dee Wallace. Garrard 1956, 166 pp.

A collection of 18 chapters that tell 15 true stories about the circus. Some are descriptions of activities (trapeze flying) or people (Emmett Kelly, a circus doctor, the Ringling Brothers). Other chapters tell of unusual occurrences; i.e., the bareback rider who was thrown off her horse into the lap of a spectator whom she later married. Some stories, such as the story of the horse trainer whose life was saved by an elephant, are exciting. Others are sad ("Blinky," the dog who was killed by an angry lion).

The authors' tone becomes condescending off and on through this collection, thus hampering its usefulness somewhat. Otherwise, it is very similar to the other Dolch books; it is a decent collection of very simplified stories. Dolch Basic Vocabulary Book series.

Interest Level: 1-4. Reading Level: 2.2. Further Search Topics: Circus-Fiction, Clowns-Fiction, Acrobats and Acrobatics-Fiction, Group 2.

DOLCH, Edward W and Dolch, Marguerite P.
Dog stories; illus by Bernette Johnson and Robert S. Kerr. Garrard 1954, 169 pp.

Although overly sentimental for most adult tastes, this collection of true dog stories appeals to young dog lovers. Eighteen chapters tell 15 stories, ranging from the first story in which dog rescues boy, to the final story in which boy rescues dog. There is a dog who played baseball, a dog who went to live at a newspaper, a dog who saved a fireman from a fire, two dogs who were lost and several more dogs who became heroes. A consistent reading level, large print and a popular topic make this a good choice to offer reluctant readers despite the Dolch books' usual unattractive illustrations. Dolch Basic Vocabulary Book series.

Interest Level: 2-4. Reading Level: 2.1. Further Search Topics: Dogs-Fiction, Courage-Fiction, Pets-Fiction.

DOLCH, Edward W, Dolch, Marguerite P. and Jackson, Beulah F.
Fairy stories; illus by Marguerite Dolch and Yolande Cuypers-Fransen. Garrard 1950, 165 pp.

A collection of mostly familiar fairy tales told in the Dolchs' very simplified manner. Because the book's purpose is not to provide the most literate version of favorite fairy tales, better versions of any of the stories can be found elsewhere. It provides instead, very accessible versions of tales young readers have enjoyed for years. Includes "Cinderella," "Hansel and Gretel," "Jack and the Bean Stalk," "Snow White," "Sleeping Beauty," and "The Elves and the Shoemaker," among others. Dolch Pleasure Reading Book series.

Interest Level: 1-4. Reading Level: 2.2. Further Search Topics: Folklore, Fairy Tales, Fantasy, Group 2.

DOLCH, Edward W and Dolch, Marguerite P.
Irish stories; illus by Carmen Mowry. Garrard 1958, 165 pp.

Besides controlling the vocabulary used in the stories, the Dolchs seem to include only stories with very uncomplicated plots. Once again they split the longer stories into two chapters. Thus, from 17 chapters there come only 12 stories. Most of the stories will be unfamiliar to readers (except perhaps those about Finn McCool), but all are pleasurable. See *Andersen Stories* for more information. Dolch Basic Vocabulary Book series.

Interest Level: 2-5. Reading Level: 2.2. Further Search Topics: Folklore, Fantasy, Ireland-Fiction, Giants-Fiction.

DOLCH, Edward W, Dolch, Marguerite P. and Jackson, Beulah F.
Robin Hood stories; illus by Carmen Mowry. Garrard 1957, 162 pp.

The illustrations are still drab, but the stories in this volume are exciting. Here we find straight-forward adventure and familiar characters: Robin Hood, Little John, Will Scarlet, Sheriff of Nottingham, Allan-a-dale and Sir Richard of Lea. The book makes a good choice for adventure lovers. Dolch Pleasure Reading Book series.

Interest Level: 2-6. Reading Level: 2.2. Further Search Topics: Robin Hood, Knights and Knighthood-Fiction, Folklore, Crime-Fiction.

DOLCH, Edward W and Dolch, Marguerite P.
Stories from France; illus by Gordon Laite. Garrard 1963, 167 pp.

It is very difficult to simplify a story and not lose at least some of its original flavor. Such is the case here and in all the Dolch retellings. Nevertheless, this collection of folktales is quite useful for the French flavor it does maintain. The stories, as they are retold, are good; not great, but good. There are 14 stories related in the 19 chapters. This is a result of splitting the longer, more complicated stories into episodes. Some frustration may arise for readers because there is no indication that a story may involve more than one chapter. The much-improved illustrations that introduce each chapter and adorn the cover help make this more attractive than the earlier books. The book ends with a list of the provinces from which the stories came as well as a pronunciation key to French names. Folklore of the World series.

Interest Level: 2-6. Reading Level: 3.1. Further Search Topics: Folklore, Fantasy, France-Fiction, Royalty-Fiction, Group 2, Knights and Knighthood-Fiction.

DOLCH, Edward W and Dolch, Marguerite P.
Stories from Old Russia; illus by James Lewicki. Garrard 1964, 168 pp.

There are 21 chapters and only nine stories in this volume. These are more robust and exciting adventure stories than many of the other Dolch collections listed here, although once again the simplified vocabulary is somewhat restrictive. A guide to pronunciation of some Russian names is included at the end of the book. More colorful illustrations than some of the other titles. Very consistent reading level. See *Stories From France* for more information. Folklore of the World series.

Interest Level: 2-6. Reading Level: 2.1. Further Search Topics: Folklore, Fantasy, Russia-Fiction, Witches-Fiction.

DOLCH, Edward W and Dolch, Marguerite P.
"Why" stories; illus by Marguerite Dolch.   Garrard
1952, 160 pp.

"Why the Bear Has a Little Tail," "Why Turkeys
Have Red Eyes," and "How the Tiger Got His Stripes"
are three titles that illustrate the type of stories found
in this collection. Seventeen short, simple folktales
explain why the world and creatures in it operate and
appear as they do. All of the tales can be found
elsewhere. However, few if any stories are likely to be
familiar to readers. This type of story is one children
often find very appealing. The stories are
understandable, logical within their own framework
and simple enough to be retold to others. The reading
level varies from 1.2 to 2.2. Dolch Basic Vocabulary
Book series.

Interest Level: 1-4. Reading Level: 2.2. Further
Search Topics: Folklore, Why Stories, Animals-Fiction,
Group 2, Creation-Fiction.

DOLCH, Marguerite P, jt. auth., see Dolch, Edward W.

EASTMAN, Philip D. Sam and the firefly.   Beginner
1958, 62 pp.

Sam, the owl, went looking for a playmate one night
but found everyone was asleep except a mischievous
firefly named Gus. When Sam showed Gus how to
write words with his light in the dark sky, Gus went
wild. First he tried to direct auto traffic, then airplane
traffic, until finally the Hot Dog Man, an angry victim of
Gus' tricks, captured him. However, when the Hot Dog
Man tried to take Gus out of town, his truck became
stuck on the railroad tracks in front of an oncoming
train. Gus, freed from the jar in which he'd been
caught, quickly wrote the word STOP in the sky and
saved everyone. Gus' silliness, the catastrophies he
caused and his final triumph should interest almost
any young child who likes humor or excitement.
Reader format.

Interest Level: 1-2. Reading Level: 1.2. Further
Search Topics: Best Sellers, Fireflies-Fiction,
Owls-Fiction, Humorous Fiction.

EYERLY, Jeannette. The seeing summer; illus by
Emily Arnold McCully.   Lippincott 1981, 153 pp.

That it attempts to be two books at the same time is
the one flaw in this book that may be noticed by
young readers. The first half of the book is an
interesting story of the growing friendship between a
sighted girl and a blind girl. Carey's delight at the idea
of a new friend next door turned to disbelief and
discomfort when she learned that Jenny was blind.
Jenny too wanted to be friends, but not if she was to
be pitied or patronized. Gradually she was able to
show Carey that being blind was a nuisance, but
nothing she was ashamed of or embarrassed about.
The second half of the book presents the contrived
and somewhat unnecessary story of Jenny's
kidnapping. When Carey's attempt to rescue Jenny
resulted in her capture too, it was, of course, Jenny's
independence and ingenuity that led the way to their
eventual rescue.

To the reader looking for a rousing story of a
kidnapping the book may be a disappointment. Half of
the book is a long time to wait for the slight adventure.
But, for those readers interested in a good story of
physical differences and friendship, this will be more
satisfying.

Interest Level: 3-6. Reading Level: 3.1. Further
Search Topics: Vision-Fiction, Friendship-Fiction,
Kidnapping-Fiction, Single Parent Family-Fiction,
Physically Handicapped-Fiction.

FALL, Thomas. Jim Thorpe; illus by John Gretzer.
Har-Row 1970, 33 pp.

Jim Thorpe was an Indian from the Oklahoma
territory who became one of the United State's
greatest athletes. He and his twin brother were trained
by their father to run and jump faster and farther than
anyone else. When Charles died, Jim couldn't face
returning to school without his twin, so his family kept
him home for a few months before sending him away
to school again. Jim ran home once more when his
father and mother both became ill. Months later he
went to still another school where he was noticed by
Pop Warner. Pop advised Joe to concentrate on track
until he was big enough to play football. His father's
death left Jim so despondent he quit school to play
professional baseball for a while. By the time he went
back to school, Jim was big enough to play
spectacular football and then to win the 1912 Olympic
decathlon competition. Unfortunately, his short time as
a paid baseball player made him ineligible for the
Olympic honor and Jim's medal was taken away.
Public sentiment was with Jim, but the rules were
against him. He went on, however, to play both
professional baseball and football. In 1982, 29 years
after his death, Thorpe's medal was finally returned to
him.

A short, meaty and readable biography of a person
who should be interesting to many sports fans.
Follows the usual format of Crowell biographies, but
looks less like a picture book than many. Crowell
Biography series.

Interest Level: 3-5. Reading Level: 3.1. Further
Search Topics: Football-Biography, Indians of North
America-Biography, Baseball-Biography, Olympic
Games, Biography, Running-Biography,
Twins-Biography.

FIFE, Dale. Follow that ghost!; illus by Joan
Drescher.   Dutton 1979, 58 pp.

In short sentences reminiscent of "Dragnet," Chuck
tells a very simple story of Chuck and Jason's first
detective case. He and Jason were practicing
following people, when their next-door-neighbor caught
them following her home. Instead of being angry at
the two boys, Glory decided to hire them to find the
ghost she and her mother were hearing at 5:00 every
morning. Despite their best attempts to capture and
bury the ghost, or a find a human cause for the
ghostly sounds, Chuck and Jason couldn't rid Glory's
apartment of its ghost. Their final effort nearly resulted
in injury to a neighbor. Ultimately, Chuck discovered
that the ghost was merely a displaced woodpecker
looking for a new home.

Not a terribly ambitious mystery, but one whose
consistent reading level, familiar urban setting and
interesting characters will please many young readers.

Interest Level: 2-4. Reading Level: 2.1. Further
Search Topics: Ghosts-Fiction, Mystery and Detective
Stories, Spies-Fiction, Humorous Fiction.

FOLEY, Louise Munro. Tackle 22; illus by John
Heinly.   Delacorte 1978, unp (43 pp).

When their quarterback came down with the mumps,
it looked like the Wildcats would have to forfeit the big
football game to the Spacemen. But Chub's little
brother Herb surprised everyone and saved the game.

Brief and somewhat predictable, the book maintains
a light touch that many young readers will like. Heavily
illustrated.

Interest Level: 1-4. Reading Level: 2.1. Further
Search Topics: Football-Fiction, Brothers and
Sisters-Fiction, Humorous Fiction, Group 2.

GIFF, Patricia Reilly. Have you seen Hyacinth Macaw?; illus by Anthony Kramer.   Delacorte 1981, 135 pp.

Abby Jones was trying very hard to be a detective, but it was difficult without any mysteries to solve. So to keep in practice, Abby filled a memo book with her notes about anything that seemed at all unusual. At the same time, Abby kept in touch with two local police detectives who gave her hints about detective work. Because of her police friends and her observations, Abby found herself involved in what seemed to be four or more mysteries. Who had moved into the apartment next door and what were the screams that came from there? What was the theft that the police were worried about? Who was Hyacinth Macaw and why had she disappeared? And why was Abby's older brother Dan acting so strangely? Was he involved in the theft?

Abby and her friend Potsie ended up trailing a suspect through the New York subway system, breaking into the next-door apartment, suspecting Abby's brother of the theft, capturing an unusual bird, releasing the bird into a pet shop and recapturing it, before they realized that all the mysteries were linked together. Hyacinth Macaw was a valuable bird stolen from Justine's Junktique Shop. The daughter of Abby's landland had taken the bird and placed it in the empty apartment next to Abby's, so that she could paint the bird's portrait. The picture was to be entered in Justine's Junktique contest. Dan and his friend Holly Monk had been secretly constructing a Purple Pigeon Purifier to enter in the contest. They needed the prize money to repair a window they had accidentally broken. By the time the mysteries were all sorted out, Dan and Holly had won a special prize; Kiki, the portrait painter, had not only been forgiven, but had also been awarded first prize; and Abby had received the reward for finding and returning the bird.

The action in this mystery is both abundant and humorous enough to make the book enjoyable to many readers. There are also some problems that need to be noted. Some readers may find the action too swift and the characters too numerous to be easily followed. Abby's memo notes are sometimes written without vowels and are almost always in incomplete sentences. The reader who is highly motivated or has help from another person will still be able to enjoy the story; however, for the others another choice may be more appropriate.

Interest Level: 4-6. Reading Level: 3.1. Further Search Topics: Mystery and Detective Stories, Humorous Fiction, Writing-Fiction, Detectives-Fiction, Birds-Fiction.

GINSBURG, Mirra. The lazies; illus by Marian Parry.   Macmillan 1973, 70 pp.

A good collection of 15 short Russian folktales all having to do with laziness. Most are humorous tales; few are well-known. In just under a third of the stories the humor may be too subtle even for older elementary school children; however, the rest of the stories can be enjoyed by almost any child between third and sixth grade. ("Who Will Wash the Pot," "Easy Bread," "Who Will Row Next," and "The Princess Who Learned to Work" are the questionable stories). Print somewhat small.

Interest Level: 3-6. Reading Level: 3.1. Further Search Topics: Folklore, Humorous Fiction, Laziness-Fiction, Russia-Fiction.

GOLDIN, Augusta. Spider silk; illus by Joseph Low. Har-Row 1964, unp (34 pp).

No gimmicks here, just straight-forward information about spider webs. Where are spider webs found? How are they formed? What are their shapes? For what are they used? How strong are they? And, what are the other uses of spider silk? In answering those questions the author also gives a bit of information about particular types of spiders. The book can easily be used through grade three. Its picture book format will turn many fourth and fifth graders away even though the book's information is still quite interesting and useful. Let's-Read- & -Find-Out Science Book series.

Interest Level: 1-5. Reading Level: 2.2. Further Search Topics: Spiders, Nature Study, Group 2.

GREEN, Phyllis. The fastest quitter in town; illus by Lorenzo Lynch.   A-W 1972, 62 pp.

Whenever Johnny played baseball and things went wrong for him, he would quit. Johnny's teammates finally grew so angry with him that they told him to leave the team. That same day, Johnny's 90-year-old great-grandfather lost a very special ring his wife had given him. Johnny's love for this great-grandfather pushed him to keep looking for the ring until days later, when everyone else had quit searching, Johnny found the ring. Having learned a hard lesson, Johnny returned to his team for one more chance. That evening Johnny went to see his great-grandfather to tell him, with legitimate pride, that he had played the entire game.

Although the lesson is pointed, the story is very satisfying. Johnny's relationship with this great-grandfather is close and supportive. His problem is one shared by many children, especially those with a weak self-image.

Interest Level: 1-4. Reading Level: 3.1. Further Search Topics: Blacks-Fiction, Challenges-Fiction, Courage-Fiction, Group 2, Baseball-Fiction, Grandparents-Fiction, Friendship-Fiction.

GREENE, Constance C. A girl called Al; illus by Byron Barton.   Viking Pr. 1969, 127 pp.

Told in the first person, this is the story of two seventh grade girls. The girls' warm friendship began the moment Al introduced herself to the narrator as a non-conformist. Al was very independent, mostly because she was on her own so much of the time. Her parents were divorced and she seldom saw either one of them. Her father only wrote her postcards and her mother was rarely home. The narrator's family and Mr. Richards, their building superintendent, became Al's family. They cooked, ate, played, fought, talked and even made bookcases together. When Mr. Richards had a heart attack, they found help for him and later went to see him in the hospital. It was his death that helped Al and her mother grow closer, just as Mr. Richards' life had helped her understand why her father never came to see her.

A satisfying, low-key story of friendship and maturation. The girls are Judy Blume-style characters with much greater innocence. Their ages are not discernible by their actions or dialogue, only by the author's statement.

Interest Level: 3-6. Reading Level: 3.1. Further Search Topics: Children-Growth-Fiction, Single Parent Family-Fiction, Friendship-Fiction, Weight-Fiction, Aging-Fiction, Death-Fiction, Divorce and Separation-Fiction, Family Problems-Fiction, Everyday Stories, Humorous Fiction.

GREENE, Constance C. I and Sproggy; illus by Emily A. McCully.   Viking Pr. 1978, 155 pp.

Ten-year-old Adam had adjusted to his parents' divorce and had even grown to like living alone with his mother. When his father came back from London with his new wife and stepdaughter Sproggy and announced that they were moving into an apartment nearby, Adam was a little worried. But when his father asked him to take care of Sproggy, Adam was furious. First of all, he didn't know Sproggy and he didn't want to know her. Secondly, she was two months older than he, taller too, and she embarrassed him in public. And finally, she didn't need his help. She got along quite well by herself; so well that she even saved Adam from a mugger and became good friends with Adam's friends behind his back. It wasn't until Sproggy proved to be vulnerable that Adam and she became friends.

A warm, realistic and humorous story whose interesting characters (even the minor ones) heighten the book's appeal.

Interest Level: 4-6. Reading Level: 3.2. Further Search Topics: Brothers and Sisters-Fiction, Divorce and Separation-Fiction, City Life-Fiction, New York City-Fiction, Humorous Fiction, Friendship-Fiction, Everyday Stories.

GREENE, Constance C. Isabelle the itch; illus by Emily A. McCully.   Viking Pr. 1973, 126 pp.

This is a loosely plotted story about a spunky, original fifth grade girl who could drive everyone around her crazy without ever tiring. Isabelle's dearest dream was to win the 50-yard dash at her school's field day. Even though she took over her brother's paper route to earn money for the Adidas track shoes she needed, Isabelle still didn't win. However, she did meet some new people, make new friends and keep those around her on their toes. A very amusing story told mostly in dialogue.

Interest Level: 4-6. Reading Level: 3.2. Further Search Topics: School Stories, Occupations-Fiction, Humorous Fiction, Everyday Stories, Running-Fiction, Individualists-Fiction, Sex Role-Fiction, Read Aloud.

GREENFIELD, Eloise. Rosa Parks; illus by Eric Marlow.   Har-Row 1973, 33 pp.

This book succumbs to the difficulty of writing for children about a subject that needs more explanation. The occasionally condescending tone combined with the Crowell Biography picture book format will keep this otherwise adequate introduction to the civil rights movement from being useful beyond fourth grade. The book should be very useful, however, for third and fourth grade social studies, history or biography units.

Rosa Parks' childhood and her feelings about the special rules for blacks make up the first half of the book. The second half is devoted to Rosa's act of defiance (refusing to give up her seat on a bus to a white man) and the repercussions of that act. Crowell Biography series.

Interest Level: 2-4. Reading Level 2.2. Further Search Topics: Blacks-Biography, Biography, Prejudice, Civil Rights, Women-Biography, Courage.

GREENFIELD, Eloise. Talk about a family; illus by James Calvin.   Lippincott 1978, 60 pp.

Genny, Kim, and Mac knew something was wrong between their parents, and fully expected that their older brother Larry would be able to fix everything when he came home from the army. But even Larry's welcome home party was almost ruined by their parents' fighting and Kim's reaction. That night, as she listened to Larry and her parents' low voices, Genny was certain that Larry was bringing her parents back together. When her father announced the next morning that he was going to move out, Genny's anger and hurt was directed at Larry. With her friend Mr. Parker's help, Genny finally realized that they were still a family; a family with a new shape, but one that would be able to adjust. A one-theme, realistic and reassuring, short book with good-sized print. Very useful

Interest Level: 3-6. Reading Level: 3.1. Further Search Topics: Divorce and Separation-Fiction, Family Problems-Fiction, Brothers and Sisters-Fiction, Best Sellers.

GREENWALD, Sheila. Give us a great big smile, Rosy Cole.   Little 1981, 76 pp.

It was Rosy's turn to be the subject of her uncle's book. He needed to earn money again and Rosy had just turned 10, the age each of her sisters had been when Uncle Ralph wrote *Anitra Dances* and *Pippa Prances* about them. However, Rosy couldn't dance like Anitra or ride horses like Pippa. In fact, Rosy had no talent that was appropriate for a book. She drew well but Uncle Ralph said that wasn't visual enough. Then Rosy's mother and uncle decided that Rosy could be *A Very Little Fiddler.*

Rosy had been taking violin lessons for two years, but only Rosy and her music teacher knew how truly untalented she was. Rosy hated the whole idea of the book at first. But as people began to treat her like a star, she found herself acting like one, until the day she heard her tape of the piece she was to play at the recital. Once again she realized that she could not play the violin and didn't want to go on with the charade. When everyone ignored her wishes, Rosy started to run away. Her route took her through the park where she thought of a brilliant idea. She ran home, changed clothes, picked up her violin, created a sign, and raced back to the park. There, with all the other street musicians Rosy set up her sign and began to play her violin. Her sign asked people to sign a petition if they felt that she should not be encouraged to play the violin anymore. Right away Rosy drew a large crowd. Before long, even her mother was one of the listeners and one of the signers. That was the end of Rosy's musical career and her uncle's book, but both were happier. Rosy went back to being normal and Uncle Ralph found another topic for his next book.

Chapters are long, but should not be a problem. Print is large. Some of the story is actually told in the illustrations, so the reader should be aware of them. Younger children may take the book more seriously than children whose sense of humor includes irony or children who were not as fond of Krementz's *Very Young* series.

Interest Level: 4-6. Reading Level: 3.1. Further Search Topics: Occupations-Fiction, Humorous Fiction, Family-Fiction, Relatives-Fiction, Talent-Fiction, Photography-Fiction, Everyday Stories.

HALL, Lynn. The mystery of Pony Hollow; illus by Ruth Sanderson.   Garrard 1978, 64 pp.

Sarah investigated strange voices only to find the skeleton of a horse that had died 40 years earlier. She was determined to find out what it was that had killed the horse and why its ghost was uneasy.

The mystery element isn't as strong here as most mystery fans would like, but the book will not disappoint many true horse story enthusiasts.

Interest Level: 3-5. Reading Level: 3.2. Further Search Topics: Horses-Fiction, Ghosts-Fiction, Mystery and Detective Stories.

HAMILTON, Virginia. Zeely; illus by Symeon Shimin.   Macmillan 1967, 122 pp.

A beautiful, almost mystical story of a black girl who learns about self-identity and pride from a statuesque neighbor whom Geeder is convinced must be a Watutsi princess. At first by chance and later at an arranged meeting, Zeely (Geeder's neighbor) gently and symbolically speaks to Geeder of her racial origins. She also tells Geeder of a young girl (Zeely as a child), too ignorant of the world around her to be able to recognize reality. It is a quietly moving story that is most likely to find an appreciative audience in the thoughtful, more mature reader.

Interest Level: 5-6. Reading Level: 5.1. Further Search Topics: Africa-Fiction, Royalty-Fiction, Blacks-Fiction, Courage-Fiction, Vacation-Fiction, Country Life-Fiction, Read Aloud.

HARRIS, Robie H. Rosie's double dare; illus by Tony DeLuna.   Knopf 1980, 112 pp.

Rosie wanted to play baseball with the Willard Street Gang, but she couldn't play well enough to play by their rules. She needed what her older brother called "shrimp rules." She couldn't hit a pitched ball, only a grounder; but grounders were "shrimp rules." In desperation Rosie agreed to take a dare that the gang made up. If she actually performed the dare, the gang would let her play with them by her rules.

The gang dared Rosie to sneak into cranky Mr. Quirk's apartment and borrow a set of his false teeth. Because Rosie couldn't find any extra false teeth, she borrowed his wig instead but that didn't satisfy the gang. They only laughed and made up another dare for Rosie. She was to untie Mrs. Samuels' dog and let it run loose. As Rosie untied him, Elmer ran away, Rosie ran off after him. One rainstorm later, Rosie caught up with him in the middle of a Red Sox game at Fenway Park. Rosie's attempt to catch Elmer stopped the game, brought her an interview on TV, and secured her a place on the Willard Street baseball team.

This very light story, made up almost entirely of action and examples of sibling rivalry, should have wide appeal through fifth grade. Beyond that, Rosie's age (almost nine) and childish behavior won't ring true. Capers series.

Interest Level: 2-5. Reading Level: 2.2. Further Search Topics: Baseball-Fiction, Humorous Fiction, Brothers and Sisters-Fiction, Challenges-Fiction, Courage-Fiction, Gangs-Fiction, Everyday Stories.

HEIDE, Florence Parry and Heide, Roxanne. Black magic at Brillstone.   A. Whitman 1981, 126 pp.

Liza is a little older, her romance with Logan has progressed to a kiss, and the book's plot is more complex than earlier Brillstone adventures. Other than those differences, the book follows Heide's standard format. The Brillstone books all center on Liza Webster and Logan Forrest, teenage partners in crime detection, who live in the Brillstone Apartments. The stories are similar enough that one could almost substitute the names Nancy Drew and Ned for Liza and Logan. Both young women are only children who live with their fathers. They are both independent, resourceful, and very concerned that justice be done. The men in their lives play approximately the same roles; their fathers are proud and supportive, but distantly preoccupied with their own business; Logan

and Ned are gallant, boyish, and devoted. Liza and Logan, like Nancy and Ned, are not distinctive characters. Instead, they are shells into which readers who want excitement and adventure can pour themselves. There is no parental interference to worry about. There is plenty of action, some suspense, and real world crime (for Liza: murder, bank robberies, etc.) rather than childish escapades. The books' success is practically guaranteed. Beware, however, of inconsistent reading levels that wander over a year's range.

Logan was first aware of strange occurrences at the Brillstone Apartments when someone entered his apartment late at night. While the person had searched the apartment, he or she had unconsciously whistled a nursery tune. Logan's neighbor, Miss Violet, said the tune reminded her of her deceased nephew. Slowly Logan and Liza realized that someone was trying to trick Miss Violet out of a substantial amount of money she had just inherited. They suspected that Bella Vine, a spiritualist, and an accomplice were trying to convince Miss Violet that her nephew was communicating from the dead and wanted Miss Violet to give her money to Bella. Not until it was almost too late did Liza and Logan realize that Bella was also posing as another possible recipient of the money and was really Miss Violet's nephew's wife. Miss Violet's nephew had only pretended to die in order to collect insurance money. When he and his wife had heard about Miss Violet's large inheritance, they had decided to reappear in order to bilk her out of the money. Brillstone Mystery series.

Interest Level: 5-6. Reading Level: 3.1. Further Search Topics: Mystery and Detective Stories, Occult-Fiction, Crime-Fiction, Ghosts-Fiction, Cats-Fiction, Detectives-Fiction, Inheritance-Fiction.

HEIDE, Florence Parry and Heide, Roxanne. Body in the Brillstone garage.   A. Whitman 1980, 127 pp.

Liza's trip into the apartment house garage late one night made her even more frightened of that dark area than she had been. As she bent to pick up an envelope she thought someone had dropped, she saw a body lying on the floor of the garage. Because of a jacket he wore, Liza was certain the dead man was Mr. Greening, a neighbor. But when she returned to the garage with the police, the body was gone. The next day Mr. Greening was very much alive. Then Liza began to suspect that Mr. Greening was a murderer, but she didn't know who or where the victim was. It could have been Mr. Feeney, another neighbor, or it might have been a stranger. When Mr. Greening's stolen car was later discovered with the body of the car thief inside, Liza began to suspect that the thief's body was the one she had discovered. When she was told that the thief's name was Sharkey, she was certain Mr. Greening had engineered Sharkey's death. Sharkey was the name used by an angry man who had said he was looking for someone at the Brillstone who owed him something.

About then Liza remembered to look in the envelope she had found in the garage. The envelope revealed a note from Sharkey to Greening stating that Sharkey had proof that Greening was a car thief and that he would keep quiet only if Greening paid him twice the money he was owed. Knowing that without proof, she couldn't convince the police that Greening was a crook, Liza went to get the proof from Sharkey's hiding place in the about-to-be-junked car. Greening followed Liza to see what she knew and made a desperate attempt to kill her when he realized that she knew enough to put him in prison. At the last minute, Logan appeared, accidentally knocked Greening out, and helped Liza prove Greening's guilt to the police.

This is a fast-paced book that should be useful with mystery readers who can handle the jump from 4.1 to an occasional 5.1 reading level. See notes included with *Black Magic at Brillstone* for more information. Brillstone Mystery series.

Interest Level: 4-6. Reading Level: 4.2. Further Search Topics: Mystery and Detective Stories, Murder-Fiction, Running-Fiction, Crime-Fiction, Detectives-Fiction.

HEIDE, Florence Parry and Heide, Roxanne.
Face at the Brillstone window.　A. Whitman 1979, 128 pp.

As Liza drove out of the garage one evening she heard a thump at the side of the car. She jumped out and found that she had accidentally hit Peter Pritchard, an insurance man and a new tenant of the apartment building. Pritchard seemed to be a very nice person who took some interest in Liza, her friends, and the criminal cases Liza's father (a journalist) was investigating. Liza was particularly interested in the case of the one-armed bandit who had been convicted of robbing and shooting a security guard. Against her father's research assistant's wishes she continued to search for evidence that would prove Robin Keck was innocent of the charges. As she interviewed the security guard, Keck's fiancee, his best friend, and the grandmother of a young girl who had had a strong crush on Keck, Liza found hints of his innocence. Young Bridgette's diary, however, held the proof she needed: an alibi. But someone else knew she had the information; someone who didn't want the information made public. Diary in hand, Liza began walking to her father's assistant's house (her father was out of town) when Pritchard offered her a ride. When Pritchard drove off in the wrong direction and then handed her a piece of incriminating evidence (gum), Liza realized she had played right into the real criminal's hands. Liza made a risky escape attempt that ended successfully with Pritchard's capture.

See *Black Magic at Brillstone* for more information about the series. Brillstone Mystery series.

Interest Level: 4-6. Reading Level: 3.2. Further Search Topics: Mystery and Detective Stories, Crime-Fiction, Detectives-Fiction.

HEIDE, Florence Parry and Heide, Roxanne.
Mystery at Southport Cinema; illus by Seymour Fleishman.　A. Whitman 1978, 128 pp.

The Spotlight Club was the name Jay, his sister Cindy, and his friend Dexter gave themselves. Their main interest was solving mysteries and just as in Sobol's Encyclopedia Brown series, Hildick's McGurk Mysteries, and Warner books about the Alden children, mysteries seem to follow them around. Their cases are more intricate and lengthy than Encyclopedia Brown's. They involve more danger than most of McGurk's, and they center on more common themes than the Alden's. The series serves much the same audience, however, as the others. It serves those children who want action, intrigue, and the challenge of a mystery, and who don't care about character development or in-depth motivation. The chapters are 8 to 12 pages long, print size is adequate, and the children are normal enough to make this a very popular series. As an added attraction, reading levels here are fairly consistent.

Thorne prided himself on doing his job well, so when the grocery store he ran for Callie (the owner) was robbed by a bearded stranger, Thorne felt responsible. Thorne ran after the thief but lost him in the darkened Southport Cinema. The Spotlight Club members also tried to track the thief. They figured that he had hidden the bag with the stolen money somewhere in the movie house because no one had been seen leaving with such a bag.

In the janitor's lost and found basket Jay found a wig the thief must have used as a disguise. The children called the wig maker to find out who had ordered it and were directed to a local post office box, Jay and Dexter were surprised to find belonged to the grocery store. Because Thorne picked up the mail each day, he became a prime suspect. In the meantime, Cindy had gone back to the cinema to look for the money. In the dark she had scuffled with someone else looking for the money and had given the person a deep scratch on the face.

At the same time that Thorne decided to pay Callie back for the stolen money, the Club members decided to tell Callie their suspicions about him. As Thorne handed his veterinary school savings to Callie, Cindy took a close enough look at Callie's face to see a new scratch and accused her of being the thief. Callie had so wanted Thorne to run the store instead of going to school, and had needed money so intensely, that she had stolen from her own business. The ending is weak but the rest of the book will hold reader interest. Spotlight Club Mystery series.

Interest Level: 3-5. Reading Level: 3.1. Further Search Topics: Mystery and Detective Stories, Gangs-Fiction, Crime-Fiction, Detectives-Fiction, Brothers and Sisters-Fiction.

HEIDE, Florence Parry and Heide, Roxanne.
Mystery of the forgotten island; illus by Seymour Fleishman.　A. Whitman 1980, 127 pp.

On a small island, unmarked on the map, the Spotlight Club members found old Mr. Whitson, who claimed that he was being kept prisoner by his granddaughter Lorrie and her husband John. Lorrie and John had told him he was being kept in the yard for his own good, so that he wouldn't wander off and get hurt or lost. They had also told him that he should will the island to them so that his daughter Cassie couldn't sell the island to a resort company for development. He was going to be forced to sign such a will unless he could get the children to help him smuggle a new will to his lawyer. Mr. Whitson wasn't convinced that Cassie wanted to sell the island, but he couldn't get in touch with her and he hadn'd had a letter from her in many months.

As the children went to secretly meet Mr. Whitson and mail his new will, they discovered that their trusted friend Guy was attempting to blackmail Lorrie and John into giving him some of the money from the sale of the island. He had evidence that Lorrie and John, not Cassie, wanted to sell the island and were tricking Mr. Whitson into signing a will in their favor. In a daring move, the children were able to free Mr. Whitson and isolate all three of the thieves so that the police could capture them.

This book involves a somewhat more complicated plot and slightly less familiar ingredients than most other Spotlight Club mysteries. One should progress to rather than begin the series with this title. Spotlight Club Mystery series.

Interest Level: 4-6. Reading Level: 3.1. Further Search Topics: Mystery and Detective Stories, Inheritance-Fiction, Gangs-Fiction, Kidnapping-Fiction, Brothers and Sisters-Fiction, Aging-Fiction, Detectives-Fiction.

HEIDE, Florence Parry and Heide, Roxanne.
Mystery of the melting snowman; illus by Seymour Fleishman.   A. Whitman 1974, 128 pp.

Hidden inside of a snowman, the Spotlight Club found what they believed was a stolen iron statue of a dog. In order to try to catch the thief, the children hid the statue again and watched to see who came to look for it. Eventually they determined that the thief or thieves was either Tom and Jenny, the amenable young couple who were helping Mrs. Wellington sell her house or Alex, the man who seemed to be a detective. After a frightening episode in which Alex almost captured Cindy, the dog, and a cache of Mrs. Wellington's diamonds (hidden in a secret compartment to which the dog held the key), Cindy managed to lock Alex in a closet long enough to enable Jay and Dexter to alert Mrs. Wellington to what was happening. The case was closed as Mrs. Wellington revealed Alex to be her greedy, young nephew, whom she had indulged once too often, but would not indulge again.

See *Mystery at Southport Cinema* for series information. Spotlight Club Mystery series.

Interest Level: 3-5. Reading Level: 2.2. Further Search Topics: Mystery and Detective Stories, Gangs-Fiction, Crime-Fiction, Brothers and Sisters-Fiction, Detectives-Fiction, Inheritance-Fiction.

HEIDE, Florence Parry and Heide, Roxanne.
Mystery of the midnight message; illus by Seymour Fleishman.   A. Whitman 1977, 128 pp.

The challenge to the Spotlight Club this time was to stop a crime before it happened. Jay and his sister Cindy were on a bus trip home when a blizzard forced the bus to stop at a motel for the night. Jay answered the room telephone late that night and heard a woman's strange and stern instructions. The instructions were to say nothing, to look in the desk drawer for directions, to expect that Bee had the other half of the instructions, and to be at the place at 8:00 the next evening. The envelope, which Jay and Cindy found, showed the location of and half the combination to someone's bedroom safe.

Early the next morning, the children found themselves fleeing in terror from the evil Scull, the man who was supposed to have received the message. Scull pursued them as they escaped in a friendly salesman's car, caught them and locked them into a cold barn without jackets. When the two were finally back on the road and reunited with Dexter and his sister Anne, they had only a few hours and fewer clues to help them find Woodvale and Jeremiah Gibbon, the intended victim.

Despite difficult driving conditions in the snow, Anne managed to get the children to their destination a few minutes before the thieves arrived. Anne and Jeremiah's secretary left the house together to get the police while the Spotlight Club members and Mr. Gibbon hid near the safe. A few tense minutes later, the case was closed; Mr. Gibbons' money was safe, the ringleader had been named (Mr. Gibbon's doctor), and the thieves had been caught.

See *Mystery at Southport Cinema* for series information. Spotlight Club Mystery series.

Interest Level: 3-5. Reading Level: 3.1. Further Search Topics: Mystery and Detective Stories, Crime-Fiction, Snow-Fiction, Disasters-Fiction, Gangs-Fiction, Brothers and Sisters-Fiction, Detectives-Fiction.

HEIDE, Florence Parry and Heide, Roxanne.
Mystery of the mummy's mask; illus by Seymour Fleishman.   A. Whitman 1979, 127 pp.

The Spotlight Club published a neighborhood newspaper. Just as the club was about to take the fourth issue to the printer, Jay discovered an ancient mummy mask hidden near Mr. Pruitt's house. Mr. Pruitt was intrigued by the discovery (he worked at the nearby museum) and he took the mask from Jay, but agreed that Jay could write about the mask for the paper. At about the same time, Dexter discovered that an old, abandoned house was being used. When the printer's office was broken into that night and only their newspaper was stolen, the three children began to suspect that something strange was going on at the abandoned house.

Dexter rode back to the house alone and was captured by Hank, one of three thieves hiding out there. Figuring that they never would have missed one item, Hank had taken the mask from the cache of goods that the other two had stolen. When he overheard Jay's conversation with Mr. Pruitt, Hank realized that his partners would find out what he had done if they ever read the newspaper article. To avoid being discovered, Hank broke into the printer's and stole the paste-up of the paper. In order to keep Dexter from escaping, Hank tied him up and placed him in a shipping crate. When he didn't return as soon as expected, Jay and Cindy realized that Dexter was in trouble, so they went out to the house to search for him. As the three escaped, Dexter and Cindy slashed the thieves' truck's tires, and Jay ran to phone for the police. After several nervous moments in which Cindy and Dexter thought Jay might not get back before they were caught, Jay finally brought the police, who captured all three thieves.

See *Mystery at Southport Cinema* for more information. Spotlight Club Mystery series.

Interest Level: 3-5. Reading Level: 3.1. Further Search Topics: Mystery and Detective Stories, Crime-Fiction, Egypt-Fiction, Archaeology-Fiction, Antiquities-Fiction, Journalism-Fiction, Gangs-Fiction, Brothers and Sisters-Fiction, Detectives-Fiction.

HEIDE, Florence Parry and Van Clief, Sylvia Worth.
The mystery of the silver tag; illus by Seymour Fleishman.   A. Whitman 1972, 127 pp.

Jay's paper route took him to one house that he wished he could avoid. It was grumpy, old Mr. Pendleton's house that Jay hated. One rainy day he spotted what he later realized was a prize Angora cat hiding on Mr. Pendleton's porch. When the cat was reported lost in that night's paper, Jay and the other members of the Spotlight Club decided to try to return the cat to its owner, Miss Horton. Their attempts to get the cat back from Mr. Pendleton meant that they had to spy on him, to sneak into his garage, and to spend the night in a treehouse overlooking his house. They were afraid that they had failed when they saw Mr. Pendleton leave with the cat. Determined to be the ones to tell Miss Horton of their failure, they went to her apartment and found Mr. Pendleton already there. Mr. Pendleton was a famous animal photographer who, upon finding the cat, had asked Miss Horton if he could photograph him. The children, thinking only that Mr. Pendleton was a mad scientist who kidnapped cats, had jumped to all the wrong conclusions, but ended with a mystery solved, new friends, and their first lesson in being detectives.

See entry with *Mystery at Southport Cinema* for series information. Spotlight Club Mystery series.

Interest Level: 3-5. Reading Level: 2.2. Further Search Topics: Mystery and Detective Stories, Brothers and Sisters-Fiction, Gangs-Fiction, Cats-Fiction, Loners-Fiction, Detectives-Fiction, Photography-Fiction, Kidnapping-Fiction.

HEIDE, Florence Parry and Heide, Roxanne.
Mystery of the vanishing visitor; illus by Seymour Fleishman.   A. Whitman 1975, 128 pp.

Cindy was hired to take care of Mrs. Widget's house, animals, and plants for a weekend. That same weekend, someone tried to find and steal something from Mrs. Widget's overcrowded house. She had very few empty spaces in her house, so it was not a surprise that the thief wasn't able to find the object of his or her search. The three Spotlight Club members were determined to figure out not only who was the thief, but also what it was that the thief, wanted. Their prime suspects included the very nasty Bertha Beaker and the charming Charley Capp.

After spending a night in Mrs. Widget's house trying to, and almost succeeding in catching the thief, the children were surprised by an early morning visit from Mr. Capp. Mr. Capp was nearly able to steal away with a painting that hid a great deal of money before Cindy figured out that he was the thief. Even after Mr. Capp had been caught, he charmed his way out of any punishment and left before anyone had second thoughts.

See entry for *Mystery at Southport Cinema* for series information. Spotlight Club Mystery series.

Interest Level: 3-5. Reading Level: 2.2. Further Search Topics: Mystery and Detective Stories, Brothers and Sisters-Fiction, Gangs-Fiction, Crime-Fiction, Antiquities-Fiction, Detectives-Fiction.

HEIDE, Roxanne, jt. auth., see Heide, Florence Parry.

HILDICK, Edmund W. The case of the bashful bank robber; illus by Lisl Weil.   Macmillan 1981, 138 pp.

The McGurk Organization is a crime fighting detective agency. Led by Jack McGurk's strong ego, they had taken on many a seemingly impossible task and had always been successful. Never before, however, had they tried to protect the seven banks in town from being robbed. The five children's first idea was to regularly patrol each bank and watch for likely looking get-away cars. When that plan only led to a nasty confrontation with their new junior high school principal, they decided to try something else. Their second plan, to photograph all suspicious looking people near the banks, didn't fare much better than their first idea. Then, without knowing it, they found themselves holding the key to solving a real bank robbery. Before they realized its importance, they had literally given away the vital clue. Using only their own memories, powers of observation, and cleverness, they were still able to solve the crime with only a little help from the FBI.

The "McGurk mysteries" are light, fast-moving, and often humorous. Clues for solving the mysteries are sometimes subtle, but always there in the plot and illustrations for the reader to find. The characters are somewhat flat but still appealing. Joey, who is handy with words and a typewriter, is the narrator of each book. Jack McGurk, dedicated mastermind of all the group's activities is shrewd, a natural leader, and egotistical. Willie has the world's most sensitive nose and an excellent memory for odors. Wanda is the best tree-climber in town and a rational influence on the group. Brains, the newest and youngest member of the group, is a scientific genius, so he runs their crime lab. The books need not be read in chronological order although most have a brief reference to an earlier story. Reading level varies within each book from 2.1 to 3.1. A few books include enough more difficult passages that their average reading level is pushed from 2.2 to 3.1. Interest level in the series, once a reader has started on it, is high. McGurk Mystery series.

Interest Level: 3-6. Reading Level: 2.2. Further Search Topics: Mystery and Detective Stories, Crime-Fiction, Detectives-Fiction, Humorous Fiction, Gangs-Fiction.

HILDICK, Edmund W. The case of the condemned cat; illus by Lisl Weil.   Macmillan 1975, 106 pp.

Ray Williams had a terrible problem when he begged the McGurk Organization for help. His cat Whiskers had been accused of killing a neighbor's pet dove. Ray's mother decided that they couldn't risk upsetting the neighbors anymore and threatened to take Whiskers to the pound unless it could be proven that he was innocent. The Organization, needing time, hid Whiskers and told Mrs. Williams that he had run away. While Whiskers was safely hidden, the group interviewed all the neighbors, surveyed the scene of the crime, and tried to decide upon the real murderer. When the remains of another bird were found while Whiskers was safely locked away, it looked as if the cat was surely innocent. But then McGurk and his detectives found out that the cat had been sprung. It wasn't until they went back over all the information they had gathered that McGurk realized who was the real culprit. The only step left was to trick old Gramp Martin (the neighborhood grouch) into confessing.

See *The Case of the Bashful Bank Robber* for series information. McGurk Mystery series.

Interest Level: 3-6. Reading Level: 2.2. Further Search Topics: Mystery and Detective Stories, Cats-Fiction, Detectives-Fiction, Humorous Fiction, Gangs-Fiction, Pets-Fiction.

HILDICK, Edmund W. The case of the four flying fingers; illus by Lisl Weil.   Macmillan 1981, 138 pp.

At first the four young strangers who were knocking over garbage cans had been merely a neighborhood nuisance. Later McGurk and his fellow detectives began to suspect that they were involved in the rash of break-ins and burglaries in the city. The Organization didn't think the "garbage gang" was actually committing the robberies, but rather that they were fingering houses for someone else to burglarize (thus their nickname: The Four Flying Fingers). It could be safely assumed by a would-be burglar that where no one picked up the spilled garbage, no one was home. It was the Organization's job to find the Thumb who was the mastermind behind the plot. When they caught up with the Fingers, McGurk and crew found out that the Flying Fingers hadn't realized what they were doing; only that a blonde lady in a camper was paying them a nickel for every driveway they left strewn with garbage. It didn't take long for the Organization to track down the woman and her accomplice. But, in one of their less intelligent moves, they played right into her hands and soon found themselves being transported out of town in her camper. When they tried to call to passing cars for help, no one took them seriously. It wasn't until Brains, bound and gagged to appear authentic, used a flashlight and Morse code to signal for help that anyone paid any attention to them. A police car finally stopped the camper for speeding apd after some clever arguments McGurk and his friends were able to convince the police that Lady Thumb was a thief.

This title is just as enjoyable as the best of the other books in the series, more exciting and universal in appeal than most, and equally humorous. It's only drawback is a very inconsistent reading level (from 2.1 to 4.1) that will discourage a reader new to McGurk. Established fans will be able to tolerate the range. McGurk Mystery series.

Interest Level: 3-6. Reading Level: 3.1. Further Search Topics: Mystery and Detective Stories, Detectives-Fiction, Humorous Fiction, Crime-Fiction, Gangs-Fiction.

HILDICK, Edmund W. The case of the invisible dog; illus by Lisl Weil. Macmillan 1977, 101 pp.

Brains Bellingham, a nine-year-old scientific genius, interrupted the McGurk Organization's Annual Picnic with an invisible dog. It was only a short time before McGurk and his friends were convinced that Brains' discovery of how to make things invisible was the greatest event since putting a man on the moon. Although they had always scorned the idea of including anyone else in the Organization, they decided to persuade Brains to join. But, before the day was over, they discovered not only that they had been duped, but exactly how Brains had made the impossible seem real. The Organization took its revenge by using Brain's own trick to make him confess. When Brains began laughing at how well his trick had been used in reverse, McGurk admitted how impressed they all had been by Brain's clever thinking. The outcome of their discussion was that Brains was invited, a second time, to become a member of the McGurk Organization.

See *The Case of the Bashful Bank Robber* for series information. McGurk Mystery series.

Interest Level: 3-6. Reading Level: 3.1. Further Search Topics: Mystery and Detective Stories, Detectives-Fiction, Gangs-Fiction, Dogs-Fiction, Supernatural-Fiction, Humorous Fiction, Jealousy-Fiction.

HILDICK, Edmund W. The case of the phantom frog; illus by Lisl Weil. Macmillan 1979, 121 pp.

The McGurk Organization would not, under ordinary circumstances, have agreed to babysit for seven-year-old Bela, but there was an unusual twist to Bela's case. Bela's aunt, who asked them to babysit while she worked in her sculpture studio, had heard the eerie sounds of a VERY large frog coming from Bela's room. At first it appeared to the group that Bela actually turned into a frog at night, a werefrog. But, upon investigation they found a very clever, very lonely, and very unhappy young boy who had invented the phantom because he was afraid that his aunt would make him give up his pet frog.

See *The Case of the Bashful Bank Robber* for series information. McGurk Mystery series.

Interest Level: 3-5. Reading Level: 3.1. Further Search Topics: Mystery and Detective Stories, Gangs-Fiction, Frogs-Fiction, Supernatural-Fiction, Transformations-Fiction, Detectives-Fiction, Babysitting-Fiction, Humorous Fiction, Occupations-Fiction.

HILDICK, Edmund W. The case of the secret scribbler; illus by Lisl Weil. Macmillan 1978, 106 pp.

Joey's discovery in a library book of a scrap of paper with part of a letter and a strange diagram on it led the McGurk Organization on a lively chase. Brains identified the diagram as that of a widely-used security system. The part of the letter that they could read told the group that there was a burglary being planned for the approaching weekend, but the youngsters knew the police would never take them seriously until they had much more evidence. By researching local alarm systems, determining who bought the unusual paper, and comparing handwriting samples, the detectives were able to convince the police of what was about to happen. In gratitude, the police loaned the Organization a police monitor so that they could listen as the thieves were caught. To all but McGurk it seemed like the perfect way to end the case: he tried to sneak into the midst of the capture, but only succeeded in getting himself in real trouble.

See *The Case of the Bashful Bank Robber* for series information. McGurk Mystery series.

Interest Level: 3-6. Reading Level: 2.2. Further Search Topics: Mystery and Detective Stories, Crime-Fiction, Gangs-Fiction, Nonverbal Communication-Fiction, Humorous Fiction, Detectives-Fiction.

HILDICK, Edmund W. The case of the snowbound spy; illus by Lisl Weil. Macmillan 1980, 132 pp.

One snowy morning McGurk called the five members of his organization together to decipher a code. The code was part of a message from someone who wanted to hire them and would pay $5.00 a day. When they broke the code and met their employer, Mr. Fitch, he gave the group another code as part of their assignment. The second code told them where to deliver a small package that Mr. Fitch gave them. They were to pick up another coded message at the same place. After three pick-ups and drops they would be finished and Mr. Fitch, an ex-government spy, would have proved he was still a trustworthy and capable person to an ex-colleague with whom he wanted to work on a book. It seemed like just the challenging kind of assignment the McGurk Organization looked for. As they worked, however, it began to look more and more as if they were being used for illegal business. While Joey and McGurk staked out the next drop-off spot, Willie, Brains and Wanda pretended to Mr. Fitch to be unsuspecting. By working quickly and cleverly and by alerting the police, the McGurk gang uncovered and stopped two industrial spies who were stealing secret information about a new copying machine.

See *The Case of the Bashful Bank Robber* for series information. McGurk Mystery series.

Interest Level: 3-6. Reading Level: 3.1. Further Search Topics: Mystery and Detective Stories, Spies-Fiction, Detectives-Fiction, Gangs-Fiction, Humorous Fiction, Nonverbal Communication-Fiction, Crime-Fiction.

HILDICK, Edmund W. The case of the treetop treasure; illus by Lisl Weil. Macmillan 1980, 121 pp.

As Wanda rescued a cat she discovered a stash of odd items tucked into a hollow high up in a tree. On top of the assortment was a sign that said simply "Beware!" The McGurk Organization suspected a thief was using the tree as a place to hide stolen goods, but until an antique silver bowl was added nothing that had been placed there was worth stealing. Shortly afterwards Wanda found out from the police that she was the prime suspect in the theft of the bowl. Brains devised a complicated system for determining the real thief while McGurk worked more from intuition. Nevertheless, it wasn't long before they both arrived at the same conclusion. The culprit was the gang's long-time enemy Sandra Ennis. Then it was just a simple matter of finding the right way to persuade Sandra to confess and apologize to her victims.

See *The Case of the Bashful Bank Robber* for series information. McGurk Mystery series.

Interest Level: 3-5. Reading Level: 3.1. Further Search Topics: Mystery and Detective Stories, Crime-Fiction, Gangs-Fiction, Detectives-Fiction, Humorous Fiction.

HILDICK, Edmund W. Deadline for McGurk; illus by Lisl Weil.   Macmillan 1975, 104 pp.

When many of the dolls in the neighborhood began disappearing, their owners went to the McGurk Organization for help. At first McGurk was reluctant to take on such a silly task as recovering lost dolls. But when a ransom note appeared and the Organization was linked to the dolls' safety, McGurk's reluctance vanished. The note stated that if, in a written public notice, the members of the Organization did not admit that they were no good, the dolls were doomed. McGurk's pride would never have allowed him to write such a notice. As the deadline approached, the group plotted a daring move designed to uncover the doll thief. The plan depended on Willie's super-sensitive nose, a particular perfume dabbed on a stolen doll, and the curiosity of the thief. Success came only minutes before the hour of doom. Once again Sandra Ennis was the culprit.

See *The Case of the Bashful Bank Robber* for series information. McGurk Mystery series.

Interest Level: 3-5. Reading Level: 2.2. Further Search Topics: Dolls-Fiction, Mystery and Detective Stories, Detectives-Fiction, Humorous Fiction, Gangs-Fiction, Jealousy-Fiction.

HILDICK, Edmund W. The great rabbit rip-off; illus by Lisl Weil.   Macmillan 1976, 101 pp.

Why would anyone want to put red paint on all of the clay lawn rabbits in town? That was the first and easier of the mysteries the McGurk Organization had to solve. The bigger mystery was who would then steal them all and why? Almost everyone in town had purchased a rabbit to help a charity drive. Donny Towers a local social worker had thought of the idea. Donny, his fiancee, Joanne, and two reformed thieves, Sam and Ferdie, had made enough rabbits for everyone. When the rabbits disappeared, the Organization began to suspect, among others, Sam and Ferdie. Then when Donny replaced each one almost immediately with rabbits smelling of paint remover, the group began to think Donny might have been involved. It was Wanda's sharp eyes that revealed Donny's motive. Joanne's engagement ring had been accidentally molded into one of the rabbits and Donny had retrieved the rabbits to find the ring. Knowing he couldn't return the paint stained rabbits without raising suspicion, Donny had removed the red paint and told everyone that he was simply replacing the stolen rabbits with new ones.

See *Case of the Bashful Bank Robber* for series information. McGurk Mystery series.

Interest Level: 3-5. Reading Level: 2.2. Further Search Topics: Mystery and Detective Stories, Detectives-Fiction, Gangs-Fiction, Rabbits-Fiction, Crime-Fiction, Humorous Fiction.

HINTON, Susan E. The outsiders.   Viking Pr. 1967, 188 pp.

When she wrote this book Susan Hinton was only 17 years old, but she had the sensitivity of someone much older. She wrote a taut story of the rivalry between two city gangs; the Socs (the rich socialites) and the Greasers (poor kids from the wrong side of town) that is more than anything a plea for understanding and tolerance. Seen through the eyes of Ponyboy (a very bright, 14-year-old Greaser), the rivalry brought on violence and an accidental killing that forced Pony and his friend Johnny to flee for their lives. Dallas, the meanest and most dangerous of the Greasers, provided them with shelter, food for a week, and a gun. At the end of that week, Johnny decided that they should turn themselves in to the police. But before they could do that, their hideout (an old church) burned in a fire which threatened the lives of four children who had been playing there. In trying to rescue the children, Johnny, Pony, and Dallas were injured; Johnny was severely burned and probably permanently crippled. A vengeance rumble was held while Johnny lay in the hospital, but the Greasers' victory was empty when Johnny died. He had been the one member of the gang whom they all loved and who had most needed them. Dallas went to pieces: he robbed a store and set himself up to be killed by the police. He had nothing left to live for after Johnny's death. Pony found support and security with his brothers (their parents were dead) and, in a note from Johnny, some hope for the future.

Hinton speaks most often through Pony (his depth of understanding of the people around him is very impressive), but through Johnny and two of the Socs as well, Randy and Cherry. Her message is clear, but at no time does she fail to maintain believable characters in a compelling plot.

Although the book looks forbidding with its 188 pages of unrelenting small print, it is an exciting story, full of adventure, realism, and room for thought. Perhaps the best way to introduce this book is to read a fair portion of it aloud. Now a motion picture too.

Interest Level: 6+ Reading Level: 5.1. Further Search Topics: Crime-Fiction, Gangs-Fiction, Murder-Fiction, Read Aloud, Friendship-Fiction, Juvenile Delinquency-Fiction, Best Sellers, City Life-Fiction, Brothers and Sisters-Fiction, Orphans-Fiction, Runaways-Fiction, Troublemakers-Fiction, Poverty-Fiction.

HOLLAND, John. The way it is.   HarBraceJ 1969, 87 pp.

For 15 boys living in a run-down area of Brooklyn, school became interesting when they were assigned to photograph whatever was meaningful to them in their neighborhood. The results, described in their own words, were developed into this fascinating documentary which is at the same time a spontaneous glimpse of the boys themselves. The book should be of particular interest to older urban children. Print slightly on the small side. Has recently gone out of print, but is worth looking for.

Interest Level: 4-6. Reading Level: 3.2. Further Search Topics: Best Sellers, City Life, Photography, Poverty, Academic Problems.

HORNBLOW, Arthur, jt. auth., see Hornblow, Leonora

HORNBLOW, Leonora and Hornblow, Arthur.

Prehistoric monsters did the strangest things; illus by Michael K. Frith.   Random 1974, 65 pp.

A basic survey of an era and its animal life forms. Animals from the earliest water creatures through Diplocaulus, Ichthyosaurs, dinosaurs (about 12 varieties) and early mammals (including the Beast of Baluchistan) to the appearance of man are introduced and illustrated. It is a brief but meaty treatment of a very popular subject that should be especially useful with second and third grade children. Reader format.

Interest Level: 1-3. Reading Level: 2.1. Further Search Topics: Prehistory, Dinosaurs, Evolution, Monsters, Group 2.

HURWITZ, Johanna. Aldo Applesauce; illus by John Wallner.   Morrow 1979, 127 pp.

Aldo Sossi, vegetarian and new kid at school, was immediately dubbed Applesauce for obvious reasons. Aldo didn't like his new name. He didn't like being teased either—not the way he was teased at school. Nothing went right for Aldo. His attempts at making friends only ended in disasters (once at a bowling alley and another time at a birthday party). He had been able to start a friendship only with a strange girl who wore a heavy, black fake moustache most of the time. After accidentally nearly ruining that friendship too, Aldo not only learned why DeDe wore the moustache, but helped her learn to live without it. DeDe, in turn, helped Aldo take himself less seriously and find more friends.

This is a comfortable, humorous story of two fourth grade children learning to be themselves. The vocabulary is occasionally difficult, but sentence length is almost always short.

Interest Level: 3-5. Reading Level: 3.1. Further Search Topics: Moving, Household-Fiction, Humorous Fiction, School Stories, Friendship-Fiction, Divorce and Separation-Fiction, Vegetarians-Fiction, Individualists-Fiction, Everyday Stories.

HURWITZ, Johanna. Aldo Ice Cream; illus by John Wallner.   Morrow 1981, 124 pp.

Aldo got his newest nickname (Ice Cream) from his friend DeDe when she heard that Aldo not only wanted to try every flavor of ice cream at the local store, but wanted to buy an ice cream freezer for his sister's birthday as well. Aldo decided his summer project would be to earn enough money for the freezer, but he soon found out that there were very few ways a nine-year-old boy could earn $49.95. In the meantime, he helped his mother deliver food for a Meals-On-Wheels project, learned to swim, found out about fish from Mr. Puccini, and shared his cat with Mrs. Nardo. As the summer came to an end he saw one last opportunity to earn enough money for the ice cream maker. A local shoe store offered a new pair of sneakers to the child who owned the most worn out pair. Aldo convinced his mother that if he won the sneakers, she should pay him the money she would otherwise have had to spend on his new sneakers. Aldo set about making sure that his already well-worn sneakers were the most dilapidated in town. A few days before the sneaker contest the hardware store lowered the price on the ice cream freezer to a point where Aldo could afford it if he won the sneakers. When Aldo did win, just as he knew he would, he and his mother bought the very last freezer in the store.

It is not as well-constructed a story as *Aldo Applesauce*, but for established Aldo fans, or those who want quiet, reassuring fiction, this is a usable title.

Interest Level: 3-4. Reading Level: 3.1. Further Search Topics: Humorous Fiction, Brothers and Sisters-Fiction, Vacation-Fiction, Occupations-Fiction, Everyday Stories, Aging-Fiction, Family-Fiction, Contests-Fiction.

HURWITZ, Johanna. Baseball fever; illus by Ray Cruz.   Morrow 1981, 128 pp.

Only baseball nuts need even consider this title, but for the die-hard baseball fan this is perfect. Much to his father's disgust, Ezra had only one interest in life. Baseball was almost all Ezra ever thought of. His father was a German-born intellectual who couldn't understand how anyone could waste so much time watching men hit a ball with a stick. He wanted Ezra to become interested in history and chess. Ezra had no interest in history except baseball history. He hated chess, not just because he always lost, but because his father continually told him how badly he played. Predictably they reach a compromise; each learns to appreciate the other's passion, but not before everyone in the family and a few people outside the family have become involved in a series of warmly humorous incidents. Includes much baseball information.

Interest Level: 3-6. Reading Level: 3.1. Further Search Topics: Baseball-Fiction, Family Problems-Fiction, Humorous Fiction.

HURWITZ, Johanna. The law of gravity; illus by Ingrid Fetz.   Morrow 1978, 192 pp.

The summer between fifth and sixth grades looked very unexciting to Margot. Her best friends were both going away for the whole summer and her father, a musician, was going to be on tour for most of the summer. Margot's very overweight mother had sworn never to go downstairs from their fifth floor walk-up apartment. Unless Margot chose to stay upstairs too, she was sure she would have a very lonely vacation. In addition, she had to work on a summer project for school. The project she finally chose was to get her mother downstairs after nine years of staying upstairs. In search of help she went to the local library where she met Bernie. Bernie was only a year older than Margot, but he seemed to know the most interesting things about the city. He showed her places Margot had never heard of before, he taught her to play chess, backgammon, and even to ride a bicycle. He was so full of fascinating ideas and information that Margot had no chance to be bored or lonely. Best of all, he even tried to help Margot with her project. None of their ideas worked, however, until Margot pretended to run away and scared her mother into going downstairs. Only then did Margot realize that she loved her mother whether or not she stayed on the fifth floor and that she couldn't simply force her mother or anyone else to change to suit her own fancy.

The book is a warm, understanding, slightly humorous treatment of the fairly common wish to change someone else. Although not many readers are likely to share Margot's exact problem, most will recognize her feelings. The book is also a virtual Chamber of Commerce advertisement for urban living. One of its other charms is its picture of a non-competitive, open, real friendship between an 11-year-old girl and a 12-year-old boy. The only drawback to the book is its inconsistent reading level which varies from 4.1 to 5.1 with a rare leap to 5.2.

Interest Level: 4-6. Reading Level: 4.2. Further Search Topics: Vacation-Fiction, Friendship-Fiction, Loners-Fiction, City Life-Fiction, Individualists-Fiction, Courage-Fiction, New York City-Fiction, Humorous Fiction, Family-Fiction, Challenges-Fiction, Weight-Fiction, Everyday Stories, Best Sellers.

HURWITZ, Johanna. Once I was a plum tree; illus by Ingrid Fetz.   Morrow 1980, 160 pp.

Ten-year-old Gerry Flam knew nothing about her religion except that she was Jewish. Her parents didn't practice their religion and only superficially observed some of the holidays. As they told Gerry, their reason was that they were assimilated Americans. In fact, they seemed to practice as many Christian as Jewish holidays. All Gerry's friends and neighbors were

Catholic, so Gerry had very little chance to learn about Judaism or the prejudice to which Jews were still being subjected in 1947 in the Bronx. A Jewish family moved into the apartment building next door, and Gerry's quiet curiosity was stimulated. From the Wulfs, Gerry began to learn about Judaism, World War II, and Hitler. As her pride in her heritage grew, Gerry also felt prejudice for the first time. After celebrating her first Passover Seder, Gerry found that despite the problems, she was truly happy to be Jewish.

Much like Chaikin's *I Should Worry, I Should Care* in tone and mood. Will be useful where there is already an interest in Judaism.

Interest Level: 3-5. Reading Level: 3.1. Further Search Topics: Religion-Fiction, Family-Fiction, Jews-Fiction, City Life-Fiction, Children-Growth-Fiction, Prejudice-Fiction.

JACKSON, Beulah F, jt. auth., see Dolch, Edward W.

JORDAN, June. Fannie Lou Hamer; illus by Albert Williams.   Har-Row 1972, 41 pp.

In 1917, Fannie Lou Hamer was the last of 20 children born to a fearless black woman. Fannie and her family grew up working on a white man's cotton plantation. Although they were kept poor and hungry by the plantation owner and the field boss, Fannie Lou grew up in her mother's image—unafraid of white people and unhappy with the poor treatment of blacks that she saw all around her. In 1962, when most other blacks in Mississippi where afraid of the consequences, Fannie registered to vote. After both she and her husband lost their jobs and their home, and after she was beaten in a Mississippi jail, Fannie Lou Hamer drew national attention to her fight for blacks' civil rights. She spoke all over the country, helped to form a new political party, and raised money to help poor people. That money was what started the 640 acre Freedom Farm Cooperative that provided work and food for more than 5,000 people. It was Mrs. Hamer's dream to see poor people work together to feed themselves rather than to accept food from others. She made her dream come true.

Another competent entry in the Crowell Biography series. Only its picture book format keeps this book from being useful through sixth grade.

Interest Level: 3-5. Reading Level: 3.2. Further Search Topics: Biography, Blacks-Biography, Civil Rights, Poverty, Women-Biography.

KALB, Jonah. The easy hockey book; illus by Bill Morrison.   HM 1977, 64 pp.

This book is exactly what the title indicates; an easy-read introduction to the sport of hockey. It does not teach one how to skate, but in a logical non-sexist manner it does carefully and thoroughly teach the rules, techniques, and skills of hockey. Common mistakes are anticipated in each section. Chapter summaries make an already serviceable text even more useful. It could have been even better with an index.

Interest Level: 2-6. Reading Level: 2.2. Further Search Topics: Hockey.

KELLEY, Sally. Trouble with explosives.   Bradbury 1976, 117 pp.

Polly Banks stuttered very badly. She wanted to stop but she couldn't. Moving, entering a new school, and facing a mean teacher who seemed in need of psychiatric help, all made Polly's stuttering worse. When Sis, Polly's new friend, rose to Polly's defense in one confrontation too many with Miss Patterson, the teacher took cruel revenge. Polly's desire to help Sis, her need to do something about her stuttering, and an understanding psychiatrist, all helped Polly learn to help herself with her speech problem. At the same time, she began to understand and have confidence in herself and her family.

Another "problem book" that older elementary school readers seem to crave. Polly and Sis are both very sympathetic characters who bring to life many of the uncertainties of growing up. Print and line spacing of only average size but otherwise a good choice.

Interest Level: 4-6. Reading Level: 3.2. Further Search Topics: Academic Problems-Fiction, Stuttering-Fiction, Psychiatrists-Fiction, School Stories, Mental Illness-Fiction, Troublemakers-Fiction, Courage-Fiction, Physically Handicapped-Fiction, Children-Growth-Fiction, Moving, Household-Fiction.

KESSLER, Leonard. Last one in is a rotten egg. Har-Row 1969, 64 pp.

Willie and Bobby could swim, but Freddy could not. After all three went to the local swimming pool and Freddy was pushed into the water by two older bullies, he was scared to try swimming again. Finally, a sympathetic lifeguard gave Freddy lessons. After much practice, Freddy became competent and confident enough to swim in the deep water and to stand up to the bullies.

A very slight plot designed to reassure new swimmers and provide a few basic rules of swimming. Reader format. A Sports-I-Can-Read-Book.

Interest Level: 1-2. Reading Level: 1.2. Further Search Topics: Courage-Fiction, Swimming-Fiction, Challenges-Fiction, Bullies-Fiction.

KIBBE, Pat. The hocus-pocus dilemma; illus by Dan Jones.   Knopf 1979, 125 pp.

Each chapter of this book is a separate episode in B.J.'s attempt to cultivate her newly-discovered ESP talents (more invented than discovered). The episodes, each of which involves a different member of B.J.'s family, are slightly outlandish, but very funny. Even the dog and the cat become involved. The dog becomes the unwitting target for a skunk. The cat accidentally starts a tape recording of speech habits that sounds like burglars breaking into the house. After nine disasters, B.J. finally concludes that she was being ridiculous to think that she had ESP, but that everyone is allowed to be ridiculous sometimes.

The nine, reasonably short episodes, the moderate size print, the sympathetic characters, and the book's humor, make this a very useful and popular title.

Interest Level: 4-6. Reading Level: 3.1. Further Search Topics: Extra Sensory Perception-Fiction, Humorous Fiction, Family-Fiction, Everyday Stories, Best Sellers, Read Aloud.

KIBBE, Pat. My mother the mayor, maybe; illus by Charles Robinson.   Knopf 1981, 165 pp.

The Pinkertons first appeared in *The Hocus-Pocus Dilemma*, a better introduction to the family than this book. Although this is a satisfactory story, its appeal is somewhat limited by its subject matter. B.J.'s mother's decision to run for town mayor meant that the whole family became involved in the political process. B.J. became her mother's unofficial public relations coordinator, a position Sam Jessup (Mrs. Pinkerton's campaign manager) didn't want to see anyone fill but himself. But because Jessup's ideas seemed suspiciously designed to insure that Mrs. Pinkerton would lose the election, B.J. continued working on her mother's behalf. Almost every day she managed to get her mother's campaign on the front page of the newspaper, although not always in a flattering light. Once B.J. was arrested for breaking into her mother's campaign headquarters. Another day she inadvertently circulated a picture of her mother in a bikini all over town. B.J. and her brothers and sisters illegally campaigned on the high school campus during Homecoming. B.J. even accidentally succeeded in blowing her mother's opponent's wig off in the middle of a campaign appearance. Mrs. Pinkerton finally lost the election, but managed to bring an important issue to light and to stage the closest and most exciting election the town had known in a long time.

Election campaigns and political issues won't lure many new reluctant readers to this book, but those youngsters who have enjoyed the Pinkerton's previous adventures and can understand a simplified version of politics at work will enjoy this humorous tale.

Interest Level: 5-6. Reading Level: 3.1. Further Search Topics: Politics-Fiction, Humorous Fiction, Sex Role-Fiction, Family-Fiction.

KLUGER, Ruth and Mann, Peggy.
The secret ship. Doubleday 1978, 136 pp.

A tense, true story about the secret transportation of hundreds of European Jews to Palestine early in World War II. The transport ship became ice-bound in a Rumanian harbor, the crew mutinied and the passengers threatened to expose their plight to the world. In complete charge of the operation was a 25-year-old woman. The book closes with a summary of the Jews' continuing fight for Israel.

The historical understanding that is necessary in order to really appreciate this excellent book make it best suited to readers no younger than sixth grade.

The paper on which this book is printed is so thin that the print shows through from one page to another and the print at the beginning and the end of the book is italicized. Both factors may distract the reader.

Interest Level: 6+ Reading Level: 3.1. Further Search Topics: World War II, Jews, Women, Sex Role, Israel, Survival, Courage.

KOBRIN, Janet, jt. auth., see Bernstein, Margery.

KREMENTZ, Jill. A very young circus flyer. Knopf 1979, unp (112 pp).

One of a series of five oversized, abundantly photographed views of unusual children. Tato Farfan is part of the Flying Farfans of Ringling Brothers and Barnum and Bailey Circus. He lives in a railroad car on a circus train with his mother, father, and older brother. The whole family performs as trapeze artists and flyers for the circus. Told as if Tato were speaking, this is the story of a fairly normal boy who also happens to be a circus flyer. Practice sessions are difficult, costumes must be readied, and time must be spent helping each other, but there is also time for Tato to watch TV, play with the clowns, play soccer, and just have fun.

In addition to Tato's story, the reader is given a behind-the-scenes tour of the circus right up to and including the performance itself (color photos used for the performance). It is an exciting world that should appeal to almost anyone who has enjoyed the circus.

Interest Level: 2-6. Reading Level: 3.2. Further Search Topics: Circus, Acrobats and Acrobatics, Best Sellers, Talent, Group 2, Gymnastics.

KREMENTZ, Jill. A very young dancer. Knopf 1976, unp (121 pp).

This was the first of the five Very Young books to be written. Like the others, it is large in format and lavishly photographed. Unlike *A Very Young Circus Flyer*, this and the remaining books in the series are written about 10-year-old girls from obviously privileged backgrounds. All the girls are high achievers in their chosen areas but they seem very determined to work still harder until they attain whatever goals they have set for themselves. The books all follow the same formula. The girls introduce themselves, tell about their start in dancing, riding etc., describe their goals, and tell the reader how close they are to those goals. The girls go on to describe their daily routines, the practice, the chores, the hours, and the fun. Then the reader is ushered through approximately a year's worth of the young star's challenges, achievements, and defeats (the latter are only lightly touched upon). Through it all, the child shows enthusiasm, pride, dedication, hard work, and finally, hopes for the future.

Young readers love this series. Despite heavy use of jargon that makes the reading levels somewhat unstable, those already interested in the subject area pour over every word and picture in the books. Perhaps it's partly hero worship, or romance. Maybe it's the inspiration the books provide, but certainly one of the reasons the books are so popular is the vicarious thrill that they provide young enthusiasts.

A Very Young Dancer differs slightly from the formula. Instead of following Stephanie through a year of dance classes at the School of American Ballet, the book concentrates on New York City Ballet Company's production of the Nutcracker, in which Stephanie has a lead role.

Interest Level: 2-5. Reading Level: 3.1. Further Search Topics: Dancing, Ballet, Talent, Best Sellers, Group 2.

KREMENTZ, Jill. A very young gymnast. Knopf 1978, unp (128 pp).

This is Torrence York's story. It includes a team trip to Germany for competition. See notes for *A Very Young Dancer* for more information.

Interest Level: 2-6. Reading Level: 3.2. Further Search Topics: Gymnastics, Talent, Acrobats and Acrobatics, Group 2, Best Sellers.

KREMENTZ, Jill. A very young rider. Knopf 1977, unp (128 pp).

Vivi Malloy is the youngest rider in a family of several other riders. Her greatest dream is to make the Olympic equestrian team. She is progressing towards her goal with daily workouts and about fifteen major horse shows each year. See *A Very Young Dancer* for more extensive notes.

Interest Level: 2-6. Reading Level: 3.2. Further Search Topics: Horses, Riding, Talent, Group 2.

KREMENTZ, Jill. A very young skater. Knopf 1979, unp (103 pp).

Katherine Healy started ice skating because her parents liked to skate and because it was easier for them to take her with them than it was to find a babysitter. From such beginnings, at age three, Katherine progressed to skating in Superskates at Madison Square Garden and ballet lessons at George Balanchine's School of American Ballet. See *A Very Young Dancer* for further explanation.

Interest Level: 2-6. Reading Level: 4.1. Further Search Topics: Ice Skating, Dancing, Ballet, Talent, Group 2, Best Sellers.

LAW, Carol Russell. The case of the Weird Street firebug; illus by Bill Morrison. Knopf 1980, 119 pp.

This is the humorous story of a Nancy Drew-type character who gets involved in a mystery before she is even half finished with her mail-order detective lessons. Steffi wanted very much to be a detective.

When she saw an ad for a local correspondence course, she tracked down the shabby office in a run-down building on Weir Street, and went to visit Jeff Dangerfield of Dangerfield Detective School. Steffi's first lesson, trailing suspects, was a disaster. She tried to pick out suspicious characters at a fire on Weir Street on her way home. The only really suspicious character (Beady Eyes) didn't go anywhere, so Steffi couldn't follow him. Her next attempts were very obvious and only resulted in her own anger and embarrassment. On her way back to seek advice from Dangerfield, Steffi literally ran into Beady Eyes again. She didn't think anything more about him until she saw him a short time later at another fire just down the street from Dangerfield's office. As the fire moved closer to Dangerfield's building, Steffi took desperate measures to try and save her friend. Steffi's efforts were interpreted by Beady Eyes as attempts to indicate that he was an arsonist. By the time Steffi figured out that Beady Eyes really was an arsonist, he had her cornered. A timely entry by the police saved both Steffi and Dangerfield. Steffi's reward for the capture of Beady Eyes was a medal from the police and a partnership with Dangerfield.

A fast-paced story, as well as slightly more original characters than most stories of this genre, make this a likely success with third through sixth grade readers. Capers series.

Interest Level: 3-6. Reading Level: 3.1. Further Search Topics: Mystery and Detective Stories, Humorous Fiction, Fire-Fiction, Detectives-Fiction, Crime-Fiction.

LESIEG, Theo. Wacky Wednesday; illus by George Booth. Beginner 1974, unp (36 pp).

A series of true picture puzzles. A little boy wakes up one Wednesday to find everything around him has gone "wacky." People are missing heads but have extra legs. Cars are being driven from the back seat. Doors are placed in the wrong places. Airplanes fly backwards. At the end of the day everything settles back to normal, but not before readers have had fun finding the numerous "wacky" things on each page.

The story is told in silly rhyme (LeSieg and Seuss are the same person). What is wrong with each picture is not always easily located, making this reader an excellent excerise in observation as well as great fun.

Interest Level: 1-3. Reading Level: 1.2. Further Search Topics: Puzzles, Humorous Fiction, Wit and Humor, Poetry, Best Sellers.

LEVY, Elizabeth. Lizzie lies a lot; illus by John Wallner. Delacorte 1976, 102 pp.

Almost any child can identify with Lizzie. She had found that it was sometimes easier to lie than to tell the truth. Her problem was that she had lost control. It seemed as if almost everything she said was a lie. She told so many lies it became difficult to keep track of them all. Lizzie wasn't even really sure why she lied so much. She knew that she sometimes lied because she thought people would be more apt to like her. Other times she lied to get herself out of trouble or to cover up her feelings when she was hurt or angry. But that didn't explain why she lied all the time. Maybe, as her grandmother said, she was a born liar.

It wasn't until Lizzie got herself caught in the middle of so many lies that she lost her only friend, that she could admit her problem to herself and to her family. After their initial shock had passed, everyone agreed to help Lizzie stop lying. Lizzie took the next step by admitting her lies to her friend Sue.

Levy has brought such an appropriately light touch to a fairly common problem that many children find this story enjoyable. Overlook the book's faults (Lizzie's grandmother is overdrawn and her mother's guilt feelings are unsupported by the story) for the fun and the message young readers get from it.

Interest Level: 3-5. Reading Level: 4.2. Further Search Topics: Honesty-Fiction, Group 2, Friendship-Fiction, Best Sellers, Everyday Stories, Family Problems-Fiction, Grandparents-Fiction, Humorous Fiction.

LEWIS, Thomas P. Hill of fire; illus by Joan Sandin. Har-Row 1971, 63 pp.

A personalized account of the volcano that suddenly erupted in the middle of a farmer's field in Mexico on February 20, 1943. Because the account is written as a story and because of its easy-reader format, the book is most useful only through third grade. An I-Can-Read-History-Book.

Interest Level: 1-3. Reading Level: 2.2. Further Search Topics: Volcanoes, Group 2, Mexico, Disasters, Historical Fiction.

LOW, Joseph. Five men under one umbrella. Macmillan 1975, 64 pp.

Twenty-nine riddles, most of which are fairly familiar. Nothing special in this collection, just an additional choice for the young comedian.

Interest Level: 1-3. Reading Level: 2.1. Further Search Topics: Riddles, Wit and Humor, Group 2.

LOWRY, Lois. Anastasia again!   HM 1981, 145 pp.

This is a sequel that is as funny and well-written as its predecessor. Because its plot involves less common experiences, this book may not enjoy quite the wide-spread success of *Anastasia Krupnik*. However, among those readers who liked their first meeting with Anastasia, this book will find many fans.

Anastasia's parents astounded her when they announced that the family was going to move from their Cambridge, Massachusetts apartment to a house in the suburbs. She didn't like the idea of leaving the apartment, but she *hated* the idea of the suburbs. The only thing that made the move bearable was the house itself. Anastasia had said she would move only if they could find a house with a tower—and they had. After she got over the shock of moving, Anastasia began to enjoy her new home. She met a neighborhood boy who became a special friend, she tried to help her cranky elderly neighbor Mrs. Stein make friends, and she even wrote a short mystery book.

Anastasia is as spunky and original as before. She is a bit precocious, but her precocity is nothing compared to that of her brother. At two-and-a-half years old, he speaks as well as many adults. As we mentioned above, the book will be most appealing to readers who want second helpings of Anastasia's adventures. The print is slightly smaller here than in the first title.

Interest Level: 4-6. Reading Level: 2.2. Further Search Topics: Moving, Household-Fiction, City Life-Fiction, Suburbia-Fiction, Humorous Fiction, Aging-Fiction, Writing-Fiction, Family-Fiction, Everyday Stories.

LOWRY, Lois. Anastasia Krupnik.   HM 1979, 113 pp.

Anastasia Krupnik led a comfortable, relatively happy life until her parents announced that she was not going to be an only child for much longer. After 10 years of enjoying that luxury, Anastasia wasn't at all pleased with the change. Babies immediately went to a prominent, and as far as Anastasia was concerned, permanent place on her list of hates. Anastasia kept two lists: one for things and people she particularly liked, and one list for what she did not like. What went on and off the lists tells much about Anastasia. Anastasia tells the rest in this perceptive, sensitive, and humorous story of growing up and adjusting to a new sibling.

Spacing between lines is slightly too narrow for the rather large print.

Interest Level: 4-6. Reading Level: 3.1. Further Search Topics: Humorous Fiction, Brothers and Sisters-Fiction, Everyday Stories, Jealousy-Fiction, Infants-Fiction, Best Sellers, Children-Growth-Fiction.

MACLACHLAN, Patricia. Arthur, for the very first time; illus by Lloyd Bloom.   Har-Row 1980, 117 pp.

A beautifully written, sensitive yet humorous story of a boy's maturation and growing awareness of the world around him. When Arthur's unhappiness at home is made more intense by the advent of a new baby, he is sent to spend the summer with his older aunt and uncle. Their eccentricities and those of their friends are at first only material for Arthur to write about in his journal. But as the summer progresses he not only learns from them, but also grows from an observer of life to a participant. His final step is helping a large and beloved pig bear her litter in a driving rain storm aided only by his independent, totally untamed young friend Moira.

The print is somewhat small, but spacing between lines is generous.

Interest Level: 4-6. Reading Level: 4.2. Further Search Topics: Read Aloud, Children-Growth-Fiction, Humorous Fiction, Friendship-Fiction, Vacation-Fiction, Relatives-Fiction, Infants-Fiction, Individualists-Fiction, Writing-Fiction, Loners-Fiction, Group 2.

MCNULTY, Faith. Woodchuck; illus by Joan Sandin. Har-Row 64 pp.

There's a great deal of information in this little book. It describes a woodchuck's physical appearance, its habits and behavior, and its life cycle. The treatment is very direct and very honest (two of four young woodchucks are killed before the first year is over). Only an overly repetitive, slightly condescending beginning, and the reader format hamper the book's usefulness beyond grade four. A Science-I-Can-Read-Book.

Interest Level: 1-4. Reading Level: 3.1. Further Search Topics: Nature Study, Groundhogs, Group 2, Woodchucks.

MADIAN, Jon. Beautiful junk: a story of the Watts Towers; photos by Barbara Jacobs, Jr. and Lou Jacobs, Jr.   Little 1968, 44 pp.

Although this book is now out of print; it is well worth trying to find. It is a fictionalized account of a young, angry black boy's encounter with the creator of Los Angeles' unusual Watts Towers. Simon Rodia, a poor tile setter, worked on the towers for 33 years until he was 75 years old. He used only his imagination, discarded materials he found around him, seashells, and sand to build three tall, fantasy-like towers in the middle of a ghetto. He created beauty where others saw only junk.

The book is illustrated with photography that makes the story more vivid and the towers and Rodia's accomplishment more impressive than they would have seemed with drawings. The print is good-sized, spacing is totally adequate. Rodia's life is quickly submarized and an update on the Towers is included at the book's end.

Interest Level: 3-6. Reading Level: 3.1. Further Search Topics: Blacks-Fiction, Read Aloud, Best Sellers, Poverty-Fiction, Rodia, Simon, Architecture, Biography, Aging-Fiction, Watts Towers, California, Poverty.

MADLEE, Dorothy, jt. auth., see Norton, Andre.

MALONE, Mary. Annie Sullivan; illus by Lydia Rosier.   Putnam 1971, 61 pp.

This is a very brief sketch of both Annie Sullivan's life and Helen Keller's life. Their lives were so intertwined that they cannot be separated. But because they are combined in such a short book, neither woman can be treated in much depth. That fact is not as harmful here as it might otherwise be, because even a bare bones description of the life of this extraordinary deaf, blind and mute woman or her near-blind, dedicated teacher, is interesting.

Interest Level: 2-5. Reading Level: 2.2. Further Search Topics: Sullivan, Annie, Keller, Helen, Vision, Biography, Physically Handicapped, Sound, Courage.

MANN, Peggy, jt. auth., see Kluger, Ruth.

MATHIS, Sharon Bell. Ray Charles; illus by George Ford.   Har-Row 1973, 33 pp.

Dominent throughout this biography of Ray Charles is the theme of overcoming adversity. The book is not just a recounting of Ray Charles' music lessons, early schooling, family life, and talent. All of that is included, but it serves to illustrate the manner in which Charles met his troubles. His problems began when he was very young. His brother died, and Ray lost one eye and then the sight in his other eye. His family was poor, but close, and he missed them when he was sent away to a school for the blind. Music was his love, but even that was work, for Charles had to learn to read and write music in Braille. He worked hard at it and eventually could play and arrange music for every instrument in the band.

Determined to be independent, when Charles was orphaned at age 15, he left school and began playing music for a living. The first record he made resulted in a $16 fine because he made it during a musician's union strike. Charles took a series of sideman and nightclub jobs until he finally had enough money to hire seven other musicians to play his music. Today Charles is very wealthy, owns his own record company, has a family, and is considered a great jazz and blues musician. None of his success came easily; only through determination, will power, pride, and hard work.

The book, interesting and serviceable enough for music or biography units, is also designed to set an example for youngsters facing their own problems. It will, of course, be popular with Ray Charles fans, too. Crowell Biography series.

Interest Level: 2-4. Reading Level: 3.1. Further Search Topics: Jazz Music, Music-Biography, Vision, Physically Handicapped, Blacks-Biography, Group 2, Biography, Pianists, Orphans, Challenges, Courage.

MAZER, Harry. The war on Villa Street.   Delacorte 1978, 182 pp.

Willis was a loner and a runner. He was a loner because he didn't want anyone to find out about his alcoholic father. He wasn't quite sure why he ran; perhaps because it was the only time he felt good. When Rabbit Slavin and his friends asked Willis to become part of their gang, he refused. He was flattered and wanted to join, but the gang wanted to meet at his house and Willis couldn't risk that. Then when he agreed to coach the local "retard" for the school's field day, Willis gave the gang the opportunity they wanted to take their revenge on him for turning them down. The gang's hatred for Willis increased still more when he beat their best runner and athlete. In payment, the gang jumped Willis and beat him badly. After he picked himself up, Willis realized that he had at least faced the worst of his fears and survived. Days later when his drunken father humiliated him, Willis realized he had to face that, too. He made peace with himself and the world by deciding he could neither continue to run away from, nor apologize for his father anymore. He was independent and strong.

There is much in this fast-paced book besides the obvious violence and action. It is written with an intuitive feel for a teenager's problems and emotions and is a sensitive portrayal of mature concepts. The print is large, but spacing between the lines should have been slightly increased.

Interest Level: 5-6. Reading Level: 5.1. Further Search Topics: Running-Fiction, Loneliness-Fiction, Alcoholism-Fiction, Loners-Fiction, Mental Retardation-Fiction, Gangs-Fiction, Child Abuse-Fiction, Bullies-Fiction, Family Problems-Fiction, Courage-Fiction.

MERIWETHER, Louise. The freedom ship of Robert Smalls; illus by Lee Jack Morton. P-H 1971, unp (30 pp).

A brief, but very interesting biography of a black man whose dreams of freedom as a young slave during the Civil War, led to a daring plan of escape. Robert Smalls sailed 16 slaves to freedom and presented the Northern Navy with a valuable gunboat of which he was eventually named captain. Smalls later went on to serve five terms in Congress.

Although the picture book format of this book prevents its confortable use much beyond fourth grade, it is a compelling enough story to interest even sixth graders. Print is somewhat small.

Interest Level: 1-4. Reading Level: 3.1. Further Search Topics: Biography, United States-History-War, Blacks-Biography, Smalls, Robert, Group 2, Slavery, Politics-Biography.

MILES, Betty. The secret life of the underwear champ; illus by Dan Jones. Kncpf 1981, 117 pp.

Larry hadn't planned it; in fact, he hadn't even really wanted it to happen. But suddenly he found himself about to make a television commercial for ChampWin Knitting Mills, makers of sports clothing and underwear. He knew his family could use the money he would make, but he certainly didn't want the whole school seeing him in his underwear. Nevertheless, Larry went ahead and made the commercial, hoping that it would never be used. He even had to skip baseball practice to make the taping. Much to his horror, the commercial appeared the night before the team's first game. Not only did the entire opposing team tease him, but so did all his own teammates. By the time he got up to bat, Larry was mad enough to slam the ball out of the park. He didn't hit the ball quite that hard, but he did make a winning home run and end the others' giggles forever. He became the true underwear champ.

This is a funny look at the embarrassments of growing up. It also deals lightly with a boy's pride, his peer relationship, and his growing awareness of girls. An appealing and broadly usable title. Capers series.

Interest Level: 3-5. Reading Level: 2.2. Further Search Topics: Baseball-Fiction, Television-Fiction,

Occupations-Fiction, School Stories, Humorous Fiction, Advertising-Fiction, Beauty-Fiction, Motion Pictures-Fiction, Best Sellers, Everyday Stories.

MILES, Miska. Annie and the old one; illus by Peter Parnall. Little 1971, 44 pp.

A quietly beautiful story that will not appeal to all readers. Annie, a young Navajo girl, had a very close relationship with her grandmother. Her grandmother announced that she would "go to Mother Earth" at the time when the new rug Annie's mother was weaving was "taken from the loom." Annie tried all she could think of to keep the rug from being finished in order to keep her grandmother alive. When her grandmother solemnly explained that Annie could not stop time, Annie listened and "understood many things" for the first time.

It will be a thoughtful, sensitive child or a child trying to understand death who will best appreciate this special book.

Interest Level: 3-6. Reading Level: 3.2. Further Search Topics: Grandparents-Fiction, Death-Fiction, Indians of North America-Fiction, Navajo Indians-Fiction.

MILLER, Mary Beth, jt. auth., see Charlip, Remy.

MONTGOMERY, Raymond A. The lost jewels of Nabooti; illus by Paul Granger. Bantam 1981, 121 pp.

See entry for *Sugarcane Island*, by Edward Packard for series information. Only available in paperback edition. Choose Your Own Adventure series.

Interest Level: 2-6. Reading Level: 3.2. Further Search Topics: Mystery and Detective Stories, Detectives-Fiction, Treasure-Fiction, Best Sellers, Group 2.

MONTGOMERY, Raymond A. Space and beyond; illus by Paul Granger. Bantam 1980, 117 pp.

See entry for *Sugarcane Island*, by Edward Packard for full annotation. Available in paperback only. Choose Your Own Adventure series

Interest Level: 2-6. Reading Level: 4.1. Further Search Topics: Science Fiction, Outer Space-Fiction, Group 2, Best Sellers.

MOORE, Lilian. The snake that went to school; illus by Mary Stevens. Random 1957, 99 pp.

Hank's pet snake Puffy disappeared from the Science Room at school and his little brother, Benjy (in first grade) became ill on the same day. Hank was so worried about finding Puffy that he hardly thought about his pesky little brother, until Puffy was found two days later. Then Hank learned that Benjy had secretly gone to visit Puffy, after being rejected by Hank and had accidentally let the snake out of its cage. Benjy had been so worried about letting the snake out that he had actually made himself ill. Hank finally realized that Benjy wasn't the pest he had thought he was, and promised to be a better older brother.

A somewhat old-fashioned but satisfying story told in ten short chapters.

Interest Level: 2-4. Reading Level: 3.1. Further Search Topics: Pets-Fiction, Snakes-Fiction, Brothers and Sisters-Fiction, School Stories.

MORRESSY, John. The drought on Ziax II, illus by Stanley Skardinsky. Walker & Co 1978, 77 pp.

Ziax II, the planet that Toren, his father, and other Earth Pioneers were helping to colonize, was suffering a severe drought. It took both cooperation with the inhabitants of Ziax II and courage to seek out the frightening creature that could save the planet.

The importance of maintaining the balance of nature is the strongest message here. Respect for the ways of others is the secondary message.

Interest Level: 3-5. Reading Level: 3.1. Further Search Topics: Science Fiction, Ecology-Fiction, Outer Space-Fiction.

NEWFIELD, Marcia. A book for Jodan; illus by Diane DeGroot.   Atheneum 1975, unp (41 pp).

Jodan found her parents' separation very hard to understand and accept. She and her mother had moved 3,000 miles away from her father and she missed him very much. When Jodan visited her father for the first time, he gave her a very special present that lessened her loneliness. He created a book just for Jodan that was filled with his thoughts and memories.

The book is a sensitive portrayal of a very common experience. Only Jodan's age (nine-years-old) and consequent actions and reactions, limit the book's probable usefulness beyond fifth grade. Print is somewhat small.

Interest Level: 2-5. Reading Level: 3.2. Further Search Topics: Group 2, Divorce and Separation-Fiction, Family Problems-Fiction, Loneliness-Fiction.

NODSET, Joan L. Go away dog; illus by Crosby Bonsall.   Har-Row 1963, unp (29 pp).

A small boy who doesn't like dogs meets a shaggy, homeless dog who wants to play. The little boy, resisting all the way, gradually gives in to the dog's charms. Finally he tells the dog to follow him home. At home, he finds out that the dog was sent to him for his birthday by his Uncle George.

The dog, the boy, and the book are irresistible. You must, however, notice the illustrations on both the dedication and title pages to fully understand the story. Since much of the story is told by the illustrations and the text is repetitive as well as simple, it is an excellent beginning-to-read story.

Interest Level: 1-2. Reading Level: 1.1. Further Search Topics: Dogs-Fiction, Humorous Fiction, Best Sellers, Pets-Fiction, Birthdays-Fiction.

NORTON, Andre and Madlee, Dorothy. Star Ka'at; illus by Bernard Colonna.   Walker & Co 1976, 122 pp.

Jim Evans and Elly Mae Brown, both orphaned and alone, met each other and two strange cats at the same time. As the children became more unhappy with their lives, they began to realize that Tiro and Mer were not usual cats. They were highly intelligent Ka'ats from another planet who had come to Earth in search of new strong stock to add to their breed. Both Ka'ats became as fond of the children as the children became of them. When the time came for the transport ship to leave, Jim and Elly contrived to go with them. However, the only way they could go was if they were accepted by the other Ka'ats and adopted by Tiro and Mer.

This is the first book in a series. Unfortunately the second book *Star Ka'at World*, has a much more difficult reading level (sixth grade) and the third title, *Star Ka'at and the Plant People*, varies from 2.1 to 4.1. Reading level of this entry varies between 4.1 and 5.1 but children seem to like the book enough to put up with the variability.

Interest Level: 3-6. Reading Level: 4.2. Further Search Topics: Science Fiction, Friendship-Fiction, Cats-Fiction, Group 2, Outer Space-Fiction, Orphans-Fiction.

O'NEILL, Mary. Hailstones and halibut bones; illus by Leonard Weisgard.   Doubleday 1961, 59 pp.

This is a classic collection of twelve poems about colors. The poems are rhymed mood pieces of two or three pages that should appeal to almost any age reader. The difficulty of the vocabulary within each poem can vary greatly; however, most stanzas are short, most of the vocabulary is at least familiar, and the rhyme scheme is consistent.

Interest Level: 1-5. Reading Level: 3.2. Further Search Topics: Poetry, Colors, Group 2.

PACKARD, Edward. The cave of time; illus by Paul Granger.   Bantam 1979, 115 pp.

Beware of the greater than usual inconsistency of reading levels within this book. Its difficulty level ranges from 2.2 to 4.2. See notes for *Sugarcane Island* for more information about the series. In paperback only. Choose Your Own Adventure series.

Interest Level: 2-6. Reading Level: 4.1. Further Search Topics: Time-Fiction, Science Fiction, Fantasy, Group 2.

PACKARD, Edward. Deadwood City; illus by Barbara Carter.   Bantam 1978, 96 pp.

See *Sugarcane Island* for full series notes. Paperback edition only. Choose Your Own Adventure series.

Interest Level: 2-6. Reading Level: 3.1. Further Search Topics: West-Fiction, Cowboys-Fiction, Crime-Fiction, Best Sellers, Group 2.

PACKARD, Edward. The mystery of Chimney Rock; illus by Paul Granger.   Bantam 1979, 121 pp.

See notes for *Sugarcane Island* for information about the series. Paperback only. Choose Your Own Adventure series.

Interest Level: 2-6. Reading Level: 3.2. Further Search Topics: Mystery and Detective Stories, Cats-Fiction, Witches-Fiction, Ghosts-Fiction, Detectives-Fiction, Best Sellers, Group 2.

PACKARD, Edward. Sugarcane Island; illus by Barbara Carter.   Archway 1976, 105 pp.

The warning on the first page, that the book should *not* be read straight through, tells you that this book is different. And different it is. It is the first of what is now a new type of book; the "Choose Your Own Adventure" story. The formula is simple and highly successful, especially with reluctant readers. The reader is made the central character of the book. After a very brief series of events that set the stage, the reader is given choices to make. Upon making a decision, the reader is instructed to proceed to another page of the book. More action is described before the reader must make another choice. The sequence of action, choice, action and choice continues until the reader has finally completed an entire story. The books can be read over and over and the reader may never repeat exactly the same story unless he/she makes all of the same choices. What distinguishes one book from another is the setting, genre, and/or author (there are three: Edward Packard, R. A. Montgomery, and D. Terman). Don't expect quality writing or consistent reading levels because you won't find either. (Reading levels vary from 2.2 to 3.2 for most titles). What you will find is dependable, action-filled, enticing, light reading. Some are available only in paperback editions where the print size is fairly small. Choose Your Own Adventure series.

Interest Level: 2-6. Reading Level: 3.1. Further Search Topics: Shipwrecks-Fiction, Best Sellers, Survival-Fiction, Group 2.

PACKARD, Edward. Your code name is Jonah; illus by Paul Granger.   Bantam 1980, 114 pp.

See *Sugarcane Island* for information about books in this series. Paperback only. Choose Your Own Adventure series.

Interest Level: 2-6. Reading Level: 3.2. Further Search Topics: Nonverbal Communication-Fiction, Best Sellers, Spies-Fiction, Group 2.

PARISH, Peggy. Clues in the woods; illus by Paul Frame.   Macmillan 1968, 154 pp.

The books about the three Roberts children share problems that are obvious to adults and felt by some young readers as well, but they continue to be popular with undemanding young readers. The characters are very white and middle class and their actions often fit out-of-date stereotypes. The plots have few surprises or suspense, but the reading levels are consistent and the very predictability of the books makes them familiar and therefore comfortable.

This particular story takes place at the end of the same summer the children solved the mystery of *The Key to the Treasure*. The children were alerted by their grandmother to the disappearance of food scraps, left outside the house. Thinking that two runaway children, about whom they had read, had taken the food, Liza, Bill, and Jed tried to find the runaways. Their attempts eventually brought them new friends and thus the solution to their mystery. It had not been the runaways who had taken the food, it was their new friends' dog.

Interest Level: 1-4. Reading Level: 2.2. Further Search Topics: Mystery and Detective Stories, Brothers and Sisters-Fiction, Vacation-Fiction, Dogs-Fiction, Runaways-Fiction, Grandparents-Fiction, Group 2.

PARISH, Peggy. Haunted house; illus by Paul Frame.   Macmillan 1971, 151 pp.

Although this is the third book about Jed, Bill and Liza Roberts, it too can be read out of order. This time the family has moved into what was locally known as a haunted house. Very shortly after they moved into the house, a coded note appeared that led them to a series of messages and unusual occurrences. Lights that flashed into Liza's room turned out to be the headlights of cars, but the messages and a secret compartment in an old clock couldn't be as easily explained. Each day took them closer to the surprise that the messages hinted would be theirs. That surprise turned out to be three kittens and a treehouse. Two of the children's best friends had planned the whole mystery just to lead to the surprises.

This book has the same faults and strong points as the others about the Roberts children. Each chapter is short; the book is episodic; reading level is consistent; there is much dialogue and action and little description, and the plot has a comfortable familiarity about it. It can be very useful to the right readers.

Interest Level: 1-4. Reading Level: 2.1. Further Search Topics: Mystery and Detective Stories. Brothers and Sisters-Fiction, Ghosts-Fiction, Moving, Household-Fiction, Nonverbal Communication-Fiction, Group 2.

PARISH, Peggy. Hermit Dan; illus by Paul Frame. Macmillan 1977, 151 pp.

When the Roberts children tried to prove that Pirate Island really had been used by pirates, they encountered more action and intrigue than they had found in any of their earlier adventures. Liza, Bill and Jed suspected that Hermit Dan knew whether or not there had been pirates on the island, but he was so gruff and apparently mean that they didn't dare ask him any questions. Instead, they trailed and spied on him and asked questions of anyone who had known Hermit Dan as a child. It was rumored that his ancestors had actually been pirates. Until a terrible fire that had destroyed all they owned, Hermit Dan's family had been very wealthy. However, no one knew how they had become so rich.

In an attempt to see what the summer residents knew about Hermit Dan, the children introduced themselves to the vacationing youngsters. Among the visitors the Roberts met Hank and Ted, brothers bent on bullying Hermit Dan. When the children were rescued from a severe sandstorm by Hermit Dan, they were surprised to find that he wasn't nearly as gruff as he appeared. In fact they began to feel quite protective of the old man. Thus when Hank and Ted stole a secret box that held all of Hermit Dan's valuables, it was the Roberts children who fought (literally) to get the box back. It was after Liza, Bill and Jed returned the box to Hermit Dan, however, that the real surprises began: these included a surprise party for Hermit Dan, his wish to be friendly, and his gift to the children of three pieces of eight that proved his family members were pirates.

This title's more interesting and involved plot makes the book more likely to be a success with older readers than the other stories about the Roberts children. Otherwise it shares the same format, faults and strengths as the other series titles.

Interest Level: 2-5. Reading Level: 2.1. Further Search Topics: Mystery and Detective Stories, Pirates-Fiction, Vacation-Fiction, Loners-Fiction, Treasure-Fiction, Bullies-Fiction, Brothers and Sisters-Fiction, Grandparents-Fiction.

PARISH, Peggy. Key to the treasure; illus by Paul Frame.   Macmillan 1966, 154 pp.

This is the first of the stories about Jed, Bill and Liza Roberts. The three children are very middle-class, the book's plots are simple and often lack suspense, but the stories still enjoy widespread popularity among unsophisticated readers.

All three children went to spend the summer with their grandparents and decided to tackle a mystery left unsolved for over 75 years. An old drawing and an authentic war bonnet provided the only clues to finding three Indian artifacts. At each step along the way there were crumbled, brittle pieces of paper bearing coded messages that led to the next clue. The search ended when the children found that a storage area in a porch piller contained an Indian doll, mask, and leather shield that had belonged to their great-grandfather.

Interest Level: 1-4. Reading Level: 2.1. Further Search Topics: Vacation-Fiction, Brothers and Sisters-Fiction, Group 2, Mystery and Detective Stories, Grandparents-Fiction, Nonverbal Communication-Fiction.

PARISH, Peggy. Pirate Island adventure; illus by Paul Frame.   Macmillan 1975, 167 pp.

Although this is the fourth book in the series about the Roberts children, none of the titles must be read in chronological order. This time the three rather privileged children spent the summer with their grandparents on a resort island. They lived in a house that their family had owned for years, explored the island, and swam in their own private cove. But, most of their time was spent trying to solve an old mystery. Their great-uncle had hidden several very special items (one for each member of his family) years earlier, and had left only one clue with their grandfather. After he gave the children that clue it was only a matter of time before they found the hidden treasures.

This book is also lengthy, but is divided into 22 very manageable chapters. It is, like the others, almost entirely dialogue and action, which makes it especially appealing to young reluctant readers.

Interest Level: 1-4. Reading Level: 2.1. Further Search Topics: Mystery and Detective Stories, Vacation-Fiction, Treasure-Fiction, Brothers and Sisters-Fiction, Grandparents-Fiction, Group 2.

PARISH, Peggy. Too many rabbits; illus by Leonard Kessler.   Macmillan 1974, 48 pp.

One day Miss Molly opened her front door to find a rabbit waiting to be invited inside. The next day Miss Molly discovered the rabbit had had baby rabbits, lots of baby rabbits. Because babies need care, Miss Molly couldn't just turn them out, so she kept them all. Before long she had more rabbits than she could handle. She tried giving them away, but all the children's mothers refused to keep them, the zoo didn't need any, and Miss Molly didn't want to sell them to the butcher. Finally a man who owned an island where they could live, asked to take all the rabbits. As Miss Molly was about to close the door after giving the rabbits to the man with an island, a cat walked right up to her and inside her house. The next day Miss Molly discovered she had kittens—lots of kittens. A very humorous story in a reader format.

Interest Level: 1-3. Reading Level: 1.2. Further Search Topics: Humorous Fiction, Rabbits-Fiction, Best Sellers.

PARK, Barbara. Don't make me smile.   Knopf 1981, 114 pp.

As far as Charlie Hickle was concerned his parents' divorce was the worst thing in the world. His parents had ruined his life and he hadn't done anything to deserve such a fate. At first he didn't say very much. Then he ran away to live in a tree. Finally he cried a lot. That was all just in the first week after his parents announced their decision. After that, both his grades at school and his behavior began to deteriorate. It wasn't until Charlie had had several talks with a helpful children's psychologist and made a disastrous attempt to reunite his parents on his birthday, that he began to realize that he didn't like the divorce, but he could live with it.

The author's use of amusing anecdotes, Charlie's very strong feelings, and the frequency of divorce make this book very popular. Its major drawbacks are its superficiality and the overdrawn portrait of Charlie's mother. The book's faults will not deter many young readers from enjoying it, however.

Interest Level: 4-6. Reading Level: 3.1. Further Search Topics: Divorce and Separation-Fiction, Family Problems-Fiction, Psychiatrists-Fiction, Everyday Stories.

PECK, Robert Newton. Mr. Little; illus by Ben Stahl. Doubleday 1979, 87 pp.

All summer long Drag and Finley had looked forward to having Miss Kellogg as their teacher, so they were extremely disappointed to find ordinary-looking Mr. Little in her place on the first day of school. Used to playing tricks on their teachers anyway, Drag and Finley decided to go all out to get even with Mr. Little for spoiling their year. But try as they might, they couldn't get an advantage over Mr. Little; he seemed to be unflappable. Finally, in their riskiest prank ever, they stole Mr. Little's underwear to dress a statue in the town square. That attempt to embarrass Mr. Little only served to get Finley and Drag in serious trouble from which Mr. Little saved them. It was his later rescue of Miss Kellogg, however, that added respect to the boys' growing feeling of friendship for Mr. Little.

Because the author's adult viewpoint is never quite lost, even though he writes in the first person, and because the rural and historic time settings are not familiar to many readers, the book may need some introduction and encouragement. It is a prime candidate for reading aloud until the young reader's interest takes over. Print is of adequate size, but spacing between lines could have been more generous.

Interest Level: 4-6. Reading Level: 5.1. Further Search Topics: Humorous Fiction, School Stories, Troublemakers-Fiction, Group 2, Read Aloud, Country Life-Fiction, Best Sellers.

PENE DU BOIS, William. Lazy Tommy Pumpkinhead.   Har-Row 1966, 32 pp.

Tommy lived a solitary life in an all-electric house. An electric bed woke Tommy and slid him into a tub full of warm water. The tub then tipped him out and into a harness that held Tommy upright while other machines dried him, combed his hair, brushed his teeth, dressed him, and fed him. But one day Tommy's life was literally turned upside down with disastrous results. His feet were cleaned and combed and his clothes were all put on upside down, but the worst part of all was that Tommy almost starved; the machine fed his feet instead of his mouth.

A tongue-in-cheek warning against laziness. The lesson is obvious but the treatment (both text and illustrations) is so enjoyable that the book is appealing to almost any reader who wants a short, funny book. Print is somewhat small but spacing between lines is more than adequate.

Interest Level: 1-6. Reading Level: 3.2. Further Search Topics: Electricity-Fiction, Robots-Fiction, Laziness-Fiction, Humorous Fiction, Group 2, Read Aloud.

PEVSNER, Stella. And you give me a pain, Elaine. HM 1978, 182 pp.

Andrea was the youngest of three children. She was very close to her brother, Joe, but he was away at college. There was only Elaine at home, but Andrea and Elaine didn't get along at all. Elaine was a troubled young woman who took so much of her parents' attention that there was none left for Andrea. This is the story of Andrea's year in eighth grade, a year in which she discovered that she was a steady and strong person. It was the year in which Andrea worked on the school play, had her first boyfriend, weathered the storms when her sister ran away, and began to understand her sister more and resent her less. It was also the year that she had to learn to live with her brother's accidental death.

The author's Judy Blume style (but with less humor) guarantees readers among older children.

Interest Level: 5-6. Reading Level: 4.1. Further Search Topics: Family Problems-Fiction, Brothers and Sisters-Fiction, Love-Fiction, Death-Fiction, Runaways-Fiction, Troublemakers-Fiction, Adolescence-Fiction.

PFEFFER, Susan Beth. Just between us; illus by Lorna Tomei.   Delacorte 1980, 116 pp.

Cass's inability to keep secrets finally became such a problem that Cass asked her mother to help her learn how to keep them. Cass's mother, a psychology student, devised a behavior modification experiment. Every day that Cass was able to figure out which bit of information she had been told was a secret and keep it, she received a dollar. After a poor start Cass did well for a while, until the day she told three secrets and made her entire family angry at her.

More determined than ever, Cass tried again. This time she found herself caught between two friends. Only Cass knew that Robin was adopted and Robin wanted it kept a secret. Jenny was so mad at Robin that she decided to spread an untrue story to hurt Robin. She told Cass not to tell anyone what she was going to do. The story Jenny was going to spread was that Robin was adopted. After hours of mental anguish Cass finally devised a way to stop Jenny and help Jenny return to being the nice person she had been before her parents' divorce.

The reading level of this book varies greatly from second grade to mid-fourth grade. Otherwise, it is good fare for Judy Blume fans. Print size just a slight bit on the small side.

Interest Level: 4-6. Reading Level: 3.2. Further Search Topics: Humorous Fiction, Everyday Stories, Friendship-Fiction, School Stories, Divorce and Separation-Fiction, Psychiatrists-Fiction, Secrets-Fiction.

PFEFFER, Susan Beth. Kid power; illus by Leigh Grant.   Watts 1977, 121 pp.

When Janie's mother lost her job, her father's salary wouldn't stretch to provide any more money for the new bicycle fund. There was enough money already set aside to pay for one new bike, but both Janie and her older sister Carol wanted a bicycle. Carol, who had saved money of her own, suggested that they each pay for half a bike and their parents contribute the money for the other half. Then Janie's only problem was how to earn money, since she had none saved. Her solution was to create a business: Kid Power. Before long, Janie's business had blossomed and she was becoming rich, but she had lost her best friend and was ruining a client's roses. When Janie finally realized that getting rich wasn't the only thing that mattered in life, she relaxed, delegated jobs to friends better able to handle them, and became their agent.

A genuinely funny book that, as a bonus, takes a realistic look at the interworkings of a family. Consistent reading level.

Interest Level: 4-6. Reading Level: 3.1. Further Search Topics: Occupations-Fiction, Everyday Stories, Vacation-Fiction, Family-Fiction, Humorous Fiction, Best Sellers, Bicycles and Bicycling-Fiction, Friendship-Fiction.

PINKWATER, Daniel Manus. Fat men from space. Dodd 1977, 57 pp.

The evening after his trip to the dentist William found that he could still hear radio programs when his radio was turned off. He was even more surprised to find that when he wired himself to a fence he could hear spacemen talking. When the spacemen discovered that William could hear them, they landed and captured him. They were on a top secret mission and couldn't risk any human knowing about their existence. The spacemen were about to invade Earth to consume all the junk food they could find. As mass panic set in on Earth, William could do nothing to save his fellow humans. He was held captive and helpless until the invaders' interest was captured by a giant potato pancake floating in outer space.

A tongue-in-check, slapstick spoof of science fiction, food fads, and junk food. Do not expect anything more.

Interest Level: 3-5. Reading Level: 3.2. Further Search Topics: Science Fiction, Humorous Fiction, Food-Fiction, Flying Saucers-Fiction, Aliens-Fiction, Best Sellers, Kidnapping-Fiction, Teeth-Fiction.

PINKWATER, Daniel Manus. The Hoboken chicken emergency.   P-H 1977, 83 pp.

Arthur's mother sent him out with $16 to buy a Thanksgiving turkey. He returned with a live 266 pound chicken on a leash. It seemed that their turkey reservation had been lost at the meat market and, because it was Thanksgiving morning, there were no other turkeys available. Arthur searched everywhere but found nothing, until a strange old professor tricked him into buying the chicken. No one could bear to kill and eat such a large and friendly chicken, so Arthur and his family named it Henrietta and kept it as a pet. Henrietta was a difficult pet to keep hidden from the neighbors When the neighbors, and later the city, saw Henrietta running loose there was general hysteria. But all ended well when Henrietta and the city calmed down and Henrietta became a kind of neighborhood mascot.

A purely absurd plot but presented with enough energy and humor that most readers thoroughly enjoy the book. Some brief introduction may be necessary to get readers beyond the first few pages.

Interest Level: 3-6. Reading Level: 2.2. Further Search Topics: Humorous Fiction, Chickens-Fiction, Pets-Fiction, Thanksgiving-Fiction, Holidays-Fiction, Read Aloud, Best Sellers.

PLACE, Marian T. The boy who saw Bigfoot.   Dodd 1979, 96 pp.

Joey and his foster mother searched for and found Bigfoot. But, when Joey told his classmates, no one would believe him. Joey's next idea was to take the entire class on a field trip to track Bigfoot.

Joey's rapid change from a difficult to a very well-adjusted child is not well supported. But interest in Bigfoot is so great that the book's flaws will be overlooked by its readers.

Interest Level: 3-6. Reading Level: 2.2. Further Search Topics: Bigfoot-Fiction, Foster Homes-Fiction, Monsters-Fiction, Troublemakers-Fiction, School Stories.

PLATT, Kin. Brogg's brain.   Lippincott 1981, 123 pp.

According to everyone else, Monty Davis should have been one of the fastest milers in the city. He had, after all, run a four minute and ten second mile in practice one day. He had run well enough that day to beat his high school's two best milers. That was a good enough performance to make the coach push him, his teacher talk about winning, and his father puff up with pride. Even the marathon runner he saw occasionally in the park and his girl friend Cindy seemed to think that he could be the best. Monty really didn't care, or he thought he didn't. Maybe he was just afraid to see how good or bad he really was. For whatever reason, he didn't want to run in the meet against Culver High School. He talked so much about not doing well, that by the time he was supposed to run, he even had his coach convinced he couldn't win. But as he ran, Monty heard a voice inside his head that sounded like the voice in a strange science fiction film that he and Cindy had just seen. The voice seemed to say that he could win, and suddenly that was what Monty wanted. The voice and his new-found determination were what pulled Monty through and gave him first place.

This book is for the track fan or the runner. Few others are likely to care about the difference between a four-twenty and a four-ten high school mile. For those who do care, this is a good choice.

Interest Level: 5-6. Reading Level: 3.1. Further Search Topics: Family Problems-Fiction, Love-Fiction, Running-Fiction, Courage-Fiction.

PLATT, Kin. Dracula, go home; illus by Frank Mayo. Watts 1979, 87 pp.

From the chapter numbers that drip blood, and the humorously grotesque illustrations, to the short sentences and chapters, this is a book designed and almost guaranteed to appeal to the reluctant reader. A sense of immediacy and involvement is created by the first person narration. Tension is created on the opening page when Larry sees a man in the cemetery who looked exactly like Dracula. When that man registered at the hotel where Larry was working, Larry decided to find out more about him. It began to look as if Mr. A. R. Claude (the letters spell Dracula) was not only a vampire, but a thief and a murderer as well. The trouble was that Larry couldn't prove anything. Even when he found the stolen jewels for which Mr. Claude had been searching, Larry still couldn't convince anyone of Claude's true identify. No one ever did believe Larry, thus Claude went free.

The author uses a light touch to treat an eerie subject. His inconclusive ending may disappoint some, but should delight many. Beware of the variability of the reading level however; it swings from high first grade to low third grade.

Interest Level: 3-6. Reading Level: 2.2. Further Search Topics: Monsters-Fiction, Horror-Fiction, Mystery and Detective Stories, Best Sellers, Murder-Fiction, Crime-Fiction, Transformations-Fiction.

PLATT, Kin. Run for your life; photos by Chuck Freedman. Watts 1977, 95 pp.

Lee almost lost his newspaper delivery job when someone began to regularly steal money and papers from the newspaper boxes along his route. Lee saw a chance for revenge if he could beat the thief in the mile race at the next track meet.

Most of the abundant dialogue is slang. The romantic interest is innocent and low keyed. The story has enough running to make that a strong appeal, but not so much that no one but a track or running enthusiast can enjoy it.

Interest Level: 5-6. Reading Level: 2.2. Further Search Topics: Running-Fiction, Love-Fiction, Occupations-Fiction, Crime-Fiction.

RENNER, Beverly. The Hideaway summer; illus by Ruth Sanderson. Har-Row 1978, 134 pp.

On their way to summer camp, Addie suddenly got off the bus and took her younger brother Clay to see the place where Addie had spent prior summer vacations. It was their grandmother's house and a small cabin called the Hideaway. The house had been sold after their grandmother had died that year, but Addie's father had decided to keep the Hideaway. Much to Addie's surprise she found the Hideaway beautifully fixed-up, just as Gram had promised she would do one day.

When they missed the last bus out of the tiny town and realized that they had enough money to buy the food they would need, Addie and Clay decided to make the Hideaway their summer home. One phone call to the camp and weekly calls to their father kept

people from worrying about them. Their discovery of two small raccoons meant that their days were filled with caring for and training the animals. In addition, they had to build a warning system so that no one would discover them and they had to get their food and provisions from town about every two weeks without being too noticeable. They even had to figure out a way to survive a wild summer storm, a flood, and poachers who hunted raccoons. By summer's end Addie and Clay had grown independent, resourceful, and very close to each other.

An exciting story whose short chapters and fairly short sentences keep the reading level reasonably low. Print is dark and of adequate size, but space between the lines is somewhat narrow.

Interest Level: 4-6. Reading Level: 3.1. Further Search Topics: Brothers and Sisters-Fiction, Runaways-Fiction, Pets-Fiction, Survival-Fiction, Vacation-Fiction, Raccoons-Fiction, Read Aloud.

ROBINSON, Barbara. The best Christmas pageant ever; illus by Judith Gwyn Brown. Har-Row 1972, 80 pp.

A truly delightful story of what happens when the meanest kids in town (they are all in one family) take over all the lead roles in the Sunday school Christmas pageant. The Herdmans (all six of them), having heard that the church was giving away free food, showed up to take some. While they were there, they heard about the Christmas pageant and decided it presented them with another perfect opportunity for food and mischief. With a little behind-the-scenes arm-twisting (literally), they managed to dissuade everyone else from showing interest in the major roles. Theirs was a completely original interpretation of the Christmas story that left nothing and no one around them untouched.

That the book's reading level will prove too high for many people is unfortunate. The story is well worth the struggle. A wonderful choice for reading aloud.

Interest Level: 3-6. Reading Level: 5.1 Further Search Topics: Christmas-Fiction, Bullies-Fiction, Troublemakers-Fiction, Humorous Fiction, Religion-Fiction, Group 2, Read Aloud, Acting-Fiction, Holidays-Fiction.

ROBINSON, Jean. The strange but wonderful cosmic awareness of Duffy Moon; illus by Lawrence Di Fiori. HM 1974, 142 pp.

Duffy was tired of being small, of always being on the losing side of fights, and of being unappreciated at home (by his ex-football star uncle). When he sent away for Mr. Flamel's Cosmic Awareness Kit, Duffy was sure he would then be able to take control over anything he wanted and direct his own life. His friend Peter, the narrator, wasn't quite so sure. Peter turned out to be right. Duffy almost made himself sick trying to build a stone wall. Babysitting two small boys and trying to bathe a Great Dane proved to be disastrous. But Duffy's biggest problem came from Boots McAfee's gang. A series of events finally brought Duffy and Peter face-to-face with the dreaded Boots. Luckily, she turned out to be a very smart girl who appreciated Duffy's true talents.

From the first to the last page this is a funny, very enjoyable book. A delightful book with a very palatable message.

Interest Level: 3-6. Reading Level: 3.2. Further Search Topics: Humorous Fiction, Bullies-Fiction, Magic-Fiction, Read Aloud, Occupations-Fiction, Sex Role-Fiction, Orphans-Fiction, Best Sellers, Gangs-Fiction, Courage-Fiction, Babysitting-Fiction.

ROBINSON, Nancy K. Wendy and the bullies; illus by Ingrid Fetz.   Hastings 1980, 128 pp.

Wendy and her best friend Karen had a very carefully mapped out route to and from school—a route that allowed them to meet up with the fewest number of bullies possible. But when Karen became sick enough to stay home from school, Wendy had to face the bullies alone. Wendy's fears escalated to panic so intense that she avoided walking to school by hiding in her basement. She finally realized that she was letting fear and anger control her life when she found herself bullying Karen. Only her new friendship with Monica, making up with Karen, and her involvement in a school project helped Wendy overcome her fears.

This is a humorous, episodic tale of a feeling and circumstances common to many children. The illustrations sometimes make Wendy and her classmates appear much younger than her actual nine years, but fortunately that doesn't happen often enough to spoil the book's appeal.

Interest Level: 3-5. Reading Level: 3.1. Further Search Topics: School Stories, Bullies-Fiction, Courage-Fiction, Best Sellers, Humorous Fiction, Friendship-Fiction, Everyday Stories.

ROCKWELL, Thomas. How to eat fried worms; illus by Emily McCully.   Watts 1973, 116 pp.

It started more as a joke than anything else, but it escalated into a strange commitment. Alan bet Billy $50 that Billy couldn't eat a worm a day for fifteen days. Billy had always been willing to take almost any dare offered and he was stubborn enough to carry them out, but when he actually faced the first worm (an enormous night crawler), he almost backed down. He and his friend Tom had to keep repeating the word "minibike" (the prize he planned to buy with the money) and smother the worm in everything imaginable in order to eat it all. After the first worm, however, the next few were easier to face. That was when Alan and his ally Joe, began using psychological warfare and almost won. In 41 very short, grotesquely funny chapters Billy becomes the proud owner of a minibike and is the first person to become hooked on worm sandwiches.

Once this book is started, it is hard to resist its gruesome fascination. Although the print is somewhat small, and there are occasionally very difficult or babytalk words, the interest is strong enough to sustain almost all readers.

Interest Level: 3-6. Reading Level: 3.1. Further Search Topics: Humorous Fiction, Worms-Fiction, Read Aloud, Best Sellers, Challenges-Fiction, Food-Fiction, Bicycles and Bicycling-Fiction.

ROY, Ron. Nightmare Island; illus by Robert MacLean.   Dutton 1981, 69 pp.

Harley didn't want to take his younger brother camping, but because he had promised his father he would, the boys packed a tent, sleeping bags, and plenty of food into a small boat and set off to nearby Little Island. Hidden in his pocket, Harley had matches and marshmallows for a midnight marshmallow roast. After they had finished the bag of marshmallows, Harley threw the last log of the fire into the water. The water erupted into flames that quickly spread around the island. As the boys fought desperately to save themselves and to find shelter, they realized that the large shape they had seen in the distance must have been an oil tanker that had spread an oil slick all around the island. With time running out Harley gave his brother the only truly secure shelter from the fire, curled up on top of a tall rock and went to sleep.

When he awoke the fire had burned itself out and help was on the way.

Most young readers will be able to suspend disbelief long enough to enjoy this as an exciting adventure and survival story, but it is hard to believe that two young boys could not only survive such a holocaust, but that they could sleep through part of it, too. It is also difficult to believe that there would not be more of a fuss made about the oil tanker blowing up. Plot problems aside, young readers seem to love the story.

Interest Level: 3-6. Reading Level: 3.2. Further Search Topics: Brothers and Sisters-Fiction, Survival-Fiction, Camping-Fiction, Disasters-Fiction, Best Sellers.

RUDEEN, Kenneth. Jackie Robinson; illus by Richard Cuffari.   Har-Row 1971, 41 pp.

Jackie Robinson was the youngest child in a large, poor family. As early as high school it was Robinson's superior athletic talent that set him apart. He could run track or play baseball, football, or basketball. He was the first student at UCLA to win a letter in all four sports. But because he wasn't happy to see the way his mother still had to struggle to earn money to live, after a year and a half at UCLA, Robinson left college to take a job. Soon after that, the United States entered World War II and Robinson went into the Army. His refusal to ride in the back of a bus in Texas resulted in a courtmartial, but he was found innocent after an uproar was made by the newspapers.

After the Army, Robinson played baseball with a Negro League team. A short time later, he was asked by the Dodger manager Branch Rickey to become the first black man to play in the major leagues. Rickey warned Robinson that it would mean he not only had to play well, but that he would also have to take all the anger and bitterness that would be directed at him. Robinson agreed. For three long years, while there were no other black players in the major leagues, Robinson played well and took everything without fighting back. Robinson was then able to stop trying to be perfect because he had successfully broken a very important color barrier and no longer had to prove to white managers, players and fans that blacks belonged in baseball just as much as whites. Robinson played for the Dodgers for ten years. When he left baseball he was elected into the Baseball Hall of Fame. He continued to fight for civil rights throughout the rest of his life, although there is only a brief mention of his activities in the book. Since the book's publication Jackie Robinson has died.

This is an excellent choice for the child who thinks of nothing but sports. It may be helpful in opening up an interest in the civil rights movement, black history, or black heroes. It is unfortunate that the traditional Crowell biography format (semi-picture book), and the author's slight tendency to be condescending, prevents the book from being useful beyond fourth grade. Crowell Biography series.

Interest Level: 2-4. Reading Level: 2.2. Further Search Topics: Civil Rights, Robinson, Jackie, Baseball-Biography, Biography, Blacks-Biography, Prejudice, Poverty.

RUDEEN, Kenneth. Roberto Clemente; illus by Frank Mullins.   Har-Row 1974, 33 pp.

A romanticized retelling of a great baseball player's life. Those already interested in baseball or in Clemente will probably not mind the romantic tone, but may notice the almost patronizing explanations of some of the basics of baseball. Crowell Biography series.

Interest Level: 2-4. Reading Level: 3.1. Further Search Topics: Baseball-Biography, Biography, Puerto Rico, Group 2, Clemente, Roberto.

RUDEEN, Kenneth. Wilt Chamberlain; illus by Frank Mullins.   Har-Row 1972, 33 pp.

A short and somewhat adoring version of Wilt Chamberlain's childhood, schooling, and professional career. Very little of Chamberlain's personality comes through in this book, but his superior talents and skills as well as his importance to the sport of basketball will be enough to prompt many basketball fans to read it. Although simplistic in style, the book is not condescending. It is, however, out of date, a fact most notable when Chamberlain's salary is quoted. Beware of juvenile format when using with older readers. Crowell Biography series.

Interest Level: 2-6. Reading Level: 3.2. Further Search Topics: Biography, Chamberlain, Wilt, Basketball-Biography, Blacks-Biography, Group 2.

SACHS, Marily. The bears' house; illus by Louis Glanzman.   Doubleday 1971, 81 pp.

Don't let the benign appearance of this book fool you. This is a disturbing, almost brutal story. It is the story of Fran Ellen, a fourth grader with more problems than anyone should have to shoulder at one time. Her father had left the family and her mother had had a mental breakdown. Fran Ellen and her older brother were left with responsibility for themselves, their mother, and three other children (including a baby). They were all ill-fed, poorly dressed, and unwashed. Neither the social worker nor Fran Ellen's teacher knew the extent of the family's problems. Fran Ellen's only happiness came from her baby sister and from a schoolroom model (of *Goldilocks and the Three Bears* and their house) into which she mentally retreated whenever she had the chance.

As the school year closed, Fran Ellen's teacher visited her home to deliver the bears' house and discovered Fran Ellen's mother and very sick baby sister. Although she hated the idea that the family might have to split up, Fran Ellen had matured enough to realize that when her teacher insisted that she would get help for the family, her teacher was taking the proper action.

The book is inappropriately illustrated to make it appear cute and even humorous. The story is far from either. It is so stark that it probably shouldn't have been illustrated at all. And because the hope that is present in the book's ending is very subtle, a review and a discussion may be necessary to help relieve some young readers' anxieties.

Interest Level: 5-6. Reading Level: 3.1. Further Search Topics: Divorce and Separation-Fiction, Challenges-Fiction, Poverty-Fiction, Family Problems-Fiction, Loners-Fiction, Survival-Fiction, Mental Illness-Fiction, Brothers and Sisters-Fiction.

ST. JOHN, Wylly Folk. The ghost next door; illus by Trina Schart Hyman.   Har-Row 1971, 178 pp.

Told by 13-year-old Lindsay, this is the story of her neighbor Miss Judith and Miss Judith's two nieces. Her niece Miranda had drowned years earlier in Miss Judith's backyard fish pond and Miss Judith had never fully recovered from her death. As the story begins, Miss Judith is about to welcome another niece (Sherry) for a summer stay. Sherry, without ever being told about Miranda, seems to sense Miranda's presence all around. Her mother laughs and says that Sherry has an imaginary friend. Miss Judith, who is a strong believer in ESP, thinks that Sherry is communicating with Miranda. As the days go on Sherry learns more and more of Miranda' secrets. When Miss Judith is scared by Sherry, Lindsay and her friend, Tammy, decide to see what sort of tricks Sherry is playing.

A believable suspense story, made even more so by the illustrations.

Interest Level: 4-6. Reading Level: 5.1. Further Search Topics: Mystery and Detective Stories, Relatives-Fiction, Group 2, Extra Sensory Perception-Fiction, Best Sellers, Ghosts-Fiction.

SARNOFF, Jane. What? A riddle book; illus by Reynold Ruffins.   Scribner 1974, 62 pp.

A good, lengthy collection of both familiar and unfamiliar riddles. Every other page is brightened by bold and humorous illustrations. The first part of the book seems to have slightly more riddles for younger readers than the rest of the book. Some of the riddles in the collection involve rather sophisticated puns; thus they are more appealing to fifth and sixth grade readers. The final three pages of the book include 35 riddles whose answers are in code. The key to the code is given on the last page of the book. It is a picture book printed in two tones. The riddles sometimes slant diagonally across the page.

Interest Level: 1-6. Reading Level: 3.1. Further Search Topics: Riddles, Wit and Humor, Group 2, Nonverbal Communication.

SCISM, Carol K. The wizard of Walnut Street; illus by Martha Alexander.   Dial 1973, 54 pp.

John and his friends had no room in their Wizard Club for Ford Owens, the new kid. John thought Ford was a conceited show-off who only wanted to make John look like a coward. It was true that John was afraid of some things, such as going down the giant slide into the lake, but he didn't want anyone else to know it. So he excluded Ford from all the club's activities until Ford pushed his way into their magic wishing-well project.

It had been John's idea to charge everyone a dime who wanted to make a wish. They could use the money to buy the few simple things that they would need to make the wishes come true. But it was Ford's eerie volcano and his large dog that had added just the right atmosphere to the trick to make people believe. Even John and Ford found themselves making wishes. John wished to be able to go down the giant slide. He didn't know what Ford wished. Much to John's initial surprise, people's wishes began to be fulfilled. Even Arthur, who had wished he could learn to dive, found he could. Then because John began to realize that the magic was in believing in himself and not in the wishing well, he tried the slide and succeeded. Once John's reason to avoid Ford was gone, he relaxed and asked Ford to join the club. At that point, even Ford's wish was granted.

Interest Level: 2-4. Reading Level: 2.1. Further Search Topics: Friendship-Fiction, Gangs-Fiction, Courage-Fiction, Magic-Fiction, Vacation-Fiction, Best Sellers.

SELSAM, Millicent E. How kittens grow; photos by Esther Bubley.   School Bk Serv 1973, unp (28 pp).

A warm picture essay that illustrates and briefly describes the first eight weeks in kittens' lives. Guaranteed to charm cat fanciers.

Interest Level: 1-3. Reading Level: 2.1. Further Search Topics: Cats, Pets, Infants, Group 2, Birth.

SEUSS, Dr. Hop on Pop.   Beginner 1963, 64pp.

Between one and four rhyming words are introduced or reviewed and used in a silly sentence on each page. The sentence is interpreted with even more amusing illustrations. It is one of the simplest of books (no story at all) and yet it is usable through second grade because of Dr. Seuss' playful style and ridiculous illustrations. Reader format.

Interest Level: 1-2. Reading Level: 1.1. Further Search Topics: Poetry, Best Sellers, Wit and Humor, Humorous Fiction, Stories in Rhyme.

SEUSS, Dr. One fish, two fish, red fish, blue fish. Beginner 1960, 63pp.

Beginning with one almost ordinary-looking fish, this is a humorous look at the "funny things that go by." When Dr. Seuss says "funny," he really means highly imaginative, whimsical, and totally nonsensical. Each of the more than 20 silly creatures are described and appropriately illustrated to appeal to a child's sense of the ridiculous. Reader.

Interest Level: 1-2. Reading Level: 1.1. Further Search Topics: Fantasy, Wit and Humor, Poetry, Humorous Fiction, Stories in Rhyme.

SEUSS, Dr. The cat in the hat.   Beginner 1957, 61 pp.

When the Cat in the Hat visits two children, a dreary, boring afternoon becomes almost too exciting. The Cat's juggling act and the two "things" he brings with him almost destroy the house. But the Cat cleans up so well that when the children's mother comes home and asks what they did all afternoon, they can't decide if they should tell her.

A funny, rhyming tale of the destruction all children can create and the boredom all children can feel. Reader format.

Interest Level: 1-3. Reading Level: 1.2. Further Search Topics: Humorous Fiction, Fantasy, Cats-Fiction, Poetry, Troublemakers-Fiction, Best Sellers, Stories in Rhyme.

SEUSS, Dr. The cat in the hat comes back. Beginner 1958, 63 pp.

Sally and her brother were doing a good job of clearing the front walk of snow when the Cat in the Hat showed up. While they worked, the Cat created a pink mess in the house. The mess only became worse when he tried to clean it. The pink spot finally covered the snow all around the house until the Cat called upon his friends Little Cats A-Z. It was Little Cat Z and his magic zoom that eventually not only cleaned the snow, but cleared the front walk as well.

Another zany, rhymed adventure of the mischievious Cat whose ability to get into trouble endears him to most children from pre-school to early third grade. Reader format.

Interest Level: 1-3. Reading Level: 1.2. Further Search Topics: Fantasy, Cats-Fiction, Troublemakers-Fiction, Humorous Fiction, Snow-Fiction, Poetry, Best Sellers, Stories in Rhyme.

SEUSS, Dr. The foot book.   Random 1968, unp (27 pp).

Left feet, right feet, big feet, small feet; with its rhyme, silly illustrations and rhythmic celebration of feet of all descriptions, this book is a sure winner with the very young. Reader format.

Interest Level 1-2. Reading Level: 1.1. Further Search Topics: Best Sellers, Feet-Fiction, Humorous Fiction, Poetry, Wit and Humor, Stories in Rhyme.

SHARMAT, Marjorie W. Getting something on Maggie Marmelstein; illus by Ben Shecter.   Har-Row 1971, 101 pp.

A curious love-hate relationship existed between Thad and Maggie. It all began when Maggie overheard Thad say she squeaked like a mouse. Then Maggie caught Thad wearing an apron and cooking. Thad was so uncomfortable with the thought that Maggie might tell his friends, that he was determined to find out Maggie's deepest secret. That meant that Thad had to take a lead role as a frog opposite Maggie as the princess in the school play. While at Maggie's apartment for a costume fitting, Thad found a love letter Maggie had written to Cary Grant. Thad decided he would read the letter to the class right after the play was over. But during the play Maggie saved Thad from what could have been one of the most embarrassing moments of his life. By the time he finally had the chance to make Maggie appear foolish, Thad had changed his mind.

Written as Thad's story, the book is funny, warm, and realistic. A good, short, story that continues to be popular. Print is of moderate size.

Interest Level: 3-6. Reading Level: 3.1. Further Search Topics: Humorous Fiction, Everyday Stories, School Stories, Best Sellers, Friendship-Fiction, Sex Role-Fiction, Acting-Fiction.

SHARMAT, Marjorie W. The Lancelot closes at five; illus by Lisl Weil.   Macmillan 1976, 120 pp.

Despite a somewhat slow beginning, this is an amusing, almost sensitive story of two friends who decided to spend the night in the model home of the new housing development in which they both lived. Hutch, a health food fanatic whose mother pronounced judgment on everything Hutch did, conceived of the idea as her way of breaking away. Abby went along for the fun of it. When the local newspaper wrote of unusual vandalism at the model home, the townspeople became engrossed in finding the culprits. As the adults became enraged about the crime wave, their children began to admire the clever idea. Soon, almost every youngster in town had confessed to spending the night in the model home. By the time Abby and Hutch got around to admitting they had slept there, no one believed them. Only a sock with Abby's name in it could tie Abby and Hutch to the scene of the crime. As the book ends, the police have begun a thorough search of the house, after a real robbery, and the sock's discovery is imminent.

Interest Level: 4-6. Reading Level: 3.2. Further Search Topics: Humorous Fiction, Suburbia-Fiction, Runaways-Fiction, Crime-Fiction, Individualists-Fiction, Family Problems-Fiction.

SHARMAT, Marjorie W. Maggie Marmelstein for President; illus by Ben Shecter.   Har-Row 1975, 122 pp.

Maggie and Thad Smith are at it again. When Thad decided to run for sixth grade president, Maggie decided to become his campaign manager. However, because Thad thought Maggie was too strong and would end up managing him much more than he wanted to be managed, he turned down her offer. Thad's refusal made Maggie so angry that she not only decided to run against Thad, but she also enlisted Noah, the smartest kid in the class, as her manager. With Noah's expert guidance Maggie's campaign went rather well, despite attempts at sabotage by a spy for Thad. But as election day drew closer, both Thad and Maggie lost track of the campaign issues and concentrated only on beating each other. Consequently the pre-election debate turned into a disastrous shouting match. The next day Noah was elected class president by write-in votes.

Not very subtle, but funny. A satisfying sequel for those who enjoyed *Getting Something on Maggie Marmelstein*.

Interest Level: 3-6. Reading Level: 3.1. Further Search Topics: Humorous Fiction, Politics-Fiction, School Stories, Friendship-Fiction, Sex Role-Fiction.

SHARMAT, Marjorie W. Nate the great goes undercover; illus by Marc Simont.   Coward 1974, 47 pp.

Nate's next door neighbor Oliver was a pest, but Oliver had a mystery for Nate to solve. Oliver's garbage can was being burglarized at night. He wanted Nate to catch the garbage snatcher. Nate quickly drew up a list of human suspects and just as quickly eliminated them all. A night spent hiding in the garbage can proved the best way to catch the thief. Much to Nate's surprise, the thief turned out to be his new dog.

Very amusing and very useful. Reader format.

Interest Level: 1-3. Reading Level: 2.1. Further Search Topics: Humorous Fiction, Mystery and Detective Stories, Group 2, Detectives-Fiction, Best Sellers.

SHARMAT, Marjorie W. Nate the great; illus by Marc Simont.   Coward 1972, 62 pp.

This is a young imitation of Humphrey Bogart solving a *Dragnet* style mystery. Annie's recently finished painting of her dog had disappeared so she hired Nate to search for it. Nate gathered all the facts, investigated his suspects, and eventually solved the mystery, but not before he had consumed plenty of pancakes (his favorite food) and solved a second mystery by accident.

A simple plot, humorous telling, and a sympathetic, likeable protagonist make this one of a very popular series. Reader format.

Interest Level: 1-3. Reading Level: 2.1. Further Search Topics: Humorous Fiction, Detectives-Fiction, Mystery and Detective Stories, Group 2, Best Sellers.

SHAW, Evelyn. Alligator; illus by Frances Zweifel. Har-Row 1972, 61 pp.

A straight-forward, respectful description of an alligator's life cycle. Emphasis is placed on the time between the mother's nest-building and the birth of the young alligators. The danger to alligators posed by man is expressed, but not stressed. Little physical description is included. An interesting and competent treatment of a narrow subject. Reader format. A Science-I-Can-Read Book series.

Interest Level: 1-4. Reading Level: 2.1. Further Search Topics: Alligators, Nature Study, Group 2.

SHEARER, John. Billy Jo Jive and the case of the missing pigeons; illus by Ted Shearer.   Delacorte 1978, 47 pp.

This is the third in a series of slight mysteries, always solved by Billy Jo Jive and his crime fighter partner, Susie Sunset. Jive and Sunset are street-wise, black youngsters who take their jobs as crime fighters very seriously, and are never detered for long from finding the criminals they seek. The crimes are always thefts, and the criminals vary from young children to neighborhood menaces. Suspense is created more by the manner in which Jive and Sunset catch the thieves, plus the determination and pace of the young detectives, than by guessing who the culprits might be. Jive, his street-slang manner of telling the first-person stories, and the urban setting will appeal to many readers. Jive and Sunset also appear on *Sesame Street*.

Jive accidentally photographed the fleeing pigeon thief as he was being chased by Flip, the victim. The photograph didn't show the thief's face, but did give Jive and Sunset a good look at what he was wearing. Jive and Sunset concluded that the thief was Snake Hips Robberts. They later realized that they had been wrong. When they looked carefully at the picture, they remembered that any dark color clothing photographs almost black in a black and white picture. Snake Hips had a black jacket, but he was innocent. The real thief was Sugar Brown. Then it was a simple matter of showing the evidence to both Flip and Sugar to get Sugar to confess.

Interest Level: 1-4. Reading Level: 2.2. Further Search Topics: Mystery and Detective Stories, Detectives-Fiction, Blacks-Fiction, City Life-Fiction, Group 2, Best Sellers.

SHEARER, John. Billy Jo Jive and the walkie-talkie caper; illus by Ted Shearer.   Delacorte 1981, 47 pp.

When Steam Boat Louis went to Jive and Sunset for help, he was desperate. Because Jive and Sunset had already solved three cases, they were the logical people to find the walkie-talkie that had been stolen from Steam Boat. The walkie-talkie was one of two that Steam Boat had been told to buy as part of a secret communication system for the Bugaloo Smackers. Even as Jive and Sunset hunted for the thief, the second walkie-talkie was stolen. Their only clue was a footprint found outside Steam Boat's fix-it shop. Eventually, after trial and error, Jive and Sunset uncovered the real thieves; Steam Boat's young twin cousins. Unhappy at being separated in school, they wanted to use the walkie-talkies to be able to talk with each other.

The high reading level of this book will make it most useful for those children who have read and enjoyed other books in the series and are willing to stretch to read one more.

Interest Level: 1-4. Reading Level: 3.2. Further Search Topics: Mystery and Detective Stories, Detectives-Fiction, Blacks-Fiction, City Life-Fiction, Group 2.

SHEARER, John. Billy Jo Jive super private eye: the case of the missing ten speed bike; illus by Ted Shearer.   Delacorte 1976, 47 pp.

Jive and Sunset began their friendship and their sleuthing career with this book. It all started when Sunset borrowed her older brother's 10-speed bicycle. Jive met Sunset while she sat at the side of the road crying, after her brother's bike had been stolen. Some careful joint detective work proved to Jive and Sunset that Dynamite Jones, jealous of Sunset's brother, had stolen the bike. The young crime fighters recovered the bicycle before Sunset's brother even knew it was missing.

This book sets the formula that all the others follow. A neighborhood person finds that something has been stolen and goes to Jive and Sunset for help. Jive and Sunset never have much trouble finding the thief even though they are sometimes misled for a short time. Often the culprit is quite obvious to the reader. After some attempts at clever detective work and an occasional bit of preaching, the crime is solved. It is the manner of the pursuit and the street-smart characters that give the stories their interest.

Interest Level: 1-4. Reading Level: 2.2. Further Search Topics: Mystery and Detective Stories, Blacks-Fiction, Detectives-Fiction, City Life-Fiction, Best Sellers, Group 2, Bicycles and Bicycling-Fiction.

SHREVE, Susan. The Nightmares of Geranium Street. Knopf 1977, 127 pp.

The Nightmares, a small neighborhood gang, had very little to do until beautiful Tess moved on the block. Tess dressed in satins, furs, and rhinestones, and sang in nightclubs. She was even more of a fascination to the gang because they had been told to stay away from her. When Amanda moved in with Tess, the Nightmares invited her to join the gang so that they would have a way of spying on Tess. Gradually her strange behavior, her moods, her bruises and shaking spells, the strangers she let in the house, and the fights she had, led the gang members to suspect that Tess dealt in drugs. When Amanda failed to show up for a picnic and the Nightmares learned the police were searching for Tess, the gang became worried enough to look for Amanda themselves. In doing so, they uncovered proof of Tess' drug dealings, put themselves in great danger, and were protected by Tess as they escaped only moments before Tess was arrested.

Despite its low reading level, the book's confusing sequence of final events, and its subject matter make it best suited to older readers. It is not great literature, but its subject has strong appeal.

Interest Level: 5-6. Reading Level: 3.1. Further Search Topics: Family Problems-Fiction, Gangs-Fiction, Drugs-Fiction, Mystery and Detective Stories, City Life-Fiction, Crime-Fiction, Philadelphia-Fiction.

SHURA, Mary Francis. The Barkley Street six-pack: illus by Gene Sparkman. Dodd 1979, 159 pp.

Jane's best friend Natalie was everything Jane wanted to be. She was self-assured, pretty, vibrant, and even possessed magical talents. Jane didn't realize at first, and she later resisted seeing, that Natalie ran Jane's life and cleverly made sure that Jane had no other friends. Natalie's move left Jane with no friends among those people she had once enjoyed. Little by little, with the help of a stray dog and the new boy on the block, Jane bagan to see how destructive Natalie had been. She finally realized that a true friendship is one in which neither party tries to control the other.

With its enticements of ESP, magic, stray dogs, and problems with peers, this is a very appealing book to many young readers. As a bonus it is a thoughtful, sympathetic, fairly well-written story.

Interest Level: 4-6. Reading Level: 4.2. Further Search Topics: Gangs-Fiction, Pets-Fiction, Dogs-Fiction, Friendship-Fiction, Honesty-Fiction, Courage-Fiction, Loneliness-Fiction, Extra Sensory Perception-Fiction, Everyday Stories.

SILMAN, Roberta. Somebody else's child; illus by Chris Conover. Warne 1976, 64 pp.

Peter was adopted, but he had never questioned his family's love for him until Puddin' Paint, the school bus driver, made a thoughtless remark. Peter's affection for the older man was strong enough to help him understand Puddin' Paint's feelings. When Puddin' Paint's two dogs disappeared and the bus driver was almost heartbroken, it was Peter who helped the old man search for the dogs. That experience helped both Peter and Puddin' Paint understand that love doesn't only extend to natural born children, but can be just as strong and deep for others.

A simple telling of a moving story. It is as useful for readers who love dogs as for those interested in adoption. Rather inconsistent reading level, tests between 1.2 and 3.1.

Interest Level: 2-5. Reading Level: 2.2. Further Search Topics: Adoption-Fiction, Dogs-Fiction, Friendship-Fiction, Love-Fiction.

SILVERSTEIN, Shel. A light in the attic. Har-Row 1981, 169 pp.

This is the second and most recent collection of Shel Silverstein's wonderfully wry poetry. No young person who has read and enjoyed *Where the Sidewalk Ends* will be disappointed in this effort. For those readers new to Silverstein or to poetry in general, this is as good a place as any to start enjoying both. Hearing a few of these poems read aloud is guaranteed to provoke loud cries of "May I read some?" from almost all listeners.

Interest Level: 2-6. Reading Level: 3.2. Further Search Topics: Poetry, Wit and Humor, Best Sellers, Group 2, Read Aloud.

SILVERSTEIN, Shel. Where the sidewalk ends. Har-Row 1974, 166 pp.

There is something here for almost everyone. It isn't always easy reading, but there are enough short, easier poems to pique almost any child's interest. Once caught, children will find the book hard to put down. The best way to encourage the use of this book is to read selections aloud so that potential readers may hear the rhythm and enjoy the humor. This method almost guarantees that they will then want to try reading the book themselves. Readers may struggle with a poem but once it is mastered, they will usually want more.

Interest Level: 2-6. Reading Level: 3.1. Further Search Topics: Poetry, Wit and Humor, Read Aloud, Group 2, Best Sellers.

SIMON, Seymour. Einstein Anderson makes up for lost time; illus by Fred Winkowski. Viking Pr 1981, 73 pp.

Adam (nicknamed Einstein) Anderson loves science. He also loves bad puns and correcting wrongs. What he does best, however, is to figure out science puzzles. Each book in this series (this is the third) presents 10 science puzzles which challenge Einstein and the reader. Clues and background are established in several pages of scene setting. Einstein regularly solves the puzzle and then the reader is asked how he did it. The answer follows on the next page. Areas of science that are drawn upon vary widely and range from animal behavior through chemistry and space science to zoology. Very palatable science reading. Print is on the small side in all four books.

Interest Level: 3-6. Reading Level: 2.2. Further Search Topics: Science, Puzzles, Mystery and Detective Stories.

SIMON, Seymour. Einstein Anderson, science sleuth; illus by Fred Winkowski. Viking Pr 1980, 73 pp.

Einstein Anderson is the scientific equivalent of Encyclopedia Brown. Einstein was the nickname that Adam Anderson earned at the age of six. Even at that early age he was a scientific genius. He seems to especially love solving scientific puzzles and mysteries and that is just what Einstein does throughout this and the other books. There are ten very brief, somewhat plotless cases that are presented to Einstein. The clues are all included in each story. The solutions are supplied at the end of each case after the reader has had a chance to try to figure out the answers. None of the cases or solutions are terribly technical. Some of the cases can be solved simply by paying careful attention to the text. The rest require a moderate knowledge of scientific principles. It is a satisfying series to the science sleuth. Print is somewhat small.

Interest Level: 3-6. Reading Level: 3.1. Further Search Topics: Mystery and Detective Stories, Science, Puzzles.

SIMON, Seymour. Einstein Anderson shocks his friends; illus by Fred Winkowski.   Viking Pr 1980, 73 pp.

Using the identical formula as that in *Einstein Anderson, Science Sleuth* the author presents 10 more science puzzles to be solved by the reader. Einstein (nee Adam) outwits a bully, discovers who broke the window on the school bus, helps the sixth grade win contests against both the seventh and the eighth grades and more. This book, as well as the others in the series, is both fun and instructive.

Interest Level: 3-6. Reading Level: 3.1. Further Search Topics: Science, Puzzles, Mystery and Detective Stories.

SIMON, Seymour. Einstein Anderson tells a comet's tale; illus by Fred Winkowski.   Viking Pr 1981, 73 pp.

Adam earned his nickname Einstein by proving over and over again that he could solve any science puzzle put to him. Ten more challenges are presented here, none of which prove to be too much for our scientific whiz kid. Like its predecessors, this book is for science sleuths who enjoy matching wits with a cocky punster.

Interest Level: 3-6. Reading Level: 3.1. Further Search Topics: Science, Puzzles, Mystery and Detective Stories.

SIMON, Seymour. The paper airplane book; illus by Byron Barton.   Viking Pr 1971, 48 pp.

For the theory as well as the practice behind successful paper airplanes, this is the book. This is as much a book about the principles of flight as it is about how to make a paper airplane. The reader is introduced to thrust, drag, lift and gravity through explanation, examples, diagrams and experiments. The effects of vertical and horizontal stabilizers, elevators, rudders, flaps, and ailerons on both paper and real airplanes, is explained and illustrated. Instructions are given for building and modifying a basic plane as each new idea is introduced. The book ends with plans for four more sophisticated planes and encouragement to try further experiments. An excellent resource for the enthusiast. Print is small.

Interest Level: 3-6. Reading Level: 3.2. Further Search Topics: Airplanes, Handicrafts, Flight.

SINGER, Marilyn. It can't hurt forever; illus by Leigh Grant.   Har-Row 1978, 186 pp.

When she was 11 years old, it was discovered that Ellie had a heart valve that hadn't closed by itself. Although her mother had promised her that she wouldn't die, Ellie was scared of the hospital and the operation she had to face. Her parents were kind and open about all that was to happen to her, but there was still much that Ellie had to learn from friends she made while she was in the hospital. There were times when she was frightened and only Sonia, a young open-heart surgery patient, could calm her. When Ellie, a special nurse, and a few other patients became close friends, Ellie learned enough from them to allow her to help another patient.

This is not a story of sweetness and light, but it is told with warmth, humor, and real understanding of a young person's fears. Thus it is not only an excellent candidate for bibliotherapy, but it is a truly satisfying story for the general reader as well.

Interest Level: 4-6. Reading Level: 2.2. Further Search Topics: Illness-Fiction, Physicians-Fiction, Medicine-Fiction, Courage-Fiction, Death-Fiction.

SKELLY, James R, jt. auth., see Zim, Herbert S.

SLEATOR, William. Into the dream; illus by Ruth Sanderson.   Dutton 1979, 137 pp.

Paul and Francine each started having what, at first, seemed like nightmares. As the dreams became more detailed and forboding, they discovered that they were sharing the same nightmare. They dreamed of a four-year-old boy, swirling lights, and a large dog. After awhile they figured out that the dog was trying to save the little boy from some unknown danger. As the pieces of the puzzle began to increase in number, Paul and Francine decided that the dream was in some way connected to a night over four years earlier when they had both been staying at the same motel. They, a pregnant woman, and a pregnant dog had all been affected by the telepathic power given off by a spaceship. The progeny of the woman and the dog had been given extraordinary mental powers; powers that a secret government agency wanted to mold and then put to their own use. The danger Paul and Francine felt came from two government agents sent to take the young boy Noah from his mother. Their attempt ended in a bizarre scene at an amusement park, where Noah levitated a broken ferris wheel chair to safety. By thus exposing his talent in public, Noah unconsciously insured against its secret and unsupervised use by the government.

A terrifying and suspense-filled psychological thriller whose main problems are a slightly overdrawn ending and a variable reading level. Reading level drops as low as 2.1 and climbs occasionally to 4.1.

Interest Level: 5-6. Reading Level: 3.2. Further Search Topics: Best Sellers, Supernatural-Fiction, Occult-Fiction, Flying Saucers-Fiction, Nonverbal Communication-Fiction, Dreams-Fiction, Survival-Fiction, Extra Sensory Perception-Fiction, Horror-Fiction.

SLOTE, Alfred. C.O.L.A.R.; illus by Anthony Kramer.   Lippincott 1981, 146 pp.

Jack, his robot twin Danny, and Jack's mother and father were forced to make an emergency landing on an uncharted planet. There they were attacked by creatures who looked like rocks and who wanted to destroy all humans. They captured Danny, led him into an underground living complex, and revealed their true identities. The creatures were robots who had escaped from their owners and the slavery in which they had lived. They kept their planet secret from all humans for fear of what would happen to them should they be discovered. Their main purpose was to free as many robots as possible and to allow robots the same pleasures humans enjoyed. Because Danny had been happy with his humans and claimed to have been treated as one of the family, the inhabitants of the planet C.O.L.A.R. felt he had to be reprogrammed to see the truth. Jack looked and acted so much like Danny that he was able to prevent Danny from being brainwashed, to save his parents from death, and to convince the other robots that some humans treated their robots quite well. In fact, he and Danny, together, were able to persuade the robot manufacturer that a great program of robot-owner re-education was needed.

This is a good adventure story which could also be useful as a lead into discussions of slavery, intelligence, and interpersonal relationships. It is a sequel to *My Robot Buddy*, but one which can be read without having read its predecessor.

Interest Level: 3-5. Reading Level: 3.1.
Robots-Fiction, Science Fiction, Outer Space-Fiction,
Kidnapping-Fiction, Brainwashing-Fiction,
Slavery-Fiction.

SLOTE, Alfred. Hang tough, Paul Mather.   Lippincott
1973, 156 pp.

Paul Mather went against his doctor's and his
parents' orders when he accepted his new neighbors'
challenge to show his pitching skill. He had been told
not to play baseball until he had been given
permission, but Paul not only loved to pitch, he was
also the best pitcher his new friends had ever seen.
Knowing full well the medical problems he could be
precipitating, Paul went ahead and pitched a
spectacular game for the Wilson Dairy team against
the Ace Appliance team. But by the end of the game,
Paul was in the hospital again, and Wilson Dairy had
been forced to forfeit the game because Paul had
played illegally. As Paul's leukemia worsened, his
determination to play baseball again grew. When the
day came that his team was to play a second game
against Ace Appliance, Paul made sure he was there.
He was in a wheelchair and weak, but he was there.
He couldn't actually play, but Paul's psychological
support insured that Wilson Dairy won the game. He
went back to the hospital proud, happy, and still
determined to fight his disease.

This is more than the usual sports story. This is a
very sensitive story of a young boy's determination to
fight leukemia. The reader looking for only a baseball
story may find this book more than he/she wants.
However, the reader who is open to a story of human
strength and courage will be well rewarded. The book
neither dwells on nor minimizes the disease. Instead it
uses both the disease and the sport to portray a
character much more completely than in most sport
stories, especially at this low a reading level. This is
an excellent book for those special readers who
respond well to thought-provoking material. Although
chapters are short and reading level is low, the print is
somewhat small. In addition, the first person style, told
as if dictated into a tape recorder (complete with
occasional interruptions), may be confusing to readers
unless it is explained.

Interest Level: 5-6+Reading Level: 3.1. Further
Search Topics: Baseball-Fiction, Death-Fiction,
Illness-Fiction, Moving, Household-Fiction,
Medicine-Fiction, Physicians-Fiction,
Challenges-Fiction, Courage-Fiction.

SLOTE, Alfred. My robot buddy; illus by Joel
Schick.   Lippincott 1975, 92 pp.

For Jack's tenth birthday he was given a robot—a
robot so real it did everything but run like a human.
The robot appeared so human that a thief, thinking he
was stealing the robot, almost kidnapped Jack by
mistake.

The few points at which the text becomes more
difficult than the reading level indicates should not
prove too intimidating to the reader. The suspense
and humor of the story and the book's high interest
subject matter should carry the reader through the
rough spots. A satisfying read-aloud for second and
third grades.

Interest Level: 2-5. Reading Level: 3.1. Further
Search Topics: Science Fiction, Robots-Fiction,
Friendship-Fiction, Kidnapping-Fiction, Read Aloud.

SMITH, Alison. Help! There's a cat washing in here!;
illus by Amy Rowen.   Dutton 1981, 152 pp.

Henry Walker agreed to care for his younger brother
and sister for two weeks so that his mother could
spend her time preparing a portfolio of her art work in
the hopes of getting a much-needed job. It was a
desperate move for Henry, but it was the only way he
could prevent his bossy Aunt Wilhemina from moving
in to run the household. Despite Henry's best efforts,
almost everything seemed to go wrong. He burned the
food, couldn't keep his brother and sister from
misbehaving, seemed to have poisoned his sister's
friend, and was faced with making a costume in one
night for a school play. The worst of it all was that his
mother wasn't pleased with what she was drawing,
and Henry only seemed to make her feel more
discouraged and unhappy. After what appeared to be
certain defeat, however, Henry's efforts were
rewarded. His mother was given the job, the family
proved they could take care of themselves, and all
ended happily.

A light, humorous tale of a young boy's growing
independence and maturation under stress and
increased responsibility.

Interest Level: 4-6. Reading Level: 3.1. Further
Search Topics: Brothers and Sisters-Fiction, Working
Parents-Fiction, Single Parent Family-Fiction,
Humorous Fiction, Family-Fiction, Challenges-Fiction,
Children-Growth-Fiction.

SMITH, Doris Buchanan. Last was Lloyd.   Viking Pr
1981, 124 pp.

Lloyd had several problems: he was overweight, his
mother was overprotective, he had no school friends,
and there was a chance he might be taken away from
home and put into foster care because he had missed
so much school. Lloyd's mother, very young and very
defensive when she had Lloyd, had done her best to
be a "good mother," but in doing so, had made Lloyd
fearful of the world. He had become the subject of his
classmates' mockery so many times that the only way
he could respond to his peers was with nastiness. The
one skill he possessed was hitting a baseball. He kept
this skill well hidden for fear of exposing himself to
further mockery. When one of his classmates
accidentally discovered how well Lloyd hit, he took the
first step to becoming Lloyd's friend. Lloyd's reaction
was to back away, but Kirby kept trying. Eventually
Kirby's attempts and those of an understanding truant
officer, helped Lloyd begin to make friends, to treat
others decently, and to pull away from his mother; in
short, he began to mature.

Because Lloyd's problems can be oversimplified too
easily, this book requires a fairly mature reader and
perhaps even discussion in order to fully understand
its subtleties.

Interest Level: 5-6+Reading Level: 4.2. Further
Search Topics: Weight-Fiction, Single Parent
Family-Fiction, Courage-Fiction, School Stories,
Loners-Fiction, Friendship-Fiction, Baseball-Fiction,
Family Problems-Fiction, Foster Homes-Fiction,
Children-Growth-Fiction.

SMITH, Doris Buchanan. A taste of blackberries; illus
by Charles Robinson.   T Y Crowell 1973, 58 pp.

A beautifully written, sensitive tale of a boy whose
best friend dies suddenly. Jamie was always joking,
so, when he fell to the ground after being stung by a
bee everyone thought he was playing. A short time
later Jamie was dead. His friend, the story's narrator,
tried to will Jamie back again until the funeral was
over and he finally realized there would be no such
miracle. The next day he accepted his feelings and
picked the newly ripened blackberries, just as he and
Jamie had planned to do. A basket full of the best

blackberries he gave to Jamie's mother and promised her that he would "slam her door" daily just as he and Jamie had done.

Eight short chapters, small print but short sentences, and a child's point of view perfectly maintained. For the lovers of sad stories and stories of friendship. Very useful when discussing death.

Interest Level: 4-6. Reading Level: 3.2. Further Search Topics: Death-Fiction, Friendship-Fiction, Read Aloud.

SMITH, Doris Buchanan. Tough Chauncey.   Morrow 1974, 222 pp.

Chauncey Childs had taught himself to be tough— very tough. Even though he was small for his age (13 years old), the only person who gave him any trouble was his sometimes-friend, Black Jack Levitt. Everyone else was scared of Chauncey. Chauncey felt that he had to be tough or he wouldn't be able to survive. He had to be tough to stand the beatings his grandfather gave him "for his own good," to put up with his mother's drinking and disappearances, and to stand the sight of his grandfather shooting the stray kittens born in their garage.

Chauncey's greatest wish was to be able to live with his mother, instead of with his grandparents. In a desperate attempt to achieve that end he accidentally fell from a moving train and badly hurt his leg. Instead of being returned to his mother he was once more taken back to his grandparents. Chauncey's unhappiness grew until he finally decided to take the one surviving stray kitten and run away. Jack helped him find an empty garage where he could hide while he figured out what to do with his future. After talking with Jack and doing more deep soul searching, Chauncey decided to reshape himself and his life. His first step was to curb his temper and his tongue when his hiding place was discovered. His second step was to see about finding a foster home where he would be treated well, and where he could get a new start.

Ugly as the story is in places, its ending is hopeful. Although it is not always realistic, Chauncey's story is compelling enough to appeal to many readers, especially those who have enjoyed *The War on Villa Street*, by Henry Mazer, *The Outsiders*, by Susan Hinton, or *Mystery of the Fat Cat*, by Frank Bonham. The book's length and its artificially low reading level (vocabulary is often difficult but sentences are very short) make this book most appropriate for an older reader whose reading level is 4.1 or higher.

Interest Level: 5-6. Reading Level: 3.2. Further Search Topics: Child Abuse-Fiction, Family Problems-Fiction, Grandparents-Fiction, Runaways-Fiction, Bullies-Fiction, Single Parent Family-Fiction, Loners-Fiction, Friendship-Fiction, Troublemakers-Fiction, Foster Homes-Fiction.

SOBOL, Donald J. Encyclopedia Brown and the case of the dead eagles; illus by Leonard Shortall. Elsevier-Nelson 1975, 96 pp.

By all rights Idaville should be declared a disaster area and Mr. Brown, the chief of police, should be fired from his job. Idaville looks like an ordinary small town, but behind its sleepy exterior there exists a crime wave that would challenge the best police departments in the country. It is true that the crimes are always solved and the criminals always caught, but not by Chief Brown. Chief Brown is frequently so stumped by his police cases that he talks about them at home, usually at dinner time. Almost always, his son, Leroy "Encyclopedia" Brown, solves the case before dinner is even over. A clear case of superior intelligence and skill.

Encyclopedia (so nicknamed because of his intellect) not only solves his father's cases, but serves as a detective for his friends, too. He is kept so busy that each slim volume in this series contains 10 short mysteries. Needless to say Encyclopedia solves them all. The question is can the reader? All necessary clues are there and specialized knowledge is rarely required. Should the reader fail to solve a mystery (they are not always as easy as one would expect), a full explanation and solution for each case is provided at the back of the book. Each title follows exactly the same formula. Although a teacher or parent may grow bored hearing of Encyclopedia's accomplishments, most young readers thoroughly enjoy them.

The books actively challenge and thus involve the reader in a way most books do not. A very popular series that does not have to be read in sequence. Reading level is consistently 2.2 to 3.1. Encyclopedia Brown series.

Interest Level: 2-6. Reading Level: 3.1. Further Search Topics: Mystery and Detective Stories, Puzzles, Best Sellers, Group 2, Detectives-Fiction.

SOBOL, Donald J. Encyclopedia Brown and the case of the midnight visitor; illus by Lillian Brandi. Elsevier-Nelson 1977, 96 pp.

See *Encyclopedia Brown and the Case of the Dead Eagles* for full annotation.

Interest Level: 2-6. Reading Level: 2.2. Further Search Topics: Mystery and Detective Stories, Puzzles, Detectives-Fiction, Best Sellers.

SOBOL, Donald J. Encyclopedia Brown and the case of the secret pitch; illus by Leonard Shortall. Elsevier-Nelson 1965, 96 pp.

See *Encyclopedia Brown and the Case of the Dead Eagles* for full annotation.

Interest Level: 2-6. Reading Level: 3.1. Further Search Topics: Group 2, Mystery and Detective Stories, Puzzles, Best Sellers, Detectives-Fiction.

SOBOL, Donald J. Encyclopedia Brown, boy detective; illus by Leonard Shortall.   Elsevier-Nelson 1963, 88 pp.

The first of a large number of books that challenge the reader to solve the same mysteries Encyclopedia Brown deciphers. See *Encyclopedia Brown and the Case of the Dead Eagles* for more information.

Interest Level: 2-6. Reading Level: 2.2. Further Search Topics: Mystery and Detective Stories, Puzzles, Best Sellers, Detectives-Fiction.

SOBOL, Donald J. Encyclopedia Brown carries on; illus by Ib Ohlsson.   Schol Bk Serv 1980, 72 pp.

See *Encyclopedia Brown and the Case of the Dead Eagle* for full annotation.

Interest Level: 2-6. Reading Level: 3.1. Further Search Topics: Mystery and Detective Stories, Puzzles, Detectives-Fiction, Group 2, Best Sellers.

SOBOL, Donald J. Encyclopedia Brown finds the clues; illus by Leonard Shortall.   Elsevier-Nelson 1966, 96 pp.

See *Encyclopedia Brown and the Case of the Dead Eagles* for full annotation.

Interest Level 2-6. Reading Level: 3.1. Further Search Topics: Mystery and Detective Stories, Puzzles, Detectives-Fiction, Best Sellers, Group 2.

SOBOL, Donald J. Encyclopedia Brown gets his man; illus by Leonard Shortall.   Elsevier-Nelson 1967, 96 pp.

See *Encyclopedia Brown and the Case of the Dead Eagles* for full annotation.

Interest Level: 2-6. Reading Level: 3.1. Further Search Topics: Mystery and Detective Stories, Puzzles, Best Sellers, Group 2, Detectives-Fiction.

SOBOL, Donald J. Encyclopedia Brown keeps the peace; illus by Leonard Shortall. Elsevier-Nelson 1969, 96 pp.

See *Encyclopedia Brown and the Case of the Dead Eagles* for full annotation.

Interest Level: 2-6. Reading Level: 2.2. Further Search Topics: Mystery and Detective Stories, Puzzles, Best Sellers, Detectives-Fiction.

SOBOL, Donald J. Encyclopedia Brown lends a hand; illus by Leonard Shortall. Elsevier-Nelson 1974, 96 pp.

See *Encyclopedia Brown and the Case of the Dead Eagles* for full annotation.

Interest Level: 2-6. Reading Level: 3.1. Further Search Topics: Mystery and Detective Stories, Puzzles, Detectives-Fiction, Best Sellers, Group 2.

SOBOL, Donald J. Encyclopedia Brown saves the day; illus by Leonard Shortall. Elsevier-Nelson 1970, 96 pp.

See *Encyclopedia Brown and the Case of the Dead Eagles* for full annotation.

Interest Level: 2-6. Reading Level: 2.2. Further Search Topics: Mystery and Detective Stories, Puzzles, Detectives-Fiction, Best Sellers.

SOBOL, Donald J. Encyclopedia Brown sets the pace; illus by Ib Ohlsson. Four Winds Pr 1982, 89 pp.

See *Encyclopedia Brown and the Case of the Dead Eagles* for full annotation.

Interest Level: 2-6. Reading Level: 3.1. Further Search Topics: Mystery and Detective Stories, Detectives-Fiction, Puzzles, Group 2, Best Sellers.

SOBOL, Donald J. Encyclopedia Brown shows the way; illus by Leonard Shortall. Elsevier-Nelson 1972, 96 pp.

See *Encyclopedia Brown and the Case of the Dead Eagles* for full annotation.

Interest Level: 2-6. Reading Level: 2.2. Further Search Topics: Mystery and Detective Stories, Puzzles, Detectives-Fiction, Best Sellers.

SOBOL, Donald J. Encyclopedia Brown solves them all; illus by Leonard Shortall. Elsevier-Nelson 1968, 96 pp.

See *Encyclopedia Brown and the Case of the Dead Eagles* for full annotation.

Interest Level: 2-6. Reading Level: 3.1. Further Search Topics: Mystery and Detective Stories, Puzzles, Detectives-Fiction, Group 2, Best Sellers.

STEVEN, Carla. Hooray for Pig!; illus by Rainey Bennett. HM 1974, 48 pp.

Pig couldn't spend the day swimming with his friend Raccoon because he didn't know how to swim. Instead Pig took a picnic to the lake by himself. At the lake, Pig met Otter, who encouraged Pig to at least try getting in the water. After several days of Otter's patient coaching, not only could Pig stay afloat, but he liked it, too!

For much the same audience as Kessler's *Last One In Is A Rotten Egg*, but because of a more interesting plot it is a little more useful. Reader format.

Interest Level: 1-2. Reading Level: 1.2. Further Search Topics: Pigs-Fiction, Courage-Fiction, Swimming-Fiction, Humorous Fiction.

STODDARD, Edward. The first book of magic; illus by Rod Slater. Watts 1977, 65 pp.

This is a good choice for readers who have already enjoyed reading and mastering an easier book of magic tricks (such as *Let's Make Magic*, by Edward Dolan, Jr.). The tricks the author includes are often too difficult for the casual beginner. They require both a good deal of practice, and the staging and poise that accompany experience. But for the magic enthusiast there are plenty of flashy tricks, hints for performing and detailed instructions. A few, but not many, are tricks found in other books. Most use easily found household objects. Print and illustrations are fairly small however.

Interest Level: 4-6. Reading Level: 3.1. Further Search Topics: Magic.

TALBOT, Charlene Joy. The Great Rat Island adventure; illus by Ruth Sanderson. Atheneum 1977, 164 pp.

Joel dreaded spending the summer with his father. His parents were divorced and Joel was sure his father didn't want him. His father only wanted to study birds. Great Rat Island, where Joel and his father were to spend the summer, was of no interest to Joel. It had no television, no one his own age, only terns. Even the assignment Joel was given (to make sure that no more tern eggs were stolen) sounded dull. It led to an adventure and a friend, however, that were anything but dull.

Joel discovered that a girl his own age was the thief of the tern eggs. Her name was Vicky Owens. She had run away from camp and was spending the summer alone on Little Rat Island. Joel kept her secret until the day of hurricane warnings. As the storm approached Joel realized that Vicky wouldn't be safe on Little Rat Island. Without telling anyone else he took the only boat around and went to look for Vicky to bring her back to Great Rat Island. He found her with her leg stuck between two rocks, unable to move. By the time Joel got her loose, it was too late to get back to the big island. Not knowing what else to do, Joel and Vicky dragged the boat inside an abandoned building where Vicky had been living. As the water rose around them and Vicky grew delirious with fever, Joel set up camp in the boat. While the building filled with water they stayed dry in the boat. Rescue and medical care for Vicky finally came the next day.

A solid, steadily-paced survival story for the reader who wants a little more than just an adventure story. Print is small.

Interest Level: 4-6. Reading Level: 3.1. Further Search Topics: Vacation-Fiction, Family Problems-Fiction, Birds-Fiction, Divorce and Separation-Fiction, Disasters-Fiction, Survival-Fiction, Runaways-Fiction.

TERMAN, Douglas. By balloons to the Sahara; illus by Paul Granger. Bantam 1979, 117 pp.

See the entry for *Sugarcane Island*, by Edward Packard for detailed information about the series. Available in paperback edition only. Choose Your Own Adventure series.

Interest Level: 2-6. Reading Level: 3.2. Further Search Topics: Voyages and Travels-Fiction, Flight-Fiction, Best Sellers, Group 2.

THOMAS, Kathleen. Out of the bug jar; illus by Tom O'Sullivan. Dodd 1981, 125 pp.

Even though 10-year-old Tom Jenkins didn't believe in the tooth fairy, when one of his teeth fell out, he placed it under his pillow just in case he was wrong.

In the middle of that night he was awakened by a small creature crawling under his pillow and grumbling. Tom quickly scooped him into a bug jar he kept nearby and thus began two years of life with Marvin, a tooth fairy. Marvin was a delightful dictator; he ruled Tom's life. He put Tom into a terrible predicament when Tom tried to charge others to see him and Marvin became invisible. Marvin insisted on being fed just what he demanded, despite the difficulties he made for Tom. He badgered Tom to do his homework, to brush his teeth, and to tell the truth. He even managed to follow Tom to school. The only other person Marvin would allow to see or hear him was Tom's friend Sammy. Tom couldn't get rid of Marvin either. Because Tom had captured him, Marvin, should he ever have been able to escape, was entitled to take *all* of Tom's teeth as compensation for being held prisoner.

Actually Marvin didn't really want to escape. He had grown tired of having to race around and collect teeth. For a while then, everyone was fairly content. Tom had all his teeth and Marvin had a rather nice home. Then quite by accident, Marvin got loose. Both Tom and Marvin wanted Tom to catch Marvin again. Tom wanted to keep his teeth and Marvin wanted to keep his comfortable lifestyle, but Marvin played by the rules and wouldn't give Tom any help at all. After more than seven days of valiant but fruitless efforts and nights of sleeping with tape over his mouth, Tom finally caught Marvin and all were happy again.

An amusing story told in short sentences and short chapters. The book should be popular with those who enjoy either fantasy or humor.

Interest Level: 3-5. Reading Level: 2.2. Further Search Topics: Fantasy, Fairies-Fiction, Humorous Fiction, Teeth-Fiction.

THOMPSON, Jean. Brother of the wolves; illus by Steve Marchesi.   Morrow 1978, 159 pp.

Shadow Fox, a Sioux medicine man, went into a wolves' den looking for special items he needed for healing, but found much more. He found a baby boy who had apparently lost his parents in an accident and then been adopted by the wolves. Winter was approaching and Shadow Fox knew the baby would not be able to survive the cold, so he took the child back to his people. The people were reluctant to accept Wolf Brother, saying that he was an evil omen, that he was unnatural, and that he would bring them trouble. But Shadow Fox's will prevailed and Wolf Brother was allowed to stay and grow up with the Sioux.

As he grew Wolf Brother continued to communicate with the wolves and thus fueled the rumors that grew about him. A very jealous young man, Looks-Away, told the people that a vision had shown him that Wolf Brother and his wolves would one day destroy the village and all its people. The people grew so suspicious of Wolf Brother that, when their horses were stolen and they faced a drought, they blamed him and drove him from the village.

For a while Wolf Brother tried to live as a wolf but found that he could not be totally happy. He wandered away to look for a tribe by whom he might be accepted. On his way, he too had a vision—a vision that told him he would find horses and buffalo for the Sioux and be welcomed home again. It was weeks later before he accidentally found his tribe's horses. In a daring move and with help from the wolves, Wolf Brother not only rescued the horses from the raiders,

but also found buffalo just as his vision had predicted. He was then, for the first time, fully welcomed by his people.

This is a taut, suspenseful and mature story about a strong and unusual character. Older readers are most likely to respond positively to the Indian culture and lore.

Interest Level: 5-6. Reading Level: 3.1. Further Search Topics: Survival-Fiction, Wolves-Fiction, Orphans-Fiction, Loners-Fiction, Indians of North America-Fiction, Sioux Indians-Fiction, Jealousy-Fiction, Best Sellers.

TOBIAS, Tobi. Marian Anderson; illus by Symeon Shimin.   Har-Row 1972, 40 pp.

Marian Anderson's beautiful, strong voice and her great range set her apart from other singers even as a child. By the time she was in high school, she was being paid to sing. However, when she tried to apply to a well-known music school, because she was black she was turned away without even being heard. Anderson's determination as well as her own and others' faith in her kept her singing and seeking better and better coaches until she met Giuseppi Boghetti. He was one of the best voice coaches in the country. With him Marian trained and traveled until she finally won the chance to sing with the New York Philharmonic Orchestra. Anderson thought that at that point she would be invited to sing in famous theaters all across the United States, but because she was black she still received no invitations. She went to Europe where she studied and played to wildly enthusiastic audiences. Her European triumphs finally convinced American theater owners and audiences that she was a serious talent. For the next 30 years Marian Anderson sang all over the world, most of the time without incident, with one notable exception in 1939, when the D.A.R. prohibited her from singing in a hall they owned in Washington, D. C. She sang instead, in front of the Lincoln Memorial, at the invitation of the United States government. During the following years Marian married, bought a farm, sang opera and was made a delegate to the United Nations. In 1956, she retired from singing to help children, young singers, and world understanding.

Crowell Biographies make excellent school report sources for reluctant readers. They are short, interesting, and not overly juvenile looking, although the quasi-picture book format may be a problem for some older readers. This biography fits that description perfectly. The series is somewhat sentimental (as are many children's biographies), however, the sentimentality is not forbidding or condescending. A useful series. Crowell Biography series.

Interest Level: 2-5. Reading Level: 3.1. Further Search Topics: Biography, Music-Biography, Blacks-Biography, Talent, Women-Biography, Singers, Prejudice, Group 2.

VAN CLIEF, Sylvia Worth, jt. auth., see Heide, Florence Parry.

VIORST, Judith. The tenth good thing about Barney; illus by Erik Blegvad.   Atheneum 1971, 25 pp.

A quiet, thoughtful book to help a child face the difficult experience of death. When a family's beloved cat Barney died, their little boy tried to find 10 good things to say about him at the funeral. Nine things came easily to mind, but it was not until he had worked in the garden with his father that the little boy realized the tenth good thing. Barney, buried in the ground, would help the flowers, trees, and grass grow.

A special picture book, small in size, but large in impact. Print is somewhat small but well-spaced.

Interest Level: 1-4. Reading Level: 2.1. Further Search Topics: Pets-Fiction, Cats-Fiction, Death-Fiction, Group 2, Read Aloud.

WAGNER, Jane. J.T; photos by Gordon Parks, Jr. Van Nostrand 1969, 64 pp.

This is a sentimental story that rarely fails to elicit a sympathetic response from young readers. J.T. is a poor black boy who saw a portable radio almost begging to be stolen and stole it. Two of the neighborhood bullies, Boomer and Claymore, saw J.T. take the radio. Though they threatened him, even poured soap in his eyes in the school bathrooms, J.T. wouldn't give them the radio as they demanded.

About the same time J.T. found a scrawny, scared little cat with only one eye. Because his mother wouldn't let him take the cat home, J.T. built it a warm but ramshackle little house in an abandoned building. He fed it by charging tuna to his mother's grocery store account without her knowledge. Bones became the only thing in J.T.'s life that he had cared about since his father had walked out.

When Boomer and Claymore found out about Bones, they taunted J.T. by throwing the cat back and forth between them until the frightened cat escaped, darted out into the street and was hit by a car. J.T.'s heart broke as he looked at Bones, but he spoke to no one to tell them of his sadness. Only time, his mother's and grandmother's love and a small kitten from Mr. Rosen, the grocer, helped him recover. On the morning that he decided to accept the kitten, J.T. returned the stolen radio, faced Boomer and Claymore without fear, and asked Mr. Rosen for a job in order to pay for cat food.

The book is oversized and illustrated with photographs from the television movie version. It is not only an excellent story to read aloud but one that will prompt listeners to want to finish it on their own or to reread it. It is now available only in paperback from Dell.

Interest Level: 3-6. Reading Level: 3.1. Further Search Topics: Read Aloud, Courage-Fiction, Best Sellers, Cats-Fiction, Single Parent Family-Fiction, Bullies-Fiction, Blacks-Fiction, Poverty-Fiction, City Life-Fiction, Christmas Stories, Crime-Fiction, Pets-Fiction, Holidays-Fiction.

WALDORF, Mary. Jake McGee and his feet; illus by Leonard Shortall.   HM 1980, 82 pp.

His severe reading difficulties made school the worst place in the world for Jake McGee. On the day that his reading tutor became so impatient with him that she sent Jake to the principal, Jake decided that he couldn't stand school any longer and ran away. He didn't actually run away, he just let his feet finally do what they wanted. His feet were always getting Jake in trouble. They walked too slowly to get him to school on time; they wouldn't stay still once he was in school; and they were always trying to trip someone.

Jake knew that in addition to having problems with his feet he had reading problems, but no one at his old school in the country had noticed. When he and his family moved to the city everything had changed. Jake's mother was always at work or tired. Jake hadn't made any friends and so was always alone. But Jake thought the biggest of all his immediate problems was his feet. The day he ran away, Jake's feet led him to a lost baby, an eccentric old woman, and a neighbor boy, all of whom helped Jake recognize and deal with his real problem.

The book is not high literary quality. The characterization is somewhat flat and the plot is fairly predictable. However, the sentences and chapters are short, the vocabulary is manageable, and Jake's feelings will be shared by many non-readers.

Interest Level: 3-5. Reading Level: 2.2. Further Search Topics: School Stories, Moving, Household-Fiction, Runaways-Fiction, Academic Problems-Fiction, Working Parents-Fiction, Loneliness-Fiction, Feet-Fiction.

WALKER, Alice. Langston Hughes, American poet; illus by Don Miller.   Har-Row 1974, 33 pp.

Langston Hughes is one of the world's most famous black poets. He spent most of his childhood in poverty and yet he shunned and was shunned by his wealthy father because his father disliked blacks. To Hughes the two most important things in the world were his heritage and his writing. His love of black history stemmed from the stories his grandmother told him. His love of language and writing grew out of the lonely hours he spent reading as a child. Hughes began to write poetry even before he was in high school and continued to write for many years. He wrote not only poems, but children's books, novels, plays and short stories. He wrote about and for blacks around the world. He was a proud and honest man who chose to share his pride in his race and his honesty through his writing.

This book is more of an inspirational tribute to a black hero than a fact-filled biography. That isn't to say that there are no facts included in the book. There are facts, but the book will not do as the sole source for a report about Langston Hughes. The book is, however, a good introduction to the man and his writing.

Interest Level: 3-5. Reading Level: 2.2. Further Search Topics: Biography, Blacks-Biography, Writing, Poverty, Divorce and Separation, Poetry.

WALLACE, Bill. A dog named Kitty.   Holiday 1980, 153 pp.

Ricky's fear of dogs was extreme but also understandable. He had been attacked by a rabid dog when he was very young. Remembering the fear, the stitches and the painful rabies shots was enough to bring tears to Ricky's eyes even years later. When a local bully told his dog to attack Ricky, Ricky's fear was discovered. About that time, a stray puppy showed up at Ricky's farm. Not quite knowing why, Ricky began to warm to the puppy, to feed it, and finally to love it. When the dog was attacked by a pack of wild dogs (a brutal scene vividly described), Ricky fully overcame his fear of dogs, went to Kitty's defense, and was barely able to save her life. When Kitty was later tragically and accidentally killed, Ricky swore that he would never have anything to do with a dog again. He almost kept his promise to himself, but eventually a second stray dog wandered into the farm and Ricky decided to try again.

This is an emotional story that should appeal to many readers. However, because of the violence and the dog's two-stage death, the book is probably best suited to fifth and sixth grade children.

Interest Level: 5-6. Reading Level: 3.1. Further Search Topics: Dogs-Fiction, Pets-Fiction, Bullies-Fiction, Death-Fiction, Oklahoma-Fiction, Courage-Fiction, Country Life-Fiction.

WARNER, Gertrude Chandler. The boxcar children; illus by L. Kate Deal.   A. Whitman 1950, 154 pp.

This is the first in a series of very early hi/lo books. Although they often bear signs of stilted "Dick and Jane"-style writing, occasionally preach to the reader, and are interrupted by frequent asides from the author, the stories are still popular with young readers. In each book the children are not simply manipulated, but control their own destiny. They fulfill many a child's dream of finding a loving home and family, becoming rich, having adventures, and solving mysteries. This is the simplest story of the series, most of the other entries assume interest in such advanced subjects as fossils, food sources, antiques, or the Revolutionary War.

The only place the four orphaned Alden children had to live was with a grandfather whom they had never met, but whom they had heard was mean. Rather than live with him, they decided to try and survive on their own. They found an abandoned railway boxcar and filled it was items that they found in a junkyard in order to make it their home. Henry, the oldest, went to work for a doctor who, in addition to money, gave him food and kept a silent but watchful eye over all the children without their knowledge. When Violet became ill, the children had no choice but to take her to Dr. Moore. He gave them all a temporary home and arranged for them to gradually get to know their grandfather. By the time Violet was almost well the children had grown to like the elderly stranger. It was a happy day when the children finally realized that the man to whom Dr. Moore had introduced them was really their grandfather.

Interest Level: 1-4. Reading Level: 2.1. Further Search Topics: Orphans-Fiction, Survival-Fiction, Runaways-Fiction, Brothers and Sisters-Fiction, Grandparents-Fiction.

WARNER, Gertrude Chandler. The lighthouse mystery; illus by David Cunningham.   A. Whitman 1963, 128 pp.

What better place for a mystery than a lighthouse late at night? Add the excitement of a storm at sea and a young man alone in a boat and the story should be unbeatable. Unfortunately this, as well as some of the other books in the series, does not quite live up to its potential. It will not attract many new readers but it will satisfy those who crave more adventures of the Alden family. The main problem with the book is its lack of definition. It isn't quite a mystery or an adventure story, it's a little of both. It is also part homespun family story, part science lesson, and part "problem story."

The Aldens rented a lighthouse in a very small fishing village one summer. Late each night their dog awoke them as he barked at a stranger who walked into or away from a closed-up building nearby. When the children investigated, they found that the surly son of a local fisherman was using the building to experiment on plankton as a food source. Harry was a brilliant young man who wanted to go to college, but whose father stubbornly refused to let him study. One night when Larry was at sea gathering samples, a terrible storm blew up. Only the Coast Guard and an improvised light in the lighthouse saved Larry from drowning. Larry's brush with death forced his father to acknowledge Larry's abilities and allow him to continue studying at college.

The sketchy illustrations in this and the following books in the series are an improvement over the silhouettes of *The Boxcar Children*. See the annotation for *The Boxcar Children* for further series information.

Interest Level: 3-6. Reading Level: 2.1. Further Search Topics: Mystery and Detective Stories, Lighthouses-Fiction, Food-Fiction, Disasters-Fiction, Vacation-Fiction.

WARNER, Gertrude Chandler. Mountain top mystery; illus by David Cunningham.   A. Whitman 1964, 128 pp.

A day's climb up and down Old Flat Top was all the Alden family had wanted. Instead, when a portion of the trail collapsed into a cave, they found themselves stranded on top of the mountain. From their vantage point that night they could see a shadowy light which they investigated the next day. They found a 90-year-old Indian woman who had a strange story to tell of treasure hidden in a cave somewhere on Old Flat Top. The treasure was rightfully hers as the last of her tribe, but she had never been able to find it. The collapse of the trail and the reopening of the cave attracted more attention than just the Alden's though. Both an expert on caves and a young Indian boy wanted to find out more about the cave. David, the Indian boy, turned out to be the old woman's grandnephew. The treasure was indeed unearthed; David and Lovan were reunited; the treasure was given to Lovan, and both David's and Lovan's futures were secured.

What in the other books is mild stereotyping becomes more noticeable here (the books are all around 20 years old). The print is smaller here than before but the spacing between the lines is adequate. See entry for *The Boxcar Children* for more information.

Interest Level: 3-6. Reading Level: 2.2. Further Search Topics: Mystery and Detective Stories, Treasure-Fiction, Survival-Fiction, Indians of North America-Fiction, Mountain Climbing-Fiction, Brothers and Sisters-Fiction.

WARNER, Gertrude Chandler. Schoolhouse mystery; illus by David Cunningham.   A. Whitman 1965, 128 pp.

On a dare, the Aldens went to a quiet fishing village to see what excitement they could find there. They found an isolated town filled with poor and unfriendly people. In their attempt to get to know the townspeople, the Aldens learned of the children's desire for schooling and the adults' anticipation of the Money Man's arrival. The Alden children took on the task of teaching school for the summer in an abandoned schoolhouse owned by Miss Gray, a recluse. The Money Man intrigued them more with each new bit of information they learned about him. They finally decided that the Money Man was a swindler who was practically stealing valuable antiques away from the villagers. By spying on the Money Man when he used the schoolhouse to store the antiques, the Aldens and an ex-FBI man were able to capture him. When the vacation was over, the Aldens had once more found excitement, Miss Gray had agreed to teach the local school, the Money Man was on his way to jail, and the townspeople knew the value of their old household items.

See the entry for *The Boxcar Children* for more information.

Interest Level: 3-5. Reading Level: 2.2. Further Search Topics: Mystery and Detective Stories, Vacation-Fiction, School Stories, Antiquities-Fiction, Crime-Fiction, Brothers and Sisters-Fiction, Challenges-Fiction.

WARNER, Gertrude Chandler. The woodshed mystery; illus by David Cunningham.   A. Whitman 1960, 159 pp.

   The four Alden children have grown since their first appearance in *The Boxcar Children* but they are still as close a family as ever. Aunt Jane's telephone message that she wanted to move near them started this adventure. Grandfather proceeded to buy and refurbish his childhood home as a surprise for Aunt Jane. It was an easy house to buy because it had been abandoned and was thought to be haunted. Even though the children and Aunt Jane weren't really worried by the stories of odd occurrences that no one quite remembered, they began to be aware of strange noises and things missing. Upon investigation they discovered Aunt Jane's old boyfriend living in the woodshed in the forest. There beneath the floor of the woodshed, they also found a store of Revolutionary War supplies and a letter from the original owners of the house. The supplies and the letter helped to explain some of the stories. Andrew, Jane's long-lost boyfriend, explained the rest.

   It is not necessary to have read any of the series in order to read this story, but those children who enjoyed *The Boxcar Children* are most likely to enjoy the Alden's further adventures. See the entry for *The Boxcar Children* for more information.

   Interest Level: 3-5. Reading Level: 2.1. Further Search Topics: Mystery and Detective Stories, United States-History-War-Fiction, Brothers and Sisters-Fiction, Ghosts-Fiction, Vacation-Fiction.

WHITE, Laurence B., Jr. Science puzzles; illus by Marc Tolon Brown.   A-W 1975, unp (46 pp).

   There are twenty four very short experiments designed to illustrate the simplest of scientific principles clearly presented here. For all but a few experiments there is not only an explanation of what happens but also an explanation of why it happened. What makes the book even more useful, is that it can also be used as a book of easy magic tricks. Any child who enjoys it as science will, with a little help, be able to see its possibilities as magic. In fact it provides a better explanation of the Knot Magic trick than can be found in *It's Magic*.

   Interest Level: 1-3. Reading Level: 1.2. Further Search Topics: Science, Magic, Puzzles, Experiments, Scientific.

WHITE, Laurence B., Jr. Science toys; illus by Marc Tolon Brown.   A-W 1975, unp (46 pp).

   This book presents 23 toys that a young child can easily make and learn from at the same time. A sundial, a drinking straw that flies, a balloon that rolls over, a ghost that sticks to the wall by itself, a water-go-round, and a paper cup that roars are a few examples of what is to be found here. The construction and use of each toy is explained and illustrated in enough detail to enable the child to work alone. And as in *Science Puzzles*, some of the toys will double as magic tricks (i.e. can you balance the rim of a paper plate on your nose?).

   Interest Level: 1-3. Reading Level: 2.1. Further Search Topics: Handicrafts, Science, Magic, Toys, Games, Group 2, Puzzles.

WISEMAN, Bernard. Morris and Boris.   Dodd 1974, 64 pp.

   This is a compilation of three silly stories about Morris the Moose and Boris the Bear. When Boris tries to interest Morris in telling riddles, Morris frustrates Boris so completely that Boris runs off angrily. Later Boris tries to teach Morris a tongue twister, but ends up running off in total confusion. Finally Boris tries to teach Morris to play hide-and-seek and that, too, is a disaster. Boris tells Morris that Morris just cannot do anything. A bird who has seen everything reminds Boris that Morris can make him very angry and that is something. When Boris agrees they all laugh happily.

   Broad, slapstick humor makes this appealing to children well into third grade. Reader format.

   Interest Level: 1-3. Reading Level: 1.2. Further Search Topics: Wit and Humor, Riddles, Tongue Twisters, Games, Humorous Fiction.

WOLKOFF, Judie. Wally.   Bradbury 1977, 199 pp.

   Michael Price agreed to take care of his friend Billy's chuckwalla for three weeks. But because his mother had declared a moratorium on any more reptiles in the house, Michael tried to hide Wally in his closet. With help from his brother Roger, Michael managed to keep Wally a secret until Wally was mistakenly left out of his box one night. Despite Michael and Roger's desperate searches, the chuckwalla did not reappear until Mr. and Mrs. Price were involved in the final negotiations for the sale of their house. Wally completely disrupted the proceedings, prevented the sale and thus made everyone happy. For as it turned out, none of the Prices had really wanted to move after all.

   A fast-paced, funny book with much reader appeal.

   Interest Level: 2-5. Reading Level: 2.2. Further Search Topics: Pets-Fiction, Humorous Fiction, Lizards-Fiction, Best Sellers, Reptiles-Fiction, Secrets-Fiction.

WYLER, Rose and Ames, Gerald.

   Funny Magic; illus by Talivaldis Stubis.   Schol Bk Serv 1972, 52 pp.

   A collection of 20 simple but effective magic tricks that require some advance preparation and practice but which are well-suited to the third through fifth grade child's coordination. Because all tricks are meant to be performed in front of an audience, there are performance hints throughout the book. Most of the tricks are impressive enough to interest even sixth grade magicians, but the book's reader format and cute tone make it difficult to use beyond grade four.

   Interest Level: 2-4. Reading Level: 2.1. Further Search Topics: Magic.

WYLER, Rose and Ames, Gerald.

   Magic secrets; illus by Talivaldis Stubis.   Har-Row 1967, 64 pp.

   Another good selection of easily performed but impressive looking magic tricks. After a short section defining magic, 13 tricks are described. Another 11 tricks are included as the authors describe how to put on a magic show. Just what differentiates the first group of tricks from the second is not clear. With a little imagination any of the tricks shown in the book could be used in a magic show. Use of the book beyond fourth grade is not likely due to its "early-reader" appearance. An I-Can-Read-Book.

   Interest Level: 1-4. Reading Level: 2.1. Further Search Topics: Magic, Group 2.

YOLEN, Jane. The boy who spoke chimp illus by David Wiesner.   Knopf 1981, 120 pp.

   Kriss was determined to prove to his father that, at 12 years old, he was perfectly capable of camping out by himself. To do so, he left home and headed up the coast of California with a sleeping bag, some food, a map and compass, and water. His plan was to camp, ride, and hike his way to his grandmother's house. On the way, the coast line was torn apart by the second great earthquake to strike California. The first had already destroyed great portions of the state. The second was even stronger. The truck he had been riding in was destroyed and everyone around Kriss was killed by the quake except for two chimpanzees. The chimps, in transit from one lab to another, were research animals who had been taught to use sign language. Kriss took the animals with him as he tried to get farther inland and finally home to Los Angeles. His trip not only confirmed his father's fears about Kriss' inadequacies but taught him how to overcome them. Kriss learned to communicate with the chimps, to find food and to live on his own until Old Chris, a hermit, happened along. Together they continued to brave the chaos brought about by the earthquake even when Old Chris' heart troubled him. When a helicopter finally spotted them, Kriss decided to let the chimps go wild and promised Old Chris that he would be back in the woods very soon. It was a mature, capable Kriss who returned home.

This is typical of the Capers series—much action, few background details, little characterization. The books, however, are on appealing topics; they move quickly and they create intriguing (if sometimes implausible) situations. They are light, enjoyable and very useful. Capers series.

Interest Level: 3-6. Reading Level: 3.1. Further Search Topics: California-Fiction, Disasters-Fiction, Survival-Fiction, Apes-Fiction, Nonverbal Communication-Fiction, Camping-Fiction, Runaways-Fiction, Best Sellers.

YOLEN, Jane. Shirlick Holmes and the case of the wandering wardrobe; illus by Anthony Rao.   Coward 1981, 80 pp.

This is a light, fast-paced story of Shirli and her four friends' attempt to solve a local mystery. Its more fully developed characters and plot make this a better literary piece than any of the *Encyclopedia Brown* stories, but it resembles them in other ways. The children live in a small, secure town. The police chief, Shirli's neighbor and George's father, is working on the same case that interests the children but the children solve it first. The mystery is real and involves danger, as opposed to many of Hildick's McGurk mysteries, the other series this book resembles.

Shirli is a fiesty figure who took up George's challenge to solve the town's latest mystery. Thieves had been systematically robbing some of the wealthy summer homes of antiques. Shirli's plan, to search each of the houses for clues, only succeeded in angering the police chief when he caught Shirli and her friends. Being intrepid detectives, however, they did not give up. Instead, they staked out a likely house and waited for the thieves. When the robbers finally arrived Shirli and George hid. Only Gloria was able to escape and go for help. The oak wardrobe in which Shirli took refuge was one of the first pieces the thieves took out of the house. When Shirli tried to get out of it, she found the wardrobe had been placed on a truck with its door against the truck's side; she was

caught. Very frightened, she stayed silent until she found herself in the middle of an antiques auction and recognized one of the voices making bids as George's father! As Shirli tumbled out of the wardrobe some of the police chief's men arrested the auctioneer for burglary and selling stolen goods. After she escaped, Gloria had told the police about the thieves, their truck, Shirli, and George, whom they found locked inside a closet still at the summer house.

A serviceable book that will be enjoyed by a wide range of readers.

Interest Level: 3-5. Reading Level: 3.1. Further Search Topics: Mystery and Detective Stories, Humorous Fiction, Friendship-Fiction, Crime-Fiction, Antiquities-Fiction, Detectives-Fiction, Challenges-Fiction.

YOUNG, Carol Beach. Remember me when I am dead.   Elsevier-Nelson 1980, 94 pp.

This is a short but taut story about the effect of their mother's death upon two young girls. For a long time Jenny, the younger and more vivacious of the sisters, refused to believe her mother had really died. Sara, quiet and serious, mourned and missed her mother, but eventually accepted her mother's sudden death as a fact. Jenny's continuing denial prompted her father and stepmother to talk of sending her away to a school where memories wouldn't be so vivid. That talk inspired Sara to develop a devious and calculated plan to insure that Jenny would indeed be sent away. All her life Sara had been given less attention than Jenny. With Jenny gone, Sara would finally have her father and stepmother's love and attention all to herself. With a Hitchcock-like twist Sara's plan proved too successful. Jenny was sent away to school, but because she didn't want to go alone and because her parents could deny Jenny nothing, Sara was to go too.

This suspenseful psychological thriller is almost guaranteed success with older readers.

Interest Level: 5-6. Reading Level: 4.2. Further Search Topics: Mystery and Detective Stories, Brothers and Sisters-Fiction, Death-Fiction, Horror-Fiction, Best Sellers, Jealousy-Fiction.

ZIM, Herbert S and Skelly, James R.
Hoists, cranes and derricks; illus by Gary Ruse. Morrow 1969, 64 pp.

This is a very thorough treatment of lifting machinery. It is a straight-forward explanation that is technical, but not so technical that it can't be understood by young enthusiasts. The text is well-supplemented by a good number of clear illustrations and diagrams including drawings of the attachments to mobile cranes, motions used by signalmen, kinds of quay cranes, types of derricks, and even charts of the capacities of cranes and derricks and load-bearing materials. A fair index helps to make the book useful for reference or report writing.

Interest Level: 3-6. Reading Level: 3.2. Further Search Topics: Construction.

SUBJECTS

AARON, HENRY

Burchard, Marshall. Sports hero: Henry Aaron. Putnam 1974, 96 pp.

Baseball's homerun king. See entry under *Sports Hero: Bill Walton* for more information. Sports Hero series.

Interest Level: 2-6. Reading Level: 3.1. Further Search Topics: Biography, Aaron, Henry, Baseball-Biography, Blacks-Biography.

ACADEMIC PROBLEMS

Holland, John. The way it is. HarBraceJ 1969, 87 pp.

For 15 boys living in a run-down area of Brooklyn, school became interesting when they were assigned to photograph whatever was meaningful to them in their neighborhood. The results, described in their own words, were developed into this fascinating documentary which is at the same time a spontaneous glimpse of the boys themselves. The book should be of particular interest to older urban children. Print slightly on the small side. Has recently gone out of print, but is worth looking for.

Interest Level: 4-6. Reading Level: 3.2. Further Search Topics: Best Sellers, City Life, Photography, Poverty, Academic Problems.

ACADEMIC PROBLEMS-FICTION

Burch, Robert. Queenie Peavy; illus by Jerry Lazare. Viking Pr. 1966, 159 pp.

Queenie was always in trouble. She could be mean, really mean, but, she was also bright, talented, independent and resilient. Queenie blamed her problems on the fact that people teased her because her father was in jail and because she was poor. She thought that she had to defend herself against the world. Queenie was proud of her poor reputation until she accidentally-on-purpose caused a classmate to break his leg. Then, when her father returned home and wasn't the person she'd hoped he'd be, Queenie realized that only she could make her life better. Being the strong person she was, she set out to do just that.

Queenie is a wonderfully alive and sympathetic character, one well worth introducing to older readers despite the book's reading level. Print somewhat small. Line spacing average width.

Interest Level: 5-6. Reading Level: 5.1. Further Search Topics: Family Problems-Fiction, Crime-Fiction, Loners-Fiction, Poverty-Fiction, Humorous Fiction, Bullies-Fiction, Troublemakers-Fiction, Academic Problems-Fiction, Read Aloud.

Cone, Molly. The amazing memory of Harvey Bean; illus by Robert MacLean. HM 1980, 83 pp.

It had been a long time since Harvey had been happy. His memory was so bad that he was always in trouble at school. And now that his parents were separating, he had trouble at home, too. Because he thought that neither one of his parents wanted him he told each one that he was going to stay with the other and instead decided to spend the summer alone. A few hours after he left home, Harry ran into Mr. and Mrs. Katz and before he completely realized it, he was living with them.

Mr. Katz couldn't stand to see anything go to waste. He collected the usable food thrown out behind grocery stores, old furniture, tools, windows and more. Mrs. Katz, whose memory was just as bad as Harvey's, loved to cook, so she could always find a way to use the food. Everything else bulged from the house and garage into the driveway and yard. Harvey spent a happy summer learning to scavenge, eating well, learning not to worry about what others thought of him and even improving his memory. When his parents finally found him, Harvey realized that they really did want him, even if they were separated. He decided to live with his mother on weekdays, his father on weekends, and the Katzs during the summers.

The plot problems that are obvious to adult readers are ones that most young readers will be able to ignore (i.e. neither parent checks on Harvey for over two months). Young readers will enjoy the humor and realism of Harvey's pain, happiness and eventual feeling of self-confidence and triumph. The ten short chapters, good-sized print and adequate space between the lines help lower the book's reading level to late fourth grade.

Interest Level: 3-6. Reading Level: 5.1. Further Search Topics: Loners-Fiction, Vacation-Fiction, Divorce and Separation-Fiction, Humorous Fiction, Group 2, Memory-Fiction, Runaways-Fiction, Academic Problems-Fiction, Individualists-Fiction.

Curtis, Philip. The invasion of the Brain Sharpeners; illus by Tony Ross. Knopf 1979, 117 pp.

This book is one of a number of books published by Albert Knopf under the series title Capers. They are meant to be (and with few exceptions are) light, easy-to-read fiction, published simultaneously in hardcover and paperback editions. Each book is about 120 pages long with chapter length varying from 9 to 14 pages. Print is plenty large and spacing between lines is always adequate. Plots are built around an idea of guaranteed appeal, descriptive passages are kept to a minimum and action (often suspenseful) abounds. This should, on the whole, be a very useful series. Some entries (i.e., *Man From the Sky* and *Who Stole the Wizard of Oz*, both by Avi) are either too difficult or too obscure to be widely appealing, but they are by far the exceptions to the rule.

Invasion of the Brain Sharpeners is the catchy science fiction story of Michael's successful, but risky, attempt to rid his fifth grade classroom of the overpowering influence of the Brain Sharpeners. The Brain Sharpeners came from another galaxy to search for humans to help them colonize their Planet Five. Humans were so lacking in brain power that the Brain Sharpeners' plan was to periodically expose each child to brain-developing rays, then put them through intensive courses of study guided by their also-exposed teacher. When the children had all learned enough to be beneficial to the Brain Sharpeners, they were to be taken from Earth to Planet Five. Michael was the only one to see the danger they were in and to attempt to stop the plot. He managed to chase the aliens away and to prevent his classmates and teacher from receiving their second dose of rays, but in doing so, he sent the principal to the spaceship. Michael's classmates were thus saved, but his principal was never heard from again. Capers series.

Interest Level: 3-6. Reading Level: 3.1. Further Search Topics: Science Fiction, Flying Saucers-Fiction, Aliens-Fiction, School Stories, Kidnapping-Fiction, Best Sellers, Academic Problems-Fiction, Brainwashing-Fiction.

Kelley, Sally. Trouble with explosives. Bradbury 1976, 117 pp.

Polly Banks stuttered very badly. She wanted to stop but she couldn't. Moving, entering a new school, and facing a mean teacher who seemed in need of psychiatric help, all made Polly's stuttering worse.

When Sis, Polly's new friend, rose to Polly's defense in one confrontation too many with Miss Patterson, the teacher took cruel revenge. Polly's desire to help Sis, her need to do something about her stuttering, and an understanding psychiatrist, all helped Polly learn to help herself with her speech problem. At the same time, she began to understand and have confidence in herself and her family.

Another "problem book" that older elementary school readers seem to crave. Polly and Sis are both very sympathetic characters who bring to life many of the uncertainties of growing up. Print and line spacing of only average size but otherwise a good choice.

Interest Level: 4-6. Reading Level: 3.2. Further Search Topics: Academic Problems-Fiction, Stuttering-Fiction, Psychiatrists-Fiction, School Stories, Mental Illness-Fiction, Troublemakers-Fiction, Courage-Fiction, Physically Handicapped-Fiction, Children-Growth-Fiction, Moving, Household-Fiction.

Waldorf, Mary. Jake McGee and his feet; illus by Leonard Shortall. HM 1980, 82 pp.

His severe reading difficulties made school the worst place in the world for Jake McGee. On the day that his reading tutor became so impatient with him that she sent Jake to the principal, Jake decided that he couldn't stand school any longer and ran away. He didn't actually run away, he just let his feet finally do what they wanted. His feet were always getting Jake in trouble. They walked too slowly to get him to school on time; they wouldn't stay still once he was in school; and they were always trying to trip someone.

Jake knew that in addition to having problems with his feet he had reading problems, but no one at his old school in the country had noticed. When he and his family moved to the city everything had changed. Jake's mother was always at work or tired. Jake hadn't made any friends and so was always alone. But Jake thought the biggest of all his immediate problems was his feet. The day he ran away, Jake's feet led him to a lost baby, an eccentric old woman, and a neighbor boy, all of whom helped Jake recognize and deal with his real problem.

The book is not high literary quality. The characterization is somewhat flat and the plot is fairly predictable. However, the sentences and chapters are short, the vocabulary is manageable, and Jake's feelings will be shared by many non-readers.

Interest Level: 3-5. Reading Level: 2.2. Further Search Topics: School Stories, Moving, Household-Fiction, Runaways-Fiction, Academic Problems-Fiction, Working Parents-Fiction, Loneliness-Fiction, Feet-Fiction.

ACROBATS AND ACROBATICS

Krementz, Jill. A very young circus flyer. Knopf 1979, unp (112 pp).

One of a series of five oversized, abundantly photographed views of unusual children. Tato Farfan is part of the Flying Farfans of Ringling Brothers and Barnum and Bailey Circus. He lives in a railroad car on a circus train with his mother, father, and older brother. The whole family performs as trapeze artists and flyers for the circus. Told as if Tato were speaking, this is the story of a fairly normal boy who also happens to be a circus flyer. Practice sessions are difficult, costumes must be readied, and time must be spent helping each other, but there is also time for Tato to watch TV, play with the clowns, play soccer, and just have fun.

In addition to Tato's story, the reader is given a behind-the-scenes tour of the circus right up to and including the performance itself (color photos used for the performance). It is an exciting world that should appeal to almost anyone who has enjoyed the circus.

Interest Level: 2-6. Reading Level: 3.2. Further Search Topics: Circus, Acrobats and Acrobatics, Best Sellers, Talent, Group 2, Gymnastics.

Krementz, Jill. A very young gymnast. Knopf 1978, unp (128 pp).

This is Torrence York's story. It includes a team trip to Germany for competition. See notes for *A Very Young Dancer* for more information.

Interest Level: 2-6. Reading Level: 3.2. Further Search Topics: Gymnastics, Talent, Acrobats and Acrobatics, Group 2, Best Sellers.

ACROBATS AND ACROBATICS-FICTION

Bulla, Clyde Robert. Dexter; illus by Glo Coalson. Har-Row 1973, 69 pp.

This is not as simple a story as it first appears. Dave, 12 years old and lonely, had hoped his new neighbors would be friends. But, the Arvin family kept very much to themselves until Dave accidentally discovered Alex, the Arvin's son, doing tricks on a trapeze in the barn. Because Dave kept the secret and shared Alex's love for Dexter, his circus pony, the boys soon became friends. Then in one horrible night, the Arvins were forced to leave the town and Dexter was so badly hurt he was believed to be dead. A week later Dave found Dexter alive, but crippled for life and so frightened that no one could get near him. The horse surprised everyone and managed to live through a very harsh winter as well as the townspeople's determination to kill him. When Alex and his father returned, almost a year later, they found Dexter and took the old and feeble horse back to a ranch with them. The story is told with sympathy, with an understanding of how it feels to be lonely, and with tension and suspense. It's appeal should last from third through sixth grade. Print size is smaller than Bulla's usual.

Interest Level: 3-6. Reading Level: 3.1. Further Search Topics: Survival-Fiction, Acrobats and Acrobatics-Fiction, Horses-Fiction, Read Aloud, Circus-Fiction, Loneliness-Fiction, Friendship-Fiction.

Dolch, Edward W. Circus stories; illus by Dee Wallace. Garrard 1956, 166 pp.

A collection of 18 chapters that tell 15 true stories about the circus. Some are descriptions of activities (trapeze flying) or people (Emmett Kelly, a circus doctor, the Ringling Brothers). Other chapters tell of unusual occurrences; i.e., the bareback rider who was thrown off her horse into the lap of a spectator whom she later married. Some stories, such as the story of the horse trainer whose life was saved by an elephant, are exciting. Others are sad ("Blinky," the dog who was killed by an angry lion).

The authors' tone becomes condescending off and on through this collection, thus hampering its usefulness somewhat. Otherwise, it is very similar to the other Dolch books; it is a decent collection of very simplified stories. Dolch Basic Vocabulary Book series.

Interest Level: 1-4. Reading Level: 2.2. Further Search Topics: Circus-Fiction, Clowns-Fiction, Acrobats and Acrobatics-Fiction, Group 2.

ACTING

Alexander, Sue. Small plays for you and a friend; illus by Olivia H. Cole. Seabury 1974, 48 pp.

Five very short and very simple plays for two actors that will be of more interest to the players than the audience. However, because the reading level is low, and because children's love of acting is strong and their tolerance of weak plot is high, this can be used through grade three. A companion volume *Small Plays for Special Days* presents seven more short plays for two characters.

Interest Level: 1-3. Reading Level: 2.1. Further Search Topics: Acting, Drama, Group 2.

Aylesworth, Thomas G. Movie monsters. Lippincott 1975, 79 pp.

If you are looking for an example of fine writing, you won't find it here. What you will find is a collection of monster movie photographs and facts. This is a wealth of trivia about eleven famous monsters (including King Kong, Godzilla, the Fly, Frankenstein's monster, the Mummy, Dracula, Wolf Man and others), their films, sequels, historic backgrounds, identifying characteristics, and more. There is an extensive index, a list of monster movies and their credits, and even brief information about famous monster actors. The book is not great literature, but it is interesting and fun.

Interest Level: 1-6. Reading Level 3.1. Further Search Topics: Acting, Motion Pictures, Monsters, Horror-Fiction, Group 2, Best Sellers.

ACTING-FICTION

Clifford, Eth. The dastardly murder of Dirty Pete; illus by George Hughes. HM 1981, 120 pp.

Although this is a sequel to *Help, I'm a Prisoner in the Library*, it does not depend on the previous title, and in fact, is likely to be the more successful introduction to Mary Rose and Jo-Beth Onetree. Given the choice, most young readers will take a mystery set in a ghost town over a mystery set in a library.

Mary Rose, Jo-Beth and their father were on their way across country when they became lost. As night grew closer, the only place they could find to stay was an old hotel in the ghost town where Sorehead Jones had allegedly killed Dirty Pete. It was Sorehead's ghost who was supposed to haunt the town, and indeed there was someone or something who was in the town with the Onetrees. To their surprise, that someone turned out to be Sourdough Sam, an aging actor who had become senile and spent his days acting out all the parts in the Dirty Pete story. The town was only a movie set and the story was only a movie script. The Onetrees discovered the truth bit by bit after a frightening venture into an abandoned gold mine, a harrowing night in the haunted hotel and a jail sentence for Mr. Onetree.

Beware of the rare, very difficult descriptive passage that may cause trouble for some readers.

Interest Level: 2-5. Reading Level: 3.1. Further Search Topics: Mystery and Detective Stories, West-Fiction, Brothers and Sisters-Fiction, Motion Pictures-Fiction, Ghosts-Fiction, Treasure-Fiction, Group 2, Acting-Fiction, Aging-Fiction, Mental Illness-Fiction.

Robinson, Barbara. The best Christmas pageant ever; illus by Judith Gwyn Brown. Har-Row 1972, 80 pp.

A truly delightful story of what happens when the meanest kids in town (they are all in one family) take over all the lead roles in the Sunday school Christmas pageant. The Herdmans (all six of them), having heard that the church was giving away free food, showed up to take some. While they were there, they heard about the Christmas pageant and decided it presented them with another perfect opportunity for food and mischief. With a little behind-the-scenes arm-twisting (literally), they managed to dissuade everyone else from showing interest in the major roles. Theirs was a completely original interpretation of the Christmas story that left nothing and no one around them untouched.

That the book's reading level will prove too high for many people is unfortunate. The story is well worth the struggle. A wonderful choice for reading aloud.

Interest Level: 3-6. Reading Level: 5.1 Further Search Topics: Christmas-Fiction, Bullies-Fiction, Troublemakers-Fiction, Humorous Fiction, Religion-Fiction, Group 2, Read Aloud, Acting-Fiction, Holidays-Fiction.

Sharmat, Marjorie W. Getting something on Maggie Marmelstein; illus by Ben Shecter. Har-Row 1971, 101 pp.

A curious love-hate relationship existed between Thad and Maggie. It all began when Maggie overheard Thad say she squeaked like a mouse. Then Maggie caught Thad wearing an apron and cooking. Thad was so uncomfortable with the thought that Maggie might tell his friends, that he was determined to find out Maggie's deepest secret. That meant that Thad had to take a lead role as a frog opposite Maggie as the princess in the school play. While at Maggie's apartment for a costume fitting, Thad found a love letter Maggie had written to Cary Grant. Thad decided he would read the letter to the class right after the play was over. But during the play Maggie saved Thad from what could have been one of the most embarrassing moments of his life. By the time he finally had the chance to make Maggie appear foolish, Thad had changed his mind.

Written as Thad's story, the book is funny, warm, and realistic. A good, short, story that continues to be popular. Print is of moderate size.

Interest Level: 3-6. Reading Level: 3.1. Further Search Topics: Humorous Fiction, Everyday Stories, School Stories, Best Sellers, Friendship-Fiction, Sex Role-Fiction, Acting-Fiction.

ADOLESCENCE-FICTION

Blume, Judy. Deenie. Bradbury 1973, 159 pp.

Deenie's mother wanted Deenie to be a model. Deenie didn't know what she wanted until she learned that she had scoliosis (curvature of the spine) and would have to wear a brace for four years. Then she knew she only wanted to be normal. She was repulsed by deformities of any kind. She couldn't stand the idea of a brace. Her mother's attitude made Deenie's adjustment even more difficult. It was her father, her doctor, her sister, and a new friend with excema who finally helped Deenie accept her brace and the idea of physical differences. Subplots include Deenie's budding romance with an eighth grade boy, her strained relationship with her mother, and her growing awareness of sex (masturbation and intercourse). Print and line spacing are similar to *Are You There God? It's Me, Margaret.*

Interest Level: 5-6. Reading Level: 3.1. Further Search Topics: Models, Fashion-Fiction, Beauty-Fiction, Scoliosis-Fiction, Physically Handicapped-Fiction, Children-Growth-Fiction, Sex-Fiction, Love-Fiction, Family Problems-Fiction, Illness-Fiction, Adolescence-Fiction.

Byars, Betsy. The Cybil war; illus by Gail Owens. Viking Pr. 1981, 126 pp.

Simon and Tony both had a crush on Cybil, but according to Tony, Cybil liked Tony better than she liked Simon. Simon was unhappily willing to accept Tony's word even though he knew Tony was a chronic liar. After all, Cybil had been the one to talk their teacher out of giving the lead in the class play about nutrition to Simon. Consequently Simon was being forced to impersonate a jar of peanut butter. In an elaborate attempt to win Cybil's affection Tony began telling Cybil lies about Simon and then set up a double date with Cybil and Harriet. On their walk home, Simon learned from Harriet that Cybil had only agreed to the date because Simon was going along. Happy at last, Simon realized he wanted no more lies and tricks; that he wanted to be truthful with Cybil and with himself. In the name of truth, he was even willing to accept the fact that his father, who had deserted the family, would not be returning.

A good story with just enough humor and romance to make it widely appealing as either a shared book (read aloud) or a personal pick. Print is fairly small.

Interest Level: 5-6. Reading Level: 4.2. Further Search Topics: Humorous Fiction, Love-Fiction, School Stories, Honesty-Fiction, Friendship-Fiction, Single Parent Family-Fiction, Read Aloud, Everyday Stories, Adolescence-Fiction.

Danziger, Paula. There's a bat in bunk five. Delacorte 1980, 150 pp.

Although this is a sequel to *The Cat Ate My Gymsuit,* it can be read alone. Marcy accepted an offer to become a junior counselor at an arts camp run by her ex-English teacher Ms. Finney and Ms. Finney's husband. After a nervous beginning, Marcy found herself enjoying the other counselors and the campers, but most of all, her first romance. Marcy's only difficulty was dealing with Ginger, a very troubled 10-year-old in Marcy's cabin. Marcy couldn't seem to get through to Ginger. When Ginger ran away, Marcy was forced to consider whether she should have spent more time with the campers and not quite so much time with Ted.

Marcy is a normal teenager whose problems, questions and activities are appealing to many teen and pre-teen readers. The characters who surround Marcy here are less stereotyped and flat than those in The Cat Ate My Gymsuit. Even Marcy's parents are more human. The author's light touch is just right for Marcy's story.

Interest Level: 5-6. Reading Level: 3.2. Further Search Topics: Humorous Fiction, Camp-Fiction, Everyday Stories, Love-Fiction, Vacation-Fiction, Occupations-Fiction, Adolescence-Fiction.

Danziger, Paula. The pistachio prescription. Delacorte 1978 154 pp.

Just as Cassie entered her freshman year in high school, the old stand-by that had helped her deal with all her problems (eating pistachio nuts) began to fail. To be sure, she did get through the class elections and was elected president. She met and started dating Bernie. She gained self-confidence. She even managed to stand up to a particularly mean teacher. But, eating pistachios didn't help at all at home where Cassie really needed them. She could hardly stand to be in the same room with her older sister. She hated the importance her mother placed on looking right and dressing well. Most of all, she hated the way her parents were constantly fighting. The only person with whom she was really confortable was her brother. But, before the year was over, Cassie's parents decided to get a divorce, she and her sister became friends and Cassie learned to accept her family.

Another Judy Blume-style author, but Danziger's portraits of adults tend to be even more one-dimensional and exaggerated than Blume's. Very popular anyway.

Interest Level: 6+. Reading Level: 5.1. Further Search Topics: Divorce and Separation-Fiction, Family Problems-Fiction, Beauty-Fiction, School Stories, Adolescence-Fiction, Love-Fiction, Brothers and Sisters-Fiction, Everyday Stories.

Pevsner, Stella. And you give me a pain, Elaine. HM 1978, 182 pp.

Andrea was the youngest of three children. She was very close to her brother, Joe, but he was away at college. There was only Elaine at home, but Andrea and Elaine didn't get along at all. Elaine was a troubled young woman who took so much of her parents' attention that there was none left for Andrea. This is the story of Andrea's year in eighth grade, a year in which she discovered that she was a steady and strong person. It was the year in which Andrea worked on the school play, had her first boyfriend, weathered the storms when her sister ran away, and began to understand her sister more and resent her less. It was also the year that she had to learn to live with her brother's accidental death.

The author's Judy Blume style (but with less humor) guarantees readers among older children.

Interest Level: 5-6. Reading Level: 4.1. Further Search Topics: Family Problems-Fiction, Brothers and Sisters-Fiction, Love-Fiction, Death-Fiction, Runaways-Fiction, Troublemakers-Fiction, Adolescence-Fiction.

ADOPTION-FICTION

Clark, Margaret Goff. Barney in space; illus by Ted Lewin. Dodd 1981, 155 pp.

This is a sequel to *Barney and the UFO,* but it stands by itself quite well. It's title is a misnomer, however, for it isn't until the last third of the book that Barney goes into space. In the previous book Barney made friends with Tibbo, a Gark from the planet Ornam. In this book Tibbo tries to save Barney from an evil Gark named Rokell. Because Barney knew about Garks, Rokell was afraid Barney would betray them and turn humans against Garks. To prevent that from happening, Rokell was determined to kidnap Barney. Tibbo was too far from Earth to do more than warn Barney of Rokell's intentions and tell him not to be alone at any time. Barney's friends Dick and Kara tried to protect Barney but only succeeded in endangering their own lives. When Kara was almost killed by Rokell, Barney decided to face Rokell alone and try to defeat him, but Rokell's powers were too strong for Barney. Against their wills both Barney and David were taken aboard a spaceship. They discovered later, to their relief, that the spaceship belonged to a friend of Tibbo's who was commanding the ship from the moon. Barney and Dick were to be taken to the moon for safety until Rokell could be controlled. Rokell didn't give up easily. He attacked the ship twice before he captured it and set it down on a remote portion of the moon. Only Barney's quick thinking stopped Rokell permanently and saved both Barney and Dick.

The preliminary sequences are more suspenseful and exciting than the space travel; however, the book will not disappoint young science fiction fans.

Interest Level: 4-6. Reading Level: 4.2. Further Search Topics: Science Fiction, Flying Saucers-Fiction, Outer Space-Fiction, Orphans-Fiction, Kidnapping-Fiction, Aliens-Fiction, Adoption-Fiction.

Clark, Margaret Goff. Barney and the UFO; illus by Ted Lewin. Dodd 1979, 159 pp.

Barney felt a strange prickly sensation several times before he discovered that it was caused by Tibbo, a

Gark from the planet Ornam. Tibbo had selected Barney as a friend who would accompany him back to Ornam. Barney was to learn the peaceful ways of Gark and then return to Earth to help persuade the world to accept the aliens. At first the idea of visiting Ornam appealed to Barney because he liked Tibbo and felt very lonely and unsure of his adoptive family's love. Those were the very reasons that Tibbo had chosen Barney: he wanted someone without strong ties to Earth and Barney's only tie when he was first contacted by Tibbo was his little brother Scott. As the time to go grew closer, Barney found a new and strong friendship with Dave, a science whiz-kid, and great love for his new parents. Tibbo, however, was determined to hold Barney to his promise. Only a last minute confrontation between Tibbo and Barney, David, Scott and Mr. and Mrs. Crandall prevented Tibbo from succeeding. But even as Tibbo left, he and Barney acknowledged their new friendship and agreed to keep in touch.

Because of its fairly slow beginning, readers must be well-introduced to this book. If they can be persuaded to be patient while the author sets the stage for about 18 pages they will be rewarded with a decent, if somewhat wordy, story of friendship, UFO's, space travel and family affection.

Interest Level: 3-6. Reading Level: 3.2. Further Search Topics: Science Fiction, Flying Saucers-Fiction, Kidnapping-Fiction, Foster Homes-Fiction, Family-Fiction, Adoption-Fiction, Aliens-Fiction, Loneliness-Fiction, Orphans-Fiction.

Silman, Roberta. Somebody else's child; illus by Chris Conover. Warne 1976, 64 pp.

Peter was adopted, but he had never questioned his family's love for him until Puddin' Paint, the school bus driver, made a thoughtless remark. Peter's affection for the older man was strong enough to help him understand Puddin' Paint's feelings. When Puddin' Paint's two dogs disappeared and the bus driver was almost heartbroken, it was Peter who helped the old man search for the dogs. That experience helped both Peter and Puddin' Paint understand that love doesn't only extend to natural born children, but can be just as strong and deep for others.

A simple telling of a moving story. It is as useful for readers who love dogs as for those interested in adoption. Rather inconsistent reading level, tests between 1.2 and 3.1.

Interest Level: 2-5. Reading Level: 2.2. Further Search Topics: Adoption-Fiction, Dogs-Fiction, Friendship-Fiction, Love-Fiction.

ADVERTISING-FICTION

Miles, Betty. The secret life of the underwear champ; illus by Dan Jones. Knopf 1981, 117 pp.

Larry hadn't planned it; in fact, he hadn't even really wanted it to happen. But suddenly he found himself about to make a television commercial for ChampWin Knitting Mills, makers of sports clothing and underwear. He knew his family could use the money he would make, but he certainly didn't want the whole school seeing him in his underwear. Nevertheless, Larry went ahead and made the commercial, hoping that it would never be used. He even had to skip baseball practice to make the taping. Much to his horror, the commercial appeared the night before the team's first game. Not only did the entire opposing team tease him, but so did all his own teammates. By the time he got up to bat, Larry was mad enough to slam the ball out of the park. He didn't hit the ball quite that hard, but he did make a winning home run

and end the others' giggles forever. He became the true underwear champ.

This is a funny look at the embarrassments of growing up. It also deals lightly with a boy's pride, his peer relationship, and his growing awareness of girls. An appealing and broadly usable title. Capers series.

Interest Level: 3-5. Reading Level: 2.2. Further Search Topics: Baseball-Fiction, Television-Fiction, Occupations-Fiction, School Stories, Humorous Fiction, Advertising-Fiction, Beauty-Fiction, Motion Pictures-Fiction, Best Sellers, Everyday Stories.

AFRICA-FICTION

Hamilton, Virginia. Zeely; illus by Symeon Shimin. Macmillan 1967, 122 pp.

A beautiful, almost mystical story of a black girl who learns about self-identity and pride from a statuesque neighbor whom Geeder is convinced must be a Watutsi princess. At first by chance and later at an arranged meeting, Zeely (Geeder's neighbor) gently and symbolically speaks to Geeder of her racial origins. She also tells Geeder of a young girl (Zeely as a child), too ignorant of the world around her to be able to recognize reality. It is a quietly moving story that is most likely to find an appreciative audience in the thoughtful, more mature reader.

Interest Level: 5-6. Reading Level: 5.1. Further Search Topics: Africa-Fiction, Royalty-Fiction, Blacks-Fiction, Courage-Fiction, Vacation-Fiction, Country Life-Fiction, Read Aloud.

AFRICA-FOLKLORE

Arkhurst, Joyce. The adventures of Spider; West African folktales; illus by Jerry Pinkney. Little 1964, 58 pp.

A delightful collection of six West African folktales about Spider. Spider is mischievous, greedy, lazy and clever. He loves to eat and he hates to work. Four of the stories tell of Spider's ill-fated attempts to get food without having to work for it ("How Spider Got a Thin Waist," "How Spider Got a Bald Head," "How Spider Helped a Fisherman," and "Why Spiders Live in Dark Corners"). One story tells of his greed ("How the World Got Wisdom"), and only one story is complimentary ("Why Spider Lives in Ceilings"). All are short, gentle, humorous, and adapt well to dramatization or retelling.

Interest Level: 2-6. Reading Level 3.1. Further Search Topics: Humorous Fiction, Spiders-Fiction, Folklore, Tricksters-Fiction, Africa-Folklore, Group 2, Read Aloud, Creation-Fiction, Drama.

Bernstein, Margery. The first morning; illus by Enid Warner Romanek. Scribner 1976, 44 pp.

Spider, Mouse, and Fly volunteered to ask the king of the sky for light to take back to earth because the animals on earth were tired of living in darkness. The king didn't want to give away any light and so he set what he thought was an impossible task for the three animals. They were able to outwit the king three times and finally return to earth with a box Mouse was sure contained light. When they opened the box all they found was a rooster. Poor Mouse was ashamed at having been so badly tricked. But then Rooster crowed up the first morning and has done so ever since. A competent retelling of an African myth, nicely complemented by bold illustrations. Good candidate for dramatization.

Interest Level: 1-3. Reading Level: 2.1. Further Search Topics: Animals-Fiction, Group 2, Mythology, Light-Fiction, Drama, Time-Fiction, Calendars-Fiction, Creation-Fiction, Africa-Folklore.

AGING-FICTION

Clifford, Eth. The dastardly murder of Dirty Pete; illus by George Hughes. HM 1981, 120 pp.

Although this is a sequel to *Help, I'm a Prisoner in the Library*, it does not depend on the previous title, and in fact, is likely to be the more successful introduction to Mary Rose and Jo-Beth Onetree. Given the choice, most young readers will take a mystery set in a ghost town over a mystery set in a library.

Mary Rose, Jo-Beth and their father were on their way across country when they became lost. As night grew closer, the only place they could find to stay was an old hotel in the ghost town where Sorehead Jones had allegedly killed Dirty Pete. It was Sorehead's ghost who was supposed to haunt the town, and indeed there was someone or something who was in the town with the Onetrees. To their surprise, that someone turned out to be Sourdough Sam, an aging actor who had become senile and spent his days acting out all the parts in the Dirty Pete story. The town was only a movie set and the story was only a movie script. The Onetrees discovered the truth bit by bit after a frightening venture into an abandoned gold mine, a harrowing night in the haunted hotel and a jail sentence for Mr. Onetree.

Beware of the rare, very difficult descriptive passage that may cause trouble for some readers.

Interest Level: 2-5. Reading Level: 3.1. Further Search Topics: Mystery and Detective Stories, West-Fiction, Brothers and Sisters-Fiction, Motion Pictures-Fiction, Ghosts-Fiction, Treasure-Fiction, Group 2, Acting-Fiction, Aging-Fiction, Mental Illness-Fiction.

Cohen, Barbara. Thank you, Jackie Robinson; illus by Richard Cuffari. Lothrop 1974, 125 pp.

This story is not for everyone, but for the right reader it is perfect. The book is a catalog of baseball facts, thus it is likely to appeal primarily to baseball fans. But it is not the typical story of a child overcoming a problem through practice and perserverance, as are most sports books. This is a sensitive story of a fatherless boy whose life centered around the New York Dodgers.

Sam could repeat the starting line-up and details of any game the Dodgers had played within the last three years; however, no one cared. In fact, most people were bored when Sam began reciting. Only Davey, the old, black cook at the inn where Sam and his family lived, took any interest. Davey was as much a fan as Sam. They began spending hours together talking and then watching baseball as Davey and his daughter took Sam to the games with them. It was Sam and Davey's dream to catch a fly ball and have it autograped by all the Dodgers, especially Jackie Robinson, the first black major league player. When Davey had a severe heart attack, Sam gathered all his courage to make that dream come true. He bought a baseball, took the subway to a game, and argued with the ushers until he was finally able to get Jackie Robinson's and the team's autographs. Just a few days before Davey died Sam took the baseball to the hospital and gave it to Davey. Sam's feelings about Davey's death are real and painful. He felt sorry for himself, lonely, angry, sad and confused. But a remark by his mother and one more Jackie Robinson hit helped Sam accept Davey's death.

Because the story is told as a first-person flashback set in the late 1940s, it may need a little introduction. It also alludes to racial problems and practices that young readers may not understand without explanation (i.e., why Davey had some hesitation about taking a white child with him to the ballpark or on a trip).

Interest Level: 4-6. Reading Level: 4.2. Further Search Topics: Baseball-Fiction, Blacks-Fiction, Aging-Fiction, Single Parent Family-Fiction, Friendship-Fiction, Death-Fiction, Robinson, Jackie.

Greene, Constance C. A girl called Al; illus by Byron Barton. Viking Pr. 1969, 127 pp.

Told in the first person, this is the story of two seventh grade girls. The girls' warm friendship began the moment Al introduced herself to the narrator as a non-conformist. Al was very independent, mostly because she was on her own so much of the time. Her parents were divorced and she seldom saw either one of them. Her father only wrote her postcards and her mother was rarely home. The narrator's family and Mr. Richards, their building superintendent, became Al's family. They cooked, ate, played, fought, talked and even made bookcases together. When Mr. Richards had a heart attack, they found help for him and later went to see him in the hospital. It was his death that helped Al and her mother grow closer, just as Mr. Richards' life had helped her understand why her father never came to see her.

A satisfying, low-key story of friendship and maturation. The girls are Judy Blume-style characters with much greater innocence. Their ages are not discernible by their actions or dialogue, only by the author's statement.

Interest Level: 3-6. Reading Level: 3.1. Further Search Topics: Children-Growth-Fiction, Single Parent Family-Fiction, Friendship-Fiction, Weight-Fiction, Aging-Fiction, Death-Fiction, Divorce and Separation-Fiction, Family Problems-Fiction, Everyday Stories, Humorous Fiction.

Heide, Florence Parry. Mystery of the forgotten island; illus by Seymour Fleishman. A. Whitman 1980, 127 pp.

On a small island, unmarked on the map, the Spotlight Club members found old Mr. Whitson, who claimed that he was being kept prisoner by his granddaughter Lorrie and her husband John. Lorrie and John had told him he was being kept in the yard for his own good, so that he wouldn't wander off and get hurt or lost. They had also told him that he should will the island to them so that his daughter Cassie couldn't sell the island to a resort company for development. He was going to be forced to sign such a will unless he could get the children to help him smuggle a new will to his lawyer. Mr. Whitson wasn't convinced that Cassie wanted to sell the island, but he couldn't get in touch with her and he hadn'd had a letter from her in many months.

As the children went to secretly meet Mr. Whitson and mail his new will, they discovered that their trusted friend Guy was attempting to blackmail Lorrie and John into giving him some of the money from the sale of the island. He had evidence that Lorrie and John, not Cassie, wanted to sell the island and were tricking Mr. Whitson into signing a will in their favor. In a daring move, the children were able to free Mr. Whitson and isolate all three of the thieves so that the police could capture them.

This book involves a somewhat more complicated plot and slightly less familiar ingredients than most other Spotlight Club mysteries. One should progress to rather than begin the series with this title. Spotlight Club Mystery series.

Interest Level: 4-6. Reading Level: 3.1. Further Search Topics: Mystery and Detective Stories, Inheritance-Fiction, Gangs-Fiction, Kidnapping-Fiction,

Brothers and Sisters-Fiction, Aging-Fiction, Detectives-Fiction.

Hurwitz, Johanna. Aldo Ice Cream; illus by John Wallner. Morrow 1981, 124 pp.

Aldo got his newest nickname (Ice Cream) from his friend DeDe when she heard that Aldo not only wanted to try every flavor of ice cream at the local store, but wanted to buy an ice cream freezer for his sister's birthday as well. Aldo decided his summer project would be to earn enough money for the freezer, but he soon found out that there were very few ways a nine-year-old boy could earn $49.95. In the meantime, he helped his mother deliver food for a Meals-On-Wheels project, learned to swim, found out about fish from Mr. Puccini, and shared his cat with Mrs. Nardo. As the summer came to an end he saw one last opportunity to earn enough money for the ice cream maker. A local shoe store offered a new pair of sneakers to the child who owned the most worn out pair. Aldo convinced his mother that if he won the sneakers, she should pay him the money she would otherwise have had to spend on his new sneakers. Aldo set about making sure that his already well-worn sneakers were the most dilapidated in town. A few days before the sneaker contest the hardware store lowered the price on the ice cream freezer to a point where Aldo could afford it if he won the sneakers. When Aldo did win, just as he knew he would, he and his mother bought the very last freezer in the store.

It is not as well-constructed a story as *Aldo Applesauce*, but for established Aldo fans, or those who want quiet, reassuring fiction, this is a usable title.

Interest Level: 3-4. Reading Level: 3.1. Further Search Topics: Humorous Fiction, Brothers and Sisters-Fiction, Vacation-Fiction, Occupations-Fiction, Everyday Stories, Aging-Fiction, Family-Fiction, Contests-Fiction.

Lowry, Lois. Anastasia again! HM 1981, 145 pp.

This is a sequel that is as funny and well-written as its predecessor. Because its plot involves less common experiences, this book may not enjoy quite the wide-spread success of *Anastasia Krupnik*. However, among those readers who liked their first meeting with Anastasia, this book will find many fans.

Anastasia's parents astounded her when they announced that the family was going to move from their Cambridge, Massachusetts apartment to a house in the suburbs. She didn't like the idea of leaving the apartment, but she *hated* the idea of the suburbs. The only thing that made the move bearable was the house itself. Anastasia had said she would move only if they could find a house with a tower—and they had. After she got over the shock of moving, Anastasia began to enjoy her new home. She met a neighborhood boy who became a special friend, she tried to help her cranky elderly neighbor Mrs. Stein make friends, and she even wrote a short mystery book.

Anastasia is as spunky and original as before. She is a bit precocious, but her precocity is nothing compared to that of her brother. At two-and-a-half years old, he speaks as well as many adults. As we mentioned above, the book will be most appealing to readers who want second helpings of Anastasia's adventures. The print is slightly smaller here than in the first title.

Interest Level: 4-6. Reading Level: 2.2. Further Search Topics: Moving, Household-Fiction, City

Life-Fiction, Suburbia-Fiction, Humorous Fiction, Aging-Fiction, Writing-Fiction, Family-Fiction, Everyday Stories.

Madian, Jon. Beautiful junk: a story of the Watts Towers; photos by Barbara Jacobs, Jr. and Lou Jacobs, Jr. Little 1968, 44 pp.

Although this book is now out of print; it is well worth trying to find. It is a fictionalized account of a young, angry black boy's encounter with the creator of Los Angeles' unusual Watts Towers. Simon Rodia, a poor tile setter, worked on the towers for 33 years until he was 75 years old. He used only his imagination, discarded materials he found around him, seashells, and sand to build three tall, fantasy-like towers in the middle of a ghetto. He created beauty where others saw only junk.

The book is illustrated with photography that makes the story more vivid and the towers and Rodia's accomplishment more impressive than they would have seemed with drawings. The print is good-sized, spacing is totally adequate. Rodia's life is quickly submarized and an update on the Towers is included at the book's end.

Interest Level: 3-6. Reading Level: 3.1. Further Search Topics: Blacks-Fiction, Read Aloud, Best Sellers, Poverty-Fiction, Rodia, Simon, Architecture, Biography, Aging-Fiction, Watts Towers, California, Poverty.

AIR
Branley, Franklyn M. Oxygen keeps you alive; illus by Don Madden. Har-Row 1971, 33 pp.

A well-explained, beginning treatment of the functions, importance, and uses of oxygen. The explanation is not limited to humans, but extends to plants and animals as well. Although the book can be stretched to use with fifth graders, its picture book format and sometimes condescending tone indicate it is most easily used through fourth grade. No index or table to contents.
Let's-Read-and-Find-Out-Science-Book series.

Interest Level: 2-4. Reading Level: 2.2. Further Search Topics: Air, Respiration, Scuba Diving, Astronauts.

AIRPLANES
Bendick, Jeanne. The first book of airplanes. Watts 1975, revised edition, 65 pp.

It will take a determined reader to get much technical information from this overview of airplanes. The first sections (thrust, lift gravity, drag, and parts of a plane) promise simple, understandable explanations of complicated topics. The next portion of the book fails to live up to that promise. The descriptions of airplane engines will be intelligible only to the reader who already knows how an engine works. The history of flight is little more than an outline. The two-page chapter on air maps and distances will do more to confuse than instruct most readers. On the other hand, the information about airports, control towers, and types and uses of aircrafts is better. The book is well-indexed and includes a four-page glossary. It is perhaps best used as a general introduction to airplanes (skip the three areas mentioned above). For technical information about flight, look elsewhere. Print size is adequate but spacing between lines could have been more generous.

Interest Level: 4-6. Reading Level: 3.2. Further Search Topics: Airports, Engines, Flight, Airplanes.

Simon, Seymour. The paper airplane book; illus by Byron Barton. Viking Pr 1971, 48 pp.

For the theory as well as the practice behind successful paper airplanes, this is the book. This is as much a book about the principles of flight as it is about how to make a paper airplane. The reader is introduced to thrust, drag, lift and gravity through explanation, examples, diagrams and experiments. The effects of vertical and horizontal stabilizers, elevators, rudders, flaps, and ailerons on both paper and real airplanes, is explained and illustrated. Instructions are given for building and modifying a basic plane as each new idea is introduced. The book ends with plans for four more sophisticated planes and encouragement to try further experiments. An excellent resource for the enthusiast. Print is small.

Interest Level: 3-6. Reading Level: 3.2. Further Search Topics: Airplanes, Handicrafts, Flight.

AIRPORTS

Bendick, Jeanne. The first book of airplanes. Watts 1975, revised edition, 65 pp.

It will take a determined reader to get much technical information from this overview of airplanes. The first sections (thrust, lift gravity, drag, and parts of a plane) promise simple, understandable explanations of complicated topics. The next portion of the book fails to live up to that promise. The descriptions of airplane engines will be intelligible only to the reader who already knows how an engine works. The history of flight is little more than an outline. The two-page chapter on air maps and distances will do more to confuse than instruct most readers. On the other hand, the information about airports, control towers, and types and uses of aircrafts is better. The book is well-indexed and includes a four-page glossary. It is perhaps best used as a general introduction to airplanes (skip the three areas mentioned above). For technical information about flight, look elsewhere. Print size is adequate but spacing between lines could have been more generous.

Interest Level: 4-6. Reading Level: 3.2. Further Search Topics: Airports, Engines, Flight, Airplanes.

ALCOHOLISM-FICTION

Mazer, Harry. The war on Villa Street. Delacorte 1978, 182 pp.

Willis was a loner and a runner. He was a loner because he didn't want anyone to find out about his alcoholic father. He wasn't quite sure why he ran; perhaps because it was the only time he felt good. When Rabbit Slavin and his friends asked Willis to become part of their gang, he refused. He was flattered and wanted to join, but the gang wanted to meet at his house and Willis couldn't risk that. Then when he agreed to coach the local "retard" for the school's field day, Willis gave the gang the opportunity they wanted to take their revenge on him for turning them down. The gang's hatred for Willis increased still more when he beat their best runner and athlete. In payment, the gang jumped Willis and beat him badly. After he picked himself up, Willis realized that he had at least faced the worst of his fears and survived. Days later when his drunken father humiliated him, Willis realized he had to face that, too. He made peace with himself and the world by deciding he could neither continue to run away from, nor apologize for his father anymore. He was independent and strong.

There is much in this fast-paced book besides the obvious violence and action. It is written with an intuitive feel for a teenager's problems and emotions and is a sensitive portrayal of mature concepts. The print is large, but spacing between the lines should have been slightly increased.

Interest Level: 5-6. Reading Level: 5.1. Further Search Topics: Running-Fiction, Loneliness-Fiction, Alcoholism-Fiction, Loners-Fiction, Mental Retardation-Fiction, Gangs-Fiction, Child Abuse-Fiction, Bullies-Fiction, Family Problems-Fiction, Courage-Fiction.

ALI, MUHAMMAD

Burchard, Marshall. Sports hero: Muhammad Ali. Putnam 1975, 95 pp.

The man who brought a quick tongue as well as fast feet and flying fists to the sport of boxing. Entry for *Sports Hero: Bill Walton* gives series notes. Ring record included here. Sports Hero series.

Interest Level: 3-6. Reading Level: 4.1. Further Search Topics: Boxing-Biography, Blacks-Biography, Ali, Muhammad, Group 2.

ALIENS-FICTION

Clark, Margaret Goff. Barney in space; illus by Ted Lewin. Dodd 1981, 155 pp.

This is a sequel to *Barney and the UFO*, but it stands by itself quite well. It's title is a misnomer, however, for it isn't until the last third of the book that Barney goes into space. In the previous book Barney made friends with Tibbo, a Gark from the planet Ornam. In this book Tibbo tries to save Barney from an evil Gark named Rokell. Because Barney knew about Garks, Rokell was afraid Barney would betray them and turn humans against Garks. To prevent that from happening, Rokell was determined to kidnap Barney. Tibbo was too far from Earth to do more than warn Barney of Rokell's intentions and tell him not to be alone at any time. Barney's friends Dick and Kara tried to protect Barney but only succeeded in endangering their own lives. When Kara was almost killed by Rokell, Barney decided to face Rokell alone and try to defeat him, but Rokell's powers were too strong for Barney. Against their wills both Barney and David were taken aboard a spaceship. They discovered later, to their relief, that the spaceship belonged to a friend of Tibbo's who was commanding the ship from the moon. Barney and Dick were to be taken to the moon for safety until Rokell could be controlled. Rokell didn't give up easily. He attacked the ship twice before he captured it and set it down on a remote portion of the moon. Only Barney's quick thinking stopped Rokell permanently and saved both Barney and Dick.

The preliminary sequences are more suspenseful and exciting than the space travel; however, the book will not disappoint young science fiction fans.

Interest Level: 4-6. Reading Level: 4.2. Further Search Topics: Science Fiction, Flying Saucers-Fiction, Outer Space-Fiction, Orphans-Fiction, Kidnapping-Fiction, Aliens-Fiction, Adoption-Fiction.

Clark, Margaret Goff. Barney and the UFO; illus by Ted Lewin. Dodd 1979, 159 pp.

Barney felt a strange prickly sensation several times before he discovered that it was caused by Tibbo, a Gark from the planet Ornam. Tibbo had selected Barney as a friend who would accompany him back to Ornam. Barney was to learn the peaceful ways of Gark and then return to Earth to help persuade the world to accept the aliens. At first the idea of visiting Ornam appealed to Barney because he liked Tibbo and felt very lonely and unsure of his adoptive family's love. Those were the very reasons that Tibbo had chosen Barney: he wanted someone without strong ties to Earth and Barney's only tie when he was first contacted by Tibbo was his little brother Scott. As the time to go grew closer, Barney found a new and strong friendship with Dave, a science whiz-kid, and great love for his new parents. Tibbo, however, was determined to hold Barney to his promise. Only a last minute confrontation between Tibbo and Barney, David, Scott and Mr. and Mrs. Crandall prevented Tibbo from succeeding. But even as Tibbo left, he and Barney acknowledged their new friendship and agreed to keep in touch.

Because of its fairly slow beginning, readers must be well-introduced to this book. If they can be persuaded to be patient while the author sets the stage for about 18 pages they will be rewarded with a decent, if somewhat wordy, story of friendship, UFO's, space travel and family affection.

Interest Level: 3-6. Reading Level: 3.2. Further Search Topics: Science Fiction, Flying Saucers-Fiction, Kidnapping-Fiction, Foster Homes-Fiction, Family-Fiction, Adoption-Fiction, Aliens-Fiction, Loneliness-Fiction, Orphans-Fiction.

Curtis, Philip. The invasion of the Brain Sharpeners; illus by Tony Ross. Knopf 1979, 117 pp.

This book is one of a number of books published by Albert Knopf under the series title Capers. They are meant to be (and with few exceptions are) light, easy-to-read fiction, published simultaneously in hardcover and paperback editions. Each book is about 120 pages long with chapter length varying from 9 to 14 pages. Print is plenty large and spacing between lines is always adequate. Plots are built around an idea of guaranteed appeal, descriptive passages are kept to a minimum and action (often suspenseful) abounds. This should, on the whole, be a very useful series. Some entries (i.e., *Man From the Sky* and *Who Stole the Wizard of Oz*, both by Avi) are either too difficult or too obscure to be widely appealing, but they are by far the exceptions to the rule.

Invasion of the Brain Sharpeners is the catchy science fiction story of Michael's successful, but risky, attempt to rid his fifth grade classroom of the overpowering influence of the Brain Sharpeners. The Brain Sharpeners came from another galaxy to search for humans to help them colonize their Planet Five. Humans were so lacking in brain power that the Brain Sharpeners' plan was to periodically expose each child to brain-developing rays, then put them through intensive courses of study guided by their also-exposed teacher. When the children had all learned enough to be beneficial to the Brain Sharpeners, they were to be taken from Earth to Planet Five. Michael was the only one to see the danger they were in and to attempt to stop the plot. He managed to chase the aliens away and to prevent his classmates and teacher from receiving their second dose of rays, but in doing so, he sent the principal to the spaceship. Michael's classmates were thus saved, but his principal was never heard from again. Capers series.

Interest Level: 3-6. Reading Level: 3.1. Further Search Topics: Science Fiction, Flying Saucers-Fiction, Aliens-Fiction, School Stories, Kidnapping-Fiction, Best Sellers, Academic Problems-Fiction, Brainwashing-Fiction.

Pinkwater, Daniel Manus. Fat men from space. Dodd 1977, 57 pp.

The evening after his trip to the dentist William found that he could still hear radio programs when his radio was turned off. He was even more surprised to find that when he wired himself to a fence he could hear spacemen talking. When the spacemen discovered that William could hear them, they landed and captured him. They were on a top secret mission and couldn't risk any human knowing about their existence. The spacemen were about to invade Earth to consume all the junk food they could find. As mass panic set in on Earth, William could do nothing to save his fellow humans. He was held captive and helpless until the invaders' interest was captured by a giant potato pancake floating in outer space.

A tongue-in-check, slapstick spoof of science fiction, food fads, and junk food. Do not expect anything more.

Interest Level: 3-5. Reading Level: 3.2. Further Search Topics: Science Fiction, Humorous Fiction, Food-Fiction, Flying Saucers-Fiction, Aliens-Fiction, Best Sellers, Kidnapping-Fiction, Teeth-Fiction.

ALLIGATORS

Shaw, Evelyn. Alligator; illus by Frances Zweifel. Har-Row 1972, 61 pp.

A straight-forward, respectful description of an alligator's life cycle. Emphasis is placed on the time between the mother's nest-building and the birth of the young alligators. The danger to alligators posed by man is expressed, but not stressed. Little physical description is included. An interesting and competent treatment of a narrow subject. Reader format. A Science-I-Can-Read Book series.

Interest Level: 1-4. Reading Level: 2.1. Further Search Topics: Alligators, Nature Study, Group 2.

ANDERSEN, HANS CHRISTIAN

Dolch, Edward W. Andersen stories; illus by Carmen Mowry. Garrard 1956, 165 pp.

The best way to be introduced to Andersen's fairy tales is to hear them told or read aloud. Because they are beautifully written literary tales they suffer tremendously when the language is simplified enough so that the stories can be included in a reader. Furthermore, episodes have been cut out of some tales ("Big Klaus and Little Klaus") and others have been divided into chapters ("The Ugly Duckling"). But, where there is a need for such an easy version of Hans Christian Andersen, this selection will do. The 18 chapters tell only 11 stories. Most of the included stories are familiar ("The Emperor's New Clothes," "The Little Mermaid," "Thumbelina" etc.); all are enjoyable. Illustrations, however, are unattractive and uninspiring. One further caution: the reading level jumps from 2.1 to 3.2. Dolch Pleasure Reading Book series.

Interest Level: 2-5. Reading Level: 3.1. Further Search Topics: Folklore, Fantasy, Group 2, Fairy Tales, Andersen, Hans Christian.

ANDRETTI, MARIO

Burchard, Marshall. Sports hero: Mario Andretti. Putnam 1977, 90 pp.

Auto racing's all-around superstar. See *Sports Hero: Bill Walton* for details about the series. Sports Hero series.

Interest Level: 3-6. Reading Level: 3.2. Further Search Topics: Biography, Andretti, Mario, Auto Racing-Biography.

ANIMALS-FICTION

Bernstein, Margery. Coyote goes hunting for fire; illus by Ed Heffernan. Scribner 1974, 40 pp.

A delightful story that can be read for fun or used as part of a unit on North American Indians. A long time ago when there was no fire, all the animals but Coyote banded together to find it. The animals left Coyote behind because he was always spoiling their plans. Coyote saw them leave, chased after them and once more tried to direct everything, but only ended up losing fire. Cartoon-like illustrations add to the humor of the story. This book should make a simple, but effective play.

Interest Level: 1-4. Reading Level 2.1. Further Search Topics: Animals-Fiction, Legends, Mythology, Fire-Fiction, Indians of North America-Legends, Coyotes-Fiction, Group 2, Creation-Fiction, Drama.

Bernstein, Margery. The first morning; illus by Enid Warner Romanek. Scribner 1976, 44 pp.

Spider, Mouse, and Fly volunteered to ask the king of the sky for light to take back to earth because the animals on earth were tired of living in darkness. The king didn't want to give away any light and so he set what he thought was an impossible task for the three animals. They were able to outwit the king three times and finally return to earth with a box Mouse was sure contained light. When they opened the box all they found was a rooster. Poor Mouse was ashamed at having been so badly tricked. But then Rooster crowed up the first morning and has done so ever since. A competent retelling of an African myth, nicely complemented by bold illustrations. Good candidate for dramatization.

Interest Level: 1-3. Reading Level: 2.1. Further Search Topics: Animals-Fiction, Group 2, Mythology, Light-Fiction, Drama, Time-Fiction, Calendars-Fiction, Creation-Fiction, Africa-Folklore.

Chew, Ruth. No such thing as a witch. Hastings 1971, 112 pp.

Despite the fact that their mother said there was no such thing as a witch, Tad and Nora were convinced that their neighbor Maggie Brown was indeed a witch. And they were right! Maggie Brown knew how to make a special kind of fudge that could make anyone into an animal-lover, enable people to talk with animals, or actually transform someone into an animal. All you had to do was to eat one, two, or three pieces of fudge respectively. But Maggie's overzealous love of animals and her disenchantment with housework eventually attracted the attention of her neighbors and the city health department. Only Tad and Nora's frantic efforts to help her saved Maggie from losing all of her animal friends.

A fairly detailed plot, the fascination of being able to change size and appearance and the intrigue involved in fooling the adults around Maggie make this one of Chew's best books.

Interest Level: 2-5. Reading Level: 2.2. Further Search Topics: Individualists-Fiction, Witches-Fiction, Animals-Fiction, Fantasy, Magic-Fiction, Brothers and Sisters-Fiction, Transformations-Fiction.

Dolch, Edward W. "Why" stories; illus by Marguerite Dolch. Garrard 1952, 160 pp.

"Why the Bear Has a Little Tail," "Why Turkeys Have Red Eyes," and "How the Tiger Got His Stripes" are three titles that illustrate the type of stories found in this collection. Seventeen short, simple folktales explain why the world and creatures in it operate and appear as they do. All of the tales can be found elsewhere. However, few if any stories are likely to be familiar to readers. This type of story is one children often find very appealing. The stories are understandable, logical within their own framework and simple enough to be retold to others. The reading level varies from 1.2 to 2.2. Dolch Basic Vocabulary Book series.

Interest Level: 1-4. Reading Level: 2.2. Further Search Topics: Folklore, Why Stories, Animals-Fiction, Group 2, Creation-Fiction.

ANTIQUITIES-FICTION

Heide, Florence Parry. Mystery of the mummy's mask; illus by Seymour Fleishman. A. Whitman 1979, 127 pp.

The Spotlight Club published a neighborhood newspaper. Just as the club was about to take the fourth issue to the printer, Jay discovered an ancient mummy mask hidden near Mr. Pruitt's house. Mr. Pruitt was intrigued by the discovery (he worked at the nearby museum) and he took the mask from Jay, but agreed that Jay could write about the mask for the paper. At about the same time, Dexter discovered that an old, abandoned house was being used. When the printer's office was broken into that night and only their newspaper was stolen, the three children began to suspect that something strange was going on at the abandoned house.

Dexter rode back to the house alone and was captured by Hank, one of three thieves hiding out there. Figuring that they never would have missed one item, Hank had taken the mask from the cache of goods that the other two had stolen. When he overheard Jay's conversation with Mr. Pruitt, Hank realized that his partners would find out what he had done if they ever read the newspaper article. To avoid being discovered, Hank broke into the printer's and stole the paste-up of the paper. In order to keep Dexter from escaping, Hank tied him up and placed him in a shipping crate. When he didn't return as soon as expected, Jay and Cindy realized that Dexter was in trouble, so they went out to the house to search for him. As the three escaped, Dexter and Cindy slashed the thieves' truck's tires, and Jay ran to phone for the police. After several nervous moments in which Cindy and Dexter thought Jay might not get back before they were caught, Jay finally brought the police, who captured all three thieves.

See *Mystery at Southport Cinema* for more information. Spotlight Club Mystery series.

Interest Level: 3-5. Reading Level: 3.1. Further Search Topics: Mystery and Detective Stories, Crime-Fiction, Egypt-Fiction, Archaeology-Fiction, Antiquities-Fiction, Journalism-Fiction, Gangs-Fiction, Brothers and Sisters-Fiction, Detectives-Fiction.

Heide, Florence Parry. Mystery of the vanishing visitor; illus by Seymour Fleishman. A. Whitman 1975, 128 pp.

Cindy was hired to take care of Mrs. Widget's house, animals, and plants for a weekend. That same weekend, someone tried to find and steal something from Mrs. Widget's overcrowded house. She had very few empty spaces in her house, so it was not a surprise that the thief wasn't able to find the object of his or her search. The three Spotlight Club members were determined to figure out not only who was the thief, but also what it was that the thief, wanted. Their prime suspects included the very nasty Bertha Beaker and the charming Charley Capp.

After spending a night in Mrs. Widget's house trying to, and almost succeeding in catching the thief, the children were surprised by an early morning visit from Mr. Capp. Mr. Capp was nearly able to steal away with a painting that hid a great deal of money before Cindy figured out that he was the thief. Even after Mr. Capp had been caught, he charmed his way out of any punishment and left before anyone had second thoughts.

See entry for *Mystery at Southport Cinema* for series information. Spotlight Club Mystery series.

Interest Level: 3-5. Reading Level: 2.2. Further Search Topics: Mystery and Detective Stories, Brothers and Sisters-Fiction, Gangs-Fiction, Crime-Fiction, Antiquities-Fiction, Detectives-Fiction. 00001944

Warner, Gertrude Chandler. Schoolhouse mystery; illus by David Cunningham. A. Whitman 1965, 128 pp.

On a dare, the Aldens went to a quiet fishing village to see what excitement they could find there. They found an isolated town filled with poor and unfriendly people. In their attempt to get to know the townspeople, the Aldens learned of the children's desire for schooling and the adults' anticipation of the Money Man's arrival. The Alden children took on the task of teaching school for the summer in an abandoned schoolhouse owned by Miss Gray, a recluse. The Money Man intrigued them more with each new bit of information they learned about him. They finally decided that the Money Man was a swindler who was practically stealing valuable antiques away from the villagers. By spying on the Money Man when he used the schoolhouse to store the antiques, the Aldens and an ex-FBI man were able to capture him. When the vacation was over, the Aldens had once more found excitement, Miss Gray had agreed to teach the local school, the Money Man was on his way to jail, and the townspeople knew the value of their old household items.

See the entry for *The Boxcar Children* for more information.

Interest Level: 3-5. Reading Level: 2.2. Further Search Topics: Mystery and Detective Stories, Vacation-Fiction, School Stories, Antiquities-Fiction, Crime-Fiction, Brothers and Sisters-Fiction, Challenges-Fiction.

Yolen, Jane. Shirlick Holmes and the case of the wandering wardrobe; illus by Anthony Rao. Coward 1981, 80 pp.

This is a light, fast-paced story of Shirli and her four friends' attempt to solve a local mystery. Its more fully developed characters and plot make this a better literary piece than any of the *Encyclopedia Brown* stories, but it resembles them in other ways. The children live in a small, secure town. The police chief, Shirli's neighbor and George's father, is working on the same case that interests the children but the children solve it first. The mystery is real and involves danger, as opposed to many of Hildick's McGurk mysteries, the other series this book resembles.

Shirli is a fiesty figure who took up George's challenge to solve the town's latest mystery. Thieves had been systematically robbing some of the wealthy summer homes of antiques. Shirli's plan, to search each of the houses for clues, only succeeded in angering the police chief when he caught Shirli and her friends. Being intrepid detectives, however, they did not give up. Instead, they staked out a likely house and waited for the thieves. When the robbers finally arrived Shirli and George hid. Only Gloria was able to escape and go for help. The oak wardrobe in which Shirli took refuge was one of the first pieces the thieves took out of the house. When Shirli tried to get out of it, she found the wardrobe had been placed on a truck with its door against the truck's side; she was caught. Very frightened, she stayed silent until she found herself in the middle of an antiques auction and recognized one of the voices making bids as George's father! As Shirli tumbled out of the wardrobe some of the police chief's men arrested the auctioneer for burglary and selling stolen goods. After she escaped, Gloria had told the police about the thieves, their truck, Shirli, and George, whom they found locked inside a closet still at the summer house.

A serviceable book that will be enjoyed by a wide range of readers.

Interest Level: 3-5. Reading Level: 3.1. Further Search Topics: Mystery and Detective Stories, Humorous Fiction, Friendship-Fiction, Crime-Fiction, Antiquities-Fiction, Detectives-Fiction, Challenges-Fiction.

APACHE INDIANS

Baylor, Byrd. And it is still that way: legends told by Arizona Indian children. Scribner 1976, 85 pp.

Byrd Baylor has collected and written notes for forty-one short American Indian legends from seven Arizona tribes whose school children were asked to write down or illustrate their favorite legend. The result is a collection that reflects the concerns, the history, religion, humor and pride of the children and their ancestors. This excellent collection is not only interesting reading, but it also fits well into social studies and language arts units.

Interest Level: 2-6. Reading Level: 3.1. Further Search Topics: Legends, Arizona-Fiction, Navajo Indians, Hopi Indians, Papago Indians, Pima Indians, Apache Indians, Quechan Indians, Cocopah Indians, Indians of North America-Legends, Mythology, Group 2.

APES

Conklin, Gladys. Little apes; illus by Joseph Cellini. Holiday 1970, unp (32pp).

An informative as well as interesting look at gorillas, chimpanzees, orangutans and gibbons. Their habits and behavior patterns are described by following a young one of each species through a full day in its natural surroundings. The text is simple without being condescending and the illustrations are so life-like that they almost walk off the pages. An excellent treatment of a popular subject makes this a very useful book.

Interest Level: 2-5. Reading Level: 2.2. Further Search Topics: Apes, Gorillas, Nature Study, Infants, Group 2.

APES-FICTION

Yolen, Jane. The boy who spoke chimp illus by David Wiesner. Knopf 1981, 120 pp.

Kriss was determined to prove to his father that, at 12 years old, he was perfectly capable of camping out by himself. To do so, he left home and headed up the coast of California with a sleeping bag, some food, a map and compass, and water. His plan was to camp, ride, and hike his way to his grandmother's house. On the way, the coast line was torn apart by the second great earthquake to strike California. The first had already destroyed great portions of the state. The second was even stronger. The truck he had been riding in was destroyed and everyone around Kriss was killed by the quake except for two chimpanzees. The chimps, in transit from one lab to another, were research animals who had been taught to use sign language. Kriss took the animals with him as he tried to get farther inland and finally home to Los Angeles. His trip not only confirmed his father's fears about Kriss' inadequacies but taught him how to overcome them. Kriss learned to communicate with the chimps, to find food and to live on his own until Old Chris, a hermit, happened along. Together they continued to brave the chaos brought about by the earthquake even when Old Chris' heart troubled him. When a helicopter finally spotted them, Kriss decided to let the chimps go wild and promised Old Chris that he would be back in the woods very soon. It was a mature, capable Kriss who returned home.

This is typical of the Capers series—much action, few background details, little characterization. The books, however, are on appealing topics; they move quickly and they create intriguing (if sometimes implausible) situations. They are light, enjoyable and very useful. Capers series.

Interest Level: 3-6. Reading Level: 3.1. Further Search Topics: California-Fiction, Disasters-Fiction, Survival-Fiction, Apes-Fiction, Nonverbal Communication-Fiction, Camping-Fiction, Runaways-Fiction, Best Sellers.

ARCHAEOLOGY-FICTION

Clymer, Eleanor. Santiago's silver mine; illus by Ingrid Fetz. Atheneum 1973, 74 pp.

Although somewhat complicated by a large number of background incidents, especially early in the book, the story is both interesting and informative. Santiago and his friend Andreas wanted to be rich. The year's harvest had been very poor, so there was little food to eat. Both of their fathers had gone to Mexico City to find jobs and their mothers worked for very few pesos near home. Andreas wanted to search the old mine in the hills outside of town for silver, but the mining company had left a guard named Jose to prevent people from getting into the mines. While up on a hill, tending a cow, Andreas found an old piece of pottery and a back entrance to the mine. As they started to enter the mine, Andreas and Santiago found a basket full of old pottery pieces that Jose had apparently dug from the hill. Not knowing what the pottery pieces were, the boys took them to the local school teacher who identified them as ancient archeological treasures that by law belonged to the government. As soon as he realized others had found out that he had been selling the pottery, Jose disappeared. Shortly afterwards, the government paved the road through town and opened the hill as an official archaeological site. The extra jobs meant that the boys' fathers could once again find work at home. Although they hadn't become exactly rich, Santiago and Andreas had certainly found treasure.

Local flavor abounds, along with some history. Useful for Social Studies units. Print size fairly small, but spaces between lines are good sized. Recently out-of-print, but still worth looking for.

Interest Level: 3-5. Reading Level: 3.1. Further Search Topics: Archaeology-Fiction, Poverty-Fiction, Mexico-Fiction, Country Life-Fiction, Treasure-Fiction, Miners-Fiction.

Heide, Florence Parry. Mystery of the mummy's mask; illus by Seymour Fleishman. A. Whitman 1979, 127 pp.

The Spotlight Club published a neighborhood newspaper. Just as the club was about to take the fourth issue to the printer, Jay discovered an ancient mummy mask hidden near Mr. Pruitt's house. Mr. Pruitt was intrigued by the discovery (he worked at the nearby museum) and he took the mask from Jay, but agreed that Jay could write about the mask for the paper. At about the same time, Dexter discovered that an old, abandoned house was being used. When the printer's office was broken into that night and only their newspaper was stolen, the three children began to suspect that something strange was going on at the abandoned house.

Dexter rode back to the house alone and was captured by Hank, one of three thieves hiding out there. Figuring that they never would have missed one item, Hank had taken the mask from the cache of goods that the other two had stolen. When he overheard Jay's conversation with Mr. Pruitt, Hank realized that his partners would find out what he had done if they ever read the newspaper article. To avoid being discovered, Hank broke into the printer's and stole the paste-up of the paper. In order to keep Dexter from escaping, Hank tied him up and placed him in a shipping crate. When he didn't return as soon as expected, Jay and Cindy realized that Dexter was in trouble, so they went out to the house to search for him. As the three escaped, Dexter and Cindy slashed the thieves' truck's tires, and Jay ran to phone for the police. After several nervous moments in which Cindy and Dexter thought Jay might not get back before they were caught, Jay finally brought the police, who captured all three thieves.

See *Mystery at Southport Cinema* for more information. Spotlight Club Mystery series.

Interest Level: 3-5. Reading Level: 3.1. Further Search Topics: Mystery and Detective Stories, Crime-Fiction, Egypt-Fiction, Archaeology-Fiction, Antiquities-Fiction, Journalism-Fiction, Gangs-Fiction, Brothers and Sisters-Fiction, Detectives-Fiction.

ARCHITECTURE

Madian, Jon. Beautiful junk: a story of the Watts Towers; photos by Barbara Jacobs, Jr. and Lou Jacobs, Jr. Little 1968, 44 pp.

Although this book is now out of print; it is well worth trying to find. It is a fictionalized account of a young, angry black boy's encounter with the creator of Los Angeles' unusual Watts Towers. Simon Rodia, a poor tile setter, worked on the towers for 33 years until he was 75 years old. He used only his imagination, discarded materials he found around him, seashells, and sand to build three tall, fantasy-like towers in the middle of a ghetto. He created beauty where others saw only junk.

The book is illustrated with photography that makes the story more vivid and the towers and Rodia's accomplishment more impressive than they would have seemed with drawings. The print is good-sized, spacing is totally adequate. Rodia's life is quickly submarized and an update on the Towers is included at the book's end.

Interest Level: 3-6. Reading Level: 3.1. Further Search Topics: Blacks-Fiction, Read Aloud, Best Sellers, Poverty-Fiction, Rodia, Simon, Architecture, Biography, Aging-Fiction, Watts Towers, California, Poverty.

ARIZONA-FICTION

Baylor, Byrd. And it is still that way: legends told by Arizona Indian children. Scribner 1976, 85 pp.

Byrd Baylor has collected and written notes for forty-one short American Indian legends from seven Arizona tribes whose school children were asked to write down or illustrate their favorite legend. The result is a collection that reflects the concerns, the history, religion, humor and pride of the children and their ancestors. This excellent collection is not only interesting reading, but it also fits well into social studies and language arts units.

Interest Level: 2-6. Reading Level: 3.1. Further Search Topics: Legends, Arizona-Fiction, Navajo Indians, Hopi Indians, Papago Indians, Pima Indians, Apache Indians, Quechan Indians, Cocopah Indians, Indians of North America-Legends, Mythology, Group 2.

ASSASSINATIONS

Adoff, Arnold. Malcolm X; illus by John Wilson. Har-Row 1970, 41 pp.

This is a simple, intellectually honest biography of a very controversial man. Taught a strong sense of self-respect by his father, Malcolm X could not accept the second-class status that white society tried to impose upon him. Instead he turned away from whites and all they stood for. He hated high school, the detention home he lived in after his father's death, and his mother's placement in a state hospital. He didn't feel comfortable until he moved to Harlem. There he found friends, but he also found crime. While he was in prison, Malcolm X began to read of great, black societies and people. His brother told him about the Nation of Islam, the Black Muslims, and Elijah Muhammad, the leader of the religion. He began corresponding with Mr. Muhammad. Shortly after he was released from prison, Malcolm X met Elijah Muhammad and eventually became a minister of the religion. There was even talk that he would be Elijah Muhammad's successor. But, as the years went on, Malcolm X began to think that black Christians as well as Muslims should be united in the fight for black rights. Despite threats against his life Malcolm X formed the Organization of Afro-American Unity. Both blacks and whites were angry with him. The threats continued until his house was firebombed; and, only a week later, at a public meeting, Malcolm X was assassinated.

An excellent overview of a complex man. The book may well prompt readers to learn more about the man and his beliefs. At the very least it will expose readers, in an interesting manner, to someone they should know. The book shares the same semi-picture book format of the others in Harper and Row/Crowell's biography series, therefore it will need a careful introduction to potential readers.

Interest Level: 3-5. Reading Level: 3.1. Further Search Topics: Blacks-Biography, Civil Rights, Biography, Crime, Religion, Assassinations, Prejudice, Poverty, Foster Homes.

ASTRONAUTS

Branley, Franklyn M. Oxygen keeps you alive; illus by Don Madden. Har-Row 1971, 33 pp.

A well-explained, beginning treatment of the functions, importance, and uses of oxygen. The explanation is not limited to humans, but extends to plants and animals as well. Although the book can be stretched to use with fifth graders, its picture book format and sometimes condescending tone indicate it is most easily used through fourth grade. No index or table to contents.
Let's-Read-and-Find-Out-Science-Book series.

Interest Level: 2-4. Reading Level: 2.2. Further Search Topics: Air, Respiration, Scuba Diving, Astronauts.

ASTRONOMY

Adrian, Mary. The fireball mystery illus by Reisie Lonette. Hastings 1977, 118 pp.

While stargazing one night, Tim and Vicky and their friend Joey saw a meteor fall onto their private island. Before they were able to find it the children realized that someone else was trying to steal the meteorite from them. As much astronomy as mystery here. Beyond fourth grade, the reader may begin to find the astronomy lesson heavy-handed and the mystery light.

Interest Level: 2-4. Reading Level: 3.1. Further Search Topics: Mystery and Detective Stories, Astronomy, Flying Saucers-Fiction, Outer Space-Fiction, Group 2.

Branley, Franklyn M. Eclipse: darkness in daytime; illus by Donald Crews. Har-Row 1973, 33 pp.

The subject is so well-explained and the book is so physically attractive, it's a shame that some older readers will be put off by this title's picture book appearance. Aside from an occasional jarring, condescending note, this is a fine introduction to an interesting subject. Use comfortably with third and fourth graders. Recommend to fifth graders with caution. No index or table of contents.
Lets-Read-and-Find-Out-Science-Book series.

Interest Level: 2-4. Reading Level: 2.2. Further Search Topics: Sun, Astronomy, Eclipses, Moon.

AUTO RACING-BIOGRAPHY

Burchard, Marshall. Sports hero: Mario Andretti. Putnam 1977, 90 pp.

Auto racing's all-around superstar. See *Sports Hero: Bill Walton* for details about the series. Sports Hero series.

Interest Level: 3-6. Reading Level: 3.2. Further Search Topics: Biography, Andretti, Mario, Auto Racing-Biography.

BABYSITTING-FICTION

Hildick, Edmund W. The case of the phantom frog; illus by Lisl Weil. Macmillan 1979, 121 pp.

The McGurk Organization would not, under ordinary circumstances, have agreed to babysit for seven-year-old Bela, but there was an unusual twist to Bela's case. Bela's aunt, who asked them to babysit while she worked in her sculpture studio, had heard the eerie sounds of a VERY large frog coming from Bela's room. At first it appeared to the group that Bela actually turned into a frog at night, a werefrog. But, upon investigation they found a very clever, very lonely, and very unhappy young boy who had invented the phantom because he was afraid that his aunt would make him give up his pet frog.

See *The Case of the Bashful Bank Robber* for series information. McGurk Mystery series.

Interest Level: 3-5. Reading Level: 3.1. Further Search Topics: Mystery and Detective Stories, Gangs-Fiction, Frogs-Fiction, Supernatural-Fiction, Transformations-Fiction, Detectives-Fiction, Babysitting-Fiction, Humorous Fiction, Occupations-Fiction.

Robinson, Jean. The strange but wonderful cosmic awareness of Duffy Moon; illus by Lawrence Di Fiori. HM 1974, 142 pp.

Duffy was tired of being small, of always being on the losing side of fights, and of being unappreciated at home (by his ex-football star uncle). When he sent away for Mr. Flamel's Cosmic Awareness Kit, Duffy was sure he would then be able to take control over anything he wanted and direct his own life. His friend Peter, the narrator, wasn't quite so sure. Peter turned out to be right. Duffy almost made himself sick trying to build a stone wall. Babysitting two small boys and trying to bathe a Great Dane proved to be disastrous. But Duffy's biggest problem came from Boots McAfee's gang. A series of events finally brought Duffy and Peter face-to-face with the dreaded Boots. Luckily, she turned out to be a very smart girl who appreciated Duffy's true talents.

From the first to the last page this is a funny, very enjoyable book. A delightful book with a very palatable message.

Interest Level: 3-6. Reading Level: 3.2. Further Search Topics: Humorous Fiction, Bullies-Fiction,

Magic-Fiction, Read Aloud, Occupations-Fiction, Sex Role-Fiction, Orphans-Fiction, Best Sellers, Gangs-Fiction, Courage-Fiction, Babysitting-Fiction.

BALLET

Krementz, Jill. A very young dancer. Knopf 1976, unp (121 pp).

This was the first of the five *Very Young* books to be written. Like the others, it is large in format and lavishly photographed. Unlike *A Very Young Circus Flyer*, this and the remaining books in the series are written about 10-year-old girls from obviously privileged backgrounds. All the girls are high achievers in their chosen areas but they seem very determined to work still harder until they attain whatever goals they have set for themselves. The books all follow the same formula. The girls introduce themselves, tell about their start in dancing, riding etc., describe their goals, and tell the reader how close they are to those goals. The girls go on to describe their daily routines, the practice, the chores, the hours, and the fun. Then the reader is ushered through approximately a year's worth of the young star's challenges, achievements, and defeats (the latter are only lightly touched upon). Through it all, the child shows enthusiasm, pride, dedication, hard work, and finally, hopes for the future.

Young readers love this series. Despite heavy use of jargon that makes the reading levels somewhat unstable, those already interested in the subject area pour over every word and picture in the books. Perhaps it's partly hero worship, or romance. Maybe it's the inspiration the books provide, but certainly one of the reasons the books are so popular is the vicarious thrill that they provide young enthusiasts.

A Very Young Dancer differs slightly from the formula. Instead of following Stephanie through a year of dance classes at the School of American Ballet, the book concentrates on New York City Ballet Company's production of the Nutcracker, in which Stephanie has a lead role.

Interest Level: 2-5. Reading Level: 3.1. Further Search Topics: Dancing, Ballet, Talent, Best Sellers, Group 2.

Krementz, Jill. A very young skater. Knopf 1979, unp (103 pp).

Katherine Healy started ice skating because her parents liked to skate and because it was easier for them to take her with them than it was to find a babysitter. From such beginnings, at age three, Katherine progressed to skating in Superskates at Madison Square Garden and ballet lessons at George Balanchine's School of American Ballet. See *A Very Young Dancer* for further explanation.

Interest Level: 2-6. Reading Level: 4.1. Further Search Topics: Ice Skating, Dancing, Ballet, Talent, Group 2, Best Sellers.

BARRY, RICK

Burchard, Marshall. Sports hero: Rick Barry. Putnam 1977, 95 pp.

Rick Barry, now a color commentator for televised basketball games, was once one of the best forwards in basketball. Details about the series with *Sports Hero: Bill Walton* entry. Sports Hero series.

Interest Level: 2-6. Reading Level: 3.1. Further Search Topics: Biography, Barry, Rick, Basketball-Biography, Group 2.

BASEBALL

Coombs, Charles. Be a winner in baseball. Morrow 1973, 127 pp.

A solid, though chauvanistic discussion of baseball basics. After a very short summary of baseball's history, the author spends a chapter emphasizing the importance of practice and physical training. From there he goes on to cover techniques of pitching, catching, hitting, running bases, playing the infield and playing the outfield. Directions are clear and often well-illustrated. There is great emphasis placed on playing correctly to avoid injury and on out-smarting the opponent. The book concludes with a reminder that the game is, above all, meant to be fun.

Although the book's reading level tests at 5.2, the jargon that influences the tests will be familiar to most baseball fans. For enthusiasts, therefore, the reading level is probably 4.2 to 5.1. Includes glossary and index.

Interest Level: 4-6. Reading Level: 5.1. Further Search Topics: Baseball.

BASEBALL-BIOGRAPHY

Burchard, Marshall. Sports hero: Joe Morgan. Putnam 1978, 93 pp.

Joe Morgan has been described as one of baseball's most complete players. He could field, hit, run and steal bases with the best. See *Sports Hero: Bill Walton* for more details about the book. Sports Hero series.

Interest Level: 2-6. Reading Level: 3.2. Further Search Topics: Biography, Morgan, Joe, Baseball-Biography, Blacks-Biography, Group 2.

Burchard, Marshall. Sports hero: Reggie Jackson. Putnam 1975, 93 pp.

Reggie Jackson was one of the big reasons why the Oakland A's won baseball's World Series three years in a row. *Sports Hero: Bill Walton* gives more information about the books in the series. Sports Hero series.

Interest Level: 2-6. Reading Level: 3.2. Further Search Topics: Biography, Jackson, Reggie, Baseball-Biography, Blacks-Biography, Group 2.

Burchard, Marshall. Sports hero: Fred Lynn. Putnam 1976, 95 pp.

Fred Lynn was baseball's first rookie to be named Most Valuable Player. Consistent reading level. See *Sports Hero: Bill Walton*. Sports Hero series.

Interest Level: 2-6. Reading Level: 3.2. Further Search Topics: Biography, Lynn, Fred, Baseball-Biography, Group 2.

Burchard, Marshall. Sports hero: Johnny Bench. Putnam 1973, 95 pp.

The youngest baseball player to receive the National League's Most Valuable Player award. See *Sports Hero: Bill Walton* for information about the book. Sports Hero series.

Interest Level: 2-6. Reading Level: 3.1. Further Search Topics: Biography, Bench, Johnny, Baseball-Biography, Group 2.

Burchard, Marshall. Sports hero: Ron Guidry. Putnam 1981, 95 pp.

The Cajun, left-handed pitcher who led the Yankees to two World Championships. See *Sports Hero: Bill Walton* for series details. Sports Hero series.

Interest Level: 3-6. Reading Level: 3.2. Further Search Topics: Baseball-Biography, Biography, Guidry, Ron.

Burchard, Marshall. Sports hero: Henry Aaron. Putnam 1974, 96 pp.

Baseball's homerun king. See entry under *Sports Hero: Bill Walton* for more information. Sports Hero series.

Interest Level: 2-6. Reading Level: 3.1. Further Search Topics: Biography, Aaron, Henry, Baseball-Biography, Blacks-Biography.

Burchard, Susan H. Sports star: Tommy John. HarBraceJ 1981, 63 pp.

Tommy John's elbow injury was severe enough that no one thought he would be able to pitch again. He proved that the skeptics were wrong. For series notes see *Sports Star: Elvin Hayes*. Sports Star series.

Interest Level: 3-6. Reading Level: 4.1. Further Search Topics: Baseball-Biography, John, Tommy, Biography, Group 2, Physically Handicapped.

Burchard, Susan H. Sports star: Jim "Catfish" Hunter. HarBraceJ 1976, 64 pp.

The pitcher who, because of contract violations by his club's owner, became the first free agent in baseball. See Marshall Burchard's *Sports Hero: Bill Walton* for information about the series. Sports Star series.

Interest Level: 2-6. Reading Level: 3.1. Further Search Topics: Biography, Baseball-Biography, Hunter, Jim "Catfish", Group 2.

Burchard, Susan H. Sports star: Mark "The Bird" Fidrych. HarBraceJ 1977, 64 pp.

Although his major league career was short, it was also notable. Mark Fidrych's way of concentrating on his pitching was by talking to the baseball. Entry for *Sports Hero: Bill Walton*, by Marshall Burchard, provides more information about the book. Sports Star series.

Interest Level: 2-6. Reading Level: 2.2. Further Search Topics: Biography, Baseball-Biography, Fidrych, Mark "The Bird."

Fall, Thomas. Jim Thorpe; illus by John Gretzer. Har-Row 1970, 33 pp.

Jim Thorpe was an Indian from the Oklahoma territory who became one of the United State's greatest athletes. He and his twin brother were trained by their father to run and jump faster and farther than anyone else. When Charles died, Jim couldn't face returning to school without his twin, so his family kept him home for a few months before sending him away to school again. Jim ran home once more when his father and mother both became ill. Months later he went to still another school where he was noticed by Pop Warner. Pop advised Joe to concentrate on track until he was big enough to play football. His father's death left Jim so despondent he quit school to play professional baseball for a while. By the time he went back to school, Jim was big enough to play spectacular football and then to win the 1912 Olympic decathlon competition. Unfortunately, his short time as a paid baseball player made him ineligible for the Olympic honor and Jim's medal was taken away. Public sentiment was with Jim, but the rules were against him. He went on, however, to play both professional baseball and football. In 1982, 29 years after his death, Thorpe's medal was finally returned to him.

A short, meaty and readable biography of a person who should be interesting to many sports fans. Follows the usual format of Crowell biographies, but looks less like a picture book than many. Crowell Biography series.

Interest Level: 3-5. Reading Level: 3.1. Further Search Topics: Football-Biography, Indians of North America-Biography, Baseball-Biography, Olympic Games, Biography, Running-Biography, Twins-Biography.

Rudeen, Kenneth. Roberto Clemente; illus by Frank Mullins. Har-Row 1974, 33 pp.

A romanticized retelling of a great baseball player's life. Those already interested in baseball or in Clemente will probably not mind the romantic tone, but may notice the almost patronizing explanations of some of the basics of baseball. Crowell Biography series.

Interest Level: 2-4. Reading Level: 3.1. Further Search Topics: Baseball-Biography, Biography, Puerto Rico, Group 2, Clemente, Roberto.

Rudeen, Kenneth. Jackie Robinson; illus by Richard Cuffari. Har-Row 1971, 41 pp.

Jackie Robinson was the youngest child in a large, poor family. As early as high school it was Robinson's superior athletic talent that set him apart. He could run track or play baseball, football, or basketball. He was the first student at UCLA to win a letter in all four sports. But because he wasn't happy to see the way his mother still had to struggle to earn money to live, after a year and a half at UCLA, Robinson left college to take a job. Soon after that, the United States entered World War II and Robinson went into the Army. His refusal to ride in the back of a bus in Texas resulted in a courtmartial, but he was found innocent after an uproar was made by the newspapers.

After the Army, Robinson played baseball with a Negro League team. A short time later, he was asked by the Dodger manager Branch Rickey to become the first black man to play in the major leagues. Rickey warned Robinson that it would mean he not only had to play well, but that he would also have to take all the anger and bitterness that would be directed at him. Robinson agreed. For three long years, while there were no other black players in the major leagues, Robinson played well and took everything without fighting back. Robinson was then able to stop trying to be perfect because he had successfully broken a very important color barrier and no longer had to prove to white managers, players and fans that blacks belonged in baseball just as much as whites. Robinson played for the Dodgers for ten years. When he left baseball he was elected into the Baseball Hall of Fame. He continued to fight for civil rights throughout the rest of his life, although there is only a brief mention of his activities in the book. Since the book's publication Jackie Robinson has died.

This is an excellent choice for the child who thinks of nothing but sports. It may be helpful in opening up an interest in the civil rights movement, black history, or black heroes. It is unfortunate that the traditional Crowell biography format (semi-picture book), and the author's slight tendency to be condescending, prevents the book from being useful beyond fourth grade. Crowell Biography series.

Interest Level: 2-4. Reading Level: 2.2. Further Search Topics: Civil Rights, Robinson, Jackie, Baseball-Biography, Biography, Blacks-Biography, Prejudice, Poverty.

BASEBALL-FICTION

Christopher, Matt. No arm in left field; illus by Byron Goto. Little 1974, 131 pp.

Matt Christopher's books are just the thing for sports junkies. The play-by-play accounts of several sports events (here it is baseball games) are loosely tied together by secondary plot developments. Usually the plot revolves around the main character's successful attempt to overcome a difficulty of some sort.

Terry was a good baseball player so, when he was invited to join a local team shortly after he moved to Pennsylvania, he was very pleased. Almost immediately, he learned that a teammate was not at all happy about playing with Terry. Terry was black and his teammate, Tony, was very prejudiced. Terry had dealt with people like Tony before, so he was able to ignore most, but not all, of Tony's unkind comments and actions. But the day finally came when Tony realized that to play well as a team, they had to work together instead of against each other.

Interest Level: 3-6. Reading Level: 3.2. Further Search Topics: Prejudice-Fiction, Baseball-Fiction, Friendship-Fiction, Challenges-Fiction.

Christopher, Matt. Wild pitch. Little 1980, 137 pp.

This is one of Christopher's better written books but it is also one that will find a smaller audience than usual. Here he has drawn interesting characters of flesh and bone rather than his normal stereotypes. The sports action is still detailed, but it is no longer the core around which a purely skeletal plot is stretched. Christopher has produced an intriguing story line here.

Eddie was a good strong pitcher who sometimes threw wild pitches. One of his wild pitches hit Phyl Monahan, the only girl playing in his league. It was well known that Eddie didn't like the idea of girls playing in the same league as the boys, so people accused him of purposely hitting Phyl. Eddie knew he hadn't meant to hit her, but he still felt very guilty that his pitch had put her into the hospital. He went to the hospital many times before he was finally able to see Phyl and apologize. When he did, he found that she was very likeable and reasonable. When she confessed that she wasn't sure she wanted to play baseball again, Eddie decided he owed it to her to help her regain her confidence. As they worked together each one gained respect for the other until theirs became a very solid friendship. The test for both was when Phyl had to hit against Eddie again.

For many baseball fans there may be too much plot here and not enough baseball. Because the problem of how to control wild pitches is never addressed, other readers may also find the book disappointing. But, for those baseball fans who are open to more than box scores and replays, this is a good story.

Interest Level: 6+. Reading Level: 4.2. Further Search Topics: Baseball-Fiction, Sex Role-Fiction, Friendship-Fiction, Courage-Fiction.

Christopher, Matt. The year mom won the pennant; illus by Foster Caddell. Little 1968, 147 pp.

When no one's father had the time to coach the Thunderballs it began to look like the team would be disbanded. They just didn't seem to be able to work together without a coach. Then Nick Vassey's mother volunteered to coach for the season. After all, she knew baseball as well as anyone else and had watched her husband coach for several years. Nick wasn't at all pleased, but had to accept the idea when his teammates voted to make his mother their coach. Nick's embarrassment was almost as great as the rival coach's skepticism, but before the season was over Nick was proud of his mother. She coached the team to first place and forced even the rival coach to admit she was a good coach. Much baseball action. See note about (*No Arm In Left Field*).

Interest Level: 2-6. Reading Level: 3.1. Further Search Topics: Group 2, Baseball-Fiction, Friendship-Fiction, Prejudice-Fiction, Sex Role-Fiction, Women-Fiction.

Cohen, Barbara. Thank you, Jackie Robinson; illus by Richard Cuffari. Lothrop 1974, 125 pp.

This story is not for everyone, but for the right reader it is perfect. The book is a catalog of baseball facts, thus it is likely to appeal primarily to baseball fans. But it is not the typical story of a child overcoming a problem through practice and perserverance, as are most sports books. This is a sensitive story of a fatherless boy whose life centered around the New York Dodgers.

Sam could repeat the starting line-up and details of any game the Dodgers had played within the last three years; however, no one cared. In fact, most people were bored when Sam began reciting. Only Davey, the old, black cook at the inn where Sam and his family lived, took any interest. Davey was as much a fan as Sam. They began spending hours together talking and then watching baseball as Davey and his daughter took Sam to the games with them. It was Sam and Davey's dream to catch a fly ball and have it autograped by all the Dodgers, especially Jackie Robinson, the first black major league player. When Davey had a severe heart attack, Sam gathered all his courage to make that dream come true. He bought a baseball, took the subway to a game, and argued with the ushers until he was finally able to get Jackie Robinson's and the team's autographs. Just a few days before Davey died Sam took the baseball to the hospital and gave it to Davey. Sam's feelings about Davey's death are real and painful. He felt sorry for himself, lonely, angry, sad and confused. But a remark by his mother and one more Jackie Robinson hit helped Sam accept Davey's death.

Because the story is told as a first-person flashback set in the late 1940s, it may need a little introduction. It also alludes to racial problems and practices that young readers may not understand without explanation (i.e., why Davey had some hesitation about taking a white child with him to the ballpark or on a trip).

Interest Level: 4-6. Reading Level: 4.2. Further Search Topics: Baseball-Fiction, Blacks-Fiction, Aging-Fiction, Single Parent Family-Fiction, Friendship-Fiction, Death-Fiction, Robinson, Jackie.

Green, Phyllis. The fastest quitter in town; illus by Lorenzo Lynch. A-W 1972, 62 pp.

Whenever Johnny played baseball and things went wrong for him, he would quit. Johnny's teammates finally grew so angry with him that they told him to leave the team. That same day, Johnny's 90-year-old great-grandfather lost a very special ring his wife had given him. Johnny's love for this great-grandfather pushed him to keep looking for the ring until days later, when everyone else had quit searching, Johnny found the ring. Having learned a hard lesson, Johnny returned to his team for one more chance. That evening Johnny went to see his great-grandfather to tell him, with legitimate pride, that he had played the entire game.

Although the lesson is pointed, the story is very satisfying. Johnny's relationship with this great-grandfather is close and supportive. His problem is one shared by many children, especially those with a weak self-image.

Interest Level: 1-4. Reading Level: 3.1. Further Search Topics: Blacks-Fiction, Challenges-Fiction, Courage-Fiction, Group 2, Baseball-Fiction, Grandparents-Fiction, Friendship-Fiction.

Harris, Robie H. Rosie's double dare; illus by Tony DeLuna. Knopf 1980, 112 pp.

Rosie wanted to play baseball with the Willard Street Gang, but she couldn't play well enough to play by their rules. She needed what her older brother called "shrimp rules." She couldn't hit a pitched ball, only a grounder; but grounders were "shrimp rules." In desperation Rosie agreed to take a dare that the gang made up. If she actually performed the dare, the gang would let her play with them by her rules.

The gang dared Rosie to sneak into cranky Mr. Quirk's apartment and borrow a set of his false teeth. Because Rosie couldn't find any extra false teeth, she borrowed his wig instead but that didn't satisfy the gang. They only laughed and made up another dare for Rosie. She was to untie Mrs. Samuels' dog and let it run loose. As Rosie untied him, Elmer ran away, Rosie ran off after him. One rainstorm later, Rosie caught up with him in the middle of a Red Sox game at Fenway Park. Rosie's attempt to catch Elmer stopped the game, brought her an interview on TV, and secured her a place on the Willard Street baseball team.

This very light story, made up almost entirely of action and examples of sibling rivalry, should have wide appeal through fifth grade. Beyond that, Rosie's age (almost nine) and childish behavior won't ring true. Capers series.

Interest Level: 2-5. Reading Level: 2.2. Further Search Topics: Baseball-Fiction, Humorous Fiction, Brothers and Sisters-Fiction, Challenges-Fiction, Courage-Fiction, Gangs-Fiction, Everyday Stories.

Hurwitz, Johanna. Baseball fever; illus by Ray Cruz. Morrow 1981, 128 pp.

Only baseball nuts need even consider this title, but for the die-hard baseball fan this is perfect. Much to his father's disgust, Ezra had only one interest in life. Baseball was almost all Ezra ever thought of. His father was a German-born intellectual who couldn't understand how anyone could waste so much time watching men hit a ball with a stick. He wanted Ezra to become interested in history and chess. Ezra had no interest in history except baseball history. He hated chess, not just because he always lost, but because his father continually told him how badly he played. Predictably they reach a compromise; each learns to appreciate the other's passion, but not before everyone in the family and a few people outside the family have become involved in a series of warmly humorous incidents. Includes much baseball information.

Interest Level: 3-6. Reading Level: 3.1. Further Search Topics: Baseball-Fiction, Family Problems-Fiction, Humorous Fiction.

Miles, Betty. The secret life of the underwear champ; illus by Dan Jones. Knopf 1981, 117 pp.

Larry hadn't planned it; in fact, he hadn't even really wanted it to happen. But suddenly he found himself about to make a television commercial for ChampWin Knitting Mills, makers of sports clothing and underwear. He knew his family could use the money he would make, but he certainly didn't want the whole school seeing him in his underwear. Nevertheless, Larry went ahead and made the commercial, hoping that it would never be used. He even had to skip baseball practice to make the taping. Much to his horror, the commercial appeared the night before the team's first game. Not only did the entire opposing team tease him, but so did all his own teammates. By the time he got up to bat, Larry was mad enough to slam the ball out of the park. He didn't hit the ball quite that hard, but he did make a winning home run and end the others' giggles forever. He became the true underwear champ.

This is a funny look at the embarrassments of growing up. It also deals lightly with a boy's pride, his peer relationship, and his growing awareness of girls. An appealing and broadly usable title. Capers series.

Interest Level: 3-5. Reading Level: 2.2. Further Search Topics: Baseball-Fiction, Television-Fiction, Occupations-Fiction, School Stories, Humorous Fiction, Advertising-Fiction, Beauty-Fiction, Motion Pictures-Fiction, Best Sellers, Everyday Stories.

Slote, Alfred. Hang tough, Paul Mather. Lippincott 1973, 156 pp.

Paul Mather went against his doctor's and his parents' orders when he accepted his new neighbors' challenge to show his pitching skill. He had been told not to play baseball until he had been given permission, but Paul not only loved to pitch, he was also the best pitcher his new friends had ever seen. Knowing full well the medical problems he could be precipitating, Paul went ahead and pitched a spectacular game for the Wilson Dairy team against the Ace Appliance team. But by the end of the game, Paul was in the hospital again, and Wilson Dairy had been forced to forfeit the game because Paul had played illegally. As Paul's leukemia worsened, his determination to play baseball again grew. When the day came that his team was to play a second game against Ace Appliance, Paul made sure he was there. He was in a wheelchair and weak, but he was there. He couldn't actually play, but Paul's psychological support insured that Wilson Dairy won the game. He went back to the hospital proud, happy, and still determined to fight his disease.

This is more than the usual sports story. This is a very sensitive story of a young boy's determination to fight leukemia. The reader looking for only a baseball story may find this book more than he/she wants. However, the reader who is open to a story of human strength and courage will be well rewarded. The book neither dwells on nor minimizes the disease. Instead it uses both the disease and the sport to portray a character much more completely than in most sport stories, especially at this low a reading level. This is an excellent book for those special readers who respond well to thought-provoking material. Although chapters are short and reading level is low, the print is somewhat small. In addition, the first person style, told as if dictated into a tape recorder (complete with occasional interruptions), may be confusing to readers unless it is explained.

Interest Level: 5-6+ Reading Level: 3.1. Further Search Topics: Baseball-Fiction, Death-Fiction, Illness-Fiction, Moving, Household-Fiction, Medicine-Fiction, Physicians-Fiction, Challenges-Fiction, Courage-Fiction.

Smith, Doris Buchanan. Last was Lloyd. Viking Pr 1981, 124 pp.

Lloyd had several problems: he was overweight, his mother was overprotective, he had no school friends, and there was a chance he might be taken away from home and put into foster care because he had missed so much school. Lloyd's mother, very young and very defensive when she had Lloyd, had done her best to be a "good mother," but in doing so, had made Lloyd fearful of the world. He had become the subject of his classmates' mockery so many times that the only way he could respond to his peers was with nastiness. The one skill he possessed was hitting a baseball. He kept this skill well hidden for fear of exposing himself to further mockery. When one of his classmates accidentally discovered how well Lloyd hit, he took the first step to becoming Lloyd's friend. Lloyd's reaction was to back away, but Kirby kept trying. Eventually Kirby's attempts and those of an understanding truant officer, helped Lloyd begin to make friends, to treat others decently, and to pull away from his mother; in short, he began to mature.

Because Lloyd's problems can be oversimplified too easily, this book requires a fairly mature reader and perhaps even discussion in order to fully understand its subtleties.

Interest Level: 5-6+Reading Level: 4.2. Further Search Topics: Weight-Fiction, Single Parent Family-Fiction, Courage-Fiction, School Stories, Loners-Fiction, Friendship-Fiction, Baseball-Fiction, Family Problems-Fiction, Foster Homes-Fiction, Children-Growth-Fiction.

BASKETBALL-BIOGRAPHY

Burchard, Marshall. Sports hero: Dr. J. Putnam 1976, 89 pp.

Julius Erving can jump higher and stay in the air longer than almost any other basketball player. He can also move around the court with the most agile of players. All in all he is a very exciting player to watch. This book includes his college and pro records (through 1975). See *Sports Hero: Bill Walton* for more information. Sports Hero series.

Interest Level: 3-6. Reading Level: 4.1. Further Search Topics: Biography, Blacks-Biography, Basketball-Biography, Erving, Julius, Group 2.

Burchard, Marshall. Sports hero: Bill Walton. Putnam 1978, 94 pp.

Burchard's series of *Sports Hero* biographies is better than many other sports biography series. Although heavy emphasis is placed on the subject's playing time, each person's life is capsulized from childhood to just before the book's publication date. Marshall and Sue Burchard (with whom he has collaborated and who writes an almost identical series called *Sports Stars*) treat each figure favorably and with enthusiasm. But, contrary to many children's writers, particularly sports biographers, these writers at least touch on those personal foibles that make players human (i.e. Joe Namath's tendency to break training is briefly described). Each book is abundantly illustrated with photographs, avoids patronizing the reader and is consistently interesting. Each is reliable, very useful and can be depended on to appeal to the sports enthusiast. Problems arise, however, with inconsistent and/or artificially inflated reading levels. The reading level of a title may vary from 2.2 to 4.2. The same passage tested on both a Spache and a Dale-Chall scale may show a similar two-year spread. The problem seems to be with jargon. Most sports jargon does not appear on either Spache's or Chall's list of familiar words and thus raises a book's reading level. But, the words may well be known to the reader (or quickly recognized after one introduction and so not truly unfamiliar). Keep in mind, therefore, that the true sports fan will often be able to read a title that tests well above his/her actual reading level.

Bill Walton's career is covered only through the end of the 1976-1977 season when the Portland Trailblazers won the NBA title. The reading level of this title is one of the most inconsistent of the series (from 2.2 to 4.2).

Interest Level: 2-6. Reading Level: 3.2. Further Search Topics: Biography, Walton, Bill, Basketball-Biography, Group 2.

Burchard, Marshall. Sports hero: Rick Barry. Putnam 1977, 95 pp.

Rick Barry, now a color commentator for televised basketball games, was once one of the best forwards in basketball. Details about the series with *Sports Hero: Bill Walton* entry. Sports Hero series.

Interest Level: 2-6. Reading Level: 3.1. Further Search Topics: Biography, Barry, Rick, Basketball-Biography, Group 2.

Burchard, Susan H. Sports star: Elvin Hayes. HarBraceJ 1980, 63 pp.

Only this and three other Sue Burchard titles listed here differ much from the format described 'or the *Sports Hero* series (see *Sports Hero: Bill Walton*). It appears that in 1979 Ms. Burchard's books took on a slick new look. The covers began to sport color photos rather than black and white. The print size became noticeably smaller, although still of adequate size. More emphasis was placed on the players early life and background, in an apparent attempt to make him or her understandable as an individual rather than just as a star. A short career summary was added at the end of each book. All-in-all, the new, flashier approach should make the books more appealing than ever to older students.

Elvin Hayes came from a very poor family who lived in a town where blacks were badly treated. He went on to become one of the best college basketball players of his time. His deep religious convictions helped him through some rough times in his early years as a pro. Now he is happy, not just when he wins, but when he knows he has played his best. Sports Star series.

Interest Level: 3-6. Reading Level: 3.1. Further Search Topics: Biography, Hayes, Elvin, Basketball-Biography, Blacks-Biography, Religion-Biography.

Burchard, Susan H. Sports star: Walt Frazier. HarBraceJ 1975, 64 pp.

Walt Frazier earned his nickname Clyde (from _ITBonnie and Clyde_ME) because of his style both on and off the basketball court. He could steal the ball from almost anyone on the court and he enjoyed high living and fancy dressing off the court. Entry for *Sports Hero: Bill Walton* gives more information about the series. Sports Star series.

Interest Level: 2-6. Reading Level: 3.1. Further Search Topics: Biography, Basketball-Biography, Frazier, Walt, Blacks-Biography.

Rudeen, Kenneth. Wilt Chamberlain; illus by Frank Mullins. Har-Row 1972, 33 pp.

A short and somewhat adoring version of Wilt Chamberlain's childhood, schooling, and professional career. Very little of Chamberlain's personality comes through in this book, but his superior talents and skills as well as his importance to the sport of basketball will be enough to prompt many basketball fans to read it. Although simplistic in style, the book is not condescending. It is, however, out of date, a fact most notable when Chamberlain's salary is quoted. Beware of juvenile format when using with older readers. Crowell Biography series.

Interest Level: 2-6. Reading Level: 3.2. Further Search Topics: Biography, Chamberlain, Wilt, Basketball-Biography, Blacks-Biography, Group 2.

BEARS-FICTION

Berenstain, Stan. Bears in the night. Random 1971, 30 pp.

This is for the very beginning reader. Only 24 words plus illustrations are used to tell the story of a bedtime adventure for seven small bears. Bravely they sneak out of the house, through the woods, and up Spook

Hill. Frightened by an owl's hoot, they run back over the same route until they are safely back in bed again.

Interest Level: K-2. Reading Level: 1.1. Further Search Topics: Bears-Fiction, Group 2, Courage-Fiction, Humorous Fiction.

BEAUTY-FICTION

Blume, Judy. Deenie. Bradbury 1973, 159 pp.

Deenie's mother wanted Deenie to be a model. Deenie didn't know what she wanted until she learned that she had scoliosis (curvature of the spine) and would have to wear a brace for four years. Then she knew she only wanted to be normal. She was repulsed by deformities of any kind. She couldn't stand the idea of a brace. Her mother's attitude made Deenie's adjustment even more difficult. It was her father, her doctor, her sister, and a new friend with excema who finally helped Deenie accept her brace and the idea of physical differences. Subplots include Deenie's budding romance with an eighth grade boy, her strained relationship with her mother, and her growing awareness of sex (masturbation and intercourse). Print and line spacing are similar to *Are You There God? It's Me, Margaret.*

Interest Level: 5-6. Reading Level: 3.1. Further Search Topics: Models, Fashion-Fiction, Beauty-Fiction, Scoliosis-Fiction, Physically Handicapped-Fiction, Children-Growth-Fiction, Sex-Fiction, Love-Fiction, Family Problems-Fiction, Illness-Fiction, Adolescence-Fiction.

Blume, Judy. Freckle juice; illus by Sonia O. Lisker. Four Winds 1971, 40 pp.

A very funny story that should appeal to almost everyone. Andrew wanted freckles so that the dirt on his skin wouldn't show as much and he wouldn't have to wash as often. As luck would have it, Sharon, the most obnoxious girl in class, had a freckle juice recipe that she was willing to sell for 50 cents. Even after drinking the brew of grape juice, vinegar, mustard, olive oil, and more, Andrew didn't see any freckles, but, he certainly was sick. Although the protagonists are younger, this book will hold even a fifth grade reader's interest.

Interest Level: 2-5. Reading Level 3.1. Further Search Topics: Humorous Fiction, Group 2, Read Aloud, Everyday Stories, Beauty-Fiction, School Stories, Magic-Fiction, Best Sellers.

Danziger, Paula. The pistachio prescription. Delacorte 1978 154 pp.

Just as Cassie entered her freshman year in high school, the old stand-by that had helped her deal with all her problems (eating pistachio nuts) began to fail. To be sure, she did get through the class elections and was elected president. She met and started dating Bernie. She gained self-confidence. She even managed to stand up to a particularly mean teacher. But, eating pistachios didn't help at all at home where Cassie really needed them. She could hardly stand to be in the same room with her older sister. She hated the importance her mother placed on looking right and dressing well. Most of all, she hated the way her parents were constantly fighting. The only person with whom she was really confortable was her brother. But, before the year was over, Cassie's parents decided to get a divorce, she and her sister became friends and Cassie learned to accept her family.

Another Judy Blume-style author, but Danziger's portraits of adults tend to be even more one-dimensional and exaggerated than Blume's. Very popular anyway.

Interest Level: 6+. Reading Level: 5.1. Further Search Topics: Divorce and Separation-Fiction, Family Problems-Fiction, Beauty-Fiction, School Stories, Adolescence-Fiction, Love-Fiction, Brothers and Sisters-Fiction, Everyday Stories.

Miles, Betty. The secret life of the underwear champ; illus by Dan Jones. Knopf 1981, 117 pp.

Larry hadn't planned it; in fact, he hadn't even really wanted it to happen. But suddenly he found himself about to make a television commercial for ChampWin Knitting Mills, makers of sports clothing and underwear. He knew his family could use the money he would make, but he certainly didn't want the whole school seeing him in his underwear. Nevertheless, Larry went ahead and made the commercial, hoping that it would never be used. He even had to skip baseball practice to make the taping. Much to his horror, the commercial appeared the night before the team's first game. Not only did the entire opposing team tease him, but so did all his own teammates. By the time he got up to bat, Larry was mad enough to slam the ball out of the park. He didn't hit the ball quite that hard, but he did make a winning home run and end the others' giggles forever. He became the true underwear champ.

This is a funny look at the embarrassments of growing up. It also deals lightly with a boy's pride, his peer relationship, and his growing awareness of girls. An appealing and broadly usable title. Capers series.

Interest Level: 3-5. Reading Level: 2.2. Further Search Topics: Baseball-Fiction, Television-Fiction, Occupations-Fiction, School Stories, Humorous Fiction, Advertising-Fiction, Beauty-Fiction, Motion Pictures-Fiction, Best Sellers, Everyday Stories.

BENCH, JOHNNY

Burchard, Marshall. Sports hero: Johnny Bench. Putnam 1973, 95 pp.

The youngest baseball player to receive the National League's Most Valuable Player award. See *Sports Hero: Bill Walton* for information about the book. Sports Hero series.

Interest Level: 2-6. Reading Level: 3.1. Further Search Topics: Biography, Bench, Johnny, Baseball-Biography, Group 2.

BEST SELLERS

Aylesworth, Thomas G. Movie monsters. Lippincott 1975, 79 pp.

If you are looking for an example of fine writing, you won't find it here. What you will find is a collection of monster movie photographs and facts. This is a wealth of trivia about eleven famous monsters (including King Kong, Godzilla, the Fly, Frankenstein's monster, the Mummy, Dracula, Wolf Man and others), their films, sequels, historic backgrounds, identifying characteristics, and more. There is an extensive index, a list of monster movies and their credits, and even brief information about famous monster actors. The book is not great literature, but it is interesting and fun.

Interest Level: 1-6. Reading Level 3.1. Further Search Topics: Acting, Motion Pictures, Monsters, Horror-Fiction, Group 2, Best Sellers.

Beame, Rona. Ladder company 108. Messner 1973, 63 pp.

The reader of this book will literally live through several days with a New York City fire company. The author's "Dragnet"-like writing style, her use of photographs, and actual people, all make the firefighters' experiences very real. It is an exciting, engrossing and satisfying book. The heavily-used jargon will be quickly understood, thus should pose no real obstacle to most readers.

Interest Level 2-6. Reading Level: 3.1. Further Search Topics: Firefighters, Occupations, City Life, New York City, Group 2, Best Sellers.

Bennett, Jay. The pigeon. Methuen 1980, 147 pp.

Despite a low testing score, this is not a truly easy book to read. The author assumes his readers are fairly sophisticated and worldly, thus he does not explain the meaning of the Iron Cross symbol or the word Aryan. The book's language varies from simple to difficult, making the reading level inconsistent (2.1 - 4.1). The setting is dark and forbidding; an underground world of fugitives and terrorists. And yet, the book will be popular with many readers in sixth grade; it will be even more popular with older readers. The tension in this story of a teenage boy, blamed for the murder of his ex-girlfriend, is almost palpable. Brian's flight from the police and his desire to find Donna's murderer take him directly into the midst of a ring of terrorists, for whom life has no meaning. In Brian's attempt to prove his innocence, two more lives are lost, but hundreds more are saved as Brian discovers and stops a bomb threat. The author has used riveting action, short, clipped sentences, and terse dialogue to create a very successful, highly suspenseful book. Print size is only moderate.

Interest Level: 6 . Reading Level: 3.2. Further Search Topics: Mystery and Detective Stories, Terrorism-Fiction, Murder-Fiction, Best Sellers, Crime-Fiction, Courage-Fiction, Survival-Fiction, Runaways-Fiction.

Blume, Judy. Are you there God? It's me, Margaret. Bradbury 1970, 149 pp.

Sixth grade was a year of growth for Margaret and her friends. They all wondered when they would start growing breasts and when they would begin menstruating. Each was kissed for the first time. It was also a year in which Margaret tried to decide whether to be Jewish or Christian and ended up neither. She simply remained friends with God, just as she was when the year began. The book is a reassuring, very open, and humorous treatment of the pains and promise of maturation. It is exceptionally popular with older elementary school readers, so the book's slightly small print and narrow lines should not impede an interested reader's progress.

Interest Level: 4-6. Reading Level: 3.2. Further Search Topics: School Stories, Family-Fiction, Children-Growth-Fiction, Religion-Fiction, Humorous Fiction, Love-Fiction, Best Sellers, Grandparents-Fiction, Everyday Stories.

Blume, Judy. Blubber. Bradbury 1974, 153 pp.

Jill, like all the other fifth graders in her class, did exactly as Wendy directed her. When Wendy nicknamed one of the class members Blubber and launched a campaign against her, Jill joined right in. It wasn't until the tables were turned and Jill became Wendy's next victim that Jill realized how much it hurt to be the target of such nastiness. It was only then that Jill could stand up to Wendy. Wendy's meanness is extreme and her classmates, without exception, actively follow her lead, yet all adult characters in the book are blind to what happens. Despite those drawbacks, the book deals with a problem very real to children and thus it has guaranteed audience appeal.

Interest Level: 4-6. Reading Level: 3.1. School Stories, Bullies-Fiction, Weight-Fiction, Loners-Fiction, Gangs-Fiction, Read Aloud, Cruelty-Fiction, Best Sellers, Troublemakers-Fiction, Friendship-Fiction.

Blume, Judy. Tales of a fourth grade nothing; illus by Roy Doty. Dutton 1972, 120 pp.

Another humorous Blume book that can be counted on to appeal to third and fourth grade readers. If fifth and sixth graders can ignore the title's reference to fourth grade, they too will love it. The story is an exaggeration of a common theme—an older child whose life is in continual turmoil because of a somewhat spoiled younger sibling. Peter's problems with three-year-old Fudge become worse with each chapter until the final disaster when Fudge swallows Peter's pet turtle. Each approximately 15-page chapter is a complete, very funny episode.

Interest Level: 3-6. Reading Level 3.1. Further Search Topics: Humorous Fiction, Turtles-Fiction, Brothers and Sisters-Fiction, Pets-Fiction, Family-Fiction, Read Aloud, Best Sellers, Everyday Stories, Troublemakers-Fiction.

Blume, Judy. Superfudge. Dutton 1980, 166 pp.

On Fudge's first day in school his older brother Peter had to rescue him from the top of the kindergarten storage cabinets. Later in the school year Fudge's eagerness to join a school guest speaker on stage almost spelled disaster. Then when Fudge unexpectedly disappeared one day everyone, including Peter, thought he had drowned. In addition to Peter's problems with Fudge, Peter had to cope with a baby sister, moving to Princeton, New Jersey, a new job for his mother, and his father's attempts to write a book. Although the book is a sequel and is best enjoyed as such, it can be read alone. It is not as amusing or well-written as it's predecessor, *Tales of a Fourth Grade Nothing*, but will still be popular with young readers.

Interest Level: 3-6. Reading Level 3.1. Further Search Topics: Brothers and Sisters-Fiction, Moving, Household-Fiction, Infants-Fiction, Working Parents-Fiction, School Stories, Family-Fiction, Best Sellers, Humorous Fiction, Everyday Stories.

Blume, Judy. Freckle juice; illus by Sonia O. Lisker. Four Winds 1971, 40 pp.

A very funny story that should appeal to almost everyone. Andrew wanted freckles so that the dirt on his skin wouldn't show as much and he wouldn't have to wash as often. As luck would have it, Sharon, the most obnoxious girl in class, had a freckle juice recipe that she was willing to sell for 50 cents. Even after drinking the brew of grape juice, vinegar, mustard, olive oil, and more, Andrew didn't see any freckles, but, he certainly was sick. Although the protagonists are younger, this book will hold even a fifth grade reader's interest.

Interest Level: 2-5. Reading Level 3.1. Further Search Topics: Humorous Fiction, Group 2, Read Aloud, Everyday Stories, Beauty-Fiction, School Stories, Magic-Fiction, Best Sellers.

Bonham, Frank. The mystery of the fat cat; illus by Alvin Smith. Dutton 1968, 160 pp.

Although noticeably dated at times, this is still an exciting story of an inner city neighborhood. Buddy, Little Pie, Rich, and Cool were among the many who used the local Boys' Club as their hangout. It was a place to stay out of trouble and off the streets, but it was also a haven for rats. The rats were big and brazen; so brazen that one attacked Buddy in the swimming pool. The club needed a new building desperately. The money was there; they just weren't able to use it. Fifteen years earlier an eccentric old woman willed the Boys' Club over $600,000, but stated that the money was first to be used to support her cat until it died. A caretaker, a lawyer, and a veterinarian all benefited as long as the cat lived. Buddy and his friends took on the job of discovering if the cat really was alive or if the Boys' Club was being cheated out of half a million dollars. It was a job that nearly killed them before they set things right. Plenty of action, some violence, a cast of street-smart characters, realistic trouble with the police, as well as a slight mystery almost insure the book's success with older readers. Moderate sized print. Line spacing somewhat narrow.

Interest Level: 6+ Reading Level: 5.1. Further Search Topics: Humorous Fiction, Cats-Fiction, Gangs-Fiction, City Life-Fiction, Mystery and Detective Stories, Poverty-Fiction, Friendship-Fiction, Juvenile Delinquency-Fiction, Crime-Fiction, Best Sellers.

Bonsall, Crosby. And I mean it, Stanley. Har-Row 1974, 32 pp.

A little girl builds "the very best thing I ever made," but all the while calls to Stanley to tell him not to look and to stay on the other side of the fence. Stanley pays attention only long enough for the "thing" to be completed - then crashes through the fence and bounds into the "thing." He draws no anger from the little girl, though, for Stanley is an enormous, loveable mutt. Told as much through pictures as words, this very easy reader will draw smiles from most first and second graders - especially dog lovers. An Early I Can Read Book.

Interest Level: 1-2. Reading Level: 1.2. Further Search Topics: Dogs-Fiction, Humorous Fiction, Best Sellers.

Bulla, Clyde Robert. The sword in the tree; illus by Paul Galdone. Har-Row 1956, 113 pp.

Shan didn't like or trust his Uncle Lionel, who had suddenly appeared at the castle gates after being away many years. Just as suddenly, Shan's father disappeared or died. Shan and his mother soon realized that Lionel wanted to take over the castle, even if it meant killing them. To save themselves, Shan and his mother fled. After walking many miles, they found a poor goat herder and his family who gave them a place to live. Sometime later Shan decided to travel to see King Arthur and ask for help in reclaiming the castle from Lionel. It wasn't until Shan was able to prove the castle was his, and Lionel lost a duel to one of Arthur's knights, that Shan was given back his home. Deep in the castle dungeon Shan found his father, still alive but imprisoned by Lionel.

This book, with its short chapters, short sentences, and steadily progressing plot should interest even the most reluctant reader from grade two through six.

Interest Level: 2-6. Reading Level: 2.2. Further Search Topics: Knights and Knighthood-Fiction, Survival-Fiction, Royalty-Fiction, Best Sellers, Courage-Fiction.

Bulla, Clyde Robert. My friend the monster; illus by Michele Chessare. Har-Row 1980, 75 pp.

Even though Hal was plain and not very clever, his disappointed parents knew that he was still a prince; thus he had to be raised as one. Hal didn't like his lonely, dull life until a new world was accidentally opened to him. A servant's child gave him an old book of monsters and told him that the monsters still lived under the distant mountains. Hal finally made a trip to the mountains, spent a day exploring, and by chance met Humbert, a young monster curious about the world. But, Hal's cruel cousin Archer captured Humbert and put him in a cage. Hal's daring rescue

attempt almost resulted in disaster for both Humbert and Hal.

This is another example of Bulla's forte; a book with an action-filled plot, short chapters, large print, wide spaces between the lines, and a low reading level. A book about monsters has almost guaranteed appeal through third grade. Although the book is useful beyond third grade, readers in fourth and fifth grade may be more sensitive to Hal's apparent youth and the fantastic elements of the story.

Interest Level: 1-3. Reading Level: 2.1. Further Search Topics: Fantasy, Monsters-Fiction, Royalty-Fiction, Group 2, Read Aloud, Best Sellers.

Bulla, Clyde Robert. Pirate's promise; illus by Peter Burchard. Har-Row 1958, 87 pp.

After their mother and father died, Tom and Dinah Pippin had nowhere to go but to their Uncle John's house. Uncle John had no place for them, so he sold Tom into bondage but kept Dinah to help his wife with housework. Tom was to be taken by ship to America where the ship's captain would sell him to the highest bidder. After several years, Tom would be free. But, Tom couldn't accept the idea of one person being another's property, so he spoke out at every opportunity. Tom spoke up to the seaman who dragged him aboard ship, to the captain, to the others who had been bonded, even to the pirate captain who captured their ship. Captain Land was so impressed by Tom's bravery that although he set everyone else he had captured adrift on a small boat, he kept Tom with him. He and Tom became good friends. He never asked Tom to become a pirate and Tom never did. Instead, they enjoyed each other's company. When the pirate ship needed work, they stopped at a safe island where Tom met and impressed Captain Red, a fierce enemy of Captain Land. Captain Red's insistence that Tom join his pirate ship led to another clash between the enemies. Although he was ill, Captain Land fought a duel with Captain Red and lost. Land's last requests were that Benjy, a freed slave who loved him, take all his gold, and that Tom go to Charlestown, South Carolina to find Land's family. Benjy led their flight from Captain Red and arranged a way for Tom to sail to Charlestown before putting Tom on his own. When Tom reached Charlestown he found Land's parents were so angry with Land that at first they didn't even want to hear about him. But, eventually, they not only asked all about their son, but also asked Tom if he and Dinah would like to live with them as their family.

There is enough excitement, danger, and warmth here to satisfy almost any arm-chair adventurer. Usual format of short, episodic chapters.

Interest Level: 3-6. Reading Level 2.1. Further Search Topics: Pirates-Fiction, Seafaring Life-Fiction, Orphans-Fiction, Slavery-Fiction, Brothers and Sisters-Fiction, Best Sellers, Courage-Fiction.

Bulla, Clyde Robert. Marco Moonlight; illus by Julia Noonan. T Y Crowell 1976, 104 pp.

No one could explain Marco's strange, recurring dream. The dream seemed to be about a brother, but Marco had no brother. He had no family but his wealthy grandparents with whom he lived. Marco loved his grandparents very much, but he couldn't help wondering about his own past. He knew only what he and his grandparents could figure out from a few clues. His mother had run away to marry and for three years Marco's grandparents had heard nothing. Then, suddenly, they received a note that she was dying, had parted from her husband, and needed them. By the time they arrived, she was dead and two-year-old Marco could tell them no more. About the time of his thirteenth birthday Marco made friends with a strange man named Flint, who later became the gardener on Marco's grandparents' estate. Rather than live in the room provided for him with the other servants, Flint chose a bleak and isolated beach cottage. Being very careful that no one should suspect, Flint locked Marco into the cottage and forced Marco to change clothes with Matt, who was Marco's long-lost identical twin. Flint and Matt planned that Matt would steal all the money he could from the estate before killing Marco and fleeing. But when Matt began to realize how nice his grandparents were, how much he liked Marco, and how evil Flint was, he decided to thwart Flint's plan. In Matt and Marco's desperate attempt to flee from Flint, Flint was accidentally killed, leaving Marco free to return home and Matt free to find a way to feel he also had the right to claim his heritage before joining Marco.

The tense and dramatic plot immediately involves the reader and the short, fast-paced chapters sustain interest to the end of the book. Readers should also appreciate the small, paperback-size format. A good choice.

Interest Level: 3-6. Reading Level: 2.1. Further Search Topics: Dreams-Fiction, Mystery and Detective Stories, Kidnapping-Fiction, Twins-Fiction, Orphans-Fiction, Grandparents-Fiction, Best Sellers, Brothers and Sisters-Fiction, Jealousy-Fiction, Courage-Fiction.

Bulla, Clyde Robert. Viking adventure; illus by Douglas Gorsline. T Y Crowell 1963, 117 pp.

An exciting story of a young Norwegian boy named Sigurd. Sigurd realized his dream when he finally set sail on a Viking ship in search of Wineland (Vinland). Leif Eriksson had told of his North American findings over 100 years earlier. Sigurd and his father's friend Grom, the captain of the ship, were sure they could find that land again. Their determination finally brought Grom's death at the hands of the ship's owner, Sigurd's near death, and the destruction of the ship.

This book, too, is true to Bulla's style of short chapters, short sentences, much action and high appeal. Although it is a little higher reading level than many of Bulla's others, it is still a good choice. Recently out of print, but worth a search.

Interest Level: 2-6. Reading Level: 3.1. Further Search Topics: Norway-Fiction, Historical Fiction, Seafaring Life-Fiction, Voyages and Travels-Fiction, Shipwrecks-Fiction, Explorers-Fiction, Vikings-Fiction, Courage-Fiction, Best Sellers, Group 2.

Bunting, Eve. The skate patrol; illus by Don Madden. Albert Whitman 1980, 40 pp.

The book is funny, clever, undemanding and short. The combination of those qualities plus its slight mystery and its consistent reading level make this a very appealing and useful book for young readers. The plot is simple: in the hopes that their neighbors would be so grateful that they would allow the boys to roller skate in the neighborhood again, two friends decided to capture a local thief. James and Milton even knew who the thief was. He was the "mysterious man" who sat in the park. They only had to capture him in the act of stealing to prove that they were correct. They watched him continuously and trailed him as he followed old ladies. Then came the day that they heard Mrs. Grump scream that her purse had been snatched. The boys sped after the "mysterious man" on their skates. They caught him and knocked him down. To their surprise he declared that he was an undercover policeman and they were letting the

real thief get away. Off they went again. This time they caught the right person and were rewarded just the way that they had hoped: Mrs. Crump (not Grump) promised that the boys would be allowed to roller skate any time they wished. A light and lively entertainment.

Interest Level: 2-4. Reading Level: 2.2. Further Search Topics: Mystery and Detective Stories, Humorous Fiction, Spies-Fiction, Roller Skating-Fiction, Crime-Fiction, Best Sellers.

Byars, Betsy. The 18th emergency; illus by Robert Grossman. Viking Pr. 1973, 126 pp.

When your best friend knows how to escape from the world's 17 worst emergencies and you're faced with the eighteenth, you're in trouble. That was the spot in which Mouse found himself one day. He had drawn an arrow towards a large picture of the Neanderthal man and written Marv Hammerman's name. Hammerman had seen him do it and was out to kill, maim, or at least beat up Mouse. Mouse finally ran out of ways to avoid Hammerman and had to face the fight. When it was over and he was once again able to stand up, Mouse realized he felt better for having allowed Hammerman to regain his honor and for having taken responsibility for his own actions.

A funny, fast-moving look at real feelings of fear, honor and responsibility. Very popular. Print is dark and of good size but lines could have been spaced farther apart.

Interest Level: 4-6. Reading Level: 3.2. Further Search Topics: Bullies-Fiction, Humorous Fiction, Courage-Fiction, Best Sellers, Challenges-Fiction, Read Aloud.

Byars, Betsy. Trouble River; illus by Rocco Negri. Viking Pr. 1969, 158 pp.

A gripping adventure story of survival. After being attacked by an Indian in the middle of the night, Dewey and his grandmother rushed to Trouble River to board a small raft which Dewey had just finished making. They thought they would only need to navigate a few miles down the river to safety at a neighbor's home, but found instead that the neighbor's cabin had been burned down. For almost 40 miles they fought against the unknown river, wolves and rapids.

This is a book that should satisfy many reluctant readers. It's frequent dialogue, fast action and high interest are only occasionally marred by an overly long sentence.

Interest Level: 3-6. Reading Level: 3.1. Further Search Topics: Courage-Fiction, Frontier and Pioneer Life-Fiction, Survival-Fiction, Grandparents-Fiction, Voyages and Travels-Fiction, Best Sellers, Read Aloud.

Clymer, Eleanor. Me and the Eggman; illus by David K. Stone. Dutton 1972, 57 pp.

As Donald's life became more and more miserable and as his chores and responsibilities around his small, overcrowded, urban apartment increased, he began to look for a way to escape. Thinking that if he could just get to the country, life would be better, Donald sneaked into a truck owned by a farmer who delivered eggs to the city. Not surprisingly the farmer, a sharp speaking, independent old man, was not at all happy to find Donald. Reluctantly, the Eggman, as the farmer was called, agreed to let Donald stay a week and help to work his rundown farm. The week stretched into a summer in which Donald learned to face and accept reality, to love the Eggman and to like himself.

This book is a surprisingly consistent success with reluctant readers, especially boys. Watch for the lack of quotation marks around the dialogue and the somewhat small print.

Interest Level: 3-6. Reading Level: 3.2. Further Search Topics: Family Problems-Fiction, Poverty-Fiction, Vacation-Fiction, Runaways-Fiction, Farm Life-Fiction, Best Sellers.

Clymer, Eleanor. Luke was there; illus by Diane de Groat. HR & W 1973, 74 pp.

Julius' father, uncle and finally his step-father had all walked out on him. Even his mother had left him, although she hadn't wanted to go. When his mother had been taken to the hospital, Julius and his younger brother Danny were sent to a children's home. Julius felt alone and cheated until he met a young, black, social worker named Luke. Luke liked and respected Julius and helped Julius learn to feel the same way about himself. When Luke, too, left Julius, Julius was so angry at the world that he stole food and then money. Afraid to go back to the children's home because he thought he'd be caught and punished, Julius ran away. It wasn't until he found an abandoned child, about Danny's age, who needed care, that Julius returned to the home. Luke was there when he arrived, just when Julius needed him most. Luke listened to Julius' unhappy feelings, arranged for him to see his mother and helped him begin to accept the fact that life is not always fair.

Julius tells his own story in a realistic, straight-forward book that will touch most readers. Only the lack of quotation marks and inadequate spacing between the lines may slow the reader.

Interest Level: 3-6. Reading Level: 2.2. Further Search Topics: Runaways-Fiction, Orphans-Fiction, Juvenile Delinquency-Fiction, Divorce and Separation-Fiction, Friendship-Fiction, Courage-Fiction, Survival-Fiction, Loneliness-Fiction, Best Sellers, Read Aloud.

Cohen, Daniel. Creatures from UFOs. Dodd 1978, 112 pp.

A series of reports about close encounters of the third kind. The author offers both sides of each story, then allows the reader to draw his or her own conclusions. Stories will intrigue even those readers not already interested in UFOs. Index. Photographs. A natural. Parts can even be read aloud.

Interest Level: 3-6. Reading Level: 3.1. Further Search Topics: Best Sellers, Flying Saucers.

Curtis, Philip. The invasion of the Brain Sharpeners; illus by Tony Ross. Knopf 1979, 117 pp.

This book is one of a number of books published by Albert Knopf under the series title Capers. They are meant to be (and with few exceptions are) light, easy-to-read fiction, published simultaneously in hardcover and paperback editions. Each book is about 120 pages long with chapter length varying from 9 to 14 pages. Print is plenty large and spacing between lines is always adequate. Plots are built around an idea of guaranteed appeal, descriptive passages are kept to a minimum and action (often suspenseful) abounds. This should, on the whole, be a very useful series. Some entries (i.e., *Man From the Sky* and *Who Stole the Wizard of Oz*, both by Avi) are either too difficult or too obscure to be widely appealing, but they are by far the exceptions to the rule.

Invasion of the Brain Sharpeners is the catchy science fiction story of Michael's successful, but risky, attempt to rid his fifth grade classroom of the overpowering influence of the Brain Sharpeners. The

Brain Sharpeners came from another galaxy to search for humans to help them colonize their Planet Five. Humans were so lacking in brain power that the Brain Sharpeners' plan was to periodically expose each child to brain-developing rays, then put them through intensive courses of study guided by their also-exposed teacher. When the children had all learned enough to be beneficial to the Brain Sharpeners, they were to be taken from Earth to Planet Five. Michael was the only one to see the danger they were in and to attempt to stop the plot. He managed to chase the aliens away and to prevent his classmates and teacher from receiving their second dose of rays, but in doing so, he sent the principal to the spaceship. Michael's classmates were thus saved, but his principal was never heard from again. Capers series.

Interest Level: 3-6. Reading Level: 3.1. Further Search Topics: Science Fiction, Flying Saucers-Fiction, Aliens-Fiction, School Stories, Kidnapping-Fiction, Best Sellers, Academic Problems-Fiction, Brainwashing-Fiction.

Dolan, Edward F., Jr. Let's make magic; photos by Jay Irving. Doubleday 1981, 96 pp.

With playing cards, coins, paper, a few commonly available odds and ends and some practice, the reader can perform most of the tricks in this book. The book is not a step-by-step description of how to put together a magic show (as some of the other titles are), but is more like a casual chat with a friend who wants to teach you to perform a few tricks. Some are simply optical illusions; some are brain teasers that involve mathematical calculations; some are card tricks; and others are much more traditional magic tricks.

Very little is said about how to use conversation as audience distraction or how to link the tricks together into a show. Instead, it is the kind of book that allows the reader to pick and choose any tricks he or she may want to learn without feeling pressured to do more than entertain a friend or two for a few moments. The tricks, with the possible exception of the mathematical brain teasers, are all easily manageable by third through sixth grade readers and yet are impressive to their peers. The use of photographs, rather than cartoon illustrations, helps to make the book a probable success, especially with older readers who like to entertain, enjoy the spotlight, or are interested in magic.

Interest Level: 3-6. Reading Level: 3.1. Further Search Topics: Magic, Optical illusions, Best Sellers.

Eastman, Philip D. Sam and the firefly. Beginner 1958, 62 pp.

Sam, the owl, went looking for a playmate one night but found everyone was asleep except a mischievous firefly named Gus. When Sam showed Gus how to write words with his light in the dark sky, Gus went wild. First he tried to direct auto traffic, then airplane traffic, until finally the Hot Dog Man, an angry victim of Gus' tricks, captured him. However, when the Hot Dog Man tried to take Gus out of town, his truck became stuck on the railroad tracks in front of an oncoming train. Gus, freed from the jar in which he'd been caught, quickly wrote the word STOP in the sky and saved everyone. Gus' silliness, the catastrophies he caused and his final triumph should interest almost any young child who likes humor or excitement. Reader format.

Interest Level: 1-2. Reading Level: 1.2. Further Search Topics: Best Sellers, Fireflies-Fiction, Owls-Fiction, Humorous Fiction.

Greenfield, Eloise. Talk about a family; illus by James Calvin. Lippincott 1978, 60 pp.

Genny, Kim, and Mac knew something was wrong between their parents, and fully expected that their older brother Larry would be able to fix everything when he came home from the army. But even Larry's welcome home party was almost ruined by their parents' fighting and Kim's reaction. That night, as she listened to Larry and her parents' low voices, Genny was certain that Larry was bringing her parents back together. When her father announced the next morning that he was going to move out, Genny's anger and hurt was directed at Larry. With her friend Mr. Parker's help, Genny finally realized that they were still a family; a family with a new shape, but one that would be able to adjust. A one-theme, realistic and reassuring, short book with good-sized print. Very useful

Interest Level: 3-6. Reading Level: 3.1. Further Search Topics: Divorce and Separation-Fiction, Family Problems-Fiction, Brothers and Sisters-Fiction, Best Sellers.

Hinton, Susan E. The outsiders. Viking Pr. 1967, 188 pp.

When she wrote this book Susan Hinton was only 17 years old, but she had the sensitivity of someone much older. She wrote a taut story of the rivalry between two city gangs; the Socs (the rich socialites) and the Greasers (poor kids from the wrong side of town) that is more than anything a plea for understanding and tolerance. Seen through the eyes of Ponyboy (a very bright, 14-year-old Greaser), the rivalry brought on violence and an accidental killing that forced Pony and his friend Johnny to flee for their lives. Dallas, the meanest and most dangerous of the Greasers, provided them with shelter, food for a week, and a gun. At the end of that week, Johnny decided that they should turn themselves in to the police. But before they could do that, their hideout (an old church) burned in a fire which threatened the lives of four children who had been playing there. In trying to rescue the children, Johnny, Pony, and Dallas were injured; Johnny was severely burned and probably permanently crippled. A vengeance rumble was held while Johnny lay in the hospital, but the Greasers' victory was empty when Johnny died. He had been the one member of the gang whom they all loved and who had most needed them. Dallas went to pieces: he robbed a store and set himself up to be killed by the police. He had nothing left to live for after Johnny's death. Pony found support and security with his brothers (their parents were dead) and, in a note from Johnny, some hope for the future.

Hinton speaks most often through Pony (his depth of understanding of the people around him is very impressive), but through Johnny and two of the Socs as well, Randy and Cherry. Her message is clear, but at no time does she fail to maintain believable characters in a compelling plot.

Although the book looks forbidding with its 188 pages of unrelenting small print, it is an exciting story, full of adventure, realism, and room for thought. Perhaps the best way to introduce this book is to read a fair portion of it aloud. Now a motion picture too.

Interest Level: 6+. Reading Level: 5.1. Further Search Topics: Crime-Fiction, Gangs-Fiction, Murder-Fiction, Read Aloud, Friendship-Fiction, Juvenile Delinquency-Fiction, Best Sellers, City Life-Fiction, Brothers and Sisters-Fiction, Orphans-Fiction, Runaways-Fiction, Troublemakers-Fiction, Poverty-Fiction.

Holland, John. The way it is. HarBraceJ 1969, 87 pp.

For 15 boys living in a run-down area of Brooklyn, school became interesting when they were assigned to photograph whatever was meaningful to them in their neighborhood. The results, described in their own words, were developed into this fascinating documentary which is at the same time a spontaneous glimpse of the boys themselves. The book should be of particular interest to older urban children. Print slightly on the small side. Has recently gone out of print, but is worth looking for.

Interest Level: 4-6. Reading Level: 3.2. Further Search Topics: Best Sellers, City Life, Photography, Poverty, Academic Problems.

Hurwitz, Johanna. The law of gravity; illus by Ingrid Fetz. Morrow 1978, 192 pp.

The summer between fifth and sixth grades looked very unexciting to Margot. Her best friends were both going away for the whole summer and her father, a musician, was going to be on tour for most of the summer. Margot's very overweight mother had sworn never to go downstairs from their fifth floor walk-up apartment. Unless Margot chose to stay upstairs too, she was sure she would have a very lonely vacation. In addition, she had to work on a summer project for school. The project she finally chose was to get her mother downstairs after nine years of staying upstairs. In search of help she went to the local library where she met Bernie. Bernie was only a year older than Margot, but he seemed to know the most interesting things about the city. He showed her places Margot had never heard of before, he taught her to play chess, backgammon, and even to ride a bicycle. He was so full of fascinating ideas and information that Margot had no chance to be bored or lonely. Best of all, he even tried to help Margot with her project. None of their ideas worked, however, until Margot pretended to run away and scared her mother into going downstairs. Only then did Margot realize that she loved her mother whether or not she stayed on the fifth floor and that she couldn't simply force her mother or anyone else to change to suit her own fancy.

The book is a warm, understanding, slightly humorous treatment of the fairly common wish to change someone else. Although not many readers are likely to share Margot's exact problem, most will recognize her feelings. The book is also a virtual Chamber of Commerce advertisement for urban living. One of its other charms is its picture of a non-competitive, open, real friendship between an 11-year-old girl and a 12-year-old boy. The only drawback to the book is its inconsistent reading level which varies from 4.1 to 5.1 with a rare leap to 5.2.

Interest Level: 4-6. Reading Level: 4.2. Further Search Topics: Vacation-Fiction, Friendship-Fiction, Loners-Fiction, City Life-Fiction, Individualists-Fiction, Courage-Fiction, New York City-Fiction, Humorous Fiction, Family-Fiction, Challenges-Fiction, Weight-Fiction, Everyday Stories, Best Sellers.

Kibbe, Pat. The hocus-pocus dilemma; illus by Dan Jones. Knopf 1979, 125 pp.

Each chapter of this book is a separate episode in B.J.'s attempt to cultivate her newly-discovered ESP talents (more invented than discovered). The episodes, each of which involves a different member of B.J.'s family, are slightly outlandish, but very funny. Even the dog and the cat become involved. The dog becomes the unwitting target for a skunk. The cat accidentally starts a tape recording of speech habits that sounds like burglars breaking into the house. After nine disasters, B.J. finally concludes that she was being ridiculous to think that she had ESP, but that everyone is allowed to be ridiculous sometimes.

The nine, reasonably short episodes, the moderate size print, the sympathetic characters, and the book's humor, make this a very useful and popular title.

Interest Level: 4-6. Reading Level: 3.1. Further Search Topics: Extra Sensory Perception-Fiction, Humorous Fiction, Family-Fiction, Everyday Stories, Best Sellers, Read Aloud.

Krementz, Jill. A very young circus flyer. Knopf 1979, unp (112 pp).

One of a series of five oversized, abundantly photographed views of unusual children. Tato Farfan is part of the Flying Farfans of Ringling Brothers and Barnum and Bailey Circus. He lives in a railroad car on a circus train with his mother, father, and older brother. The whole family performs as trapeze artists and flyers for the circus. Told as if Tato were speaking, this is the story of a fairly normal boy who also happens to be a circus flyer. Practice sessions are difficult, costumes must be readied, and time must be spent helping each other, but there is also time for Tato to watch TV, play with the clowns, play soccer, and just have fun.

In addition to Tato's story, the reader is given a behind-the-scenes tour of the circus right up to and including the performance itself (color photos used for the performance). It is an exciting world that should appeal to almost anyone who has enjoyed the circus.

Interest Level: 2-6. Reading Level: 3.2. Further Search Topics: Circus, Acrobats and Acrobatics, Best Sellers, Talent, Group 2, Gymnastics.

Krementz, Jill. A very young dancer. Knopf 1976, unp (121 pp).

This was the first of the five *Very Young* books to be written. Like the others, it is large in format and lavishly photographed. Unlike *A Very Young Circus Flyer*, this and the remaining books in the series are written about 10-year-old girls from obviously privileged backgrounds. All the girls are high achievers in their chosen areas but they seem very determined to work still harder until they attain whatever goals they have set for themselves. The books all follow the same formula. The girls introduce themselves, tell about their start in dancing, riding etc., describe their goals, and tell the reader how close they are to those goals. The girls go on to describe their daily routines, the practice, the chores, the hours, and the fun. Then the reader is ushered through approximately a year's worth of the young star's challenges, achievements, and defeats (the latter are only lightly touched upon). Through it all, the child shows enthusiasm, pride, dedication, hard work, and finally, hopes for the future.

Young readers love this series. Despite heavy use of jargon that makes the reading levels somewhat unstable, those already interested in the subject area pour over every word and picture in the books. Perhaps it's partly hero worship, or romance. Maybe it's the inspiration the books provide, but certainly one of the reasons the books are so popular is the vicarious thrill that they provide young enthusiasts.

A Very Young Dancer differs slightly from the formula. Instead of following Stephanie through a year of dance classes at the School of American Ballet, the book concentrates on New York City Ballet Company's production of the Nutcracker, in which Stephanie has a lead role.

Interest Level: 2-5. Reading Level: 3.1. Further Search Topics: Dancing, Ballet, Talent, Best Sellers, Group 2.

Krementz, Jill. A very young skater. Knopf 1979, unp (103 pp).

Katherine Healy started ice skating because her parents liked to skate and because it was easier for them to take her with them than it was to find a babysitter. From such beginnings, at age three, Katherine progressed to skating in Superskates at Madison Square Garden and ballet lessons at George Balanchine's School of American Ballet. See *A Very Young Dancer* for further explanation.

Interest Level: 2-6. Reading Level: 4.1. Further Search Topics: Ice Skating, Dancing, Ballet, Talent, Group 2, Best Sellers.

Krementz, Jill. A very young gymnast. Knopf 1978, unp (128 pp).

This is Torrence York's story. It includes a team trip to Germany for competition. See notes for *A Very Young Dancer* for more information.

Interest Level: 2-6. Reading Level: 3.2. Further Search Topics: Gymnastics, Talent, Acrobats and Acrobatics, Group 2, Best Sellers.

LeSieg, Theo. Wacky Wednesday; illus by George Booth. Beginner 1974, unp (36 pp).

A series of true picture puzzles. A little boy wakes up one Wednesday to find everything around him has gone "wacky." People are missing heads but have extra legs. Cars are being driven from the back seat. Doors are placed in the wrong places. Airplanes fly backwards. At the end of the day everything settles back to normal, but not before readers have had fun finding the numerous "wacky" things on each page.

The story is told in silly rhyme (LeSieg and Seuss are the same person). What is wrong with each picture is not always easily located, making this reader an excellent excerise in observation as well as great fun.

Interest Level: 1-3. Reading Level: 1.2. Further Search Topics: Puzzles, Humorous Fiction, Wit and Humor, Poetry, Best Sellers.

Levy, Elizabeth. Lizzie lies a lot; illus by John Wallner. Delacorte 1976, 102 pp.

Almost any child can identify with Lizzie. She had found that it was sometimes easier to lie than to tell the truth. Her problem was that she had lost control. It seemed as if almost everything she said was a lie. She told so many lies it became difficult to keep track of them all. Lizzie wasn't even really sure why she lied so much. She knew that she sometimes lied because she thought people would be more apt to like her. Other times she lied to get herself out of trouble or to cover up her feelings when she was hurt or angry. But that didn't explain why she lied all the time. Maybe, as her grandmother said, she was a born liar.

It wasn't until Lizzie got herself caught in the middle of so many lies that she lost her only friend, that she could admit her problem to herself and to her family. After their initial shock had passed, everyone agreed to help Lizzie stop lying. Lizzie took the next step by admitting her lies to her friend Sue.

Levy has brought such an appropriately light touch to a fairly common problem that many children find this story enjoyable. Overlook the book's faults (Lizzie's grandmother is overdrawn and her mother's guilt feelings are unsupported by the story) for the fun and the message young readers get from it.

Interest Level: 3-5. Reading Level: 4.2. Further Search Topics: Honesty-Fiction, Group 2, Friendship-Fiction, Best Sellers, Everyday Stories, Family Problems-Fiction, Grandparents-Fiction, Humorous Fiction.

Lowry, Lois. Anastasia Krupnik. HM 1979, 113 pp.
Anastasia Krupnik led a comfortable, relatively happy life until her parents announced that she was not going to be an only child for much longer. After 10 years of enjoying that luxury, Anastasia wasn't at all pleased with the change. Babies immediately went to a prominent, and as far as Anastasia was concerned, permanent place on her list of hates. Anastasia kept two lists: one for things and people she particularly liked, and one list for what she did not like. What went on and off the lists tells much about Anastasia. Anastasia tells the rest in this perceptive, sensitive, and humorous story of growing up and adjusting to a new sibling.
Spacing between lines is slightly too narrow for the rather large print.
Interest Level: 4-6. Reading Level: 3.1. Further Search Topics: Humorous Fiction, Brothers and Sisters-Fiction, Everyday Stories, Jealousy-Fiction, Infants-Fiction, Best Sellers, Children-Growth-Fiction.

Madian, Jon. Beautiful junk: a story of the Watts Towers; photos by Barbara Jacobs, Jr. and Lou Jacobs, Jr. Little 1968, 44 pp.
Although this book is now out of print; it is well worth trying to find. It is a fictionalized account of a young, angry black boy's encounter with the creator of Los Angeles' unusual Watts Towers. Simon Rodia, a poor tile setter, worked on the towers for 33 years until he was 75 years old. He used only his imagination, discarded materials he found around him, seashells, and sand to build three tall, fantasy-like towers in the middle of a ghetto. He created beauty where others saw only junk.
The book is illustrated with photography that makes the story more vivid and the towers and Rodia's accomplishment more impressive than they would have seemed with drawings. The print is good-sized, spacing is totally adequate. Rodia's life is quickly submarized and an update on the Towers is included at the book's end.
Interest Level: 3-6. Reading Level: 3.1. Further Search Topics: Blacks-Fiction, Read Aloud, Best Sellers, Poverty-Fiction, Rodia, Simon, Architecture, Biography, Aging-Fiction, Watts Towers, California, Poverty.

Miles, Betty. The secret life of the underwear champ; illus by Dan Jones. Knopf 1981, 117 pp.
Larry hadn't planned it; in fact, he hadn't even really wanted it to happen. But suddenly he found himself about to make a television commercial for ChampWin Knitting Mills, makers of sports clothing and underwear. He knew his family could use the money he would make, but he certainly didn't want the whole school seeing him in his underwear. Nevertheless, Larry went ahead and made the commercial, hoping that it would never be used. He even had to skip baseball practice to make the taping. Much to his horror, the commercial appeared the night before the team's first game. Not only did the entire opposing team tease him, but so did all his own teammates. By the time he got up to bat, Larry was mad enough to slam the ball out of the park. He didn't hit the ball quite that hard, but he did make a winning home run and end the others' giggles forever. He became the true underwear champ.

This is a funny look at the embarrassments of growing up. It also deals lightly with a boy's pride, his peer relationship, and his growing awareness of girls. An appealing and broadly usable title. Capers series.
Interest Level: 3-5. Reading Level: 2.2. Further Search Topics: Baseball-Fiction, Television-Fiction, Occupations-Fiction, School Stories, Humorous Fiction, Advertising-Fiction, Beauty-Fiction, Motion Pictures-Fiction, Best Sellers, Everyday Stories.

Montgomery, Raymond A. Space and beyond; illus by Paul Granger. Bantam 1980, 117 pp.
See entry for *Sugarcane Island*, by Edward Packard for full annotation. Available in paperback only. Choose Your Own Adventure series
Interest Level: 2-6. Reading Level: 4.1. Further Search Topics: Science Fiction, Outer Space-Fiction, Group 2, Best Sellers.

Montgomery, Raymond A. The lost jewels of Nabooti; illus by Paul Granger. Bantam 1981, 121 pp.
See entry for *Sugarcane Island*, by Edward Packard for series information. Only available in paperback edition. Choose Your Own Adventure series.
Interest Level: 2-6. Reading Level: 3.2. Further Search Topics: Mystery and Detective Stories, Detectives-Fiction, Treasure-Fiction, Best Sellers, Group 2.

Nodset, Joan L. Go away dog; illus by Crosby Bonsall. Har-Row 1963, unp (29 pp).
A small boy who doesn't like dogs meets a shaggy, homeless dog who wants to play. The little boy, resisting all the way, gradually gives in to the dog's charms. Finally he tells the dog to follow him home. At home, he finds out that the dog was sent to him for his birthday by his Uncle George.
The dog, the boy, and the book are irresistible. You must, however, notice the illustrations on both the dedication and title pages to fully understand the story. Since much of the story is told by the illustrations and the text is repetitive as well as simple, it is an excellent beginning-to-read story.
Interest Level: 1-2. Reading Level: 1.1. Further Search Topics: Dogs-Fiction, Humorous Fiction, Best Sellers, Pets-Fiction, Birthdays-Fiction.

Packard, Edward. Sugarcane Island; illus by Barbara Carter. Archway 1976, 105 pp.
The warning on the first page, that the book should *not* be read straight through, tells you that this book is different. And different it is. It is the first of what is now a new type of book; the "Choose Your Own Adventure" story. The formula is simple and highly successful, especially with reluctant readers. The reader is made the central character of the book. After a very brief series of events that set the stage, the reader is given choices to make. Upon making a decision, the reader is instructed to proceed to another page of the book. More action is described before the reader must make another choice. The sequence of action, choice, action and choice continues until the reader has finally completed an entire story. The books can be read over and over and the reader may never repeat exactly the same story unless he/she makes all of the same choices. What distinguishes one book from another is the setting, genre, and/or author (there are three: Edward Packard, R. A. Montgomery, and D. Terman). Don't expect quality writing or consistent reading levels because you won't find either. (Reading levels vary from 2.2 to 3.2 for most titles). What you will find is dependable, action-filled, enticing, light reading. Some are available only in paperback editions where the

print size is fairly small. Choose Your Own Adventure series.

Interest Level: 2-6. Reading Level: 3.1. Further Search Topics: Shipwrecks-Fiction, Best Sellers, Survival-Fiction, Group 2.

Packard, Edward. Your code name is Jonah; illus by Paul Granger. Bantam 1980, 114 pp.

See *Sugarcane Island* for information about books in this series. Paperback only. Choose Your Own Adventure series.

Interest Level: 2-6. Reading Level: 3.2. Further Search Topics: Nonverbal Communication-Fiction, Best Sellers, Spies-Fiction, Group 2.

Packard, Edward. The mystery of Chimney Rock; illus by Paul Granger. Bantam 1979, 121 pp.

See notes for *Sugarcane Island* for information about the series. Paperback only. Choose Your Own Adventure series.

Interest Level: 2-6. Reading Level: 3.2. Further Search Topics: Mystery and Detective Stories, Cats-Fiction, Witches-Fiction, Ghosts-Fiction, Detectives-Fiction, Best Sellers, Group 2.

Packard, Edward. Deadwood City; illus by Barbara Carter. Bantam 1978, 96 pp.

See *Sugarcane Island* for full series notes. Paperback edition only. Choose Your Own Adventure series.

Interest Level: 2-6. Reading Level: 3.1. Further Search Topics: West-Fiction, Cowboys-Fiction, Crime-Fiction, Best Sellers, Group 2.

Parish, Peggy. Too many rabbits; illus by Leonard Kessler. Macmillan 1974, 48 pp.

One day Miss Molly opened her front door to find a rabbit waiting to be invited inside. The next day Miss Molly discovered the rabbit had had baby rabbits, lots of baby rabbits. Because babies need care, Miss Molly couldn't just turn them out, so she kept them all. Before long she had more rabbits than she could handle. She tried giving them away, but all the children's mothers refused to keep them, the zoo didn't need any, and Miss Molly didn't want to sell them to the butcher. Finally a man who owned an island where they could live, asked to take all the rabbits. As Miss Molly was about to close the door after giving the rabbits to the man with an island, a cat walked right up to her and inside her house. The next day Miss Molly discovered she had kittens—lots of kittens. A very humorous story in a reader format.

Interest Level: 1-3. Reading Level: 1.2. Further Search Topics: Humorous Fiction, Rabbits-Fiction, Best Sellers.

Peck, Robert Newton. Mr. Little; illus by Ben Stahl. Doubleday 1979, 87 pp.

All summer long Drag and Finley had looked forward to having Miss Kellogg as their teacher, so they were extremely disappointed to find ordinary-looking Mr. Little in her place on the first day of school. Used to playing tricks on their teachers anyway, Drag and Finley decided to go all out to get even with Mr. Little for spoiling their year. But try as they might, they couldn't get an advantage over Mr. Little; he seemed to be unflappable. Finally, in their riskiest prank ever, they stole Mr. Little's underwear to dress a statue in the town square. That attempt to embarrass Mr. Little only served to get Finley and Drag in serious trouble from which Mr. Little saved them. It was his later rescue of Miss Kellogg, however, that added respect to the boys' growing feeling of friendship for Mr. Little.

Because the author's adult viewpoint is never quite lost, even though he writes in the first person, and because the rural and historic time settings are not familiar to many readers, the book may need some introduction and encouragement. It is a prime candidate for reading aloud until the young reader's interest takes over. Print is of adequate size, but spacing between lines could have been more generous.

Interest Level: 4-6. Reading Level: 5.1. Further Search Topics: Humorous Fiction, School Stories, Troublemakers-Fiction, Group 2, Read Aloud, Country Life-Fiction, Best Sellers.

Pfeffer, Susan Beth. Kid power; illus by Leigh Grant. Watts 1977, 121 pp.

When Janie's mother lost her job, her father's salary wouldn't stretch to provide any more money for the new bicycle fund. There was enough money already set aside to pay for one new bike, but both Janie and her older sister Carol wanted a bicycle. Carol, who had saved money of her own, suggested that they each pay for half a bike and their parents contribute the money for the other half. Then Janie's only problem was how to earn money, since she had none saved. Her solution was to create a business: Kid Power. Before long, Janie's business had blossomed and she was becoming rich, but she had lost her best friend and was ruining a client's roses. When Janie finally realized that getting rich wasn't the only thing that mattered in life, she relaxed, delegated jobs to friends better able to handle them, and became their agent.

A genuinely funny book that, as a bonus, takes a realistic look at the interworkings of a family. Consistent reading level.

Interest Level: 4-6. Reading Level: 3.1. Further Search Topics: Occupations-Fiction, Everyday Stories, Vacation-Fiction, Family-Fiction, Humorous Fiction, Best Sellers, Bicycles and Bicycling-Fiction, Friendship-Fiction.

Pinkwater, Daniel Manus. Fat men from space. Dodd 1977, 57 pp.

The evening after his trip to the dentist William found that he could still hear radio programs when his radio was turned off. He was even more surprised to find that when he wired himself to a fence he could hear spacemen talking. When the spacemen discovered that William could hear them, they landed and captured him. They were on a top secret mission and couldn't risk any human knowing about their existence. The spacemen were about to invade Earth to consume all the junk food they could find. As mass panic set in on Earth, William could do nothing to save his fellow humans. He was held captive and helpless until the invaders' interest was captured by a giant potato pancake floating in outer space.

A tongue-in-check, slapstick spoof of science fiction, food fads, and junk food. Do not expect anything more.

Interest Level: 3-5. Reading Level: 3.2. Further Search Topics: Science Fiction, Humorous Fiction, Food-Fiction, Flying Saucers-Fiction, Aliens-Fiction, Best Sellers, Kidnapping-Fiction, Teeth-Fiction.

Pinkwater, Daniel Manus. The Hoboken chicken emergency. P-H 1977, 83 pp.

Arthur's mother sent him out with $16 to buy a Thanksgiving turkey. He returned with a live 266 pound chicken on a leash. It seemed that their turkey reservation had been lost at the meat market and, because it was Thanksgiving morning, there were no other turkeys available. Arthur searched everywhere but found nothing, until a strange old professor tricked him into buying the chicken. No one could bear to kill and eat such a large and friendly chicken, so Arthur and his family named it Henrietta and kept it as a pet. Henrietta was a difficult pet to keep hidden from the neighbors When the neighbors, and later the city, saw Henrietta running loose there was general hysteria. But all ended well when Henrietta and the city calmed down and Henrietta became a kind of neighborhood mascot.

A purely absurd plot but presented with enough energy and humor that most readers thoroughly enjoy the book. Some brief introduction may be necessary to get readers beyond the first few pages.

Interest Level: 3-6. Reading Level: 2.2. Further Search Topics: Humorous Fiction, Chickens-Fiction, Pets-Fiction, Thanksgiving-Fiction, Holidays-Fiction, Read Aloud, Best Sellers.

Platt, Kin. Dracula, go home; illus by Frank Mayo. Watts 1979, 87 pp.

From the chapter numbers that drip blood, and the humorously grotesque illustrations, to the short sentences and chapters, this is a book designed and almost guaranteed to appeal to the reluctant reader. A sense of immediacy and involvement is created by the first person narration. Tension is created on the opening page when Larry sees a man in the cemetery who looked exactly like Dracula. When that man registered at the hotel where Larry was working, Larry decided to find out more about him. It began to look as if Mr. A. R. Claude (the letters spell Dracula) was not only a vampire, but a thief and a murderer as well. The trouble was that Larry couldn't prove anything. Even when he found the stolen jewels for which Mr. Claude had been searching, Larry still couldn't convince anyone of Claude's true identify. No one ever did believe Larry, thus Claude went free.

The author uses a light touch to treat an eerie subject. His inconclusive ending may disappoint some, but should delight many. Beware of the variability of the reading level however; it swings from high first grade to low third grade.

Interest Level: 3-6. Reading Level: 2.2. Further Search Topics: Monsters-Fiction, Horror-Fiction, Mystery and Detective Stories, Best Sellers, Murder-Fiction, Crime-Fiction, Transformations-Fiction.

Robinson, Jean. The strange but wonderful cosmic awareness of Duffy Moon; illus by Lawrence Di Fiori. HM 1974, 142 pp.

Duffy was tired of being small, of always being on the losing side of fights, and of being unappreciated at home (by his ex-football star uncle). When he sent away for Mr. Flamel's Cosmic Awareness Kit, Duffy was sure he would then be able to take control over anything he wanted and direct his own life. His friend Peter, the narrator, wasn't quite so sure. Peter turned out to be right. Duffy almost made himself sick trying to build a stone wall. Babysitting two small boys and trying to bathe a Great Dane proved to be disastrous. But Duffy's biggest problem came from Boots McAfee's gang. A series of events finally brought Duffy and Peter face-to-face with the dreaded Boots. Luckily, she turned out to be a very smart girl who appreciated Duffy's true talents.

From the first to the last page this is a funny, very enjoyable book. A delightful book with a very palatable message.

Interest Level: 3-6. Reading Level: 3.2. Further Search Topics: Humorous Fiction, Bullies-Fiction, Magic-Fiction, Read Aloud, Occupations-Fiction, Sex Role-Fiction, Orphans-Fiction, Best Sellers, Gangs-Fiction, Courage-Fiction, Babysitting-Fiction.

Robinson, Nancy K. Wendy and the bullies; illus by Ingrid Fetz. Hastings 1980, 128 pp.

Wendy and her best friend Karen had a very carefully mapped out route to and from school—a route that allowed them to meet up with the fewest number of bullies possible. But when Karen became sick enough to stay home from school, Wendy had to face the bullies alone. Wendy's fears escalated to panic so intense that she avoided walking to school by hiding in her basement. She finally realized that she was letting fear and anger control her life when she found herself bullying Karen. Only her new friendship with Monica, making up with Karen, and her involvement in a school project helped Wendy overcome her fears.

This is a humorous, episodic tale of a feeling and circumstances common to many children. The illustrations sometimes make Wendy and her classmates appear much younger than her actual nine years, but fortunately that doesn't happen often enough to spoil the book's appeal.

Interest Level: 3-5. Reading Level: 3.1. Further Search Topics: School Stories, Bullies-Fiction, Courage-Fiction, Best Sellers, Humorous Fiction, Friendship-Fiction, Everyday Stories.

Rockwell, Thomas. How to eat fried worms; illus by Emily McCully. Watts 1973, 116 pp.

It started more as a joke than anything else, but it escalated into a strange commitment. Alan bet Billy $50 that Billy couldn't eat a worm a day for fifteen days. Billy had always been willing to take almost any dare offered and he was stubborn enough to carry them out, but when he actually faced the first worm (an enormous night crawler), he almost backed down. He and his friend Tom had to keep repeating the word "minibike" (the prize he planned to buy with the money) and smother the worm in everything imaginable in order to eat it all. After the first worm, however, the next few were easier to face. That was when Alan and his ally Joe, began using psychological warfare and almost won. In 41 very short, grotesquely funny chapters Billy becomes the proud owner of a minibike and is the first person to become hooked on worm sandwiches.

Once this book is started, it is hard to resist its gruesome fascination. Although the print is somewhat small, and there are occasionally very difficult or babytalk words, the interest is strong enough to sustain almost all readers.

Interest Level: 3-6. Reading Level: 3.1. Further Search Topics: Humorous Fiction, Worms-Fiction, Read Aloud, Best Sellers, Challenges-Fiction, Food-Fiction, Bicycles and Bicycling-Fiction.

Roy, Ron. Nightmare Island; illus by Robert MacLean. Dutton 1981, 69 pp.

Harley didn't want to take his younger brother camping, but because he had promised his father he would, the boys packed a tent, sleeping bags, and plenty of food into a small boat and set off to nearby Little Island. Hidden in his pocket, Harley had matches and marshmallows for a midnight marshmallow roast. After they had finished the bag of marshmallows, Harley threw the last log of the fire into the water. The water erupted into flames that quickly spread around the island. As the boys fought desperately to save themselves and to find shelter, they realized that the large shape they had seen in the distance must have been an oil tanker that had spread an oil slick all around the island. With time running out Harley gave his brother the only truly secure shelter from the fire, curled up on top of a tall rock and went to sleep. When he awoke the fire had burned itself out and help was on the way.

Most young readers will be able to suspend disbelief long enough to enjoy this as an exciting adventure and survival story, but it is hard to believe that two young boys could not only survive such a holocaust, but that they could sleep through part of it, too. It is also difficult to believe that there would not be more of a fuss made about the oil tanker blowing up. Plot problems aside, young readers seem to love the story.

Interest Level: 3-6. Reading Level: 3.2. Further Search Topics: Brothers and Sisters-Fiction, Survival-Fiction, Camping-Fiction, Disasters-Fiction, Best Sellers.

St. John, Wylly Folk. The ghost next door; illus by Trina Schart Hyman. Har-Row 1971, 178 pp.

Told by 13-year-old Lindsay, this is the story of her neighbor Miss Judith and Miss Judith's two nieces. Her niece Miranda had drowned years earlier in Miss Judith's backyard fish pond and Miss Judith had never fully recovered from her death. As the story begins, Miss Judith is about to welcome another niece (Sherry) for a summer stay. Sherry, without ever being told about Miranda, seems to sense Miranda's presence all around. Her mother laughs and says that Sherry has an imaginary friend. Miss Judith, who is a strong believer in ESP, thinks that Sherry is communicating with Miranda. As the days go on Sherry learns more and more of Miranda' secrets. When Miss Judith is scared by Sherry, Lindsay and her friend, Tammy, decide to see what sort of tricks Sherry is playing.

A believable suspense story, made even more so by the illustrations.

Interest Level: 4-6. Reading Level: 5.1. Further Search Topics: Mystery and Detective Stories, Relatives-Fiction, Group 2, Extra Sensory Perception-Fiction, Best Sellers, Ghosts-Fiction.

Scism, Carol K. The wizard of Walnut Street; illus by Martha Alexander. Dial 1973, 54 pp.

John and his friends had no room in their Wizard Club for Ford Owens, the new kid. John thought Ford was a conceited show-off who only wanted to make John look like a coward. It was true that John was afraid of some things, such as going down the giant slide into the lake, but he didn't want anyone else to know it. So he excluded Ford from all the club's activities until Ford pushed his way into their magic wishing-well project.

It had been John's idea to charge everyone a dime who wanted to make a wish. They could use the money to buy the few simple things that they would need to make the wishes come true. But it was Ford's eerie volcano and his large dog that had added just the right atmosphere to the trick to make people believe. Even John and Ford found themselves making wishes. John wished to be able to go down the giant slide. He didn't know what Ford wished. Much to John's initial surprise, people's wishes began to be fulfilled. Even Arthur, who had wished he could learn to dive, found he could. Then because John began to realize that the magic was in believing in himself and not in the wishing well, he tried the slide and succeeded. Once John's reason to avoid Ford was gone, he relaxed and asked Ford to join the club. At that point, even Ford's wish was granted.

Interest Level: 2-4. Reading Level: 2.1. Further Search Topics: Friendship-Fiction, Gangs-Fiction, Courage-Fiction, Magic-Fiction, Vacation-Fiction, Best Sellers.

Seuss, Dr. Hop on Pop. Beginner 1963, 64pp.

Between one and four rhyming words are introduced or reviewed and used in a silly sentence on each page. The sentence is interpreted with even more amusing illustrations. It is one of the simplest of books (no story at all) and yet it is usable through second grade because of Dr. Seuss' playful style and ridiculous illustrations. Reader format.

Interest Level: 1-2. Reading Level: 1.1. Further Search Topics: Poetry, Best Sellers, Wit and Humor, Humorous Fiction, Stories in Rhyme.

Seuss, Dr. The cat in the hat. Beginner 1957, 61 pp.

When the Cat in the Hat visits two children, a dreary, boring afternoon becomes almost too exciting. The Cat's juggling act and the two "things" he brings with him almost destroy the house. But the Cat cleans up so well that when the children's mother comes home and asks what they did all afternoon, they can't decide if they should tell her.

A funny, rhyming tale of the destruction all children can create and the boredom all children can feel. Reader format.

Interest Level: 1-3. Reading Level: 1.2. Further Search Topics: Humorous Fiction, Fantasy, Cats-Fiction, Poetry, Troublemakers-Fiction, Best Sellers, Stories in Rhyme.

Seuss, Dr. The cat in the hat comes back. Beginner 1958, 63 pp.

Sally and her brother were doing a good job of clearing the front walk of snow when the Cat in the Hat showed up. While they worked, the Cat created a pink mess in the house. The mess only became worse when he tried to clean it. The pink spot finally covered the snow all around the house until the Cat called upon his friends Little Cats A-Z. It was Little Cat Z and his magic zoom that eventually not only cleaned the snow, but cleared the front walk as well.

Another zany, rhymed adventure of the mischievious Cat whose ability to get into trouble endears him to most children from pre-school to early third grade. Reader format.

Interest Level: 1-3. Reading Level: 1.2. Further Search Topics: Fantasy, Cats-Fiction, Troublemakers-Fiction, Humorous Fiction, Snow-Fiction, Poetry, Best Sellers, Stories in Rhyme.

Seuss, Dr. The foot book. Random 1968, unp (27 pp).

Left feet, right feet, big feet, small feet; with its rhyme, silly illustrations and rhythmic celebration of feet of all descriptions, this book is a sure winner with the very young. Reader format.

Interest Level 1-2. Reading Level: 1.1. Further Search Topics: Best Sellers, Feet-Fiction, Humorous Fiction, Poetry, Wit and Humor, Stories in Rhyme.

Sharmat, Marjorie W. Nate the great goes undercover; illus by Marc Simont. Coward 1974, 47 pp.

Nate's next door neighbor Oliver was a pest, but Oliver had a mystery for Nate to solve. Oliver's garbage can was being burglarized at night. He wanted Nate to catch the garbage snatcher. Nate quickly drew up a list of human suspects and just as quickly eliminated them all. A night spent hiding in the garbage can proved the best way to catch the thief.

Much to Nate's surprise, the thief turned out to be his new dog.

Very amusing and very useful. Reader format.

Interest Level: 1-3. Reading Level: 2.1. Further Search Topics: Humorous Fiction, Mystery and Detective Stories, Group 2, Detectives-Fiction, Best Sellers.

Sharmat, Marjorie W. Nate the great; illus by Marc Simont. Coward 1972, 62 pp.

This is a young imitation of Humphrey Bogart solving a *Dragnet* style mystery. Annie's recently finished painting of her dog had disappeared so she hired Nate to search for it. Nate gathered all the facts, investigated his suspects, and eventually solved the mystery, but not before he had consumed plenty of pancakes (his favorite food) and solved a second mystery by accident.

A simple plot, humorous telling, and a sympathetic, likeable protagonist make this one of a very popular series. Reader format.

Interest Level: 1-3. Reading Level: 2.1. Further Search Topics: Humorous Fiction, Detectives-Fiction, Mystery and Detective Stories, Group 2, Best Sellers.

Sharmat, Marjorie W. Getting something on Maggie Marmelstein; illus by Ben Shecter. Har-Row 1971, 101 pp.

A curious love-hate relationship existed between Thad and Maggie. It all began when Maggie overheard Thad say she squeaked like a mouse. Then Maggie caught Thad wearing an apron and cooking. Thad was so uncomfortable with the thought that Maggie might tell his friends, that he was determined to find out Maggie's deepest secret. That meant that Thad had to take a lead role as a frog opposite Maggie as the princess in the school play. While at Maggie's apartment for a costume fitting, Thad found a love letter Maggie had written to Cary Grant. Thad decided he would read the letter to the class right after the play was over. But during the play Maggie saved Thad from what could have been one of the most embarrassing moments of his life. By the time he finally had the chance to make Maggie appear foolish, Thad had changed his mind.

Written as Thad's story, the book is funny, warm, and realistic. A good, short, story that continues to be popular. Print is of moderate size.

Interest Level: 3-6. Reading Level: 3.1. Further Search Topics: Humorous Fiction, Everyday Stories, School Stories, Best Sellers, Friendship-Fiction, Sex Role-Fiction, Acting-Fiction.

Shearer, John. Billy Jo Jive and the case of the missing pigeons; illus by Ted Shearer. Delacorte 1978, 47 pp.

This is the third in a series of slight mysteries, always solved by Billy Jo Jive and his crime fighter partner, Susie Sunset. Jive and Sunset are street-wise, black youngsters who take their jobs as crime fighters very seriously, and are never detered for long from finding the criminals they seek. The crimes are always thefts, and the criminals vary from young children to neighborhood menaces. Suspense is created more by the manner in which Jive and Sunset catch the thieves, plus the determination and pace of the young detectives, than by guessing who the culprits might be. Jive, his street-slang manner of telling the first-person stories, and the urban setting will appeal to many readers. Jive and Sunset also appear on *Sesame Street*.

Jive accidentally photographed the fleeing pigeon thief as he was being chased by Flip, the victim. The photograph didn't show the thief's face, but did give Jive and Sunset a good look at what he was wearing. Jive and Sunset concluded that the thief was Snake Hips Robberts. They later realized that they had been wrong. When they looked carefully at the picture, they remembered that any dark color clothing photographs almost black in a black and white picture. Snake Hips had a black jacket, but he was innocent. The real thief was Sugar Brown. Then it was a simple matter of showing the evidence to both Flip and Sugar to get Sugar to confess.

Interest Level: 1-4. Reading Level: 2.2. Further Search Topics: Mystery and Detective Stories, Detectives-Fiction, Blacks-Fiction, City Life-Fiction, Group 2, Best Sellers.

Shearer, John. Billy Jo Jive super private eye: the case of the missing ten speed bike; illus by Ted Shearer. Delacorte 1976, 47 pp.

Jive and Sunset began their friendship and their sleuthing career with this book. It all started when Sunset borrowed her older brother's 10-speed bicycle. Jive met Sunset while she sat at the side of the road crying, after her brother's bike had been stolen. Some careful joint detective work proved to Jive and Sunset that Dynamite Jones, jealous of Sunset's brother, had stolen the bike. The young crime fighters recovered the bicycle before Sunset's brother even knew it was missing.

This book sets the formula that all the others follow. A neighborhood person finds that something has been stolen and goes to Jive and Sunset for help. Jive and Sunset never have much trouble finding the thief even though they are sometimes misled for a short time. Often the culprit is quite obvious to the reader. After some attempts at clever detective work and an occasional bit of preaching, the crime is solved. It is the manner of the pursuit and the street-smart characters that give the stories their interest.

Interest Level: 1-4. Reading Level: 2.2. Further Search Topics: Mystery and Detective Stories, Blacks-Fiction, Detectives-Fiction, City Life-Fiction, Best Sellers, Group 2, Bicycles and Bicycling-Fiction.

Silverstein, Shel. Where the sidewalk ends. Har-Row 1974, 166 pp.

There is something here for almost everyone. It isn't always easy reading, but there are enough short, easier poems to pique almost any child's interest. Once caught, children will find the book hard to put down. The best way to encourage the use of this book is to read selections aloud so that potential readers may hear the rhythm and enjoy the humor. This method almost guarantees that they will then want to try reading the book themselves. Readers may struggle with a poem but once it is mastered, they will usually want more.

Interest Level: 2-6. Reading Level: 3.1. Further Search Topics: Poetry, Wit and Humor, Read Aloud, Group 2, Best Sellers.

Silverstein, Shel. A light in the attic. Har-Row 1981, 169 pp.

This is the second and most recent collection of Shel Silverstein's wonderfully wry poetry. No young person who has read and enjoyed *Where the Sidewalk Ends* will be disappointed in this effort. For those readers new to Silverstein or to poetry in general, this is as good a place as any to start enjoying both. Hearing a few of these poems read aloud is guaranteed to provoke loud cries of "May I read some?" from almost all listeners.

Interest Level: 2-6. Reading Level: 3.2. Further Search Topics: Poetry, Wit and Humor, Best Sellers, Group 2, Read Aloud.

Sleator, William. Into the dream; illus by Ruth Sanderson. Dutton 1979, 137 pp.

Paul and Francine each started having what, at first, seemed like nightmares. As the dreams became more detailed and forboding, they discovered that they were sharing the same nightmare. They dreamed of a four-year-old boy, swirling lights, and a large dog. After awhile they figured out that the dog was trying to save the little boy from some unknown danger. As the pieces of the puzzle began to increase in number, Paul and Francine decided that the dream was in some way connected to a night over four years earlier when they had both been staying at the same motel. They, a pregnant woman, and a pregnant dog had all been affected by the telepathic power given off by a spaceship. The progeny of the woman and the dog had been given extraordinary mental powers; powers that a secret government agency wanted to mold and then put to their own use. The danger Paul and Francine felt came from two government agents sent to take the young boy Noah from his mother. Their attempt ended in a bizarre scene at an amusement park, where Noah levitated a broken ferris wheel chair to safety. By thus exposing his talent in public, Noah unconsciously insured against its secret and unsupervised use by the government.

A terrifying and suspense-filled psychological thriller whose main problems are a slightly overdrawn ending and a variable reading level. Reading level drops as low as 2.1 and climbs occasionally to 4.1.

Interest Level: 5-6. Reading Level: 3.2. Further Search Topics: Best Sellers, Supernatural-Fiction, Occult-Fiction, Flying Saucers-Fiction, Nonverbal Communication-Fiction, Dreams-Fiction, Survival-Fiction, Extra Sensory Perception-Fiction, Horror-Fiction.

Sobol, Donald J. Encyclopedia Brown, boy detective; illus by Leonard Shortall. Elsevier-Nelson 1963, 88 pp.

The first of a large number of books that challenge the reader to solve the same mysteries Encyclopedia Brown deciphers. See *Encyclopedia Brown and the Case of the Dead Eagles* for more information.

Interest Level: 2-6. Reading Level: 2.2. Further Search Topics: Mystery and Detective Stories, Puzzles, Best Sellers, Detectives-Fiction.

Sobol, Donald J. Encyclopedia Brown and the case of the dead eagles; illus by Leonard Shortall. Elsevier-Nelson 1975, 96 pp.

By all rights Idaville should be declared a disaster area and Mr. Brown, the chief of police, should be fired from his job. Idaville looks like an ordinary small town, but behind its sleepy exterior there exists a crime wave that would challenge the best police departments in the country. It is true that the crimes are always solved and the criminals always caught, but not by Chief Brown. Chief Brown is frequently so stumped by his police cases that he talks about them at home, usually at dinner time. Almost always, his son, Leroy "Encyclopedia" Brown, solves the case before dinner is even over. A clear case of superior intelligence and skill.

Encyclopedia (so nicknamed because of his intellect) not only solves his father's cases, but serves as a detective for his friends, too. He is kept so busy that each slim volume in this series contains 10 short mysteries. Needless to say Encyclopedia solves them

all. The question is can the reader? All necessary clues are there and specialized knowledge is rarely required. Should the reader fail to solve a mystery (they are not always as easy as one would expect), a full explanation and solution for each case is provided at the back of the book. Each title follows exactly the same formula. Although a teacher or parent may grow bored hearing of Encyclopedia's accomplishments, most young readers thoroughly enjoy them.

The books actively challenge and thus involve the reader in a way most books do not. A very popular series that does not have to be read in sequence. Reading level is consistently 2.2 to 3.1. Encyclopedia Brown series.

Interest Level: 2-6. Reading Level: 3.1. Further Search Topics: Mystery and Detective Stories, Puzzles, Best Sellers, Group 2, Detectives-Fiction.

Sobol, Donald J. Encyclopedia Brown and the case of the midnight visitor; illus by Lillian Brandi. Elsevier-Nelson 1977, 96 pp.

See *Encyclopedia Brown and the Case of the Dead Eagles* for full annotation.

Interest Level: 2-6. Reading Level: 2.2. Further Search Topics: Mystery and Detective Stories, Puzzles, Detectives-Fiction, Best Sellers.

Sobol, Donald J. Encyclopedia Brown and the case of the secret pitch; illus by Leonard Shortall. Elsevier-Nelson 1965, 96 pp.

See *Encyclopedia Brown and the Case of the Dead Eagles* for full annotation.

Interest Level: 2-6. Reading Level: 3.1. Further Search Topics: Group 2, Mystery and Detective Stories, Puzzles, Best Sellers, Detectives-Fiction.

Sobol, Donald J. Encyclopedia Brown finds the clues; illus by Leonard Shortall. Elsevier-Nelson 1966, 96 pp.

See *Encyclopedia Brown and the Case of the Dead Eagles* for full annotation.

Interest Level 2-6. Reading Level: 3.1. Further Search Topics: Mystery and Detective Stories, Puzzles, Detectives-Fiction, Best Sellers, Group 2.

Sobol, Donald J. Encyclopedia Brown gets his man; illus by Leonard Shortall. Elsevier-Nelson 1967, 96 pp.

See *Encyclopedia Brown and the Case of the Dead Eagles* for full annotation.

Interest Level: 2-6. Reading Level: 3.1. Further Search Topics: Mystery and Detective Stories, Puzzles, Best Sellers, Group 2, Detectives-Fiction.

Sobol, Donald J. Encyclopedia Brown keeps the peace; illus by Leonard Shortall. Elsevier-Nelson 1969, 96 pp.

See *Encyclopedia Brown and the Case of the Dead Eagles* for full annotation.

Interest Level: 2-6. Reading Level: 2.2. Further Search Topics: Mystery and Detective Stories, Puzzles, Best Sellers, Detectives-Fiction.

Sobol, Donald J. Encyclopedia Brown lends a hand; illus by Leonard Shortall. Elsevier-Nelson 1974, 96 pp.

See *Encyclopedia Brown and the Case of the Dead Eagles* for full annotation.

Interest Level: 2-6. Reading Level: 3.1. Further Search Topics: Mystery and Detective Stories, Puzzles, Detectives-Fiction, Best Sellers, Group 2.

Sobol, Donald J. Encyclopedia Brown saves the day; illus by Leonard Shortall. Elsevier-Nelson 1970, 96 pp.

See *Encyclopedia Brown and the Case of the Dead Eagles* for full annotation.
Interest Level: 2-6. Reading Level: 2.2. Further Search Topics: Mystery and Detective Stories, Puzzles, Detectives-Fiction, Best Sellers.

Sobol, Donald J. Encyclopedia Brown shows the way; illus by Leonard Shortall. Elsevier-Nelson 1972, 96 pp.
See *Encyclopedia Brown and the Case of the Dead Eagles* for full annotation.
Interest Level: 2-6. Reading Level: 2.2. Further Search Topics: Mystery and Detective Stories, Puzzles, Detectives-Fiction, Best Sellers.

Sobol, Donald J. Encyclopedia Brown solves them all; illus by Leonard Shortall. Elsevier-Nelson 1968, 96 pp.
See *Encyclopedia Brown and the Case of the Dead Eagles* for full annotation.
Interest Level: 2-6. Reading Level: 3.1. Further Search Topics: Mystery and Detective Stories, Puzzles, Detectives-Fiction, Group 2, Best Sellers.

Sobol, Donald J. Encyclopedia Brown sets the pace; illus by Ib Ohlsson. Four Winds Pr 1982, 89 pp.
See *Encyclopedia Brown and the Case of the Dead Eagles* for full annotation.
Interest Level: 2-6. Reading Level: 3.1. Further Search Topics: Mystery and Detective Stories, Detectives-Fiction, Puzzles, Group 2, Best Sellers.

Sobol, Donald J. Encyclopedia Brown carries on; illus by Ib Ohlsson. Schol Bk Serv 1980, 72 pp.
See *Encyclopedia Brown and the Case of the Dead Eagle* for full annotation.
Interest Level: 2-6. Reading Level: 3.1. Further Search Topics: Mystery and Detective Stories, Puzzles, Detectives-Fiction, Group 2, Best Sellers.

Terman, Douglas. By balloons to the Sahara; illus by Paul Granger. Bantam 1979, 117 pp.
See the entry for *Sugarcane Island*, by Edward Packard for detailed information about the series. Available in paperback edition only. Choose Your Own Adventure series.
Interest Level: 2-6. Reading Level: 3.2. Further Search Topics: Voyages and Travels-Fiction, Flight-Fiction, Best Sellers, Group 2.

Thompson, Jean. Brother of the wolves; illus by Steve Marchesi. Morrow 1978, 159 pp.
Shadow Fox, a Sioux medicine man, went into a wolves' den looking for special items he needed for healing, but found much more. He found a baby boy who had apparently lost his parents in an accident and then been adopted by the wolves. Winter was approaching and Shadow Fox knew the baby would not be able to survive the cold, so he took the child back to his people. The people were reluctant to accept Wolf Brother, saying that he was an evil omen, that he was unnatural, and that he would bring them trouble. But Shadow Fox's will prevailed and Wolf Brother was allowed to stay and grow up with the Sioux.
As he grew Wolf Brother continued to communicate with the wolves and thus fueled the rumors that grew about him. A very jealous young man, Looks-Away, told the people that a vision had shown him that Wolf Brother and his wolves would one day destroy the village and all its people. The people grew so suspicious of Wolf Brother that, when their horses were stolen and they faced a drought, they blamed him and drove him from the village.

For a while Wolf Brother tried to live as a wolf but found that he could not be totally happy. He wandered away to look for a tribe by whom he might be accepted. On his way, he too had a vision—a vision that told him he would find horses and buffalo for the Sioux and be welcomed home again. It was weeks later before he accidentally found his tribe's horses. In a daring move and with help from the wolves, Wolf Brother not only rescued the horses from the raiders, but also found buffalo just as his vision had predicted. He was then, for the first time, fully welcomed by his people.
This is a taut, suspenseful and mature story about a strong and unusual character. Older readers are most likely to respond positively to the Indian culture and lore.
Interest Level: 5-6. Reading Level: 3.1. Further Search Topics: Survival-Fiction, Wolves-Fiction, Orphans-Fiction, Loners-Fiction, Indians of North America-Fiction, Sioux Indians-Fiction, Jealousy-Fiction, Best Sellers.

Wagner, Jane. J.T; photos by Gordon Parks, Jr. Van Nostrand 1969, 64 pp.
This is a sentimental story that rarely fails to elicit a sympathetic response from young readers. J.T. is a poor black boy who saw a portable radio almost begging to be stolen and stole it. Two of the neighborhood bullies, Boomer and Claymore, saw J.T. take the radio. Though they threatened him, even poured soap in his eyes in the school bathrooms, J.T. wouldn't give them the radio as they demanded.
About the same time J.T. found a scrawny, scared little cat with only one eye. Because his mother wouldn't let him take the cat home, J.T. built it a warm but ramshackle little house in an abandoned building. He fed it by charging tuna to his mother's grocery store account without her knowledge. Bones became the only thing in J.T.'s life that he had cared about since his father had walked out.
When Boomer and Claymore found out about Bones, they taunted J.T. by throwing the cat back and forth between them until the frightened cat escaped, darted out into the street and was hit by a car. J.T.'s heart broke as he looked at Bones, but he spoke to no one to tell them of his sadness. Only time, his mother's and grandmother's love and a small kitten from Mr. Rosen, the grocer, helped him recover. On the morning that he decided to accept the kitten, J.T. returned the stolen radio, faced Boomer and Claymore without fear, and asked Mr. Rosen for a job in order to pay for cat food.
The book is oversized and illustrated with photographs from the television movie version. It is not only an excellent story to read aloud but one that will prompt listeners to want to finish it on their own or to reread it. It is now available only in paperback from Dell.
Interest Level: 3-6. Reading Level: 3.1. Further Search Topics: Read Aloud, Courage-Fiction, Best Sellers, Cats-Fiction, Single Parent Family-Fiction, Bullies-Fiction, Blacks-Fiction, Poverty-Fiction, City Life-Fiction, Christmas Stories, Crime-Fiction, Pets-Fiction, Holidays-Fiction.

Wolkoff, Judie. Wally. Bradbury 1977, 199 pp.
Michael Price agreed to take care of his friend Billy's chuckwalla for three weeks. But because his mother had declared a moratorium on any more reptiles in the house, Michael tried to hide Wally in his closet. With help from his brother Roger, Michael managed to keep Wally a secret until Wally was mistakenly left out of his box one night. Despite Michael and Roger's

desperate searches, the chuckwalla did not reappear until Mr. and Mrs. Price were involved in the final negotiations for the sale of their house. Wally completely disrupted the proceedings, prevented the sale and thus made everyone happy. For as it turned out, none of the Prices had really wanted to move after all.

A fast-paced, funny book with much reader appeal. Interest Level: 2-5. Reading Level: 2.2. Further Search Topics: Pets-Fiction, Humorous Fiction, Lizards-Fiction, Best Sellers, Reptiles-Fiction, Secrets-Fiction.

Yolen, Jane. The boy who spoke chimp illus by David Wiesner. Knopf 1981, 120 pp.

Kriss was determined to prove to his father that, at 12 years old, he was perfectly capable of camping out by himself. To do so, he left home and headed up the coast of California with a sleeping bag, some food, a map and compass, and water. His plan was to camp, ride, and hike his way to his grandmother's house. On the way, the coast line was torn apart by the second great earthquake to strike California. The first had already destroyed great portions of the state. The second was even stronger. The truck he had been riding in was destroyed and everyone around Kriss was killed by the quake except for two chimpanzees. The chimps, in transit from one lab to another, were research animals who had been taught to use sign language. Kriss took the animals with him as he tried to get farther inland and finally home to Los Angeles. His trip not only confirmed his father's fears about Kriss' inadequacies but taught him how to overcome them. Kriss learned to communicate with the chimps, to find food and to live on his own until Old Chris, a hermit, happened along. Together they continued to brave the chaos brought about by the earthquake even when Old Chris' heart troubled him. When a helicopter finally spotted them, Kriss decided to let the chimps go wild and promised Old Chris that he would be back in the woods very soon. It was a mature, capable Kriss who returned home.

This is typical of the Capers series—much action, few background details, little characterization. The books, however, are on appealing topics; they move quickly and they create intriguing (if sometimes implausible) situations. They are light, enjoyable and very useful. Capers series.

Interest Level: 3-6. Reading Level: 3.1. Further Search Topics: California-Fiction, Disasters-Fiction, Survival-Fiction, Apes-Fiction, Nonverbal Communication-Fiction, Camping-Fiction, Runaways-Fiction, Best Sellers.

Young, Carol Beach. Remember me when I am dead. Elsevier-Nelson 1980, 94 pp.

This is a short but taut story about the effect of their mother's death upon two young girls. For a long time Jenny, the younger and more vivacious of the sisters, refused to believe her mother had really died. Sara, quiet and serious, mourned and missed her mother, but eventually accepted her mother's sudden death as a fact. Jenny's continuing denial prompted her father and stepmother to talk of sending her away to a school where memories wouldn't be so vivid. That talk inspired Sara to develop a devious and calculated plan to insure that Jenny would indeed be sent away. All her life Sara had been given less attention than Jenny. With Jenny gone, Sara would finally have her father and stepmother's love and attention all to herself. With a Hitchcock-like twist Sara's plan proved too successful. Jenny was sent away to school, but because she didn't want to go alone and because her parents could deny Jenny nothing, Sara was to go too.

This suspenseful psychological thriller is almost guaranteed success with older readers.

Interest Level: 5-6. Reading Level: 4.2. Further Search Topics: Mystery and Detective Stories, Brothers and Sisters-Fiction, Death-Fiction, Horror-Fiction, Best Sellers, Jealousy-Fiction.

BICYCLES AND BICYCLING-FICTION

Avi. No more magic. Pantheon 1975, 138 pp.

Avi has woven a mixture of mystery and magic to produce an excellent story. Chris' belief in magic is bolstered when his new bicycle disappears on Halloween night. Chris, his best friend Eddie, and a new friend, Muffin, eventually decide that strange Mr. Bullen, the junk dealer, has magical powers. In order to keep his powers a secret, Mr. Bullen had to steal back the magical bike he sold Chris. With plenty of intriguing complications along the way, the three children attempt to prove their theory correct but only prove themselves wrong. The age of the protagonists (fourth grade) is touched on so lightly and the plot is interesting enough that even sixth grade readers should find the book enjoyable.

Interest Level: 3-6. Reading Level: 4.2. Further Search Topics: Divorce and Separation-Fiction, Mystery and Detective Stories, Magic-Fiction, Halloween-Fiction, Witches-Fiction, Group 2, Read Aloud, Bicycles and Bicycling–Fiction.

Berenstain, Stan. The bike lesson. Beginner 1964, 61 pp.

This story of a bumbling father trying to teach his eager son how to ride a bike is pure silliness. Much of the action is shown in the humorous illustrations. The rhymed text adds dialogue and description. Good fun.

Interest Level: K-3. Reading Level: 1.2. Further Search Topics: Humorous Fiction, Bicycles and Bicycling-Fiction, Stories in Rhyme, Group 2.

Cleary, Beverly. Henry and Beezus; illus by Louis Darling. Morrow 1952, 192 pp.

When Henry's dog Ribsy stole the meat from a neighbor's barbecue, a friend rode after Ribsy on his bike and saved the meat. Henry was so embarrassed and jealous that he boasted about an even nicer bike that he was going to get. At first Henry thought he'd be able to earn money to buy a bike in a very short time (he found 49 boxes of bubble gum that he could sell). When that scheme fell through, Henry tried taking over a friend's paper route, but Ribsy kept retrieving the newspapers Henry delivered. Eventually Henry decided to buy a used bike at the police department auction. Beezus, who made a bid for Henry, ended up buying him a beaten-up girl's bike that was hardly worth fixing. The money finally appeared when Henry least expected it; he won $50.00 worth of work at a beauty salon.

Although all seven chapters continue the same story, Chapters 1, 2, 3 and 7, can each stand alone. Henry is definitely old-fashioned, but children still enjoy his humorous escapades and empathize with his desire for a bicycle. The revised paperback cover makes the book's physical appearance less dated. Reading level is somewhat inconsistent: from 2.2 to 3.2.

Interest Level: 2-5. Reading Level: 3.1. Further Search Topics: Humorous Fiction, Occupations-Fiction, Everyday Stories, Bicycles and Bicycling-Fiction, Read Aloud, Group 2.

Pfeffer, Susan Beth. Kid power; illus by Leigh Grant. Watts 1977, 121 pp.

When Janie's mother lost her job, her father's salary wouldn't stretch to provide any more money for the new bicycle fund. There was enough money already set aside to pay for one new bike, but both Janie and her older sister Carol wanted a bicycle. Carol, who had saved money of her own, suggested that they each pay for half a bike and their parents contribute the money for the other half. Then Janie's only problem was how to earn money, since she had none saved. Her solution was to create a business: Kid Power. Before long, Janie's business had blossomed and she was becoming rich, but she had lost her best friend and was ruining a client's roses. When Janie finally realized that getting rich wasn't the only thing that mattered in life, she relaxed, delegated jobs to friends better able to handle them, and became their agent.

A genuinely funny book that, as a bonus, takes a realistic look at the interworkings of a family. Consistent reading level.

Interest Level: 4-6. Reading Level: 3.1. Further Search Topics: Occupations-Fiction, Everyday Stories, Vacation-Fiction, Family-Fiction, Humorous Fiction, Best Sellers, Bicycles and Bicycling-Fiction, Friendship-Fiction.

Rockwell, Thomas. How to eat fried worms; illus by Emily McCully. Watts 1973, 116 pp.

It started more as a joke than anything else, but it escalated into a strange commitment. Alan bet Billy $50 that Billy couldn't eat a worm a day for fifteen days. Billy had always been willing to take almost any dare offered and he was stubborn enough to carry them out, but when he actually faced the first worm (an enormous night crawler), he almost backed down. He and his friend Tom had to keep repeating the word "minibike" (the prize he planned to buy with the money) and smother the worm in everything imaginable in order to eat it all. After the first worm, however, the next few were easier to face. That was when Alan and his ally Joe, began using psychological warfare and almost won. In 41 very short, grotesquely funny chapters Billy becomes the proud owner of a minibike and is the first person to become hooked on worm sandwiches.

Once this book is started, it is hard to resist its gruesome fascination. Although the print is somewhat small, and there are occasionally very difficult or babytalk words, the interest is strong enough to sustain almost all readers.

Interest Level: 3-6. Reading Level: 3.1. Further Search Topics: Humorous Fiction, Worms-Fiction, Read Aloud, Best Sellers, Challenges-Fiction, Food-Fiction, Bicycles and Bicycling-Fiction.

Shearer, John. Billy Jo Jive super private eye: the case of the missing ten speed bike; illus by Ted Shearer. Delacorte 1976, 47 pp.

Jive and Sunset began their friendship and their sleuthing career with this book. It all started when Sunset borrowed her older brother's 10-speed bicycle. Jive met Sunset while she sat at the side of the road crying, after her brother's bike had been stolen. Some careful joint detective work proved to Jive and Sunset that Dynamite Jones, jealous of Sunset's brother, had stolen the bike. The young crime fighters recovered the bicycle before Sunset's brother even knew it was missing.

This book sets the formula that all the others follow. A neighborhood person finds that something has been stolen and goes to Jive and Sunset for help. Jive and Sunset never have much trouble finding the thief even though they are sometimes misled for a short time. Often the culprit is quite obvious to the reader. After some attempts at clever detective work and an occasional bit of preaching, the crime is solved. It is the manner of the pursuit and the street-smart characters that give the stories their interest.

Interest Level: 1-4. Reading Level: 2.2. Further Search Topics: Mystery and Detective Stories, Blacks-Fiction, Detectives-Fiction, City Life-Fiction, Best Sellers, Group 2, Bicycles and Bicycling-Fiction.

BIGFOOT-FICTION

Place, Marian T. The boy who saw Bigfoot. Dodd 1979, 96 pp.

Joey and his foster mother searched for and found Bigfoot. But, when Joey told his classmates, no one would believe him. Joey's next idea was to take the entire class on a field trip to track Bigfoot.

Joey's rapid change from a difficult to a very well-adjusted child is not well supported. But interest in Bigfoot is so great that the book's flaws will be overlooked by its readers.

Interest Level: 3-6. Reading Level: 2.2. Further Search Topics: Bigfoot-Fiction, Foster Homes-Fiction, Monsters-Fiction, Troublemakers-Fiction, School Stories.

BIOGRAPHY

Adoff, Arnold. Malcolm X; illus by John Wilson. Har-Row 1970, 41 pp.

This is a simple, intellectually honest biography of a very controversial man. Taught a strong sense of self-respect by his father, Malcolm X could not accept the second-class status that white society tried to impose upon him. Instead he turned away from whites and all they stood for. He hated high school, the detention home he lived in after his father's death, and his mother's placement in a state hospital. He didn't feel comfortable until he moved to Harlem. There he found friends, but he also found crime. While he was in prison, Malcolm X began to read of great, black societies and people. His brother told him about the Nation of Islam, the Black Muslims, and Elijah Muhammad, the leader of the religion. He began corresponding with Mr. Muhammad. Shortly after he was released from prison, Malcolm X met Elijah Muhammad and eventually became a minister of the religion. There was even talk that he would be Elijah Muhammad's successor. But, as the years went on, Malcolm X began to think that black Christians as well as Muslims should be united in the fight for black rights. Despite threats against his life Malcolm X formed the Organization of Afro-American Unity. Both blacks and whites were angry with him. The threats continued until his house was firebombed; and, only a week later, at a public meeting, Malcolm X was assassinated.

An excellent overview of a complex man. The book may well prompt readers to learn more about the man and his beliefs. At the very least it will expose readers, in an interesting manner, to someone they should know. The book shares the same semi-picture book format of the others in Harper and Row/Crowell's biography series, therefore it will need a careful introduction to potential readers.

Interest Level: 3-5. Reading Level: 3.1. Further Search Topics: Blacks-Biography, Civil Rights, Biography, Crime, Religion, Assassinations, Prejudice, Poverty, Foster Homes.

Bales, Carol Ann. Chinatown Sunday; the story of Lillian Der. Contemp Bks. 1973, 32 pp.

A short, personal visit with a fifth grade Chinese-American girl who lives in a Chicago suburb. The author transcribed taped interviews with Lillian Der to produce a first-person description of Lillian's daily life. The uniquely Chinese-American features of Lillian's life are casually intertwined with experiences common to most American children. Month-old parties, the celebration of Chinese New Year, lucky money, old-age birthday parties, Girl Scout meetings, homework, and being a tomboy are all important to Lillian. Not only is this an interesting portrait of Lillian, but it can be a useful part of a multi-ethnic unit or an introduction to autobiography. The book's usefulness is further extended by its introduction to Chinese immigration and by the glossary, which explains terms such as "abacus," "Chinese calendar," and "sea cucumber." The author saves the over-sized book from looking like a picture book by using photographs instead of drawings, thus she makes the book comfortable even for a sixth grade reader.

Interest Level: 3-6. Reading Level: 3.1. Further Search Topics: Ethnic Groups, Chinese-Americans, Biography, Chicago, Immigration and Emigration.

Bryant, Bernice. George Gershwin: young composer; illus by Nathan Goldstein. Bobbs 1965, 200 pp.

Even when George Gershwin was very young he loved music, showed signs of musical talent, and longed to play the piano. However, any boy who played the piano in George's neighborhood was called a sissy and George didn't like being teased in that way. When he was no longer able to keep his music lessons a secret, he stopped them for fear of the teasing. But each time George quit playing the piano, he always went back to it, even when his parents pressured him not to waste his time at the piano. A young teacher told George that he would never be a musician. One of George's teachers actually taught him to play poorly, instead of well. In time, however, George learned to play well and to compose his own music. Then came the hard work of determining his own style. Gradually, more and more people heard and appreciated his American jazz, until George Gershwin's music was heard all around the world.

Another adequate entry in the *Childhood of Famous Americans* series. Includes the usual glossary, bibliography, time line, and follow-up questions. It is most likely to appeal to the reader already interested in music. Childhood of Famous Americans series.

Interest Level: 3-6. Reading Level: 3.1. Further Search Topics: Biography, Composers, Immigration and Emigration-Biography, Jazz Music, Bullies, Music-Biography, Pianists.

Burchard, Marshall. Sports hero: Dr. J. Putnam 1976, 89 pp.

Julius Erving can jump higher and stay in the air longer than almost any other basketball player. He can also move around the court with the most agile of players. All in all he is a very exciting player to watch. This book includes his college and pro records (through 1975). See *Sports Hero: Bill Walton* for more information. Sports Hero series.

Interest Level: 3-6. Reading Level: 4.1. Further Search Topics: Biography, Blacks-Biography, Basketball-Biography, Erving, Julius, Group 2.

Burchard, Marshall. Sports hero: Mario Andretti. Putnam 1977, 90 pp.

Auto racing's all-around superstar. See *Sports Hero: Bill Walton* for details about the series. Sports Hero series.

Interest Level: 3-6. Reading Level: 3.2. Further Search Topics: Biography, Andretti, Mario, Auto Racing-Biography.

Burchard, Marshall. Sports hero: Joe Morgan. Putnam 1978, 93 pp.

Joe Morgan has been described as one of baseball's most complete players. He could field, hit, run and steal bases with the best. See *Sports Hero: Bill Walton* for more details about the book. Sports Hero series.

Interest Level: 2-6. Reading Level: 3.2. Further Search Topics: Biography, Morgan, Joe, Baseball-Biography, Blacks-Biography, Group 2.

Burchard, Marshall. Sports hero: Reggie Jackson. Putnam 1975, 93 pp.

Reggie Jackson was one of the big reasons why the Oakland A's won baseball's World Series three years in a row. *Sports Hero: Bill Walton* gives more information about the books in the series. Sports Hero series.

Interest Level: 2-6. Reading Level: 3.2. Further Search Topics: Biography, Jackson, Reggie, Baseball-Biography, Blacks-Biography, Group 2.

Burchard, Marshall. Sports hero: Bill Walton. Putnam 1978, 94 pp.

Burchard's series of *Sports Hero* biographies is better than many other sports biography series. Although heavy emphasis is placed on the subject's playing time, each person's life is capsulized from childhood to just before the book's publication date. Marshall and Sue Burchard (with whom he has collaborated and who writes an almost identical series called *Sports Stars*) treat each figure favorably and with enthusiasm. But, contrary to many children's writers, particularly sports biographers, these writers at least touch on those personal foibles that make players human (i.e. Joe Namath's tendency to break training is briefly described). Each book is abundantly illustrated with photographs, avoids patronizing the reader and is consistently interesting. Each is reliable, very useful and can be depended on to appeal to the sports enthusiast. Problems arise, however, with inconsistent and/or artificially inflated reading levels. The reading level of a title may vary from 2.2 to 4.2. The same passage tested on both a Spache and a Dale-Chall scale may show a similar two-year spread. The problem seems to be with jargon. Most sports jargon does not appear on either Spache's or Chall's list of familiar words and thus raises a book's reading level. But, the words may well be known to the reader (or quickly recognized after one introduction and so not truly unfamiliar). Keep in mind, therefore, that the true sports fan will often be able to read a title that tests well above his/her actual reading level.

Bill Walton's career is covered only through the end of the 1976-1977 season when the Portland Trailblazers won the NBA title. The reading level of this title is one of the most inconsistent of the series (from 2.2 to 4.2).

Interest Level: 2-6. Reading Level: 3.2. Further Search Topics: Biography, Walton, Bill, Basketball-Biography, Group 2.

Burchard, Marshall. Sports hero: Billie Jean King. Putnam 1975, 95 pp.

Winner of every major women's tennis title and a very important person to women's professional sports. Consistent reading level. Book includes glossary of tennis terms. See entry under *Sports Hero: Bill Walton* Sports Hero series.

Interest Level: 3-6. Reading Level: 3.2. Further Search Topics: Biography, King, Billie Jean, Tennis-Biography, Women-Biography.

Burchard, Marshall. Sports hero: Fran Tarkenton. Putnam 1977, 95 pp.

From a strict religious background where athletics were not encouraged, Fran went on to set every NFL passing record possible See *Sports Hero: Bill Walton.* Sports Hero series.

Interest Level: 3-6. Reading Level: 3.2. Further Search Topics: Biography, Tarkenton, Fran, Football-Biography, Religion-Biography.

Burchard, Marshall. Sports hero: Fred Lynn. Putnam 1976, 95 pp.

Fred Lynn was baseball's first rookie to be named Most Valuable Player. Consistent reading level. See *Sports Hero: Bill Walton.* Sports Hero series.

Interest Level: 2-6. Reading Level: 3.2. Further Search Topics: Biography, Lynn, Fred, Baseball-Biography, Group 2.

Burchard, Marshall. Sports hero: Joe Namath. Putnam 1971, 95 pp.

One of football's best and flashiest quarterbacks. See *Sports Hero: Bill Walton* entry. Sports Hero series.

Interest Level: 2-6. Reading Level: 2.2. Further Search Topics: Biography, Namath, Joe, Football-Biography.

Burchard, Marshall. Sports hero: Johnny Bench. Putnam 1973, 95 pp.

The youngest baseball player to receive the National League's Most Valuable Player award. See *Sports Hero: Bill Walton* for information about the book. Sports Hero series.

Interest Level: 2-6. Reading Level: 3.1. Further Search Topics: Biography, Bench, Johnny, Baseball-Biography, Group 2.

Burchard, Marshall. Sports hero: Larry Csonka. Putnam 1975, 95 pp.

Larry Csonka was almost the stereotype of a football player; big, fearless and driving. For more information about the books in the series see *Sports Hero: Bill Walton.* Sports Hero series.

Interest Level: 2-6. Reading Level: 3.1. Further Search Topics: Biography, Csonka, Larry, Football-Biography, Group 2.

Burchard, Marshall. Sports hero: Muhammad Ali. Putnam 1975, 95 pp.

The man who brought a quick tongue as well as fast feet and flying fists to the sport of boxing. Entry for *Sports Hero: Bill Walton* gives series notes. Ring record included here. Sports Hero series.

Interest Level: 3-6. Reading Level: 4.1. Further Search Topics: Boxing-Biography, Blacks-Biography, Ali, Muhammad, Group 2.

Burchard, Marshall. Sports Hero: O.J. Simpson. Putnam 1975, 95 pp.

O.J. Simpson, who now flies through airports, still holds at least three NFL records, including most yards gained in a single season. See *Sports Hero: Bill Walton* for series information. Sports Hero series.

Interest Level: 2-6. Reading Level: 3.2. Further Search Topics: Biography, Simpson, O.J., Football-Biography, Blacks-Biography, Group 2.

Burchard, Marshall. Sports hero: Rick Barry. Putnam 1977, 95 pp.

Rick Barry, now a color commentator for televised basketball games, was once one of the best forwards in basketball. Details about the series with *Sports Hero: Bill Walton* entry. Sports Hero series.

Interest Level: 2-6. Reading Level: 3.1. Further Search Topics: Biography, Barry, Rick, Basketball-Biography, Group 2.

Burchard, Marshall. Sports hero: Ron Guidry. Putnam 1981, 95 pp.

The Cajun, left-handed pitcher who led the Yankees to two World Championships. See *Sports Hero: Bill Walton* for series details. Sports Hero series.

Interest Level: 3-6. Reading Level: 3.2. Further Search Topics: Baseball-Biography, Biography, Guidry, Ron.

Burchard, Marshall. Sports hero: Terry Bradshaw. Putnam 1980, 95 pp.

Once labeled a "dumb hick," Terry Bradshaw went on to prove he was a talented and thinking quarterback, good enough to be named NFL Player of the Year. He is also a deeply religious man. Reading level of this title varies from 3.1 to 4.1. For more details about the series, see *Sports Hero: Bill Walton.* Sports Hero series.

Interest Level: 3-6. Reading Level: 3.2. Further Search Topics: Biography, Bradshaw, Terry, Football-Biography, Religion-Biography.

Burchard, Marshall. Sports hero: Henry Aaron. Putnam 1974, 96 pp.

Baseball's homerun king. See entry under *Sports Hero: Bill Walton* for more information. Sports Hero series.

Interest Level: 2-6. Reading Level: 3.1. Further Search Topics: Biography, Aaron, Henry, Baseball-Biography, Blacks-Biography.

Burchard, Susan H. Sports star: Pele. HarBrace J 1976, 64 pp.

At age 35, when many people thought he might be "past his prime," Pele proved he could still play superior soccer. More details about the series in *Sports Hero: Bill Walton* entry, by Marshall Burchard. Sports Star series.

Interest Level: 2-6. Reading Level: 3.1. Further Search Topics: Biography, Soccer-Biography, Pele, Group 2.

Burchard, Susan H. Sports star: Dorothy Hamill. HarBraceJ 1978, 63 pp.

Although written by Susan Burchard, this and most of the following listings are true to Marshall Burchard's *Sports Hero* format. For more explanation see *Sports Hero: Bill Walton.*

Dorothy Hamill was the darling of ice skating in 1976 and is now a top professional figure skater. This makes her rise to stardom sound romantic and glamorous. Skating jargon pushes the reading level from 3.1 to 3.2. Sports Star series.

Interest Level: 2-6. Reading Level: 3.2. Further Search Topics: Hamill, Dorothy, Ice Skating-Biography, Women-Biography, Biography, Group 2.

Burchard, Susan H. Sports star: Earl Campbell. HarBraceJ 1980, 63 pp.

The Houston Oiler's star running back, probably the best in football, has only been out of college a few years. He should have a long career ahead of him. *Sports Star: Elvin Hayes* includes series notes. Sports Star series.

Interest Level: 3-6. Reading Level: 3.1. Further Search Topics: Football-Biography, Blacks-Biography, Campbell, Earl, Biography.

Burchard, Susan H. Sports star: Elvin Hayes. HarBraceJ 1980, 63 pp.

Only this and three other Sue Burchard titles listed here differ much from the format described for the *Sports Hero* series (see *Sports Hero: Bill Walton*). It appears that in 1979 Ms. Burchard's books took on a slick new look. The covers began to sport color photos rather than black and white. The print size became noticeably smaller, although still of adequate size. More emphasis was placed on the players early life and background, in an apparent attempt to make him or her understandable as an individual rather than just as a star. A short career summary was added at the end of each book. All-in-all, the new, flashier approach should make the books more appealing than ever to older students.

Elvin Hayes came from a very poor family who lived in a town where blacks were badly treated. He went on to become one of the best college basketball players of his time. His deep religious convictions helped him through some rough times in his early years as a pro. Now he is happy, not just when he wins, but when he knows he has played his best. Sports Star series.

Interest Level: 3-6. Reading Level: 3.1. Further Search Topics: Biography, Hayes, Elvin, Basketball-Biography, Blacks-Biography, Religion-Biography.

Burchard, Susan H. Sports star: John McEnroe. HarBraceJ 1979, 63 pp.

In 1977, feisty John McEnroe became the youngest semi-finalist ever to play at Wimbledon. Both before and since then, he has been noted almost as often for his temper as his talent. The level of difficulty of this book varies from 3.1 to 4.1. See *Sports Star: Elvin Hayes* for more details about the book. Sports Star series.

Interest Level: 3-6. Reading Level: 3.2. Further Search Topics: Biography, Tennis-Biography, McEnroe, John.

Burchard, Susan H. Sports star: Tommy John. HarBraceJ 1981, 63 pp.

Tommy John's elbow injury was severe enough that no one thought he would be able to pitch again. He proved that the skeptics were wrong. For series notes see *Sports Star: Elvin Hayes*. Sports Star series.

Interest Level: 3-6. Reading Level: 4.1. Further Search Topics: Baseball-Biography, John, Tommy, Biography, Group 2, Physically Handicapped.

Burchard, Susan H. Sports star: Franco Harris. HarBraceJ 1976, 64 pp.

Franco is the talented son of a black Army man and his Italian wife. He became a hero to thousands of Pittsburgh Steeler fans, who called themselves Franco's Italian Army. See *Sports Hero: Bill Walton*, by Marshall Burchard for series details. Sports Star series.

Interest Level: 2-6. Reading Level: 3.1. Further Search Topics: Biography, Group 2, Harris, Franco, Football-Biography, Blacks-Biography.

Burchard, Susan H. Sports star: Jim "Catfish" Hunter. HarBraceJ 1976, 64 pp.

The pitcher who, because of contract violations by his club's owner, became the first free agent in baseball. See Marshall Burchard's *Sports Hero: Bill Walton* for information about the series. Sports Star series.

Interest Level: 2-6. Reading Level: 3.1. Further Search Topics: Biography, Baseball-Biography, Hunter, Jim "Catfish", Group 2.

Burchard, Susan H. Sports star: Mark "The Bird" Fidrych. HarBraceJ 1977, 64 pp.

Although his major league career was short, it was also notable. Mark Fidrych's way of concentrating on his pitching was by talking to the baseball. Entry for *Sports Hero: Bill Walton*, by Marshall Burchard, provides more information about the book. Sports Star series.

Interest Level: 2-6. Reading Level: 2.2. Further Search Topics: Biography, Baseball-Biography, Fidrych, Mark "The Bird."

Burchard, Susan H. Sports star: "Mean" Joe Greene. HarBraceJ 1976, 64 pp.

"Mean" Joe Greene's nickname is appropriate. He is big, "mean" on the playing field, and likes to win. He usually does. More details about the book under *Sports Hero: Bill Walton*, by Marshall Burchard. Sports Star series.

Interest Level: 2-6. Reading Level: 3.2. Further Search Topics: Biography, Football-Biography, Greene, "Mean" Joe, Blacks-Biography, Group 2.

Burchard, Susan H. Sports star: Tony Dorsett. HarBraceJ 1978, 64 pp.

One year after he set the college rushing record and won the Heisman Trophy, Tony Dorsett was named the NFL's Rookie of the Year and found himself playing in the Super Bowl. Reading level of this title varies from 2.2 to 3.2. For more information about the series see the entry for Marshall Burchard's *Sports Hero: Bill Walton*. Sports Star series.

Interest Level: 2-6. Reading Level: 3.2. Further Search Topics: Biography, Football-Biography, Dorsett, Tony, Blacks-Biography, Group 2.

Burchard, Susan H. Sports star: Walt Frazier. HarBraceJ 1975, 64 pp.

Walt Frazier earned his nickname Clyde (from *Bonnie and Clyde*) because of his style both on and off the basketball court. He could steal the ball from almost anyone on the court and he enjoyed high living and fancy dressing off the court. Entry for *Sports Hero: Bill Walton* gives more information about the series. Sports Star series.

Interest Level: 2-6. Reading Level: 3.1. Further Search Topics: Biography, Basketball-Biography, Frazier, Walt, Blacks-Biography.

Cone, Molly. Leonard Bernstein; illus by Robert Galster. Har-Row 1970, 33 pp.

This is a bare bones outline that will appeal to music enthusiasts but will not attract anyone else. The reader catches very little of Bernstein's personality, but *is* awed by an impressive list of his accomplishments. The few attempts made to recreate the real person may have to be explained (i.e., references to Bernstein forgetting to get his hair cut because he was so busy). Picture book format of the hardback may deter some readers. Now published in paperback edition only. Crowell Biography series.

Interest Level: 2-4. Reading Level: 2.2. Further

Search Topics: Music-Biography, Biography, Conductors, Composers, Pianists, Group 2.

Fall, Thomas. Jim Thorpe; illus by John Gretzer. Har-Row 1970, 33 pp.

Jim Thorpe was an Indian from the Oklahoma territory who became one of the United State's greatest athletes. He and his twin brother were trained by their father to run and jump faster and farther than anyone else. When Charles died, Jim couldn't face returning to school without his twin, so his family kept him home for a few months before sending him away to school again. Jim ran home once more when his father and mother both became ill. Months later he went to still another school where he was noticed by Pop Warner. Pop advised Joe to concentrate on track until he was big enough to play football. His father's death left Jim so despondent he quit school to play professional baseball for a while. By the time he went back to school, Jim was big enough to play spectacular football and then to win the 1912 Olympic decathlon competition. Unfortunately, his short time as a paid baseball player made him ineligible for the Olympic honor and Jim's medal was taken away. Public sentiment was with Jim, but the rules were against him. He went on, however, to play both professional baseball and football. In 1982, 29 years after his death, Thorpe's medal was finally returned to him.

A short, meaty and readable biography of a person who should be interesting to many sports fans. Follows the usual format of Crowell biographies, but looks less like a picture book than many. Crowell Biography series.

Interest Level: 3-5. Reading Level: 3.1. Further Search Topics: Football-Biography, Indians of North America-Biography, Baseball-Biography, Olympic Games, Biography, Running-Biography, Twins-Biography.

Greenfield, Eloise. Rosa Parks; illus by Eric Marlow. Har-Row 1973, 33 pp.

This book succumbs to the difficulty of writing for children about a subject that needs more explanation. The occasionally condescending tone combined with the Crowell Biography picture book format will keep this otherwise adequate introduction to the civil rights movement from being useful beyond fourth grade. The book should be very useful, however, for third and fourth grade social studies, history or biography units.

Rosa Parks' childhood and her feelings about the special rules for blacks make up the first half of the book. The second half is devoted to Rosa's act of defiance (refusing to give up her seat on a bus to a white man) and the repercussions of that act. Crowell Biography series.

Interest Level: 2-4. Reading Level 2.2. Further Search Topics: Blacks-Biography, Biography, Prejudice, Civil Rights, Women-Biography, Courage.

Jordan, June. Fannie Lou Hamer; illus by Albert Williams. Har-Row 1972, 41 pp.

In 1917, Fannie Lou Hamer was the last of 20 children born to a fearless black woman. Fannie and her family grew up working on a white man's cotton plantation. Although they were kept poor and hungry by the plantation owner and the field boss, Fannie Lou grew up in her mother's image—unafraid of white people and unhappy with the poor treatment of blacks that she saw all around her. In 1962, when most other blacks in Mississippi where afraid of the consequences, Fannie registered to vote. After both she and her husband lost their jobs and their home, and after she was beaten in a Mississippi jail, Fannie Lou Hamer drew national attention to her fight for blacks' civil rights. She spoke all over the country, helped to form a new political party, and raised money to help poor people. That money was what started the 640 acre Freedom Farm Cooperative that provided work and food for more than 5,000 people. It was Mrs. Hamer's dream to see poor people work together to feed themselves rather than to accept food from others. She made her dream come true.

Another competent entry in the Crowell Biography series. Only its picture book format keeps this book from being useful through sixth grade.

Interest Level: 3-5. Reading Level: 3.2. Further Search Topics: Biography, Blacks-Biography, Civil Rights, Poverty, Women-Biography.

Madian, Jon. Beautiful junk: a story of the Watts Towers; photos by Barbara Jacobs, Jr. and Lou Jacobs, Jr. Little 1968, 44 pp.

Although this book is now out of print; it is well worth trying to find. It is a fictionalized account of a young, angry black boy's encounter with the creator of Los Angeles' unusual Watts Towers. Simon Rodia, a poor tile setter, worked on the towers for 33 years until he was 75 years old. He used only his imagination, discarded materials he found around him, seashells, and sand to build three tall, fantasy-like towers in the middle of a ghetto. He created beauty where others saw only junk.

The book is illustrated with photography that makes the story more vivid and the towers and Rodia's accomplishment more impressive than they would have seemed with drawings. The print is good-sized, spacing is totally adequate. Rodia's life is quickly submarized and an update on the Towers is included at the book's end.

Interest Level: 3-6. Reading Level: 3.1. Further Search Topics: Blacks-Fiction, Read Aloud, Best Sellers, Poverty-Fiction, Rodia, Simon, Architecture, Biography, Aging-Fiction, Watts Towers, California, Poverty.

Malone, Mary. Annie Sullivan; illus by Lydia Rosier. Putnam 1971, 61 pp.

This is a very brief sketch of both Annie Sullivan's life and Helen Keller's life. Their lives were so intertwined that they cannot be separated. But because they are combined in such a short book, neither woman can be treated in much depth. That fact is not as harmful here as it might otherwise be, because even a bare bones description of the life of this extraordinary deaf, blind and mute woman or her near-blind, dedicated teacher, is interesting.

Interest Level: 2-5. Reading Level: 2.2. Further Search Topics: Sullivan, Annie, Keller, Helen, Vision, Biography, Physically Handicapped, Sound, Courage.

Mathis, Sharon Bell. Ray Charles; illus by George Ford. Har-Row 1973, 33 pp.

Dominent throughout this biography of Ray Charles is the theme of overcoming adversity. The book is not just a recounting of Ray Charles' music lessons, early schooling, family life, and talent. All of that is included, but it serves to illustrate the manner in which Charles met his troubles. His problems began when he was very young. His brother died, and Ray lost one eye and then the sight in his other eye. His family was poor, but close, and he missed them when he was sent away to a school for the blind. Music was his love, but even that was work, for Charles had to learn to read and write music in Braille. He worked hard at it and eventually could play and arrange music for every instrument in the band.

Determined to be independent, when Charles was orphaned at age 15, he left school and began playing music for a living. The first record he made resulted in a $16 fine because he made it during a musician's union strike. Charles took a series of sideman and nightclub jobs until he finally had enough money to hire seven other musicians to play his music. Today Charles is very wealthy, owns his own record company, has a family, and is considered a great jazz and blues musician. None of his success came easily; only through determination, will power, pride, and hard work.

The book, interesting and serviceable enough for music or biography units, is also designed to set an example for youngsters facing their own problems. It will, of course, be popular with Ray Charles fans, too. Crowell Biography series.

Interest Level: 2-4. Reading Level: 3.1. Further Search Topics: Jazz Music, Music-Biography, Vision, Physically Handicapped, Blacks-Biography, Group 2, Biography, Pianists, Orphans, Challenges, Courage.

Meriwether, Louise. The freedom ship of Robert Smalls; illus by Lee Jack Morton. P-H 1971, unp (30 pp).

A brief, but very interesting biography of a black man whose dreams of freedom as a young slave during the Civil War, led to a daring plan of escape. Robert Smalls sailed 16 slaves to freedom and presented the Northern Navy with a valuable gunboat of which he was eventually named captain. Smalls later went on to serve five terms in Congress.

Although the picture book format of this book prevents its confortable use much beyond fourth grade, it is a compelling enough story to interest even sixth graders. Print is somewhat small.

Interest Level: 1-4. Reading Level: 3.1. Further Search Topics: Biography, United States-History-War, Blacks-Biography, Smalls, Robert, Group 2, Slavery, Politics-Biography.

Rudeen, Kenneth. Roberto Clemente; illus by Frank Mullins. Har-Row 1974, 33 pp.

A romanticized retelling of a great baseball player's life. Those already interested in baseball or in Clemente will probably not mind the romantic tone, but may notice the almost patronizing explanations of some of the basics of baseball. Crowell Biography series.

Interest Level: 2-4. Reading Level: 3.1. Further Search Topics: Baseball-Biography, Biography, Puerto Rico, Group 2, Clemente, Roberto.

Rudeen, Kenneth. Wilt Chamberlain; illus by Frank Mullins. Har-Row 1972, 33 pp.

A short and somewhat adoring version of Wilt Chamberlain's childhood, schooling, and professional career. Very little of Chamberlain's personality comes through in this book, but his superior talents and skills as well as his importance to the sport of basketball will be enough to prompt many basketball fans to read it. Although simplistic in style, the book is not condescending. It is, however, out of date, a fact most notable when Chamberlain's salary is quoted. Beware of juvenile format when using with older readers. Crowell Biography series.

Interest Level: 2-6. Reading Level: 3.2. Further Search Topics: Biography, Chamberlain, Wilt, Basketball-Biography, Blacks-Biography, Group 2.

Rudeen, Kenneth. Jackie Robinson; illus by Richard Cuffari. Har-Row 1971, 41 pp.

Jackie Robinson was the youngest child in a large, poor family. As early as high school it was Robinson's superior athletic talent that set him apart. He could run track or play baseball, football, or basketball. He was the first student at UCLA to win a letter in all four sports. But because he wasn't happy to see the way his mother still had to struggle to earn money to live, after a year and a half at UCLA, Robinson left college to take a job. Soon after that, the United States entered World War II and Robinson went into the Army. His refusal to ride in the back of a bus in Texas resulted in a courtmartial, but he was found innocent after an uproar was made by the newspapers.

After the Army, Robinson played baseball with a Negro League team. A short time later, he was asked by the Dodger manager Branch Rickey to become the first black man to play in the major leagues. Rickey warned Robinson that it would mean he not only had to play well, but that he would also have to take all the anger and bitterness that would be directed at him. Robinson agreed. For three long years, while there were no other black players in the major leagues, Robinson played well and took everything without fighting back. Robinson was then able to stop trying to be perfect because he had successfully broken a very important color barrier and no longer had to prove to white managers, players and fans that blacks belonged in baseball just as much as whites. Robinson played for the Dodgers for ten years. When he left baseball he was elected into the Baseball Hall of Fame. He continued to fight for civil rights throughout the rest of his life, although there is only a brief mention of his activities in the book. Since the book's publication Jackie Robinson has died.

This is an excellent choice for the child who thinks of nothing but sports. It may be helpful in opening up an interest in the civil rights movement, black history, or black heroes. It is unfortunate that the traditional Crowell biography format (semi-picture book), and the author's slight tendency to be condescending, prevents the book from being useful beyond fourth grade. Crowell Biography series.

Interest Level: 2-4. Reading Level: 2.2. Further Search Topics: Civil Rights, Robinson, Jackie, Baseball-Biography, Biography, Blacks-Biography, Prejudice, Poverty.

Tobias, Tobi. Marian Anderson; illus by Symeon Shimin. Har-Row 1972, 40 pp.

Marian Anderson's beautiful, strong voice and her great range set her apart from other singers even as a child. By the time she was in high school, she was being paid to sing. However, when she tried to apply to a well-known music school, because she was black she was turned away without even being heard. Anderson's determination as well as her own and others' faith in her kept her singing and seeking better and better coaches until she met Giuseppi Boghetti. He was one of the best voice coaches in the country. With him Marian trained and traveled until she finally won the chance to sing with the New York Philharmonic Orchestra. Anderson thought that at that point she would be invited to sing in famous theaters all across the United States, but because she was black she still received no invitations. She went to Europe where she studied and played to wildly enthusiastic audiences. Her European triumphs finally convinced American theater owners and audiences that she was a serious talent. For the next 30 years Marian Anderson sang all over the world, most of the time without incident, with one notable exception in 1939, when the D.A.R. prohibited her from singing in a hall they owned in Washington, D. C. She sang instead, in front of the Lincoln Memorial, at the invitation of the United States government. During the following years Marian married, bought a farm, sang opera and was made a delegate to the United Nations. In 1956, she retired from singing to help children, young singers, and world understanding.

Crowell Biographies make excellent school report sources for reluctant readers. They are short, interesting, and not overly juvenile looking, although the quasi-picture book format may be a problem for some older readers. This biography fits that description perfectly. The series is somewhat sentimental (as are many children's biographies), however, the sentimentality is not forbidding or condescending. A useful series. Crowell Biography series.

Interest Level: 2-5. Reading Level: 3.1. Further Search Topics: Biography, Music-Biography, Blacks-Biography, Talent, Women-Biography, Singers, Prejudice, Group 2.

Walker, Alice. Langston Hughes, American poet; illus by Don Miller. Har-Row 1974, 33 pp.

Langston Hughes is one of the world's most famous black poets. He spent most of his childhood in poverty and yet he shunned and was shunned by his wealthy father because his father disliked blacks. To Hughes the two most important things in the world were his heritage and his writing. His love of black history stemmed from the stories his grandmother told him. His love of language and writing grew out of the lonely hours he spent reading as a child. Hughes began to write poetry even before he was in high school and continued to write for many years. He wrote not only poems, but children's books, novels, plays and short stories. He wrote about and for blacks around the world. He was a proud and honest man who chose to share his pride in his race and his honesty through his writing.

This book is more of an inspirational tribute to a black hero than a fact-filled biography. That isn't to say that there are no facts included in the book. There are facts, but the book will not do as the sole source for a report about Langston Hughes. The book is, however, a good introduction to the man and his writing.

Interest Level: 3-5. Reading Level: 2.2. Further Search Topics: Biography, Blacks-Biography, Writing, Poverty, Divorce and Separation, Poetry.

BIRDS

Brenner, Barbara. Baltimore Orioles; illus by J. Winslow Higginbottom. Har-Row 1974, 62 pp.

An impressive combination of very easy, as well as interesting and informative reading. Within the barest skeleton of a story the author gives a great deal of information about young Baltimore Orioles and the mating and hatching cycle of the older birds. Unfortunately its easy reader format will discourage use beyond third grade. Use freely until that point. Science I Can Read Book series.

Interest Level: 1-3. Reading Level 1.2. Further Search Topics: Birds, Nature Study.

BIRDS-FICTION

Bulla, Clyde Robert. White bird; illus by Leonard Weisgard. T Y Crowell 1966, 79 pp.

This book is meant for a special reader. It will not appeal to the reader who wants only action and excitement from a book. It is a story of complex human relationships and differing definitions of love. John Thomas lost his parents in a river accident when he was just a baby. His cradle had been pulled from the river and he had been raised by reclusive Luke Vail. Luke placed no trust in the world or in people outside his tiny valley home and so forbade John Thomas to have anything to do with either one. Luke didn't allow John Thomas a pet either because he thought that John Thomas would only be hurt when he no longer had the animal. Despite Luke's argument, when he found an injured white crow, John Thomas kept it and tended it until the crow was stolen by three strangers as Luke stood by. Angry at Luke as much as at the strangers, John Thomas ran away to search for the bird, but found that it had been shot. Far from being fruitless, however, John Thomas's trip out of the valley gave him an entirely different view of people than the one Luke had shown him. Upon a friend's encouragement, John Thomas returned to Luke to share that view.

Subtle and unusual, this book needs a mature, sensitive reader and/or discussion in order to be fully appreciated.

Interest Level: 4-6. Reading Level 2.1. Further Search Topics: Pets-Fiction, Orphans-Fiction, Runaways-Fiction, Birds-Fiction, Love-Fiction, Loners-Fiction, Courage-Fiction.

Byars, Betsy. The house of wings; illus by Daniel Schwarts. Viking Pr. 1972, 142 pp.

Sammy was the youngest of eight children. His parents were tired of raising children when Sammy was born, so they almost let Sammy raise himself. That meant that he grew up to be independent. It didn't mean it was any easier for Sammy to accept being left behind unexpectedly with his strange grandfather when his parents moved to Detroit. His reaction when his grandfather told him that his parents had gone was to deny it and to run away. He ran until he could run no more. When he stopped running, the old man stopped chasing him and they found a wild but blind crane in desperate need of help. Helping the crane heal and find the desire to live again taught Sammy and his grandfather respect and, most of all, love for each other.

The parallels between Sammy and the crane are strong but subtle. The story is a compelling one, but may need a brief introductory note to alleviate confusion in the first two chapters.

Interest Level: 5-6. Reading Level: 4.2. Further Search Topics: Grandparents-Fiction, Birds-Fiction, Family Problems-Fiction, Poverty-Fiction, Physically Handicapped-Fiction, Runaways-Fiction.

Chew, Ruth. Witch's broom. Dodd 1977, 128 pp.

Amy's mother was the one who found the blue broom, but Amy and her friend Jean were the ones who learned it was magical. One night the broom flew Amy into a mountain cave where a coven of witches was meeting. It even forced Amy to answer the roll call for someone named Beryl. But it wasn't until it took both Amy and Jean back to the cave that they discovered the broom's connection to the strange bluejay that had been following them. The bluejay was really Beryl, a young and headstrong witch who had turned herself into the bluejay and then couldn't turn herself back. With the girls' unwitting help, Beryl found the charm to turn herself back into a witch and flew off on a scrawny old broom, leaving the blue broom for Amy and Jean.

What youngster wouldn't want a flying broomstick and the misadventures that go with owning one? Wish fulfillment can never be overrated as an appeal of Ruth Chew's books.

Interest Level: 2-5. Reading Level: 3.1. Further Search Topics: Witches-Fiction, Magic-Fiction, Fantasy, Birds-Fiction, Group 2, Transformations-Fiction.

Giff, Patricia Reilly. Have you seen Hyacinth Macaw?; illus by Anthony Kramer. Delacorte 1981, 135 pp.

Abby Jones was trying very hard to be a detective, but it was difficult without any mysteries to solve. So to keep in practice, Abby filled a memo book with her notes about anything that seemed at all unusual. At the same time, Abby kept in touch with two local police detectives who gave her hints about detective work. Because of her police friends and her observations, Abby found herself involved in what seemed to be four or more mysteries. Who had moved into the apartment next door and what were the screams that came from there? What was the theft that the police were worried about? Who was Hyacinth Macaw and why had she disappeared? And why was Abby's older brother Dan acting so strangely? Was he involved in the theft?

Abby and her friend Potsie ended up trailing a suspect through the New York subway system, breaking into the next-door apartment, suspecting Abby's brother of the theft, capturing an unusual bird, releasing the bird into a pet shop and recapturing it, before they realized that all the mysteries were linked together. Hyacinth Macaw was a valuable bird stolen from Justine's Junktique Shop. The daughter of Abby's landland had taken the bird and placed it in the empty apartment next to Abby's, so that she could paint the bird's portrait. The picture was to be entered in Justine's Junktique contest. Dan and his friend Holly Monk had been secretly constructing a Purple Pigeon Purifier to enter in the contest. They needed the prize money to repair a window they had accidentally broken. By the time the mysteries were all sorted out, Dan and Holly had won a special prize; Kiki, the portrait painter, had not only been forgiven, but had also been awarded first prize; and Abby had received the reward for finding and returning the bird.

The action in this mystery is both abundant and humorous enough to make the book enjoyable to many readers. There are also some problems that need to be noted. Some readers may find the action too swift and the characters too numerous to be easily followed. Abby's memo notes are sometimes written without vowels and are almost always in incomplete sentences. The reader who is highly motivated or has help from another person will still be able to enjoy the story; however, for the others another choice may be more appropriate.

Interest Level: 4-6. Reading Level: 3.1. Further Search Topics: Mystery and Detective Stories, Humorous Fiction, Writing-Fiction, Detectives-Fiction, Birds-Fiction.

Talbot, Charlene Joy. The Great Rat Island adventure; illus by Ruth Sanderson. Atheneum 1977, 164 pp.

Joel dreaded spending the summer with his father. His parents were divorced and Joel was sure his father didn't want him. His father only wanted to study birds. Great Rat Island, where Joel and his father were to spend the summer, was of no interest to Joel. It had no television, no one his own age, only terns. Even the assignment Joel was given (to make sure

that no more tern eggs were stolen) sounded dull. It led to an adventure and a friend, however, that were anything but dull.

Joel discovered that a girl his own age was the thief of the tern eggs. Her name was Vicky Owens. She had run away from camp and was spending the summer alone on Little Rat Island. Joel kept her secret until the day of hurricane warnings. As the storm approached Joel realized that Vicky wouldn't be safe on Little Rat Island. Without telling anyone else he took the only boat around and went to look for Vicky to bring her back to Great Rat Island. He found her with her leg stuck between two rocks, unable to move. By the time Joel got her loose, it was too late to get back to the big island. Not knowing what else to do, Joel and Vicky dragged the boat inside an abandoned building where Vicky had been living. As the water rose around them and Vicky grew delirious with fever, Joel set up camp in the boat. While the building filled with water they stayed dry in the boat. Rescue and medical care for Vicky finally came the next day.

A solid, steadily-paced survival story for the reader who wants a little more than just an adventure story. Print is small.

Interest Level: 4-6. Reading Level: 3.1. Further Search Topics: Vacation-Fiction, Family Problems-Fiction, Birds-Fiction, Divorce and Separation-Fiction, Disasters-Fiction, Survival-Fiction, Runaways-Fiction.

BIRTH

Cole, Joanna. My puppy is born; photos by Jerome Wexler. Morrow 1973, unp (38 pp).

This is an unadorned description of a dachshund puppy's birth and first eight weeks of growth. The black and white photographs are large, sometimes graphic, and most often charming. The text is direct, carefully worded, concise and interesting. It is only the intrusion of an obviously young narrator that keeps this excellent book from being useful beyond third grade.

Interest Level: 1-3. Reading Level: 2.1. Further Search Topics: Group 2, Infants, Dogs, Pets, Birth.

Selsam, Millicent E. How kittens grow; photos by Esther Bubley. School Bk Serv 1973, unp (28 pp).

A warm picture essay that illustrates and briefly describes the first eight weeks in kittens' lives. Guaranteed to charm cat fanciers.

Interest Level: 1-3. Reading Level: 2.1. Further Search Topics: Cats, Pets, Infants, Group 2, Birth.

BIRTHDAYS-FICTION

Nodset, Joan L. Go away dog; illus by Crosby Bonsall. Har-Row 1963, unp (29 pp).

A small boy who doesn't like dogs meets a shaggy, homeless dog who wants to play. The little boy, resisting all the way, gradually gives in to the dog's charms. Finally he tells the dog to follow him home. At home, he finds out that the dog was sent to him for his birthday by his Uncle George.

The dog, the boy, and the book are irresistible. You must, however, notice the illustrations on both the dedication and title pages to fully understand the story. Since much of the story is told by the illustrations and the text is repetitive as well as simple, it is an excellent beginning-to-read story.

Interest Level: 1-2. Reading Level: 1.1. Further Search Topics: Dogs-Fiction, Humorous Fiction, Best Sellers, Pets-Fiction, Birthdays-Fiction.

BLACKS-BIOGRAPHY

Adoff, Arnold. Malcolm X; illus by John Wilson. Har-Row 1970, 41 pp.

This is a simple, intellectually honest biography of a very controversial man. Taught a strong sense of self-respect by his father, Malcolm X could not accept the second-class status that white society tried to impose upon him. Instead he turned away from whites and all they stood for. He hated high school, the detention home he lived in after his father's death, and his mother's placement in a state hospital. He didn't feel comfortable until he moved to Harlem. There he found friends, but he also found crime. While he was in prison, Malcolm X began to read of great, black societies and people. His brother told him about the Nation of Islam, the Black Muslims, and Elijah Muhammad, the leader of the religion. He began corresponding with Mr. Muhammad. Shortly after he was released from prison, Malcolm X met Elijah Muhammad and eventually became a minister of the religion. There was even talk that he would be Elijah Muhammad's successor. But, as the years went on, Malcolm X began to think that black Christians as well as Muslims should be united in the fight for black rights. Despite threats against his life Malcolm X formed the Organization of Afro-American Unity. Both blacks and whites were angry with him. The threats continued until his house was firebombed; and, only a week later, at a public meeting, Malcolm X was assassinated.

An excellent overview of a complex man. The book may well prompt readers to learn more about the man and his beliefs. At the very least it will expose readers, in an interesting manner, to someone they should know. The book shares the same semi-picture book format of the others in Harper and Row/Crowell's biography series, therefore it will need a careful introduction to potential readers.

Interest Level: 3-5. Reading Level: 3.1. Further Search Topics: Blacks-Biography, Civil Rights, Biography, Crime, Religion, Assassinations, Prejudice, Poverty, Foster Homes.

Burchard, Marshall. Sports hero: Dr. J. Putnam 1976, 89 pp.

Julius Erving can jump higher and stay in the air longer than almost any other basketball player. He can also move around the court with the most agile of players. All in all he is a very exciting player to watch. This book includes his college and pro records (through 1975). See *Sports Hero: Bill Walton* for more information. Sports Hero series.

Interest Level: 3-6. Reading Level: 4.1. Further Search Topics: Biography, Blacks-Biography, Basketball-Biography, Erving, Julius, Group 2.

Burchard, Marshall. Sports hero: Joe Morgan. Putnam 1978, 93 pp.

Joe Morgan has been described as one of baseball's most complete players. He could field, hit, run and steal bases with the best. See *Sports Hero: Bill Walton* for more details about the book. Sports Hero series.

Interest Level: 2-6. Reading Level: 3.2. Further Search Topics: Biography, Morgan, Joe, Baseball-Biography, Blacks-Biography, Group 2.

Burchard, Marshall. Sports hero: Reggie Jackson. Putnam 1975, 93 pp.

Reggie Jackson was one of the big reasons why the Oakland A's won baseball's World Series three years in a row. *Sports Hero: Bill Walton* gives more information about the books in the series. Sports Hero series.

Interest Level: 2-6. Reading Level: 3.2. Further Search Topics: Biography, Jackson, Reggie, Baseball-Biography, Blacks-Biography, Group 2.

Burchard, Marshall. Sports hero: Muhammad Ali. Putnam 1975, 95 pp.

The man who brought a quick tongue as well as fast feet and flying fists to the sport of boxing. Entry for *Sports Hero: Bill Walton* gives series notes. Ring record included here. Sports Hero series.

Interest Level: 3-6. Reading Level: 4.1. Further Search Topics: Boxing-Biography, Blacks-Biography, Ali, Muhammad, Group 2.

Burchard, Marshall. Sports Hero: O.J. Simpson. Putnam 1975, 95 pp.

O.J. Simpson, who now flies through airports, still holds at least three NFL records, including most yards gained in a single season. See *Sports Hero: Bill Walton* for series information. Sports Hero series.

Interest Level: 2-6. Reading Level: 3.2. Further Search Topics: Biography, Simpson, O.J., Football-Biography, Blacks-Biography, Group 2.

Burchard, Marshall. Sports hero: Henry Aaron. Putnam 1974, 96 pp.

Baseball's homerun king. See entry under *Sports Hero: Bill Walton* for more information. Sports Hero series.

Interest Level: 2-6. Reading Level: 3.1. Further Search Topics: Biography, Aaron, Henry, Baseball-Biography, Blacks-Biography.

Burchard, Susan H. Sports star: Earl Campbell. HarBraceJ 1980, 63 pp.

The Houston Oiler's star running back, probably the best in football, has only been out of college a few years. He should have a long career ahead of him. *Sports Star: Elvin Hayes* includes series notes. Sports Star series.

Interest Level: 3-6. Reading Level: 3.1. Further Search Topics: Football-Biography, Blacks-Biography, Campbell, Earl, Biography.

Burchard, Susan H. Sports star: Elvin Hayes. HarBraceJ 1980, 63 pp.

Only this and three other Sue Burchard titles listed here differ much from the format described for the *Sports Hero* series (see *Sports Hero: Bill Walton*). It appears that in 1979 Ms. Burchard's books took on a slick new look. The covers began to sport color photos rather than black and white. The print size became noticeably smaller, although still of adequate size. More emphasis was placed on the players early life and background, in an apparent attempt to make him or her understandable as an individual rather than just as a star. A short career summary was added at the end of each book. All-in-all, the new, flashier approach should make the books more appealing than ever to older students.

Elvin Hayes came from a very poor family who lived in a town where blacks were badly treated. He went on to become one of the best college basketball players of his time. His deep religious convictions helped him through some rough times in his early years as a pro. Now he is happy, not just when he wins, but when he knows he has played his best. Sports Star series.

Interest Level: 3-6. Reading Level: 3.1. Further Search Topics: Biography, Hayes, Elvin, Basketball-Biography, Blacks-Biography, Religion-Biography.

Burchard, Susan H. Sports star: Franco Harris. HarBraceJ 1976, 64 pp.

Franco is the talented son of a black Army man and his Italian wife. He became a hero to thousands of Pittsburgh Steeler fans, who called themselves Franco's Italian Army. See *Sports Hero: Bill Walton*, by Marshall Burchard for series details. Sports Star series.

Interest Level: 2-6. Reading Level: 3.1. Further Search Topics: Biography, Group 2, Harris, Franco, Football-Biography, Blacks-Biography.

Burchard, Susan H. Sports star: "Mean" Joe Greene. HarBraceJ 1976, 64 pp.

"Mean" Joe Greene's nickname is appropriate. He is big, "mean" on the playing field, and likes to win. He usually does. More details about the book under *Sports Hero: Bill Walton*, by Marshall Burchard. Sports Star series.

Interest Level: 2-6. Reading Level: 3.2. Further Search Topics: Biography, Football-Biography, Greene, "Mean" Joe, Blacks-Biography, Group 2.

Burchard, Susan H. Sports star: Tony Dorsett. HarBraceJ 1978, 64 pp.

One year after he set the college rushing record and won the Heisman Trophy, Tony Dorsett was named the NFL's Rookie of the Year and found himself playing in the Super Bowl. Reading level of this title varies from 2.2 to 3.2. For more information about the series see the entry for Marshall Burchard's *Sports Hero: Bill Walton*. Sports Star series.

Interest Level: 2-6. Reading Level: 3.2. Further Search Topics: Biography, Football-Biography, Dorsett, Tony, Blacks-Biography, Group 2.

Burchard, Susan H. Sports star: Walt Frazier. HarBraceJ 1975, 64 pp.

Walt Frazier earned his nickname Clyde (from *Bonnie and Clyde*) because of his style both on and off the basketball court. He could steal the ball from almost anyone on the court and he enjoyed high living and fancy dressing off the court. Entry for *Sports Hero: Bill Walton* gives more information about the series. Sports Star series.

Interest Level: 2-6. Reading Level: 3.1. Further Search Topics: Biography, Basketball-Biography, Frazier, Walt, Blacks-Biography.

Greenfield, Eloise. Rosa Parks; illus by Eric Marlow. Har-Row 1973, 33 pp.

This book succumbs to the difficulty of writing for children about a subject that needs more explanation. The occasionally condescending tone combined with the Crowell Biography picture book format will keep this otherwise adequate introduction to the civil rights movement from being useful beyond fourth grade. The book should be very useful, however, for third and fourth grade social studies, history or biography units.

Rosa Parks' childhood and her feelings about the special rules for blacks make up the first half of the book. The second half is devoted to Rosa's act of defiance (refusing to give up her seat on a bus to a white man) and the repercussions of that act. Crowell Biography series.

Interest Level: 2-4. Reading Level 2.2. Further Search Topics: Blacks-Biography, Biography, Prejudice, Civil Rights, Women-Biography, Courage.

Jordan, June. Fannie Lou Hamer; illus by Albert Williams. Har-Row 1972, 41 pp.

In 1917, Fannie Lou Hamer was the last of 20 children born to a fearless black woman. Fannie and her family grew up working on a white man's cotton plantation. Although they were kept poor and hungry by the plantation owner and the field boss, Fannie Lou grew up in her mother's image—unafraid of white people and unhappy with the poor treatment of blacks that she saw all around her. In 1962, when most other blacks in Mississippi where afraid of the consequences, Fannie registered to vote. After both she and her husband lost their jobs and their home, and after she was beaten in a Mississippi jail, Fannie Lou Hamer drew national attention to her fight for blacks' civil rights. She spoke all over the country, helped to form a new political party, and raised money to help poor people. That money was what started the 640 acre Freedom Farm Cooperative that provided work and food for more than 5,000 people. It was Mrs. Hamer's dream to see poor people work together to feed themselves rather than to accept food from others. She made her dream come true.

Another competent entry in the Crowell Biography series. Only its picture book format keeps this book from being useful through sixth grade.

Interest Level: 3-5. Reading Level: 3.2. Further Search Topics: Biography, Blacks-Biography, Civil Rights, Poverty, Women-Biography,

Mathis, Sharon Bell. Ray Charles; illus by George Ford. Har-Row 1973, 33 pp.

Dominent throughout this biography of Ray Charles is the theme of overcoming adversity. The book is not just a recounting of Ray Charles' music lessons, early schooling, family life, and talent. All of that is included, but it serves to illustrate the manner in which Charles met his troubles. His problems began when he was very young. His brother died, and Ray lost one eye and then the sight in his other eye. His family was poor, but close, and he missed them when he was sent away to a school for the blind. Music was his love, but even that was work, for Charles had to learn to read and write music in Braille. He worked hard at it and eventually could play and arrange music for every instrument in the band.

Determined to be independent, when Charles was orphaned at age 15, he left school and began playing music for a living. The first record he made resulted in a $16 fine because he made it during a musician's union strike. Charles took a series of sideman and nightclub jobs until he finally had enough money to hire seven other musicians to play his music. Today Charles is very wealthy, owns his own record company, has a family, and is considered a great jazz and blues musician. None of his success came easily; only through determination, will power, pride, and hard work.

The book, interesting and serviceable enough for music or biography units, is also designed to set an example for youngsters facing their own problems. It will, of course, be popular with Ray Charles fans, too. Crowell Biography series.

Interest Level: 2-4. Reading Level: 3.1. Further Search Topics: Jazz Music, Music-Biography, Vision, Physically Handicapped, Blacks-Biography, Group 2, Biography, Pianists, Orphans, Challenges, Courage.

Meriwether, Louise. The freedom ship of Robert Smalls; illus by Lee Jack Morton. P-H 1971, unp (30 pp).

A brief, but very interesting biography of a black man whose dreams of freedom as a young slave during the Civil War, led to a daring plan of escape. Robert Smalls sailed 16 slaves to freedom and presented the Northern Navy with a valuable gunboat of which he was eventually named captain. Smalls later went on to serve five terms in Congress.

Although the picture book format of this book prevents its confortable use much beyond fourth grade, it is a compelling enough story to interest even sixth graders. Print is somewhat small.

Interest Level: 1-4. Reading Level: 3.1. Further Search Topics: Biography, United States-History-War, Blacks-Biography, Smalls, Robert, Group 2, Slavery, Politics-Biography.

Rudeen, Kenneth. Wilt Chamberlain; illus by Frank Mullins. Har-Row 1972, 33 pp.

A short and somewhat adoring version of Wilt Chamberlain's childhood, schooling, and professional career. Very little of Chamberlain's personality comes through in this book, but his superior talents and skills as well as his importance to the sport of basketball will be enough to prompt many basketball fans to read it. Although simplistic in style, the book is not condescending. It is, however, out of date, a fact most notable when Chamberlain's salary is quoted. Beware of juvenile format when using with older readers. Crowell Biography series.

Interest Level: 2-6. Reading Level: 3.2. Further Search Topics: Biography, Chamberlain, Wilt, Basketball-Biography, Blacks-Biography, Group 2.

Rudeen, Kenneth. Jackie Robinson; illus by Richard Cuffari. Har-Row 1971, 41 pp.

Jackie Robinson was the youngest child in a large, poor family. As early as high school it was Robinson's superior athletic talent that set him apart. He could run track or play baseball, football, or basketball. He was the first student at UCLA to win a letter in all four sports. But because he wasn't happy to see the way his mother still had to struggle to earn money to live, after a year and a half at UCLA, Robinson left college to take a job. Soon after that, the United States entered World War II and Robinson went into the Army. His refusal to ride in the back of a bus in Texas resulted in a courtmartial, but he was found innocent after an uproar was made by the newspapers.

After the Army, Robinson played baseball with a Negro League team. A short time later, he was asked by the Dodger manager Branch Rickey to become the first black man to play in the major leagues. Rickey warned Robinson that it would mean he not only had to play well, but that he would also have to take all the anger and bitterness that would be directed at him. Robinson agreed. For three long years, while there were no other black players in the major leagues, Robinson played well and took everything without fighting back. Robinson was then able to stop trying to be perfect because he had successfully broken a very important color barrier and no longer had to prove to white managers, players and fans that blacks belonged in baseball just as much as whites. Robinson played for the Dodgers for ten years. When he left baseball he was elected into the Baseball Hall of Fame. He continued to fight for civil rights throughout the rest of his life, although there is only a brief mention of his activities in the book. Since the book's publication Jackie Robinson has died.

This is an excellent choice for the child who thinks of nothing but sports. It may be helpful in opening up an interest in the civil rights movement, black history, or black heroes. It is unfortunate that the traditional Crowell biography format (semi-picture book), and the author's slight tendency to be condescending, prevents the book from being useful beyond fourth grade. Crowell Biography series.

Interest Level: 2-4. Reading Level: 2.2. Further Search Topics: Civil Rights, Robinson, Jackie, Baseball-Biography, Biography, Blacks-Biography, Prejudice, Poverty.

Tobias, Tobi. Marian Anderson; illus by Symeon Shimin. Har-Row 1972, 40 pp.

Marian Anderson's beautiful, strong voice and her great range set her apart from other singers even as a child. By the time she was in high school, she was being paid to sing. However, when she tried to apply to a well-known music school, because she was black she was turned away without even being heard. Anderson's determination as well as her own and others' faith in her kept her singing and seeking better and better coaches until she met Giuseppi Boghetti. He was one of the best voice coaches in the country. With him Marian trained and traveled until she finally won the chance to sing with the New York Philharmonic Orchestra. Anderson thought that at that point she would be invited to sing in famous theaters all across the United States, but because she was black she still received no invitations. She went to Europe where she studied and played to wildly enthusiastic audiences. Her European triumphs finally convinced American theater owners and audiences that she was a serious talent. For the next 30 years Marian Anderson sang all over the world, most of the time without incident, with one notable exception in 1939, when the D.A.R. prohibited her from singing in a hall they owned in Washington, D. C. She sang instead, in front of the Lincoln Memorial, at the invitation of the United States government. During the following years Marian married, bought a farm, sang opera and was made a delegate to the United Nations. In 1956, she retired from singing to help children, young singers, and world understanding.

Crowell Biographies make excellent school report sources for reluctant readers. They are short, interesting, and not overly juvenile looking, although the quasi-picture book format may be a problem for some older readers. This biography fits that description perfectly. The series is somewhat sentimental (as are many children's biographies), however, the sentimentality is not forbidding or condescending. A useful series. Crowell Biography series.

Interest Level: 2-5. Reading Level: 3.1. Further Search Topics: Biography, Music-Biography, Blacks-Biography, Talent, Women-Biography, Singers, Prejudice, Group 2.

Walker, Alice. Langston Hughes, American poet; illus by Don Miller. Har-Row 1974, 33 pp.

Langston Hughes is one of the world's most famous black poets. He spent most of his childhood in poverty and yet he shunned and was shunned by his wealthy father because his father disliked blacks. To Hughes the two most important things in the world were his heritage and his writing. His love of black history stemmed from the stories his grandmother told him. His love of language and writing grew out of the lonely hours he spent reading as a child. Hughes began to write poetry even before he was in high school and continued to write for many years. He wrote not only poems, but children's books, novels, plays and short stories. He wrote about and for blacks around the world. He was a proud and honest man who chose to share his pride in his race and his honesty through his writing.

This book is more of an inspirational tribute to a black hero than a fact-filled biography. That isn't to say that there are no facts included in the book. There are facts, but the book will not do as the sole source for a report about Langston Hughes. The book is, however, a good introduction to the man and his writing.

Interest Level: 3-5. Reading Level: 2.2. Further Search Topics: Biography, Blacks-Biography, Writing, Poverty, Divorce and Separation, Poetry.

BLACKS-FICTION

Cohen, Barbara. Thank you, Jackie Robinson; illus by Richard Cuffari. Lothrop 1974, 125 pp.

This story is not for everyone, but for the right reader it is perfect. The book is a catalog of baseball facts, thus it is likely to appeal primarily to baseball fans. But it is not the typical story of a child overcoming a problem through practice and perserverance, as are most sports books. This is a sensitive story of a fatherless boy whose life centered around the New York Dodgers.

Sam could repeat the starting line-up and details of any game the Dodgers had played within the last three years; however, no one cared. In fact, most people were bored when Sam began reciting. Only Davey, the old, black cook at the inn where Sam and his family lived, took any interest. Davey was as much a fan as Sam. They began spending hours together talking and then watching baseball as Davey and his daughter took Sam to the games with them. It was Sam and Davey's dream to catch a fly ball and have it autograped by all the Dodgers, especially Jackie Robinson, the first black major league player. When Davey had a severe heart attack, Sam gathered all his courage to make that dream come true. He bought a baseball, took the subway to a game, and argued with the ushers until he was finally able to get Jackie Robinson's and the team's autographs. Just a few days before Davey died Sam took the baseball to the hospital and gave it to Davey. Sam's feelings about Davey's death are real and painful. He felt sorry for himself, lonely, angry, sad and confused. But a remark by his mother and one more Jackie Robinson hit helped Sam accept Davey's death.

Because the story is told as a first-person flashback set in the late 1940s, it may need a little introduction. It also alludes to racial problems and practices that young readers may not understand without explanation (i.e., why Davey had some hesitation about taking a white child with him to the ballpark or on a trip).

Interest Level: 4-6. Reading Level: 4.2. Further Search Topics: Baseball-Fiction, Blacks-Fiction, Aging-Fiction, Single Parent Family-Fiction, Friendship-Fiction, Death-Fiction, Robinson, Jackie.

Green, Phyllis. The fastest quitter in town; illus by Lorenzo Lynch. A-W 1972, 62 pp.

Whenever Johnny played baseball and things went wrong for him, he would quit. Johnny's teammates finally grew so angry with him that they told him to leave the team. That same day, Johnny's 90-year-old great-grandfather lost a very special ring his wife had given him. Johnny's love for this great-grandfather pushed him to keep looking for the ring until days later, when everyone else had quit searching, Johnny found the ring. Having learned a hard lesson, Johnny returned to his team for one more chance. That evening Johnny went to see his great-grandfather to tell him, with legitimate pride, that he had played the entire game.

Although the lesson is pointed, the story is very satisfying. Johnny's relationship with this great-grandfather is close and supportive. His problem is one shared by many children, especially those with a weak self-image.

Interest Level: 1-4. Reading Level: 3.1. Further Search Topics: Blacks-Fiction, Challenges-Fiction, Courage-Fiction, Group 2, Baseball-Fiction, Grandparents-Fiction, Friendship-Fiction.

Hamilton, Virginia. Zeely; illus by Symeon Shimin. Macmillan 1967, 122 pp.

A beautiful, almost mystical story of a black girl who learns about self-identity and pride from a statuesque neighbor whom Geeder is convinced must be a Watutsi princess. At first by chance and later at an arranged meeting, Zeely (Geeder's neighbor) gently and symbolically speaks to Geeder of her racial origins. She also tells Geeder of a young girl (Zeely as a child), too ignorant of the world around her to be able to recognize reality. It is a quietly moving story that is most likely to find an appreciative audience in the thoughtful, more mature reader.

Interest Level: 5-6. Reading Level: 5.1. Further Search Topics: Africa-Fiction, Royalty-Fiction, Blacks-Fiction, Courage-Fiction, Vacation-Fiction, Country Life-Fiction, Read Aloud.

Madian, Jon. Beautiful junk: a story of the Watts Towers; photos by Barbara Jacobs, Jr. and Lou Jacobs, Jr. Little 1968, 44 pp.

Although this book is now out of print; it is well worth trying to find. It is a fictionalized account of a young, angry black boy's encounter with the creator of Los Angeles' unusual Watts Towers. Simon Rodia, a poor tile setter, worked on the towers for 33 years until he was 75 years old. He used only his imagination, discarded materials he found around him, seashells, and sand to build three tall, fantasy-like towers in the middle of a ghetto. He created beauty where others saw only junk.

The book is illustrated with photography that makes the story more vivid and the towers and Rodia's accomplishment more impressive than they would have seemed with drawings. The print is good-sized, spacing is totally adequate. Rodia's life is quickly submarized and an update on the Towers is included at the book's end.

Interest Level: 3-6. Reading Level: 3.1. Further Search Topics: Blacks-Fiction, Read Aloud, Best Sellers, Poverty-Fiction, Rodia, Simon, Architecture, Biography, Aging-Fiction, Watts Towers, California, Poverty.

Shearer, John. Billy Jo Jive and the case of the missing pigeons; illus by Ted Shearer. Delacorte 1978, 47 pp.

This is the third in a series of slight mysteries, always solved by Billy Jo Jive and his crime fighter partner, Susie Sunset. Jive and Sunset are street-wise, black youngsters who take their jobs as crime fighters very seriously, and are never detered for long from finding the criminals they seek. The crimes are always thefts, and the criminals vary from young children to neighborhood menaces. Suspense is created more by the manner in which Jive and Sunset catch the thieves, plus the determination and pace of the young detectives, than by guessing who the culprits might be. Jive, his street-slang manner of telling the first-person stories, and the urban setting will appeal to many readers. Jive and Sunset also appear on *Sesame Street*.

Jive accidentally photographed the fleeing pigeon thief as he was being chased by Flip, the victim. The photograph didn't show the thief's face, but did give Jive and Sunset a good look at what he was wearing. Jive and Sunset concluded that the thief was Snake Hips Robberts. They later realized that they had been wrong. When they looked carefully at the picture, they remembered that any dark color clothing photographs almost black in a black and white picture. Snake Hips had a black jacket, but he was innocent. The real thief was Sugar Brown. Then it was a simple matter of showing the evidence to both Flip and Sugar to get Sugar to confess.

Interest Level: 1-4. Reading Level: 2.2. Further Search Topics: Mystery and Detective Stories, Detectives-Fiction, Blacks-Fiction, City Life-Fiction, Group 2, Best Sellers.

Shearer, John. Billy Jo Jive and the walkie-talkie caper; illus by Ted Shearer. Delacorte 1981, 47 pp.

When Steam Boat Louis went to Jive and Sunset for help, he was desperate. Because Jive and Sunset had already solved three cases, they were the logical people to find the walkie-talkie that had been stolen from Steam Boat. The walkie-talkie was one of two that Steam Boat had been told to buy as part of a secret communication system for the Bugaloo Smackers. Even as Jive and Sunset hunted for the thief, the second walkie-talkie was stolen. Their only clue was a footprint found outside Steam Boat's fix-it shop. Eventually, after trial and error, Jive and Sunset uncovered the real thieves; Steam Boat's young twin cousins. Unhappy at being separated in school, they wanted to use the walkie-talkies to be able to talk with each other.

The high reading level of this book will make it most useful for those children who have read and enjoyed other books in the series and are willing to stretch to read one more.

Interest Level: 1-4. Reading Level: 3.2. Further Search Topics: Mystery and Detective Stories, Detectives-Fiction, Blacks-Fiction, City Life-Fiction, Group 2.

Shearer, John. Billy Jo Jive super private eye: the case of the missing ten speed bike; illus by Ted Shearer. Delacorte 1976, 47 pp.

Jive and Sunset began their friendship and their sleuthing career with this book. It all started when Sunset borrowed her older brother's 10-speed bicycle. Jive met Sunset while she sat at the side of the road crying, after her brother's bike had been stolen. Some careful joint detective work proved to Jive and Sunset that Dynamite Jones, jealous of Sunset's brother, had stolen the bike. The young crime fighters recovered the bicycle before Sunset's brother even knew it was missing.

This book sets the formula that all the others follow. A neighborhood person finds that something has been stolen and goes to Jive and Sunset for help. Jive and Sunset never have much trouble finding the thief even though they are sometimes misled for a short time. Often the culprit is quite obvious to the reader. After some attempts at clever detective work and an occasional bit of preaching, the crime is solved. It is the manner of the pursuit and the street-smart characters that give the stories their interest.

Interest Level: 1-4. Reading Level: 2.2. Further Search Topics: Mystery and Detective Stories, Blacks-Fiction, Detectives-Fiction, City Life-Fiction, Best Sellers, Group 2, Bicycles and Bicycling-Fiction.

Wagner, Jane. J.T; photos by Gordon Parks, Jr. Van Nostrand 1969, 64 pp.

This is a sentimental story that rarely fails to elicit a sympathetic response from young readers. J.T. is a poor black boy who saw a portable radio almost begging to be stolen and stole it. Two of the neighborhood bullies, Boomer and Claymore, saw J.T. take the radio. Though they threatened him, even poured soap in his eyes in the school bathrooms, J.T. wouldn't give them the radio as they demanded.

About the same time J.T. found a scrawny, scared little cat with only one eye. Because his mother wouldn't let him take the cat home, J.T. built it a warm but ramshackle little house in an abandoned building. He fed it by charging tuna to his mother's grocery store account without her knowledge. Bones became the only thing in J.T.'s life that he had cared about since his father had walked out.

When Boomer and Claymore found out about Bones, they taunted J.T. by throwing the cat back and forth between them until the frightened cat escaped, darted out into the street and was hit by a car. J.T.'s heart broke as he looked at Bones, but he spoke to no one to tell them of his sadness. Only time, his mother's and grandmother's love and a small kitten from Mr. Rosen, the grocer, helped him recover. On the morning that he decided to accept the kitten, J.T. returned the stolen radio, faced Boomer and Claymore without fear, and asked Mr. Rosen for a job in order to pay for cat food.

The book is oversized and illustrated with photographs from the television movie version. It is not only an excellent story to read aloud but one that will prompt listeners to want to finish it on their own or to reread it. It is now available only in paperback from Dell.

Interest Level: 3-6. Reading Level: 3.1. Further Search Topics: Read Aloud, Courage-Fiction, Best Sellers, Cats-Fiction, Single Parent Family-Fiction, Bullies-Fiction, Blacks-Fiction, Poverty-Fiction, City Life-Fiction, Christmas Stories, Crime-Fiction, Pets-Fiction, Holidays-Fiction.

BOTANY
Branley, Franklyn M. Roots are food finders; illus by Joseph Low. Har-Row 1975, 33 pp.

It really is a shame that the picture book format of this and other *Let's-Read-and-Find-Out-Science-Books* will prevent older children from using them. There is much good information here that is thoroughly and logically explained without patronizing the reader. Functions and types of roots are described. Experiments to show root growth, root hairs, and absorption are given. A very useful book through third grade and possibly fourth grade. Beyond fourth grade children will certainly balk at the book's "babyish" appearance. Let's-Read-and-Find-Out-Science-Book series.

Interest Level: 1-4. Reading Level: 2.2. Further Search Topics: Nature Study, Botany, Group 2, Experiments, Scientific.

BOXING-BIOGRAPHY
Burchard, Marshall. Sports hero: Muhammad Ali. Putnam 1975, 95 pp.

The man who brought a quick tongue as well as fast feet and flying fists to the sport of boxing. Entry for *Sports Hero: Bill Walton* gives series notes. Ring record included here. Sports Hero series.

Interest Level: 3-6. Reading Level: 4.1. Further Search Topics: Boxing-Biography, Blacks-Biography, Ali, Muhammad, Group 2.

BRADSHAW, TERRY

Burchard, Marshall. Sports hero: Terry Bradshaw. Putnam 1980, 95 pp.

Once labeled a "dumb hick," Terry Bradshaw went on to prove he was a talented and thinking quarterback, good enough to be named NFL Player of the Year. He is also a deeply religious man. Reading level of this title varies from 3.1 to 4.1. For more details about the series, see *Sports Hero: Bill Walton.* Sports Hero series.

Interest Level: 3-6. Reading Level: 3.2. Further Search Topics: Biography, Bradshaw, Terry, Football-Biography, Religion-Biography.

BRAINWASHING-FICTION

Curtis, Philip. The invasion of the Brain Sharpeners; illus by Tony Ross. Knopf 1979, 117 pp.

This book is one of a number of books published by Albert Knopf under the series title Capers. They are meant to be (and with few exceptions are) light, easy-to-read fiction, published simultaneously in hardcover and paperback editions. Each book is about 120 pages long with chapter length varying from 9 to 14 pages. Print is plenty large and spacing between lines is always adequate. Plots are built around an idea of guaranteed appeal, descriptive passages are kept to a minimum and action (often suspenseful) abounds. This should, on the whole, be a very useful series. Some entries (i.e., *Man From the Sky* and *Who Stole the Wizard of Oz*, both by Avi) are either too difficult or too obscure to be widely appealing, but they are by far the exceptions to the rule.

Invasion of the Brain Sharpeners is the catchy science fiction story of Michael's successful, but risky, attempt to rid his fifth grade classroom of the overpowering influence of the Brain Sharpeners. The Brain Sharpeners came from another galaxy to search for humans to help them colonize their Planet Five. Humans were so lacking in brain power that the Brain Sharpeners' plan was to periodically expose each child to brain-developing rays, then put them through intensive courses of study guided by their also-exposed teacher. When the children had all learned enough to be beneficial to the Brain Sharpeners, they were to be taken from Earth to Planet Five. Michael was the only one to see the danger they were in and to attempt to stop the plot. He managed to chase the aliens away and to prevent his classmates and teacher from receiving their second dose of rays, but in doing so, he sent the principal to the spaceship. Michael's classmates were thus saved, but his principal was never heard from again. Capers series.

Interest Level: 3-6. Reading Level: 3.1. Further Search Topics: Science Fiction, Flying Saucers-Fiction, Aliens-Fiction, School Stories, Kidnapping-Fiction, Best Sellers, Academic Problems-Fiction, Brainwashing-Fiction.

Slote, Alfred. C.O.L.A.R.; illus by Anthony Kramer. Lippincott 1981, 146 pp.

Jack, his robot twin Danny, and Jack's mother and father were forced to make an emergency landing on an uncharted planet. There they were attacked by creatures who looked like rocks and who wanted to destroy all humans. They captured Danny, led him into an underground living complex, and revealed their true identities. The creatures were robots who had escaped from their owners and the slavery in which they had lived. They kept their planet secret from all humans for fear of what would happen to them should they be discovered. Their main purpose was to free as many robots as possible and to allow robots the same pleasures humans enjoyed. Because Danny had been happy with his humans and claimed to have been treated as one of the family, the inhabitants of the planet C.O.L.A.R. felt he had to be reprogrammed to see the truth. Jack looked and acted so much like Danny that he was able to prevent Danny from being brainwashed, to save his parents from death, and to convince the other robots that some humans treated their robots quite well. In fact, he and Danny, together, were able to persuade the robot manufacturer that a great program of robot-owner re-education was needed.

This is a good adventure story which could also be useful as a lead into discussions of slavery, intelligence, and interpersonal relationships. It is a sequel to *My Robot Buddy*, but one which can be read without having read its predecessor.

Interest Level: 3-5. Reading Level: 3.1. Robots-Fiction, Science Fiction, Outer Space-Fiction, Kidnapping-Fiction, Brainwashing-Fiction, Slavery-Fiction.

BROTHERS AND SISTERS-FICTION

Blume, Judy. Tales of a fourth grade nothing; illus by Roy Doty. Dutton 1972, 120 pp.

Another humorous Blume book that can be counted on to appeal to third and fourth grade readers. If fifth and sixth graders can ignore the title's reference to fourth grade, they too will love it. The story is an exaggeration of a common theme—an older child whose life is in continual turmoil because of a somewhat spoiled younger sibling. Peter's problems with three-year-old Fudge become worse with each chapter until the final disaster when Fudge swallows Peter's pet turtle. Each approximately 15-page chapter is a complete, very funny episode.

Interest Level: 3-6. Reading Level 3.1. Further Search Topics: Humorous Fiction, Turtles-Fiction, Brothers and Sisters-Fiction, Pets-Fiction, Family-Fiction, Read Aloud, Best Sellers, Everyday Stories, Troublemakers-Fiction.

Blume, Judy. Otherwise known as Sheila the great. Dutton 1972, 128 pp.

Sheila first appears in *Tales of a Fourth Grade Nothing* as Peter Thatcher's neighbor. Sheila was a bundle of fears. She was afraid of dogs, thunderstorms, spiders, horses, putting her face in water, and strange noises at night. The summer she and her family rented a house in Tarrytown, New York, she confronted each one of her fears, even mastered one (putting her face in the water) and learned how to swim. That gave her the self-confidence to face a dog without running away. Sheila's progress was aided by her friend Mouse's steadfast belief that a person should always be honest about herself. Sheila's problems are treated realistically and with dignity, yet humorously. Reading level varies greatly from 1.2 - 4.1, therefore, the book is *most* suitable to grades four through six.

Interest Level: 3-6. Reading Level: 3.1. Further Search Topics: Humorous Fiction, Courage-Fiction, Camp-Fiction, Group 2, Vacation-Fiction, Swimming-Fiction, Brothers and Sisters-Fiction, Friendship-Fiction, Everyday Stories.

Blume, Judy. Superfudge. Dutton 1980, 166 pp.

On Fudge's first day in school his older brother Peter had to rescue him from the top of the kindergarten storage cabinets. Later in the school year Fudge's eagerness to join a school guest speaker on stage almost spelled disaster. Then when Fudge unexpectedly disappeared one day everyone, including Peter, thought he had drowned. In addition to Peter's problems with Fudge, Peter had to cope with a baby sister, moving to Princeton, New Jersey, a new job for his mother, and his father's attempts to write a book. Although the book is a sequel and is best enjoyed as such, it can be read alone. It is not as amusing or well-written as it's predecessor, *Tales of a Fourth Grade Nothing*, but will still be popular with young readers.

Interest Level: 3-6. Reading Level 3.1. Further Search Topics: Brothers and Sisters-Fiction, Moving, Household-Fiction, Infants-Fiction, Working Parents-Fiction, School Stories, Family-Fiction, Best Sellers, Humorous Fiction, Everyday Stories.

Bonsall, Crosby. The day I had to play with my sister. Har-Row 1972, 32 pp.

A very easy reader, only slightly less universally appealing and humorous than *And I Mean It, Stanley*. This time a little boy tries very hard to teach his younger sister to play hide-and-seek. He is totally unsuccessful and thoroughly frustrated. Again the story is told as much with pictures as with words. Useful through second grade. Reader format. An Early I Can Read Book.

Interest Level: 1-2. Reading Level: 1.1. Further Search Topics: Humorous Fiction, Games-Fiction, Brothers and Sisters-Fiction, Everyday Stories.

Bulla, Clyde Robert. The ghost of windy hill; illus by Don Bolognese. Har-Row 168, 84 pp.

If the reader doesn't expect a high adventure ghost story, he or she will not be disappointed by this low-keyed tale of a family who goes to live in a house that is supposedly haunted. Mr. Giddings asked the Carver family to move into his country home while he and his wife stayed in Boston. His intent was that the Carvers should either prove to his wife that the house was not haunted or drive the ghost out. The Carvers found no ghosts—at first—only an interesting group of neighbors. There was shy Miss Miggie who drifted around in a long, white dress and wore a flower-covered hat. Bruno was the gruff beggar boy who couldn't walk and had no friends but a goat, until the Carver children came along. Near the end of their stay Lorna Carver mentioned that because they had seen no ghosts the family would soon leave and the Giddings would return. Strange occurrences began almost immediately after Lorna's statement and ended only when the Carvers caught Bruno trying to convince them that he was the ghost. Lorna and Jamie were his only friends, so he had risked his guardians wrath and given up the pretense of being lame to trick the Carvers into staying. All ends well as Bruno's cruel guardian is run off, the Carvers take responsibility for Bruno's care, and Mrs. Giddings admits she made up the ghost story because she hated living in the country and had wanted to return to the city. Another serviceable book in the very successful Bulla style.

Interest Level: 2-5. Reading Level: 2.1. Further Search Topics: Ghosts-Fiction, Brothers and Sisters-Fiction, Orphans-Fiction, Country Life-Fiction, Courage-Fiction, Challenges-Fiction, Friendship-Fiction.

Bulla, Clyde Robert. Pirate's promise; illus by Peter Burchard. Har-Row 1958, 87 pp.

After their mother and father died, Tom and Dinah Pippin had nowhere to go but to their Uncle John's house. Uncle John had no place for them, so he sold Tom into bondage but kept Dinah to help his wife with housework. Tom was to be taken by ship to America where the ship's captain would sell him to the highest bidder. After several years, Tom would be free. But, Tom couldn't accept the idea of one person being another's property, so he spoke out at every opportunity. Tom spoke up to the seaman who dragged him aboard ship, to the captain, to the others who had been bonded, even to the pirate captain who captured their ship. Captain Land was so impressed by Tom's bravery that although he set everyone else he had captured adrift on a small boat, he kept Tom with him. He and Tom became good friends. He never asked Tom to become a pirate and Tom never did. Instead, they enjoyed each other's company. When the pirate ship needed work, they stopped at a safe island where Tom met and impressed Captain Red, a fierce enemy of Captain Land. Captain Red's insistence that Tom join his pirate ship led to another clash between the enemies. Although he was ill, Captain Land fought a duel with Captain Red and lost. Land's last requests were that Benjy, a freed slave who loved him, take all his gold, and that Tom go to Charlestown, South Carolina to find Land's family. Benjy led their flight from Captain Red and arranged a way for Tom to sail to Charlestown before putting Tom on his own. When Tom reached Charlestown he found Land's parents were so angry with Land that at first they didn't even want to hear about him. But, eventually, they not only asked all about their son, but also asked Tom if he and Dinah would like to live with them as their family.

There is enough excitement, danger, and warmth here to satisfy almost any arm-chair adventurer. Usual format of short, episodic chapters.

Interest Level: 3-6. Reading Level 2.1. Further Search Topics: Pirates-Fiction, Seafaring Life-Fiction, Orphans-Fiction, Slavery-Fiction, Brothers and Sisters-Fiction, Best Sellers, Courage-Fiction.

Bulla, Clyde Robert. Marco Moonlight; illus by Julia Noonan. T Y Crowell 1976, 104 pp.

No one could explain Marco's strange, recurring dream. The dream seemed to be about a brother, but Marco had no brother. He had no family but his wealthy grandparents with whom he lived. Marco loved his grandparents very much, but he couldn't help wondering about his own past. He knew only what he and his grandparents could figure out from a few clues. His mother had run away to marry and for three years Marco's grandparents had heard nothing. Then, suddenly, they received a note that she was dying, had parted from her husband, and needed them. By the time they arrived, she was dead and two-year-old Marco could tell them no more. About the time of his thirteenth birthday Marco made friends with a strange man named Flint, who later became the gardener on Marco's grandparents' estate. Rather than live in the room provided for him with the other servants, Flint chose a bleak and isolated beach cottage. Being very careful that no one should suspect, Flint locked Marco into the cottage and forced Marco to change clothes with Matt, who was Marco's long-lost identical twin. Flint and Matt planned that Matt would steal all the money he could from the estate before killing Marco and fleeing. But when Matt began to realize how nice his grandparents were, how much he liked Marco, and how evil Flint was, he decided to thwart Flint's plan. In Matt and Marco's desperate attempt to flee from Flint, Flint was accidentally killed, leaving Marco free to return home and Matt free to find a way to feel he also had the right to claim his heritage before joining Marco.

The tense and dramatic plot immediately involves the reader and the short, fast-paced chapters sustain interest to the end of the book. Readers should also appreciate the small, paperback-size format. A good choice.

Interest Level: 3-6. Reading Level: 2.1. Further Search Topics: Dreams-Fiction, Mystery and Detective Stories, Kidnapping-Fiction, Twins-Fiction, Orphans-Fiction, Grandparents-Fiction, Best Sellers, Brothers and Sisters-Fiction, Jealousy-Fiction, Courage-Fiction.

Bulla, Clyde Robert. Open the door and see all the people; illus by Wendy Watson. T Y Crowell 1972, 69 pp.

A slight story that makes up for its lack of excitement with warmth. When Joann, Teeney and Mama were burned out of their house in the country, they decided it was time to move to the city. With the help of a friend, Mama was quickly able to find a job and an apartment. Only Teeney was noticeably unhappy. She missed her doll and resented anyone else who had one. Then the girls learned about the Toy House, a place to borrow or adopt toys. Both girls found dolls they wanted to adopt. Just before the end of the six week trial period Tenney lost her doll and almost lost her chance to adopt it. After the doll was found and repaired, the people at the Toy House realized how much she wanted the doll and let Teeney keep it.

Because of the ages of the characters, (six and eight), and the subject matter, the book's appeal is doubtful beyond third grade. Print size slightly smaller than usual for Bulla.

Interest Level: 1-3. Reading Level: 2.1. Further Search Topics: Dolls-Fiction, Brothers and Sisters-Fiction, Moving, Household-Fiction, Family-Fiction, Group 2.

Chew, Ruth. No such thing as a witch. Hastings 1971, 112 pp.

Despite the fact that their mother said there was no such thing as a witch, Tad and Nora were convinced that their neighbor Maggie Brown was indeed a witch. And they were right! Maggie Brown knew how to make a special kind of fudge that could make anyone into an animal-lover, enable people to talk with animals, or actually transform someone into an animal. All you had to do was to eat one, two, or three pieces of fudge respectively. But Maggie's overzealous love of animals and her disenchantment with housework eventually attracted the attention of her neighbors and the city health department. Only Tad and Nora's frantic efforts to help her saved Maggie from losing all of her animal friends.

A fairly detailed plot, the fascination of being able to change size and appearance and the intrigue involved in fooling the adults around Maggie make this one of Chew's best books.

Interest Level: 2-5. Reading Level: 2.2. Further Search Topics: Individualists-Fiction, Witches-Fiction, Animals-Fiction, Fantasy, Magic-Fiction, Brothers and Sisters-Fiction, Transformations-Fiction.

Chew, Ruth. The witch's garden. Hastings 1978, 112 pp.

Although its elements seem to promise an exciting adventure story, this is a disappointing book. The witch who moved into the dark, old home next door to Josh and Susan, was trying to improve her overgrown garden when Susan and Josh offered to help. The children accidentally splashed themselves with the witch's newest brew and found they suddenly became very tiny inhabitants of a dense and threatening jungle (the garden). After they regained their normal size, they dug into other areas of the garden. One hole they dug opened into an underground tunnel that they found was inhabited by a fire-breathing dragon. When the dragon cornered Mrs. Muldoon, Susan and Josh ran out of the tunnel, found the brew and splashed it onto the dragon. The dragon shrank away, Mrs. Muldoon was safe and the tunnel closed over.

Because there is little more suspense than in this description, the book fails to live up to its promise. In addition, the children's first sudden size change is just subtle enough to be confusing. Despite its problems the book is popular with Ruth Chew fans and therefore useful.

Interest Level: 2-5. Reading Level: 2.2. Further Search Topics: Witches-Fiction, Brothers and Sisters-Fiction, Magic-Fiction, Fantasy, Dragons-Fiction, Transformations-Fiction.

Chew, Ruth. The would-be witch. Hastings 1976, 112 pp.

Robin and her brother Andy took a liking to the clumsy white cat they saw in Zelda's Antique Shop. The cat apparently liked them, too, for it followed them home. Not having enough money to offer to buy Pearl from Zelda, the children tried to polish up an old pair of silver birds to trade for the cat. The polish turned out to be magical and made the birds real. When they tried the polish on a broom in Zelda's store, the broom began to fly. Upon discovering that Zelda wanted to be a witch but had failed the coven entrance exam, Rob helped her learn to fly and told her of the witches' meeting place that she and Andy had discovered. But the 12 witches who had been turned into cats were wicked enough to want to use Zelda to regain their human form and turn *her* into a cat. In attempting to prevent such a fate, Rob, Andy and Zelda set fire to the abandoned building being used as a meeting place. The 12 witches were rescued from the fire but charged with arson, which meant probable jail sentences for all of them. Zelda, finally a happy and capable witch, gave Pearl to Rob and Andy to thank them for their help.

A better-crafted story than many of the others, this also has a more evil cast of characters to provide additional interest.

Interest Level: 2-5. Reading Level: 2.2. Further Search Topics: Witches-Fiction, Brothers and Sisters-Fiction, Magic-Fiction, Fantasy, Transformations-Fiction, Cats-Fiction.

Chew, Ruth. Earthstar magic. Hastings 1979, 128 pp.

This is one of a series of similar stories by Ruth Chew. Each story involves two children and an old woman they usually suspect is a witch. As their suspicions become convictions they also find that, contrary to their expectation, the witch is very nice and often in need of help.

The children in this tale are brother and sister. Ben and Elizabeth first saw and then didn't see Trudy as she searched for a magical mushroom called an earthstar. Accidentally thrown together again, Ben and Elizabeth took a liking to Trudy, especially when she explained that she had been thrown out of her coven because she was so inept. In fact, she wasn't even able to control the earthstar. The earthstar manages to get all three in and out of adventures (including becoming tiny, flying and almost being eaten) before they learn to control its power. As the story ends, Trudy, finally respected by the other witches, flies off with a promise that Ben and Elizabeth will see her again.

Very lightweight but also very popular with young lovers of witch stories. There seems to be just the right amount of adventure to make up for the very benign witch.

Interest Level: 2-5. Reading Level: 2.2. Further Search Topics: Witches-Fiction, Magic-Fiction, Fantasy, Vacation-Fiction, Brothers and Sisters-Fiction, Transformations-Fiction.

Chew, Ruth. The wishing tree. Hastings 1980, 142 pp.

Peggy and Brian's discovery of a talking cat, a bird with a beautiful song, and a strange and frightening tree led them to a shopping bag lady, a giant named Fred, a gold key and a magical tablecloth. In a rather complicated series of events, the children and the cat finally succeeded in retrieving the tablecloth from Annie (the old woman to whom Puss had loaned it) and giving it back to Fred, who needed it to help satisfy his gigantic appetite. In addition, they returned Fred to normal human size, rescued Annie from a fall on the ice, introduced the two characters and encouraged them to live together in Fred's castle.

Complicated enough already, the story's lengthy adventure that leads up to the discovery of the key (climbing into the magical tree and swimming in a pond) makes the plot even more complex. If a reader doesn't expect more than benign fantasy and fun this is an adequate choice.

Interest Level: 2-5. Reading Level: 2.2. Further Search Topics: Magic-Fiction, Fantasy, Brothers and Sisters-Fiction, Giants-Fiction, Cats-Fiction.

Clifford, Eth. Help, I'm a prisoner in the library; illus by George Hughes. HM 1979, 103 pp.

When their car stopped, Mary Rose and Jo-Beth were left alone in a strange city while their father went to find some gas. Jo-Beth needed to use the bathroom, so the sisters headed for the closest public building they could see, the library. No one saw them go in, so no one knew that they were locked inside when the librarian secured the building for the night. With the lights out and a blizzard outside, the library was a very spooky place. The girls tried calling the police, but the police wouldn't take them seriously. Then they heard groans and eerie moans from the second floor. Gathering all their courage, the girls went to investigate, only to discover the librarian lying hurt and unconscious. Their ingenuity and imagination helped the sisters through the difficult hours before they were all rescued.

Don't read it too carefully or the book's implausibilities will become very evident. Most young readers, however, will enjoy this story for its suspense, spooky atmosphere and adventurous girls, and they will ignore its weaknesses.

Interest Level: 2-5. Reading Level: 3.1. Further Search Topics: Disasters-Fiction, Snow-Fiction, Brothers and Sisters-Fiction, Libraries-Fiction, Survival-Fiction, Courage-Fiction, Group 2.

Clifford, Eth. The dastardly murder of Dirty Pete; illus by George Hughes. HM 1981, 120 pp.

Although this is a sequel to *Help, I'm a Prisoner in the Library*, it does not depend on the previous title, and in fact, is likely to be the more successful introduction to Mary Rose and Jo-Beth Onetree. Given the choice, most young readers will take a mystery set in a ghost town over a mystery set in a library.

Mary Rose, Jo-Beth and their father were on their way across country when they became lost. As night grew closer, the only place they could find to stay was an old hotel in the ghost town where Sorehead Jones had allegedly killed Dirty Pete. It was Sorehead's ghost who was supposed to haunt the town, and indeed there was someone or something who was in the town with the Onetrees. To their surprise, that someone turned out to be Sourdough Sam, an aging actor who had become senile and spent his days acting out all the parts in the Dirty Pete story. The town was only a movie set and the story was only a movie script. The Onetrees discovered the truth bit by bit after a frightening venture into an abandoned gold mine, a harrowing night in the haunted hotel and a jail sentence for Mr. Onetree.

Beware of the rare, very difficult descriptive passage that may cause trouble for some readers.

Interest Level: 2-5. Reading Level: 3.1. Further Search Topics: Mystery and Detective Stories, West-Fiction, Brothers and Sisters-Fiction, Motion Pictures-Fiction, Ghosts-Fiction, Treasure-Fiction, Group 2, Acting-Fiction, Aging-Fiction, Mental Illness-Fiction.

Cohen, Barbara. The carp in the bathtub; illus by Joan Halpern. Lothrop 1972, 48 pp.

Leah and Harry couldn't face the prospect of seeing Joe, their pet carp, made into gefilte fish, even for such a special occasion as the Seder on the first night of Passover. The large, friendly carp had lived in the family's bathtub for over a week. It even swam right over to Leah and Harry to be fed everytime they went into the bathroom. At a time when most children in New York didn't have pets, Joe was as close to being a pet as possible. So, Leah and Harry hid Joe in a neighbor's apartment until their father discovered what they had done. When Joe's destiny was fulfilled, the children had to face a difficult fact of life. A week later, however, their despair became delight, when their father brought home a pet cat.

A short, warm and satisfying story.

Interest Level: 2-5. Reading Level: 3.1. Further Search Topics: Group 2, Jews-Fiction, Religion-Fiction, Pets-Fiction, Passover-Fiction, Family-Fiction, Holidays-Fiction, Read Aloud, Brothers and Sisters-Fiction.

Conford, Ellen. The luck of Pokey Bloom; illus by Bernice Loewenstein. Little 1975, 135 pp.

Pokey Bloom's passion was entering contests. She entered every contest she heard of and always thought she would win. Unfortunately, she never won anything. She even went so far as to practice concentrating three times each day on winning every contest she had entered. Someone who had been interviewed on the radio had *guaranteed* she would win that way. She didn't! It only made more trouble for her at school and at home. Pokey had enough trouble getting along with her older brother and didn't need any more problems at home.

There isn't much plot or direction to this story, but it does have some amusing moments. It is an extra book for the reader who enjoys Judy Blume-type books and wants another story about "regular kids."

Interest Level: 4-6. Reading Level: 3.1. Further Search Topics: Family-Fiction, Contests-Fiction, Brothers and Sisters-Fiction, Humorous Fiction, Everyday Stories.

Danziger, Paula. The pistachio prescription. Delacorte 1978 154 pp.

Just as Cassie entered her freshman year in high school, the old stand-by that had helped her deal with all her problems (eating pistachio nuts) began to fail. To be sure, she did get through the class elections and was elected president. She met and started dating Bernie. She gained self-confidence. She even managed to stand up to a particularly mean teacher. But, eating pistachios didn't help at all at home where Cassie really needed them. She could hardly stand to be in the same room with her older sister. She hated the importance her mother placed on looking right and dressing well. Most of all, she hated the way her parents were constantly fighting. The only person with whom she was really confortable was her brother. But, before the year was over, Cassie's parents decided to get a divorce, she and her sister became friends and Cassie learned to accept her family.

Another Judy Blume-style author, but Danziger's portraits of adults tend to be even more one-dimensional and exaggerated than Blume's. Very popular anyway.

Interest Level: 6+. Reading Level: 5.1. Further Search Topics: Divorce and Separation-Fiction, Family Problems-Fiction, Beauty-Fiction, School Stories, Adolescence-Fiction, Love-Fiction, Brothers and Sisters-Fiction, Everyday Stories.

Foley, Louise Munro. Tackle 22; illus by John Heinly. Delacorte 1978, unp (43 pp).

When their quarterback came down with the mumps, it looked like the Wildcats would have to forfeit the big football game to the Spacemen. But Chub's little brother Herb surprised everyone and saved the game.

Brief and somewhat predictable, the book maintains a light touch that many young readers will like. Heavily illustrated.

Interest Level: 1-4. Reading Level: 2.1. Further Search Topics: Football-Fiction, Brothers and Sisters-Fiction, Humorous Fiction, Group 2.

Greene, Constance C. I and Sproggy; illus by Emily A. McCully. Viking Pr. 1978, 155 pp.

Ten-year-old Adam had adjusted to his parents' divorce and had even grown to like living alone with his mother. When his father came back from London with his new wife and stepdaughter Sproggy and announced that they were moving into an apartment nearby, Adam was a little worried. But when his father asked him to take care of Sproggy, Adam was furious. First of all, he didn't know Sproggy and he didn't want to know her. Secondly, she was two months older than he, taller too, and she embarrassed him in public. And finally, she didn't need his help. She got along quite well by herself; so well that she even saved Adam from a mugger and became good friends with Adam's friends behind his back. It wasn't until Sproggy proved to be vulnerable that Adam and she became friends.

A warm, realistic and humorous story whose interesting characters (even the minor ones) heighten the book's appeal.

Interest Level: 4-6. Reading Level: 3.2. Further Search Topics: Brothers and Sisters-Fiction, Divorce and Separation-Fiction, City Life-Fiction, New York City-Fiction, Humorous Fiction, Friendship-Fiction, Everyday Stories.

Greenfield, Eloise. Talk about a family; illus by James Calvin. Lippincott 1978, 60 pp.

Genny, Kim, and Mac knew something was wrong between their parents, and fully expected that their older brother Larry would be able to fix everything when he came home from the army. But even Larry's welcome home party was almost ruined by their parents' fighting and Kim's reaction. That night, as she listened to Larry and her parents' low voices, Genny was certain that Larry was bringing her parents back together. When her father announced the next morning that he was going to move out, Genny's anger and hurt was directed at Larry. With her friend Mr. Parker's help, Genny finally realized that they were still a family; a family with a new shape, but one that would be able to adjust. A one-theme, realistic and reassuring, short book with good-sized print. Very useful

Interest Level: 3-6. Reading Level: 3.1. Further Search Topics: Divorce and Separation-Fiction, Family Problems-Fiction, Brothers and Sisters-Fiction, Best Sellers.

Harris, Robie H. Rosie's double dare; illus by Tony DeLuna. Knopf 1980, 112 pp.

Rosie wanted to play baseball with the Willard Street Gang, but she couldn't play well enough to play by their rules. She needed what her older brother called "shrimp rules." She couldn't hit a pitched ball, only a grounder; but grounders were "shrimp rules." In desperation Rosie agreed to take a dare that the gang made up. If she actually performed the dare, the gang would let her play with them by her rules.

The gang dared Rosie to sneak into cranky Mr. Quirk's apartment and borrow a set of his false teeth. Because Rosie couldn't find any extra false teeth, she borrowed his wig instead but that didn't satisfy the gang. They only laughed and made up another dare for Rosie. She was to untie Mrs. Samuels' dog and let it run loose. As Rosie untied him, Elmer ran away, Rosie ran off after him. One rainstorm later, Rosie caught up with him in the middle of a Red Sox game at Fenway Park. Rosie's attempt to catch Elmer stopped the game, brought her an interview on TV, and secured her a place on the Willard Street baseball team.

This very light story, made up almost entirely of action and examples of sibling rivalry, should have wide appeal through fifth grade. Beyond that, Rosie's age (almost nine) and childish behavior won't ring true. Capers series.

Interest Level: 2-5. Reading Level: 2.2. Further Search Topics: Baseball-Fiction, Humorous Fiction, Brothers and Sisters-Fiction, Challenges-Fiction, Courage-Fiction, Gangs-Fiction, Everyday Stories.

Heide, Florence Parry. Mystery of the forgotten island; illus by Seymour Fleishman. A. Whitman 1980, 127 pp.

On a small island, unmarked on the map, the Spotlight Club members found old Mr. Whitson, who claimed that he was being kept prisoner by his granddaughter Lorrie and her husband John. Lorrie and John had told him he was being kept in the yard for his own good, so that he wouldn't wander off and get hurt or lost. They had also told him that he should will the island to them so that his daughter Cassie couldn't sell the island to a resort company for development. He was going to be forced to sign such a will unless he could get the children to help him smuggle a new will to his lawyer. Mr. Whitson wasn't convinced that Cassie wanted to sell the island, but he couldn't get in touch with her and he hadn'd had a letter from her in many months.

As the children went to secretly meet Mr. Whitson and mail his new will, they discovered that their trusted friend Guy was attempting to blackmail Lorrie and John into giving him some of the money from the sale of the island. He had evidence that Lorrie and John, not Cassie, wanted to sell the island and were tricking Mr. Whitson into signing a will in their favor. In a daring move, the children were able to free Mr. Whitson and isolate all three of the thieves so that the police could capture them.

This book involves a somewhat more complicated plot and slightly less familiar ingredients than most other Spotlight Club mysteries. One should progress to rather than begin the series with this title. Spotlight Club Mystery series.

Interest Level: 4-6. Reading Level: 3.1. Further Search Topics: Mystery and Detective Stories, Inheritance-Fiction, Gangs-Fiction, Kidnapping-Fiction, Brothers and Sisters-Fiction, Aging-Fiction, Detectives-Fiction.

Heide, Florence Parry. Mystery of the mummy's mask; illus by Seymour Fleishman. A. Whitman 1979, 127 pp.

The Spotlight Club published a neighborhood newspaper. Just as the club was about to take the fourth issue to the printer, Jay discovered an ancient mummy mask hidden near Mr. Pruitt's house. Mr. Pruitt was intrigued by the discovery (he worked at the nearby museum) and he took the mask from Jay, but agreed that Jay could write about the mask for the paper. At about the same time, Dexter discovered that an old, abandoned house was being used. When the printer's office was broken into that night and only their newspaper was stolen, the three children began to suspect that something strange was going on at the abandoned house.

Dexter rode back to the house alone and was captured by Hank, one of three thieves hiding out there. Figuring that they never would have missed one item, Hank had taken the mask from the cache of goods that the other two had stolen. When he overheard Jay's conversation with Mr. Pruitt, Hank realized that his partners would find out what he had done if they ever read the newspaper article. To avoid being discovered, Hank broke into the printer's and stole the paste-up of the paper. In order to keep Dexter from escaping, Hank tied him up and placed him in a shipping crate. When he didn't return as soon as expected, Jay and Cindy realized that Dexter was in trouble, so they went out to the house to search for him. As the three escaped, Dexter and Cindy slashed the thieves' truck's tires, and Jay ran to phone for the police. After several nervous moments in which Cindy and Dexter thought Jay might not get back before they were caught, Jay finally brought the police, who captured all three thieves.

See *Mystery at Southport Cinema* for more information. Spotlight Club Mystery series.

Interest Level: 3-5. Reading Level: 3.1. Further Search Topics: Mystery and Detective Stories, Crime-Fiction, Egypt-Fiction, Archaeology-Fiction, Antiquities-Fiction, Journalism-Fiction, Gangs-Fiction, Brothers and Sisters-Fiction, Detectives-Fiction.

Heide, Florence Parry. The mystery of the silver tag; illus by Seymour Fleishman. A. Whitman 1972, 127 pp.

Jay's paper route took him to one house that he wished he could avoid. It was grumpy, old Mr. Pendleton's house that Jay hated. One rainy day he spotted what he later realized was a prize Angora cat hiding on Mr. Pendleton's porch. When the cat was reported lost in that night's paper, Jay and the other members of the Spotlight Club decided to try to return the cat to its owner, Miss Horton. Their attempts to get the cat back from Mr. Pendleton meant that they had to spy on him, to sneak into his garage, and to spend the night in a treehouse overlooking his house. They were afraid that they had failed when they saw Mr. Pendleton leave with the cat. Determined to be the ones to tell Miss Horton of their failure, they went to her apartment and found Mr. Pendleton already there. Mr. Pendleton was a famous animal photographer who, upon finding the cat, had asked Miss Horton if he could photograph him. The children, thinking only that Mr. Pendleton was a mad scientist who kidnapped cats, had jumped to all the wrong conclusions, but ended with a mystery solved, new friends, and their first lesson in being detectives.

See entry with *Mystery at Southport Cinema* for series information. Spotlight Club Mystery series.

Interest Level: 3-5. Reading Level: 2.2. Further Search Topics: Mystery and Detective Stories, Brothers and Sisters-Fiction, Gangs-Fiction, Cats-Fiction, Loners-Fiction, Detectives-Fiction, Photography-Fiction, Kidnapping-Fiction.

Heide, Florence Parry. Mystery at Southport Cinema; illus by Seymour Fleishman. A. Whitman 1978, 128 pp.

The Spotlight Club was the name Jay, his sister Cindy, and his friend Dexter gave themselves. Their main interest was solving mysteries and just as in Sobol's Encyclopedia Brown series, Hildick's McGurk Mysteries, and Warner books about the Alden children, mysteries seem to follow them around. Their cases are more intricate and lengthy than Encyclopedia Brown's. They involve more danger than most of McGurk's, and they center on more common themes than the Alden's. The series serves much the same audience, however, as the others. It serves those children who want action, intrigue, and the challenge of a mystery, and who don't care about character development or in-depth motivation. The chapters are 8 to 12 pages long, print size is adequate, and the children are normal enough to make this a very popular series. As an added attraction, reading levels here are fairly consistent.

Thorne prided himself on doing his job well, so when the grocery store he ran for Callie (the owner) was robbed by a bearded stranger, Thorne felt responsible. Thorne ran after the thief but lost him in the darkened Southport Cinema. The Spotlight Club members also tried to track the thief. They figured that he had hidden the bag with the stolen money somewhere in the movie house because no one had been seen leaving with such a bag.

In the janitor's lost and found basket Jay found a wig the thief must have used as a disguise. The children called the wig maker to find out who had ordered it and were directed to a local post office box, Jay and Dexter were surprised to find belonged to the grocery store. Because Thorne picked up the mail each day, he became a prime suspect. In the meantime, Cindy had gone back to the cinema to look for the money. In the dark she had scuffled with someone else looking for the money and had given the person a deep scratch on the face.

At the same time that Thorne decided to pay Callie back for the stolen money, the Club members decided to tell Callie their suspicions about him. As Thorne handed his veterinary school savings to Callie, Cindy took a close enough look at Callie's face to see a new scratch and accused her of being the thief. Callie had so wanted Thorne to run the store instead of going to school, and had needed money so intensely, that she had stolen from her own business. The ending is weak but the rest of the book will hold reader interest. Spotlight Club Mystery series.

Interest Level: 3-5. Reading Level: 3.1. Further Search Topics: Mystery and Detective Stories, Gangs-Fiction, Crime-Fiction, Detectives-Fiction, Brothers and Sisters-Fiction.

Heide, Florence Parry. Mystery of the melting snowman; illus by Seymour Fleishman. A. Whitman 1974, 128 pp.

Hidden inside of a snowman, the Spotlight Club found what they believed was a stolen iron statue of a dog. In order to try to catch the thief, the children hid the statue again and watched to see who came to look for it. Eventually they determined that the thief or thieves was either Tom and Jenny, the amenable young couple who were helping Mrs. Wellington sell her house or Alex, the man who seemed to be a detective. After a frightening episode in which Alex almost captured Cindy, the dog, and a cache of Mrs. Wellington's diamonds (hidden in a secret compartment to which the dog held the key), Cindy managed to lock Alex in a closet long enough to enable Jay and Dexter to alert Mrs. Wellington to what was happening. The case was closed as Mrs. Wellington revealed Alex to be her greedy, young nephew, whom she had indulged once too often, but would not indulge again.

See *Mystery at Southport Cinema* for series information. Spotlight Club Mystery series.

Interest Level: 3-5. Reading Level: 2.2. Further Search Topics: Mystery and Detective Stories, Gangs-Fiction, Crime-Fiction, Brothers and Sisters-Fiction, Detectives-Fiction, Inheritance-Fiction.

Heide, Florence Parry. Mystery of the midnight message; illus by Seymour Fleishman. A. Whitman 1977, 128 pp.

The challenge to the Spotlight Club this time was to stop a crime before it happened. Jay and his sister Cindy were on a bus trip home when a blizzard forced the bus to stop at a motel for the night. Jay answered the room telephone late that night and heard a woman's strange and stern instructions. The instructions were to say nothing, to look in the desk drawer for directions, to expect that Bee had the other half of the instructions, and to be at the place at 8:00 the next evening. The envelope, which Jay and Cindy found, showed the location of and half the combination to someone's bedroom safe.

Early the next morning, the children found themselves fleeing in terror from the evil Scull, the man who was supposed to have received the message. Scull pursued them as they escaped in a friendly salesman's car, caught them and locked them into a cold barn without jackets. When the two were finally back on the road and reunited with Dexter and his sister Anne, they had only a few hours and fewer clues to help them find Woodvale and Jeremiah Gibbon, the intended victim.

Despite difficult driving conditions in the snow, Anne managed to get the children to their destination a few minutes before the thieves arrived. Anne and Jeremiah's secretary left the house together to get the police while the Spotlight Club members and Mr. Gibbon hid near the safe. A few tense minutes later, the case was closed; Mr. Gibbons' money was safe, the ringleader had been named (Mr. Gibbon's doctor), and the thieves had been caught.

See *Mystery at Southport Cinema* for series information. Spotlight Club Mystery series.

Interest Level: 3-5. Reading Level: 3.1. Further Search Topics: Mystery and Detective Stories, Crime-Fiction, Snow-Fiction, Disasters-Fiction, Gangs-Fiction, Brothers and Sisters-Fiction, Detectives-Fiction.

Heide, Florence Parry. Mystery of the vanishing visitor; illus by Seymour Fleishman. A. Whitman 1975, 128 pp.

Cindy was hired to take care of Mrs. Widget's house, animals, and plants for a weekend. That same weekend, someone tried to find and steal something from Mrs. Widget's overcrowded house. She had very few empty spaces in her house, so it was not a surprise that the thief wasn't able to find the object of his or her search. The three Spotlight Club members were determined to figure out not only who was the thief, but also what it was that the thief, wanted. Their prime suspects included the very nasty Bertha Beaker and the charming Charley Capp.

After spending a night in Mrs. Widget's house trying to, and almost succeeding in catching the thief, the children were surprised by an early morning visit from Mr. Capp. Mr. Capp was nearly able to steal away with a painting that hid a great deal of money before Cindy figured out that he was the thief. Even after Mr. Capp had been caught, he charmed his way out of any punishment and left before anyone had second thoughts.

See entry for *Mystery at Southport Cinema* for series information. Spotlight Club Mystery series.

Interest Level: 3-5. Reading Level: 2.2. Further Search Topics: Mystery and Detective Stories, Brothers and Sisters-Fiction, Gangs-Fiction, Crime-Fiction, Antiquities-Fiction, Detectives-Fiction.

Hinton, Susan E. The outsiders. Viking Pr. 1967, 188 pp.

When she wrote this book Susan Hinton was only 17 years old, but she had the sensitivity of someone much older. She wrote a taut story of the rivalry between two city gangs; the Socs (the rich socialites) and the Greasers (poor kids from the wrong side of town) that is more than anything a plea for understanding and tolerance. Seen through the eyes of Ponyboy (a very bright, 14-year-old Greaser), the rivalry brought on violence and an accidental killing that forced Pony and his friend Johnny to flee for their lives. Dallas, the meanest and most dangerous of the Greasers, provided them with shelter, food for a week, and a gun. At the end of that week, Johnny decided that they should turn themselves in to the police. But before they could do that, their hideout (an old church) burned in a fire which threatened the lives of four children who had been playing there. In trying to rescue the children, Johnny, Pony, and Dallas were injured; Johnny was severely burned and probably permanently crippled. A vengeance rumble was held while Johnny lay in the hospital, but the Greasers' victory was empty when Johnny died. He had been the one member of the gang whom they all loved and who had most needed them. Dallas went to pieces: he robbed a store and set himself up to be killed by the police. He had nothing left to live for after Johnny's death. Pony found support and security with his brothers (their parents were dead) and, in a note from Johnny, some hope for the future.

Hinton speaks most often through Pony (his depth of understanding of the people around him is very impressive), but through Johnny and two of the Socs as well, Randy and Cherry. Her message is clear, but at no time does she fail to maintain believable characters in a compelling plot.

Although the book looks forbidding with its 188 pages of unrelenting small print, it is an exciting story, full of adventure, realism, and room for thought. Perhaps the best way to introduce this book is to read a fair portion of it aloud. Now a motion picture too.

Interest Level: 6+. Reading Level: 5.1. Further Search Topics: Crime-Fiction, Gangs-Fiction, Murder-Fiction, Read Aloud, Friendship-Fiction, Juvenile Delinquency-Fiction, Best Sellers, City Life-Fiction, Brothers and Sisters-Fiction, Orphans-Fiction, Runaways-Fiction, Troublemakers-Fiction, Poverty-Fiction.

Hurwitz, Johanna. Aldo Ice Cream; illus by John Wallner. Morrow 1981, 124 pp.

Aldo got his newest nickname (Ice Cream) from his friend DeDe when she heard that Aldo not only wanted to try every flavor of ice cream at the local store, but wanted to buy an ice cream freezer for his sister's birthday as well. Aldo decided his summer project would be to earn enough money for the freezer, but he soon found out that there were very few ways a nine-year-old boy could earn $49.95. In the meantime, he helped his mother deliver food for a Meals-On-Wheels project, learned to swim, found out about fish from Mr. Puccini, and shared his cat with Mrs. Nardo. As the summer came to an end he saw one last opportunity to earn enough money for the ice cream maker. A local shoe store offered a new pair of sneakers to the child who owned the most worn out pair. Aldo convinced his mother that if he won the sneakers, she should pay him the money she would otherwise have had to spend on his new sneakers. Aldo set about making sure that his already well-worn sneakers were the most dilapidated in town. A few days before the sneaker contest the hardware store lowered the price on the ice cream freezer to a point where Aldo could afford it if he won the sneakers. When Aldo did win, just as he knew he would, he and his mother bought the very last freezer in the store.

It is not as well-constructed a story as *Aldo Applesauce*, but for established Aldo fans, or those who want quiet, reassuring fiction, this is a usable title.

Interest Level: 3-4. Reading Level: 3.1. Further Search Topics: Humorous Fiction, Brothers and Sisters-Fiction, Vacation-Fiction, Occupations-Fiction, Everyday Stories, Aging-Fiction, Family-Fiction, Contests-Fiction.

Lowry, Lois. Anastasia Krupnik. HM 1979, 113 pp.

Anastasia Krupnik led a comfortable, relatively happy life until her parents announced that she was not going to be an only child for much longer. After 10 years of enjoying that luxury, Anastasia wasn't at all pleased with the change. Babies immediately went to a prominent, and as far as Anastasia was concerned, permanent place on her list of hates. Anastasia kept two lists: one for things and people she particularly liked, and one list for what she did not like. What went on and off the lists tells much about Anastasia. Anastasia tells the rest in this perceptive, sensitive, and humorous story of growing up and adjusting to a new sibling.

Spacing between lines is slightly too narrow for the rather large print.

Interest Level: 4-6. Reading Level: 3.1. Further Search Topics: Humorous Fiction, Brothers and Sisters-Fiction, Everyday Stories, Jealousy-Fiction, Infants-Fiction, Best Sellers, Children-Growth-Fiction.

Moore, Lilian. The snake that went to school; illus by Mary Stevens. Random 1957, 99 pp.

Hank's pet snake Puffy disappeared from the Science Room at school and his little brother, Benjy (in first grade) became ill on the same day. Hank was so worried about finding Puffy that he hardly thought about his pesky little brother, until Puffy was found two days later. Then Hank learned that Benjy had secretly gone to visit Puffy, after being rejected by Hank and had accidentally let the snake out of its cage. Benjy had been so worried about letting the snake out that he had actually made himself ill. Hank finally realized that Benjy wasn't the pest he had thought he was, and promised to be a better older brother.

A somewhat old-fashioned but satisfying story told in ten short chapters.

Interest Level: 2-4. Reading Level: 3.1. Further Search Topics: Pets-Fiction, Snakes-Fiction, Brothers and Sisters-Fiction, School Stories.

Parish, Peggy. Haunted house; illus by Paul Frame. Macmillan 1971, 151 pp.

Although this is the third book about Jed, Bill and Liza Roberts, it too can be read out of order. This time the family has moved into what was locally known as a haunted house. Very shortly after they moved into the house, a coded note appeared that led them to a series of messages and unusual occurrences. Lights that flashed into Liza's room turned out to be the headlights of cars, but the messages and a secret compartment in an old clock couldn't be as easily explained. Each day took them closer to the surprise that the messages hinted would be theirs. That surprise turned out to be three kittens and a treehouse. Two of the children's best friends had planned the whole mystery just to lead to the surprises.

This book has the same faults and strong points as the others about the Roberts children. Each chapter is short; the book is episodic; reading level is consistent; there is much dialogue and action and little description, and the plot has a comfortable familiarity about it. It can be very useful to the right readers.

Interest Level: 1-4. Reading Level: 2.1. Further Search Topics: Mystery and Detective Stories. Brothers and Sisters-Fiction, Ghosts-Fiction, Moving, Household-Fiction, Nonverbal Communication-Fiction, Group 2.

Parish, Peggy. Hermit Dan; illus by Paul Frame. Macmillan 1977, 151 pp.

When the Roberts children tried to prove that Pirate Island really had been used by pirates, they encountered more action and intrigue than they had found in any of their earlier adventures. Liza, Bill and Jed suspected that Hermit Dan knew whether or not there had been pirates on the island, but he was so gruff and apparently mean that they didn't dare ask him any questions. Instead, they trailed and spied on him and asked questions of anyone who had known Hermit Dan as a child. It was rumored that his ancestors had actually been pirates. Until a terrible fire that had destroyed all they owned, Hermit Dan's family had been very wealthy. However, no one knew how they had become so rich.

In an attempt to see what the summer residents knew about Hermit Dan, the children introduced themselves to the vacationing youngsters. Among the visitors the Roberts met Hank and Ted, brothers bent on bullying Hermit Dan. When the children were rescued from a severe sandstorm by Hermit Dan, they were surprised to find that he wasn't nearly as gruff as he appeared. In fact they began to feel quite protective of the old man. Thus when Hank and Ted stole a secret box that held all of Hermit Dan's valuables, it was the Roberts children who fought (literally) to get the box back. It was after Liza, Bill and Jed returned the box to Hermit Dan, however, that the real surprises began: these included a surprise party for Hermit Dan, his wish to be friendly, and his gift to the children of three pieces of eight that proved his family members were pirates.

This title's more interesting and involved plot makes the book more likely to be a success with older readers than the other stories about the Roberts children. Otherwise it shares the same format, faults and strengths as the other series titles.

Interest Level: 2-5. Reading Level: 2.1. Further Search Topics: Mystery and Detective Stories, Pirates-Fiction, Vacation-Fiction, Loners-Fiction, Treasure-Fiction, Bullies-Fiction, Brothers and Sisters-Fiction, Grandparents-Fiction.

Parish, Peggy. Clues in the woods; illus by Paul Frame. Macmillan 1968, 154 pp.

The books about the three Roberts children share problems that are obvious to adults and felt by some young readers as well, but they continue to be popular with undemanding young readers. The characters are very white and middle class and their actions often fit out-of-date stereotypes. The plots have few surprises or suspense, but the reading levels are consistent and the very predictability of the books makes them familiar and therefore comfortable.

This particular story takes place at the end of the same summer the children solved the mystery of *The Key to the Treasure*. The children were alerted by their grandmother to the disappearance of food scraps, left outside the house. Thinking that two runaway children, about whom they had read, had taken the food, Liza, Bill, and Jed tried to find the runaways. Their attempts eventually brought them new friends and thus the solution to their mystery. It had not been the runaways who had taken the food, it was their new friends' dog.

Interest Level: 1-4. Reading Level: 2.2. Further Search Topics: Mystery and Detective Stories, Brothers and Sisters-Fiction, Vacation-Fiction, Dogs-Fiction, Runaways-Fiction, Grandparents-Fiction, Group 2.

Parish, Peggy. Key to the treasure; illus by Paul Frame. Macmillan 1966, 154 pp.

This is the first of the stories about Jed, Bill and Liza Roberts. The three children are very middle-class, the book's plots are simple and often lack suspense, but the stories still enjoy widespread popularity among unsophisticated readers.

All three children went to spend the summer with their grandparents and decided to tackle a mystery left unsolved for over 75 years. An old drawing and an authentic war bonnet provided the only clues to finding three Indian artifacts. At each step along the way there were crumbled, brittle pieces of paper bearing coded messages that led to the next clue. The search ended when the children found that a storage area in a porch piller contained an Indian doll, mask, and leather shield that had belonged to their great-grandfather.

Interest Level: 1-4. Reading Level: 2.1. Further Search Topics: Vacation-Fiction, Brothers and Sisters-Fiction, Group 2, Mystery and Detective Stories, Grandparents-Fiction, Nonverbal Communication-Fiction.

Parish, Peggy. Pirate Island adventure; illus by Paul Frame. Macmillan 1975, 167 pp.

Although this is the fourth book in the series about the Roberts children, none of the titles must be read in chronological order. This time the three rather privileged children spent the summer with their grandparents on a resort island. They lived in a house that their family had owned for years, explored the island, and swam in their own private cove. But, most of their time was spent trying to solve an old mystery. Their great-uncle had hidden several very special items (one for each member of his family) years earlier, and had left only one clue with their grandfather. After he gave the children that clue it was only a matter of time before they found the hidden treasures.

This book is also lengthy, but is divided into 22 very manageable chapters. It is, like the others, almost entirely dialogue and action, which makes it especially appealing to young reluctant readers.

Interest Level: 1-4. Reading Level: 2.1. Further Search Topics: Mystery and Detective Stories, Vacation-Fiction, Treasure-Fiction, Brothers and Sisters-Fiction, Grandparents-Fiction, Group 2.

Pevsner, Stella. And you give me a pain, Elaine. HM 1978, 182 pp.

Andrea was the youngest of three children. She was very close to her brother, Joe, but he was away at college. There was only Elaine at home, but Andrea and Elaine didn't get along at all. Elaine was a troubled young woman who took so much of her parents' attention that there was none left for Andrea. This is the story of Andrea's year in eighth grade, a year in which she discovered that she was a steady and strong person. It was the year in which Andrea worked on the school play, had her first boyfriend, weathered the storms when her sister ran away, and began to understand her sister more and resent her less. It was also the year that she had to learn to live with her brother's accidental death.

The author's Judy Blume style (but with less humor) guarantees readers among older children.

Interest Level: 5-6. Reading Level: 4.1. Further Search Topics: Family Problems-Fiction, Brothers and Sisters-Fiction, Love-Fiction, Death-Fiction, Runaways-Fiction, Troublemakers-Fiction, Adolescence-Fiction.

Renner, Beverly. The Hideaway summer; illus by Ruth Sanderson. Har-Row 1978, 134 pp.

On their way to summer camp, Addie suddenly got off the bus and took her younger brother Clay to see the place where Addie had spent prior summer vacations. It was their grandmother's house and a small cabin called the Hideaway. The house had been sold after their grandmother had died that year, but Addie's father had decided to keep the Hideaway. Much to Addie's surprise she found the Hideaway beautifully fixed-up, just as Gram had promised she would do one day.

When they missed the last bus out of the tiny town and realized that they had enough money to buy the food they would need, Addie and Clay decided to make the Hideaway their summer home. One phone call to the camp and weekly calls to their father kept people from worrying about them. Their discovery of two small raccoons meant that their days were filled with caring for and training the animals. In addition, they had to build a warning system so that no one would discover them and they had to get their food and provisions from town about every two weeks without being too noticeable. They even had to figure out a way to survive a wild summer storm, a flood, and poachers who hunted raccoons. By summer's end Addie and Clay had grown independent, resourceful, and very close to each other.

An exciting story whose short chapters and fairly short sentences keep the reading level reasonably low. Print is dark and of adequate size, but space between the lines is somewhat narrow.

Interest Level: 4-6. Reading Level: 3.1. Further Search Topics: Brothers and Sisters-Fiction, Runaways-Fiction, Pets-Fiction, Survival-Fiction, Vacation-Fiction, Raccoons-Fiction, Read Aloud.

Roy, Ron. Nightmare Island; illus by Robert MacLean. Dutton 1981, 69 pp.

Harley didn't want to take his younger brother camping, but because he had promised his father he would, the boys packed a tent, sleeping bags, and plenty of food into a small boat and set off to nearby Little Island. Hidden in his pocket, Harley had matches and marshmallows for a midnight marshmallow roast. After they had finished the bag of marshmallows, Harley threw the last log of the fire into the water. The water erupted into flames that quickly spread around the island. As the boys fought desperately to save themselves and to find shelter, they realized that the large shape they had seen in the distance must have been an oil tanker that had spread an oil slick all around the island. With time running out Harley gave his brother the only truly secure shelter from the fire, curled up on top of a tall rock and went to sleep. When he awoke the fire had burned itself out and help was on the way.

Most young readers will be able to suspend disbelief long enough to enjoy this as an exciting adventure and survival story, but it is hard to believe that two young boys could not only survive such a holocaust, but that they could sleep through part of it, too. It is also difficult to believe that there would not be more of a fuss made about the oil tanker blowing up. Plot problems aside, young readers seem to love the story.

Interest Level: 3-6. Reading Level: 3.2. Further Search Topics: Brothers and Sisters-Fiction, Survival-Fiction, Camping-Fiction, Disasters-Fiction, Best Sellers.

Sachs, Marily. The bears' house; illus by Louis Glanzman. Doubleday 1971, 81 pp.

Don't let the benign appearance of this book fool you. This is a disturbing, almost brutal story. It is the story of Fran Ellen, a fourth grader with more problems than anyone should have to shoulder at one time. Her father had left the family and her mother had had a mental breakdown. Fran Ellen and her older brother were left with responsibility for themselves, their mother, and three other children (including a baby). They were all ill-fed, poorly dressed, and unwashed. Neither the social worker nor Fran Ellen's teacher knew the extent of the family's problems. Fran Ellen's only happiness came from her baby sister and from a schoolroom model (of *Goldilocks and the Three Bears* and their house) into which she mentally retreated whenever she had the chance.

As the school year closed, Fran Ellen's teacher visited her home to deliver the bears' house and discovered Fran Ellen's mother and very sick baby sister. Although she hated the idea that the family might have to split up, Fran Ellen had matured enough to realize that when her teacher insisted that she would get help for the family, her teacher was taking the proper action.

The book is inappropriately illustrated to make it appear cute and even humorous. The story is far from either. It is so stark that it probably shouldn't have been illustrated at all. And because the hope that is present in the book's ending is very subtle, a review and a discussion may be necessary to help relieve some young readers' anxieties.

Interest Level: 5-6. Reading Level: 3.1. Further Search Topics: Divorce and Separation-Fiction, Challenges-Fiction, Poverty-Fiction, Family Problems-Fiction, Loners-Fiction, Survival-Fiction, Mental Illness-Fiction, Brothers and Sisters-Fiction.

Smith, Alison. Help! There's a cat washing in here!; illus by Amy Rowen. Dutton 1981, 152 pp.

Henry Walker agreed to care for his younger brother and sister for two weeks so that his mother could spend her time preparing a portfolio of her art work in the hopes of getting a much-needed job. It was a desperate move for Henry, but it was the only way he could prevent his bossy Aunt Wilhemina from moving in to run the household. Despite Henry's best efforts, almost everything seemed to go wrong. He burned the food, couldn't keep his brother and sister from misbehaving, seemed to have poisoned his sister's friend, and was faced with making a costume in one night for a school play. The worst of it all was that his mother wasn't pleased with what she was drawing, and Henry only seemed to make her feel more discouraged and unhappy. After what appeared to be certain defeat, however, Henry's efforts were rewarded. His mother was given the job, the family proved they could take care of themselves, and all ended happily.

A light, humorous tale of a young boy's growing independence and maturation under stress and increased responsibility.

Interest Level: 4-6. Reading Level: 3.1. Further Search Topics: Brothers and Sisters-Fiction, Working Parents-Fiction, Single Parent Family-Fiction, Humorous Fiction, Family-Fiction, Challenges-Fiction, Children-Growth-Fiction.

Warner, Gertrude Chandler. Mountain top mystery; illus by David Cunningham. A. Whitman 1964, 128 pp.

A day's climb up and down Old Flat Top was all the Alden family had wanted. Instead, when a portion of the trail collapsed into a cave, they found themselves stranded on top of the mountain. From their vantage point that night they could see a shadowy light which they investigated the next day. They found a 90-year-old Indian woman who had a strange story to tell of treasure hidden in a cave somewhere on Old Flat Top. The treasure was rightfully hers as the last of her tribe, but she had never been able to find it. The collapse of the trail and the reopening of the cave attracted more attention than just the Alden's though. Both an expert on caves and a young Indian boy wanted to find out more about the cave. David, the Indian boy, turned out to be the old woman's grandnephew. The treasure was indeed unearthed; David and Lovan were reunited; the treasure was given to Lovan, and both David's and Lovan's futures were secured.

What in the other books is mild stereotyping becomes more noticeable here (the books are all around 20 years old). The print is smaller here than before but the spacing between the lines is adequate. See entry for *The Boxcar Children* for more information.

Interest Level: 3-6. Reading Level: 2.2. Further Search Topics: Mystery and Detective Stories, Treasure-Fiction, Survival-Fiction, Indians of North

America-Fiction, Mountain Climbing-Fiction, Brothers and Sisters-Fiction.

Warner, Gertrude Chandler. Schoolhouse mystery; illus by David Cunningham. A. Whitman 1965, 128 pp.

On a dare, the Aldens went to a quiet fishing village to see what excitement they could find there. They found an isolated town filled with poor and unfriendly people. In their attempt to get to know the townspeople, the Aldens learned of the children's desire for schooling and the adults' anticipation of the Money Man's arrival. The Alden children took on the task of teaching school for the summer in an abandoned schoolhouse owned by Miss Gray, a recluse. The Money Man intrigued them more with each new bit of information they learned about him. They finally decided that the Money Man was a swindler who was practically stealing valuable antiques away from the villagers. By spying on the Money Man when he used the schoolhouse to store the antiques, the Aldens and an ex-FBI man were able to capture him. When the vacation was over, the Aldens had once more found excitement, Miss Gray had agreed to teach the local school, the Money Man was on his way to jail, and the townspeople knew the value of their old household items.

See the entry for *The Boxcar Children* for more information.

Interest Level: 3-5. Reading Level: 2.2. Further Search Topics: Mystery and Detective Stories, Vacation-Fiction, School Stories, Antiquities-Fiction, Crime-Fiction, Brothers and Sisters-Fiction, Challenges-Fiction.

Warner, Gertrude Chandler. The boxcar children; illus by L. Kate Deal. A. Whitman 1950, 154 pp.

This is the first in a series of very early hi/lo books. Although they often bear signs of stilted "Dick and Jane"-style writing, occasionally preach to the reader, and are interrupted by frequent asides from the author, the stories are still popular with young readers. In each book the children are not simply manipulated, but control their own destiny. They fulfill many a child's dream of finding a loving home and family, becoming rich, having adventures, and solving mysteries. This is the simplest story of the series, most of the other entries assume interest in such advanced subjects as fossils, food sources, antiques, or the Revolutionary War.

The only place the four orphaned Alden children had to live was with a grandfather whom they had never met, but whom they had heard was mean. Rather than live with him, they decided to try and survive on their own. They found an abandoned railway boxcar and filled it was items that they found in a junkyard in order to make it their home. Henry, the oldest, went to work for a doctor who, in addition to money, gave him food and kept a silent but watchful eye over all the children without their knowledge. When Violet became ill, the children had no choice but to take her to Dr. Moore. He gave them all a temporary home and arranged for them to gradually get to know their grandfather. By the time Violet was almost well the children had grown to like the elderly stranger. It was a happy day when the children finally realized that the man to whom Dr. Moore had introduced them was really their grandfather.

Interest Level: 1-4. Reading Level: 2.1. Further Search Topics: Orphans-Fiction, Survival-Fiction, Runaways-Fiction, Brothers and Sisters-Fiction, Grandparents-Fiction.

Warner, Gertrude Chandler. The woodshed mystery; illus by David Cunningham. A. Whitman 1960, 159 pp.

The four Alden children have grown since their first appearance in *The Boxcar Children* but they are still as close a family as ever. Aunt Jane's telephone message that she wanted to move near them started this adventure. Grandfather proceeded to buy and refurbish his childhood home as a surprise for Aunt Jane. It was an easy house to buy because it had been abandoned and was thought to be haunted. Even though the children and Aunt Jane weren't really worried by the stories of odd occurrences that no one quite remembered, they began to be aware of strange noises and things missing. Upon investigation they discovered Aunt Jane's old boyfriend living in the woodshed in the forest. There beneath the floor of the woodshed, they also found a store of Revolutionary War supplies and a letter from the original owners of the house. The supplies and the letter helped to explain some of the stories. Andrew, Jane's long-lost boyfriend, explained the rest.

It is not necessary to have read any of the series in order to read this story, but those children who enjoyed *The Boxcar Children* are most likely to enjoy the Alden's further adventures. See the entry for *The Boxcar Children* for more information.

Interest Level: 3-5. Reading Level: 2.1. Further Search Topics: Mystery and Detective Stories, United States-History-War-Fiction, Brothers and Sisters-Fiction, Ghosts-Fiction, Vacation-Fiction.

Young, Carol Beach. Remember me when I am dead. Elsevier-Nelson 1980, 94 pp.

This is a short but taut story about the effect of their mother's death upon two young girls. For a long time Jenny, the younger and more vivacious of the sisters, refused to believe her mother had really died. Sara, quiet and serious, mourned and missed her mother, but eventually accepted her mother's sudden death as a fact. Jenny's continuing denial prompted her father and stepmother to talk of sending her away to a school where memories wouldn't be so vivid. That talk inspired Sara to develop a devious and calculated plan to insure that Jenny would indeed be sent away. All her life Sara had been given less attention than Jenny. With Jenny gone, Sara would finally have her father and stepmother's love and attention all to herself. With a Hitchcock-like twist Sara's plan proved too successful. Jenny was sent away to school, but because she didn't want to go alone and because her parents could deny Jenny nothing, Sara was to go too.

This suspenseful psychological thriller is almost guaranteed success with older readers.

Interest Level: 5-6. Reading Level: 4.2. Further Search Topics: Mystery and Detective Stories, Brothers and Sisters-Fiction, Death-Fiction, Horror-Fiction, Best Sellers, Jealousy-Fiction.

BULLIES

Bryant, Bernice. George Gershwin: young composer; illus by Nathan Goldstein. Bobbs 1965, 200 pp.

Even when George Gershwin was very young he loved music, showed signs of musical talent, and longed to play the piano. However, any boy who played the piano in George's neighborhood was called a sissy and George didn't like being teased in that way. When he was no longer able to keep his music lessons a secret, he stopped them for fear of the teasing. But each time George quit playing the piano, he always went back to it, even when his parents pressured him not to waste his time at the piano. A young teacher told George that he would never be a musician. One of George's teachers actually taught him to play poorly, instead of well. In time, however, George learned to play well and to compose his own music. Then came the hard work of determining his own style. Gradually, more and more people heard and appreciated his American jazz, until George Gershwin's music was heard all around the world.

Another adequate entry in the *Childhood of Famous Americans* series. Includes the usual glossary, bibliography, time line, and follow-up questions. It is most likely to appeal to the reader already interested in music. Childhood of Famous Americans series.

Interest Level: 3-6. Reading Level: 3.1. Further Search Topics: Biography, Composers, Immigration and Emigration-Biography, Jazz Music, Bullies, Music-Biography, Pianists.

BULLIES-FICTION

Blume, Judy. Blubber. Bradbury 1974, 153 pp.

Jill, like all the other fifth graders in her class, did exactly as Wendy directed her. When Wendy nicknamed one of the class members Blubber and launched a campaign against her, Jill joined right in. It wasn't until the tables were turned and Jill became Wendy's next victim that Jill realized how much it hurt to be the target of such nastiness. It was only then that Jill could stand up to Wendy. Wendy's meanness is extreme and her classmates, without exception, actively follow her lead, yet all adult characters in the book are blind to what happens. Despite those drawbacks, the book deals with a problem very real to children and thus it has guaranteed audience appeal.

Interest Level: 4-6. Reading Level: 3.1. School Stories, Bullies-Fiction, Weight-Fiction, Loners-Fiction, Gangs-Fiction, Read Aloud, Cruelty-Fiction, Best Sellers, Troublemakers-Fiction, Friendship-Fiction.

Burch, Robert. Queenie Peavy; illus by Jerry Lazare. Viking Pr. 1966, 159 pp.

Queenie was always in trouble. She could be mean, really mean, but, she was also bright, talented, independent and resilient. Queenie blamed her problems on the fact that people teased her because her father was in jail and because she was poor. She thought that she had to defend herself against the world. Queenie was proud of her poor reputation until she accidentally-on-purpose caused a classmate to break his leg. Then, when her father returned home and wasn't the person she'd hoped he'd be, Queenie realized that only she could make her life better. Being the strong person she was, she set out to do just that.

Queenie is a wonderfully alive and sympathetic character, one well worth introducing to older readers despite the book's reading level. Print somewhat small. Line spacing average width.

Interest Level: 5-6. Reading Level: 5.1. Further Search Topics: Family Problems-Fiction, Crime-Fiction, Loners-Fiction, Poverty-Fiction, Humorous Fiction, Bullies-Fiction, Troublemakers-Fiction, Academic Problems-Fiction, Read Aloud.

Byars, Betsy. The 18th emergency; illus by Robert Grossman. Viking Pr. 1973, 126 pp.

When your best friend knows how to escape from the world's 17 worst emergencies and you're faced with the eighteenth, you're in trouble. That was the spot in which Mouse found himself one day. He had drawn an arrow towards a large picture of the Neanderthal man and written Marv Hammerman's name. Hammerman had seen him do it and was out to kill, maim, or at least beat up Mouse. Mouse finally

ran out of ways to avoid Hammerman and had to face the fight. When it was over and he was once again able to stand up, Mouse realized he felt better for having allowed Hammerman to regain his honor and for having taken responsibility for his own actions.

A funny, fast-moving look at real feelings of fear, honor and responsibility. Very popular. Print is dark and of good size but lines could have been spaced farther apart.

Interest Level: 4-6. Reading Level: 3.2. Further Search Topics: Bullies-Fiction, Humorous Fiction, Courage-Fiction, Best Sellers, Challenges-Fiction, Read Aloud.

Conford, Ellen. The revenge of the incredible Dr. Rancid and his youthful assistant, Jeffrey. Little 1980, 119 pp.

There were two people Jeff hated and feared: Dewey Belasco, the sixth grade bully and Lana McCabe, Dewey's female counterpart. Only in his imagination could Jeff stand up to them. In the stories Jeff wrote in a notebook, he and his friend Dr. Rancid were superheroes who rid the world of such scum as Lana and Dewey. In real life, Jeff ran from bullies rather than face them; even if it meant that an eight-year-old boy and a girl Jeff's age were left to stand up to Dewey by themselves. Although the way Jeff took care of an injured child soon had most everyone thinking of Jeff as a hero, he saw that, too, as an indication of his failings at first. Finally, something inside Jeff snapped and he answered Dewey back when Dewey insulted him. Before long Jeff found himself flat on his back with a bloody nose and so many pains he couldn't count them. But, he had finally faced Dewey and showed Dewey that he was no longer afraid. Jeff felt good.

Similar to *The 18th Emergency* but a higher reading level. The notebook stories will appeal to fans of superheroes, but because they are stories within a story, they may also cause difficulties. Spacing between lines is somewhat narrow.

Interest Level: 5-6. Reading Level: 4.2. Further Search Topics: Courage-Fiction, Bullies-Fiction, Writing-Fiction, School Stories, Superheroes-Fiction, Humorous Fiction.

Corbett, Scott. The lemonade trick; illus by Paul Galdone. Little 1960, 103 pp.

This is the first book in a series of quite enjoyable stories (most of which are, unfortunately, too difficult to recommend here). Kerby was given an odd chemistry set by a strange old woman whom he helped one day. When he used the set to put together a brew, Kerby found himself completely under its spell. The sweet-smelling liquid he had concocted forced him to be good, so good that his parents began to worry about him. Luckily the spell wore off in a short time. But, Kerby kept experimenting with it: on himself, on his dog, on his friend, on his enemy and finally in desperation, on the entire boy's choir at church.

A succession of innocently humorous incidents are woven together into a satisfying story. Print size is on the small side.

Interest Level: 3-6. Reading Level: 3.1. Further Search Topics: Humorous Fiction, Bullies-Fiction, Magic-Fiction, Magicians-Fiction, Chemistry-Fiction, Read Aloud.

Kessler, Leonard. Last one in is a rotten egg. Har-Row 1969, 64 pp.

Willie and Bobby could swim, but Freddy could not. After all three went to the local swimming pool and

Freddy was pushed into the water by two older bullies, he was scared to try swimming again. Finally, a sympathetic lifeguard gave Freddy lessons. After much practice, Freddy became competent and confident enough to swim in the deep water and to stand up to the bullies.

A very slight plot designed to reassure new swimmers and provide a few basic rules of swimming. Reader format. A Sports-I-Can-Read-Book.

Interest Level: 1-2. Reading Level: 1.2. Further Search Topics: Courage-Fiction, Swimming-Fiction, Challenges-Fiction, Bullies-Fiction.

Mazer, Harry. The war on Villa Street. Delacorte 1978, 182 pp.

Willis was a loner and a runner. He was a loner because he didn't want anyone to find out about his alcoholic father. He wasn't quite sure why he ran; perhaps because it was the only time he felt good. When Rabbit Slavin and his friends asked Willis to become part of their gang, he refused. He was flattered and wanted to join, but the gang wanted to meet at his house and Willis couldn't risk that. Then when he agreed to coach the local "retard" for the school's field day, Willis gave the gang the opportunity they wanted to take their revenge on him for turning them down. The gang's hatred for Willis increased still more when he beat their best runner and athlete. In payment, the gang jumped Willis and beat him badly. After he picked himself up, Willis realized that he had at least faced the worst of his fears and survived. Days later when his drunken father humiliated him, Willis realized he had to face that, too. He made peace with himself and the world by deciding he could neither continue to run away from, nor apologize for his father anymore. He was independent and strong.

There is much in this fast-paced book besides the obvious violence and action. It is written with an intuitive feel for a teenager's problems and emotions and is a sensitive portrayal of mature concepts. The print is large, but spacing between the lines should have been slightly increased.

Interest Level: 5-6. Reading Level: 5.1. Further Search Topics: Running-Fiction, Loneliness-Fiction, Alcoholism-Fiction, Loners-Fiction, Mental Retardation-Fiction, Gangs-Fiction, Child Abuse-Fiction, Bullies-Fiction, Family Problems-Fiction, Courage-Fiction.

Parish, Peggy. Hermit Dan; illus by Paul Frame. Macmillan 1977, 151 pp.

When the Roberts children tried to prove that Pirate Island really had been used by pirates, they encountered more action and intrigue than they had found in any of their earlier adventures. Liza, Bill and Jed suspected that Hermit Dan knew whether or not there had been pirates on the island, but he was so gruff and apparently mean that they didn't dare ask him any questions. Instead, they trailed and spied on him and asked questions of anyone who had known Hermit Dan as a child. It was rumored that his ancestors had actually been pirates. Until a terrible fire that had destroyed all they owned, Hermit Dan's family had been very wealthy. However, no one knew how they had become so rich.

In an attempt to see what the summer residents knew about Hermit Dan, the children introduced themselves to the vacationing youngsters. Among the visitors the Roberts met Hank and Ted, brothers bent on bullying Hermit Dan. When the children were rescued from a severe sandstorm by Hermit Dan, they were surprised to find that he wasn't nearly as gruff as he appeared. In fact they began to feel quite

protective of the old man. Thus when Hank and Ted stole a secret box that held all of Hermit Dan's valuables, it was the Roberts children who fought (literally) to get the box back. It was after Liza, Bill and Jed returned the box to Hermit Dan, however, that the real surprises began: these included a surprise party for Hermit Dan, his wish to be friendly, and his gift to the children of three pieces of eight that proved his family members were pirates.

This title's more interesting and involved plot makes the book more likely to be a success with older readers than the other stories about the Roberts children. Otherwise it shares the same format, faults and strengths as the other series titles.

Interest Level: 2-5. Reading Level: 2.1. Further Search Topics: Mystery and Detective Stories, Pirates-Fiction, Vacation-Fiction, Loners-Fiction, Treasure-Fiction, Bullies-Fiction, Brothers and Sisters-Fiction, Grandparents-Fiction.

Robinson, Barbara. The best Christmas pageant ever; illus by Judith Gwyn Brown. Har-Row 1972, 80 pp.

A truly delightful story of what happens when the meanest kids in town (they are all in one family) take over all the lead roles in the Sunday school Christmas pageant. The Herdmans (all six of them), having heard that the church was giving away free food, showed up to take some. While they were there, they heard about the Christmas pageant and decided it presented them with another perfect opportunity for food and mischief. With a little behind-the-scenes arm-twisting (literally), they managed to dissuade everyone else from showing interest in the major roles. Theirs was a completely original interpretation of the Christmas story that left nothing and no one around them untouched.

That the book's reading level will prove too high for many people is unfortunate. The story is well worth the struggle. A wonderful choice for reading aloud.

Interest Level: 3-6. Reading Level: 5.1 Further Search Topics: Christmas-Fiction, Bullies-Fiction, Troublemakers-Fiction, Humorous Fiction, Religion-Fiction, Group 2, Read Aloud, Acting-Fiction, Holidays-Fiction.

Robinson, Jean. The strange but wonderful cosmic awareness of Duffy Moon; illus by Lawrence Di Fiori. HM 1974, 142 pp.

Duffy was tired of being small, of always being on the losing side of fights, and of being unappreciated at home (by his ex-football star uncle). When he sent away for Mr. Flamel's Cosmic Awareness Kit, Duffy was sure he would then be able to take control over anything he wanted and direct his own life. His friend Peter, the narrator, wasn't quite so sure. Peter turned out to be right. Duffy almost made himself sick trying to build a stone wall. Babysitting two small boys and trying to bathe a Great Dane proved to be disastrous. But Duffy's biggest problem came from Boots McAfee's gang. A series of events finally brought Duffy and Peter face-to-face with the dreaded Boots. Luckily, she turned out to be a very smart girl who appreciated Duffy's true talents.

From the first to the last page this is a funny, very enjoyable book. A delightful book with a very palatable message.

Interest Level: 3-6. Reading Level: 3.2. Further Search Topics: Humorous Fiction, Bullies-Fiction, Magic-Fiction, Read Aloud, Occupations-Fiction, Sex Role-Fiction, Orphans-Fiction, Best Sellers, Gangs-Fiction, Courage-Fiction, Babysitting-Fiction.

Robinson, Nancy K. Wendy and the bullies; illus by Ingrid Fetz. Hastings 1980, 128 pp.

Wendy and her best friend Karen had a very carefully mapped out route to and from school—a route that allowed them to meet up with the fewest number of bullies possible. But when Karen became sick enough to stay home from school, Wendy had to face the bullies alone. Wendy's fears escalated to panic so intense that she avoided walking to school by hiding in her basement. She finally realized that she was letting fear and anger control her life when she found herself bullying Karen. Only her new friendship with Monica, making up with Karen, and her involvement in a school project helped Wendy overcome her fears.

This is a humorous, episodic tale of a feeling and circumstances common to many children. The illustrations sometimes make Wendy and her classmates appear much younger than her actual nine years, but fortunately that doesn't happen often enough to spoil the book's appeal.

Interest Level: 3-5. Reading Level: 3.1. Further Search Topics: School Stories, Bullies-Fiction, Courage-Fiction, Best Sellers, Humorous Fiction, Friendship-Fiction, Everyday Stories.

Smith, Doris Buchanan. Tough Chauncey. Morrow 1974, 222 pp.

Chauncey Childs had taught himself to be tough—very tough. Even though he was small for his age (13 years old), the only person who gave him any trouble was his sometimes-friend, Black Jack Levitt. Everyone else was scared of Chauncey. Chauncey felt that he had to be tough or he wouldn't be able to survive. He had to be tough to stand the beatings his grandfather gave him "for his own good," to put up with his mother's drinking and disappearances, and to stand the sight of his grandfather shooting the stray kittens born in their garage.

Chauncey's greatest wish was to be able to live with his mother, instead of with his grandparents. In a desperate attempt to achieve that end he accidentally fell from a moving train and badly hurt his leg. Instead of being returned to his mother he was once more taken back to his grandparents. Chauncey's unhappiness grew until he finally decided to take the one surviving stray kitten and run away. Jack helped him find an empty garage where he could hide while he figured out what to do with his future. After talking with Jack and doing more deep soul searching, Chauncey decided to reshape himself and his life. His first step was to curb his temper and his tongue when his hiding place was discovered. His second step was to see about finding a foster home where he would be treated well, and where he could get a new start.

Ugly as the story is in places, its ending is hopeful. Although it is not always realistic, Chauncey's story is compelling enough to appeal to many readers, especially those who have enjoyed *The War on Villa Street*, by Henry Mazer, *The Outsiders*, by Susan Hinton, or *Mystery of the Fat Cat*, by Frank Bonham. The book's length and its artificially low reading level (vocabulary is often difficult but sentences are very short) make this book most appropriate for an older reader whose reading level is 4.1 or higher.

Interest Level: 5-6. Reading Level: 3.2. Further Search Topics: Child Abuse-Fiction, Family Problems-Fiction, Grandparents-Fiction, Runaways-Fiction, Bullies-Fiction, Single Parent Family-Fiction, Loners-Fiction, Friendship-Fiction, Troublemakers-Fiction, Foster Homes-Fiction.

Wagner, Jane. J.T; photos by Gordon Parks, Jr. Van Nostrand 1969, 64 pp.

This is a sentimental story that rarely fails to elicit a sympathetic response from young readers. J.T. is a poor black boy who saw a portable radio almost begging to be stolen and stole it. Two of the neighborhood bullies, Boomer and Claymore, saw J.T. take the radio. Though they threatened him, even poured soap in his eyes in the school bathrooms, J.T. wouldn't give them the radio as they demanded.

About the same time J.T. found a scrawny, scared little cat with only one eye. Because his mother wouldn't let him take the cat home, J.T. built it a warm but ramshackle little house in an abandoned building. He fed it by charging tuna to his mother's grocery store account without her knowledge. Bones became the only thing in J.T.'s life that he had cared about since his father had walked out.

When Boomer and Claymore found out about Bones, they taunted J.T. by throwing the cat back and forth between them until the frightened cat escaped, darted out into the street and was hit by a car. J.T.'s heart broke as he looked at Bones, but he spoke to no one to tell them of his sadness. Only time, his mother's and grandmother's love and a small kitten from Mr. Rosen, the grocer, helped him recover. On the morning that he decided to accept the kitten, J.T. returned the stolen radio, faced Boomer and Claymore without fear, and asked Mr. Rosen for a job in order to pay for cat food.

The book is oversized and illustrated with photographs from the television movie version. It is not only an excellent story to read aloud but one that will prompt listeners to want to finish it on their own or to reread it. It is now available only in paperback from Dell.

Interest Level: 3-6. Reading Level: 3.1. Further Search Topics: Read Aloud, Courage-Fiction, Best Sellers, Cats-Fiction, Single Parent Family-Fiction, Bullies-Fiction, Blacks-Fiction, Poverty-Fiction, City Life-Fiction, Christmas Stories, Crime-Fiction, Pets-Fiction, Holidays-Fiction.

Wallace, Bill. A dog named Kitty. Holiday 1980, 153 pp.

Ricky's fear of dogs was extreme but also understandable. He had been attacked by a rabid dog when he was very young. Remembering the fear, the stitches and the painful rabies shots was enough to bring tears to Ricky's eyes even years later. When a local bully told his dog to attack Ricky, Ricky's fear was discovered. About that time, a stray puppy showed up at Ricky's farm. Not quite knowing why, Ricky began to warm to the puppy, to feed it, and finally to love it. When the dog was attacked by a pack of wild dogs (a brutal scene vividly described), Ricky fully overcame his fear of dogs, went to Kitty's defense, and was barely able to save her life. When Kitty was later tragically and accidentally killed, Ricky swore that he would never have anything to do with a dog again. He almost kept his promise to himself, but eventually a second stray dog wandered into the farm and Ricky decided to try again.

This is an emotional story that should appeal to many readers. However, because of the violence and the dog's two-stage death, the book is probably best suited to fifth and sixth grade children.

Interest Level: 5-6. Reading Level: 3.1. Further Search Topics: Dogs-Fiction, Pets-Fiction, Bullies-Fiction, Death-Fiction, Oklahoma-Fiction, Courage-Fiction, Country Life-Fiction.

CALENDARS-FICTION

Bernstein, Margery. The first morning; illus by Enid Warner Romanek. Scribner 1976, 44 pp.

Spider, Mouse, and Fly volunteered to ask the king of the sky for light to take back to earth because the animals on earth were tired of living in darkness. The king didn't want to give away any light and so he set what he thought was an impossible task for the three animals. They were able to outwit the king three times and finally return to earth with a box Mouse was sure contained light. When they opened the box all they found was a rooster. Poor Mouse was ashamed at having been so badly tricked. But then Rooster crowed up the first morning and has done so ever since. A competent retelling of an African myth, nicely complemented by bold illustrations. Good candidate for dramatization.

Interest Level: 1-3. Reading Level: 2.1. Further Search Topics: Animals-Fiction, Group 2, Mythology, Light-Fiction, Drama, Time-Fiction, Calendars-Fiction, Creation-Fiction, Africa-Folklore.

CALIFORNIA

Madian, Jon. Beautiful junk: a story of the Watts Towers; photos by Barbara Jacobs, Jr. and Lou Jacobs, Jr. Little 1968, 44 pp.

Although this book is now out of print; it is well worth trying to find. It is a fictionalized account of a young, angry black boy's encounter with the creator of Los Angeles' unusual Watts Towers. Simon Rodia, a poor tile setter, worked on the towers for 33 years until he was 75 years old. He used only his imagination, discarded materials he found around him, seashells, and sand to build three tall, fantasy-like towers in the middle of a ghetto. He created beauty where others saw only junk.

The book is illustrated with photography that makes the story more vivid and the towers and Rodia's accomplishment more impressive than they would have seemed with drawings. The print is good-sized, spacing is totally adequate. Rodia's life is quickly submarized and an update on the Towers is included at the book's end.

Interest Level: 3-6. Reading Level: 3.1. Further Search Topics: Blacks-Fiction, Read Aloud, Best Sellers, Poverty-Fiction, Rodia, Simon, Architecture, Biography, Aging-Fiction, Watts Towers, California, Poverty.

CALIFORNIA-FICTION

Bulla, Clyde Robert. Ghost town treasure; illus by Don Freeman. Har-Row 1957, 87 pp.

A very simple story whose title is somewhat misleading. Instead of a mystery or an exciting story of buried treasure, Bulla has written a very pleasant story of a family whose fortunes are reversed by the accidental discovery of a nearby cave. Young Ty Jackson and his family were the last people living in Gold Rock, California. Everyone else had moved out when the new highway had bypassed the town. The Jacksons had been able to stay on only because some of the nearby ranchers had continued to buy food and supplies from the Jacksons' store. Just as they, too, were preparing to move out, Ty's pen pals wrote that they were coming to visit the town. Their grandfather had died there, years earlier, during his search for gold. When Paul and Nora arrived, they brought with them their grandfather's diary. The last entry in the journal seemed to indicate that their grandfather had found gold in an isolated cave in the nearby canyon. After a long search, the children discovered the cave, but no gold. Ty's disappointment changed to joy when tourists started arriving to see the new natural attraction. Once again his parents could sell their groceries, the hotel could be reopened and Gold Rock would flourish.

Interest Level: 2-5. Reading Level: 2.2. Further Search Topics: Treasure-Fiction, Family Problems-Fiction, West-Fiction, California-Fiction, Family-Fiction, Pen Pals-Fiction.

CAMP-FICTION

Blume, Judy. Otherwise known as Sheila the great. Dutton 1972, 128 pp.

Sheila first appears in *Tales of a Fourth Grade Nothing* as Peter Thatcher's neighbor. Sheila was a bundle of fears. She was afraid of dogs, thunderstorms, spiders, horses, putting her face in water, and strange noises at night. The summer she and her family rented a house in Tarrytown, New York, she confronted each one of her fears, even mastered one (putting her face in the water) and learned how to swim. That gave her the self-confidence to face a dog without running away. Sheila's progress was aided by her friend Mouse's steadfast belief that a person should always be honest about herself. Sheila's problems are treated realistically and with dignity, yet humorously. Reading level varies greatly from 1.2 - 4.1, therefore, the book is *most* suitable to grades four through six.

Interest Level: 3-6. Reading Level: 3.1. Further Search Topics: Humorous Fiction, Courage-Fiction, Camp-Fiction, Group 2, Vacation-Fiction, Swimming-Fiction, Brothers and Sisters-Fiction, Friendship-Fiction, Everyday Stories.

Danziger, Paula. There's a bat in bunk five. Delacorte 1980, 150 pp.

Although this is a sequel to *The Cat Ate My Gymsuit,* it can be read alone. Marcy accepted an offer to become a junior counselor at an arts camp run by her ex-English teacher Ms. Finney and Ms. Finney's husband. After a nervous beginning, Marcy found herself enjoying the other counselors and the campers, but most of all, her first romance. Marcy's only difficulty was dealing with Ginger, a very troubled 10-year-old in Marcy's cabin. Marcy couldn't seem to get through to Ginger. When Ginger ran away, Marcy was forced to consider whether she should have spent more time with the campers and not quite so much time with Ted.

Marcy is a normal teenager whose problems, questions and activities are appealing to many teen and pre-teen readers. The characters who surround Marcy here are less stereotyped and flat than those in The Cat Ate My Gymsuit. Even Marcy's parents are more human. The author's light touch is just right for Marcy's story.

Interest Level: 5-6. Reading Level: 3.2. Further Search Topics: Humorous Fiction, Camp-Fiction, Everyday Stories, Love-Fiction, Vacation-Fiction, Occupations-Fiction, Adolescence-Fiction.

CAMPBELL, EARL

Burchard, Susan H. Sports star: Earl Campbell. HarBraceJ 1980, 63 pp.

The Houston Oiler's star running back, probably the best in football, has only been out of college a few years. He should have a long career ahead of him. *Sports Star: Elvin Hayes* includes series notes. Sports Star series.

Interest Level: 3-6. Reading Level: 3.1. Further Search Topics: Football-Biography, Blacks-Biography, Campbell, Earl, Biography.

CAMPING-FICTION

Roy, Ron. Nightmare Island; illus by Robert MacLean. Dutton 1981, 69 pp.

Harley didn't want to take his younger brother camping, but because he had promised his father he would, the boys packed a tent, sleeping bags, and plenty of food into a small boat and set off to nearby Little Island. Hidden in his pocket, Harley had matches and marshmallows for a midnight marshmallow roast. After they had finished the bag of marshmallows, Harley threw the last log of the fire into the water. The water erupted into flames that quickly spread around the island. As the boys fought desperately to save themselves and to find shelter, they realized that the large shape they had seen in the distance must have been an oil tanker that had spread an oil slick all around the island. With time running out Harley gave his brother the only truly secure shelter from the fire, curled up on top of a tall rock and went to sleep. When he awoke the fire had burned itself out and help was on the way.

Most young readers will be able to suspend disbelief long enough to enjoy this as an exciting adventure and survival story, but it is hard to believe that two young boys could not only survive such a holocaust, but that they could sleep through part of it, too. It is also difficult to believe that there would not be more of a fuss made about the oil tanker blowing up. Plot problems aside, young readers seem to love the story.

Interest Level: 3-6. Reading Level: 3.2. Further Search Topics: Brothers and Sisters-Fiction, Survival-Fiction, Camping-Fiction, Disasters-Fiction, Best Sellers.

Yolen, Jane. The boy who spoke chimp illus by David Wiesner. Knopf 1981, 120 pp.

Kriss was determined to prove to his father that, at 12 years old, he was perfectly capable of camping out by himself. To do so, he left home and headed up the coast of California with a sleeping bag, some food, a map and compass, and water. His plan was to camp, ride, and hike his way to his grandmother's house. On the way, the coast line was torn apart by the second great earthquake to strike California. The first had already destroyed great portions of the state. The second was even stronger. The truck he had been riding in was destroyed and everyone around Kriss was killed by the quake except for two chimpanzees. The chimps, in transit from one lab to another, were research animals who had been taught to use sign language. Kriss took the animals with him as he tried to get farther inland and finally home to Los Angeles. His trip not only confirmed his father's fears about Kriss' inadequacies but taught him how to overcome them. Kriss learned to communicate with the chimps, to find food and to live on his own until Old Chris, a hermit, happened along. Together they continued to brave the chaos brought about by the earthquake even when Old Chris' heart troubled him. When a helicopter finally spotted them, Kriss decided to let the chimps go wild and promised Old Chris that he would be back in the woods very soon. It was a mature, capable Kriss who returned home.

This is typical of the Capers series—much action, few background details, little characterization. The books, however, are on appealing topics; they move quickly and they create intriguing (if sometimes implausible) situations. They are light, enjoyable and very useful. Capers series.

Interest Level: 3-6. Reading Level: 3.1. Further Search Topics: California-Fiction, Disasters-Fiction, Survival-Fiction, Apes-Fiction, Nonverbal

Communication-Fiction, Camping-Fiction, Runaways-Fiction, Best Sellers.

CATS

Selsam, Millicent E. How kittens grow; photos by Esther Bubley. School Bk Serv 1973, unp (28 pp).

A warm picture essay that illustrates and briefly describes the first eight weeks in kittens' lives. Guaranteed to charm cat fanciers.

Interest Level: 1-3. Reading Level: 2.1. Further Search Topics: Cats, Pets, Infants, Group 2, Birth.

CATS-FICTION

Bonham, Frank. The mystery of the fat cat; illus by Alvin Smith. Dutton 1968, 160 pp.

Although noticeably dated at times, this is still an exciting story of an inner city neighborhood. Buddy, Little Pie, Rich, and Cool were among the many who used the local Boys' Club as their hangout. It was a place to stay out of trouble and off the streets, but it was also a haven for rats. The rats were big and brazen; so brazen that one attacked Buddy in the swimming pool. The club needed a new building desperately. The money was there; they just weren't able to use it. Fifteen years earlier an eccentric old woman willed the Boys' Club over $600,000, but stated that the money was first to be used to support her cat until it died. A caretaker, a lawyer, and a veterinarian all benefited as long as the cat lived. Buddy and his friends took on the job of discovering if the cat really was alive or if the Boys' Club was being cheated out of half a million dollars. It was a job that nearly killed them before they set things right. Plenty of action, some violence, a cast of street-smart characters, realistic trouble with the police, as well as a slight mystery almost insure the book's success with older readers. Moderate sized print. Line spacing somewhat narrow.

Interest Level: 6+. Reading Level: 5.1. Further Search Topics: Humorous Fiction, Cats-Fiction, Gangs-Fiction, City Life-Fiction, Mystery and Detective Stories, Poverty-Fiction, Friendship-Fiction, Juvenile Delinquency-Fiction, Crime-Fiction, Best Sellers.

Chew, Ruth. The would-be witch. Hastings 1976, 112 pp.

Robin and her brother Andy took a liking to the clumsy white cat they saw in Zelda's Antique Shop. The cat apparently liked them, too, for it followed them home. Not having enough money to offer to buy Pearl from Zelda, the children tried to polish up an old pair of silver birds to trade for the cat. The polish turned out to be magical and made the birds real. When they tried the polish on a broom in Zelda's store, the broom began to fly. Upon discovering that Zelda wanted to be a witch but had failed the coven entrance exam, Rob helped her learn to fly and told her of the witches' meeting place that she and Andy had discovered. But the 12 witches who had been turned into cats were wicked enough to want to use Zelda to regain their human form and turn *her* into a cat. In attempting to prevent such a fate, Rob, Andy and Zelda set fire to the abandoned building being used as a meeting place. The 12 witches were rescued from the fire but charged with arson, which meant probable jail sentences for all of them. Zelda, finally a happy and capable witch, gave Pearl to Rob and Andy to thank them for their help.

A better-crafted story than many of the others, this also has a more evil cast of characters to provide additional interest.

Interest Level: 2-5. Reading Level: 2.2. Further Search Topics: Witches-Fiction, Brothers and

Sisters-Fiction, Magic-Fiction, Fantasy, Transformations-Fiction, Cats-Fiction.

Chew, Ruth. The wishing tree. Hastings 1980, 142 pp.

Peggy and Brian's discovery of a talking cat, a bird with a beautiful song, and a strange and frightening tree led them to a shopping bag lady, a giant named Fred, a gold key and a magical tablecloth. In a rather complicated series of events, the children and the cat finally succeeded in retrieving the tablecloth from Annie (the old woman to whom Puss had loaned it) and giving it back to Fred, who needed it to help satisfy his gigantic appetite. In addition, they returned Fred to normal human size, rescued Annie from a fall on the ice, introduced the two characters and encouraged them to live together in Fred's castle.

Complicated enough already, the story's lengthy adventure that leads up to the discovery of the key (climbing into the magical tree and swimming in a pond) makes the plot even more complex. If a reader doesn't expect more than benign fantasy and fun this is an adequate choice.

Interest Level: 2-5. Reading Level: 2.2. Further Search Topics: Magic-Fiction, Fantasy, Brothers and Sisters-Fiction, Giants-Fiction, Cats-Fiction.

Heide, Florence Parry. Black magic at Brillstone. A. Whitman 1981, 126 pp.

Liza is a little older, her romance with Logan has progressed to a kiss, and the book's plot is more complex than earlier Brillstone adventures. Other than those differences, the book follows Heide's standard format. The Brillstone books all center on Liza Webster and Logan Forrest, teenage partners in crime detection, who live in the Brillstone Apartments. The stories are similar enough that one could almost substitute the names Nancy Drew and Ned for Liza and Logan. Both young women are only children who live with their fathers. They are both independent, resourceful, and very concerned that justice be done. The men in their lives play approximately the same roles; their fathers are proud and supportive, but distantly preoccupied with their own business; Logan and Ned are gallant, boyish, and devoted. Liza and Logan, like Nancy and Ned, are not distinctive characters. Instead, they are shells into which readers who want excitement and adventure can pour themselves. There is no parental interference to worry about. There is plenty of action, some suspense, and real world crime (for Liza: murder, bank robberies, etc.) rather than childish escapades. The books' success is practically guaranteed. Beware, however, of inconsistent reading levels that wander over a year's range.

Logan was first aware of strange occurrences at the Brillstone Apartments when someone entered his apartment late at night. While the person had searched the apartment, he or she had unconsciously whistled a nursery tune. Logan's neighbor, Miss Violet, said the tune reminded her of her deceased nephew. Slowly Logan and Liza realized that someone was trying to trick Miss Violet out of a substantial amount of money she had just inherited. They suspected that Bella Vine, a spiritualist, and an accomplice were trying to convince Miss Violet that her nephew was communicating from the dead and wanted Miss Violet to give her money to Bella. Not until it was almost too late did Liza and Logan realize that Bella was also posing as another possible recipient of the money and was really Miss Violet's nephew's wife. Miss Violet's nephew had only pretended to die in order to collect insurance money. When he and his wife had heard

about Miss Violet's large inheritance, they had decided to reappear in order to bilk her out of the money. Brillstone Mystery series.

Interest Level: 5-6. Reading Level: 3.1. Further Search Topics: Mystery and Detective Stories, Occult-Fiction, Crime-Fiction, Ghosts-Fiction, Cats-Fiction, Detectives-Fiction, Inheritance-Fiction.

Heide, Florence Parry. The mystery of the silver tag; illus by Seymour Fleishman. A. Whitman 1972, 127 pp.

Jay's paper route took him to one house that he wished he could avoid. It was grumpy, old Mr. Pendleton's house that Jay hated. One rainy day he spotted what he later realized was a prize Angora cat hiding on Mr. Pendleton's porch. When the cat was reported lost in that night's paper, Jay and the other members of the Spotlight Club decided to try to return the cat to its owner, Miss Horton. Their attempts to get the cat back from Mr. Pendleton meant that they had to spy on him, to sneak into his garage, and to spend the night in a treehouse overlooking his house. They were afraid that they had failed when they saw Mr. Pendleton leave with the cat. Determined to be the ones to tell Miss Horton of their failure, they went to her apartment and found Mr. Pendleton already there. Mr. Pendleton was a famous animal photographer who, upon finding the cat, had asked Miss Horton if he could photograph him. The children, thinking only that Mr. Pendleton was a mad scientist who kidnapped cats, had jumped to all the wrong conclusions, but ended with a mystery solved, new friends, and their first lesson in being detectives.

See entry with *Mystery at Southport Cinema* for series information. Spotlight Club Mystery series.

Interest Level: 3-5. Reading Level: 2.2. Further Search Topics: Mystery and Detective Stories, Brothers and Sisters-Fiction, Gangs-Fiction, Cats-Fiction, Loners-Fiction, Detectives-Fiction, Photography-Fiction, Kidnapping-Fiction.

Hildick, Edmund W. The case of the condemned cat; illus by Lisl Weil. Macmillan 1975, 106 pp.

Ray Williams had a terrible problem when he begged the McGurk Organization for help. His cat Whiskers had been accused of killing a neighbor's pet dove. Ray's mother decided that they couldn't risk upsetting the neighbors anymore and threatened to take Whiskers to the pound unless it could be proven that he was innocent. The Organization, needing time, hid Whiskers and told Mrs. Williams that he had run away. While Whiskers was safely hidden, the group interviewed all the neighbors, surveyed the scene of the crime, and tried to decide upon the real murderer. When the remains of another bird were found while Whiskers was safely locked away, it looked as if the cat was surely innocent. But then McGurk and his detectives found out that the cat had been sprung. It wasn't until they went back over all the information they had gathered that McGurk realized who was the real culprit. The only step left was to trick old Gramp Martin (the neighborhood grouch) into confessing.

See *The Case of the Bashful Bank Robber* for series information. McGurk Mystery series.

Interest Level: 3-6. Reading Level: 2.2. Further Search Topics: Mystery and Detective Stories, Cats-Fiction, Detectives-Fiction, Humorous Fiction, Gangs-Fiction, Pets-Fiction.

Norton, Andre. Star Ka'at; illus by Bernard Colonna. Walker & Co 1976, 122 pp.

Jim Evans and Elly Mae Brown, both orphaned and alone, met each other and two strange cats at the same time. As the children became more unhappy with their lives, they began to realize that Tiro and Mer were not usual cats. They were highly intelligent Ka'ats from another planet who had come to Earth in search of new strong stock to add to their breed. Both Ka'ats became as fond of the children as the children became of them. When the time came for the transport ship to leave, Jim and Elly contrived to go with them. However, the only way they could go was if they were accepted by the other Ka'ats and adopted by Tiro and Mer.

This is the first book in a series. Unfortunately the second book *Star Ka'at World*, has a much more difficult reading level (sixth grade) and the third title, *Star Ka'at and the Plant People*, varies from 2.1 to 4.1. Reading level of this entry varies between 4.1 and 5.1 but children seem to like the book enough to put up with the variability.

Interest Level: 3-6. Reading Level: 4.2. Further Search Topics: Science Fiction, Friendship-Fiction, Cats-Fiction, Group 2, Outer Space-Fiction, Orphans-Fiction.

Packard, Edward. The mystery of Chimney Rock; illus by Paul Granger. Bantam 1979, 121 pp.

See notes for *Sugarcane Island* for information about the series. Paperback only. Choose Your Own Adventure series.

Interest Level: 2-6. Reading Level: 3.2. Further Search Topics: Mystery and Detective Stories, Cats-Fiction, Witches-Fiction, Ghosts-Fiction, Detectives-Fiction, Best Sellers, Group 2.

Seuss, Dr. The cat in the hat. Beginner 1957, 61 pp.

When the Cat in the Hat visits two children, a dreary, boring afternoon becomes almost too exciting. The Cat's juggling act and the two "things" he brings with him almost destroy the house. But the Cat cleans up so well that when the children's mother comes home and asks what they did all afternoon, they can't decide if they should tell her.

A funny, rhyming tale of the destruction all children can create and the boredom all children can feel. Reader format.

Interest Level: 1-3. Reading Level: 1.2. Further Search Topics: Humorous Fiction, Fantasy, Cats-Fiction, Poetry, Troublemakers-Fiction, Best Sellers, Stories in Rhyme.

Seuss, Dr. The cat in the hat comes back. Beginner 1958, 63 pp.

Sally and her brother were doing a good job of clearing the front walk of snow when the Cat in the Hat showed up. While they worked, the Cat created a pink mess in the house. The mess only became worse when he tried to clean it. The pink spot finally covered the snow all around the house until the Cat called upon his friends Little Cats A-Z. It was Little Cat Z and his magic zoom that eventually not only cleaned the snow, but cleared the front walk as well.

Another zany, rhymed adventure of the mischievious Cat whose ability to get into trouble endears him to most children from pre-school to early third grade. Reader format.

Interest Level: 1-3. Reading Level: 1.2. Further Search Topics: Fantasy, Cats-Fiction, Troublemakers-Fiction, Humorous Fiction, Snow-Fiction, Poetry, Best Sellers, Stories in Rhyme.

Viorst, Judith. The tenth good thing about Barney; illus by Erik Blegvad. Atheneum 1971, 25 pp.

A quiet, thoughtful book to help a child face the difficult experience of death. When a family's beloved cat Barney died, their little boy tried to find 10 good things to say about him at the funeral. Nine things came easily to mind, but it was not until he had worked in the garden with his father that the little boy realized the tenth good thing. Barney, buried in the ground, would help the flowers, trees, and grass grow. A special picture book, small in size, but large in impact. Print is somewhat small but well-spaced.

Interest Level: 1-4. Reading Level: 2.1. Further Search Topics: Pets-Fiction, Cats-Fiction, Death-Fiction, Group 2, Read Aloud.

Wagner, Jane. J.T; photos by Gordon Parks, Jr. Van Nostrand 1969, 64 pp.

This is a sentimental story that rarely fails to elicit a sympathetic response from young readers. J.T. is a poor black boy who saw a portable radio almost begging to be stolen and stole it. Two of the neighborhood bullies, Boomer and Claymore, saw J.T. take the radio. Though they threatened him, even poured soap in his eyes in the school bathrooms, J.T. wouldn't give them the radio as they demanded.

About the same time J.T. found a scrawny, scared little cat with only one eye. Because his mother wouldn't let him take the cat home, J.T. built it a warm but ramshackle little house in an abandoned building. He fed it by charging tuna to his mother's grocery store account without her knowledge. Bones became the only thing in J.T.'s life that he had cared about since his father had walked out.

When Boomer and Claymore found out about Bones, they taunted J.T. by throwing the cat back and forth between them until the frightened cat escaped, darted out into the street and was hit by a car. J.T.'s heart broke as he looked at Bones, but he spoke to no one to tell them of his sadness. Only time, his mother's and grandmother's love and a small kitten from Mr. Rosen, the grocer, helped him recover. On the morning that he decided to accept the kitten, J.T. returned the stolen radio, faced Boomer and Claymore without fear, and asked Mr. Rosen for a job in order to pay for cat food.

The book is oversized and illustrated with photographs from the television movie version. It is not only an excellent story to read aloud but one that will prompt listeners to want to finish it on their own or to reread it. It is now available only in paperback from Dell.

Interest Level: 3-6. Reading Level: 3.1. Further Search Topics: Read Aloud, Courage-Fiction, Best Sellers, Cats-Fiction, Single Parent Family-Fiction, Bullies-Fiction, Blacks-Fiction, Poverty-Fiction, City Life-Fiction, Christmas Stories, Crime-Fiction, Pets-Fiction, Holidays-Fiction.

CHALLENGES

Mathis, Sharon Bell. Ray Charles; illus by George Ford. Har-Row 1973, 33 pp.

Dominent throughout this biography of Ray Charles is the theme of overcoming adversity. The book is not just a recounting of Ray Charles' music lessons, early schooling, family life, and talent. All of that is included, but it serves to illustrate the manner in which Charles met his troubles. His problems began when he was very young. His brother died, and Ray lost one eye and then the sight in his other eye. His family was poor, but close, and he missed them when he was sent away to a school for the blind. Music was his love, but even that was work, for Charles had to learn to read and write music in Braille. He worked hard at it and eventually could play and arrange music for every instrument in the band.

Determined to be independent, when Charles was orphaned at age 15, he left school and began playing music for a living. The first record he made resulted in a $16 fine because he made it during a musician's union strike. Charles took a series of sideman and nightclub jobs until he finally had enough money to hire seven other musicians to play his music. Today Charles is very wealthy, owns his own record company, has a family, and is considered a great jazz and blues musician. None of his success came easily; only through determination, will power, pride, and hard work.

The book, interesting and serviceable enough for music or biography units, is also designed to set an example for youngsters facing their own problems. It will, of course, be popular with Ray Charles fans, too. Crowell Biography series.

Interest Level: 2-4. Reading Level: 3.1. Further Search Topics: Jazz Music, Music-Biography, Vision, Physically Handicapped, Blacks-Biography, Group 2, Biography, Pianists, Orphans, Challenges, Courage.

CHALLENGES-FICTION

Bulla, Clyde Robert. The ghost of windy hill; illus by Don Bolognese. Har-Row 168, 84 pp.

If the reader doesn't expect a high adventure ghost story, he or she will not be disappointed by this low-keyed tale of a family who goes to live in a house that is supposedly haunted. Mr. Giddings asked the Carver family to move into his country home while he and his wife stayed in Boston. His intent was that the Carvers should either prove to his wife that the house was not haunted or drive the ghost out. The Carvers found no ghosts—at first—only an interesting group of neighbors. There was shy Miss Miggie who drifted around in a long, white dress and wore a flower-covered hat. Bruno was the gruff beggar boy who couldn't walk and had no friends but a goat, until the Carver children came along. Near the end of their stay Lorna Carver mentioned that because they had seen no ghosts the family would soon leave and the Giddings would return. Strange occurrences began almost immediately after Lorna's statement and ended only when the Carvers caught Bruno trying to convince them that he was the ghost. Lorna and Jamie were his only friends, so he had risked his guardians wrath and given up the pretense of being lame to trick the Carvers into staying. All ends well as Bruno's cruel guardian is run off, the Carvers take responsibility for Bruno's care, and Mrs. Giddings admits she made up the ghost story because she hated living in the country and had wanted to return to the city. Another serviceable book in the very successful Bulla style.

Interest Level: 2-5. Reading Level: 2.1. Further Search Topics: Ghosts-Fiction, Brothers and Sisters-Fiction, Orphans-Fiction, Country Life-Fiction, Courage-Fiction, Challenges-Fiction, Friendship-Fiction.

Byars, Betsy. The 18th emergency; illus by Robert Grossman. Viking Pr. 1973, 126 pp.

When your best friend knows how to escape from the world's 17 worst emergencies and you're faced with the eighteenth, you're in trouble. That was the spot in which Mouse found himself one day. He had drawn an arrow towards a large picture of the Neanderthal man and written Marv Hammerman's name. Hammerman had seen him do it and was out to kill, maim, or at least beat up Mouse. Mouse finally ran out of ways to avoid Hammerman and had to face the fight. When it was over and he was once again able to stand up, Mouse realized he felt better for having allowed Hammerman to regain his honor and for having taken responsibility for his own actions.

A funny, fast-moving look at real feelings of fear, honor and responsibility. Very popular. Print is dark and of good size but lines could have been spaced farther apart.

Interest Level: 4-6. Reading Level: 3.2. Further Search Topics: Bullies-Fiction, Humorous Fiction, Courage-Fiction, Best Sellers, Challenges-Fiction, Read Aloud.

Christopher, Matt. No arm in left field; illus by Byron Goto. Little 1974, 131 pp.

Matt Christopher's books are just the thing for sports junkies. The play-by-play accounts of several sports events (here it is baseball games) are loosely tied together by secondary plot developments. Usually the plot revolves around the main character's successful attempt to overcome a difficulty of some sort.

Terry was a good baseball player so, when he was invited to join a local team shortly after he moved to Pennsylvania, he was very pleased. Almost immediately, he learned that a teammate was not at all happy about playing with Terry. Terry was black and his teammate, Tony, was very prejudiced. Terry had dealt with people like Tony before, so he was able to ignore most, but not all, of Tony's unkind comments and actions. But the day finally came when Tony realized that to play well as a team, they had to work together instead of against each other.

Interest Level: 3-6. Reading Level: 3.2. Further Search Topics: Prejudice-Fiction, Baseball-Fiction, Friendship-Fiction, Challenges-Fiction.

Danziger, Paula. The cat ate my gymsuit. Delacorte 1974, 147 pp.

Another book for fans of Judy Blume. Marcy was shy and insecure, unhappy at school and unhappy at home. She was self-conscious about being heavy and sure she would never have a date. Only Ms. Finney (a new teacher), her English class and Smedley (a communications group) meant anything to Marcy. When Ms. Finney was fired because of her refusal to recite the pledge of allegiance and her unorthodox teaching methods, Marcy began to organize a protest movement. Marcy's commitment brought more problems at school and at home, but eventually resulted in Ms. Finney's vindication and Marcy's and her mother's growth and understanding.

Don't expect much depth of characterization. Most of the characters are flat and stereotypical, but the book will have great appeal in spite of its faults, for Marcy's insecurities are ones with which many young readers can identify.

Interest Level: 5-6. Reading Level: 5.1. Further Search Topics: School Stories, Everyday Stories, Family Problems-Fiction, Challenges-Fiction, Weight-Fiction, Courage-Fiction, Individualists-Fiction, Sex Role-Fiction.

Green, Phyllis. The fastest quitter in town; illus by Lorenzo Lynch. A-W 1972, 62 pp.

Whenever Johnny played baseball and things went wrong for him, he would quit. Johnny's teammates finally grew so angry with him that they told him to leave the team. That same day, Johnny's 90-year-old great-grandfather lost a very special ring his wife had given him. Johnny's love for this great-grandfather pushed him to keep looking for the ring until days later, when everyone else had quit searching, Johnny found the ring. Having learned a hard lesson, Johnny returned to his team for one more chance. That evening Johnny went to see his great-grandfather to tell him, with legitimate pride, that he had played the entire game.

Although the lesson is pointed, the story is very satisfying. Johnny's relationship with this great-grandfather is close and supportive. His problem is one shared by many children, especially those with a weak self-image.

Interest Level: 1-4. Reading Level: 3.1. Further Search Topics: Blacks-Fiction, Challenges-Fiction, Courage-Fiction, Group 2, Baseball-Fiction, Grandparents-Fiction, Friendship-Fiction.

Harris, Robie H. Rosie's double dare; illus by Tony DeLuna. Knopf 1980, 112 pp.

Rosie wanted to play baseball with the Willard Street Gang, but she couldn't play well enough to play by their rules. She needed what her older brother called "shrimp rules." She couldn't hit a pitched ball, only a grounder; but grounders were "shrimp rules." In desperation Rosie agreed to take a dare that the gang made up. If she actually performed the dare, the gang would let her play with them by her rules.

The gang dared Rosie to sneak into cranky Mr. Quirk's apartment and borrow a set of his false teeth. Because Rosie couldn't find any extra false teeth, she borrowed his wig instead but that didn't satisfy the gang. They only laughed and made up another dare for Rosie. She was to untie Mrs. Samuels' dog and let it run loose. As Rosie untied him, Elmer ran away, Rosie ran off after him. One rainstorm later, Rosie caught up with him in the middle of a Red Sox game at Fenway Park. Rosie's attempt to catch Elmer stopped the game, brought her an interview on TV, and secured her a place on the Willard Street baseball team.

This very light story, made up almost entirely of action and examples of sibling rivalry, should have wide appeal through fifth grade. Beyond that, Rosie's age (almost nine) and childish behavior won't ring true. Capers series.

Interest Level: 2-5. Reading Level: 2.2. Further Search Topics: Baseball-Fiction, Humorous Fiction, Brothers and Sisters-Fiction, Challenges-Fiction, Courage-Fiction, Gangs-Fiction, Everyday Stories.

Hurwitz, Johanna. The law of gravity; illus by Ingrid Fetz. Morrow 1978, 192 pp.

The summer between fifth and sixth grades looked very unexciting to Margot. Her best friends were both going away for the whole summer and her father, a musician, was going to be on tour for most of the summer. Margot's very overweight mother had sworn never to go downstairs from their fifth floor walk-up apartment. Unless Margot chose to stay upstairs too, she was sure she would have a very lonely vacation. In addition, she had to work on a summer project for school. The project she finally chose was to get her mother downstairs after nine years of staying upstairs. In search of help she went to the local library where she met Bernie. Bernie was only a year older than Margot, but he seemed to know the most interesting things about the city. He showed her places Margot had never heard of before, he taught her to play chess, backgammon, and even to ride a bicycle. He was so full of fascinating ideas and information that Margot had no chance to be bored or lonely. Best of all, he even tried to help Margot with her project. None of their ideas worked, however, until Margot pretended to run away and scared her mother into

going downstairs. Only then did Margot realize that she loved her mother whether or not she stayed on the fifth floor and that she couldn't simply force her mother or anyone else to change to suit her own fancy.

The book is a warm, understanding, slightly humorous treatment of the fairly common wish to change someone else. Although not many readers are likely to share Margot's exact problem, most will recognize her feelings. The book is also a virtual Chamber of Commerce advertisement for urban living. One of its other charms is its picture of a non-competitive, open, real friendship between an 11-year-old girl and a 12-year-old boy. The only drawback to the book is its inconsistent reading level which varies from 4.1 to 5.1 with a rare leap to 5.2.

Interest Level: 4-6. Reading Level: 4.2. Further Search Topics: Vacation-Fiction, Friendship-Fiction, Loners-Fiction, City Life-Fiction, Individualists-Fiction, Courage-Fiction, New York City-Fiction, Humorous Fiction, Family-Fiction, Challenges-Fiction, Weight-Fiction, Everyday Stories, Best Sellers.

Kessler, Leonard. Last one in is a rotten egg. Har-Row 1969, 64 pp.

Willie and Bobby could swim, but Freddy could not. After all three went to the local swimming pool and Freddy was pushed into the water by two older bullies, he was scared to try swimming again. Finally, a sympathetic lifeguard gave Freddy lessons. After much practice, Freddy became competent and confident enough to swim in the deep water and to stand up to the bullies.

A very slight plot designed to reassure new swimmers and provide a few basic rules of swimming. Reader format. A Sports-I-Can-Read-Book.

Interest Level: 1-2. Reading Level: 1.2. Further Search Topics: Courage-Fiction, Swimming-Fiction, Challenges-Fiction, Bullies-Fiction.

Rockwell, Thomas. How to eat fried worms; illus by Emily McCully. Watts 1973, 116 pp.

It started more as a joke than anything else, but it escalated into a strange commitment. Alan bet Billy $50 that Billy couldn't eat a worm a day for fifteen days. Billy had always been willing to take almost any dare offered and he was stubborn enough to carry them out, but when he actually faced the first worm (an enormous night crawler), he almost backed down. He and his friend Tom had to keep repeating the word "minibike" (the prize he planned to buy with the money) and smother the worm in everything imaginable in order to eat it all. After the first worm, however, the next few were easier to face. That was when Alan and his ally Joe, began using psychological warfare and almost won. In 41 very short, grotesquely funny chapters Billy becomes the proud owner of a minibike and is the first person to become hooked on worm sandwiches.

Once this book is started, it is hard to resist its gruesome fascination. Although the print is somewhat small, and there are occasionally very difficult or babytalk words, the interest is strong enough to sustain almost all readers.

Interest Level: 3-6. Reading Level: 3.1. Further Search Topics: Humorous Fiction, Worms-Fiction, Read Aloud, Best Sellers, Challenges-Fiction, Food-Fiction, Bicycles and Bicycling-Fiction.

Sachs, Marily. The bears' house; illus by Louis Glanzman. Doubleday 1971, 81 pp.

Don't let the benign appearance of this book fool you. This is a disturbing, almost brutal story. It is the story of Fran Ellen, a fourth grader with more problems than anyone should have to shoulder at one time. Her father had left the family and her mother had had a mental breakdown. Fran Ellen and her older brother were left with responsibility for themselves, their mother, and three other children (including a baby). They were all ill-fed, poorly dressed, and unwashed. Neither the social worker nor Fran Ellen's teacher knew the extent of the family's problems. Fran Ellen's only happiness came from her baby sister and from a schoolroom model (of *Goldilocks and the Three Bears* and their house) into which she mentally retreated whenever she had the chance.

As the school year closed, Fran Ellen's teacher visited her home to deliver the bears' house and discovered Fran Ellen's mother and very sick baby sister. Although she hated the idea that the family might have to split up, Fran Ellen had matured enough to realize that when her teacher insisted that she would get help for the family, her teacher was taking the proper action.

The book is inappropriately illustrated to make it appear cute and even humorous. The story is far from either. It is so stark that it probably shouldn't have been illustrated at all. And because the hope that is present in the book's ending is very subtle, a review and a discussion may be necessary to help relieve some young readers' anxieties.

Interest Level: 5-6. Reading Level: 3.1. Further Search Topics: Divorce and Separation-Fiction, Challenges-Fiction, Poverty-Fiction, Family Problems-Fiction, Loners-Fiction, Survival-Fiction, Mental Illness-Fiction, Brothers and Sisters-Fiction.

Slote, Alfred. Hang tough, Paul Mather. Lippincott 1973, 156 pp.

Paul Mather went against his doctor's and his parents' orders when he accepted his new neighbors' challenge to show his pitching skill. He had been told not to play baseball until he had been given permission, but Paul not only loved to pitch, he was also the best pitcher his new friends had ever seen. Knowing full well the medical problems he could be precipitating, Paul went ahead and pitched a spectacular game for the Wilson Dairy team against the Ace Appliance team. But by the end of the game, Paul was in the hospital again, and Wilson Dairy had been forced to forfeit the game because Paul had played illegally. As Paul's leukemia worsened, his determination to play baseball again grew. When the day came that his team was to play a second game against Ace Appliance, Paul made sure he was there. He was in a wheelchair and weak, but he was there. He couldn't actually play, but Paul's psychological support insured that Wilson Dairy won the game. He went back to the hospital proud, happy, and still determined to fight his disease.

This is more than the usual sports story. This is a very sensitive story of a young boy's determination to fight leukemia. The reader looking for only a baseball story may find this book more than he/she wants. However, the reader who is open to a story of human strength and courage will be well rewarded. The book neither dwells on nor minimizes the disease. Instead it uses both the disease and the sport to portray a character much more completely than in most sport stories, especially at this low a reading level. This is an excellent book for those special readers who respond well to thought-provoking material. Although chapters are short and reading level is low, the print is somewhat small. In addition, the first person style, told

as if dictated into a tape recorder (complete with occasional interruptions), may be confusing to readers unless it is explained.

Interest Level: 5-6+Reading Level: 3.1. Further Search Topics: Baseball-Fiction, Death-Fiction, Illness-Fiction, Moving, Household-Fiction, Medicine-Fiction, Physicians-Fiction, Challenges-Fiction, Courage-Fiction.

Smith, Alison. Help! There's a cat washing in here!; illus by Amy Rowen. Dutton 1981, 152 pp.

Henry Walker agreed to care for his younger brother and sister for two weeks so that his mother could spend her time preparing a portfolio of her art work in the hopes of getting a much-needed job. It was a desperate move for Henry, but it was the only way he could prevent his bossy Aunt Wilhemina from moving in to run the household. Despite Henry's best efforts, almost everything seemed to go wrong. He burned the food, couldn't keep his brother and sister from misbehaving, seemed to have poisoned his sister's friend, and was faced with making a costume in one night for a school play. The worst of it all was that his mother wasn't pleased with what she was drawing, and Henry only seemed to make her feel more discouraged and unhappy. After what appeared to be certain defeat, however, Henry's efforts were rewarded. His mother was given the job, the family proved they could take care of themselves, and all ended happily.

A light, humorous tale of a young boy's growing independence and maturation under stress and increased responsibility.

Interest Level: 4-6. Reading Level: 3.1. Further Search Topics: Brothers and Sisters-Fiction, Working Parents-Fiction, Single Parent Family-Fiction, Humorous Fiction, Family-Fiction, Challenges-Fiction, Children-Growth-Fiction.

Warner, Gertrude Chandler. Schoolhouse mystery; illus by David Cunningham. A. Whitman 1965, 128 pp.

On a dare, the Aldens went to a quiet fishing village to see what excitement they could find there. They found an isolated town filled with poor and unfriendly people. In their attempt to get to know the townspeople, the Aldens learned of the children's desire for schooling and the adults' anticipation of the Money Man's arrival. The Alden children took on the task of teaching school for the summer in an abandoned schoolhouse owned by Miss Gray, a recluse. The Money Man intrigued them more with each new bit of information they learned about him. They finally decided that the Money Man was a swindler who was practically stealing valuable antiques away from the villagers. By spying on the Money Man when he used the schoolhouse to store the antiques, the Aldens and an ex-FBI man were able to capture him. When the vacation was over, the Aldens had once more found excitement, Miss Gray had agreed to teach the local school, the Money Man was on his way to jail, and the townspeople knew the value of their old household items.

See the entry for *The Boxcar Children* for more information.

Interest Level: 3-5. Reading Level: 2.2. Further Search Topics: Mystery and Detective Stories, Vacation-Fiction, School Stories, Antiquities-Fiction, Crime-Fiction, Brothers and Sisters-Fiction, Challenges-Fiction.

Yolen, Jane. Shirlick Holmes and the case of the wandering wardrobe; illus by Anthony Rao. Coward 1981, 80 pp.

This is a light, fast-paced story of Shirli and her four friends' attempt to solve a local mystery. Its more fully developed characters and plot make this a better literary piece than any of the *Encyclopedia Brown* stories, but it resembles them in other ways. The children live in a small, secure town. The police chief, Shirli's neighbor and George's father, is working on the same case that interests the children but the children solve it first. The mystery is real and involves danger, as opposed to many of Hildick's McGurk mysteries, the other series this book resembles.

Shirli is a fiesty figure who took up George's challenge to solve the town's latest mystery. Thieves had been systematically robbing some of the wealthy summer homes of antiques. Shirli's plan, to search each of the houses for clues, only succeeded in angering the police chief when he caught Shirli and her friends. Being intrepid detectives, however, they did not give up. Instead, they staked out a likely house and waited for the thieves. When the robbers finally arrived Shirli and George hid. Only Gloria was able to escape and go for help. The oak wardrobe in which Shirli took refuge was one of the first pieces the thieves took out of the house. When Shirli tried to get out of it, she found the wardrobe had been placed on a truck with its door against the truck's side; she was caught. Very frightened, she stayed silent until she found herself in the middle of an antiques auction and recognized one of the voices making bids as George's father! As Shirli tumbled out of the wardrobe some of the police chief's men arrested the auctioneer for burglary and selling stolen goods. After she escaped, Gloria had told the police about the thieves, their truck, Shirli, and George, whom they found locked inside a closet still at the summer house.

A serviceable book that will be enjoyed by a wide range of readers.

Interest Level: 3-5. Reading Level: 3.1. Further Search Topics: Mystery and Detective Stories, Humorous Fiction, Friendship-Fiction, Crime-Fiction, Antiquities-Fiction, Detectives-Fiction, Challenges-Fiction.

CHAMBERLAIN, WILT

Rudeen, Kenneth. Wilt Chamberlain; illus by Frank Mullins. Har-Row 1972, 33 pp.

A short and somewhat adoring version of Wilt Chamberlain's childhood, schooling, and professional career. Very little of Chamberlain's personality comes through in this book, but his superior talents and skills as well as his importance to the sport of basketball will be enough to prompt many basketball fans to read it. Although simplistic in style, the book is not condescending. It is, however, out of date, a fact most notable when Chamberlain's salary is quoted. Beware of juvenile format when using with older readers. Crowell Biography series.

Interest Level: 2-6. Reading Level: 3.2. Further Search Topics: Biography, Chamberlain, Wilt, Basketball-Biography, Blacks-Biography, Group 2.

CHEMISTRY-FICTION

Corbett, Scott. The lemonade trick; illus by Paul Galdone. Little 1960, 103 pp.

This is the first book in a series of quite enjoyable stories (most of which are, unfortunately, too difficult to recommend here). Kerby was given an odd chemistry set by a strange old woman whom he helped one day. When he used the set to put together a brew, Kerby found himself completely under its spell. The sweet-smelling liquid he had concocted forced him to be good, so good that his parents began to worry about him. Luckily the spell wore off in a short time. But, Kerby kept experimenting with it: on himself, on his dog, on his friend, on his enemy and finally in desperation, on the entire boy's choir at church.

A succession of innocently humorous incidents are woven together into a satisfying story. Print size is on the small side.

Interest Level: 3-6. Reading Level: 3.1. Further Search Topics: Humorous Fiction, Bullies-Fiction, Magic-Fiction, Magicians-Fiction, Chemistry-Fiction, Read Aloud.

CHICAGO

Bales, Carol Ann. Chinatown Sunday; the story of Lillian Der. Contemp Bks. 1973, 32 pp.

A short, personal visit with a fifth grade Chinese-American girl who lives in a Chicago suburb. The author transcribed taped interviews with Lillian Der to produce a first-person description of Lillian's daily life. The uniquely Chinese-American features of Lillian's life are casually intertwined with experiences common to most American children. Month-old parties, the celebration of Chinese New Year, lucky money, old-age birthday parties, Girl Scout meetings, homework, and being a tomboy are all important to Lillian. Not only is this an interesting portrait of Lillian, but it can be a useful part of a multi-ethnic unit or an introduction to autobiography. The book's usefulness is further extended by its introduction to Chinese immigration and by the glossary, which explains terms such as "abacus," "Chinese calendar," and "sea cucumber." The author saves the over-sized book from looking like a picture book by using photographs instead of drawings, thus she makes the book comfortable even for a sixth grade reader.

Interest Level: 3-6. Reading Level: 3.1. Further Search Topics: Ethnic Groups, Chinese-Americans, Biography, Chicago, Immigration and Emigration.

CHICKENS-FICTION

Pinkwater, Daniel Manus. The Hoboken chicken emergency. P-H 1977, 83 pp.

Arthur's mother sent him out with $16 to buy a Thanksgiving turkey. He returned with a live 266 pound chicken on a leash. It seemed that their turkey reservation had been lost at the meat market and, because it was Thanksgiving morning, there were no other turkeys available. Arthur searched everywhere but found nothing, until a strange old professor tricked him into buying the chicken. No one could bear to kill and eat such a large and friendly chicken, so Arthur and his family named it Henrietta and kept it as a pet. Henrietta was a difficult pet to keep hidden from the neighbors When the neighbors, and later the city, saw Henrietta running loose there was general hysteria. But all ended well when Henrietta and the city calmed down and Henrietta became a kind of neighborhood mascot.

A purely absurd plot but presented with enough energy and humor that most readers thoroughly enjoy the book. Some brief introduction may be necessary to get readers beyond the first few pages.

Interest Level: 3-6. Reading Level: 2.2. Further Search Topics: Humorous Fiction, Chickens-Fiction, Pets-Fiction, Thanksgiving-Fiction, Holidays-Fiction, Read Aloud, Best Sellers.

CHILD ABUSE-FICTION

Mazer, Harry. The war on Villa Street. Delacorte 1978, 182 pp.

Willis was a loner and a runner. He was a loner because he didn't want anyone to find out about his alcoholic father. He wasn't quite sure why he ran;

perhaps because it was the only time he felt good. When Rabbit Slavin and his friends asked Willis to become part of their gang, he refused. He was flattered and wanted to join, but the gang wanted to meet at his house and Willis couldn't risk that. Then when he agreed to coach the local "retard" for the school's field day, Willis gave the gang the opportunity they wanted to take their revenge on him for turning them down. The gang's hatred for Willis increased still more when he beat their best runner and athlete. In payment, the gang jumped Willis and beat him badly. After he picked himself up, Willis realized that he had at least faced the worst of his fears and survived. Days later when his drunken father humiliated him, Willis realized he had to face that, too. He made peace with himself and the world by deciding he could neither continue to run away from, nor apologize for his father anymore. He was independent and strong.

There is much in this fast-paced book besides the obvious violence and action. It is written with an intuitive feel for a teenager's problems and emotions and is a sensitive portrayal of mature concepts. The print is large, but spacing between the lines should have been slightly increased.

Interest Level: 5-6. Reading Level: 5.1. Further Search Topics: Running-Fiction, Loneliness-Fiction, Alcoholism-Fiction, Loners-Fiction, Mental Retardation-Fiction, Gangs-Fiction, Child Abuse-Fiction, Bullies-Fiction, Family Problems-Fiction, Courage-Fiction.

Smith, Doris Buchanan. Tough Chauncey. Morrow 1974, 222 pp.

Chauncey Childs had taught himself to be tough— very tough. Even though he was small for his age (13 years old), the only person who gave him any trouble was his sometimes-friend, Black Jack Levitt. Everyone else was scared of Chauncey. Chauncey felt that he had to be tough or he wouldn't be able to survive. He had to be tough to stand the beatings his grandfather gave him "for his own good," to put up with his mother's drinking and disappearances, and to stand the sight of his grandfather shooting the stray kittens born in their garage.

Chauncey's greatest wish was to be able to live with his mother, instead of with his grandparents. In a desperate attempt to achieve that end he accidentally fell from a moving train and badly hurt his leg. Instead of being returned to his mother he was once more taken back to his grandparents. Chauncey's unhappiness grew until he finally decided to take the one surviving stray kitten and run away. Jack helped him find an empty garage where he could hide while he figured out what to do with his future. After talking with Jack and doing more deep soul searching, Chauncey decided to reshape himself and his life. His first step was to curb his temper and his tongue when his hiding place was discovered. His second step was to see about finding a foster home where he would be treated well, and where he could get a new start.

Ugly as the story is in places, its ending is hopeful. Although it is not always realistic, Chauncey's story is compelling enough to appeal to many readers, especially those who have enjoyed *The War on Villa Street*, by Henry Mazer, *The Outsiders*, by Susan Hinton, or *Mystery of the Fat Cat*, by Frank Bonham. The book's length and its artificially low reading level (vocabulary is often difficult but sentences are very short) make this book most appropriate for an older reader whose reading level is 4.1 or higher.

Interest Level: 5-6. Reading Level: 3.2. Further Search Topics: Child Abuse-Fiction, Family

Problems-Fiction, Grandparents-Fiction, Runaways-Fiction, Bullies-Fiction, Single Parent Family-Fiction, Loners-Fiction, Friendship-Fiction, Troublemakers-Fiction, Foster Homes-Fiction.

CHILDREN-GROWTH-FICTION

Blume, Judy. Are you there God? It's me, Margaret. Bradbury 1970, 149 pp.

Sixth grade was a year of growth for Margaret and her friends. They all wondered when they would start growing breasts and when they would begin menstruating. Each was kissed for the first time. It was also a year in which Margaret tried to decide whether to be Jewish or Christian and ended up neither. She simply remained friends with God, just as she was when the year began. The book is a reassuring, very open, and humorous treatment of the pains and promise of maturation. It is exceptionally popular with older elementary school readers, so the book's slightly small print and narrow lines should not impede an interested reader's progress.

Interest Level: 4-6. Reading Level: 3.2. Further Search Topics: School Stories, Family-Fiction, Children-Growth-Fiction, Religion-Fiction, Humorous Fiction, Love-Fiction, Best Sellers, Grandparents-Fiction, Everyday Stories.

Blume, Judy. Deenie. Bradbury 1973, 159 pp.

Deenie's mother wanted Deenie to be a model. Deenie didn't know what she wanted until she learned that she had scoliosis (curvature of the spine) and would have to wear a brace for four years. Then she knew she only wanted to be normal. She was repulsed by deformities of any kind. She couldn't stand the idea of a brace. Her mother's attitude made Deenie's adjustment even more difficult. It was her father, her doctor, her sister, and a new friend with excema who finally helped Deenie accept her brace and the idea of physical differences. Subplots include Deenie's budding romance with an eighth grade boy, her strained relationship with her mother, and her growing awareness of sex (masturbation and intercourse). Print and line spacing are similar to *Are You There God? It's Me, Margaret.*

Interest Level: 5-6. Reading Level: 3.1. Further Search Topics: Models, Fashion-Fiction, Beauty-Fiction, Scoliosis-Fiction, Physically Handicapped-Fiction, Children-Growth-Fiction, Sex-Fiction, Love-Fiction, Family Problems-Fiction, Illness-Fiction, Adolescence-Fiction.

Bulla, Clyde Robert. Shoeshine girl; illus by Leigh Grant. Har-Row 1975, 84 pp.

A well-written, realistic story of 10-year-old Sarah who was sent to spend the summer with her Aunt Claudia. Sarah's parents felt that Sarah put too much importance on money and so insisted that Aunt Claudia give her no allowance for the summer. Sure that Aunt Claudia would call her bluff, Sarah threatened to get a job. Instead, Aunt Claudia thought it was a good idea. Sarah's experience as a shoeshine girl forced her to grow, to learn to like working, and finally to take responsibility for the stand when her boss was hit by a car. Told with quiet humor. For the reader who enjoys Judy Blume's books.

Interest Level: 2-5. Reading Level: 2.2. Further Search Topics: Children-Growth-Fiction, Family Problems-Fiction, Vacation-Fiction, Occupations-Fiction, Everyday Stories.

Greene, Constance C. A girl called Al; illus by Byron Barton. Viking Pr. 1969, 127 pp.

Told in the first person, this is the story of two seventh grade girls. The girls' warm friendship began the moment Al introduced herself to the narrator as a non-conformist. Al was very independent, mostly because she was on her own so much of the time. Her parents were divorced and she seldom saw either one of them. Her father only wrote her postcards and her mother was rarely home. The narrator's family and Mr. Richards, their building superintendent, became Al's family. They cooked, ate, played, fought, talked and even made bookcases together. When Mr. Richards had a heart attack, they found help for him and later went to see him in the hospital. It was his death that helped Al and her mother grow closer, just as Mr. Richards' life had helped her understand why her father never came to see her.

A satisfying, low-key story of friendship and maturation. The girls are Judy Blume-style characters with much greater innocence. Their ages are not discernible by their actions or dialogue, only by the author's statement.

Interest Level: 3-6. Reading Level: 3.1. Further Search Topics: Children-Growth-Fiction, Single Parent Family-Fiction, Friendship-Fiction, Weight-Fiction, Aging-Fiction, Death-Fiction, Divorce and Separation-Fiction, Family Problems-Fiction, Everyday Stories, Humorous Fiction.

Hurwitz, Johanna. Once I was a plum tree; illus by Ingrid Fetz. Morrow 1980, 160 pp.

Ten-year-old Gerry Flam knew nothing about her religion except that she was Jewish. Her parents didn't practice their religion and only superficially observed some of the holidays. As they told Gerry, their reason was that they were assimilated Americans. In fact, they seemed to practice as many Christian as Jewish holidays. All Gerry's friends and neighbors were Catholic, so Gerry had very little chance to learn about Judaism or the prejudice to which Jews were still being subjected in 1947 in the Bronx. A Jewish family moved into the apartment building next door, and Gerry's quiet curiosity was stimulated. From the Wulfs, Gerry began to learn about Judaism, World War II, and Hitler. As her pride in her heritage grew, Gerry also felt prejudice for the first time. After celebrating her first Passover Seder, Gerry found that despite the problems, she was truly happy to be Jewish.

Much like Chaikin's *I Should Worry, I Should Care* in tone and mood. Will be useful where there is already an interest in Judaism.

Interest Level: 3-5. Reading Level: 3.1. Further Search Topics: Religion-Fiction, Family-Fiction, Jews-Fiction, City Life-Fiction, Children-Growth-Fiction, Prejudice-Fiction.

Kelley, Sally. Trouble with explosives. Bradbury 1976, 117 pp.

Polly Banks stuttered very badly. She wanted to stop but she couldn't. Moving, entering a new school, and facing a mean teacher who seemed in need of psychiatric help, all made Polly's stuttering worse. When Sis, Polly's new friend, rose to Polly's defense in one confrontation too many with Miss Patterson, the teacher took cruel revenge. Polly's desire to help Sis, her need to do something about her stuttering, and an understanding psychiatrist, all helped Polly learn to help herself with her speech problem. At the same time, she began to understand and have confidence in herself and her family.

Another "problem book" that older elementary school readers seem to crave. Polly and Sis are both very sympathetic characters who bring to life many of the uncertainties of growing up. Print and line spacing of only average size but otherwise a good choice.

Interest Level: 4-6. Reading Level: 3.2. Further Search Topics: Academic Problems-Fiction, Stuttering-Fiction, Psychiatrists-Fiction, School Stories, Mental Illness-Fiction, Troublemakers-Fiction, Courage-Fiction, Physically Handicapped-Fiction, Children-Growth-Fiction, Moving, Household-Fiction.

Lowry, Lois. Anastasia Krupnik. HM 1979, 113 pp.

Anastasia Krupnik led a comfortable, relatively happy life until her parents announced that she was not going to be an only child for much longer. After 10 years of enjoying that luxury, Anastasia wasn't at all pleased with the change. Babies immediately went to a prominent, and as far as Anastasia was concerned, permanent place on her list of hates. Anastasia kept two lists: one for things and people she particularly liked, and one list for what she did not like. What went on and off the lists tells much about Anastasia. Anastasia tells the rest in this perceptive, sensitive, and humorous story of growing up and adjusting to a new sibling.

Spacing between lines is slightly too narrow for the rather large print.

Interest Level: 4-6. Reading Level: 3.1. Further Search Topics: Humorous Fiction, Brothers and Sisters-Fiction, Everyday Stories, Jealousy-Fiction, Infants-Fiction, Best Sellers, Children-Growth-Fiction.

MacLachlan, Patricia. Arthur, for the very first time; illus by Lloyd Bloom. Har-Row 1980, 117 pp.

A beautifully written, sensitive yet humorous story of a boy's maturation and growing awareness of the world around him. When Arthur's unhappiness at home is made more intense by the advent of a new baby, he is sent to spend the summer with his older aunt and uncle. Their eccentricities and those of their friends are at first only material for Arthur to write about in his journal. But as the summer progresses he not only learns from them, but also grows from an observer of life to a participant. His final step is helping a large and beloved pig bear her litter in a driving rain storm aided only by his independent, totally untamed young friend Moira.

The print is somewhat small, but spacing between lines is generous.

Interest Level: 4-6. Reading Level: 4.2. Further Search Topics: Read Aloud, Children-Growth-Fiction, Humorous Fiction, Friendship-Fiction, Vacation-Fiction, Relatives-Fiction, Infants-Fiction, Individualists-Fiction, Writing-Fiction, Loners-Fiction, Group 2.

Smith, Alison. Help! There's a cat washing in here!; illus by Amy Rowen. Dutton 1981, 152 pp.

Henry Walker agreed to care for his younger brother and sister for two weeks so that his mother could spend her time preparing a portfolio of her art work in the hopes of getting a much-needed job. It was a desperate move for Henry, but it was the only way he could prevent his bossy Aunt Wilhemina from moving in to run the household. Despite Henry's best efforts, almost everything seemed to go wrong. He burned the food, couldn't keep his brother and sister from misbehaving, seemed to have poisoned his sister's friend, and was faced with making a costume in one night for a school play. The worst of it all was that his mother wasn't pleased with what she was drawing, and Henry only seemed to make her feel more discouraged and unhappy. After what appeared to be certain defeat, however, Henry's efforts were rewarded. His mother was given the job, the family proved they could take care of themselves, and all ended happily.

A light, humorous tale of a young boy's growing independence and maturation under stress and increased responsibility.

Interest Level: 4-6. Reading Level: 3.1. Further Search Topics: Brothers and Sisters-Fiction, Working Parents-Fiction, Single Parent Family-Fiction, Humorous Fiction, Family-Fiction, Challenges-Fiction, Children-Growth-Fiction.

Smith, Doris Buchanan. Last was Lloyd. Viking Pr 1981, 124 pp.

Lloyd had several problems: he was overweight, his mother was overprotective, he had no school friends, and there was a chance he might be taken away from home and put into foster care because he had missed so much school. Lloyd's mother, very young and very defensive when she had Lloyd, had done her best to be a "good mother," but in doing so, had made Lloyd fearful of the world. He had become the subject of his classmates' mockery so many times that the only way he could respond to his peers was with nastiness. The one skill he possessed was hitting a baseball. He kept this skill well hidden for fear of exposing himself to further mockery. When one of his classmates accidentally discovered how well Lloyd hit, he took the first step to becoming Lloyd's friend. Lloyd's reaction was to back away, but Kirby kept trying. Eventually Kirby's attempts and those of an understanding truant officer, helped Lloyd begin to make friends, to treat others decently, and to pull away from his mother; in short, he began to mature.

Because Lloyd's problems can be oversimplified too easily, this book requires a fairly mature reader and perhaps even discussion in order to fully understand its subtleties.

Interest Level: 5-6+Reading Level: 4.2. Further Search Topics: Weight-Fiction, Single Parent Family-Fiction, Courage-Fiction, School Stories, Loners-Fiction, Friendship-Fiction, Baseball-Fiction, Family Problems-Fiction, Foster Homes-Fiction, Children-Growth-Fiction.

CHINESE-AMERICANS

Bales, Carol Ann. Chinatown Sunday; the story of Lillian Der. Contemp Bks. 1973, 32 pp.

A short, personal visit with a fifth grade Chinese-American girl who lives in a Chicago suburb. The author transcribed taped interviews with Lillian Der to produce a first-person description of Lillian's daily life. The uniquely Chinese-American features of Lillian's life are casually intertwined with experiences common to most American children. Month-old parties, the celebration of Chinese New Year, lucky money, old-age birthday parties, Girl Scout meetings, homework, and being a tomboy are all important to Lillian. Not only is this an interesting portrait of Lillian, but it can be a useful part of a multi-ethnic unit or an introduction to autobiography. The book's usefulness is further extended by its introduction to Chinese immigration and by the glossary, which explains terms such as "abacus," "Chinese calendar," and "sea cucumber." The author saves the over-sized book from looking like a picture book by using photographs instead of drawings, thus she makes the book comfortable even for a sixth grade reader.

Interest Level: 3-6. Reading Level: 3.1. Further Search Topics: Ethnic Groups, Chinese-Americans, Biography, Chicago, Immigration and Emigration.

CHRISTMAS-FICTION

Robinson, Barbara. The best Christmas pageant ever; illus by Judith Gwyn Brown. Har-Row 1972, 80 pp.

A truly delightful story of what happens when the meanest kids in town (they are all in one family) take over all the lead roles in the Sunday school Christmas pageant. The Herdmans (all six of them), having heard that the church was giving away free food, showed up to take some. While they were there, they heard about the Christmas pageant and decided it presented them with another perfect opportunity for food and mischief. With a little behind-the-scenes arm-twisting (literally), they managed to dissuade everyone else from showing interest in the major roles. Theirs was a completely original interpretation of the Christmas story that left nothing and no one around them untouched.

That the book's reading level will prove too high for many people is unfortunate. The story is well worth the struggle. A wonderful choice for reading aloud.

Interest Level: 3-6. Reading Level: 5.1 Further Search Topics: Christmas-Fiction, Bullies-Fiction, Troublemakers-Fiction, Humorous Fiction, Religion-Fiction, Group 2, Read Aloud, Acting-Fiction, Holidays-Fiction.

CHRISTMAS STORIES

Wagner, Jane. J.T; photos by Gordon Parks, Jr. Van Nostrand 1969, 64 pp.

This is a sentimental story that rarely fails to elicit a sympathetic response from young readers. J.T. is a poor black boy who saw a portable radio almost begging to be stolen and stole it. Two of the neighborhood bullies, Boomer and Claymore, saw J.T. take the radio. Though they threatened him, even poured soap in his eyes in the school bathrooms, J.T. wouldn't give them the radio as they demanded.

About the same time J.T. found a scrawny, scared little cat with only one eye. Because his mother wouldn't let him take the cat home, J.T. built it a warm but ramshackle little house in an abandoned building. He fed it by charging tuna to his mother's grocery store account without her knowledge. Bones became the only thing in J.T.'s life that he had cared about since his father had walked out.

When Boomer and Claymore found out about Bones, they taunted J.T. by throwing the cat back and forth between them until the frightened cat escaped, darted out into the street and was hit by a car. J.T.'s heart broke as he looked at Bones, but he spoke to no one to tell them of his sadness. Only time, his mother's and grandmother's love and a small kitten from Mr. Rosen, the grocer, helped him recover. On the morning that he decided to accept the kitten, J.T. returned the stolen radio, faced Boomer and Claymore without fear, and asked Mr. Rosen for a job in order to pay for cat food.

The book is oversized and illustrated with photographs from the television movie version. It is not only an excellent story to read aloud but one that will prompt listeners to want to finish it on their own or to reread it. It is now available only in paperback from Dell.

Interest Level: 3-6. Reading Level: 3.1. Further Search Topics: Read Aloud, Courage-Fiction, Best Sellers, Cats-Fiction, Single Parent Family-Fiction, Bullies-Fiction, Blacks-Fiction, Poverty-Fiction, City Life-Fiction, Christmas Stories, Crime-Fiction, Pets-Fiction, Holidays-Fiction.

CIRCUS

Krementz, Jill. A very young circus flyer. Knopf 1979, unp (112 pp).

One of a series of five oversized, abundantly photographed views of unusual children. Tato Farfan is part of the Flying Farfans of Ringling Brothers and Barnum and Bailey Circus. He lives in a railroad car on a circus train with his mother, father, and older brother. The whole family performs as trapeze artists and flyers for the circus. Told as if Tato were speaking, this is the story of a fairly normal boy who also happens to be a circus flyer. Practice sessions are difficult, costumes must be readied, and time must be spent helping each other, but there is also time for Tato to watch TV, play with the clowns, play soccer, and just have fun.

In addition to Tato's story, the reader is given a behind-the-scenes tour of the circus right up to and including the performance itself (color photos used for the performance). It is an exciting world that should appeal to almost anyone who has enjoyed the circus.

Interest Level: 2-6. Reading Level: 3.2. Further Search Topics: Circus, Acrobats and Acrobatics, Best Sellers, Talent, Group 2, Gymnastics.

CIRCUS-FICTION

Bulla, Clyde Robert . Dexter; illus by Glo Coalson. Har-Row 1973, 69 pp.

This is not as simple a story as it first appears. Dave, 12 years old and lonely, had hoped his new neighbors would be friends. But, the Arvin family kept very much to themselves until Dave accidentally discovered Alex, the Arvin's son, doing tricks on a trapeze in the barn. Because Dave kept the secret and shared Alex's love for Dexter, his circus pony, the boys soon became friends. Then in one horrible night, the Arvins were forced to leave the town and Dexter was so badly hurt he was believed to be dead. A week later Dave found Dexter alive, but crippled for life and so frightened that no one could get near him. The horse surprised everyone and managed to live through a very harsh winter as well as the townspeople's determination to kill him. When Alex and his father returned, almost a year later, they found Dexter and took the old and feeble horse back to a ranch with them. The story is told with sympathy, with an understanding of how it feels to be lonely, and with tension and suspense. It's appeal should last from third through sixth grade. Print size is smaller than Bulla's usual.

Interest Level: 3-6. Reading Level: 3.1. Further Search Topics: Survival-Fiction, Acrobats and Acrobatics-Fiction, Horses-Fiction, Read Aloud, Circus-Fiction, Loneliness-Fiction, Friendship-Fiction.

Dolch, Edward W. Circus stories; illus by Dee Wallace. Garrard 1956, 166 pp.

A collection of 18 chapters that tell 15 true stories about the circus. Some are descriptions of activities (trapeze flying) or people (Emmett Kelly, a circus doctor, the Ringling Brothers). Other chapters tell of unusual occurrences; i.e., the bareback rider who was thrown off her horse into the lap of a spectator whom she later married. Some stories, such as the story of the horse trainer whose life was saved by an elephant, are exciting. Others are sad ("Blinky," the dog who was killed by an angry lion).

The authors' tone becomes condescending off and on through this collection, thus hampering its usefulness somewhat. Otherwise, it is very similar to the other Dolch books; it is a decent collection of very simplified stories. Dolch Basic Vocabulary Book series.

Interest Level: 1-4. Reading Level: 2.2. Further Search Topics: Circus-Fiction, Clowns-Fiction, Acrobats and Acrobatics-Fiction, Group 2.

CITY LIFE

Beame, Rona. Ladder company 108. Messner 1973, 63 pp.

The reader of this book will literally live through several days with a New York City fire company. The author's "Dragnet"-like writing style, her use of photographs, and actual people, all make the firefighters' experiences very real. It is an exciting, engrossing and satisfying book. The heavily-used jargon will be quickly understood, thus should pose no real obstacle to most readers.

Interest Level 2-6. Reading Level: 3.1. Further Search Topics: Firefighters, Occupations, City Life, New York City, Group 2, Best Sellers.

Holland, John. The way it is. HarBraceJ 1969, 87 pp.

For 15 boys living in a run-down area of Brooklyn, school became interesting when they were assigned to photograph whatever was meaningful to them in their neighborhood. The results, described in their own words, were developed into this fascinating documentary which is at the same time a spontaneous glimpse of the boys themselves. The book should be of particular interest to older urban children. Print slightly on the small side. Has recently gone out of print, but is worth looking for.

Interest Level: 4-6. Reading Level: 3.2. Further Search Topics: Best Sellers, City Life, Photography, Poverty, Academic Problems.

CITY LIFE-FICTION

Berends, Polly Berrien. The case of the elevator duck; illus by James K. Washburn. Random 1973, 54 pp.

Although it would be stretching the meaning of the word to call this a mystery, it is a story of an 11-year-old detective. Albert tells his own story in a clipped style that resembles adult detective novels. One morning Albert found a duck abandoned in the apartment house elevator. He was determined to find the owner of the duck and return it. He had to be very careful as he searched because pets were absolutely forbidden in the housing projects. Anyone who saw him with the duck might report him. Albert and his parents had waited too long to get into the projects to be kicked out because of a duck. When Albert finally found the duck's owner (a young, sad child named Julio), Julio's sister forced Albert to take the duck back. Still angry at Julio's sister, Albert took the duck to the project's day care center, where the teacher agreed to formally adopt the duck. Albert stayed at the center long enough to see Julio's happy surprise when he arrived and found the duck. Its appealing characters, the tension created by the writing style, and the book's humor make this a delightful story.

Interest Level: 2-5. Reading Level 2.2. Further Search Topics: Humorous Fiction, City Life-Fiction, Housing Projects-Fiction, Detectives-Fiction, Pets-Fiction, Ducks-Fiction, Read Aloud.

Bonham, Frank. The mystery of the fat cat; illus by Alvin Smith. Dutton 1968, 160 pp.

Although noticeably dated at times, this is still an exciting story of an inner city neighborhood. Buddy, Little Pie, Rich, and Cool were among the many who used the local Boys' Club as their hangout. It was a place to stay out of trouble and off the streets, but it was also a haven for rats. The rats were big and brazen; so brazen that one attacked Buddy in the swimming pool. The club needed a new building desperately. The money was there; they just weren't able to use it. Fifteen years earlier an eccentric old woman willed the Boys' Club over $600,000, but stated that the money was first to be used to support her cat until it died. A caretaker, a lawyer, and a veterinarian all benefited as long as the cat lived. Buddy and his friends took on the job of discovering if the cat really was alive or if the Boys' Club was being cheated out of half a million dollars. It was a job that nearly killed them before they set things right. Plenty of action, some violence, a cast of street-smart characters, realistic trouble with the police, as well as a slight mystery almost insure the book's success with older readers. Moderate sized print. Line spacing somewhat narrow.

Interest Level: 6+. Reading Level: 5.1. Further Search Topics: Humorous Fiction, Cats-Fiction, Gangs-Fiction, City Life-Fiction, Mystery and Detective Stories, Poverty-Fiction, Friendship-Fiction, Juvenile Delinquency-Fiction, Crime-Fiction, Best Sellers.

Bulla, Clyde Robert. Indian hill; illus by James J. Spanfeller. T Y Crowell 1963, 74 pp.

A very low-key story of a Navajo family who moved from the reservation to a city because they could no longer support themselves on the reservation. The move was necessary, but it was not appreciated by young Kee and his mother. They hated their ugly apartment and the crowded city, and wanted to go home. When an excuse to return to the reservation arose, Kee and his mother left the city. However, by the time Kee's father arrived to tell them he had been wrong to force them to move, Kee and his mother had realized they never gave their new home a chance. They were ready to try again. No excitement here, only an understanding look at the difficulties of moving.

Interest Level: 2-5. Reading Level: 2.1. Further Search Topics: Indians of North America-Fiction, Navajo Indians-Fiction, City Life-Fiction, Moving, Household-Fiction.

Chaikin, Miriam. I should worry, I should care; illus by Richard Egielski. Har-Row 1979, 103 pp.

A warm, well-written story about life in a Jewish family in Brooklyn just before World War II. This is the story of young Molly's adjustment to moving, to leaving old friends, to making and losing new friends (one by death) and to the small happenings that make up her life. In the background, but always there, is Hitler's ever-increasing threat to the world.

A comfortable, truthful look at a close-knit family. Also useful for its picture of the times and the place. An occasional Yiddish expression may slow the reader but adds to the book's authenticity. Print is slightly lighter and smaller than *Finders Weepers*.

Interest Level: 3-5. Reading Level: 2.2. Further Search Topics: Moving, Household-Fiction, Friendship-Fiction, City Life-Fiction, Jews-Fiction, Family-Fiction.

Greene, Constance C. I and Sproggy; illus by Emily A. McCully. Viking Pr. 1978, 155 pp.

Ten-year-old Adam had adjusted to his parents' divorce and had even grown to like living alone with his mother. When his father came back from London with his new wife and stepdaughter Sproggy and announced that they were moving into an apartment nearby, Adam was a little worried. But when his father asked him to take care of Sproggy, Adam was furious. First of all, he didn't know Sproggy and he didn't want to know her. Secondly, she was two months older

than he, taller too, and she embarrassed him in public. And finally, she didn't need his help. She got along quite well by herself; so well that she even saved Adam from a mugger and became good friends with Adam's friends behind his back. It wasn't until Sproggy proved to be vulnerable that Adam and she became friends.

A warm, realistic and humorous story whose interesting characters (even the minor ones) heighten the book's appeal.

Interest Level: 4-6. Reading Level: 3.2. Further Search Topics: Brothers and Sisters-Fiction, Divorce and Separation-Fiction, City Life-Fiction, New York City-Fiction, Humorous Fiction, Friendship-Fiction, Everyday Stories.

Hinton, Susan E. The outsiders. Viking Pr. 1967, 188 pp.

When she wrote this book Susan Hinton was only 17 years old, but she had the sensitivity of someone much older. She wrote a taut story of the rivalry between two city gangs; the Socs (the rich socialites) and the Greasers (poor kids from the wrong side of town) that is more than anything a plea for understanding and tolerance. Seen through the eyes of Ponyboy (a very bright, 14-year-old Greaser), the rivalry brought on violence and an accidental killing that forced Pony and his friend Johnny to flee for their lives. Dallas, the meanest and most dangerous of the Greasers, provided them with shelter, food for a week, and a gun. At the end of that week, Johnny decided that they should turn themselves in to the police. But before they could do that, their hideout (an old church) burned in a fire which threatened the lives of four children who had been playing there. In trying to rescue the children, Johnny, Pony, and Dallas were injured; Johnny was severely burned and probably permanently crippled. A vengeance rumble was held while Johnny lay in the hospital, but the Greasers' victory was empty when Johnny died. He had been the one member of the gang whom they all loved and who had most needed them. Dallas went to pieces: he robbed a store and set himself up to be killed by the police. He had nothing left to live for after Johnny's death. Pony found support and security with his brothers (their parents were dead) and, in a note from Johnny, some hope for the future.

Hinton speaks most often through Pony (his depth of understanding of the people around him is very impressive), but through Johnny and two of the Socs as well, Randy and Cherry. Her message is clear, but at no time does she fail to maintain believable characters in a compelling plot.

Although the book looks forbidding with its 188 pages of unrelenting small print, it is an exciting story, full of adventure, realism, and room for thought. Perhaps the best way to introduce this book is to read a fair portion of it aloud. Now a motion picture too.

Interest Level: 6+. Reading Level: 5.1. Further Search Topics: Crime-Fiction, Gangs-Fiction, Murder-Fiction, Read Aloud, Friendship-Fiction, Juvenile Delinquency-Fiction, Best Sellers, City Life-Fiction, Brothers and Sisters-Fiction, Orphans-Fiction, Runaways-Fiction, Troublemakers-Fiction, Poverty-Fiction.

Hurwitz, Johanna. Once I was a plum tree; illus by Ingrid Fetz. Morrow 1980, 160 pp.

Ten-year-old Gerry Flam knew nothing about her religion except that she was Jewish. Her parents didn't practice their religion and only superficially observed some of the holidays. As they told Gerry, their reason was that they were assimilated Americans. In fact, they seemed to practice as many Christian as Jewish holidays. All Gerry's friends and neighbors were Catholic, so Gerry had very little chance to learn about Judaism or the prejudice to which Jews were still being subjected in 1947 in the Bronx. A Jewish family moved into the apartment building next door, and Gerry's quiet curiosity was stimulated. From the Wulfs, Gerry began to learn about Judaism, World War II, and Hitler. As her pride in her heritage grew, Gerry also felt prejudice for the first time. After celebrating her first Passover Seder, Gerry found that despite the problems, she was truly happy to be Jewish.

Much like Chaikin's *I Should Worry, I Should Care* in tone and mood. Will be useful where there is already an interest in Judaism.

Interest Level: 3-5. Reading Level: 3.1. Further Search Topics: Religion-Fiction, Family-Fiction, Jews-Fiction, City Life-Fiction, Children-Growth-Fiction, Prejudice-Fiction.

Hurwitz, Johanna. The law of gravity; illus by Ingrid Fetz. Morrow 1978, 192 pp.

The summer between fifth and sixth grades looked very unexciting to Margot. Her best friends were both going away for the whole summer and her father, a musician, was going to be on tour for most of the summer. Margot's very overweight mother had sworn never to go downstairs from their fifth floor walk-up apartment. Unless Margot chose to stay upstairs too, she was sure she would have a very lonely vacation. In addition, she had to work on a summer project for school. The project she finally chose was to get her mother downstairs after nine years of staying upstairs. In search of help she went to the local library where she met Bernie. Bernie was only a year older than Margot, but he seemed to know the most interesting things about the city. He showed her places Margot had never heard of before, he taught her to play chess, backgammon, and even to ride a bicycle. He was so full of fascinating ideas and information that Margot had no chance to be bored or lonely. Best of all, he even tried to help Margot with her project. None of their ideas worked, however, until Margot pretended to run away and scared her mother into going downstairs. Only then did Margot realize that she loved her mother whether or not she stayed on the fifth floor and that she couldn't simply force her mother or anyone else to change to suit her own fancy.

The book is a warm, understanding, slightly humorous treatment of the fairly common wish to change someone else. Although not many readers are likely to share Margot's exact problem, most will recognize her feelings. The book is also a virtual Chamber of Commerce advertisement for urban living. One of its other charms is its picture of a non-competitive, open, real friendship between an 11-year-old girl and a 12-year-old boy. The only drawback to the book is its inconsistent reading level which varies from 4.1 to 5.1 with a rare leap to 5.2.

Interest Level: 4-6. Reading Level: 4.2. Further Search Topics: Vacation-Fiction, Friendship-Fiction, Loners-Fiction, City Life-Fiction, Individualists-Fiction, Courage-Fiction, New York City-Fiction, Humorous Fiction, Family-Fiction, Challenges-Fiction, Weight-Fiction, Everyday Stories, Best Sellers.

Lowry, Lois. Anastasia again! HM 1981, 145 pp.

This is a sequel that is as funny and well-written as its predecessor. Because its plot involves less common experiences, this book may not enjoy quite the wide-spread success of *Anastasia Krupnik.*

However, among those readers who liked their first meeting with Anastasia, this book will find many fans.

Anastasia's parents astounded her when they announced that the family was going to move from their Cambridge, Massachusetts apartment to a house in the suburbs. She didn't like the idea of leaving the apartment, but she *hated* the idea of the suburbs. The only thing that made the move bearable was the house itself. Anastasia had said she would move only if they could find a house with a tower—and they had. After she got over the shock of moving, Anastasia began to enjoy her new home. She met a neighborhood boy who became a special friend, she tried to help her cranky elderly neighbor Mrs. Stein make friends, and she even wrote a short mystery book.

Anastasia is as spunky and original as before. She is a bit precocious, but her precocity is nothing compared to that of her brother. At two-and-a-half years old, he speaks as well as many adults. As we mentioned above, the book will be most appealing to readers who want second helpings of Anastasia's adventures. The print is slightly smaller here than in the first title.

Interest Level: 4-6. Reading Level: 2.2. Further Search Topics: Moving, Household-Fiction, City Life-Fiction, Suburbia-Fiction, Humorous Fiction, Aging-Fiction, Writing-Fiction, Family-Fiction, Everyday Stories.

Shearer, John. Billy Jo Jive and the case of the missing pigeons; illus by Ted Shearer. Delacorte 1978, 47 pp.

This is the third in a series of slight mysteries, always solved by Billy Jo Jive and his crime fighter partner, Susie Sunset. Jive and Sunset are street-wise, black youngsters who take their jobs as crime fighters very seriously, and are never detered for long from finding the criminals they seek. The crimes are always thefts, and the criminals vary from young children to neighborhood menaces. Suspense is created more by the manner in which Jive and Sunset catch the thieves, plus the determination and pace of the young detectives, than by guessing who the culprits might be. Jive, his street-slang manner of telling the first-person stories, and the urban setting will appeal to many readers. Jive and Sunset also appear on *Sesame Street*.

Jive accidentally photographed the fleeing pigeon thief as he was being chased by Flip, the victim. The photograph didn't show the thief's face, but did give Jive and Sunset a good look at what he was wearing. Jive and Sunset concluded that the thief was Snake Hips Robberts. They later realized that they had been wrong. When they looked carefully at the picture, they remembered that any dark color clothing photographs almost black in a black and white picture. Snake Hips had a black jacket, but he was innocent. The real thief was Sugar Brown. Then it was a simple matter of showing the evidence to both Flip and Sugar to get Sugar to confess.

Interest Level: 1-4. Reading Level: 2.2. Further Search Topics: Mystery and Detective Stories, Detectives-Fiction, Blacks-Fiction, City Life-Fiction, Group 2, Best Sellers.

Shearer, John. Billy Jo Jive and the walkie-talkie caper; illus by Ted Shearer. Delacorte 1981, 47 pp.

When Steam Boat Louis went to Jive and Sunset for help, he was desperate. Because Jive and Sunset had already solved three cases, they were the logical people to find the walkie-talkie that had been stolen from Steam Boat. The walkie-talkie was one of two that Steam Boat had been told to buy as part of a secret communication system for the Bugaloo Smackers. Even as Jive and Sunset hunted for the thief, the second walkie-talkie was stolen. Their only clue was a footprint found outside Steam Boat's fix-it shop. Eventually, after trial and error, Jive and Sunset uncovered the real thieves; Steam Boat's young twin cousins. Unhappy at being separated in school, they wanted to use the walkie-talkies to be able to talk with each other.

The high reading level of this book will make it most useful for those children who have read and enjoyed other books in the series and are willing to stretch to read one more.

Interest Level: 1-4. Reading Level: 3.2. Further Search Topics: Mystery and Detective Stories, Detectives-Fiction, Blacks-Fiction, City Life-Fiction, Group 2.

Shearer, John. Billy Jo Jive super private eye: the case of the missing ten speed bike; illus by Ted Shearer. Delacorte 1976, 47 pp.

Jive and Sunset began their friendship and their sleuthing career with this book. It all started when Sunset borrowed her older brother's 10-speed bicycle. Jive met Sunset while she sat at the side of the road crying, after her brother's bike had been stolen. Some careful joint detective work proved to Jive and Sunset that Dynamite Jones, jealous of Sunset's brother, had stolen the bike. The young crime fighters recovered the bicycle before Sunset's brother even knew it was missing.

This book sets the formula that all the others follow. A neighborhood person finds that something has been stolen and goes to Jive and Sunset for help. Jive and Sunset never have much trouble finding the thief even though they are sometimes misled for a short time. Often the culprit is quite obvious to the reader. After some attempts at clever detective work and an occasional bit of preaching, the crime is solved. It is the manner of the pursuit and the street-smart characters that give the stories their interest.

Interest Level: 1-4. Reading Level: 2.2. Further Search Topics: Mystery and Detective Stories, Blacks-Fiction, Detectives-Fiction, City Life-Fiction, Best Sellers, Group 2, Bicycles and Bicycling-Fiction.

Shreve, Susan. The Nightmares of Geranium Street. Knopf 1977, 127 pp.

The Nightmares, a small neighborhood gang, had very little to do until beautiful Tess moved on the block. Tess dressed in satins, furs, and rhinestones, and sang in nightclubs. She was even more of a fascination to the gang because they had been told to stay away from her. When Amanda moved in with Tess, the Nightmares invited her to join the gang so that they would have a way of spying on Tess. Gradually her strange behavior, her moods, her bruises and shaking spells, the strangers she let in the house, and the fights she had, led the gang members to suspect that Tess dealt in drugs. When Amanda failed to show up for a picnic and the Nightmares learned the police were searching for Tess, the gang became worried enough to look for Amanda themselves. In doing so, they uncovered proof of Tess' drug dealings, put themselves in great danger, and were protected by Tess as they escaped only moments before Tess was arrested.

Despite its low reading level, the book's confusing sequence of final events, and its subject matter make it best suited to older readers. It is not great literature, but its subject has strong appeal.

Interest Level: 5-6. Reading Level: 3.1. Further Search Topics: Family Problems-Fiction, Gangs-Fiction, Drugs-Fiction, Mystery and Detective Stories, City Life-Fiction, Crime-Fiction, Philadelphia-Fiction.

Wagner, Jane. J.T; photos by Gordon Parks, Jr. Van Nostrand 1969, 64 pp.

This is a sentimental story that rarely fails to elicit a sympathetic response from young readers. J.T. is a poor black boy who saw a portable radio almost begging to be stolen and stole it. Two of the neighborhood bullies, Boomer and Claymore, saw J.T. take the radio. Though they threatened him, even poured soap in his eyes in the school bathrooms, J.T. wouldn't give them the radio as they demanded.

About the same time J.T. found a scrawny, scared little cat with only one eye. Because his mother wouldn't let him take the cat home, J.T. built it a warm but ramshackle little house in an abandoned building. He fed it by charging tuna to his mother's grocery store account without her knowledge. Bones became the only thing in J.T.'s life that he had cared about since his father had walked out.

When Boomer and Claymore found out about Bones, they taunted J.T. by throwing the cat back and forth between them until the frightened cat escaped, darted out into the street and was hit by a car. J.T.'s heart broke as he looked at Bones, but he spoke to no one to tell them of his sadness. Only time, his mother's and grandmother's love and a small kitten from Mr. Rosen, the grocer, helped him recover. On the morning that he decided to accept the kitten, J.T. returned the stolen radio, faced Boomer and Claymore without fear, and asked Mr. Rosen for a job in order to pay for cat food.

The book is oversized and illustrated with photographs from the television movie version. It is not only an excellent story to read aloud but one that will prompt listeners to want to finish it on their own or to reread it. It is now available only in paperback from Dell.

Interest Level: 3-6. Reading Level: 3.1. Further Search Topics: Read Aloud, Courage-Fiction, Best Sellers, Cats-Fiction, Single Parent Family-Fiction, Bullies-Fiction, Blacks-Fiction, Poverty-Fiction, City Life-Fiction, Christmas Stories, Crime-Fiction, Pets-Fiction, Holidays-Fiction.

CIVIL RIGHTS

Adoff, Arnold. Malcolm X; illus by John Wilson. Har-Row 1970, 41 pp.

This is a simple, intellectually honest biography of a very controversial man. Taught a strong sense of self-respect by his father, Malcolm X could not accept the second-class status that white society tried to impose upon him. Instead he turned away from whites and all they stood for. He hated high school, the detention home he lived in after his father's death, and his mother's placement in a state hospital. He didn't feel comfortable until he moved to Harlem. There he found friends, but he also found crime. While he was in prison, Malcolm X began to read of great, black societies and people. His brother told him about the Nation of Islam, the Black Muslims, and Elijah Muhammad, the leader of the religion. He began corresponding with Mr. Muhammad. Shortly after he was released from prison, Malcolm X met Elijah Muhammad and eventually became a minister of the religion. There was even talk that he would be Elijah Muhammad's successor. But, as the years went on, Malcolm X began to think that black Christians as well as Muslims should be united in the fight for black rights. Despite threats against his life Malcolm X formed the Organization of Afro-American Unity. Both blacks and whites were angry with him. The threats continued until his house was firebombed; and, only a week later, at a public meeting, Malcolm X was assassinated.

An excellent overview of a complex man. The book may well prompt readers to learn more about the man and his beliefs. At the very least it will expose readers, in an interesting manner, to someone they should know. The book shares the same semi-picture book format of the others in Harper and Row/Crowell's biography series, therefore it will need a careful introduction to potential readers.

Interest Level: 3-5. Reading Level: 3.1. Further Search Topics: Blacks-Biography, Civil Rights, Biography, Crime, Religion, Assassinations, Prejudice, Poverty, Foster Homes.

Greenfield, Eloise. Rosa Parks; illus by Eric Marlow. Har-Row 1973, 33 pp.

This book succumbs to the difficulty of writing for children about a subject that needs more explanation. The occasionally condescending tone combined with the Crowell Biography picture book format will keep this otherwise adequate introduction to the civil rights movement from being useful beyond fourth grade. The book should be very useful, however, for third and fourth grade social studies, history or biography units.

Rosa Parks' childhood and her feelings about the special rules for blacks make up the first half of the book. The second half is devoted to Rosa's act of defiance (refusing to give up her seat on a bus to a white man) and the repercussions of that act. Crowell Biography series.

Interest Level: 2-4. Reading Level 2.2. Further Search Topics: Blacks-Biography, Biography, Prejudice, Civil Rights, Women-Biography, Courage.

Jordan, June. Fannie Lou Hamer; illus by Albert Williams. Har-Row 1972, 41 pp.

In 1917, Fannie Lou Hamer was the last of 20 children born to a fearless black woman. Fannie and her family grew up working on a white man's cotton plantation. Although they were kept poor and hungry by the plantation owner and the field boss, Fannie Lou grew up in her mother's image—unafraid of white people and unhappy with the poor treatment of blacks that she saw all around her. In 1962, when most other blacks in Mississippi where afraid of the consequences, Fannie registered to vote. After both she and her husband lost their jobs and their home, and after she was beaten in a Mississippi jail, Fannie Lou Hamer drew national attention to her fight for blacks' civil rights. She spoke all over the country, helped to form a new political party, and raised money to help poor people. That money was what started the 640 acre Freedom Farm Cooperative that provided work and food for more than 5,000 people. It was Mrs. Hamer's dream to see poor people work together to feed themselves rather than to accept food from others. She made her dream come true.

Another competent entry in the Crowell Biography series. Only its picture book format keeps this book from being useful through sixth grade.

Interest Level: 3-5. Reading Level: 3.2. Further Search Topics: Biography, Blacks-Biography, Civil Rights, Poverty, Women-Biography,

Rudeen, Kenneth. Jackie Robinson; illus by Richard Cuffari. Har-Row 1971, 41 pp.

Jackie Robinson was the youngest child in a large, poor family. As early as high school it was Robinson's superior athletic talent that set him apart. He could run track or play baseball, football, or basketball. He was the first student at UCLA to win a letter in all four sports. But because he wasn't happy to see the way his mother still had to struggle to earn money to live, after a year and a half at UCLA, Robinson left college to take a job. Soon after that, the United States entered World War II and Robinson went into the Army. His refusal to ride in the back of a bus in Texas resulted in a courtmartial, but he was found innocent after an uproar was made by the newspapers.

After the Army, Robinson played baseball with a Negro League team. A short time later, he was asked by the Dodger manager Branch Rickey to become the first black man to play in the major leagues. Rickey warned Robinson that it would mean he not only had to play well, but that he would also have to take all the anger and bitterness that would be directed at him. Robinson agreed. For three long years, while there were no other black players in the major leagues, Robinson played well and took everything without fighting back. Robinson was then able to stop trying to be perfect because he had successfully broken a very important color barrier and no longer had to prove to white managers, players and fans that blacks belonged in baseball just as much as whites. Robinson played for the Dodgers for ten years. When he left baseball he was elected into the Baseball Hall of Fame. He continued to fight for civil rights throughout the rest of his life, although there is only a brief mention of his activities in the book. Since the book's publication Jackie Robinson has died.

This is an excellent choice for the child who thinks of nothing but sports. It may be helpful in opening up an interest in the civil rights movement, black history, or black heroes. It is unfortunate that the traditional Crowell biography format (semi-picture book), and the author's slight tendency to be condescending, prevents the book from being useful beyond fourth grade. Crowell Biography series.

Interest Level: 2-4. Reading Level: 2.2. Further Search Topics: Civil Rights, Robinson, Jackie, Baseball-Biography, Biography, Blacks-Biography, Prejudice, Poverty.

CLEMENTE, ROBERTO

Rudeen, Kenneth. Roberto Clemente; illus by Frank Mullins. Har-Row 1974, 33 pp.

A romanticized retelling of a great baseball player's life. Those already interested in baseball or in Clemente will probably not mind the romantic tone, but may notice the almost patronizing explanations of some of the basics of baseball. Crowell Biography series.

Interest Level: 2-4. Reading Level: 3.1. Further Search Topics: Baseball-Biography, Biography, Puerto Rico, Group 2, Clemente, Roberto.

CLOCKS AND WATCHES

Berger, Melvin. Time after time; illus by Richard Cuffari. Coward 1975, 45 pp.

The book begins with a description of inner clocks, proceeds into measurement of time, the seasons, and finally demonstrates the making of a simple clock. The explanations are simple but interesting. One point logically follows from another. It is a solid, serviceable tool limited only somewhat by the fact that it looks like a cross between a picture book and a reader. A brief index is included.

Interest Level: 1-4. Reading Level: 2.2. Further Search Topics: Time, Clocks and Watches, Seasons, Group 2.

CLOWNS-FICTION

Dolch, Edward W. Circus stories; illus by Dee Wallace. Garrard 1956, 166 pp.

A collection of 18 chapters that tell 15 true stories about the circus. Some are descriptions of activities (trapeze flying) or people (Emmett Kelly, a circus doctor, the Ringling Brothers). Other chapters tell of unusual occurrences; i.e., the bareback rider who was thrown off her horse into the lap of a spectator whom she later married. Some stories, such as the story of the horse trainer whose life was saved by an elephant, are exciting. Others are sad ("Blinky," the dog who was killed by an angry lion).

The authors' tone becomes condescending off and on through this collection, thus hampering its usefulness somewhat. Otherwise, it is very similar to the other Dolch books; it is a decent collection of very simplified stories. Dolch Basic Vocabulary Book series.

Interest Level: 1-4. Reading Level: 2.2. Further Search Topics: Circus-Fiction, Clowns-Fiction, Acrobats and Acrobatics-Fiction, Group 2.

COCOPAH INDIANS

Baylor, Byrd. And it is still that way: legends told by Arizona Indian children. Scribner 1976, 85 pp.

Byrd Baylor has collected and written notes for forty-one short American Indian legends from seven Arizona tribes whose school children were asked to write down or illustrate their favorite legend. The result is a collection that reflects the concerns, the history, religion, humor and pride of the children and their ancestors. This excellent collection is not only interesting reading, but it also fits well into social studies and language arts units.

Interest Level: 2-6. Reading Level: 3.1. Further Search Topics: Legends, Arizona-Fiction, Navajo Indians, Hopi Indians, Papago Indians, Pima Indians, Apache Indians, Quechan Indians, Cocopah Indians, Indians of North America-Legends, Mythology, Group 2.

COLORS

O'Neill, Mary. Hailstones and halibut bones; illus by Leonard Weisgard. Doubleday 1961, 59 pp.

This is a classic collection of twelve poems about colors. The poems are rhymed mood pieces of two or three pages that should appeal to almost any age reader. The difficulty of the vocabulary within each poem can vary greatly; however, most stanzas are short, most of the vocabulary is at least familiar, and the rhyme scheme is consistent.

Interest Level: 1-5. Reading Level: 3.2. Further Search Topics: Poetry, Colors, Group 2.

COMMUNICATION

Amon, Aline. Talking hands: Indian sign language. Doubleday 1968, 80 pp.

If you can ignore the author's patronizing tone and air of self-satisfaction, this is a book with great appeal. Children love ways of communicating privately, be it Pig Latin, codes and ciphers, or just whispering. This book appeals to that love by clearly, though unattractively, demonstrating over 200 words in American Indian sign language. By the time the young reader finishes the book, he/she will not only have had the fun of learning another method of communication, but will have learned a few simple generalities about North American Indians. The index is detailed enough that any word can be quickly checked. The book is useful for history, social studies, or language arts units, as well as for fun.

Interest Level: 2-6. Reading Level: 2.2. Further Search Topics: Indians of North America-Sign Language, Communication, Nonverbal Communication, Ethnic Groups.

Charlip, Remy. Handtalk; an ABC of finger spelling and sign language; photos by George Ancona. Schol. Bk. Serv. 1974, 42 pp.

This is not a book to be read and put away. It is a challenge to learn finger spelling (forming words letter by letter with the fingers) and signing (forming whole words or ideas by making a picture using one or both hands). It is a challenge that appeals to almost any child, reader and non-reader. One letter of the manual alphabet is shown at the top of each page. At the bottom of the page is a series of pictures that spell out a word which begins with the letter for that page. In the center of the page a model signs that same word. Only the first few words are explained, although there are hints for some of the more difficult words. The rest must be deciphered by the reader. In addition, the book includes over 25 more signs and a sentence about a very ugly vampire. The entire manual alphabet is also shown on a quick-reference, double page spread. The book provides an enjoyable and successful experience with language, especially if two or more children work with the book together. Although its picture book format would ordinarily turn older children away, interest in the book remains high through sixth grade. Because there are so few words that a child needs to read to enjoy this book, its reading level is an estimate.

Interest Level: 2-6. Reading Level: 2.1. Further Search Topics: Nonverbal Communication, Physically Handicapped, Communication.

COMPOSERS

Bryant, Bernice. George Gershwin: young composer; illus by Nathan Goldstein. Bobbs 1965, 200 pp.

Even when George Gershwin was very young he loved music, showed signs of musical talent, and longed to play the piano. However, any boy who played the piano in George's neighborhood was called a sissy and George didn't like being teased in that way. When he was no longer able to keep his music lessons a secret, he stopped them for fear of the teasing. But each time George quit playing the piano, he always went back to it, even when his parents pressured him not to waste his time at the piano. A young teacher told George that he would never be a musician. One of George's teachers actually taught him to play poorly, instead of well. In time, however, George learned to play well and to compose his own music. Then came the hard work of determining his own style. Gradually, more and more people heard and appreciated his American jazz, until George Gershwin's music was heard all around the world.

Another adequate entry in the *Childhood of Famous Americans* series. Includes the usual glossary, bibliography, time line, and follow-up questions. It is most likely to appeal to the reader already interested in music. Childhood of Famous Americans series.

Interest Level: 3-6. Reading Level: 3.1. Further Search Topics: Biography, Composers, Immigration and Emigration-Biography, Jazz Music, Bullies, Music-Biography, Pianists.

Cone, Molly. Leonard Bernstein; illus by Robert Galster. Har-Row 1970, 33 pp.

This is a bare bones outline that will appeal to music enthusiasts but will not attract anyone else. The reader catches very little of Bernstein's personality, but *is* awed by an impressive list of his accomplishments. The few attempts made to recreate the real person may have to be explained (i.e., references to Bernstein forgetting to get his hair cut because he was so busy). Picture book format of the hardback may deter some readers. Now published in paperback edition only. Crowell Biography series.

Interest Level: 2-4. Reading Level: 2.2. Further Search Topics: Music-Biography, Biography, Conductors, Composers, Pianists, Group 2.

COMPUTERS-FICTION

Butterworth, William E. Next stop, Earth; illus by Paul Frame. Walker 1978, 80 pp.

After two years on a desolate planet, 12-year-old Charley and his family were anticipating their return to Earth. But when Charley was awakened from sleep by a spaceship robot, he learned that an asteroid disturbance had caused several key systems on the ship to malfunction. Of 24 passengers on board the spaceship, only 10 were still alive and only Charley and his sister were able to be awakened. It was up to Charley to pilot the ship to its landing on Earth. The controls were all in an adjacent room which a faulty robot kept Charley from entering. Without someone at the controls the ship would burn up when re-entering Earth's atmosphere. By tricking the robot and commanding the ship's main computer, Charley was able to get to the control panel just in time to wake his father, help with reentry and save the ship.

Though the story tends to be heavy with conversations between Charley and various computers and robots, it is also that dialogue that helps maintain suspense. It is a story for the confirmed science fiction fan, not for the inductee.

Interest Level: 3-6. Reading Level: 2.2. Further Search Topics: Science Fiction, Outer Space-Fiction, Voyages and Travels-Fiction, Robots-Fiction, Computers-Fiction.

CONDUCTORS

Cone, Molly. Leonard Bernstein; illus by Robert Galster. Har-Row 1970, 33 pp.

This is a bare bones outline that will appeal to music enthusiasts but will not attract anyone else. The reader catches very little of Bernstein's personality, but *is* awed by an impressive list of his accomplishments. The few attempts made to recreate the real person may have to be explained (i.e., references to Bernstein forgetting to get his hair cut because he was so busy). Picture book format of the hardback may deter some readers. Now published in paperback edition only. Crowell Biography series.

Interest Level: 2-4. Reading Level: 2.2. Further Search Topics: Music-Biography, Biography, Conductors, Composers, Pianists, Group 2.

CONSTRUCTION

Zim, Herbert S. Hoists, cranes and derricks; illus by Gary Ruse. Morrow 1969, 64 pp.

This is a very thorough treatment of lifting machinery. It is a straight-forward explanation that is technical, but not so technical that it can't be understood by young enthusiasts. The text is well-supplemented by a good number of clear illustrations and diagrams including drawings of the attachments to mobile cranes, motions used by signalmen, kinds of quay cranes, types of derricks, and even charts of the capacities of cranes and derricks and load-bearing materials. A fair index helps to make the book useful for reference or report writing.

Interest Level: 3-6. Reading Level: 3.2. Further Search Topics: Construction.

CONTESTS-FICTION

Conford, Ellen. The luck of Pokey Bloom; illus by Bernice Loewenstein. Little 1975, 135 pp.

Pokey Bloom's passion was entering contests. She entered every contest she heard of and always thought she would win. Unfortunately, she never won anything. She even went so far as to practice concentrating three times each day on winning every contest she had entered. Someone who had been interviewed on the radio had *guaranteed* she would win that way. She didn't! It only made more trouble for her at school and at home. Pokey had enough trouble getting along with her older brother and didn't need any more problems at home.

There isn't much plot or direction to this story, but it does have some amusing moments. It is an extra book for the reader who enjoys Judy Blume-type books and wants another story about "regular kids."

Interest Level: 4-6. Reading Level: 3.1. Further Search Topics: Family-Fiction, Contests-Fiction, Brothers and Sisters-Fiction, Humorous Fiction, Everyday Stories.

Hurwitz, Johanna. Aldo Ice Cream; illus by John Wallner. Morrow 1981, 124 pp.

Aldo got his newest nickname (Ice Cream) from his friend DeDe when she heard that Aldo not only wanted to try every flavor of ice cream at the local store, but wanted to buy an ice cream freezer for his sister's birthday as well. Aldo decided his summer project would be to earn enough money for the freezer, but he soon found out that there were very few ways a nine-year-old boy could earn $49.95. In the meantime, he helped his mother deliver food for a Meals-On-Wheels project, learned to swim, found out about fish from Mr. Puccini, and shared his cat with Mrs. Nardo. As the summer came to an end he saw one last opportunity to earn enough money for the ice cream maker. A local shoe store offered a new pair of sneakers to the child who owned the most worn out pair. Aldo convinced his mother that if he won the sneakers, she should pay him the money she would otherwise have had to spend on his new sneakers. Aldo set about making sure that his already well-worn sneakers were the most dilapidated in town. A few days before the sneaker contest the hardware store lowered the price on the ice cream freezer to a point where Aldo could afford it if he won the sneakers. When Aldo did win, just as he knew he would, he and his mother bought the very last freezer in the store.

It is not as well-constructed a story as *Aldo Applesauce*, but for established Aldo fans, or those who want quiet, reassuring fiction, this is a usable title.

Interest Level: 3-4. Reading Level: 3.1. Further Search Topics: Humorous Fiction, Brothers and Sisters-Fiction, Vacation-Fiction, Occupations-Fiction, Everyday Stories, Aging-Fiction, Family-Fiction, Contests-Fiction.

COUNTRY LIFE-FICTION

Bulla, Clyde Robert. The ghost of windy hill; illus by Don Bolognese. Har-Row 168, 84 pp.

If the reader doesn't expect a high adventure ghost story, he or she will not be disappointed by this low-keyed tale of a family who goes to live in a house that is supposedly haunted. Mr. Giddings asked the Carver family to move into his country home while he and his wife stayed in Boston. His intent was that the Carvers should either prove to his wife that the house was not haunted or drive the ghost out. The Carvers found no ghosts—at first—only an interesting group of neighbors. There was shy Miss Miggie who drifted around in a long, white dress and wore a flower-covered hat. Bruno was the gruff beggar boy who couldn't walk and had no friends but a goat, until the Carver children came along. Near the end of their stay Lorna Carver mentioned that because they had seen no ghosts the family would soon leave and the Giddings would return. Strange occurrences began almost immediately after Lorna's statement and ended only when the Carvers caught Bruno trying to convince them that he was the ghost. Lorna and Jamie were his only friends, so he had risked his guardians wrath and given up the pretense of being lame to trick the Carvers into staying. All ends well as Bruno's cruel guardian is run off, the Carvers take responsibility for Bruno's care, and Mrs. Giddings admits she made up the ghost story because she hated living in the country and had wanted to return to the city. Another serviceable book in the very successful Bulla style.

Interest Level: 2-5. Reading Level: 2.1. Further Search Topics: Ghosts-Fiction, Brothers and Sisters-Fiction, Orphans-Fiction, Country Life-Fiction, Courage-Fiction, Challenges-Fiction, Friendship-Fiction.

Clymer, Eleanor. Santiago's silver mine; illus by Ingrid Fetz. Atheneum 1973, 74 pp.

Although somewhat complicated by a large number of background incidents, especially early in the book, the story is both interesting and informative. Santiago and his friend Andreas wanted to be rich. The year's harvest had been very poor, so there was little food to eat. Both of their fathers had gone to Mexico City to find jobs and their mothers worked for very few pesos near home. Andreas wanted to search the old mine in the hills outside of town for silver, but the mining company had left a guard named Jose to prevent people from getting into the mines. While up on a hill, tending a cow, Andreas found an old piece of pottery and a back entrance to the mine. As they started to enter the mine, Andreas and Santiago found a basket full of old pottery pieces that Jose had apparently dug from the hill. Not knowing what the pottery pieces were, the boys took them to the local school teacher who identified them as ancient archeological treasures that by law belonged to the government. As soon as he realized others had found out that he had been selling the pottery, Jose disappeared. Shortly afterwards, the government paved the road through town and opened the hill as an official archaeological site. The extra jobs meant that the boys' fathers could once again find work at home. Although they hadn't become exactly rich, Santiago and Andreas had certainly found treasure.

Local flavor abounds, along with some history. Useful for Social Studies units. Print size fairly small, but spaces between lines are good sized. Recently out-of-print, but still worth looking for.

Interest Level: 3-5. Reading Level: 3.1. Further Search Topics: Archaeology-Fiction, Poverty-Fiction, Mexico-Fiction, Country Life-Fiction, Treasure-Fiction, Miners-Fiction.

Hamilton, Virginia. Zeely; illus by Symeon Shimin. Macmillan 1967, 122 pp.

A beautiful, almost mystical story of a black girl who learns about self-identity and pride from a statuesque neighbor whom Geeder is convinced must be a Watutsi princess. At first by chance and later at an arranged meeting, Zeely (Geeder's neighbor) gently and symbolically speaks to Geeder of her racial origins. She also tells Geeder of a young girl (Zeely as a child), too ignorant of the world around her to be able to recognize reality. It is a quietly moving story that is most likely to find an appreciative audience in the thoughtful, more mature reader.

Interest Level: 5-6. Reading Level: 5.1. Further Search Topics: Africa-Fiction, Royalty-Fiction, Blacks-Fiction, Courage-Fiction, Vacation-Fiction, Country Life-Fiction, Read Aloud.

Peck, Robert Newton. Mr. Little; illus by Ben Stahl. Doubleday 1979, 87 pp.

All summer long Drag and Finley had looked forward to having Miss Kellogg as their teacher, so they were extremely disappointed to find ordinary-looking Mr. Little in her place on the first day of school. Used to playing tricks on their teachers anyway, Drag and Finley decided to go all out to get even with Mr. Little for spoiling their year. But try as they might, they couldn't get an advantage over Mr. Little; he seemed to be unflappable. Finally, in their riskiest prank ever, they stole Mr. Little's underwear to dress a statue in the town square. That attempt to embarrass Mr. Little only served to get Finley and Drag in serious trouble from which Mr. Little saved them. It was his later rescue of Miss Kellogg, however, that added respect to the boys' growing feeling of friendship for Mr. Little.

Because the author's adult viewpoint is never quite lost, even though he writes in the first person, and because the rural and historic time settings are not familiar to many readers, the book may need some introduction and encouragement. It is a prime candidate for reading aloud until the young reader's interest takes over. Print is of adequate size, but spacing between lines could have been more generous.

Interest Level: 4-6. Reading Level: 5.1. Further Search Topics: Humorous Fiction, School Stories, Troublemakers-Fiction, Group 2, Read Aloud, Country Life-Fiction, Best Sellers.

Wallace, Bill. A dog named Kitty. Holiday 1980, 153 pp.

Ricky's fear of dogs was extreme but also understandable. He had been attacked by a rabid dog when he was very young. Remembering the fear, the stitches and the painful rabies shots was enough to bring tears to Ricky's eyes even years later. When a local bully told his dog to attack Ricky, Ricky's fear was discovered. About that time, a stray puppy showed up at Ricky's farm. Not quite knowing why, Ricky began to warm to the puppy, to feed it, and finally to love it. When the dog was attacked by a pack of wild dogs (a brutal scene vividly described), Ricky fully overcame his fear of dogs, went to Kitty's defense, and was barely able to save her life. When Kitty was later tragically and accidentally killed, Ricky swore that he would never have anything to do with a dog again. He almost kept his promise to himself, but eventually a second stray dog wandered into the farm and Ricky decided to try again.

This is an emotional story that should appeal to many readers. However, because of the violence and the dog's two-stage death, the book is probably best suited to fifth and sixth grade children.

Interest Level: 5-6. Reading Level: 3.1. Further Search Topics: Dogs-Fiction, Pets-Fiction, Bullies-Fiction, Death-Fiction, Oklahoma-Fiction, Courage-Fiction, Country Life-Fiction.

COURAGE

Greenfield, Eloise. Rosa Parks; illus by Eric Marlow. Har-Row 1973, 33 pp.

This book succumbs to the difficulty of writing for children about a subject that needs more explanation. The occasionally condescending tone combined with the Crowell Biography picture book format will keep this otherwise adequate introduction to the civil rights movement from being useful beyond fourth grade. The book should be very useful, however, for third and fourth grade social studies, history or biography units.

Rosa Parks' childhood and her feelings about the special rules for blacks make up the first half of the book. The second half is devoted to Rosa's act of defiance (refusing to give up her seat on a bus to a white man) and the repercussions of that act. Crowell Biography series.

Interest Level: 2-4. Reading Level 2.2. Further Search Topics: Blacks-Biography, Biography, Prejudice, Civil Rights, Women-Biography, Courage.

Kluger, Ruth. The secret ship. Doubleday 1978, 136 pp.

A tense, true story about the secret transportation of hundreds of European Jews to Palestine early in World War II. The transport ship became ice-bound in a Rumanian harbor, the crew mutinied and the passengers threatened to expose their plight to the world. In complete charge of the operation was a 25-year-old woman. The book closes with a summary of the Jews' continuing fight for Israel.

The historical understanding that is necessary in order to really appreciate this excellent book make it best suited to readers no younger than sixth grade.

The paper on which this book is printed is so thin that the print shows through from one page to another and the print at the beginning and the end of the book is italicized. Both factors may distract the reader.

Interest Level: 6+. Reading Level: 3.1. Further Search Topics: World War II, Jews, Women, Sex Role, Israel, Survival, Courage.

Malone, Mary. Annie Sullivan; illus by Lydia Rosier. Putnam 1971, 61 pp.

This is a very brief sketch of both Annie Sullivan's life and Helen Keller's life. Their lives were so intertwined that they cannot be separated. But because they are combined in such a short book, neither woman can be treated in much depth. That fact is not as harmful here as it might otherwise be, because even a bare bones description of the life of this extraordinary deaf, blind and mute woman or her near-blind, dedicated teacher, is interesting.

Interest Level: 2-5. Reading Level: 2.2. Further Search Topics: Sullivan, Annie, Keller, Helen, Vision, Biography, Physically Handicapped, Sound, Courage.

Mathis, Sharon Bell. Ray Charles; illus by George Ford. Har-Row 1973, 33 pp.

Dominent throughout this biography of Ray Charles is the theme of overcoming adversity. The book is not just a recounting of Ray Charles' music lessons, early schooling, family life, and talent. All of that is included, but it serves to illustrate the manner in which Charles met his troubles. His problems began when he was very young. His brother died, and Ray lost one eye and then the sight in his other eye. His family was poor, but close, and he missed them when he was sent away to a school for the blind. Music was his love, but even that was work, for Charles had to learn to read and write music in Braille. He worked hard at it and eventually could play and arrange music for every instrument in the band.

Determined to be independent, when Charles was orphaned at age 15, he left school and began playing music for a living. The first record he made resulted in a $16 fine because he made it during a musician's union strike. Charles took a series of sideman and nightclub jobs until he finally had enough money to hire seven other musicians to play his music. Today Charles is very wealthy, owns his own record company, has a family, and is considered a great jazz and blues musician. None of his success came easily; only through determination, will power, pride, and hard work.

The book, interesting and serviceable enough for music or biography units, is also designed to set an example for youngsters facing their own problems. It will, of course, be popular with Ray Charles fans, too. Crowell Biography series.

Interest Level: 2-4. Reading Level: 3.1. Further Search Topics: Jazz Music, Music-Biography, Vision, Physically Handicapped, Blacks-Biography, Group 2, Biography, Pianists, Orphans, Challenges, Courage.

COURAGE-FICTION

Benchley, Nathaniel. Sam the Minutemen; illus by Arnold Lobel. Har-Row 1969, 62 pp.

A good but limited book. It is a simple, personalized account of the beginning of the Revolutionary War as seen by the young son of a Minuteman. The book is a fairly exciting, uncomplicated and enjoyable story. Its limitations rest in its format (it's designed as a reader), the apparent young age of the main character, and the fact that it is told as a story. Its usefulness extends no further than grade three. An I Can Read History Book

Interest Level: 1-3. Reading Level: 2.2. Further Search Topics: United States-History-War-Fiction, Historical Fiction, War-Fiction, Group 2, Courage-Fiction.

Bennett, Jay. The pigeon. Methuen 1980, 147 pp.

Despite a low testing score, this is not a truly easy book to read. The author assumes his readers are fairly sophisticated and worldly, thus he does not explain the meaning of the Iron Cross symbol or the word Aryan. The book's language varies from simple to difficult, making the reading level inconsistent (2.1 - 4.1). The setting is dark and forbidding; an underground world of fugitives and terrorists. And yet, the book will be popular with many readers in sixth grade; it will be even more popular with older readers. The tension in this story of a teenage boy, blamed for the murder of his ex-girlfriend, is almost palpable. Brian's flight from the police and his desire to find Donna's murderer take him directly into the midst of a ring of terrorists, for whom life has no meaning. In Brian's attempt to prove his innocence, two more lives are lost, but hundreds more are saved as Brian discovers and stops a bomb threat. The author has used riveting action, short, clipped sentences, and terse dialogue to create a very successful, highly suspenseful book. Print size is only moderate.

Interest Level: 6 . Reading Level: 3.2. Further Search Topics: Mystery and Detective Stories, Terrorism-Fiction, Murder-Fiction, Best Sellers, Crime-Fiction, Courage-Fiction, Survival-Fiction, Runaways-Fiction.

Berenstain, Stan. Bears in the night. Random 1971, 30 pp.

This is for the very beginning reader. Only 24 words plus illustrations are used to tell the story of a bedtime adventure for seven small bears. Bravely they sneak out of the house, through the woods, and up Spook Hill. Frightened by an owl's hoot, they run back over the same route until they are safely back in bed again.

Interest Level: K-2. Reading Level: 1.1. Further Search Topics: Bears-Fiction, Group 2, Courage-Fiction, Humorous Fiction.

Blume, Judy. Otherwise known as Sheila the great. Dutton 1972, 128 pp.

Sheila first appears in *Tales of a Fourth Grade Nothing* as Peter Thatcher's neighbor. Sheila was a bundle of fears. She was afraid of dogs, thunderstorms, spiders, horses, putting her face in water, and strange noises at night. The summer she and her family rented a house in Tarrytown, New York, she confronted each one of her fears, even mastered one (putting her face in the water) and learned how to swim. That gave her the self-confidence to face a dog without running away. Sheila's progress was aided by her friend Mouse's steadfast belief that a person should always be honest about herself. Sheila's problems are treated realistically and with dignity, yet humorously. Reading level varies greatly from 1.2 - 4.1, therefore, the book is *most* suitable to grades four through six.

Interest Level: 3-6. Reading Level: 3.1. Further Search Topics: Humorous Fiction, Courage-Fiction, Camp-Fiction, Group 2, Vacation-Fiction, Swimming-Fiction, Brothers and Sisters-Fiction, Friendship-Fiction, Everyday Stories.

Bulla, Clyde Robert. The sword in the tree; illus by Paul Galdone. Har-Row 1956, 113 pp.

Shan didn't like or trust his Uncle Lionel, who had suddenly appeared at the castle gates after being away many years. Just as suddenly, Shan's father disappeared or died. Shan and his mother soon realized that Lionel wanted to take over the castle, even if it meant killing them. To save themselves, Shan and his mother fled. After walking many miles, they found a poor goat herder and his family who gave them a place to live. Sometime later Shan decided to travel to see King Arthur and ask for help in reclaiming the castle from Lionel. It wasn't until Shan was able to prove the castle was his, and Lionel lost a duel to one of Arthur's knights, that Shan was given back his home. Deep in the castle dungeon Shan found his father, still alive but imprisoned by Lionel.

This book, with its short chapters, short sentences, and steadily progressing plot should interest even the most reluctant reader from grade two through six.

Interest Level: 2-6. Reading Level: 2.2. Further Search Topics: Knights and Knighthood-Fiction, Survival-Fiction, Royalty-Fiction, Best Sellers, Courage-Fiction.

Bulla, Clyde Robert. A lion to guard us; illus by Michele Chessare. Har-Row 1981, 117 pp.

Bulla's writing isn't quite as successful here as elsewhere. This story of three London children's attempt to go to their father in Jamestown, Virginia, has danger, adventure, daring and promise. It also has too many characters to allow the reader to get to know any of them well. There are also too many very short chapters to allow plot development (23 chapters

and 117 pages). The short sentences help to keep the reading level low, but a glossary would have been useful to fully explain the many unfamiliar terms.

Despite its problems, the book is still useful. The story is based on the 1609 voyage of the Sea Adventure. Blown far off course and badly damaged by a storm, the ship landed at Bermuda rather than Jamestown. The survivors were unable to sail again for over nine months. When they reached Jamestown, they found that few people had survived the very harsh year.

The three Freebold children are the focus of this story. When their mother died they left London to find their father in the New World. Having no money of their own, they were lucky to find a doctor friend to pay their ship's passage and to go with them. Halfway across the ocean, the doctor was swept overboard and drowned. From that time until they found their father barely alive, the children were on their own, even though they were still with the ship's passengers.

Although not the best of Bulla, this is still serviceable as a piece of historical fiction (hard to get children to read), or as a choice for the lover of survival and/or sea stories.

Interest Level: 3-5. Reading Level: 2.1. Further Search Topics: United States-History-Fiction, Historical Fiction, Courage-Fiction, Survival-Fiction, Shipwrecks-Fiction, Voyages and Travels-Fiction, Seafaring Life-Fiction.

Bulla, Clyde Robert. The ghost of windy hill; illus by Don Bolognese. Har-Row 168, 84 pp.

If the reader doesn't expect a high adventure ghost story, he or she will not be disappointed by this low-keyed tale of a family who goes to live in a house that is supposedly haunted. Mr. Giddings asked the Carver family to move into his country home while he and his wife stayed in Boston. His intent was that the Carvers should either prove to his wife that the house was not haunted or drive the ghost out. The Carvers found no ghosts—at first—only an interesting group of neighbors. There was shy Miss Miggie who drifted around in a long, white dress and wore a flower-covered hat. Bruno was the gruff beggar boy who couldn't walk and had no friends but a goat, until the Carver children came along. Near the end of their stay Lorna Carver mentioned that because they had seen no ghosts the family would soon leave and the Giddings would return. Strange occurrences began almost immediately after Lorna's statement and ended only when the Carvers caught Bruno trying to convince them that he was the ghost. Lorna and Jamie were his only friends, so he had risked his guardians wrath and given up the pretense of being lame to trick the Carvers into staying. All ends well as Bruno's cruel guardian is run off, the Carvers take responsibility for Bruno's care, and Mrs. Giddings admits she made up the ghost story because she hated living in the country and had wanted to return to the city. Another serviceable book in the very successful Bulla style.

Interest Level: 2-5. Reading Level: 2.1. Further Search Topics: Ghosts-Fiction, Brothers and Sisters-Fiction, Orphans-Fiction, Country Life-Fiction, Courage-Fiction, Challenges-Fiction, Friendship-Fiction.

Bulla, Clyde Robert. Pirate's promise; illus by Peter Burchard. Har-Row 1958, 87 pp.

After their mother and father died, Tom and Dinah Pippin had nowhere to go but to their Uncle John's house. Uncle John had no place for them, so he sold Tom into bondage but kept Dinah to help his wife with housework. Tom was to be taken by ship to America where the ship's captain would sell him to the highest bidder. After several years, Tom would be free. But, Tom couldn't accept the idea of one person being another's property, so he spoke out at every opportunity. Tom spoke up to the seaman who dragged him aboard ship, to the captain, to the others who had been bonded, even to the pirate captain who captured their ship. Captain Land was so impressed by Tom's bravery that although he set everyone else he had captured adrift on a small boat, he kept Tom with him. He and Tom became good friends. He never asked Tom to become a pirate and Tom never did. Instead, they enjoyed each other's company. When the pirate ship needed work, they stopped at a safe island where Tom met and impressed Captain Red, a fierce enemy of Captain Land. Captain Red's insistence that Tom join his pirate ship led to another clash between the enemies. Although he was ill, Captain Land fought a duel with Captain Red and lost. Land's last requests were that Benjy, a freed slave who loved him, take all his gold, and that Tom go to Charlestown, South Carolina to find Land's family. Benjy led their flight from Captain Red and arranged a way for Tom to sail to Charlestown before putting Tom on his own. When Tom reached Charlestown he found Land's parents were so angry with Land that at first they didn't even want to hear about him. But, eventually, they not only asked all about their son, but also asked Tom if he and Dinah would like to live with them as their family.

There is enough excitement, danger, and warmth here to satisfy almost any arm-chair adventurer. Usual format of short, episodic chapters.

Interest Level: 3-6. Reading Level 2.1. Further Search Topics: Pirates-Fiction, Seafaring Life-Fiction, Orphans-Fiction, Slavery-Fiction, Brothers and Sisters-Fiction, Best Sellers, Courage-Fiction.

Bulla, Clyde Robert. Riding the pony express; illus by Grace Paull. Har-Row 1948, 95 pp.

Although somewhat marred by the stereotyped speech of a young Indian boy, this is otherwise an exciting piece of historical fiction set in the 1860s. Dick was sent from New York City to join his father in St. Joseph, Missouri, only to find his father had moved to Nebraska to become a pony express rider. When Dick finally found his father, after a long stagecoach ride, he thought his father didn't want him. Dick stayed at the way station and helped with the chores because he didn't know what else to do. Then one day the house was burned, his father was shot, and the horses were almost stolen. There was no one around who could carry the mail, except Dick. Despite a wolf pack at his heels, Dick rode to the next way station. On his way home he realized his father really did want him and he no longer wanted to leave his father. Chapters are short with separate episodes that tie them together. A few simple songs appear between the chapters.

Interest Level: 2-5. Reading Level: 2.1. Further Search Topics: Horses-Fiction, West-Fiction, United States-History-Fiction, Historical Fiction, Voyages and Travels-Fiction, Courage-Fiction, Frontier and Pioneer Life-Fiction.

Bulla, Clyde Robert. Marco Moonlight; illus by Julia Noonan. T Y Crowell 1976, 104 pp.

No one could explain Marco's strange, recurring dream. The dream seemed to be about a brother, but Marco had no brother. He had no family but his wealthy grandparents with whom he lived. Marco loved his grandparents very much, but he couldn't

help wondering about his own past. He knew only what he and his grandparents could figure out from a few clues. His mother had run away to marry and for three years Marco's grandparents had heard nothing. Then, suddenly, they received a note that she was dying, had parted from her husband, and needed them. By the time they arrived, she was dead and two-year-old Marco could tell them no more. About the time of his thirteenth birthday Marco made friends with a strange man named Flint, who later became the gardener on Marco's grandparents' estate. Rather than live in the room provided for him with the other servants, Flint chose a bleak and isolated beach cottage. Being very careful that no one should suspect, Flint locked Marco into the cottage and forced Marco to change clothes with Matt, who was Marco's long-lost identical twin. Flint and Matt planned that Matt would steal all the money he could from the estate before killing Marco and fleeing. But when Matt began to realize how nice his grandparents were, how much he liked Marco, and how evil Flint was, he decided to thwart Flint's plan. In Matt and Marco's desperate attempt to flee from Flint, Flint was accidentally killed, leaving Marco free to return home and Matt free to find a way to feel he also had the right to claim his heritage before joining Marco.

The tense and dramatic plot immediately involves the reader and the short, fast-paced chapters sustain interest to the end of the book. Readers should also appreciate the small, paperback-size format. A good choice.

Interest Level: 3-6. Reading Level: 2.1. Further Search Topics: Dreams-Fiction, Mystery and Detective Stories, Kidnapping-Fiction, Twins-Fiction, Orphans-Fiction, Grandparents-Fiction, Best Sellers, Brothers and Sisters-Fiction, Jealousy-Fiction, Courage-Fiction.

Bulla, Clyde Robert. Viking adventure; illus by Douglas Gorsline. T Y Crowell 1963, 117 pp.

An exciting story of a young Norwegian boy named Sigurd. Sigurd realized his dream when he finally set sail on a Viking ship in search of Wineland (Vinland). Leif Eriksson had told of his North American findings over 100 years earlier. Sigurd and his father's friend Grom, the captain of the ship, were sure they could find that land again. Their determination finally brought Grom's death at the hands of the ship's owner, Sigurd's near death, and the destruction of the ship.

This book, too, is true to Bulla's style of short chapters, short sentences, much action and high appeal. Although it is a little higher reading level than many of Bulla's others, it is still a good choice. Recently out of print, but worth a search.

Interest Level: 2-6. Reading Level: 3.1. Further Search Topics: Norway-Fiction, Historical Fiction, Seafaring Life-Fiction, Voyages and Travels-Fiction, Shipwrecks-Fiction, Explorers-Fiction, Vikings-Fiction, Courage-Fiction, Best Sellers, Group 2.

Bulla, Clyde Robert. White bird; illus by Leonard Weisgard. T Y Crowell 1966, 79 pp.

This book is meant for a special reader. It will not appeal to the reader who wants only action and excitement from a book. It is a story of complex human relationships and differing definitions of love. John Thomas lost his parents in a river accident when he was just a baby. His cradle had been pulled from the river and he had been raised by reclusive Luke Vail. Luke placed no trust in the world or in people outside his tiny valley home and so forbade John Thomas to have anything to do with either one. Luke didn't allow John Thomas a pet either because he thought that John Thomas would only be hurt when he no longer had the animal. Despite Luke's argument, when he found an injured white crow, John Thomas kept it and tended it until the crow was stolen by three strangers as Luke stood by. Angry at Luke as much as at the strangers, John Thomas ran away to search for the bird, but found that it had been shot. Far from being fruitless, however, John Thomas's trip out of the valley gave him an entirely different view of people than the one Luke had shown him. Upon a friend's encouragement, John Thomas returned to Luke to share that view.

Subtle and unusual, this book needs a mature, sensitive reader and/or discussion in order to be fully appreciated.

Interest Level: 4-6. Reading Level 2.1. Further Search Topics: Pets-Fiction, Orphans-Fiction, Runaways-Fiction, Birds-Fiction, Love-Fiction, Loners-Fiction, Courage-Fiction.

Byars, Betsy. After the goat man; illus by Ronald Himler. Viking Pr. 1974, 126 pp.

Harold was fat and over-sensitive. Ada was serious and independent. Figgy was lonely, poor and in need of help. Figgy and his grandfather, the Goat Man, had been forced to move from their cabin to make room for a highway. The Goat Man had returned to the cabin with a shotgun, vowing to defend his right to live there. Figgy knew he had to persuade his grandfather to leave or someone would be hurt. But, in the children's hurry to reach the Goat Man, it was Figgy who was hurt and Harold who rescued both Figgy and the Goat Man. Harold grew up that day. He stopped dreaming about the way he wanted things to be and faced life realistically for the first time.

The book is very much a character study. Realistic characters are treated with sympathy and dignity and given a chance to grow. Introspective readers will understand and enjoy the book more than those looking for adventure. Print size is fairly large, but lines are separated by only average width.

Interest Level: 4-6. Reading Level: 3.2. Further Search Topics: Loneliness-Fiction, Weight-Fiction, Moving, Household-Fiction, Courage-Fiction, Grandparents-Fiction, Orphans-Fiction.

Byars, Betsy. The 18th emergency; illus by Robert Grossman. Viking Pr. 1973, 126 pp.

When your best friend knows how to escape from the world's 17 worst emergencies and you're faced with the eighteenth, you're in trouble. That was the spot in which Mouse found himself one day. He had drawn an arrow towards a large picture of the Neanderthal man and written Marv Hammerman's name. Hammerman had seen him do it and was out to kill, maim, or at least beat up Mouse. Mouse finally ran out of ways to avoid Hammerman and had to face the fight. When it was over and he was once again able to stand up, Mouse realized he felt better for having allowed Hammerman to regain his honor and for having taken responsibility for his own actions.

A funny, fast-moving look at real feelings of fear, honor and responsibility. Very popular. Print is dark and of good size but lines could have been spaced farther apart.

Interest Level: 4-6. Reading Level: 3.2. Further Search Topics: Bullies-Fiction, Humorous Fiction, Courage-Fiction, Best Sellers, Challenges-Fiction, Read Aloud.

Byars, Betsy. Trouble River; illus by Rocco Negri. Viking Pr. 1969, 158 pp.

A gripping adventure story of survival. After being attacked by an Indian in the middle of the night, Dewey and his grandmother rushed to Trouble River to board a small raft which Dewey had just finished making. They thought they would only need to navigate a few miles down the river to safety at a neighbor's home, but found instead that the neighbor's cabin had been burned down. For almost 40 miles they fought against the unknown river, wolves and rapids.

This is a book that should satisfy many reluctant readers. It's frequent dialogue, fast action and high interest are only occasionally marred by an overly long sentence.

Interest Level: 3-6. Reading Level: 3.1. Further Search Topics: Courage-Fiction, Frontier and Pioneer Life-Fiction, Survival-Fiction, Grandparents-Fiction, Voyages and Travels-Fiction, Best Sellers, Read Aloud.

Christopher, Matt. Face-off; illus by Harvey Kidder. Little 1972, 131 pp.

Christopher sticks strictly to the sports story formula here. The characters seem to have no time or thoughts for anything but sports. They epitomize the macho image, and once their problems with sports are solved everything in life seems to fall into place. But, for the young sports enthusiast who doesn't really like to read, this formula of much sports action and very little else is successful.

Scott had never played hockey but he was an extremely fast skater. When Del and Skinny asked him to join their hockey team and to be one of the Three Icekateers, Scott was thrilled. But Scott's performance was less than inspiring and Del's patience with his failures was short. The two almost came to blows when Scott discovered that he was puck-shy and would duck every time someone took a shot near him. Their coach's advice to both of them helped clear up Scott's problem and Del's impatience. All ends happily as Scott played well and he and Del became friends once more.

Interest Level: 3-6. Reading Level: 3.1. Further Search Topics: Hockey-Fiction, Ice Skating-Fiction, Courage-Fiction, Friendship-Fiction.

Christopher, Matt. Wild pitch. Little 1980, 137 pp.

This is one of Christopher's better written books but it is also one that will find a smaller audience than usual. Here he has drawn interesting characters of flesh and bone rather than his normal stereotypes. The sports action is still detailed, but it is no longer the core around which a purely skeletal plot is stretched. Christopher has produced an intriguing story line here.

Eddie was a good strong pitcher who sometimes threw wild pitches. One of his wild pitches hit Phyl Monahan, the only girl playing in his league. It was well known that Eddie didn't like the idea of girls playing in the same league as the boys, so people accused him of purposely hitting Phyl. Eddie knew he hadn't meant to hit her, but he still felt very guilty that his pitch had put her into the hospital. He went to the hospital many times before he was finally able to see Phyl and apologize. When he did, he found that she was very likeable and reasonable. When she confessed that she wasn't sure she wanted to play baseball again, Eddie decided he owed it to her to help her regain her confidence. As they worked together each one gained respect for the other until theirs became a very solid friendship. The test for both was when Phyl had to hit against Eddie again.

For many baseball fans there may be too much plot here and not enough baseball. Because the problem of how to control wild pitches is never addressed, other readers may also find the book disappointing. But, for those baseball fans who are open to more than box scores and replays, this is a good story.

Interest Level: 6+. Reading Level: 4.2. Further Search Topics: Baseball-Fiction, Sex Role-Fiction, Friendship-Fiction, Courage-Fiction.

Clifford, Eth. Help, I'm a prisoner in the library; illus by George Hughes. HM 1979, 103 pp.

When their car stopped, Mary Rose and Jo-Beth were left alone in a strange city while their father went to find some gas. Jo-Beth needed to use the bathroom, so the sisters headed for the closest public building they could see, the library. No one saw them go in, so no one knew that they were locked inside when the librarian secured the building for the night. With the lights out and a blizzard outside, the library was a very spooky place. The girls tried calling the police, but the police wouldn't take them seriously. Then they heard groans and eerie moans from the second floor. Gathering all their courage, the girls went to investigate, only to discover the librarian lying hurt and unconscious. Their ingenuity and imagination helped the sisters through the difficult hours before they were all rescued.

Don't read it too carefully or the book's implausibilities will become very evident. Most young readers, however, will enjoy this story for its suspense, spooky atmosphere and adventurous girls, and they will ignore its weaknesses.

Interest Level: 2-5. Reading Level: 3.1. Further Search Topics: Disasters-Fiction, Snow-Fiction, Brothers and Sisters-Fiction, Libraries-Fiction, Survival-Fiction, Courage-Fiction, Group 2.

Clymer, Eleanor. Chipmunk in the forest; illus by Ingrid Fetz. Atheneum 1965, 56 pp.

A simple story of an Indian boy who learned the meaning of the word "courage". Chipmunk had never admitted to anyone that he was afraid of the forest. But when his uncle tried to teach him to hunt, Chipmunk was too frightened to be quiet, and thus he scared away all the animals. He returned to the village in disgrace to do "women's work." One of his jobs was to watch Little Brother. When Little Brother disappeared, Chipmunk went in search of him. It began to snow as Chipmunk went farther and farther into the forest, but even though he was frightened, Chipmunk kept on looking. By the time he found Little Brother, the snow had covered their tracks. Chipmunk had to use all that he had learned from his uncle to get them safely home. When he arrived back at the village, Chipmunk had finally proven that he was brave.

Interest Level: 2-4. Reading Level: 2.1. Further Search Topics: Indians of North America-Fiction, Courage-Fiction, Snow-Fiction, Hunting-Fiction, Survival-Fiction.

Clymer, Eleanor. Luke was there; illus by Diane de Groat. HR & W 1973, 74 pp.

Julius' father, uncle and finally his step-father had all walked out on him. Even his mother had left him, although she hadn't wanted to go. When his mother had been taken to the hospital, Julius and his younger brother Danny were sent to a children's home. Julius felt alone and cheated until he met a young, black, social worker named Luke. Luke liked and respected Julius and helped Julius learn to feel the same way about himself. When Luke, too, left Julius, Julius was so angry at the world that he stole food and then money. Afraid to go back to the children's home because he thought he'd be caught and punished, Julius ran away. It wasn't until he found an abandoned child, about Danny's age, who needed care, that Julius returned to the home. Luke was there when he arrived, just when Julius needed him most. Luke listened to Julius' unhappy feelings, arranged for him to see his mother and helped him begin to accept the fact that life is not always fair.

Julius tells his own story in a realistic, straight-forward book that will touch most readers. Only the lack of quotation marks and inadequate spacing between the lines may slow the reader.

Interest Level: 3-6. Reading Level: 2.2. Further Search Topics: Runaways-Fiction, Orphans-Fiction, Juvenile Delinquency-Fiction, Divorce and Separation-Fiction, Friendship-Fiction, Courage-Fiction, Survival-Fiction, Loneliness-Fiction, Best Sellers, Read Aloud.

Conford, Ellen. The revenge of the incredible Dr. Rancid and his youthful assistant, Jeffrey. Little 1980, 119 pp.

There were two people Jeff hated and feared: Dewey Belasco, the sixth grade bully and Lana McCabe, Dewey's female counterpart. Only in his imagination could Jeff stand up to them. In the stories Jeff wrote in a notebook, he and his friend Dr. Rancid were superheroes who rid the world of such scum as Lana and Dewey. In real life, Jeff ran from bullies rather than face them; even if it meant that an eight-year-old boy and a girl Jeff's age were left to stand up to Dewey by themselves. Although the way Jeff took care of an injured child soon had most everyone thinking of Jeff as a hero, he saw that, too, as an indication of his failings at first. Finally, something inside Jeff snapped and he answered Dewey back when Dewey insulted him. Before long Jeff found himself flat on his back with a bloody nose and so many pains he couldn't count them. But, he had finally faced Dewey and showed Dewey that he was no longer afraid. Jeff felt good.

Similar to *The 18th Emergency* but a higher reading level. The notebook stories will appeal to fans of superheroes, but because they are stories within a story, they may also cause difficulties. Spacing between lines is somewhat narrow.

Interest Level: 5-6. Reading Level: 4.2. Further Search Topics: Courage-Fiction, Bullies-Fiction, Writing-Fiction, School Stories, Superheroes-Fiction, Humorous Fiction.

Conford, Ellen. And this is Laura. Little 1977, 179 pp.

As a member of a family of high-achievers, Laura was convinced that she was unloved and worthless because she had no talents. Then, suddenly Laura discovered she had very special psychic powers; powers she began to exploit. At first it was fun to give readings after school each day. Gradually, however, as Laura foresaw her friend hurt and her brother missing, she realized that having ESP was also a frightening responsibility. Finally, her ESP became the vehicle that made it possible for Laura to tell her parents her true feelings and to understand that they loved her for herself, not for her achievements.

The author treats a common concern with sensitivity and humor. An especially good choice for Judy Blume lovers. Print somewhat small.

Interest Level: 4-6. Reading Level: 4.2. Further Search Topics: Occult-Fiction, Courage-Fiction, Extra Sensory Perception-Fiction, Family-Fiction, Humorous Fiction, Everyday Stories, Talent-Fiction.

Danziger, Paula. The cat ate my gymsuit. Delacorte 1974, 147 pp.

Another book for fans of Judy Blume. Marcy was shy and insecure, unhappy at school and unhappy at home. She was self-conscious about being heavy and sure she would never have a date. Only Ms. Finney (a new teacher), her English class and Smedley (a communications group) meant anything to Marcy. When Ms. Finney was fired because of her refusal to recite the pledge of allegiance and her unorthodox teaching methods, Marcy began to organize a protest movement. Marcy's commitment brought more problems at school and at home, but eventually resulted in Ms. Finney's vindication and Marcy's and her mother's growth and understanding.

Don't expect much depth of characterization. Most of the characters are flat and stereotypical, but the book will have great appeal in spite of its faults, for Marcy's insecurities are ones with which many young readers can identify.

Interest Level: 5-6. Reading Level: 5.1. Further Search Topics: School Stories, Everyday Stories, Family Problems-Fiction, Challenges-Fiction, Weight-Fiction, Courage-Fiction, Individualists-Fiction, Sex Role-Fiction.

Dolch, Edward W. Dog stories; illus by Bernette Johnson and Robert S. Kerr. Garrard 1954, 169 pp.

Although overly sentimental for most adult tastes, this collection of true dog stories appeals to young dog lovers. Eighteen chapters tell 15 stories, ranging from the first story in which dog rescues boy, to the final story in which boy rescues dog. There is a dog who played baseball, a dog who went to live at a newspaper, a dog who saved a fireman from a fire, two dogs who were lost and several more dogs who became heroes. A consistent reading level, large print and a popular topic make this a good choice to offer reluctant readers despite the Dolch books' usual unattractive illustrations. Dolch Basic Vocabulary Book series.

Interest Level: 2-4. Reading Level: 2.1. Further Search Topics: Dogs-Fiction, Courage-Fiction, Pets-Fiction.

Green, Phyllis. The fastest quitter in town; illus by Lorenzo Lynch. A-W 1972, 62 pp.

Whenever Johnny played baseball and things went wrong for him, he would quit. Johnny's teammates finally grew so angry with him that they told him to leave the team. That same day, Johnny's 90-year-old great-grandfather lost a very special ring his wife had given him. Johnny's love for this great-grandfather pushed him to keep looking for the ring until days later, when everyone else had quit searching, Johnny found the ring. Having learned a hard lesson, Johnny returned to his team for one more chance. That evening Johnny went to see his great-grandfather to tell him, with legitimate pride, that he had played the entire game.

Although the lesson is pointed, the story is very satisfying. Johnny's relationship with this great-grandfather is close and supportive. His problem is one shared by many children, especially those with a weak self-image.

Interest Level: 1-4. Reading Level: 3.1. Further Search Topics: Blacks-Fiction, Challenges-Fiction, Courage-Fiction, Group 2, Baseball-Fiction, Grandparents-Fiction, Friendship-Fiction.

Hamilton, Virginia. Zeely; illus by Symeon Shimin. Macmillan 1967, 122 pp.

A beautiful, almost mystical story of a black girl who learns about self-identity and pride from a statuesque neighbor whom Geeder is convinced must be a Watutsi princess. At first by chance and later at an arranged meeting, Zeely (Geeder's neighbor) gently and symbolically speaks to Geeder of her racial origins. She also tells Geeder of a young girl (Zeely as a child), too ignorant of the world around her to be able to recognize reality. It is a quietly moving story that is most likely to find an appreciative audience in the thoughtful, more mature reader.

Interest Level: 5-6. Reading Level: 5.1. Further Search Topics: Africa-Fiction, Royalty-Fiction, Blacks-Fiction, Courage-Fiction, Vacation-Fiction, Country Life-Fiction, Read Aloud.

Harris, Robie H. Rosie's double dare; illus by Tony DeLuna. Knopf 1980, 112 pp.

Rosie wanted to play baseball with the Willard Street Gang, but she couldn't play well enough to play by their rules. She needed what her older brother called "shrimp rules." She couldn't hit a pitched ball, only a grounder; but grounders were "shrimp rules." In desperation Rosie agreed to take a dare that the gang made up. If she actually performed the dare, the gang would let her play with them by her rules.

The gang dared Rosie to sneak into cranky Mr. Quirk's apartment and borrow a set of his false teeth. Because Rosie couldn't find any extra false teeth, she borrowed his wig instead but that didn't satisfy the gang. They only laughed and made up another dare for Rosie. She was to untie Mrs. Samuels' dog and let it run loose. As Rosie untied him, Elmer ran away, Rosie ran off after him. One rainstorm later, Rosie caught up with him in the middle of a Red Sox game at Fenway Park. Rosie's attempt to catch Elmer stopped the game, brought her an interview on TV, and secured her a place on the Willard Street baseball team.

This very light story, made up almost entirely of action and examples of sibling rivalry, should have wide appeal through fifth grade. Beyond that, Rosie's age (almost nine) and childish behavior won't ring true. Capers series.

Interest Level: 2-5. Reading Level: 2.2. Further Search Topics: Baseball-Fiction, Humorous Fiction, Brothers and Sisters-Fiction, Challenges-Fiction, Courage-Fiction, Gangs-Fiction, Everyday Stories.

Hurwitz, Johanna. The law of gravity; illus by Ingrid Fetz. Morrow 1978, 192 pp.

The summer between fifth and sixth grades looked very unexciting to Margot. Her best friends were both going away for the whole summer and her father, a musician, was going to be on tour for most of the summer. Margot's very overweight mother had sworn never to go downstairs from their fifth floor walk-up apartment. Unless Margot chose to stay upstairs too, she was sure she would have a very lonely vacation. In addition, she had to work on a summer project for school. The project she finally chose was to get her mother downstairs after nine years of staying upstairs. In search of help she went to the local library where she met Bernie. Bernie was only a year older than Margot, but he seemed to know the most interesting things about the city. He showed her places Margot had never heard of before, he taught her to play chess, backgammon, and even to ride a bicycle. He was so full of fascinating ideas and information that Margot had no chance to be bored or lonely. Best of all, he even tried to help Margot with her project. None of their ideas worked, however, until Margot pretended to run away and scared her mother into going downstairs. Only then did Margot realize that she loved her mother whether or not she stayed on the fifth floor and that she couldn't simply force her mother or anyone else to change to suit her own fancy.

The book is a warm, understanding, slightly humorous treatment of the fairly common wish to change someone else. Although not many readers are likely to share Margot's exact problem, most will recognize her feelings. The book is also a virtual Chamber of Commerce advertisement for urban living. One of its other charms is its picture of a non-competitive, open, real friendship between an 11-year-old girl and a 12-year-old boy. The only drawback to the book is its inconsistent reading level which varies from 4.1 to 5.1 with a rare leap to 5.2.

Interest Level: 4-6. Reading Level: 4.2. Further Search Topics: Vacation-Fiction, Friendship-Fiction, Loners-Fiction, City Life-Fiction, Individualists-Fiction, Courage-Fiction, New York City-Fiction, Humorous Fiction, Family-Fiction, Challenges-Fiction, Weight-Fiction, Everyday Stories, Best Sellers.

Kelley, Sally. Trouble with explosives. Bradbury 1976, 117 pp.

Polly Banks stuttered very badly. She wanted to stop but she couldn't. Moving, entering a new school, and facing a mean teacher who seemed in need of psychiatric help, all made Polly's stuttering worse. When Sis, Polly's new friend, rose to Polly's defense in one confrontation too many with Miss Patterson, the teacher took cruel revenge. Polly's desire to help Sis, her need to do something about her stuttering, and an understanding psychiatrist, all helped Polly learn to help herself with her speech problem. At the same time, she began to understand and have confidence in herself and her family.

Another "problem book" that older elementary school readers seem to crave. Polly and Sis are both very sympathetic characters who bring to life many of the uncertainties of growing up. Print and line spacing of only average size but otherwise a good choice.

Interest Level: 4-6. Reading Level: 3.2. Further Search Topics: Academic Problems-Fiction, Stuttering-Fiction, Psychiatrists-Fiction, School Stories, Mental Illness-Fiction, Troublemakers-Fiction, Courage-Fiction, Physically Handicapped-Fiction, Children-Growth-Fiction, Moving, Household-Fiction.

Kessler, Leonard. Last one in is a rotten egg. Har-Row 1969, 64 pp.

Willie and Bobby could swim, but Freddy could not. After all three went to the local swimming pool and Freddy was pushed into the water by two older bullies, he was scared to try swimming again. Finally, a sympathetic lifeguard gave Freddy lessons. After much practice, Freddy became competent and confident enough to swim in the deep water and to stand up to the bullies.

A very slight plot designed to reassure new swimmers and provide a few basic rules of swimming. Reader format. A Sports-I-Can-Read-Book.

Interest Level: 1-2. Reading Level: 1.2. Further Search Topics: Courage-Fiction, Swimming-Fiction, Challenges-Fiction, Bullies-Fiction.

Mazer, Harry. The war on Villa Street. Delacorte 1978, 182 pp.

Willis was a loner and a runner. He was a loner because he didn't want anyone to find out about his alcoholic father. He wasn't quite sure why he ran; perhaps because it was the only time he felt good. When Rabbit Slavin and his friends asked Willis to become part of their gang, he refused. He was flattered and wanted to join, but the gang wanted to meet at his house and Willis couldn't risk that. Then when he agreed to coach the local "retard" for the school's field day, Willis gave the gang the opportunity they wanted to take their revenge on him for turning them down. The gang's hatred for Willis increased still more when he beat their best runner and athlete. In payment, the gang jumped Willis and beat him badly. After he picked himself up, Willis realized that he had at least faced the worst of his fears and survived. Days later when his drunken father humiliated him, Willis realized he had to face that, too. He made peace with himself and the world by deciding he could neither continue to run away from, nor apologize for his father anymore. He was independent and strong.

There is much in this fast-paced book besides the obvious violence and action. It is written with an intuitive feel for a teenager's problems and emotions and is a sensitive portrayal of mature concepts. The print is large, but spacing between the lines should have been slightly increased.

Interest Level: 5-6. Reading Level: 5.1. Further Search Topics: Running-Fiction, Loneliness-Fiction, Alcoholism-Fiction, Loners-Fiction, Mental Retardation-Fiction, Gangs-Fiction, Child Abuse-Fiction, Bullies-Fiction, Family Problems-Fiction, Courage-Fiction.

Platt, Kin. Brogg's brain. Lippincott 1981, 123 pp.

According to everyone else, Monty Davis should have been one of the fastest milers in the city. He had, after all, run a four minute and ten second mile in practice one day. He had run well enough that day to beat his high school's two best milers. That was a good enough performance to make the coach push him, his teacher talk about winning, and his father puff up with pride. Even the marathon runner he saw occasionally in the park and his girl friend Cindy seemed to think that he could be the best. Monty really didn't care, or he thought he didn't. Maybe he was just afraid to see how good or bad he really was. For whatever reason, he didn't want to run in the meet against Culver High School. He talked so much about not doing well, that by the time he was supposed to run, he even had his coach convinced he couldn't win. But as he ran, Monty heard a voice inside his head that sounded like the voice in a strange science fiction film that he and Cindy had just seen. The voice seemed to say that he could win, and suddenly that was what Monty wanted. The voice and his new-found determination were what pulled Monty through and gave him first place.

This book is for the track fan or the runner. Few others are likely to care about the difference between a four-twenty and a four-ten high school mile. For those who do care, this is a good choice.

Interest Level: 5-6. Reading Level: 3.1. Further Search Topics: Family Problems-Fiction, Love-Fiction, Running-Fiction, Courage-Fiction.

Robinson, Jean. The strange but wonderful cosmic awareness of Duffy Moon; illus by Lawrence Di Fiori. HM 1974, 142 pp.

Duffy was tired of being small, of always being on the losing side of fights, and of being unappreciated at home (by his ex-football star uncle). When he sent away for Mr. Flamel's Cosmic Awareness Kit, Duffy was sure he would then be able to take control over anything he wanted and direct his own life. His friend Peter, the narrator, wasn't quite so sure. Peter turned out to be right. Duffy almost made himself sick trying to build a stone wall. Babysitting two small boys and trying to bathe a Great Dane proved to be disastrous. But Duffy's biggest problem came from Boots McAfee's gang. A series of events finally brought Duffy and Peter face-to-face with the dreaded Boots. Luckily, she turned out to be a very smart girl who appreciated Duffy's true talents.

From the first to the last page this is a funny, very enjoyable book. A delightful book with a very palatable message.

Interest Level: 3-6. Reading Level: 3.2. Further Search Topics: Humorous Fiction, Bullies-Fiction, Magic-Fiction, Read Aloud, Occupations-Fiction, Sex Role-Fiction, Orphans-Fiction, Best Sellers, Gangs-Fiction, Courage-Fiction, Babysitting-Fiction.

Robinson, Nancy K. Wendy and the bullies; illus by Ingrid Fetz. Hastings 1980, 128 pp.

Wendy and her best friend Karen had a very carefully mapped out route to and from school—a route that allowed them to meet up with the fewest number of bullies possible. But when Karen became sick enough to stay home from school, Wendy had to face the bullies alone. Wendy's fears escalated to panic so intense that she avoided walking to school by hiding in her basement. She finally realized that she was letting fear and anger control her life when she found herself bullying Karen. Only her new friendship with Monica, making up with Karen, and her involvement in a school project helped Wendy overcome her fears.

This is a humorous, episodic tale of a feeling and circumstances common to many children. The illustrations sometimes make Wendy and her classmates appear much younger than her actual nine years, but fortunately that doesn't happen often enough to spoil the book's appeal.

Interest Level: 3-5. Reading Level: 3.1. Further Search Topics: School Stories, Bullies-Fiction, Courage-Fiction, Best Sellers, Humorous Fiction, Friendship-Fiction, Everyday Stories.

Scism, Carol K. The wizard of Walnut Street; illus by Martha Alexander. Dial 1973, 54 pp.

John and his friends had no room in their Wizard Club for Ford Owens, the new kid. John thought Ford was a conceited show-off who only wanted to make John look like a coward. It was true that John was afraid of some things, such as going down the giant slide into the lake, but he didn't want anyone else to know it. So he excluded Ford from all the club's activities until Ford pushed his way into their magic wishing-well project.

It had been John's idea to charge everyone a dime who wanted to make a wish. They could use the money to buy the few simple things that they would need to make the wishes come true. But it was Ford's eerie volcano and his large dog that had added just the right atmosphere to the trick to make people believe. Even John and Ford found themselves making wishes. John wished to be able to go down the giant slide. He didn't know what Ford wished. Much to John's initial surprise, people's wishes began to be fulfilled. Even Arthur, who had wished he could learn to dive, found he could. Then because John

began to realize that the magic was in believing in himself and not in the wishing well, he tried the slide and succeeded. Once John's reason to avoid Ford was gone, he relaxed and asked Ford to join the club. At that point, even Ford's wish was granted.

Interest Level: 2-4. Reading Level: 2.1. Further Search Topics: Friendship-Fiction, Gangs-Fiction, Courage-Fiction, Magic-Fiction, Vacation-Fiction, Best Sellers.

Shura, Mary Francis. The Barkley Street six-pack: illus by Gene Sparkman. Dodd 1979, 159 pp.

Jane's best friend Natalie was everything Jane wanted to be. She was self-assured, pretty, vibrant, and even possessed magical talents. Jane didn't realize at first, and she later resisted seeing, that Natalie ran Jane's life and cleverly made sure that Jane had no other friends. Natalie's move left Jane with no friends among those people she had once enjoyed. Little by little, with the help of a stray dog and the new boy on the block, Jane bagan to see how destructive Natalie had been. She finally realized that a true friendship is one in which neither party tries to control the other.

With its enticements of ESP, magic, stray dogs, and problems with peers, this is a very appealing book to many young readers. As a bonus it is a thoughtful, sympathetic, fairly well-written story.

Interest Level: 4-6. Reading Level: 4.2. Further Search Topics: Gangs-Fiction, Pets-Fiction, Dogs-Fiction, Friendship-Fiction, Honesty-Fiction, Courage-Fiction, Loneliness-Fiction, Extra Sensory Perception-Fiction, Everyday Stories.

Singer, Marilyn. It can't hurt forever; illus by Leigh Grant. Har-Row 1978, 186 pp.

When she was 11 years old, it was discovered that Ellie had a heart valve that hadn't closed by itself. Although her mother had promised her that she wouldn't die, Ellie was scared of the hospital and the operation she had to face. Her parents were kind and open about all that was to happen to her, but there was still much that Ellie had to learn from friends she made while she was in the hospital. There were times when she was frightened and only Sonia, a young open-heart surgery patient, could calm her. When Ellie, a special nurse, and a few other patients became close friends, Ellie learned enough from them to allow her to help another patient.

This is not a story of sweetness and light, but it is told with warmth, humor, and real understanding of a young person's fears. Thus it is not only an excellent candidate for bibliotherapy, but it is a truly satisfying story for the general reader as well.

Interest Level: 4-6. Reading Level: 2.2. Further Search Topics: Illness-Fiction, Physicians-Fiction, Medicine-Fiction, Courage-Fiction, Death-Fiction.

Slote, Alfred. Hang tough, Paul Mather. Lippincott 1973, 156 pp.

Paul Mather went against his doctor's and his parents' orders when he accepted his new neighbors' challenge to show his pitching skill. He had been told not to play baseball until he had been given permission, but Paul not only loved to pitch, he was also the best pitcher his new friends had ever seen. Knowing full well the medical problems he could be precipitating, Paul went ahead and pitched a spectacular game for the Wilson Dairy team against the Ace Appliance team. But by the end of the game, Paul was in the hospital again, and Wilson Dairy had been forced to forfeit the game because Paul had played illegally. As Paul's leukemia worsened, his determination to play baseball again grew. When the day came that his team was to play a second game against Ace Appliance, Paul made sure he was there. He was in a wheelchair and weak, but he was there. He couldn't actually play, but Paul's psychological support insured that Wilson Dairy won the game. He went back to the hospital proud, happy, and still determined to fight his disease.

This is more than the usual sports story. This is a very sensitive story of a young boy's determination to fight leukemia. The reader looking for only a baseball story may find this book more than he/she wants. However, the reader who is open to a story of human strength and courage will be well rewarded. The book neither dwells on nor minimizes the disease. Instead it uses both the disease and the sport to portray a character much more completely than in most sport stories, especially at this low a reading level. This is an excellent book for those special readers who respond well to thought-provoking material. Although chapters are short and reading level is low, the print is somewhat small. In addition, the first person style, told as if dictated into a tape recorder (complete with occasional interruptions), may be confusing to readers unless it is explained.

Interest Level: 5-6+Reading Level: 3.1. Further Search Topics: Baseball-Fiction, Death-Fiction, Illness-Fiction, Moving, Household-Fiction, Medicine-Fiction, Physicians-Fiction, Challenges-Fiction, Courage-Fiction.

Smith, Doris Buchanan. Last was Lloyd. Viking Pr 1981, 124 pp.

Lloyd had several problems: he was overweight, his mother was overprotective, he had no school friends, and there was a chance he might be taken away from home and put into foster care because he had missed so much school. Lloyd's mother, very young and very defensive when she had Lloyd, had done her best to be a "good mother," but in doing so, had made Lloyd fearful of the world. He had become the subject of his classmates' mockery so many times that the only way he could respond to his peers was with nastiness. The one skill he possessed was hitting a baseball. He kept this skill well hidden for fear of exposing himself to further mockery. When one of his classmates accidentally discovered how well Lloyd hit, he took the first step to becoming Lloyd's friend. Lloyd's reaction was to back away, but Kirby kept trying. Eventually Kirby's attempts and those of an understanding truant officer, helped Lloyd begin to make friends, to treat others decently, and to pull away from his mother; in short, he began to mature.

Because Lloyd's problems can be oversimplified too easily, this book requires a fairly mature reader and perhaps even discussion in order to fully understand its subtleties.

Interest Level: 5-6+Reading Level: 4.2. Further Search Topics: Weight-Fiction, Single Parent Family-Fiction, Courage-Fiction, School Stories, Loners-Fiction, Friendship-Fiction, Baseball-Fiction, Family Problems-Fiction, Foster Homes-Fiction, Children-Growth-Fiction.

Steven, Carla. Hooray for Pig!; illus by Rainey Bennett. HM 1974, 48 pp.

Pig couldn't spend the day swimming with his friend Raccoon because he didn't know how to swim. Instead Pig took a picnic to the lake by himself. At the lake, Pig met Otter, who encouraged Pig to at least try getting in the water. After several days of Otter's patient coaching, not only could Pig stay afloat, but he liked it, too!

For much the same audience as Kessler's *Last One In Is A Rotten Egg*, but because of a more interesting plot it is a little more useful. Reader format.

Interest Level: 1-2. Reading Level: 1.2. Further Search Topics: Pigs-Fiction, Courage-Fiction, Swimming-Fiction, Humorous Fiction.

Wagner, Jane. J.T; photos by Gordon Parks, Jr. Van Nostrand 1969, 64 pp.

This is a sentimental story that rarely fails to elicit a sympathetic response from young readers. J.T. is a poor black boy who saw a portable radio almost begging to be stolen and stole it. Two of the neighborhood bullies, Boomer and Claymore, saw J.T. take the radio. Though they threatened him, even poured soap in his eyes in the school bathrooms, J.T. wouldn't give them the radio as they demanded.

About the same time J.T. found a scrawny, scared little cat with only one eye. Because his mother wouldn't let him take the cat home, J.T. built it a warm but ramshackle little house in an abandoned building. He fed it by charging tuna to his mother's grocery store account without her knowledge. Bones became the only thing in J.T.'s life that he had cared about since his father had walked out.

When Boomer and Claymore found out about Bones, they taunted J.T. by throwing the cat back and forth between them until the frightened cat escaped, darted out into the street and was hit by a car. J.T.'s heart broke as he looked at Bones, but he spoke to no one to tell them of his sadness. Only time, his mother's and grandmother's love and a small kitten from Mr. Rosen, the grocer, helped him recover. On the morning that he decided to accept the kitten, J.T. returned the stolen radio, faced Boomer and Claymore without fear, and asked Mr. Rosen for a job in order to pay for cat food.

The book is oversized and illustrated with photographs from the television movie version. It is not only an excellent story to read aloud but one that will prompt listeners to want to finish it on their own or to reread it. It is now available only in paperback from Dell.

Interest Level: 3-6. Reading Level: 3.1. Further Search Topics: Read Aloud, Courage-Fiction, Best Sellers, Cats-Fiction, Single Parent Family-Fiction, Bullies-Fiction, Blacks-Fiction, Poverty-Fiction, City Life-Fiction, Christmas Stories, Crime-Fiction, Pets-Fiction, Holidays-Fiction.

Wallace, Bill. A dog named Kitty. Holiday 1980, 153 pp.

Ricky's fear of dogs was extreme but also understandable. He had been attacked by a rabid dog when he was very young. Remembering the fear, the stitches and the painful rabies shots was enough to bring tears to Ricky's eyes even years later. When a local bully told his dog to attack Ricky, Ricky's fear was discovered. About that time, a stray puppy showed up at Ricky's farm. Not quite knowing why, Ricky began to warm to the puppy, to feed it, and finally to love it. When the dog was attacked by a pack of wild dogs (a brutal scene vividly described), Ricky fully overcame his fear of dogs, went to Kitty's defense, and was barely able to save her life. When Kitty was later tragically and accidentally killed, Ricky swore that he would never have anything to do with a dog again. He almost kept his promise to himself, but eventually a second stray dog wandered into the farm and Ricky decided to try again.

This is an emotional story that should appeal to many readers. However, because of the violence and the dog's two-stage death, the book is probably best suited to fifth and sixth grade children.

Interest Level: 5-6. Reading Level: 3.1. Further Search Topics: Dogs-Fiction, Pets-Fiction, Bullies-Fiction, Death-Fiction, Oklahoma-Fiction, Courage-Fiction, Country Life-Fiction.

COWBOYS-FICTION

Packard, Edward. Deadwood City; illus by Barbara Carter. Bantam 1978, 96 pp.

See *Sugarcane Island* for full series notes. Paperback edition only. Choose Your Own Adventure series.

Interest Level: 2-6. Reading Level: 3.1. Further Search Topics: West-Fiction, Cowboys-Fiction, Crime-Fiction, Best Sellers, Group 2.

COYOTES-FICTION

Bernstein, Margery. Coyote goes hunting for fire; illus by Ed Heffernan. Scribner 1974, 40 pp.

A delightful story that can be read for fun or used as part of a unit on North American Indians. A long time ago when there was no fire, all the animals but Coyote banded together to find it. The animals left Coyote behind because he was always spoiling their plans. Coyote saw them leave, chased after them and once more tried to direct everything, but only ended up losing fire. Cartoon-like illustrations add to the humor of the story. This book should make a simple, but effective play.

Interest Level: 1-4. Reading Level 2.1. Further Search Topics: Animals-Fiction, Legends, Mythology, Fire-Fiction, Indians of North America-Legends, Coyotes-Fiction, Group 2, Creation-Fiction, Drama.

CREATION-FICTION

Arkhurst, Joyce. The adventures of Spider; West African folktales; illus by Jerry Pinkney. Little 1964, 58 pp.

A delightful collection of six West African folktales about Spider. Spider is mischievous, greedy, lazy and clever. He loves to eat and he hates to work. Four of the stories tell of Spider's ill-fated attempts to get food without having to work for it ("How Spider Got a Thin Waist," "How Spider Got a Bald Head," "How Spider Helped a Fisherman," and "Why Spiders Live in Dark Corners"). One story tells of his greed ("How the World Got Wisdom"), and only one story is complimentary ("Why Spider Lives in Ceilings"). All are short, gentle, humorous, and adapt well to dramatization or retelling.

Interest Level: 2-6. Reading Level 3.1. Further Search Topics: Humorous Fiction, Spiders-Fiction, Folklore, Tricksters-Fiction, Africa-Folklore, Group 2, Read Aloud, Creation-Fiction, Drama.

Bernstein, Margery. Coyote goes hunting for fire; illus by Ed Heffernan. Scribner 1974, 40 pp.

A delightful story that can be read for fun or used as part of a unit on North American Indians. A long time ago when there was no fire, all the animals but Coyote banded together to find it. The animals left Coyote behind because he was always spoiling their plans. Coyote saw them leave, chased after them and once more tried to direct everything, but only ended up losing fire. Cartoon-like illustrations add to the humor of the story. This book should make a simple, but effective play.

Interest Level: 1-4. Reading Level 2.1. Further Search Topics: Animals-Fiction, Legends, Mythology, Fire-Fiction, Indians of North America-Legends, Coyotes-Fiction, Group 2, Creation-Fiction, Drama.

Bernstein, Margery. The first morning; illus by Enid Warner Romanek. Scribner 1976, 44 pp.

Spider, Mouse, and Fly volunteered to ask the king of the sky for light to take back to earth because the animals on earth were tired of living in darkness. The king didn't want to give away any light and so he set what he thought was an impossible task for the three animals. They were able to outwit the king three times and finally return to earth with a box Mouse was sure contained light. When they opened the box all they found was a rooster. Poor Mouse was ashamed at having been so badly tricked. But then Rooster crowed up the first morning and has done so ever since. A competent retelling of an African myth, nicely complemented by bold illustrations. Good candidate for dramatization.

Interest Level: 1-3. Reading Level: 2.1. Further Search Topics: Animals-Fiction, Group 2, Mythology, Light-Fiction, Drama, Time-Fiction, Calendars-Fiction, Creation-Fiction, Africa-Folklore.

Dolch, Edward W. "Why" stories; illus by Marguerite Dolch. Garrard 1952, 160 pp.

"Why the Bear Has a Little Tail," "Why Turkeys Have Red Eyes," and "How the Tiger Got His Stripes" are three titles that illustrate the type of stories found in this collection. Seventeen short, simple folktales explain why the world and creatures in it operate and appear as they do. All of the tales can be found elsewhere. However, few if any stories are likely to be familiar to readers. This type of story is one children often find very appealing. The stories are understandable, logical within their own framework and simple enough to be retold to others. The reading level varies from 1.2 to 2.2. Dolch Basic Vocabulary Book series.

Interest Level: 1-4. Reading Level: 2.2. Further Search Topics: Folklore, Why Stories, Animals-Fiction, Group 2, Creation-Fiction.

CRIME

Adoff, Arnold. Malcolm X; illus by John Wilson. Har-Row 1970, 41 pp.

This is a simple, intellectually honest biography of a very controversial man. Taught a strong sense of self-respect by his father, Malcolm X could not accept the second-class status that white society tried to impose upon him. Instead he turned away from whites and all they stood for. He hated high school, the detention home he lived in after his father's death, and his mother's placement in a state hospital. He didn't feel comfortable until he moved to Harlem. There he found friends, but he also found crime. While he was in prison, Malcolm X began to read of great, black societies and people. His brother told him about the Nation of Islam, the Black Muslims, and Elijah Muhammad, the leader of the religion. He began corresponding with Mr. Muhammad. Shortly after he was released from prison, Malcolm X met Elijah Muhammad and eventually became a minister of the religion. There was even talk that he would be Elijah Muhammad's successor. But, as the years went on, Malcolm X began to think that black Christians as well as Muslims should be united in the fight for black rights. Despite threats against his life Malcolm X formed the Organization of Afro-American Unity. Both blacks and whites were angry with him. The threats continued until his house was firebombed; and, only a week later, at a public meeting, Malcolm X was assassinated.

An excellent overview of a complex man. The book may well prompt readers to learn more about the man and his beliefs. At the very least it will expose readers, in an interesting manner, to someone they should know. The book shares the same semi-picture book format of the others in Harper and Row/Crowell's biography series, therefore it will need a careful introduction to potential readers.

Interest Level: 3-5. Reading Level: 3.1. Further Search Topics: Blacks-Biography, Civil Rights, Biography, Crime, Religion, Assassinations, Prejudice, Poverty, Foster Homes.

CRIME-FICTION

Bennett, Jay. The pigeon. Methuen 1980, 147 pp.

Despite a low testing score, this is not a truly easy book to read. The author assumes his readers are fairly sophisticated and worldly, thus he does not explain the meaning of the Iron Cross symbol or the word Aryan. The book's language varies from simple to difficult, making the reading level inconsistent (2.1 - 4.1). The setting is dark and forbidding; an underground world of fugitives and terrorists. And yet, the book will be popular with many readers in sixth grade; it will be even more popular with older readers. The tension in this story of a teenage boy, blamed for the murder of his ex-girlfriend, is almost palpable. Brian's flight from the police and his desire to find Donna's murderer take him directly into the midst of a ring of terrorists, for whom life has no meaning. In Brian's attempt to prove his innocence, two more lives are lost, but hundreds more are saved as Brian discovers and stops a bomb threat. The author has used riveting action, short, clipped sentences, and terse dialogue to create a very successful, highly suspenseful book. Print size is only moderate.

Interest Level: 6 . Reading Level: 3.2. Further Search Topics: Mystery and Detective Stories, Terrorism-Fiction, Murder-Fiction, Best Sellers, Crime-Fiction, Courage-Fiction, Survival-Fiction, Runaways-Fiction.

Bonham, Frank. The mystery of the fat cat; illus by Alvin Smith. Dutton 1968, 160 pp.

Although noticeably dated at times, this is still an exciting story of an inner city neighborhood. Buddy, Little Pie, Rich, and Cool were among the many who used the local Boys' Club as their hangout. It was a place to stay out of trouble and off the streets, but it was also a haven for rats. The rats were big and brazen; so brazen that one attacked Buddy in the swimming pool. The club needed a new building desperately. The money was there; they just weren't able to use it. Fifteen years earlier an eccentric old woman willed the Boys' Club over $600,000, but stated that the money was first to be used to support her cat until it died. A caretaker, a lawyer, and a veterinarian all benefited as long as the cat lived. Buddy and his friends took on the job of discovering if the cat really was alive or if the Boys' Club was being cheated out of half a million dollars. It was a job that nearly killed them before they set things right. Plenty of action, some violence, a cast of street-smart characters, realistic trouble with the police, as well as a slight mystery almost insure the book's success with older readers. Moderate sized print. Line spacing somewhat narrow.

Interest Level: 6+. Reading Level: 5.1. Further Search Topics: Humorous Fiction, Cats-Fiction, Gangs-Fiction, City Life-Fiction, Mystery and Detective Stories, Poverty-Fiction, Friendship-Fiction, Juvenile Delinquency-Fiction, Crime-Fiction, Best Sellers.

Bunting, Eve. The skate patrol; illus by Don Madden. Albert Whitman 1980, 40 pp.

The book is funny, clever, undemanding and short. The combination of those qualities plus its slight mystery and its consistent reading level make this a very appealing and useful book for young readers. The plot is simple: in the hopes that their neighbors would be so grateful that they would allow the boys to roller skate in the neighborhood again, two friends decided to capture a local thief. James and Milton even knew who the thief was. He was the "mysterious man" who sat in the park. They only had to capture him in the act of stealing to prove that they were correct. They watched him continuously and trailed him as he followed old ladies. Then came the day that they heard Mrs. Grump scream that her purse had been snatched. The boys sped after the "mysterious man" on their skates. They caught him and knocked him down. To their surprise he declared that he was an undercover policeman and they were letting the real thief get away. Off they went again. This time they caught the right person and were rewarded just the way that they had hoped: Mrs. Crump (not Grump) promised that the boys would be allowed to roller skate any time they wished. A light and lively entertainment.

Interest Level: 2-4. Reading Level: 2.2. Further Search Topics: Mystery and Detective Stories, Humorous Fiction, Spies-Fiction, Roller Skating-Fiction, Crime-Fiction, Best Sellers.

Burch, Robert. Queenie Peavy; illus by Jerry Lazare. Viking Pr. 1966, 159 pp.

Queenie was always in trouble. She could be mean, really mean, but, she was also bright, talented, independent and resilient. Queenie blamed her problems on the fact that people teased her because her father was in jail and because she was poor. She thought that she had to defend herself against the world. Queenie was proud of her poor reputation until she accidentally-on-purpose caused a classmate to break his leg. Then, when her father returned home and wasn't the person she'd hoped he'd be, Queenie realized that only she could make her life better. Being the strong person she was, she set out to do just that.

Queenie is a wonderfully alive and sympathetic character, one well worth introducing to older readers despite the book's reading level. Print somewhat small. Line spacing average width.

Interest Level: 5-6. Reading Level: 5.1. Further Search Topics: Family Problems-Fiction, Crime-Fiction, Loners-Fiction, Poverty-Fiction, Humorous Fiction, Bullies-Fiction, Troublemakers-Fiction, Academic Problems-Fiction, Read Aloud.

Dolch, Edward W. Robin Hood stories; illus by Carmen Mowry. Garrard 1957, 162 pp.

The illustrations are still drab, but the stories in this volume are exciting. Here we find straight-forward adventure and familiar characters: Robin Hood, Little John, Will Scarlet, Sheriff of Nottingham, Allan-a-dale and Sir Richard of Lea. The book makes a good choice for adventure lovers. Dolch Pleasure Reading Book series.

Interest Level: 2-6. Reading Level: 2.2. Further Search Topics: Robin Hood, Knights and Knighthood-Fiction, Folklore, Crime-Fiction.

Heide, Florence Parry. Black magic at Brillstone. A. Whitman 1981, 126 pp.

Liza is a little older, her romance with Logan has progressed to a kiss, and the book's plot is more complex than earlier Brillstone adventures. Other than those differences, the book follows Heide's standard format. The Brillstone books all center on Liza Webster and Logan Forrest, teenage partners in crime detection, who live in the Brillstone Apartments. The stories are similar enough that one could almost substitute the names Nancy Drew and Ned for Liza and Logan. Both young women are only children who live with their fathers. They are both independent, resourceful, and very concerned that justice be done. The men in their lives play approximately the same roles; their fathers are proud and supportive, but distantly preoccupied with their own business; Logan and Ned are gallant, boyish, and devoted. Liza and Logan, like Nancy and Ned, are not distinctive characters. Instead, they are shells into which readers who want excitement and adventure can pour themselves. There is no parental interference to worry about. There is plenty of action, some suspense, and real world crime (for Liza: murder, bank robberies, etc.) rather than childish escapades. The books' success is practically guaranteed. Beware, however, of inconsistent reading levels that wander over a year's range.

Logan was first aware of strange occurrences at the Brillstone Apartments when someone entered his apartment late at night. While the person had searched the apartment, he or she had unconsciously whistled a nursery tune. Logan's neighbor, Miss Violet, said the tune reminded her of her deceased nephew. Slowly Logan and Liza realized that someone was trying to trick Miss Violet out of a substantial amount of money she had just inherited. They suspected that Bella Vine, a spiritualist, and an accomplice were trying to convince Miss Violet that her nephew was communicating from the dead and wanted Miss Violet to give her money to Bella. Not until it was almost too late did Liza and Logan realize that Bella was also posing as another possible recipient of the money and was really Miss Violet's nephew's wife. Miss Violet's nephew had only pretended to die in order to collect insurance money. When he and his wife had heard about Miss Violet's large inheritance, they had decided to reappear in order to bilk her out of the money. Brillstone Mystery series.

Interest Level: 5-6. Reading Level: 3.1. Further Search Topics: Mystery and Detective Stories, Occult-Fiction, Crime-Fiction, Ghosts-Fiction, Cats-Fiction, Detectives-Fiction, Inheritance-Fiction.

Heide, Florence Parry. Body in the Brillstone garage. A. Whitman 1980, 127 pp.

Liza's trip into the apartment house garage late one night made her even more frightened of that dark area than she had been. As she bent to pick up an envelope she thought someone had dropped, she saw a body lying on the floor of the garage. Because of a jacket he wore, Liza was certain the dead man was Mr. Greening, a neighbor. But when she returned to the garage with the police, the body was gone. The next day Mr. Greening was very much alive. Then Liza began to suspect that Mr. Greening was a murderer, but she didn't know who or where the victim was. It could have been Mr. Feeney, another neighbor, or it might have been a stranger. When Mr. Greening's stolen car was later discovered with the body of the car thief inside, Liza began to suspect that the thief's body was the one she had discovered. When she was told that the thief's name was Sharkey, she was certain Mr. Greening had engineered Sharkey's death. Sharkey was the name used by an angry man who had said he was looking for someone at the Brillstone who owed him something.

About then Liza remembered to look in the envelope she had found in the garage. The envelope revealed a note from Sharkey to Greening stating that Sharkey had proof that Greening was a car thief and that he would keep quiet only if Greening paid him twice the money he was owed. Knowing that without proof, she couldn't convince the police that Greening was a crook, Liza went to get the proof from Sharkey's hiding place in the about-to-be-junked car. Greening followed Liza to see what she knew and made a desperate attempt to kill her when he realized that she knew enough to put him in prison. At the last minute, Logan appeared, accidentally knocked Greening out, and helped Liza prove Greening's guilt to the police.

This is a fast-paced book that should be useful with mystery readers who can handle the jump from 4.1 to an occasional 5.1 reading level. See notes included with *Black Magic at Brillstone* for more information. Brillstone Mystery series.

Interest Level: 4-6. Reading Level: 4.2. Further Search Topics: Mystery and Detective Stories, Murder-Fiction, Running-Fiction, Crime-Fiction, Detectives-Fiction.

Heide, Florence Parry. Mystery of the mummy's mask; illus by Seymour Fleishman. A. Whitman 1979, 127 pp.

The Spotlight Club published a neighborhood newspaper. Just as the club was about to take the fourth issue to the printer, Jay discovered an ancient mummy mask hidden near Mr. Pruitt's house. Mr. Pruitt was intrigued by the discovery (he worked at the nearby museum) and he took the mask from Jay, but agreed that Jay could write about the mask for the paper. At about the same time, Dexter discovered that an old, abandoned house was being used. When the printer's office was broken into that night and only their newspaper was stolen, the three children began to suspect that something strange was going on at the abandoned house.

Dexter rode back to the house alone and was captured by Hank, one of three thieves hiding out there. Figuring that they never would have missed one item, Hank had taken the mask from the cache of goods that the other two had stolen. When he overheard Jay's conversation with Mr. Pruitt, Hank realized that his partners would find out what he had done if they ever read the newspaper article. To avoid being discovered, Hank broke into the printer's and stole the paste-up of the paper. In order to keep Dexter from escaping, Hank tied him up and placed him in a shipping crate. When he didn't return as soon as expected, Jay and Cindy realized that Dexter was in trouble, so they went out to the house to search for him. As the three escaped, Dexter and Cindy slashed the thieves' truck's tires, and Jay ran to phone for the police. After several nervous moments in which Cindy and Dexter thought Jay might not get back before they were caught, Jay finally brought the police, who captured all three thieves.

See *Mystery at Southport Cinema* for more information. Spotlight Club Mystery series.

Interest Level: 3-5. Reading Level: 3.1. Further Search Topics: Mystery and Detective Stories, Crime-Fiction, Egypt-Fiction, Archaeology-Fiction, Antiquities-Fiction, Journalism-Fiction, Gangs-Fiction, Brothers and Sisters-Fiction, Detectives-Fiction.

Heide, Florence Parry. Face at the Brillstone window. A. Whitman 1979, 128 pp.

As Liza drove out of the garage one evening she heard a thump at the side of the car. She jumped out and found that she had accidentally hit Peter

Pritchard, an insurance man and a new tenant of the apartment building. Pritchard seemed to be a very nice person who took some interest in Liza, her friends, and the criminal cases Liza's father (a journalist) was investigating. Liza was particularly interested in the case of the one-armed bandit who had been convicted of robbing and shooting a security guard. Against her father's research assistant's wishes she continued to search for evidence that would prove Robin Keck was innocent of the charges. As she interviewed the security guard, Keck's fiancee, his best friend, and the grandmother of a young girl who had had a strong crush on Keck, Liza found hints of his innocence. Young Bridgette's diary, however, held the proof she needed: an alibi. But someone else knew she had the information; someone who didn't want the information made public. Diary in hand, Liza began walking to her father's assistant's house (her father was out of town) when Pritchard offered her a ride. When Pritchard drove off in the wrong direction and then handed her a piece of incriminating evidence (gum), Liza realized she had played right into the real criminal's hands. Liza made a risky escape attempt that ended successfully with Pritchard's capture.

See *Black Magic at Brillstone* for more information about the series. Brillstone Mystery series.

Interest Level: 4-6. Reading Level: 3.2. Further Search Topics: Mystery and Detective Stories, Crime-Fiction, Detectives-Fiction.

Heide, Florence Parry. Mystery at Southport Cinema; illus by Seymour Fleishman. A. Whitman 1978, 128 pp.

The Spotlight Club was the name Jay, his sister Cindy, and his friend Dexter gave themselves. Their main interest was solving mysteries and just as in Sobol's Encyclopedia Brown series, Hildick's McGurk Mysteries, and Warner books about the Alden children, mysteries seem to follow them around. Their cases are more intricate and lengthy than Encyclopedia Brown's. They involve more danger than most of McGurk's, and they center on more common themes than the Alden's. The series serves much the same audience, however, as the others. It serves those children who want action, intrigue, and the challenge of a mystery, and who don't care about character development or in-depth motivation. The chapters are 8 to 12 pages long, print size is adequate, and the children are normal enough to make this a very popular series. As an added attraction, reading levels here are fairly consistent.

Thorne prided himself on doing his job well, so when the grocery store he ran for Callie (the owner) was robbed by a bearded stranger, Thorne felt responsible. Thorne ran after the thief but lost him in the darkened Southport Cinema. The Spotlight Club members also tried to track the thief. They figured that he had hidden the bag with the stolen money somewhere in the movie house because no one had been seen leaving with such a bag.

In the janitor's lost and found basket Jay found a wig the thief must have used as a disguise. The children called the wig maker to find out who had ordered it and were directed to a local post office box, Jay and Dexter were surprised to find belonged to the grocery store. Because Thorne picked up the mail each day, he became a prime suspect. In the meantime, Cindy had gone back to the cinema to look for the money. In the dark she had scuffled with someone else looking for the money and had given the person a deep scratch on the face.

At the same time that Thorne decided to pay Callie back for the stolen money, the Club members decided to tell Callie their suspicions about him. As Thorne handed his veterinary school savings to Callie, Cindy took a close enough look at Callie's face to see a new scratch and accused her of being the thief. Callie had so wanted Thorne to run the store instead of going to school, and had needed money so intensely, that she had stolen from her own business. The ending is weak but the rest of the book will hold reader interest. Spotlight Club Mystery series.

Interest Level: 3-5. Reading Level: 3.1. Further Search Topics: Mystery and Detective Stories, Gangs-Fiction, Crime-Fiction, Detectives-Fiction, Brothers and Sisters-Fiction.

Heide, Florence Parry. Mystery of the melting snowman; illus by Seymour Fleishman. A. Whitman 1974, 128 pp.

Hidden inside of a snowman, the Spotlight Club found what they believed was a stolen iron statue of a dog. In order to try to catch the thief, the children hid the statue again and watched to see who came to look for it. Eventually they determined that the thief or thieves was either Tom and Jenny, the amenable young couple who were helping Mrs. Wellington sell her house or Alex, the man who seemed to be a detective. After a frightening episode in which Alex almost captured Cindy, the dog, and a cache of Mrs. Wellington's diamonds (hidden in a secret compartment to which the dog held the key), Cindy managed to lock Alex in a closet long enough to enable Jay and Dexter to alert Mrs. Wellington to what was happening. The case was closed as Mrs. Wellington revealed Alex to be her greedy, young nephew, whom she had indulged once too often, but would not indulge again.

See *Mystery at Southport Cinema* for series information. Spotlight Club Mystery series.

Interest Level: 3-5. Reading Level: 2.2. Further Search Topics: Mystery and Detective Stories, Gangs-Fiction, Crime-Fiction, Brothers and Sisters-Fiction, Detectives-Fiction, Inheritance-Fiction.

Heide, Florence Parry. Mystery of the midnight message; illus by Seymour Fleishman. A. Whitman 1977, 128 pp.

The challenge to the Spotlight Club this time was to stop a crime before it happened. Jay and his sister Cindy were on a bus trip home when a blizzard forced the bus to stop at a motel for the night. Jay answered the room telephone late that night and heard a woman's strange and stern instructions. The instructions were to say nothing, to look in the desk drawer for directions, to expect that Bee had the other half of the instructions, and to be at the place at 8:00 the next evening. The envelope, which Jay and Cindy found, showed the location of and half the combination to someone's bedroom safe.

Early the next morning, the children found themselves fleeing in terror from the evil Scull, the man who was supposed to have received the message. Scull pursued them as they escaped in a friendly salesman's car, caught them and locked them into a cold barn without jackets. When the two were finally back on the road and reunited with Dexter and his sister Anne, they had only a few hours and fewer clues to help them find Woodvale and Jeremiah Gibbon, the intended victim.

Despite difficult driving conditions in the snow, Anne managed to get the children to their destination a few minutes before the thieves arrived. Anne and Jeremiah's secretary left the house together to get the police while the Spotlight Club members and Mr. Gibbon hid near the safe. A few tense minutes later, the case was closed; Mr. Gibbons' money was safe, the ringleader had been named (Mr. Gibbon's doctor), and the thieves had been caught.

See *Mystery at Southport Cinema* for series information. Spotlight Club Mystery series.

Interest Level: 3-5. Reading Level: 3.1. Further Search Topics: Mystery and Detective Stories, Crime-Fiction, Snow-Fiction, Disasters-Fiction, Gangs-Fiction, Brothers and Sisters-Fiction, Detectives-Fiction.

Heide, Florence Parry. Mystery of the vanishing visitor; illus by Seymour Fleishman. A. Whitman 1975, 128 pp.

Cindy was hired to take care of Mrs. Widget's house, animals, and plants for a weekend. That same weekend, someone tried to find and steal something from Mrs. Widget's overcrowded house. She had very few empty spaces in her house, so it was not a surprise that the thief wasn't able to find the object of his or her search. The three Spotlight Club members were determined to figure out not only who was the thief, but also what it was that the thief, wanted. Their prime suspects included the very nasty Bertha Beaker and the charming Charley Capp.

After spending a night in Mrs. Widget's house trying to, and almost succeeding in catching the thief, the children were surprised by an early morning visit from Mr. Capp. Mr. Capp was nearly able to steal away with a painting that hid a great deal of money before Cindy figured out that he was the thief. Even after Mr. Capp had been caught, he charmed his way out of any punishment and left before anyone had second thoughts.

See entry for *Mystery at Southport Cinema* for series information. Spotlight Club Mystery series.

Interest Level: 3-5. Reading Level: 2.2. Further Search Topics: Mystery and Detective Stories, Brothers and Sisters-Fiction, Gangs-Fiction, Crime-Fiction, Antiquities-Fiction, Detectives-Fiction. 00001944

Hildick, Edmund W. The great rabbit rip-off; illus by Lisl Weil. Macmillan 1976, 101 pp.

Why would anyone want to put red paint on all of the clay lawn rabbits in town? That was the first and easier of the mysteries the McGurk Organization had to solve. The bigger mystery was who would then steal them all and why? Almost everyone in town had purchased a rabbit to help a charity drive. Donny Towers a local social worker had thought of the idea. Donny, his fiancee, Joanne, and two reformed thieves, Sam and Ferdie, had made enough rabbits for everyone. When the rabbits disappeared, the Organization began to suspect, among others, Sam and Ferdie. Then when Donny replaced each one almost immediately with rabbits smelling of paint remover, the group began to think Donny might have been involved. It was Wanda's sharp eyes that revealed Donny's motive. Joanne's engagement ring had been accidentally molded into one of the rabbits and Donny had retrieved the rabbits to find the ring. Knowing he couldn't return the paint stained rabbits without raising suspicion, Donny had removed the red paint and told everyone that he was simply replacing the stolen rabbits with new ones.

See Case of the Bashful Bank Robber for series information. McGurk Mystery series.

Interest Level: 3-5. Reading Level: 2.2. Further Search Topics: Mystery and Detective Stories, Detectives-Fiction, Gangs-Fiction, Rabbits-Fiction, Crime-Fiction, Humorous Fiction.

Hildick, Edmund W. The case of the secret scribbler; illus by Lisl Weil. Macmillan 1978, 106 pp.

Joey's discovery in a library book of a scrap of paper with part of a letter and a strange diagram on it led the McGurk Organization on a lively chase. Brains identified the diagram as that of a widely-used security system. The part of the letter that they could read told the group that there was a burglary being planned for the approaching weekend, but the youngsters knew the police would never take them seriously until they had much more evidence. By researching local alarm systems, determining who bought the unusual paper, and comparing handwriting samples, the detectives were able to convince the police of what was about to happen. In gratitude, the police loaned the Organization a police monitor so that they could listen as the thieves were caught. To all but McGurk it seemed like the perfect way to end the case: he tried to sneak into the midst of the capture, but only succeeded in getting himself in real trouble.

See *Case of the Bashful Bank Robber* for series information. McGurk Mystery series.

Interest Level: 3-6. Reading Level: 2.2. Further Search Topics: Mystery and Detective Stories, Crime-Fiction, Gangs-Fiction, Nonverbal Communication-Fiction, Humorous Fiction, Detectives-Fiction.

Hildick, Edmund W. The case of the treetop treasure; illus by Lisl Weil. Macmillan 1980, 121 pp.

As Wanda rescued a cat she discovered a stash of odd items tucked into a hollow high up in a tree. On top of the assortment was a sign that said simply "Beware!" The McGurk Organization suspected a thief was using the tree as a place to hide stolen goods, but until an antique silver bowl was added nothing that had been placed there was worth stealing. Shortly afterwards Wanda found out from the police that she was the prime suspect in the theft of the bowl. Brains devised a complicated system for determining the real thief while McGurk worked more from intuition. Nevertheless, it wasn't long before they both arrived at the same conclusion. The culprit was the gang's long-time enemy Sandra Ennis. Then it was just a simple matter of finding the right way to persuade Sandra to confess and apologize to her victims.

See *The Case of the Bashful Bank Robber* for series information. McGurk Mystery series.

Interest Level: 3-5. Reading Level: 3.1. Further Search Topics: Mystery and Detective Stories, Crime-Fiction, Gangs-Fiction, Detectives-Fiction, Humorous Fiction.

Hildick, Edmund W. The case of the snowbound spy; illus by Lisl Weil. Macmillan 1980, 132 pp.

One snowy morning McGurk called the five members of his organization together to decipher a code. The code was part of a message from someone who wanted to hire them and would pay $5.00 a day. When they broke the code and met their employer, Mr. Fitch, he gave the group another code as part of their assignment. The second code told them where to deliver a small package that Mr. Fitch gave them. They were to pick up another coded message at the same place. After three pick-ups and drops they would be finished and Mr. Fitch, an ex-government spy, would have proved he was still a trustworthy and capable person to an ex-colleague with whom he wanted to work on a book. It seemed like just the challenging kind of assignment the McGurk Organization looked for. As they worked, however, it began to look more and more as if they were being used for illegal business. While Joey and McGurk staked out the next drop-off spot, Willie, Brains and Wanda pretended to Mr. Fitch to be unsuspecting. By working quickly and cleverly and by alerting the police, the McGurk gang uncovered and stopped two industrial spies who were stealing secret information about a new copying machine.

See *The Case of the Bashful Bank Robber* for series information. McGurk Mystery series.

Interest Level: 3-6. Reading Level: 3.1. Further Search Topics: Mystery and Detective Stories, Spies-Fiction, Detectives-Fiction, Gangs-Fiction, Humorous Fiction, Nonverbal Communication-Fiction, Crime-Fiction.

Hildick, Edmund W. The case of the bashful bank robber; illus by Lisl Weil. Macmillan 1981, 138 pp.

The McGurk Organization is a crime fighting detective agency. Led by Jack McGurk's strong ego, they had taken on many a seemingly impossible task and had always been successful. Never before, however, had they tried to protect the seven banks in town from being robbed. The five children's first idea was to regularly patrol each bank and watch for likely looking get-away cars. When that plan only led to a nasty confrontation with their new junior high school principal, they decided to try something else. Their second plan, to photograph all suspicious looking people near the banks, didn't fare much better than their first idea. Then, without knowing it, they found themselves holding the key to solving a real bank robbery. Before they realized its importance, they had literally given away the vital clue. Using only their own memories, powers of observation, and cleverness, they were still able to solve the crime with only a little help from the FBI.

The "McGurk mysteries" are light, fast-moving, and often humorous. Clues for solving the mysteries are sometimes subtle, but always there in the plot and illustrations for the reader to find. The characters are somewhat flat but still appealing. Joey, who is handy with words and a typewriter, is the narrator of each book. Jack McGurk, dedicated mastermind of all the group's activities is shrewd, a natural leader, and egotistical. Willie has the world's most sensitive nose and an excellent memory for odors. Wanda is the best tree-climber in town and a rational influence on the group. Brains, the newest and youngest member of the group, is a scientific genius, so he runs their crime lab. The books need not be read in chronological order although most have a brief reference to an earlier story. Reading level varies within each book from 2.1 to 3.1. A few books include enough more difficult passages that their average reading level is pushed from 2.2 to 3.1. Interest level in the series, once a reader has started on it, is high. McGurk Mystery series.

Interest Level: 3-6. Reading Level: 2.2. Further Search Topics: Mystery and Detective Stories, Crime-Fiction, Detectives-Fiction, Humorous Fiction, Gangs-Fiction.

Hildick, Edmund W. The case of the four flying fingers; illus by Lisl Weil. Macmillan 1981, 138 pp.

At first the four young strangers who were knocking over garbage cans had been merely a neighborhood nuisance. Later McGurk and his fellow detectives began to suspect that they were involved in the rash of break-ins and burglaries in the city. The Organization didn't think the "garbage gang" was actually committing the robberies, but rather that they were fingering houses for someone else to burglarize (thus their nickname: The Four Flying Fingers). It could be safely assumed by a would-be burglar that where no one picked up the spilled garbage, no one was home. It was the Organization's job to find the Thumb who was the mastermind behind the plot. When they caught up with the Fingers, McGurk and crew found out that the Flying Fingers hadn't realized what they were doing; only that a blonde lady in a camper was paying them a nickel for every driveway they left strewn with garbage. It didn't take long for the Organization to track down the woman and her accomplice. But, in one of their less intelligent moves, they played right into her hands and soon found themselves being transported out of town in her camper. When they tried to call to passing cars for help, no one took them seriously. It wasn't until Brains, bound and gagged to appear authentic, used a flashlight and Morse code to signal for help that anyone paid any attention to them. A police car finally stopped the camper for speeding apd after some clever arguments McGurk and his friends were able to convince the police that Lady Thumb was a thief.

This title is just as enjoyable as the best of the other books in the series, more exciting and universal in appeal than most, and equally humorous. It's only drawback is a very inconsistent reading level (from 2.1 to 4.1) that will discourage a reader new to McGurk. Established fans will be able to tolerate the range. McGurk Mystery series.

Interest Level: 3-6. Reading Level: 3.1. Further Search Topics: Mystery and Detective Stories, Detectives-Fiction, Humorous Fiction, Crime-Fiction, Gangs-Fiction.

Hinton, Susan E. The outsiders. Viking Pr. 1967, 188 pp.

When she wrote this book Susan Hinton was only 17 years old, but she had the sensitivity of someone much older. She wrote a taut story of the rivalry between two city gangs; the Socs (the rich socialites) and the Greasers (poor kids from the wrong side of town) that is more than anything a plea for understanding and tolerance. Seen through the eyes of Ponyboy (a very bright, 14-year-old Greaser), the rivalry brought on violence and an accidental killing that forced Pony and his friend Johnny to flee for their lives. Dallas, the meanest and most dangerous of the Greasers, provided them with shelter, food for a week, and a gun. At the end of that week, Johnny decided that they should turn themselves in to the police. But before they could do that, their hideout (an old church) burned in a fire which threatened the lives of four children who had been playing there. In trying to rescue the children, Johnny, Pony, and Dallas were injured; Johnny was severely burned and probably permanently crippled. A vengeance rumble was held while Johnny lay in the hospital, but the Greasers' victory was empty when Johnny died. He had been the one member of the gang whom they all loved and who had most needed them. Dallas went to pieces: he robbed a store and set himself up to be killed by the police. He had nothing left to live for after Johnny's death. Pony found support and security with his brothers (their parents were dead) and, in a note from Johnny, some hope for the future.

Hinton speaks most often through Pony (his depth of understanding of the people around him is very impressive), but through Johnny and two of the Socs as well, Randy and Cherry. Her message is clear, but at no time does she fail to maintain believable characters in a compelling plot.

Although the book looks forbidding with its 188 pages of unrelenting small print, it is an exciting story, full of adventure, realism, and room for thought. Perhaps the best way to introduce this book is to read a fair portion of it aloud. Now a motion picture too.

Interest Level: 6+. Reading Level: 5.1. Further Search Topics: Crime-Fiction, Gangs-Fiction, Murder-Fiction, Read Aloud, Friendship-Fiction, Juvenile Delinquency-Fiction, Best Sellers, City Life-Fiction, Brothers and Sisters-Fiction, Orphans-Fiction, Runaways-Fiction, Troublemakers-Fiction, Poverty-Fiction.

Law, Carol Russell. The case of the Weird Street firebug; illus by Bill Morrison. Knopf 1980, 119 pp.

This is the humorous story of a Nancy Drew-type character who gets involved in a mystery before she is even half finished with her mail-order detective lessons. Steffi wanted very much to be a detective. When she saw an ad for a local correspondence course, she tracked down the shabby office in a run-down building on Weir Street, and went to visit Jeff Dangerfield of Dangerfield Detective School. Steffi's first lesson, trailing suspects, was a disaster. She tried to pick out suspicious characters at a fire on Weir Street on her way home. The only really suspicious character (Beady Eyes) didn't go anywhere, so Steffi couldn't follow him. Her next attempts were very obvious and only resulted in her own anger and embarrassment. On her way back to seek advice from Dangerfield, Steffi literally ran into Beady Eyes again. She didn't think anything more about him until she saw him a short time later at another fire just down the street from Dangerfield's office. As the fire moved closer to Dangerfield's building, Steffi took desperate measures to try and save her friend. Steffi's efforts were interpreted by Beady Eyes as attempts to indicate that he was an arsonist. By the time Steffi figured out that Beady Eyes really was an arsonist, he had her cornered. A timely entry by the police saved both Steffi and Dangerfield. Steffi's reward for the capture of Beady Eyes was a medal from the police and a partnership with Dangerfield.

A fast-paced story, as well as slightly more original characters than most stories of this genre, make this a likely success with third through sixth grade readers. Capers series.

Interest Level: 3-6. Reading Level: 3.1. Further Search Topics: Mystery and Detective Stories, Humorous Fiction, Fire-Fiction, Detectives-Fiction, Crime-Fiction.

Packard, Edward. Deadwood City; illus by Barbara Carter. Bantam 1978, 96 pp.

See *Sugarcane Island* for full series notes. Paperback edition only. Choose Your Own Adventure series.

Interest Level: 2-6. Reading Level: 3.1. Further Search Topics: West-Fiction, Cowboys-Fiction, Crime-Fiction, Best Sellers, Group 2.

Platt, Kin. Dracula, go home; illus by Frank Mayo. Watts 1979, 87 pp.

From the chapter numbers that drip blood, and the humorously grotesque illustrations, to the short sentences and chapters, this is a book designed and almost guaranteed to appeal to the reluctant reader. A sense of immediacy and involvement is created by the first person narration. Tension is created on the opening page when Larry sees a man in the cemetery who looked exactly like Dracula. When that man registered at the hotel where Larry was working, Larry decided to find out more about him. It began to look as if Mr. A. R. Claude (the letters spell Dracula) was not only a vampire, but a thief and a murderer as well. The trouble was that Larry couldn't prove anything. Even when he found the stolen jewels for which Mr. Claude had been searching, Larry still couldn't convince anyone of Claude's true identify. No one ever did believe Larry, thus Claude went free.

The author uses a light touch to treat an eerie subject. His inconclusive ending may disappoint some, but should delight many. Beware of the variability of the reading level however; it swings from high first grade to low third grade.

Interest Level: 3-6. Reading Level: 2.2. Further Search Topics: Monsters-Fiction, Horror-Fiction, Mystery and Detective Stories, Best Sellers, Murder-Fiction, Crime-Fiction, Transformations-Fiction.

Platt, Kin. Run for your life; photos by Chuck Freedman. Watts 1977, 95 pp.

Lee almost lost his newspaper delivery job when someone began to regularly steal money and papers from the newspaper boxes along his route. Lee saw a chance for revenge if he could beat the thief in the mile race at the next track meet.

Most of the abundant dialogue is slang. The romantic interest is innocent and low keyed. The story has enough running to make that a strong appeal, but not so much that no one but a track or running enthusiast can enjoy it.

Interest Level: 5-6. Reading Level: 2.2. Further Search Topics: Running-Fiction, Love-Fiction, Occupations-Fiction, Crime-Fiction.

Sharmat, Marjorie W. The Lancelot closes at five; illus by Lisl Weil. Macmillan 1976, 120 pp.

Despite a somewhat slow beginning, this is an amusing, almost sensitive story of two friends who decided to spend the night in the model home of the new housing development in which they both lived. Hutch, a health food fanatic whose mother pronounced judgment on everything Hutch did, conceived of the idea as her way of breaking away. Abby went along for the fun of it. When the local newspaper wrote of unusual vandalism at the model home, the townspeople became engrossed in finding the culprits. As the adults became enraged about the crime wave, their children began to admire the clever idea. Soon, almost every youngster in town had confessed to spending the night in the model home. By the time Abby and Hutch got around to admitting they had slept there, no one believed them. Only a sock with Abby's name in it could tie Abby and Hutch to the scene of the crime. As the book ends, the police have begun a thorough search of the house, after a real robbery, and the sock's discovery is imminent.

Interest Level: 4-6. Reading Level: 3.2. Further Search Topics: Humorous Fiction, Suburbia-Fiction, Runaways-Fiction, Crime-Fiction, Individualists-Fiction, Family Problems-Fiction.

Shreve, Susan. The Nightmares of Geranium Street. Knopf 1977, 127 pp.

The Nightmares, a small neighborhood gang, had very little to do until beautiful Tess moved on the block. Tess dressed in satins, furs, and rhinestones, and sang in nightclubs. She was even more of a fascination to the gang because they had been told to stay away from her. When Amanda moved in with Tess, the Nightmares invited her to join the gang so that they would have a way of spying on Tess. Gradually her strange behavior, her moods, her bruises and shaking spells, the strangers she let in the house, and the fights she had, led the gang members to suspect that Tess dealt in drugs. When Amanda failed to show up for a picnic and the Nightmares learned the police were searching for Tess, the gang became worried enough to look for Amanda themselves. In doing so, they uncovered proof of Tess' drug dealings, put themselves in great danger, and were protected by Tess as they escaped only moments before Tess was arrested.

Despite its low reading level, the book's confusing sequence of final events, and its subject matter make it best suited to older readers. It is not great literature, but its subject has strong appeal.

Interest Level: 5-6. Reading Level: 3.1. Further Search Topics: Family Problems-Fiction, Gangs-Fiction, Drugs-Fiction, Mystery and Detective Stories, City Life-Fiction, Crime-Fiction, Philadelphia-Fiction.

Wagner, Jane. J.T; photos by Gordon Parks, Jr. Van Nostrand 1969, 64 pp.

This is a sentimental story that rarely fails to elicit a sympathetic response from young readers. J.T. is a poor black boy who saw a portable radio almost begging to be stolen and stole it. Two of the neighborhood bullies, Boomer and Claymore, saw J.T. take the radio. Though they threatened him, even poured soap in his eyes in the school bathrooms, J.T. wouldn't give them the radio as they demanded.

About the same time J.T. found a scrawny, scared little cat with only one eye. Because his mother wouldn't let him take the cat home, J.T. built it a warm but ramshackle little house in an abandoned building. He fed it by charging tuna to his mother's grocery store account without her knowledge. Bones became the only thing in J.T.'s life that he had cared about since his father had walked out.

When Boomer and Claymore found out about Bones, they taunted J.T. by throwing the cat back and forth between them until the frightened cat escaped, darted out into the street and was hit by a car. J.T.'s heart broke as he looked at Bones, but he spoke to no one to tell them of his sadness. Only time, his mother's and grandmother's love and a small kitten from Mr. Rosen, the grocer, helped him recover. On the morning that he decided to accept the kitten, J.T. returned the stolen radio, faced Boomer and Claymore without fear, and asked Mr. Rosen for a job in order to pay for cat food.

The book is oversized and illustrated with photographs from the television movie version. It is not only an excellent story to read aloud but one that will prompt listeners to want to finish it on their own or to reread it. It is now available only in paperback from Dell.

Interest Level: 3-6. Reading Level: 3.1. Further Search Topics: Read Aloud, Courage-Fiction, Best Sellers, Cats-Fiction, Single Parent Family-Fiction, Bullies-Fiction, Blacks-Fiction, Poverty-Fiction, City Life-Fiction, Christmas Stories, Crime-Fiction, Pets-Fiction, Holidays-Fiction.

Warner, Gertrude Chandler. Schoolhouse mystery; illus by David Cunningham. A. Whitman 1965, 128 pp.

On a dare, the Aldens went to a quiet fishing village to see what excitement they could find there. They found an isolated town filled with poor and unfriendly people. In their attempt to get to know the townspeople, the Aldens learned of the children's desire for schooling and the adults' anticipation of the Money Man's arrival. The Alden children took on the task of teaching school for the summer in an abandoned schoolhouse owned by Miss Gray, a recluse. The Money Man intrigued them more with each new bit of information they learned about him. They finally decided that the Money Man was a swindler who was practically stealing valuable antiques away from the villagers. By spying on the Money Man when he used the schoolhouse to store the antiques, the Aldens and an ex-FBI man were able to capture him. When the vacation was over, the Aldens had once more found excitement, Miss Gray had agreed to teach the local school, the Money Man was on his way to jail, and the townspeople knew the value of their old household items.

See the entry for *The Boxcar Children* for more information.

Interest Level: 3-5. Reading Level: 2.2. Further Search Topics: Mystery and Detective Stories, Vacation-Fiction, School Stories, Antiquities-Fiction, Crime-Fiction, Brothers and Sisters-Fiction, Challenges-Fiction.

Yolen, Jane. Shirlick Holmes and the case of the wandering wardrobe; illus by Anthony Rao. Coward 1981, 80 pp.

This is a light, fast-paced story of Shirli and her four friends' attempt to solve a local mystery. Its more fully developed characters and plot make this a better literary piece than any of the *Encyclopedia Brown* stories, but it resembles them in other ways. The children live in a small, secure town. The police chief, Shirli's neighbor and George's father, is working on the same case that interests the children but the children solve it first. The mystery is real and involves danger, as opposed to many of Hildick's McGurk mysteries, the other series this book resembles.

Shirli is a fiesty figure who took up George's challenge to solve the town's latest mystery. Thieves had been systematically robbing some of the wealthy summer homes of antiques. Shirli's plan, to search each of the houses for clues, only succeeded in angering the police chief when he caught Shirli and her friends. Being intrepid detectives, however, they did not give up. Instead, they staked out a likely house and waited for the thieves. When the robbers finally arrived Shirli and George hid. Only Gloria was able to escape and go for help. The oak wardrobe in which Shirli took refuge was one of the first pieces the thieves took out of the house. When Shirli tried to get out of it, she found the wardrobe had been placed on a truck with its door against the truck's side; she was caught. Very frightened, she stayed silent until she found herself in the middle of an antiques auction and recognized one of the voices making bids as George's father! As Shirli tumbled out of the wardrobe some of the police chief's men arrested the auctioneer for burglary and selling stolen goods. After she escaped, Gloria had told the police about the thieves, their truck, Shirli, and George, whom they found locked inside a closet still at the summer house.

A serviceable book that will be enjoyed by a wide range of readers.

Interest Level: 3-5. Reading Level: 3.1. Further Search Topics: Mystery and Detective Stories, Humorous Fiction, Friendship-Fiction, Crime-Fiction, Antiquities-Fiction, Detectives-Fiction, Challenges-Fiction.

CRUELTY-FICTION
Blume, Judy. Blubber. Bradbury 1974, 153 pp.

Jill, like all the other fifth graders in her class, did exactly as Wendy directed her. When Wendy nicknamed one of the class members Blubber and launched a campaign against her, Jill joined right in. It wasn't until the tables were turned and Jill became Wendy's next victim that Jill realized how much it hurt to be the target of such nastiness. It was only then that Jill could stand up to Wendy. Wendy's meanness is extreme and her classmates, without exception, actively follow her lead, yet all adult characters in the book are blind to what happens. Despite those drawbacks, the book deals with a problem very real to children and thus it has guaranteed audience appeal.

Interest Level: 4-6. Reading Level: 3.1. School Stories, Bullies-Fiction, Weight-Fiction, Loners-Fiction, Gangs-Fiction, Read Aloud, Cruelty-Fiction, Best Sellers, Troublemakers-Fiction, Friendship-Fiction.

CSONKA, LARRY

Burchard, Marshall. Sports hero: Larry Csonka. Putnam 1975, 95 pp.

Larry Csonka was almost the stereotype of a football player; big, fearless and driving. For more information about the books in the series see *Sports Hero: Bill Walton*. Sports Hero series.

Interest Level: 2-6. Reading Level: 3.1. Further Search Topics: Biography, Csonka, Larry, Football-Biography, Group 2.

DANCING

Baylor, Byrd. Sometimes I dance mountains; illus by Ken Longtemps and Bill Sears. Scribner 1973, 42 pp.

The author feels strongly that dance is a creative personal statement. That feeling becomes very clear in this combination of photographs and drawings. The photographs record a young girl's dance interpretation of the author's prose. The background drawings enlarge upon the poetic mood of the sparse text. For the dance enthusiast.

Interest Level: 2-6. Reading Level: 2.2. Further Search Topics: Dancing.

Krementz, Jill. A very young dancer. Knopf 1976, unp (121 pp).

This was the first of the five *Very Young* books to be written. Like the others, it is large in format and lavishly photographed. Unlike *A Very Young Circus Flyer*, this and the remaining books in the series are written about 10-year-old girls from obviously privileged backgrounds. All the girls are high achievers in their chosen areas but they seem very determined to work still harder until they attain whatever goals they have set for themselves. The books all follow the same formula. The girls introduce themselves, tell about their start in dancing, riding etc., describe their goals, and tell the reader how close they are to those goals. The girls go on to describe their daily routines, the practice, the chores, the hours, and the fun. Then the reader is ushered through approximately a year's worth of the young star's challenges, achievements, and defeats (the latter are only lightly touched upon). Through it all, the child shows enthusiasm, pride, dedication, hard work, and finally, hopes for the future.

Young readers love this series. Despite heavy use of jargon that makes the reading levels somewhat unstable, those already interested in the subject area pour over every word and picture in the books. Perhaps it's partly hero worship, or romance. Maybe it's the inspiration the books provide, but certainly one of the reasons the books are so popular is the vicarious thrill that they provide young enthusiasts.

A Very Young Dancer differs slightly from the formula. Instead of following Stephanie through a year of dance classes at the School of American Ballet, the book concentrates on New York City Ballet Company's production of the Nutcracker, in which Stephanie has a lead role.

Interest Level: 2-5. Reading Level: 3.1. Further Search Topics: Dancing, Ballet, Talent, Best Sellers, Group 2.

Krementz, Jill. A very young skater. Knopf 1979, unp (103 pp).

Katherine Healy started ice skating because her parents liked to skate and because it was easier for them to take her with them than it was to find a babysitter. From such beginnings, at age three, Katherine progressed to skating in Superskates at Madison Square Garden and ballet lessons at George Balanchine's School of American Ballet. See *A Very Young Dancer* for further explanation.

Interest Level: 2-6. Reading Level: 4.1. Further Search Topics: Ice Skating, Dancing, Ballet, Talent, Group 2, Best Sellers.

DEATH-FICTION

Blume, Judy. Tiger eyes. Bradbury 1981, 206 pp.

Davey's father's death was a shock that for awhile separated Davey from her mother. They occupied the same space, but Davey felt herself unable to communicate with her mother or with her aunt and uncle with whom they were living. The horror of the night her father was shot in a robbery attempt was too great for Davey to confront. It was too much for Davey's mother too, and so instead of growing closer, they draw apart. They let Davey's aunt and uncle direct their lives for almost a year before each was able to accept Mr. Wexler's death. During that time Davey's closest, most helpful friend was a loner named only Wolf. With him Davey lost enough fear and hatred that she was finally able to begin to talk about her father.

The setting (New Mexico) is much more important than in most of Blume's stories, the book's reading level is considerably more difficult, and the plot is about experiences more unique than usual. It will not fail to draw crowds of older readers however, for in most other respects the book follows Blume's successful formula.

Interest Level: 6+ Reading Level 5.1. Further Search Topics: Death-Fiction, Moving, Household-Fiction, Love-Fiction, Single Parent Family-Fiction, Family Problems-Fiction.

Coerr, Eleanor. Sadako and the thousand paper cranes; illus by Ronand Himler. Putnam 1977, 64 pp.

This is a beautiful and very sad story of a young girl who was only two years old when the atomic bomb was dropped on Hiroshima. Ten years later she contracted leukemia and died a slow, painful death. A fast and enthusiastic runner, she had been full of life and energy before her illness. Soon after she became sick Sadako's best friend folded a paper crane for her and reminded her of an old story: If someone folded 1000 paper cranes, the gods would give that person good health again. Sadako was able to fold only 644 before she died. After her death her classmates made 356 more in order that she could be buried with all 1000 paper cranes. About three years later, a statue, erected in Peace Park in Hiroshima, was dedicated to Sadako and to a hope for world peace.

Because of the theme and its straight-forward handling, this book needs a fairly mature reader.

Interest Level: 4-6. Reading Level: 3.1. Further Search Topics: Japan-Fiction, Historical Fiction, World War II-Fiction, Death-Fiction, Illness-Fiction, War-Fiction, Running-Fiction, Origami-Fiction, Read Aloud.

Cohen, Barbara. Thank you, Jackie Robinson; illus by Richard Cuffari. Lothrop 1974, 125 pp.

This story is not for everyone, but for the right reader it is perfect. The book is a catalog of baseball facts, thus it is likely to appeal primarily to baseball fans. But it is not the typical story of a child overcoming a problem through practice and perserverance, as are most sports books. This is a sensitive story of a fatherless boy whose life centered around the New York Dodgers.

Sam could repeat the starting line-up and details of any game the Dodgers had played within the last three years; however, no one cared. In fact, most people were bored when Sam began reciting. Only Davey, the old, black cook at the inn where Sam and his family lived, took any interest. Davey was as much a fan as Sam. They began spending hours together talking and then watching baseball as Davey and his daughter took Sam to the games with them. It was Sam and Davey's dream to catch a fly ball and have it autograped by all the Dodgers, especially Jackie Robinson, the first black major league player. When Davey had a severe heart attack, Sam gathered all his courage to make that dream come true. He bought a baseball, took the subway to a game, and argued with the ushers until he was finally able to get Jackie Robinson's and the team's autographs. Just a few days before Davey died Sam took the baseball to the hospital and gave it to Davey. Sam's feelings about Davey's death are real and painful. He felt sorry for himself, lonely, angry, sad and confused. But a remark by his mother and one more Jackie Robinson hit helped Sam accept Davey's death.

Because the story is told as a first-person flashback set in the late 1940s, it may need a little introduction. It also alludes to racial problems and practices that young readers may not understand without explanation (i.e., why Davey had some hesitation about taking a white child with him to the ballpark or on a trip).

Interest Level: 4-6. Reading Level: 4.2. Further Search Topics: Baseball-Fiction, Blacks-Fiction, Aging-Fiction, Single Parent Family-Fiction, Friendship-Fiction, Death-Fiction, Robinson, Jackie.

Greene, Constance C. A girl called Al; illus by Byron Barton. Viking Pr. 1969, 127 pp.

Told in the first person, this is the story of two seventh grade girls. The girls' warm friendship began the moment Al introduced herself to the narrator as a non-conformist. Al was very independent, mostly because she was on her own so much of the time. Her parents were divorced and she seldom saw either one of them. Her father only wrote her postcards and her mother was rarely home. The narrator's family and Mr. Richards, their building superintendent, became Al's family. They cooked, ate, played, fought, talked and even made bookcases together. When Mr. Richards had a heart attack, they found help for him and later went to see him in the hospital. It was his death that helped Al and her mother grow closer, just as Mr. Richards' life had helped her understand why her father never came to see her.

A satisfying, low-key story of friendship and maturation. The girls are Judy Blume-style characters with much greater innocence. Their ages are not discernible by their actions or dialogue, only by the author's statement.

Interest Level: 3-6. Reading Level: 3.1. Further Search Topics: Children-Growth-Fiction, Single Parent Family-Fiction, Friendship-Fiction, Weight-Fiction, Aging-Fiction, Death-Fiction, Divorce and Separation-Fiction, Family Problems-Fiction, Everyday Stories, Humorous Fiction.

Miles, Miska. Annie and the old one; illus by Peter Parnall. Little 1971, 44 pp.

A quietly beautiful story that will not appeal to all readers. Annie, a young Navajo girl, had a very close relationship with her grandmother. Her grandmother announced that she would "go to Mother Earth" at the time when the new rug Annie's mother was weaving was "taken from the loom." Annie tried all she could think of to keep the rug from being finished in order to keep her grandmother alive. When her grandmother solemnly explained that Annie could not stop time, Annie listened and "understood many things" for the first time.

It will be a thoughtful, sensitive child or a child trying to understand death who will best appreciate this special book.

Interest Level: 3-6. Reading Level: 3.2. Further Search Topics: Grandparents-Fiction, Death-Fiction, Indians of North America-Fiction, Navajo Indians-Fiction.

Pevsner, Stella. And you give me a pain, Elaine. HM 1978, 182 pp.

Andrea was the youngest of three children. She was very close to her brother, Joe, but he was away at college. There was only Elaine at home, but Andrea and Elaine didn't get along at all. Elaine was a troubled young woman who took so much of her parents' attention that there was none left for Andrea. This is the story of Andrea's year in eighth grade, a year in which she discovered that she was a steady and strong person. It was the year in which Andrea worked on the school play, had her first boyfriend, weathered the storms when her sister ran away, and began to understand her sister more and resent her less. It was also the year that she had to learn to live with her brother's accidental death.

The author's Judy Blume style (but with less humor) guarantees readers among older children.

Interest Level: 5-6. Reading Level: 4.1. Further Search Topics: Family Problems-Fiction, Brothers and Sisters-Fiction, Love-Fiction, Death-Fiction, Runaways-Fiction, Troublemakers-Fiction, Adolescence-Fiction.

Singer, Marilyn. It can't hurt forever; illus by Leigh Grant. Har-Row 1978, 186 pp.

When she was 11 years old, it was discovered that Ellie had a heart valve that hadn't closed by itself. Although her mother had promised her that she wouldn't die, Ellie was scared of the hospital and the operation she had to face. Her parents were kind and open about all that was to happen to her, but there was still much that Ellie had to learn from friends she made while she was in the hospital. There were times when she was frightened and only Sonia, a young open-heart surgery patient, could calm her. When Ellie, a special nurse, and a few other patients became close friends, Ellie learned enough from them to allow her to help another patient.

This is not a story of sweetness and light, but it is told with warmth, humor, and real understanding of a young person's fears. Thus it is not only an excellent candidate for bibliotherapy, but it is a truly satisfying story for the general reader as well.

Interest Level: 4-6. Reading Level: 2.2. Further Search Topics: Illness-Fiction, Physicians-Fiction, Medicine-Fiction, Courage-Fiction, Death-Fiction.

Slote, Alfred. Hang tough, Paul Mather. Lippincott 1973, 156 pp.

Paul Mather went against his doctor's and his parents' orders when he accepted his new neighbors' challenge to show his pitching skill. He had been told not to play baseball until he had been given permission, but Paul not only loved to pitch, he was also the best pitcher his new friends had ever seen. Knowing full well the medical problems he could be precipitating, Paul went ahead and pitched a spectacular game for the Wilson Dairy team against the Ace Appliance team. But by the end of the game, Paul was in the hospital again, and Wilson Dairy had been forced to forfeit the game because Paul had played illegally. As Paul's leukemia worsened, his determination to play baseball again grew. When the day came that his team was to play a second game against Ace Appliance, Paul made sure he was there. He was in a wheelchair and weak, but he was there. He couldn't actually play, but Paul's psychological support insured that Wilson Dairy won the game. He went back to the hospital proud, happy, and still determined to fight his disease.

This is more than the usual sports story. This is a very sensitive story of a young boy's determination to fight leukemia. The reader looking for only a baseball story may find this book more than he/she wants. However, the reader who is open to a story of human strength and courage will be well rewarded. The book neither dwells on nor minimizes the disease. Instead it uses both the disease and the sport to portray a character much more completely than in most sport stories, especially at this low a reading level. This is an excellent book for those special readers who respond well to thought-provoking material. Although chapters are short and reading level is low, the print is somewhat small. In addition, the first person style, told as if dictated into a tape recorder (complete with occasional interruptions), may be confusing to readers unless it is explained.

Interest Level: 5-6+Reading Level: 3.1. Further Search Topics: Baseball-Fiction, Death-Fiction, Illness-Fiction, Moving, Household-Fiction, Medicine-Fiction, Physicians-Fiction, Challenges-Fiction, Courage-Fiction.

Smith, Doris Buchanan. A taste of blackberries; illus by Charles Robinson. T Y Crowell 1973, 58 pp.

A beautifully written, sensitive tale of a boy whose best friend dies suddenly. Jamie was always joking, so, when he fell to the ground after being stung by a bee everyone thought he was playing. A short time later Jamie was dead. His friend, the story's narrator, tried to will Jamie back again until the funeral was over and he finally realized there would be no such miracle. The next day he accepted his feelings and picked the newly ripened blackberries, just as he and Jamie had planned to do. A basket full of the best blackberries he gave to Jamie's mother and promised her that he would "slam her door" daily just as he and Jamie had done.

Eight short chapters, small print but short sentences, and a child's point of view perfectly maintained. For the lovers of sad stories and stories of friendship. Very useful when discussing death.

Interest Level: 4-6. Reading Level: 3.2. Further Search Topics: Death-Fiction, Friendship-Fiction, Read Aloud.

Viorst, Judith. The tenth good thing about Barney; illus by Erik Blegvad. Atheneum 1971, 25 pp.

A quiet, thoughtful book to help a child face the difficult experience of death. When a family's beloved cat Barney died, their little boy tried to find 10 good things to say about him at the funeral. Nine things came easily to mind, but it was not until he had worked in the garden with his father that the little boy realized the tenth good thing. Barney, buried in the ground, would help the flowers, trees, and grass grow. A special picture book, small in size, but large in impact. Print is somewhat small but well-spaced.

Interest Level: 1-4. Reading Level: 2.1. Further Search Topics: Pets-Fiction, Cats-Fiction, Death-Fiction, Group 2, Read Aloud.

Wallace, Bill. A dog named Kitty. Holiday 1980, 153 pp.

Ricky's fear of dogs was extreme but also understandable. He had been attacked by a rabid dog when he was very young. Remembering the fear, the stitches and the painful rabies shots was enough to bring tears to Ricky's eyes even years later. When a local bully told his dog to attack Ricky, Ricky's fear was discovered. About that time, a stray puppy showed up at Ricky's farm. Not quite knowing why, Ricky began to warm to the puppy, to feed it, and finally to love it. When the dog was attacked by a pack of wild dogs (a brutal scene vividly described), Ricky fully overcame his fear of dogs, went to Kitty's defense, and was barely able to save her life. When Kitty was later tragically and accidentally killed, Ricky swore that he would never have anything to do with a dog again. He almost kept his promise to himself, but eventually a second stray dog wandered into the farm and Ricky decided to try again.

This is an emotional story that should appeal to many readers. However, because of the violence and the dog's two-stage death, the book is probably best suited to fifth and sixth grade children.

Interest Level: 5-6. Reading Level: 3.1. Further Search Topics: Dogs-Fiction, Pets-Fiction, Bullies-Fiction, Death-Fiction, Oklahoma-Fiction, Courage-Fiction, Country Life-Fiction.

Young, Carol Beach. Remember me when I am dead. Elsevier-Nelson 1980, 94 pp.

This is a short but taut story about the effect of their mother's death upon two young girls. For a long time Jenny, the younger and more vivacious of the sisters, refused to believe her mother had really died. Sara, quiet and serious, mourned and missed her mother, but eventually accepted her mother's sudden death as a fact. Jenny's continuing denial prompted her father and stepmother to talk of sending her away to a school where memories wouldn't be so vivid. That talk inspired Sara to develop a devious and calculated plan to insure that Jenny would indeed be sent away. All her life Sara had been given less attention than Jenny. With Jenny gone, Sara would finally have her father and stepmother's love and attention all to herself. With a Hitchcock-like twist Sara's plan proved too successful. Jenny was sent away to school, but because she didn't want to go alone and because her parents could deny Jenny nothing, Sara was to go too.

This suspenseful psychological thriller is almost guaranteed success with older readers.

Interest Level: 5-6. Reading Level: 4.2. Further Search Topics: Mystery and Detective Stories, Brothers and Sisters-Fiction, Death-Fiction, Horror-Fiction, Best Sellers, Jealousy-Fiction.

DETECTIVES-FICTION

Berends, Polly Berrien. The case of the elevator duck; illus by James K. Washburn. Random 1973, 54 pp.

Although it would be stretching the meaning of the word to call this a mystery, it is a story of an 11-year-old detective. Albert tells his own story in a clipped style that resembles adult detective novels. One morning Albert found a duck abandoned in the apartment house elevator. He was determined to find the owner of the duck and return it. He had to be very careful as he searched because pets were absolutely forbidden in the housing projects. Anyone who saw him with the duck might report him. Albert and his parents had waited too long to get into the projects to be kicked out because of a duck. When Albert finally found the duck's owner (a young, sad child named Julio), Julio's sister forced Albert to take the duck back. Still angry at Julio's sister, Albert took the duck to the project's day care center, where the teacher agreed to formally adopt the duck. Albert stayed at the center long enough to see Julio's happy surprise when he arrived and found the duck. Its appealing characters, the tension created by the writing style, and the book's humor make this a delightful story.

Interest Level: 2-5. Reading Level 2.2. Further Search Topics: Humorous Fiction, City Life-Fiction, Housing Projects-Fiction, Detectives-Fiction, Pets-Fiction, Ducks-Fiction, Read Aloud.

Giff, Patricia Reilly. Have you seen Hyacinth Macaw?; illus by Anthony Kramer. Delacorte 1981, 135 pp.

Abby Jones was trying very hard to be a detective, but it was difficult without any mysteries to solve. So to keep in practice, Abby filled a memo book with her notes about anything that seemed at all unusual. At the same time, Abby kept in touch with two local police detectives who gave her hints about detective work. Because of her police friends and her observations, Abby found herself involved in what seemed to be four or more mysteries. Who had moved into the apartment next door and what were the screams that came from there? What was the theft that the police were worried about? Who was Hyacinth Macaw and why had she disappeared? And why was Abby's older brother Dan acting so strangely? Was he involved in the theft?

Abby and her friend Potsie ended up trailing a suspect through the New York subway system, breaking into the next-door apartment, suspecting Abby's brother of the theft, capturing an unusual bird, releasing the bird into a pet shop and recapturing it, before they realized that all the mysteries were linked together. Hyacinth Macaw was a valuable bird stolen from Justine's Junktique Shop. The daughter of Abby's landland had taken the bird and placed it in the empty apartment next to Abby's, so that she could paint the bird's portrait. The picture was to be entered in Justine's Junktique contest. Dan and his friend Holly Monk had been secretly constructing a Purple Pigeon Purifier to enter in the contest. They needed the prize money to repair a window they had accidentally broken. By the time the mysteries were all sorted out, Dan and Holly had won a special prize; Kiki, the portrait painter, had not only been forgiven, but had also been awarded first prize; and Abby had received the reward for finding and returning the bird.

The action in this mystery is both abundant and humorous enough to make the book enjoyable to many readers. There are also some problems that need to be noted. Some readers may find the action too swift and the characters too numerous to be easily followed. Abby's memo notes are sometimes written without vowels and are almost always in incomplete sentences. The reader who is highly motivated or has help from another person will still be able to enjoy the story; however, for the others another choice may be more appropriate.

Interest Level: 4-6. Reading Level: 3.1. Further Search Topics: Mystery and Detective Stories, Humorous Fiction, Writing-Fiction, Detectives-Fiction, Birds-Fiction.

Heide, Florence Parry. Black magic at Brillstone. A. Whitman 1981, 126 pp.

Liza is a little older, her romance with Logan has progressed to a kiss, and the book's plot is more complex than earlier Brillstone adventures. Other than those differences, the book follows Heide's standard format. The Brillstone books all center on Liza Webster and Logan Forrest, teenage partners in crime detection, who live in the Brillstone Apartments. The stories are similar enough that one could almost substitute the names Nancy Drew and Ned for Liza and Logan. Both young women are only children who live with their fathers. They are both independent, resourceful, and very concerned that justice be done. The men in their lives play approximately the same roles; their fathers are proud and supportive, but distantly preoccupied with their own business; Logan and Ned are gallant, boyish, and devoted. Liza and Logan, like Nancy and Ned, are not distinctive characters. Instead, they are shells into which readers who want excitement and adventure can pour themselves. There is no parental interference to worry about. There is plenty of action, some suspense, and real world crime (for Liza: murder, bank robberies, etc.) rather than childish escapades. The books' success is practically guaranteed. Beware, however, of inconsistent reading levels that wander over a year's range.

Logan was first aware of strange occurrences at the Brillstone Apartments when someone entered his apartment late at night. While the person had searched the apartment, he or she had unconsciously whistled a nursery tune. Logan's neighbor, Miss Violet, said the tune reminded her of her deceased nephew. Slowly Logan and Liza realized that someone was trying to trick Miss Violet out of a substantial amount of money she had just inherited. They suspected that Bella Vine, a spiritualist, and an accomplice were trying to convince Miss Violet that her nephew was communicating from the dead and wanted Miss Violet to give her money to Bella. Not until it was almost too late did Liza and Logan realize that Bella was also posing as another possible recipient of the money and was really Miss Violet's nephew's wife. Miss Violet's nephew had only pretended to die in order to collect insurance money. When he and his wife had heard about Miss Violet's large inheritance, they had decided to reappear in order to bilk her out of the money. Brillstone Mystery series.

Interest Level: 5-6. Reading Level: 3.1. Further Search Topics: Mystery and Detective Stories, Occult-Fiction, Crime-Fiction, Ghosts-Fiction, Cats-Fiction, Detectives-Fiction, Inheritance-Fiction.

Heide, Florence Parry. Body in the Brillstone garage. A. Whitman 1980, 127 pp.

Liza's trip into the apartment house garage late one night made her even more frightened of that dark area than she had been. As she bent to pick up an envelope she thought someone had dropped, she saw a body lying on the floor of the garage. Because of a jacket he wore, Liza was certain the dead man was Mr. Greening, a neighbor. But when she returned to the garage with the police, the body was gone. The next day Mr. Greening was very much alive. Then Liza began to suspect that Mr. Greening was a murderer, but she didn't know who or where the victim was. It could have been Mr. Feeney, another neighbor, or it might have been a stranger. When Mr. Greening's stolen car was later discovered with the body of the car thief inside, Liza began to suspect that the thief's body was the one she had discovered. When she was told that the thief's name was Sharkey, she was certain Mr. Greening had engineered Sharkey's death. Sharkey was the name used by an angry man who had said he was looking for someone at the Brillstone who owed him something.

About then Liza remembered to look in the envelope she had found in the garage. The envelope revealed a note from Sharkey to Greening stating that Sharkey had proof that Greening was a car thief and that he would keep quiet only if Greening paid him twice the money he was owed. Knowing that without proof, she couldn't convince the police that Greening was a crook, Liza went to get the proof from Sharkey's hiding place in the about-to-be-junked car. Greening followed Liza to see what she knew and made a desperate attempt to kill her when he realized that she knew enough to put him in prison. At the last minute, Logan appeared, accidentally knocked Greening out, and helped Liza prove Greening's guilt to the police.

This is a fast-paced book that should be useful with mystery readers who can handle the jump from 4.1 to an occasional 5.1 reading level. See notes included with *Black Magic at Brillstone* for more information. Brillstone Mystery series.

Interest Level: 4-6. Reading Level: 4.2. Further Search Topics: Mystery and Detective Stories, Murder-Fiction, Running-Fiction, Crime-Fiction, Detectives-Fiction.

Heide, Florence Parry. Mystery of the forgotten island; illus by Seymour Fleishman. A. Whitman 1980, 127 pp.

On a small island, unmarked on the map, the Spotlight Club members found old Mr. Whitson, who claimed that he was being kept prisoner by his granddaughter Lorrie and her husband John. Lorrie and John had told him he was being kept in the yard for his own good, so that he wouldn't wander off and get hurt or lost. They had also told him that he should will the island to them so that his daughter Cassie couldn't sell the island to a resort company for development. He was going to be forced to sign such a will unless he could get the children to help him smuggle a new will to his lawyer. Mr. Whitson wasn't convinced that Cassie wanted to sell the island, but he couldn't get in touch with her and he hadn'd had a letter from her in many months.

As the children went to secretly meet Mr. Whitson and mail his new will, they discovered that their trusted friend Guy was attempting to blackmail Lorrie and John into giving him some of the money from the sale of the island. He had evidence that Lorrie and John, not Cassie, wanted to sell the island and were tricking Mr. Whitson into signing a will in their favor. In

a daring move, the children were able to free Mr. Whitson and isolate all three of the thieves so that the police could capture them.

This book involves a somewhat more complicated plot and slightly less familiar ingredients than most other Spotlight Club mysteries. One should progress to rather than begin the series with this title. Spotlight Club Mystery series.

Interest Level: 4-6. Reading Level: 3.1. Further Search Topics: Mystery and Detective Stories, Inheritance-Fiction, Gangs-Fiction, Kidnapping-Fiction, Brothers and Sisters-Fiction, Aging-Fiction, Detectives-Fiction.

Heide, Florence Parry. Mystery of the mummy's mask; illus by Seymour Fleishman. A. Whitman 1979, 127 pp.

The Spotlight Club published a neighborhood newspaper. Just as the club was about to take the fourth issue to the printer, Jay discovered an ancient mummy mask hidden near Mr. Pruitt's house. Mr. Pruitt was intrigued by the discovery (he worked at the nearby museum) and he took the mask from Jay, but agreed that Jay could write about the mask for the paper. At about the same time, Dexter discovered that an old, abandoned house was being used. When the printer's office was broken into that night and only their newspaper was stolen, the three children began to suspect that something strange was going on at the abandoned house.

Dexter rode back to the house alone and was captured by Hank, one of three thieves hiding out there. Figuring that they never would have missed one item, Hank had taken the mask from the cache of goods that the other two had stolen. When he overheard Jay's conversation with Mr. Pruitt, Hank realized that his partners would find out what he had done if they ever read the newspaper article. To avoid being discovered, Hank broke into the printer's and stole the paste-up of the paper. In order to keep Dexter from escaping, Hank tied him up and placed him in a shipping crate. When he didn't return as soon as expected, Jay and Cindy realized that Dexter was in trouble, so they went out to the house to search for him. As the three escaped, Dexter and Cindy slashed the thieves' truck's tires, and Jay ran to phone for the police. After several nervous moments in which Cindy and Dexter thought Jay might not get back before they were caught, Jay finally brought the police, who captured all three thieves.

See *Mystery at Southport Cinema* for more information. Spotlight Club Mystery series.

Interest Level: 3-5. Reading Level: 3.1. Further Search Topics: Mystery and Detective Stories, Crime-Fiction, Egypt-Fiction, Archaeology-Fiction, Antiquities-Fiction, Journalism-Fiction, Gangs-Fiction, Brothers and Sisters-Fiction, Detectives-Fiction.

Heide, Florence Parry. The mystery of the silver tag; illus by Seymour Fleishman. A. Whitman 1972, 127 pp.

Jay's paper route took him to one house that he wished he could avoid. It was grumpy, old Mr. Pendleton's house that Jay hated. One rainy day he spotted what he later realized was a prize Angora cat hiding on Mr. Pendleton's porch. When the cat was reported lost in that night's paper, Jay and the other members of the Spotlight Club decided to try to return the cat to its owner, Miss Horton. Their attempts to get the cat back from Mr. Pendleton meant that they had to spy on him, to sneak into his garage, and to spend the night in a treehouse overlooking his house. They were afraid that they had failed when they saw

Mr. Pendleton leave with the cat. Determined to be the ones to tell Miss Horton of their failure, they went to her apartment and found Mr. Pendleton already there. Mr. Pendleton was a famous animal photographer who, upon finding the cat, had asked Miss Horton if he could photograph him. The children, thinking only that Mr. Pendleton was a mad scientist who kidnapped cats, had jumped to all the wrong conclusions, but ended with a mystery solved, new friends, and their first lesson in being detectives.

See entry with *Mystery at Southport Cinema* for series information. Spotlight Club Mystery series.

Interest Level: 3-5. Reading Level: 2.2. Further Search Topics: Mystery and Detective Stories, Brothers and Sisters-Fiction, Gangs-Fiction, Cats-Fiction, Loners-Fiction, Detectives-Fiction, Photography-Fiction, Kidnapping-Fiction.

Heide, Florence Parry. Face at the Brillstone window. A. Whitman 1979, 128 pp.

As Liza drove out of the garage one evening she heard a thump at the side of the car. She jumped out and found that she had accidentally hit Peter Pritchard, an insurance man and a new tenant of the apartment building. Pritchard seemed to be a very nice person who took some interest in Liza, her friends, and the criminal cases Liza's father (a journalist) was investigating. Liza was particularly interested in the case of the one-armed bandit who had been convicted of robbing and shooting a security guard. Against her father's research assistant's wishes she continued to search for evidence that would prove Robin Keck was innocent of the charges. As she interviewed the security guard, Keck's fiancee, his best friend, and the grandmother of a young girl who had had a strong crush on Keck, Liza found hints of his innocence. Young Bridgette's diary, however, held the proof she needed: an alibi. But someone else knew she had the information; someone who didn't want the information made public. Diary in hand, Liza began walking to her father's assistant's house (her father was out of town) when Pritchard offered her a ride. When Pritchard drove off in the wrong direction and then handed her a piece of incriminating evidence (gum), Liza realized she had played right into the real criminal's hands. Liza made a risky escape attempt that ended successfully with Pritchard's capture.

See *Black Magic at Brillstone* for more information about the series. Brillstone Mystery series.

Interest Level: 4-6. Reading Level: 3.2. Further Search Topics: Mystery and Detective Stories, Crime-Fiction, Detectives-Fiction.

Heide, Florence Parry. Mystery at Southport Cinema; illus by Seymour Fleishman. A. Whitman 1978, 128 pp.

The Spotlight Club was the name Jay, his sister Cindy, and his friend Dexter gave themselves. Their main interest was solving mysteries and just as in Sobol's Encyclopedia Brown series, Hildick's McGurk Mysteries, and Warner books about the Alden children, mysteries seem to follow them around. Their cases are more intricate and lengthy than Encyclopedia Brown's. They involve more danger than most of McGurk's, and they center on more common themes than the Alden's. The series serves much the same audience, however, as the others. It serves those children who want action, intrigue, and the challenge of a mystery, and who don't care about character development or in-depth motivation. The chapters are 8 to 12 pages long, print size is

adequate, and the children are normal enough to make this a very popular series. As an added attraction, reading levels here are fairly consistent.

Thorne prided himself on doing his job well, so when the grocery store he ran for Callie (the owner) was robbed by a bearded stranger, Thorne felt responsible. Thorne ran after the thief but lost him in the darkened Southport Cinema. The Spotlight Club members also tried to track the thief. They figured that he had hidden the bag with the stolen money somewhere in the movie house because no one had been seen leaving with such a bag.

In the janitor's lost and found basket Jay found a wig the thief must have used as a disguise. The children called the wig maker to find out who had ordered it and were directed to a local post office box, Jay and Dexter were surprised to find belonged to the grocery store. Because Thorne picked up the mail each day, he became a prime suspect. In the meantime, Cindy had gone back to the cinema to look for the money. In the dark she had scuffled with someone else looking for the money and had given the person a deep scratch on the face.

At the same time that Thorne decided to pay Callie back for the stolen money, the Club members decided to tell Callie their suspicions about him. As Thorne handed his veterinary school savings to Callie, Cindy took a close enough look at Callie's face to see a new scratch and accused her of being the thief. Callie had so wanted Thorne to run the store instead of going to school, and had needed money so intensely, that she had stolen from her own business. The ending is weak but the rest of the book will hold reader interest. Spotlight Club Mystery series.

Interest Level: 3-5. Reading Level: 3.1. Further Search Topics: Mystery and Detective Stories, Gangs-Fiction, Crime-Fiction, Detectives-Fiction, Brothers and Sisters-Fiction.

Heide, Florence Parry. Mystery of the melting snowman; illus by Seymour Fleishman. A. Whitman 1974, 128 pp.

Hidden inside of a snowman, the Spotlight Club found what they believed was a stolen iron statue of a dog. In order to try to catch the thief, the children hid the statue again and watched to see who came to look for it. Eventually they determined that the thief or thieves was either Tom and Jenny, the amenable young couple who were helping Mrs. Wellington sell her house or Alex, the man who seemed to be a detective. After a frightening episode in which Alex almost captured Cindy, the dog, and a cache of Mrs. Wellington's diamonds (hidden in a secret compartment to which the dog held the key), Cindy managed to lock Alex in a closet long enough to enable Jay and Dexter to alert Mrs. Wellington to what was happening. The case was closed as Mrs. Wellington revealed Alex to be her greedy, young nephew, whom she had indulged once too often, but would not indulge again.

See *Mystery at Southport Cinema* for series information. Spotlight Club Mystery series.

Interest Level: 3-5. Reading Level: 2.2. Further Search Topics: Mystery and Detective Stories, Gangs-Fiction, Crime-Fiction, Brothers and Sisters-Fiction, Detectives-Fiction, Inheritance-Fiction.

Heide, Florence Parry. Mystery of the midnight message; illus by Seymour Fleishman. A. Whitman 1977, 128 pp.

The challenge to the Spotlight Club this time was to stop a crime before it happened. Jay and his sister Cindy were on a bus trip home when a blizzard forced the bus to stop at a motel for the night. Jay answered the room telephone late that night and heard a woman's strange and stern instructions. The instructions were to say nothing, to look in the desk drawer for directions, to expect that Bee had the other half of the instructions, and to be at the place at 8:00 the next evening. The envelope, which Jay and Cindy found, showed the location of and half the combination to someone's bedroom safe.

Early the next morning, the children found themselves fleeing in terror from the evil Scull, the man who was supposed to have received the message. Scull pursued them as they escaped in a friendly salesman's car, caught them and locked them into a cold barn without jackets. When the two were finally back on the road and reunited with Dexter and his sister Anne, they had only a few hours and fewer clues to help them find Woodvale and Jeremiah Gibbon, the intended victim.

Despite difficult driving conditions in the snow, Anne managed to get the children to their destination a few minutes before the thieves arrived. Anne and Jeremiah's secretary left the house together to get the police while the Spotlight Club members and Mr. Gibbon hid near the safe. A few tense minutes later, the case was closed; Mr. Gibbons' money was safe, the ringleader had been named (Mr. Gibbon's doctor), and the thieves had been caught.

See *Mystery at Southport Cinema* for series information. Spotlight Club Mystery series.

Interest Level: 3-5. Reading Level: 3.1. Further Search Topics: Mystery and Detective Stories, Crime-Fiction, Snow-Fiction, Disasters-Fiction, Gangs-Fiction, Brothers and Sisters-Fiction, Detectives-Fiction.

Hildick, Edmund W. The case of the invisible dog; illus by Lisl Weil. Macmillan 1977, 101 pp.

Brains Bellingham, a nine-year-old scientific genius, interrupted the McGurk Organization's Annual Picnic with an invisible dog. It was only a short time before McGurk and his friends were convinced that Brains' discovery of how to make things invisible was the greatest event since putting a man on the moon. Although they had always scorned the idea of including anyone else in the Organization, they decided to persuade Brains to join. But, before the day was over, they discovered not only that they had been duped, but exactly how Brains had made the impossible seem real. The Organization took its revenge by using Brain's own trick to make him confess. When Brains began laughing at how well his trick had been used in reverse, McGurk admitted how impressed they all had been by Brain's clever thinking. The outcome of their discussion was that Brains was invited, a second time, to become a member of the McGurk Organization.

See *The Case of the Bashful Bank Robber* for series information. McGurk Mystery series.

Interest Level: 3-6. Reading Level: 3.1. Further Search Topics: Mystery and Detective Stories, Detectives-Fiction, Gangs-Fiction, Dogs-Fiction, Supernatural-Fiction, Humorous Fiction, Jealousy-Fiction.

Hildick, Edmund W. The great rabbit rip-off; illus by Lisl Weil. Macmillan 1976, 101 pp.

Why would anyone want to put red paint on all of the clay lawn rabbits in town? That was the first and easier of the mysteries the McGurk Organization had to solve. The bigger mystery was who would then steal them all and why? Almost everyone in town had purchased a rabbit to help a charity drive. Donny

Towers a local social worker had thought of the idea. Donny, his fiancee, Joanne, and two reformed thieves, Sam and Ferdie, had made enough rabbits for everyone. When the rabbits disappeared, the Organization began to suspect, among others, Sam and Ferdie. Then when Donny replaced each one almost immediately with rabbits smelling of paint remover, the group began to think Donny might have been involved. It was Wanda's sharp eyes that revealed Donny's motive. Joanne's engagement ring had been accidentally molded into one of the rabbits and Donny had retrieved the rabbits to find the ring. Knowing he couldn't return the paint stained rabbits without raising suspicion, Donny had removed the red paint and told everyone that he was simply replacing the stolen rabbits with new ones.

See Case of the Bashful Bank Robber for series information. McGurk Mystery series.

Interest Level: 3-5. Reading Level: 2.2. Further Search Topics: Mystery and Detective Stories, Detectives-Fiction, Gangs-Fiction, Rabbits-Fiction, Crime-Fiction, Humorous Fiction.

Hildick, Edmund W. Deadline for McGurk; illus by Lisl Weil. Macmillan 1975, 104 pp.

When many of the dolls in the neighborhood began disappearing, their owners went to the McGurk Organization for help. At first McGurk was reluctant to take on such a silly task as recovering lost dolls. But when a ransom note appeared and the Organization was linked to the dolls' safety, McGurk's reluctance vanished. The note stated that if, in a written public notice, the members of the Organization did not admit that they were no good, the dolls were doomed. McGurk's pride would never have allowed him to write such a notice. As the deadline approached, the group plotted a daring move designed to uncover the doll thief. The plan depended on Willie's super-sensitive nose, a particular perfume dabbed on a stolen doll, and the curiosity of the thief. Success came only minutes before the hour of doom. Once again Sandra Ennis was the culprit.

See *The Case of the Bashful Bank Robber* for series information. McGurk Mystery series.

Interest Level: 3-5. Reading Level: 2.2. Further Search Topics: Dolls-Fiction, Mystery and Detective Stories, Detectives-Fiction, Humorous Fiction, Gangs-Fiction, Jealousy-Fiction.

Hildick, Edmund W. The case of the condemned cat; illus by Lisl Weil. Macmillan 1975, 106 pp.

Ray Williams had a terrible problem when he begged the McGurk Organization for help. His cat Whiskers had been accused of killing a neighbor's pet dove. Ray's mother decided that they couldn't risk upsetting the neighbors anymore and threatened to take Whiskers to the pound unless it could be proven that he was innocent. The Organization, needing time, hid Whiskers and told Mrs. Williams that he had run away. While Whiskers was safely hidden, the group interviewed all the neighbors, surveyed the scene of the crime, and tried to decide upon the real murderer. When the remains of another bird were found while Whiskers was safely locked away, it looked as if the cat was surely innocent. But then McGurk and his detectives found out that the cat had been sprung. It wasn't until they went back over all the information they had gathered that McGurk realized who was the real culprit. The only step left was to trick old Gramp Martin (the neighborhood grouch) into confessing.

See *The Case of the Bashful Bank Robber* for series information. McGurk Mystery series.

Interest Level: 3-6. Reading Level: 2.2. Further Search Topics: Mystery and Detective Stories, Cats-Fiction, Detectives-Fiction, Humorous Fiction, Gangs-Fiction, Pets-Fiction.

Hildick, Edmund W. The case of the secret scribbler; illus by Lisl Weil. Macmillan 1978, 106 pp.

Joey's discovery in a library book of a scrap of paper with part of a letter and a strange diagram on it led the McGurk Organization on a lively chase. Brains identified the diagram as that of a widely-used security system. The part of the letter that they could read told the group that there was a burglary being planned for the approaching weekend, but the youngsters knew the police would never take them seriously until they had much more evidence. By researching local alarm systems, determining who bought the unusual paper, and comparing handwriting samples, the detectives were able to convince the police of what was about to happen. In gratitude, the police loaned the Organization a police monitor so that they could listen as the thieves were caught. To all but McGurk it seemed like the perfect way to end the case: he tried to sneak into the midst of the capture, but only succeeded in getting himself in real trouble.

See *The Case of the Bashful Bank Robber* for series information. McGurk Mystery series.

Interest Level: 3-6. Reading Level: 2.2. Further Search Topics: Mystery and Detective Stories, Crime-Fiction, Gangs-Fiction, Nonverbal Communication-Fiction, Humorous Fiction, Detectives-Fiction.

Hildick, Edmund W. The case of the phantom frog; illus by Lisl Weil. Macmillan 1979, 121 pp.

The McGurk Organization would not, under ordinary circumstances, have agreed to babysit for seven-year-old Bela, but there was an unusual twist to Bela's case. Bela's aunt, who asked them to babysit while she worked in her sculpture studio, had heard the eerie sounds of a VERY large frog coming from Bela's room. At first it appeared to the group that Bela actually turned into a frog at night, a werefrog. But, upon investigation they found a very clever, very lonely, and very unhappy young boy who had invented the phantom because he was afraid that his aunt would make him give up his pet frog.

See *The Case of the Bashful Bank Robber* for series information. McGurk Mystery series.

Interest Level: 3-5. Reading Level: 3.1. Further Search Topics: Mystery and Detective Stories, Gangs-Fiction, Frogs-Fiction, Supernatural-Fiction, Transformations-Fiction, Detectives-Fiction, Babysitting-Fiction, Humorous Fiction, Occupations-Fiction.

Hildick, Edmund W. The case of the treetop treasure; illus by Lisl Weil. Macmillan 1980, 121 pp.

As Wanda rescued a cat she discovered a stash of odd items tucked into a hollow high up in a tree. On top of the assortment was a sign that said simply "Beware!" The McGurk Organization suspected a thief was using the tree as a place to hide stolen goods, but until an antique silver bowl was added nothing that had been placed there was worth stealing. Shortly afterwards Wanda found out from the police that she was the prime suspect in the theft of the bowl. Brains devised a complicated system for determining the real thief while McGurk worked more from intuition. Nevertheless, it wasn't long before they both arrived at the same conclusion. The culprit was the gang's

long-time enemy Sandra Ennis. Then it was just a simple matter of finding the right way to persuade Sandra to confess and apologize to her victims.

See *The Case of the Bashful Bank Robber* for series information. McGurk Mystery series.

Interest Level: 3-5. Reading Level: 3.1. Further Search Topics: Mystery and Detective Stories, Crime-Fiction, Gangs-Fiction, Detectives-Fiction, Humorous Fiction.

Hildick, Edmund W. The case of the snowbound spy; illus by Lisl Weil. Macmillan 1980, 132 pp.

One snowy morning McGurk called the five members of his organization together to decipher a code. The code was part of a message from someone who wanted to hire them and would pay $5.00 a day. When they broke the code and met their employer, Mr. Fitch, he gave the group another code as part of their assignment. The second code told them where to deliver a small package that Mr. Fitch gave them. They were to pick up another coded message at the same place. After three pick-ups and drops they would be finished and Mr. Fitch, an ex-government spy, would have proved he was still a trustworthy and capable person to an ex-colleague with whom he wanted to work on a book. It seemed like just the challenging kind of assignment the McGurk Organization looked for. As they worked, however, it began to look more and more as if they were being used for illegal business. While Joey and McGurk staked out the next drop-off spot, Willie, Brains and Wanda pretended to Mr. Fitch to be unsuspecting. By working quickly and cleverly and by alerting the police, the McGurk gang uncovered and stopped two industrial spies who were stealing secret information about a new copying machine.

See *The Case of the Bashful Bank Robber* for series information. McGurk Mystery series.

Interest Level: 3-6. Reading Level: 3.1. Further Search Topics: Mystery and Detective Stories, Spies-Fiction, Detectives-Fiction, Gangs-Fiction, Humorous Fiction, Nonverbal Communication-Fiction, Crime-Fiction.

Hildick, Edmund W. The case of the bashful bank robber; illus by Lisl Weil. Macmillan 1981, 138 pp.

The McGurk Organization is a crime fighting detective agency. Led by Jack McGurk's strong ego, they had taken on many a seemingly impossible task and had always been successful. Never before, however, had they tried to protect the seven banks in town from being robbed. The five children's first idea was to regularly patrol each bank and watch for likely looking get-away cars. When that plan only led to a nasty confrontation with their new junior high school principal, they decided to try something else. Their second plan, to photograph all suspicious looking people near the banks, didn't fare much better than their first idea. Then, without knowing it, they found themselves holding the key to solving a real bank robbery. Before they realized its importance, they had literally given away the vital clue. Using only their own memories, powers of observation, and cleverness, they were still able to solve the crime with only a little help from the FBI.

The "McGurk mysteries" are light, fast-moving, and often humorous. Clues for solving the mysteries are sometimes subtle, but always there in the plot and illustrations for the reader to find. The characters are somewhat flat but still appealing. Joey, who is handy with words and a typewriter, is the narrator of each book. Jack McGurk, dedicated mastermind of all the group's activities is shrewd, a natural leader, and egotistical. Willie has the world's most sensitive nose and an excellent memory for odors. Wanda is the best tree-climber in town and a rational influence on the group. Brains, the newest and youngest member of the group, is a scientific genius, so he runs their crime lab. The books need not be read in chronological order although most have a brief reference to an earlier story. Reading level varies within each book from 2.1 to 3.1. A few books include enough more difficult passages that their average reading level is pushed from 2.2 to 3.1. Interest level in the series, once a reader has started on it, is high. McGurk Mystery series.

Interest Level: 3-6. Reading Level: 2.2. Further Search Topics: Mystery and Detective Stories, Crime-Fiction, Detectives-Fiction, Humorous Fiction, Gangs-Fiction.

Hildick, Edmund W. The case of the four flying fingers; illus by Lisl Weil. Macmillan 1981, 138 pp.

At first the four young strangers who were knocking over garbage cans had been merely a neighborhood nuisance. Later McGurk and his fellow detectives began to suspect that they were involved in the rash of break-ins and burglaries in the city. The Organization didn't think the "garbage gang" was actually committing the robberies, but rather that they were fingering houses for someone else to burglarize (thus their nickname: The Four Flying Fingers). It could be safely assumed by a would-be burglar that where no one picked up the spilled garbage, no one was home. It was the Organization's job to find the Thumb who was the mastermind behind the plot. When they caught up with the Fingers, McGurk and crew found out that the Flying Fingers hadn't realized what they were doing; only that a blonde lady in a camper was paying them a nickel for every driveway they left strewn with garbage. It didn't take long for the Organization to track down the woman and her accomplice. But, in one of their less intelligent moves, they played right into her hands and soon found themselves being transported out of town in her camper. When they tried to call to passing cars for help, no one took them seriously. It wasn't until Brains, bound and gagged to appear authentic, used a flashlight and Morse code to signal for help that anyone paid any attention to them. A police car finally stopped the camper for speeding apd after some clever arguments McGurk and his friends were able to convince the police that Lady Thumb was a thief.

This title is just as enjoyable as the best of the other books in the series, more exciting and universal in appeal than most, and equally humorous. It's only drawback is a very inconsistent reading level (from 2.1 to 4.1) that will discourage a reader new to McGurk. Established fans will be able to tolerate the range. McGurk Mystery series.

Interest Level: 3-6. Reading Level: 3.1. Further Search Topics: Mystery and Detective Stories, Detectives-Fiction, Humorous Fiction, Crime-Fiction, Gangs-Fiction.

Law, Carol Russell. The case of the Weird Street firebug; illus by Bill Morrison. Knopf 1980, 119 pp.

This is the humorous story of a Nancy Drew-type character who gets involved in a mystery before she is even half finished with her mail-order detective lessons. Steffi wanted very much to be a detective. When she saw an ad for a local correspondence course, she tracked down the shabby office in a run-down building on Weir Street, and went to visit Jeff Dangerfield of Dangerfield Detective School. Steffi's first lesson, trailing suspects, was a disaster.

She tried to pick out suspicious characters at a fire on Weir Street on her way home. The only really suspicious character (Beady Eyes) didn't go anywhere, so Steffi couldn't follow him. Her next attempts were very obvious and only resulted in her own anger and embarrassment. On her way back to seek advice from Dangerfield, Steffi literally ran into Beady Eyes again. She didn't think anything more about him until she saw him a short time later at another fire just down the street from Dangerfield's office. As the fire moved closer to Dangerfield's building, Steffi took desperate measures to try and save her friend. Steffi's efforts were interpreted by Beady Eyes as attempts to indicate that he was an arsonist. By the time Steffi figured out that Beady Eyes really was an arsonist, he had her cornered. A timely entry by the police saved both Steffi and Dangerfield. Steffi's reward for the capture of Beady Eyes was a medal from the police and a partnership with Dangerfield.

A fast-paced story, as well as slightly more original characters than most stories of this genre, make this a likely success with third through sixth grade readers. Capers series.

Interest Level: 3-6. Reading Level: 3.1. Further Search Topics: Mystery and Detective Stories, Humorous Fiction, Fire-Fiction, Detectives-Fiction, Crime-Fiction.

Montgomery, Raymond A. The lost jewels of Nabooti; illus by Paul Granger. Bantam 1981, 121 pp.

See entry for *Sugarcane Island*, by Edward Packard for series information. Only available in paperback edition. Choose Your Own Adventure series.

Interest Level: 2-6. Reading Level: 3.2. Further Search Topics: Mystery and Detective Stories, Detectives-Fiction, Treasure-Fiction, Best Sellers, Group 2.

Packard, Edward. The mystery of Chimney Rock; illus by Paul Granger. Bantam 1979, 121 pp.

See notes for *Sugarcane Island* for information about the series. Paperback only. Choose Your Own Adventure series.

Interest Level: 2-6. Reading Level: 3.2. Further Search Topics: Mystery and Detective Stories, Cats-Fiction, Witches-Fiction, Ghosts-Fiction, Detectives-Fiction, Best Sellers, Group 2.

Sharmat, Marjorie W. Nate the great goes undercover; illus by Marc Simont. Coward 1974, 47 pp.

Nate's next door neighbor Oliver was a pest, but Oliver had a mystery for Nate to solve. Oliver's garbage can was being burglarized at night. He wanted Nate to catch the garbage snatcher. Nate quickly drew up a list of human suspects and just as quickly eliminated them all. A night spent hiding in the garbage can proved the best way to catch the thief. Much to Nate's surprise, the thief turned out to be his new dog.

Very amusing and very useful. Reader format.

Interest Level: 1-3. Reading Level: 2.1. Further Search Topics: Humorous Fiction, Mystery and Detective Stories, Group 2, Detectives-Fiction, Best Sellers.

Sharmat, Marjorie W. Nate the great; illus by Marc Simont. Coward 1972, 62 pp.

This is a young imitation of Humphrey Bogart solving a *Dragnet* style mystery. Annie's recently finished painting of her dog had disappeared so she hired Nate to search for it. Nate gathered all the facts, investigated his suspects, and eventually solved the mystery, but not before he had consumed plenty of pancakes (his favorite food) and solved a second mystery by accident.

A simple plot, humorous telling, and a sympathetic, likeable protagonist make this one of a very popular series. Reader format.

Interest Level: 1-3. Reading Level: 2.1. Further Search Topics: Humorous Fiction, Detectives-Fiction, Mystery and Detective Stories, Group 2, Best Sellers.

Shearer, John. Billy Jo Jive and the case of the missing pigeons; illus by Ted Shearer. Delacorte 1978, 47 pp.

This is the third in a series of slight mysteries, always solved by Billy Jo Jive and his crime fighter partner, Susie Sunset. Jive and Sunset are street-wise, black youngsters who take their jobs as crime fighters very seriously, and are never detered for long from finding the criminals they seek. The crimes are always thefts, and the criminals vary from young children to neighborhood menaces. Suspense is created more by the manner in which Jive and Sunset catch the thieves, plus the determination and pace of the young detectives, than by guessing who the culprits might be. Jive, his street-slang manner of telling the first-person stories, and the urban setting will appeal to many readers. Jive and Sunset also appear on *Sesame Street*.

Jive accidentally photographed the fleeing pigeon thief as he was being chased by Flip, the victim. The photograph didn't show the thief's face, but did give Jive and Sunset a good look at what he was wearing. Jive and Sunset concluded that the thief was Snake Hips Robberts. They later realized that they had been wrong. When they looked carefully at the picture, they remembered that any dark color clothing photographs almost black in a black and white picture. Snake Hips had a black jacket, but he was innocent. The real thief was Sugar Brown. Then it was a simple matter of showing the evidence to both Flip and Sugar to get Sugar to confess.

Interest Level: 1-4. Reading Level: 2.2. Further Search Topics: Mystery and Detective Stories, Detectives-Fiction, Blacks-Fiction, City Life-Fiction, Group 2, Best Sellers.

Shearer, John. Billy Jo Jive and the walkie-talkie caper; illus by Ted Shearer. Delacorte 1981, 47 pp.

When Steam Boat Louis went to Jive and Sunset for help, he was desperate. Because Jive and Sunset had already solved three cases, they were the logical people to find the walkie-talkie that had been stolen from Steam Boat. The walkie-talkie was one of two that Steam Boat had been told to buy as part of a secret communication system for the Bugaloo Smackers. Even as Jive and Sunset hunted for the thief, the second walkie-talkie was stolen. Their only clue was a footprint found outside Steam Boat's fix-it shop. Eventually, after trial and error, Jive and Sunset uncovered the real thieves; Steam Boat's young twin cousins. Unhappy at being separated in school, they wanted to use the walkie-talkies to be able to talk with each other.

The high reading level of this book will make it most useful for those children who have read and enjoyed other books in the series and are willing to stretch to read one more.

Interest Level: 1-4. Reading Level: 3.2. Further Search Topics: Mystery and Detective Stories, Detectives-Fiction, Blacks-Fiction, City Life-Fiction, Group 2.

Shearer, John. Billy Jo Jive super private eye: the case of the missing ten speed bike; illus by Ted Shearer. Delacorte 1976, 47 pp.

Jive and Sunset began their friendship and their sleuthing career with this book. It all started when Sunset borrowed her older brother's 10-speed bicycle. Jive met Sunset while she sat at the side of the road crying, after her brother's bike had been stolen. Some careful joint detective work proved to Jive and Sunset that Dynamite Jones, jealous of Sunset's brother, had stolen the bike. The young crime fighters recovered the bicycle before Sunset's brother even knew it was missing.

This book sets the formula that all the others follow. A neighborhood person finds that something has been stolen and goes to Jive and Sunset for help. Jive and Sunset never have much trouble finding the thief even though they are sometimes misled for a short time. Often the culprit is quite obvious to the reader. After some attempts at clever detective work and an occasional bit of preaching, the crime is solved. It is the manner of the pursuit and the street-smart characters that give the stories their interest.

Interest Level: 1-4. Reading Level: 2.2. Further Search Topics: Mystery and Detective Stories, Blacks-Fiction, Detectives-Fiction, City Life-Fiction, Best Sellers, Group 2, Bicycles and Bicycling-Fiction.

Sobol, Donald J. Encyclopedia Brown, boy detective; illus by Leonard Shortall. Elsevier-Nelson 1963, 88 pp.

The first of a large number of books that challenge the reader to solve the same mysteries Encyclopedia Brown deciphers. See *Encyclopedia Brown and the Case of the Dead Eagles* for more information.

Interest Level: 2-6. Reading Level: 2.2. Further Search Topics: Mystery and Detective Stories, Puzzles, Best Sellers, Detectives-Fiction.

Sobol, Donald J. Encyclopedia Brown and the case of the dead eagles; illus by Leonard Shortall. Elsevier-Nelson 1975, 96 pp.

By all rights Idaville should be declared a disaster area and Mr. Brown, the chief of police, should be fired from his job. Idaville looks like an ordinary small town, but behind its sleepy exterior there exists a crime wave that would challenge the best police departments in the country. It is true that the crimes are always solved and the criminals always caught, but not by Chief Brown. Chief Brown is frequently so stumped by his police cases that he talks about them at home, usually at dinner time. Almost always, his son, Leroy "Encyclopedia" Brown, solves the case before dinner is even over. A clear case of superior intelligence and skill.

Encyclopedia (so nicknamed because of his intellect) not only solves his father's cases, but serves as a detective for his friends, too. He is kept so busy that each slim volume in this series contains 10 short mysteries. Needless to say Encyclopedia solves them all. The question is can the reader? All necessary clues are there and specialized knowledge is rarely required. Should the reader fail to solve a mystery (they are not always as easy as one would expect), a full explanation and solution for each case is provided at the back of the book. Each title follows exactly the same formula. Although a teacher or parent may grow bored hearing of Encyclopedia's accomplishments, most young readers thoroughly enjoy them.

The books actively challenge and thus involve the reader in a way most books do not. A very popular

series that does not have to be read in sequence. Reading level is consistently 2.2 to 3.1. Encyclopedia Brown series.
Interest Level: 2-6. Reading Level: 3.1. Further Search Topics: Mystery and Detective Stories, Puzzles, Best Sellers, Group 2, Detectives-Fiction.

Sobol, Donald J. Encyclopedia Brown and the case of the midnight visitor; illus by Lillian Brandi. Elsevier-Nelson 1977, 96 pp.
See *Encyclopedia Brown and the Case of the Dead Eagles* for full annotation.
Interest Level: 2-6. Reading Level: 2.2. Further Search Topics: Mystery and Detective Stories, Puzzles, Detectives-Fiction, Best Sellers.

Sobol, Donald J. Encyclopedia Brown and the case of the secret pitch; illus by Leonard Shortall. Elsevier-Nelson 1965, 96 pp.
See *Encyclopedia Brown and the Case of the Dead Eagles* for full annotation.
Interest Level: 2-6. Reading Level: 3.1. Further Search Topics: Group 2, Mystery and Detective Stories, Puzzles, Best Sellers, Detectives-Fiction.

Sobol, Donald J. Encyclopedia Brown finds the clues; illus by Leonard Shortall. Elsevier-Nelson 1966, 96 pp.
See *Encyclopedia Brown and the Case of the Dead Eagles* for full annotation.
Interest Level 2-6. Reading Level: 3.1. Further Search Topics: Mystery and Detective Stories, Puzzles, Detectives-Fiction, Best Sellers, Group 2.

Sobol, Donald J. Encyclopedia Brown gets his man; illus by Leonard Shortall. Elsevier-Nelson 1967, 96 pp.
See *Encyclopedia Brown and the Case of the Dead Eagles* for full annotation.
Interest Level: 2-6. Reading Level: 3.1. Further Search Topics: Mystery and Detective Stories, Puzzles, Best Sellers, Group 2, Detectives-Fiction.

Sobol, Donald J. Encyclopedia Brown keeps the peace; illus by Leonard Shortall. Elsevier-Nelson 1969, 96 pp.
See *Encyclopedia Brown and the Case of the Dead Eagles* for full annotation.
Interest Level: 2-6. Reading Level: 2.2. Further Search Topics: Mystery and Detective Stories, Puzzles, Best Sellers, Detectives-Fiction.

Sobol, Donald J. Encyclopedia Brown lends a hand; illus by Leonard Shortall. Elsevier-Nelson 1974, 96 pp.
See *Encyclopedia Brown and the Case of the Dead Eagles* for full annotation.
Interest Level: 2-6. Reading Level: 3.1. Further Search Topics: Mystery and Detective Stories, Puzzles, Detectives-Fiction, Best Sellers, Group 2.

Sobol, Donald J. Encyclopedia Brown saves the day; illus by Leonard Shortall. Elsevier-Nelson 1970, 96 pp.
See *Encyclopedia Brown and the Case of the Dead Eagles* for full annotation.
Interest Level: 2-6. Reading Level: 2.2. Further Search Topics: Mystery and Detective Stories, Puzzles, Detectives-Fiction, Best Sellers.

Sobol, Donald J. Encyclopedia Brown shows the way; illus by Leonard Shortall. Elsevier-Nelson 1972, 96 pp.
See *Encyclopedia Brown and the Case of the Dead Eagles* for full annotation.

Interest Level: 2-6. Reading Level: 2.2. Further Search Topics: Mystery and Detective Stories, Puzzles, Detectives-Fiction, Best Sellers.

Sobol, Donald J. Encyclopedia Brown solves them all; illus by Leonard Shortall. Elsevier-Nelson 1968, 96 pp.
See *Encyclopedia Brown and the Case of the Dead Eagles* for full annotation.
Interest Level: 2-6. Reading Level: 3.1. Further Search Topics: Mystery and Detective Stories, Puzzles, Detectives-Fiction, Group 2, Best Sellers.

Sobol, Donald J. Encyclopedia Brown sets the pace; illus by Ib Ohlsson. Four Winds Pr 1982, 89 pp.
See *Encyclopedia Brown and the Case of the Dead Eagles* for full annotation.
Interest Level: 2-6. Reading Level: 3.1. Further Search Topics: Mystery and Detective Stories, Detectives-Fiction, Puzzles, Group 2, Best Sellers.

Sobol, Donald J. Encyclopedia Brown carries on; illus by Ib Ohlsson. Schol Bk Serv 1980, 72 pp.
See *Encyclopedia Brown and the Case of the Dead Eagle* for full annotation.
Interest Level: 2-6. Reading Level: 3.1. Further Search Topics: Mystery and Detective Stories, Puzzles, Detectives-Fiction, Group 2, Best Sellers.

Yolen, Jane. Shirlick Holmes and the case of the wandering wardrobe; illus by Anthony Rao. Coward 1981, 80 pp.
This is a light, fast-paced story of Shirli and her four friends' attempt to solve a local mystery. Its more fully developed characters and plot make this a better literary piece than any of the *Encyclopedia Brown* stories, but it resembles them in other ways. The children live in a small, secure town. The police chief, Shirli's neighbor and George's father, is working on the same case that interests the children but the children solve it first. The mystery is real and involves danger, as opposed to many of Hildick's McGurk mysteries, the other series this book resembles.
Shirli is a fiesty figure who took up George's challenge to solve the town's latest mystery. Thieves had been systematically robbing some of the wealthy summer homes of antiques. Shirli's plan, to search each of the houses for clues, only succeeded in angering the police chief when he caught Shirli and her friends. Being intrepid detectives, however, they did not give up. Instead, they staked out a likely house and waited for the thieves. When the robbers finally arrived Shirli and George hid. Only Gloria was able to escape and go for help. The oak wardrobe in which Shirli took refuge was one of the first pieces the thieves took out of the house. When Shirli tried to get out of it, she found the wardrobe had been placed on a truck with its door against the truck's side; she was caught. Very frightened, she stayed silent until she found herself in the middle of an antiques auction and recognized one of the voices making bids as George's father! As Shirli tumbled out of the wardrobe some of the police chief's men arrested the auctioneer for burglary and selling stolen goods. After she escaped, Gloria had told the police about the thieves, their truck, Shirli, and George, whom they found locked inside a closet still at the summer house.
A serviceable book that will be enjoyed by a wide range of readers.
Interest Level: 3-5. Reading Level: 3.1. Further Search Topics: Mystery and Detective Stories, Humorous Fiction, Friendship-Fiction, Crime-Fiction, Antiquities-Fiction, Detectives-Fiction, Challenges-Fiction.

DINOSAURS

Cole, Joanna. Dinosaur story; illus by Mort Kunstler. Morrow 1974, unp (30 pp).

A general introduction to eight dinosaurs: Brontosaurus, Allosaurus, Stegosaurus, Ornitholestes, Protoceratops, Triceratops, Tyrannosaurus rex and Duckbills. Although not a wealth of information, there is more than enough interesting material here to attract a young dinosaur enthusiast. Because of the short sentences, the text is somewhat plodding. The subject matter's great appeal and the appropriately fierce-looking illustrations, however, make up for that problem.

Interest Level: 1-3. Reading Level: 2.1. Further Search Topics: Group 2, Dinosaurs, Prehistory.

Hornblow, Leonora. Prehistoric monsters did the strangest things; illus by Michael K. Frith. Random 1974, 65 pp.

A basic survey of an era and its animal life forms. Animals from the earliest water creatures through Diplocaulus, Ichthyosaurs, dinosaurs (about 12 varieties) and early mammals (including the Beast of Baluchistan) to the appearance of man are introduced and illustrated. It is a brief but meaty treatment of a very popular subject that should be especially useful with second and third grade children. Reader format.

Interest Level: 1-3. Reading Level: 2.1. Further Search Topics: Prehistory, Dinosaurs, Evolution, Monsters, Group 2.

DISASTERS

Lewis, Thomas P. Hill of fire; illus by Joan Sandin. Har-Row 1971, 63 pp.

A personalized account of the volcano that suddenly erupted in the middle of a farmer's field in Mexico on February 20, 1943. Because the account is written as a story and because of its easy-reader format, the book is most useful only through third grade. An I-Can-Read-History-Book.

Interest Level: 1-3. Reading Level: 2.2. Further Search Topics: Volcanoes, Group 2, Mexico, Disasters, Historical Fiction.

DISASTERS-FICTION

Clifford, Eth. Help, I'm a prisoner in the library; illus by George Hughes. HM 1979, 103 pp.

When their car stopped, Mary Rose and Jo-Beth were left alone in a strange city while their father went to find some gas. Jo-Beth needed to use the bathroom, so the sisters headed for the closest public building they could see, the library. No one saw them go in, so no one knew that they were locked inside when the librarian secured the building for the night. With the lights out and a blizzard outside, the library was a very spooky place. The girls tried calling the police, but the police wouldn't take them seriously. Then they heard groans and eerie moans from the second floor. Gathering all their courage, the girls went to investigate, only to discover the librarian lying hurt and unconscious. Their ingenuity and imagination helped the sisters through the difficult hours before they were all rescued.

Don't read it too carefully or the book's implausibilities will become very evident. Most young readers, however, will enjoy this story for its suspense, spooky atmosphere and adventurous girls, and they will ignore its weaknesses.

Interest Level: 2-5. Reading Level: 3.1. Further Search Topics: Disasters-Fiction, Snow-Fiction, Brothers and Sisters-Fiction, Libraries-Fiction, Survival-Fiction, Courage-Fiction, Group 2.

Heide, Florence Parry. Mystery of the midnight message; illus by Seymour Fleishman. A. Whitman 1977, 128 pp.

The challenge to the Spotlight Club this time was to stop a crime before it happened. Jay and his sister Cindy were on a bus trip home when a blizzard forced the bus to stop at a motel for the night. Jay answered the room telephone late that night and heard a woman's strange and stern instructions. The instructions were to say nothing, to look in the desk drawer for directions, to expect that Bee had the other half of the instructions, and to be at the place at 8:00 the next evening. The envelope, which Jay and Cindy found, showed the location of and half the combination to someone's bedroom safe.

Early the next morning, the children found themselves fleeing in terror from the evil Scull, the man who was supposed to have received the message. Scull pursued them as they escaped in a friendly salesman's car, caught them and locked them into a cold barn without jackets. When the two were finally back on the road and reunited with Dexter and his sister Anne, they had only a few hours and fewer clues to help them find Woodvale and Jeremiah Gibbon, the intended victim.

Despite difficult driving conditions in the snow, Anne managed to get the children to their destination a few minutes before the thieves arrived. Anne and Jeremiah's secretary left the house together to get the police while the Spotlight Club members and Mr. Gibbon hid near the safe. A few tense minutes later, the case was closed; Mr. Gibbons' money was safe, the ringleader had been named (Mr. Gibbon's doctor), and the thieves had been caught.

See *Mystery at Southport Cinema* for series information. Spotlight Club Mystery series.

Interest Level: 3-5. Reading Level: 3.1. Further Search Topics: Mystery and Detective Stories, Crime-Fiction, Snow-Fiction, Disasters-Fiction, Gangs-Fiction, Brothers and Sisters-Fiction, Detectives-Fiction.

Roy, Ron. Nightmare Island; illus by Robert MacLean. Dutton 1981, 69 pp.

Harley didn't want to take his younger brother camping, but because he had promised his father he would, the boys packed a tent, sleeping bags, and plenty of food into a small boat and set off to nearby Little Island. Hidden in his pocket, Harley had matches and marshmallows for a midnight marshmallow roast. After they had finished the bag of marshmallows, Harley threw the last log of the fire into the water. The water erupted into flames that quickly spread around the island. As the boys fought desperately to save themselves and to find shelter, they realized that the large shape they had seen in the distance must have been an oil tanker that had spread an oil slick all around the island. With time running out Harley gave his brother the only truly secure shelter from the fire, curled up on top of a tall rock and went to sleep. When he awoke the fire had burned itself out and help was on the way.

Most young readers will be able to suspend disbelief long enough to enjoy this as an exciting adventure and survival story, but it is hard to believe that two young boys could not only survive such a holocaust, but that they could sleep through part of it, too. It is also difficult to believe that there would not be more of a fuss made about the oil tanker blowing up. Plot problems aside, young readers seem to love the story.

Interest Level: 3-6. Reading Level: 3.2. Further Search Topics: Brothers and Sisters-Fiction,

Survival-Fiction, Camping-Fiction, Disasters-Fiction, Best Sellers.

Talbot, Charlene Joy. The Great Rat Island adventure; illus by Ruth Sanderson. Atheneum 1977, 164 pp.

Joel dreaded spending the summer with his father. His parents were divorced and Joel was sure his father didn't want him. His father only wanted to study birds. Great Rat Island, where Joel and his father were to spend the summer, was of no interest to Joel. It had no television, no one his own age, only terns. Even the assignment Joel was given (to make sure that no more tern eggs were stolen) sounded dull. It led to an adventure and a friend, however, that were anything but dull.

Joel discovered that a girl his own age was the thief of the tern eggs. Her name was Vicky Owens. She had run away from camp and was spending the summer alone on Little Rat Island. Joel kept her secret until the day of hurricane warnings. As the storm approached Joel realized that Vicky wouldn't be safe on Little Rat Island. Without telling anyone else he took the only boat around and went to look for Vicky to bring her back to Great Rat Island. He found her with her leg stuck between two rocks, unable to move. By the time Joel got her loose, it was too late to get back to the big island. Not knowing what else to do, Joel and Vicky dragged the boat inside an abandoned building where Vicky had been living. As the water rose around them and Vicky grew delirious with fever, Joel set up camp in the boat. While the building filled with water they stayed dry in the boat. Rescue and medical care for Vicky finally came the next day.

A solid, steadily-paced survival story for the reader who wants a little more than just an adventure story. Print is small.

Interest Level: 4-6. Reading Level: 3.1. Further Search Topics: Vacation-Fiction, Family Problems-Fiction, Birds-Fiction, Divorce and Separation-Fiction, Disasters-Fiction, Survival-Fiction, Runaways-Fiction.

Warner, Gertrude Chandler. The lighthouse mystery; illus by David Cunningham. A. Whitman 1963, 128 pp.

What better place for a mystery than a lighthouse late at night? Add the excitement of a storm at sea and a young man alone in a boat and the story should be unbeatable. Unfortunately this, as well as some of the other books in the series, does not quite live up to its potential. It will not attract many new readers but it will satisfy those who crave more adventures of the Alden family. The main problem with the book is its lack of definition. It isn't quite a mystery or an adventure story, it's a little of both. It is also part homespun family story, part science lesson, and part "problem story."

The Aldens rented a lighthouse in a very small fishing village one summer. Late each night their dog awoke them as he barked at a stranger who walked into or away from a closed-up building nearby. When the children investigated, they found that the surly son of a local fisherman was using the building to experiment on plankton as a food source. Harry was a brilliant young man who wanted to go to college, but whose father stubbornly refused to let him study. One night when Larry was at sea gathering samples, a terrible storm blew up. Only the Coast Guard and an improvised light in the lighthouse saved Larry from drowning. Larry's brush with death forced his father to acknowledge Larry's abilities and allow him to continue studying at college.

The sketchy illustrations in this and the following books in the series are an improvement over the silhouettes of *The Boxcar Children*. See the annotation for *The Boxcar Children* for further series information.

Interest Level: 3-6. Reading Level: 2.1. Further Search Topics: Mystery and Detective Stories, Lighthouses-Fiction, Food-Fiction, Disasters-Fiction, Vacation-Fiction.

Yolen, Jane. The boy who spoke chimp illus by David Wiesner. Knopf 1981, 120 pp.

Kriss was determined to prove to his father that, at 12 years old, he was perfectly capable of camping out by himself. To do so, he left home and headed up the coast of California with a sleeping bag, some food, a map and compass, and water. His plan was to camp, ride, and hike his way to his grandmother's house. On the way, the coast line was torn apart by the second great earthquake to strike California. The first had already destroyed great portions of the state. The second was even stronger. The truck he had been riding in was destroyed and everyone around Kriss was killed by the quake except for two chimpanzees. The chimps, in transit from one lab to another, were research animals who had been taught to use sign language. Kriss took the animals with him as he tried to get farther inland and finally home to Los Angeles. His trip not only confirmed his father's fears about Kriss' inadequacies but taught him how to overcome them. Kriss learned to communicate with the chimps, to find food and to live on his own until Old Chris, a hermit, happened along. Together they continued to brave the chaos brought about by the earthquake even when Old Chris' heart troubled him. When a helicopter finally spotted them, Kriss decided to let the chimps go wild and promised Old Chris that he would be back in the woods very soon. It was a mature, capable Kriss who returned home.

This is typical of the Capers series—much action, few background details, little characterization. The books, however, are on appealing topics; they move quickly and they create intriguing (if sometimes implausible) situations. They are light, enjoyable and very useful. Capers series.

Interest Level: 3-6. Reading Level: 3.1. Further Search Topics: California-Fiction, Disasters-Fiction, Survival-Fiction, Apes-Fiction, Nonverbal Communication-Fiction, Camping-Fiction, Runaways-Fiction, Best Sellers.

DIVORCE AND SEPARATION

Walker, Alice. Langston Hughes, American poet; illus by Don Miller. Har-Row 1974, 33 pp.

Langston Hughes is one of the world's most famous black poets. He spent most of his childhood in poverty and yet he shunned and was shunned by his wealthy father because his father disliked blacks. To Hughes the two most important things in the world were his heritage and his writing. His love of black history stemmed from the stories his grandmother told him. His love of language and writing grew out of the lonely hours he spent reading as a child. Hughes began to write poetry even before he was in high school and continued to write for many years. He wrote not only poems, but children's books, novels, plays and short stories. He wrote about and for blacks around the world. He was a proud and honest man who chose to share his pride in his race and his honesty through his writing.

This book is more of an inspirational tribute to a black hero than a fact-filled biography. That isn't to say that there are no facts included in the book. There are facts, but the book will not do as the sole source for a report about Langston Hughes. The book is, however, a good introduction to the man and his writing.

Interest Level: 3-5. Reading Level: 2.2. Further Search Topics: Biography, Blacks-Biography, Writing, Poverty, Divorce and Separation, Poetry.

DIVORCE AND SEPARATION-FICTION

Avi. No more magic. Pantheon 1975, 138 pp.

Avi has woven a mixture of mystery and magic to produce an excellent story. Chris' belief in magic is bolstered when his new bicycle disappears on Halloween night. Chris, his best friend Eddie, and a new friend, Muffin, eventually decide that strange Mr. Bullen, the junk dealer, has magical powers. In order to keep his powers a secret, Mr. Bullen had to steal back the magical bike he sold Chris. With plenty of intriguing complications along the way, the three children attempt to prove their theory correct but only prove themselves wrong. The age of the protagonists (fourth grade) is touched on so lightly and the plot is interesting enough that even sixth grade readers should find the book enjoyable.

Interest Level: 3-6. Reading Level: 4.2. Further Search Topics: Divorce and Separation-Fiction, Mystery and Detective Stories, Magic-Fiction, Halloween-Fiction, Witches-Fiction, Group 2, Read Aloud, Bicycles and Bicycling-Fiction.

Blume, Judy. It's not the end of the world. Bradbury 1972, 169 pp.

This is a one theme book (as are many of Judy Blume's titles). It is the story of 11-year-old Karen's attempt to prevent her parents' divorce and then to accept it. In this first-person story she tells of her disappointment, anger, fear, and lack of understanding. She describes her parents' fights and her brother's and sister's reactions, too. It is a book with an obvious and mostly reassuring message to its readers, but it is not just for readers whose families may be in similar situations. It is also a book that will be enjoyed by any Judy Blume enthusiast.

Interest Level: 4-6. Reading Level: 3.1. Further Search Topics: Divorce and Separation-Fiction, Family Problems-Fiction, Everyday Stories.

Clymer, Eleanor. Luke was there; illus by Diane de Groat. HR & W 1973, 74 pp.

Julius' father, uncle and finally his step-father had all walked out on him. Even his mother had left him, although she hadn't wanted to go. When his mother had been taken to the hospital, Julius and his younger brother Danny were sent to a children's home. Julius felt alone and cheated until he met a young, black, social worker named Luke. Luke liked and respected Julius and helped Julius learn to feel the same way about himself. When Luke, too, left Julius, Julius was so angry at the world that he stole food and then money. Afraid to go back to the children's home because he thought he'd be caught and punished, Julius ran away. It wasn't until he found an abandoned child, about Danny's age, who needed care, that Julius returned to the home. Luke was there when he arrived, just when Julius needed him most. Luke listened to Julius' unhappy feelings, arranged for him to see his mother and helped him begin to accept the fact that life is not always fair.

Julius tells his own story in a realistic, straight-forward book that will touch most readers. Only the lack of quotation marks and inadequate spacing between the lines may slow the reader.

Interest Level: 3-6. Reading Level: 2.2. Further Search Topics: Runaways-Fiction, Orphans-Fiction, Juvenile Delinquency-Fiction, Divorce and Separation-Fiction, Friendship-Fiction, Courage-Fiction, Survival-Fiction, Loneliness-Fiction, Best Sellers, Read Aloud.

Cone, Molly. The amazing memory of Harvey Bean; illus by Robert MacLean. HM 1980, 83 pp.

It had been a long time since Harvey had been happy. His memory was so bad that he was always in trouble at school. And now that his parents were separating, he had trouble at home, too. Because he thought that neither one of his parents wanted him he told each one that he was going to stay with the other and instead decided to spend the summer alone. A few hours after he left home, Harry ran into Mr. and Mrs. Katz and before he completely realized it, he was living with them.

Mr. Katz couldn't stand to see anything go to waste. He collected the usable food thrown out behind grocery stores, old furniture, tools, windows and more. Mrs. Katz, whose memory was just as bad as Harvey's, loved to cook, so she could always find a way to use the food. Everything else bulged from the house and garage into the driveway and yard. Harvey spent a happy summer learning to scavenge, eating well, learning not to worry about what others thought of him and even improving his memory. When his parents finally found him, Harvey realized that they really did want him, even if they were separated. He decided to live with his mother on weekdays, his father on weekends, and the Katzs during the summers.

The plot problems that are obvious to adult readers are ones that most young readers will be able to ignore (i.e. neither parent checks on Harvey for over two months). Young readers will enjoy the humor and realism of Harvey's pain, happiness and eventual feeling of self-confidence and triumph. The ten short chapters, good-sized print and adequate space between the lines help lower the book's reading level to late fourth grade.

Interest Level: 3-6. Reading Level: 5.1. Further Search Topics: Loners-Fiction, Vacation-Fiction, Divorce and Separation-Fiction, Humorous Fiction, Group 2, Memory-Fiction, Runaways-Fiction, Academic Problems-Fiction, Individualists-Fiction.

Danziger, Paula. The pistachio prescription. Delacorte 1978 154 pp.

Just as Cassie entered her freshman year in high school, the old stand-by that had helped her deal with all her problems (eating pistachio nuts) began to fail. To be sure, she did get through the class elections and was elected president. She met and started dating Bernie. She gained self-confidence. She even managed to stand up to a particularly mean teacher. But, eating pistachios didn't help at all at home where Cassie really needed them. She could hardly stand to be in the same room with her older sister. She hated the importance her mother placed on looking right and dressing well. Most of all, she hated the way her parents were constantly fighting. The only person with whom she was really confortable was her brother. But, before the year was over, Cassie's parents decided to get a divorce, she and her sister became friends and Cassie learned to accept her family.

Another Judy Blume-style author, but Danziger's portraits of adults tend to be even more one-dimensional and exaggerated than Blume's. Very popular anyway.

Interest Level: 6+. Reading Level: 5.1. Further Search Topics: Divorce and Separation-Fiction, Family Problems-Fiction, Beauty-Fiction, School Stories, Adolescence-Fiction, Love-Fiction, Brothers and Sisters-Fiction, Everyday Stories.

Greene, Constance C. A girl called Al; illus by Byron Barton. Viking Pr. 1969, 127 pp.

Told in the first person, this is the story of two seventh grade girls. The girls' warm friendship began the moment Al introduced herself to the narrator as a non-conformist. Al was very independent, mostly because she was on her own so much of the time. Her parents were divorced and she seldom saw either one of them. Her father only wrote her postcards and her mother was rarely home. The narrator's family and Mr. Richards, their building superintendent, became Al's family. They cooked, ate, played, fought, talked and even made bookcases together. When Mr. Richards had a heart attack, they found help for him and later went to see him in the hospital. It was his death that helped Al and her mother grow closer, just as Mr. Richards' life had helped her understand why her father never came to see her.

A satisfying, low-key story of friendship and maturation. The girls are Judy Blume-style characters with much greater innocence. Their ages are not discernible by their actions or dialogue, only by the author's statement.

Interest Level: 3-6. Reading Level: 3.1. Further Search Topics: Children-Growth-Fiction, Single Parent Family-Fiction, Friendship-Fiction, Weight-Fiction, Aging-Fiction, Death-Fiction, Divorce and Separation-Fiction, Family Problems-Fiction, Everyday Stories, Humorous Fiction.

Greene, Constance C. I and Sproggy; illus by Emily A. McCully. Viking Pr. 1978, 155 pp.

Ten-year-old Adam had adjusted to his parents' divorce and had even grown to like living alone with his mother. When his father came back from London with his new wife and stepdaughter Sproggy and announced that they were moving into an apartment nearby, Adam was a little worried. But when his father asked him to take care of Sproggy, Adam was furious. First of all, he didn't know Sproggy and he didn't want to know her. Secondly, she was two months older than he, taller too, and she embarrassed him in public. And finally, she didn't need his help. She got along quite well by herself; so well that she even saved Adam from a mugger and became good friends with Adam's friends behind his back. It wasn't until Sproggy proved to be vulnerable that Adam and she became friends.

A warm, realistic and humorous story whose interesting characters (even the minor ones) heighten the book's appeal.

Interest Level: 4-6. Reading Level: 3.2. Further Search Topics: Brothers and Sisters-Fiction, Divorce and Separation-Fiction, City Life-Fiction, New York City-Fiction, Humorous Fiction, Friendship-Fiction, Everyday Stories.

Greenfield, Eloise. Talk about a family; illus by James Calvin. Lippincott 1978, 60 pp.

Genny, Kim, and Mac knew something was wrong between their parents, and fully expected that their older brother Larry would be able to fix everything when he came home from the army. But even Larry's welcome home party was almost ruined by their parents' fighting and Kim's reaction. That night, as she listened to Larry and her parents' low voices, Genny was certain that Larry was bringing her parents back

together. When her father announced the next morning that he was going to move out, Genny's anger and hurt was directed at Larry. With her friend Mr. Parker's help, Genny finally realized that they were still a family; a family with a new shape, but one that would be able to adjust. A one-theme, realistic and reassuring, short book with good-sized print. Very useful

Interest Level: 3-6. Reading Level: 3.1. Further Search Topics: Divorce and Separation-Fiction, Family Problems-Fiction, Brothers and Sisters-Fiction, Best Sellers.

Hurwitz, Johanna. Aldo Applesauce; illus by John Wallner. Morrow 1979, 127 pp.

Aldo Sossi, vegetarian and new kid at school, was immediately dubbed Applesauce for obvious reasons. Aldo didn't like his new name. He didn't like being teased either—not the way he was teased at school. Nothing went right for Aldo. His attempts at making friends only ended in disasters (once at a bowling alley and another time at a birthday party). He had been able to start a friendship only with a strange girl who wore a heavy, black fake moustache most of the time. After accidentally nearly ruining that friendship too, Aldo not only learned why DeDe wore the moustache, but helped her learn to live without it. DeDe, in turn, helped Aldo take himself less seriously and find more friends.

This is a comfortable, humorous story of two fourth grade children learning to be themselves. The vocabulary is occasionally difficult, but sentence length is almost always short.

Interest Level: 3-5. Reading Level: 3.1. Further Search Topics: Moving, Household-Fiction, Humorous Fiction, School Stories, Friendship-Fiction, Divorce and Separation-Fiction, Vegetarians-Fiction, Individualists-Fiction, Everyday Stories.

Newfield, Marcia. A book for Jodan; illus by Diane DeGroot. Atheneum 1975, unp (41 pp).

Jodan found her parents' separation very hard to understand and accept. She and her mother had moved 3,000 miles away from her father and she missed him very much. When Jodan visited her father for the first time, he gave her a very special present that lessened her loneliness. He created a book just for Jodan that was filled with his thoughts and memories.

The book is a sensitive portrayal of a very common experience. Only Jodan's age (nine-years-old) and consequent actions and reactions, limit the book's probable usefulness beyond fifth grade. Print is somewhat small.

Interest Level: 2-5. Reading Level: 3.2. Further Search Topics: Group 2, Divorce and Separation-Fiction, Family Problems-Fiction, Loneliness-Fiction.

Park, Barbara. Don't make me smile. Knopf 1981, 114 pp.

As far as Charlie Hickle was concerned his parents' divorce was the worst thing in the world. His parents had ruined his life and he hadn't done anything to deserve such a fate. At first he didn't say very much. Then he ran away to live in a tree. Finally he cried a lot. That was all just in the first week after his parents announced their decision. After that, both his grades at school and his behavior began to deteriorate. It wasn't until Charlie had had several talks with a helpful children's psychologist and made a disastrous attempt to reunite his parents on his birthday, that he began to realize that he didn't like the divorce, but he could live with it.

The author's use of amusing anecdotes, Charlie's very strong feelings, and the frequency of divorce make this book very popular. Its major drawbacks are its superficiality and the overdrawn portrait of Charlie's mother. The book's faults will not deter many young readers from enjoying it, however.

Interest Level: 4-6. Reading Level: 3.1. Further Search Topics: Divorce and Separation-Fiction, Family Problems-Fiction, Psychiatrists-Fiction, Everyday Stories.

Pfeffer, Susan Beth. Just between us; illus by Lorna Tomei. Delacorte 1980, 116 pp.

Cass's inability to keep secrets finally became such a problem that Cass asked her mother to help her learn how to keep them. Cass's mother, a psychology student, devised a behavior modification experiment. Every day that Cass was able to figure out which bit of information she had been told was a secret and keep it, she received a dollar. After a poor start Cass did well for a while, until the day she told three secrets and made her entire family angry at her.

More determined than ever, Cass tried again. This time she found herself caught between two friends. Only Cass knew that Robin was adopted and Robin wanted it kept a secret. Jenny was so mad at Robin that she decided to spread an untrue story to hurt Robin. She told Cass not to tell anyone what she was going to do. The story Jenny was going to spread was that Robin was adopted. After hours of mental anguish Cass finally devised a way to stop Jenny and help Jenny return to being the nice person she had been before her parents' divorce.

The reading level of this book varies greatly from second grade to mid-fourth grade. Otherwise, it is good fare for Judy Blume fans. Print size just a slight bit on the small side.

Interest Level: 4-6. Reading Level: 3.2. Further Search Topics: Humorous Fiction, Everyday Stories, Friendship-Fiction, School Stories, Divorce and Separation-Fiction, Psychiatrists-Fiction, Secrets-Fiction.

Sachs, Marily. The bears' house; illus by Louis Glanzman. Doubleday 1971, 81 pp.

Don't let the benign appearance of this book fool you. This is a disturbing, almost brutal story. It is the story of Fran Ellen, a fourth grader with more problems than anyone should have to shoulder at one time. Her father had left the family and her mother had had a mental breakdown. Fran Ellen and her older brother were left with responsibility for themselves, their mother, and three other children (including a baby). They were all ill-fed, poorly dressed, and unwashed. Neither the social worker nor Fran Ellen's teacher knew the extent of the family's problems. Fran Ellen's only happiness came from her baby sister and from a schoolroom model (of *Goldilocks and the Three Bears* and their house) into which she mentally retreated whenever she had the chance.

As the school year closed, Fran Ellen's teacher visited her home to deliver the bears' house and discovered Fran Ellen's mother and very sick baby sister. Although she hated the idea that the family might have to split up, Fran Ellen had matured enough to realize that when her teacher insisted that she would get help for the family, her teacher was taking the proper action.

The book is inappropriately illustrated to make it appear cute and even humorous. The story is far from either. It is so stark that it probably shouldn't have been illustrated at all. And because the hope that is present in the book's ending is very subtle, a review and a discussion may be necessary to help relieve some young readers' anxieties.

Interest Level: 5-6. Reading Level: 3.1. Further Search Topics: Divorce and Separation-Fiction, Challenges-Fiction, Poverty-Fiction, Family Problems-Fiction, Loners-Fiction, Survival-Fiction, Mental Illness-Fiction, Brothers and Sisters-Fiction.

Talbot, Charlene Joy. The Great Rat Island adventure; illus by Ruth Sanderson. Atheneum 1977, 164 pp.

Joel dreaded spending the summer with his father. His parents were divorced and Joel was sure his father didn't want him. His father only wanted to study birds. Great Rat Island, where Joel and his father were to spend the summer, was of no interest to Joel. It had no television, no one his own age, only terns. Even the assignment Joel was given (to make sure that no more tern eggs were stolen) sounded dull. It led to an adventure and a friend, however, that were anything but dull.

Joel discovered that a girl his own age was the thief of the tern eggs. Her name was Vicky Owens. She had run away from camp and was spending the summer alone on Little Rat Island. Joel kept her secret until the day of hurricane warnings. As the storm approached Joel realized that Vicky wouldn't be safe on Little Rat Island. Without telling anyone else he took the only boat around and went to look for Vicky to bring her back to Great Rat Island. He found her with her leg stuck between two rocks, unable to move. By the time Joel got her locse, it was too late to get back to the big island. Not knowing what else to do, Joel and Vicky dragged the boat inside an abandoned building where Vicky had been living. As the water rose around them and Vicky grew delirious with fever, Joel set up camp in the boat. While the building filled with water they stayed dry in the boat. Rescue and medical care for Vicky finally came the next day.

A solid, steadily-paced survival story for the reader who wants a little more than just an adventure story. Print is small.

Interest Level: 4-6. Reading Level: 3.1. Further Search Topics: Vacation-Fiction, Family Problems-Fiction, Birds-Fiction, Divorce and Separation-Fiction, Disasters-Fiction, Survival-Fiction, Runaways-Fiction.

DOGS

Cole, Joanna. My puppy is born; photos by Jerome Wexler. Morrow 1973, unp (38 pp).

This is an unadorned description of a dachshund puppy's birth and first eight weeks of growth. The black and white photographs are large, sometimes graphic, and most often charming. The text is direct, carefully worded, concise and interesting. It is only the intrusion of an obviously young narrator that keeps this excellent book from being useful beyond third grade.

Interest Level: 1-3. Reading Level: 2.1. Further Search Topics: Group 2, Infants, Dogs, Pets, Birth.

Dolch, Edward W. Dog stories; illus by Bernette Johnson and Robert S. Kerr. Garrard 1954, 169 pp.

Although overly sentimental for most adult tastes, this collection of true dog stories appeals to young dog lovers. Eighteen chapters tell 15 stories, ranging from the first story in which dog rescues boy, to the final story in which boy rescues dog. There is a dog who played baseball, a dog who went to live at a newspaper, a dog who saved a fireman from a fire, two dogs who were lost and several more dogs who became heroes. A consistent reading level, large print and a popular topic make this a good choice to offer reluctant readers despite the Dolch books' usual unattractive illustrations. Dolch Basic Vocabulary Book series.

Interest Level: 2-4. Reading Level: 2.1. Further Search Topics: Dogs-Fiction, Courage-Fiction, Pets-Fiction.

DOGS-FICTION

Bonsall, Crosby. And I mean it, Stanley. Har-Row 1974, 32 pp.

A little girl builds "the very best thing I ever made," but all the while calls to Stanley to tell him not to look and to stay on the other side of the fence. Stanley pays attention only long enough for the "thing" to be completed - then crashes through the fence and bounds into the "thing." He draws no anger from the little girl, though, for Stanley is an enormous, loveable mutt. Told as much through pictures as words, this very easy reader will draw smiles from most first and second graders - especially dog lovers. An Early I Can Read Book.

Interest Level: 1-2. Reading Level: 1.2. Further Search Topics: Dogs-Fiction, Humorous Fiction, Best Sellers.

Cleary, Beverly. Henry Huggins; illus by Louis Darling. Morrow 1950, 155 pp.

Henry Huggins is over 30 years old now, so if he occasionally seems a little old-fashioned, it is not surprising. What is surprising is how well he has withstood the years. His antics are innocent, but humorous and realistic. The book's six chapters are six separate stories that follow the same cast of characters through an entire year.

In the first chapter, Henry finds a stray dog (Ribsy) whom he must then transport home on a bus. Ribsy was too large and too frisky not to get into trouble, so before Henry finally gets him home, they have been kicked off of three buses and have ridden in a police car. The second chapter describes what happens when Henry buys two guppies and ends up with millions. In the third chapter Henry accidentally throws his friend's football into the back seat of a speeding car and tries to earn the money to replace it by catching and selling 1,331 night crawlers. The fourth chapter involves Henry's attempts to get out of playing the lead in a school Christmas play. His last minute rescue comes in the form of a can of green paint that spills all over him. It is Ribsy's turn to change colors in Chapter 5. Henry tries to cover Ribsy's dirt spots with talcolm powder for a dog show, but only succeeds in turning Ribsy pink. And in Chapter 6, Ribsy's original owner finally finds him and wants him back, but Ribsy chooses to stay with Henry. Only the occasional extra cute expression and Henry's age (third grade) keep this from being enjoyed beyond fourth grade.

Interest Level: 1-4. Reading Level: 2.2. Further Search Topics: Humorous Fiction, Everyday Stories, Read Aloud Pets-Fiction, Dogs-Fiction, Group 2.

Hildick, Edmund W. The case of the invisible dog; illus by Lisl Weil. Macmillan 1977, 101 pp.

Brains Bellingham, a nine-year-old scientific genius, interrupted the McGurk Organization's Annual Picnic with an invisible dog. It was only a short time before McGurk and his friends were convinced that Brains' discovery of how to make things invisible was the greatest event since putting a man on the moon. Although they had always scorned the idea of including anyone else in the Organization, they decided to persuade Brains to join. But, before the day was over, they discovered not only that they had been duped, but exactly how Brains had made the impossible seem real. The Organization took its revenge by using Brain's own trick to make him confess. When Brains began laughing at how well his trick had been used in reverse, McGurk admitted how impressed they all had been by Brain's clever thinking. The outcome of their discussion was that Brains was invited, a second time, to become a member of the McGurk Organization.

See *Case of the Bashful Bank Robber* for series information. McGurk Mystery series.

Interest Level: 3-6. Reading Level: 3.1. Further Search Topics: Mystery and Detective Stories, Detectives-Fiction, Gangs-Fiction, Dogs-Fiction, Supernatural-Fiction, Humorous Fiction, Jealousy-Fiction.

Nodset, Joan L. Go away dog; illus by Crosby Bonsall. Har-Row 1963, unp (29 pp).

A small boy who doesn't like dogs meets a shaggy, homeless dog who wants to play. The little boy, resisting all the way, gradually gives in to the dog's charms. Finally he tells the dog to follow him home. At home, he finds out that the dog was sent to him for his birthday by his Uncle George.

The dog, the boy, and the book are irresistible. You must, however, notice the illustrations on both the dedication and title pages to fully understand the story. Since much of the story is told by the illustrations and the text is repetitive as well as simple, it is an excellent beginning-to-read story.

Interest Level: 1-2. Reading Level: 1.1. Further Search Topics: Dogs-Fiction, Humorous Fiction, Best Sellers, Pets-Fiction, Birthdays-Fiction.

Parish, Peggy. Clues in the woods; illus by Paul Frame. Macmillan 1968, 154 pp.

The books about the three Roberts children share problems that are obvious to adults and felt by some young readers as well, but they continue to be popular with undemanding young readers. The characters are very white and middle class and their actions often fit out-of-date stereotypes. The plots have few surprises or suspense, but the reading levels are consistent and the very predictability of the books makes them familiar and therefore comfortable.

This particular story takes place at the end of the same summer the children solved the mystery of *The Key to the Treasure*. The children were alerted by their grandmother to the disappearance of food scraps, left outside the house. Thinking that two runaway children, about whom they had read, had taken the food, Liza, Bill, and Jed tried to find the runaways. Their attempts eventually brought them new friends and thus the solution to their mystery. It had not been the runaways who had taken the food, it was their new friends' dog.

Interest Level: 1-4. Reading Level: 2.2. Further Search Topics: Mystery and Detective Stories, Brothers and Sisters-Fiction, Vacation-Fiction, Dogs-Fiction, Runaways-Fiction, Grandparents-Fiction, Group 2.

Shura, Mary Francis. The Barkley Street six-pack: illus by Gene Sparkman. Dodd 1979, 159 pp.

Jane's best friend Natalie was everything Jane wanted to be. She was self-assured, pretty, vibrant, and even possessed magical talents. Jane didn't realize at first, and she later resisted seeing, that Natalie ran Jane's life and cleverly made sure that Jane had no other friends. Natalie's move left Jane with no friends among those people she had once enjoyed. Little by little, with the help of a stray dog and the new boy on the block, Jane bagan to see how destructive Natalie had been. She finally realized that a true friendship is one in which neither party tries to control the other.

With its enticements of ESP, magic, stray dogs, and problems with peers, this is a very appealing book to many young readers. As a bonus it is a thoughtful, sympathetic, fairly well-written story.

Interest Level: 4-6. Reading Level: 4.2. Further Search Topics: Gangs-Fiction, Pets-Fiction, Dogs-Fiction, Friendship-Fiction, Honesty-Fiction, Courage-Fiction, Loneliness-Fiction, Extra Sensory Perception-Fiction, Everyday Stories.

Silman, Roberta. Somebody else's child; illus by Chris Conover. Warne 1976, 64 pp.

Peter was adopted, but he had never questioned his family's love for him until Puddin' Paint, the school bus driver, made a thoughtless remark. Peter's affection for the older man was strong enough to help him understand Puddin' Paint's feelings. When Puddin' Paint's two dogs disappeared and the bus driver was almost heartbroken, it was Peter who helped the old man search for the dogs. That experience helped both Peter and Puddin' Paint understand that love doesn't only extend to natural born children, but can be just as strong and deep for others.

A simple telling of a moving story. It is as useful for readers who love dogs as for those interested in adoption. Rather inconsistent reading level, tests between 1.2 and 3.1.

Interest Level: 2-5. Reading Level: 2.2. Further Search Topics: Adoption-Fiction, Dogs-Fiction, Friendship-Fiction, Love-Fiction.

Wallace, Bill. A dog named Kitty. Holiday 1980, 153 pp.

Ricky's fear of dogs was extreme but also understandable. He had been attacked by a rabid dog when he was very young. Remembering the fear, the stitches and the painful rabies shots was enough to bring tears to Ricky's eyes even years later. When a local bully told his dog to attack Ricky, Ricky's fear was discovered. About that time, a stray puppy showed up at Ricky's farm. Not quite knowing why, Ricky began to warm to the puppy, to feed it, and finally to love it. When the dog was attacked by a pack of wild dogs (a brutal scene vividly described), Ricky fully overcame his fear of dogs, went to Kitty's defense, and was barely able to save her life. When Kitty was later tragically and accidentally killed, Ricky swore that he would never have anything to do with a dog again. He almost kept his promise to himself, but eventually a second stray dog wandered into the farm and Ricky decided to try again.

This is an emotional story that should appeal to many readers. However, because of the violence and the dog's two-stage death, the book is probably best suited to fifth and sixth grade children.

Interest Level: 5-6. Reading Level: 3.1. Further Search Topics: Dogs-Fiction, Pets-Fiction, Bullies-Fiction, Death-Fiction, Oklahoma-Fiction, Courage-Fiction, Country Life-Fiction.

DOLLS-FICTION

Bulla, Clyde Robert. Open the door and see all the people; illus by Wendy Watson. T Y Crowell 1972, 69 pp.

A slight story that makes up for its lack of excitement with warmth. When Joann, Teeney and Mama were burned out of their house in the country, they decided it was time to move to the city. With the help of a friend, Mama was quickly able to find a job and an apartment. Only Teeney was noticeably unhappy. She missed her doll and resented anyone else who had one. Then the girls learned about the Toy House, a place to borrow or adopt toys. Both girls found dolls they wanted to adopt. Just before the end of the six week trial period Tenney lost her doll and almost lost her chance to adopt it. After the doll was found and repaired, the people at the Toy House realized how much she wanted the doll and let Teeney keep it.

Because of the ages of the characters, (six and eight), and the subject matter, the book's appeal is doubtful beyond third grade. Print size slightly smaller than usual for Bulla.

Interest Level: 1-3. Reading Level: 2.1. Further Search Topics: Dolls-Fiction, Brothers and Sisters-Fiction, Moving, Household-Fiction, Family-Fiction, Group 2.

Hildick, Edmund W. Deadline for McGurk; illus by Lisl Weil. Macmillan 1975, 104 pp.

When many of the dolls in the neighborhood began disappearing, their owners went to the McGurk Organization for help. At first McGurk was reluctant to take on such a silly task as recovering lost dolls. But when a ransom note appeared and the Organization was linked to the dolls' safety, McGurk's reluctance vanished. The note stated that if, in a written public notice, the members of the Organization did not admit that they were no good, the dolls were doomed. McGurk's pride would never have allowed him to write such a notice. As the deadline approached, the group plotted a daring move designed to uncover the doll thief. The plan depended on Willie's super-sensitive nose, a particular perfume dabbed on a stolen doll, and the curiosity of the thief. Success came only minutes before the hour of doom. Once again Sandra Ennis was the culprit.

See *The Case of the Bashful Bank Robber* for series information. McGurk Mystery series.

Interest Level: 3-5. Reading Level: 2.2. Further Search Topics: Dolls-Fiction, Mystery and Detective Stories, Detectives-Fiction, Humorous Fiction, Gangs-Fiction, Jealousy-Fiction.

DOLPHINS

Davidson, Margaret. Nine true dolphin stories: illus by Roger Wilson. Hastings 1974, 67 pp.

Nine short stories about dolphins preceded by a brief description of their physical characteristics, their habits and their behavior. Each story is true, although some are more anecdotes than stories. Most are amusing; all are interesting. Satisfying to the dolphin enthusiast from grades two through five.

Interest Level: 2-5. Reading Level: 3.1. Further Search Topics: Dolphins, Group 2.

DOLPHINS-FICTION

Davidson, Carson. Fast-talking dolphin; illus by Sylvia Stone. Dodd 1978, 127 pp.

After a rather slow start, this story develops into a well-paced adventure-fantasy with touches of warmth and humor. Eric wasn't just surprised when he found a dolphin in the 10-foot fish pond, he was astonished.

Not only had there never been a dolphin there before, but this dolphin spoke in poetry. His name was Wallingford Ullingham Lowell III; Wallingford for short. He was elegant, proud and cultured; but as Eric soon found out, he was very impractical. He didn't seem to realize that he needed salt water and more fish than those in the pond in order to live. It was Eric who figured out a way to keep salt flowing into the pond and a supply of fresh fish. He also kept Wallingford's presence a secret, just as Wallingford requested. The day that Wallingford was discovered was the day that Eric had to break his promise. In order to find out who else had found out about Wallingford, Eric talked with his brother. Together they scouted the town before they realized that Herbert Benson was the only other person who had seen Wallingford.

Herbert reluctantly admitted that he had told his father about the dolphin. Eric knew enough about Mr. Benson to realize that he was just crazy enough to want to harm the dolphin. Eric and his brother gathered all the local children together to shield Wallingford from Mr. Benson. Even Herbert dared to defy his father for the first time. As Mr. Benson struggled with Eric and his brother, he fell, hit his head and rolled into the pond. Wallingford dove to save him, but his leg was caught between two rocks. With the others' help, Wallingford, Eric and his brother Karl were able to save Mr. Benson from drowning.

A few days later Eric, with new-found skills, spontaneously recited a poem about friendship to Wallingford. Wallingford answered with a rare compliment and for the first time used Eric's name (a show of respect). They were such true friends that when Wallingford was helicopter-lifted out of the pond and taken back to his research project, Eric couldn't understand why his father didn't tell him of Wallingford's departure. Eventually he realized that his father had been right; he would rather remember Wallingford swimming in the pond than in a helicopter's sling. Also, Wallingford would have been embarrassed to be seen making so undignified a departure. Wallingford's final message to Eric was a note that Eric found scratched in the dirt thanking him for the salt and the fish and saying that they would one day meet again.

Don't take the plot too seriously or peruse it too carefully for it won't stand up to scrutiny. This is merely a pleasant story with enough humor, action and originality to intrigue many readers. The book's major drawback is the poetry Wallingford spouts: the poetic form and somewhat difficult language will throw some readers. On the other hand, the book could be very useful in a classroom unit about poetry.

Interest Level: 3-5. Reading Level: 3.1. Further Search Topics: Poetry, Dolphins-Fiction, Pets-Fiction, Fantasy, Friendship-Fiction, Humorous Fiction.

DORSETT, TONY

Burchard, Susan H. Sports star: Tony Dorsett. HarBraceJ 1978, 64 pp.

One year after he set the college rushing record and won the Heisman Trophy, Tony Dorsett was named the NFL's Rookie of the Year and found himself playing in the Super Bowl. Reading level of this title varies from 2.2 to 3.2. For more information about the series see the entry for Marshall Burchard's *Sports Hero: Bill Walton*. Sports Star series.

Interest Level: 2-6. Reading Level: 3.2. Further Search Topics: Biography, Football-Biography, Dorsett, Tony, Blacks-Biography, Group 2.

DRAGONS-FICTION

Chew, Ruth. The witch's garden. Hastings 1978, 112 pp.

Although its elements seem to promise an exciting adventure story, this is a disappointing book. The witch who moved into the dark, old home next door to Josh and Susan, was trying to improve her overgrown garden when Susan and Josh offered to help. The children accidentally splashed themselves with the witch's newest brew and found they suddenly became very tiny inhabitants of a dense and threatening jungle (the garden). After they regained their normal size, they dug into other areas of the garden. One hole they dug opened into an underground tunnel that they found was inhabited by a fire-breathing dragon. When the dragon cornered Mrs. Muldoon, Susan and Josh ran out of the tunnel, found the brew and splashed it onto the dragon. The dragon shrank away, Mrs. Muldoon was safe and the tunnel closed over.

Because there is little more suspense than in this description, the book fails to live up to its promise. In addition, the children's first sudden size change is just subtle enough to be confusing. Despite its problems the book is popular with Ruth Chew fans and therefore useful.

Interest Level: 2-5. Reading Level: 2.2. Further Search Topics: Witches-Fiction, Brothers and Sisters-Fiction, Magic-Fiction, Fantasy, Dragons-Fiction, Transformations-Fiction.

DRAMA

Alexander, Sue. Small plays for you and a friend; illus by Olivia H. Cole. Seabury 1974, 48 pp.

Five very short and very simple plays for two actors that will be of more interest to the players than the audience. However, because the reading level is low, and because children's love of acting is strong and their tolerance of weak plot is high, this can be used through grade three. A companion volume *Small Plays for Special Days* presents seven more short plays for two characters.

Interest Level: 1-3. Reading Level: 2.1. Further Search Topics: Acting, Drama, Group 2.

Arkhurst, Joyce. The adventures of Spider; West African folktales; illus by Jerry Pinkney. Little 1964, 58 pp.

A delightful collection of six West African folktales about Spider. Spider is mischievous, greedy, lazy and clever. He loves to eat and he hates to work. Four of the stories tell of Spider's ill-fated attempts to get food without having to work for it ("How Spider Got a Thin Waist," "How Spider Got a Bald Head," "How Spider Helped a Fisherman," and "Why Spiders Live in Dark Corners"). One story tells of his greed ("How the World Got Wisdom"), and only one story is complimentary ("Why Spider Lives in Ceilings"). All are short, gentle, humorous, and adapt well to dramatization or retelling.

Interest Level: 2-6. Reading Level 3.1. Further Search Topics: Humorous Fiction, Spiders-Fiction, Folklore, Tricksters-Fiction, Africa-Folklore, Group 2, Read Aloud, Creation-Fiction, Drama.

Bernstein, Margery. Coyote goes hunting for fire; illus by Ed Heffernan. Scribner 1974, 40 pp.

A delightful story that can be read for fun or used as part of a unit on North American Indians. A long time ago when there was no fire, all the animals but Coyote banded together to find it. The animals left Coyote behind because he was always spoiling their plans. Coyote saw them leave, chased after them and once more tried to direct everything, but only ended up losing fire. Cartoon-like illustrations add to the humor of the story. This book should make a simple, but effective play.

Interest Level: 1-4. Reading Level 2.1. Further Search Topics: Animals-Fiction, Legends, Mythology, Fire-Fiction, Indians of North America-Legends, Coyotes-Fiction, Group 2, Creation-Fiction, Drama.

Bernstein, Margery. The first morning; illus by Enid Warner Romanek. Scribner 1976, 44 pp.

Spider, Mouse, and Fly volunteered to ask the king of the sky for light to take back to earth because the animals on earth were tired of living in darkness. The king didn't want to give away any light and so he set what he thought was an impossible task for the three animals. They were able to outwit the king three times and finally return to earth with a box Mouse was sure contained light. When they opened the box all they found was a rooster. Poor Mouse was ashamed at having been so badly tricked. But then Rooster crowed up the first morning and has done so ever since. A competent retelling of an African myth, nicely complemented by bold illustrations. Good candidate for dramatization.

Interest Level: 1-3. Reading Level: 2.1. Further Search Topics: Animals-Fiction, Group 2, Mythology, Light-Fiction, Drama, Time-Fiction, Calendars-Fiction, Creation-Fiction, Africa-Folklore.

DREAMS-FICTION
Bulla, Clyde Robert. Marco Moonlight; illus by Julia Noonan. T Y Crowell 1976, 104 pp.

No one could explain Marco's strange, recurring dream. The dream seemed to be about a brother, but Marco had no brother. He had no family but his wealthy grandparents with whom he lived. Marco loved his grandparents very much, but he couldn't help wondering about his own past. He knew only what he and his grandparents could figure out from a few clues. His mother had run away to marry and for three years Marco's grandparents had heard nothing. Then, suddenly, they received a note that she was dying, had parted from her husband, and needed them. By the time they arrived, she was dead and two-year-old Marco could tell them no more. About the time of his thirteenth birthday Marco made friends with a strange man named Flint, who later became the gardener on Marco's grandparents' estate. Rather than live in the room provided for him with the other servants, Flint chose a bleak and isolated beach cottage. Being very careful that no one should suspect, Flint locked Marco into the cottage and forced Marco to change clothes with Matt, who was Marco's long-lost identical twin. Flint and Matt planned that Matt would steal all the money he could from the estate before killing Marco and fleeing. But when Matt began to realize how nice his grandparents were, how much he liked Marco, and how evil Flint was, he decided to thwart Flint's plan. In Matt and Marco's desperate attempt to flee from Flint, Flint was accidentally killed, leaving Marco free to return home and Matt free to find a way to feel he also had the right to claim his heritage before joining Marco.

The tense and dramatic plot immediately involves the reader and the short, fast-paced chapters sustain interest to the end of the book. Readers should also appreciate the small, paperback-size format. A good choice.

Interest Level: 3-6. Reading Level: 2.1. Further Search Topics: Dreams-Fiction, Mystery and Detective Stories, Kidnapping-Fiction, Twins-Fiction, Orphans-Fiction, Grandparents-Fiction, Best Sellers, Brothers and Sisters-Fiction, Jealousy-Fiction, Courage-Fiction.

Sleator, William. Into the dream; illus by Ruth Sanderson. Dutton 1979, 137 pp.

Paul and Francine each started having what, at first, seemed like nightmares. As the dreams became more detailed and forboding, they discovered that they were sharing the same nightmare. They dreamed of a four-year-old boy, swirling lights, and a large dog. After awhile they figured out that the dog was trying to save the little boy from some unknown danger. As the pieces of the puzzle began to increase in number, Paul and Francine decided that the dream was in some way connected to a night over four years earlier when they had both been staying at the same motel. They, a pregnant woman, and a pregnant dog had all been affected by the telepathic power given off by a spaceship. The progeny of the woman and the dog had been given extraordinary mental powers; powers that a secret government agency wanted to mold and then put to their own use. The danger Paul and Francine felt came from two government agents sent to take the young boy Noah from his mother. Their attempt ended in a bizarre scene at an amusement park, where Noah levitated a broken ferris wheel chair to safety. By thus exposing his talent in public, Noah unconsciously insured against its secret and unsupervised use by the government.

A terrifying and suspense-filled psychological thriller whose main problems are a slightly overdrawn ending and a variable reading level. Reading level drops as low as 2.1 and climbs occasionally to 4.1.

Interest Level: 5-6. Reading Level: 3.2. Further Search Topics: Best Sellers, Supernatural-Fiction, Occult-Fiction, Flying Saucers-Fiction, Nonverbal Communication-Fiction, Dreams-Fiction, Survival-Fiction, Extra Sensory Perception-Fiction, Horror-Fiction.

DRUGS-FICTION
Shreve, Susan. The Nightmares of Geranium Street. Knopf 1977, 127 pp.

The Nightmares, a small neighborhood gang, had very little to do until beautiful Tess moved on the block. Tess dressed in satins, furs, and rhinestones, and sang in nightclubs. She was even more of a fascination to the gang because they had been told to stay away from her. When Amanda moved in with Tess, the Nightmares invited her to join the gang so that they would have a way of spying on Tess. Gradually her strange behavior, her moods, her bruises and shaking spells, the strangers she let in the house, and the fights she had, led the gang members to suspect that Tess dealt in drugs. When Amanda failed to show up for a picnic and the Nightmares learned the police were searching for Tess, the gang became worried enough to look for Amanda themselves. In doing so, they uncovered proof of Tess' drug dealings, put themselves in great danger, and were protected by Tess as they escaped only moments before Tess was arrested.

Despite its low reading level, the book's confusing sequence of final events, and its subject matter make it best suited to older readers. It is not great literature, but its subject has strong appeal.

Interest Level: 5-6. Reading Level: 3.1. Further Search Topics: Family Problems-Fiction, Gangs-Fiction, Drugs-Fiction, Mystery and Detective Stories, City Life-Fiction, Crime-Fiction, Philadelphia-Fiction.

DUCKS-FICTION

Berends, Polly Berrien. The case of the elevator duck; illus by James K. Washburn. Random 1973, 54 pp.

Although it would be stretching the meaning of the word to call this a mystery, it is a story of an 11-year-old detective. Albert tells his own story in a clipped style that resembles adult detective novels. One morning Albert found a duck abandoned in the apartment house elevator. He was determined to find the owner of the duck and return it. He had to be very careful as he searched because pets were absolutely forbidden in the housing projects. Anyone who saw him with the duck might report him. Albert and his parents had waited too long to get into the projects to be kicked out because of a duck. When Albert finally found the duck's owner (a young, sad child named Julio), Julio's sister forced Albert to take the duck back. Still angry at Julio's sister, Albert took the duck to the project's day care center, where the teacher agreed to formally adopt the duck. Albert stayed at the center long enough to see Julio's happy surprise when he arrived and found the duck. Its appealing characters, the tension created by the writing style, and the book's humor make this a delightful story.

Interest Level: 2-5. Reading Level 2.2. Further Search Topics: Humorous Fiction, City Life-Fiction, Housing Projects-Fiction, Detectives-Fiction, Pets-Fiction, Ducks-Fiction, Read Aloud.

ECLIPSES

Branley, Franklyn M. Eclipse: darkness in daytime; illus by Donald Crews. Har-Row 1973, 33 pp.

The subject is so well-explained and the book is so physically attractive, it's a shame that some older readers will be put off by this title's picture book appearance. Aside from an occasional jarring, condescending note, this is a fine introduction to an interesting subject. Use comfortably with third and fourth graders. Recommend to fifth graders with caution. No index or table of contents. Lets-Read-and-Find-Out-Science-Book series.

Interest Level: 2-4. Reading Level: 2.2. Further Search Topics: Sun, Astronomy, Eclipses, Moon.

ECOLOGY-FICTION

Morressy, John. The drought on Ziax II, illus by Stanley Skardinsky. Walker & Co 1978, 77 pp.

Ziax II, the planet that Toren, his father, and other Earth Pioneers were helping to colonize, was suffering a severe drought. It took both cooperation with the inhabitants of Ziax II and courage to seek out the frightening creature that could save the planet.

The importance of maintaining the balance of nature is the strongest message here. Respect for the ways of others is the secondary message.

Interest Level: 3-5. Reading Level: 3.1. Further Search Topics: Science Fiction, Ecology-Fiction, Outer Space-Fiction.

EGYPT-FICTION

Heide, Florence Parry. Mystery of the mummy's mask; illus by Seymour Fleishman. A. Whitman 1979, 127 pp.

The Spotlight Club published a neighborhood newspaper. Just as the club was about to take the fourth issue to the printer, Jay discovered an ancient mummy mask hidden near Mr. Pruitt's house. Mr. Pruitt was intrigued by the discovery (he worked at the nearby museum) and he took the mask from Jay, but agreed that Jay could write about the mask for the paper. At about the same time, Dexter discovered that an old, abandoned house was being used. When the printer's office was broken into that night and only their newspaper was stolen, the three children began to suspect that something strange was going on at the abandoned house.

Dexter rode back to the house alone and was captured by Hank, one of three thieves hiding out there. Figuring that they never would have missed one item, Hank had taken the mask from the cache of goods that the other two had stolen. When he overheard Jay's conversation with Mr. Pruitt, Hank realized that his partners would find out what he had done if they ever read the newspaper article. To avoid being discovered, Hank broke into the printer's and stole the paste-up of the paper. In order to keep Dexter from escaping, Hank tied him up and placed him in a shipping crate. When he didn't return as soon as expected, Jay and Cindy realized that Dexter was in trouble, so they went out to the house to search for him. As the three escaped, Dexter and Cindy slashed the thieves' truck's tires, and Jay ran to phone for the police. After several nervous moments in which Cindy and Dexter thought Jay might not get back before they were caught, Jay finally brought the police, who captured all three thieves.

See *Mystery at Southport Cinema* for more information. Spotlight Club Mystery series.

Interest Level: 3-5. Reading Level: 3.1. Further Search Topics: Mystery and Detective Stories, Crime-Fiction, Egypt-Fiction, Archaeology-Fiction, Antiquities-Fiction, Journalism-Fiction, Gangs-Fiction, Brothers and Sisters-Fiction, Detectives-Fiction.

ELECTRICITY-FICTION

Pene du Bois, William. Lazy Tommy Pumpkinhead. Har-Row 1966, 32 pp.

Tommy lived a solitary life in an all-electric house. An electric bed woke Tommy and slid him into a tub full of warm water. The tub then tipped him out and into a harness that held Tommy upright while other machines dried him, combed his hair, brushed his teeth, dressed him, and fed him. But one day Tommy's life was literally turned upside down with disastrous results. His feet were cleaned and combed and his clothes were all put on upside down, but the worst part of all was that Tommy almost starved; the machine fed his feet instead of his mouth.

A tongue-in-cheek warning against laziness. The lesson is obvious but the treatment (both text and illustrations) is so enjoyable that the book is appealing to almost any reader who wants a short, funny book. Print is somewhat small but spacing between lines is more than adequate.

Interest Level: 1-6. Reading Level: 3.2. Further Search Topics: Electricity-Fiction, Robots-Fiction, Laziness-Fiction, Humorous Fiction, Group 2, Read Aloud.

ENGINES

Bendick, Jeanne. The first book of airplanes. Watts 1975, revised edition, 65 pp.

It will take a determined reader to get much technical information from this overview of airplanes. The first sections (thrust, lift gravity, drag, and parts of a plane) promise simple, understandable explanations of complicated topics. The next portion of the book fails to live up to that promise. The descriptions of airplane engines will be intelligible only to the reader who already knows how an engine works. The history of flight is little more than an outline. The two-page chapter on air maps and distances will do more to confuse than instruct most readers. On the other hand, the information about airports, control towers, and types and uses of aircrafts is better. The book is well-indexed and includes a four-page glossary. It is perhaps best used as a general introduction to airplanes (skip the three areas mentioned above). For technical information about flight, look elsewhere. Print size is adequate but spacing between lines could have been more generous.

Interest Level: 4-6. Reading Level: 3.2. Further Search Topics: Airports, Engines, Flight, Airplanes.

ERVING, JULIUS

Burchard, Marshall. Sports hero: Dr. J. Putnam 1976, 89 pp.

Julius Erving can jump higher and stay in the air longer than almost any other basketball player. He can also move around the court with the most agile of players. All in all he is a very exciting player to watch. This book includes his college and pro records (through 1975). See *Sports Hero: Bill Walton* for more information. Sports Hero series.

Interest Level: 3-6. Reading Level: 4.1. Further Search Topics: Biography, Blacks-Biography, Basketball-Biography, Erving, Julius, Group 2.

ETHNIC GROUPS

Amon, Aline. Talking hands: Indian sign language. Doubleday 1968, 80 pp.

If you can ignore the author's patronizing tone and air of self-satisfaction, this is a book with great appeal. Children love ways of communicating privately, be it Pig Latin, codes and ciphers, or just whispering. This book appeals to that love by clearly, though unattractively, demonstrating over 200 words in American Indian sign language. By the time the young reader finishes the book, he/she will not only have had the fun of learning another method of communication, but will have learned a few simple generalities about North American Indians. The index is detailed enough that any word can be quickly checked. The book is useful for history, social studies, or language arts units, as well as for fun.

Interest Level: 2-6. Reading Level: 2.2. Further Search Topics: Indians of North America-Sign Language, Communication, Nonverbal Communication, Ethnic Groups.

Bales, Carol Ann. Chinatown Sunday; the story of Lillian Der. Contemp Bks. 1973, 32 pp.

A short, personal visit with a fifth grade Chinese-American girl who lives in a Chicago suburb. The author transcribed taped interviews with Lillian Der to produce a first-person description of Lillian's daily life. The uniquely Chinese-American features of Lillian's life are casually intertwined with experiences common to most American children. Month-old parties, the celebration of Chinese New Year, lucky money, old-age birthday parties, Girl Scout meetings, homework, and being a tomboy are all important to Lillian. Not only is this an interesting portrait of Lillian, but it can be a useful part of a multi-ethnic unit or an introduction to autobiography. The book's usefulness is further extended by its introduction to Chinese immigration and by the glossary, which explains terms such as "abacus," "Chinese calendar," and "sea cucumber." The author saves the over-sized book from looking like a picture book by using photographs instead of drawings, thus she makes the book comfortable even for a sixth grade reader.

Interest Level: 3-6. Reading Level: 3.1. Further Search Topics: Ethnic Groups, Chinese-Americans, Biography, Chicago, Immigration and Emigration.

Buckley, Peter. I am from Puerto Rico. S ËAN S 1971, 127 pp.

Federico Ramirez had enjoyed his two years in New York City and didn't like the idea of moving back to Puerto Rico. When he arrived, he had no friends, no T.V., and nothing to do. Then Neri taught Federico the local games, showed him the sights and introduced him to Narciso, a special fisherman. Narcisco took Federico through the wonders of the coral reefs. He taught him how to dive and fish. Within several months Federico was thoroughly at home in the water and loved Puerto Rico.

There is so much information about Puerto Rico and marine life that the book is never dry. Federico tells his own story as a series of fascinating experiences (meeting up with a shark, playing pinball, scuba diving at night, keeping a large turtle as a pet, etc.). There are abundant black and white photographs. An excellent choice for research (no index) or recreational reading. The print size is slightly on the small side, but the space between lines is good. Recently out of print, but worth looking for.

Interest Level: 5-6. Reading Level: 5.1. Further Search Topics: Puerto Rico, Fishing, Moving, Household-Fiction, Marine Biology, Scuba Diving, Ethnic Groups.

EVERYDAY STORIES

Blegvad, Lenore. The great hamster hunt; illus by Erik Blegvad. HarBraceJ 1969, 32 pp.

Nicholas wanted a hamster; but, because his mother didn't like them, he couldn't have one. She did, however, agree to let Nicholas take care of his friend Tony's hamster for a week. It was a good and happy week for Nicholas until the evening before Tony was to return for his hamster. Nicholas accidentally broke the glass front of Harvey's cage and temporarily replaced it with cardboard. By morning Harvey had chewed through the cardbroad and was gone. Nicholas and his family searched all day but couldn't find Harvey. They finally bought another hamster and waited for Tony to arrive. As evening came Nicholas realized that hamsters are nocturnal and began to look for Harvey once more. This time Harvey was awake and active. The happy result was that Harvey was found and the new hampster became Nicholas' own pet. A simple, satisfying story even to fourth grade readers.

Interest Level: 1-4. Reading Level: 2.2. Further Search Topics: Pets-Fiction, Hamsters-Fiction, Group 2, Everyday Stories.

Blume, Judy. Are you there God? It's me, Margaret. Bradbury 1970, 149 pp.

Sixth grade was a year of growth for Margaret and her friends. They all wondered when they would start growing breasts and when they would begin menstruating. Each was kissed for the first time. It was also a year in which Margaret tried to decide whether to be Jewish or Christian and ended up neither. She simply remained friends with God, just as she was when the year began. The book is a reassuring, very open, and humorous treatment of the pains and promise of maturation. It is exceptionally popular with older elementary school readers, so the book's slightly small print and narrow lines should not impede an interested reader's progress.

Interest Level: 4-6. Reading Level: 3.2. Further Search Topics: School Stories, Family-Fiction, Children-Growth-Fiction, Religion-Fiction, Humorous Fiction, Love-Fiction, Best Sellers, Grandparents-Fiction, Everyday Stories.

Blume, Judy. It's not the end of the world. Bradbury 1972, 169 pp.

This is a one theme book (as are many of Judy Blume's titles). It is the story of 11-year-old Karen's attempt to prevent her parents' divorce and then to accept it. In this first-person story she tells of her disappointment, anger, fear, and lack of understanding. She describes her parents' fights and her brother's and sister's reactions, too. It is a book with an obvious and mostly reassuring message to its readers, but it is not just for readers whose families may be in similar situations. It is also a book that will be enjoyed by any Judy Blume enthusiast.

Interest Level: 4-6. Reading Level: 3.1. Further Search Topics: Divorce and Separation-Fiction, Family Problems-Fiction, Everyday Stories.

Blume, Judy. Tales of a fourth grade nothing; illus by Roy Doty. Dutton 1972, 120 pp.

Another humorous Blume book that can be counted on to appeal to third and fourth grade readers. If fifth and sixth graders can ignore the title's reference to fourth grade, they too will love it. The story is an exaggeration of a common theme—an older child whose life is in continual turmoil because of a somewhat spoiled younger sibling. Peter's problems with three-year-old Fudge become worse with each chapter until the final disaster when Fudge swallows Peter's pet turtle. Each approximately 15-page chapter is a complete, very funny episode.

Interest Level: 3-6. Reading Level 3.1. Further Search Topics: Humorous Fiction, Turtles-Fiction, Brothers and Sisters-Fiction, Pets-Fiction, Family-Fiction, Read Aloud, Best Sellers, Everyday Stories, Troublemakers-Fiction.

Blume, Judy. Otherwise known as Sheila the great. Dutton 1972, 128 pp.

Sheila first appears in *Tales of a Fourth Grade Nothing* as Peter Thatcher's neighbor. Sheila was a bundle of fears. She was afraid of dogs, thunderstorms, spiders, horses, putting her face in water, and strange noises at night. The summer she and her family rented a house in Tarrytown, New York, she confronted each one of her fears, even mastered one (putting her face in the water) and learned how to swim. That gave her the self-confidence to face a dog without running away. Sheila's progress was aided by her friend Mouse's steadfast belief that a person should always be honest about herself. Sheila's problems are treated realistically and with dignity, yet humorously. Reading level varies greatly from 1.2 - 4.1, therefore, the book is *most* suitable to grades four through six.

Interest Level: 3-6. Reading Level: 3.1. Further Search Topics: Humorous Fiction, Courage-Fiction, Camp-Fiction, Group 2, Vacation-Fiction, Swimming-Fiction, Brothers and Sisters-Fiction, Friendship-Fiction, Everyday Stories.

Blume, Judy. Superfudge. Dutton 1980, 166 pp.

On Fudge's first day in school his older brother Peter had to rescue him from the top of the kindergarten storage cabinets. Later in the school year Fudge's eagerness to join a school guest speaker on stage almost spelled disaster. Then when Fudge unexpectedly disappeared one day everyone, including Peter, thought he had drowned. In addition to Peter's problems with Fudge, Peter had to cope with a baby sister, moving to Princeton, New Jersey, a new job for his mother, and his father's attempts to write a book. Although the book is a sequel and is best enjoyed as such, it can be read alone. It is not

as amusing or well-written as it's predecessor, *Tales of a Fourth Grade Nothing*, but will still be popular with young readers.

Interest Level: 3-6. Reading Level 3.1. Further Search Topics: Brothers and Sisters-Fiction, Moving, Household-Fiction, Infants-Fiction, Working Parents-Fiction, School Stories, Family-Fiction, Best Sellers, Humorous Fiction, Everyday Stories.

Blume, Judy. Freckle juice; illus by Sonia O. Lisker. Four Winds 1971, 40 pp.

A very funny story that should appeal to almost everyone. Andrew wanted freckles so that the dirt on his skin wouldn't show as much and he wouldn't have to wash as often. As luck would have it, Sharon, the most obnoxious girl in class, had a freckle juice recipe that she was willing to sell for 50 cents. Even after drinking the brew of grape juice, vinegar, mustard, olive oil, and more, Andrew didn't see any freckles, but, he certainly was sick. Although the protagonists are younger, this book will hold even a fifth grade reader's interest.

Interest Level: 2-5. Reading Level 3.1. Further Search Topics: Humorous Fiction, Group 2, Read Aloud, Everyday Stories, Beauty-Fiction, School Stories, Magic-Fiction, Best Sellers.

Bonsall, Crosby. The day I had to play with my sister. Har-Row 1972, 32 pp.

A very easy reader, only slightly less universally appealing and humorous than *And I Mean It, Stanley*. This time a little boy tries very hard to teach his younger sister to play hide-and-seek. He is totally unsuccessful and thoroughly frustrated. Again the story is told as much with pictures as with words. Useful through second grade. Reader format. An Early I Can Read Book.

Interest Level: 1-2. Reading Level: 1.1. Further Search Topics: Humorous Fiction, Games-Fiction, Brothers and Sisters-Fiction, Everyday Stories.

Bulla, Clyde Robert. Shoeshine girl; illus by Leigh Grant. Har-Row 1975, 84 pp.

A well-written, realistic story of 10-year-old Sarah who was sent to spend the summer with her Aunt Claudia. Sarah's parents felt that Sarah put too much importance on money and so insisted that Aunt Claudia give her no allowance for the summer. Sure that Aunt Claudia would call her bluff, Sarah threatened to get a job. Instead, Aunt Claudia thought it was a good idea. Sarah's experience as a shoeshine girl forced her to grow, to learn to like working, and finally to take responsibility for the stand when her boss was hit by a car. Told with quiet humor. For the reader who enjoys Judy Blume's books.

Interest Level: 2-5. Reading Level: 2.2. Further Search Topics: Children-Growth-Fiction, Family Problems-Fiction, Vacation-Fiction, Occupations-Fiction, Everyday Stories.

Byars, Betsy. The Cybil war; illus by Gail Owens. Viking Pr. 1981, 126 pp.

Simon and Tony both had a crush on Cybil, but according to Tony, Cybil liked Tony better than she liked Simon. Simon was unhappily willing to accept Tony's word even though he knew Tony was a chronic liar. After all, Cybil had been the one to talk their teacher out of giving the lead in the class play about nutrition to Simon. Consequently Simon was being forced to impersonate a jar of peanut butter. In an elaborate attempt to win Cybil's affection Tony began telling Cybil lies about Simon and then set up a double date with Cybil and Harriet. On their walk home, Simon learned from Harriet that Cybil had only agreed to the date because Simon was going along. Happy at last, Simon realized he wanted no more lies and tricks; that he wanted to be truthful with Cybil and with himself. In the name of truth, he was even willing to accept the fact that his father, who had deserted the family, would not be returning.

A good story with just enough humor and romance to make it widely appealing as either a shared book (read aloud) or a personal pick. Print is fairly small.

Interest Level: 5-6. Reading Level: 4.2. Further Search Topics: Humorous Fiction, Love-Fiction, School Stories, Honesty-Fiction, Friendship-Fiction, Single Parent Family-Fiction, Read Aloud, Everyday Stories, Adolescence-Fiction.

Cleary, Beverly. Henry Huggins; illus by Louis Darling. Morrow 1950, 155 pp.

Henry Huggins is over 30 years old now, so if he occasionally seems a little old-fashioned, it is not surprising. What is surprising is how well he has withstood the years. His antics are innocent, but humorous and realistic. The book's six chapters are six separate stories that follow the same cast of characters through an entire year.

In the first chapter, Henry finds a stray dog (Ribsy) whom he must then transport home on a bus. Ribsy was too large and too frisky not to get into trouble, so before Henry finally gets him home, they have been kicked off of three buses and have ridden in a police car. The second chapter describes what happens when Henry buys two guppies and ends up with millions. In the third chapter Henry accidentally throws his friend's football into the back seat of a speeding car and tries to earn the money to replace it by catching and selling 1,331 night crawlers. The fourth chapter involves Henry's attempts to get out of playing the lead in a school Christmas play. His last minute rescue comes in the form of a can of green paint that spills all over him. It is Ribsy's turn to change colors in Chapter 5. Henry tries to cover Ribsy's dirt spots with talcolm powder for a dog show, but only succeeds in turning Ribsy pink. And in Chapter 6, Ribsy's original owner finally finds him and wants him back, but Ribsy chooses to stay with Henry. Only the occasional extra cute expression and Henry's age (third grade) keep this from being enjoyed beyond fourth grade.

Interest Level: 1-4. Reading Level: 2.2. Further Search Topics: Humorous Fiction, Everyday Stories, Read Aloud Pets-Fiction, Dogs-Fiction, Group 2.

Cleary, Beverly. Otis Spofford; illus by Louis Darling. Morrow 1953, 191 pp.

Here are six separate humorous adventures that link together, but can be read separately and out of order. Otis' favorite activity was "stirring up a little excitement," but his definition of excitement usually meant trouble. The school fiesta turned into a disaster when Otis decided to rechoreograph the bullfight and make the bull win. His attempt to liven up the reading lesson about Indians meant he almost scalped a classmate. However, a wild day at the skating pond finally gave everyone a chance to take revenge for all the things Otis had done to them. The remaining three chapters (2, 3 and 4) are slightly less exciting, but useful if a reader has enjoyed the others. There is much humor in Otis' antics and his tendency to act on every thought that comes to mind is one many readers can appreciate.

Interest Level: 2-6. Reading Level: 5.1. Further Search Topics: Troublemakers-Fiction, Group 2, Read Aloud, Everyday Stories, Humorous Fiction, School Stories.

Cleary, Beverly. Henry and Beezus; illus by Louis Darling. Morrow 1952, 192 pp.

When Henry's dog Ribsy stole the meat from a neighbor's barbecue, a friend rode after Ribsy on his bike and saved the meat. Henry was so embarrassed and jealous that he boasted about an even nicer bike that he was going to get. At first Henry thought he'd be able to earn money to buy a bike in a very short time (he found 49 boxes of bubble gum that he could sell). When that scheme fell through, Henry tried taking over a friend's paper route, but Ribsy kept retrieving the newspapers Henry delivered. Eventually Henry decided to buy a used bike at the police department auction. Beezus, who made a bid for Henry, ended up buying him a beaten-up girl's bike that was hardly worth fixing. The money finally appeared when Henry least expected it; he won $50.00 worth of work at a beauty salon.

Although all seven chapters continue the same story, Chapters 1, 2, 3 and 7, can each stand alone. Henry is definitely old-fashioned, but children still enjoy his humorous escapades and empathize with his desire for a bicycle. The revised paperback cover makes the book's physical appearance less dated. Reading level is somewhat inconsistent: from 2.2 to 3.2.

Interest Level: 2-5. Reading Level: 3.1. Further Search Topics: Humorous Fiction, Occupations-Fiction, Everyday Stories, Bicycles and Bicycling-Fiction, Read Aloud, Group 2.

Conford, Ellen. The luck of Pokey Bloom; illus by Bernice Loewenstein. Little 1975, 135 pp.

Pokey Bloom's passion was entering contests. She entered every contest she heard of and always thought she would win. Unfortunately, she never won anything. She even went so far as to practice concentrating three times each day on winning every contest she had entered. Someone who had been interviewed on the radio had *guaranteed* she would win that way. She didn't! It only made more trouble for her at school and at home. Pokey had enough trouble getting along with her older brother and didn't need any more problems at home.

There isn't much plot or direction to this story, but it does have some amusing moments. It is an extra book for the reader who enjoys Judy Blume-type books and wants another story about "regular kids."

Interest Level: 4-6. Reading Level: 3.1. Further Search Topics: Family-Fiction, Contests-Fiction, Brothers and Sisters-Fiction, Humorous Fiction, Everyday Stories.

Conford, Ellen. And this is Laura. Little 1977, 179 pp.

As a member of a family of high-achievers, Laura was convinced that she was unloved and worthless because she had no talents. Then, suddenly Laura discovered she had very special psychic powers; powers she began to exploit. At first it was fun to give readings after school each day. Gradually, however, as Laura foresaw her friend hurt and her brother missing, she realized that having ESP was also a frightening responsibility. Finally, her ESP became the vehicle that made it possible for Laura to tell her parents her true feelings and to understand that they loved her for herself, not for her achievements.

The author treats a common concern with sensitivity and humor. An especially good choice for Judy Blume lovers. Print somewhat small.

Interest Level: 4-6. Reading Level: 4.2. Further Search Topics: Occult-Fiction, Courage-Fiction, Extra Sensory Perception-Fiction, Family-Fiction, Humorous Fiction, Everyday Stories, Talent-Fiction.

Danziger, Paula. The cat ate my gymsuit. Delacorte 1974, 147 pp.

Another book for fans of Judy Blume. Marcy was shy and insecure, unhappy at school and unhappy at home. She was self-conscious about being heavy and sure she would never have a date. Only Ms. Finney (a new teacher), her English class and Smedley (a communications group) meant anything to Marcy. When Ms. Finney was fired because of her refusal to recite the pledge of allegiance and her unorthodox teaching methods, Marcy began to organize a protest movement. Marcy's commitment brought more problems at school and at home, but eventually resulted in Ms. Finney's vindication and Marcy's and her mother's growth and understanding.

Don't expect much depth of characterization. Most of the characters are flat and stereotypical, but the book will have great appeal in spite of its faults, for Marcy's insecurities are ones with which many young readers can identify.

Interest Level: 5-6. Reading Level: 5.1. Further Search Topics: School Stories, Everyday Stories, Family Problems-Fiction, Challenges-Fiction, Weight-Fiction, Courage-Fiction, Individualists-Fiction, Sex Role-Fiction.

Danziger, Paula. There's a bat in bunk five. Delacorte 1980, 150 pp.

Although this is a sequel to *The Cat Ate My Gymsuit*, it can be read alone. Marcy accepted an offer to become a junior counselor at an arts camp run by her ex-English teacher Ms. Finney and Ms. Finney's husband. After a nervous beginning, Marcy found herself enjoying the other counselors and the campers, but most of all, her first romance. Marcy's only difficulty was dealing with Ginger, a very troubled 10-year-old in Marcy's cabin. Marcy couldn't seem to get through to Ginger. When Ginger ran away, Marcy was forced to consider whether she should have spent more time with the campers and not quite so much time with Ted.

Marcy is a normal teenager whose problems, questions and activities are appealing to many teen and pre-teen readers. The characters who surround Marcy here are less stereotyped and flat than those in The Cat Ate My Gymsuit. Even Marcy's parents are more human. The author's light touch is just right for Marcy's story.

Interest Level: 5-6. Reading Level: 3.2. Further Search Topics: Humorous Fiction, Camp-Fiction, Everyday Stories, Love-Fiction, Vacation-Fiction, Occupations-Fiction, Adolescence-Fiction.

Danziger, Paula. The pistachio prescription. Delacorte 1978 154 pp.

Just as Cassie entered her freshman year in high school, the old stand-by that had helped her deal with all her problems (eating pistachio nuts) began to fail. To be sure, she did get through the class elections and was elected president. She met and started dating Bernie. She gained self-confidence. She even managed to stand up to a particularly mean teacher. But, eating pistachios didn't help at all at home where Cassie really needed them. She could hardly stand to be in the same room with her older sister. She hated the importance her mother placed on looking right and dressing well. Most of all, she hated the way her parents were constantly fighting. The only person with whom she was really confortable was her brother. But, before the year was over, Cassie's parents decided to get a divorce, she and her sister became friends and Cassie learned to accept her family.

Another Judy Blume-style author, but Danziger's portraits of adults tend to be even more one-dimensional and exaggerated than Blume's. Very popular anyway.

Interest Level: 6+. Reading Level: 5.1. Further Search Topics: Divorce and Separation-Fiction, Family Problems-Fiction, Beauty-Fiction, School Stories, Adolescence-Fiction, Love-Fiction, Brothers and Sisters-Fiction, Everyday Stories.

Greene, Constance C. Isabelle the itch; illus by Emily A. McCully. Viking Pr. 1973, 126 pp.

This is a loosely plotted story about a spunky, original fifth grade girl who could drive everyone around her crazy without ever tiring. Isabelle's dearest dream was to win the 50-yard dash at her school's field day. Even though she took over her brother's paper route to earn money for the Adidas track shoes she needed, Isabelle still didn't win. However, she did meet some new people, make new friends and keep those around her on their toes. A very amusing story told mostly in dialogue.

Interest Level: 4-6. Reading Level: 3.2. Further Search Topics: School Stories, Occupations-Fiction, Humorous Fiction, Everyday Stories, Running-Fiction, Individualists-Fiction, Sex Role-Fiction, Read Aloud.

Greene, Constance C. A girl called Al; illus by Byron Barton. Viking Pr. 1969, 127 pp.

Told in the first person, this is the story of two seventh grade girls. The girls' warm friendship began the moment Al introduced herself to the narrator as a non-conformist. Al was very independent, mostly because she was on her own so much of the time. Her parents were divorced and she seldom saw either one of them. Her father only wrote her postcards and her mother was rarely home. The narrator's family and Mr. Richards, their building superintendent, became Al's family. They cooked, ate, played, fought, talked and even made bookcases together. When Mr. Richards had a heart attack, they found help for him and later went to see him in the hospital. It was his death that helped Al and her mother grow closer, just as Mr. Richards' life had helped her understand why her father never came to see her.

A satisfying, low-key story of friendship and maturation. The girls are Judy Blume-style characters with much greater innocence. Their ages are not discernible by their actions or dialogue, only by the author's statement.

Interest Level: 3-6. Reading Level: 3.1. Further Search Topics: Children-Growth-Fiction, Single Parent Family-Fiction, Friendship-Fiction, Weight-Fiction, Aging-Fiction, Death-Fiction, Divorce and Separation-Fiction, Family Problems-Fiction, Everyday Stories, Humorous Fiction.

Greene, Constance C. I and Sproggy; illus by Emily A. McCully. Viking Pr. 1978, 155 pp.

Ten-year-old Adam had adjusted to his parents' divorce and had even grown to like living alone with his mother. When his father came back from London with his new wife and stepdaughter Sproggy and announced that they were moving into an apartment nearby, Adam was a little worried. But when his father asked him to take care of Sproggy, Adam was furious. First of all, he didn't know Sproggy and he didn't want to know her. Secondly, she was two months older than he, taller too, and she embarrassed him in public. And finally, she didn't need his help. She got along quite well by herself; so well that she even saved Adam from a mugger and became good friends with Adam's friends behind his back. It wasn't until Sproggy proved to be vulnerable that Adam and she became friends.

A warm, realistic and humorous story whose interesting characters (even the minor ones) heighten the book's appeal.

Interest Level: 4-6. Reading Level: 3.2. Further Search Topics: Brothers and Sisters-Fiction, Divorce and Separation-Fiction, City Life-Fiction, New York City-Fiction, Humorous Fiction, Friendship-Fiction, Everyday Stories.

Greenwald, Sheila. Give us a great big smile, Rosy Cole. Little 1981, 76 pp.

It was Rosy's turn to be the subject of her uncle's book. He needed to earn money again and Rosy had just turned 10, the age each of her sisters had been when Uncle Ralph wrote *Anitra Dances* and *Pippa Prances* about them. However, Rosy couldn't dance like Anitra or ride horses like Pippa. In fact, Rosy had no talent that was appropriate for a book. She drew well but Uncle Ralph said that wasn't visual enough. Then Rosy's mother and uncle decided that Rosy could be *A Very Little Fiddler*.

Rosy had been taking violin lessons for two years, but only Rosy and her music teacher knew how truly untalented she was. Rosy hated the whole idea of the book at first. But as people began to treat her like a star, she found herself acting like one, until the day she heard her tape of the piece she was to play at the recital. Once again she realized that she could not play the violin and didn't want to go on with the charade. When everyone ignored her wishes, Rosy started to run away. Her route took her through the park where she thought of a brilliant idea. She ran home, changed clothes, picked up her violin, created a sign, and raced back to the park. There, with all the other street musicians Rosy set up her sign and began to play her violin. Her sign asked people to sign a petition if they felt that she should not be encouraged to play the violin anymore. Right away Rosy drew a large crowd. Before long, even her mother was one of the listeners and one of the signers. That was the end of Rosy's musical career and her uncle's book, but both were happier. Rosy went back to being normal and Uncle Ralph found another topic for his next book.

Chapters are long, but should not be a problem. Print is large. Some of the story is actually told in the illustrations, so the reader should be aware of them. Younger children may take the book more seriously than children whose sense of humor includes irony or children who were not as fond of Krementz's *Very Young* series.

Interest Level: 4-6. Reading Level: 3.1. Further Search Topics: Occupations-Fiction, Humorous Fiction, Family-Fiction, Relatives-Fiction, Talent-Fiction, Photography-Fiction, Everyday Stories.

Harris, Robie H. Rosie's double dare; illus by Tony DeLuna. Knopf 1980, 112 pp.

Rosie wanted to play baseball with the Willard Street Gang, but she couldn't play well enough to play by their rules. She needed what her older brother called "shrimp rules." She couldn't hit a pitched ball, only a grounder; but grounders were "shrimp rules." In desperation Rosie agreed to take a dare that the gang made up. If she actually performed the dare, the gang would let her play with them by her rules.

The gang dared Rosie to sneak into cranky Mr. Quirk's apartment and borrow a set of his false teeth. Because Rosie couldn't find any extra false teeth, she borrowed his wig instead but that didn't satisfy the gang. They only laughed and made up another dare for Rosie. She was to untie Mrs. Samuels' dog and let it run loose. As Rosie untied him, Elmer ran away, Rosie ran off after him. One rainstorm later, Rosie caught up with him in the middle of a Red Sox game at Fenway Park. Rosie's attempt to catch Elmer stopped the game, brought her an interview on TV, and secured her a place on the Willard Street baseball team.

This very light story, made up almost entirely of action and examples of sibling rivalry, should have wide appeal through fifth grade. Beyond that, Rosie's age (almost nine) and childish behavior won't ring true. Capers series.

Interest Level: 2-5. Reading Level: 2.2. Further Search Topics: Baseball-Fiction, Humorous Fiction, Brothers and Sisters-Fiction, Challenges-Fiction, Courage-Fiction, Gangs-Fiction, Everyday Stories.

Hurwitz, Johanna. Aldo Ice Cream; illus by John Wallner. Morrow 1981, 124 pp.

Aldo got his newest nickname (Ice Cream) from his friend DeDe when she heard that Aldo not only wanted to try every flavor of ice cream at the local store, but wanted to buy an ice cream freezer for his sister's birthday as well. Aldo decided his summer project would be to earn enough money for the freezer, but he soon found out that there were very few ways a nine-year-old boy could earn $49.95. In the meantime, he helped his mother deliver food for a Meals-On-Wheels project, learned to swim, found out about fish from Mr. Puccini, and shared his cat with Mrs. Nardo. As the summer came to an end he saw one last opportunity to earn enough money for the ice cream maker. A local shoe store offered a new pair of sneakers to the child who owned the most worn out pair. Aldo convinced his mother that if he won the sneakers, she should pay him the money she would otherwise have had to spend on his new sneakers. Aldo set about making sure that his already well-worn sneakers were the most dilapidated in town. A few days before the sneaker contest the hardware store lowered the price on the ice cream freezer to a point where Aldo could afford it if he won the sneakers. When Aldo did win, just as he knew he would, he and his mother bought the very last freezer in the store.

It is not as well-constructed a story as *Aldo Applesauce*, but for established Aldo fans, or those who want quiet, reassuring fiction, this is a usable title.

Interest Level: 3-4. Reading Level: 3.1. Further Search Topics: Humorous Fiction, Brothers and Sisters-Fiction, Vacation-Fiction, Occupations-Fiction, Everyday Stories, Aging-Fiction, Family-Fiction, Contests-Fiction.

Hurwitz, Johanna. Aldo Applesauce; illus by John Wallner. Morrow 1979, 127 pp.

Aldo Sossi, vegetarian and new kid at school, was immediately dubbed Applesauce for obvious reasons. Aldo didn't like his new name. He didn't like being teased either—not the way he was teased at school. Nothing went right for Aldo. His attempts at making friends only ended in disasters (once at a bowling alley and another time at a birthday party). He had been able to start a friendship only with a strange girl who wore a heavy, black fake moustache most of the time. After accidentally nearly ruining that friendship too, Aldo not only learned why DeDe wore the moustache, but helped her learn to live without it. DeDe, in turn, helped Aldo take himself less seriously and find more friends.

This is a comfortable, humorous story of two fourth grade children learning to be themselves. The vocabulary is occasionally difficult, but sentence length is almost always short.

Interest Level: 3-5. Reading Level: 3.1. Further Search Topics: Moving, Household-Fiction, Humorous Fiction, School Stories, Friendship-Fiction, Divorce and Separation-Fiction, Vegetarians-Fiction, Individualists-Fiction, Everyday Stories.

Hurwitz, Johanna. The law of gravity; illus by Ingrid Fetz. Morrow 1978, 192 pp.

The summer between fifth and sixth grades looked very unexciting to Margot. Her best friends were both going away for the whole summer and her father, a musician, was going to be on tour for most of the summer. Margot's very overweight mother had sworn never to go downstairs from their fifth floor walk-up apartment. Unless Margot chose to stay upstairs too, she was sure she would have a very lonely vacation. In addition, she had to work on a summer project for school. The project she finally chose was to get her mother downstairs after nine years of staying upstairs. In search of help she went to the local library where she met Bernie. Bernie was only a year older than Margot, but he seemed to know the most interesting things about the city. He showed her places Margot had never heard of before, he taught her to play chess, backgammon, and even to ride a bicycle. He was so full of fascinating ideas and information that Margot had no chance to be bored or lonely. Best of all, he even tried to help Margot with her project. None of their ideas worked, however, until Margot pretended to run away and scared her mother into going downstairs. Only then did Margot realize that she loved her mother whether or not she stayed on the fifth floor and that she couldn't simply force her mother or anyone else to change to suit her own fancy.

The book is a warm, understanding, slightly humorous treatment of the fairly common wish to change someone else. Although not many readers are likely to share Margot's exact problem, most will recognize her feelings. The book is also a virtual Chamber of Commerce advertisement for urban living. One of its other charms is its picture of a non-competitive, open, real friendship between an 11-year-old girl and a 12-year-old boy. The only drawback to the book is its inconsistent reading level which varies from 4.1 to 5.1 with a rare leap to 5.2.

Interest Level: 4-6. Reading Level: 4.2. Further Search Topics: Vacation-Fiction, Friendship-Fiction, Loners-Fiction, City Life-Fiction, Individualists-Fiction, Courage-Fiction, New York City-Fiction, Humorous Fiction, Family-Fiction, Challenges-Fiction, Weight-Fiction, Everyday Stories, Best Sellers.

Kibbe, Pat. The hocus-pocus dilemma; illus by Dan Jones. Knopf 1979, 125 pp.

Each chapter of this book is a separate episode in B.J.'s attempt to cultivate her newly-discovered ESP talents (more invented than discovered). The episodes, each of which involves a different member of B.J.'s family, are slightly outlandish, but very funny. Even the dog and the cat become involved. The dog becomes the unwitting target for a skunk. The cat accidentally starts a tape recording of speech habits that sounds like burglars breaking into the house.

After nine disasters, B.J. finally concludes that she was being ridiculous to think that she had ESP, but that everyone is allowed to be ridiculous sometimes.

The nine, reasonably short episodes, the moderate size print, the sympathetic characters, and the book's humor, make this a very useful and popular title.

Interest Level: 4-6. Reading Level: 3.1. Further Search Topics: Extra Sensory Perception-Fiction, Humorous Fiction, Family-Fiction, Everyday Stories, Best Sellers, Read Aloud.

Levy, Elizabeth. Lizzie lies a lot; illus by John Wallner. Delacorte 1976, 102 pp.

Almost any child can identify with Lizzie. She had found that it was sometimes easier to lie than to tell the truth. Her problem was that she had lost control. It seemed as if almost everything she said was a lie. She told so many lies it became difficult to keep track of them all. Lizzie wasn't even really sure why she lied so much. She knew that she sometimes lied because she thought people would be more apt to like her. Other times she lied to get herself out of trouble or to cover up her feelings when she was hurt or angry. But that didn't explain why she lied all the time. Maybe, as her grandmother said, she was a born liar.

It wasn't until Lizzie got herself caught in the middle of so many lies that she lost her only friend, that she could admit her problem to herself and to her family. After their initial shock had passed, everyone agreed to help Lizzie stop lying. Lizzie took the next step by admitting her lies to her friend Sue.

Levy has brought such an appropriately light touch to a fairly common problem that many children find this story enjoyable. Overlook the book's faults (Lizzie's grandmother is overdrawn and her mother's guilt feelings are unsupported by the story) for the fun and the message young readers get from it.

Interest Level: 3-5. Reading Level: 4.2. Further Search Topics: Honesty-Fiction, Group 2, Friendship-Fiction, Best Sellers, Everyday Stories, Family Problems-Fiction, Grandparents-Fiction, Humorous Fiction.

Lowry, Lois. Anastasia Krupnik. HM 1979, 113 pp.

Anastasia Krupnik led a comfortable, relatively happy life until her parents announced that she was not going to be an only child for much longer. After 10 years of enjoying that luxury, Anastasia wasn't at all pleased with the change. Babies immediately went to a prominent, and as far as Anastasia was concerned, permanent place on her list of hates. Anastasia kept two lists: one for things and people she particularly liked, and one list for what she did not like. What went on and off the lists tells much about Anastasia. Anastasia tells the rest in this perceptive, sensitive, and humorous story of growing up and adjusting to a new sibling.

Spacing between lines is slightly too narrow for the rather large print.

Interest Level: 4-6. Reading Level: 3.1. Further Search Topics: Humorous Fiction, Brothers and Sisters-Fiction, Everyday Stories, Jealousy-Fiction, Infants-Fiction, Best Sellers, Children-Growth-Fiction.

Lowry, Lois. Anastasia again! HM 1981, 145 pp.

This is a sequel that is as funny and well-written as its predecessor. Because its plot involves less common experiences, this book may not enjoy quite the wide-spread success of *Anastasia Krupnik*. However, among those readers who liked their first meeting with Anastasia, this book will find many fans.

Anastasia's parents astounded her when they announced that the family was going to move from their Cambridge, Massachusetts apartment to a house in the suburbs. She didn't like the idea of leaving the apartment, but she *hated* the idea of the suburbs. The only thing that made the move bearable was the house itself. Anastasia had said she would move only if they could find a house with a tower—and they had. After she got over the shock of moving, Anastasia began to enjoy her new home. She met a neighborhood boy who became a special friend, she tried to help her cranky elderly neighbor Mrs. Stein make friends, and she even wrote a short mystery book.

Anastasia is as spunky and original as before. She is a bit precocious, but her precocity is nothing compared to that of her brother. At two-and-a-half years old, he speaks as well as many adults. As we mentioned above, the book will be most appealing to readers who want second helpings of Anastasia's adventures. The print is slightly smaller here than in the first title.

Interest Level: 4-6. Reading Level: 2.2. Further Search Topics: Moving, Household-Fiction, City Life-Fiction, Suburbia-Fiction, Humorous Fiction, Aging-Fiction, Writing-Fiction, Family-Fiction, Everyday Stories.

Miles, Betty. The secret life of the underwear champ; illus by Dan Jones. Knopf 1981, 117 pp.

Larry hadn't planned it; in fact, he hadn't even really wanted it to happen. But suddenly he found himself about to make a television commercial for ChampWin Knitting Mills, makers of sports clothing and underwear. He knew his family could use the money he would make, but he certainly didn't want the whole school seeing him in his underwear. Nevertheless, Larry went ahead and made the commercial, hoping that it would never be used. He even had to skip baseball practice to make the taping. Much to his horror, the commercial appeared the night before the team's first game. Not only did the entire opposing team tease him, but so did all his own teammates. By the time he got up to bat, Larry was mad enough to slam the ball out of the park. He didn't hit the ball quite that hard, but he did make a winning home run and end the others' giggles forever. He became the true underwear champ.

This is a funny look at the embarrassments of growing up. It also deals lightly with a boy's pride, his peer relationship, and his growing awareness of girls. An appealing and broadly usable title. Capers series.

Interest Level: 3-5. Reading Level: 2.2. Further Search Topics: Baseball-Fiction, Television-Fiction, Occupations-Fiction, School Stories, Humorous Fiction, Advertising-Fiction, Beauty-Fiction, Motion Pictures-Fiction, Best Sellers, Everyday Stories.

Park, Barbara. Don't make me smile. Knopf 1981, 114 pp.

As far as Charlie Hickle was concerned his parents' divorce was the worst thing in the world. His parents had ruined his life and he hadn't done anything to deserve such a fate. At first he didn't say very much. Then he ran away to live in a tree. Finally he cried a lot. That was all just in the first week after his parents announced their decision. After that, both his grades at school and his behavior began to deteriorate. It wasn't until Charlie had had several talks with a helpful children's psychologist and made a disastrous attempt to reunite his parents on his birthday, that he began to realize that he didn't like the divorce, but he could live with it.

The author's use of amusing anecdotes, Charlie's very strong feelings, and the frequency of divorce make this book very popular. Its major drawbacks are its superficiality and the overdrawn portrait of Charlie's mother. The book's faults will not deter many young readers from enjoying it, however.

Interest Level: 4-6. Reading Level: 3.1. Further Search Topics: Divorce and Separation-Fiction, Family Problems-Fiction, Psychiatrists-Fiction, Everyday Stories.

Pfeffer, Susan Beth. Just between us; illus by Lorna Tomei. Delacorte 1980, 116 pp.

Cass's inability to keep secrets finally became such a problem that Cass asked her mother to help her learn how to keep them. Cass's mother, a psychology student, devised a behavior modification experiment. Every day that Cass was able to figure out which bit of information she had been told was a secret and keep it, she received a dollar. After a poor start Cass did well for a while, until the day she told three secrets and made her entire family angry at her.

More determined than ever, Cass tried again. This time she found herself caught between two friends. Only Cass knew that Robin was adopted and Robin wanted it kept a secret. Jenny was so mad at Robin that she decided to spread an untrue story to hurt Robin. She told Cass not to tell anyone what she was going to do. The story Jenny was going to spread was that Robin was adopted. After hours of mental anguish Cass finally devised a way to stop Jenny and help Jenny return to being the nice person she had been before her parents' divorce.

The reading level of this book varies greatly from second grade to mid-fourth grade. Otherwise, it is good fare for Judy Blume fans. Print size just a slight bit on the small side.

Interest Level: 4-6. Reading Level: 3.2. Further Search Topics: Humorous Fiction, Everyday Stories, Friendship-Fiction, School Stories, Divorce and Separation-Fiction, Psychiatrists-Fiction, Secrets-Fiction.

Pfeffer, Susan Beth. Kid power; illus by Leigh Grant. Watts 1977, 121 pp.

When Janie's mother lost her job, her father's salary wouldn't stretch to provide any more money for the new bicycle fund. There was enough money already set aside to pay for one new bike, but both Janie and her older sister Carol wanted a bicycle. Carol, who had saved money of her own, suggested that they each pay for half a bike and their parents contribute the money for the other half. Then Janie's only problem was how to earn money, since she had none saved. Her solution was to create a business: Kid Power. Before long, Janie's business had blossomed and she was becoming rich, but she had lost her best friend and was ruining a client's roses. When Janie finally realized that getting rich wasn't the only thing that mattered in life, she relaxed, delegated jobs to friends better able to handle them, and became their agent.

A genuinely funny book that, as a bonus, takes a realistic look at the interworkings of a family. Consistent reading level.

Interest Level: 4-6. Reading Level: 3.1. Further Search Topics: Occupations-Fiction, Everyday Stories, Vacation-Fiction, Family-Fiction, Humorous Fiction, Best Sellers, Bicycles and Bicycling-Fiction, Friendship-Fiction.

Robinson, Nancy K. Wendy and the bullies; illus by Ingrid Fetz. Hastings 1980, 128 pp.

Wendy and her best friend Karen had a very carefully mapped out route to and from school—a route that allowed them to meet up with the fewest number of bullies possible. But when Karen became sick enough to stay home from school, Wendy had to face the bullies alone. Wendy's fears escalated to panic so intense that she avoided walking to school by hiding in her basement. She finally realized that she was letting fear and anger control her life when she found herself bullying Karen. Only her new friendship with Monica, making up with Karen, and her involvement in a school project helped Wendy overcome her fears.

This is a humorous, episodic tale of a feeling and circumstances common to many children. The illustrations sometimes make Wendy and her classmates appear much younger than her actual nine years, but fortunately that doesn't happen often enough to spoil the book's appeal.

Interest Level: 3-5. Reading Level: 3.1. Further Search Topics: School Stories, Bullies-Fiction, Courage-Fiction, Best Sellers, Humorous Fiction, Friendship-Fiction, Everyday Stories.

Sharmat, Marjorie W. Getting something on Maggie Marmelstein; illus by Ben Shecter. Har-Row 1971, 101 pp.

A curious love-hate relationship existed between Thad and Maggie. It all began when Maggie overheard Thad say she squeaked like a mouse. Then Maggie caught Thad wearing an apron and cooking. Thad was so uncomfortable with the thought that Maggie might tell his friends, that he was determined to find out Maggie's deepest secret. That meant that Thad had to take a lead role as a frog opposite Maggie as the princess in the school play. While at Maggie's apartment for a costume fitting, Thad found a love letter Maggie had written to Cary Grant. Thad decided he would read the letter to the class right after the play was over. But during the play Maggie saved Thad from what could have been one of the most embarrassing moments of his life. By the time he finally had the chance to make Maggie appear foolish, Thad had changed his mind.

Written as Thad's story, the book is funny, warm, and realistic. A good, short, story that continues to be popular. Print is of moderate size.

Interest Level: 3-6. Reading Level: 3.1. Further Search Topics: Humorous Fiction, Everyday Stories, School Stories, Best Sellers, Friendship-Fiction, Sex Role-Fiction, Acting-Fiction.

Shura, Mary Francis. The Barkley Street six-pack; illus by Gene Sparkman. Dodd 1979, 159 pp.

Jane's best friend Natalie was everything Jane wanted to be. She was self-assured, pretty, vibrant, and even possessed magical talents. Jane didn't realize at first, and she later resisted seeing, that Natalie ran Jane's life and cleverly made sure that Jane had no other friends. Natalie's move left Jane with no friends among those people she had once enjoyed. Little by little, with the help of a stray dog and the new boy on the block, Jane bagan to see how destructive Natalie had been. She finally realized that a true friendship is one in which neither party tries to control the other.

With its enticements of ESP, magic, stray dogs, and problems with peers, this is a very appealing book to many young readers. As a bonus it is a thoughtful, sympathetic, fairly well-written story.

Interest Level: 4-6. Reading Level: 4.2. Further Search Topics: Gangs-Fiction, Pets-Fiction, Dogs-Fiction, Friendship-Fiction, Honesty-Fiction, Courage-Fiction, Loneliness-Fiction, Extra Sensory Perception-Fiction, Everyday Stories.

EVOLUTION

Hornblow, Leonora. Prehistoric monsters did the strangest things; illus by Michael K. Frith. Random 1974, 65 pp.

A basic survey of an era and its animal life forms. Animals from the earliest water creatures through Diplocaulus, Ichthyosaurs, dinosaurs (about 12 varieties) and early mammals (including the Beast of Baluchistan) to the appearance of man are introduced and illustrated. It is a brief but meaty treatment of a very popular subject that should be especially useful with second and third grade children. Reader format.

Interest Level: 1-3. Reading Level: 2.1. Further Search Topics: Prehistory, Dinosaurs, Evolution, Monsters, Group 2.

EXPERIMENTS, SCIENTIFIC

Branley, Franklyn M. Roots are food finders; illus by Joseph Low. Har-Row 1975, 33 pp.

It really is a shame that the picture book format of this and other *Let's-Read-and-Find-Out-Science-Books* will prevent older children from using them. There is much good information here that is thoroughly and logically explained without patronizing the reader. Functions and types of roots are described. Experiments to show root growth, root hairs, and absorption are given. A very useful book through third grade and possibly fourth grade. Beyond fourth grade children will certainly balk at the book's "babyish" appearance. Let's-Read-and-Find-Out-Science-Book series.

Interest Level: 1-4. Reading Level: 2.2. Further Search Topics: Nature Study, Botany, Group 2, Experiments, Scientific.

Branley, Franklyn M. High sounds, low sounds; illus by Paul Galdone. Har-Row 1967, 35 pp.

A no-nonsense, informative, thorough introduction to sound, sound waves, and hearing. Includes a couple of simple, illustrative experiments. Useful through third and fourth grade with no problems. The picture book format and opening and closing questions to the reader may turn away fifth and sixth grade users. Worth trying anyway. No index or table of contents. Let's-Read-and-Find-Out-Science-Book series.

Interest Level: 2-4. Reading Level: 2.2. Further Search Topics: Sound, Experiments, Scientific.

White, Laurence B., Jr. Science puzzles; illus by Marc Tolon Brown. A-W 1975, unp (46 pp).

There are twenty four very short experiments designed to illustrate the simplest of scientific principles clearly presented here. For all but a few experiments there is not only an explanation of what happens but also an explanation of why it happened. What makes the book even more useful, is that it can also be used as a book of easy magic tricks. Any child who enjoys it as science will, with a little help, be able to see its possibilities as magic. In fact it provides a better explanation of the Knot Magic trick than can be found in *It's Magic*.

Interest Level: 1-3. Reading Level: 1.2. Further Search Topics: Science, Magic, Puzzles, Experiments, Scientific.

EXPLORERS-FICTION

Bulla, Clyde Robert. Viking adventure; illus by Douglas Gorsline. T Y Crowell 1963, 117 pp.

An exciting story of a young Norwegian boy named Sigurd. Sigurd realized his dream when he finally set sail on a Viking ship in search of Wineland (Vinland). Leif Eriksson had told of his North American findings over 100 years earlier. Sigurd and his father's friend Grom, the captain of the ship, were sure they could find that land again. Their determination finally brought Grom's death at the hands of the ship's owner, Sigurd's near death, and the destruction of the ship.

This book, too, is true to Bulla's style of short chapters, short sentences, much action and high appeal. Although it is a little higher reading level than many of Bulla's others, it is still a good choice. Recently out of print, but worth a search.

Interest Level: 2-6. Reading Level: 3.1. Further Search Topics: Norway-Fiction, Historical Fiction, Seafaring Life-Fiction, Voyages and Travels-Fiction, Shipwrecks-Fiction, Explorers-Fiction, Vikings-Fiction, Courage-Fiction, Best Sellers, Group 2.

EXTRA SENSORY PERCEPTION-FICTION

Conford, Ellen. And this is Laura. Little 1977, 179 pp.

As a member of a family of high-achievers, Laura was convinced that she was unloved and worthless because she had no talents. Then, suddenly Laura discovered she had very special psychic powers; powers she began to exploit. At first it was fun to give readings after school each day. Gradually, however, as Laura foresaw her friend hurt and her brother missing, she realized that having ESP was also a frightening responsibility. Finally, her ESP became the vehicle that made it possible for Laura to tell her parents her true feelings and to understand that they loved her for herself, not for her achievements.

The author treats a common concern with sensitivity and humor. An especially good choice for Judy Blume lovers. Print somewhat small.

Interest Level: 4-6. Reading Level: 4.2. Further Search Topics: Occult-Fiction, Courage-Fiction, Extra Sensory Perception-Fiction, Family-Fiction, Humorous Fiction, Everyday Stories, Talent-Fiction.

Kibbe, Pat. The hocus-pocus dilemma; illus by Dan Jones. Knopf 1979, 125 pp.

Each chapter of this book is a separate episode in B.J.'s attempt to cultivate her newly-discovered ESP talents (more invented than discovered). The episodes, each of which involves a different member of B.J.'s family, are slightly outlandish, but very funny. Even the dog and the cat become involved. The dog becomes the unwitting target for a skunk. The cat accidentally starts a tape recording of speech habits that sounds like burglars breaking into the house. After nine disasters, B.J. finally concludes that she was being ridiculous to think that she had ESP, but that everyone is allowed to be ridiculous sometimes.

The nine, reasonably short episodes, the moderate size print, the sympathetic characters, and the book's humor, make this a very useful and popular title.

Interest Level: 4-6. Reading Level: 3.1. Further Search Topics: Extra Sensory Perception-Fiction, Humorous Fiction, Family-Fiction, Everyday Stories, Best Sellers, Read Aloud.

St. John, Wylly Folk. The ghost next door; illus by Trina Schart Hyman. Har-Row 1971, 178 pp.

Told by 13-year-old Lindsay, this is the story of her neighbor Miss Judith and Miss Judith's two nieces. Her niece Miranda had drowned years earlier in Miss Judith's backyard fish pond and Miss Judith had never fully recovered from her death. As the story begins, Miss Judith is about to welcome another niece (Sherry) for a summer stay. Sherry, without ever being told about Miranda, seems to sense Miranda's presence all around. Her mother laughs and says that Sherry has an imaginary friend. Miss Judith, who is a strong believer in ESP, thinks that Sherry is communicating with Miranda. As the days go on Sherry learns more and more of Miranda' secrets. When Miss Judith is scared by Sherry, Lindsay and her friend, Tammy, decide to see what sort of tricks Sherry is playing.

A believable suspense story, made even more so by the illustrations.

Interest Level: 4-6. Reading Level: 5.1. Further Search Topics: Mystery and Detective Stories, Relatives-Fiction, Group 2, Extra Sensory Perception-Fiction, Best Sellers, Ghosts-Fiction.

Shura, Mary Francis. The Barkley Street six-pack: illus by Gene Sparkman. Dodd 1979, 159 pp.

Jane's best friend Natalie was everything Jane wanted to be. She was self-assured, pretty, vibrant, and even possessed magical talents. Jane didn't realize at first, and she later resisted seeing, that Natalie ran Jane's life and cleverly made sure that Jane had no other friends. Natalie's move left Jane with no friends among those people she had once enjoyed. Little by little, with the help of a stray dog and the new boy on the block, Jane bagan to see how destructive Natalie had been. She finally realized that a true friendship is one in which neither party tries to control the other.

With its enticements of ESP, magic, stray dogs, and problems with peers, this is a very appealing book to many young readers. As a bonus it is a thoughtful, sympathetic, fairly well-written story.

Interest Level: 4-6. Reading Level: 4.2. Further Search Topics: Gangs-Fiction, Pets-Fiction, Dogs-Fiction, Friendship-Fiction, Honesty-Fiction, Courage-Fiction, Loneliness-Fiction, Extra Sensory Perception-Fiction, Everyday Stories.

Sleator, William. Into the dream; illus by Ruth Sanderson. Dutton 1979, 137 pp.

Paul and Francine each started having what, at first, seemed like nightmares. As the dreams became more detailed and forboding, they discovered that they were sharing the same nightmare. They dreamed of a four-year-old boy, swirling lights, and a large dog. After awhile they figured out that the dog was trying to save the little boy from some unknown danger. As the pieces of the puzzle began to increase in number, Paul and Francine decided that the dream was in some way connected to a night over four years earlier when they had both been staying at the same motel. They, a pregnant woman, and a pregnant dog had all been affected by the telepathic power given off by a spaceship. The progeny of the woman and the dog had been given extraordinary mental powers; powers that a secret government agency wanted to mold and then put to their own use. The danger Paul and Francine felt came from two government agents sent to take the young boy Noah from his mother. Their attempt ended in a bizarre scene at an amusement park, where Noah levitated a broken ferris wheel chair to safety. By thus exposing his talent in public, Noah unconsciously insured against its secret and unsupervised use by the government.

A terrifying and suspense-filled psychological thriller whose main problems are a slightly overdrawn ending and a variable reading level. Reading level drops as low as 2.1 and climbs occasionally to 4.1.

Interest Level: 5-6. Reading Level: 3.2. Further Search Topics: Best Sellers, Supernatural-Fiction, Occult-Fiction, Flying Saucers-Fiction, Nonverbal Communication-Fiction, Dreams-Fiction, Survival-Fiction, Extra Sensory Perception-Fiction, Horror-Fiction.

FABLES

Aesop. Aesop's Fables; retold by Ann Terry White; illus by Helen Siegl. Random 1964, 77 pp.

An attractive, appealing-looking collection of forty of Aesop's fables. Children without a background in folklore are not likely to read these short tales without encouragement. Where there is such encouragement, or a curricular need, this is an excellent source. The use of many proper nouns in the text means the book tests artificially low at 2.2. It is probably more appropriate to consider it 3.1.

Interest Level: 2-6. Reading Level: 3.1. Further Search Topics: Fables, Folklore, Group 2.

FAIRIES-FICTION

Thomas, Kathleen. Out of the bug jar; illus by Tom O'Sullivan. Dodd 1981, 125 pp.

Even though 10-year-old Tom Jenkins didn't believe in the tooth fairy, when one of his teeth fell out, he placed it under his pillow just in case he was wrong. In the middle of that night he was awakened by a small creature crawling under his pillow and grumbling. Tom quickly scooped him into a bug jar he kept nearby and thus began two years of life with Marvin, a tooth fairy. Marvin was a delightful dictator; he ruled Tom's life. He put Tom into a terrible predicament when Tom tried to charge others to see him and Marvin became invisible. Marvin insisted on being fed just what he demanded, despite the difficulties he made for Tom. He badgered Tom to do his homework, to brush his teeth, and to tell the truth. He even managed to follow Tom to school. The only other person Marvin would allow to see or hear him was Tom's friend Sammy. Tom couldn't get rid of Marvin either. Because Tom had captured him, Marvin, should he ever have been able to escape, was entitled to take *all* of Tom's teeth as compensation for being held prisoner.

Actually Marvin didn't really want to escape. He had grown tired of having to race around and collect teeth. For a while then, everyone was fairly content. Tom had all his teeth and Marvin had a rather nice home. Then quite by accident, Marvin got loose. Both Tom and Marvin wanted Tom to catch Marvin again. Tom wanted to keep his teeth and Marvin wanted to keep his comfortable lifestyle, but Marvin played by the rules and wouldn't give Tom any help at all. After more than seven days of valient but fruitless efforts and nights of sleeping with tape over his mouth, Tom finally caught Marvin and all were happy again.

An amusing story told in short sentences and short chapters. The book should be popular with those who enjoy either fantasy or humor.

Interest Level: 3-5. Reading Level: 2.2. Further Search Topics: Fantasy, Fairies-Fiction, Humorous Fiction, Teeth-Fiction.

FAIRY TALES

Dolch, Edward W. Andersen stories; illus by Carmen Mowry. Garrard 1956, 165 pp.

The best way to be introduced to Andersen's fairy tales is to hear them told or read aloud. Because they are beautifully written literary tales they suffer tremendously when the language is simplified enough so that the stories can be included in a reader. Furthermore, episodes have been cut out of some

tales ("Big Klaus and Little Klaus") and others have been divided into chapters ("The Ugly Duckling"). But, where there is a need for such an easy version of Hans Christian Andersen, this selection will do. The 18 chapters tell only 11 stories. Most of the included stories are familiar ("The Emperor's New Clothes," "The Little Mermaid," "Thumbelina" etc.); all are enjoyable. Illustrations, however, are unattractive and uninspiring. One further caution: the reading level jumps from 2.1 to 3.2. Dolch Pleasure Reading Book series.

Interest Level: 2-5. Reading Level: 3.1. Further Search Topics: Folklore, Fantasy, Group 2, Fairy Tales, Andersen, Hans Christian.

Dolch, Edward W. Fairy stories; illus by Marguerite Dolch and Yolande Cuypers-Fransen. Garrard 1950, 165 pp.

A collection of mostly familiar fairy tales told in the Dolchs' very simplified manner. Because the book's purpose is not to provide the most literate version of favorite fairy tales, better versions of any of the stories can be found elsewhere. It provides instead, very accessible versions of tales young readers have enjoyed for years. Includes "Cinderella," "Hansel and Gretel," "Jack and the Bean Stalk," "Snow White," "Sleeping Beauty," and "The Elves and the Shoemaker," among others. Dolch Pleasure Reading Book series.

Interest Level: 1-4. Reading Level: 2.2. Further Search Topics: Folklore, Fairy Tales, Fantasy, Group 2.

FAMILY-FICTION

Allen, Linda. Lionel and the spy next door; illus by Margot Apple. Morrow 1980, 94 pp.

No one in Lionel's family understood why he wanted to be a spy; but then, he couldn't understand why they were anthropologists and motorcycle freaks. Even though he wasn't supposed to do any more spying (especially while his parents were away) Lionel couldn't resist watching the man who moved into Miss Bannister's house, next-door. Mark Shakespeare was his name. His name was suspicious enough, but his actions firmly convinced Lionel that Mark was a spy. Lionel's attempts to trail Shakespeare only succeeded in angering others in the neighborhood. He interrupted a bird watcher and irritated a woman walking a large dog. She was already angry with Lionel's grandfather for disturbing the quiet neighborhood with his motorcycles. The closer Lionel got to finding proof that Mark was a spy, the friendlier Mark became. Mark even gave Lionel the old clock which Lionel and Miss Bannister had carefully wound each week until the old woman's death. When Lionel's grandfather finally convinced Lionel that Mark should be left alone, Mark enlisted Lionel's help in a project that left Lionel wondering again. Much to Lionel's surprise, he learned that the papers and secret documents he and Mark had burned had all belonged to Miss Bannister, Mark's great-aunt. Forty years earlier she, not Mark, had been a spy. Lionel had been wrong about who it was, but right about a spy living next-door.

Here we find a slightly anti-climactic ending to an otherwise enjoyable book. A grandfather who rides with motorcycle gangs and the intrigue of spying should be of interest to many readers. Readers may need a little help with the few British phrases that dot the book, but otherwise, the book has an impressively consistent reading level.

Interest Level: 4-6. Reading Level: 3.1. Further Search Topics: Spies-Fiction, Family-Fiction, Mystery and Detective Stories, Individualists-Fiction, Motorcycles-Fiction, Occupations-Fiction.

Angell, Judie. Dear Lola; or how to build your own family. Bradbury 1980, 166 pp.

Arthur (age 18), James (13), Annie and Al-Willie (twins, age 10), Edmund (9), and Ben (5) wanted to run away from the orphanage and find a place where they could be a real family. After waiting months, their chance arrived one night. They escaped in a van and began living on the road. It was weeks before they found a house in which they thought they could live. They didn't want trouble with local authorities, so most of the children enrolled in school and pretended to be living with their widowed grandfather. Only James (who never left his room) and Arthur stayed home. Arthur was the anonymous author of a nationally syndicated newspaper advice column. It was with the income from his "Dear Lola" column that Arthur was able to support the "family." When the townspeople eventually began to wonder about the "strange" behavior of the children, they investigated and found no adult in charge of the household. Arthur went to court to be appointed the childrens' guardian, but the judge ruled against him. Rather than be sent to foster homes again, Arthur and the children raced from the courtroom. The book ends as the family is once more together and on their own. An unusual cast of characters in a surprisingly warm and humorous book.

Interest Level: 4-6. Reading Level 3.1. Further Search Topics: Loners-Fiction, Runaways-Fiction, Orphans-Fiction, Survival-Fiction, Family Problems-Fiction, Family-Fiction, Read Aloud, Foster Homes-Fiction, Individualists-Fiction, Humorous Fiction.

Blume, Judy. Are you there God? It's me, Margaret. Bradbury 1970, 149 pp.

Sixth grade was a year of growth for Margaret and her friends. They all wondered when they would start growing breasts and when they would begin menstruating. Each was kissed for the first time. It was also a year in which Margaret tried to decide whether to be Jewish or Christian and ended up neither. She simply remained friends with God, just as she was when the year began. The book is a reassuring, very open, and humorous treatment of the pains and promise of maturation. It is exceptionally popular with older elementary school readers, so the book's slightly small print and narrow lines should not impede an interested reader's progress.

Interest Level: 4-6. Reading Level: 3.2. Further Search Topics: School Stories, Family-Fiction, Children-Growth-Fiction, Religion-Fiction, Humorous Fiction, Love-Fiction, Best Sellers, Grandparents-Fiction, Everyday Stories.

Blume, Judy. Tales of a fourth grade nothing; illus by Roy Doty. Dutton 1972, 120 pp.

Another humorous Blume book that can be counted on to appeal to third and fourth grade readers. If fifth and sixth graders can ignore the title's reference to fourth grade, they too will love it. The story is an exaggeration of a common theme—an older child whose life is in continual turmoil because of a somewhat spoiled younger sibling. Peter's problems with three-year-old Fudge become worse with each chapter until the final disaster when Fudge swallows Peter's pet turtle. Each approximately 15-page chapter is a complete, very funny episode.

Interest Level: 3-6. Reading Level 3.1. Further Search Topics: Humorous Fiction, Turtles-Fiction, Brothers and Sisters-Fiction, Pets-Fiction, Family-Fiction, Read Aloud, Best Sellers, Everyday Stories, Troublemakers-Fiction.

Blume, Judy. Superfudge. Dutton 1980, 166 pp.

On Fudge's first day in school his older brother Peter had to rescue him from the top of the kindergarten storage cabinets. Later in the school year Fudge's eagerness to join a school guest speaker on stage almost spelled disaster. Then when Fudge unexpectedly disappeared one day everyone, including Peter, thought he had drowned. In addition to Peter's problems with Fudge, Peter had to cope with a baby sister, moving to Princeton, New Jersey, a new job for his mother, and his father's attempts to write a book. Although the book is a sequel and is best enjoyed as such, it can be read alone. It is not as amusing or well-written as it's predecessor, *Tales of a Fourth Grade Nothing*, but will still be popular with young readers.

Interest Level: 3-6. Reading Level 3.1. Further Search Topics: Brothers and Sisters-Fiction, Moving, Household-Fiction, Infants-Fiction, Working Parents-Fiction, School Stories, Family-Fiction, Best Sellers, Humorous Fiction, Everyday Stories.

Bulla, Clyde Robert. Ghost town treasure; illus by Don Freeman. Har-Row 1957, 87 pp.

A very simple story whose title is somewhat misleading. Instead of a mystery or an exciting story of buried treasure, Bulla has written a very pleasant story of a family whose fortunes are reversed by the accidental discovery of a nearby cave. Young Ty Jackson and his family were the last people living in Gold Rock, California. Everyone else had moved out when the new highway had bypassed the town. The Jacksons had been able to stay on only because some of the nearby ranchers had continued to buy food and supplies from the Jacksons' store. Just as they, too, were preparing to move out, Ty's pen pals wrote that they were coming to visit the town. Their grandfather had died there, years earlier, during his search for gold. When Paul and Nora arrived, they brought with them their grandfather's diary. The last entry in the journal seemed to indicate that their grandfather had found gold in an isolated cave in the nearby canyon. After a long search, the children discovered the cave, but no gold. Ty's disappointment changed to joy when tourists started arriving to see the new natural attraction. Once again his parents could sell their groceries, the hotel could be reopened and Gold Rock would flourish.

Interest Level: 2-5. Reading Level: 2.2. Further Search Topics: Treasure-Fiction, Family Problems-Fiction, West-Fiction, California-Fiction, Family-Fiction, Pen Pals-Fiction.

Bulla, Clyde Robert. Open the door and see all the people; illus by Wendy Watson. T Y Crowell 1972, 69 pp.

A slight story that makes up for its lack of excitement with warmth. When Joann, Teeney and Mama were burned out of their house in the country, they decided it was time to move to the city. With the help of a friend, Mama was quickly able to find a job and an apartment. Only Teeney was noticeably unhappy. She missed her doll and resented anyone else who had one. Then the girls learned about the Toy House, a place to borrow or adopt toys. Both girls found dolls they wanted to adopt. Just before the end of the six week trial period Tenney lost her doll and almost lost her chance to adopt it. After the doll was found and repaired, the people at the Toy House realized how much she wanted the doll and let Teeney keep it.

Because of the ages of the characters, (six and eight), and the subject matter, the book's appeal is doubtful beyond third grade. Print size slightly smaller than usual for Bulla.

Interest Level: 1-3. Reading Level: 2.1. Further Search Topics: Dolls-Fiction, Brothers and Sisters-Fiction, Moving, Household-Fiction, Family-Fiction, Group 2.

Chaikin, Miriam. I should worry, I should care; illus by Richard Egielski. Har-Row 1979, 103 pp.

A warm, well-written story about life in a Jewish family in Brooklyn just before World War II. This is the story of young Molly's adjustment to moving, to leaving old friends, to making and losing new friends (one by death) and to the small happenings that make up her life. In the background, but always there, is Hitler's ever-increasing threat to the world.

A comfortable, truthful look at a close-knit family. Also useful for its picture of the times and the place. An occasional Yiddish expression may slow the reader but adds to the book's authenticity. Print is slightly lighter and smaller than *Finders Weepers*.

Interest Level: 3-5. Reading Level: 2.2. Further Search Topics: Moving, Household-Fiction, Friendship-Fiction, City Life-Fiction, Jews-Fiction, Family-Fiction.

Chaikin, Miriam. Finders weepers; illus Richard Egielski. Har-Row 1980, 120 pp.

The children most likely to read this are those who have enjoyed *I Should Worry, I Should Care*. On her way home from school one day, Molly found a ring. Rather than try to find its owner, she made up excuses to keep the ring. Molly knew it was a sin to keep something that belonged to someone else, she even knew who *did* own the ring. When she finally decided to return it, the ring had become stuck on Molly's finger and wouldn't come off. With Yom Kippur just a few days away, Molly became convinced that all the unpleasant things happening around her were punishments for her sin. She finally had to have the ring cut off her finger. After she prayed for forgiveness life immediately went back to normal.

There's enough guilt here to satisfy even the most demanding reader. There is also the same solid family group that appeared in the first book. But this book probably lacks enough excitement and/or empathy to interest a reader new to Molly and her family. Print is dark but spacing between lines could have been wider.

Interest Level: 3-5. Reading Level: 3.1. Further Search Topics: Family-Fiction, Jews-Fiction, Honesty-Fiction, Holidays-Fiction, Religion-Fiction.

Clark, Margaret Goff. Barney and the UFO; illus by Ted Lewin. Dodd 1979, 159 pp.

Barney felt a strange prickly sensation several times before he discovered that it was caused by Tibbo, a Gark from the planet Ornam. Tibbo had selected Barney as a friend who would accompany him back to Ornam. Barney was to learn the peaceful ways of Gark and then return to Earth to help persuade the world to accept the aliens. At first the idea of visiting Ornam appealed to Barney because he liked Tibbo and felt very lonely and unsure of his adoptive family's love. Those were the very reasons that Tibbo had chosen Barney: he wanted someone without strong ties to Earth and Barney's only tie when he was first contacted by Tibbo was his little brother Scott. As the time to go grew closer, Barney found a new and strong friendship with Dave, a science whiz-kid, and great love for his new parents. Tibbo, however, was determined to hold Barney to his promise. Only a last minute confrontation between Tibbo and Barney, David, Scott and Mr. and Mrs. Crandall prevented Tibbo from succeeding. But even as Tibbo left, he and Barney acknowledged their new friendship and agreed to keep in touch.

Because of its fairly slow beginning, readers must be well-introduced to this book. If they can be persuaded to be patient while the author sets the stage for about 18 pages they will be rewarded with a decent, if somewhat wordy, story of friendship, UFO's, space travel and family affection.

Interest Level: 3-6. Reading Level: 3.2. Further Search Topics: Science Fiction, Flying Saucers-Fiction, Kidnapping-Fiction, Foster Homes-Fiction, Family-Fiction, Adoption-Fiction, Aliens-Fiction, Loneliness-Fiction, Orphans-Fiction.

Cohen, Barbara. The carp in the bathtub; illus by Joan Halpern. Lothrop 1972, 48 pp.

Leah and Harry couldn't face the prospect of seeing Joe, their pet carp, made into gefilte fish, even for such a special occasion as the Seder on the first night of Passover. The large, friendly carp had lived in the family's bathtub for over a week. It even swam right over to Leah and Harry to be fed everytime they went into the bathroom. At a time when most children in New York didn't have pets, Joe was as close to being a pet as possible. So, Leah and Harry hid Joe in a neighbor's apartment until their father discovered what they had done. When Joe's destiny was fulfilled, the children had to face a difficult fact of life. A week later, however, their despair became delight, when their father brought home a pet cat.

A short, warm and satisfying story.

Interest Level: 2-5. Reading Level: 3.1. Further Search Topics: Group 2, Jews-Fiction, Religion-Fiction, Pets-Fiction, Passover-Fiction, Family-Fiction, Holidays-Fiction, Read Aloud, Brothers and Sisters-Fiction.

Conford, Ellen. The luck of Pokey Bloom; illus by Bernice Loewenstein. Little 1975, 135 pp.

Pokey Bloom's passion was entering contests. She entered every contest she heard of and always thought she would win. Unfortunately, she never won anything. She even went so far as to practice concentrating three times each day on winning every contest she had entered. Someone who had been interviewed on the radio had *guaranteed* she would win that way. She didn't! It only made more trouble for her at school and at home. Pokey had enough trouble getting along with her older brother and didn't need any more problems at home.

There isn't much plot or direction to this story, but it does have some amusing moments. It is an extra book for the reader who enjoys Judy Blume-type books and wants another story about "regular kids."

Interest Level: 4-6. Reading Level: 3.1. Further Search Topics: Family-Fiction, Contests-Fiction, Brothers and Sisters-Fiction, Humorous Fiction, Everyday Stories.

Conford, Ellen. And this is Laura. Little 1977, 179 pp.

As a member of a family of high-achievers, Laura was convinced that she was unloved and worthless because she had no talents. Then, suddenly Laura discovered she had very special psychic powers;

powers she began to exploit. At first it was fun to give readings after school each day. Gradually, however, as Laura foresaw her friend hurt and her brother missing, she realized that having ESP was also a frightening responsibility. Finally, her ESP became the vehicle that made it possible for Laura to tell her parents her true feelings and to understand that they loved her for herself, not for her achievements.

The author treats a common concern with sensitivity and humor. An especially good choice for Judy Blume lovers. Print somewhat small.

Interest Level: 4-6. Reading Level: 4.2. Further Search Topics: Occult-Fiction, Courage-Fiction, Extra Sensory Perception-Fiction, Family-Fiction, Humorous Fiction, Everyday Stories, Talent-Fiction.

Greenwald, Sheila. Give us a great big smile, Rosy Cole. Little 1981, 76 pp.

It was Rosy's turn to be the subject of her uncle's book. He needed to earn money again and Rosy had just turned 10, the age each of her sisters had been when Uncle Ralph wrote *Anitra Dances* and *Pippa Prances* about them. However, Rosy couldn't dance like Anitra or ride horses like Pippa. In fact, Rosy had no talent that was appropriate for a book. She drew well but Uncle Ralph said that wasn't visual enough. Then Rosy's mother and uncle decided that Rosy could be *A Very Little Fiddler*.

Rosy had been taking violin lessons for two years, but only Rosy and her music teacher knew how truly untalented she was. Rosy hated the whole idea of the book at first. But as people began to treat her like a star, she found herself acting like one, until the day she heard her tape of the piece she was to play at the recital. Once again she realized that she could not play the violin and didn't want to go on with the charade. When everyone ignored her wishes, Rosy started to run away. Her route took her through the park where she thought of a brilliant idea. She ran home, changed clothes, picked up her violin, created a sign, and raced back to the park. There, with all the other street musicians Rosy set up her sign and began to play her violin. Her sign asked people to sign a petition if they felt that she should not be encouraged to play the violin anymore. Right away Rosy drew a large crowd. Before long, even her mother was one of the listeners and one of the signers. That was the end of Rosy's musical career and her uncle's book, but both were happier. Rosy went back to being normal and Uncle Ralph found another topic for his next book.

Chapters are long, but should not be a problem. Print is large. Some of the story is actually told in the illustrations, so the reader should be aware of them. Younger children may take the book more seriously than children whose sense of humor includes irony or children who were not as fond of Krementz's *Very Young* series.

Interest Level: 4-6. Reading Level: 3.1. Further Search Topics: Occupations-Fiction, Humorous Fiction, Family-Fiction, Relatives-Fiction, Talent-Fiction, Photography-Fiction, Everyday Stories.

Hurwitz, Johanna. Aldo Ice Cream; illus by John Wallner. Morrow 1981, 124 pp.

Aldo got his newest nickname (Ice Cream) from his friend DeDe when she heard that Aldo not only wanted to try every flavor of ice cream at the local store, but wanted to buy an ice cream freezer for his sister's birthday as well. Aldo decided his summer project would be to earn enough money for the freezer, but he soon found out that there were very few ways a nine-year-old boy could earn $49.95. In the meantime, he helped his mother deliver food for a Meals-On-Wheels project, learned to swim, found out about fish from Mr. Puccini, and shared his cat with Mrs. Nardo. As the summer came to an end he saw one last opportunity to earn enough money for the ice cream maker. A local shoe store offered a new pair of sneakers to the child who owned the most worn out pair. Aldo convinced his mother that if he won the sneakers, she should pay him the money she would otherwise have had to spend on his new sneakers. Aldo set about making sure that his already well-worn sneakers were the most dilapidated in town. A few days before the sneaker contest the hardware store lowered the price on the ice cream freezer to a point where Aldo could afford it if he won the sneakers. When Aldo did win, just as he knew he would, he and his mother bought the very last freezer in the store.

It is not as well-constructed a story as *Aldo Applesauce*, but for established Aldo fans, or those who want quiet, reassuring fiction, this is a usable title.

Interest Level: 3-4. Reading Level: 3.1. Further Search Topics: Humorous Fiction, Brothers and Sisters-Fiction, Vacation-Fiction, Occupations-Fiction, Everyday Stories, Aging-Fiction, Family-Fiction, Contests-Fiction.

Hurwitz, Johanna. Once I was a plum tree; illus by Ingrid Fetz. Morrow 1980, 160 pp.

Ten-year-old Gerry Flam knew nothing about her religion except that she was Jewish. Her parents didn't practice their religion and only superficially observed some of the holidays. As they told Gerry, their reason was that they were assimilated Americans. In fact, they seemed to practice as many Christian as Jewish holidays. All Gerry's friends and neighbors were Catholic, so Gerry had very little chance to learn about Judaism or the prejudice to which Jews were still being subjected in 1947 in the Bronx. A Jewish family moved into the apartment building next door, and Gerry's quiet curiosity was stimulated. From the Wulfs, Gerry began to learn about Judaism, World War II, and Hitler. As her pride in her heritage grew, Gerry also felt prejudice for the first time. After celebrating her first Passover Seder, Gerry found that despite the problems, she was truly happy to be Jewish.

Much like Chaikin's *I Should Worry, I Should Care* in tone and mood. Will be useful where there is already an interest in Judaism.

Interest Level: 3-5. Reading Level: 3.1. Further Search Topics: Religion-Fiction, Family-Fiction, Jews-Fiction, City Life-Fiction, Children-Growth-Fiction, Prejudice-Fiction.

Hurwitz, Johanna. The law of gravity; illus by Ingrid Fetz. Morrow 1978, 192 pp.

The summer between fifth and sixth grades looked very unexciting to Margot. Her best friends were both going away for the whole summer and her father, a musician, was going to be on tour for most of the summer. Margot's very overweight mother had sworn never to go downstairs from their fifth floor walk-up apartment. Unless Margot chose to stay upstairs too, she was sure she would have a very lonely vacation. In addition, she had to work on a summer project for school. The project she finally chose was to get her mother downstairs after nine years of staying upstairs. In search of help she went to the local library where she met Bernie. Bernie was only a year older than Margot, but he seemed to know the most interesting things about the city. He showed her places Margot had never heard of before, he taught her to play chess, backgammon, and even to ride a bicycle. He was so full of fascinating ideas and information that Margot had no chance to be bored or lonely. Best of all, he even tried to help Margot with her project. None of their ideas worked, however, until Margot pretended to run away and scared her mother into going downstairs. Only then did Margot realize that she loved her mother whether or not she stayed on the fifth floor and that she couldn't simply force her mother or anyone else to change to suit her own fancy.

The book is a warm, understanding, slightly humorous treatment of the fairly common wish to change someone else. Although not many readers are likely to share Margot's exact problem, most will recognize her feelings. The book is also a virtual Chamber of Commerce advertisement for urban living. One of its other charms is its picture of a non-competitive, open, real friendship between an 11-year-old girl and a 12-year-old boy. The only drawback to the book is its inconsistent reading level which varies from 4.1 to 5.1 with a rare leap to 5.2.

Interest Level: 4-6. Reading Level: 4.2. Further Search Topics: Vacation-Fiction, Friendship-Fiction, Loners-Fiction, City Life-Fiction, Individualists-Fiction, Courage-Fiction, New York City-Fiction, Humorous Fiction, Family-Fiction, Challenges-Fiction, Weight-Fiction, Everyday Stories, Best Sellers.

Kibbe, Pat. The hocus-pocus dilemma; illus by Dan Jones. Knopf 1979, 125 pp.

Each chapter of this book is a separate episode in B.J.'s attempt to cultivate her newly-discovered ESP talents (more invented than discovered). The episodes, each of which involves a different member of B.J.'s family, are slightly outlandish, but very funny. Even the dog and the cat become involved. The dog becomes the unwitting target for a skunk. The cat accidentally starts a tape recording of speech habits that sounds like burglars breaking into the house. After nine disasters, B.J. finally concludes that she was being ridiculous to think that she had ESP, but that everyone is allowed to be ridiculous sometimes.

The nine, reasonably short episodes, the moderate size print, the sympathetic characters, and the book's humor, make this a very useful and popular title.

Interest Level: 4-6. Reading Level: 3.1. Further Search Topics: Extra Sensory Perception-Fiction, Humorous Fiction, Family-Fiction, Everyday Stories, Best Sellers, Read Aloud.

Kibbe, Pat. My mother the mayor, maybe; illus by Charles Robinson. Knopf 1981, 165 pp.

The Pinkertons first appeared in *The Hocus-Pocus Dilemma*, a better introduction to the family than this book. Although this is a satisfactory story, its appeal is somewhat limited by its subject matter. B.J.'s mother's decision to run for town mayor meant that the whole family became involved in the political process. B.J. became her mother's unofficial public relations coordinator, a position Sam Jessup (Mrs. Pinkerton's campaign manager) didn't want to see anyone fill but himself. But because Jessup's ideas seemed suspiciously designed to insure that Mrs. Pinkerton would lose the election, B.J. continued working on her mother's behalf. Almost every day she managed to get her mother's campaign on the front page of the newspaper, although not always in a flattering light. Once B.J. was arrested for breaking into her mother's campaign headquarters. Another day she inadvertently circulated a picture of her mother in a bikini all over town. B.J. and her brothers and sisters illegally campaigned on the high school campus during Homecoming. B.J. even accidentally succeeded in blowing her mother's opponent's wig off in the middle of a campaign appearance. Mrs. Pinkerton finally lost the election, but managed to bring an important issue to light and to stage the closest and most exciting election the town had known in a long time.

Election campaigns and political issues won't lure many new reluctant readers to this book, but those youngsters who have enjoyed the Pinkerton's previous adventures and can understand a simplified version of politics at work will enjoy this humorous tale.

Interest Level: 5-6. Reading Level: 3.1. Further Search Topics: Politics-Fiction, Humorous Fiction, Sex Role-Fiction, Family-Fiction.

Lowry, Lois. Anastasia again! HM 1981, 145 pp.

This is a sequel that is as funny and well-written as its predecessor. Because its plot involves less common experiences, this book may not enjoy quite the wide-spread success of *Anastasia Krupnik*. However, among those readers who liked their first meeting with Anastasia, this book will find many fans.

Anastasia's parents astounded her when they announced that the family was going to move from their Cambridge, Massachusetts apartment to a house in the suburbs. She didn't like the idea of leaving the apartment, but she *hated* the idea of the suburbs. The only thing that made the move bearable was the house itself. Anastasia had said she would move only if they could find a house with a tower—and they had. After she got over the shock of moving, Anastasia began to enjoy her new home. She met a neighborhood boy who became a special friend, she tried to help her cranky elderly neighbor Mrs. Stein make friends, and she even wrote a short mystery book.

Anastasia is as spunky and original as before. She is a bit precocious, but her precocity is nothing compared to that of her brother. At two-and-a-half years old, he speaks as well as many adults. As we mentioned above, the book will be most appealing to readers who want second helpings of Anastasia's adventures. The print is slightly smaller here than in the first title.

Interest Level: 4-6. Reading Level: 2.2. Further Search Topics: Moving, Household-Fiction, City Life-Fiction, Suburbia-Fiction, Humorous Fiction, Aging-Fiction, Writing-Fiction, Family-Fiction, Everyday Stories.

Parish, Peggy. Clues in the woods; illus by Paul Frame. Macmillan 1968, 154 pp.

The books about the three Roberts children share problems that are obvious to adults and felt by some young readers as well, but they continue to be popular with undemanding young readers. The characters are very white and middle class and their actions often fit out-of-date stereotypes. The plots have few surprises or suspense, but the reading levels are consistent and the very predictability of the books makes them familiar and therefore comfortable.

This particular story takes place at the end of the same summer the children solved the mystery of *The Key to the Treasure*. The children were alerted by their grandmother to the disappearance of food scraps, left outside the house. Thinking that two runaway children, about whom they had read, had taken the food, Liza, Bill, and Jed tried to find the runaways. Their attempts eventually brought them new friends and thus the solution to their mystery. It had not been the runaways who had taken the food, it was their new friends' dog.

Interest Level: 1-4. Reading Level: 2.2. Further Search Topics: Mystery and Detective Stories, Brothers and Sisters-Fiction, Vacation-Fiction, Dogs-Fiction, Runaways-Fiction, Grandparents-Fiction, Group 2.

Pfeffer, Susan Beth. Kid power; illus by Leigh Grant. Watts 1977, 121 pp.

When Janie's mother lost her job, her father's salary wouldn't stretch to provide any more money for the new bicycle fund. There was enough money already set aside to pay for one new bike, but both Janie and her older sister Carol wanted a bicycle. Carol, who had saved money of her own, suggested that they each pay for half a bike and their parents contribute the money for the other half. Then Janie's only problem was how to earn money, since she had none saved. Her solution was to create a business: Kid Power. Before long, Janie's business had blossomed and she was becoming rich, but she had lost her best friend and was ruining a client's roses. When Janie finally realized that getting rich wasn't the only thing that mattered in life, she relaxed, delegated jobs to friends better able to handle them, and became their agent.

A genuinely funny book that, as a bonus, takes a realistic look at the interworkings of a family. Consistent reading level.

Interest Level: 4-6. Reading Level: 3.1. Further Search Topics: Occupations-Fiction, Everyday Stories, Vacation-Fiction, Family-Fiction, Humorous Fiction, Best Sellers, Bicycles and Bicycling-Fiction, Friendship-Fiction.

Smith, Alison. Help! There's a cat washing in here!; illus by Amy Rowen. Dutton 1981, 152 pp.

Henry Walker agreed to care for his younger brother and sister for two weeks so that his mother could spend her time preparing a portfolio of her art work in the hopes of getting a much-needed job. It was a desperate move for Henry, but it was the only way he could prevent his bossy Aunt Wilhemina from moving in to run the household. Despite Henry's best efforts, almost everything seemed to go wrong. He burned the food, couldn't keep his brother and sister from misbehaving, seemed to have poisoned his sister's friend, and was faced with making a costume in one night for a school play. The worst of it all was that his mother wasn't pleased with what she was drawing, and Henry only seemed to make her feel more discouraged and unhappy. After what appeared to be certain defeat, however, Henry's efforts were rewarded. His mother was given the job, the family proved they could take care of themselves, and all ended happily.

A light, humorous tale of a young boy's growing independence and maturation under stress and increased responsibility.

Interest Level: 4-6. Reading Level: 3.1. Further Search Topics: Brothers and Sisters-Fiction, Working Parents-Fiction, Single Parent Family-Fiction, Humorous Fiction, Family-Fiction, Challenges-Fiction, Children-Growth-Fiction.

FAMILY PROBLEMS-FICTION

Angell, Judie. Dear Lola; or how to build your own family. Bradbury 1980, 166 pp.

Arthur (age 18), James (13), Annie and Al-Willie (twins, age 10), Edmund (9), and Ben (5) wanted to run away from the orphanage and find a place where they could be a real family. After waiting months, their chance arrived one night. They escaped in a van and began living on the road. It was weeks before they

found a house in which they thought they could live. They didn't want trouble with local authorities, so most of the children enrolled in school and pretended to be living with their widowed grandfather. Only James (who never left his room) and Arthur stayed home. Arthur was the anonymous author of a nationally syndicated newspaper advice column. It was with the income from his "Dear Lola" column that Arthur was able to support the "family." When the townspeople eventually began to wonder about the "strange" behavior of the children, they investigated and found no adult in charge of the household. Arthur went to court to be appointed the childrens' guardian, but the judge ruled against him. Rather than be sent to foster homes again, Arthur and the children raced from the courtroom. The book ends as the family is once more together and on their own. An unusual cast of characters in a surprisingly warm and humorous book.

Interest Level: 4-6. Reading Level 3.1. Further Search Topics: Loners-Fiction, Runaways-Fiction, Orphans-Fiction, Survival-Fiction, Family Problems-Fiction, Family-Fiction, Read Aloud, Foster Homes-Fiction, Individualists-Fiction, Humorous Fiction.

Blume, Judy. Deenie. Bradbury 1973, 159 pp.

Deenie's mother wanted Deenie to be a model. Deenie didn't know what she wanted until she learned that she had scoliosis (curvature of the spine) and would have to wear a brace for four years. Then she knew she only wanted to be normal. She was repulsed by deformities of any kind. She couldn't stand the idea of a brace. Her mother's attitude made Deenie's adjustment even more difficult. It was her father, her doctor, her sister, and a new friend with excema who finally helped Deenie accept her brace and the idea of physical differences. Subplots include Deenie's budding romance with an eighth grade boy, her strained relationship with her mother, and her growing awareness of sex (masturbation and intercourse). Print and line spacing are similar to *Are You There God? It's Me, Margaret.*

Interest Level: 5-6. Reading Level: 3.1. Further Search Topics: Models, Fashion-Fiction, Beauty-Fiction, Scoliosis-Fiction, Physically Handicapped-Fiction, Children-Growth-Fiction, Sex-Fiction, Love-Fiction, Family Problems-Fiction, Illness-Fiction, Adolescence-Fiction.

Blume, Judy. It's not the end of the world. Bradbury 1972, 169 pp.

This is a one theme book (as are many of Judy Blume's titles). It is the story of 11-year-old Karen's attempt to prevent her parents' divorce and then to accept it. In this first-person story she tells of her disappointment, anger, fear, and lack of understanding. She describes her parents' fights and her brother's and sister's reactions, too. It is a book with an obvious and mostly reassuring message to its readers, but it is not just for readers whose families may be in similar situations. It is also a book that will be enjoyed by any Judy Blume enthusiast.

Interest Level: 4-6. Reading Level: 3.1. Further Search Topics: Divorce and Separation-Fiction, Family Problems-Fiction, Everyday Stories.

Blume, Judy. Tiger eyes. Bradbury 1981, 206 pp.

Davey's father's death was a shock that for awhile separated Davey from her mother. They occupied the same space, but Davey felt herself unable to communicate with her mother or with her aunt and uncle with whom they were living. The horror of the night her father was shot in a robbery attempt was too great for Davey to confront. It was too much for Davey's mother too, and so instead of growing closer, they draw apart. They let Davey's aunt and uncle direct their lives for almost a year before each was able to accept Mr. Wexler's death. During that time Davey's closest, most helpful friend was a loner named only Wolf. With him Davey lost enough fear and hatred that she was finally able to begin to talk about her father.

The setting (New Mexico) is much more important than in most of Blume's stories, the book's reading level is considerably more difficult, and the plot is about experiences more unique than usual. It will not fail to draw crowds of older readers however, for in most other respects the book follows Blume's successful formula.

Interest Level: 6+. Reading Level 5.1. Further Search Topics: Death-Fiction, Moving, Household-Fiction, Love-Fiction, Single Parent Family-Fiction, Family Problems-Fiction.

Bulla, Clyde Robert. Shoeshine girl; illus by Leigh Grant. Har-Row 1975, 84 pp.

A well-written, realistic story of 10-year-old Sarah who was sent to spend the summer with her Aunt Claudia. Sarah's parents felt that Sarah put too much importance on money and so insisted that Aunt Claudia give her no allowance for the summer. Sure that Aunt Claudia would call her bluff, Sarah threatened to get a job. Instead, Aunt Claudia thought it was a good idea. Sarah's experience as a shoeshine girl forced her to grow, to learn to like working, and finally to take responsibility for the stand when her boss was hit by a car. Told with quiet humor. For the reader who enjoys Judy Blume's books.

Interest Level: 2-5. Reading Level: 2.2. Further Search Topics: Children-Growth-Fiction, Family Problems-Fiction, Vacation-Fiction, Occupations-Fiction, Everyday Stories.

Bulla, Clyde Robert. Ghost town treasure; illus by Don Freeman. Har-Row 1957, 87 pp.

A very simple story whose title is somewhat misleading. Instead of a mystery or an exciting story of buried treasure, Bulla has written a very pleasant story of a family whose fortunes are reversed by the accidental discovery of a nearby cave. Young Ty Jackson and his family were the last people living in Gold Rock, California. Everyone else had moved out when the new highway had bypassed the town. The Jacksons had been able to stay on only because some of the nearby ranchers had continued to buy food and supplies from the Jacksons' store. Just as they, too, were preparing to move out, Ty's pen pals wrote that they were coming to visit the town. Their grandfather had died there, years earlier, during his search for gold. When Paul and Nora arrived, they brought with them their grandfather's diary. The last entry in the journal seemed to indicate that their grandfather had found gold in an isolated cave in the nearby canyon. After a long search, the children discovered the cave, but no gold. Ty's disappointment changed to joy when tourists started arriving to see the new natural attraction. Once again his parents could sell their groceries, the hotel could be reopened and Gold Rock would flourish.

Interest Level: 2-5. Reading Level: 2.2. Further Search Topics: Treasure-Fiction, Family Problems-Fiction, West-Fiction, California-Fiction, Family-Fiction, Pen Pals-Fiction.

Bulla, Clyde Robert. The sugar pear tree; illus by Taro Yashima. T Y Crowell 1960, 54 pp.

Lonnie lived with his mother and his grandfather in a house owned by the state. A new highway was to be built that would force the family to move, but Gramp refused to acknowledge that the state could force them out of their home. He chased away every state representative who came to warn the family that they should move. Lonnie's mother had always been at work when the representatives came and so knew nothing about the warnings until she came home to find their belongings on the sidewalk and their house on wheels. The only person they could turn to was their friend Nick. Nick owned a nursery in town and a small house with a large yard in the country. He had become a friend of Lonnie's when he gave Lonnie first prize in a school essay contest on the topic of "favorite trees." Lonnie's prize had been a sugar pear tree, his favorite. Nick had next become Lonnie's mother's friend. Nick arranged for them to stay in the greenhouse at his country place. The longer they stayed, the better friends Nick and Lonnie's mother became. Gramp was the only person who didn't adjust to the move. He stopped speaking the moment he was carried out of his old home. In a final and successful attempt to make Gramp happy, Nick bought the old house and had it moved out to his country lot.

The idea of a state government being able to force a family to move may need some explaining. The story's warmth and very consistent early second grade reading level make this a particularly useful book with quiet readers.

Interest Level: 2-4. Reading Level: 2.1. Further Search Topics: Trees-Fiction, Moving, Household-Fiction, Family Problems-Fiction, Grandparents-Fiction, Poverty-Fiction.

Burch, Robert. Queenie Peavy; illus by Jerry Lazare. Viking Pr. 1966, 159 pp.

Queenie was always in trouble. She could be mean, really mean, but, she was also bright, talented, independent and resilient. Queenie blamed her problems on the fact that people teased her because her father was in jail and because she was poor. She thought that she had to defend herself against the world. Queenie was proud of her poor reputation until she accidentally-on-purpose caused a classmate to break his leg. Then, when her father returned home and wasn't the person she'd hoped he'd be, Queenie realized that only she could make her life better. Being the strong person she was, she set out to do just that.

Queenie is a wonderfully alive and sympathetic character, one well worth introducing to older readers despite the book's reading level. Print somewhat small. Line spacing average width.

Interest Level: 5-6. Reading Level: 5.1. Further Search Topics: Family Problems-Fiction, Crime-Fiction, Loners-Fiction, Poverty-Fiction, Humorous Fiction, Bullies-Fiction, Troublemakers-Fiction, Academic Problems-Fiction, Read Aloud.

Byars, Betsy. The house of wings; illus by Daniel Schwarts. Viking Pr. 1972, 142 pp.

Sammy was the youngest of eight children. His parents were tired of raising children when Sammy was born, so they almost let Sammy raise himself. That meant that he grew up to be independent. It didn't mean it was any easier for Sammy to accept being left behind unexpectedly with his strange grandfather when his parents moved to Detroit. His reaction when his grandfather told him that his parents had gone was to deny it and to run away. He ran until he could run no more. When he stopped running, the old man stopped chasing him and they found a wild but blind crane in desperate need of help. Helping the crane heal and find the desire to live again taught Sammy and his grandfather respect and, most of all, love for each other.

The parallels between Sammy and the crane are strong but subtle. The story is a compelling one, but may need a brief introductory note to alleviate confusion in the first two chapters.

Interest Level: 5-6. Reading Level: 4.2. Further Search Topics: Grandparents-Fiction, Birds-Fiction, Family Problems-Fiction, Poverty-Fiction, Physically Handicapped-Fiction, Runaways-Fiction.

Christopher, Matt. Football fugitive; illus by Larry Johnson. Little 1976, 119 pp.

Larry had been writing to the great football player Yancey Roote for about two years when his letters suddenly went unanswered. Because his relationship with his father was cool and distant, Larry's friendship with Yancey had meant a great deal to him. Shortly after Larry learned that Yancey was in legal trouble, Yancey showed up in town to ask Larry's father, a famous lawyer, to defend him in court. The court case and Yancey helped to bring Larry and his father closer together and to provide each one with new respect for the other. Lots of football action plus a realistic and somewhat common problem (though an unrealistic solution) make this a useful selection.

Interest Level: 3-6. Reading Level: 3.1. Further Search Topics: Football-Fiction, Lawyers-Fiction, Family Problems-Fiction.

Clymer, Eleanor. Me and the Eggman; illus by David K. Stone. Dutton 1972, 57 pp.

As Donald's life became more and more miserable and as his chores and responsibilities around his small, overcrowded, urban apartment increased, he began to look for a way to escape. Thinking that if he could just get to the country, life would be better, Donald sneaked into a truck owned by a farmer who delivered eggs to the city. Not surprisingly the farmer, a sharp speaking, independent old man, was not at all happy to find Donald. Reluctantly, the Eggman, as the farmer was called, agreed to let Donald stay a week and help to work his rundown farm. The week stretched into a summer in which Donald learned to face and accept reality, to love the Eggman and to like himself.

This book is a surprisingly consistent success with reluctant readers, especially boys. Watch for the lack of quotation marks around the dialogue and the somewhat small print.

Interest Level: 3-6. Reading Level: 3.2. Further Search Topics: Family Problems-Fiction, Poverty-Fiction, Vacation-Fiction, Runaways-Fiction, Farm Life-Fiction, Best Sellers.

Danziger, Paula. The cat ate my gymsuit. Delacorte 1974, 147 pp.

Another book for fans of Judy Blume. Marcy was shy and insecure, unhappy at school and unhappy at home. She was self-conscious about being heavy and sure she would never have a date. Only Ms. Finney (a new teacher), her English class and Smedley (a communications group) meant anything to Marcy. When Ms. Finney was fired because of her refusal to recite the pledge of allegiance and her unorthodox teaching methods, Marcy began to organize a protest movement. Marcy's commitment brought more problems at school and at home, but eventually resulted in Ms. Finney's vindication and Marcy's and her mother's growth and understanding.

Don't expect much depth of characterization. Most of the characters are flat and stereotypical, but the book will have great appeal in spite of its faults, for Marcy's insecurities are ones with which many young readers can identify.

Interest Level: 5-6. Reading Level: 5.1. Further Search Topics: School Stories, Everyday Stories, Family Problems-Fiction, Challenges-Fiction, Weight-Fiction, Courage-Fiction, Individualists-Fiction, Sex Role-Fiction.

Danziger, Paula. The pistachio prescription. Delacorte 1978 154 pp.

Just as Cassie entered her freshman year in high school, the old stand-by that had helped her deal with all her problems (eating pistachio nuts) began to fail. To be sure, she did get through the class elections and was elected president. She met and started dating Bernie. She gained self-confidence. She even managed to stand up to a particularly mean teacher. But, eating pistachios didn't help at all at home where Cassie really needed them. She could hardly stand to be in the same room with her older sister. She hated the importance her mother placed on looking right and dressing well. Most of all, she hated the way her parents were constantly fighting. The only person with whom she was really confortable was her brother. But, before the year was over, Cassie's parents decided to get a divorce, she and her sister became friends and Cassie learned to accept her family.

Another Judy Blume-style author, but Danziger's portraits of adults tend to be even more one-dimensional and exaggerated than Blume's. Very popular anyway.

Interest Level: 6+. Reading Level: 5.1. Further Search Topics: Divorce and Separation-Fiction, Family Problems-Fiction, Beauty-Fiction, School Stories, Adolescence-Fiction, Love-Fiction, Brothers and Sisters-Fiction, Everyday Stories.

Greene, Constance C. A girl called Al; illus by Byron Barton. Viking Pr. 1969, 127 pp.

Told in the first person, this is the story of two seventh grade girls. The girls' warm friendship began the moment Al introduced herself to the narrator as a non-conformist. Al was very independent, mostly because she was on her own so much of the time. Her parents were divorced and she seldom saw either one of them. Her father only wrote her postcards and her mother was rarely home. The narrator's family and Mr. Richards, their building superintendent, became Al's family. They cooked, ate, played, fought, talked and even made bookcases together. When Mr. Richards had a heart attack, they found help for him and later went to see him in the hospital. It was his death that helped Al and her mother grow closer, just as Mr. Richards' life had helped her understand why her father never came to see her.

A satisfying, low-key story of friendship and maturation. The girls are Judy Blume-style characters with much greater innocence. Their ages are not discernible by their actions or dialogue, only by the author's statement.

Interest Level: 3-6. Reading Level: 3.1. Further Search Topics: Children-Growth-Fiction, Single Parent Family-Fiction, Friendship-Fiction, Weight-Fiction, Aging-Fiction, Death-Fiction, Divorce and Separation-Fiction, Family Problems-Fiction, Everyday Stories, Humorous Fiction.

Greenfield, Eloise. Talk about a family; illus by James Calvin. Lippincott 1978, 60 pp.

Genny, Kim, and Mac knew something was wrong between their parents, and fully expected that their older brother Larry would be able to fix everything when he came home from the army. But even Larry's welcome home party was almost ruined by their parents' fighting and Kim's reaction. That night, as she listened to Larry and her parents' low voices, Genny was certain that Larry was bringing her parents back together. When her father announced the next morning that he was going to move out, Genny's anger and hurt was directed at Larry. With her friend Mr. Parker's help, Genny finally realized that they were still a family; a family with a new shape, but one that would be able to adjust. A one-theme, realistic and reassuring, short book with good-sized print. Very useful

Interest Level: 3-6. Reading Level: 3.1. Further Search Topics: Divorce and Separation-Fiction, Family Problems-Fiction, Brothers and Sisters-Fiction, Best Sellers.

Hurwitz, Johanna. Baseball fever; illus by Ray Cruz. Morrow 1981, 128 pp.

Only baseball nuts need even consider this title, but for the die-hard baseball fan this is perfect. Much to his father's disgust, Ezra had only one interest in life. Baseball was almost all Ezra ever thought of. His father was a German-born intellectual who couldn't understand how anyone could waste so much time watching men hit a ball with a stick. He wanted Ezra to become interested in history and chess. Ezra had no interest in history except baseball history. He hated chess, not just because he always lost, but because his father continually told him how badly he played. Predictably they reach a compromise; each learns to appreciate the other's passion, but not before everyone in the family and a few people outside the family have become involved in a series of warmly humorous incidents. Includes much baseball information.

Interest Level: 3-6. Reading Level: 3.1. Further Search Topics: Baseball-Fiction, Family Problems-Fiction, Humorous Fiction.

Levy, Elizabeth. Lizzie lies a lot; illus by John Wallner. Delacorte 1976, 102 pp.

Almost any child can identify with Lizzie. She had found that it was sometimes easier to lie than to tell the truth. Her problem was that she had lost control. It seemed as if almost everything she said was a lie. She told so many lies it became difficult to keep track of them all. Lizzie wasn't even really sure why she lied so much. She knew that she sometimes lied because she thought people would be more apt to like her. Other times she lied to get herself out of trouble or to cover up her feelings when she was hurt or angry. But that didn't explain why she lied all the time. Maybe, as her grandmother said, she was a born liar.

It wasn't until Lizzie got herself caught in the middle of so many lies that she lost her only friend, that she could admit her problem to herself and to her family. After their initial shock had passed, everyone agreed to help Lizzie stop lying. Lizzie took the next step by admitting her lies to her friend Sue.

Levy has brought such an appropriately light touch to a fairly common problem that many children find this story enjoyable. Overlook the book's faults (Lizzie's grandmother is overdrawn and her mother's guilt feelings are unsupported by the story) for the fun and the message young readers get from it.

Interest Level: 3-5. Reading Level: 4.2. Further Search Topics: Honesty-Fiction, Group 2, Friendship-Fiction, Best Sellers, Everyday Stories, Family Problems-Fiction, Grandparents-Fiction, Humorous Fiction.

Mazer, Harry. The war on Villa Street. Delacorte 1978, 182 pp.

Willis was a loner and a runner. He was a loner because he didn't want anyone to find out about his alcoholic father. He wasn't quite sure why he ran; perhaps because it was the only time he felt good. When Rabbit Slavin and his friends asked Willis to become part of their gang, he refused. He was flattered and wanted to join, but the gang wanted to meet at his house and Willis couldn't risk that. Then when he agreed to coach the local "retard" for the school's field day, Willis gave the gang the opportunity they wanted to take their revenge on him for turning them down. The gang's hatred for Willis increased still more when he beat their best runner and athlete. In payment, the gang jumped Willis and beat him badly. After he picked himself up, Willis realized that he had at least faced the worst of his fears and survived. Days later when his drunken father humiliated him, Willis realized he had to face that, too. He made peace with himself and the world by deciding he could neither continue to run away from, nor apologize for his father anymore. He was independent and strong.

There is much in this fast-paced book besides the obvious violence and action. It is written with an intuitive feel for a teenager's problems and emotions and is a sensitive portrayal of mature concepts. The print is large, but spacing between the lines should have been slightly increased.

Interest Level: 5-6. Reading Level: 5.1. Further Search Topics: Running-Fiction, Loneliness-Fiction, Alcoholism-Fiction, Loners-Fiction, Mental Retardation-Fiction, Gangs-Fiction, Child Abuse-Fiction, Bullies-Fiction, Family Problems-Fiction, Courage-Fiction.

Newfield, Marcia. A book for Jodan; illus by Diane DeGroot. Atheneum 1975, unp (41 pp).

Jodan found her parents' separation very hard to understand and accept. She and her mother had moved 3,000 miles away from her father and she missed him very much. When Jodan visited her father for the first time, he gave her a very special present that lessened her loneliness. He created a book just for Jodan that was filled with his thoughts and memories.

The book is a sensitive portrayal of a very common experience. Only Jodan's age (nine-years-old) and consequent actions and reactions, limit the book's probable usefulness beyond fifth grade. Print is somewhat small.

Interest Level: 2-5. Reading Level: 3.2. Further Search Topics: Group 2, Divorce and Separation-Fiction, Family Problems-Fiction, Loneliness-Fiction.

Park, Barbara. Don't make me smile. Knopf 1981, 114 pp.

As far as Charlie Hickle was concerned his parents' divorce was the worst thing in the world. His parents had ruined his life and he hadn't done anything to deserve such a fate. At first he didn't say very much. Then he ran away to live in a tree. Finally he cried a lot. That was all just in the first week after his parents announced their decision. After that, both his grades at school and his behavior began to deteriorate. It wasn't until Charlie had had several talks with a helpful children's psychologist and made a disastrous attempt to reunite his parents on his birthday, that he began to realize that he didn't like the divorce, but he could live with it.

The author's use of amusing anecdotes, Charlie's very strong feelings, and the frequency of divorce make this book very popular. Its major drawbacks are its superficiality and the overdrawn portrait of Charlie's mother. The book's faults will not deter many young readers from enjoying it, however.

Interest Level: 4-6. Reading Level: 3.1. Further Search Topics: Divorce and Separation-Fiction, Family Problems-Fiction, Psychiatrists-Fiction, Everyday Stories.

Pevsner, Stella. And you give me a pain, Elaine. HM 1978, 182 pp.

Andrea was the youngest of three children. She was very close to her brother, Joe, but he was away at college. There was only Elaine at home, but Andrea and Elaine didn't get along at all. Elaine was a troubled young woman who took so much of her parents' attention that there was none left for Andrea. This is the story of Andrea's year in eighth grade, a year in which she discovered that she was a steady and strong person. It was the year in which Andrea worked on the school play, had her first boyfriend, weathered the storms when her sister ran away, and began to understand her sister more and resent her less. It was also the year that she had to learn to live with her brother's accidental death.

The author's Judy Blume style (but with less humor) guarantees readers among older children.

Interest Level: 5-6. Reading Level: 4.1. Further Search Topics: Family Problems-Fiction, Brothers and Sisters-Fiction, Love-Fiction, Death-Fiction, Runaways-Fiction, Troublemakers-Fiction, Adolescence-Fiction.

Platt, Kin. Brogg's brain. Lippincott 1981, 123 pp.

According to everyone else, Monty Davis should have been one of the fastest milers in the city. He had, after all, run a four minute and ten second mile in practice one day. He had run well enough that day to beat his high school's two best milers. That was a good enough performance to make the coach push him, his teacher talk about winning, and his father puff up with pride. Even the marathon runner he saw occasionally in the park and his girl friend Cindy seemed to think that he could be the best. Monty really didn't care, or he thought he didn't. Maybe he was just afraid to see how good or bad he really was. For whatever reason, he didn't want to run in the meet against Culver High School. He talked so much about not doing well, that by the time he was supposed to run, he even had his coach convinced he couldn't win. But as he ran, Monty heard a voice inside his head that sounded like the voice in a strange science fiction film that he and Cindy had just seen. The voice seemed to say that he could win, and suddenly that was what Monty wanted. The voice and his new-found determination were what pulled Monty through and gave him first place.

This book is for the track fan or the runner. Few others are likely to care about the difference between a four-twenty and a four-ten high school mile. For those who do care, this is a good choice.

Interest Level: 5-6. Reading Level: 3.1. Further Search Topics: Family Problems-Fiction, Love-Fiction, Running-Fiction, Courage-Fiction.

Sachs, Marily. The bears' house; illus by Louis Glanzman. Doubleday 1971, 81 pp.

Don't let the benign appearance of this book fool you. This is a disturbing, almost brutal story. It is the story of Fran Ellen, a fourth grader with more problems than anyone should have to shoulder at one time. Her father had left the family and her mother had had a mental breakdown. Fran Ellen and her older brother were left with responsibility for themselves, their mother, and three other children (including a baby). They were all ill-fed, poorly dressed, and unwashed. Neither the social worker nor Fran Ellen's teacher knew the extent of the family's problems. Fran Ellen's only happiness came from her baby sister and from a schoolroom model (of *Goldilocks and the Three Bears* and their house) into which she mentally retreated whenever she had the chance.

As the school year closed, Fran Ellen's teacher visited her home to deliver the bears' house and discovered Fran Ellen's mother and very sick baby sister. Although she hated the idea that the family might have to split up, Fran Ellen had matured enough to realize that when her teacher insisted that she would get help for the family, her teacher was taking the proper action.

The book is inappropriately illustrated to make it appear cute and even humorous. The story is far from either. It is so stark that it probably shouldn't have been illustrated at all. And because the hope that is present in the book's ending is very subtle, a review and a discussion may be necessary to help relieve some young readers' anxieties.

Interest Level: 5-6. Reading Level: 3.1. Further Search Topics: Divorce and Separation-Fiction, Challenges-Fiction, Poverty-Fiction, Family Problems-Fiction, Loners-Fiction, Survival-Fiction, Mental Illness-Fiction, Brothers and Sisters-Fiction.

Sharmat, Marjorie W. The Lancelot closes at five; illus by Lisl Weil. Macmillan 1976, 120 pp.

Despite a somewhat slow beginning, this is an amusing, almost sensitive story of two friends who decided to spend the night in the model home of the new housing development in which they both lived. Hutch, a health food fanatic whose mother pronounced judgment on everything Hutch did, conceived of the idea as her way of breaking away. Abby went along for the fun of it. When the local newspaper wrote of unusual vandalism at the model home, the townspeople became engrossed in finding the culprits. As the adults became enraged about the crime wave, their children began to admire the clever idea. Soon, almost every youngster in town had confessed to spending the night in the model home. By the time Abby and Hutch got around to admitting they had slept there, no one believed them. Only a sock with Abby's name in it could tie Abby and Hutch to the scene of the crime. As the book ends, the police have begun a thorough search of the house, after a real robbery, and the sock's discovery is imminent.

Interest Level: 4-6. Reading Level: 3.2. Further Search Topics: Humorous Fiction, Suburbia-Fiction, Runaways-Fiction, Crime-Fiction, Individualists-Fiction, Family Problems-Fiction.

Shreve, Susan. The Nightmares of Geranium Street. Knopf 1977, 127 pp.

The Nightmares, a small neighborhood gang, had very little to do until beautiful Tess moved on the block. Tess dressed in satins, furs, and rhinestones, and sang in nightclubs. She was even more of a fascination to the gang because they had been told to stay away from her. When Amanda moved in with Tess, the Nightmares invited her to join the gang so that they would have a way of spying on Tess. Gradually her strange behavior, her moods, her bruises and shaking spells, the strangers she let in the house, and the fights she had, led the gang members to suspect that Tess dealt in drugs. When Amanda failed to show up for a picnic and the Nightmares learned the police were searching for Tess, the gang became worried enough to look for Amanda themselves. In doing so, they uncovered proof of Tess' drug dealings, put themselves in great danger, and were protected by Tess as they escaped only moments before Tess was arrested.

Despite its low reading level, the book's confusing sequence of final events, and its subject matter make it best suited to older readers. It is not great literature, but its subject has strong appeal.

Interest Level: 5-6. Reading Level: 3.1. Further Search Topics: Family Problems-Fiction, Gangs-Fiction, Drugs-Fiction, Mystery and Detective Stories, City Life-Fiction, Crime-Fiction, Philadelphia-Fiction.

Smith, Doris Buchanan. Tough Chauncey. Morrow 1974, 222 pp.

Chauncey Childs had taught himself to be tough— very tough. Even though he was small for his age (13 years old), the only person who gave him any trouble was his sometimes-friend, Black Jack Levitt. Everyone else was scared of Chauncey. Chauncey felt that he had to be tough or he wouldn't be able to survive. He had to be tough to stand the beatings his grandfather gave him "for his own good," to put up with his mother's drinking and disappearances, and to stand the sight of his grandfather shooting the stray kittens born in their garage.

Chauncey's greatest wish was to be able to live with his mother, instead of with his grandparents. In a desperate attempt to achieve that end he accidentally fell from a moving train and badly hurt his leg. Instead of being returned to his mother he was once more taken back to his grandparents. Chauncey's unhappiness grew until he finally decided to take the one surviving stray kitten and run away. Jack helped him find an empty garage where he could hide while he figured out what to do with his future. After talking with Jack and doing more deep soul searching, Chauncey decided to reshape himself and his life. His first step was to curb his temper and his tongue when his hiding place was discovered. His second step was to see about finding a foster home where he would be treated well, and where he could get a new start.

Ugly as the story is in places, its ending is hopeful. Although it is not always realistic, Chauncey's story is compelling enough to appeal to many readers, especially those who have enjoyed *The War on Villa Street*, by Henry Mazer, *The Outsiders*, by Susan Hinton, or *Mystery of the Fat Cat*, by Frank Bonham. The book's length and its artificially low reading level (vocabulary is often difficult but sentences are very short) make this book most appropriate for an older reader whose reading level is 4.1 or higher.

Interest Level: 5-6. Reading Level: 3.2. Further Search Topics: Child Abuse-Fiction, Family Problems-Fiction, Grandparents-Fiction, Runaways-Fiction, Bullies-Fiction, Single Parent Family-Fiction, Loners-Fiction, Friendship-Fiction, Troublemakers-Fiction, Foster Homes-Fiction.

Smith, Doris Buchanan. Last was Lloyd. Viking Pr 1981, 124 pp.

Lloyd had several problems: he was overweight, his mother was overprotective, he had no school friends, and there was a chance he might be taken away from home and put into foster care because he had missed so much school. Lloyd's mother, very young and very defensive when she had Lloyd, had done her best to be a "good mother," but in doing so, had made Lloyd fearful of the world. He had become the subject of his classmates' mockery so many times that the only way he could respond to his peers was with nastiness. The one skill he possessed was hitting a baseball. He kept this skill well hidden for fear of exposing himself to further mockery. When one of his classmates accidentally discovered how well Lloyd hit, he·took the first step to becoming Lloyd's friend. Lloyd's reaction was to back away, but Kirby kept trying. Eventually Kirby's attempts and those of an understanding truant officer, helped Lloyd begin to make friends, to treat others decently, and to pull away from his mother; in short, he began to mature.

Because Lloyd's problems can be oversimplified too easily, this book requires a fairly mature reader and perhaps even discussion in order to fully understand its subtleties.

Interest Level: 5-6+Reading Level: 4.2. Further Search Topics: Weight-Fiction, Single Parent Family-Fiction, Courage-Fiction, School Stories, Loners-Fiction, Friendship-Fiction, Baseball-Fiction, Family Problems-Fiction, Foster Homes-Fiction, Children-Growth-Fiction.

Talbot, Charlene Joy. The Great Rat Island adventure; illus by Ruth Sanderson. Atheneum 1977, 164 pp.

Joel dreaded spending the summer with his father. His parents were divorced and Joel was sure his father didn't want him. His father only wanted to study birds. Great Rat Island, where Joel and his father were to spend the summer, was of no interest to Joel. It had no television, no one his own age, only terns. Even the assignment Joel was given (to make sure that no more tern eggs were stolen) sounded dull. It led to an adventure and a friend, however, that were anything but dull.

Joel discovered that a girl his own age was the thief of the tern eggs. Her name was Vicky Owens. She had run away from camp and was spending the summer alone on Little Rat Island. Joel kept her secret until the day of hurricane warnings. As the storm approached Joel realized that Vicky wouldn't be safe on Little Rat Island. Without telling anyone else he took the only boat around and went to look for Vicky to bring her back to Great Rat Island. He found her with her leg stuck between two rocks, unable to move. By the time Joel got her loose, it was too late to get back to the big island. Not knowing what else to do, Joel and Vicky dragged the boat inside an abandoned building where Vicky had been living. As the water rose around them and Vicky grew delirious with fever, Joel set up camp in the boat. While the building filled with water they stayed dry in the boat. Rescue and medical care for Vicky finally came the next day.

A solid, steadily-paced survival story for the reader who wants a little more than just an adventure story. Print is small.

Interest Level: 4-6. Reading Level: 3.1. Further Search Topics: Vacation-Fiction, Family

Problems-Fiction, Birds-Fiction, Divorce and Separation-Fiction, Disasters-Fiction, Survival-Fiction, Runaways-Fiction.

FANTASY

Bulla, Clyde Robert. My friend the monster; illus by Michele Chessare. Har-Row 1980, 75 pp.

Even though Hal was plain and not very clever, his disappointed parents knew that he was still a prince; thus he had to be raised as one. Hal didn't like his lonely, dull life until a new world was accidentally opened to him. A servant's child gave him an old book of monsters and told him that the monsters still lived under the distant mountains. Hal finally made a trip to the mountains, spent a day exploring, and by chance met Humbert, a young monster curious about the world. But, Hal's cruel cousin Archer captured Humbert and put him in a cage. Hal's daring rescue attempt almost resulted in disaster for both Humbert and Hal.

This is another example of Bulla's forte; a book with an action-filled plot, short chapters, large print, wide spaces between the lines, and a low reading level. A book about monsters has almost guaranteed appeal through third grade. Although the book is useful beyond third grade, readers in fourth and fifth grade may be more sensitive to Hal's apparent youth and the fantastic elements of the story.

Interest Level: 1-3. Reading Level: 2.1. Further Search Topics: Fantasy, Monsters-Fiction, Royalty-Fiction, Group 2, Read Aloud, Best Sellers.

Chew, Ruth. Witch's broom. Dodd 1977, 128 pp.

Amy's mother was the one who found the blue broom, but Amy and her friend Jean were the ones who learned it was magical. One night the broom flew Amy into a mountain cave where a coven of witches was meeting. It even forced Amy to answer the roll call for someone named Beryl. But it wasn't until it took both Amy and Jean back to the cave that they discovered the broom's connection to the strange bluejay that had been following them. The bluejay was really Beryl, a young and headstrong witch who had turned herself into the bluejay and then couldn't turn herself back. With the girls' unwitting help, Beryl found the charm to turn herself back into a witch and flew off on a scrawny old broom, leaving the blue broom for Amy and Jean.

What youngster wouldn't want a flying broomstick and the misadventures that go with owning one? Wish fulfillment can never be overrated as an appeal of Ruth Chew's books.

Interest Level: 2-5. Reading Level: 3.1. Further Search Topics: Witches-Fiction, Magic-Fiction, Fantasy, Birds-Fiction, Group 2, Transformations-Fiction.

Chew, Ruth. No such thing as a witch. Hastings 1971, 112 pp.

Despite the fact that their mother said there was no such thing as a witch, Tad and Nora were convinced that their neighbor Maggie Brown was indeed a witch. And they were right! Maggie Brown knew how to make a special kind of fudge that could make anyone into an animal-lover, enable people to talk with animals, or actually transform someone into an animal. All you had to do was to eat one, two, or three pieces of fudge respectively. But Maggie's overzealous love of animals and her disenchantment with housework eventually attracted the attention of her neighbors and the city health department. Only Tad and Nora's frantic efforts to help her saved Maggie from losing all of her animal friends.

A fairly detailed plot, the fascination of being able to change size and appearance and the intrigue involved in fooling the adults around Maggie make this one of Chew's best books.

Interest Level: 2-5. Reading Level: 2.2. Further Search Topics: Individualists-Fiction, Witches-Fiction, Animals-Fiction, Fantasy, Magic-Fiction, Brothers and Sisters-Fiction, Transformations-Fiction.

Chew, Ruth. The witch's garden. Hastings 1978, 112 pp.

Although its elements seem to promise an exciting adventure story, this is a disappointing book. The witch who moved into the dark, old home next door to Josh and Susan, was trying to improve her overgrown garden when Susan and Josh offered to help. The children accidentally splashed themselves with the witch's newest brew and found they suddenly became very tiny inhabitants of a dense and threatening jungle (the garden). After they regained their normal size, they dug into other areas of the garden. One hole they dug opened into an underground tunnel that they found was inhabited by a fire-breathing dragon. When the dragon cornered Mrs. Muldoon, Susan and Josh ran out of the tunnel, found the brew and splashed it onto the dragon. The dragon shrank away, Mrs. Muldoon was safe and the tunnel closed over.

Because there is little more suspense than in this description, the book fails to live up to its promise. In addition, the children's first sudden size change is just subtle enough to be confusing. Despite its problems the book is popular with Ruth Chew fans and therefore useful.

Interest Level: 2-5. Reading Level: 2.2. Further Search Topics: Witches-Fiction, Brothers and Sisters-Fiction, Magic-Fiction, Fantasy, Dragons-Fiction, Transformations-Fiction.

Chew, Ruth. The would-be witch. Hastings 1976, 112 pp.

Robin and her brother Andy took a liking to the clumsy white cat they saw in Zelda's Antique Shop. The cat apparently liked them, too, for it followed them home. Not having enough money to offer to buy Pearl from Zelda, the children tried to polish up an old pair of silver birds to trade for the cat. The polish turned out to be magical and made the birds real. When they tried the polish on a broom in Zelda's store, the broom began to fly. Upon discovering that Zelda wanted to be a witch but had failed the coven entrance exam, Rob helped her learn to fly and told her of the witches' meeting place that she and Andy had discovered. But the 12 witches who had been turned into cats were wicked enough to want to use Zelda to regain their human form and turn *her* into a cat. In attempting to prevent such a fate, Rob, Andy and Zelda set fire to the abandoned building being used as a meeting place. The 12 witches were rescued from the fire but charged with arson, which meant probable jail sentences for all of them. Zelda, finally a happy and capable witch, gave Pearl to Rob and Andy to thank them for their help.

A better-crafted story than many of the others, this also has a more evil cast of characters to provide additional interest.

Interest Level: 2-5. Reading Level: 2.2. Further Search Topics: Witches-Fiction, Brothers and Sisters-Fiction, Magic-Fiction, Fantasy, Transformations-Fiction, Cats-Fiction.

Chew, Ruth. Earthstar magic. Hastings 1979, 128 pp.

This is one of a series of similar stories by Ruth Chew. Each story involves two children and an old woman they usually suspect is a witch. As their suspicions become convictions they also find that, contrary to their expectation, the witch is very nice and often in need of help.

The children in this tale are brother and sister. Ben and Elizabeth first saw and then didn't see Trudy as she searched for a magical mushroom called an earthstar. Accidentally thrown together again, Ben and Elizabeth took a liking to Trudy, especially when she explained that she had been thrown out of her coven because she was so inept. In fact, she wasn't even able to control the earthstar. The earthstar manages to get all three in and out of adventures (including becoming tiny, flying and almost being eaten) before they learn to control its power. As the story ends, Trudy, finally respected by the other witches, flies off with a promise that Ben and Elizabeth will see her again.

Very lightweight but also very popular with young lovers of witch stories. There seems to be just the right amount of adventure to make up for the very benign witch.

Interest Level: 2-5. Reading Level: 2.2. Further Search Topics: Witches-Fiction, Magic-Fiction, Fantasy, Vacation-Fiction, Brothers and Sisters-Fiction, Transformations-Fiction.

Chew, Ruth. What the witch left. Hastings 1973, 128 pp.

One afternoon Katy and Louise decided to search through the locked drawer of an old dresser. Inside they found strange-looking gloves, an old robe, boots, a mirror and a tin box. The girls quickly learned that each item was magical. With the gloves on, the girls could draw, play piano, weave or write. They thought their new talents were wonderful until they each wrote identical school compositions. When she wore the robe for the school play, Louise found out that it made people invisible. The boots, which travelled 21 miles with each step, took the girls to Mexico, but made them late for lunch at home. The mirror showed them anything they wanted to see, and the box "found" everything that was lost. A very light story for children who don't need high adventure but like a mixture of humor and magic.

Interest Level: 3-5. Reading Level: 3.1. Further Search Topics: Magic-Fiction, Mexico-Fiction, Witches-Fiction, Fantasy, Humorous Fiction.

Chew, Ruth. The wishing tree. Hastings 1980, 142 pp.

Peggy and Brian's discovery of a talking cat, a bird with a beautiful song, and a strange and frightening tree led them to a shopping bag lady, a giant named Fred, a gold key and a magical tablecloth. In a rather complicated series of events, the children and the cat finally succeeded in retrieving the tablecloth from Annie (the old woman to whom Puss had loaned it) and giving it back to Fred, who needed it to help satisfy his gigantic appetite. In addition, they returned Fred to normal human size, rescued Annie from a fall on the ice, introduced the two characters and encouraged them to live together in Fred's castle.

Complicated enough already, the story's lengthy adventure that leads up to the discovery of the key (climbing into the magical tree and swimming in a pond) makes the plot even more complex. If a reader doesn't expect more than benign fantasy and fun this is an adequate choice.

Interest Level: 2-5. Reading Level: 2.2. Further Search Topics: Magic-Fiction, Fantasy, Brothers and Sisters-Fiction, Giants-Fiction, Cats-Fiction.

Davidson, Carson. Fast-talking dolphin; illus by Sylvia Stone. Dodd 1978, 127 pp.

After a rather slow start, this story develops into a well-paced adventure-fantasy with touches of warmth and humor. Eric wasn't just surprised when he found a dolphin in the 10-foot fish pond, he was astonished. Not only had there never been a dolphin there before, but this dolphin spoke in poetry. His name was Wallingford Ullingham Lowell III; Wallingford for short. He was elegant, proud and cultured; but as Eric soon found out, he was very impractical. He didn't seem to realize that he needed salt water and more fish than those in the pond in order to live. It was Eric who figured out a way to keep salt flowing into the pond and a supply of fresh fish. He also kept Wallingford's presence a secret, just as Wallingford requested. The day that Wallingford was discovered was the day that Eric had to break his promise. In order to find out who else had found out about Wallingford, Eric talked with his brother. Together they scouted the town before they realized that Herbert Benson was the only other person who had seen Wallingford.

Herbert reluctantly admitted that he had told his father about the dolphin. Eric knew enough about Mr. Benson to realize that he was just crazy enough to want to harm the dolphin. Eric and his brother gathered all the local children together to shield Wallingford from Mr. Benson. Even Herbert dared to defy his father for the first time. As Mr. Benson struggled with Eric and his brother, he fell, hit his head and rolled into the pond. Wallingford dove to save him, but his leg was caught between two rocks. With the others' help, Wallingford, Eric and his brother Karl were able to save Mr. Benson from drowning.

A few days later Eric, with new-found skills, spontaneously recited a poem about friendship to Wallingford. Wallingford answered with a rare compliment and for the first time used Eric's name (a show of respect). They were such true friends that when Wallingford was helicopter-lifted out of the pond and taken back to his research project, Eric couldn't understand why his father didn't tell him of Wallingford's departure. Eventually he realized that his father had been right; he would rather remember Wallingford swimming in the pond than in a helicopter's sling. Also, Wallingford would have been embarrassed to be seen making so undignified a departure. Wallingford's final message to Eric was a note that Eric found scratched in the dirt thanking him for the salt and the fish and saying that they would one day meet again.

Don't take the plot too seriously or peruse it too carefully for it won't stand up to scrutiny. This is merely a pleasant story with enough humor, action and originality to intrigue many readers. The book's major drawback is the poetry Wallingford spouts: the poetic form and somewhat difficult language will throw some readers. On the other hand, the book could be very useful in a classroom unit about poetry.

Interest Level: 3-5. Reading Level: 3.1. Further Search Topics: Poetry, Dolphins-Fiction, Pets-Fiction, Fantasy, Friendship-Fiction, Humorous Fiction.

Dolch, Edward W. Andersen stories; illus by Carmen Mowry. Garrard 1956, 165 pp.

The best way to be introduced to Andersen's fairy tales is to hear them told or read aloud. Because they are beautifully written literary tales they suffer tremendously when the language is simplified enough so that the stories can be included in a reader. Furthermore, episodes have been cut out of some tales ("Big Klaus and Little Klaus") and others have been divided into chapters ("The Ugly Duckling"). But, where there is a need for such an easy version of Hans Christian Andersen, this selection will do. The 18 chapters tell only 11 stories. Most of the included stories are familiar ("The Emperor's New Clothes," "The Little Mermaid," "Thumbelina" etc.); all are enjoyable. Illustrations, however, are unattractive and uninspiring. One further caution: the reading level jumps from 2.1 to 3.2. Dolch Pleasure Reading Book series.

Interest Level: 2-5. Reading Level: 3.1. Further Search Topics: Folklore, Fantasy, Group 2, Fairy Tales, Andersen, Hans Christian.

Dolch, Edward W. Fairy stories; illus by Marguerite Dolch and Yolande Cuypers-Fransen. Garrard 1950, 165 pp.

A collection of mostly familiar fairy tales told in the Dolchs' very simplified manner. Because the book's purpose is not to provide the most literate version of favorite fairy tales, better versions of any of the stories can be found elsewhere. It provides instead, very accessible versions of tales young readers have enjoyed for years. Includes "Cinderella," "Hansel and Gretel," "Jack and the Bean Stalk," "Snow White," "Sleeping Beauty," and "The Elves and the Shoemaker," among others. Dolch Pleasure Reading Book series.

Interest Level: 1-4. Reading Level: 2.2. Further Search Topics: Folklore, Fairy Tales, Fantasy, Group 2.

Dolch, Edward W. Irish stories; illus by Carmen Mowry. Garrard 1958, 165 pp.

Besides controlling the vocabulary used in the stories, the Dolchs seem to include only stories with very uncomplicated plots. Once again they split the longer stories into two chapters. Thus, from 17 chapters there come only 12 stories. Most of the stories will be unfamiliar to readers (except perhaps those about Finn McCool), but all are pleasurable. See *Andersen Stories* for more information. Dolch Basic Vocabulary Book series.

Interest Level: 2-5. Reading Level: 2.2. Further Search Topics: Folklore, Fantasy, Ireland-Fiction, Giants-Fiction.

Dolch, Edward W. Stories from France; illus by Gordon Laite. Garrard 1963, 167 pp.

It is very difficult to simplify a story and not lose at least some of its original flavor. Such is the case here and in all the Dolch retellings. Nevertheless, this collection of folktales is quite useful for the French flavor it does maintain. The stories, as they are retold, are good; not great, but good. There are 14 stories related in the 19 chapters. This is a result of splitting the longer, more complicated stories into episodes. Some frustration may arise for readers because there is no indication that a story may involve more than one chapter. The much-improved illustrations that introduce each chapter and adorn the cover help make this more attractive than the earlier books. The book ends with a list of the provinces from which the stories came as well as a pronunciation key to French names. Folklore of the World series.

Interest Level: 2-6. Reading Level: 3.1. Further Search Topics: Folklore, Fantasy, France-Fiction, Royalty-Fiction, Group 2, Knights and Knighthood-Fiction.

Dolch, Edward W. Stories from Old Russia; illus by James Lewicki. Garrard 1964, 168 pp.

There are 21 chapters and only nine stories in this volume. These are more robust and exciting adventure stories than many of the other Dolch collections listed here, although once again the simplified vocabulary is somewhat restrictive. A guide to pronounciation of some Russian names is included at the end of the book. More colorful illustrations than some of the other titles. Very consistent reading level. See *Stories From France* for more information. Folklore of the World series.

Interest Level: 2-6. Reading Level: 2.1. Further Search Topics: Folklore, Fantasy, Russia-Fiction, Witches-Fiction.

Packard, Edward. The cave of time; illus by Paul Granger. Bantam 1979, 115 pp.

Beware of the greater than usual inconsistency of reading levels within this book. Its difficulty level ranges from 2.2 to 4.2. See notes for *Sugarcane Island* for more information about the series. In paperback only. Choose Your Own Adventure series.

Interest Level: 2-6. Reading Level: 4.1. Further Search Topics: Time-Fiction, Science Fiction, Fantasy, Group 2.

Seuss, Dr. One fish, two fish, red fish, blue fish. Beginner 1960, 63pp.

Beginning with one almost ordinary-looking fish, this is a humorous look at the "funny things that go by." When Dr. Seuss says "funny," he really means highly imaginative, whimsical, and totally nonsensical. Each of the more than 20 silly creatures are described and appropriately illustrated to appeal to a child's sense of the ridiculous. Reader.

Interest Level: 1-2. Reading Level: 1.1. Further Search Topics: Fantasy, Wit and Humor, Poetry, Humorous Fiction, Stories in Rhyme.

Seuss, Dr. The cat in the hat. Beginner 1957, 61 pp.

When the Cat in the Hat visits two children, a dreary, boring afternoon becomes almost too exciting. The Cat's juggling act and the two "things" he brings with him almost destroy the house. But the Cat cleans up so well that when the children's mother comes home and asks what they did all afternoon, they can't decide if they should tell her.

A funny, rhyming tale of the destruction all children can create and the boredom all children can feel. Reader format.

Interest Level: 1-3. Reading Level: 1.2. Further Search Topics: Humorous Fiction, Fantasy, Cats-Fiction, Poetry, Troublemakers-Fiction, Best Sellers, Stories in Rhyme.

Seuss, Dr. The cat in the hat comes back. Beginner 1958, 63 pp.

Sally and her brother were doing a good job of clearing the front walk of snow when the Cat in the Hat showed up. While they worked, the Cat created a pink mess in the house. The mess only became worse when he tried to clean it. The pink spot finally covered the snow all around the house until the Cat called upon his friends Little Cats A-Z. It was Little Cat Z and his magic zoom that eventually not only cleaned the snow, but cleared the front walk as well.

Another zany, rhymed adventure of the mischievious Cat whose ability to get into trouble endears him to most children from pre-school to early third grade. Reader format.

Interest Level: 1-3. Reading Level: 1.2. Further Search Topics: Fantasy, Cats-Fiction, Troublemakers-Fiction, Humorous Fiction, Snow-Fiction, Poetry, Best Sellers, Stories in Rhyme.

Thomas, Kathleen. Out of the bug jar; illus by Tom O'Sullivan. Dodd 1981, 125 pp.

Even though 10-year-old Tom Jenkins didn't believe in the tooth fairy, when one of his teeth fell out, he placed it under his pillow just in case he was wrong. In the middle of that night he was awakened by a small creature crawling under his pillow and grumbling. Tom quickly scooped him into a bug jar he kept nearby and thus began two years of life with Marvin, a tooth fairy. Marvin was a delightful dictator; he ruled Tom's life. He put Tom into a terrible predicament when Tom tried to charge others to see him and Marvin became invisible. Marvin insisted on being fed just what he demanded, despite the difficulties he made for Tom. He badgered Tom to do his homework, to brush his teeth, and to tell the truth. He even managed to follow Tom to school. The only other person Marvin would allow to see or hear him was Tom's friend Sammy. Tom couldn't get rid of Marvin either. Because Tom had captured him, Marvin, should he ever have been able to escape, was entitled to take *all* of Tom's teeth as compensation for being held prisoner.

Actually Marvin didn't really want to escape. He had grown tired of having to race around and collect teeth. For a while then, everyone was fairly content. Tom had all his teeth and Marvin had a rather nice home. Then quite by accident, Marvin got loose. Both Tom and Marvin wanted Tom to catch Marvin again. Tom wanted to keep his teeth and Marvin wanted to keep his comfortable lifestyle, but Marvin played by the rules and wouldn't give Tom any help at all. After more than seven days of valient but fruitless efforts and nights of sleeping with tape over his mouth, Tom finally caught Marvin and all were happy again.

An amusing story told in short sentences and short chapters. The book should be popular with those who enjoy either fantasy or humor.

Interest Level: 3-5. Reading Level: 2.2. Further Search Topics: Fantasy, Fairies-Fiction, Humorous Fiction, Teeth-Fiction.

FARM LIFE-FICTION

Clymer, Eleanor. Me and the Eggman; illus by David K. Stone. Dutton 1972, 57 pp.

As Donald's life became more and more miserable and as his chores and responsibilities around his small, overcrowded, urban apartment increased, he began to look for a way to escape. Thinking that if he could just get to the country, life would be better, Donald sneaked into a truck owned by a farmer who delivered eggs to the city. Not surprisingly the farmer, a sharp speaking, independent old man, was not at all happy to find Donald. Reluctantly, the Eggman, as the farmer was called, agreed to let Donald stay a week and help to work his rundown farm. The week stretched into a summer in which Donald learned to face and accept reality, to love the Eggman and to like himself.

This book is a surprisingly consistent success with reluctant readers, especially boys. Watch for the lack of quotation marks around the dialogue and the somewhat small print.

Interest Level: 3-6. Reading Level: 3.2. Further Search Topics: Family Problems-Fiction, Poverty-Fiction, Vacation-Fiction, Runaways-Fiction, Farm Life-Fiction, Best Sellers.

FEET-FICTION

Seuss, Dr. The foot book. Random 1968, unp (27 pp).

Left feet, right feet, big feet, small feet; with its rhyme, silly illustrations and rhythmic celebration of feet of all descriptions, this book is a sure winner with the very young. Reader format.

Interest Level 1-2. Reading Level: 1.1. Further Search Topics: Best Sellers, Feet-Fiction, Humorous Fiction, Poetry, Wit and Humor, Stories in Rhyme.

Waldorf, Mary. Jake McGee and his feet; illus by Leonard Shortall. HM 1980, 82 pp.

His severe reading difficulties made school the worst place in the world for Jake McGee. On the day that his reading tutor became so impatient with him that she sent Jake to the principal, Jake decided that he couldn't stand school any longer and ran away. He didn't actually run away, he just let his feet finally do what they wanted. His feet were always getting Jake in trouble. They walked too slowly to get him to school on time; they wouldn't stay still once he was in school; and they were always trying to trip someone.

Jake knew that in addition to having problems with his feet he had reading problems, but no one at his old school in the country had noticed. When he and his family moved to the city everything had changed. Jake's mother was always at work or tired. Jake hadn't made any friends and so was always alone. But Jake thought the biggest of all his immediate problems was his feet. The day he ran away, Jake's feet led him to a lost baby, an eccentric old woman, and a neighbor boy, all of whom helped Jake recognize and deal with his real problem.

The book is not high literary quality. The characterization is somewhat flat and the plot is fairly predictable. However, the sentences and chapters are short, the vocabulary is manageable, and Jake's feelings will be shared by many non-readers.

Interest Level: 3-5. Reading Level: 2.2. Further Search Topics: School Stories, Moving, Household-Fiction, Runaways-Fiction, Academic Problems-Fiction, Working Parents-Fiction, Loneliness-Fiction, Feet-Fiction.

FIDRYCH, MARK "THE BIRD"

Burchard, Susan H. Sports star: Mark "The Bird" Fidrych. HarBraceJ 1977, 64 pp.

Although his major league career was short, it was also notable. Mark Fidrych's way of concentrating on his pitching was by talking to the baseball. Entry for *Sports Hero: Bill Walton*, by Marshall Burchard, provides more information about the book. Sports Star series.

Interest Level: 2-6. Reading Level: 2.2. Further Search Topics: Biography, Baseball-Biography, Fidrych, Mark "The Bird."

FIRE-FICTION

Bernstein, Margery. Coyote goes hunting for fire; illus by Ed Heffernan. Scribner 1974, 40 pp.

A delightful story that can be read for fun or used as part of a unit on North American Indians. A long time ago when there was no fire, all the animals but Coyote banded together to find it. The animals left Coyote behind because he was always spoiling their plans. Coyote saw them leave, chased after them and once more tried to direct everything, but only ended up losing fire. Cartoon-like illustrations add to the humor of the story. This book should make a simple, but effective play.

Interest Level: 1-4. Reading Level 2.1. Further Search Topics: Animals-Fiction, Legends, Mythology,

Fire-Fiction, Indians of North America-Legends, Coyotes-Fiction, Group 2, Creation-Fiction, Drama.

Law, Carol Russell. The case of the Weird Street firebug; illus by Bill Morrison. Knopf 1980, 119 pp.

This is the humorous story of a Nancy Drew-type character who gets involved in a mystery before she is even half finished with her mail-order detective lessons. Steffi wanted very much to be a detective. When she saw an ad for a local correspondence course, she tracked down the shabby office in a run-down building on Weir Street, and went to visit Jeff Dangerfield of Dangerfield Detective School. Steffi's first lesson, trailing suspects, was a disaster. She tried to pick out suspicious characters at a fire on Weir Street on her way home. The only really suspicious character (Beady Eyes) didn't go anywhere, so Steffi couldn't follow him. Her next attempts were very obvious and only resulted in her own anger and embarrassment. On her way back to seek advice from Dangerfield, Steffi literally ran into Beady Eyes again. She didn't think anything more about him until she saw him a short time later at another fire just down the street from Dangerfield's office. As the fire moved closer to Dangerfield's building, Steffi took desperate measures to try and save her friend. Steffi's efforts were interpreted by Beady Eyes as attempts to indicate that he was an arsonist. By the time Steffi figured out that Beady Eyes really was an arsonist, he had her cornered. A timely entry by the police saved both Steffi and Dangerfield. Steffi's reward for the capture of Beady Eyes was a medal from the police and a partnership with Dangerfield.

A fast-paced story, as well as slightly more original characters than most stories of this genre, make this a likely success with third through sixth grade readers. Capers series.

Interest Level: 3-6. Reading Level: 3.1. Further Search Topics: Mystery and Detective Stories, Humorous Fiction, Fire-Fiction, Detectives-Fiction, Crime-Fiction.

FIREFIGHTERS

Beame, Rona. Ladder company 108. Messner 1973, 63 pp.

The reader of this book will literally live through several days with a New York City fire company. The author's "Dragnet"-like writing style, her use of photographs, and actual people, all make the firefighters' experiences very real. It is an exciting, engrossing and satisfying book. The heavily-used jargon will be quickly understood, thus should pose no real obstacle to most readers.

Interest Level 2-6. Reading Level: 3.1. Further Search Topics: Firefighters, Occupations, City Life, New York City, Group 2, Best Sellers.

FIREFLIES-FICTION

Eastman, Philip D. Sam and the firefly. Beginner 1958, 62 pp.

Sam, the owl, went looking for a playmate one night but found everyone was asleep except a mischievous firefly named Gus. When Sam showed Gus how to write words with his light in the dark sky, Gus went wild. First he tried to direct auto traffic, then airplane traffic, until finally the Hot Dog Man, an angry victim of Gus' tricks, captured him. However, when the Hot Dog Man tried to take Gus out of town, his truck became stuck on the railroad tracks in front of an oncoming train. Gus, freed from the jar in which he'd been caught, quickly wrote the word STOP in the sky and saved everyone. Gus' silliness, the catastrophies he

caused and his final triumph should interest almost any young child who likes humor or excitement. Reader format.

Interest Level: 1-2. Reading Level: 1.2. Further Search Topics: Best Sellers, Fireflies-Fiction, Owls-Fiction, Humorous Fiction.

FISHING

Buckley, Peter. I am from Puerto Rico. S ËAN S 1971, 127 pp.

Federico Ramirez had enjoyed his two years in New York City and didn't like the idea of moving back to Puerto Rico. When he arrived, he had no friends, no T.V., and nothing to do. Then Neri taught Federico the local games, showed him the sights and introduced him to Narcisco, a special fisherman. Narcisco took Federico through the wonders of the coral reefs. He taught him how to dive and fish. Within several months Federico was thoroughly at home in the water and loved Puerto Rico.

There is so much information about Puerto Rico and marine life that the book is never dry. Federico tells his own story as a series of fascinating experiences (meeting up with a shark, playing pinball, scuba diving at night, keeping a large turtle as a pet, etc.). There are abundant black and white photographs. An excellent choice for research (no index) or recreational reading. The print size is slightly on the small side, but the space between lines is good. Recently out of print, but worth looking for.

Interest Level: 5-6. Reading Level: 5.1. Further Search Topics: Puerto Rico, Fishing, Moving, Household-Fiction, Marine Biology, Scuba Diving, Ethnic Groups.

FLIGHT

Bendick, Jeanne. The first book of airplanes. Watts 1975, revised edition, 65 pp.

It will take a determined reader to get much technical information from this overview of airplanes. The first sections (thrust, lift gravity, drag, and parts of a plane) promise simple, understandable explanations of complicated topics. The next portion of the book fails to live up to that promise. The descriptions of airplane engines will be intelligible only to the reader who already knows how an engine works. The history of flight is little more than an outline. The two-page chapter on air maps and distances will do more to confuse than instruct most readers. On the other hand, the information about airports, control towers, and types and uses of aircrafts is better. The book is well-indexed and includes a four-page glossary. It is perhaps best used as a general introduction to airplanes (skip the three areas mentioned above). For technical information about flight, look elsewhere. Print size is adequate but spacing between lines could have been more generous.

Interest Level: 4-6. Reading Level: 3.2. Further Search Topics: Airports, Engines, Flight, Airplanes.

Simon, Seymour. The paper airplane book; illus by Byron Barton. Viking Pr 1971, 48 pp.

For the theory as well as the practice behind successful paper airplanes, this is the book. This is as much a book about the principles of flight as it is about how to make a paper airplane. The reader is introduced to thrust, drag, lift and gravity through explanation, examples, diagrams and experiments. The effects of vertical and horizontal stabilizers, elevators, rudders, flaps, and ailerons on both paper and real airplanes, is explained and illustrated. Instructions are given for building and modifying a basic plane as each new idea is introduced. The book ends with plans for four more sophisticated planes and encouragement to try further experiments. An excellent resource for the enthusiast. Print is small.

Interest Level: 3-6. Reading Level: 3.2. Further Search Topics: Airplanes, Handicrafts, Flight.

FLIGHT-FICTION

Terman, Douglas. By balloons to the Sahara; illus by Paul Granger. Bantam 1979, 117 pp.

See the entry for *Sugarcane Island*, by Edward Packard for detailed information about the series. Available in paperback edition only. Choose Your Own Adventure series.

Interest Level: 2-6. Reading Level: 3.2. Further Search Topics: Voyages and Travels-Fiction, Flight-Fiction, Best Sellers, Group 2.

FLYING SAUCERS

Cohen, Daniel. Creatures from UFOs. Dodd 1978, 112 pp.

A series of reports about close encounters of the third kind. The author offers both sides of each story, then allows the reader to draw his or her own conclusions. Stories will intrigue even those readers not already interested in UFOs. Index. Photographs. A natural. Parts can even be read aloud.

Interest Level: 3-6. Reading Level: 3.1. Further Search Topics: Best Sellers, Flying Saucers.

FLYING SAUCERS-FICTION

Adrian, Mary. The fireball mystery illus by Reisie Lonette. Hastings 1977, 118 pp.

While stargazing one night, Tim and Vicky and their friend Joey saw a meteor fall onto their private island. Before they were able to find it the children realized that someone else was trying to steal the meteorite from them. As much astronomy as mystery here. Beyond fourth grade, the reader may begin to find the astronomy lesson heavy-handed and the mystery light.

Interest Level: 2-4. Reading Level: 3.1. Further Search Topics: Mystery and Detective Stories, Astronomy, Flying Saucers-Fiction, Outer Space-Fiction, Group 2.

Clark, Margaret Goff. Barney in space; illus by Ted Lewin. Dodd 1981, 155 pp.

This is a sequel to *Barney and the UFO*, but it stands by itself quite well. It's title is a misnomer, however, for it isn't until the last third of the book that Barney goes into space. In the previous book Barney made friends with Tibbo, a Gark from the planet Ornam. In this book Tibbo tries to save Barney from an evil Gark named Rokell. Because Barney knew about Garks, Rokell was afraid Barney would betray them and turn humans against Garks. To prevent that from happening, Rokell was determined to kidnap Barney. Tibbo was too far from Earth to do more than warn Barney of Rokell's intentions and tell him not to be alone at any time. Barney's friends Dick and Kara tried to protect Barney but only succeeded in endangering their own lives. When Kara was almost killed by Rokell, Barney decided to face Rokell alone and try to defeat him, but Rokell's powers were too strong for Barney. Against their wills both Barney and David were taken aboard a spaceship. They discovered later, to their relief, that the spaceship belonged to a friend of Tibbo's who was commanding the ship from the moon. Barney and Dick were to be taken to the moon for safety until Rokell could be controlled. Rokell didn't give up easily. He attacked the ship twice before he captured it and set it down on a remote portion of the moon. Only Barney's quick thinking stopped Rokell permanently and saved both Barney and Dick.

The preliminary sequences are more suspenseful and exciting than the space travel; however, the book will not disappoint young science fiction fans.

Interest Level: 4-6. Reading Level: 4.2. Further Search Topics: Science Fiction, Flying Saucers-Fiction, Outer Space-Fiction, Orphans-Fiction, Kidnapping-Fiction, Aliens-Fiction, Adoption-Fiction.

Clark, Margaret Goff. Barney and the UFO; illus by Ted Lewin. Dodd 1979, 159 pp.

Barney felt a strange prickly sensation several times before he discovered that it was caused by Tibbo, a Gark from the planet Ornam. Tibbo had selected Barney as a friend who would accompany him back to Ornam. Barney was to learn the peaceful ways of Gark and then return to Earth to help persuade the world to accept the aliens. At first the idea of visiting Ornam appealed to Barney because he liked Tibbo and felt very lonely and unsure of his adoptive family's love. Those were the very reasons that Tibbo had chosen Barney: he wanted someone without strong ties to Earth and Barney's only tie when he was first contacted by Tibbo was his little brother Scott. As the time to go grew closer, Barney found a new and strong friendship with Dave, a science whiz-kid, and great love for his new parents. Tibbo, however, was determined to hold Barney to his promise. Only a last minute confrontation between Tibbo and Barney, David, Scott and Mr. and Mrs. Crandall prevented Tibbo from succeeding. But even as Tibbo left, he and Barney acknowledged their new friendship and agreed to keep in touch.

Because of its fairly slow beginning, readers must be well-introduced to this book. If they can be persuaded to be patient while the author sets the stage for about 18 pages they will be rewarded with a decent, if somewhat wordy, story of friendship, UFO's, space travel and family affection.

Interest Level: 3-6. Reading Level: 3.2. Further Search Topics: Science Fiction, Flying Saucers-Fiction, Kidnapping-Fiction, Foster Homes-Fiction, Family-Fiction, Adoption-Fiction, Aliens-Fiction, Loneliness-Fiction, Orphans-Fiction.

Curtis, Philip. The invasion of the Brain Sharpeners; illus by Tony Ross. Knopf 1979, 117 pp.

This book is one of a number of books published by Albert Knopf under the series title Capers. They are meant to be (and with few exceptions are) light, easy-to-read fiction, published simultaneously in hardcover and paperback editions. Each book is about 120 pages long with chapter length varying from 9 to 14 pages. Print is plenty large and spacing between lines is always adequate. Plots are built around an idea of guaranteed appeal, descriptive passages are kept to a minimum and action (often suspenseful) abounds. This should, on the whole, be a very useful series. Some entries (i.e., *Man From the Sky* and *Who Stole the Wizard of Oz*, both by Avi) are either too difficult or too obscure to be widely appealing, but they are by far the exceptions to the rule.

Invasion of the Brain Sharpeners is the catchy science fiction story of Michael's successful, but risky, attempt to rid his fifth grade classroom of the overpowering influence of the Brain Sharpeners. The Brain Sharpeners came from another galaxy to search for humans to help them colonize their Planet Five. Humans were so lacking in brain power that the Brain Sharpeners' plan was to periodically expose each child to brain-developing rays, then put them through intensive courses of study guided by their also-exposed teacher. When the children had all learned enough to be beneficial to the Brain

Sharpeners, they were to be taken from Earth to Planet Five. Michael was the only one to see the danger they were in and to attempt to stop the plot. He managed to chase the aliens away and to prevent his classmates and teacher from receiving their second dose of rays, but in doing so, he sent the principal to the spaceship. Michael's classmates were thus saved, but his principal was never heard from again. Capers series.

Interest Level: 3-6. Reading Level: 3.1. Further Search Topics: Science Fiction, Flying Saucers-Fiction, Aliens-Fiction, School Stories, Kidnapping-Fiction, Best Sellers, Academic Problems-Fiction, Brainwashing-Fiction.

Pinkwater, Daniel Manus. Fat men from space. Dodd 1977, 57 pp.

The evening after his trip to the dentist William found that he could still hear radio programs when his radio was turned off. He was even more surprised to find that when he wired himself to a fence he could hear spacemen talking. When the spacemen discovered that William could hear them, they landed and captured him. They were on a top secret mission and couldn't risk any human knowing about their existence. The spacemen were about to invade Earth to consume all the junk food they could find. As mass panic set in on Earth, William could do nothing to save his fellow humans. He was held captive and helpless until the invaders' interest was captured by a giant potato pancake floating in outer space.

A tongue-in-check, slapstick spoof of science fiction, food fads, and junk food. Do not expect anything more.

Interest Level: 3-5. Reading Level: 3.2. Further Search Topics: Science Fiction, Humorous Fiction, Food-Fiction, Flying Saucers-Fiction, Aliens-Fiction, Best Sellers, Kidnapping-Fiction, Teeth-Fiction.

Sleator, William. Into the dream; illus by Ruth Sanderson. Dutton 1979, 137 pp.

Paul and Francine each started having what, at first, seemed like nightmares. As the dreams became more detailed and forboding, they discovered that they were sharing the same nightmare. They dreamed of a four-year-old boy, swirling lights, and a large dog. After awhile they figured out that the dog was trying to save the little boy from some unknown danger. As the pieces of the puzzle began to increase in number, Paul and Francine decided that the dream was in some way connected to a night over four years earlier when they had both been staying at the same motel. They, a pregnant woman, and a pregnant dog had all been affected by the telepathic power given off by a spaceship. The progeny of the woman and the dog had been given extraordinary mental powers; powers that a secret government agency wanted to mold and then put to their own use. The danger Paul and Francine felt came from two government agents sent to take the young boy Noah from his mother. Their attempt ended in a bizarre scene at an amusement park, where Noah levitated a broken ferris wheel chair to safety. By thus exposing his talent in public, Noah unconsciously insured against its secret and unsupervised use by the government.

A terrifying and suspense-filled psychological thriller whose main problems are a slightly overdrawn ending and a variable reading level. Reading level drops as low as 2.1 and climbs occasionally to 4.1.

Interest Level: 5-6. Reading Level: 3.2. Further Search Topics: Best Sellers, Supernatural-Fiction, Occult-Fiction, Flying Saucers-Fiction, Nonverbal Communication-Fiction, Dreams-Fiction, Survival-Fiction, Extra Sensory Perception-Fiction, Horror-Fiction.

FOLKLORE

Aesop. Aesop's Fables; retold by Ann Terry White; illus by Helen Siegl. Random 1964, 77 pp.

An attractive, appealing-looking collection of forty of Aesop's fables. Children without a background in folklore are not likely to read these short tales without encouragement. Where there is such encouragement, or a curricular need, this is an excellent source. The use of many proper nouns in the text means the book tests artificially low at 2.2. It is probably more appropriate to consider it 3.1.

Interest Level: 2-6. Reading Level: 3.1. Further Search Topics: Fables, Folklore, Group 2.

Arkhurst, Joyce. The adventures of Spider; West African folktales; illus by Jerry Pinkney. Little 1964, 58 pp.

A delightful collection of six West African folktales about Spider. Spider is mischievous, greedy, lazy and clever. He loves to eat and he hates to work. Four of the stories tell of Spider's ill-fated attempts to get food without having to work for it ("How Spider Got a Thin Waist," "How Spider Got a Bald Head," "How Spider Helped a Fisherman," and "Why Spiders Live in Dark Corners"). One story tells of his greed ("How the World Got Wisdom"), and only one story is complimentary ("Why Spider Lives in Ceilings"). All are short, gentle, humorous, and adapt well to dramatization or retelling.

Interest Level: 2-6. Reading Level 3.1. Further Search Topics: Humorous Fiction, Spiders-Fiction, Folklore, Tricksters-Fiction, Africa-Folklore, Group 2, Read Aloud, Creation-Fiction, Drama.

Dolch, Edward W. "Why" stories; illus by Marguerite Dolch. Garrard 1952, 160 pp.

"Why the Bear Has a Little Tail," "Why Turkeys Have Red Eyes," and "How the Tiger Got His Stripes" are three titles that illustrate the type of stories found in this collection. Seventeen short, simple folktales explain why the world and creatures in it operate and appear as they do. All of the tales can be found elsewhere. However, few if any stories are likely to be familiar to readers. This type of story is one children often find very appealing. The stories are understandable, logical within their own framework and simple enough to be retold to others. The reading level varies from 1.2 to 2.2. Dolch Basic Vocabulary Book series.

Interest Level: 1-4. Reading Level: 2.2. Further Search Topics: Folklore, Why Stories, Animals-Fiction, Group 2, Creation-Fiction.

Dolch, Edward W. Robin Hood stories; illus by Carmen Mowry. Garrard 1957, 162 pp.

The illustrations are still drab, but the stories in this volume are exciting. Here we find straight-forward adventure and familiar characters: Robin Hood, Little John, Will Scarlet, Sheriff of Nottingham, Allan-a-dale and Sir Richard of Lea. The book makes a good choice for adventure lovers. Dolch Pleasure Reading Book series.

Interest Level: 2-6. Reading Level: 2.2. Further Search Topics: Robin Hood, Knights and Knighthood-Fiction, Folklore, Crime-Fiction.

Dolch, Edward W. Andersen stories; illus by Carmen Mowry. Garrard 1956, 165 pp.

The best way to be introduced to Andersen's fairy tales is to hear them told or read aloud. Because they are beautifully written literary tales they suffer tremendously when the language is simplified enough so that the stories can be included in a reader. Furthermore, episodes have been cut out of some tales ("Big Klaus and Little Klaus") and others have been divided into chapters ("The Ugly Duckling"). But, where there is a need for such an easy version of Hans Christian Andersen, this selection will do. The 18 chapters tell only 11 stories. Most of the included stories are familiar ("The Emperor's New Clothes," "The Little Mermaid," "Thumbelina" etc.); all are enjoyable. Illustrations, however, are unattractive and uninspiring. One further caution: the reading level jumps from 2.1 to 3.2. Dolch Pleasure Reading Book series.

Interest Level: 2-5. Reading Level: 3.1. Further Search Topics: Folklore, Fantasy, Group 2, Fairy Tales, Andersen, Hans Christian.

Dolch, Edward W. Fairy stories; illus by Marguerite Dolch and Yolande Cuypers-Fransen. Garrard 1950, 165 pp.

A collection of mostly familiar fairy tales told in the Dolchs' very simplified manner. Because the book's purpose is not to provide the most literate version of favorite fairy tales, better versions of any of the stories can be found elsewhere. It provides instead, very accessible versions of tales young readers have enjoyed for years. Includes "Cinderella," "Hansel and Gretel," "Jack and the Bean Stalk," "Snow White," "Sleeping Beauty," and "The Elves and the Shoemaker," among others. Dolch Pleasure Reading Book series.

Interest Level: 1-4. Reading Level: 2.2. Further Search Topics: Folklore, Fairy Tales, Fantasy, Group 2.

Dolch, Edward W. Irish stories; illus by Carmen Mowry. Garrard 1958, 165 pp.

Besides controlling the vocabulary used in the stories, the Dolchs seem to include only stories with very uncomplicated plots. Once again they split the longer stories into two chapters. Thus, from 17 chapters there come only 12 stories. Most of the stories will be unfamiliar to readers (except perhaps those about Finn McCool), but all are pleasurable. See *Andersen Stories* for more information. Dolch Basic Vocabulary Book series.

Interest Level: 2-5. Reading Level: 2.2. Further Search Topics: Folklore, Fantasy, Ireland-Fiction, Giants-Fiction.

Dolch, Edward W. Stories from France; illus by Gordon Laite. Garrard 1963, 167 pp.

It is very difficult to simplify a story and not lose at least some of its original flavor. Such is the case here and in all the Dolch retellings. Nevertheless, this collection of folktales is quite useful for the French flavor it does maintain. The stories, as they are retold, are good; not great, but good. There are 14 stories related in the 19 chapters. This is a result of splitting the longer, more complicated stories into episodes. Some frustration may arise for readers because there is no indication that a story may involve more than one chapter. The much-improved illustrations that introduce each chapter and adorn the cover help make this more attractive than the earlier books. The book ends with a list of the provinces from which the stories came as well as a pronunciation key to French names. Folklore of the World series.

Interest Level: 2-6. Reading Level: 3.1. Further Search Topics: Folklore, Fantasy, France-Fiction, Royalty-Fiction, Group 2, Knights and Knighthood-Fiction.

Dolch, Edward W. Stories from Old Russia; illus by James Lewicki. Garrard 1964, 168 pp.

There are 21 chapters and only nine stories in this volume. These are more robust and exciting adventure stories than many of the other Dolch collections listed here, although once again the simplified vocabulary is somewhat restrictive. A guide to pronounciation of some Russian names is included at the end of the book. More colorful illustrations than some of the other titles. Very consistent reading level. See *Stories From France* for more information. Folklore of the World series.

Interest Level: 2-6. Reading Level: 2.1. Further Search Topics: Folklore, Fantasy, Russia-Fiction, Witches-Fiction.

Ginsburg, Mirra. The lazies; illus by Marian Parry. Macmillan 1973, 70 pp.

A good collection of 15 short Russian folktales all having to do with laziness. Most are humorous tales; few are well-known. In just under a third of the stories the humor may be too subtle even for older elementary school children; however, the rest of the stories can be enjoyed by almost any child between third and sixth grade. ("Who Will Wash the Pot," "Easy Bread," "Who Will Row Next," and "The Princess Who Learned to Work" are the questionable stories). Print somewhat small.

Interest Level: 3-6. Reading Level: 3.1. Further Search Topics: Folklore, Humorous Fiction, Laziness-Fiction, Russia-Fiction.

FOOD-FICTION

Pinkwater, Daniel Manus. Fat men from space. Dodd 1977, 57 pp.

The evening after his trip to the dentist William found that he could still hear radio programs when his radio was turned off. He was even more surprised to find that when he wired himself to a fence he could hear spacemen talking. When the spacemen discovered that William could hear them, they landed and captured him. They were on a top secret mission and couldn't risk any human knowing about their existence. The spacemen were about to invade Earth to consume all the junk food they could find. As mass panic set in on Earth, William could do nothing to save his fellow humans. He was held captive and helpless until the invaders' interest was captured by a giant potato pancake floating in outer space.

A tongue-in-check, slapstick spoof of science fiction, food fads, and junk food. Do not expect anything more.

Interest Level: 3-5. Reading Level: 3.2. Further Search Topics: Science Fiction, Humorous Fiction, Food-Fiction, Flying Saucers-Fiction, Aliens-Fiction, Best Sellers, Kidnapping-Fiction, Teeth-Fiction.

Rockwell, Thomas. How to eat fried worms; illus by Emily McCully. Watts 1973, 116 pp.

It started more as a joke than anything else, but it escalated into a strange commitment. Alan bet Billy $50 that Billy couldn't eat a worm a day for fifteen days. Billy had always been willing to take almost any dare offered and he was stubborn enough to carry them out, but when he actually faced the first worm (an enormous night crawler), he almost backed down. He and his friend Tom had to keep repeating the word "minibike" (the prize he planned to buy with the money) and smother the worm in everything imaginable in order to eat it all. After the first worm, however, the next few were easier to face. That was when Alan and his ally Joe, began using psychological warfare and almost won. In 41 very short, grotesquely funny chapters Billy becomes the proud owner of a minibike and is the first person to become hooked on worm sandwiches.

Once this book is started, it is hard to resist its gruesome fascination. Although the print is somewhat small, and there are occasionally very difficult or babytalk words, the interest is strong enough to sustain almost all readers.

Interest Level: 3-6. Reading Level: 3.1. Further Search Topics: Humorous Fiction, Worms-Fiction, Read Aloud, Best Sellers, Challenges-Fiction, Food-Fiction, Bicycles and Bicycling-Fiction.

Warner, Gertrude Chandler. The lighthouse mystery; illus by David Cunningham. A. Whitman 1963, 128 pp.

What better place for a mystery than a lighthouse late at night? Add the excitement of a storm at sea and a young man alone in a boat and the story should be unbeatable. Unfortunately this, as well as some of the other books in the series, does not quite live up to its potential. It will not attract many new readers but it will satisfy those who crave more adventures of the Alden family. The main problem with the book is its lack of definition. It isn't quite a mystery or an adventure story, it's a little of both. It is also part homespun family story, part science lesson, and part "problem story."

The Aldens rented a lighthouse in a very small fishing village one summer. Late each night their dog awoke them as he barked at a stranger who walked into or away from a closed-up building nearby. When the children investigated, they found that the surly son of a local fisherman was using the building to experiment on plankton as a food source. Harry was a brilliant young man who wanted to go to college, but whose father stubbornly refused to let him study. One night when Larry was at sea gathering samples, a terrible storm blew up. Only the Coast Guard and an improvised light in the lighthouse saved Larry from drowning. Larry's brush with death forced his father to acknowledge Larry's abilities and allow him to continue studying at college.

The sketchy illustrations in this and the following books in the series are an improvement over the silhouettes of *The Boxcar Children*. See the annotation for *The Boxcar Children* for further series information.

Interest Level: 3-6. Reading Level: 2.1. Further Search Topics: Mystery and Detective Stories, Lighthouses-Fiction, Food-Fiction, Disasters-Fiction, Vacation-Fiction.

FOOTBALL-BIOGRAPHY

Burchard, Marshall. Sports hero: Fran Tarkenton. Putnam 1977, 95 pp.

From a strict religious background where athletics were not encouraged, Fran went on to set every NFL passing record possible See *Sports Hero: Bill Walton*. Sports Hero series.

Interest Level: 3-6. Reading Level: 3.2. Further Search Topics: Biography, Tarkenton, Fran, Football-Biography, Religion-Biography.

Burchard, Marshall. Sports hero: Joe Namath. Putnam 1971, 95 pp.

One of football's best and flashiest quarterbacks. See *Sports Hero: Bill Walton* entry. Sports Hero series.

Interest Level: 2-6. Reading Level: 2.2. Further Search Topics: Biography, Namath, Joe, Football-Biography.

Burchard, Marshall. Sports hero: Larry Csonka. Putnam 1975, 95 pp.

Larry Csonka was almost the stereotype of a football player; big, fearless and driving. For more information about the books in the series see *Sports Hero: Bill Walton*. Sports Hero series.

Interest Level: 2-6. Reading Level: 3.1. Further Search Topics: Biography, Csonka, Larry, Football-Biography, Group 2.

Burchard, Marshall. Sports Hero: O.J. Simpson. Putnam 1975, 95 pp.

O.J. Simpson, who now flies through airports, still holds at least three NFL records, including most yards gained in a single season. See *Sports Hero: Bill Walton* for series information. Sports Hero series.

Interest Level: 2-6. Reading Level: 3.2. Further Search Topics: Biography, Simpson, O.J., Football-Biography, Blacks-Biography, Group 2.

Burchard, Marshall. Sports hero: Terry Bradshaw. Putnam 1980, 95 pp.

Once labeled a "dumb hick," Terry Bradshaw went on to prove he was a talented and thinking quarterback, good enough to be named NFL Player of the Year. He is also a deeply religious man. Reading level of this title varies from 3.1 to 4.1. For more details about the series, see *Sports Hero: Bill Walton*. Sports Hero series.

Interest Level: 3-6. Reading Level: 3.2. Further Search Topics: Biography, Bradshaw, Terry, Football-Biography, Religion-Biography.

Burchard, Susan H. Sports star: Earl Campbell. HarBraceJ 1980, 63 pp.

The Houston Oiler's star running back, probably the best in football, has only been out of college a few years. He should have a long career ahead of him. *Sports Star: Elvin Hayes* includes series notes. Sports Star series.

Interest Level: 3-6. Reading Level: 3.1. Further Search Topics: Football-Biography, Blacks-Biography, Campbell, Earl, Biography.

Burchard, Susan H. Sports star: Franco Harris. HarBraceJ 1976, 64 pp.

Franco is the talented son of a black Army man and his Italian wife. He became a hero to thousands of Pittsburgh Steeler fans, who called themselves Franco's Italian Army. See *Sports Hero: Bill Walton*, by Marshall Burchard for series details. Sports Star series.

Interest Level: 2-6. Reading Level: 3.1. Further Search Topics: Biography, Group 2, Harris, Franco, Football-Biography, Blacks-Biography.

Burchard, Susan H. Sports star: "Mean" Joe Greene. HarBraceJ 1976, 64 pp.

"Mean" Joe Greene's nickname is appropriate. He is big, "mean" on the playing field, and likes to win. He usually does. More details about the book under *Sports Hero: Bill Walton*, by Marshall Burchard. Sports Star series.

Interest Level: 2-6. Reading Level: 3.2. Further Search Topics: Biography, Football-Biography, Greene, "Mean" Joe, Blacks-Biography, Group 2.

Burchard, Susan H. Sports star: Tony Dorsett. HarBraceJ 1978, 64 pp.

One year after he set the college rushing record and won the Heisman Trophy, Tony Dorsett was named the NFL's Rookie of the Year and found himself playing in the Super Bowl. Reading level of this title varies from 2.2 to 3.2. For more information about the series see the entry for Marshall Burchard's *Sports Hero: Bill Walton*. Sports Star series.

Interest Level: 2-6. Reading Level: 3.2. Further Search Topics: Biography, Football-Biography, Dorsett, Tony, Blacks-Biography, Group 2.

Fall, Thomas. Jim Thorpe; illus by John Gretzer. Har-Row 1970, 33 pp.

Jim Thorpe was an Indian from the Oklahoma territory who became one of the United State's greatest athletes. He and his twin brother were trained by their father to run and jump faster and farther than anyone else. When Charles died, Jim couldn't face returning to school without his twin, so his family kept him home for a few months before sending him away to school again. Jim ran home once more when his father and mother both became ill. Months later he went to still another school where he was noticed by Pop Warner. Pop advised Joe to concentrate on track until he was big enough to play football. His father's death left Jim so despondent he quit school to play professional baseball for a while. By the time he went back to school, Jim was big enough to play spectacular football and then to win the 1912 Olympic decathlon competition. Unfortunately, his short time as a paid baseball player made him ineligible for the Olympic honor and Jim's medal was taken away. Public sentiment was with Jim, but the rules were against him. He went on, however, to play both professional baseball and football. In 1982, 29 years after his death, Thorpe's medal was finally returned to him.

A short, meaty and readable biography of a person who should be interesting to many sports fans. Follows the usual format of Crowell biographies, but looks less like a picture book than many. Crowell Biography series.

Interest Level: 3-5. Reading Level: 3.1. Further Search Topics: Football-Biography, Indians of North America-Biography, Baseball-Biography, Olympic Games, Biography, Running-Biography, Twins-Biography.

FOOTBALL-FICTION

Christopher, Matt. Football fugitive; illus by Larry Johnson. Little 1976, 119 pp.

Larry had been writing to the great football player Yancey Roote for about two years when his letters suddenly went unanswered. Because his relationship with his father was cool and distant, Larry's friendship with Yancey had meant a great deal to him. Shortly after Larry learned that Yancey was in legal trouble, Yancey showed up in town to ask Larry's father, a famous lawyer, to defend him in court. The court case and Yancey helped to bring Larry and his father closer together and to provide each one with new respect for the other. Lots of football action plus a realistic and somewhat common problem (though an unrealistic solution) make this a useful selection.

Interest Level: 3-6. Reading Level: 3.1. Further Search Topics: Football-Fiction, Lawyers-Fiction, Family Problems-Fiction.

Foley, Louise Munro. Tackle 22; illus by John Heinly. Delacorte 1978, unp (43 pp).

When their quarterback came down with the mumps, it looked like the Wildcats would have to forfeit the big football game to the Spacemen. But Chub's little brother Herb surprised everyone and saved the game.

Brief and somewhat predictable, the book maintains a light touch that many young readers will like. Heavily illustrated.

Interest Level: 1-4. Reading Level: 2.1. Further Search Topics: Football-Fiction, Brothers and Sisters-Fiction, Humorous Fiction, Group 2.

FOSTER HOMES

Adoff, Arnold. Malcolm X; illus by John Wilson. Har-Row 1970, 41 pp.

This is a simple, intellectually honest biography of a very controversial man. Taught a strong sense of self-respect by his father, Malcolm X could not accept the second-class status that white society tried to impose upon him. Instead he turned away from whites and all they stood for. He hated high school, the detention home he lived in after his father's death, and his mother's placement in a state hospital. He didn't feel comfortable until he moved to Harlem. There he found friends, but he also found crime. While he was in prison, Malcolm X began to read of great, black societies and people. His brother told him about the Nation of Islam, the Black Muslims, and Elijah Muhammad, the leader of the religion. He began corresponding with Mr. Muhammad. Shortly after he was released from prison, Malcolm X met Elijah Muhammad and eventually became a minister of the religion. There was even talk that he would be Elijah Muhammad's successor. But, as the years went on, Malcolm X began to think that black Christians as well as Muslims should be united in the fight for black rights. Despite threats against his life Malcolm X formed the Organization of Afro-American Unity. Both blacks and whites were angry with him. The threats continued until his house was firebombed; and, only a week later, at a public meeting, Malcolm X was assassinated.

An excellent overview of a complex man. The book may well prompt readers to learn more about the man and his beliefs. At the very least it will expose readers, in an interesting manner, to someone they should know. The book shares the same semi-picture book format of the others in Harper and Row/Crowell's biography series, therefore it will need a careful introduction to potential readers.

Interest Level: 3-5. Reading Level: 3.1. Further Search Topics: Blacks-Biography, Civil Rights, Biography, Crime, Religion, Assassinations, Prejudice, Poverty, Foster Homes.

FOSTER HOMES-FICTION

Angell, Judie. Dear Lola; or how to build your own family. Bradbury 1980, 166 pp.

Arthur (age 18), James (13), Annie and Al-Willie (twins, age 10), Edmund (9), and Ben (5) wanted to run away from the orphanage and find a place where they could be a real family. After waiting months, their chance arrived one night. They escaped in a van and began living on the road. It was weeks before they found a house in which they thought they could live. They didn't want trouble with local authorities, so most of the children enrolled in school and pretended to be living with their widowed grandfather. Only James (who never left his room) and Arthur stayed home. Arthur was the anonymous author of a nationally syndicated newspaper advice column. It was with the income from his "Dear Lola" column that Arthur was able to support the "family." When the townspeople eventually began to wonder about the "strange" behavior of the children, they investigated and found no adult in charge of the household. Arthur went to court to be appointed the childrens' guardian, but the judge ruled against him. Rather than be sent to foster homes again, Arthur and the children raced from the courtroom. The book ends as the family is once more together and on their own. An unusual cast of characters in a surprisingly warm and humorous book.

Interest Level: 4-6. Reading Level 3.1. Further Search Topics: Loners-Fiction, Runaways-Fiction, Orphans-Fiction, Survival-Fiction, Family Problems-Fiction, Family-Fiction, Read Aloud, Foster Homes-Fiction, Individualists-Fiction, Humorous Fiction.

Clark, Margaret Goff. Barney and the UFO; illus by Ted Lewin. Dodd 1979, 159 pp.

Barney felt a strange prickly sensation several times before he discovered that it was caused by Tibbo, a Gark from the planet Ornam. Tibbo had selected Barney as a friend who would accompany him back to Ornam. Barney was to learn the peaceful ways of Gark and then return to Earth to help persuade the world to accept the aliens. At first the idea of visiting Ornam appealed to Barney because he liked Tibbo and felt very lonely and unsure of his adoptive family's love. Those were the very reasons that Tibbo had chosen Barney: he wanted someone without strong ties to Earth and Barney's only tie when he was first contacted by Tibbo was his little brother Scott. As the time to go grew closer, Barney found a new and strong friendship with Dave, a science whiz-kid, and great love for his new parents. Tibbo, however, was determined to hold Barney to his promise. Only a last minute confrontation between Tibbo and Barney, David, Scott and Mr. and Mrs. Crandall prevented Tibbo from succeeding. But even as Tibbo left, he and Barney acknowledged their new friendship and agreed to keep in touch.

Because of its fairly slow beginning, readers must be well-introduced to this book. If they can be persuaded to be patient while the author sets the stage for about 18 pages they will be rewarded with a decent, if somewhat wordy, story of friendship, UFO's, space travel and family affection.

Interest Level: 3-6. Reading Level: 3.2. Further Search Topics: Science Fiction, Flying Saucers-Fiction, Kidnapping-Fiction, Foster Homes-Fiction, Family-Fiction, Adoption-Fiction, Aliens-Fiction, Loneliness-Fiction, Orphans-Fiction.

Place, Marian T. The boy who saw Bigfoot. Dodd 1979, 96 pp.

Joey and his foster mother searched for and found Bigfoot. But, when Joey told his classmates, no one would believe him. Joey's next idea was to take the entire class on a field trip to track Bigfoot.

Joey's rapid change from a difficult to a very well-adjusted child is not well supported. But interest in Bigfoot is so great that the book's flaws will be overlooked by its readers.

Interest Level: 3-6. Reading Level: 2.2. Further Search Topics: Bigfoot-Fiction, Foster Homes-Fiction, Monsters-Fiction, Troublemakers-Fiction, School Stories.

Smith, Doris Buchanan. Tough Chauncey. Morrow 1974, 222 pp.

Chauncey Childs had taught himself to be tough— very tough. Even though he was small for his age (13 years old), the only person who gave him any trouble was his sometimes-friend, Black Jack Levitt. Everyone else was scared of Chauncey. Chauncey felt that he had to be tough or he wouldn't be able to survive. He had to be tough to stand the beatings his grandfather gave him "for his own good," to put up with his

mother's drinking and disappearances, and to stand the sight of his grandfather shooting the stray kittens born in their garage.

Chauncey's greatest wish was to be able to live with his mother, instead of with his grandparents. In a desperate attempt to achieve that end he accidentally fell from a moving train and badly hurt his leg. Instead of being returned to his mother he was once more taken back to his grandparents. Chauncey's unhappiness grew until he finally decided to take the one surviving stray kitten and run away. Jack helped him find an empty garage where he could hide while he figured out what to do with his future. After talking with Jack and doing more deep soul searching, Chauncey decided to reshape himself and his life. His first step was to curb his temper and his tongue when his hiding place was discovered. His second step was to see about finding a foster home where he would be treated well, and where he could get a new start.

Ugly as the story is in places, its ending is hopeful. Although it is not always realistic, Chauncey's story is compelling enough to appeal to many readers, especially those who have enjoyed *The War on Villa Street*, by Henry Mazer, *The Outsiders*, by Susan Hinton, or *Mystery of the Fat Cat*, by Frank Bonham. The book's length and its artificially low reading level (vocabulary is often difficult but sentences are very short) make this book most appropriate for an older reader whose reading level is 4.1 or higher.

Interest Level: 5-6. Reading Level: 3.2. Further Search Topics: Child Abuse-Fiction, Family Problems-Fiction, Grandparents-Fiction, Runaways-Fiction, Bullies-Fiction, Single Parent Family-Fiction, Loners-Fiction, Friendship-Fiction, Troublemakers-Fiction, Foster Homes-Fiction.

Smith, Doris Buchanan. Last was Lloyd. Viking Pr 1981, 124 pp.

Lloyd had several problems: he was overweight, his mother was overprotective, he had no school friends, and there was a chance he might be taken away from home and put into foster care because he had missed so much school. Lloyd's mother, very young and very defensive when she had Lloyd, had done her best to be a "good mother," but in doing so, had made Lloyd fearful of the world. He had become the subject of his classmates' mockery so many times that the only way he could respond to his peers was with nastiness. The one skill he possessed was hitting a baseball. He kept this skill well hidden for fear of exposing himself to further mockery. When one of his classmates accidentally discovered how well Lloyd hit, he took the first step to becoming Lloyd's friend. Lloyd's reaction was to back away, but Kirby kept trying. Eventually Kirby's attempts and those of an understanding truant officer, helped Lloyd begin to make friends, to treat others decently, and to pull away from his mother; in short, he began to mature.

Because Lloyd's problems can be oversimplified too easily, this book requires a fairly mature reader and perhaps even discussion in order to fully understand its subtleties.

Interest Level: 5-6+Reading Level: 4.2. Further Search Topics: Weight-Fiction, Single Parent Family-Fiction, Courage-Fiction, School Stories, Loners-Fiction, Friendship-Fiction, Baseball-Fiction, Family Problems-Fiction, Foster Homes-Fiction, Children-Growth-Fiction.

FRANCE-FICTION
Dolch, Edward W. Stories from France; illus by Gordon Laite. Garrard 1963, 167 pp.

It is very difficult to simplify a story and not lose at least some of its original flavor. Such is the case here and in all the Dolch retellings. Nevertheless, this collection of folktales is quite useful for the French flavor it does maintain. The stories, as they are retold, are good; not great, but good. There are 14 stories related in the 19 chapters. This is a result of splitting the longer, more complicated stories into episodes. Some frustration may arise for readers because there is no indication that a story may involve more than one chapter. The much-improved illustrations that introduce each chapter and adorn the cover help make this more attractive than the earlier books. The book ends with a list of the provinces from which the stories came as well as a pronounciation key to French names. Folklore of the World series.

Interest Level: 2-6. Reading Level: 3.1. Further Search Topics: Folklore, Fantasy, France-Fiction, Royalty-Fiction, Group 2, Knights and Knighthood-Fiction.

FRAZIER, WALT

Burchard, Susan H. Sports star: Walt Frazier. HarBraceJ 1975, 64 pp.

Walt Frazier earned his nickname Clyde (from *Bonnie and Clyde*) because of his style both on and off the basketball court. He could steal the ball from almost anyone on the court and he enjoyed high living and fancy dressing off the court. Entry for *Sports Hero: Bill Walton* gives more information about the series. Sports Star series.

Interest Level: 2-6. Reading Level: 3.1. Further Search Topics: Biography, Basketball-Biography, Frazier, Walt, Blacks-Biography.

FRIENDSHIP-FICTION

Blume, Judy. Blubber. Bradbury 1974, 153 pp.

Jill, like all the other fifth graders in her class, did exactly as Wendy directed her. When Wendy nicknamed one of the class members Blubber and launched a campaign against her, Jill joined right in. It wasn't until the tables were turned and Jill became Wendy's next victim that Jill realized how much it hurt to be the target of such nastiness. It was only then that Jill could stand up to Wendy. Wendy's meanness is extreme and her classmates, without exception, actively follow her lead, yet all adult characters in the book are blind to what happens. Despite those drawbacks, the book deals with a problem very real to children and thus it has guaranteed audience appeal.

Interest Level: 4-6. Reading Level: 3.1. School Stories, Bullies-Fiction, Weight-Fiction, Loners-Fiction, Gangs-Fiction, Read Aloud, Cruelty-Fiction, Best Sellers, Troublemakers-Fiction, Friendship-Fiction.

Blume, Judy. Otherwise known as Sheila the great. Dutton 1972, 128 pp.

Sheila first appears in *Tales of a Fourth Grade Nothing* as Peter Thatcher's neighbor. Sheila was a bundle of fears. She was afraid of dogs, thunderstorms, spiders, horses, putting her face in water, and strange noises at night. The summer she and her family rented a house in Tarrytown, New York, she confronted each one of her fears, even mastered one (putting her face in the water) and learned how to swim. That gave her the self-confidence to face a dog without running away. Sheila's progress was aided by her friend Mouse's steadfast belief that a person should always be honest about herself. Sheila's problems are treated realistically and with dignity, yet humorously. Reading level varies greatly from 1.2 - 4.1, therefore, the book is *most* suitable to grades four through six.

Interest Level: 3-6. Reading Level: 3.1. Further Search Topics: Humorous Fiction, Courage-Fiction, Camp-Fiction, Group 2, Vacation-Fiction, Swimming-Fiction, Brothers and Sisters-Fiction, Friendship-Fiction, Everyday Stories.

Bonham, Frank. The mystery of the fat cat; illus by Alvin Smith. Dutton 1968, 160 pp.

Although noticeably dated at times, this is still an exciting story of an inner city neighborhood. Buddy, Little Pie, Rich, and Cool were among the many who used the local Boys' Club as their hangout. It was a place to stay out of trouble and off the streets, but it was also a haven for rats. The rats were big and brazen; so brazen that one attacked Buddy in the swimming pool. The club needed a new building desperately. The money was there; they just weren't able to use it. Fifteen years earlier an eccentric old woman willed the Boys' Club over $600,000, but stated that the money was first to be used to support her cat until it died. A caretaker, a lawyer, and a veterinarian all benefited as long as the cat lived. Buddy and his friends took on the job of discovering if the cat really was alive or if the Boys' Club was being cheated out of half a million dollars. It was a job that nearly killed them before they set things right. Plenty of action, some violence, a cast of street-smart characters, realistic trouble with the police, as well as a slight mystery almost insure the book's success with older readers. Moderate sized print. Line spacing somewhat narrow.

Interest Level: 6+. Reading Level: 5.1. Further Search Topics: Humorous Fiction, Cats-Fiction, Gangs-Fiction, City Life-Fiction, Mystery and Detective Stories, Poverty-Fiction, Friendship-Fiction, Juvenile Delinquency-Fiction, Crime-Fiction, Best Sellers.

Bulla, Clyde Robert. Dexter; illus by Glo Coalson. Har-Row 1973, 69 pp.

This is not as simple a story as it first appears. Dave, 12 years old and lonely, had hoped his new neighbors would be friends. But, the Arvin family kept very much to themselves until Dave accidentally discovered Alex, the Arvin's son, doing tricks on a trapeze in the barn. Because Dave kept the secret and shared Alex's love for Dexter, his circus pony, the boys soon became friends. Then in one horrible night, the Arvins were forced to leave the town and Dexter was so badly hurt he was believed to be dead. A week later Dave found Dexter alive, but crippled for life and so frightened that no one could get near him. The horse surprised everyone and managed to live through a very harsh winter as well as the townspeople's determination to kill him. When Alex and his father returned, almost a year later, they found Dexter and took the old and feeble horse back to a ranch with them. The story is told with sympathy, with an understanding of how it feels to be lonely, and with tension and suspense. It's appeal should last from third through sixth grade. Print size is smaller than Bulla's usual.

Interest Level: 3-6. Reading Level: 3.1. Further Search Topics: Survival-Fiction, Acrobats and Acrobatics-Fiction, Horses-Fiction, Read Aloud, Circus-Fiction, Loneliness-Fiction, Friendship-Fiction.

Bulla, Clyde Robert. The ghost of windy hill; illus by Don Bolognese. Har-Row 168, 84 pp.

If the reader doesn't expect a high adventure ghost story, he or she will not be disappointed by this low-keyed tale of a family who goes to live in a house that is supposedly haunted. Mr. Giddings asked the Carver family to move into his country home while he and his wife stayed in Boston. His intent was that the Carvers should either prove to his wife that the house was not haunted or drive the ghost out. The Carvers found no ghosts—at first—only an interesting group of neighbors. There was shy Miss Miggie who drifted around in a long, white dress and wore a flower-covered hat. Bruno was the gruff beggar boy who couldn't walk and had no friends but a goat, until the Carver children came along. Near the end of their stay Lorna Carver mentioned that because they had seen no ghosts the family would soon leave and the Giddings would return. Strange occurrences began almost immediately after Lorna's statement and ended only when the Carvers caught Bruno trying to convince them that he was the ghost. Lorna and Jamie were his only friends, so he had risked his guardians wrath and given up the pretense of being lame to trick the Carvers into staying. All ends well as Bruno's cruel guardian is run off, the Carvers take responsibility for Bruno's care, and Mrs. Giddings admits she made up the ghost story because she hated living in the country and had wanted to return to the city. Another serviceable book in the very successful Bulla style.

Interest Level: 2-5. Reading Level: 2.1. Further Search Topics: Ghosts-Fiction, Brothers and Sisters-Fiction, Orphans-Fiction, Country Life-Fiction, Courage-Fiction, Challenges-Fiction, Friendship-Fiction.

Byars, Betsy. The Cybil war; illus by Gail Owens. Viking Pr. 1981, 126 pp.

Simon and Tony both had a crush on Cybil, but according to Tony, Cybil liked Tony better than she liked Simon. Simon was unhappily willing to accept Tony's word even though he knew Tony was a chronic liar. After all, Cybil had been the one to talk their teacher out of giving the lead in the class play about nutrition to Simon. Consequently Simon was being forced to impersonate a jar of peanut butter. In an elaborate attempt to win Cybil's affection Tony began telling Cybil lies about Simon and then set up a double date with Cybil and Harriet. On their walk home, Simon learned from Harriet that Cybil had only agreed to the date because Simon was going along. Happy at last, Simon realized he wanted no more lies and tricks; that he wanted to be truthful with Cybil and with himself. In the name of truth, he was even willing to accept the fact that his father, who had deserted the family, would not be returning.

A good story with just enough humor and romance to make it widely appealing as either a shared book (read aloud) or a personal pick. Print is fairly small.

Interest Level: 5-6. Reading Level: 4.2. Further Search Topics: Humorous Fiction, Love-Fiction, School Stories, Honesty-Fiction, Friendship-Fiction, Single Parent Family-Fiction, Read Aloud, Everyday Stories, Adolescence-Fiction.

Chaikin, Miriam. I should worry, I should care; illus by Richard Egielski. Har-Row 1979, 103 pp.

A warm, well-written story about life in a Jewish family in Brooklyn just before World War II. This is the story of young Molly's adjustment to moving, to leaving old friends, to making and losing new friends (one by death) and to the small happenings that make up her life. In the background, but always there, is Hitler's ever-increasing threat to the world.

A comfortable, truthful look at a close-knit family. Also useful for its picture of the times and the place. An occasional Yiddish expression may slow the reader but adds to the book's authenticity. Print is slightly lighter and smaller than *Finders Weepers*.

Interest Level: 3-5. Reading Level: 2.2. Further Search Topics: Moving, Household-Fiction, Friendship-Fiction, City Life-Fiction, Jews-Fiction, Family-Fiction.

Christopher, Matt. Face-off; illus by Harvey Kidder. Little 1972, 131 pp.

Christopher sticks strictly to the sports story formula here. The characters seem to have no time or thoughts for anything but sports. They epitomize the macho image, and once their problems with sports are solved everything in life seems to fall into place. But, for the young sports enthusiast who doesn't really like to read, this formula of much sports action and very little else is successful.

Scott had never played hockey but he was an extremely fast skater. When Del and Skinny asked him to join their hockey team and to be one of the Three Icekateers, Scott was thrilled. But Scott's performance was less than inspiring and Del's patience with his failures was short. The two almost came to blows when Scott discovered that he was puck-shy and would duck every time someone took a shot near him. Their coach's advice to both of them helped clear up Scott's problem and Del's impatience. All ends happily as Scott played well and he and Del became friends once more.

Interest Level: 3-6. Reading Level: 3.1. Further Search Topics: Hockey-Fiction, Ice Skating-Fiction, Courage-Fiction, Friendship-Fiction.

Christopher, Matt. No arm in left field; illus by Byron Goto. Little 1974, 131 pp.

Matt Christopher's books are just the thing for sports junkies. The play-by-play accounts of several sports events (here it is baseball games) are loosely tied together by secondary plot developments. Usually the plot revolves around the main character's successful attempt to overcome a difficulty of some sort.

Terry was a good baseball player so, when he was invited to join a local team shortly after he moved to Pennsylvania, he was very pleased. Almost immediately, he learned that a teammate was not at all happy about playing with Terry. Terry was black and his teammate, Tony, was very prejudiced. Terry had dealt with people like Tony before, so he was able to ignore most, but not all, of Tony's unkind comments and actions. But the day finally came when Tony realized that to play well as a team, they had to work together instead of against each other.

Interest Level: 3-6. Reading Level: 3.2. Further Search Topics: Prejudice-Fiction, Baseball-Fiction, Friendship-Fiction, Challenges-Fiction.

Christopher, Matt. Wild pitch. Little 1980, 137 pp.

This is one of Christopher's better written books but it is also one that will find a smaller audience than usual. Here he has drawn interesting characters of flesh and bone rather than his normal stereotypes. The sports action is still detailed, but it is no longer the core around which a purely skeletal plot is stretched. Christopher has produced an intriguing story line here.

Eddie was a good strong pitcher who sometimes threw wild pitches. One of his wild pitches hit Phyl Monahan, the only girl playing in his league. It was well known that Eddie didn't like the idea of girls playing in the same league as the boys, so people accused him of purposely hitting Phyl. Eddie knew he hadn't meant to hit her, but he still felt very guilty that his pitch had put her into the hospital. He went to the hospital many times before he was finally able to see Phyl and apologize. When he did, he found that she was very likeable and reasonable. When she confessed that she wasn't sure she wanted to play baseball again, Eddie decided he owed it to her to help her regain her confidence. As they worked together each one gained respect for the other until theirs became a very solid friendship. The test for both was when Phyl had to hit against Eddie again.

For many baseball fans there may be too much plot here and not enough baseball. Because the problem of how to control wild pitches is never addressed, other readers may also find the book disappointing. But, for those baseball fans who are open to more than box scores and replays, this is a good story.

Interest Level: 6+. Reading Level: 4.2. Further Search Topics: Baseball-Fiction, Sex Role-Fiction, Friendship-Fiction, Courage-Fiction.

Christopher, Matt. The year mom won the pennant; illus by Foster Caddell. Little 1968, 147 pp.

When no one's father had the time to coach the Thunderballs it began to look like the team would be disbanded. They just didn't seem to be able to work together without a coach. Then Nick Vassey's mother volunteered to coach for the season. After all, she knew baseball as well as anyone else and had watched her husband coach for several years. Nick wasn't at all pleased, but had to accept the idea when his teammates voted to make his mother their coach. Nick's embarrassment was almost as great as the rival coach's skepticism, but before the season was over Nick was proud of his mother. She coached the team to first place and forced even the rival coach to admit she was a good coach. Much baseball action. See note about (*No Arm In Left Field*).

Interest Level: 2-6. Reading Level: 3.1. Further Search Topics: Group 2, Baseball-Fiction, Friendship-Fiction, Prejudice-Fiction, Sex Role-Fiction, Women-Fiction.

Clymer, Eleanor. Luke was there; illus by Diane de Groat. HR & W 1973, 74 pp.

Julius' father, uncle and finally his step-father had all walked out on him. Even his mother had left him, although she hadn't wanted to go. When his mother had been taken to the hospital, Julius and his younger brother Danny were sent to a children's home. Julius felt alone and cheated until he met a young, black, social worker named Luke. Luke liked and respected Julius and helped Julius learn to feel the same way about himself. When Luke, too, left Julius, Julius was so angry at the world that he stole food and then money. Afraid to go back to the children's home because he thought he'd be caught and punished, Julius ran away. It wasn't until he found an abandoned child, about Danny's age, who needed care, that Julius returned to the home. Luke was there when he arrived, just when Julius needed him most. Luke listened to Julius' unhappy feelings, arranged for him to see his mother and helped him begin to accept the fact that life is not always fair.

Julius tells his own story in a realistic, straight-forward book that will touch most readers. Only the lack of quotation marks and inadequate spacing between the lines may slow the reader.

Interest Level: 3-6. Reading Level: 2.2. Further Search Topics: Runaways-Fiction, Orphans-Fiction, Juvenile Delinquency-Fiction, Divorce and Separation-Fiction, Friendship-Fiction, Courage-Fiction, Survival-Fiction, Loneliness-Fiction, Best Sellers, Read Aloud.

Cohen, Barbara. Thank you, Jackie Robinson; illus by Richard Cuffari. Lothrop 1974, 125 pp.

This story is not for everyone, but for the right reader it is perfect. The book is a catalog of baseball facts, thus it is likely to appeal primarily to baseball fans. But it is not the typical story of a child overcoming a problem through practice and perserverance, as are most sports books. This is a sensitive story of a fatherless boy whose life centered around the New York Dodgers.

Sam could repeat the starting line-up and details of any game the Dodgers had played within the last three years; however, no one cared. In fact, most people were bored when Sam began reciting. Only Davey, the old, black cook at the inn where Sam and his family lived, took any interest. Davey was as much a fan as Sam. They began spending hours together talking and then watching baseball as Davey and his daughter took Sam to the games with them. It was Sam and Davey's dream to catch a fly ball and have it autograped by all the Dodgers, especially Jackie Robinson, the first black major league player. When Davey had a severe heart attack, Sam gathered all his courage to make that dream come true. He bought a baseball, took the subway to a game, and argued with the ushers until he was finally able to get Jackie Robinson's and the team's autographs. Just a few days before Davey died Sam took the baseball to the hospital and gave it to Davey. Sam's feelings about Davey's death are real and painful. He felt sorry for himself, lonely, angry, sad and confused. But a remark by his mother and one more Jackie Robinson hit helped Sam accept Davey's death.

Because the story is told as a first-person flashback set in the late 1940s, it may need a little introduction. It also alludes to racial problems and practices that young readers may not understand without explanation (i.e., why Davey had some hesitation about taking a white child with him to the ballpark or on a trip).

Interest Level: 4-6. Reading Level: 4.2. Further Search Topics: Baseball-Fiction, Blacks-Fiction, Aging-Fiction, Single Parent Family-Fiction, Friendship-Fiction, Death-Fiction, Robinson, Jackie.

Davidson, Carson. Fast-talking dolphin; illus by Sylvia Stone. Dodd 1978, 127 pp.

After a rather slow start, this story develops into a well-paced adventure-fantasy with touches of warmth and humor. Eric wasn't just surprised when he found a dolphin in the 10-foot fish pond, he was astonished. Not only had there never been a dolphin there before, but this dolphin spoke in poetry. His name was Wallingford Ullingham Lowell III; Wallingford for short. He was elegant, proud and cultured; but as Eric soon found out, he was very impractical. He didn't seem to realize that he needed salt water and more fish than those in the pond in order to live. It was Eric who figured out a way to keep salt flowing into the pond and a supply of fresh fish. He also kept Wallingford's presence a secret, just as Wallingford requested. The day that Wallingford was discovered was the day that Eric had to break his promise. In order to find out who else had found out about Wallingford, Eric talked with his brother. Together they scouted the town before they realized that Herbert Benson was the only other person who had seen Wallingford.

Herbert reluctantly admitted that he had told his father about the dolphin. Eric knew enough about Mr. Benson to realize that he was just crazy enough to want to harm the dolphin. Eric and his brother gathered all the local children together to shield

Wallingford from Mr. Benson. Even Herbert dared to defy his father for the first time. As Mr. Benson struggled with Eric and his brother, he fell, hit his head and rolled into the pond. Wallingford dove to save him, but his leg was caught between two rocks. With the others' help, Wallingford, Eric and his brother Karl were able to save Mr. Benson from drowning.

A few days later Eric, with new-found skills, spontaneously recited a poem about friendship to Wallingford. Wallingford answered with a rare compliment and for the first time used Eric's name (a show of respect). They were such true friends that when Wallingford was helicopter-lifted out of the pond and taken back to his research project, Eric couldn't understand why his father didn't tell him of Wallingford's departure. Eventually he realized that his father had been right; he would rather remember Wallingford swimming in the pond than in a helicopter's sling. Also, Wallingford would have been embarrassed to be seen making so undignified a departure. Wallingford's final message to Eric was a note that Eric found scratched in the dirt thanking him for the salt and the fish and saying that they would one day meet again.

Don't take the plot too seriously or peruse it too carefully for it won't stand up to scrutiny. This is merely a pleasant story with enough humor, action and originality to intrigue many readers. The book's major drawback is the poetry Wallingford spouts: the poetic form and somewhat difficult language will throw some readers. On the other hand, the book could be very useful in a classroom unit about poetry.

Interest Level: 3-5. Reading Level: 3.1. Further Search Topics: Poetry, Dolphins-Fiction, Pets-Fiction, Fantasy, Friendship-Fiction, Humorous Fiction.

Eyerly, Jeannette. The seeing summer; illus by Emily Arnold McCully. Lippincott 1981, 153 pp.

That it attempts to be two books at the same time is the one flaw in this book that may be noticed by young readers. The first half of the book is an interesting story of the growing friendship between a sighted girl and a blind girl. Carey's delight at the idea of a new friend next door turned to disbelief and discomfort when she learned that Jenny was blind. Jenny too wanted to be friends, but not if she was to be pitied or patronized. Gradually she was able to show Carey that being blind was a nuisance, but nothing she was ashamed of or embarrassed about. The second half of the book presents the contrived and somewhat unnecessary story of Jenny's kidnapping. When Carey's attempt to rescue Jenny resulted in her capture too, it was, of course, Jenny's independence and ingenuity that led the way to their eventual rescue.

To the reader looking for a rousing story of a kidnapping the book may be a disappointment. Half of the book is a long time to wait for the slight adventure. But, for those readers interested in a good story of physical differences and friendship, this will be more satisfying.

Interest Level: 3-6. Reading Level: 3.1. Further Search Topics: Vision-Fiction, Friendship-Fiction, Kidnapping-Fiction, Single Parent Family-Fiction, Physically Handicapped-Fiction.

Green, Phyllis. The fastest quitter in town; illus by Lorenzo Lynch. A-W 1972, 62 pp.

Whenever Johnny played baseball and things went wrong for him, he would quit. Johnny's teammates finally grew so angry with him that they told him to leave the team. That same day, Johnny's 90-year-old great-grandfather lost a very special ring his wife had given him. Johnny's love for this great-grandfather pushed him to keep looking for the ring until days later, when everyone else had quit searching, Johnny found the ring. Having learned a hard lesson, Johnny returned to his team for one more chance. That evening Johnny went to see his great-grandfather to tell him, with legitimate pride, that he had played the entire game.

Although the lesson is pointed, the story is very satisfying. Johnny's relationship with this great-grandfather is close and supportive. His problem is one shared by many children, especially those with a weak self-image.

Interest Level: 1-4. Reading Level: 3.1. Further Search Topics: Blacks-Fiction, Challenges-Fiction, Courage-Fiction, Group 2, Baseball-Fiction, Grandparents-Fiction, Friendship-Fiction.

Greene, Constance C. A girl called Al; illus by Byron Barton. Viking Pr. 1969, 127 pp.

Told in the first person, this is the story of two seventh grade girls. The girls' warm friendship began the moment Al introduced herself to the narrator as a non-conformist. Al was very independent, mostly because she was on her own so much of the time. Her parents were divorced and she seldom saw either one of them. Her father only wrote her postcards and her mother was rarely home. The narrator's family and Mr. Richards, their building superintendent, became Al's family. They cooked, ate, played, fought, talked and even made bookcases together. When Mr. Richards had a heart attack, they found help for him and later went to see him in the hospital. It was his death that helped Al and her mother grow closer, just as Mr. Richards' life had helped her understand why her father never came to see her.

A satisfying, low-key story of friendship and maturation. The girls are Judy Blume-style characters with much greater innocence. Their ages are not discernible by their actions or dialogue, only by the author's statement.

Interest Level: 3-6. Reading Level: 3.1. Further Search Topics: Children-Growth-Fiction, Single Parent Family-Fiction, Friendship-Fiction, Weight-Fiction, Aging-Fiction, Death-Fiction, Divorce and Separation-Fiction, Family Problems-Fiction, Everyday Stories, Humorous Fiction.

Greene, Constance C. I and Sproggy; illus by Emily A. McCully. Viking Pr. 1978, 155 pp.

Ten-year-old Adam had adjusted to his parents' divorce and had even grown to like living alone with his mother. When his father came back from London with his new wife and stepdaughter Sproggy and announced that they were moving into an apartment nearby, Adam was a little worried. But when his father asked him to take care of Sproggy, Adam was furious. First of all, he didn't know Sproggy and he didn't want to know her. Secondly, she was two months older than he, taller too, and she embarrassed him in public. And finally, she didn't need his help. She got along quite well by herself; so well that she even saved Adam from a mugger and became good friends with Adam's friends behind his back. It wasn't until Sproggy proved to be vulnerable that Adam and she became friends.

A warm, realistic and humorous story whose interesting characters (even the minor ones) heighten the book's appeal.

Interest Level: 4-6. Reading Level: 3.2. Further Search Topics: Brothers and Sisters-Fiction, Divorce and Separation-Fiction, City Life-Fiction, New York City-Fiction, Humorous Fiction, Friendship-Fiction, Everyday Stories.

Hinton, Susan E. The outsiders. Viking Pr. 1967, 188 pp.

When she wrote this book Susan Hinton was only 17 years old, but she had the sensitivity of someone much older. She wrote a taut story of the rivalry between two city gangs; the Socs (the rich socialites) and the Greasers (poor kids from the wrong side of town) that is more than anything a plea for understanding and tolerance. Seen through the eyes of Ponyboy (a very bright, 14-year-old Greaser), the rivalry brought on violence and an accidental killing that forced Pony and his friend Johnny to flee for their lives. Dallas, the meanest and most dangerous of the Greasers, provided them with shelter, food for a week, and a gun. At the end of that week, Johnny decided that they should turn themselves in to the police. But before they could do that, their hideout (an old church) burned in a fire which threatened the lives of four children who had been playing there. In trying to rescue the children, Johnny, Pony, and Dallas were injured; Johnny was severely burned and probably permanently crippled. A vengeance rumble was held while Johnny lay in the hospital, but the Greasers' victory was empty when Johnny died. He had been the one member of the gang whom they all loved and who had most needed them. Dallas went to pieces: he robbed a store and set himself up to be killed by the police. He had nothing left to live for after Johnny's death. Pony found support and security with his brothers (their parents were dead) and, in a note from Johnny, some hope for the future.

Hinton speaks most often through Pony (his depth of understanding of the people around him is very impressive), but through Johnny and two of the Socs as well, Randy and Cherry. Her message is clear, but at no time does she fail to maintain believable characters in a compelling plot.

Although the book looks forbidding with its 188 pages of unrelenting small print, it is an exciting story, full of adventure, realism, and room for thought. Perhaps the best way to introduce this book is to read a fair portion of it aloud. Now a motion picture too.

Interest Level: 6+. Reading Level: 5.1. Further Search Topics: Crime-Fiction, Gangs-Fiction, Murder-Fiction, Read Aloud, Friendship-Fiction, Juvenile Delinquency-Fiction, Best Sellers, City Life-Fiction, Brothers and Sisters-Fiction, Orphans-Fiction, Runaways-Fiction, Troublemakers-Fiction, Poverty-Fiction.

Hurwitz, Johanna. Aldo Applesauce; illus by John Wallner. Morrow 1979, 127 pp.

Aldo Sossi, vegetarian and new kid at school, was immediately dubbed Applesauce for obvious reasons. Aldo didn't like his new name. He didn't like being teased either—not the way he was teased at school. Nothing went right for Aldo. His attempts at making friends only ended in disasters (once at a bowling alley and another time at a birthday party). He had been able to start a friendship only with a strange girl who wore a heavy, black fake moustache most of the time. After accidentally nearly ruining that friendship too, Aldo not only learned why DeDe wore the moustache, but helped her learn to live without it. DeDe, in turn, helped Aldo take himself less seriously and find more friends.

This is a comfortable, humorous story of two fourth grade children learning to be themselves. The vocabulary is occasionally difficult, but sentence length is almost always short.

Interest Level: 3-5. Reading Level: 3.1. Further Search Topics: Moving, Household-Fiction, Humorous Fiction, School Stories, Friendship-Fiction, Divorce and Separation-Fiction, Vegetarians-Fiction, Individualists-Fiction, Everyday Stories.

Hurwitz, Johanna. The law of gravity; illus by Ingrid Fetz. Morrow 1978, 192 pp.

The summer between fifth and sixth grades looked very unexciting to Margot. Her best friends were both going away for the whole summer and her father, a musician, was going to be on tour for most of the summer. Margot's very overweight mother had sworn never to go downstairs from their fifth floor walk-up apartment. Unless Margot chose to stay upstairs too, she was sure she would have a very lonely vacation. In addition, she had to work on a summer project for school. The project she finally chose was to get her mother downstairs after nine years of staying upstairs. In search of help she went to the local library where she met Bernie. Bernie was only a year older than Margot, but he seemed to know the most interesting things about the city. He showed her places Margot had never heard of before, he taught her to play chess, backgammon, and even to ride a bicycle. He was so full of fascinating ideas and information that Margot had no chance to be bored or lonely. Best of all, he even tried to help Margot with her project. None of their ideas worked, however, until Margot pretended to run away and scared her mother into going downstairs. Only then did Margot realize that she loved her mother whether or not she stayed on the fifth floor and that she couldn't simply force her mother or anyone else to change to suit her own fancy.

The book is a warm, understanding, slightly humorous treatment of the fairly common wish to change someone else. Although not many readers are likely to share Margot's exact problem, most will recognize her feelings. The book is also a virtual Chamber of Commerce advertisement for urban living. One of its other charms is its picture of a non-competitive, open, real friendship between an 11-year-old girl and a 12-year-old boy. The only drawback to the book is its inconsistent reading level which varies from 4.1 to 5.1 with a rare leap to 5.2.

Interest Level: 4-6. Reading Level: 4.2. Further Search Topics: Vacation-Fiction, Friendship-Fiction, Loners-Fiction, City Life-Fiction, Individualists-Fiction, Courage-Fiction, New York City-Fiction, Humorous Fiction, Family-Fiction, Challenges-Fiction, Weight-Fiction, Everyday Stories, Best Sellers.

Levy, Elizabeth. Lizzie lies a lot; illus by John Wallner. Delacorte 1976, 102 pp.

Almost any child can identify with Lizzie. She had found that it was sometimes easier to lie than to tell the truth. Her problem was that she had lost control. It seemed as if almost everything she said was a lie. She told so many lies it became difficult to keep track of them all. Lizzie wasn't even really sure why she lied so much. She knew that she sometimes lied because she thought people would be more apt to like her. Other times she lied to get herself out of trouble or to cover up her feelings when she was hurt or angry. But that didn't explain why she lied all the time. Maybe, as her grandmother said, she was a born liar.

It wasn't until Lizzie got herself caught in the middle of so many lies that she lost her only friend, that she could admit her problem to herself and to her family. After their initial shock had passed, everyone agreed to help Lizzie stop lying. Lizzie took the next step by admitting her lies to her friend Sue.

Levy has brought such an appropriately light touch to a fairly common problem that many children find this story enjoyable. Overlook the book's faults (Lizzie's grandmother is overdrawn and her mother's guilt feelings are unsupported by the story) for the fun and the message young readers get from it.

Interest Level: 3-5. Reading Level: 4.2. Further Search Topics: Honesty-Fiction, Group 2, Friendship-Fiction, Best Sellers, Everyday Stories, Family Problems-Fiction, Grandparents-Fiction, Humorous Fiction.

MacLachlan, Patricia. Arthur, for the very first time; illus by Lloyd Bloom. Har-Row 1980, 117 pp.

A beautifully written, sensitive yet humorous story of a boy's maturation and growing awareness of the world around him. When Arthur's unhappiness at home is made more intense by the advent of a new baby, he is sent to spend the summer with his older aunt and uncle. Their eccentricities and those of their friends are at first only material for Arthur to write about in his journal. But as the summer progresses he not only learns from them, but also grows from an observer of life to a participant. His final step is helping a large and beloved pig bear her litter in a driving rain storm aided only by his independent, totally untamed young friend Moira.

The print is somewhat small, but spacing between lines is generous.

Interest Level: 4-6. Reading Level: 4.2. Further Search Topics: Read Aloud, Children-Growth-Fiction, Humorous Fiction, Friendship-Fiction, Vacation-Fiction, Relatives-Fiction, Infants-Fiction, Individualists-Fiction, Writing-Fiction, Loners-Fiction, Group 2.

Norton, Andre. Star Ka'at; illus by Bernard Colonna. Walker & Co 1976, 122 pp.

Jim Evans and Elly Mae Brown, both orphaned and alone, met each other and two strange cats at the same time. As the children became more unhappy with their lives, they began to realize that Tiro and Mer were not usual cats. They were highly intelligent Ka'ats from another planet who had come to Earth in search of new strong stock to add to their breed. Both Ka'ats became as fond of the children as the children became of them. When the time came for the transport ship to leave, Jim and Elly contrived to go with them. However, the only way they could go was if they were accepted by the other Ka'ats and adopted by Tiro and Mer.

This is the first book in a series. Unfortunately the second book *Star Ka'at World*, has a much more difficult reading level (sixth grade) and the third title, *Star Ka'at and the Plant People*, varies from 2.1 to 4.1. Reading level of this entry varies between 4.1 and 5.1 but children seem to like the book enough to put up with the variability.

Interest Level: 3-6. Reading Level: 4.2. Further Search Topics: Science Fiction, Friendship-Fiction, Cats-Fiction, Group 2, Outer Space-Fiction, Orphans-Fiction.

Pfeffer, Susan Beth. Just between us; illus by Lorna Tomei. Delacorte 1980, 116 pp.

Cass's inability to keep secrets finally became such a problem that Cass asked her mother to help her learn how to keep them. Cass's mother, a psychology student, devised a behavior modification experiment. Every day that Cass was able to figure out which bit of information she had been told was a secret and keep it, she received a dollar. After a poor start Cass did well for a while, until the day she told three secrets and made her entire family angry at her.

More determined than ever, Cass tried again. This time she found herself caught between two friends. Only Cass knew that Robin was adopted and Robin wanted it kept a secret. Jenny was so mad at Robin that she decided to spread an untrue story to hurt Robin. She told Cass not to tell anyone what she was going to do. The story Jenny was going to spread was that Robin was adopted. After hours of mental anguish Cass finally devised a way to stop Jenny and help Jenny return to being the nice person she had been before her parents' divorce.

The reading level of this book varies greatly from second grade to mid-fourth grade. Otherwise, it is good fare for Judy Blume fans. Print size just a slight bit on the small side.

Interest Level: 4-6. Reading Level: 3.2. Further Search Topics: Humorous Fiction, Everyday Stories, Friendship-Fiction, School Stories, Divorce and Separation-Fiction, Psychiatrists-Fiction, Secrets-Fiction.

Pfeffer, Susan Beth. Kid power; illus by Leigh Grant. Watts 1977, 121 pp.

When Janie's mother lost her job, her father's salary wouldn't stretch to provide any more money for the new bicycle fund. There was enough money already set aside to pay for one new bike, but both Janie and her older sister Carol wanted a bicycle. Carol, who had saved money of her own, suggested that they each pay for half a bike and their parents contribute the money for the other half. Then Janie's only problem was how to earn money, since she had none saved. Her solution was to create a business: Kid Power. Before long, Janie's business had blossomed and she was becoming rich, but she had lost her best friend and was ruining a client's roses. When Janie finally realized that getting rich wasn't the only thing that mattered in life, she relaxed, delegated jobs to friends better able to handle them, and became their agent.

A genuinely funny book that, as a bonus, takes a realistic look at the interworkings of a family. Consistent reading level.

Interest Level: 4-6. Reading Level: 3.1. Further Search Topics: Occupations-Fiction, Everyday Stories, Vacation-Fiction, Family-Fiction, Humorous Fiction, Best Sellers, Bicycles and Bicycling-Fiction, Friendship-Fiction.

Robinson, Nancy K. Wendy and the bullies; illus by Ingrid Fetz. Hastings 1980, 128 pp.

Wendy and her best friend Karen had a very carefully mapped out route to and from school—a route that allowed them to meet up with the fewest number of bullies possible. But when Karen became sick enough to stay home from school, Wendy had to face the bullies alone. Wendy's fears escalated to panic so intense that she avoided walking to school by hiding in her basement. She finally realized that she was letting fear and anger control her life when she found herself bullying Karen. Only her new friendship with Monica, making up with Karen, and her involvement in a school project helped Wendy overcome her fears.

This is a humorous, episodic tale of a feeling and circumstances common to many children. The illustrations sometimes make Wendy and her classmates appear much younger than her actual nine years, but fortunately that doesn't happen often enough to spoil the book's appeal.

Interest Level: 3-5. Reading Level: 3.1. Further Search Topics: School Stories, Bullies-Fiction, Courage-Fiction, Best Sellers, Humorous Fiction, Friendship-Fiction, Everyday Stories.

Scism, Carol K. The wizard of Walnut Street; illus by Martha Alexander. Dial 1973, 54 pp.

John and his friends had no room in their Wizard Club for Ford Owens, the new kid. John thought Ford was a conceited show-off who only wanted to make John look like a coward. It was true that John was afraid of some things, such as going down the giant slide into the lake, but he didn't want anyone else to know it. So he excluded Ford from all the club's activities until Ford pushed his way into their magic wishing-well project.

It had been John's idea to charge everyone a dime who wanted to make a wish. They could use the money to buy the few simple things that they would need to make the wishes come true. But it was Ford's eerie volcano and his large dog that had added just the right atmosphere to the trick to make people believe. Even John and Ford found themselves making wishes. John wished to be able to go down the giant slide. He didn't know what Ford wished. Much to John's initial surprise, people's wishes began to be fulfilled. Even Arthur, who had wished he could learn to dive, found he could. Then because John began to realize that the magic was in believing in himself and not in the wishing well, he tried the slide and succeeded. Once John's reason to avoid Ford was gone, he relaxed and asked Ford to join the club. At that point, even Ford's wish was granted.

Interest Level: 2-4. Reading Level: 2.1. Further Search Topics: Friendship-Fiction, Gangs-Fiction, Courage-Fiction, Magic-Fiction, Vacation-Fiction, Best Sellers.

Sharmat, Marjorie W. Getting something on Maggie Marmelstein; illus by Ben Shecter. Har-Row 1971, 101 pp.

A curious love-hate relationship existed between Thad and Maggie. It all began when Maggie overheard Thad say she squeaked like a mouse. Then Maggie caught Thad wearing an apron and cooking. Thad was so uncomfortable with the thought that Maggie might tell his friends, that he was determined to find out Maggie's deepest secret. That meant that Thad had to take a lead role as a frog opposite Maggie as the princess in the school play. While at Maggie's apartment for a costume fitting, Thad found a love letter Maggie had written to Cary Grant. Thad decided he would read the letter to the class right after the play was over. But during the play Maggie saved Thad from what could have been one of the most embarrassing moments of his life. By the time he finally had the chance to make Maggie appear foolish, Thad had changed his mind.

Written as Thad's story, the book is funny, warm, and realistic. A good, short, story that continues to be popular. Print is of moderate size.

Interest Level: 3-6. Reading Level: 3.1. Further Search Topics: Humorous Fiction, Everyday Stories, School Stories, Best Sellers, Friendship-Fiction, Sex Role-Fiction, Acting-Fiction.

Sharmat, Marjorie W. Maggie Marmelstein for President; illus by Ben Shecter. Har-Row 1975, 122 pp.

Maggie and Thad Smith are at it again. When Thad decided to run for sixth grade president, Maggie decided to become his campaign manager. However, because Thad thought Maggie was too strong and would end up managing him much more than he wanted to be managed, he turned down her offer. Thad's refusal made Maggie so angry that she not only decided to run against Thad, but she also enlisted Noah, the smartest kid in the class, as her manager. With Noah's expert guidance Maggie's campaign went rather well, despite attempts at sabotage by a spy for Thad. But as election day drew closer, both Thad and Maggie lost track of the campaign issues and concentrated only on beating each other. Consequently the pre-election debate turned into a disastrous shouting match. The next day Noah was elected class president by write-in votes.

Not very subtle, but funny. A satisfying sequel for those who enjoyed *Getting Something on Maggie Marmelstein*.

Interest Level: 3-6. Reading Level: 3.1. Further Search Topics: Humorous Fiction, Politics-Fiction, School Stories, Friendship-Fiction, Sex Role-Fiction.

Shura, Mary Francis. The Barkley Street six-pack: illus by Gene Sparkman. Dodd 1979, 159 pp.

Jane's best friend Natalie was everything Jane wanted to be. She was self-assured, pretty, vibrant, and even possessed magical talents. Jane didn't realize at first, and she later resisted seeing, that Natalie ran Jane's life and cleverly made sure that Jane had no other friends. Natalie's move left Jane with no friends among those people she had once enjoyed. Little by little, with the help of a stray dog and the new boy on the block, Jane bagan to see how destructive Natalie had been. She finally realized that a true friendship is one in which neither party tries to control the other.

With its enticements of ESP, magic, stray dogs, and problems with peers, this is a very appealing book to many young readers. As a bonus it is a thoughtful, sympathetic, fairly well-written story.

Interest Level: 4-6. Reading Level: 4.2. Further Search Topics: Gangs-Fiction, Pets-Fiction, Dogs-Fiction, Friendship-Fiction, Honesty-Fiction, Courage-Fiction, Loneliness-Fiction, Extra Sensory Perception-Fiction, Everyday Stories.

Silman, Roberta. Somebody else's child; illus by Chris Conover. Warne 1976, 64 pp.

Peter was adopted, but he had never questioned his family's love for him until Puddin' Paint, the school bus driver, made a thoughtless remark. Peter's affection for the older man was strong enough to help him understand Puddin' Paint's feelings. When Puddin' Paint's two dogs disappeared and the bus driver was almost heartbroken, it was Peter who helped the old man search for the dogs. That experience helped both Peter and Puddin' Paint understand that love doesn't only extend to natural born children, but can be just as strong and deep for others.

A simple telling of a moving story. It is as useful for readers who love dogs as for those interested in adoption. Rather inconsistent reading level, tests between 1.2 and 3.1.

Interest Level: 2-5. Reading Level: 2.2. Further Search Topics: Adoption-Fiction, Dogs-Fiction, Friendship-Fiction, Love-Fiction.

Slote, Alfred. My robot buddy; illus by Joel Schick. Lippincott 1975, 92 pp.

For Jack's tenth birthday he was given a robot—a robot so real it did everything but run like a human. The robot appeared so human that a thief, thinking he was stealing the robot, almost kidnapped Jack by mistake.

The few points at which the text becomes more difficult than the reading level indicates should not prove too intimidating to the reader. The suspense and humor of the story and the book's high interest subject matter should carry the reader through the rough spots. A satisfying read-aloud for second and third grades.

Interest Level: 2-5. Reading Level: 3.1. Further Search Topics: Science Fiction, Robots-Fiction, Friendship-Fiction, Kidnapping-Fiction, Read Aloud.

Smith, Doris Buchanan. Tough Chauncey. Morrow 1974, 222 pp.

Chauncey Childs had taught himself to be tough—very tough. Even though he was small for his age (13 years old), the only person who gave him any trouble was his sometimes-friend, Black Jack Levitt. Everyone else was scared of Chauncey. Chauncey felt that he had to be tough or he wouldn't be able to survive. He had to be tough to stand the beatings his grandfather gave him "for his own good," to put up with his mother's drinking and disappearances, and to stand the sight of his grandfather shooting the stray kittens born in their garage.

Chauncey's greatest wish was to be able to live with his mother, instead of with his grandparents. In a desperate attempt to achieve that end he accidentally fell from a moving train and badly hurt his leg. Instead of being returned to his mother he was once more taken back to his grandparents. Chauncey's unhappiness grew until he finally decided to take the one surviving stray kitten and run away. Jack helped him find an empty garage where he could hide while he figured out what to do with his future. After talking with Jack and doing more deep soul searching, Chauncey decided to reshape himself and his life. His first step was to curb his temper and his tongue when his hiding place was discovered. His second step was to see about finding a foster home where he would be treated well, and where he could get a new start.

Ugly as the story is in places, its ending is hopeful. Although it is not always realistic, Chauncey's story is compelling enough to appeal to many readers, especially those who have enjoyed *The War on Villa Street*, by Henry Mazer, *The Outsiders*, by Susan Hinton, or *Mystery of the Fat Cat*, by Frank Bonham. The book's length and its artificially low reading level (vocabulary is often difficult but sentences are very short) make this book most appropriate for an older reader whose reading level is 4.1 or higher.

Interest Level: 5-6. Reading Level: 3.2. Further Search Topics: Child Abuse-Fiction, Family Problems-Fiction, Grandparents-Fiction, Runaways-Fiction, Bullies-Fiction, Single Parent Family-Fiction, Loners-Fiction, Friendship-Fiction, Troublemakers-Fiction, Foster Homes-Fiction.

Smith, Doris Buchanan. A taste of blackberries; illus by Charles Robinson. T Y Crowell 1973, 58 pp.

A beautifully written, sensitive tale of a boy whose best friend dies suddenly. Jamie was always joking, so, when he fell to the ground after being stung by a bee everyone thought he was playing. A short time later Jamie was dead. His friend, the story's narrator, tried to will Jamie back again until the funeral was over and he finally realized there would be no such miracle. The next day he accepted his feelings and picked the newly ripened blackberries, just as he and Jamie had planned to do. A basket full of the best blackberries he gave to Jamie's mother and promised her that he would "slam her door" daily just as he and Jamie had done.

Eight short chapters, small print but short sentences, and a child's point of view perfectly maintained. For the lovers of sad stories and stories of friendship. Very useful when discussing death.

Interest Level: 4-6. Reading Level: 3.2. Further Search Topics: Death-Fiction, Friendship-Fiction, Read Aloud.

Smith, Doris Buchanan. Last was Lloyd. Viking Pr 1981, 124 pp.

Lloyd had several problems: he was overweight, his mother was overprotective, he had no school friends, and there was a chance he might be taken away from home and put into foster care because he had missed so much school. Lloyd's mother, very young and very defensive when she had Lloyd, had done her best to be a "good mother," but in doing so, had made Lloyd fearful of the world. He had become the subject of his classmates' mockery so many times that the only way he could respond to his peers was with nastiness. The one skill he possessed was hitting a baseball. He kept this skill well hidden for fear of exposing himself to further mockery. When one of his classmates accidentally discovered how well Lloyd hit, he took the first step to becoming Lloyd's friend. Lloyd's reaction was to back away, but Kirby kept trying. Eventually Kirby's attempts and those of an understanding truant officer, helped Lloyd begin to make friends, to treat others decently, and to pull away from his mother; in short, he began to mature.

Because Lloyd's problems can be oversimplified too easily, this book requires a fairly mature reader and perhaps even discussion in order to fully understand its subtleties.

Interest Level: 5-6+Reading Level: 4.2. Further Search Topics: Weight-Fiction, Single Parent Family-Fiction, Courage-Fiction, School Stories, Loners-Fiction, Friendship-Fiction, Baseball-Fiction, Family Problems-Fiction, Foster Homes-Fiction, Children-Growth-Fiction.

Yolen, Jane. Shirlick Holmes and the case of the wandering wardrobe; illus by Anthony Rao. Coward 1981, 80 pp.

This is a light, fast-paced story of Shirli and her four friends' attempt to solve a local mystery. Its more fully developed characters and plot make this a better literary piece than any of the *Encyclopedia Brown* stories, but it resembles them in other ways. The children live in a small, secure town. The police chief, Shirli's neighbor and George's father, is working on the same case that interests the children but the children solve it first. The mystery is real and involves danger, as opposed to many of Hildick's McGurk mysteries, the other series this book resembles.

Shirli is a fiesty figure who took up George's challenge to solve the town's latest mystery. Thieves had been systematically robbing some of the wealthy summer homes of antiques. Shirli's plan, to search each of the houses for clues, only succeeded in angering the police chief when he caught Shirli and her friends. Being intrepid detectives, however, they did not give up. Instead, they staked out a likely house and waited for the thieves. When the robbers finally arrived Shirli and George hid. Only Gloria was able to escape and go for help. The oak wardrobe in which Shirli took refuge was one of the first pieces the thieves took out of the house. When Shirli tried to get out of it, she found the wardrobe had been placed on a truck with its door against the truck's side; she was caught. Very frightened, she stayed silent until she found herself in the middle of an antiques auction and recognized one of the voices making bids as George's father! As Shirli tumbled out of the wardrobe some of the police chief's men arrested the auctioneer for burglary and selling stolen goods. After she escaped, Gloria had told the police about the thieves, their truck, Shirli, and George, whom they found locked inside a closet still at the summer house.

A serviceable book that will be enjoyed by a wide range of readers.

Interest Level: 3-5. Reading Level: 3.1. Further Search Topics: Mystery and Detective Stories, Humorous Fiction, Friendship-Fiction, Crime-Fiction, Antiquities-Fiction, Detectives-Fiction, Challenges-Fiction.

FROGS

Allen, Gertrude. Everyday turtles, toads and their kin. HM 1970, 48 pp.

Straight-forward, short, chapter discussions of turtles, lizards, snakes, salamanders, toads, frogs and tree toads. Black and white drawings done by the author amplify the text. The major part of the book is simple enough to be understood at second grade, but should still be interesting to fourth and fifth graders. A few terms may need explanation: i.e., venomous, prey. The chapters on the turtle, lizard, frog and tree frog are the easiest. No index, but still useful for reports.

Interest Level: 2-5. Reading Level: 2.2. Further Search Topics: Turtles, Reptiles, Lizards, Toads, Frogs, Snakes, Salamanders.

FROGS-FICTION

Hildick, Edmund W. The case of the phantom frog; illus by Lisl Weil. Macmillan 1979, 121 pp.

The McGurk Organization would not, under ordinary circumstances, have agreed to babysit for seven-year-old Bela, but there was an unusual twist to Bela's case. Bela's aunt, who asked them to babysit while she worked in her sculpture studio, had heard the eerie sounds of a VERY large frog coming from Bela's room. At first it appeared to the group that Bela actually turned into a frog at night, a werefrog. But, upon investigation they found a very clever, very lonely, and very unhappy young boy who had invented the phantom because he was afraid that his aunt would make him give up his pet frog.

See *The Case of the Bashful Bank Robber* for series information. McGurk Mystery series.

Interest Level: 3-5. Reading Level: 3.1. Further Search Topics: Mystery and Detective Stories, Gangs-Fiction, Frogs-Fiction, Supernatural-Fiction, Transformations-Fiction, Detectives-Fiction, Babysitting-Fiction, Humorous Fiction, Occupations-Fiction.

FRONTIER AND PIONEER LIFE-FICTION

Byars, Betsy. Trouble River; illus by Rocco Negri. Viking Pr. 1969, 158 pp.

A gripping adventure story of survival. After being attacked by an Indian in the middle of the night, Dewey and his grandmother rushed to Trouble River to board a small raft which Dewey had just finished making. They thought they would only need to navigate a few miles down the river to safety at a neighbor's home, but found instead that the neighbor's cabin had been burned down. For almost 40 miles they fought against the unknown river, wolves and rapids.

This is a book that should satisfy many reluctant readers. It's frequent dialogue, fast action and high interest are only occasionally marred by an overly long sentence.

Interest Level: 3-6. Reading Level: 3.1. Further Search Topics: Courage-Fiction, Frontier and Pioneer Life-Fiction, Survival-Fiction, Grandparents-Fiction, Voyages and Travels-Fiction, Best Sellers, Read Aloud.

GAMES

Charosh, Mannis. Mathematical games for one or two; illus by Lois Ehlert. T Y Crowell 1975, 33 pp.

It will take a very special reader to appreciate this book, one who is excited by math puzzles and games and who is also willing to overlook the book's picture book format. Starting with a very simple, one-player game, the book progresses through six types of games, each progressively more taxing mentally. Each type of game is introduced by a very simple example that is thoroughly explained. For the up-and-coming Einstein.

Interest Level: 3-4. Reading Level: 2.2. Further Search Topics: Mathematics, Puzzles, Games.

White, Laurence B., Jr. Science toys; illus by Marc Tolon Brown. A-W 1975, unp (46 pp).

This book presents 23 toys that a young child can easily make and learn from at the same time. A sundial, a drinking straw that flies, a balloon that rolls over, a ghost that sticks to the wall by itself, a water-go-round, and a paper cup that roars are a few examples of what is to be found here. The construction and use of each toy is explained and illustrated in enough detail to enable the child to work alone. And as in *Science Puzzles*, some of the toys will double as magic tricks (i.e. can you balance the rim of a paper plate on your nose?).

Interest Level: 1-3. Reading Level: 2.1. Further Search Topics: Handicrafts, Science, Magic, Toys, Games, Group 2, Puzzles.

Wiseman, Bernard. Morris and Boris. Dodd 1974, 64 pp.

This is a compilation of three silly stories about Morris the Moose and Boris the Bear. When Boris tries to interest Morris in telling riddles, Morris frustrates Boris so completely that Boris runs off angrily. Later Boris tries to teach Morris a tongue twister, but ends up running off in total confusion. Finally Boris tries to teach Morris to play hide-and-seek and that, too, is a disaster. Boris tells Morris that Morris just cannot do anything. A bird who has seen everything reminds Boris that Morris can make him very angry and that is something. When Boris agrees they all laugh happily.

Broad, slapstick humor makes this appealing to children well into third grade. Reader format.

Interest Level: 1-3. Reading Level: 1.2. Further Search Topics: Wit and Humor, Riddles, Tongue Twisters, Games, Humorous Fiction.

GAMES-FICTION

Bonsall, Crosby. The day I had to play with my sister. Har-Row 1972, 32 pp.

A very easy reader, only slightly less universally appealing and humorous than *And I Mean It, Stanley*. This time a little boy tries very hard to teach his younger sister to play hide-and-seek. He is totally unsuccessful and thoroughly frustrated. Again the story is told as much with pictures as with words. Useful through second grade. Reader format. An Early I Can Read Book.

Interest Level: 1-2. Reading Level: 1.1. Further Search Topics: Humorous Fiction, Games-Fiction, Brothers and Sisters-Fiction, Everyday Stories.

GANGS-FICTION

Blume, Judy. Blubber. Bradbury 1974, 153 pp.

Jill, like all the other fifth graders in her class, did exactly as Wendy directed her. When Wendy nicknamed one of the class members Blubber and launched a campaign against her, Jill joined right in. It wasn't until the tables were turned and Jill became Wendy's next victim that Jill realized how much it hurt to be the target of such nastiness. It was only then that Jill could stand up to Wendy. Wendy's meanness is extreme and her classmates, without exception, actively follow her lead, yet all adult characters in the book are blind to what happens. Despite those drawbacks, the book deals with a problem very real to children and thus it has guaranteed audience appeal.

Interest Level: 4-6. Reading Level: 3.1. School Stories, Bullies-Fiction, Weight-Fiction, Loners-Fiction, Gangs-Fiction, Read Aloud, Cruelty-Fiction, Best Sellers, Troublemakers-Fiction, Friendship-Fiction.

Bonham, Frank. The mystery of the fat cat; illus by Alvin Smith. Dutton 1968, 160 pp.

Although noticeably dated at times, this is still an exciting story of an inner city neighborhood. Buddy, Little Pie, Rich, and Cool were among the many who used the local Boys' Club as their hangout. It was a place to stay out of trouble and off the streets, but it was also a haven for rats. The rats were big and brazen; so brazen that one attacked Buddy in the swimming pool. The club needed a new building desperately. The money was there; they just weren't able to use it. Fifteen years earlier an eccentric old woman willed the Boys' Club over $600,000, but stated that the money was first to be used to support her cat until it died. A caretaker, a lawyer, and a veterinarian all benefited as long as the cat lived. Buddy and his friends took on the job of discovering if the cat really was alive or if the Boys' Club was being cheated out of half a million dollars. It was a job that nearly killed them before they set things right. Plenty of action, some violence, a cast of street-smart characters, realistic trouble with the police, as well as a slight mystery almost insure the book's success with older readers. Moderate sized print. Line spacing somewhat narrow.

Interest Level: 6+. Reading Level: 5.1. Further Search Topics: Humorous Fiction, Cats-Fiction, Gangs-Fiction, City Life-Fiction, Mystery and Detective Stories, Poverty-Fiction, Friendship-Fiction, Juvenile Delinquency-Fiction, Crime-Fiction, Best Sellers.

Harris, Robie H. Rosie's double dare; illus by Tony DeLuna. Knopf 1980, 112 pp.

Rosie wanted to play baseball with the Willard Street Gang, but she couldn't play well enough to play by their rules. She needed what her older brother called "shrimp rules." She couldn't hit a pitched ball, only a grounder; but grounders were "shrimp rules." In desperation Rosie agreed to take a dare that the gang made up. If she actually performed the dare, the gang would let her play with them by her rules.

The gang dared Rosie to sneak into cranky Mr. Quirk's apartment and borrow a set of his false teeth. Because Rosie couldn't find any extra false teeth, she borrowed his wig instead but that didn't satisfy the gang. They only laughed and made up another dare for Rosie. She was to untie Mrs. Samuels' dog and let it run loose. As Rosie untied him, Elmer ran away, Rosie ran off after him. One rainstorm later, Rosie

caught up with him in the middle of a Red Sox game at Fenway Park. Rosie's attempt to catch Elmer stopped the game, brought her an interview on TV, and secured her a place on the Willard Street baseball team.

This very light story, made up almost entirely of action and examples of sibling rivalry, should have wide appeal through fifth grade. Beyond that, Rosie's age (almost nine) and childish behavior won't ring true. Capers series.

Interest Level: 2-5. Reading Level: 2.2. Further Search Topics: Baseball-Fiction, Humorous Fiction, Brothers and Sisters-Fiction, Challenges-Fiction, Courage-Fiction, Gangs-Fiction, Everyday Stories.

Heide, Florence Parry. Mystery of the forgotten island; illus by Seymour Fleishman. A. Whitman 1980, 127 pp.

On a small island, unmarked on the map, the Spotlight Club members found old Mr. Whitson, who claimed that he was being kept prisoner by his granddaughter Lorrie and her husband John. Lorrie and John had told him he was being kept in the yard for his own good, so that he wouldn't wander off and get hurt or lost. They had also told him that he should will the island to them so that his daughter Cassie couldn't sell the island to a resort company for development. He was going to be forced to sign such a will unless he could get the children to help him smuggle a new will to his lawyer. Mr. Whitson wasn't convinced that Cassie wanted to sell the island, but he couldn't get in touch with her and he hadn'd had a letter from her in many months.

As the children went to secretly meet Mr. Whitson and mail his new will, they discovered that their trusted friend Guy was attempting to blackmail Lorrie and John into giving him some of the money from the sale of the island. He had evidence that Lorrie and John, not Cassie, wanted to sell the island and were tricking Mr. Whitson into signing a will in their favor. In a daring move, the children were able to free Mr. Whitson and isolate all three of the thieves so that the police could capture them.

This book involves a somewhat more complicated plot and slightly less familiar ingredients than most other Spotlight Club mysteries. One should progress to rather than begin the series with this title. Spotlight Club Mystery series.

Interest Level: 4-6. Reading Level: 3.1. Further Search Topics: Mystery and Detective Stories, Inheritance-Fiction, Gangs-Fiction, Kidnapping-Fiction, Brothers and Sisters-Fiction, Aging-Fiction, Detectives-Fiction.

Heide, Florence Parry. Mystery of the mummy's mask; illus by Seymour Fleishman. A. Whitman 1979, 127 pp.

The Spotlight Club published a neighborhood newspaper. Just as the club was about to take the fourth issue to the printer, Jay discovered an ancient mummy mask hidden near Mr. Pruitt's house. Mr. Pruitt was intrigued by the discovery (he worked at the nearby museum) and he took the mask from Jay, but agreed that Jay could write about the mask for the paper. At about the same time, Dexter discovered that an old, abandoned house was being used. When the printer's office was broken into that night and only their newspaper was stolen, the three children began to suspect that something strange was going on at the abandoned house.

Dexter rode back to the house alone and was captured by Hank, one of three thieves hiding out there. Figuring that they never would have missed one item, Hank had taken the mask from the cache of goods that the other two had stolen. When he overheard Jay's conversation with Mr. Pruitt, Hank realized that his partners would find out what he had done if they ever read the newspaper article. To avoid being discovered, Hank broke into the printer's and stole the paste-up of the paper. In order to keep Dexter from escaping, Hank tied him up and placed him in a shipping crate. When he didn't return as soon as expected, Jay and Cindy realized that Dexter was in trouble, so they went out to the house to search for him. As the three escaped, Dexter and Cindy slashed the thieves' truck's tires, and Jay ran to phone for the police. After several nervous moments in which Cindy and Dexter thought Jay might not get back before they were caught, Jay finally brought the police, who captured all three thieves.

See *Mystery at Southport Cinema* for more information. Spotlight Club Mystery series.

Interest Level: 3-5. Reading Level: 3.1. Further Search Topics: Mystery and Detective Stories, Crime-Fiction, Egypt-Fiction, Archaeology-Fiction, Antiquities-Fiction, Journalism-Fiction, Gangs-Fiction, Brothers and Sisters-Fiction, Detectives-Fiction.

Heide, Florence Parry. The mystery of the silver tag; illus by Seymour Fleishman. A. Whitman 1972, 127 pp.

Jay's paper route took him to one house that he wished he could avoid. It was grumpy, old Mr. Pendleton's house that Jay hated. One rainy day he spotted what he later realized was a prize Angora cat hiding on Mr. Pendleton's porch. When the cat was reported lost in that night's paper, Jay and the other members of the Spotlight Club decided to try to return the cat to its owner, Miss Horton. Their attempts to get the cat back from Mr. Pendleton meant that they had to spy on him, to sneak into his garage, and to spend the night in a treehouse overlooking his house. They were afraid that they had failed when they saw Mr. Pendleton leave with the cat. Determined to be the ones to tell Miss Horton of their failure, they went to her apartment and found Mr. Pendleton already there. Mr. Pendleton was a famous animal photographer who, upon finding the cat, had asked Miss Horton if he could photograph him. The children, thinking only that Mr. Pendleton was a mad scientist who kidnapped cats, had jumped to all the wrong conclusions, but ended with a mystery solved, new friends, and their first lesson in being detectives.

See entry with *Mystery at Southport Cinema* for series information. Spotlight Club Mystery series.

Interest Level: 3-5. Reading Level: 2.2. Further Search Topics: Mystery and Detective Stories, Brothers and Sisters-Fiction, Gangs-Fiction, Cats-Fiction, Loners-Fiction, Detectives-Fiction, Photography-Fiction, Kidnapping-Fiction.

Heide, Florence Parry. Mystery at Southport Cinema; illus by Seymour Fleishman. A. Whitman 1978, 128 pp.

The Spotlight Club was the name Jay, his sister Cindy, and his friend Dexter gave themselves. Their main interest was solving mysteries and just as in Sobol's Encyclopedia Brown series, Hildick's McGurk Mysteries, and Warner books about the Alden children, mysteries seem to follow them around. Their cases are more intricate and lengthy than Encyclopedia Brown's. They involve more danger than most of McGurk's, and they center on more common themes than the Alden's. The series serves much the same audience, however, as the others. It serves those children who want action, intrigue, and the

challenge of a mystery, and who don't care about character development or in-depth motivation. The chapters are 8 to 12 pages long, print size is adequate, and the children are normal enough to make this a very popular series. As an added attraction, reading levels here are fairly consistent.

Thorne prided himself on doing his job well, so when the grocery store he ran for Callie (the owner) was robbed by a bearded stranger, Thorne felt responsible. Thorne ran after the thief but lost him in the darkened Southport Cinema. The Spotlight Club members also tried to track the thief. They figured that he had hidden the bag with the stolen money somewhere in the movie house because no one had been seen leaving with such a bag.

In the janitor's lost and found basket Jay found a wig the thief must have used as a disguise. The children called the wig maker to find out who had ordered it and were directed to a local post office box, Jay and Dexter were surprised to find belonged to the grocery store. Because Thorne picked up the mail each day, he became a prime suspect. In the meantime, Cindy had gone back to the cinema to look for the money. In the dark she had scuffled with someone else looking for the money and had given the person a deep scratch on the face.

At the same time that Thorne decided to pay Callie back for the stolen money, the Club members decided to tell Callie their suspicions about him. As Thorne handed his veterinary school savings to Callie, Cindy took a close enough look at Callie's face to see a new scratch and accused her of being the thief. Callie had so wanted Thorne to run the store instead of going to school, and had needed money so intensely, that she had stolen from her own business. The ending is weak but the rest of the book will hold reader interest. Spotlight Club Mystery series.

Interest Level: 3-5. Reading Level: 3.1. Further Search Topics: Mystery and Detective Stories, Gangs-Fiction, Crime-Fiction, Detectives-Fiction, Brothers and Sisters-Fiction.

Heide, Florence Parry. Mystery of the melting snowman; illus by Seymour Fleishman. A. Whitman 1974, 128 pp.

Hidden inside of a snowman, the Spotlight Club found what they believed was a stolen iron statue of a dog. In order to try to catch the thief, the children hid the statue again and watched to see who came to look for it. Eventually they determined that the thief or thieves was either Tom and Jenny, the amenable young couple who were helping Mrs. Wellington sell her house or Alex, the man who seemed to be a detective. After a frightening episode in which Alex almost captured Cindy, the dog, and a cache of Mrs. Wellington's diamonds (hidden in a secret compartment to which the dog held the key), Cindy managed to lock Alex in a closet long enough to enable Jay and Dexter to alert Mrs. Wellington to what was happening. The case was closed as Mrs. Wellington revealed Alex to be her greedy, young nephew, whom she had indulged once too often, but would not indulge again.

See *Mystery at Southport Cinema* for series information. Spotlight Club Mystery series.

Interest Level: 3-5. Reading Level: 2.2. Further Search Topics: Mystery and Detective Stories, Gangs-Fiction, Crime-Fiction, Brothers and Sisters-Fiction, Detectives-Fiction, Inheritance-Fiction.

Heide, Florence Parry. Mystery of the midnight message; illus by Seymour Fleishman. A. Whitman 1977, 128 pp.

The challenge to the Spotlight Club this time was to stop a crime before it happened. Jay and his sister Cindy were on a bus trip home when a blizzard forced the bus to stop at a motel for the night. Jay answered the room telephone late that night and heard a woman's strange and stern instructions. The instructions were to say nothing, to look in the desk drawer for directions, to expect that Bee had the other half of the instructions, and to be at the place at 8:00 the next evening. The envelope, which Jay and Cindy found, showed the location of and half the combination to someone's bedroom safe.

Early the next morning, the children found themselves fleeing in terror from the evil Scull, the man who was supposed to have received the message. Scull pursued them as they escaped in a friendly salesman's car, caught them and locked them into a cold barn without jackets. When the two were finally back on the road and reunited with Dexter and his sister Anne, they had only a few hours and fewer clues to help them find Woodvale and Jeremiah Gibbon, the intended victim.

Despite difficult driving conditions in the snow, Anne managed to get the children to their destination a few minutes before the thieves arrived. Anne and Jeremiah's secretary left the house together to get the police while the Spotlight Club members and Mr. Gibbon hid near the safe. A few tense minutes later, the case was closed; Mr. Gibbons' money was safe, the ringleader had been named (Mr. Gibbon's doctor), and the thieves had been caught.

See *Mystery at Southport Cinema* for series information. Spotlight Club Mystery series.

Interest Level: 3-5. Reading Level: 3.1. Further Search Topics: Mystery and Detective Stories, Crime-Fiction, Snow-Fiction, Disasters-Fiction, Gangs-Fiction, Brothers and Sisters-Fiction, Detectives-Fiction.

Heide, Florence Parry. Mystery of the vanishing visitor; illus by Seymour Fleishman. A. Whitman 1975, 128 pp.

Cindy was hired to take care of Mrs. Widget's house, animals, and plants for a weekend. That same weekend, someone tried to find and steal something from Mrs. Widget's overcrowded house. She had very few empty spaces in her house, so it was not a surprise that the thief wasn't able to find the object of his or her search. The three Spotlight Club members were determined to figure out not only who was the thief, but also what it was that the thief, wanted. Their prime suspects included the very nasty Bertha Beaker and the charming Charley Capp.

After spending a night in Mrs. Widget's house trying to, and almost succeeding in catching the thief, the children were surprised by an early morning visit from Mr. Capp. Mr. Capp was nearly able to steal away with a painting that hid a great deal of money before Cindy figured out that he was the thief. Even after Mr. Capp had been caught, he charmed his way out of any punishment and left before anyone had second thoughts.

See entry for *Mystery at Southport Cinema* for series information. Spotlight Club Mystery series.

Interest Level: 3-5. Reading Level: 2.2. Further Search Topics: Mystery and Detective Stories, Brothers and Sisters-Fiction, Gangs-Fiction, Crime-Fiction, Antiquities-Fiction, Detectives-Fiction.

Hildick, Edmund W. The case of the invisible dog; illus by Lisl Weil. Macmillan 1977, 101 pp.

Brains Bellingham, a nine-year-old scientific genius, interrupted the McGurk Organization's Annual Picnic with an invisible dog. It was only a short time before McGurk and his friends were convinced that Brains' discovery of how to make things invisible was the greatest event since putting a man on the moon. Although they had always scorned the idea of including anyone else in the Organization, they decided to persuade Brains to join. But, before the day was over, they discovered not only that they had been duped, but exactly how Brains had made the impossible seem real. The Organization took its revenge by using Brain's own trick to make him confess. When Brains began laughing at how well his trick had been used in reverse, McGurk admitted how impressed they all had been by Brain's clever thinking. The outcome of their discussion was that Brains was invited, a second time, to become a member of the McGurk Organization.

See *The Case of the Bashful Bank Robber* for series information. McGurk Mystery series.

Interest Level: 3-6. Reading Level: 3.1. Further Search Topics: Mystery and Detective Stories, Detectives-Fiction, Gangs-Fiction, Dogs-Fiction, Supernatural-Fiction, Humorous Fiction, Jealousy-Fiction.

Hildick, Edmund W. The great rabbit rip-off; illus by Lisl Weil. Macmillan 1976, 101 pp.

Why would anyone want to put red paint on all of the clay lawn rabbits in town? That was the first and easier of the mysteries the McGurk Organization had to solve. The bigger mystery was who would then steal them all and why? Almost everyone in town had purchased a rabbit to help a charity drive. Donny Towers a local social worker had thought of the idea. Donny, his fiancee, Joanne, and two reformed thieves, Sam and Ferdie, had made enough rabbits for everyone. When the rabbits disappeared, the Organization began to suspect, among others, Sam and Ferdie. Then when Donny replaced each one almost immediately with rabbits smelling of paint remover, the group began to think Donny might have been involved. It was Wanda's sharp eyes that revealed Donny's motive. Joanne's engagement ring had been accidentally molded into one of the rabbits and Donny had retrieved the rabbits to find the ring. Knowing he couldn't return the paint stained rabbits without raising suspicion, Donny had removed the red paint and told everyone that he was simply replacing the stolen rabbits with new ones.

See *Case of the Bashful Bank Robber* for series information. McGurk Mystery series.

Interest Level: 3-5. Reading Level: 2.2. Further Search Topics: Mystery and Detective Stories, Detectives-Fiction, Gangs-Fiction, Rabbits-Fiction, Crime-Fiction, Humorous Fiction.

Hildick, Edmund W. Deadline for McGurk; illus by Lisl Weil. Macmillan 1975, 104 pp.

When many of the dolls in the neighborhood began disappearing, their owners went to the McGurk Organization for help. At first McGurk was reluctant to take on such a silly task as recovering lost dolls. But when a ransom note appeared and the Organization was linked to the dolls' safety, McGurk's reluctance vanished. The note stated that if, in a written public notice, the members of the Organization did not admit that they were no good, the dolls were doomed. McGurk's pride would never have allowed him to write such a notice. As the deadline approached, the group plotted a daring move designed to uncover the doll thief. The plan depended on Willie's super-sensitive nose, a particular perfume dabbed on a stolen doll, and the curiosity of the thief. Success came only minutes before the hour of doom. Once again Sandra Ennis was the culprit.

See *The Case of the Bashful Bank Robber* for series information. McGurk Mystery series.

Interest Level: 3-5. Reading Level: 2.2. Further Search Topics: Dolls-Fiction, Mystery and Detective Stories, Detectives-Fiction, Humorous Fiction, Gangs-Fiction, Jealousy-Fiction.

Hildick, Edmund W. The case of the condemned cat; illus by Lisl Weil. Macmillan 1975, 106 pp.

Ray Williams had a terrible problem when he begged the McGurk Organization for help. His cat Whiskers had been accused of killing a neighbor's pet dove. Ray's mother decided that they couldn't risk upsetting the neighbors anymore and threatened to take Whiskers to the pound unless it could be proven that he was innocent. The Organization, needing time, hid Whiskers and told Mrs. Williams that he had run away. While Whiskers was safely hidden, the group interviewed all the neighbors, surveyed the scene of the crime, and tried to decide upon the real murderer. When the remains of another bird were found while Whiskers was safely locked away, it looked as if the cat was surely innocent. But then McGurk and his detectives found out that the cat had been sprung. It wasn't until they went back over all the information they had gathered that McGurk realized who was the real culprit. The only step left was to trick old Gramp Martin (the neighborhood grouch) into confessing.

See *The Case of the Bashful Bank Robber* for series information. McGurk Mystery series.

Interest Level: 3-6. Reading Level: 2.2. Further Search Topics: Mystery and Detective Stories, Cats-Fiction, Detectives-Fiction, Humorous Fiction, Gangs-Fiction, Pets-Fiction.

Hildick, Edmund W. The case of the secret scribbler; illus by Lisl Weil. Macmillan 1978, 106 pp.

Joey's discovery in a library book of a scrap of paper with part of a letter and a strange diagram on it led the McGurk Organization on a lively chase. Brains identified the diagram as that of a widely-used security system. The part of the letter that they could read told the group that there was a burglary being planned for the approaching weekend, but the youngsters knew the police would never take them seriously until they had much more evidence. By researching local alarm systems, determining who bought the unusual paper, and comparing handwriting samples, the detectives were able to convince the police of what was about to happen. In gratitude, the police loaned the Organization a police monitor so that they could listen as the thieves were caught. To all but McGurk it seemed like the perfect way to end the case: he tried to sneak into the midst of the capture, but only succeeded in getting himself in real trouble.

See *The Case of the Bashful Bank Robber* for series information. McGurk Mystery series.

Interest Level: 3-6. Reading Level: 2.2. Further Search Topics: Mystery and Detective Stories, Crime-Fiction, Gangs-Fiction, Nonverbal Communication-Fiction, Humorous Fiction, Detectives-Fiction.

Hildick, Edmund W. The case of the phantom frog; illus by Lisl Weil. Macmillan 1979, 121 pp.

The McGurk Organization would not, under ordinary circumstances, have agreed to babysit for seven-year-old Bela, but there was an unusual twist to Bela's case. Bela's aunt, who asked them to babysit while she worked in her sculpture studio, had heard the eerie sounds of a VERY large frog coming from Bela's room. At first it appeared to the group that Bela actually turned into a frog at night, a werefrog. But, upon investigation they found a very clever, very lonely, and very unhappy young boy who had invented the phantom because he was afraid that his aunt would make him give up his pet frog.

See *The Case of the Bashful Bank Robber* for series information. McGurk Mystery series.

Interest Level: 3-5. Reading Level: 3.1. Further Search Topics: Mystery and Detective Stories, Gangs-Fiction, Frogs-Fiction, Supernatural-Fiction, Transformations-Fiction, Detectives-Fiction, Babysitting-Fiction, Humorous Fiction, Occupations-Fiction.

Hildick, Edmund W. The case of the treetop treasure; illus by Lisl Weil. Macmillan 1980, 121 pp.

As Wanda rescued a cat she discovered a stash of odd items tucked into a hollow high up in a tree. On top of the assortment was a sign that said simply "Beware!" The McGurk Organization suspected a thief was using the tree as a place to hide stolen goods, but until an antique silver bowl was added nothing that had been placed there was worth stealing. Shortly afterwards Wanda found out from the police that she was the prime suspect in the theft of the bowl. Brains devised a complicated system for determining the real thief while McGurk worked more from intuition. Nevertheless, it wasn't long before they both arrived at the same conclusion. The culprit was the gang's long-time enemy Sandra Ennis. Then it was just a simple matter of finding the right way to persuade Sandra to confess and apologize to her victims.

See *The Case of the Bashful Bank Robber* for series information. McGurk Mystery series.

Interest Level: 3-5. Reading Level: 3.1. Further Search Topics: Mystery and Detective Stories, Crime-Fiction, Gangs-Fiction, Detectives-Fiction, Humorous Fiction.

Hildick, Edmund W. The case of the snowbound spy; illus by Lisl Weil. Macmillan 1980, 132 pp.

One snowy morning McGurk called the five members of his organization together to decipher a code. The code was part of a message from someone who wanted to hire them and would pay $5.00 a day. When they broke the code and met their employer, Mr. Fitch, he gave the group another code as part of their assignment. The second code told them where to deliver a small package that Mr. Fitch gave them. They were to pick up another coded message at the same place. After three pick-ups and drops they would be finished and Mr. Fitch, an ex-government spy, would have proved he was still a trustworthy and capable person to an ex-colleague with whom he wanted to work on a book. It seemed like just the challenging kind of assignment the McGurk Organization looked for. As they worked, however, it began to look more and more as if they were being used for illegal business. While Joey and McGurk staked out the next drop-off spot, Willie, Brains and Wanda pretended to Mr. Fitch to be unsuspecting. By working quickly and cleverly and by alerting the police, the McGurk gang uncovered and stopped two industrial spies who were stealing secret information about a new copying machine.

See *The Case of the Bashful Bank Robber* for series information. McGurk Mystery series.

Interest Level: 3-6. Reading Level: 3.1. Further Search Topics: Mystery and Detective Stories, Spies-Fiction, Detectives-Fiction, Gangs-Fiction, Humorous Fiction, Nonverbal Communication-Fiction, Crime-Fiction.

Hildick, Edmund W. The case of the bashful bank robber; illus by Lisl Weil. Macmillan 1981, 138 pp.

The McGurk Organization is a crime fighting detective agency. Led by Jack McGurk's strong ego, they had taken on many a seemingly impossible task and had always been successful. Never before, however, had they tried to protect the seven banks in town from being robbed. The five children's first idea was to regularly patrol each bank and watch for likely looking get-away cars. When that plan only led to a nasty confrontation with their new junior high school principal, they decided to try something else. Their second plan, to photograph all suspicious looking people near the banks, didn't fare much better than their first idea. Then, without knowing it, they found themselves holding the key to solving a real bank robbery. Before they realized its importance, they had literally given away the vital clue. Using only their own memories, powers of observation, and cleverness, they were still able to solve the crime with only a little help from the FBI.

The "McGurk mysteries" are light, fast-moving, and often humorous. Clues for solving the mysteries are sometimes subtle, but always there in the plot and illustrations for the reader to find. The characters are somewhat flat but still appealing. Joey, who is handy with words and a typewriter, is the narrator of each book. Jack McGurk, dedicated mastermind of all the group's activities is shrewd, a natural leader, and egotistical. Willie has the world's most sensitive nose and an excellent memory for odors. Wanda is the best tree-climber in town and a rational influence on the group. Brains, the newest and youngest member of the group, is a scientific genius, so he runs their crime lab. The books need not be read in chronological order although most have a brief reference to an earlier story. Reading level varies within each book from 2.1 to 3.1. A few books include enough more difficult passages that their average reading level is pushed from 2.2 to 3.1. Interest level in the series, once a reader has started on it, is high. McGurk Mystery series.

Interest Level: 3-6. Reading Level: 2.2. Further Search Topics: Mystery and Detective Stories, Crime-Fiction, Detectives-Fiction, Humorous Fiction, Gangs-Fiction.

Hildick, Edmund W. The case of the four flying fingers; illus by Lisl Weil. Macmillan 1981, 138 pp.

At first the four young strangers who were knocking over garbage cans had been merely a neighborhood nuisance. Later McGurk and his fellow detectives began to suspect that they were involved in the rash of break-ins and burglaries in the city. The Organization didn't think the "garbage gang" was actually committing the robberies, but rather that they were fingering houses for someone else to burglarize (thus their nickname: The Four Flying Fingers). It could be safely assumed by a would-be burglar that where no one picked up the spilled garbage, no one was home. It was the Organization's job to find the Thumb who was the mastermind behind the plot. When they caught up with the Fingers, McGurk and crew found out that the Flying Fingers hadn't realized what they were doing; only that a blonde lady in a camper was paying them a nickel for every driveway they left strewn with garbage. It didn't take long for the

Organization to track down the woman and her accomplice. But, in one of their less intelligent moves, they played right into her hands and soon found themselves being transported out of town in her camper. When they tried to call to passing cars for help, no one took them seriously. It wasn't until Brains, bound and gagged to appear authentic, used a flashlight and Morse code to signal for help that anyone paid any attention to them. A police car finally stopped the camper for speeding apd after some clever arguments McGurk and his friends were able to convince the police that Lady Thumb was a thief.

This title is just as enjoyable as the best of the other books in the series, more exciting and universal in appeal than most, and equally humorous. It's only drawback is a very inconsistent reading level (from 2.1 to 4.1) that will discourage a reader new to McGurk. Established fans will be able to tolerate the range. McGurk Mystery series.

Interest Level: 3-6. Reading Level: 3.1. Further Search Topics: Mystery and Detective Stories, Detectives-Fiction, Humorous Fiction, Crime-Fiction, Gangs-Fiction.

Hinton, Susan E. The outsiders. Viking Pr. 1967, 188 pp.

When she wrote this book Susan Hinton was only 17 years old, but she had the sensitivity of someone much older. She wrote a taut story of the rivalry between two city gangs; the Socs (the rich socialites) and the Greasers (poor kids from the wrong side of town) that is more than anything a plea for understanding and tolerance. Seen through the eyes of Ponyboy (a very bright, 14-year-old Greaser), the rivalry brought on violence and an accidental killing that forced Pony and his friend Johnny to flee for their lives. Dallas, the meanest and most dangerous of the Greasers, provided them with shelter, food for a week, and a gun. At the end of that week, Johnny decided that they should turn themselves in to the police. But before they could do that, their hideout (an old church) burned in a fire which threatened the lives of four children who had been playing there. In trying to rescue the children, Johnny, Pony, and Dallas were injured; Johnny was severely burned and probably permanently crippled. A vengeance rumble was held while Johnny lay in the hospital, but the Greasers' victory was empty when Johnny died. He had been the one member of the gang whom they all loved and who had most needed them. Dallas went to pieces: he robbed a store and set himself up to be killed by the police. He had nothing left to live for after Johnny's death. Pony found support and security with his brothers (their parents were dead) and, in a note from Johnny, some hope for the future.

Hinton speaks most often through Pony (his depth of understanding of the people around him is very impressive), but through Johnny and two of the Socs as well, Randy and Cherry. Her message is clear, but at no time does she fail to maintain believable characters in a compelling plot.

Although the book looks forbidding with its 188 pages of unrelenting small print, it is an exciting story, full of adventure, realism, and room for thought. Perhaps the best way to introduce this book is to read a fair portion of it aloud. Now a motion picture too.

Interest Level: 6+. Reading Level: 5.1. Further Search Topics: Crime-Fiction, Gangs-Fiction, Murder-Fiction, Read Aloud, Friendship-Fiction, Juvenile Delinquency-Fiction, Best Sellers, City

Life-Fiction, Brothers and Sisters-Fiction, Orphans-Fiction, Runaways-Fiction, Troublemakers-Fiction, Poverty-Fiction.

Mazer, Harry. The war on Villa Street. Delacorte 1978, 182 pp.

Willis was a loner and a runner. He was a loner because he didn't want anyone to find out about his alcoholic father. He wasn't quite sure why he ran; perhaps because it was the only time he felt good. When Rabbit Slavin and his friends asked Willis to become part of their gang, he refused. He was flattered and wanted to join, but the gang wanted to meet at his house and Willis couldn't risk that. Then when he agreed to coach the local "retard" for the school's field day, Willis gave the gang the opportunity they wanted to take their revenge on him for turning them down. The gang's hatred for Willis increased still more when he beat their best runner and athlete. In payment, the gang jumped Willis and beat him badly. After he picked himself up, Willis realized that he had at least faced the worst of his fears and survived. Days later when his drunken father humiliated him, Willis realized he had to face that, too. He made peace with himself and the world by deciding he could neither continue to run away from, nor apologize for his father anymore. He was independent and strong.

There is much in this fast-paced book besides the obvious violence and action. It is written with an intuitive feel for a teenager's problems and emotions and is a sensitive portrayal of mature concepts. The print is large, but spacing between the lines should have been slightly increased.

Interest Level: 5-6. Reading Level: 5.1. Further Search Topics: Running-Fiction, Loneliness-Fiction, Alcoholism-Fiction, Loners-Fiction, Mental Retardation-Fiction, Gangs-Fiction, Child Abuse-Fiction, Bullies-Fiction, Family Problems-Fiction, Courage-Fiction.

Robinson, Jean. The strange but wonderful cosmic awareness of Duffy Moon; illus by Lawrence Di Fiori. HM 1974, 142 pp.

Duffy was tired of being small, of always being on the losing side of fights, and of being unappreciated at home (by his ex-football star uncle). When he sent away for Mr. Flamel's Cosmic Awareness Kit, Duffy was sure he would then be able to take control over anything he wanted and direct his own life. His friend Peter, the narrator, wasn't quite so sure. Peter turned out to be right. Duffy almost made himself sick trying to build a stone wall. Babysitting two small boys and trying to bathe a Great Dane proved to be disastrous. But Duffy's biggest problem came from Boots McAfee's gang. A series of events finally brought Duffy and Peter face-to-face with the dreaded Boots. Luckily, she turned out to be a very smart girl who appreciated Duffy's true talents.

From the first to the last page this is a funny, very enjoyable book. A delightful book with a very palatable message.

Interest Level: 3-6. Reading Level: 3.2. Further Search Topics: Humorous Fiction, Bullies-Fiction, Magic-Fiction, Read Aloud, Occupations-Fiction, Sex Role-Fiction, Orphans-Fiction, Best Sellers, Gangs-Fiction, Courage-Fiction, Babysitting-Fiction.

Scism, Carol K. The wizard of Walnut Street; illus by Martha Alexander. Dial 1973, 54 pp.

John and his friends had no room in their Wizard Club for Ford Owens, the new kid. John thought Ford was a conceited show-off who only wanted to make John look like a coward. It was true that John was afraid of some things, such as going down the giant slide into the lake, but he didn't want anyone else to know it. So he excluded Ford from all the club's activities until Ford pushed his way into their magic wishing-well project.

It had been John's idea to charge everyone a dime who wanted to make a wish. They could use the money to buy the few simple things that they would need to make the wishes come true. But it was Ford's eerie volcano and his large dog that had added just the right atmosphere to the trick to make people believe. Even John and Ford found themselves making wishes. John wished to be able to go down the giant slide. He didn't know what Ford wished. Much to John's initial surprise, people's wishes began to be fulfilled. Even Arthur, who had wished he could learn to dive, found he could. Then because John began to realize that the magic was in believing in himself and not in the wishing well, he tried the slide and succeeded. Once John's reason to avoid Ford was gone, he relaxed and asked Ford to join the club. At that point, even Ford's wish was granted.

Interest Level: 2-4. Reading Level: 2.1. Further Search Topics: Friendship-Fiction, Gangs-Fiction, Courage-Fiction, Magic-Fiction, Vacation-Fiction, Best Sellers.

Shreve, Susan. The Nightmares of Geranium Street. Knopf 1977, 127 pp.

The Nightmares, a small neighborhood gang, had very little to do until beautiful Tess moved on the block. Tess dressed in satins, furs, and rhinestones, and sang in nightclubs. She was even more of a fascination to the gang because they had been told to stay away from her. When Amanda moved in with Tess, the Nightmares invited her to join the gang so that they would have a way of spying on Tess. Gradually her strange behavior, her moods, her bruises and shaking spells, the strangers she let in the house, and the fights she had, led the gang members to suspect that Tess dealt in drugs. When Amanda failed to show up for a picnic and the Nightmares learned the police were searching for Tess, the gang became worried enough to look for Amanda themselves. In doing so, they uncovered proof of Tess' drug dealings, put themselves in great danger, and were protected by Tess as they escaped only moments before Tess was arrested.

Despite its low reading level, the book's confusing sequence of final events, and its subject matter make it best suited to older readers. It is not great literature, but its subject has strong appeal.

Interest Level: 5-6. Reading Level: 3.1. Further Search Topics: Family Problems-Fiction, Gangs-Fiction, Drugs-Fiction, Mystery and Detective Stories, City Life-Fiction, Crime-Fiction, Philadelphia-Fiction.

Shura, Mary Francis. The Barkley Street six-pack: illus by Gene Sparkman. Dodd 1979, 159 pp.

Jane's best friend Natalie was everything Jane wanted to be. She was self-assured, pretty, vibrant, and even possessed magical talents. Jane didn't realize at first, and she later resisted seeing, that Natalie ran Jane's life and cleverly made sure that Jane had no other friends. Natalie's move left Jane with no friends among those people she had once enjoyed. Little by little, with the help of a stray dog and the new boy on the block, Jane bagan to see how destructive Natalie had been. She finally realized that a true friendship is one in which neither party tries to control the other.

With its enticements of ESP, magic, stray dogs, and problems with peers, this is a very appealing book to many young readers. As a bonus it is a thoughtful, sympathetic, fairly well-written story.

Interest Level: 4-6. Reading Level: 4.2. Further Search Topics: Gangs-Fiction, Pets-Fiction, Dogs-Fiction, Friendship-Fiction, Honesty-Fiction, Courage-Fiction, Loneliness-Fiction, Extra Sensory Perception-Fiction, Everyday Stories.

GERBILS-FICTION

Dobrin, Arnold. Jillions of gerbils. Lothrop 1973, 64 pp.

Right after his family moved into a big and very old house, David's gerbil disappeared. Before long, the replacement gerbil disappeared also. The house was very old and did have strange creakings. Could there also have been secret hiding places for ghosts, maybe? Determined to find out, David searched the entire house until he really did find a secret room. And in that room he found his two gerbils with their new family — the beginnings of David's millions and billions and jillions of gerbils.

A comfortable, somewhat old-fashioned book that is neatly divided into six short chapters. It includes a page of facts about gerbils at the end. A good choice to follow the very easy readers; it is easy, but not "too babyish."

Interest Level: 1-4. Reading Level: 2.1. Further Search Topics: Gerbils-Fiction, Pets-Fiction, Group 2, Humorous Fiction.

GHOSTS-FICTION

Bulla, Clyde Robert. The ghost of windy hill; illus by Don Bolognese. Har-Row 168, 84 pp.

If the reader doesn't expect a high adventure ghost story, he or she will not be disappointed by this low-keyed tale of a family who goes to live in a house that is supposedly haunted. Mr. Giddings asked the Carver family to move into his country home while he and his wife stayed in Boston. His intent was that the Carvers should either prove to his wife that the house was not haunted or drive the ghost out. The Carvers found no ghosts—at first—only an interesting group of neighbors. There was shy Miss Miggie who drifted around in a long, white dress and wore a flower-covered hat. Bruno was the gruff beggar boy who couldn't walk and had no friends but a goat, until the Carver children came along. Near the end of their stay Lorna Carver mentioned that because they had seen no ghosts the family would soon leave and the Giddings would return. Strange occurrences began almost immediately after Lorna's statement and ended only when the Carvers caught Bruno trying to convince them that he was the ghost. Lorna and Jamie were his only friends, so he had risked his guardians wrath and given up the pretense of being lame to trick the Carvers into staying. All ends well as Bruno's cruel guardian is run off, the Carvers take responsibility for Bruno's care, and Mrs. Giddings admits she made up the ghost story because she hated living in the country and had wanted to return to the city. Another serviceable book in the very successful Bulla style.

Interest Level: 2-5. Reading Level: 2.1. Further Search Topics: Ghosts-Fiction, Brothers and Sisters-Fiction, Orphans-Fiction, Country Life-Fiction, Courage-Fiction, Challenges-Fiction, Friendship-Fiction.

Christopher, Matt. Devil pony; illus by Lorence Bjorkland. Little 1977, 103 pp.

This book is a bit of a change from the usual Matt Christopher story line. There is no sports interest here; instead there is a good suspense story about a boy, his cousin and a horse. Stu had watched the black Morgan named Midnight being born and had fallen in love with him. A year later he returned to his aunt and uncle's ranch to claim the horse, as he had been promised he could, but strange things began to happen around him. His cousin Wilbur warned him that he had probably annoyed the ranch poltergeist by deciding to take Midnight away. The bizarre occurrences escalated until Stu was almost tempted to leave Midnight at the ranch. Then Stu discovered Wilbur had been orchestrating everything that had happened because he had wanted to keep the horse himself. Although Stu decided to take Midnight home as he had planned, their new honesty led Stu to believe that he and Wilbur could be friends after all. A surprisingly good story with strong reader appeal.

Interest Level: 3-6. Reading Level: 3.1. Further Search Topics: Horses-Fiction, Supernatural-Fiction, Ghosts-Fiction, Jealousy-Fiction, Relatives-Fiction.

Clifford, Eth. The dastardly murder of Dirty Pete; illus by George Hughes. HM 1981, 120 pp.

Although this is a sequel to *Help, I'm a Prisoner in the Library*, it does not depend on the previous title, and in fact, is likely to be the more successful introduction to Mary Rose and Jo-Beth Onetree. Given the choice, most young readers will take a mystery set in a ghost town over a mystery set in a library.

Mary Rose, Jo-Beth and their father were on their way across country when they became lost. As night grew closer, the only place they could find to stay was an old hotel in the ghost town where Sorehead Jones had allegedly killed Dirty Pete. It was Sorehead's ghost who was supposed to haunt the town, and indeed there was someone or something who was in the town with the Onetrees. To their surprise, that someone turned out to be Sourdough Sam, an aging actor who had become senile and spent his days acting out all the parts in the Dirty Pete story. The town was only a movie set and the story was only a movie script. The Onetrees discovered the truth bit by bit after a frightening venture into an abandoned gold mine, a harrowing night in the haunted hotel and a jail sentence for Mr. Onetree.

Beware of the rare, very difficult descriptive passage that may cause trouble for some readers.

Interest Level: 2-5. Reading Level: 3.1. Further Search Topics: Mystery and Detective Stories, West-Fiction, Brothers and Sisters-Fiction, Motion Pictures-Fiction, Ghosts-Fiction, Treasure-Fiction, Group 2, Acting-Fiction, Aging-Fiction, Mental Illness-Fiction.

Fife, Dale. Follow that ghost!; illus by Joan Drescher. Dutton 1979, 58 pp.

In short sentences reminiscent of "Dragnet," Chuck tells a very simple story of Chuck and Jason's first detective case. He and Jason were practicing following people, when their next-door-neighbor caught them following her home. Instead of being angry at the two boys, Glory decided to hire them to find the ghost she and her mother were hearing at 5:00 every morning. Despite their best attempts to capture and bury the ghost, or a find a human cause for the ghostly sounds, Chuck and Jason couldn't rid Glory's apartment of its ghost. Their final effort nearly resulted in injury to a neighbor. Ultimately, Chuck discovered that the ghost was merely a displaced woodpecker looking for a new home.

Not a terribly ambitious mystery, but one whose consistent reading level, familiar urban setting and interesting characters will please many young readers.

Interest Level: 2-4. Reading Level: 2.1. Further Search Topics: Ghosts-Fiction, Mystery and Detective Stories, Spies-Fiction, Humorous Fiction.

Hall, Lynn. The mystery of Pony Hollow; illus by Ruth Sanderson. Garrard 1978, 64 pp.

Sarah investigated strange voices only to find the skeleton of a horse that had died 40 years earlier. She was determined to find out what it was that had killed the horse and why its ghost was uneasy.

The mystery element isn't as strong here as most mystery fans would like, but the book will not disappoint many true horse story enthusiasts.

Interest Level: 3-5. Reading Level: 3.2. Further Search Topics: Horses-Fiction, Ghosts-Fiction, Mystery and Detective Stories.

Heide, Florence Parry. Black magic at Brillstone. A. Whitman 1981, 126 pp.

Liza is a little older, her romance with Logan has progressed to a kiss, and the book's plot is more complex than earlier Brillstone adventures. Other than those differences, the book follows Heide's standard format. The Brillstone books all center on Liza Webster and Logan Forrest, teenage partners in crime detection, who live in the Brillstone Apartments. The stories are similar enough that one could almost substitute the names Nancy Drew and Ned for Liza and Logan. Both young women are only children who live with their fathers. They are both independent, resourceful, and very concerned that justice be done. The men in their lives play approximately the same roles; their fathers are proud and supportive, but distantly preoccupied with their own business; Logan and Ned are gallant, boyish, and devoted. Liza and Logan, like Nancy and Ned, are not distinctive characters. Instead, they are shells into which readers who want excitement and adventure can pour themselves. There is no parental interference to worry about. There is plenty of action, some suspense, and real world crime (for Liza: murder, bank robberies, etc.) rather than childish escapades. The books' success is practically guaranteed. Beware, however, of inconsistent reading levels that wander over a year's range.

Logan was first aware of strange occurrences at the Brillstone Apartments when someone entered his apartment late at night. While the person had searched the apartment, he or she had unconsciously whistled a nursery tune. Logan's neighbor, Miss Violet, said the tune reminded her of her deceased nephew. Slowly Logan and Liza realized that someone was trying to trick Miss Violet out of a substantial amount of money she had just inherited. They suspected that Bella Vine, a spiritualist, and an accomplice were trying to convince Miss Violet that her nephew was communicating from the dead and wanted Miss Violet to give her money to Bella. Not until it was almost too late did Liza and Logan realize that Bella was also posing as another possible recipient of the money and was really Miss Violet's nephew's wife. Miss Violet's nephew had only pretended to die in order to collect insurance money. When he and his wife had heard about Miss Violet's large inheritance, they had decided to reappear in order to bilk her out of the money. Brillstone Mystery series.

Interest Level: 5-6. Reading Level: 3.1. Further Search Topics: Mystery and Detective Stories, Occult-Fiction, Crime-Fiction, Ghosts-Fiction, Cats-Fiction, Detectives-Fiction, Inheritance-Fiction.

Packard, Edward. The mystery of Chimney Rock; illus by Paul Granger. Bantam 1979, 121 pp.

See notes for *Sugarcane Island* for information about the series. Paperback only. Choose Your Own Adventure series.

Interest Level: 2-6. Reading Level: 3.2. Further Search Topics: Mystery and Detective Stories, Cats-Fiction, Witches-Fiction, Ghosts-Fiction, Detectives-Fiction, Best Sellers, Group 2.

Parish, Peggy. Haunted house; illus by Paul Frame. Macmillan 1971, 151 pp.

Although this is the third book about Jed, Bill and Liza Roberts, it too can be read out of order. This time the family has moved into what was locally known as a haunted house. Very shortly after they moved into the house, a coded note appeared that led them to a series of messages and unusual occurrences. Lights that flashed into Liza's room turned out to be the headlights of cars, but the messages and a secret compartment in an old clock couldn't be as easily explained. Each day took them closer to the surprise that the messages hinted would be theirs. That surprise turned out to be three kittens and a treehouse. Two of the children's best friends had planned the whole mystery just to lead to the surprises.

This book has the same faults and strong points as the others about the Roberts children. Each chapter is short; the book is episodic; reading level is consistent; there is much dialogue and action and little description, and the plot has a comfortable familiarity about it. It can be very useful to the right readers.

Interest Level: 1-4. Reading Level: 2.1. Further Search Topics: Mystery and Detective Stories. Brothers and Sisters-Fiction, Ghosts-Fiction, Moving, Household-Fiction, Nonverbal Communication-Fiction, Group 2.

St. John, Wylly Folk. The ghost next door; illus by Trina Schart Hyman. Har-Row 1971, 178 pp.

Told by 13-year-old Lindsay, this is the story of her neighbor Miss Judith and Miss Judith's two nieces. Her niece Miranda had drowned years earlier in Miss Judith's backyard fish pond and Miss Judith had never fully recovered from her death. As the story begins, Miss Judith is about to welcome another niece (Sherry) for a summer stay. Sherry, without ever being told about Miranda, seems to sense Miranda's presence all around. Her mother laughs and says that Sherry has an imaginary friend. Miss Judith, who is a strong believer in ESP, thinks that Sherry is communicating with Miranda. As the days go on Sherry learns more and more of Miranda' secrets. When Miss Judith is scared by Sherry, Lindsay and her friend, Tammy, decide to see what sort of tricks Sherry is playing.

A believable suspense story, made even more so by the illustrations.

Interest Level: 4-6. Reading Level: 5.1. Further Search Topics: Mystery and Detective Stories, Relatives-Fiction, Group 2, Extra Sensory Perception-Fiction, Best Sellers, Ghosts-Fiction.

Warner, Gertrude Chandler. The woodshed mystery; illus by David Cunningham. A. Whitman 1960, 159 pp.

The four Alden children have grown since their first appearance in *The Boxcar Children* but they are still as close a family as ever. Aunt Jane's telephone message that she wanted to move near them started this adventure. Grandfather proceeded to buy and refurbish his childhood home as a surprise for Aunt Jane. It was an easy house to buy because it had been abandoned and was thought to be haunted. Even though the children and Aunt Jane weren't really worried by the stories of odd occurrences that no one quite remembered, they began to be aware of strange noises and things missing. Upon investigation they discovered Aunt Jane's old boyfriend living in the woodshed in the forest. There beneath the floor of the woodshed, they also found a store of Revolutionary War supplies and a letter from the original owners of the house. The supplies and the letter helped to explain some of the stories. Andrew, Jane's long-lost boyfriend, explained the rest.

It is not necessary to have read any of the series in order to read this story, but those children who enjoyed *The Boxcar Children* are most likely to enjoy the Alden's further adventures. See the entry for *The Boxcar Children* for more information.

Interest Level: 3-5. Reading Level: 2.1. Further Search Topics: Mystery and Detective Stories, United States-History-War-Fiction, Brothers and Sisters-Fiction, Ghosts-Fiction, Vacation-Fiction.

GIANTS-FICTION

Chew, Ruth. The wishing tree. Hastings 1980, 142 pp.

Peggy and Brian's discovery of a talking cat, a bird with a beautiful song, and a strange and frightening tree led them to a shopping bag lady, a giant named Fred, a gold key and a magical tablecloth. In a rather complicated series of events, the children and the cat finally succeeded in retrieving the tablecloth from Annie (the old woman to whom Puss had loaned it) and giving it back to Fred, who needed it to help satisfy his gigantic appetite. In addition, they returned Fred to normal human size, rescued Annie from a fall on the ice, introduced the two characters and encouraged them to live together in Fred's castle.

Complicated enough already, the story's lengthy adventure that leads up to the discovery of the key (climbing into the magical tree and swimming in a pond) makes the plot even more complex. If a reader doesn't expect more than benign fantasy and fun this is an adequate choice.

Interest Level: 2-5. Reading Level: 2.2. Further Search Topics: Magic-Fiction, Fantasy, Brothers and Sisters-Fiction, Giants-Fiction, Cats-Fiction.

Dolch, Edward W. Irish stories; illus by Carmen Mowry. Garrard 1958, 165 pp.

Besides controlling the vocabulary used in the stories, the Dolchs seem to include only stories with very uncomplicated plots. Once again they split the longer stories into two chapters. Thus, from 17 chapters there come only 12 stories. Most of the stories will be unfamiliar to readers (except perhaps those about Finn McCool), but all are pleasurable. See *Andersen Stories* for more information. Dolch Basic Vocabulary Book series.

Interest Level: 2-5. Reading Level: 2.2. Further Search Topics: Folklore, Fantasy, Ireland-Fiction, Giants-Fiction.

GORILLAS

Conklin, Gladys. Little apes; illus by Joseph Cellini. Holiday 1970, unp (32pp).

An informative as well as interesting look at gorillas, chimpanzees, orangutans and gibbons. Their habits and behavior patterns are described by following a young one of each species through a full day in its natural surroundings. The text is simple without being condescending and the illustrations are so life-like that they almost walk off the pages. An excellent treatment of a popular subject makes this a very useful book.

Interest Level: 2-5. Reading Level: 2.2. Further Search Topics: Apes, Gorillas, Nature Study, Infants, Group 2.

GRANDPARENTS-FICTION

Blume, Judy. Are you there God? It's me, Margaret. Bradbury 1970, 149 pp.

Sixth grade was a year of growth for Margaret and her friends. They all wondered when they would start growing breasts and when they would begin menstruating. Each was kissed for the first time. It was also a year in which Margaret tried to decide whether to be Jewish or Christian and ended up neither. She simply remained friends with God, just as she was when the year began. The book is a reassuring, very open, and humorous treatment of the pains and promise of maturation. It is exceptionally popular with older elementary school readers, so the book's slightly small print and narrow lines should not impede an interested reader's progress.

Interest Level: 4-6. Reading Level: 3.2. Further Search Topics: School Stories, Family-Fiction, Children-Growth-Fiction, Religion-Fiction, Humorous Fiction, Love-Fiction, Best Sellers, Grandparents-Fiction, Everyday Stories.

Bulla, Clyde Robert. Marco Moonlight; illus by Julia Noonan. T Y Crowell 1976, 104 pp.

No one could explain Marco's strange, recurring dream. The dream seemed to be about a brother, but Marco had no brother. He had no family but his wealthy grandparents with whom he lived. Marco loved his grandparents very much, but he couldn't help wondering about his own past. He knew only what he and his grandparents could figure out from a few clues. His mother had run away to marry and for three years Marco's grandparents had heard nothing. Then, suddenly, they received a note that she was dying, had parted from her husband, and needed them. By the time they arrived, she was dead and two-year-old Marco could tell them no more. About the time of his thirteenth birthday Marco made friends with a strange man named Flint, who later became the gardener on Marco's grandparents' estate. Rather than live in the room provided for him with the other servants, Flint chose a bleak and isolated beach cottage. Being very careful that no one should suspect, Flint locked Marco into the cottage and forced Marco to change clothes with Matt, who was Marco's long-lost identical twin. Flint and Matt planned that Matt would steal all the money he could from the estate before killing Marco and fleeing. But when Matt began to realize how nice his grandparents were, how much he liked Marco, and how evil Flint was, he decided to thwart Flint's plan. In Matt and Marco's desperate attempt to flee from Flint, Flint was accidentally killed, leaving Marco free to return home and Matt free to find a way to feel he also had the right to claim his heritage before joining Marco.

The tense and dramatic plot immediately involves the reader and the short, fast-paced chapters sustain interest to the end of the book. Readers should also appreciate the small, paperback-size format. A good choice.

Interest Level: 3-6. Reading Level: 2.1. Further Search Topics: Dreams-Fiction, Mystery and Detective Stories, Kidnapping-Fiction, Twins-Fiction, Orphans-Fiction, Grandparents-Fiction, Best Sellers, Brothers and Sisters-Fiction, Jealousy-Fiction, Courage-Fiction.

Bulla, Clyde Robert. The sugar pear tree; illus by Taro Yashima. T Y Crowell 1960, 54 pp.

Lonnie lived with his mother and his grandfather in a house owned by the state. A new highway was to be built that would force the family to move, but Gramp refused to acknowledge that the state could force them out of their home. He chased away every state representative who came to warn the family that they should move. Lonnie's mother had always been at work when the representatives came and so knew nothing about the warnings until she came home to find their belongings on the sidewalk and their house on wheels. The only person they could turn to was their friend Nick. Nick owned a nursery in town and a small house with a large yard in the country. He had become a friend of Lonnie's when he gave Lonnie first prize in a school essay contest on the topic of "favorite trees." Lonnie's prize had been a sugar pear tree, his favorite. Nick had next become Lonnie's mother's friend. Nick arranged for them to stay in the greenhouse at his country place. The longer they stayed, the better friends Nick and Lonnie's mother became. Gramp was the only person who didn't adjust to the move. He stopped speaking the moment he was carried out of his old home. In a final and successful attempt to make Gramp happy, Nick bought the old house and had it moved out to his country lot.

The idea of a state government being able to force a family to move may need some explaining. The story's warmth and very consistent early second grade reading level make this a particularly useful book with quiet readers.

Interest Level: 2-4. Reading Level: 2.1. Further Search Topics: Trees-Fiction, Moving, Household-Fiction, Family Problems-Fiction, Grandparents-Fiction, Poverty-Fiction.

Byars, Betsy. After the goat man; illus by Ronald Himler. Viking Pr. 1974, 126 pp.

Harold was fat and over-sensitive. Ada was serious and independent. Figgy was lonely, poor and in need of help. Figgy and his grandfather, the Goat Man, had been forced to move from their cabin to make room for a highway. The Goat Man had returned to the cabin with a shotgun, vowing to defend his right to live there. Figgy knew he had to persuade his grandfather to leave or someone would be hurt. But, in the children's hurry to reach the Goat Man, it was Figgy who was hurt and Harold who rescued both Figgy and the Goat Man. Harold grew up that day. He stopped dreaming about the way he wanted things to be and faced life realistically for the first time.

The book is very much a character study. Realistic characters are treated with sympathy and dignity and given a chance to grow. Introspective readers will understand and enjoy the book more than those looking for adventure. Print size is fairly large, but lines are separated by only average width.

Interest Level: 4-6. Reading Level: 3.2. Further Search Topics: Loneliness-Fiction, Weight-Fiction, Moving, Household-Fiction, Courage-Fiction, Grandparents-Fiction, Orphans-Fiction.

Byars, Betsy. The house of wings; illus by Daniel Schwarts. Viking Pr. 1972, 142 pp.

Sammy was the youngest of eight children. His parents were tired of raising children when Sammy was born, so they almost let Sammy raise himself. That meant that he grew up to be independent. It didn't mean it was any easier for Sammy to accept being left behind unexpectedly with his strange grandfather when his parents moved to Detroit. His reaction when his grandfather told him that his parents had gone was to deny it and to run away. He ran until he could run no more. When he stopped running, the old man stopped chasing him and they found a wild but blind crane in desperate need of help. Helping the crane heal and find the desire to live again taught Sammy and his grandfather respect and, most of all, love for each other.

The parallels between Sammy and the crane are strong but subtle. The story is a compelling one, but may need a brief introductory note to alleviate confusion in the first two chapters.

Interest Level: 5-6. Reading Level: 4.2. Further Search Topics: Grandparents-Fiction, Birds-Fiction, Family Problems-Fiction, Poverty-Fiction, Physically Handicapped-Fiction, Runaways-Fiction.

Byars, Betsy. Trouble River; illus by Rocco Negri. Viking Pr. 1969, 158 pp.

A gripping adventure story of survival. After being attacked by an Indian in the middle of the night, Dewey and his grandmother rushed to Trouble River to board a small raft which Dewey had just finished making. They thought they would only need to navigate a few miles down the river to safety at a neighbor's home, but found instead that the neighbor's cabin had been burned down. For almost 40 miles they fought against the unknown river, wolves and rapids.

This is a book that should satisfy many reluctant readers. It's frequent dialogue, fast action and high interest are only occasionally marred by an overly long sentence.

Interest Level: 3-6. Reading Level: 3.1. Further Search Topics: Courage-Fiction, Frontier and Pioneer Life-Fiction, Survival-Fiction, Grandparents-Fiction, Voyages and Travels-Fiction, Best Sellers, Read Aloud.

Green, Phyllis. The fastest quitter in town; illus by Lorenzo Lynch. A-W 1972, 62 pp.

Whenever Johnny played baseball and things went wrong for him, he would quit. Johnny's teammates finally grew so angry with him that they told him to leave the team. That same day, Johnny's 90-year-old great-grandfather lost a very special ring his wife had given him. Johnny's love for this great-grandfather pushed him to keep looking for the ring until days later, when everyone else had quit searching, Johnny found the ring. Having learned a hard lesson, Johnny returned to his team for one more chance. That evening Johnny went to see his great-grandfather to tell him, with legitimate pride, that he had played the entire game.

Although the lesson is pointed, the story is very satisfying. Johnny's relationship with this great-grandfather is close and supportive. His problem is one shared by many children, especially those with a weak self-image.

Interest Level: 1-4. Reading Level: 3.1. Further Search Topics: Blacks-Fiction, Challenges-Fiction, Courage-Fiction, Group 2, Baseball-Fiction, Grandparents-Fiction, Friendship-Fiction.

Levy, Elizabeth. Lizzie lies a lot; illus by John Wallner. Delacorte 1976, 102 pp.

Almost any child can identify with Lizzie. She had found that it was sometimes easier to lie than to tell the truth. Her problem was that she had lost control. It seemed as if almost everything she said was a lie. She told so many lies it became difficult to keep track of them all. Lizzie wasn't even really sure why she lied so much. She knew that she sometimes lied because she thought people would be more apt to like her. Other times she lied to get herself out of trouble or to cover up her feelings when she was hurt or angry. But that didn't explain why she lied all the time. Maybe, as her grandmother said, she was a born liar.

It wasn't until Lizzie got herself caught in the middle of so many lies that she lost her only friend, that she could admit her problem to herself and to her family. After their initial shock had passed, everyone agreed to help Lizzie stop lying. Lizzie took the next step by admitting her lies to her friend Sue.

Levy has brought such an appropriately light touch to a fairly common problem that many children find this story enjoyable. Overlook the book's faults (Lizzie's grandmother is overdrawn and her mother's guilt feelings are unsupported by the story) for the fun and the message young readers get from it.

Interest Level: 3-5. Reading Level: 4.2. Further Search Topics: Honesty-Fiction, Group 2, Friendship-Fiction, Best Sellers, Everyday Stories, Family Problems-Fiction, Grandparents-Fiction, Humorous Fiction.

Miles, Miska. Annie and the old one; illus by Peter Parnall. Little 1971, 44 pp.

A quietly beautiful story that will not appeal to all readers. Annie, a young Navajo girl, had a very close relationship with her grandmother. Her grandmother announced that she would "go to Mother Earth" at the time when the new rug Annie's mother was weaving was "taken from the loom." Annie tried all she could think of to keep the rug from being finished in order to keep her grandmother alive. When her grandmother solemnly explained that Annie could not stop time, Annie listened and "understood many things" for the first time.

It will be a thoughtful, sensitive child or a child trying to understand death who will best appreciate this special book.

Interest Level: 3-6. Reading Level: 3.2. Further Search Topics: Grandparents-Fiction, Death-Fiction, Indians of North America-Fiction, Navajo Indians-Fiction.

Parish, Peggy. Hermit Dan; illus by Paul Frame. Macmillan 1977, 151 pp.

When the Roberts children tried to prove that Pirate Island really had been used by pirates, they encountered more action and intrigue than they had found in any of their earlier adventures. Liza, Bill and Jed suspected that Hermit Dan knew whether or not there had been pirates on the island, but he was so gruff and apparently mean that they didn't dare ask him any questions. Instead, they trailed and spied on him and asked questions of anyone who had known Hermit Dan as a child. It was rumored that his ancestors had actually been pirates. Until a terrible fire that had destroyed all they owned, Hermit Dan's family had been very wealthy. However, no one knew how they had become so rich.

In an attempt to see what the summer residents knew about Hermit Dan, the children introduced themselves to the vacationing youngsters. Among the visitors the Roberts met Hank and Ted, brothers bent on bullying Hermit Dan. When the children were rescued from a severe sandstorm by Hermit Dan, they were surprised to find that he wasn't nearly as gruff as he appeared. In fact they began to feel quite protective of the old man. Thus when Hank and Ted stole a secret box that held all of Hermit Dan's valuables, it was the Roberts children who fought (literally) to get the box back. It was after Liza, Bill and Jed returned the box to Hermit Dan, however, that the

real surprises began: these included a surprise party for Hermit Dan, his wish to be friendly, and his gift to the children of three pieces of eight that proved his family members were pirates.

This title's more interesting and involved plot makes the book more likely to be a success with older readers than the other stories about the Roberts children. Otherwise it shares the same format, faults and strengths as the other series titles.

Interest Level: 2-5. Reading Level: 2.1. Further Search Topics: Mystery and Detective Stories, Pirates-Fiction, Vacation-Fiction, Loners-Fiction, Treasure-Fiction, Bullies-Fiction, Brothers and Sisters-Fiction, Grandparents-Fiction.

Parish, Peggy. Key to the treasure; illus by Paul Frame. Macmillan 1966, 154 pp.

This is the first of the stories about Jed, Bill and Liza Roberts. The three children are very middle-class, the book's plots are simple and often lack suspense, but the stories still enjoy widespread popularity among unsophisticated readers.

All three children went to spend the summer with their grandparents and decided to tackle a mystery left unsolved for over 75 years. An old drawing and an authentic war bonnet provided the only clues to finding three Indian artifacts. At each step along the way there were crumbled, brittle pieces of paper bearing coded messages that led to the next clue. The search ended when the children found that a storage area in a porch piller contained an Indian doll, mask, and leather shield that had belonged to their great-grandfather.

Interest Level: 1-4. Reading Level: 2.1. Further Search Topics: Vacation-Fiction, Brothers and Sisters-Fiction, Group 2, Mystery and Detective Stories, Grandparents-Fiction, Nonverbal Communication-Fiction.

Parish, Peggy. Pirate Island adventure; illus by Paul Frame. Macmillan 1975, 167 pp.

Although this is the fourth book in the series about the Roberts children, none of the titles must be read in chronological order. This time the three rather privileged children spent the summer with their grandparents on a resort island. They lived in a house that their family had owned for years, explored the island, and swam in their own private cove. But, most of their time was spent trying to solve an old mystery. Their great-uncle had hidden several very special items (one for each member of his family) years earlier, and had left only one clue with their grandfather. After he gave the children that clue it was only a matter of time before they found the hidden treasures.

This book is also lengthy, but is divided into 22 very manageable chapters. It is, like the others, almost entirely dialogue and action, which makes it especially appealing to young reluctant readers.

Interest Level: 1-4. Reading Level: 2.1. Further Search Topics: Mystery and Detective Stories, Vacation-Fiction, Treasure-Fiction, Brothers and Sisters-Fiction, Grandparents-Fiction, Group 2.

Smith, Doris Buchanan. Tough Chauncey. Morrow 1974, 222 pp.

Chauncey Childs had taught himself to be tough— very tough. Even though he was small for his age (13 years old), the only person who gave him any trouble was his sometimes-friend, Black Jack Levitt. Everyone else was scared of Chauncey. Chauncey felt that he had to be tough or he wouldn't be able to survive. He had to be tough to stand the beatings his grandfather gave him "for his own good," to put up with his mother's drinking and disappearances, and to stand the sight of his grandfather shooting the stray kittens born in their garage.

Chauncey's greatest wish was to be able to live with his mother, instead of with his grandparents. In a desperate attempt to achieve that end he accidentally fell from a moving train and badly hurt his leg. Instead of being returned to his mother he was once more taken back to his grandparents. Chauncey's unhappiness grew until he finally decided to take the one surviving stray kitten and run away. Jack helped him find an empty garage where he could hide while he figured out what to do with his future. After talking with Jack and doing more deep soul searching, Chauncey decided to reshape himself and his life. His first step was to curb his temper and his tongue when his hiding place was discovered. His second step was to see about finding a foster home where he would be treated well, and where he could get a new start.

Ugly as the story is in places, its ending is hopeful. Although it is not always realistic, Chauncey's story is compelling enough to appeal to many readers, especially those who have enjoyed *The War on Villa Street*, by Henry Mazer, *The Outsiders*, by Susan Hinton, or *Mystery of the Fat Cat*, by Frank Bonham. The book's length and its artificially low reading level (vocabulary is often difficult but sentences are very short) make this book most appropriate for an older reader whose reading level is 4.1 or higher.

Interest Level: 5-6. Reading Level: 3.2. Further Search Topics: Child Abuse-Fiction, Family Problems-Fiction, Grandparents-Fiction, Runaways-Fiction, Bullies-Fiction, Single Parent Family-Fiction, Loners-Fiction, Friendship-Fiction, Troublemakers-Fiction, Foster Homes-Fiction.

Warner, Gertrude Chandler. The boxcar children; illus by L. Kate Deal. A. Whitman 1950, 154 pp.

This is the first in a series of very early hi/lo books. Although they often bear signs of stilted "Dick and Jane"-style writing, occasionally preach to the reader, and are interrupted by frequent asides from the author, the stories are still popular with young readers. In each book the children are not simply manipulated, but control their own destiny. They fulfill many a child's dream of finding a loving home and family, becoming rich, having adventures, and solving mysteries. This is the simplest story of the series, most of the other entries assume interest in such advanced subjects as fossils, food sources, antiques, or the Revolutionary War.

The only place the four orphaned Alden children had to live was with a grandfather whom they had never met, but whom they had heard was mean. Rather than live with him, they decided to try and survive on their own. They found an abandoned railway boxcar and filled it was items that they found in a junkyard in order to make it their home. Henry, the oldest, went to work for a doctor who, in addition to money, gave him food and kept a silent but watchful eye over all the children without their knowledge. When Violet became ill, the children had no choice but to take her to Dr. Moore. He gave them all a temporary home and arranged for them to gradually get to know their grandfather. By the time Violet was almost well the children had grown to like the elderly stranger. It was a happy day when the children finally realized that the man to whom Dr. Moore had introduced them was really their grandfather.

Interest Level: 1-4. Reading Level: 2.1. Further Search Topics: Orphans-Fiction, Survival-Fiction, Runaways-Fiction, Brothers and Sisters-Fiction, Grandparents-Fiction.

GREAT BRITAIN-HISTORY-FICTION

Baker, Betty. The pig war; illus by Robert Lopshire. Har-Row 1969, 64 pp.

A brief, fictionalized account of an 1859 land squabble between the United States and Britain. The incident, which took place in what is now the state of Washington, became known as the Pig War. Frightened British pigs destroyed the American farmers' gardens. When the farmers shot one of the pigs, the war began. Simply told and humorously illustrated. Should appeal to history or military fans. Early reader format.

Interest Level: 2-4. Reading Level: 2.1. Further Search Topics: United States-History-War-Fiction, Great Britain-History-Fiction, War-Fiction, Washington (state)-Fiction, Historical Fiction, Pigs-Fiction.

GREENE, "MEAN" JOE

Burchard, Susan H. Sports star: "Mean" Joe Greene. HarBraceJ 1976, 64 pp.

"Mean" Joe Greene's nickname is appropriate. He is big, "mean" on the playing field, and likes to win. He usually does. More details about the book under *Sports Hero: Bill Walton*, by Marshall Burchard. Sports Star series.

Interest Level: 2-6. Reading Level: 3.2. Further Search Topics: Biography, Football-Biography, Greene, "Mean" Joe, Blacks-Biography, Group 2.

GROUNDHOGS

McNulty, Faith. Woodchuck; illus by Joan Sandin. Har-Row 64 pp.

There's a great deal of information in this little book. It describes a woodchuck's physical appearance, its habits and behavior, and its life cycle. The treatment is very direct and very honest (two of four young woodchucks are killed before the first year is over). Only an overly repetitive, slightly condescending beginning, and the reader format hamper the book's usefulness beyond grade four. A Science-I-Can-Read-Book.

Interest Level: 1-4. Reading Level: 3.1. Further Search Topics: Nature Study, Groundhogs, Group 2, Woodchucks.

GROUP 2

Adler, Irving. Your eyes. John Day 1962, 48 pp.

Getting a young reader past this book's unattractive appearance may be difficult. Everything about the book's physical appearance screams "old." Some of the information and lack of information conveys the same message (e.g. no mention of contact lenses). For basic material about eyes and sight however, there is much here that is accessible and interesting to readers in grades two to six. Includes pronunciation guide, glossary, and detailed table of contents. No index. The Reason Why Series

Interest Level: 2-6. Reading Level: 3.1. Further Search Topics: Vision, Physically Handicapped, Group 2.

Adrian, Mary. The fireball mystery illus by Reisie Lonette. Hastings 1977, 118 pp.

While stargazing one night, Tim and Vicky and their friend Joey saw a meteor fall onto their private island. Before they were able to find it the children realized that someone else was trying to steal the meteorite from them. As much astronomy as mystery here. Beyond fourth grade, the reader may begin to find the astronomy lesson heavy-handed and the mystery light.

Interest Level: 2-4. Reading Level: 3.1. Further Search Topics: Mystery and Detective Stories, Astronomy, Flying Saucers-Fiction, Outer Space-Fiction, Group 2.

Aesop. Aesop's Fables; retold by Ann Terry White; illus by Helen Siegl. Random 1964, 77 pp.

An attractive, appealing-looking collection of forty of Aesop's fables. Children without a background in folklore are not likely to read these short tales without encouragement. Where there is such encouragement, or a curricular need, this is an excellent source. The use of many proper nouns in the text means the book tests artificially low at 2.2. It is probably more appropriate to consider it 3.1.

Interest Level: 2-6. Reading Level: 3.1. Further Search Topics: Fables, Folklore, Group 2.

Alexander, Sue. Small plays for you and a friend; illus by Olivia H. Cole. Seabury 1974, 48 pp.

Five very short and very simple plays for two actors that will be of more interest to the players than the audience. However, because the reading level is low, and because children's love of acting is strong and their tolerance of weak plot is high, this can be used through grade three. A companion volume *Small Plays for Special Days* presents seven more short plays for two characters.

Interest Level: 1-3. Reading Level: 2.1. Further Search Topics: Acting, Drama, Group 2.

Arkhurst, Joyce. The adventures of Spider; West African folktales; illus by Jerry Pinkney. Little 1964, 58 pp.

A delightful collection of six West African folktales about Spider. Spider is mischievous, greedy, lazy and clever. He loves to eat and he hates to work. Four of the stories tell of Spider's ill-fated attempts to get food without having to work for it ("How Spider Got a Thin Waist," "How Spider Got a Bald Head," "How Spider Helped a Fisherman," and "Why Spiders Live in Dark Corners"). One story tells of his greed ("How the World Got Wisdom"), and only one story is complimentary ("Why Spider Lives in Ceilings"). All are short, gentle, humorous, and adapt well to dramatization or retelling.

Interest Level: 2-6. Reading Level 3.1. Further Search Topics: Humorous Fiction, Spiders-Fiction, Folklore, Tricksters-Fiction, Africa-Folklore, Group 2, Read Aloud, Creation-Fiction, Drama.

Avi. No more magic. Pantheon 1975, 138 pp.

Avi has woven a mixture of mystery and magic to produce an excellent story. Chris' belief in magic is bolstered when his new bicycle disappears on Halloween night. Chris, his best friend Eddie, and a new friend, Muffin, eventually decide that strange Mr. Bullen, the junk dealer, has magical powers. In order to keep his powers a secret, Mr. Bullen had to steal back the magical bike he sold Chris. With plenty of intriguing complications along the way, the three children attempt to prove their theory correct but only prove themselves wrong. The age of the protagonists (fourth grade) is touched on so lightly and the plot is interesting enough that even sixth grade readers should find the book enjoyable.

Interest Level: 3-6. Reading Level: 4.2. Further Search Topics: Divorce and Separation-Fiction, Mystery and Detective Stories, Magic-Fiction, Halloween-Fiction, Witches-Fiction, Group 2, Read Aloud, Bicycles and Bicycling–Fiction.

Aylesworth, Thomas G. Movie monsters. Lippincott 1975, 79 pp.

If you are looking for an example of fine writing, you won't find it here. What you will find is a collection of monster movie photographs and facts. This is a wealth of trivia about eleven famous monsters (including King Kong, Godzilla, the Fly, Frankenstein's monster, the Mummy, Dracula, Wolf Man and others), their films, sequels, historic backgrounds, identifying characteristics, and more. There is an extensive index, a list of monster movies and their credits, and even brief information about famous monster actors. The book is not great literature, but it is interesting and fun.

Interest Level: 1-6. Reading Level 3.1. Further Search Topics: Acting, Motion Pictures, Monsters, Horror-Fiction, Group 2, Best Sellers.

Baylor, Byrd. And it is still that way: legends told by Arizona Indian children. Scribner 1976, 85 pp.

Byrd Baylor has collected and written notes for forty-one short American Indian legends from seven Arizona tribes whose school children were asked to write down or illustrate their favorite legend. The result is a collection that reflects the concerns, the history, religion, humor and pride of the children and their ancestors. This excellent collection is not only interesting reading, but it also fits well into social studies and language arts units.

Interest Level: 2-6. Reading Level: 3.1. Further Search Topics: Legends, Arizona-Fiction, Navajo Indians, Hopi Indians, Papago Indians, Pima Indians, Apache Indians, Quechan Indians, Cocopah Indians, Indians of North America-Legends, Mythology, Group 2.

Beame, Rona. Ladder company 108. Messner 1973, 63 pp.

The reader of this book will literally live through several days with a New York City fire company. The author's "Dragnet"-like writing style, her use of photographs, and actual people, all make the firefighters' experiences very real. It is an exciting, engrossing and satisfying book. The heavily-used jargon will be quickly understood, thus should pose no real obstacle to most readers.

Interest Level 2-6. Reading Level: 3.1. Further Search Topics: Firefighters, Occupations, City Life, New York City, Group 2, Best Sellers.

Benchley, Nathaniel. Sam the Minutemen; illus by Arnold Lobel. Har-Row 1969, 62 pp.

A good but limited book. It is a simple, personalized account of the beginning of the Revolutionary War as seen by the young son of a Minuteman. The book is a fairly exciting, uncomplicated and enjoyable story. Its limitations rest in its format (it's designed as a reader), the apparent young age of the main character, and the fact that it is told as a story. Its usefulness extends no further than grade three. An I Can Read History Book

Interest Level: 1-3. Reading Level: 2.2. Further Search Topics: United States-History-War-Fiction, Historical Fiction, War-Fiction, Group 2, Courage-Fiction.

Benchley, Nathaniel. Small Wolf; illus by Joan Sandin. Har-Row 1972, 64 pp.

A straight-forward telling of white man's purchase of Manhattan and the resulting displacement of the Indians. The text is simple. The tone is sympathetic to the plight of the Indians. The reader is neither lectured

nor patronized, but the early-reader format will prevent using the book comfortably beyond fourth grade. An I Can Read History Book.
Interest Level: 1-4. Reading Level 2.2. Further Search Topics: Historical Fiction, New York City-Fiction, United States-History-Fiction, Indians of North America-Fiction, Group 2.

Berenstain, Stan. The bike lesson. Beginner 1964, 61 pp.
This story of a bumbling father trying to teach his eager son how to ride a bike is pure silliness. Much of the action is shown in the humorous illustrations. The rhymed text adds dialogue and description. Good fun.
Interest Level: K-3. Reading Level: 1.2. Further Search Topics: Humorous Fiction, Bicycles and Bicycling-Fiction, Stories in Rhyme, Group 2.

Berenstain, Stan. Bears in the night. Random 1971, 30 pp.
This is for the very beginning reader. Only 24 words plus illustrations are used to tell the story of a bedtime adventure for seven small bears. Bravely they sneak out of the house, through the woods, and up Spook Hill. Frightened by an owl's hoot, they run back over the same route until they are safely back in bed again.
Interest Level: K-2. Reading Level: 1.1. Further Search Topics: Bears-Fiction, Group 2, Courage-Fiction, Humorous Fiction.

Berger, Melvin. Time after time; illus by Richard Cuffari. Coward 1975, 45 pp.
The book begins with a description of inner clocks, proceeds into measurement of time, the seasons, and finally demonstrates the making of a simple clock. The explanations are simple but interesting. One point logically follows from another. It is a solid, serviceable tool limited only somewhat by the fact that it looks like a cross between a picture book and a reader. A brief index is included.
Interest Level: 1-4. Reading Level: 2.2. Further Search Topics: Time, Clocks and Watches, Seasons, Group 2.

Bernstein, Margery. Coyote goes hunting for fire; illus by Ed Heffernan. Scribner 1974, 40 pp.
A delightful story that can be read for fun or used as part of a unit on North American Indians. A long time ago when there was no fire, all the animals but Coyote banded together to find it. The animals left Coyote behind because he was always spoiling their plans. Coyote saw them leave, chased after them and once more tried to direct everything, but only ended up losing fire. Cartoon-like illustrations add to the humor of the story. This book should make a simple, but effective play.
Interest Level: 1-4. Reading Level 2.1. Further Search Topics: Animals-Fiction, Legends, Mythology, Fire-Fiction, Indians of North America-Legends, Coyotes-Fiction, Group 2, Creation-Fiction, Drama.

Bernstein, Margery. The first morning; illus by Enid Warner Romanek. Scribner 1976, 44 pp.
Spider, Mouse, and Fly volunteered to ask the king of the sky for light to take back to earth because the animals on earth were tired of living in darkness. The king didn't want to give away any light and so he set what he thought was an impossible task for the three animals. They were able to outwit the king three times and finally return to earth with a box Mouse was sure contained light. When they opened the box all they found was a rooster. Poor Mouse was ashamed at having been so badly tricked. But then Rooster crowed up the first morning and has done so ever since. A competent retelling of an African myth, nicely complemented by bold illustrations. Good candidate for dramatization.
Interest Level: 1-3. Reading Level: 2.1. Further Search Topics: Animals-Fiction, Group 2, Mythology, Light-Fiction, Drama, Time-Fiction, Calendars-Fiction, Creation-Fiction, Africa-Folklore.

Blegvad, Lenore. The great hamster hunt; illus by Erik Blegvad. HarBraceJ 1969, 32 pp.
Nicholas wanted a hamster; but, because his mother didn't like them, he couldn't have one. She did, however, agree to let Nicholas take care of his friend Tony's hamster for a week. It was a good and happy week for Nicholas until the evening before Tony was to return for his hamster. Nicholas accidentally broke the glass front of Harvey's cage and temporarily replaced it with cardboard. By morning Harvey had chewed through the cardbroad and was gone. Nicholas and his family searched all day but couldn't find Harvey. They finally bought another hamster and waited for Tony to arrive. As evening came Nicholas realized that hamsters are nocturnal and began to look for Harvey once more. This time Harvey was awake and active. The happy result was that Harvey was found and the new hampster became Nicholas' own pet. A simple, satisfying story even to fourth grade readers.
Interest Level: 1-4. Reading Level: 2.2. Further Search Topics: Pets-Fiction, Hamsters-Fiction, Group 2, Everyday Stories.

Blume, Judy. Otherwise known as Sheila the great. Dutton 1972, 128 pp.
Sheila first appears in *Tales of a Fourth Grade Nothing* as Peter Thatcher's neighbor. Sheila was a bundle of fears. She was afraid of dogs, thunderstorms, spiders, horses, putting her face in water, and strange noises at night. The summer she and her family rented a house in Tarrytown, New York, she confronted each one of her fears, even mastered one (putting her face in the water) and learned how to swim. That gave her the self-confidence to face a dog without running away. Sheila's progress was aided by her friend Mouse's steadfast belief that a person should always be honest about herself. Sheila's problems are treated realistically and with dignity, yet humorously. Reading level varies greatly from 1.2 - 4.1, therefore, the book is *most* suitable to grades four through six.
Interest Level: 3-6. Reading Level: 3.1. Further Search Topics: Humorous Fiction, Courage-Fiction, Camp-Fiction, Group 2, Vacation-Fiction, Swimming-Fiction, Brothers and Sisters-Fiction, Friendship-Fiction, Everyday Stories.

Blume, Judy. Freckle juice; illus by Sonia O. Lisker. Four Winds 1971, 40 pp.
A very funny story that should appeal to almost everyone. Andrew wanted freckles so that the dirt on his skin wouldn't show as much and he wouldn't have to wash as often. As luck would have it, Sharon, the most obnoxious girl in class, had a freckle juice recipe that she was willing to sell for 50 cents. Even after drinking the brew of grape juice, vinegar, mustard, olive oil, and more, Andrew didn't see any freckles, but, he certainly was sick. Although the protagonists are younger, this book will hold even a fifth grade reader's interest.
Interest Level: 2-5. Reading Level: 3.1. Further Search Topics: Humorous Fiction, Group 2, Read Aloud, Everyday Stories, Beauty-Fiction, School Stories, Magic-Fiction, Best Sellers.

Branley, Franklyn M. Roots are food finders; illus by Joseph Low. Har-Row 1975, 33 pp.

It really is a shame that the picture book format of this and other *Let's-Read-and-Find-Out-Science-Books* will prevent older children from using them. There is much good information here that is thoroughly and logically explained without patronizing the reader. Functions and types of roots are described. Experiments to show root growth, root hairs, and absorption are given. A very useful book through third grade and possibly fourth grade. Beyond fourth grade children will certainly balk at the book's "babyish" appearance. Let's-Read-and-Find-Out-Science-Book series.

Interest Level: 1-4. Reading Level: 2.2. Further Search Topics: Nature Study, Botany, Group 2, Experiments, Scientific.

Bulla, Clyde Robert. My friend the monster; illus by Michele Chessare. Har-Row 1980, 75 pp.

Even though Hal was plain and not very clever, his disappointed parents knew that he was still a prince; thus he had to be raised as one. Hal didn't like his lonely, dull life until a new world was accidentally opened to him. A servant's child gave him an old book of monsters and told him that the monsters still lived under the distant mountains. Hal finally made a trip to the mountains, spent a day exploring, and by chance met Humbert, a young monster curious about the world. But, Hal's cruel cousin Archer captured Humbert and put him in a cage. Hal's daring rescue attempt almost resulted in disaster for both Humbert and Hal.

This is another example of Bulla's forte; a book with an action-filled plot, short chapters, large print, wide spaces between the lines, and a low reading level. A book about monsters has almost guaranteed appeal through third grade. Although the book is useful beyond third grade, readers in fourth and fifth grade may be more sensitive to Hal's apparent youth and the fantastic elements of the story.

Interest Level: 1-3. Reading Level: 2.1. Further Search Topics: Fantasy, Monsters-Fiction, Royalty-Fiction, Group 2, Read Aloud, Best Sellers.

Bulla, Clyde Robert. Viking adventure; illus by Douglas Gorsline. T Y Crowell 1963, 117 pp.

An exciting story of a young Norwegian boy named Sigurd. Sigurd realized his dream when he finally set sail on a Viking ship in search of Wineland (Vinland). Leif Eriksson had told of his North American findings over 100 years earlier. Sigurd and his father's friend Grom, the captain of the ship, were sure they could find that land again. Their determination finally brought Grom's death at the hands of the ship's owner, Sigurd's near death, and the destruction of the ship.

This book, too, is true to Bulla's style of short chapters, short sentences, much action and high appeal. Although it is a little higher reading level than many of Bulla's others, it is still a good choice. Recently out of print, but worth a search.

Interest Level: 2-6. Reading Level: 3.1. Further Search Topics: Norway-Fiction, Historical Fiction, Seafaring Life-Fiction, Voyages and Travels-Fiction, Shipwrecks-Fiction, Explorers-Fiction, Vikings-Fiction, Courage-Fiction, Best Sellers, Group 2.

Bulla, Clyde Robert. Open the door and see all the people; illus by Wendy Watson. T Y Crowell 1972, 69 pp.

A slight story that makes up for its lack of excitement with warmth. When Joann, Teeney and Mama were burned out of their house in the country,

they decided it was time to move to the city. With the help of a friend, Mama was quickly able to find a job and an apartment. Only Teeney was noticeably unhappy. She missed her doll and resented anyone else who had one. Then the girls learned about the Toy House, a place to borrow or adopt toys. Both girls found dolls they wanted to adopt. Just before the end of the six week trial period Tenney lost her doll and almost lost her chance to adopt it. After the doll was found and repaired, the people at the Toy House realized how much she wanted the doll and let Teeney keep it.

Because of the ages of the characters, (six and eight), and the subject matter, the book's appeal is doubtful beyond third grade. Print size slightly smaller than usual for Bulla.

Interest Level: 1-3. Reading Level: 2.1. Further Search Topics: Dolls-Fiction, Brothers and Sisters-Fiction, Moving, Household-Fiction, Family-Fiction, Group 2.

Burchard, Marshall. Sports hero: Dr. J. Putnam 1976, 89 pp.

Julius Erving can jump higher and stay in the air longer than almost any other basketball player. He can also move around the court with the most agile of players. All in all he is a very exciting player to watch. This book includes his college and pro records (through 1975). See *Sports Hero: Bill Walton* for more information. Sports Hero series.

Interest Level: 3-6. Reading Level: 4.1. Further Search Topics: Biography, Blacks-Biography, Basketball-Biography, Erving, Julius, Group 2.

Burchard, Marshall. Sports hero: Joe Morgan. Putnam 1978, 93 pp.

Joe Morgan has been described as one of baseball's most complete players. He could field, hit, run and steal bases with the best. See *Sports Hero: Bill Walton* for more details about the book. Sports Hero series.

Interest Level: 2-6. Reading Level: 3.2. Further Search Topics: Biography, Morgan, Joe, Baseball-Biography, Blacks-Biography, Group 2.

Burchard, Marshall. Sports hero: Reggie Jackson. Putnam 1975, 93 pp.

Reggie Jackson was one of the big reasons why the Oakland A's won baseball's World Series three years in a row. *Sports Hero: Bill Walton* gives more information about the books in the series. Sports Hero series.

Interest Level: 2-6. Reading Level: 3.2. Further Search Topics: Biography, Jackson, Reggie, Baseball-Biography, Blacks-Biography, Group 2.

Burchard, Marshall. Sports hero: Bill Walton. Putnam 1978, 94 pp.

Burchard's series of *Sports Hero* biographies is better than many other sports biography series. Although heavy emphasis is placed on the subject's playing time, each person's life is capsulized from childhood to just before the book's publication date. Marshall and Sue Burchard (with whom he has collaborated and who writes an almost identical series called *Sports Stars*) treat each figure favorably and with enthusiasm. But, contrary to many children's writers, particularly sports biographers, these writers at least touch on those personal foibles that make players human (i.e. Joe Namath's tendency to break training is briefly described). Each book is abundantly illustrated with photographs, avoids patronizing the reader and is consistently interesting. Each is reliable, very useful and can be depended on to appeal to the sports enthusiast. Problems arise, however, with inconsistent and/or artificially inflated reading levels. The reading level of a title may vary from 2.2 to 4.2. The same passage tested on both a Spache and a Dale-Chall scale may show a similar two-year spread. The problem seems to be with jargon. Most sports jargon does not appear on either Spache's or Chall's list of familiar words and thus raises a book's reading level. But, the words may well be known to the reader (or quickly recognized after one introduction and so not truly unfamiliar). Keep in mind, therefore, that the true sports fan will often be able to read a title that tests well above his/her actual reading level.

Bill Walton's career is covered only through the end of the 1976-1977 season when the Portland Trailblazers won the NBA title. The reading level of this title is one of the most inconsistent of the series (from 2.2 to 4.2).

Interest Level: 2-6. Reading Level: 3.2. Further Search Topics: Biography, Walton, Bill, Basketball-Biography, Group 2.

Burchard, Marshall. Sports hero: Fred Lynn. Putnam 1976, 95 pp.

Fred Lynn was baseball's first rookie to be named Most Valuable Player. Consistent reading level. See *Sports Hero: Bill Walton*. Sports Hero series.

Interest Level: 2-6. Reading Level: 3.2. Further Search Topics: Biography, Lynn, Fred, Baseball-Biography, Group 2.

Burchard, Marshall. Sports hero: Johnny Bench. Putnam 1973, 95 pp.

The youngest baseball player to receive the National League's Most Valuable Player award. See *Sports Hero: Bill Walton* for information about the book. Sports Hero series.

Interest Level: 2-6. Reading Level: 3.1. Further Search Topics: Biography, Bench, Johnny, Baseball-Biography, Group 2.

Burchard, Marshall. Sports hero: Larry Csonka. Putnam 1975, 95 pp.

Larry Csonka was almost the stereotype of a football player; big, fearless and driving. For more information about the books in the series see *Sports Hero: Bill Walton*. Sports Hero series.

Interest Level: 2-6. Reading Level: 3.1. Further Search Topics: Biography, Csonka, Larry, Football-Biography, Group 2.

Burchard, Marshall. Sports hero: Muhammad Ali. Putnam 1975, 95 pp.

The man who brought a quick tongue as well as fast feet and flying fists to the sport of boxing. Entry for *Sports Hero: Bill Walton* gives series notes. Ring record included here. Sports Hero series.

Interest Level: 3-6. Reading Level: 4.1. Further Search Topics: Boxing-Biography, Blacks-Biography, Ali, Muhammad, Group 2.

Burchard, Marshall. Sports Hero: O.J. Simpson. Putnam 1975, 95 pp.

O.J. Simpson, who now flies through airports, still holds at least three NFL records, including most yards gained in a single season. See *Sports Hero: Bill Walton* for series information. Sports Hero series.

Interest Level: 2-6. Reading Level: 3.2. Further Search Topics: Biography, Simpson, O.J., Football-Biography, Blacks-Biography, Group 2.

Burchard, Marshall. Sports hero: Rick Barry. Putnam 1977, 95 pp.

Rick Barry, now a color commentator for televised basketball games, was once one of the best forwards in basketball. Details about the series with *Sports Hero: Bill Walton* entry. Sports Hero series.

Interest Level: 2-6. Reading Level: 3.1. Further Search Topics: Biography, Barry, Rick, Basketball-Biography, Group 2.

Burchard, Susan H. Sports star: Pele. HarBrace J 1976, 64 pp.

At age 35, when many people thought he might be "past his prime," Pele proved he could still play superior soccer. More details about the series in *Sports Hero: Bill Walton* entry, by Marshall Burchard. Sports Star series.

Interest Level: 2-6. Reading Level: 3.1. Further Search Topics: Biography, Soccer-Biography, Pele, Group 2.

Burchard, Susan H. Sports star: Dorothy Hamill. HarBraceJ 1978, 63 pp.

Although written by Susan Burchard, this and most of the following listings are true to Marshall Burchard's *Sports Hero* format. For more explanation see *Sports Hero: Bill Walton*.

Dorothy Hamill was the darling of ice skating in 1976 and is now a top professional figure skater. This makes her rise to stardom sound romantic and glamorous. Skating jargon pushes the reading level from 3.1 to 3.2. Sports Star series.

Interest Level: 2-6. Reading Level: 3.2. Further Search Topics: Hamill, Dorothy, Ice Skating-Biography, Women-Biography, Biography, Group 2.

Burchard, Susan H. Sports star: Tommy John. HarBraceJ 1981, 63 pp.

Tommy John's elbow injury was severe enough that no one thought he would be able to pitch again. He proved that the skeptics were wrong. For series notes see *Sports Star: Elvin Hayes*. Sports Star series.

Interest Level: 3-6. Reading Level: 4.1. Further Search Topics: Baseball-Biography, John, Tommy, Biography, Group 2, Physically Handicapped.

Burchard, Susan H. Sports star: Franco Harris. HarBraceJ 1976, 64 pp.

Franco is the talented son of a black Army man and his Italian wife. He became a hero to thousands of Pittsburgh Steeler fans, who called themselves Franco's Italian Army. See *Sports Hero: Bill Walton*, by Marshall Burchard for series details. Sports Star series.

Interest Level: 2-6. Reading Level: 3.1. Further Search Topics: Biography, Group 2, Harris, Franco, Football-Biography, Blacks-Biography.

Burchard, Susan H. Sports star: Jim "Catfish" Hunter. HarBraceJ 1976, 64 pp.

The pitcher who, because of contract violations by his club's owner, became the first free agent in baseball. See Marshall Burchard's *Sports Hero: Bill Walton* for information about the series. Sports Star series.

Interest Level: 2-6. Reading Level: 3.1. Further Search Topics: Biography, Baseball-Biography, Hunter, Jim "Catfish", Group 2.

Burchard, Susan H. Sports star: "Mean" Joe Greene. HarBraceJ 1976, 64 pp.

"Mean" Joe Greene's nickname is appropriate. He is big, "mean" on the playing field, and likes to win. He usually does. More details about the book under *Sports Hero: Bill Walton*, by Marshall Burchard. Sports Star series.

Interest Level: 2-6. Reading Level: 3.2. Further Search Topics: Biography, Football-Biography, Greene, "Mean" Joe, Blacks-Biography, Group 2.

Burchard, Susan H. Sports star: Tony Dorsett. HarBraceJ 1978, 64 pp.

One year after he set the college rushing record and won the Heisman Trophy, Tony Dorsett was named the NFL's Rookie of the Year and found himself playing in the Super Bowl. Reading level of this title varies from 2.2 to 3.2. For more information about the series see the entry for Marshall Burchard's *Sports Hero: Bill Walton*. Sports Star series.

Interest Level: 2-6. Reading Level: 3.2. Further Search Topics: Biography, Football-Biography, Dorsett, Tony, Blacks-Biography, Group 2.

Cerf, Bennett. Bennett Cerf's book of animal riddles; illus by Roy McKie. Beginner 1964, 62 pp.

A slightly more difficult selection of riddles than the following listing. The riddles are longer and less familiar, but still very useful. See *Bennett Cerf's Book of Riddles* for more explanation. Reader format.

Interest Level: 1-3. Reading Level: 2.1. Further Search Topics: Riddles, Wit and Humor, Group 2.

Cerf, Bennett. Bennett Cerf's book of riddles; illus by Roy McKie. Beginner 1960, 64 pp.

Simple, well-known riddles that are always popular with children. The riddle is introduced on one page and answered on the reverse side of the page. Silly drawings illustrate each riddle and answer. Because each riddle and answer stands alone, even the most problematic of readers can have the satisfaction of completing a unit in a short time. That satisfaction, plus the universal appeal of humor make this book and the preceding listing useful through grade four, despite the book's reader format.

Interest Level: 1-4. Reading Level: 2.1. Further Search Topics: Riddles, Wit and Humor, Group 2.

Chenery, Janet. Wolfie; illus by Marc Simont. Har-Row 1969, 64 pp.

This slight but satisfying story is the vehicle for much information about spiders. Harry caught a wolf spider. To keep his sister Polly out of the way, Harry and his friend George told her she could see the spider only after she caught 100 flies to feed it. In the meantime, they took the spider to the nature center where they were treated to a fascinating lesson about insects and spiders (especially wolf spiders). It's too bad that the book's cartoon style illustrations prevent this book from being very useful beyond grade three.

Interest Level: 1-3. Reading Level: 2.1. Further Search Topics: Spiders, Pets, Nature Study, Group 2.

Chew, Ruth. Witch's broom. Dodd 1977, 128 pp.

Amy's mother was the one who found the blue broom, but Amy and her friend Jean were the ones who learned it was magical. One night the broom flew Amy into a mountain cave where a coven of witches was meeting. It even forced Amy to answer the roll call for someone named Beryl. But it wasn't until it took both Amy and Jean back to the cave that they discovered the broom's connection to the strange bluejay that had been following them. The bluejay was really Beryl, a young and headstrong witch who had turned herself into the bluejay and then couldn't turn herself back. With the girls' unwitting help, Beryl found the charm to turn herself back into a witch and flew off on a scrawny old broom, leaving the blue broom for Amy and Jean.

What youngster wouldn't want a flying broomstick and the misadventures that go with owning one? Wish

fulfillment can never be overrated as an appeal of Ruth Chew's books.

Interest Level: 2-5. Reading Level: 3.1. Further Search Topics: Witches-Fiction, Magic-Fiction, Fantasy, Birds-Fiction, Group 2, Transformations-Fiction.

Christopher, Matt. The year mom won the pennant; illus by Foster Caddell. Little 1968, 147 pp.

When no one's father had the time to coach the Thunderballs it began to look like the team would be disbanded. They just didn't seem to be able to work together without a coach. Then Nick Vassey's mother volunteered to coach for the season. After all, she knew baseball as well as anyone else and had watched her husband coach for several years. Nick wasn't at all pleased, but had to accept the idea when his teammates voted to make his mother their coach. Nick's embarrassment was almost as great as the rival coach's skepticism, but before the season was over Nick was proud of his mother. She coached the team to first place and forced even the rival coach to admit she was a good coach. Much baseball action. See note about (*No Arm In Left Field*).

Interest Level: 2-6. Reading Level: 3.1. Further Search Topics: Group 2, Baseball-Fiction, Friendship-Fiction, Prejudice-Fiction, Sex Role-Fiction, Women-Fiction.

Ciardi, John. I met a man; illus by Robert Osborn. HM 1961, 74 pp.

Ciardi's poems are pure fun. About half are riddle poems (poems that describe something without naming it until the end) and the rest are humorous descriptions or nonsense poems. There is a problem, however, with the riddle poems: they are somewhat more difficult to read than the other poems, but of interest to younger rather than older readers. For that reason pages 1-21 (primarily nonsense verse) can be recommended for grades one through five. The remainder of the book, although enjoyable to the very young, needs to be read to them or needs a strong young reader.

Interest Level: 1-5. Reading Level: 2.2. Further Search Topics: Wit and Humor, Poetry, Riddles, Group 2.

Cleary, Beverly. Henry Huggins; illus by Louis Darling. Morrow 1950, 155 pp.

Henry Huggins is over 30 years old now, so if he occasionally seems a little old-fashioned, it is not surprising. What is surprising is how well he has withstood the years. His antics are innocent, but humorous and realistic. The book's six chapters are six separate stories that follow the same cast of characters through an entire year.

In the first chapter, Henry finds a stray dog (Ribsy) whom he must then transport home on a bus. Ribsy was too large and too frisky not to get into trouble, so before Henry finally gets him home, they have been kicked off of three buses and have ridden in a police car. The second chapter describes what happens when Henry buys two guppies and ends up with millions. In the third chapter Henry accidentally throws his friend's football into the back seat of a speeding car and tries to earn the money to replace it by catching and selling 1,331 night crawlers. The fourth chapter involves Henry's attempts to get out of playing the lead in a school Christmas play. His last minute rescue comes in the form of a can of green paint that spills all over him. It is Ribsy's turn to change colors in Chapter 5. Henry tries to cover Ribsy's dirt spots with talcom powder for a dog show, but only succeeds in turning Ribsy pink. And in Chapter 6, Ribsy's original owner finally finds him and wants him back, but Ribsy chooses to stay with Henry. Only the occasional extra cute expression and Henry's age (third grade) keep this from being enjoyed beyond fourth grade.

Interest Level: 1-4. Reading Level: 2.2. Further Search Topics: Humorous Fiction, Everyday Stories, Read Aloud Pets-Fiction, Dogs-Fiction, Group 2.

Cleary, Beverly. Otis Spofford; illus by Louis Darling. Morrow 1953, 191 pp.

Here are six separate humorous adventures that link together, but can be read separately and out of order. Otis' favorite activity was "stirring up a little excitement," but his definition of excitement usually meant trouble. The school fiesta turned into a disaster when Otis decided to rechoreograph the bullfight and make the bull win. His attempt to liven up the reading lesson about Indians meant he almost scalped a classmate. However, a wild day at the skating pond finally gave everyone a chance to take revenge for all the things Otis had done to them. The remaining three chapters (2, 3 and 4) are slightly less exciting, but useful if a reader has enjoyed the others. There is much humor in Otis' antics and his tendency to act on every thought that comes to mind is one many readers can appreciate.

Interest Level: 2-6. Reading Level: 5.1. Further Search Topics: Troublemakers-Fiction, Group 2, Read Aloud, Everyday Stories, Humorous Fiction, School Stories.

Cleary, Beverly. Henry and Beezus; illus by Louis Darling. Morrow 1952, 192 pp.

When Henry's dog Ribsy stole the meat from a neighbor's barbecue, a friend rode after Ribsy on his bike and saved the meat. Henry was so embarrassed and jealous that he boasted about an even nicer bike that he was going to get. At first Henry thought he'd be able to earn money to buy a bike in a very short time (he found 49 boxes of bubble gum that he could sell). When that scheme fell through, Henry tried taking over a friend's paper route, but Ribsy kept retrieving the newspapers Henry delivered. Eventually Henry decided to buy a used bike at the police department auction. Beezus, who made a bid for Henry, ended up buying him a beaten-up girl's bike that was hardly worth fixing. The money finally appeared when Henry least expected it; he won $50.00 worth of work at a beauty salon.

Although all seven chapters continue the same story, Chapters 1, 2, 3 and 7, can each stand alone. Henry is definitely old-fashioned, but children still enjoy his humorous escapades and empathize with his desire for a bicycle. The revised paperback cover makes the book's physical appearance less dated. Reading level is somewhat inconsistent: from 2.2 to 3.2.

Interest Level: 2-5. Reading Level: 3.1. Further Search Topics: Humorous Fiction, Occupations-Fiction, Everyday Stories, Bicycles and Bicycling-Fiction, Read Aloud, Group 2.

Clifford, Eth. Help, I'm a prisoner in the library; illus by George Hughes. HM 1979, 103 pp.

When their car stopped, Mary Rose and Jo-Beth were left alone in a strange city while their father went to find some gas. Jo-Beth needed to use the bathroom, so the sisters headed for the closest public building they could see, the library. No one saw them go in, so no one knew that they were locked inside when the librarian secured the building for the night. With the lights out and a blizzard outside, the library was a very spooky place. The girls tried calling the police, but the police wouldn't take them seriously. Then they heard groans and eerie moans from the second floor. Gathering all their courage, the girls went to investigate, only to discover the librarian lying hurt and unconscious. Their ingenuity and imagination helped the sisters through the difficult hours before they were all rescued.

Don't read it too carefully or the book's implausibilities will become very evident. Most young readers, however, will enjoy this story for its suspense, spooky atmosphere and adventurous girls, and they will ignore its weaknesses.

Interest Level: 2-5. Reading Level: 3.1. Further Search Topics: Disasters-Fiction, Snow-Fiction, Brothers and Sisters-Fiction, Libraries-Fiction, Survival-Fiction, Courage-Fiction, Group 2.

Clifford, Eth. The dastardly murder of Dirty Pete; illus by George Hughes. HM 1981, 120 pp.

Although this is a sequel to *Help, I'm a Prisoner in the Library*, it does not depend on the previous title, and in fact, is likely to be the more successful introduction to Mary Rose and Jo-Beth Onetree. Given the choice, most young readers will take a mystery set in a ghost town over a mystery set in a library.

Mary Rose, Jo-Beth and their father were on their way across country when they became lost. As night grew closer, the only place they could find to stay was an old hotel in the ghost town where Sorehead Jones had allegedly killed Dirty Pete. It was Sorehead's ghost who was supposed to haunt the town, and indeed there was someone or something who was in the town with the Onetrees. To their surprise, that someone turned out to be Sourdough Sam, an aging actor who had become senile and spent his days acting out all the parts in the Dirty Pete story. The town was only a movie set and the story was only a movie script. The Onetrees discovered the truth bit by bit after a frightening venture into an abandoned gold mine, a harrowing night in the haunted hotel and a jail sentence for Mr. Onetree.

Beware of the rare, very difficult descriptive passage that may cause trouble for some readers.

Interest Level: 2-5. Reading Level: 3.1. Further Search Topics: Mystery and Detective Stories, West-Fiction, Brothers and Sisters-Fiction, Motion Pictures-Fiction, Ghosts-Fiction, Treasure-Fiction, Group 2, Acting-Fiction, Aging-Fiction, Mental Illness-Fiction.

Cohen, Barbara. The carp in the bathtub; illus by Joan Halpern. Lothrop 1972, 48 pp.

Leah and Harry couldn't face the prospect of seeing Joe, their pet carp, made into gefilte fish, even for such a special occasion as the Seder on the first night of Passover. The large, friendly carp had lived in the family's bathtub for over a week. It even swam right over to Leah and Harry to be fed everytime they went into the bathroom. At a time when most children in New York didn't have pets, Joe was as close to being a pet as possible. So, Leah and Harry hid Joe in a neighbor's apartment until their father discovered what they had done. When Joe's destiny was fulfilled, the children had to face a difficult fact of life. A week later, however, their despair became delight, when their father brought home a pet cat.

A short, warm and satisfying story.

Interest Level: 2-5. Reading Level: 3.1. Further Search Topics: Group 2, Jews-Fiction, Religion-Fiction, Pets-Fiction, Passover-Fiction, Family-Fiction, Holidays-Fiction, Read Aloud, Brothers and Sisters-Fiction.

Cole, Joanna. Dinosaur story; illus by Mort Kunstler. Morrow 1974, unp (30 pp).

A general introduction to eight dinosaurs: Brontosaurus, Allosaurus, Stegosaurus, Ornitholestes, Protoceratops, Triceratops, Tyrannosaurus rex and Duckbills. Although not a wealth of information, there is more than enough interesting material here to attract a young dinosaur enthusiast. Because of the short sentences, the text is somewhat plodding. The subject matter's great appeal and the appropriately fierce-looking illustrations, however, make up for that problem.

Interest Level: 1-3. Reading Level: 2.1. Further Search Topics: Group 2, Dinosaurs, Prehistory.

Cole, Joanna. My puppy is born; photos by Jerome Wexler. Morrow 1973, unp (38 pp).

This is an unadorned description of a dachshund puppy's birth and first eight weeks of growth. The black and white photographs are large, sometimes graphic, and most often charming. The text is direct, carefully worded, concise and interesting. It is only the intrusion of an obviously young narrator that keeps this excellent book from being useful beyond third grade.

Interest Level: 1-3. Reading Level: 2.1. Further Search Topics: Group 2, Infants, Dogs, Pets, Birth.

Cone, Molly. Leonard Bernstein; illus by Robert Galster. Har-Row 1970, 33 pp.

This is a bare bones outline that will appeal to music enthusiasts but will not attract anyone else. The reader catches very little of Bernstein's personality, but *is* awed by an impressive list of his accomplishments. The few attempts made to recreate the real person may have to be explained (i.e., references to Bernstein forgetting to get his hair cut because he was so busy). Picture book format of the hardback may deter some readers. Now published in paperback edition only. Crowell Biography series.

Interest Level: 2-4. Reading Level: 2.2. Further Search Topics: Music-Biography, Biography, Conductors, Composers, Pianists, Group 2.

Cone, Molly. The amazing memory of Harvey Bean; illus by Robert MacLean. HM 1980, 83 pp.

It had been a long time since Harvey had been happy. His memory was so bad that he was always in trouble at school. And now that his parents were separating, he had trouble at home, too. Because he thought that neither one of his parents wanted him he told each one that he was going to stay with the other and instead decided to spend the summer alone. A few hours after he left home, Harry ran into Mr. and Mrs. Katz and before he completely realized it, he was living with them.

Mr. Katz couldn't stand to see anything go to waste. He collected the usable food thrown out behind grocery stores, old furniture, tools, windows and more. Mrs. Katz, whose memory was just as bad as Harvey's, loved to cook, so she could always find a way to use the food. Everything else bulged from the house and garage into the driveway and yard. Harvey spent a happy summer learning to scavenge, eating well, learning not to worry about what others thought of him and even improving his memory. When his parents finally found him, Harvey realized that they really did want him, even if they were separated. He decided to live with his mother on weekdays, his father on weekends, and the Katzs during the summers.

The plot problems that are obvious to adult readers are ones that most young readers will be able to ignore (i.e. neither parent checks on Harvey for over two months). Young readers will enjoy the humor and realism of Harvey's pain, happiness and eventual feeling of self-confidence and triumph. The ten short chapters, good-sized print and adequate space between the lines help lower the book's reading level to late fourth grade.

Interest Level: 3-6. Reading Level: 5.1. Further Search Topics: Loners-Fiction, Vacation-Fiction, Divorce and Separation-Fiction, Humorous Fiction, Group 2, Memory-Fiction, Runaways-Fiction, Academic Problems-Fiction, Individualists-Fiction.

Conklin, Gladys. Little apes; illus by Joseph Cellini. Holiday 1970, unp (32pp).

An informative as well as interesting look at gorillas, chimpanzees, orangutans and gibbons. Their habits and behavior patterns are described by following a young one of each species through a full day in its natural surroundings. The text is simple without being condescending and the illustrations are so life-like that they almost walk off the pages. An excellent treatment of a popular subject makes this a very useful book.

Interest Level: 2-5. Reading Level: 2.2. Further Search Topics: Apes, Gorillas, Nature Study, Infants, Group 2.

Davidson, Margaret. Nine true dolphin stories: illus by Roger Wilson. Hastings 1974, 67 pp.

Nine short stories about dolphins preceded by a brief description of their physical characteristics, their habits and their behavior. Each story is true, although some are more anecdotes than stories. Most are amusing; all are interesting. Satisfying to the dolphin enthusiast from grades two through five.

Interest Level: 2-5. Reading Level: 3.1. Further Search Topics: Dolphins, Group 2.

Dobrin, Arnold. Jillions of gerbils. Lothrop 1973, 64 pp.

Right after his family moved into a big and very old house, David's gerbil disappeared. Before long, the replacement gerbil disappeared also. The house was very old and did have strange creakings. Could there also have been secret hiding places for ghosts, maybe? Determined to find out, David searched the entire house until he really did find a secret room. And in that room he found his two gerbils with their new family — the beginnings of David's millions and billions and jillions of gerbils.

A comfortable, somewhat old-fashioned book that is neatly divided into six short chapters. It includes a page of facts about gerbils at the end. A good choice to follow the very easy readers; it is easy, but not "too babyish."

Interest Level: 1-4. Reading Level: 2.1. Further Search Topics: Gerbils-Fiction, Pets-Fiction, Group 2, Humorous Fiction.

Dolch, Edward W. "Why" stories; illus by Marguerite Dolch. Garrard 1952, 160 pp.

"Why the Bear Has a Little Tail," "Why Turkeys Have Red Eyes," and "How the Tiger Got His Stripes" are three titles that illustrate the type of stories found in this collection. Seventeen short, simple folktales explain why the world and creatures in it operate and appear as they do. All of the tales can be found elsewhere. However, few if any stories are likely to be familiar to readers. This type of story is one children often find very appealing. The stories are understandable, logical within their own framework and simple enough to be retold to others. The reading level varies from 1.2 to 2.2. Dolch Basic Vocabulary Book series.

Interest Level: 1-4. Reading Level: 2.2. Further Search Topics: Folklore, Why Stories, Animals-Fiction, Group 2, Creation-Fiction.

Dolch, Edward W. Andersen stories; illus by Carmen Mowry. Garrard 1956, 165 pp.

The best way to be introduced to Andersen's fairy tales is to hear them told or read aloud. Because they are beautifully written literary tales they suffer tremendously when the language is simplified enough so that the stories can be included in a reader. Furthermore, episodes have been cut out of some tales ("Big Klaus and Little Klaus") and others have been divided into chapters ("The Ugly Duckling"). But, where there is a need for such an easy version of Hans Christian Andersen, this selection will do. The 18 chapters tell only 11 stories. Most of the included stories are familiar ("The Emperor's New Clothes," "The Little Mermaid," "Thumbelina" etc.); all are enjoyable. Illustrations, however, are unattractive and uninspiring. One further caution: the reading level jumps from 2.1 to 3.2. Dolch Pleasure Reading Book series.

Interest Level: 2-5. Reading Level: 3.1. Further Search Topics: Folklore, Fantasy, Group 2, Fairy Tales, Andersen, Hans Christian.

Dolch, Edward W. Fairy stories; illus by Marguerite Dolch and Yolande Cuypers-Fransen. Garrard 1950, 165 pp.

A collection of mostly familiar fairy tales told in the Dolchs' very simplified manner. Because the book's purpose is not to provide the most literate version of favorite fairy tales, better versions of any of the stories can be found elsewhere. It provides instead, very accessible versions of tales young readers have enjoyed for years. Includes "Cinderella," "Hansel and Gretel," "Jack and the Bean Stalk," "Snow White," "Sleeping Beauty," and "The Elves and the Shoemaker," among others. Dolch Pleasure Reading Book series.

Interest Level: 1-4. Reading Level: 2.2. Further Search Topics: Folklore, Fairy Tales, Fantasy, Group 2.

Dolch, Edward W. Circus stories; illus by Dee Wallace. Garrard 1956, 166 pp.

A collection of 18 chapters that tell 15 true stories about the circus. Some are descriptions of activities (trapeze flying) or people (Emmett Kelly, a circus doctor, the Ringling Brothers). Other chapters tell of unusual occurrences; i.e., the bareback rider who was thrown off her horse into the lap of a spectator whom she later married. Some stories, such as the story of the horse trainer whose life was saved by an elephant, are exciting. Others are sad ("Blinky," the dog who was killed by an angry lion).

The authors' tone becomes condescending off and on through this collection, thus hampering its usefulness somewhat. Otherwise, it is very similar to the other Dolch books; it is a decent collection of very simplified stories. Dolch Basic Vocabulary Book series.

Interest Level: 1-4. Reading Level: 2.2. Further Search Topics: Circus-Fiction, Clowns-Fiction, Acrobats and Acrobatics-Fiction, Group 2.

Dolch, Edward W. Stories from France; illus by Gordon Laite. Garrard 1963, 167 pp.

It is very difficult to simplify a story and not lose at least some of its original flavor. Such is the case here and in all the Dolch retellings. Nevertheless, this collection of folktales is quite useful for the French flavor it does maintain. The stories, as they are retold, are good; not great, but good. There are 14 stories related in the 19 chapters. This is a result of splitting the longer, more complicated stories into episodes. Some frustration may arise for readers because there is no indication that a story may involve more than one chapter. The much-improved illustrations that introduce each chapter and adorn the cover help make this more attractive than the earlier books. The book ends with a list of the provinces from which the stories came as well as a pronounciation key to French names. Folklore of the World series.

Interest Level: 2-6. Reading Level: 3.1. Further Search Topics: Folklore, Fantasy, France-Fiction, Royalty-Fiction, Group 2, Knights and Knighthood-Fiction.

Foley, Louise Munro. Tackle 22; illus by John Heinly. Delacorte 1978, unp (43 pp).

When their quarterback came down with the mumps, it looked like the Wildcats would have to forfeit the big football game to the Spacemen. But Chub's little brother Herb surprised everyone and saved the game.

Brief and somewhat predictable, the book maintains a light touch that many young readers will like. Heavily illustrated.

Interest Level: 1-4. Reading Level: 2.1. Further Search Topics: Football-Fiction, Brothers and Sisters-Fiction, Humorous Fiction, Group 2.

Goldin, Augusta. Spider silk; illus by Joseph Low. Har-Row 1964, unp (34 pp).

No gimmicks here, just straight-forward information about spider webs. Where are spider webs found? How are they formed? What are their shapes? For what are they used? How strong are they? And, what are the other uses of spider silk? In answering those questions the author also gives a bit of information about particular types of spiders. The book can easily be used through grade three. Its picture book format will turn many fourth and fifth graders away even though the book's information is still quite interesting and useful. Let's-Read- & -Find-Out Science Book series.

Interest Level: 1-5. Reading Level: 2.2. Further Search Topics: Spiders, Nature Study, Group 2.

Green, Phyllis. The fastest quitter in town; illus by Lorenzo Lynch. A-W 1972, 62 pp.

Whenever Johnny played baseball and things went wrong for him, he would quit. Johnny's teammates finally grew so angry with him that they told him to leave the team. That same day, Johnny's 90-year-old great-grandfather lost a very special ring his wife had given him. Johnny's love for this great-grandfather pushed him to keep looking for the ring until days later, when everyone else had quit searching, Johnny found the ring. Having learned a hard lesson, Johnny returned to his team for one more chance. That evening Johnny went to see his great-grandfather to tell him, with legitimate pride, that he had played the entire game.

Although the lesson is pointed, the story is very satisfying. Johnny's relationship with this great-grandfather is close and supportive. His problem is one shared by many children, especially those with a weak self-image.

Interest Level: 1-4. Reading Level: 3.1. Further Search Topics: Blacks-Fiction, Challenges-Fiction, Courage-Fiction, Group 2, Baseball-Fiction, Grandparents-Fiction, Friendship-Fiction.

Hornblow, Leonora. Prehistoric monsters did the strangest things; illus by Michael K. Frith. Random 1974, 65 pp.

A basic survey of an era and its animal life forms. Animals from the earliest water creatures through Diplocaulus, Ichthyosaurs, dinosaurs (about 12 varieties) and early mammals (including the Beast of Baluchistan) to the appearance of man are introduced and illustrated. It is a brief but meaty treatment of a very popular subject that should be especially useful with second and third grade children. Reader format.

Interest Level: 1-3. Reading Level: 2.1. Further Search Topics: Prehistory, Dinosaurs, Evolution, Monsters, Group 2.

Krementz, Jill. A very young circus flyer. Knopf 1979, unp (112 pp).

One of a series of five oversized, abundantly photographed views of unusual children. Tato Farfan is part of the Flying Farfans of Ringling Brothers and Barnum and Bailey Circus. He lives in a railroad car on a circus train with his mother, father, and older brother. The whole family performs as trapeze artists and flyers for the circus. Told as if Tato were speaking, this is the story of a fairly normal boy who also happens to be a circus flyer. Practice sessions are difficult, costumes must be readied, and time must be spent helping each other, but there is also time for Tato to watch TV, play with the clowns, play soccer, and just have fun.

In addition to Tato's story, the reader is given a behind-the-scenes tour of the circus right up to and including the performance itself (color photos used for the performance). It is an exciting world that should appeal to almost anyone who has enjoyed the circus.

Interest Level: 2-6. Reading Level: 3.2. Further Search Topics: Circus, Acrobats and Acrobatics, Best Sellers, Talent, Group 2, Gymnastics.

Krementz, Jill. A very young dancer. Knopf 1976, unp (121 pp).

This was the first of the five *Very Young* books to be written. Like the others, it is large in format and lavishly photographed. Unlike *A Very Young Circus Flyer*, this and the remaining books in the series are written about 10-year-old girls from obviously privileged backgrounds. All the girls are high achievers in their chosen areas but they seem very determined to work still harder until they attain whatever goals they have set for themselves. The books all follow the same formula. The girls introduce themselves, tell about their start in dancing, riding etc., describe their goals, and tell the reader how close they are to those goals. The girls go on to describe their daily routines, the practice, the chores, the hours, and the fun. Then the reader is ushered through approximately a year's worth of the young star's challenges, achievements, and defeats (the latter are only lightly touched upon). Through it all, the child shows enthusiasm, pride, dedication, hard work, and finally, hopes for the future.

Young readers love this series. Despite heavy use of jargon that makes the reading levels somewhat unstable, those already interested in the subject area pour over every word and picture in the books. Perhaps it's partly hero worship, or romance. Maybe it's the inspiration the books provide, but certainly one of the reasons the books are so popular is the vicarious thrill that they provide young enthusiasts.

A Very Young Dancer differs slightly from the formula. Instead of following Stephanie through a year of dance classes at the School of American Ballet, the book concentrates on New York City Ballet

Company's production of the Nutcracker, in which Stephanie has a lead role.

Interest Level: 2-5. Reading Level: 3.1. Further Search Topics: Dancing, Ballet, Talent, Best Sellers, Group 2.

Krementz, Jill. A very young skater. Knopf 1979, unp (103 pp).

Katherine Healy started ice skating because her parents liked to skate and because it was easier for them to take her with them than it was to find a babysitter. From such beginnings, at age three, Katherine progressed to skating in Superskates at Madison Square Garden and ballet lessons at George Balanchine's School of American Ballet. See *A Very Young Dancer* for further explanation.

Interest Level: 2-6. Reading Level: 4.1. Further Search Topics: Ice Skating, Dancing, Ballet, Talent, Group 2, Best Sellers.

Krementz, Jill. A very young gymnast. Knopf 1978, unp (128 pp).

This is Torrence York's story. It includes a team trip to Germany for competition. See notes for *A Very Young Dancer* for more information.

Interest Level: 2-6. Reading Level: 3.2. Further Search Topics: Gymnastics, Talent, Acrobats and Acrobatics, Group 2, Best Sellers.

Krementz, Jill. A very young rider. Knopf 1977, unp (128 pp).

Vivi Malloy is the youngest rider in a family of several other riders. Her greatest dream is to make the Olympic equestrian team. She is progressing towards her goal with daily workouts and about fifteen major horse shows each year. See *A Very Young Dancer* for more extensive notes.

Interest Level: 2-6. Reading Level: 3.2. Further Search Topics: Horses, Riding, Talent, Group 2.

Levy, Elizabeth. Lizzie lies a lot; illus by John Wallner. Delacorte 1976, 102 pp.

Almost any child can identify with Lizzie. She had found that it was sometimes easier to lie than to tell the truth. Her problem was that she had lost control. It seemed as if almost everything she said was a lie. She told so many lies it became difficult to keep track of them all. Lizzie wasn't even really sure why she lied so much. She knew that she sometimes lied because she thought people would be more apt to like her. Other times she lied to get herself out of trouble or to cover up her feelings when she was hurt or angry. But that didn't explain why she lied all the time. Maybe, as her grandmother said, she was a born liar.

It wasn't until Lizzie got herself caught in the middle of so many lies that she lost her only friend, that she could admit her problem to herself and to her family. After their initial shock had passed, everyone agreed to help Lizzie stop lying. Lizzie took the next step by admitting her lies to her friend Sue.

Levy has brought such an appropriately light touch to a fairly common problem that many children find this story enjoyable. Overlook the book's faults (Lizzie's grandmother is overdrawn and her mother's guilt feelings are unsupported by the story) for the fun and the message young readers get from it.

Interest Level: 3-5. Reading Level: 4.2. Further Search Topics: Honesty-Fiction, Group 2, Friendship-Fiction, Best Sellers, Everyday Stories, Family Problems-Fiction, Grandparents-Fiction, Humorous Fiction.

Lewis, Thomas P. Hill of fire; illus by Joan Sandin. Har-Row 1971, 63 pp.

A personalized account of the volcano that suddenly erupted in the middle of a farmer's field in Mexico on February 20, 1943. Because the account is written as a story and because of its easy-reader format, the book is most useful only through third grade. An I-Can-Read-History-Book.

Interest Level: 1-3. Reading Level: 2.2. Further Search Topics: Volcanoes, Group 2, Mexico, Disasters, Historical Fiction.

Low, Joseph. Five men under one umbrella. Macmillan 1975, 64 pp.

Twenty-nine riddles, most of which are fairly familiar. Nothing special in this collection, just an additional choice for the young comedian.

Interest Level: 1-3. Reading Level: 2.1. Further Search Topics: Riddles, Wit and Humor, Group 2.

MacLachlan, Patricia. Arthur, for the very first time; illus by Lloyd Bloom. Har-Row 1980, 117 pp.

A beautifully written, sensitive yet humorous story of a boy's maturation and growing awareness of the world around him. When Arthur's unhappiness at home is made more intense by the advent of a new baby, he is sent to spend the summer with his older aunt and uncle. Their eccentricities and those of their friends are at first only material for Arthur to write about in his journal. But as the summer progresses he not only learns from them, but also grows from an observer of life to a participant. His final step is helping a large and beloved pig bear her litter in a driving rain storm aided only by his independent, totally untamed young friend Moira.

The print is somewhat small, but spacing between lines is generous.

Interest Level: 4-6. Reading Level: 4.2. Further Search Topics: Read Aloud, Children-Growth-Fiction, Humorous Fiction, Friendship-Fiction, Vacation-Fiction, Relatives-Fiction, Infants-Fiction, Individualists-Fiction, Writing-Fiction, Loners-Fiction, Group 2.

McNulty, Faith. Woodchuck; illus by Joan Sandin. Har-Row 64 pp.

There's a great deal of information in this little book. It describes a woodchuck's physical appearance, its habits and behavior, and its life cycle. The treatment is very direct and very honest (two of four young woodchucks are killed before the first year is over). Only an overly repetitive, slightly condescending beginning, and the reader format hamper the book's usefulness beyond grade four. A Science-I-Can-Read-Book.

Interest Level: 1-4. Reading Level: 3.1. Further Search Topics: Nature Study, Groundhogs, Group 2, Woodchucks.

Mathis, Sharon Bell. Ray Charles; illus by George Ford. Har-Row 1973, 33 pp.

Dominent throughout this biography of Ray Charles is the theme of overcoming adversity. The book is not just a recounting of Ray Charles' music lessons, early schooling, family life, and talent. All of that is included, but it serves to illustrate the manner in which Charles met his troubles. His problems began when he was very young. His brother died, and Ray lost one eye and then the sight in his other eye. His family was poor, but close, and he missed them when he was sent away to a school for the blind. Music was his love, but even that was work, for Charles had to learn to read and write music in Braille. He worked hard at it and eventually could play and arrange music for every instrument in the band.

Determined to be independent, when Charles was orphaned at age 15, he left school and began playing music for a living. The first record he made resulted in a $16 fine because he made it during a musician's union strike. Charles took a series of sideman and nightclub jobs until he finally had enough money to hire seven other musicians to play his music. Today Charles is very wealthy, owns his own record company, has a family, and is considered a great jazz and blues musician. None of his success came easily; only through determination, will power, pride, and hard work.

The book, interesting and serviceable enough for music or biography units, is also designed to set an example for youngsters facing their own problems. It will, of course, be popular with Ray Charles fans, too. Crowell Biography series.

Interest Level: 2-4. Reading Level: 3.1. Further Search Topics: Jazz Music, Music-Biography, Vision, Physically Handicapped, Blacks-Biography, Group 2, Charles, Ray, Biography, Pianists, Orphans, Challenges, Courage.

Meriwether, Louise. The freedom ship of Robert Smalls; illus by Lee Jack Morton. P-H 1971, unp (30 pp).

A brief, but very interesting biography of a black man whose dreams of freedom as a young slave during the Civil War, led to a daring plan of escape. Robert Smalls sailed 16 slaves to freedom and presented the Northern Navy with a valuable gunboat of which he was eventually named captain. Smalls later went on to serve five terms in Congress.

Although the picture book format of this book prevents its confortable use much beyond fourth grade, it is a compelling enough story to interest even sixth graders. Print is somewhat small.

Interest Level: 1-4. Reading Level: 3.1. Further Search Topics: Biography, United States-History-War, Blacks-Biography, Smalls, Robert, Group 2, Slavery, Politics-Biography.

Montgomery, Raymond A. Space and beyond; illus by Paul Granger. Bantam 1980, 117 pp.

See entry for *Sugarcane Island*, by Edward Packard for full annotation. Available in paperback only. Choose Your Own Adventure series

Interest Level: 2-6. Reading Level: 4.1. Further Search Topics: Science Fiction, Outer Space-Fiction, Group 2, Best Sellers.

Montgomery, Raymond A. The lost jewels of Nabooti; illus by Paul Granger. Bantam 1981, 121 pp.

See entry for *Sugarcane Island*, by Edward Packard for series information. Only available in paperback edition. Choose Your Own Adventure series.

Interest Level: 2-6. Reading Level: 3.2. Further Search Topics: Mystery and Detective Stories, Detectives-Fiction, Treasure-Fiction, Best Sellers, Group 2.

Newfield, Marcia. A book for Jodan; illus by Diane DeGroot. Atheneum 1975, unp (41 pp).

Jodan found her parents' separation very hard to understand and accept. She and her mother had moved 3,000 miles away from her father and she missed him very much. When Jodan visited her father for the first time, he gave her a very special present that lessened her loneliness. He created a book just for Jodan that was filled with his thoughts and memories.

The book is a sensitive portrayal of a very common experience. Only Jodan's age (nine-years-old) and consequent actions and reactions, limit the book's probable usefulness beyond fifth grade. Print is somewhat small.

Interest Level: 2-5. Reading Level: 3.2. Further Search Topics: Group 2, Divorce and Separation-Fiction, Family Problems-Fiction, Loneliness-Fiction.

Norton, Andre. Star Ka'at; illus by Bernard Colonna. Walker & Co 1976, 122 pp.

Jim Evans and Elly Mae Brown, both orphaned and alone, met each other and two strange cats at the same time. As the children became more unhappy with their lives, they began to realize that Tiro and Mer were not usual cats. They were highly intelligent Ka'ats from another planet who had come to Earth in search of new strong stock to add to their breed. Both Ka'ats became as fond of the children as the children became of them. When the time came for the transport ship to leave, Jim and Elly contrived to go with them. However, the only way they could go was if they were accepted by the other Ka'ats and adopted by Tiro and Mer.

This is the first book in a series. Unfortunately the second book *Star Ka'at World*, has a much more difficult reading level (sixth grade) and the third title, *Star Ka'at and the Plant People*, varies from 2.1 to 4.1. Reading level of this entry varies between 4.1 and 5.1 but children seem to like the book enough to put up with the variability.

Interest Level: 3-6. Reading Level: 4.2. Further Search Topics: Science Fiction, Friendship-Fiction, Cats-Fiction, Group 2, Outer Space-Fiction, Orphans-Fiction.

O'Neill, Mary. Hailstones and halibut bones; illus by Leonard Weisgard. Doubleday 1961, 59 pp.

This is a classic collection of twelve poems about colors. The poems are rhymed mood pieces of two or three pages that should appeal to almost any age reader. The difficulty of the vocabulary within each poem can vary greatly; however, most stanzas are short, most of the vocabulary is at least familiar, and the rhyme scheme is consistent.

Interest Level: 1-5. Reading Level: 3.2. Further Search Topics: Poetry, Colors, Group 2.

Packard, Edward. Sugarcane Island; illus by Barbara Carter. Archway 1976, 105 pp.

The warning on the first page, that the book should *not* be read straight through, tells you that this book is different. And different it is. It is the first of what is now a new type of book; the "Choose Your Own Adventure" story. The formula is simple and highly successful, especially with reluctant readers. The reader is made the central character of the book. After a very brief series of events that set the stage, the reader is given choices to make. Upon making a decision, the reader is instructed to proceed to another page of the book. More action is described before the reader must make another choice. The sequence of action, choice, action and choice continues until the reader has finally completed an entire story. The books can be read over and over and the reader may never repeat exactly the same story unless he/she makes all of the same choices. What distinguishes one book from another is the setting, genre, and/or author (there are three: Edward Packard, R. A. Montgomery, and D. Terman). Don't expect quality writing or consistent reading levels because you won't find either. (Reading levels vary from 2.2 to 3.2 for most titles). What you will find is dependable, action-filled, enticing, light reading. Some are available only in paperback editions where the

print size is fairly small. Choose Your Own Adventure series.

Interest Level: 2-6. Reading Level: 3.1. Further Search Topics: Shipwrecks-Fiction, Best Sellers, Survival-Fiction, Group 2.

Packard, Edward. Your code name is Jonah; illus by Paul Granger. Bantam 1980, 114 pp.

See *Sugarcane Island* for information about books in this series. Paperback only. Choose Your Own Adventure series.

Interest Level: 2-6. Reading Level: 3.2. Further Search Topics: Nonverbal Communication-Fiction, Best Sellers, Spies-Fiction, Group 2.

Packard, Edward. The cave of time; illus by Paul Granger. Bantam 1979, 115 pp.

Beware of the greater than usual inconsistency of reading levels within this book. Its difficulty level ranges from 2.2 to 4.2. See notes for *Sugarcane Island* for more information about the series. In paperback only. Choose Your Own Adventure series.

Interest Level: 2-6. Reading Level: 4.1. Further Search Topics: Time-Fiction, Science Fiction, Fantasy, Group 2.

Packard, Edward. The mystery of Chimney Rock; illus by Paul Granger. Bantam 1979, 121 pp.

See notes for *Sugarcane Island* for information about the series. Paperback only. Choose Your Own Adventure series.

Interest Level: 2-6. Reading Level: 3.2. Further Search Topics: Mystery and Detective Stories, Cats-Fiction, Witches-Fiction, Ghosts-Fiction, Detectives-Fiction, Best Sellers, Group 2.

Packard, Edward. Deadwood City; illus by Barbara Carter. Bantam 1978, 96 pp.

See *Sugarcane Island* for full series notes. Paperback edition only. Choose Your Own Adventure series.

Interest Level: 2-6. Reading Level: 3.1. Further Search Topics: West-Fiction, Cowboys-Fiction, Crime-Fiction, Best Sellers, Group 2.

Parish, Peggy. Haunted house; illus by Paul Frame. Macmillan 1971, 151 pp.

Although this is the third book about Jed, Bill and Liza Roberts, it too can be read out of order. This time the family has moved into what was locally known as a haunted house. Very shortly after they moved into the house, a coded note appeared that led them to a series of messages and unusual occurrences. Lights that flashed into Liza's room turned out to be the headlights of cars, but the messages and a secret compartment in an old clock couldn't be as easily explained. Each day took them closer to the surprise that the messages hinted would be theirs. That surprise turned out to be three kittens and a treehouse. Two of the children's best friends had planned the whole mystery just to lead to the surprises.

This book has the same faults and strong points as the others about the Roberts children. Each chapter is short; the book is episodic; reading level is consistent; there is much dialogue and action and little description, and the plot has a comfortable familiarity about it. It can be very useful to the right readers.

Interest Level: 1-4. Reading Level: 2.1. Further Search Topics: Mystery and Detective Stories, Brothers and Sisters-Fiction, Ghosts-Fiction, Moving, Household-Fiction, Nonverbal Communication-Fiction, Group 2.

Parish, Peggy. Clues in the woods; illus by Paul Frame. Macmillan 1968, 154 pp.

The books about the three Roberts children share problems that are obvious to adults and felt by some young readers as well, but they continue to be popular with undemanding young readers. The characters are very white and middle class and their actions often fit out-of-date stereotypes. The plots have few surprises or suspense, but the reading levels are consistent and the very predictability of the books makes them familiar and therefore comfortable.

This particular story takes place at the end of the same summer the children solved the mystery of *The Key to the Treasure*. The children were alerted by their grandmother to the disappearance of food scraps, left outside the house. Thinking that two runaway children, about whom they had read, had taken the food, Liza, Bill, and Jed tried to find the runaways. Their attempts eventually brought them new friends and thus the solution to their mystery. It had not been the runaways who had taken the food, it was their new friends' dog.

Interest Level: 1-4. Reading Level: 2.2. Further Search Topics: Mystery and Detective Stories, Brothers and Sisters-Fiction, Vacation-Fiction, Dogs-Fiction, Runaways-Fiction, Grandparents-Fiction, Group 2.

Parish, Peggy. Key to the treasure; illus by Paul Frame. Macmillan 1966, 154 pp.

This is the first of the stories about Jed, Bill and Liza Roberts. The three children are very middle-class, the book's plots are simple and often lack suspense, but the stories still enjoy widespread popularity among unsophisticated readers.

All three children went to spend the summer with their grandparents and decided to tackle a mystery left unsolved for over 75 years. An old drawing and an authentic war bonnet provided the only clues to finding three Indian artifacts. At each step along the way there were crumbled, brittle pieces of paper bearing coded messages that led to the next clue. The search ended when the children found that a storage area in a porch piller contained an Indian doll, mask, and leather shield that had belonged to their great-grandfather.

Interest Level: 1-4. Reading Level: 2.1. Further Search Topics: Vacation-Fiction, Brothers and Sisters-Fiction, Group 2, Mystery and Detective Stories, Grandparents-Fiction, Nonverbal Communication-Fiction.

Parish, Peggy. Pirate Island adventure; illus by Paul Frame. Macmillan 1975, 167 pp.

Although this is the fourth book in the series about the Roberts children, none of the titles must be read in chronological order. This time the three rather privileged children spent the summer with their grandparents on a resort island. They lived in a house that their family had owned for years, explored the island, and swam in their own private cove. But, most of their time was spent trying to solve an old mystery. Their great-uncle had hidden several very special items (one for each member of his family) years earlier, and had left only one clue with their grandfather. After he gave the children that clue it was only a matter of time before they found the hidden treasures.

This book is also lengthy, but is divided into 22 very manageable chapters. It is, like the others, almost entirely dialogue and action, which makes it especially appealing to young reluctant readers.

Interest Level: 1-4. Reading Level: 2.1. Further Search Topics: Mystery and Detective Stories, Vacation-Fiction, Treasure-Fiction, Brothers and Sisters-Fiction, Grandparents-Fiction, Group 2.

Peck, Robert Newton. Mr. Little; illus by Ben Stahl. Doubleday 1979, 87 pp.

All summer long Drag and Finley had looked forward to having Miss Kellogg as their teacher, so they were extremely disappointed to find ordinary-looking Mr. Little in her place on the first day of school. Used to playing tricks on their teachers anyway, Drag and Finley decided to go all out to get even with Mr. Little for spoiling their year. But try as they might, they couldn't get an advantage over Mr. Little; he seemed to be unflappable. Finally, in their riskiest prank ever, they stole Mr. Little's underwear to dress a statue in the town square. That attempt to embarrass Mr. Little only served to get Finley and Drag in serious trouble from which Mr. Little saved them. It was his later rescue of Miss Kellogg, however, that added respect to the boys' growing feeling of friendship for Mr. Little.

Because the author's adult viewpoint is never quite lost, even though he writes in the first person, and because the rural and historic time settings are not familiar to many readers, the book may need some introduction and encouragement. It is a prime candidate for reading aloud until the young reader's interest takes over. Print is of adequate size, but spacing between lines could have been more generous.

Interest Level: 4-6. Reading Level: 5.1. Further Search Topics: Humorous Fiction, School Stories, Troublemakers-Fiction, Group 2, Read Aloud, Country Life-Fiction, Best Sellers.

Pene du Bois, William. Lazy Tommy Pumpkinhead. Har-Row 1966, 32 pp.

Tommy lived a solitary life in an all-electric house. An electric bed woke Tommy and slid him into a tub full of warm water. The tub then tipped him out and into a harness that held Tommy upright while other machines dried him, combed his hair, brushed his teeth, dressed him, and fed him. But one day Tommy's life was literally turned upside down with disastrous results. His feet were cleaned and combed and his clothes were all put on upside down, but the worst part of all was that Tommy almost starved; the machine fed his feet instead of his mouth.

A tongue-in-cheek warning against laziness. The lesson is obvious but the treatment (both text and illustrations) is so enjoyable that the book is appealing to almost any reader who wants a short, funny book. Print is somewhat small but spacing between lines is more than adequate.

Interest Level: 1-6. Reading Level: 3.2. Further Search Topics: Electricity-Fiction, Robots-Fiction, Laziness-Fiction, Humorous Fiction, Group 2, Read Aloud.

Robinson, Barbara. The best Christmas pageant ever; illus by Judith Gwyn Brown. Har-Row 1972, 80 pp.

A truly delightful story of what happens when the meanest kids in town (they are all in one family) take over all the lead roles in the Sunday school Christmas pageant. The Herdmans (all six of them), having heard that the church was giving away free food, showed up to take some. While they were there, they heard about the Christmas pageant and decided it presented them with another perfect opportunity for food and mischief. With a little behind-the-scenes arm-twisting (literally), they managed to dissuade everyone else from showing interest in the major roles. Theirs was a completely original interpretation of the Christmas story that left nothing and no one around them untouched.

That the book's reading level will prove too high for many people is unfortunate. The story is well worth the struggle. A wonderful choice for reading aloud.

Interest Level: 3-6. Reading Level: 5.1 Further Search Topics: Christmas-Fiction, Bullies-Fiction, Troublemakers-Fiction, Humorous Fiction, Religion-Fiction, Group 2, Read Aloud, Acting-Fiction, Holidays-Fiction.

Rudeen, Kenneth. Roberto Clemente; illus by Frank Mullins. Har-Row 1974, 33 pp.

A romanticized retelling of a great baseball player's life. Those already interested in baseball or in Clemente will probably not mind the romantic tone, but may notice the almost patronizing explanations of some of the basics of baseball. Crowell Biography series.

Interest Level: 2-4. Reading Level: 3.1. Further Search Topics: Baseball-Biography, Biography, Puerto Rico, Group 2, Clemente, Roberto.

Rudeen, Kenneth. Wilt Chamberlain; illus by Frank Mullins. Har-Row 1972, 33 pp.

A short and somewhat adoring version of Wilt Chamberlain's childhood, schooling, and professional career. Very little of Chamberlain's personality comes through in this book, but his superior talents and skills as well as his importance to the sport of basketball will be enough to prompt many basketball fans to read it. Although simplistic in style, the book is not condescending. It is, however, out of date, a fact most notable when Chamberlain's salary is quoted. Beware of juvenile format when using with older readers. Crowell Biography series.

Interest Level: 2-6. Reading Level: 3.2. Further Search Topics: Biography, Chamberlain, Wilt, Basketball-Biography, Blacks-Biography, Group 2.

St. John, Wylly Folk. The ghost next door; illus by Trina Schart Hyman. Har-Row 1971, 178 pp.

Told by 13-year-old Lindsay, this is the story of her neighbor Miss Judith and Miss Judith's two nieces. Her niece Miranda had drowned years earlier in Miss Judith's backyard fish pond and Miss Judith had never fully recovered from her death. As the story begins, Miss Judith is about to welcome another niece (Sherry) for a summer stay. Sherry, without ever being told about Miranda, seems to sense Miranda's presence all around. Her mother laughs and says that Sherry has an imaginary friend. Miss Judith, who is a strong believer in ESP, thinks that Sherry is communicating with Miranda. As the days go on Sherry learns more and more of Miranda' secrets. When Miss Judith is scared by Sherry, Lindsay and her friend, Tammy, decide to see what sort of tricks Sherry is playing.

A believable suspense story, made even more so by the illustrations.

Interest Level: 4-6. Reading Level: 5.1. Further Search Topics: Mystery and Detective Stories, Relatives-Fiction, Group 2, Extra Sensory Perception-Fiction, Best Sellers, Ghosts-Fiction.

Sarnoff, Jane. What? A riddle book; illus by Reynold Ruffins. Scribner 1974, 62 pp.

A good, lengthy collection of both familiar and unfamiliar riddles. Every other page is brightened by bold and humorous illustrations. The first part of the book seems to have slightly more riddles for younger readers than the rest of the book. Some of the riddles in the collection involve rather sophisticated puns; thus they are more appealing to fifth and sixth grade readers. The final three pages of the book include 35 riddles whose answers are in code. The key to the code is given on the last page of the book. It is a picture book printed in two tones. The riddles sometimes slant diagonally across the page.

Interest Level: 1-6. Reading Level: 3.1. Further Search Topics: Riddles, Wit and Humor, Group 2, Nonverbal Communication.

Selsam, Millicent E. How kittens grow; photos by Esther Bubley. School Bk Serv 1973, unp (28 pp).

A warm picture essay that illustrates and briefly describes the first eight weeks in kittens' lives. Guaranteed to charm cat fanciers.

Interest Level: 1-3. Reading Level: 2.1. Further Search Topics: Cats, Pets, Infants, Group 2, Birth.

Sharmat, Marjorie W. Nate the great goes undercover; illus by Marc Simont. Coward 1974, 47 pp.

Nate's next door neighbor Oliver was a pest, but Oliver had a mystery for Nate to solve. Oliver's garbage can was being burglarized at night. He wanted Nate to catch the garbage snatcher. Nate quickly drew up a list of human suspects and just as quickly eliminated them all. A night spent hiding in the garbage can proved the best way to catch the thief. Much to Nate's surprise, the thief turned out to be his new dog.

Very amusing and very useful. Reader format.

Interest Level: 1-3. Reading Level: 2.1. Further Search Topics: Humorous Fiction, Mystery and Detective Stories, Group 2, Detectives-Fiction, Best Sellers.

Sharmat, Marjorie W. Nate the great; illus by Marc Simont. Coward 1972, 62 pp.

This is a young imitation of Humphrey Bogart solving a *Dragnet* style mystery. Annie's recently finished painting of her dog had disappeared so she hired Nate to search for it. Nate gathered all the facts, investigated his suspects, and eventually solved the mystery, but not before he had consumed plenty of pancakes (his favorite food) and solved a second mystery by accident.

A simple plot, humorous telling, and a sympathetic, likeable protagonist make this one of a very popular series. Reader format.

Interest Level: 1-3. Reading Level: 2.1. Further Search Topics: Humorous Fiction, Detectives-Fiction, Mystery and Detective Stories, Group 2, Best Sellers.

Shaw, Evelyn. Alligator; illus by Frances Zweifel. Har-Row 1972, 61 pp.

A straight-forward, respectful description of an alligator's life cycle. Emphasis is placed on the time between the mother's nest-building and the birth of the young alligators. The danger to alligators posed by man is expressed, but not stressed. Little physical description is included. An interesting and competent treatment of a narrow subject. Reader format. A Science-I-Can-Read Book series.

Interest Level: 1-4. Reading Level: 2.1. Further Search Topics: Alligators, Nature Study, Group 2.

Shearer, John. Billy Jo Jive and the case of the missing pigeons; illus by Ted Shearer. Delacorte 1978, 47 pp.

This is the third in a series of slight mysteries, always solved by Billy Jo Jive and his crime fighter partner, Susie Sunset. Jive and Sunset are street-wise, black youngsters who take their jobs as crime fighters very seriously, and are never detered for long from finding the criminals they seek. The crimes are always thefts, and the criminals vary from young children to neighborhood menaces. Suspense is created more by the manner in which Jive and Sunset catch the thieves, plus the determination and pace of the young detectives, than by guessing who the culprits might be. Jive, his street-slang manner of telling the first-person stories, and the urban setting will appeal to many readers. Jive and Sunset also appear on *Sesame Street.*

Jive accidentally photographed the fleeing pigeon thief as he was being chased by Flip, the victim. The photograph didn't show the thief's face, but did give Jive and Sunset a good look at what he was wearing. Jive and Sunset concluded that the thief was Snake Hips Robberts. They later realized that they had been wrong. When they looked carefully at the picture, they remembered that any dark color clothing photographs almost black in a black and white picture. Snake Hips had a black jacket, but he was innocent. The real thief was Sugar Brown. Then it was a simple matter of showing the evidence to both Flip and Sugar to get Sugar to confess.

Interest Level: 1-4. Reading Level: 2.2. Further Search Topics: Mystery and Detective Stories, Detectives-Fiction, Blacks-Fiction, City Life-Fiction, Group 2, Best Sellers.

Shearer, John. Billy Jo Jive and the walkie-talkie caper; illus by Ted Shearer. Delacorte 1981, 47 pp.

When Steam Boat Louis went to Jive and Sunset for help, he was desperate. Because Jive and Sunset had already solved three cases, they were the logical people to find the walkie-talkie that had been stolen from Steam Boat. The walkie-talkie was one of two that Steam Boat had been told to buy as part of a secret communication system for the Bugaloo Smackers. Even as Jive and Sunset hunted for the thief, the second walkie-talkie was stolen. Their only clue was a footprint found outside Steam Boat's fix-it shop. Eventually, after trial and error, Jive and Sunset uncovered the real thieves; Steam Boat's young twin cousins. Unhappy at being separated in school, they wanted to use the walkie-talkies to be able to talk with each other.

The high reading level of this book will make it most useful for those children who have read and enjoyed other books in the series and are willing to stretch to read one more.

Interest Level: 1-4. Reading Level: 3.2. Further Search Topics: Mystery and Detective Stories, Detectives-Fiction, Blacks-Fiction, City Life-Fiction, Group 2.

Shearer, John. Billy Jo Jive super private eye: the case of the missing ten speed bike; illus by Ted Shearer. Delacorte 1976, 47 pp.

Jive and Sunset began their friendship and their sleuthing career with this book. It all started when Sunset borrowed her older brother's 10-speed bicycle. Jive met Sunset while she sat at the side of the road crying, after her brother's bike had been stolen. Some careful joint detective work proved to Jive and Sunset that Dynamite Jones, jealous of Sunset's brother, had stolen the bike. The young crime fighters recovered the bicycle before Sunset's brother even knew it was missing.

This book sets the formula that all the others follow. A neighborhood person finds that something has been stolen and goes to Jive and Sunset for help. Jive and Sunset never have much trouble finding the thief even though they are sometimes misled for a short time. Often the culprit is quite obvious to the reader. After some attempts at clever detective work and an occasional bit of preaching, the crime is solved. It is the manner of the pursuit and the street-smart characters that give the stories their interest.

Interest Level: 1-4. Reading Level: 2.2. Further Search Topics: Mystery and Detective Stories, Blacks-Fiction, Detectives-Fiction, City Life-Fiction, Best Sellers, Group 2, Bicycles and Bicycling-Fiction.

Silverstein, Shel. Where the sidewalk ends. Har-Row 1974, 166 pp.

There is something here for almost everyone. It isn't always easy reading, but there are enough short, easier poems to pique almost any child's interest. Once caught, children will find the book hard to put down. The best way to encourage the use of this book is to read selections aloud so that potential readers may hear the rhythm and enjoy the humor. This method almost guarantees that they will then want to try reading the book themselves. Readers may struggle with a poem but once it is mastered, they will usually want more.

Interest Level: 2-6. Reading Level: 3.1. Further Search Topics: Poetry, Wit and Humor, Read Aloud, Group 2, Best Sellers.

Silverstein, Shel. A light in the attic. Har-Row 1981, 169 pp.

This is the second and most recent collection of Shel Silverstein's wonderfully wry poetry. No young person who has read and enjoyed *Where the Sidewalk Ends* will be disappointed in this effort. For those readers new to Silverstein or to poetry in general, this is as good a place as any to start enjoying both. Hearing a few of these poems read aloud is guaranteed to provoke loud cries of "May I read some?" from almost all listeners.

Interest Level: 2-6. Reading Level: 3.2. Further Search Topics: Poetry, Wit and Humor, Best Sellers, Group 2, Read Aloud.

Sobol, Donald J. Encyclopedia Brown and the case of the dead eagles; illus by Leonard Shortall. Elsevier-Nelson 1975, 96 pp.

By all rights Idaville should be declared a disaster area and Mr. Brown, the chief of police, should be fired from his job. Idaville looks like an ordinary small town, but behind its sleepy exterior there exists a crime wave that would challenge the best police departments in the country. It is true that the crimes are always solved and the criminals always caught, but not by Chief Brown. Chief Brown is frequently so stumped by his police cases that he talks about them at home, usually at dinner time. Almost always, his son, Leroy "Encyclopedia" Brown, solves the case before dinner is even over. A clear case of superior intelligence and skill.

Encyclopedia (so nicknamed because of his intellect) not only solves his father's cases, but serves as a detective for his friends, too. He is kept so busy that each slim volume in this series contains 10 short mysteries. Needless to say Encyclopedia solves them all. The question is can the reader? All necessary clues are there and specialized knowledge is rarely required. Should the reader fail to solve a mystery (they are not always as easy as one would expect), a full explanation and solution for each case is provided at the back of the book. Each title follows exactly the same formula. Although a teacher or parent may grow bored hearing of Encyclopedia's accomplishments, most young readers thoroughly enjoy them.

The books actively challenge and thus involve the reader in a way most books do not. A very popular series that does not have to be read in sequence. Reading level is consistently 2.2 to 3.1. Encyclopedia Brown series.
Interest Level: 2-6. Reading Level: 3.1. Further Search Topics: Mystery and Detective Stories, Puzzles, Best Sellers, Group 2, Detectives-Fiction.

Sobol, Donald J. Encyclopedia Brown and the case of the secret pitch; illus by Leonard Shortall. Elsevier-Nelson 1965, 96 pp.
See *Encyclopedia Brown and the Case of the Dead Eagles* for full annotation.
Interest Level: 2-6. Reading Level: 3.1. Further Search Topics: Group 2, Mystery and Detective Stories, Puzzles, Best Sellers, Detectives-Fiction.

Sobol, Donald J. Encyclopedia Brown finds the clues; illus by Leonard Shortall. Elsevier-Nelson 1966, 96 pp.
See *Encyclopedia Brown and the Case of the Dead Eagles* for full annotation.
Interest Level 2-6. Reading Level: 3.1. Further Search Topics: Mystery and Detective Stories, Puzzles, Detectives-Fiction, Best Sellers, Group 2.

Sobol, Donald J. Encyclopedia Brown gets his man; illus by Leonard Shortall. Elsevier-Nelson 1967, 96 pp.
See *Encyclopedia Brown and the Case of the Dead Eagles* for full annotation.
Interest Level: 2-6. Reading Level: 3.1. Further Search Topics: Mystery and Detective Stories, Puzzles, Best Sellers, Group 2, Detectives-Fiction.

Sobol, Donald J. Encyclopedia Brown lends a hand; illus by Leonard Shortall. Elsevier-Nelson 1974, 96 pp.
See *Encyclopedia Brown and the Case of the Dead Eagles* for full annotation.
Interest Level: 2-6. Reading Level: 3.1. Further Search Topics: Mystery and Detective Stories, Puzzles, Detectives-Fiction, Best Sellers, Group 2.

Sobol, Donald J. Encyclopedia Brown solves them all; illus by Leonard Shortall. Elsevier-Nelson 1968, 96 pp.
See *Encyclopedia Brown and the Case of the Dead Eagles* for full annotation.
Interest Level: 2-6. Reading Level: 3.1. Further Search Topics: Mystery and Detective Stories, Puzzles, Detectives-Fiction, Group 2, Best Sellers.

Sobol, Donald J. Encyclopedia Brown sets the pace; illus by Ib Ohlsson. Four Winds Pr 1982, 89 pp.
See *Encyclopedia Brown and the Case of the Dead Eagles* for full annotation.
Interest Level: 2-6. Reading Level: 3.1. Further Search Topics: Mystery and Detective Stories, Detectives-Fiction, Puzzles, Group 2, Best Sellers.

Sobol, Donald J. Encyclopedia Brown carries on; illus by Ib Ohlsson. Schol Bk Serv 1980, 72 pp.
See *Encyclopedia Brown and the Case of the Dead Eagle* for full annotation.
Interest Level: 2-6. Reading Level: 3.1. Further Search Topics: Mystery and Detective Stories, Puzzles, Detectives-Fiction, Group 2, Best Sellers.

Terman, Douglas. By balloons to the Sahara; illus by Paul Granger. Bantam 1979, 117 pp.
See the entry for *Sugarcane Island*, by Edward Packard for detailed information about the series. Available in paperback edition only. Choose Your Own Adventure series.

Interest Level: 2-6. Reading Level: 3.2. Further Search Topics: Voyages and Travels-Fiction, Flight-Fiction, Best Sellers, Group 2.

Tobias, Tobi. Marian Anderson; illus by Symeon Shimin. Har-Row 1972, 40 pp.
Marian Anderson's beautiful, strong voice and her great range set her apart from other singers even as a child. By the time she was in high school, she was being paid to sing. However, when she tried to apply to a well-known music school, because she was black she was turned away without even being heard. Anderson's determination as well as her own and others' faith in her kept her singing and seeking better and better coaches until she met Giuseppi Boghetti. He was one of the best voice coaches in the country. With him Marian trained and traveled until she finally won the chance to sing with the New York Philharmonic Orchestra. Anderson thought that at that point she would be invited to sing in famous theaters all across the United States, but because she was black she still received no invitations. She went to Europe where she studied and played to wildly enthusiastic audiences. Her European triumphs finally convinced American theater owners and audiences that she was a serious talent. For the next 30 years Marian Anderson sang all over the world, most of the time without incident, with one notable exception in 1939, when the D.A.R. prohibited her from singing in a hall they owned in Washington, D. C. She sang instead, in front of the Lincoln Memorial, at the invitation of the United States government. During the following years Marian married, bought a farm, sang opera and was made a delegate to the United Nations. In 1956, she retired from singing to help children, young singers, and world understanding.
Crowell Biographies make excellent school report sources for reluctant readers. They are short, interesting, and not overly juvenile looking, although the quasi-picture book format may be a problem for some older readers. This biography fits that description perfectly. The series is somewhat sentimental (as are many children's biographies), however, the sentimentality is not forbidding or condescending. A useful series. Crowell Biography series.
Interest Level: 2-5. Reading Level: 3.1. Further Search Topics: Biography, Music-Biography, Blacks-Biography, Talent, Women-Biography, Singers, Prejudice, Group 2.

Viorst, Judith. The tenth good thing about Barney; illus by Erik Blegvad. Atheneum 1971, 25 pp.
A quiet, thoughtful book to help a child face the difficult experience of death. When a family's beloved cat Barney died, their little boy tried to find 10 good things to say about him at the funeral. Nine things came easily to mind, but it was not until he had worked in the garden with his father that the little boy realized the tenth good thing. Barney, buried in the ground, would help the flowers, trees, and grass grow. A special picture book, small in size, but large in impact. Print is somewhat small but well-spaced.
Interest Level: 1-4. Reading Level: 2.1. Further Search Topics: Pets-Fiction, Cats-Fiction, Death-Fiction, Group 2, Read Aloud.

White, Laurence B., Jr. Science toys; illus by Marc Tolon Brown. A-W 1975, unp (46 pp).
This book presents 23 toys that a young child can easily make and learn from at the same time. A sundial, a drinking straw that flies, a balloon that rolls over, a ghost that sticks to the wall by itself, a

water-go-round, and a paper cup that roars are a few examples of what is to be found here. The construction and use of each toy is explained and illustrated in enough detail to enable the child to work alone. And as in *Science Puzzles*, some of the toys will double as magic tricks (i.e. can you balance the rim of a paper plate on your nose?).

Interest Level: 1-3. Reading Level: 2.1. Further Search Topics: Handicrafts, Science, Magic, Toys, Games, Group 2, Puzzles.

Wyler, Rose. Magic secrets; illus by Talivaldis Stubis. Har-Row 1967, 64 pp.

Another good selection of easily performed but impressive looking magic tricks. After a short section defining magic, 13 tricks are described. Another 11 tricks are included as the authors describe how to put on a magic show. Just what differentiates the first group of tricks from the second is not clear. With a little imagination any of the tricks shown in the book could be used in a magic show. Use of the book beyond fourth grade is not likely due to its "early-reader" appearance. An I-Can-Read-Book.

Interest Level: 1-4. Reading Level: 2.1. Further Search Topics: Magic, Group 2.

GUIDRY, RON

Burchard, Marshall. Sports hero: Ron Guidry. Putnam 1981, 95 pp.

The Cajun, left-handed pitcher who led the Yankees to two World Championships. See *Sports Hero: Bill Walton* for series details. Sports Hero series.

Interest Level: 3-6. Reading Level: 3.2. Further Search Topics: Baseball-Biography, Biography, Guidry, Ron.

GYMNASTICS

Krementz, Jill. A very young circus flyer. Knopf 1979, unp (112 pp).

One of a series of five oversized, abundantly photographed views of unusual children. Tato Farfan is part of the Flying Farfans of Ringling Brothers and Barnum and Bailey Circus. He lives in a railroad car on a circus train with his mother, father, and older brother. The whole family performs as trapeze artists and flyers for the circus. Told as if Tato were speaking, this is the story of a fairly normal boy who also happens to be a circus flyer. Practice sessions are difficult, costumes must be readied, and time must be spent helping each other, but there is also time for Tato to watch TV, play with the clowns, play soccer, and just have fun.

In addition to Tato's story, the reader is given a behind-the-scenes tour of the circus right up to and including the performance itself (color photos used for the performance). It is an exciting world that should appeal to almost anyone who has enjoyed the circus.

Interest Level: 2-6. Reading Level: 3.2. Further Search Topics: Circus, Acrobats and Acrobatics, Best Sellers, Talent, Group 2, Gymnastics.

Krementz, Jill. A very young gymnast. Knopf 1978, unp (128 pp).

This is Torrence York's story. It includes a team trip to Germany for competition. See notes for *A Very Young Dancer* for more information.

Interest Level: 2-6. Reading Level: 3.2. Further Search Topics: Gymnastics, Talent, Acrobats and Acrobatics, Group 2, Best Sellers.

HALLOWEEN-FICTION

Avi. No more magic. Pantheon 1975, 138 pp.

Avi has woven a mixture of mystery and magic to produce an excellent story. Chris' belief in magic is bolstered when his new bicycle disappears on Halloween night. Chris, his best friend Eddie, and a new friend, Muffin, eventually decide that strange Mr. Bullen, the junk dealer, has magical powers. In order to keep his powers a secret, Mr. Bullen had to steal back the magical bike he sold Chris. With plenty of intriguing complications along the way, the three children attempt to prove their theory correct but only prove themselves wrong. The age of the protagonists (fourth grade) is touched on so lightly and the plot is interesting enough that even sixth grade readers should find the book enjoyable.

Interest Level: 3-6. Reading Level: 4.2. Further Search Topics: Divorce and Separation-Fiction, Mystery and Detective Stories, Magic-Fiction, Halloween-Fiction, Witches-Fiction, Group 2, Read Aloud, Bicycles and Bicycling-Fiction.

HAMILL, DOROTHY

Burchard, Susan H. Sports star: Dorothy Hamill. HarBraceJ 1978, 63 pp.

Although written by Susan Burchard, this and most of the following listings are true to Marshall Burchard's *Sports Hero* format. For more explanation see *Sports Hero: Bill Walton*.

Dorothy Hamill was the darling of ice skating in 1976 and is now a top professional figure skater. This makes her rise to stardom sound romantic and glamorous. Skating jargon pushes the reading level from 3.1 to 3.2. Sports Star series.

Interest Level: 2-6. Reading Level: 3.2. Further Search Topics: Hamill, Dorothy, Ice Skating-Biography, Women-Biography, Biography, Group 2.

HAMSTERS-FICTION

Blegvad, Lenore. The great hamster hunt; illus by Erik Blegvad. HarBraceJ 1969, 32 pp.

Nicholas wanted a hamster; but, because his mother didn't like them, he couldn't have one. She did, however, agree to let Nicholas take care of his friend Tony's hamster for a week. It was a good and happy week for Nicholas until the evening before Tony was to return for his hamster. Nicholas accidentally broke the glass front of Harvey's cage and temporarily replaced it with cardboard. By morning Harvey had chewed through the cardbroad and was gone. Nicholas and his family searched all day but couldn't find Harvey. They finally bought another hamster and waited for Tony to arrive. As evening came Nicholas realized that hamsters are nocturnal and began to look for Harvey once more. This time Harvey was awake and active. The happy result was that Harvey was found and the new hampster became Nicholas' own pet. A simple, satisfying story even to fourth grade readers.

Interest Level: 1-4. Reading Level: 2.2. Further Search Topics: Pets-Fiction, Hamsters-Fiction, Group 2, Everyday Stories.

HANDICRAFTS

Simon, Seymour. The paper airplane book; illus by Byron Barton. Viking Pr 1971, 48 pp.

For the theory as well as the practice behind successful paper airplanes, this is the book. This is as much a book about the principles of flight as it is about how to make a paper airplane. The reader is introduced to thrust, drag, lift and gravity through explanation, examples, diagrams and experiments. The effects of vertical and horizontal stabilizers, elevators, rudders, flaps, and ailerons on both paper and real airplanes, is explained and illustrated. Instructions are given for building and modifying a basic plane as each new idea is introduced. The book ends with plans for four more sophisticated planes and encouragement to try further experiments. An excellent resource for the enthusiast. Print is small.

Interest Level: 3-6. Reading Level: 3.2. Further Search Topics: Airplanes, Handicrafts, Flight.

White, Laurence B., Jr. Science toys; illus by Marc Tolon Brown. A-W 1975, unp (46 pp).

This book presents 23 toys that a young child can easily make and learn from at the same time. A sundial, a drinking straw that flies, a balloon that rolls over, a ghost that sticks to the wall by itself, a water-go-round, and a paper cup that roars are a few examples of what is to be found here. The construction and use of each toy is explained and illustrated in enough detail to enable the child to work alone. And as in *Science Puzzles*, some of the toys will double as magic tricks (i.e. can you balance the rim of a paper plate on your nose?).

Interest Level: 1-3. Reading Level: 2.1. Further Search Topics: Handicrafts, Science, Magic, Toys, Games, Group 2, Puzzles.

HARRIS, FRANCO

Burchard, Susan H. Sports star: Franco Harris. HarBraceJ 1976, 64 pp.

Franco is the talented son of a black Army man and his Italian wife. He became a hero to thousands of Pittsburgh Steeler fans, who called themselves Franco's Italian Army. See *Sports Hero: Bill Walton*, by Marshall Burchard for series details. Sports Star series.

Interest Level: 2-6. Reading Level: 3.1. Further Search Topics: Biography, Group 2, Harris, Franco, Football-Biography, Blacks-Biography.

HAYES, ELVIN

Burchard, Susan H. Sports star: Elvin Hayes. HarBraceJ 1980, 63 pp.

Only this and three other Sue Burchard titles listed here differ much from the format described for the *Sports Hero* series (see *Sports Hero: Bill Walton*). It appears that in 1979 Ms. Burchard's books took on a slick new look. The covers began to sport color photos rather than black and white. The print size became noticeably smaller, although still of adequate size. More emphasis was placed on the players early life and background, in an apparent attempt to make him or her understandable as an individual rather than just as a star. A short career summary was added at the end of each book. All-in-all, the new, flashier approach should make the books more appealing than ever to older students.

Elvin Hayes came from a very poor family who lived in a town where blacks were badly treated. He went on to become one of the best college basketball players of his time. His deep religious convictions helped him through some rough times in his early years as a pro. Now he is happy, not just when he wins, but when he knows he has played his best. Sports Star series.

Interest Level: 3-6. Reading Level: 3.1. Further Search Topics: Biography, Hayes, Elvin, Basketball-Biography, Blacks-Biography, Religion-Biography.

HISTORICAL FICTION

Baker, Betty. The pig war; illus by Robert Lopshire. Har-Row 1969, 64 pp.

A brief, fictionalized account of an 1859 land squabble between the United States and Britain. The incident, which took place in what is now the state of Washington, became known as the Pig War.

Frightened British pigs destroyed the American farmers' gardens. When the farmers shot one of the pigs, the war began. Simply told and humorously illustrated. Should appeal to history or military fans. Early reader format.

Interest Level: 2-4. Reading Level: 2.1. Further Search Topics: United States-History-War-Fiction, Great Britain-History-Fiction, War-Fiction, Washington (state)-Fiction, Historical Fiction, Pigs-Fiction.

Benchley, Nathaniel. Sam the Minutemen; illus by Arnold Lobel. Har-Row 1969, 62 pp.

A good but limited book. It is a simple, personalized account of the beginning of the Revolutionary War as seen by the young son of a Minuteman. The book is a fairly exciting, uncomplicated and enjoyable story. Its limitations rest in its format (it's designed as a reader), the apparent young age of the main character, and the fact that it is told as a story. Its usefulness extends no further than grade three. An I Can Read History Book

Interest Level: 1-3. Reading Level: 2.2. Further Search Topics: United States-History-War-Fiction, Historical Fiction, War-Fiction, Group 2, Courage-Fiction.

Benchley, Nathaniel. Small Wolf; illus by Joan Sandin. Har-Row 1972, 64 pp.

A straight-forward telling of white man's purchase of Manhattan and the resulting displacement of the Indians. The text is simple. The tone is sympathetic to the plight of the Indians. The reader is neither lectured nor patronized, but the early-reader format will prevent using the book comfortably beyond fourth grade. An I Can Read History Book.

Interest Level: 1-4. Reading Level 2.2. Further Search Topics: Historical Fiction, New York City-Fiction, United States-History-Fiction, Indians of North America-Fiction, Group 2.

Bulla, Clyde Robert. A lion to guard us; illus by Michele Chessare. Har-Row 1981, 117 pp.

Bulla's writing isn't quite as successful here as elsewhere. This story of three London children's attempt to go to their father in Jamestown, Virginia, has danger, adventure, daring and promise. It also has too many characters to allow the reader to get to know any of them well. There are also too many very short chapters to allow plot development (23 chapters and 117 pages). The short sentences help to keep the reading level low, but a glossary would have been useful to fully explain the many unfamiliar terms.

Despite its problems, the book is still useful. The story is based on the 1609 voyage of the Sea Adventure. Blown far off course and badly damaged by a storm, the ship landed at Bermuda rather than Jamestown. The survivors were unable to sail again for over nine months. When they reached Jamestown, they found that few people had survived the very harsh year.

The three Freebold children are the focus of this story. When their mother died they left London to find their father in the New World. Having no money of their own, they were lucky to find a doctor friend to pay their ship's passage and to go with them. Halfway across the ocean, the doctor was swept overboard and drowned. From that time until they found their father barely alive, the children were on their own, even though they were still with the ship's passengers.

Although not the best of Bulla, this is still serviceable as a piece of historical fiction (hard to get children to read), or as a choice for the lover of survival and/or sea stories.

Interest Level: 3-5. Reading Level: 2.1. Further Search Topics: United States-History-Fiction, Historical Fiction, Courage-Fiction, Survival-Fiction, Shipwrecks-Fiction, Voyages and Travels-Fiction, Seafaring Life-Fiction.

Bulla, Clyde Robert. John Billington, friend of Squanto; illus by Peter Burchard. Har-Row 1956, 88 pp.

This historical novel about the Mayflower voyage and the Pilgrims' first year at Plymouth centers on young John Billington. John was considered the troublemaker of the children. His problems are woven around the events of the year, including the Pilgrims' first meetings with the Wampanoag Indians. It was finally John, however, who was responsible for bringing peace between the Pilgrims and the Wampanoag tribe who lived further down Cape Cod. The book is not as exciting or convincing as Bulla's books are generally. It also contains a few minor historical inaccuracies; yet it remains useful as both an introduction to American history and historical fiction.

Interest Level: 2-5. Reading Level: 2.1. Further Search Topics: Pilgrims-Fiction, Historical Fiction, United States-History-Fiction, Thanksgiving-Fiction, Troublemakers-Fiction, Indians of North America-Fiction.

Bulla, Clyde Robert. Riding the pony express; illus by Grace Paull. Har-Row 1948, 95 pp.

Although somewhat marred by the stereotyped speech of a young Indian boy, this is otherwise an exciting piece of historical fiction set in the 1860s. Dick was sent from New York City to join his father in St. Joseph, Missouri, only to find his father had moved to Nebraska to become a pony express rider. When Dick finally found his father, after a long stagecoach ride, he thought his father didn't want him. Dick stayed at the way station and helped with the chores because he didn't know what else to do. Then one day the house was burned, his father was shot, and the horses were almost stolen. There was no one around who could carry the mail, except Dick. Despite a wolf pack at his heels, Dick rode to the next way station. On his way home he realized his father really did want him and he no longer wanted to leave his father. Chapters are short with separate episodes that tie them together. A few simple songs appear between the chapters.

Interest Level: 2-5. Reading Level: 2.1. Further Search Topics: Horses-Fiction, West-Fiction, United States-History-Fiction, Historical Fiction, Voyages and Travels-Fiction, Courage-Fiction, Frontier and Pioneer Life-Fiction.

Bulla, Clyde Robert. Viking adventure; illus by Douglas Gorsline. T Y Crowell 1963, 117 pp.

An exciting story of a young Norwegian boy named Sigurd. Sigurd realized his dream when he finally set sail on a Viking ship in search of Wineland (Vinland). Leif Eriksson had told of his North American findings over 100 years earlier. Sigurd and his father's friend Grom, the captain of the ship, were sure they could find that land again. Their determination finally brought Grom's death at the hands of the ship's owner, Sigurd's near death, and the destruction of the ship.

This book, too, is true to Bulla's style of short chapters, short sentences, much action and high appeal. Although it is a little higher reading level than many of Bulla's others, it is still a good choice. Recently out of print, but worth a search.

Interest Level: 2-6. Reading Level: 3.1. Further Search Topics: Norway-Fiction, Historical Fiction, Seafaring Life-Fiction, Voyages and Travels-Fiction, Shipwrecks-Fiction, Explorers-Fiction, Vikings-Fiction, Courage-Fiction, Best Sellers, Group 2.

Coerr, Eleanor. Sadako and the thousand paper cranes; illus by Ronand Himler. Putnam 1977, 64 pp.

This is a beautiful and very sad story of a young girl who was only two years old when the atomic bomb was dropped on Hiroshima. Ten years later she contracted leukemia and died a slow, painful death. A fast and enthusiastic runner, she had been full of life and energy before her illness. Soon after she became sick Sadako's best friend folded a paper crane for her and reminded her of an old story: If someone folded 1000 paper cranes, the gods would give that person good health again. Sadako was able to fold only 644 before she died. After her death her classmates made 356 more in order that she could be buried with all 1000 paper cranes. About three years later, a statue, erected in Peace Park in Hiroshima, was dedicated to Sadako and to a hope for world peace.

Because of the theme and its straight-forward handling, this book needs a fairly mature reader.

Interest Level: 4-6. Reading Level: 3.1. Further Search Topics: Japan-Fiction, Historical Fiction, World War II-Fiction, Death-Fiction, Illness-Fiction, War-Fiction, Running-Fiction, Origami-Fiction, Read Aloud.

Lewis, Thomas P. Hill of fire; illus by Joan Sandin. Har-Row 1971, 63 pp.

A personalized account of the volcano that suddenly erupted in the middle of a farmer's field in Mexico on February 20, 1943. Because the account is written as a story and because of its easy-reader format, the book is most useful only through third grade. An I-Can-Read-History-Book.

Interest Level: 1-3. Reading Level: 2.2. Further Search Topics: Volcanoes, Group 2, Mexico, Disasters, Historical Fiction.

HOCKEY

Kalb, Jonah. The easy hockey book; illus by Bill Morrison. HM 1977, 64 pp.

This book is exactly what the title indicates; an easy-read introduction to the sport of hockey. It does not teach one how to skate, but in a logical non-sexist manner it does carefully and thoroughly teach the rules, techniques, and skills of hockey. Common mistakes are anticipated in each section. Chapter summaries make an already serviceable text even more useful. It could have been even better with an index.

Interest Level: 2-6. Reading Level: 2.2. Further Search Topics: Hockey.

HOCKEY-FICTION

Christopher, Matt. Face-off; illus by Harvey Kidder. Little 1972, 131 pp.

Christopher sticks strictly to the sports story formula here. The characters seem to have no time or thoughts for anything but sports. They epitomize the macho image, and once their problems with sports are solved everything in life seems to fall into place. But, for the young sports enthusiast who doesn't really like to read, this formula of much sports action and very little else is successful.

Scott had never played hockey but he was an extremely fast skater. When Del and Skinny asked him to join their hockey team and to be one of the Three Icekateers, Scott was thrilled. But Scott's performance was less than inspiring and Del's patience with his failures was short. The two almost came to blows when Scott discovered that he was puck-shy and would duck every time someone took a shot near him. Their coach's advice to both of them helped clear up Scott's problem and Del's impatience. All ends happily as Scott played well and he and Del became friends once more.

Interest Level: 3-6. Reading Level: 3.1. Further Search Topics: Hockey-Fiction, Ice Skating-Fiction, Courage-Fiction, Friendship-Fiction.

HOLIDAYS-FICTION

Chaikin, Miriam. Finders weepers; illus Richard Egielski. Har-Row 1980, 120 pp.

The children most likely to read this are those who have enjoyed *I Should Worry, I Should Care*. On her way home from school one day, Molly found a ring. Rather than try to find its owner, she made up excuses to keep the ring. Molly knew it was a sin to keep something that belonged to someone else, she even knew who *did* own the ring. When she finally decided to return it, the ring had become stuck on Molly's finger and wouldn't come off. With Yom Kippur just a few days away, Molly became convinced that all the unpleasant things happening around her were punishments for her sin. She finally had to have the ring cut off her finger. After she prayed for forgiveness life immediately went back to normal.

There's enough guilt here to satisfy even the most demanding reader. There is also the same solid family group that appeared in the first book. But this book probably lacks enough excitement and/or empathy to interest a reader new to Molly and her family. Print is dark but spacing between lines could have been wider.

Interest Level: 3-5. Reading Level: 3.1. Further Search Topics: Family-Fiction, Jews-Fiction, Honesty-Fiction, Holidays-Fiction, Religion-Fiction.

Cohen, Barbara. The carp in the bathtub; illus by Joan Halpern. Lothrop 1972, 48 pp.

Leah and Harry couldn't face the prospect of seeing Joe, their pet carp, made into gefilte fish, even for such a special occasion as the Seder on the first night of Passover. The large, friendly carp had lived in the family's bathtub for over a week. It even swam right over to Leah and Harry to be fed everytime they went into the bathroom. At a time when most children in New York didn't have pets, Joe was as close to being a pet as possible. So, Leah and Harry hid Joe in a neighbor's apartment until their father discovered what they had done. When Joe's destiny was fulfilled, the children had to face a difficult fact of life. A week later, however, their despair became delight, when their father brought home a pet cat.

A short, warm and satisfying story.

Interest Level: 2-5. Reading Level: 3.1. Further Search Topics: Group 2, Jews-Fiction, Religion-Fiction, Pets-Fiction, Passover-Fiction, Family-Fiction, Holidays-Fiction, Read Aloud, Brothers and Sisters-Fiction.

Pinkwater, Daniel Manus. The Hoboken chicken emergency. P-H 1977, 83 pp.

Arthur's mother sent him out with $16 to buy a Thanksgiving turkey. He returned with a live 266 pound chicken on a leash. It seemed that their turkey reservation had been lost at the meat market and, because it was Thanksgiving morning, there were no other turkeys available. Arthur searched everywhere but found nothing, until a strange old professor tricked him into buying the chicken. No one could bear to kill and eat such a large and friendly chicken, so Arthur

and his family named it Henrietta and kept it as a pet. Henrietta was a difficult pet to keep hidden from the neighbors When the neighbors, and later the city, saw Henrietta running loose there was general hysteria. But all ended well when Henrietta and the city calmed down and Henrietta became a kind of neighborhood mascot.

A purely absurd plot but presented with enough energy and humor that most readers thoroughly enjoy the book. Some brief introduction may be necessary to get readers beyond the first few pages.

Interest Level: 3-6. Reading Level: 2.2. Further Search Topics: Humorous Fiction, Chickens-Fiction, Pets-Fiction, Thanksgiving-Fiction, Holidays-Fiction, Read Aloud, Best Sellers.

Robinson, Barbara. The best Christmas pageant ever; illus by Judith Gwyn Brown. Har-Row 1972, 80 pp.

A truly delightful story of what happens when the meanest kids in town (they are all in one family) take over all the lead roles in the Sunday school Christmas pageant. The Herdmans (all six of them), having heard that the church was giving away free food, showed up to take some. While they were there, they heard about the Christmas pageant and decided it presented them with another perfect opportunity for food and mischief. With a little behind-the-scenes arm-twisting (literally), they managed to dissuade everyone else from showing interest in the major roles. Theirs was a completely original interpretation of the Christmas story that left nothing and no one around them untouched.

That the book's reading level will prove too high for many people is unfortunate. The story is well worth the struggle. A wonderful choice for reading aloud.

Interest Level: 3-6. Reading Level: 5.1 Further Search Topics: Christmas-Fiction, Bullies-Fiction, Troublemakers-Fiction, Humorous Fiction, Religion-Fiction, Group 2, Read Aloud, Acting-Fiction, Holidays-Fiction.

Wagner, Jane. J.T; photos by Gordon Parks, Jr. Van Nostrand 1969, 64 pp.

This is a sentimental story that rarely fails to elicit a sympathetic response from young readers. J.T. is a poor black boy who saw a portable radio almost begging to be stolen and stole it. Two of the neighborhood bullies, Boomer and Claymore, saw J.T. take the radio. Though they threatened him, even poured soap in his eyes in the school bathrooms, J.T. wouldn't give them the radio as they demanded.

About the same time J.T. found a scrawny, scared little cat with only one eye. Because his mother wouldn't let him take the cat home, J.T. built it a warm but ramshackle little house in an abandoned building. He fed it by charging tuna to his mother's grocery store account without her knowledge. Bones became the only thing in J.T.'s life that he had cared about since his father had walked out.

When Boomer and Claymore found out about Bones, they taunted J.T. by throwing the cat back and forth between them until the frightened cat escaped, darted out into the street and was hit by a car. J.T.'s heart broke as he looked at Bones, but he spoke to no one to tell them of his sadness. Only time, his mother's and grandmother's love and a small kitten from Mr. Rosen, the grocer, helped him recover. On the morning that he decided to accept the kitten, J.T. returned the stolen radio, faced Boomer and Claymore without fear, and asked Mr. Rosen for a job in order to pay for cat food.

The book is oversized and illustrated with photographs from the television movie version. It is not only an excellent story to read aloud but one that will prompt listeners to want to finish it on their own or to reread it. It is now available only in paperback from Dell.

Interest Level: 3-6. Reading Level: 3.1. Further Search Topics: Read Aloud, Courage-Fiction, Best Sellers, Cats-Fiction, Single Parent Family-Fiction, Bullies-Fiction, Blacks-Fiction, Poverty-Fiction, City Life-Fiction, Christmas Stories, Crime-Fiction, Pets-Fiction, Holidays-Fiction.

HONESTY-FICTION

Byars, Betsy. The Cybil war; illus by Gail Owens. Viking Pr. 1981, 126 pp.

Simon and Tony both had a crush on Cybil, but according to Tony, Cybil liked Tony better than she liked Simon. Simon was unhappily willing to accept Tony's word even though he knew Tony was a chronic liar. After all, Cybil had been the one to talk their teacher out of giving the lead in the class play about nutrition to Simon. Consequently Simon was being forced to impersonate a jar of peanut butter. In an elaborate attempt to win Cybil's affection Tony began telling Cybil lies about Simon and then set up a double date with Cybil and Harriet. On their walk home, Simon learned from Harriet that Cybil had only agreed to the date because Simon was going along. Happy at last, Simon realized he wanted no more lies and tricks; that he wanted to be truthful with Cybil and with himself. In the name of truth, he was even willing to accept the fact that his father, who had deserted the family, would not be returning.

A good story with just enough humor and romance to make it widely appealing as either a shared book (read aloud) or a personal pick. Print is fairly small.

Interest Level: 5-6. Reading Level: 4.2. Further Search Topics: Humorous Fiction, Love-Fiction, School Stories, Honesty-Fiction, Friendship-Fiction, Single Parent Family-Fiction, Read Aloud, Everyday Stories, Adolescence-Fiction.

Chaikin, Miriam. Finders weepers; illus Richard Egielski. Har-Row 1980, 120 pp.

The children most likely to read this are those who have enjoyed *I Should Worry, I Should Care*. On her way home from school one day, Molly found a ring. Rather than try to find its owner, she made up excuses to keep the ring. Molly knew it was a sin to keep something that belonged to someone else, she even knew who *did* own the ring. When she finally decided to return it, the ring had become stuck on Molly's finger and wouldn't come off. With Yom Kippur just a few days away, Molly became convinced that all the unpleasant things happening around her were punishments for her sin. She finally had to have the ring cut off her finger. After she prayed for forgiveness life immediately went back to normal.

There's enough guilt here to satisfy even the most demanding reader. There is also the same solid family group that appeared in the first book. But this book probably lacks enough excitement and/or empathy to interest a reader new to Molly and her family. Print is dark but spacing between lines could have been wider.

Interest Level: 3-5. Reading Level: 3.1. Further Search Topics: Family-Fiction, Jews-Fiction, Honesty-Fiction, Holidays-Fiction, Religion-Fiction.

Levy, Elizabeth. Lizzie lies a lot; illus by John Wallner. Delacorte 1976, 102 pp.

Almost any child can identify with Lizzie. She had found that it was sometimes easier to lie than to tell the truth. Her problem was that she had lost control. It seemed as if almost everything she said was a lie. She told so many lies it became difficult to keep track of them all. Lizzie wasn't even really sure why she lied so much. She knew that she sometimes lied because she thought people would be more apt to like her. Other times she lied to get herself out of trouble or to cover up her feelings when she was hurt or angry. But that didn't explain why she lied all the time. Maybe, as her grandmother said, she was a born liar.

It wasn't until Lizzie got herself caught in the middle of so many lies that she lost her only friend, that she could admit her problem to herself and to her family. After their initial shock had passed, everyone agreed to help Lizzie stop lying. Lizzie took the next step by admitting her lies to her friend Sue.

Levy has brought such an appropriately light touch to a fairly common problem that many children find this story enjoyable. Overlook the book's faults (Lizzie's grandmother is overdrawn and her mother's guilt feelings are unsupported by the story) for the fun and the message young readers get from it.

Interest Level: 3-5. Reading Level: 4.2. Further Search Topics: Honesty-Fiction, Group 2, Friendship-Fiction, Best Sellers, Everyday Stories, Family Problems-Fiction, Grandparents-Fiction, Humorous Fiction.

Shura, Mary Francis. The Barkley Street six-pack: illus by Gene Sparkman. Dodd 1979, 159 pp.

Jane's best friend Natalie was everything Jane wanted to be. She was self-assured, pretty, vibrant, and even possessed magical talents. Jane didn't realize at first, and she later resisted seeing, that Natalie ran Jane's life and cleverly made sure that Jane had no other friends. Natalie's move left Jane with no friends among those people she had once enjoyed. Little by little, with the help of a stray dog and the new boy on the block, Jane bagan to see how destructive Natalie had been. She finally realized that a true friendship is one in which neither party tries to control the other.

With its enticements of ESP, magic, stray dogs, and problems with peers, this is a very appealing book to many young readers. As a bonus it is a thoughtful, sympathetic, fairly well-written story.

Interest Level: 4-6. Reading Level: 4.2. Further Search Topics: Gangs-Fiction, Pets-Fiction, Dogs-Fiction, Friendship-Fiction, Honesty-Fiction, Courage-Fiction, Loneliness-Fiction, Extra Sensory Perception-Fiction, Everyday Stories.

HOPI INDIANS

Baylor, Byrd. And it is still that way: legends told by Arizona Indian children. Scribner 1976, 85 pp.

Byrd Baylor has collected and written notes for forty-one short American Indian legends from seven Arizona tribes whose school children were asked to write down or illustrate their favorite legend. The result is a collection that reflects the concerns, the history, religion, humor and pride of the children and their ancestors. This excellent collection is not only interesting reading, but it also fits well into social studies and language arts units.

Interest Level: 2-6. Reading Level: 3.1. Further Search Topics: Legends, Arizona-Fiction, Navajo Indians, Hopi Indians, Papago Indians, Pima Indians, Apache Indians, Quechan Indians, Cocopah Indians, Indians of North America-Legends, Mythology, Group 2.

HORROR-FICTION

Aylesworth, Thomas G. Movie monsters. Lippincott 1975, 79 pp.

If you are looking for an example of fine writing, you won't find it here. What you will find is a collection of monster movie photographs and facts. This is a wealth of trivia about eleven famous monsters (including King Kong, Godzilla, the Fly, Frankenstein's monster, the Mummy, Dracula, Wolf Man and others), their films, sequels, historic backgrounds, identifying characteristics, and more. There is an extensive index, a list of monster movies and their credits, and even brief information about famous monster actors. The book is not great literature, but it is interesting and fun.

Interest Level: 1-6. Reading Level 3.1. Further Search Topics: Acting, Motion Pictures, Monsters, Horror-Fiction, Group 2, Best Sellers.

Platt, Kin. Dracula, go home; illus by Frank Mayo. Watts 1979, 87 pp.

From the chapter numbers that drip blood, and the humorously grotesque illustrations, to the short sentences and chapters, this is a book designed and almost guaranteed to appeal to the reluctant reader. A sense of immediacy and involvement is created by the first person narration. Tension is created on the opening page when Larry sees a man in the cemetery who looked exactly like Dracula. When that man registered at the hotel where Larry was working, Larry decided to find out more about him. It began to look as if Mr. A. R. Claude (the letters spell Dracula) was not only a vampire, but a thief and a murderer as well. The trouble was that Larry couldn't prove anything. Even when he found the stolen jewels for which Mr. Claude had been searching, Larry still couldn't convince anyone of Claude's true identify. No one ever did believe Larry, thus Claude went free.

The author uses a light touch to treat an eerie subject. His inconclusive ending may disappoint some, but should delight many. Beware of the variability of the reading level however; it swings from high first grade to low third grade.

Interest Level: 3-6. Reading Level: 2.2. Further Search Topics: Monsters-Fiction, Horror-Fiction, Mystery and Detective Stories, Best Sellers, Murder-Fiction, Crime-Fiction, Transformations-Fiction.

Sleator, William. Into the dream; illus by Ruth Sanderson. Dutton 1979, 137 pp.

Paul and Francine each started having what, at first, seemed like nightmares. As the dreams became more detailed and forboding, they discovered that they were sharing the same nightmare. They dreamed of a four-year-old boy, swirling lights, and a large dog. After awhile they figured out that the dog was trying to save the little boy from some unknown danger. As the pieces of the puzzle began to increase in number, Paul and Francine decided that the dream was in some way connected to a night over four years earlier when they had both been staying at the same motel. They, a pregnant woman, and a pregnant dog had all been affected by the telepathic power given off by a spaceship. The progeny of the woman and the dog had been given extraordinary mental powers; powers that a secret government agency wanted to mold and then put to their own use. The danger Paul and Francine felt came from two government agents sent to take the young boy Noah from his mother. Their attempt ended in a bizarre scene at an amusement park, where Noah levitated a broken ferris wheel chair to safety. By thus exposing his talent in public, Noah unconsciously insured against its secret and unsupervised use by the government.

A terrifying and suspense-filled psychological thriller whose main problems are a slightly overdrawn ending and a variable reading level. Reading level drops as low as 2.1 and climbs occasionally to 4.1.

Interest Level: 5-6. Reading Level: 3.2. Further Search Topics: Best Sellers, Supernatural-Fiction, Occult-Fiction, Flying Saucers-Fiction, Nonverbal Communication-Fiction, Dreams-Fiction, Survival-Fiction, Extra Sensory Perception-Fiction, Horror-Fiction.

Young, Carol Beach. Remember me when I am dead. Elsevier-Nelson 1980, 94 pp.

This is a short but taut story about the effect of their mother's death upon two young girls. For a long time Jenny, the younger and more vivacious of the sisters, refused to believe her mother had really died. Sara, quiet and serious, mourned and missed her mother, but eventually accepted her mother's sudden death as a fact. Jenny's continuing denial prompted her father and stepmother to talk of sending her away to a school where memories wouldn't be so vivid. That talk inspired Sara to develop a devious and calculated plan to insure that Jenny would indeed be sent away. All her life Sara had been given less attention than Jenny. With Jenny gone, Sara would finally have her father and stepmother's love and attention all to herself. With a Hitchcock-like twist Sara's plan proved too successful. Jenny was sent away to school, but because she didn't want to go alone and because her parents could deny Jenny nothing, Sara was to go too.

This suspenseful psychological thriller is almost guaranteed success with older readers.

Interest Level: 5-6. Reading Level: 4.2. Further Search Topics: Mystery and Detective Stories, Brothers and Sisters-Fiction, Death-Fiction, Horror-Fiction, Best Sellers, Jealousy-Fiction.

HORSES

Krementz, Jill. A very young rider. Knopf 1977, unp (128 pp).

Vivi Malloy is the youngest rider in a family of several other riders. Her greatest dream is to make the Olympic equestrian team. She is progressing towards her goal with daily workouts and about fifteen major horse shows each year. See *A Very Young Dancer* for more extensive notes.

Interest Level: 2-6. Reading Level: 3.2. Further Search Topics: Horses, Riding, Talent, Group 2.

HORSES-FICTION

Anderson, C. S. The blind Connemara. Macmillan 1971, 80 pp.

Rhonda, not wealthy enough to own a horse of her own, was given a beautiful Connemara pony. Unfortunately, it had begun to go blind. A blind pony is usually put away, but Rhonda loved this pony too much to let that happen. Against all odds, Rhonda not only taught Pony to trot, canter, and even jump with confidence, but went on to win a ribbon at an important horse show. Though sentimental and predictable, this book is an almost insured success with lovers of horses and champions of the underdog. Be alert to the occasional descriptive passage that is both longer and more difficult than the rest of the text.

Interest Level: 4-6. Reading Level: 3.2. Further Search Topics: Vision-Fiction, Physically Handicapped-Fiction, Horses-Fiction.

Bulla, Clyde Robert. Dexter; illus by Glo Coalson. Har-Row 1973, 69 pp.

This is not as simple a story as it first appears. Dave, 12 years old and lonely, had hoped his new neighbors would be friends. But, the Arvin family kept very much to themselves until Dave accidentally discovered Alex, the Arvin's son, doing tricks on a trapeze in the barn. Because Dave kept the secret and shared Alex's love for Dexter, his circus pony, the boys soon became friends. Then in one horrible night, the Arvins were forced to leave the town and Dexter was so badly hurt he was believed to be dead. A week later Dave found Dexter alive, but crippled for life and so frightened that no one could get near him. The horse surprised everyone and managed to live through a very harsh winter as well as the townspeople's determination to kill him. When Alex and his father returned, almost a year later, they found Dexter and took the old and feeble horse back to a ranch with them. The story is told with sympathy, with an understanding of how it feels to be lonely, and with tension and suspense. It's appeal should last from third through sixth grade. Print size is smaller than Bulla's usual.

Interest Level: 3-6. Reading Level: 3.1. Further Search Topics: Survival-Fiction, Acrobats and Acrobatics-Fiction, Horses-Fiction, Read Aloud, Circus-Fiction, Loneliness-Fiction, Friendship-Fiction.

Bulla, Clyde Robert. Riding the pony express; illus by Grace Paull. Har-Row 1948, 95 pp.

Although somewhat marred by the stereotyped speech of a young Indian boy, this is otherwise an exciting piece of historical fiction set in the 1860s. Dick was sent from New York City to join his father in St. Joseph, Missouri, only to find his father had moved to Nebraska to become a pony express rider. When Dick finally found his father, after a long stagecoach ride, he thought his father didn't want him. Dick stayed at the way station and helped with the chores because he didn't know what else to do. Then one day the house was burned, his father was shot, and the horses were almost stolen. There was no one around who could carry the mail, except Dick. Despite a wolf pack at his heels, Dick rode to the next way station. On his way home he realized his father really did want him and he no longer wanted to leave his father. Chapters are short with separate episodes that tie them together. A few simple songs appear between the chapters.

Interest Level: 2-5. Reading Level: 2.1. Further Search Topics: Horses-Fiction, West-Fiction, United States-History-Fiction, Historical Fiction, Voyages and Travels-Fiction, Courage-Fiction, Frontier and Pioneer Life-Fiction.

Christopher, Matt. Devil pony; illus by Lorence Bjorkland. Little 1977, 103 pp.

This book is a bit of a change from the usual Matt Christopher story line. There is no sports interest here; instead there is a good suspense story about a boy, his cousin and a horse. Stu had watched the black Morgan named Midnight being born and had fallen in love with him. A year later he returned to his aunt and uncle's ranch to claim the horse, as he had been promised he could, but strange things began to happen around him. His cousin Wilbur warned him that he had probably annoyed the ranch poltergeist by deciding to take Midnight away. The bizarre occurrences escalated until Stu was almost tempted to leave Midnight at the ranch. Then Stu discovered Wilbur had been orchestrating everything that had happened because he had wanted to keep the horse

himself. Although Stu decided to take Midnight home as he had planned, their new honesty led Stu to believe that he and Wilbur could be friends after all. A surprisingly good story with strong reader appeal.

Interest Level: 3-6. Reading Level: 3.1. Further Search Topics: Horses-Fiction, Supernatural-Fiction, Ghosts-Fiction, Jealousy-Fiction, Relatives-Fiction.

Hall, Lynn. The mystery of Pony Hollow; illus by Ruth Sanderson. Garrard 1978, 64 pp.

Sarah investigated strange voices only to find the skeleton of a horse that had died 40 years earlier. She was determined to find out what it was that had killed the horse and why its ghost was uneasy.

The mystery element isn't as strong here as most mystery fans would like, but the book will not disappoint many true horse story enthusiasts.

Interest Level: 3-5. Reading Level: 3.2. Further Search Topics: Horses-Fiction, Ghosts-Fiction, Mystery and Detective Stories.

HOUSING PROJECTS-FICTION

Berends, Polly Berrien. The case of the elevator duck; illus by James K. Washburn. Random 1973, 54 pp.

Although it would be stretching the meaning of the word to call this a mystery, it is a story of an 11-year-old detective. Albert tells his own story in a clipped style that resembles adult detective novels. One morning Albert found a duck abandoned in the apartment house elevator. He was determined to find the owner of the duck and return it. He had to be very careful as he searched because pets were absolutely forbidden in the housing projects. Anyone who saw him with the duck might report him. Albert and his parents had waited too long to get into the projects to be kicked out because of a duck. When Albert finally found the duck's owner (a young, sad child named Julio), Julio's sister forced Albert to take the duck back. Still angry at Julio's sister, Albert took the duck to the project's day care center, where the teacher agreed to formally adopt the duck. Albert stayed at the center long enough to see Julio's happy surprise when he arrived and found the duck. Its appealing characters, the tension created by the writing style, and the book's humor make this a delightful story.

Interest Level: 2-5. Reading Level 2.2. Further Search Topics: Humorous Fiction, City Life-Fiction, Housing Projects-Fiction, Detectives-Fiction, Pets-Fiction, Ducks-Fiction, Read Aloud.

HUMOROUS FICTION

Angell, Judie. Dear Lola; or how to build your own family. Bradbury 1980, 166 pp.

Arthur (age 18), James (13), Annie and Al-Willie (twins, age 10), Edmund (9), and Ben (5) wanted to run away from the orphanage and find a place where they could be a real family. After waiting months, their chance arrived one night. They escaped in a van and began living on the road. It was weeks before they found a house in which they thought they could live. They didn't want trouble with local authorities, so most of the children enrolled in school and pretended to be living with their widowed grandfather. Only James (who never left his room) and Arthur stayed home. Arthur was the anonymous author of a nationally syndicated newspaper advice column. It was with the income from his "Dear Lola" column that Arthur was able to support the "family." When the townspeople eventually began to wonder about the "strange" behavior of the children, they investigated and found no adult in charge of the household. Arthur went to court to be appointed the childrens' guardian, but the judge ruled against him. Rather than be sent to foster homes again, Arthur and the children raced from the courtroom. The book ends as the family is once more together and on their own. An unusual cast of characters in a surprisingly warm and humorous book.

Interest Level: 4-6. Reading Level 3.1. Further Search Topics: Loners-Fiction, Runaways-Fiction, Orphans-Fiction, Survival-Fiction, Family Problems-Fiction, Family-Fiction, Read Aloud, Foster Homes-Fiction, Individualists-Fiction, Humorous Fiction.

Arkhurst, Joyce. The adventures of Spider; West African folktales; illus by Jerry Pinkney. Little 1964, 58 pp.

A delightful collection of six West African folktales about Spider. Spider is mischievous, greedy, lazy and clever. He loves to eat and he hates to work. Four of the stories tell of Spider's ill-fated attempts to get food without having to work for it ("How Spider Got a Thin Waist," "How Spider Got a Bald Head," "How Spider Helped a Fisherman," and "Why Spiders Live in Dark Corners"). One story tells of his greed ("How the World Got Wisdom"), and only one story is complimentary ("Why Spider Lives in Ceilings"). All are short, gentle, humorous, and adapt well to dramatization or retelling.

Interest Level: 2-6. Reading Level 3.1. Further Search Topics: Humorous Fiction, Spiders-Fiction, Folklore, Tricksters-Fiction, Africa-Folklore, Group 2, Read Aloud, Creation-Fiction, Drama.

Berends, Polly Berrien. The case of the elevator duck; illus by James K. Washburn. Random 1973, 54 pp.

Although it would be stretching the meaning of the word to call this a mystery, it is a story of an 11-year-old detective. Albert tells his own story in a clipped style that resembles adult detective novels. One morning Albert found a duck abandoned in the apartment house elevator. He was determined to find the owner of the duck and return it. He had to be very careful as he searched because pets were absolutely forbidden in the housing projects. Anyone who saw him with the duck might report him. Albert and his parents had waited too long to get into the projects to be kicked out because of a duck. When Albert finally found the duck's owner (a young, sad child named Julio), Julio's sister forced Albert to take the duck back. Still angry at Julio's sister, Albert took the duck to the project's day care center, where the teacher agreed to formally adopt the duck. Albert stayed at the center long enough to see Julio's happy surprise when he arrived and found the duck. Its appealing characters, the tension created by the writing style, and the book's humor make this a delightful story.

Interest Level: 2-5. Reading Level 2.2. Further Search Topics: Humorous Fiction, City Life-Fiction, Housing Projects-Fiction, Detectives-Fiction, Pets-Fiction, Ducks-Fiction, Read Aloud.

Berenstain, Stan. The bike lesson. Beginner 1964, 61 pp.

This story of a bumbling father trying to teach his eager son how to ride a bike is pure silliness. Much of the action is shown in the humorous illustrations. The rhymed text adds dialogue and description. Good fun.

Interest Level: K-3. Reading Level: 1.2. Further Search Topics: Humorous Fiction, Bicycles and Bicycling-Fiction, Stories in Rhyme, Group 2.

Berenstain, Stan. Bears in the night. Random 1971, 30 pp.

This is for the very beginning reader. Only 24 words plus illustrations are used to tell the story of a bedtime adventure for seven small bears. Bravely they sneak out of the house, through the woods, and up Spook Hill. Frightened by an owl's hoot, they run back over the same route until they are safely back in bed again.

Interest Level: K-2. Reading Level: 1.1. Further Search Topics: Bears-Fiction, Group 2, Courage-Fiction, Humorous Fiction.

Blume, Judy. Are you there God? It's me, Margaret. Bradbury 1970, 149 pp.

Sixth grade was a year of growth for Margaret and her friends. They all wondered when they would start growing breasts and when they would begin menstruating. Each was kissed for the first time. It was also a year in which Margaret tried to decide whether to be Jewish or Christian and ended up neither. She simply remained friends with God, just as she was when the year began. The book is a reassuring, very open, and humorous treatment of the pains and promise of maturation. It is exceptionally popular with older elementary school readers, so the book's slightly small print and narrow lines should not impede an interested reader's progress.

Interest Level: 4-6. Reading Level: 3.2. Further Search Topics: School Stories, Family-Fiction, Children-Growth-Fiction, Religion-Fiction, Humorous Fiction, Love-Fiction, Best Sellers, Grandparents-Fiction, Everyday Stories.

Blume, Judy. Tales of a fourth grade nothing; illus by Roy Doty. Dutton 1972, 120 pp.

Another humorous Blume book that can be counted on to appeal to third and fourth grade readers. If fifth and sixth graders can ignore the title's reference to fourth grade, they too will love it. The story is an exaggeration of a common theme—an older child whose life is in continual turmoil because of a somewhat spoiled younger sibling. Peter's problems with three-year-old Fudge become worse with each chapter until the final disaster when Fudge swallows Peter's pet turtle. Each approximately 15-page chapter is a complete, very funny episode.

Interest Level: 3-6. Reading Level 3.1. Further Search Topics: Humorous Fiction, Turtles-Fiction, Brothers and Sisters-Fiction, Pets-Fiction, Family-Fiction, Read Aloud, Best Sellers, Everyday Stories, Troublemakers-Fiction.

Blume, Judy. Otherwise known as Sheila the great. Dutton 1972, 128 pp.

Sheila first appears in *Tales of a Fourth Grade Nothing* as Peter Thatcher's neighbor. Sheila was a bundle of fears. She was afraid of dogs, thunderstorms, spiders, horses, putting her face in water, and strange noises at night. The summer she and her family rented a house in Tarrytown, New York, she confronted each one of her fears, even mastered one (putting her face in the water) and learned how to swim. That gave her the self-confidence to face a dog without running away. Sheila's progress was aided by her friend Mouse's steadfast belief that a person should always be honest about herself. Sheila's problems are treated realistically and with dignity, yet humorously. Reading level varies greatly from 1.2 - 4.1, therefore, the book is *most* suitable to grades four through six.

Interest Level: 3-6. Reading Level: 3.1. Further Search Topics: Humorous Fiction, Courage-Fiction, Camp-Fiction, Group 2, Vacation-Fiction,

Swimming-Fiction, Brothers and Sisters-Fiction, Friendship-Fiction, Everyday Stories.

Blume, Judy. Superfudge. Dutton 1980, 166 pp.
On Fudge's first day in school his older brother Peter had to rescue him from the top of the kindergarten storage cabinets. Later in the school year Fudge's eagerness to join a school guest speaker on stage almost spelled disaster. Then when Fudge unexpectedly disappeared one day everyone, including Peter, thought he had drowned. In addition to Peter's problems with Fudge, Peter had to cope with a baby sister, moving to Princeton, New Jersey, a new job for his mother, and his father's attempts to write a book. Although the book is a sequel and is best enjoyed as such, it can be read alone. It is not as amusing or well-written as it's predecessor, *Tales of a Fourth Grade Nothing*, but will still be popular with young readers.
Interest Level: 3-6. Reading Level 3.1. Further Search Topics: Brothers and Sisters-Fiction, Moving, Household-Fiction, Infants-Fiction, Working Parents-Fiction, School Stories, Family-Fiction, Best Sellers, Humorous Fiction, Everyday Stories.

Blume, Judy. Freckle juice; illus by Sonia O. Lisker. Four Winds 1971, 40 pp.
A very funny story that should appeal to almost everyone. Andrew wanted freckles so that the dirt on his skin wouldn't show as much and he wouldn't have to wash as often. As luck would have it, Sharon, the most obnoxious girl in class, had a freckle juice recipe that she was willing to sell for 50 cents. Even after drinking the brew of grape juice, vinegar, mustard, olive oil, and more, Andrew didn't see any freckles, but, he certainly was sick. Although the protagonists are younger, this book will hold even a fifth grade reader's interest.
Interest Level: 2-5. Reading Level 3.1. Further Search Topics: Humorous Fiction, Group 2, Read Aloud, Everyday Stories, Beauty-Fiction, School Stories, Magic-Fiction, Best Sellers.

Bonham, Frank. The mystery of the fat cat; illus by Alvin Smith. Dutton 1968, 160 pp.
Although noticeably dated at times, this is still an exciting story of an inner city neighborhood. Buddy, Little Pie, Rich, and Cool were among the many who used the local Boys' Club as their hangout. It was a place to stay out of trouble and off the streets, but it was also a haven for rats. The rats were big and brazen; so brazen that one attacked Buddy in the swimming pool. The club needed a new building desperately. The money was there; they just weren't able to use it. Fifteen years earlier an eccentric old woman willed the Boys' Club over $600,000, but stated that the money was first to be used to support her cat until it died. A caretaker, a lawyer, and a veterinarian all benefited as long as the cat lived. Buddy and his friends took on the job of discovering if the cat really was alive or if the Boys' Club was being cheated out of half a million dollars. It was a job that nearly killed them before they set things right. Plenty of action, some violence, a cast of street-smart characters, realistic trouble with the police, as well as a slight mystery almost insure the book's success with older readers. Moderate sized print. Line spacing somewhat narrow.
Interest Level: 6+. Reading Level: 5.1. Further Search Topics: Humorous Fiction, Cats-Fiction, Gangs-Fiction, City Life-Fiction, Mystery and Detective Stories, Poverty-Fiction, Friendship-Fiction, Juvenile Delinquency-Fiction, Crime-Fiction, Best Sellers.

Bonsall, Crosby. And I mean it, Stanley. Har-Row 1974, 32 pp.
A little girl builds "the very best thing I ever made," but all the while calls to Stanley to tell him not to look and to stay on the other side of the fence. Stanley pays attention only long enough for the "thing" to be completed - then crashes through the fence and bounds into the "thing." He draws no anger from the little girl, though, for Stanley is an enormous, loveable mutt. Told as much through pictures as words, this very easy reader will draw smiles from most first and second graders - especially dog lovers. An Early I Can Read Book.
Interest Level: 1-2. Reading Level: 1.2. Further Search Topics: Dogs-Fiction, Humorous Fiction, Best Sellers.

Bonsall, Crosby. The day I had to play with my sister. Har-Row 1972, 32 pp.
A very easy reader, only slightly less universally appealing and humorous than *And I Mean It, Stanley*. This time a little boy tries very hard to teach his younger sister to play hide-and-seek. He is totally unsuccessful and thoroughly frustrated. Again the story is told as much with pictures as with words. Useful through second grade. Reader format. An Early I Can Read Book.
Interest Level: 1-2. Reading Level: 1.1. Further Search Topics: Humorous Fiction, Games-Fiction, Brothers and Sisters-Fiction, Everyday Stories.

Bunting, Eve. The skate patrol; illus by Don Madden. Albert Whitman 1980, 40 pp.
The book is funny, clever, undemanding and short. The combination of those qualities plus its slight mystery and its consistent reading level make this a very appealing and useful book for young readers. The plot is simple: in the hopes that their neighbors would be so grateful that they would allow the boys to roller skate in the neighborhood again, two friends decided to capture a local thief. James and Milton even knew who the thief was. He was the "mysterious man" who sat in the park. They only had to capture him in the act of stealing to prove that they were correct. They watched him continuously and trailed him as he followed old ladies. Then came the day that they heard Mrs. Grump scream that her purse had been snatched. The boys sped after the "mysterious man" on their skates. They caught him and knocked him down. To their surprise he declared that he was an undercover policeman and they were letting the real thief get away. Off they went again. This time they caught the right person and were rewarded just the way that they had hoped: Mrs. Crump (not Grump) promised that the boys would be allowed to roller skate any time they wished. A light and lively entertainment.
Interest Level: 2-4. Reading Level: 2.2. Further Search Topics: Mystery and Detective Stories, Humorous Fiction, Spies-Fiction, Roller Skating-Fiction, Crime-Fiction, Best Sellers.

Burch, Robert. Queenie Peavy; illus by Jerry Lazare. Viking Pr. 1966, 159 pp.
Queenie was always in trouble. She could be mean, really mean, but, she was also bright, talented, independent and resilient. Queenie blamed her problems on the fact that people teased her because her father was in jail and because she was poor. She thought that she had to defend herself against the world. Queenie was proud of her poor reputation until she accidentally-on-purpose caused a classmate to break his leg. Then, when her father returned home

and wasn't the person she'd hoped he'd be, Queenie realized that only she could make her life better. Being the strong person she was, she set out to do just that.

Queenie is a wonderfully alive and sympathetic character, one well worth introducing to older readers despite the book's reading level. Print somewhat small. Line spacing average width.

Interest Level: 5-6. Reading Level: 5.1. Further Search Topics: Family Problems-Fiction, Crime-Fiction, Loners-Fiction, Poverty-Fiction, Humorous Fiction, Bullies-Fiction, Troublemakers-Fiction, Academic Problems-Fiction, Read Aloud.

Byars, Betsy. The Cybil war; illus by Gail Owens. Viking Pr. 1981, 126 pp.

Simon and Tony both had a crush on Cybil, but according to Tony, Cybil liked Tony better than she liked Simon. Simon was unhappily willing to accept Tony's word even though he knew Tony was a chronic liar. After all, Cybil had been the one to talk their teacher out of giving the lead in the class play about nutrition to Simon. Consequently Simon was being forced to impersonate a jar of peanut butter. In an elaborate attempt to win Cybil's affection Tony began telling Cybil lies about Simon and then set up a double date with Cybil and Harriet. On their walk home, Simon learned from Harriet that Cybil had only agreed to the date because Simon was going along. Happy at last, Simon realized he wanted no more lies and tricks; that he wanted to be truthful with Cybil and with himself. In the name of truth, he was even willing to accept the fact that his father, who had deserted the family, would not be returning.

A good story with just enough humor and romance to make it widely appealing as either a shared book (read aloud) or a personal pick. Print is fairly small.

Interest Level: 5-6. Reading Level: 4.2. Further Search Topics: Humorous Fiction, Love-Fiction, School Stories, Honesty-Fiction, Friendship-Fiction, Single Parent Family-Fiction, Read Aloud, Everyday Stories, Adolescence-Fiction.

Byars, Betsy. The 18th emergency; illus by Robert Grossman. Viking Pr. 1973, 126 pp.

When your best friend knows how to escape from the world's 17 worst emergencies and you're faced with the eighteenth, you're in trouble. That was the spot in which Mouse found himself one day. He had drawn an arrow towards a large picture of the Neanderthal man and written Marv Hammerman's name. Hammerman had seen him do it and was out to kill, maim, or at least beat up Mouse. Mouse finally ran out of ways to avoid Hammerman and had to face the fight. When it was over and he was once again able to stand up, Mouse realized he felt better for having allowed Hammerman to regain his honor and for having taken responsibility for his own actions.

A funny, fast-moving look at real feelings of fear, honor and responsibility. Very popular. Print is dark and of good size but lines could have been spaced farther apart.

Interest Level: 4-6. Reading Level: 3.2. Further Search Topics: Bullies-Fiction, Humorous Fiction, Courage-Fiction, Best Sellers, Challenges-Fiction, Read Aloud.

Chew, Ruth. What the witch left. Hastings 1973, 128 pp.

One afternoon Katy and Louise decided to search through the locked drawer of an old dresser. Inside they found strange-looking gloves, an old robe, boots, a mirror and a tin box. The girls quickly learned that each item was magical. With the gloves on, the girls could draw, play piano, weave or write. They thought their new talents were wonderful until they each wrote identical school compositions. When she wore the robe for the school play, Louise found out that it made people invisible. The boots, which travelled 21 miles with each step, took the girls to Mexico, but made them late for lunch at home. The mirror showed them anything they wanted to see, and the box "found" everything that was lost. A very light story for children who don't need high adventure but like a mixture of humor and magic.

Interest Level: 3-5. Reading Level: 3.1. Further Search Topics: Magic-Fiction, Mexico-Fiction, Witches-Fiction, Fantasy, Humorous Fiction.

Cleary, Beverly. Henry Huggins; illus by Louis Darling. Morrow 1950, 155 pp.

Henry Huggins is over 30 years old now, so if he occasionally seems a little old-fashioned, it is not surprising. What is surprising is how well he has withstood the years. His antics are innocent, but humorous and realistic. The book's six chapters are six separate stories that follow the same cast of characters through an entire year.

In the first chapter, Henry finds a stray dog (Ribsy) whom he must then transport home on a bus. Ribsy was too large and too frisky not to get into trouble, so before Henry finally gets him home, they have been kicked off of three buses and have ridden in a police car. The second chapter describes what happens when Henry buys two guppies and ends up with millions. In the third chapter Henry accidentally throws his friend's football into the back seat of a speeding car and tries to earn the money to replace it by catching and selling 1,331 night crawlers. The fourth chapter involves Henry's attempts to get out of playing the lead in a school Christmas play. His last minute rescue comes in the form of a can of green paint that spills all over him. It is Ribsy's turn to change colors in Chapter 5. Henry tries to cover Ribsy's dirt spots with talcolm powder for a dog show, but only succeeds in turning Ribsy pink. And in Chapter 6, Ribsy's original owner finally finds him and wants him back, but Ribsy chooses to stay with Henry. Only the occasional extra cute expression and Henry's age (third grade) keep this from being enjoyed beyond fourth grade.

Interest Level: 1-4. Reading Level: 2.2. Further Search Topics: Humorous Fiction, Everyday Stories, Read Aloud Pets-Fiction, Dogs-Fiction, Group 2.

Cleary, Beverly. Otis Spofford; illus by Louis Darling. Morrow 1953, 191 pp.

Here are six separate humorous adventures that link together, but can be read separately and out of order. Otis' favorite activity was "stirring up a little excitement," but his definition of excitement usually meant trouble. The school fiesta turned into a disaster when Otis decided to rechoreograph the bullfight and make the bull win. His attempt to liven up the reading lesson about Indians meant he almost scalped a classmate. However, a wild day at the skating pond finally gave everyone a chance to take revenge for all the things Otis had done to them. The remaining three chapters (2, 3 and 4) are slightly less exciting, but useful if a reader has enjoyed the others. There is much humor in Otis' antics and his tendency to act on every thought that comes to mind is one many readers can appreciate.

Interest Level: 2-6. Reading Level: 5.1. Further Search Topics: Troublemakers-Fiction, Group 2, Read Aloud, Everyday Stories, Humorous Fiction, School Stories.

Cleary, Beverly. Henry and Beezus; illus by Louis Darling. Morrow 1952, 192 pp.

When Henry's dog Ribsy stole the meat from a neighbor's barbecue, a friend rode after Ribsy on his bike and saved the meat. Henry was so embarrassed and jealous that he boasted about an even nicer bike that he was going to get. At first Henry thought he'd be able to earn money to buy a bike in a very short time (he found 49 boxes of bubble gum that he could sell). When that scheme fell through, Henry tried taking over a friend's paper route, but Ribsy kept retrieving the newspapers Henry delivered. Eventually Henry decided to buy a used bike at the police department auction. Beezus, who made a bid for Henry, ended up buying him a beaten-up girl's bike that was hardly worth fixing. The money finally appeared when Henry least expected it; he won $50.00 worth of work at a beauty salon.

Although all seven chapters continue the same story, Chapters 1, 2, 3 and 7, can each stand alone. Henry is definitely old-fashioned, but children still enjoy his humorous escapades and empathize with his desire for a bicycle. The revised paperback cover makes the book's physical appearance less dated. Reading level is somewhat inconsistent: from 2.2 to 3.2.

Interest Level: 2-5. Reading Level: 3.1. Further Search Topics: Humorous Fiction, Occupations-Fiction, Everyday Stories, Bicycles and Bicycling-Fiction, Read Aloud, Group 2.

Cone, Molly. The amazing memory of Harvey Bean; illus by Robert MacLean. HM 1980, 83 pp.

It had been a long time since Harvey had been happy. His memory was so bad that he was always in trouble at school. And now that his parents were separating, he had trouble at home, too. Because he thought that neither one of his parents wanted him he told each one that he was going to stay with the other and instead decided to spend the summer alone. A few hours after he left home, Harry ran into Mr. and Mrs. Katz and before he completely realized it, he was living with them.

Mr. Katz couldn't stand to see anything go to waste. He collected the usable food thrown out behind grocery stores, old furniture, tools, windows and more. Mrs. Katz, whose memory was just as bad as Harvey's, loved to cook, so she could always find a way to use the food. Everything else bulged from the house and garage into the driveway and yard. Harvey spent a happy summer learning to scavenge, eating well, learning not to worry about what others thought of him and even improving his memory. When his parents finally found him, Harvey realized that they really did want him, even if they were separated. He decided to live with his mother on weekdays, his father on weekends, and the Katzs during the summers.

The plot problems that are obvious to adult readers are ones that most young readers will be able to ignore (i.e. neither parent checks on Harvey for over two months). Young readers will enjoy the humor and realism of Harvey's pain, happiness and eventual feeling of self-confidence and triumph. The ten short chapters, good-sized print and adequate space between the lines help lower the book's reading level to late fourth grade.

Interest Level: 3-6. Reading Level: 5.1. Further Search Topics: Loners-Fiction, Vacation-Fiction, Divorce and Separation-Fiction, Humorous Fiction, Group 2, Memory-Fiction, Runaways-Fiction, Academic Problems-Fiction, Individualists-Fiction.

Conford, Ellen. The revenge of the incredible Dr. Rancid and his youthful assistant, Jeffrey. Little 1980, 119 pp.

There were two people Jeff hated and feared: Dewey Belasco, the sixth grade bully and Lana McCabe, Dewey's female counterpart. Only in his imagination could Jeff stand up to them. In the stories Jeff wrote in a notebook, he and his friend Dr. Rancid were superheroes who rid the world of such scum as Lana and Dewey. In real life, Jeff ran from bullies rather than face them; even if it meant that an eight-year-old boy and a girl Jeff's age were left to stand up to Dewey by themselves. Although the way Jeff took care of an injured child soon had most everyone thinking of Jeff as a hero, he saw that, too, as an indication of his failings at first. Finally, something inside Jeff snapped and he answered Dewey back when Dewey insulted him. Before long Jeff found himself flat on his back with a bloody nose and so many pains he couldn't count them. But, he had finally faced Dewey and showed Dewey that he was no longer afraid. Jeff felt good.

Similar to *The 18th Emergency* but a higher reading level. The notebook stories will appeal to fans of superheroes, but because they are stories within a story, they may also cause difficulties. Spacing between lines is somewhat narrow.

Interest Level: 5-6. Reading Level: 4.2. Further Search Topics: Courage-Fiction, Bullies-Fiction, Writing-Fiction, School Stories, Superheroes-Fiction, Humorous Fiction.

Conford, Ellen. The luck of Pokey Bloom; illus by Bernice Loewenstein. Little 1975, 135 pp.

Pokey Bloom's passion was entering contests. She entered every contest she heard of and always thought she would win. Unfortunately, she never won anything. She even went so far as to practice concentrating three times each day on winning every contest she had entered. Someone who had been interviewed on the radio had *guaranteed* she would win that way. She didn't! It only made more trouble for her at school and at home. Pokey had enough trouble getting along with her older brother and didn't need any more problems at home.

There isn't much plot or direction to this story, but it does have some amusing moments. It is an extra book for the reader who enjoys Judy Blume-type books and wants another story about "regular kids."

Interest Level: 4-6. Reading Level: 3.1. Further Search Topics: Family-Fiction, Contests-Fiction, Brothers and Sisters-Fiction, Humorous Fiction, Everyday Stories.

Conford, Ellen. And this is Laura. Little 1977, 179 pp.

As a member of a family of high-achievers, Laura was convinced that she was unloved and worthless because she had no talents. Then, suddenly Laura discovered she had very special psychic powers; powers she began to exploit. At first it was fun to give readings after school each day. Gradually, however, as Laura foresaw her friend hurt and her brother missing, she realized that having ESP was also a frightening responsibility. Finally, her ESP became the vehicle that made it possible for Laura to tell her parents her true feelings and to understand that they loved her for herself, not for her achievements.

The author treats a common concern with sensitivity and humor. An especially good choice for Judy Blume lovers. Print somewhat small.

Interest Level: 4-6. Reading Level: 4.2. Further Search Topics: Occult-Fiction, Courage-Fiction, Extra Sensory Perception-Fiction, Family-Fiction, Humorous Fiction, Everyday Stories, Talent-Fiction.

Corbett, Scott. The lemonade trick; illus by Paul Galdone. Little 1960, 103 pp.

This is the first book in a series of quite enjoyable stories (most of which are, unfortunately, too difficult to recommend here). Kerby was given an odd chemistry set by a strange old woman whom he helped one day. When he used the set to put together a brew, Kerby found himself completely under its spell. The sweet-smelling liquid he had concocted forced him to be good, so good that his parents began to worry about him. Luckily the spell wore off in a short time. But, Kerby kept experimenting with it: on himself, on his dog, on his friend, on his enemy and finally in desperation, on the entire boy's choir at church.

A succession of innocently humorous incidents are woven together into a satisfying story. Print size is on the small side.

Interest Level: 3-6. Reading Level: 3.1. Further Search Topics: Humorous Fiction, Bullies-Fiction, Magic-Fiction, Magicians-Fiction, Chemistry-Fiction, Read Aloud.

Danziger, Paula. There's a bat in bunk five. Delacorte 1980, 150 pp.

Although this is a sequel to *The Cat Ate My Gymsuit,* it can be read alone. Marcy accepted an offer to become a junior counselor at an arts camp run by her ex-English teacher Ms. Finney and Ms. Finney's husband. After a nervous beginning, Marcy found herself enjoying the other counselors and the campers, but most of all, her first romance. Marcy's only difficulty was dealing with Ginger, a very troubled 10-year-old in Marcy's cabin. Marcy couldn't seem to get through to Ginger. When Ginger ran away, Marcy was forced to consider whether she should have spent more time with the campers and not quite so much time with Ted.

Marcy is a normal teenager whose problems, questions and activities are appealing to many teen and pre-teen readers. The characters who surround Marcy here are less stereotyped and flat than those in The Cat Ate My Gymsuit. Even Marcy's parents are more human. The author's light touch is just right for Marcy's story.

Interest Level: 5-6. Reading Level: 3.2. Further Search Topics: Humorous Fiction, Camp-Fiction, Everyday Stories, Love-Fiction, Vacation-Fiction, Occupations-Fiction, Adolescence-Fiction.

Davidson, Carson. Fast-talking dolphin; illus by Sylvia Stone. Dodd 1978, 127 pp.

After a rather slow start, this story develops into a well-paced adventure-fantasy with touches of warmth and humor. Eric wasn't just surprised when he found a dolphin in the 10-foot fish pond, he was astonished. Not only had there never been a dolphin there before, but this dolphin spoke in poetry. His name was Wallingford Ullingham Lowell III; Wallingford for short. He was elegant, proud and cultured; but as Eric soon found out, he was very impractical. He didn't seem to realize that he needed salt water and more fish than those in the pond in order to live. It was Eric who figured out a way to keep salt flowing into the pond and a supply of fresh fish. He also kept Wallingford's presence a secret, just as Wallingford requested. The day that Wallingford was discovered was the day that Eric had to break his promise. In order to find out who else had found out about Wallingford, Eric talked with his brother. Together they scouted the town before they realized that Herbert Benson was the only other person who had seen Wallingford.

Herbert reluctantly admitted that he had told his father about the dolphin. Eric knew enough about Mr. Benson to realize that he was just crazy enough to want to harm the dolphin. Eric and his brother gathered all the local children together to shield Wallingford from Mr. Benson. Even Herbert dared to defy his father for the first time. As Mr. Benson struggled with Eric and his brother, he fell, hit his head and rolled into the pond. Wallingford dove to save him, but his leg was caught between two rocks. With the others' help, Wallingford, Eric and his brother Karl were able to save Mr. Benson from drowning.

A few days later Eric, with new-found skills, spontaneously recited a poem about friendship to Wallingford. Wallingford answered with a rare compliment and for the first time used Eric's name (a show of respect). They were such true friends that when Wallingford was helicopter-lifted out of the pond and taken back to his research project, Eric couldn't understand why his father didn't tell him of Wallingford's departure. Eventually he realized that his father had been right; he would rather remember Wallingford swimming in the pond than in a helicopter's sling. Also, Wallingford would have been embarrassed to be seen making so undignified a departure. Wallingford's final message to Eric was a note that Eric found scratched in the dirt thanking him for the salt and the fish and saying that they would one day meet again.

Don't take the plot too seriously or peruse it too carefully for it won't stand up to scrutiny. This is merely a pleasant story with enough humor, action and originality to intrigue many readers. The book's major drawback is the poetry Wallingford spouts: the poetic form and somewhat difficult language will throw some readers. On the other hand, the book could be very useful in a classroom unit about poetry.

Interest Level: 3-5. Reading Level: 3.1. Further Search Topics: Poetry, Dolphins-Fiction, Pets-Fiction, Fantasy, Friendship-Fiction, Humorous Fiction.

Dobrin, Arnold. Jillions of gerbils. Lothrop 1973, 64 pp.

Right after his family moved into a big and very old house, David's gerbil disappeared. Before long, the replacement gerbil disappeared also. The house was very old and did have strange creakings. Could there also have been secret hiding places for ghosts, maybe? Determined to find out, David searched the entire house until he really did find a secret room. And in that room he found his two gerbils with their new family — the beginnings of David's millions and billions and jillions of gerbils.

A comfortable, somewhat old-fashioned book that is neatly divided into six short chapters. It includes a page of facts about gerbils at the end. A good choice to follow the very easy readers; it is easy, but not "too babyish."

Interest Level: 1-4. Reading Level: 2.1. Further Search Topics: Gerbils-Fiction, Pets-Fiction, Group 2, Humorous Fiction.

Eastman, Philip D. Sam and the firefly. Beginner 1958, 62 pp.

Sam, the owl, went looking for a playmate one night but found everyone was asleep except a mischievous firefly named Gus. When Sam showed Gus how to write words with his light in the dark sky, Gus went wild. First he tried to direct auto traffic, then airplane traffic, until finally the Hot Dog Man, an angry victim of Gus' tricks, captured him. However, when the Hot Dog Man tried to take Gus out of town, his truck became stuck on the railroad tracks in front of an oncoming train. Gus, freed from the jar in which he'd been caught, quickly wrote the word STOP in the sky and saved everyone. Gus' silliness, the catastrophies he caused and his final triumph should interest almost any young child who likes humor or excitement. Reader format.

Interest Level: 1-2. Reading Level: 1.2. Further Search Topics: Best Sellers, Fireflies-Fiction, Owls-Fiction, Humorous Fiction.

Fife, Dale. Follow that ghost!; illus by Joan Drescher. Dutton 1979, 58 pp.

In short sentences reminiscent of "Dragnet," Chuck tells a very simple story of Chuck and Jason's first detective case. He and Jason were practicing following people, when their next-door-neighbor caught them following her home. Instead of being angry at the two boys, Glory decided to hire them to find the ghost she and her mother were hearing at 5:00 every morning. Despite their best attempts to capture and bury the ghost, or a find a human cause for the ghostly sounds, Chuck and Jason couldn't rid Glory's apartment of its ghost. Their final effort nearly resulted in injury to a neighbor. Ultimately, Chuck discovered that the ghost was merely a displaced woodpecker looking for a new home.

Not a terribly ambitious mystery, but one whose consistent reading level, familiar urban setting and interesting characters will please many young readers.

Interest Level: 2-4. Reading Level: 2.1. Further Search Topics: Ghosts-Fiction, Mystery and Detective Stories, Spies-Fiction, Humorous Fiction.

Foley, Louise Munro. Tackle 22; illus by John Heinly. Delacorte 1978, unp (43 pp).

When their quarterback came down with the mumps, it looked like the Wildcats would have to forfeit the big football game to the Spacemen. But Chub's little brother Herb surprised everyone and saved the game.

Brief and somewhat predictable, the book maintains a light touch that many young readers will like. Heavily illustrated.

Interest Level: 1-4. Reading Level: 2.1. Further Search Topics: Football-Fiction, Brothers and Sisters-Fiction, Humorous Fiction, Group 2.

Giff, Patricia Reilly. Have you seen Hyacinth Macaw?; illus by Anthony Kramer. Delacorte 1981, 135 pp.

Abby Jones was trying very hard to be a detective, but it was difficult without any mysteries to solve. So to keep in practice, Abby filled a memo book with her notes about anything that seemed at all unusual. At the same time, Abby kept in touch with two local police detectives who gave her hints about detective work. Because of her police friends and her observations, Abby found herself involved in what seemed to be four or more mysteries. Who had moved into the apartment next door and what were the screams that came from there? What was the theft that the police were worried about? Who was Hyacinth Macaw and why had she disappeared? And why was Abby's older brother Dan acting so strangely? Was he involved in the theft?

Abby and her friend Potsie ended up trailing a suspect through the New York subway system, breaking into the next-door apartment, suspecting Abby's brother of the theft, capturing an unusual bird, releasing the bird into a pet shop and recapturing it, before they realized that all the mysteries were linked together. Hyacinth Macaw was a valuable bird stolen from Justine's Junktique Shop. The daughter of Abby's landland had taken the bird and placed it in the empty apartment next to Abby's, so that she could paint the bird's portrait. The picture was to be entered in Justine's Junktique contest. Dan and his friend Holly Monk had been secretly constructing a Purple Pigeon Purifier to enter in the contest. They needed the prize money to repair a window they had accidentally broken. By the time the mysteries were all sorted out, Dan and Holly had won a special prize; Kiki, the portrait painter, had not only been forgiven, but had also been awarded first prize; and Abby had received the reward for finding and returning the bird.

The action in this mystery is both abundant and humorous enough to make the book enjoyable to many readers. There are also some problems that need to be noted. Some readers may find the action too swift and the characters too numerous to be easily followed. Abby's memo notes are sometimes written without vowels and are almost always in incomplete sentences. The reader who is highly motivated or has help from another person will still be able to enjoy the story; however, for the others another choice may be more appropriate.

Interest Level: 4-6. Reading Level: 3.1. Further Search Topics: Mystery and Detective Stories, Humorous Fiction, Writing-Fiction, Detectives-Fiction, Birds-Fiction.

Ginsburg, Mirra. The lazies; illus by Marian Parry. Macmillan 1973, 70 pp.

A good collection of 15 short Russian folktales all having to do with laziness. Most are humorous tales; few are well-known. In just under a third of the stories the humor may be too subtle even for older elementary school children; however, the rest of the stories can be enjoyed by almost any child between third and sixth grade. ("Who Will Wash the Pot," "Easy Bread," "Who Will Row Next," and "The Princess Who Learned to Work" are the questionable stories). Print somewhat small.

Interest Level: 3-6. Reading Level: 3.1. Further Search Topics: Folklore, Humorous Fiction, Laziness-Fiction, Russia-Fiction.

Greene, Constance C. Isabelle the itch; illus by Emily A. McCully. Viking Pr. 1973, 126 pp.

This is a loosely plotted story about a spunky, original fifth grade girl who could drive everyone around her crazy without ever tiring. Isabelle's dearest dream was to win the 50-yard dash at her school's field day. Even though she took over her brother's paper route to earn money for the Adidas track shoes she needed, Isabelle still didn't win. However, she did meet some new people, make new friends and keep those around her on their toes. A very amusing story told mostly in dialogue.

Interest Level: 4-6. Reading Level: 3.2. Further Search Topics: School Stories, Occupations-Fiction, Humorous Fiction, Everyday Stories, Running-Fiction, Individualists-Fiction, Sex Role-Fiction, Read Aloud.

Greene, Constance C. A girl called Al; illus by Byron Barton. Viking Pr. 1969, 127 pp.

Told in the first person, this is the story of two seventh grade girls. The girls' warm friendship began the moment Al introduced herself to the narrator as a non-conformist. Al was very independent, mostly because she was on her own so much of the time. Her parents were divorced and she seldom saw either one of them. Her father only wrote her postcards and her mother was rarely home. The narrator's family and Mr. Richards, their building superintendent, became Al's family. They cooked, ate, played, fought, talked and even made bookcases together. When Mr. Richards had a heart attack, they found help for him and later went to see him in the hospital. It was his death that helped Al and her mother grow closer, just as Mr. Richards' life had helped her understand why her father never came to see her.

A satisfying, low-key story of friendship and maturation. The girls are Judy Blume-style characters with much greater innocence. Their ages are not discernible by their actions or dialogue, only by the author's statement.

Interest Level: 3-6. Reading Level: 3.1. Further Search Topics: Children-Growth-Fiction, Single Parent Family-Fiction, Friendship-Fiction, Weight-Fiction, Aging-Fiction, Death-Fiction, Divorce and Separation-Fiction, Family Problems-Fiction, Everyday Stories, Humorous Fiction.

Greene, Constance C. I and Sproggy; illus by Emily A. McCully. Viking Pr. 1978, 155 pp.

Ten-year-old Adam had adjusted to his parents' divorce and had even grown to like living alone with his mother. When his father came back from London with his new wife and stepdaughter Sproggy and announced that they were moving into an apartment nearby, Adam was a little worried. But when his father asked him to take care of Sproggy, Adam was furious. First of all, he didn't know Sproggy and he didn't want to know her. Secondly, she was two months older than he, taller too, and she embarrassed him in public. And finally, she didn't need his help. She got along quite well by herself; so well that she even saved Adam from a mugger and became good friends with Adam's friends behind his back. It wasn't until Sproggy proved to be vulnerable that Adam and she became friends.

A warm, realistic and humorous story whose interesting characters (even the minor ones) heighten the book's appeal.

Interest Level: 4-6. Reading Level: 3.2. Further Search Topics: Brothers and Sisters-Fiction, Divorce and Separation-Fiction, City Life-Fiction, New York City-Fiction, Humorous Fiction, Friendship-Fiction, Everyday Stories.

Greenwald, Sheila. Give us a great big smile, Rosy Cole. Little 1981, 76 pp.

It was Rosy's turn to be the subject of her uncle's book. He needed to earn money again and Rosy had just turned 10, the age each of her sisters had been when Uncle Ralph wrote *Anitra Dances* and *Pippa Prances* about them. However, Rosy couldn't dance like Anitra or ride horses like Pippa. In fact, Rosy had no talent that was appropriate for a book. She drew well but Uncle Ralph said that wasn't visual enough. Then Rosy's mother and uncle decided that Rosy could be *A Very Little Fiddler*.

Rosy had been taking violin lessons for two years, but only Rosy and her music teacher knew how truly untalented she was. Rosy hated the whole idea of the book at first. But as people began to treat her like a star, she found herself acting like one, until the day she heard her tape of the piece she was to play at the recital. Once again she realized that she could not play the violin and didn't want to go on with the charade. When everyone ignored her wishes, Rosy started to run away. Her route took her through the park where she thought of a brilliant idea. She ran home, changed clothes, picked up her violin, created a sign, and raced back to the park. There, with all the other street musicians Rosy set up her sign and began to play her violin. Her sign asked people to sign a petition if they felt that she should not be encouraged to play the violin anymore. Right away Rosy drew a large crowd. Before long, even her mother was one of the listeners and one of the signers. That was the end of Rosy's musical career and her uncle's book, but both were happier. Rosy went back to being normal and Uncle Ralph found another topic for his next book.

Chapters are long, but should not be a problem. Print is large. Some of the story is actually told in the illustrations, so the reader should be aware of them. Younger children may take the book more seriously than children whose sense of humor includes irony or children who were not as fond of Krementz's *Very Young* series.

Interest Level: 4-6. Reading Level: 3.1. Further Search Topics: Occupations-Fiction, Humorous Fiction, Family-Fiction, Relatives-Fiction, Talent-Fiction, Photography-Fiction, Everyday Stories.

Harris, Robie H. Rosie's double dare; illus by Tony DeLuna. Knopf 1980, 112 pp.

Rosie wanted to play baseball with the Willard Street Gang, but she couldn't play well enough to play by their rules. She needed what her older brother called "shrimp rules." She couldn't hit a pitched ball, only a grounder; but grounders were "shrimp rules." In desperation Rosie agreed to take a dare that the gang made up. If she actually performed the dare, the gang would let her play with them by her rules.

The gang dared Rosie to sneak into cranky Mr. Quirk's apartment and borrow a set of his false teeth. Because Rosie couldn't find any extra false teeth, she borrowed his wig instead but that didn't satisfy the gang. They only laughed and made up another dare for Rosie. She was to untie Mrs. Samuels' dog and let it run loose. As Rosie untied him, Elmer ran away, Rosie ran off after him. One rainstorm later, Rosie caught up with him in the middle of a Red Sox game at Fenway Park. Rosie's attempt to catch Elmer stopped the game, brought her an interview on TV, and secured her a place on the Willard Street baseball team.

This very light story, made up almost entirely of action and examples of sibling rivalry, should have wide appeal through fifth grade. Beyond that, Rosie's age (almost nine) and childish behavior won't ring true. Capers series.

Interest Level: 2-5. Reading Level: 2.2. Further Search Topics: Baseball-Fiction, Humorous Fiction, Brothers and Sisters-Fiction, Challenges-Fiction, Courage-Fiction, Gangs-Fiction, Everyday Stories.

Hildick, Edmund W. The case of the invisible dog; illus by Lisl Weil. Macmillan 1977, 101 pp.

Brains Bellingham, a nine-year-old scientific genius, interrupted the McGurk Organization's Annual Picnic with an invisible dog. It was only a short time before McGurk and his friends were convinced that Brains' discovery of how to make things invisible was the greatest event since putting a man on the moon. Although they had always scorned the idea of including anyone else in the Organization, they decided to persuade Brains to join. But, before the day was over, they discovered not only that they had been duped, but exactly how Brains had made the impossible seem real. The Organization took its revenge by using Brain's own trick to make him confess. When Brains began laughing at how well his trick had been used in reverse, McGurk admitted how impressed they all had been by Brain's clever thinking. The outcome of their discussion was that Brains was invited, a second time, to become a member of the McGurk Organization.

See *The Case of the Bashful Bank Robber* for series information. McGurk Mystery series.

Interest Level: 3-6. Reading Level: 3.1. Further Search Topics: Mystery and Detective Stories, Detectives-Fiction, Gangs-Fiction, Dogs-Fiction, Supernatural-Fiction, Humorous Fiction, Jealousy-Fiction.

Hildick, Edmund W. The great rabbit rip-off; illus by Lisl Weil. Macmillan 1976, 101 pp.

Why would anyone want to put red paint on all of the clay lawn rabbits in town? That was the first and easier of the mysteries the McGurk Organization had to solve. The bigger mystery was who would then steal them all and why? Almost everyone in town had purchased a rabbit to help a charity drive. Donny Towers a local social worker had thought of the idea. Donny, his fiancee, Joanne, and two reformed thieves, Sam and Ferdie, had made enough rabbits for everyone. When the rabbits disappeared, the Organization began to suspect, among others, Sam and Ferdie. Then when Donny replaced each one almost immediately with rabbits smelling of paint remover, the group began to think Donny might have been involved. It was Wanda's sharp eyes that revealed Donny's motive. Joanne's engagement ring had been accidentally molded into one of the rabbits and Donny had retrieved the rabbits to find the ring. Knowing he couldn't return the paint stained rabbits without raising suspicion, Donny had removed the red paint and told everyone that he was simply replacing the stolen rabbits with new ones.

See *Case of the Bashful Bank Robber* for series information. McGurk Mystery series.

Interest Level: 3-5. Reading Level: 2.2. Further Search Topics: Mystery and Detective Stories, Detectives-Fiction, Gangs-Fiction, Rabbits-Fiction, Crime-Fiction, Humorous Fiction.

Hildick, Edmund W. Deadline for McGurk; illus by Lisl Weil. Macmillan 1975, 104 pp.

When many of the dolls in the neighborhood began disappearing, their owners went to the McGurk Organization for help. At first McGurk was reluctant to take on such a silly task as recovering lost dolls. But when a ransom note appeared and the Organization was linked to the dolls' safety, McGurk's reluctance vanished. The note stated that if, in a written public notice, the members of the Organization did not admit that they were no good, the dolls were doomed. McGurk's pride would never have allowed him to write such a notice. As the deadline approached, the group plotted a daring move designed to uncover the doll thief. The plan depended on Willie's super-sensitive nose, a particular perfume dabbed on a stolen doll, and the curiosity of the thief. Success came only minutes before the hour of doom. Once again Sandra Ennis was the culprit.

See *The Case of the Bashful Bank Robber* for series information. McGurk Mystery series.

Interest Level: 3-5. Reading Level: 2.2. Further Search Topics: Dolls-Fiction, Mystery and Detective Stories, Detectives-Fiction, Humorous Fiction, Gangs-Fiction, Jealousy-Fiction.

Hildick, Edmund W. The case of the condemned cat; illus by Lisl Weil. Macmillan 1975, 106 pp.

Ray Williams had a terrible problem when he begged the McGurk Organization for help. His cat Whiskers had been accused of killing a neighbor's pet dove. Ray's mother decided that they couldn't risk upsetting the neighbors anymore and threatened to take Whiskers to the pound unless it could be proven that he was innocent. The Organization, needing time, hid Whiskers and told Mrs. Williams that he had run away. While Whiskers was safely hidden, the group interviewed all the neighbors, surveyed the scene of the crime, and tried to decide upon the real murderer. When the remains of another bird were found while Whiskers was safely locked away, it looked as if the cat was surely innocent. But then McGurk and his detectives found out that the cat had been sprung. It wasn't until they went back over all the information they had gathered that McGurk realized who was the real culprit. The only step left was to trick old Gramp Martin (the neighborhood grouch) into confessing.

See *The Case of the Bashful Bank Robber* for series information. McGurk Mystery series.

Interest Level: 3-6. Reading Level: 2.2. Further Search Topics: Mystery and Detective Stories, Cats-Fiction, Detectives-Fiction, Humorous Fiction, Gangs-Fiction, Pets-Fiction.

Hildick, Edmund W. The case of the secret scribbler; illus by Lisl Weil. Macmillan 1978, 106 pp.

Joey's discovery in a library book of a scrap of paper with part of a letter and a strange diagram on it led the McGurk Organization on a lively chase. Brains identified the diagram as that of a widely-used security system. The part of the letter that they could read told the group that there was a burglary being planned for the approaching weekend, but the youngsters knew the police would never take them seriously until they had much more evidence. By researching local alarm systems, determining who bought the unusual paper, and comparing handwriting samples, the detectives were able to convince the police of what was about to happen. In gratitude, the police loaned the Organization a police monitor so that they could listen as the thieves were caught. To all but McGurk it seemed like the perfect way to end the case: he tried to sneak into the midst of the capture, but only succeeded in getting himself in real trouble.

See *The Case of the Bashful Bank Robber* for series information. McGurk Mystery series.

Interest Level: 3-6. Reading Level: 2.2. Further Search Topics: Mystery and Detective Stories, Crime-Fiction, Gangs-Fiction, Nonverbal Communication-Fiction, Humorous Fiction, Detectives-Fiction.

Hildick, Edmund W. The case of the phantom frog; illus by Lisl Weil. Macmillan 1979, 121 pp.

The McGurk Organization would not, under ordinary circumstances, have agreed to babysit for seven-year-old Bela, but there was an unusual twist to Bela's case. Bela's aunt, who asked them to babysit while she worked in her sculpture studio, had heard the eerie sounds of a VERY large frog coming from Bela's room. At first it appeared to the group that Bela actually turned into a frog at night, a werefrog. But, upon investigation they found a very clever, very lonely, and very unhappy young boy who had invented the phantom because he was afraid that his aunt would make him give up his pet frog.

See *The Case of the Bashful Bank Robber* for series information. McGurk Mystery series.

Interest Level: 3-5. Reading Level: 3.1. Further Search Topics: Mystery and Detective Stories, Gangs-Fiction, Frogs-Fiction, Supernatural-Fiction, Transformations-Fiction, Detectives-Fiction, Babysitting-Fiction, Humorous Fiction, Occupations-Fiction.

Hildick, Edmund W. The case of the treetop treasure; illus by Lisl Weil. Macmillan 1980, 121 pp.

As Wanda rescued a cat she discovered a stash of odd items tucked into a hollow high up in a tree. On top of the assortment was a sign that said simply "Beware!" The McGurk Organization suspected a thief was using the tree as a place to hide stolen goods, but until an antique silver bowl was added nothing that had been placed there was worth stealing. Shortly afterwards Wanda found out from the police that she was the prime suspect in the theft of the bowl. Brains devised a complicated system for determining the real thief while McGurk worked more from intuition. Nevertheless, it wasn't long before they both arrived at the same conclusion. The culprit was the gang's long-time enemy Sandra Ennis. Then it was just a simple matter of finding the right way to persuade Sandra to confess and apologize to her victims.

See *The Case of the Bashful Bank Robber* for series information. McGurk Mystery series.

Interest Level: 3-5. Reading Level: 3.1. Further Search Topics: Mystery and Detective Stories, Crime-Fiction, Gangs-Fiction, Detectives-Fiction, Humorous Fiction.

Hildick, Edmund W. The case of the snowbound spy; illus by Lisl Weil. Macmillan 1980, 132 pp.

One snowy morning McGurk called the five members of his organization together to decipher a code. The code was part of a message from someone who wanted to hire them and would pay $5.00 a day. When they broke the code and met their employer, Mr. Fitch, he gave the group another code as part of their assignment. The second code told them where to deliver a small package that Mr. Fitch gave them. They were to pick up another coded message at the same place. After three pick-ups and drops they would be finished and Mr. Fitch, an ex-government spy, would have proved he was still a trustworthy and capable person to an ex-colleague with whom he wanted to work on a book. It seemed like just the challenging kind of assignment the McGurk Organization looked for. As they worked, however, it began to look more and more as if they were being used for illegal business. While Joey and McGurk staked out the next drop-off spot, Willie, Brains and Wanda pretended to Mr. Fitch to be unsuspecting. By working quickly and cleverly and by alerting the police, the McGurk gang uncovered and stopped two industrial spies who were stealing secret information about a new copying machine.

See *The Case of the Bashful Bank Robber* for series information. McGurk Mystery series.

Interest Level: 3-6. Reading Level: 3.1. Further Search Topics: Mystery and Detective Stories, Spies-Fiction, Detectives-Fiction, Gangs-Fiction, Humorous Fiction, Nonverbal Communication-Fiction, Crime-Fiction.

Hildick, Edmund W. The case of the bashful bank robber; illus by Lisl Weil. Macmillan 1981, 138 pp.

The McGurk Organization is a crime fighting detective agency. Led by Jack McGurk's strong ego, they had taken on many a seemingly impossible task and had always been successful. Never before, however, had they tried to protect the seven banks in town from being robbed. The five children's first idea was to regularly patrol each bank and watch for likely looking get-away cars. When that plan only led to a nasty confrontation with their new junior high school principal, they decided to try something else. Their second plan, to photograph all suspicious looking people near the banks, didn't fare much better than their first idea. Then, without knowing it, they found themselves holding the key to solving a real bank robbery. Before they realized its importance, they had literally given away the vital clue. Using only their own memories, powers of observation, and cleverness, they were still able to solve the crime with only a little help from the FBI.

The "McGurk mysteries" are light, fast-moving, and often humorous. Clues for solving the mysteries are sometimes subtle, but always there in the plot and illustrations for the reader to find. The characters are somewhat flat but still appealing. Joey, who is handy with words and a typewriter, is the narrator of each book. Jack McGurk, dedicated mastermind of all the group's activities is shrewd, a natural leader, and egotistical. Willie has the world's most sensitive nose and an excellent memory for odors. Wanda is the best tree-climber in town and a rational influence on the group. Brains, the newest and youngest member of the group, is a scientific genius, so he runs their crime lab. The books need not be read in chronological order although most have a brief reference to an earlier story. Reading level varies within each book from 2.1 to 3.1. A few books include enough more difficult passages that their average reading level is pushed from 2.2 to 3.1. Interest level in the series, once a reader has started on it, is high. McGurk Mystery series.

Interest Level: 3-6. Reading Level: 2.2. Further Search Topics: Mystery and Detective Stories, Crime-Fiction, Detectives-Fiction, Humorous Fiction, Gangs-Fiction.

Hildick, Edmund W. The case of the four flying fingers; illus by Lisl Weil. Macmillan 1981, 138 pp.

At first the four young strangers who were knocking over garbage cans had been merely a neighborhood nuisance. Later McGurk and his fellow detectives began to suspect that they were involved in the rash of break-ins and burglaries in the city. The Organization didn't think the "garbage gang" was actually committing the robberies, but rather that they were fingering houses for someone else to burglarize (thus their nickname: The Four Flying Fingers). It could be safely assumed by a would-be burglar that where no one picked up the spilled garbage, no one was home. It was the Organization's job to find the Thumb who was the mastermind behind the plot. When they caught up with the Fingers, McGurk and crew found out that the Flying Fingers hadn't realized what they were doing; only that a blonde lady in a camper was paying them a nickel for every driveway they left strewn with garbage. It didn't take long for the Organization to track down the woman and her accomplice. But, in one of their less intelligent moves, they played right into her hands and soon found themselves being transported out of town in her camper. When they tried to call to passing cars for help, no one took them seriously. It wasn't until Brains, bound and gagged to appear authentic, used a flashlight and Morse code to signal for help that anyone paid any attention to them. A police car finally stopped the camper for speeding apd after some clever arguments McGurk and his friends were able to convince the police that Lady Thumb was a thief.

This title is just as enjoyable as the best of the other books in the series, more exciting and universal in appeal than most, and equally humorous. It's only drawback is a very inconsistent reading level (from 2.1 to 4.1) that will discourage a reader new to McGurk. Established fans will be able to tolerate the range. McGurk Mystery series.

Interest Level: 3-6. Reading Level: 3.1. Further Search Topics: Mystery and Detective Stories, Detectives-Fiction, Humorous Fiction, Crime-Fiction, Gangs-Fiction.

Hurwitz, Johanna. Aldo Ice Cream; illus by John Wallner. Morrow 1981, 124 pp.

Aldo got his newest nickname (Ice Cream) from his friend DeDe when she heard that Aldo not only wanted to try every flavor of ice cream at the local store, but wanted to buy an ice cream freezer for his sister's birthday as well. Aldo decided his summer project would be to earn enough money for the freezer, but he soon found out that there were very few ways a nine-year-old boy could earn $49.95. In the meantime, he helped his mother deliver food for a Meals-On-Wheels project, learned to swim, found out about fish from Mr. Puccini, and shared his cat with Mrs. Nardo. As the summer came to an end he saw one last opportunity to earn enough money for the ice cream maker. A local shoe store offered a new pair of sneakers to the child who owned the most worn out pair. Aldo convinced his mother that if he won the sneakers, she should pay him the money she would otherwise have had to spend on his new sneakers. Aldo set about making sure that his already well-worn sneakers were the most dilapidated in town. A few days before the sneaker contest the hardware store lowered the price on the ice cream freezer to a point where Aldo could afford it if he won the sneakers. When Aldo did win, just as he knew he would, he and his mother bought the very last freezer in the store.

It is not as well-constructed a story as *Aldo Applesauce*, but for established Aldo fans, or those who want quiet, reassuring fiction, this is a usable title.

Interest Level: 3-4. Reading Level: 3.1. Further Search Topics: Humorous Fiction, Brothers and Sisters-Fiction, Vacation-Fiction, Occupations-Fiction, Everyday Stories, Aging-Fiction, Family-Fiction, Contests-Fiction.

Hurwitz, Johanna. Aldo Applesauce; illus by John Wallner. Morrow 1979, 127 pp.

Aldo Sossi, vegetarian and new kid at school, was immediately dubbed Applesauce for obvious reasons. Aldo didn't like his new name. He didn't like being teased either—not the way he was teased at school. Nothing went right for Aldo. His attempts at making friends only ended in disasters (once at a bowling alley and another time at a birthday party). He had been able to start a friendship only with a strange girl who wore a heavy, black fake moustache most of the time. After accidentally nearly ruining that friendship too, Aldo not only learned why DeDe wore the moustache, but helped her learn to live without it. DeDe, in turn, helped Aldo take himself less seriously and find more friends.

This is a comfortable, humorous story of two fourth grade children learning to be themselves. The vocabulary is occasionally difficult, but sentence length is almost always short.

Interest Level: 3-5. Reading Level: 3.1. Further Search Topics: Moving, Household-Fiction, Humorous Fiction, School Stories, Friendship-Fiction, Divorce and Separation-Fiction, Vegetarians-Fiction, Individualists-Fiction, Everyday Stories.

Hurwitz, Johanna. Baseball fever; illus by Ray Cruz. Morrow 1981, 128 pp.

Only baseball nuts need even consider this title, but for the die-hard baseball fan this is perfect. Much to his father's disgust, Ezra had only one interest in life. Baseball was almost all Ezra ever thought of. His father was a German-born intellectual who couldn't understand how anyone could waste so much time watching men hit a ball with a stick. He wanted Ezra to become interested in history and chess. Ezra had no interest in history except baseball history. He hated chess, not just because he always lost, but because his father continually told him how badly he played. Predictably they reach a compromise; each learns to appreciate the other's passion, but not before everyone in the family and a few people outside the family have become involved in a series of warmly humorous incidents. Includes much baseball information.

Interest Level: 3-6. Reading Level: 3.1. Further Search Topics: Baseball-Fiction, Family Problems-Fiction, Humorous Fiction.

Hurwitz, Johanna. The law of gravity; illus by Ingrid Fetz. Morrow 1978, 192 pp.

The summer between fifth and sixth grades looked very unexciting to Margot. Her best friends were both going away for the whole summer and her father, a musician, was going to be on tour for most of the summer. Margot's very overweight mother had sworn never to go downstairs from their fifth floor walk-up apartment. Unless Margot chose to stay upstairs too, she was sure she would have a very lonely vacation. In addition, she had to work on a summer project for school. The project she finally chose was to get her mother downstairs after nine years of staying upstairs. In search of help she went to the local library where she met Bernie. Bernie was only a year older than Margot, but he seemed to know the most interesting things about the city. He showed her places Margot had never heard of before, he taught her to play chess, backgammon, and even to ride a bicycle. He was so full of fascinating ideas and information that Margot had no chance to be bored or lonely. Best of all, he even tried to help Margot with her project. None of their ideas worked, however, until Margot pretended to run away and scared her mother into going downstairs. Only then did Margot realize that she loved her mother whether or not she stayed on the fifth floor and that she couldn't simply force her mother or anyone else to change to suit her own fancy.

The book is a warm, understanding, slightly humorous treatment of the fairly common wish to change someone else. Although not many readers are likely to share Margot's exact problem, most will recognize her feelings. The book is also a virtual Chamber of Commerce advertisement for urban living. One of its other charms is its picture of a non-competitive, open, real friendship between an 11-year-old girl and a 12-year-old boy. The only drawback to the book is its inconsistent reading level which varies from 4.1 to 5.1 with a rare leap to 5.2.

Interest Level: 4-6. Reading Level: 4.2. Further Search Topics: Vacation-Fiction, Friendship-Fiction, Loners-Fiction, City Life-Fiction, Individualists-Fiction, Courage-Fiction, New York City-Fiction, Humorous Fiction, Family-Fiction, Challenges-Fiction, Weight-Fiction, Everyday Stories, Best Sellers.

Kibbe, Pat. The hocus-pocus dilemma; illus by Dan Jones. Knopf 1979, 125 pp.

Each chapter of this book is a separate episode in B.J.'s attempt to cultivate her newly-discovered ESP talents (more invented than discovered). The episodes, each of which involves a different member of B.J.'s family, are slightly outlandish, but very funny. Even the dog and the cat become involved. The dog becomes the unwitting target for a skunk. The cat accidentally starts a tape recording of speech habits that sounds like burglars breaking into the house. After nine disasters, B.J. finally concludes that she was being ridiculous to think that she had ESP, but that everyone is allowed to be ridiculous sometimes.

The nine, reasonably short episodes, the moderate size print, the sympathetic characters, and the book's humor, make this a very useful and popular title.

Interest Level: 4-6. Reading Level: 3.1. Further Search Topics: Extra Sensory Perception-Fiction, Humorous Fiction, Family-Fiction, Everyday Stories, Best Sellers, Read Aloud.

Kibbe, Pat. My mother the mayor, maybe; illus by Charles Robinson. Knopf 1981, 165 pp.

The Pinkertons first appeared in *The Hocus-Pocus Dilemma*, a better introduction to the family than this book. Although this is a satisfactory story, its appeal is somewhat limited by its subject matter. B.J.'s mother's decision to run for town mayor meant that the whole family became involved in the political process. B.J. became her mother's unofficial public relations coordinator, a position Sam Jessup (Mrs. Pinkerton's campaign manager) didn't want to see anyone fill but himself. But because Jessup's ideas seemed suspiciously designed to insure that Mrs. Pinkerton would lose the election, B.J. continued working on her mother's behalf. Almost every day she managed to get her mother's campaign on the front page of the newspaper, although not always in a flattering light. Once B.J. was arrested for breaking into her mother's campaign headquarters. Another day she inadvertently circulated a picture of her mother in a bikini all over town. B.J. and her brothers and sisters illegally campaigned on the high school campus during Homecoming. B.J. even accidentally succeeded in blowing her mother's opponent's wig off in the middle of a campaign appearance. Mrs. Pinkerton finally lost the election, but managed to bring an important issue to light and to stage the closest and most exciting election the town had known in a long time.

Election campaigns and political issues won't lure many new reluctant readers to this book, but those youngsters who have enjoyed the Pinkerton's previous adventures and can understand a simplified version of politics at work will enjoy this humorous tale.

Interest Level: 5-6. Reading Level: 3.1. Further Search Topics: Politics-Fiction, Humorous Fiction, Sex Role-Fiction, Family-Fiction.

Law, Carol Russell. The case of the Weird Street firebug; illus by Bill Morrison. Knopf 1980, 119 pp.

This is the humorous story of a Nancy Drew-type character who gets involved in a mystery before she is even half finished with her mail-order detective lessons. Steffi wanted very much to be a detective. When she saw an ad for a local correspondence course, she tracked down the shabby office in a run-down building on Weir Street, and went to visit Jeff Dangerfield of Dangerfield Detective School. Steffi's first lesson, trailing suspects, was a disaster. She tried to pick out suspicious characters at a fire on Weir Street on her way home. The only really suspicious character (Beady Eyes) didn't go anywhere, so Steffi couldn't follow him. Her next attempts were very obvious and only resulted in her own anger and embarrassment. On her way back to seek advice from Dangerfield, Steffi literally ran into Beady Eyes again. She didn't think anything more about him until she saw him a short time later at another fire just down the street from Dangerfield's office. As the fire moved closer to Dangerfield's building, Steffi took desperate measures to try and save her friend. Steffi's efforts were interpreted by Beady Eyes as attempts to indicate that he was an arsonist. By the time Steffi figured out that Beady Eyes really was an arsonist, he had her cornered. A timely entry by the police saved both Steffi and Dangerfield. Steffi's reward for the capture of Beady Eyes was a medal from the police and a partnership with Dangerfield.

A fast-paced story, as well as slightly more original characters than most stories of this genre, make this a likely success with third through sixth grade readers. Capers series.

Interest Level: 3-6. Reading Level: 3.1. Further Search Topics: Mystery and Detective Stories, Humorous Fiction, Fire-Fiction, Detectives-Fiction, Crime-Fiction.

LeSieg, Theo. Wacky Wednesday; illus by George Booth. Beginner 1974, unp (36 pp).

A series of true picture puzzles. A little boy wakes up one Wednesday to find everything around him has gone "wacky." People are missing heads but have extra legs. Cars are being driven from the back seat. Doors are placed in the wrong places. Airplanes fly backwards. At the end of the day everything settles back to normal, but not before readers have had fun finding the numerous "wacky" things on each page.

The story is told in silly rhyme (LeSieg and Seuss are the same person). What is wrong with each picture is not always easily located, making this reader an excellent excerise in observation as well as great fun.

Interest Level: 1-3. Reading Level: 1.2. Further Search Topics: Puzzles, Humorous Fiction, Wit and Humor, Poetry, Best Sellers.

Levy, Elizabeth. Lizzie lies a lot; illus by John Wallner. Delacorte 1976, 102 pp.

Almost any child can identify with Lizzie. She had found that it was sometimes easier to lie than to tell the truth. Her problem was that she had lost control. It seemed as if almost everything she said was a lie. She told so many lies it became difficult to keep track of them all. Lizzie wasn't even really sure why she lied so much. She knew that she sometimes lied because she thought people would be more apt to like her. Other times she lied to get herself out of trouble or to cover up her feelings when she was hurt or angry. But that didn't explain why she lied all the time. Maybe, as her grandmother said, she was a born liar.

It wasn't until Lizzie got herself caught in the middle of so many lies that she lost her only friend, that she could admit her problem to herself and to her family. After their initial shock had passed, everyone agreed to help Lizzie stop lying. Lizzie took the next step by admitting her lies to her friend Sue.

Levy has brought such an appropriately light touch to a fairly common problem that many children find this story enjoyable. Overlook the book's faults (Lizzie's grandmother is overdrawn and her mother's guilt feelings are unsupported by the story) for the fun and the message young readers get from it.

Interest Level: 3-5. Reading Level: 4.2. Further Search Topics: Honesty-Fiction, Group 2, Friendship-Fiction, Best Sellers, Everyday Stories, Family Problems-Fiction, Grandparents-Fiction, Humorous Fiction.

Lowry, Lois. Anastasia Krupnik. HM 1979, 113 pp.
Anastasia Krupnik led a comfortable, relatively happy life until her parents announced that she was not going to be an only child for much longer. After 10 years of enjoying that luxury, Anastasia wasn't at all pleased with the change. Babies immediately went to a prominent, and as far as Anastasia was concerned, permanent place on her list of hates. Anastasia kept two lists: one for things and people she particularly liked, and one list for what she did not like. What went on and off the lists tells much about Anastasia. Anastasia tells the rest in this perceptive, sensitive, and humorous story of growing up and adjusting to a new sibling.

Spacing between lines is slightly too narrow for the rather large print.

Interest Level: 4-6. Reading Level: 3.1. Further Search Topics: Humorous Fiction, Brothers and Sisters-Fiction, Everyday Stories, Jealousy-Fiction, Infants-Fiction, Best Sellers, Children-Growth-Fiction.

Lowry, Lois. Anastasia again! HM 1981, 145 pp.
This is a sequel that is as funny and well-written as its predecessor. Because its plot involves less common experiences, this book may not enjoy quite the wide-spread success of *Anastasia Krupnik*. However, among those readers who liked their first meeting with Anastasia, this book will find many fans.

Anastasia's parents astounded her when they announced that the family was going to move from their Cambridge, Massachusetts apartment to a house in the suburbs. She didn't like the idea of leaving the apartment, but she *hated* the idea of the suburbs. The only thing that made the move bearable was the house itself. Anastasia had said she would move only if they could find a house with a tower—and they had. After she got over the shock of moving, Anastasia began to enjoy her new home. She met a neighborhood boy who became a special friend, she tried to help her cranky elderly neighbor Mrs. Stein make friends, and she even wrote a short mystery book.

Anastasia is as spunky and original as before. She is a bit precocious, but her precocity is nothing compared to that of her brother. At two-and-a-half years old, he speaks as well as many adults. As we mentioned above, the book will be most appealing to readers who want second helpings of Anastasia's adventures. The print is slightly smaller here than in the first title.

Interest Level: 4-6. Reading Level: 2.2. Further Search Topics: Moving, Household-Fiction, City Life-Fiction, Suburbia-Fiction, Humorous Fiction, Aging-Fiction, Writing-Fiction, Family-Fiction, Everyday Stories.

MacLachlan, Patricia. Arthur, for the very first time; illus by Lloyd Bloom. Har-Row 1980, 117 pp.
A beautifully written, sensitive yet humorous story of a boy's maturation and growing awareness of the world around him. When Arthur's unhappiness at home is made more intense by the advent of a new baby, he is sent to spend the summer with his older aunt and uncle. Their eccentricities and those of their friends are at first only material for Arthur to write about in his journal. But as the summer progresses he not only learns from them, but also grows from an observer of life to a participant. His final step is helping a large and beloved pig bear her litter in a driving rain storm aided only by his independent, totally untamed young friend Moira.

The print is somewhat small, but spacing between lines is generous.

Interest Level: 4-6. Reading Level: 4.2. Further Search Topics: Read Aloud, Children-Growth-Fiction, Humorous Fiction, Friendship-Fiction, Vacation-Fiction, Relatives-Fiction, Infants-Fiction, Individualists-Fiction, Writing-Fiction, Loners-Fiction, Group 2.

Miles, Betty. The secret life of the underwear champ; illus by Dan Jones. Knopf 1981, 117 pp.
Larry hadn't planned it; in fact, he hadn't even really wanted it to happen. But suddenly he found himself about to make a television commercial for ChampWin Knitting Mills, makers of sports clothing and underwear. He knew his family could use the money he would make, but he certainly didn't want the whole school seeing him in his underwear. Nevertheless, Larry went ahead and made the commercial, hoping that it would never be used. He even had to skip baseball practice to make the taping. Much to his horror, the commercial appeared the night before the team's first game. Not only did the entire opposing team tease him, but so did all his own teammates. By the time he got up to bat, Larry was mad enough to slam the ball out of the park. He didn't hit the ball quite that hard, but he did make a winning home run and end the others' giggles forever. He became the true underwear champ.

This is a funny look at the embarrassments of growing up. It also deals lightly with a boy's pride, his peer relationship, and his growing awareness of girls. An appealing and broadly usable title. Capers series.

Interest Level: 3-5. Reading Level: 2.2. Further Search Topics: Baseball-Fiction, Television-Fiction, Occupations-Fiction, School Stories, Humorous Fiction, Advertising-Fiction, Beauty-Fiction, Motion Pictures-Fiction, Best Sellers, Everyday Stories.

Nodset, Joan L. Go away dog; illus by Crosby Bonsall. Har-Row 1963, unp (29 pp).
A small boy who doesn't like dogs meets a shaggy, homeless dog who wants to play. The little boy, resisting all the way, gradually gives in to the dog's charms. Finally he tells the dog to follow him home. At home, he finds out that the dog was sent to him for his birthday by his Uncle George.

The dog, the boy, and the book are irresistible. You must, however, notice the illustrations on both the dedication and title pages to fully understand the story. Since much of the story is told by the illustrations and the text is repetitive as well as simple, it is an excellent beginning-to-read story.

Interest Level: 1-2. Reading Level: 1.1. Further Search Topics: Dogs-Fiction, Humorous Fiction, Best Sellers, Pets-Fiction, Birthdays-Fiction.

Parish, Peggy. Too many rabbits; illus by Leonard Kessler. Macmillan 1974, 48 pp.
One day Miss Molly opened her front door to find a rabbit waiting to be invited inside. The next day Miss Molly discovered the rabbit had had baby rabbits, lots of baby rabbits. Because babies need care, Miss Molly couldn't just turn them out, so she kept them all.

Before long she had more rabbits than she could handle. She tried giving them away, but all the children's mothers refused to keep them, the zoo didn't need any, and Miss Molly didn't want to sell them to the butcher. Finally a man who owned an island where they could live, asked to take all the rabbits. As Miss Molly was about to close the door after giving the rabbits to the man with an island, a cat walked right up to her and inside her house. The next day Miss Molly discovered she had kittens—lots of kittens. A very humorous story in a reader format.

Interest Level: 1-3. Reading Level: 1.2. Further Search Topics: Humorous Fiction, Rabbits-Fiction, Best Sellers.

Peck, Robert Newton. Mr. Little; illus by Ben Stahl. Doubleday 1979, 87 pp.

All summer long Drag and Finley had looked forward to having Miss Kellogg as their teacher, so they were extremely disappointed to find ordinary-looking Mr. Little in her place on the first day of school. Used to playing tricks on their teachers anyway, Drag and Finley decided to go all out to get even with Mr. Little for spoiling their year. But try as they might, they couldn't get an advantage over Mr. Little; he seemed to be unflappable. Finally, in their riskiest prank ever, they stole Mr. Little's underwear to dress a statue in the town square. That attempt to embarrass Mr. Little only served to get Finley and Drag in serious trouble from which Mr. Little saved them. It was his later rescue of Miss Kellogg, however, that added respect to the boys' growing feeling of friendship for Mr. Little.

Because the author's adult viewpoint is never quite lost, even though he writes in the first person, and because the rural and historic time settings are not familiar to many readers, the book may need some introduction and encouragement. It is a prime candidate for reading aloud until the young reader's interest takes over. Print is of adequate size, but spacing between lines could have been more generous.

Interest Level: 4-6. Reading Level: 5.1. Further Search Topics: Humorous Fiction, School Stories, Troublemakers-Fiction, Group 2, Read Aloud, Country Life-Fiction, Best Sellers.

Pene du Bois, William. Lazy Tommy Pumpkinhead. Har-Row 1966, 32 pp.

Tommy lived a solitary life in an all-electric house. An electric bed woke Tommy and slid him into a tub full of warm water. The tub then tipped him out and into a harness that held Tommy upright while other machines dried him, combed his hair, brushed his teeth, dressed him, and fed him. But one day Tommy's life was literally turned upside down with disastrous results. His feet were cleaned and combed and his clothes were all put on upside down, but the worst part of all was that Tommy almost starved; the machine fed his feet instead of his mouth.

A tongue-in-cheek warning against laziness. The lesson is obvious but the treatment (both text and illustrations) is so enjoyable that the book is appealing to almost any reader who wants a short, funny book. Print is somewhat small but spacing between lines is more than adequate.

Interest Level: 1-6. Reading Level: 3.2. Further Search Topics: Electricity-Fiction, Robots-Fiction, Laziness-Fiction, Humorous Fiction, Group 2, Read Aloud.

Pfeffer, Susan Beth. Just between us; illus by Lorna Tomei. Delacorte 1980, 116 pp.

Cass's inability to keep secrets finally became such a problem that Cass asked her mother to help her learn how to keep them. Cass's mother, a psychology student, devised a behavior modification experiment. Every day that Cass was able to figure out which bit of information she had been told was a secret and keep it, she received a dollar. After a poor start Cass did well for a while, until the day she told three secrets and made her entire family angry at her.

More determined than ever, Cass tried again. This time she found herself caught between two friends. Only Cass knew that Robin was adopted and Robin wanted it kept a secret. Jenny was so mad at Robin that she decided to spread an untrue story to hurt Robin. She told Cass not to tell anyone what she was going to do. The story Jenny was going to spread was that Robin was adopted. After hours of mental anguish Cass finally devised a way to stop Jenny and help Jenny return to being the nice person she had been before her parents' divorce.

The reading level of this book varies greatly from second grade to mid-fourth grade. Otherwise, it is good fare for Judy Blume fans. Print size just a slight bit on the small side.

Interest Level: 4-6. Reading Level: 3.2. Further Search Topics: Humorous Fiction, Everyday Stories, Friendship-Fiction, School Stories, Divorce and Separation-Fiction, Psychiatrists-Fiction, Secrets-Fiction.

Pfeffer, Susan Beth. Kid power; illus by Leigh Grant. Watts 1977, 121 pp.

When Janie's mother lost her job, her father's salary wouldn't stretch to provide any more money for the new bicycle fund. There was enough money already set aside to pay for one new bike, but both Janie and her older sister Carol wanted a bicycle. Carol, who had saved money of her own, suggested that they each pay for half a bike and their parents contribute the money for the other half. Then Janie's only problem was how to earn money, since she had none saved. Her solution was to create a business: Kid Power. Before long, Janie's business had blossomed and she was becoming rich, but she had lost her best friend and was ruining a client's roses. When Janie finally realized that getting rich wasn't the only thing that mattered in life, she relaxed, delegated jobs to friends better able to handle them, and became their agent.

A genuinely funny book that, as a bonus, takes a realistic look at the interworkings of a family. Consistent reading level.

Interest Level: 4-6. Reading Level: 3.1. Further Search Topics: Occupations-Fiction, Everyday Stories, Vacation-Fiction, Family-Fiction, Humorous Fiction, Best Sellers, Bicycles and Bicycling-Fiction, Friendship-Fiction.

Pinkwater, Daniel Manus. Fat men from space. Dodd 1977, 57 pp.

The evening after his trip to the dentist William found that he could still hear radio programs when his radio was turned off. He was even more surprised to find that when he wired himself to a fence he could hear spacemen talking. When the spacemen discovered that William could hear them, they landed and captured him. They were on a top secret mission and couldn't risk any human knowing about their existence. The spacemen were about to invade Earth to consume all the junk food they could find. As mass panic set in on Earth, William could do nothing to save his fellow humans. He was held captive and helpless until the invaders' interest was captured by a giant potato pancake floating in outer space.

A tongue-in-check, slapstick spoof of science fiction, food fads, and junk food. Do not expect anything more.

Interest Level: 3-5. Reading Level: 3.2. Further Search Topics: Science Fiction, Humorous Fiction, Food-Fiction, Flying Saucers-Fiction, Aliens-Fiction, Best Sellers, Kidnapping-Fiction, Teeth-Fiction.

Pinkwater, Daniel Manus. The Hoboken chicken emergency. P-H 1977, 83 pp.

Arthur's mother sent him out with $16 to buy a Thanksgiving turkey. He returned with a live 266 pound chicken on a leash. It seemed that their turkey reservation had been lost at the meat market and, because it was Thanksgiving morning, there were no other turkeys available. Arthur searched everywhere but found nothing, until a strange old professor tricked him into buying the chicken. No one could bear to kill and eat such a large and friendly chicken, so Arthur and his family named it Henrietta and kept it as a pet. Henrietta was a difficult pet to keep hidden from the neighbors When the neighbors, and later the city, saw Henrietta running loose there was general hysteria. But all ended well when Henrietta and the city calmed down and Henrietta became a kind of neighborhood mascot.

A purely absurd plot but presented with enough energy and humor that most readers thoroughly enjoy the book. Some brief introduction may be necessary to get readers beyond the first few pages.

Interest Level: 3-6. Reading Level: 2.2. Further Search Topics: Humorous Fiction, Chickens-Fiction, Pets-Fiction, Thanksgiving-Fiction, Holidays-Fiction, Read Aloud, Best Sellers.

Robinson, Barbara. The best Christmas pageant ever; illus by Judith Gwyn Brown. Har-Row 1972, 80 pp.

A truly delightful story of what happens when the meanest kids in town (they are all in one family) take over all the lead roles in the Sunday school Christmas pageant. The Herdmans (all six of them), having heard that the church was giving away free food, showed up to take some. While they were there, they heard about the Christmas pageant and decided it presented them with another perfect opportunity for food and mischief. With a little behind-the-scenes arm-twisting (literally), they managed to dissuade everyone else from showing interest in the major roles. Theirs was a completely original interpretation of the Christmas story that left nothing and no one around them untouched.

That the book's reading level will prove too high for many people is unfortunate. The story is well worth the struggle. A wonderful choice for reading aloud.

Interest Level: 3-6. Reading Level: 5.1 Further Search Topics: Christmas-Fiction, Bullies-Fiction, Troublemakers-Fiction, Humorous Fiction, Religion-Fiction, Group 2, Read Aloud, Acting-Fiction, Holidays-Fiction.

Robinson, Jean. The strange but wonderful cosmic awareness of Duffy Moon; illus by Lawrence Di Fiori. HM 1974, 142 pp.

Duffy was tired of being small, of always being on the losing side of fights, and of being unappreciated at home (by his ex-football star uncle). When he sent away for Mr. Flamel's Cosmic Awareness Kit, Duffy was sure he would then be able to take control over anything he wanted and direct his own life. His friend

Peter, the narrator, wasn't quite so sure. Peter turned out to be right. Duffy almost made himself sick trying to build a stone wall. Babysitting two small boys and trying to bathe a Great Dane proved to be disastrous. But Duffy's biggest problem came from Boots McAfee's gang. A series of events finally brought Duffy and Peter face-to-face with the dreaded Boots. Luckily, she turned out to be a very smart girl who appreciated Duffy's true talents.

From the first to the last page this is a funny, very enjoyable book. A delightful book with a very palatable message.

Interest Level: 3-6. Reading Level: 3.2. Further Search Topics: Humorous Fiction, Bullies-Fiction, Magic-Fiction, Read Aloud, Occupations-Fiction, Sex Role-Fiction, Orphans-Fiction, Best Sellers, Gangs-Fiction, Courage-Fiction, Babysitting-Fiction.

Robinson, Nancy K. Wendy and the bullies; illus by Ingrid Fetz. Hastings 1980, 128 pp.

Wendy and her best friend Karen had a very carefully mapped out route to and from school—a route that allowed them to meet up with the fewest number of bullies possible. But when Karen became sick enough to stay home from school, Wendy had to face the bullies alone. Wendy's fears escalated to panic so intense that she avoided walking to school by hiding in her basement. She finally realized that she was letting fear and anger control her life when she found herself bullying Karen. Only her new friendship with Monica, making up with Karen, and her involvement in a school project helped Wendy overcome her fears.

This is a humorous, episodic tale of a feeling and circumstances common to many children. The illustrations sometimes make Wendy and her classmates appear much younger than her actual nine years, but fortunately that doesn't happen often enough to spoil the book's appeal.

Interest Level: 3-5. Reading Level: 3.1. Further Search Topics: School Stories, Bullies-Fiction, Courage-Fiction, Best Sellers, Humorous Fiction, Friendship-Fiction, Everyday Stories.

Rockwell, Thomas. How to eat fried worms; illus by Emily McCully. Watts 1973, 116 pp.

It started more as a joke than anything else, but it escalated into a strange commitment. Alan bet Billy $50 that Billy couldn't eat a worm a day for fifteen days. Billy had always been willing to take almost any dare offered and he was stubborn enough to carry them out, but when he actually faced the first worm (an enormous night crawler), he almost backed down. He and his friend Tom had to keep repeating the word "minibike" (the prize he planned to buy with the money) and smother the worm in everything imaginable in order to eat it all. After the first worm, however, the next few were easier to face. That was when Alan and his ally Joe, began using psychological warfare and almost won. In 41 very short, grotesquely funny chapters Billy becomes the proud owner of a minibike and is the first person to become hooked on worm sandwiches.

Once this book is started, it is hard to resist its gruesome fascination. Although the print is somewhat small, and there are occasionally very difficult or babytalk words, the interest is strong enough to sustain almost all readers.

Interest Level: 3-6. Reading Level: 3.1. Further Search Topics: Humorous Fiction, Worms-Fiction, Read Aloud, Best Sellers, Challenges-Fiction, Food-Fiction, Bicycles and Bicycling-Fiction.

Seuss, Dr.. One fish, two fish, red fish, blue fish. Beginner 1960, 63pp.

Beginning with one almost ordinary-looking fish, this is a humorous look at the "funny things that go by." When Dr. Seuss says "funny," he really means highly imaginative, whimsical, and totally nonsensical. Each of the more than 20 silly creatures are described and appropriately illustrated to appeal to a child's sense of the ridiculous. Reader.

Interest Level: 1-2. Reading Level: 1.1. Further Search Topics: Fantasy, Wit and Humor, Poetry, Humorous Fiction, Stories in Rhyme.

Seuss, Dr. Hop on Pop. Beginner 1963, 64pp.

Between one and four rhyming words are introduced or reviewed and used in a silly sentence on each page. The sentence is interpreted with even more amusing illustrations. It is one of the simplest of books (no story at all) and yet it is usable through second grade because of Dr. Seuss' playful style and ridiculous illustrations. Reader format.

Interest Level: 1-2. Reading Level: 1.1. Further Search Topics: Poetry, Best Sellers, Wit and Humor, Humorous Fiction, Stories in Rhyme.

Seuss, Dr. The cat in the hat. Beginner 1957, 61 pp.

When the Cat in the Hat visits two children, a dreary, boring afternoon becomes almost too exciting. The Cat's juggling act and the two "things" he brings with him almost destroy the house. But the Cat cleans up so well that when the children's mother comes home and asks what they did all afternoon, they can't decide if they should tell her.

A funny, rhyming tale of the destruction all children can create and the boredom all children can feel. Reader format.

Interest Level: 1-3. Reading Level: 1.2. Further Search Topics: Humorous Fiction, Fantasy, Cats-Fiction, Poetry, Troublemakers-Fiction, Best Sellers, Stories in Rhyme.

Seuss, Dr. The cat in the hat comes back. Beginner 1958, 63 pp.

Sally and her brother were doing a good job of clearing the front walk of snow when the Cat in the Hat showed up. While they worked, the Cat created a pink mess in the house. The mess only became worse when he tried to clean it. The pink spot finally covered the snow all around the house until the Cat called upon his friends Little Cats A-Z. It was Little Cat Z and his magic zoom that eventually not only cleaned the snow, but cleared the front walk as well.

Another zany, rhymed adventure of the mischievious Cat whose ability to get into trouble endears him to most children from pre-school to early third grade. Reader format.

Interest Level: 1-3. Reading Level: 1.2. Further Search Topics: Fantasy, Cats-Fiction, Troublemakers-Fiction, Humorous Fiction, Snow-Fiction, Poetry, Best Sellers, Stories in Rhyme.

Seuss, Dr. The foot book. Random 1968, unp (27 pp).

Left feet, right feet, big feet, small feet; with its rhyme, silly illustrations and rhythmic celebration of feet of all descriptions, this book is a sure winner with the very young. Reader format.

Interest Level 1-2. Reading Level: 1.1. Further Search Topics: Best Sellers, Feet-Fiction, Humorous Fiction, Poetry, Wit and Humor, Stories in Rhyme.

Sharmat, Marjorie W. Nate the great goes undercover; illus by Marc Simont. Coward 1974, 47 pp.

Nate's next door neighbor Oliver was a pest, but Oliver had a mystery for Nate to solve. Oliver's garbage can was being burglarized at night. He wanted Nate to catch the garbage snatcher. Nate quickly drew up a list of human suspects and just as quickly eliminated them all. A night spent hiding in the garbage can proved the best way to catch the thief. Much to Nate's surprise, the thief turned out to be his new dog.

Very amusing and very useful. Reader format.

Interest Level: 1-3. Reading Level: 2.1. Further Search Topics: Humorous Fiction, Mystery and Detective Stories, Group 2, Detectives-Fiction, Best Sellers.

Sharmat, Marjorie W. Nate the great; illus by Marc Simont. Coward 1972, 62 pp.

This is a young imitation of Humphrey Bogart solving a *Dragnet* style mystery. Annie's recently finished painting of her dog had disappeared so she hired Nate to search for it. Nate gathered all the facts, investigated his suspects, and eventually solved the mystery, but not before he had consumed plenty of pancakes (his favorite food) and solved a second mystery by accident.

A simple plot, humorous telling, and a sympathetic, likeable protagonist make this one of a very popular series. Reader format.

Interest Level: 1-3. Reading Level: 2.1. Further Search Topics: Humorous Fiction, Detectives-Fiction, Mystery and Detective Stories, Group 2, Best Sellers.

Sharmat, Marjorie W. Getting something on Maggie Marmelstein; illus by Ben Shecter. Har-Row 1971, 101 pp.

A curious love-hate relationship existed between Thad and Maggie. It all began when Maggie overheard Thad say she squeaked like a mouse. Then Maggie caught Thad wearing an apron and cooking. Thad was so uncomfortable with the thought that Maggie might tell his friends, that he was determined to find out Maggie's deepest secret. That meant that Thad had to take a lead role as a frog opposite Maggie as the princess in the school play. While at Maggie's apartment for a costume fitting, Thad found a love letter Maggie had written to Cary Grant. Thad decided he would read the letter to the class right after the play was over. But during the play Maggie saved Thad from what could have been one of the most embarrassing moments of his life. By the time he finally had the chance to make Maggie appear foolish, Thad had changed his mind.

Written as Thad's story, the book is funny, warm, and realistic. A good, short, story that continues to be popular. Print is of moderate size.

Interest Level: 3-6. Reading Level: 3.1. Further Search Topics: Humorous Fiction, Everyday Stories, School Stories, Best Sellers, Friendship-Fiction, Sex Role-Fiction, Acting-Fiction.

Sharmat, Marjorie W. Maggie Marmelstein for President; illus by Ben Shecter. Har-Row 1975, 122 pp.

Maggie and Thad Smith are at it again. When Thad decided to run for sixth grade president, Maggie decided to become his campaign manager. However, because Thad thought Maggie was too strong and would end up managing him much more than he wanted to be managed, he turned down her offer. Thad's refusal made Maggie so angry that she not only decided to run against Thad, but she also enlisted Noah, the smartest kid in the class, as her manager. With Noah's expert guidance Maggie's campaign went rather well, despite attempts at sabotage by a spy for Thad. But as election day drew closer, both Thad and Maggie lost track of the campaign issues and concentrated only on beating each other. Consequently the pre-election debate turned into a disastrous shouting match. The next day Noah was elected class president by write-in votes.

Not very subtle, but funny. A satisfying sequel for those who enjoyed *Getting Something on Maggie Marmelstein.*

Interest Level: 3-6. Reading Level: 3.1. Further Search Topics: Humorous Fiction, Politics-Fiction, School Stories, Friendship-Fiction, Sex Role-Fiction.

Sharmat, Marjorie W. The Lancelot closes at five; illus by Lisl Weil. Macmillan 1976, 120 pp.

Despite a somewhat slow beginning, this is an amusing, almost sensitive story of two friends who decided to spend the night in the model home of the new housing development in which they both lived. Hutch, a health food fanatic whose mother pronounced judgment on everything Hutch did, conceived of the idea as her way of breaking away. Abby went along for the fun of it. When the local newspaper wrote of unusual vandalism at the model home, the townspeople became engrossed in finding the culprits. As the adults became enraged about the crime wave, their children began to admire the clever idea. Soon, almost every youngster in town had confessed to spending the night in the model home. By the time Abby and Hutch got around to admitting they had slept there, no one believed them. Only a sock with Abby's name in it could tie Abby and Hutch to the scene of the crime. As the book ends, the police have begun a thorough search of the house, after a real robbery, and the sock's discovery is imminent.

Interest Level: 4-6. Reading Level: 3.2. Further Search Topics: Humorous Fiction, Suburbia-Fiction, Runaways-Fiction, Crime-Fiction, Individualists-Fiction, Family Problems-Fiction.

Smith, Alison. Help! There's a cat washing in here!; illus by Amy Rowen. Dutton 1981, 152 pp.

Henry Walker agreed to care for his younger brother and sister for two weeks so that his mother could spend her time preparing a portfolio of her art work in the hopes of getting a much-needed job. It was a desperate move for Henry, but it was the only way he could prevent his bossy Aunt Wilhemina from moving in to run the household. Despite Henry's best efforts, almost everything seemed to go wrong. He burned the food, couldn't keep his brother and sister from misbehaving, seemed to have poisoned his sister's friend, and was faced with making a costume in one night for a school play. The worst of it all was that his mother wasn't pleased with what she was drawing, and Henry only seemed to make her feel more discouraged and unhappy. After what appeared to be certain defeat, however, Henry's efforts were rewarded. His mother was given the job, the family proved they could take care of themselves, and all ended happily.

A light, humorous tale of a young boy's growing independence and maturation under stress and increased responsibility.

Interest Level: 4-6. Reading Level: 3.1. Further Search Topics: Brothers and Sisters-Fiction, Working Parents-Fiction, Single Parent Family-Fiction, Humorous Fiction, Family-Fiction, Challenges-Fiction, Children-Growth-Fiction.

Steven, Carla. Hooray for Pig!; illus by Rainey Bennett. HM 1974, 48 pp.

Pig couldn't spend the day swimming with his friend Raccoon because he didn't know how to swim. Instead Pig took a picnic to the lake by himself. At the lake, Pig met Otter, who encouraged Pig to at least try getting in the water. After several days of Otter's patient coaching, not only could Pig stay afloat, but he liked it, too!

For much the same audience as Kessler's *Last One In Is A Rotten Egg,* but because of a more interesting plot it is a little more useful. Reader format.

Interest Level: 1-2. Reading Level: 1.2. Further Search Topics: Pigs-Fiction, Courage-Fiction, Swimming-Fiction, Humorous Fiction.

Thomas, Kathleen. Out of the bug jar; illus by Tom O'Sullivan. Dodd 1981, 125 pp.

Even though 10-year-old Tom Jenkins didn't believe in the tooth fairy, when one of his teeth fell out, he placed it under his pillow just in case he was wrong. In the middle of that night he was awakened by a small creature crawling under his pillow and grumbling. Tom quickly scooped him into a bug jar he kept nearby and thus began two years of life with Marvin, a tooth fairy. Marvin was a delightful dictator; he ruled Tom's life. He put Tom into a terrible predicament when Tom tried to charge others to see him and Marvin became invisible. Marvin insisted on being fed just what he demanded, despite the difficulties he made for Tom. He badgered Tom to do his homework, to brush his teeth, and to tell the truth. He even managed to follow Tom to school. The only other person Marvin would allow to see or hear him was Tom's friend Sammy. Tom couldn't get rid of Marvin either. Because Tom had captured him, Marvin, should he ever have been able to escape, was entitled to take *all* of Tom's teeth as compensation for being held prisoner.

Actually Marvin didn't really want to escape. He had grown tired of having to race around and collect teeth. For a while then, everyone was fairly content. Tom had all his teeth and Marvin had a rather nice home. Then quite by accident, Marvin got loose. Both Tom and Marvin wanted Tom to catch Marvin again. Tom wanted to keep his teeth and Marvin wanted to keep his comfortable lifestyle, but Marvin played by the rules and wouldn't give Tom any help at all. After more than seven days of valient but fruitless efforts and nights of sleeping with tape over his mouth, Tom finally caught Marvin and all were happy again.

An amusing story told in short sentences and short chapters. The book should be popular with those who enjoy either fantasy or humor.

Interest Level: 3-5. Reading Level: 2.2. Further Search Topics: Fantasy, Fairies-Fiction, Humorous Fiction, Teeth-Fiction.

Wiseman, Bernard. Morris and Boris. Dodd 1974, 64 pp.

This is a compilation of three silly stories about Morris the Moose and Boris the Bear. When Boris tries to interest Morris in telling riddles, Morris frustrates Boris so completely that Boris runs off angrily. Later Boris tries to teach Morris a tongue twister, but ends up running off in total confusion. Finally Boris tries to teach Morris to play hide-and-seek and that, too, is a disaster. Boris tells Morris that Morris just cannot do anything. A bird who has seen everything reminds Boris that Morris can make him very angry and that is something. When Boris agrees they all laugh happily.

Broad, slapstick humor makes this appealing to children well into third grade. Reader format.

Interest Level: 1-3. Reading Level: 1.2. Further Search Topics: Wit and Humor, Riddles, Tongue Twisters, Games, Humorous Fiction.

Wolkoff, Judie. Wally. Bradbury 1977, 199 pp.

Michael Price agreed to take care of his friend Billy's chuckwalla for three weeks. But because his mother had declared a moratorium on any more reptiles in the house, Michael tried to hide Wally in his closet. With help from his brother Roger, Michael managed to keep Wally a secret until Wally was mistakenly left out of his box one night. Despite Michael and Roger's desperate searches, the chuckwalla did not reappear until Mr. and Mrs. Price were involved in the final negotiations for the sale of their house. Wally completely disrupted the proceedings, prevented the sale and thus made everyone happy. For as it turned out, none of the Prices had really wanted to move after all.

A fast-paced, funny book with much reader appeal.

Interest Level: 2-5. Reading Level: 2.2. Further Search Topics: Pets-Fiction, Humorous Fiction, Lizards-Fiction, Best Sellers, Reptiles-Fiction, Secrets-Fiction.

Yolen, Jane. Shirlick Holmes and the case of the wandering wardrobe; illus by Anthony Rao. Coward 1981, 80 pp.

This is a light, fast-paced story of Shirli and her four friends' attempt to solve a local mystery. Its more fully developed characters and plot make this a better literary piece than any of the *Encyclopedia Brown* stories, but it resembles them in other ways. The children live in a small, secure town. The police chief, Shirli's neighbor and George's father, is working on the same case that interests the children but the children solve it first. The mystery is real and involves danger, as opposed to many of Hildick's McGurk mysteries, the other series this book resembles.

Shirli is a fiesty figure who took up George's challenge to solve the town's latest mystery. Thieves had been systematically robbing some of the wealthy summer homes of antiques. Shirli's plan, to search each of the houses for clues, only succeeded in angering the police chief when he caught Shirli and her friends. Being intrepid detectives, however, they did not give up. Instead, they staked out a likely house and waited for the thieves. When the robbers finally arrived Shirli and George hid. Only Gloria was able to escape and go for help. The oak wardrobe in which Shirli took refuge was one of the first pieces the thieves took out of the house. When Shirli tried to get out of it, she found the wardrobe had been placed on a truck with its door against the truck's side; she was caught. Very frightened, she stayed silent until she found herself in the middle of an antiques auction and recognized one of the voices making bids as George's father! As Shirli tumbled out of the wardrobe some of the police chief's men arrested the auctioneer for burglary and selling stolen goods. After she escaped, Gloria had told the police about the thieves, their truck, Shirli, and George, whom they found locked inside a closet still at the summer house.

A serviceable book that will be enjoyed by a wide range of readers.

Interest Level: 3-5. Reading Level: 3.1. Further Search Topics: Mystery and Detective Stories, Humorous Fiction, Friendship-Fiction, Crime-Fiction, Antiquities-Fiction, Detectives-Fiction, Challenges-Fiction.

HUNTER, JIM "CATFISH"

Burchard, Susan H. Sports star: Jim "Catfish" Hunter. HarBraceJ 1976, 64 pp.

The pitcher who, because of contract violations by his club's owner, became the first free agent in baseball. See Marshall Burchard's *Sports Hero: Bill Walton* for information about the series. Sports Star series.

Interest Level: 2-6. Reading Level: 3.1. Further Search Topics: Biography, Baseball-Biography, Hunter, Jim "Catfish", Group 2.

HUNTING-FICTION

Clymer, Eleanor. Chipmunk in the forest; illus by Ingrid Fetz. Atheneum 1965, 56 pp.

A simple story of an Indian boy who learned the meaning of the word "courage". Chipmunk had never admitted to anyone that he was afraid of the forest. But when his uncle tried to teach him to hunt, Chipmunk was too frightened to be quiet, and thus he scared away all the animals. He returned to the village in disgrace to do "women's work." One of his jobs was to watch Little Brother. When Little Brother disappeared, Chipmunk went in search of him. It began to snow as Chipmunk went farther and farther into the forest, but even though he was frightened, Chipmunk kept on looking. By the time he found Little Brother, the snow had covered their tracks. Chipmunk had to use all that he had learned from his uncle to get them safely home. When he arrived back at the village, Chipmunk had finally proven that he was brave.

Interest Level: 2-4. Reading Level: 2.1. Further Search Topics: Indians of North America-Fiction, Courage-Fiction, Snow-Fiction, Hunting-Fiction, Survival-Fiction.

ICE SKATING

Krementz, Jill. A very young skater. Knopf 1979, unp (103 pp).

Katherine Healy started ice skating because her parents liked to skate and because it was easier for them to take her with them than it was to find a babysitter. From such beginnings, at age three, Katherine progressed to skating in Superskates at Madison Square Garden and ballet lessons at George Balanchine's School of American Ballet. See *A Very Young Dancer* for further explanation.

Interest Level: 2-6. Reading Level: 4.1. Further Search Topics: Ice Skating, Dancing, Ballet, Talent, Group 2, Best Sellers.

ICE SKATING-BIOGRAPHY

Burchard, Susan H. Sports star: Dorothy Hamill. HarBraceJ 1978, 63 pp.

Although written by Susan Burchard, this and most of the following listings are true to Marshall Burchard's *Sports Hero* format. For more explanation see *Sports Hero: Bill Walton*.

Dorothy Hamill was the darling of ice skating in 1976 and is now a top professional figure skater. This makes her rise to stardom sound romantic and glamorous. Skating jargon pushes the reading level from 3.1 to 3.2. Sports Star series.

Interest Level: 2-6. Reading Level: 3.2. Further Search Topics: Hamill, Dorothy, Ice Skating-Biography, Women-Biography, Biography, Group 2.

ICE SKATING-FICTION

Christopher, Matt. Face-off; illus by Harvey Kidder. Little 1972, 131 pp.

Christopher sticks strictly to the sports story formula here. The characters seem to have no time or thoughts for anything but sports. They epitomize the macho image, and once their problems with sports are solved everything in life seems to fall into place. But, for the young sports enthusiast who doesn't really like to read, this formula of much sports action and very little else is successful.

Scott had never played hockey but he was an extremely fast skater. When Del and Skinny asked him to join their hockey team and to be one of the Three Icekateers, Scott was thrilled. But Scott's performance was less than inspiring and Del's patience with his failures was short. The two almost came to blows when Scott discovered that he was puck-shy and would duck every time someone took a shot near him. Their coach's advice to both of them helped clear up Scott's problem and Del's impatience. All ends happily as Scott played well and he and Del became friends once more.

Interest Level: 3-6. Reading Level: 3.1. Further Search Topics: Hockey-Fiction, Ice Skating-Fiction, Courage-Fiction, Friendship-Fiction.

ILLNESS-FICTION

Blume, Judy. Deenie. Bradbury 1973, 159 pp.

Deenie's mother wanted Deenie to be a model. Deenie didn't know what she wanted until she learned that she had scoliosis (curvature of the spine) and would have to wear a brace for four years. Then she knew she only wanted to be normal. She was repulsed by deformities of any kind. She couldn't stand the idea of a brace. Her mother's attitude made Deenie's adjustment even more difficult. It was her father, her doctor, her sister, and a new friend with excema who finally helped Deenie accept her brace and the idea of physical differences. Subplots include Deenie's budding romance with an eighth grade boy, her strained relationship with her mother, and her growing awareness of sex (masturbation and intercourse). Print and line spacing are similar to *Are You There God? It's Me, Margaret.*

Interest Level: 5-6. Reading Level: 3.1. Further Search Topics: Models, Fashion-Fiction, Beauty-Fiction, Scoliosis-Fiction, Physically Handicapped-Fiction, Children-Growth-Fiction, Sex-Fiction, Love-Fiction, Family Problems-Fiction, Illness-Fiction, Adolescence-Fiction.

Coerr, Eleanor. Sadako and the thousand paper cranes; illus by Ronand Himler. Putnam 1977, 64 pp.

This is a beautiful and very sad story of a young girl who was only two years old when the atomic bomb was dropped on Hiroshima. Ten years later she contracted leukemia and died a slow, painful death. A fast and enthusiastic runner, she had been full of life and energy before her illness. Soon after she became sick Sadako's best friend folded a paper crane for her and reminded her of an old story: If someone folded 1000 paper cranes, the gods would give that person good health again. Sadako was able to fold only 644 before she died. After her death her classmates made 356 more in order that she could be buried with all 1000 paper cranes. About three years later, a statue, erected in Peace Park in Hiroshima, was dedicated to Sadako and to a hope for world peace.

Because of the theme and its straight-forward handling, this book needs a fairly mature reader.

Interest Level: 4-6. Reading Level: 3.1. Further Search Topics: Japan-Fiction, Historical Fiction, World War II-Fiction, Death-Fiction, Illness-Fiction, War-Fiction, Running-Fiction, Origami-Fiction, Read Aloud.

Singer, Marilyn. It can't hurt forever; illus by Leigh Grant. Har-Row 1978, 186 pp.

When she was 11 years old, it was discovered that Ellie had a heart valve that hadn't closed by itself. Although her mother had promised her that she wouldn't die, Ellie was scared of the hospital and the operation she had to face. Her parents were kind and open about all that was to happen to her, but there was still much that Ellie had to learn from friends she made while she was in the hospital. There were times when she was frightened and only Sonia, a young open-heart surgery patient, could calm her. When Ellie, a special nurse, and a few other patients became close friends, Ellie learned enough from them to allow her to help another patient.

This is not a story of sweetness and light, but it is told with warmth, humor, and real understanding of a young person's fears. Thus it is not only an excellent candidate for bibliotherapy, but it is a truly satisfying story for the general reader as well.

Interest Level: 4-6. Reading Level: 2.2. Further Search Topics: Illness-Fiction, Physicians-Fiction, Medicine-Fiction, Courage-Fiction, Death-Fiction.

Slote, Alfred. Hang tough, Paul Mather. Lippincott 1973, 156 pp.

Paul Mather went against his doctor's and his parents' orders when he accepted his new neighbors' challenge to show his pitching skill. He had been told not to play baseball until he had been given permission, but Paul not only loved to pitch, he was also the best pitcher his new friends had ever seen. Knowing full well the medical problems he could be precipitating, Paul went ahead and pitched a spectacular game for the Wilson Dairy team against the Ace Appliance team. But by the end of the game, Paul was in the hospital again, and Wilson Dairy had been forced to forfeit the game because Paul had played illegally. As Paul's leukemia worsened, his determination to play baseball again grew. When the day came that his team was to play a second game against Ace Appliance, Paul made sure he was there. He was in a wheelchair and weak, but he was there. He couldn't actually play, but Paul's psychological support insured that Wilson Dairy won the game. He went back to the hospital proud, happy, and still determined to fight his disease.

This is more than the usual sports story. This is a very sensitive story of a young boy's determination to fight leukemia. The reader looking for only a baseball story may find this book more than he/she wants. However, the reader who is open to a story of human strength and courage will be well rewarded. The book neither dwells on nor minimizes the disease. Instead it uses both the disease and the sport to portray a character much more completely than in most sport stories, especially at this low a reading level. This is an excellent book for those special readers who respond well to thought-provoking material. Although chapters are short and reading level is low, the print is somewhat small. In addition, the first person style, told as if dictated into a tape recorder (complete with occasional interruptions), may be confusing to readers unless it is explained.

Interest Level: 5-6+Reading Level: 3.1. Further Search Topics: Baseball-Fiction, Death-Fiction, Illness-Fiction, Moving, Household-Fiction,

Medicine-Fiction, Physicians-Fiction,
Challenges-Fiction, Courage-Fiction.

IMMIGRATION AND EMIGRATION

Bales, Carol Ann. Chinatown Sunday; the story of
Lillian Der. Contemp Bks. 1973, 32 pp.

A short, personal visit with a fifth grade
Chinese-American girl who lives in a Chicago suburb.
The author transcribed taped interviews with Lillian
Der to produce a first-person description of Lillian's
daily life. The uniquely Chinese-American features of
Lillian's life are casually intertwined with experiences
common to most American children. Month-old parties,
the celebration of Chinese New Year, lucky money,
old-age birthday parties, Girl Scout meetings,
homework, and being a tomboy are all important to
Lillian. Not only is this an interesting portrait of Lillian,
but it can be a useful part of a multi-ethnic unit or an
introduction to autobiography. The book's usefulness
is further extended by its introduction to Chinese
immigration and by the glossary, which explains terms
such as "abacus," "Chinese calendar," and "sea
cucumber." The author saves the over-sized book
from looking like a picture book by using photographs
instead of drawings, thus she makes the book
comfortable even for a sixth grade reader.

Interest Level: 3-6. Reading Level: 3.1. Further
Search Topics: Ethnic Groups, Chinese-Americans,
Biography, Chicago, Immigration and Emigration.

IMMIGRATION AND EMIGRATION-BIOGRAPHY

Bryant, Bernice. George Gershwin: young composer;
illus by Nathan Goldstein. Bobbs 1965, 200 pp.

Even when George Gershwin was very young he
loved music, showed signs of musical talent, and
longed to play the piano. However, any boy who
played the piano in George's neighborhood was called
a sissy and George didn't like being teased in that
way. When he was no longer able to keep his music
lessons a secret, he stopped them for fear of the
teasing. But each time George quit playing the piano,
he always went back to it, even when his parents
pressured him not to waste his time at the piano. A
young teacher told George that he would never be a
musician. One of George's teachers actually taught
him to play poorly, instead of well. In time, however,
George learned to play well and to compose his own
music. Then came the hard work of determining his
own style. Gradually, more and more people heard
and appreciated his American jazz, until George
Gershwin's music was heard all around the world.

Another adequate entry in the *Childhood of Famous
Americans* series. Includes the usual glossary,
bibliography, time line, and follow-up questions. It is
most likely to appeal to the reader already interested
in music. Childhood of Famous Americans series.

Interest Level: 3-6. Reading Level: 3.1. Further
Search Topics: Biography, Composers, Immigration
and Emigration-Biography, Jazz Music, Bullies,
Music-Biography, Pianists.

INDIANS OF NORTH AMERICA-BIOGRAPHY

Fall, Thomas. Jim Thorpe; illus by John Gretzer.
Har-Row 1970, 33 pp.

Jim Thorpe was an Indian from the Oklahoma
territory who became one of the United State's
greatest athletes. He and his twin brother were trained
by their father to run and jump faster and farther than
anyone else. When Charles died, Jim couldn't face
returning to school without his twin, so his family kept
him home for a few months before sending him away
to school again. Jim ran home once more when his
father and mother both became ill. Months later he

went to still another school where he was noticed by
Pop Warner. Pop advised Joe to concentrate on track
until he was big enough to play football. His father's
death left Jim so despondent he quit school to play
professional baseball for a while. By the time he went
back to school, Jim was big enough to play
spectacular football and then to win the 1912 Olympic
decathlon competition. Unfortunately, his short time as
a paid baseball player made him ineligible for the
Olympic honor and Jim's medal was taken away.
Public sentiment was with Jim, but the rules were
against him. He went on, however, to play both
professional baseball and football. In 1982, 29 years
after his death, Thorpe's medal was finally returned to
him.

A short, meaty and readable biography of a person
who should be interesting to many sports fans.
Follows the usual format of Crowell biographies, but
looks less like a picture book than many. Crowell
Biography series.

Interest Level: 3-5. Reading Level: 3.1. Further
Search Topics: Football-Biography, Indians of North
America-Biography, Baseball-Biography, Olympic
Games, Biography, Running-Biography,
Twins-Biography, Thorpe, Jim.

INDIANS OF NORTH AMERICA-FICTION

Benchley, Nathaniel. Small Wolf; illus by Joan
Sandin. Har-Row 1972, 64 pp.

A straight-forward telling of white man's purchase of
Manhattan and the resulting displacement of the
Indians. The text is simple. The tone is sympathetic to
the plight of the Indians. The reader is neither lectured
nor patronized, but the early-reader format will prevent
using the book comfortably beyond fourth grade. An I
Can Read History Book.

Interest Level: 1-4. Reading Level 2.2. Further
Search Topics: Historical Fiction, New York
City-Fiction, United States-History-Fiction, Indians of
North America-Fiction, Group 2.

Bulla, Clyde Robert. John Billington, friend of
Squanto; illus by Peter Burchard. Har-Row 1956, 88
pp.

This historical novel about the Mayflower voyage
and the Pilgrims' first year at Plymouth centers on
young John Billington. John was considered the
troublemaker of the children. His problems are woven
around the events of the year, including the Pilgrims'
first meetings with the Wampanoag Indians. It was
finally John, however, who was responsible for
bringing peace between the Pilgrims and the
Wampanoag tribe who lived further down Cape Cod.
The book is not as exciting or convincing as Bulla's
books are generally. It also contains a few minor
historical inaccuracies; yet it remains useful as both
an introduction to American history and historical
fiction.

Interest Level: 2-5. Reading Level: 2.1. Further
Search Topics: Pilgrims-Fiction, Historical Fiction,
United States-History-Fiction, Thanksgiving-Fiction,
Troublemakers-Fiction, Indians of North
America-Fiction.

Bulla, Clyde Robert. Indian hill; illus by James J.
Spanfeller. T Y Crowell 1963, 74 pp.

A very low-key story of a Navajo family who moved
from the reservation to a city because they could no
longer support themselves on the reservation. The
move was necessary, but it was not appreciated by
young Kee and his mother. They hated their ugly
apartment and the crowded city, and wanted to go
home. When an excuse to return to the reservation

arose, Kee and his mother left the city. However, by the time Kee's father arrived to tell them he had been wrong to force them to move, Kee and his mother had realized they never gave their new home a chance. They were ready to try again. No excitement here, only an understanding look at the difficulties of moving.

Interest Level: 2-5. Reading Level: 2.1. Further Search Topics: Indians of North America-Fiction, Navajo Indians-Fiction, City Life-Fiction, Moving, Household-Fiction.

Clymer, Eleanor. Chipmunk in the forest; illus by Ingrid Fetz. Atheneum 1965, 56 pp.

A simple story of an Indian boy who learned the meaning of the word "courage". Chipmunk had never admitted to anyone that he was afraid of the forest. But when his uncle tried to teach him to hunt, Chipmunk was too frightened to be quiet, and thus he scared away all the animals. He returned to the village in disgrace to do "women's work." One of his jobs was to watch Little Brother. When Little Brother disappeared, Chipmunk went in search of him. It began to snow as Chipmunk went farther and farther into the forest, but even though he was frightened, Chipmunk kept on looking. By the time he found Little Brother, the snow had covered their tracks. Chipmunk had to use all that he had learned from his uncle to get them safely home. When he arrived back at the village, Chipmunk had finally proven that he was brave.

Interest Level: 2-4. Reading Level: 2.1. Further Search Topics: Indians of North America-Fiction, Courage-Fiction, Snow-Fiction, Hunting-Fiction, Survival-Fiction.

Miles, Miska. Annie and the old one; illus by Peter Parnall. Little 1971, 44 pp.

A quietly beautiful story that will not appeal to all readers. Annie, a young Navajo girl, had a very close relationship with her grandmother. Her grandmother announced that she would "go to Mother Earth" at the time when the new rug Annie's mother was weaving was "taken from the loom." Annie tried all she could think of to keep the rug from being finished in order to keep her grandmother alive. When her grandmother solemnly explained that Annie could not stop time, Annie listened and "understood many things" for the first time.

It will be a thoughtful, sensitive child or a child trying to understand death who will best appreciate this special book.

Interest Level: 3-6. Reading Level: 3.2. Further Search Topics: Grandparents-Fiction, Death-Fiction, Indians of North America-Fiction, Navajo Indians-Fiction.

Thompson, Jean. Brother of the wolves; illus by Steve Marchesi. Morrow 1978, 159 pp.

Shadow Fox, a Sioux medicine man, went into a wolves' den looking for special items he needed for healing, but found much more. He found a baby boy who had apparently lost his parents in an accident and then been adopted by the wolves. Winter was approaching and Shadow Fox knew the baby would not be able to survive the cold, so he took the child back to his people. The people were reluctant to accept Wolf Brother, saying that he was an evil omen, that he was unnatural, and that he would bring them trouble. But Shadow Fox's will prevailed and Wolf Brother was allowed to stay and grow up with the Sioux.

As he grew Wolf Brother continued to communicate with the wolves and thus fueled the rumors that grew about him. A very jealous young man, Looks-Away, told the people that a vision had shown him that Wolf Brother and his wolves would one day destroy the village and all its people. The people grew so suspicious of Wolf Brother that, when their horses were stolen and they faced a drought, they blamed him and drove him from the village.

For a while Wolf Brother tried to live as a wolf but found that he could not be totally happy. He wandered away to look for a tribe by whom he might be accepted. On his way, he too had a vision—a vision that told him he would find horses and buffalo for the Sioux and be welcomed home again. It was weeks later before he accidentally found his tribe's horses. In a daring move and with help from the wolves, Wolf Brother not only rescued the horses from the raiders, but also found buffalo just as his vision had predicted. He was then, for the first time, fully welcomed by his people.

This is a taut, suspenseful and mature story about a strong and unusual character. Older readers are most likely to respond positively to the Indian culture and lore.

Interest Level: 5-6. Reading Level: 3.1. Further Search Topics: Survival-Fiction, Wolves-Fiction, Orphans-Fiction, Loners-Fiction, Indians of North America-Fiction, Sioux Indians-Fiction, Jealousy-Fiction, Best Sellers.

Warner, Gertrude Chandler. Mountain top mystery; illus by David Cunningham. A. Whitman 1964, 128 pp.

A day's climb up and down Old Flat Top was all the Alden family had wanted. Instead, when a portion of the trail collapsed into a cave, they found themselves stranded on top of the mountain. From their vantage point that night they could see a shadowy light which they investigated the next day. They found a 90-year-old Indian woman who had a strange story to tell of treasure hidden in a cave somewhere on Old Flat Top. The treasure was rightfully hers as the last of her tribe, but she had never been able to find it. The collapse of the trail and the reopening of the cave attracted more attention than just the Alden's though. Both an expert on caves and a young Indian boy wanted to find out more about the cave. David, the Indian boy, turned out to be the old woman's grandnephew. The treasure was indeed unearthed; David and Lovan were reunited; the treasure was given to Lovan, and both David's and Lovan's futures were secured.

What in the other books is mild stereotyping becomes more noticeable here (the books are all around 20 years old). The print is smaller here than before but the spacing between the lines is adequate. See entry for *The Boxcar Children* for more information.

Interest Level: 3-6. Reading Level: 2.2. Further Search Topics: Mystery and Detective Stories, Treasure-Fiction, Survival-Fiction, Indians of North America-Fiction, Mountain Climbing-Fiction, Brothers and Sisters-Fiction.

INDIANS OF NORTH AMERICA-LEGENDS

Baylor, Byrd. And it is still that way: legends told by Arizona Indian children. Scribner 1976, 85 pp.

Byrd Baylor has collected and written notes for forty-one short American Indian legends from seven Arizona tribes whose school children were asked to write down or illustrate their favorite legend. The result is a collection that reflects the concerns, the history, religion, humor and pride of the children and their ancestors. This excellent collection is not only interesting reading, but it also fits well into social studies and language arts units.

Interest Level: 2-6. Reading Level: 3.1. Further Search Topics: Legends, Arizona-Fiction, Navajo Indians, Hopi Indians, Papago Indians, Pima Indians, Apache Indians, Quechan Indians, Cocopah Indians, Indians of North America-Legends, Mythology, Group 2.

Bernstein, Margery. Coyote goes hunting for fire; illus by Ed Heffernan. Scribner 1974, 40 pp.

A delightful story that can be read for fun or used as part of a unit on North American Indians. A long time ago when there was no fire, all the animals but Coyote banded together to find it. The animals left Coyote behind because he was always spoiling their plans. Coyote saw them leave, chased after them and once more tried to direct everything, but only ended up losing fire. Cartoon-like illustrations add to the humor of the story. This book should make a simple, but effective play.

Interest Level: 1-4. Reading Level 2.1. Further Search Topics: Animals-Fiction, Legends, Mythology, Fire-Fiction, Indians of North America-Legends, Coyotes-Fiction, Group 2, Creation-Fiction, Drama.

INDIANS OF NORTH AMERICA-SIGN LANGUAGE

Amon, Aline. Talking hands: Indian sign language. Doubleday 1968, 80 pp.

If you can ignore the author's patronizing tone and air of self-satisfaction, this is a book with great appeal. Children love ways of communicating privately, be it Pig Latin, codes and ciphers, or just whispering. This book appeals to that love by clearly, though unattractively, demonstrating over 200 words in American Indian sign language. By the time the young reader finishes the book, he/she will not only have had the fun of learning another method of communication, but will have learned a few simple generalities about North American Indians. The index is detailed enough that any word can be quickly checked. The book is useful for history, social studies, or language arts units, as well as for fun.

Interest Level: 2-6. Reading Level: 2.2. Further Search Topics: Indians of North America-Sign Language, Communication, Nonverbal Communication, Ethnic Groups.

INDIVIDUALISTS-FICTION

Allen, Linda. Lionel and the spy next door; illus by Margot Apple. Morrow 1980, 94 pp.

No one in Lionel's family understood why he wanted to be a spy; but then, he couldn't understand why they were anthropologists and motorcycle freaks. Even though he wasn't supposed to do any more spying (especially while his parents were away) Lionel couldn't resist watching the man who moved into Miss Bannister's house, next-door. Mark Shakespeare was his name. His name was suspicious enough, but his actions firmly convinced Lionel that Mark was a spy. Lionel's attempts to trail Shakespeare only succeeded in angering others in the neighborhood. He interrupted a bird watcher and irritated a woman walking a large dog. She was already angry with Lionel's grandfather for disturbing the quiet neighborhood with his motorcycles. The closer Lionel got to finding proof that Mark was a spy, the friendlier Mark became. Mark even gave Lionel the old clock which Lionel and Miss Bannister had carefully wound each week until the old woman's death. When Lionel's grandfather finally convinced Lionel that Mark should be left alone, Mark enlisted Lionel's help in a project that left Lionel

wondering again. Much to Lionel's surprise, he learned that the papers and secret documents he and Mark had burned had all belonged to Miss Bannister, Mark's great-aunt. Forty years earlier she, not Mark, had been a spy. Lionel had been wrong about who it was, but right about a spy living next-door.

Here we find a slightly anti-climactic ending to an otherwise enjoyable book. A grandfather who rides with motorcycle gangs and the intrigue of spying should be of interest to many readers. Readers may need a little help with the few British phrases that dot the book, but otherwise, the book has an impressively consistent reading level.

Interest Level: 4-6. Reading Level: 3.1. Further Search Topics: Spies-Fiction, Family-Fiction, Mystery and Detective Stories, Individualists-Fiction, Motorcycles-Fiction, Occupations-Fiction.

Angell, Judie. Dear Lola; or how to build your own family. Bradbury 1980, 166 pp.

Arthur (age 18), James (13), Annie and Al-Willie (twins, age 10), Edmund (9), and Ben (5) wanted to run away from the orphanage and find a place where they could be a real family. After waiting months, their chance arrived one night. They escaped in a van and began living on the road. It was weeks before they found a house in which they thought they could live. They didn't want trouble with local authorities, so most of the children enrolled in school and pretended to be living with their widowed grandfather. Only James (who never left his room) and Arthur stayed home. Arthur was the anonymous author of a nationally syndicated newspaper advice column. It was with the income from his "Dear Lola" column that Arthur was able to support the "family." When the townspeople eventually began to wonder about the "strange" behavior of the children, they investigated and found no adult in charge of the household. Arthur went to court to be appointed the childrens' guardian, but the judge ruled against him. Rather than be sent to foster homes again, Arthur and the children raced from the courtroom. The book ends as the family is once more together and on their own. An unusual cast of characters in a surprisingly warm and humorous book.

Interest Level: 4-6. Reading Level 3.1. Further Search Topics: Loners-Fiction, Runaways-Fiction, Orphans-Fiction, Survival-Fiction, Family Problems-Fiction, Family-Fiction, Read Aloud, Foster Homes-Fiction, Individualists-Fiction, Humorous Fiction.

Chew, Ruth. No such thing as a witch. Hastings 1971, 112 pp.

Despite the fact that their mother said there was no such thing as a witch, Tad and Nora were convinced that their neighbor Maggie Brown was indeed a witch. And they were right! Maggie Brown knew how to make a special kind of fudge that could make anyone into an animal-lover, enable people to talk with animals, or actually transform someone into an animal. All you had to do was to eat one, two, or three pieces of fudge respectively. But Maggie's overzealous love of animals and her disenchantment with housework eventually attracted the attention of her neighbors and the city health department. Only Tad and Nora's frantic efforts to help her saved Maggie from losing all of her animal friends.

A fairly detailed plot, the fascination of being able to change size and appearance and the intrigue involved in fooling the adults around Maggie make this one of Chew's best books.

Interest Level: 2-5. Reading Level: 2.2. Further Search Topics: Individualists-Fiction, Witches-Fiction, Animals-Fiction, Fantasy, Magic-Fiction, Brothers and Sisters-Fiction, Transformations-Fiction.

Cone, Molly. The amazing memory of Harvey Bean; illus by Robert MacLean. HM 1980, 83 pp.

It had been a long time since Harvey had been happy. His memory was so bad that he was always in trouble at school. And now that his parents were separating, he had trouble at home, too. Because he thought that neither one of his parents wanted him he told each one that he was going to stay with the other and instead decided to spend the summer alone. A few hours after he left home, Harry ran into Mr. and Mrs. Katz and before he completely realized it, he was living with them.

Mr. Katz couldn't stand to see anything go to waste. He collected the usable food thrown out behind grocery stores, old furniture, tools, windows and more. Mrs. Katz, whose memory was just as bad as Harvey's, loved to cook, so she could always find a way to use the food. Everything else bulged from the house and garage into the driveway and yard. Harvey spent a happy summer learning to scavenge, eating well, learning not to worry about what others thought of him and even improving his memory. When his parents finally found him, Harvey realized that they really did want him, even if they were separated. He decided to live with his mother on weekdays, his father on weekends, and the Katzs during the summers.

The plot problems that are obvious to adult readers are ones that most young readers will be able to ignore (i.e. neither parent checks on Harvey for over two months). Young readers will enjoy the humor and realism of Harvey's pain, happiness and eventual feeling of self-confidence and triumph. The ten short chapters, good-sized print and adequate space between the lines help lower the book's reading level to late fourth grade.

Interest Level: 3-6. Reading Level: 5.1. Further Search Topics: Loners-Fiction, Vacation-Fiction, Divorce and Separation-Fiction, Humorous Fiction, Group 2, Memory-Fiction, Runaways-Fiction, Academic Problems-Fiction, Individualists-Fiction.

Danziger, Paula. The cat ate my gymsuit. Delacorte 1974, 147 pp.

Another book for fans of Judy Blume. Marcy was shy and insecure, unhappy at school and unhappy at home. She was self-conscious about being heavy and sure she would never have a date. Only Ms. Finney (a new teacher), her English class and Smedley (a communications group) meant anything to Marcy. When Ms. Finney was fired because of her refusal to recite the pledge of allegiance and her unorthodox teaching methods, Marcy began to organize a protest movement. Marcy's commitment brought more problems at school and at home, but eventually resulted in Ms. Finney's vindication and Marcy's and her mother's growth and understanding.

Don't expect much depth of characterization. Most of the characters are flat and stereotypical, but the book will have great appeal in spite of its faults, for Marcy's insecurities are ones with which many young readers can identify.

Interest Level: 5-6. Reading Level: 5.1. Further Search Topics: School Stories, Everyday Stories, Family Problems-Fiction, Challenges-Fiction, Weight-Fiction, Courage-Fiction, Individualists-Fiction, Sex Role-Fiction.

Greene, Constance C. Isabelle the itch; illus by Emily A. McCully. Viking Pr. 1973, 126 pp.

This is a loosely plotted story about a spunky, original fifth grade girl who could drive everyone around her crazy without ever tiring. Isabelle's dearest dream was to win the 50-yard dash at her school's field day. Even though she took over her brother's paper route to earn money for the Adidas track shoes she needed, Isabelle still didn't win. However, she did meet some new people, make new friends and keep those around her on their toes. A very amusing story told mostly in dialogue.

Interest Level: 4-6. Reading Level: 3.2. Further Search Topics: School Stories, Occupations-Fiction, Humorous Fiction, Everyday Stories, Running-Fiction, Individualists-Fiction, Sex Role-Fiction, Read Aloud.

Hurwitz, Johanna. Aldo Applesauce; illus by John Wallner. Morrow 1979, 127 pp.

Aldo Sossi, vegetarian and new kid at school, was immediately dubbed Applesauce for obvious reasons. Aldo didn't like his new name. He didn't like being teased either—not the way he was teased at school. Nothing went right for Aldo. His attempts at making friends only ended in disasters (once at a bowling alley and another time at a birthday party). He had been able to start a friendship only with a strange girl who wore a heavy, black fake moustache most of the time. After accidentally nearly ruining that friendship too, Aldo not only learned why DeDe wore the moustache, but helped her learn to live without it. DeDe, in turn, helped Aldo take himself less seriously and find more friends.

This is a comfortable, humorous story of two fourth grade children learning to be themselves. The vocabulary is occasionally difficult, but sentence length is almost always short.

Interest Level: 3-5. Reading Level: 3.1. Further Search Topics: Moving, Household-Fiction, Humorous Fiction, School Stories, Friendship-Fiction, Divorce and Separation-Fiction, Vegetarians-Fiction, Individualists-Fiction, Everyday Stories.

Hurwitz, Johanna. The law of gravity; illus by Ingrid Fetz. Morrow 1978, 192 pp.

The summer between fifth and sixth grades looked very unexciting to Margot. Her best friends were both going away for the whole summer and her father, a musician, was going to be on tour for most of the summer. Margot's very overweight mother had sworn never to go downstairs from their fifth floor walk-up apartment. Unless Margot chose to stay upstairs too, she was sure she would have a very lonely vacation. In addition, she had to work on a summer project for school. The project she finally chose was to get her mother downstairs after nine years of staying upstairs. In search of help she went to the local library where she met Bernie. Bernie was only a year older than Margot, but he seemed to know the most interesting things about the city. He showed her places Margot had never heard of before, he taught her to play chess, backgammon, and even to ride a bicycle. He was so full of fascinating ideas and information that Margot had no chance to be bored or lonely. Best of all, he even tried to help Margot with her project. None of their ideas worked, however, until Margot pretended to run away and scared her mother into going downstairs. Only then did Margot realize that she loved her mother whether or not she stayed on the fifth floor and that she couldn't simply force her mother or anyone else to change to suit her own fancy.

The book is a warm, understanding, slightly humorous treatment of the fairly common wish to change someone else. Although not many readers are likely to share Margot's exact problem, most will recognize her feelings. The book is also a virtual Chamber of Commerce advertisement for urban living. One of its other charms is its picture of a non-competitive, open, real friendship between an 11-year-old girl and a 12-year-old boy. The only drawback to the book is its inconsistent reading level which varies from 4.1 to 5.1 with a rare leap to 5.2.

Interest Level: 4-6. Reading Level: 4.2. Further Search Topics: Vacation-Fiction, Friendship-Fiction, Loners-Fiction, City Life-Fiction, Individualists-Fiction, Courage-Fiction, New York City-Fiction, Humorous Fiction, Family-Fiction, Challenges-Fiction, Weight-Fiction, Everyday Stories, Best Sellers.

MacLachlan, Patricia. Arthur, for the very first time; illus by Lloyd Bloom. Har-Row 1980, 117 pp.

A beautifully written, sensitive yet humorous story of a boy's maturation and growing awareness of the world around him. When Arthur's unhappiness at home is made more intense by the advent of a new baby, he is sent to spend the summer with his older aunt and uncle. Their eccentricities and those of their friends are at first only material for Arthur to write about in his journal. But as the summer progresses he not only learns from them, but also grows from an observer of life to a participant. His final step is helping a large and beloved pig bear her litter in a driving rain storm aided only by his independent, totally untamed young friend Moira.

The print is somewhat small, but spacing between lines is generous.

Interest Level: 4-6. Reading Level: 4.2. Further Search Topics: Read Aloud, Children-Growth-Fiction, Humorous Fiction, Friendship-Fiction, Vacation-Fiction, Relatives-Fiction, Infants-Fiction, Individualists-Fiction, Writing-Fiction, Loners-Fiction, Group 2.

Sharmat, Marjorie W. The Lancelot closes at five; illus by Lisl Weil. Macmillan 1976, 120 pp.

Despite a somewhat slow beginning, this is an amusing, almost sensitive story of two friends who decided to spend the night in the model home of the new housing development in which they both lived. Hutch, a health food fanatic whose mother pronounced judgment on everything Hutch did, conceived of the idea as her way of breaking away. Abby went along for the fun of it. When the local newspaper wrote of unusual vandalism at the model home, the townspeople became engrossed in finding the culprits. As the adults became enraged about the crime wave, their children began to admire the clever idea. Soon, almost every youngster in town had confessed to spending the night in the model home. By the time Abby and Hutch got around to admitting they had slept there, no one believed them. Only a sock with Abby's name in it could tie Abby and Hutch to the scene of the crime. As the book ends, the police have begun a thorough search of the house, after a real robbery, and the sock's discovery is imminent.

Interest Level: 4-6. Reading Level: 3.2. Further Search Topics: Humorous Fiction, Suburbia-Fiction, Runaways-Fiction, Crime-Fiction, Individualists-Fiction, Family Problems-Fiction.

INFANTS

Cole, Joanna. My puppy is born; photos by Jerome Wexler. Morrow 1973, unp (38 pp).

This is an unadorned description of a dachshund puppy's birth and first eight weeks of growth. The black and white photographs are large, sometimes graphic, and most often charming. The text is direct, carefully worded, concise and interesting. It is only the intrusion of an obviously young narrator that keeps this excellent book from being useful beyond third grade.

Interest Level: 1-3. Reading Level: 2.1. Further Search Topics: Group 2, Infants, Dogs, Pets, Birth.

Conklin, Gladys. Little apes; illus by Joseph Cellini. Holiday 1970, unp (32pp).

An informative as well as interesting look at gorillas, chimpanzees, orangutans and gibbons. Their habits and behavior patterns are described by following a young one of each species through a full day in its natural surroundings. The text is simple without being condescending and the illustrations are so life-like that they almost walk off the pages. An excellent treatment of a popular subject makes this a very useful book.

Interest Level: 2-5. Reading Level: 2.2. Further Search Topics: Apes, Gorillas, Nature Study, Infants, Group 2.

Selsam, Millicent E. How kittens grow; photos by Esther Bubley. School Bk Serv 1973, unp (28 pp).

A warm picture essay that illustrates and briefly describes the first eight weeks in kittens' lives. Guaranteed to charm cat fanciers.

Interest Level: 1-3. Reading Level: 2.1. Further Search Topics: Cats, Pets, Infants, Group 2, Birth.

INFANTS-FICTION

Blume, Judy. Superfudge. Dutton 1980, 166 pp.

On Fudge's first day in school his older brother Peter had to rescue him from the top of the kindergarten storage cabinets. Later in the school year Fudge's eagerness to join a school guest speaker on stage almost spelled disaster. Then when Fudge unexpectedly disappeared one day everyone, including Peter, thought he had drowned. In addition to Peter's problems with Fudge, Peter had to cope with a baby sister, moving to Princeton, New Jersey, a new job for his mother, and his father's attempts to write a book. Although the book is a sequel and is best enjoyed as such, it can be read alone. It is not as amusing or well-written as it's predecessor, *Tales of a Fourth Grade Nothing*, but will still be popular with young readers.

Interest Level: 3-6. Reading Level 3.1. Further Search Topics: Brothers and Sisters-Fiction, Moving, Household-Fiction, Infants-Fiction, Working Parents-Fiction, School Stories, Family-Fiction, Best Sellers, Humorous Fiction, Everyday Stories.

Lowry, Lois. Anastasia Krupnik. HM 1979, 113 pp.

Anastasia Krupnik led a comfortable, relatively happy life until her parents announced that she was not going to be an only child for much longer. After 10 years of enjoying that luxury, Anastasia wasn't at all pleased with the change. Babies immediately went to a prominent, and as far as Anastasia was concerned, permanent place on her list of hates. Anastasia kept two lists: one for things and people she particularly liked, and one list for what she did not like. What went on and off the lists tells much about Anastasia. Anastasia tells the rest in this perceptive, sensitive, and humorous story of growing up and adjusting to a new sibling.

Spacing between lines is slightly too narrow for the rather large print.

Interest Level: 4-6. Reading Level: 3.1. Further Search Topics: Humorous Fiction, Brothers and Sisters-Fiction, Everyday Stories, Jealousy-Fiction, Infants-Fiction, Best Sellers, Children-Growth-Fiction.

MacLachlan, Patricia. Arthur, for the very first time; illus by Lloyd Bloom. Har-Row 1980, 117 pp.

A beautifully written, sensitive yet humorous story of a boy's maturation and growing awareness of the world around him. When Arthur's unhappiness at home is made more intense by the advent of a new baby, he is sent to spend the summer with his older aunt and uncle. Their eccentricities and those of their friends are at first only material for Arthur to write about in his journal. But as the summer progresses he not only learns from them, but also grows from an observer of life to a participant. His final step is helping a large and beloved pig bear her litter in a driving rain storm aided only by his independent, totally untamed young friend Moira.

The print is somewhat small, but spacing between lines is generous.

Interest Level: 4-6. Reading Level: 4.2. Further Search Topics: Read Aloud, Children-Growth-Fiction, Humorous Fiction, Friendship-Fiction, Vacation-Fiction, Relatives-Fiction, Infants-Fiction, Individualists-Fiction, Writing-Fiction, Loners-Fiction, Group 2.

INHERITANCE-FICTION

Heide, Florence Parry. Black magic at Brillstone. A. Whitman 1981, 126 pp.

Liza is a little older, her romance with Logan has progressed to a kiss, and the book's plot is more complex than earlier Brillstone adventures. Other than those differences, the book follows Heide's standard format. The Brillstone books all center on Liza Webster and Logan Forrest, teenage partners in crime detection, who live in the Brillstone Apartments. The stories are similar enough that one could almost substitute the names Nancy Drew and Ned for Liza and Logan. Both young women are only children who live with their fathers. They are both independent, resourceful, and very concerned that justice be done. The men in their lives play approximately the same roles; their fathers are proud and supportive, but distantly preoccupied with their own business; Logan and Ned are gallant, boyish, and devoted. Liza and Logan, like Nancy and Ned, are not distinctive characters. Instead, they are shells into which readers who want excitement and adventure can pour themselves. There is no parental interference to worry about. There is plenty of action, some suspense, and real world crime (for Liza: murder, bank robberies, etc.) rather than childish escapades. The books' success is practically guaranteed. Beware, however, of inconsistent reading levels that wander over a year's range.

Logan was first aware of strange occurrences at the Brillstone Apartments when someone entered his apartment late at night. While the person had searched the apartment, he or she had unconsciously whistled a nursery tune. Logan's neighbor, Miss Violet, said the tune reminded her of her deceased nephew. Slowly Logan and Liza realized that someone was trying to trick Miss Violet out of a substantial amount of money she had just inherited. They suspected that Bella Vine, a spiritualist, and an accomplice were trying to convince Miss Violet that her nephew was communicating from the dead and wanted Miss Violet to give her money to Bella. Not until it was almost too late did Liza and Logan realize that Bella was also posing as another possible recipient of the money and was really Miss Violet's nephew's wife. Miss Violet's nephew had only pretended to die in order to collect insurance money. When he and his wife had heard about Miss Violet's large inheritance, they had decided to reappear in order to bilk her out of the money. Brillstone Mystery series.

Interest Level: 5-6. Reading Level: 3.1. Further Search Topics: Mystery and Detective Stories, Occult-Fiction, Crime-Fiction, Ghosts-Fiction, Cats-Fiction, Detectives-Fiction, Inheritance-Fiction.

Heide, Florence Parry. Mystery of the forgotten island; illus by Seymour Fleishman. A. Whitman 1980, 127 pp.

On a small island, unmarked on the map, the Spotlight Club members found old Mr. Whitson, who claimed that he was being kept prisoner by his granddaughter Lorrie and her husband John. Lorrie and John had told him he was being kept in the yard for his own good, so that he wouldn't wander off and get hurt or lost. They had also told him that he should will the island to them so that his daughter Cassie couldn't sell the island to a resort company for development. He was going to be forced to sign such a will unless he could get the children to help him smuggle a new will to his lawyer. Mr. Whitson wasn't convinced that Cassie wanted to sell the island, but he couldn't get in touch with her and he hadn'd had a letter from her in many months.

As the children went to secretly meet Mr. Whitson and mail his new will, they discovered that their trusted friend Guy was attempting to blackmail Lorrie and John into giving him some of the money from the sale of the island. He had evidence that Lorrie and John, not Cassie, wanted to sell the island and were tricking Mr. Whitson into signing a will in their favor. In a daring move, the children were able to free Mr. Whitson and isolate all three of the thieves so that the police could capture them.

This book involves a somewhat more complicated plot and slightly less familiar ingredients than most other Spotlight Club mysteries. One should progress to rather than begin the series with this title. Spotlight Club Mystery series.

Interest Level: 4-6. Reading Level: 3.1. Further Search Topics: Mystery and Detective Stories, Inheritance-Fiction, Gangs-Fiction, Kidnapping-Fiction, Brothers and Sisters-Fiction, Aging-Fiction, Detectives-Fiction.

Heide, Florence Parry. Mystery of the melting snowman; illus by Seymour Fleishman. A. Whitman 1974, 128 pp.

Hidden inside of a snowman, the Spotlight Club found what they believed was a stolen iron statue of a dog. In order to try to catch the thief, the children hid the statue again and watched to see who came to look for it. Eventually they determined that the thief or thieves was either Tom and Jenny, the amenable young couple who were helping Mrs. Wellington sell her house or Alex, the man who seemed to be a detective. After a frightening episode in which Alex almost captured Cindy, the dog, and a cache of Mrs. Wellington's diamonds (hidden in a secret compartment to which the dog held the key), Cindy managed to lock Alex in a closet long enough to enable Jay and Dexter to alert Mrs. Wellington to what was happening. The case was closed as Mrs. Wellington revealed Alex to be her greedy, young nephew, whom she had indulged once too often, but would not indulge again.

See *Mystery at Southport Cinema* for series information. Spotlight Club Mystery series.

Interest Level: 3-5. Reading Level: 2.2. Further Search Topics: Mystery and Detective Stories, Gangs-Fiction, Crime-Fiction, Brothers and Sisters-Fiction, Detectives-Fiction, Inheritance-Fiction.

INTEREST LEVEL K-2

Berenstain, Stan. Bears in the night. Random 1971, 30 pp.

This is for the very beginning reader. Only 24 words plus illustrations are used to tell the story of a bedtime adventure for seven small bears. Bravely they sneak out of the house, through the woods, and up Spook Hill. Frightened by an owl's hoot, they run back over the same route until they are safely back in bed again.

Interest Level: K-2. Reading Level: 1.1. Further Search Topics: Bears-Fiction, Group 2, Courage-Fiction, Humorous Fiction.

INTEREST LEVEL K-3

Berenstain, Stan. The bike lesson. Beginner 1964, 61 pp.

This story of a bumbling father trying to teach his eager son how to ride a bike is pure silliness. Much of the action is shown in the humorous illustrations. The rhymed text adds dialogue and description. Good fun.

Interest Level: K-3. Reading Level: 1.2. Further Search Topics: Humorous Fiction, Bicycles and Bicycling-Fiction, Stories in Rhyme, Group 2.

INTEREST LEVEL 1-2

Bonsall, Crosby. And I mean it, Stanley. Har-Row 1974, 32 pp.

A little girl builds "the very best thing I ever made," but all the while calls to Stanley to tell him not to look and to stay on the other side of the fence. Stanley pays attention only long enough for the "thing" to be completed - then crashes through the fence and bounds into the "thing." He draws no anger from the little girl, though, for Stanley is an enormous, loveable mutt. Told as much through pictures as words, this very easy reader will draw smiles from most first and second graders - especially dog lovers. An Early I Can Read Book.

Interest Level: 1-2. Reading Level: 1.2. Further Search Topics: Dogs-Fiction, Humorous Fiction, Best Sellers.

Bonsall, Crosby. The day I had to play with my sister. Har-Row 1972, 32 pp.

A very easy reader, only slightly less universally appealing and humorous than *And I Mean It, Stanley*. This time a little boy tries very hard to teach his younger sister to play hide-and-seek. He is totally unsuccessful and thoroughly frustrated. Again the story is told as much with pictures as with words. Useful through second grade. Reader format. An Early I Can Read Book.

Interest Level: 1-2. Reading Level: 1.1. Further Search Topics: Humorous Fiction, Games-Fiction, Brothers and Sisters-Fiction, Everyday Stories.

Eastman, Philip D. Sam and the firefly. Beginner 1958, 62 pp.

Sam, the owl, went looking for a playmate one night but found everyone was asleep except a mischievous firefly named Gus. When Sam showed Gus how to write words with his light in the dark sky, Gus went wild. First he tried to direct auto traffic, then airplane traffic, until finally the Hot Dog Man, an angry victim of Gus' tricks, captured him. However, when the Hot Dog Man tried to take Gus out of town, his truck became stuck on the railroad tracks in front of an oncoming train. Gus, freed from the jar in which he'd been caught, quickly wrote the word STOP in the sky and

saved everyone. Gus' silliness, the catastrophies he caused and his final triumph should interest almost any young child who likes humor or excitement. Reader format.

Interest Level: 1-2. Reading Level: 1.2. Further Search Topics: Best Sellers, Fireflies-Fiction, Owls-Fiction, Humorous Fiction.

Kessler, Leonard. Last one in is a rotten egg. Har-Row 1969, 64 pp.

Willie and Bobby could swim, but Freddy could not. After all three went to the local swimming pool and Freddy was pushed into the water by two older bullies, he was scared to try swimming again. Finally, a sympathetic lifeguard gave Freddy lessons. After much practice, Freddy became competent and confident enough to swim in the deep water and to stand up to the bullies.

A very slight plot designed to reassure new swimmers and provide a few basic rules of swimming. Reader format. A Sports-I-Can-Read-Book.

Interest Level: 1-2. Reading Level: 1.2. Further Search Topics: Courage-Fiction, Swimming-Fiction, Challenges-Fiction, Bullies-Fiction.

Nodset, Joan L. Go away dog; illus by Crosby Bonsall. Har-Row 1963, unp (29 pp).

A small boy who doesn't like dogs meets a shaggy, homeless dog who wants to play. The little boy, resisting all the way, gradually gives in to the dog's charms. Finally he tells the dog to follow him home. At home, he finds out that the dog was sent to him for his birthday by his Uncle George.

The dog, the boy, and the book are irresistible. You must, however, notice the illustrations on both the dedication and title pages to fully understand the story. Since much of the story is told by the illustrations and the text is repetitive as well as simple, it is an excellent beginning-to-read story.

Interest Level: 1-2. Reading Level: 1.1. Further Search Topics: Dogs-Fiction, Humorous Fiction, Best Sellers, Pets-Fiction, Birthdays-Fiction.

Seuss, Dr.. One fish, two fish, red fish, blue fish. Beginner 1960, 63pp.

Beginning with one almost ordinary-looking fish, this is a humorous look at the "funny things that go by." When Dr. Seuss says "funny," he really means highly imaginative, whimsical, and totally nonsensical. Each of the more than 20 silly creatures are described and appropriately illustrated to appeal to a child's sense of the ridiculous. Reader.

Interest Level: 1-2. Reading Level: 1.1. Further Search Topics: Fantasy, Wit and Humor, Poetry, Humorous Fiction, Stories in Rhyme.

Seuss, Dr. Hop on Pop. Beginner 1963, 64pp.

Between one and four rhyming words are introduced or reviewed and used in a silly sentence on each page. The sentence is interpreted with even more amusing illustrations. It is one of the simplest of books (no story at all) and yet it is usable through second grade because of Dr. Seuss' playful style and ridiculous illustrations. Reader format.

Interest Level: 1-2. Reading Level: 1.1. Further Search Topics: Poetry, Best Sellers, Wit and Humor, Humorous Fiction, Stories in Rhyme.

Seuss, Dr. The foot book. Random 1968, unp (27 pp).

Left feet, right feet, big feet, small feet; with its rhyme, silly illustrations and rhythmic celebration of feet of all descriptions, this book is a sure winner with the very young. Reader format.

Interest Level 1-2. Reading Level: 1.1. Further Search Topics: Best Sellers, Feet-Fiction, Humorous Fiction, Poetry, Wit and Humor, Stories in Rhyme.

Steven, Carla. Hooray for Pig!; illus by Rainey Bennett. HM 1974, 48 pp.

Pig couldn't spend the day swimming with his friend Raccoon because he didn't know how to swim. Instead Pig took a picnic to the lake by himself. At the lake, Pig met Otter, who encouraged Pig to at least try getting in the water. After several days of Otter's patient coaching, not only could Pig stay afloat, but he liked it, too!

For much the same audience as Kessler's *Last One In Is A Rotten Egg*, but because of a more interesting plot it is a little more useful. Reader format.

Interest Level: 1-2. Reading Level: 1.2. Further Search Topics: Pigs-Fiction, Courage-Fiction, Swimming-Fiction, Humorous Fiction.

INTEREST LEVEL 1-3

Alexander, Sue. Small plays for you and a friend; illus by Olivia H. Cole. Seabury 1974, 48 pp.

Five very short and very simple plays for two actors that will be of more interest to the players than the audience. However, because the reading level is low, and because children's love of acting is strong and their tolerance of weak plot is high, this can be used through grade three. A companion volume *Small Plays for Special Days* presents seven more short plays for two characters.

Interest Level: 1-3. Reading Level: 2.1. Further Search Topics: Acting, Drama, Group 2.

Benchley, Nathaniel. Sam the Minutemen; illus by Arnold Lobel. Har-Row 1969, 62 pp.

A good but limited book. It is a simple, personalized account of the beginning of the Revolutionary War as seen by the young son of a Minuteman. The book is a fairly exciting, uncomplicated and enjoyable story. Its limitations rest in its format (it's designed as a reader), the apparent young age of the main character, and the fact that it is told as a story. Its usefulness extends no further than grade three. An I Can Read History Book

Interest Level: 1-3. Reading Level: 2.2. Further Search Topics: United States-History-War-Fiction, Historical Fiction, War-Fiction, Group 2, Courage-Fiction.

Bernstein, Margery. The first morning; illus by Enid Warner Romanek. Scribner 1976, 44 pp.

Spider, Mouse, and Fly volunteered to ask the king of the sky for light to take back to earth because the animals on earth were tired of living in darkness. The king didn't want to give away any light and so he set what he thought was an impossible task for the three animals. They were able to outwit the king three times and finally return to earth with a box Mouse was sure contained light. When they opened the box all they found was a rooster. Poor Mouse was ashamed at having been so badly tricked. But then Rooster crowed up the first morning and has done so ever since. A competent retelling of an African myth, nicely complemented by bold illustrations. Good candidate for dramatization.

Interest Level: 1-3. Reading Level: 2.1. Further Search Topics: Animals-Fiction, Group 2, Mythology, Light-Fiction, Drama, Time-Fiction, Calendars-Fiction, Creation-Fiction, Africa-Folklore.

Brenner, Barbara. Baltimore Orioles; illus by J. Winslow Higginbottom. Har-Row 1974, 62 pp.

An impressive combination of very easy, as well as interesting and informative reading. Within the barest skeleton of a story the author gives a great deal of information about young Baltimore Orioles and the mating and hatching cycle of the older birds. Unfortunately its easy reader format will discourage use beyond third grade. Use freely until that point. Science I Can Read Book series.

Interest Level: 1-3. Reading Level 1.2. Further Search Topics: Birds, Nature Study.

Bulla, Clyde Robert. My friend the monster; illus by Michele Chessare. Har-Row 1980, 75 pp.

Even though Hal was plain and not very clever, his disappointed parents knew that he was still a prince; thus he had to be raised as one. Hal didn't like his lonely, dull life until a new world was accidentally opened to him. A servant's child gave him an old book of monsters and told him that the monsters still lived under the distant mountains. Hal finally made a trip to the mountains, spent a day exploring, and by chance met Humbert, a young monster curious about the world. But, Hal's cruel cousin Archer captured Humbert and put him in a cage. Hal's daring rescue attempt almost resulted in disaster for both Humbert and Hal.

This is another example of Bulla's forte; a book with an action-filled plot, short chapters, large print, wide spaces between the lines, and a low reading level. A book about monsters has almost guaranteed appeal through third grade. Although the book is useful beyond third grade, readers in fourth and fifth grade may be more sensitive to Hal's apparent youth and the fantastic elements of the story.

Interest Level: 1-3. Reading Level: 2.1. Further Search Topics: Fantasy, Monsters-Fiction, Royalty-Fiction, Group 2, Read Aloud, Best Sellers.

Bulla, Clyde Robert. Open the door and see all the people; illus by Wendy Watson. T Y Crowell 1972, 69 pp.

A slight story that makes up for its lack of excitement with warmth. When Joann, Teeney and Mama were burned out of their house in the country, they decided it was time to move to the city. With the help of a friend, Mama was quickly able to find a job and an apartment. Only Teeney was noticeably unhappy. She missed her doll and resented anyone else who had one. Then the girls learned about the Toy House, a place to borrow or adopt toys. Both girls found dolls they wanted to adopt. Just before the end of the six week trial period Tenney lost her doll and almost lost her chance to adopt it. After the doll was found and repaired, the people at the Toy House realized how much she wanted the doll and let Teeney keep it.

Because of the ages of the characters, (six and eight), and the subject matter, the book's appeal is doubtful beyond third grade. Print size slightly smaller than usual for Bulla.

Interest Level: 1-3. Reading Level: 2.1. Further Search Topics: Dolls-Fiction, Brothers and Sisters-Fiction, Moving, Household-Fiction, Family-Fiction, Group 2.

Cerf, Bennett. Bennett Cerf's book of animal riddles; illus by Roy McKie. Beginner 1964, 62 pp.

A slightly more difficult selection of riddles than the following listing. The riddles are longer and less familiar, but still very useful. See *Bennett Cerf's Book of Riddles* for more explanation. Reader format.

Interest Level: 1-3. Reading Level: 2.1. Further Search Topics: Riddles, Wit and Humor, Group 2.

Chenery, Janet. Wolfie; illus by Marc Simont. Har-Row 1969, 64 pp.

This slight but satisfying story is the vehicle for much information about spiders. Harry caught a wolf spider. To keep his sister Polly out of the way, Harry and his friend George told her she could see the spider only after she caught 100 flies to feed it. In the meantime, they took the spider to the nature center where they were treated to a fascinating lesson about insects and spiders (especially wolf spiders). It's too bad that the book's cartoon style illustrations prevent this book from being very useful beyond grade three.

Interest Level: 1-3. Reading Level: 2.1. Further Search Topics: Spiders, Pets, Nature Study, Group 2.

Cole, Joanna. Dinosaur story; illus by Mort Kunstler. Morrow 1974, unp (30 pp).

A general introduction to eight dinosaurs: Brontosaurus, Allosaurus, Stegosaurus, Ornitholestes, Protoceratops, Triceratops, Tyrannosaurus rex and Duckbills. Although not a wealth of information, there is more than enough interesting material here to attract a young dinosaur enthusiast. Because of the short sentences, the text is somewhat plodding. The subject matter's great appeal and the appropriately fierce-looking illustrations, however, make up for that problem.

Interest Level: 1-3. Reading Level: 2.1. Further Search Topics: Group 2, Dinosaurs, Prehistory.

Cole, Joanna. My puppy is born; photos by Jerome Wexler. Morrow 1973, unp (38 pp).

This is an unadorned description of a dachshund puppy's birth and first eight weeks of growth. The black and white photographs are large, sometimes graphic, and most often charming. The text is direct, carefully worded, concise and interesting. It is only the intrusion of an obviously young narrator that keeps this excellent book from being useful beyond third grade.

Interest Level: 1-3. Reading Level: 2.1. Further Search Topics: Group 2, Infants, Dogs, Pets, Birth.

Hornblow, Leonora. Prehistoric monsters did the strangest things; illus by Michael K. Frith. Random 1974, 65 pp.

A basic survey of an era and its animal life forms. Animals from the earliest water creatures through Diplocaulus, Ichthyosaurs, dinosaurs (about 12 varieties) and early mammals (including the Beast of Baluchistan) to the appearance of man are introduced and illustrated. It is a brief but meaty treatment of a very popular subject that should be especially useful with second and third grade children. Reader format.

Interest Level: 1-3. Reading Level: 2.1. Further Search Topics: Prehistory, Dinosaurs, Evolution, Monsters, Group 2.

LeSieg, Theo. Wacky Wednesday; illus by George Booth. Beginner 1974, unp (36 pp).

A series of true picture puzzles. A little boy wakes up one Wednesday to find everything around him has gone "wacky." People are missing heads but have extra legs. Cars are being driven from the back seat. Doors are placed in the wrong places. Airplanes fly backwards. At the end of the day everything settles back to normal, but not before readers have had fun finding the numerous "wacky" things on each page.

The story is told in silly rhyme (LeSieg and Seuss are the same person). What is wrong with each picture is not always easily located, making this reader an excellent excerise in observation as well as great fun.

Interest Level: 1-3. Reading Level: 1.2. Further Search Topics: Puzzles, Humorous Fiction, Wit and Humor, Poetry, Best Sellers.

Lewis, Thomas P. Hill of fire; illus by Joan Sandin. Har-Row 1971, 63 pp.

A personalized account of the volcano that suddenly erupted in the middle of a farmer's field in Mexico on February 20, 1943. Because the account is written as a story and because of its easy-reader format, the book is most useful only through third grade. An I-Can-Read-History-Book.

Interest Level: 1-3. Reading Level: 2.2. Further Search Topics: Volcanoes, Group 2, Mexico, Disasters, Historical Fiction.

Low, Joseph. Five men under one umbrella. Macmillan 1975, 64 pp.

Twenty-nine riddles, most of which are fairly familiar. Nothing special in this collection, just an additional choice for the young comedian.

Interest Level: 1-3. Reading Level: 2.1. Further Search Topics: Riddles, Wit and Humor, Group 2.

Parish, Peggy. Too many rabbits; illus by Leonard Kessler. Macmillan 1974, 48 pp.

One day Miss Molly opened her front door to find a rabbit waiting to be invited inside. The next day Miss Molly discovered the rabbit had had baby rabbits, lots of baby rabbits. Because babies need care, Miss Molly couldn't just turn them out, so she kept them all. Before long she had more rabbits than she could handle. She tried giving them away, but all the children's mothers refused to keep them, the zoo didn't need any, and Miss Molly didn't want to sell them to the butcher. Finally a man who owned an island where they could live, asked to take all the rabbits. As Miss Molly was about to close the door after giving the rabbits to the man with an island, a cat walked right up to her and inside her house. The next day Miss Molly discovered she had kittens—lots of kittens. A very humorous story in a reader format.

Interest Level: 1-3. Reading Level: 1.2. Further Search Topics: Humorous Fiction, Rabbits-Fiction, Best Sellers.

Selsam, Millicent E. How kittens grow; photos by Esther Bubley. School Bk Serv 1973, unp (28 pp).

A warm picture essay that illustrates and briefly describes the first eight weeks in kittens' lives. Guaranteed to charm cat fanciers.

Interest Level: 1-3. Reading Level: 2.1. Further Search Topics: Cats, Pets, Infants, Group 2, Birth.

Seuss, Dr. The cat in the hat. Beginner 1957, 61 pp.

When the Cat in the Hat visits two children, a dreary, boring afternoon becomes almost too exciting. The Cat's juggling act and the two "things" he brings with him almost destroy the house. But the Cat cleans up so well that when the children's mother comes home and asks what they did all afternoon, they can't decide if they should tell her.

A funny, rhyming tale of the destruction all children can create and the boredom all children can feel. Reader format.

Interest Level: 1-3. Reading Level: 1.2. Further Search Topics: Humorous Fiction, Fantasy, Cats-Fiction, Poetry, Troublemakers-Fiction, Best Sellers, Stories in Rhyme.

Seuss, Dr. The cat in the hat comes back. Beginner 1958, 63 pp.

Sally and her brother were doing a good job of clearing the front walk of snow when the Cat in the Hat showed up. While they worked, the Cat created a pink mess in the house. The mess only became worse when he tried to clean it. The pink spot finally covered the snow all around the house until the Cat called upon his friends Little Cats A-Z. It was Little Cat Z and his magic zoom that eventually not only cleaned the snow, but cleared the front walk as well.

Another zany, rhymed adventure of the mischievious Cat whose ability to get into trouble endears him to most children from pre-school to early third grade. Reader format.

Interest Level: 1-3. Reading Level: 1.2. Further Search Topics: Fantasy, Cats-Fiction, Troublemakers-Fiction, Humorous Fiction, Snow-Fiction, Poetry, Best Sellers, Stories in Rhyme.

Sharmat, Marjorie W. Nate the great goes undercover; illus by Marc Simont. Coward 1974, 47 pp.

Nate's next door neighbor Oliver was a pest, but Oliver had a mystery for Nate to solve. Oliver's garbage can was being burglarized at night. He wanted Nate to catch the garbage snatcher. Nate quickly drew up a list of human suspects and just as quickly eliminated them all. A night spent hiding in the garbage can proved the best way to catch the thief. Much to Nate's surprise, the thief turned out to be his new dog.

Very amusing and very useful. Reader format.

Interest Level: 1-3. Reading Level: 2.1. Further Search Topics: Humorous Fiction, Mystery and Detective Stories, Group 2, Detectives-Fiction, Best Sellers.

Sharmat, Marjorie W. Nate the great; illus by Marc Simont. Coward 1972, 62 pp.

This is a young imitation of Humphrey Bogart solving a *Dragnet* style mystery. Annie's recently finished painting of her dog had disappeared so she hired Nate to search for it. Nate gathered all the facts, investigated his suspects, and eventually solved the mystery, but not before he had consumed plenty of pancakes (his favorite food) and solved a second mystery by accident.

A simple plot, humorous telling, and a sympathetic, likeable protagonist make this one of a very popular series. Reader format.

Interest Level: 1-3. Reading Level: 2.1. Further Search Topics: Humorous Fiction, Detectives-Fiction, Mystery and Detective Stories, Group 2, Best Sellers.

White, Laurence B., Jr. Science puzzles; illus by Marc Tolon Brown. A-W 1975, unp (46 pp).

There are twenty four very short experiments designed to illustrate the simplest of scientific principles clearly presented here. For all but a few experiments there is not only an explanation of what happens but also an explanation of why it happened. What makes the book even more useful, is that it can also be used as a book of easy magic tricks. Any child who enjoys it as science will, with a little help, be able to see its possibilities as magic. In fact it provides a better explanation of the Knot Magic trick than can be found in *It's Magic*.

Interest Level: 1-3. Reading Level: 1.2. Further Search Topics: Science, Magic, Puzzles, Experiments, Scientific.

White, Laurence B., Jr. Science toys; illus by Marc Tolon Brown. A-W 1975, unp (46 pp).

This book presents 23 toys that a young child can easily make and learn from at the same time. A sundial, a drinking straw that flies, a balloon that rolls over, a ghost that sticks to the wall by itself, a water-go-round, and a paper cup that roars are a few examples of what is to be found here. The construction and use of each toy is explained and illustrated in enough detail to enable the child to work alone. And as in *Science Puzzles*, some of the toys will double as magic tricks (i.e. can you balance the rim of a paper plate on your nose?).

Interest Level: 1-3. Reading Level: 2.1. Further Search Topics: Handicrafts, Science, Magic, Toys, Games, Group 2, Puzzles.

Wiseman, Bernard. Morris and Boris. Dodd 1974, 64 pp.

This is a compilation of three silly stories about Morris the Moose and Boris the Bear. When Boris tries to interest Morris in telling riddles, Morris frustrates Boris so completely that Boris runs off angrily. Later Boris tries to teach Morris a tongue twister, but ends up running off in total confusion. Finally Boris tries to teach Morris to play hide-and-seek and that, too, is a disaster. Boris tells Morris that Morris just cannot do anything. A bird who has seen everything reminds Boris that Morris can make him very angry and that is something. When Boris agrees they all laugh happily.

Broad, slapstick humor makes this appealing to children well into third grade. Reader format.

Interest Level: 1-3. Reading Level: 1.2. Further Search Topics: Wit and Humor, Riddles, Tongue Twisters, Games, Humorous Fiction.

INTEREST LEVEL 1-4

Benchley, Nathaniel. Small Wolf; illus by Joan Sandin. Har-Row 1972, 64 pp.

A straight-forward telling of white man's purchase of Manhattan and the resulting displacement of the Indians. The text is simple. The tone is sympathetic to the plight of the Indians. The reader is neither lectured nor patronized, but the early-reader format will prevent using the book comfortably beyond fourth grade. An I Can Read History Book.

Interest Level: 1-4. Reading Level 2.2. Further Search Topics: Historical Fiction, New York City-Fiction, United States-History-Fiction, Indians of North America-Fiction, Group 2.

Berger, Melvin. Time after time; illus by Richard Cuffari. Coward 1975, 45 pp.

The book begins with a description of inner clocks, proceeds into measurement of time, the seasons, and finally demonstrates the making of a simple clock. The explanations are simple but interesting. One point logically follows from another. It is a solid, serviceable tool limited only somewhat by the fact that it looks like a cross between a picture book and a reader. A brief index is included.

Interest Level: 1-4. Reading Level: 2.2. Further Search Topics: Time, Clocks and Watches, Seasons, Group 2.

Bernstein, Margery. Coyote goes hunting for fire; illus by Ed Heffernan. Scribner 1974, 40 pp.

A delightful story that can be read for fun or used as part of a unit on North American Indians. A long time ago when there was no fire, all the animals but Coyote banded together to find it. The animals left Coyote behind because he was always spoiling their plans. Coyote saw them leave, chased after them and once more tried to direct everything, but only ended up losing fire. Cartoon-like illustrations add to the humor of the story. This book should make a simple, but effective play.

Interest Level: 1-4. Reading Level 2.1. Further Search Topics: Animals-Fiction, Legends, Mythology, Fire-Fiction, Indians of North America-Legends, Coyotes-Fiction, Group 2, Creation-Fiction, Drama.

Blegvad, Lenore. The great hamster hunt; illus by Erik Blegvad. HarBraceJ 1969, 32 pp.

Nicholas wanted a hamster; but, because his mother didn't like them, he couldn't have one. She did, however, agree to let Nicholas take care of his friend Tony's hamster for a week. It was a good and happy week for Nicholas until the evening before Tony was to return for his hamster. Nicholas accidentally broke the glass front of Harvey's cage and temporarily replaced it with cardboard. By morning Harvey had chewed through the cardbroad and was gone. Nicholas and his family searched all day but couldn't find Harvey. They finally bought another hamster and waited for Tony to arrive. As evening came Nicholas realized that hamsters are nocturnal and began to look for Harvey once more. This time Harvey was awake and active. The happy result was that Harvey was found and the new hampster became Nicholas' own pet. A simple, satisfying story even to fourth grade readers.

Interest Level: 1-4. Reading Level: 2.2. Further Search Topics: Pets-Fiction, Hamsters-Fiction, Group 2, Everyday Stories.

Branley, Franklyn M. Roots are food finders; illus by Joseph Low. Har-Row 1975, 33 pp.

It really is a shame that the picture book format of this and other *Let's-Read-and-Find-Out-Science-Books* will prevent older children from using them. There is much good information here that is thoroughly and logically explained without patronizing the reader. Functions and types of roots are described. Experiments to show root growth, root hairs, and absorption are given. A very useful book through third grade and possibly fourth grade. Beyond fourth grade children will certainly balk at the book's "babyish" appearance. Let's-Read-and-Find-Out-Science-Book series.

Interest Level: 1-4. Reading Level: 2.2. Further Search Topics: Nature Study, Botany, Group 2, Experiments, Scientific.

Cerf, Bennett. Bennett Cerf's book of riddles; illus by Roy McKie. Beginner 1960, 64 pp.

Simple, well-known riddles that are always popular with children. The riddle is introduced on one page and answered on the reverse side of the page. Silly drawings illustrate each riddle and answer. Because each riddle and answer stands alone, even the most problematic of readers can have the satisfaction of completing a unit in a short time. That satisfaction, plus the universal appeal of humor make this book and the preceding listing useful through grade four, despite the book's reader format.

Interest Level: 1-4. Reading Level: 2.1. Further Search Topics: Riddles, Wit and Humor, Group 2.

Cleary, Beverly. Henry Huggins; illus by Louis Darling. Morrow 1950, 155 pp.

Henry Huggins is over 30 years old now, so if he occasionally seems a little old-fashioned, it is not surprising. What is surprising is how well he has withstood the years. His antics are innocent, but humorous and realistic. The book's six chapters are six separate stories that follow the same cast of characters through an entire year.

In the first chapter, Henry finds a stray dog (Ribsy) whom he must then transport home on a bus. Ribsy was too large and too frisky not to get into trouble, so before Henry finally gets him home, they have been kicked off of three buses and have ridden in a police car. The second chapter describes what happens when Henry buys two guppies and ends up with millions. In the third chapter Henry accidentally throws his friend's football into the back seat of a speeding car and tries to earn the money to replace it by catching and selling 1,331 night crawlers. The fourth chapter involves Henry's attempts to get out of playing the lead in a school Christmas play. His last minute rescue comes in the form of a can of green paint that spills all over him. It is Ribsy's turn to change colors in Chapter 5. Henry tries to cover Ribsy's dirt spots with talcolm powder for a dog show, but only succeeds in turning Ribsy pink. And in Chapter 6, Ribsy's original owner finally finds him and wants him back, but Ribsy chooses to stay with Henry. Only the occasional extra cute expression and Henry's age (third grade) keep this from being enjoyed beyond fourth grade.

Interest Level: 1-4. Reading Level: 2.2. Further Search Topics: Humorous Fiction, Everyday Stories, Read Aloud Pets-Fiction, Dogs-Fiction, Group 2.

Dobrin, Arnold. Jillions of gerbils. Lothrop 1973, 64 pp.

Right after his family moved into a big and very old house, David's gerbil disappeared. Before long, the replacement gerbil disappeared also. The house was very old and did have strange creakings. Could there also have been secret hiding places for ghosts, maybe? Determined to find out, David searched the entire house until he really did find a secret room. And in that room he found his two gerbils with their new family — the beginnings of David's millions and billions and jillions of gerbils.

A comfortable, somewhat old-fashioned book that is neatly divided into six short chapters. It includes a page of facts about gerbils at the end. A good choice to follow the very easy readers; it is easy, but not "too babyish."

Interest Level: 1-4. Reading Level: 2.1. Further Search Topics: Gerbils-Fiction, Pets-Fiction, Group 2, Humorous Fiction.

Dolch, Edward W. "Why" stories; illus by Marguerite Dolch. Garrard 1952, 160 pp.

"Why the Bear Has a Little Tail," "Why Turkeys Have Red Eyes," and "How the Tiger Got His Stripes" are three titles that illustrate the type of stories found in this collection. Seventeen short, simple folktales explain why the world and creatures in it operate and appear as they do. All of the tales can be found elsewhere. However, few if any stories are likely to be familiar to readers. This type of story is one children often find very appealing. The stories are understandable, logical within their own framework and simple enough to be retold to others. The reading level varies from 1.2 to 2.2. Dolch Basic Vocabulary Book series.

Interest Level: 1-4. Reading Level: 2.2. Further Search Topics: Folklore, Why Stories, Animals-Fiction, Group 2, Creation-Fiction.

Dolch, Edward W. Fairy stories; illus by Marguerite Dolch and Yolande Cuypers-Fransen. Garrard 1950, 165 pp.

A collection of mostly familiar fairy tales told in the Dolchs' very simplified manner. Because the book's purpose is not to provide the most literate version of favorite fairy tales, better versions of any of the stories can be found elsewhere. It provides instead, very accessible versions of tales young readers have enjoyed for years. Includes "Cinderella," "Hansel and Gretel," "Jack and the Bean Stalk," "Snow White," "Sleeping Beauty," and "The Elves and the Shoemaker," among others. Dolch Pleasure Reading Book series.

Interest Level: 1-4. Reading Level: 2.2. Further Search Topics: Folklore, Fairy Tales, Fantasy, Group 2.

Dolch, Edward W. Circus stories; illus by Dee Wallace. Garrard 1956, 166 pp.

A collection of 18 chapters that tell 15 true stories about the circus. Some are descriptions of activities (trapeze flying) or people (Emmett Kelly, a circus doctor, the Ringling Brothers). Other chapters tell of unusual occurrences; i.e., the bareback rider who was thrown off her horse into the lap of a spectator whom she later married. Some stories, such as the story of the horse trainer whose life was saved by an elephant, are exciting. Others are sad ("Blinky," the dog who was killed by an angry lion).

The authors' tone becomes condescending off and on through this collection, thus hampering its usefulness somewhat. Otherwise, it is very similar to the other Dolch books; it is a decent collection of very simplified stories. Dolch Basic Vocabulary Book series.

Interest Level: 1-4. Reading Level: 2.2. Further Search Topics: Circus-Fiction, Clowns-Fiction, Acrobats and Acrobatics-Fiction, Group 2.

Foley, Louise Munro. Tackle 22; illus by John Heinly. Delacorte 1978, unp (43 pp).

When their quarterback came down with the mumps, it looked like the Wildcats would have to forfeit the big football game to the Spacemen. But Chub's little brother Herb surprised everyone and saved the game.

Brief and somewhat predictable, the book maintains a light touch that many young readers will like. Heavily illustrated.

Interest Level: 1-4. Reading Level: 2.1. Further Search Topics: Football-Fiction, Brothers and Sisters-Fiction, Humorous Fiction, Group 2.

Green, Phyllis. The fastest quitter in town; illus by Lorenzo Lynch. A-W 1972, 62 pp.

Whenever Johnny played baseball and things went wrong for him, he would quit. Johnny's teammates finally grew so angry with him that they told him to leave the team. That same day, Johnny's 90-year-old great-grandfather lost a very special ring his wife had given him. Johnny's love for this great-grandfather pushed him to keep looking for the ring until days later, when everyone else had quit searching, Johnny found the ring. Having learned a hard lesson, Johnny returned to his team for one more chance. That evening Johnny went to see his great-grandfather to tell him, with legitimate pride, that he had played the entire game.

Although the lesson is pointed, the story is very satisfying. Johnny's relationship with this great-grandfather is close and supportive. His problem is one shared by many children, especially those with a weak self-image.

Interest Level: 1-4. Reading Level: 3.1. Further Search Topics: Blacks-Fiction, Challenges-Fiction, Courage-Fiction, Group 2, Baseball-Fiction, Grandparents-Fiction, Friendship-Fiction.

McNulty, Faith. Woodchuck; illus by Joan Sandin. Har-Row 64 pp.

There's a great deal of information in this little book. It describes a woodchuck's physical appearance, its habits and behavior, and its life cycle. The treatment is very direct and very honest (two of four young woodchucks are killed before the first year is over). Only an overly repetitive, slightly condescending beginning, and the reader format hamper the book's usefulness beyond grade four. A Science-I-Can-Read-Book.

Interest Level: 1-4. Reading Level: 3.1. Further Search Topics: Nature Study, Groundhogs, Group 2, Woodchucks.

Meriwether, Louise. The freedom ship of Robert Smalls; illus by Lee Jack Morton. P-H 1971, unp (30 pp).

A brief, but very interesting biography of a black man whose dreams of freedom as a young slave during the Civil War, led to a daring plan of escape. Robert Smalls sailed 16 slaves to freedom and presented the Northern Navy with a valuable gunboat of which he was eventually named captain. Smalls later went on to serve five terms in Congress.

Although the picture book format of this book prevents its confortable use much beyond fourth grade, it is a compelling enough story to interest even sixth graders. Print is somewhat small.

Interest Level: 1-4. Reading Level: 3.1. Further Search Topics: Biography, United States-History-War, Blacks-Biography, Smalls, Robert, Group 2, Slavery, Politics-Biography.

Parish, Peggy. Haunted house; illus by Paul Frame. Macmillan 1971, 151 pp.

Although this is the third book about Jed, Bill and Liza Roberts, it too can be read out of order. This time the family has moved into what was locally known as a haunted house. Very shortly after they moved into the house, a coded note appeared that led them to a series of messages and unusual occurrences. Lights that flashed into Liza's room turned out to be the headlights of cars, but the messages and a secret compartment in an old clock couldn't be as easily explained. Each day took them closer to the surprise that the messages hinted would be theirs. That surprise turned out to be three kittens and a treehouse. Two of the children's best friends had planned the whole mystery just to lead to the surprises.

This book has the same faults and strong points as the others about the Roberts children. Each chapter is short; the book is episodic; reading level is consistent; there is much dialogue and action and little description, and the plot has a comfortable familiarity about it. It can be very useful to the right readers.

Interest Level: 1-4. Reading Level: 2.1. Further Search Topics: Mystery and Detective Stories. Brothers and Sisters-Fiction, Ghosts-Fiction, Moving, Household-Fiction, Nonverbal Communication-Fiction, Group 2.

Parish, Peggy. Clues in the woods; illus by Paul Frame. Macmillan 1968, 154 pp.

The books about the three Roberts children share problems that are obvious to adults and felt by some young readers as well, but they continue to be popular with undemanding young readers. The characters are very white and middle class and their actions often fit out-of-date stereotypes. The plots have few surprises or suspense, but the reading levels are consistent and the very predictability of the books makes them familiar and therefore comfortable.

This particular story takes place at the end of the same summer the children solved the mystery of *The Key to the Treasure*. The children were alerted by their grandmother to the disappearance of food scraps, left outside the house. Thinking that two runaway children, about whom they had read, had taken the food, Liza, Bill, and Jed tried to find the runaways. Their attempts eventually brought them new friends and thus the solution to their mystery. It had not been the runaways who had taken the food, it was their new friends' dog.

Interest Level: 1-4. Reading Level: 2.2. Further Search Topics: Mystery and Detective Stories, Brothers and Sisters-Fiction, Vacation-Fiction, Dogs-Fiction, Runaways-Fiction, Grandparents-Fiction, Group 2.

Parish, Peggy. Key to the treasure; illus by Paul Frame. Macmillan 1966, 154 pp.

This is the first of the stories about Jed, Bill and Liza Roberts. The three children are very middle-class, the book's plots are simple and often lack suspense, but the stories still enjoy widespread popularity among unsophisticated readers.

All three children went to spend the summer with their grandparents and decided to tackle a mystery left unsolved for over 75 years. An old drawing and an authentic war bonnet provided the only clues to finding three Indian artifacts. At each step along the way there were crumbled, brittle pieces of paper bearing coded messages that led to the next clue. The search ended when the children found that a storage area in a porch piller contained an Indian doll, mask, and leather shield that had belonged to their great-grandfather.

Interest Level: 1-4. Reading Level: 2.1. Further Search Topics: Vacation-Fiction, Brothers and Sisters-Fiction, Group 2, Mystery and Detective Stories, Grandparents-Fiction, Nonverbal Communication-Fiction.

Parish, Peggy. Pirate Island adventure; illus by Paul Frame. Macmillan 1975, 167 pp.

Although this is the fourth book in the series about the Roberts children, none of the titles must be read in chronological order. This time the three rather privileged children spent the summer with their grandparents on a resort island. They lived in a house that their family had owned for years, explored the island, and swam in their own private cove. But, most of their time was spent trying to solve an old mystery. Their great-uncle had hidden several very special items (one for each member of his family) years earlier, and had left only one clue with their grandfather. After he gave the children that clue it was only a matter of time before they found the hidden treasures.

This book is also lengthy, but is divided into 22 very manageable chapters. It is, like the others, almost entirely dialogue and action, which makes it especially appealing to young reluctant readers.

Interest Level: 1-4. Reading Level: 2.1. Further Search Topics: Mystery and Detective Stories, Vacation-Fiction, Treasure-Fiction, Brothers and Sisters-Fiction, Grandparents-Fiction, Group 2.

Shaw, Evelyn. Alligator; illus by Frances Zweifel. Har-Row 1972, 61 pp.

A straight-forward, respectful description of an alligator's life cycle. Emphasis is placed on the time between the mother's nest-building and the birth of the young alligators. The danger to alligators posed by man is expressed, but not stressed. Little physical description is included. An interesting and competent treatment of a narrow subject. Reader format. A Science-I-Can-Read Book series.

Interest Level: 1-4. Reading Level: 2.1. Further Search Topics: Alligators, Nature Study, Group 2.

Shearer, John. Billy Jo Jive and the case of the missing pigeons; illus by Ted Shearer. Delacorte 1978, 47 pp.

This is the third in a series of slight mysteries, always solved by Billy Jo Jive and his crime fighter partner, Susie Sunset. Jive and Sunset are street-wise, black youngsters who take their jobs as crime fighters very seriously, and are never detered for long from finding the criminals they seek. The crimes are always thefts, and the criminals vary from young children to neighborhood menaces. Suspense is created more by the manner in which Jive and Sunset catch the thieves, plus the determination and pace of the young detectives, than by guessing who the culprits might be. Jive, his street-slang manner of telling the first-person stories, and the urban setting will appeal to many readers. Jive and Sunset also appear on *Sesame Street*.

Jive accidentally photographed the fleeing pigeon thief as he was being chased by Flip, the victim. The photograph didn't show the thief's face, but did give Jive and Sunset a good look at what he was wearing. Jive and Sunset concluded that the thief was Snake Hips Robberts. They later realized that they had been wrong. When they looked carefully at the picture, they remembered that any dark color clothing photographs almost black in a black and white picture. Snake Hips had a black jacket, but he was innocent. The real thief was Sugar Brown. Then it was a simple matter of showing the evidence to both Flip and Sugar to get Sugar to confess.

Interest Level: 1-4. Reading Level: 2.2. Further Search Topics: Mystery and Detective Stories, Detectives-Fiction, Blacks-Fiction, City Life-Fiction, Group 2, Best Sellers.

Shearer, John. Billy Jo Jive and the walkie-talkie caper; illus by Ted Shearer. Delacorte 1981, 47 pp.

When Steam Boat Louis went to Jive and Sunset for help, he was desperate. Because Jive and Sunset had already solved three cases, they were the logical people to find the walkie-talkie that had been stolen from Steam Boat. The walkie-talkie was one of two that Steam Boat had been told to buy as part of a secret communication system for the Bugaloo Smackers. Even as Jive and Sunset hunted for the thief, the second walkie-talkie was stolen. Their only clue was a footprint found outside Steam Boat's fix-it shop. Eventually, after trial and error, Jive and Sunset uncovered the real thieves; Steam Boat's young twin cousins. Unhappy at being separated in school, they wanted to use the walkie-talkies to be able to talk with each other.

The high reading level of this book will make it most useful for those children who have read and enjoyed other books in the series and are willing to stretch to read one more.

Interest Level: 1-4. Reading Level: 3.2. Further Search Topics: Mystery and Detective Stories, Detectives-Fiction, Blacks-Fiction, City Life-Fiction, Group 2.

Shearer, John. Billy Jo Jive super private eye: the case of the missing ten speed bike; illus by Ted Shearer. Delacorte 1976, 47 pp.

Jive and Sunset began their friendship and their sleuthing career with this book. It all started when Sunset borrowed her older brother's 10-speed bicycle. Jive met Sunset while she sat at the side of the road crying, after her brother's bike had been stolen. Some careful joint detective work proved to Jive and Sunset that Dynamite Jones, jealous of Sunset's brother, had stolen the bike. The young crime fighters recovered the bicycle before Sunset's brother even knew it was missing.

This book sets the formula that all the others follow. A neighborhood person finds that something has been stolen and goes to Jive and Sunset for help. Jive and Sunset never have much trouble finding the thief even though they are sometimes misled for a short time. Often the culprit is quite obvious to the reader. After some attempts at clever detective work and an occasional bit of preaching, the crime is solved. It is the manner of the pursuit and the street-smart characters that give the stories their interest.

Interest Level: 1-4. Reading Level: 2.2. Further Search Topics: Mystery and Detective Stories, Blacks-Fiction, Detectives-Fiction, City Life-Fiction, Best Sellers, Group 2, Bicycles and Bicycling-Fiction.

Viorst, Judith. The tenth good thing about Barney; illus by Erik Blegvad. Atheneum 1971, 25 pp.

A quiet, thoughtful book to help a child face the difficult experience of death. When a family's beloved cat Barney died, their little boy tried to find 10 good things to say about him at the funeral. Nine things came easily to mind, but it was not until he had worked in the garden with his father that the little boy realized the tenth good thing. Barney, buried in the ground, would help the flowers, trees, and grass grow. A special picture book, small in size, but large in impact. Print is somewhat small but well-spaced.

Interest Level: 1-4. Reading Level: 2.1. Further Search Topics: Pets-Fiction, Cats-Fiction, Death-Fiction, Group 2, Read Aloud.

Warner, Gertrude Chandler. The boxcar children; illus by L. Kate Deal. A. Whitman 1950, 154 pp.

This is the first in a series of very early hi/lo books. Although they often bear signs of stilted "Dick and Jane"-style writing, occasionally preach to the reader, and are interrupted by frequent asides from the author, the stories are still popular with young readers. In each book the children are not simply manipulated, but control their own destiny. They fulfill many a child's dream of finding a loving home and family, becoming rich, having adventures, and solving mysteries. This is the simplest story of the series, most of the other entries assume interest in such advanced subjects as fossils, food sources, antiques, or the Revolutionary War.

The only place the four orphaned Alden children had to live was with a grandfather whom they had never met, but whom they had heard was mean. Rather than live with him, they decided to try and survive on their own. They found an abandoned railway boxcar and filled it was items that they found in a junkyard in order to make it their home. Henry, the oldest, went to work for a doctor who, in addition to money, gave him food and kept a silent but watchful eye over all the children without their knowledge. When Violet became ill, the children had no choice but to take her to Dr. Moore. He gave them all a temporary home and arranged for them to gradually get to know their grandfather. By the time Violet was almost well the children had grown to like the elderly stranger. It was a happy day when the children finally realized that the man to whom Dr. Moore had introduced them was really their grandfather.

Interest Level: 1-4. Reading Level: 2.1. Further Search Topics: Orphans-Fiction, Survival-Fiction, Runaways-Fiction, Brothers and Sisters-Fiction, Grandparents-Fiction.

Wyler, Rose. Magic secrets; illus by Talivaldis Stubis. Har-Row 1967, 64 pp.

Another good selection of easily performed but impressive looking magic tricks. After a short section defining magic, 13 tricks are described. Another 11 tricks are included as the authors describe how to put on a magic show. Just what differentiates the first group of tricks from the second is not clear. With a little imagination any of the tricks shown in the book could be used in a magic show. Use of the book beyond fourth grade is not likely due to its "early-reader" appearance. An I-Can-Read-Book.

Interest Level: 1-4. Reading Level: 2.1. Further Search Topics: Magic, Group 2.

INTEREST LEVEL 1-5

Ciardi, John. I met a man; illus by Robert Osborn. HM 1961, 74 pp.

Ciardi's poems are pure fun. About half are riddle poems (poems that describe something without naming it until the end) and the rest are humorous descriptions or nonsense poems. There is a problem, however, with the riddle poems: they are somewhat more difficult to read than the other poems, but of interest to younger rather than older readers. For that reason pages 1-21 (primarily nonsense verse) can be recommended for grades one through five. The remainder of the book, although enjoyable to the very young, needs to be read to them or needs a strong young reader.

Interest Level: 1-5. Reading Level: 2.2. Further Search Topics: Wit and Humor, Poetry, Riddles, Group 2.

Goldin, Augusta. Spider silk; illus by Joseph Low. Har-Row 1964, unp (34 pp).

No gimmicks here, just straight-forward information about spider webs. Where are spider webs found? How are they formed? What are their shapes? For what are they used? How strong are they? And, what are the other uses of spider silk? In answering those questions the author also gives a bit of information about particular types of spiders. The book can easily be used through grade three. Its picture book format will turn many fourth and fifth graders away even though the book's information is still quite interesting and useful. Let's-Read- & -Find-Out Science Book series.

Interest Level: 1-5. Reading Level: 2.2. Further Search Topics: Spiders, Nature Study, Group 2.

O'Neill, Mary. Hailstones and halibut bones; illus by Leonard Weisgard. Doubleday 1961, 59 pp.

This is a classic collection of twelve poems about colors. The poems are rhymed mood pieces of two or three pages that should appeal to almost any age reader. The difficulty of the vocabulary within each poem can vary greatly; however, most stanzas are short, most of the vocabulary is at least familiar, and the rhyme scheme is consistent.

Interest Level: 1-5. Reading Level: 3.2. Further Search Topics: Poetry, Colors, Group 2.

INTEREST LEVEL 1-6

Aylesworth, Thomas G. Movie monsters. Lippincott 1975, 79 pp.

If you are looking for an example of fine writing, you won't find it here. What you will find is a collection of monster movie photographs and facts. This is a wealth of trivia about eleven famous monsters (including King Kong, Godzilla, the Fly, Frankenstein's monster, the Mummy, Dracula, Wolf Man and others), their films, sequels, historic backgrounds, identifying characteristics, and more. There is an extensive index, a list of monster movies and their credits, and even brief information about famous monster actors. The book is not great literature, but it is interesting and fun.

Interest Level: 1-6. Reading Level 3.1. Further Search Topics: Acting, Motion Pictures, Monsters, Horror-Fiction, Group 2, Best Sellers.

Pene du Bois, William. Lazy Tommy Pumpkinhead. Har-Row 1966, 32 pp.

Tommy lived a solitary life in an all-electric house. An electric bed woke Tommy and slid him into a tub full of warm water. The tub then tipped him out and into a harness that held Tommy upright while other machines dried him, combed his hair, brushed his teeth, dressed him, and fed him. But one day Tommy's life was literally turned upside down with disastrous results. His feet were cleaned and combed and his clothes were all put on upside down, but the worst part of all was that Tommy almost starved; the machine fed his feet instead of his mouth.

A tongue-in-cheek warning against laziness. The lesson is obvious but the treatment (both text and illustrations) is so enjoyable that the book is appealing to almost any reader who wants a short, funny book. Print is somewhat small but spacing between lines is more than adequate.

Interest Level: 1-6. Reading Level: 3.2. Further Search Topics: Electricity-Fiction, Robots-Fiction, Laziness-Fiction, Humorous Fiction, Group 2, Read Aloud.

Sarnoff, Jane. What? A riddle book; illus by Reynold Ruffins. Scribner 1974, 62 pp.

A good, lengthy collection of both familiar and unfamiliar riddles. Every other page is brightened by bold and humorous illustrations. The first part of the book seems to have slightly more riddles for younger readers than the rest of the book. Some of the riddles in the collection involve rather sophisticated puns; thus they are more appealing to fifth and sixth grade readers. The final three pages of the book include 35 riddles whose answers are in code. The key to the code is given on the last page of the book. It is a picture book printed in two tones. The riddles sometimes slant diagonally across the page.

Interest Level: 1-6. Reading Level: 3.1. Further Search Topics: Riddles, Wit and Humor, Group 2, Nonverbal Communication.

INTEREST LEVEL 2-4

Adrian, Mary. The fireball mystery illus by Reisie Lonette. Hastings 1977, 118 pp.

While stargazing one night, Tim and Vicky and their friend Joey saw a meteor fall onto their private island. Before they were able to find it the children realized that someone else was trying to steal the meteorite from them. As much astronomy as mystery here. Beyond fourth grade, the reader may begin to find the astronomy lesson heavy-handed and the mystery light.

Interest Level: 2-4. Reading Level: 3.1. Further Search Topics: Mystery and Detective Stories, Astronomy, Flying Saucers-Fiction, Outer Space-Fiction, Group 2.

Baker, Betty. The pig war; illus by Robert Lopshire. Har-Row 1969, 64 pp.

A brief, fictionalized account of an 1859 land squabble between the United States and Britain. The incident, which took place in what is now the state of Washington, became known as the Pig War. Frightened British pigs destroyed the American farmers' gardens. When the farmers shot one of the pigs, the war began. Simply told and humorously illustrated. Should appeal to history or military fans. Early reader format.

Interest Level: 2-4. Reading Level: 2.1. Further Search Topics: United States-History-War-Fiction, Great Britain-History-Fiction, War-Fiction, Washington (state)-Fiction, Historical Fiction, Pigs-Fiction.

Branley, Franklyn M. Eclipse: darkness in daytime; illus by Donald Crews. Har-Row 1973, 33 pp.

The subject is so well-explained and the book is so physically attractive, it's a shame that some older readers will be put off by this title's picture book appearance. Aside from an occasional jarring, condescending note, this is a fine introduction to an interesting subject. Use comfortably with third and fourth graders. Recommend to fifth graders with caution. No index or table of contents. Lets-Read-and-Find-Out-Science-Book series.

Interest Level: 2-4. Reading Level: 2.2. Further Search Topics: Sun, Astronomy, Eclipses, Moon.

Branley, Franklyn M. Oxygen keeps you alive; illus by Don Madden. Har-Row 1971, 33 pp.

A well-explained, beginning treatment of the functions, importance, and uses of oxygen. The explanation is not limited to humans, but extends to plants and animals as well. Although the book can be stretched to use with fifth graders, its picture book format and sometimes condescending tone indicate it is most easily used through fourth grade. No index or table to contents. Let's-Read-and-Find-Out-Science-Book series.

Interest Level: 2-4. Reading Level: 2.2. Further Search Topics: Air, Respiration, Scuba Diving, Astronauts.

Branley, Franklyn M. High sounds, low sounds; illus by Paul Galdone. Har-Row 1967, 35 pp.

A no-nonsense, informative, thorough introduction to sound, sound waves, and hearing. Includes a couple of simple, illustrative experiments. Useful through third and fourth grade with no problems. The picture book format and opening and closing questions to the reader may turn away fifth and sixth grade users. Worth trying anyway. No index or table of contents. Let's-Read-and-Find-Out-Science-Book series.

Interest Level: 2-4. Reading Level: 2.2. Further Search Topics: Sound, Experiments, Scientific.

Bulla, Clyde Robert. The sugar pear tree; illus by Taro Yashima. T Y Crowell 1960, 54 pp.

Lonnie lived with his mother and his grandfather in a house owned by the state. A new highway was to be built that would force the family to move, but Gramp refused to acknowledge that the state could force them out of their home. He chased away every state representative who came to warn the family that they should move. Lonnie's mother had always been at work when the representatives came and so knew nothing about the warnings until she came home to find their belongings on the sidewalk and their house on wheels. The only person they could turn to was their friend Nick. Nick owned a nursery in town and a small house with a large yard in the country. He had become a friend of Lonnie's when he gave Lonnie first prize in a school essay contest on the topic of "favorite trees." Lonnie's prize had been a sugar pear tree, his favorite. Nick had next become Lonnie's mother's friend. Nick arranged for them to stay in the greenhouse at his country place. The longer they stayed, the better friends Nick and Lonnie's mother became. Gramp was the only person who didn't adjust to the move. He stopped speaking the moment he was carried out of his old home. In a final and successful attempt to make Gramp happy, Nick bought the old house and had it moved out to his country lot.

The idea of a state government being able to force a family to move may need some explaining. The story's warmth and very consistent early second grade reading level make this a particularly useful book with quiet readers.

Interest Level: 2-4. Reading Level: 2.1. Further Search Topics: Trees-Fiction, Moving, Household-Fiction, Family Problems-Fiction, Grandparents-Fiction, Poverty-Fiction.

Bunting, Eve. The skate patrol; illus by Don Madden. Albert Whitman 1980, 40 pp.

The book is funny, clever, undemanding and short. The combination of those qualities plus its slight mystery and its consistent reading level make this a very appealing and useful book for young readers. The plot is simple: in the hopes that their neighbors would be so grateful that they would allow the boys to roller skate in the neighborhood again, two friends decided to capture a local thief. James and Milton even knew who the thief was. He was the "mysterious man" who sat in the park. They only had to capture him in the act of stealing to prove that they were correct. They watched him continuously and trailed him as he followed old ladies. Then came the day that they heard Mrs. Grump scream that her purse had been snatched. The boys sped after the "mysterious man" on their skates. They caught him and knocked him down. To their surprise he declared that he was an undercover policeman and they were letting the real thief get away. Off they went again. This time they caught the right person and were rewarded just the way that they had hoped: Mrs. Crump (not Grump) promised that the boys would be allowed to roller skate any time they wished. A light and lively entertainment.

Interest Level: 2-4. Reading Level: 2.2. Further Search Topics: Mystery and Detective Stories, Humorous Fiction, Spies-Fiction, Roller Skating-Fiction, Crime-Fiction, Best Sellers.

Clymer, Eleanor. Chipmunk in the forest; illus by Ingrid Fetz. Atheneum 1965, 56 pp.

A simple story of an Indian boy who learned the meaning of the word "courage". Chipmunk had never admitted to anyone that he was afraid of the forest. But when his uncle tried to teach him to hunt, Chipmunk was too frightened to be quiet, and thus he scared away all the animals. He returned to the village in disgrace to do "women's work." One of his jobs was to watch Little Brother. When Little Brother disappeared, Chipmunk went in search of him. It began to snow as Chipmunk went farther and farther into the forest, but even though he was frightened, Chipmunk kept on looking. By the time he found Little Brother, the snow had covered their tracks. Chipmunk had to use all that he had learned from his uncle to get them safely home. When he arrived back at the

village, Chipmunk had finally proven that he was brave.

Interest Level: 2-4. Reading Level: 2.1. Further Search Topics: Indians of North America-Fiction, Courage-Fiction, Snow-Fiction, Hunting-Fiction, Survival-Fiction.

Cone, Molly. Leonard Bernstein; illus by Robert Galster. Har-Row 1970, 33 pp.

This is a bare bones outline that will appeal to music enthusiasts but will not attract anyone else. The reader catches very little of Bernstein's personality, but *is* awed by an impressive list of his accomplishments. The few attempts made to recreate the real person may have to be explained (i.e., references to Bernstein forgetting to get his hair cut because he was so busy). Picture book format of the hardback may deter some readers. Now published in paperback edition only. Crowell Biography series.

Interest Level: 2-4. Reading Level: 2.2. Further Search Topics: Music-Biography, Biography, Conductors, Composers, Pianists, Group 2.

Dolch, Edward W. Dog stories; illus by Bernette Johnson and Robert S. Kerr. Garrard 1954, 169 pp.

Although overly sentimental for most adult tastes, this collection of true dog stories appeals to young dog lovers. Eighteen chapters tell 15 stories, ranging from the first story in which dog rescues boy, to the final story in which boy rescues dog. There is a dog who played baseball, a dog who went to live at a newspaper, a dog who saved a fireman from a fire, two dogs who were lost and several more dogs who became heroes. A consistent reading level, large print and a popular topic make this a good choice to offer reluctant readers despite the Dolch books' usual unattractive illustrations. Dolch Basic Vocabulary Book series.

Interest Level: 2-4. Reading Level: 2.1. Further Search Topics: Dogs-Fiction, Courage-Fiction, Pets-Fiction.

Fife, Dale. Follow that ghost!; illus by Joan Drescher. Dutton 1979, 58 pp.

In short sentences reminiscent of "Dragnet," Chuck tells a very simple story of Chuck and Jason's first detective case. He and Jason were practicing following people, when their next-door-neighbor caught them following her home. Instead of being angry at the two boys, Glory decided to hire them to find the ghost she and her mother were hearing at 5:00 every morning. Despite their best attempts to capture and bury the ghost, or a find a human cause for the ghostly sounds, Chuck and Jason couldn't rid Glory's apartment of its ghost. Their final effort nearly resulted in injury to a neighbor. Ultimately, Chuck discovered that the ghost was merely a displaced woodpecker looking for a new home.

Not a terribly ambitious mystery, but one whose consistent reading level, familiar urban setting and interesting characters will please many young readers.

Interest Level: 2-4. Reading Level: 2.1. Further Search Topics: Ghosts-Fiction, Mystery and Detective Stories, Spies-Fiction, Humorous Fiction.

Greenfield, Eloise. Rosa Parks; illus by Eric Marlow. Har-Row 1973, 33 pp.

This book succumbs to the difficulty of writing for children about a subject that needs more explanation. The occasionally condescending tone combined with the Crowell Biography picture book format will keep this otherwise adequate introduction to the civil rights movement from being useful beyond fourth grade. The book should be very useful, however, for third and fourth grade social studies, history or biography units.

Rosa Parks' childhood and her feelings about the special rules for blacks make up the first half of the book. The second half is devoted to Rosa's act of defiance (refusing to give up her seat on a bus to a white man) and the repercussions of that act. Crowell Biography series.

Interest Level: 2-4. Reading Level 2.2. Further Search Topics: Blacks-Biography, Biography, Prejudice, Civil Rights, Women-Biography, Courage.

Mathis, Sharon Bell. Ray Charles; illus by George Ford. Har-Row 1973, 33 pp.

Dominent throughout this biography of Ray Charles is the theme of overcoming adversity. The book is not just a recounting of Ray Charles' music lessons, early schooling, family life, and talent. All of that is included, but it serves to illustrate the manner in which Charles met his troubles. His problems began when he was very young. His brother died, and Ray lost one eye and then the sight in his other eye. His family was poor, but close, and he missed them when he was sent away to a school for the blind. Music was his love, but even that was work, for Charles had to learn to read and write music in Braille. He worked hard at it and eventually could play and arrange music for every instrument in the band.

Determined to be independent, when Charles was orphaned at age 15, he left school and began playing music for a living. The first record he made resulted in a $16 fine because he made it during a musician's union strike. Charles took a series of sideman and nightclub jobs until he finally had enough money to hire seven other musicians to play his music. Today Charles is very wealthy, owns his own record company, has a family, and is considered a great jazz and blues musician. None of his success came easily; only through determination, will power, pride, and hard work.

The book, interesting and serviceable enough for music or biography units, is also designed to set an example for youngsters facing their own problems. It will, of course, be popular with Ray Charles fans, too. Crowell Biography series.

Interest Level: 2-4. Reading Level: 3.1. Further Search Topics: Jazz Music, Music-Biography, Vision, Physically Handicapped, Blacks-Biography, Group 2, Biography, Pianists, Orphans, Challenges, Courage.

Moore, Lilian. The snake that went to school; illus by Mary Stevens. Random 1957, 99 pp.

Hank's pet snake Puffy disappeared from the Science Room at school and his little brother, Benjy (in first grade) became ill on the same day. Hank was so worried about finding Puffy that he hardly thought about his pesky little brother, until Puffy was found two days later. Then Hank learned that Benjy had secretly gone to visit Puffy, after being rejected by Hank and had accidentally let the snake out of its cage. Benjy had been so worried about letting the snake out that he had actually made himself ill. Hank finally realized that Benjy wasn't the pest he had thought he was, and promised to be a better older brother.

A somewhat old-fashioned but satisfying story told in ten short chapters.

Interest Level: 2-4. Reading Level: 3.1. Further Search Topics: Pets-Fiction, Snakes-Fiction, Brothers and Sisters-Fiction, School Stories.

Rudeen, Kenneth. Roberto Clemente; illus by Frank Mullins. Har-Row 1974, 33 pp.

A romanticized retelling of a great baseball player's life. Those already interested in baseball or in Clemente will probably not mind the romantic tone, but may notice the almost patronizing explanations of some of the basics of baseball. Crowell Biography series.

Interest Level: 2-4. Reading Level: 3.1. Further Search Topics: Baseball-Biography, Biography, Puerto Rico, Group 2, Clemente, Roberto.

Rudeen, Kenneth. Jackie Robinson; illus by Richard Cuffari. Har-Row 1971, 41 pp.

Jackie Robinson was the youngest child in a large, poor family. As early as high school it was Robinson's superior athletic talent that set him apart. He could run track or play baseball, football, or basketball. He was the first student at UCLA to win a letter in all four sports. But because he wasn't happy to see the way his mother still had to struggle to earn money to live, after a year and a half at UCLA, Robinson left college to take a job. Soon after that, the United States entered World War II and Robinson went into the Army. His refusal to ride in the back of a bus in Texas resulted in a courtmartial, but he was found innocent after an uproar was made by the newspapers.

After the Army, Robinson played baseball with a Negro League team. A short time later, he was asked by the Dodger manager Branch Rickey to become the first black man to play in the major leagues. Rickey warned Robinson that it would mean he not only had to play well, but that he would also have to take all the anger and bitterness that would be directed at him. Robinson agreed. For three long years, while there were no other black players in the major leagues, Robinson played well and took everything without fighting back. Robinson was then able to stop trying to be perfect because he had successfully broken a very important color barrier and no longer had to prove to white managers, players and fans that blacks belonged in baseball just as much as whites. Robinson played for the Dodgers for ten years. When he left baseball he was elected into the Baseball Hall of Fame. He continued to fight for civil rights throughout the rest of his life, although there is only a brief mention of his activities in the book. Since the book's publication Jackie Robinson has died.

This is an excellent choice for the child who thinks of nothing but sports. It may be helpful in opening up an interest in the civil rights movement, black history, or black heroes. It is unfortunate that the traditional Crowell biography format (semi-picture book), and the author's slight tendency to be condescending, prevents the book from being useful beyond fourth grade. Crowell Biography series.

Interest Level: 2-4. Reading Level: 2.2. Further Search Topics: Civil Rights, Robinson, Jackie, Baseball-Biography, Biography, Blacks-Biography, Prejudice, Poverty.

Scism, Carol K. The wizard of Walnut Street; illus by Martha Alexander. Dial 1973, 54 pp.

John and his friends had no room in their Wizard Club for Ford Owens, the new kid. John thought Ford was a conceited show-off who only wanted to make John look like a coward. It was true that John was afraid of some things, such as going down the giant slide into the lake, but he didn't want anyone else to know it. So he excluded Ford from all the club's activities until Ford pushed his way into their magic wishing-well project.

It had been John's idea to charge everyone a dime who wanted to make a wish. They could use the money to buy the few simple things that they would need to make the wishes come true. But it was Ford's eerie volcano and his large dog that had added just the right atmosphere to the trick to make people believe. Even John and Ford found themselves making wishes. John wished to be able to go down the giant slide. He didn't know what Ford wished. Much to John's initial surprise, people's wishes began to be fulfilled. Even Arthur, who had wished he could learn to dive, found he could. Then because John began to realize that the magic was in believing in himself and not in the wishing well, he tried the slide and succeeded. Once John's reason to avoid Ford was gone, he relaxed and asked Ford to join the club. At that point, even Ford's wish was granted.

Interest Level: 2-4. Reading Level: 2.1. Further Search Topics: Friendship-Fiction, Gangs-Fiction, Courage-Fiction, Magic-Fiction, Vacation-Fiction, Best Sellers.

Wyler, Rose. Funny Magic; illus by Talivaldis Stubis. Schol Bk Serv 1972, 52 pp.

A collection of 20 simple but effective magic tricks that require some advance preparation and practice but which are well-suited to the third through fifth grade child's coordination. Because all tricks are meant to be performed in front of an audience, there are performance hints throughout the book. Most of the tricks are impressive enough to interest even sixth grade magicians, but the book's reader format and cute tone make it difficult to use beyond grade four.

Interest Level: 2-4. Reading Level: 2.1. Further Search Topics: Magic.

INTEREST LEVEL 2-5

Allen, Gertrude. Everyday turtles, toads and their kin. HM 1970, 48 pp.

Straight-forward, short, chapter discussions of turtles, lizards, snakes, salamanders, toads, frogs and tree toads. Black and white drawings done by the author amplify the text. The major part of the book is simple enough to be understood at second grade, but should still be interesting to fourth and fifth graders. A few terms may need explanation: i.e., venomous, prey. The chapters on the turtle, lizard, frog and tree frog are the easiest. No index, but still useful for reports.

Interest Level: 2-5. Reading Level: 2.2. Further Search Topics: Turtles, Reptiles, Lizards, Toads, Frogs, Snakes, Salamanders.

Berends, Polly Berrien. The case of the elevator duck; illus by James K. Washburn. Random 1973, 54 pp.

Although it would be stretching the meaning of the word to call this a mystery, it is a story of an 11-year-old detective. Albert tells his own story in a clipped style that resembles adult detective novels. One morning Albert found a duck abandoned in the apartment house elevator. He was determined to find the owner of the duck and return it. He had to be very careful as he searched because pets were absolutely forbidden in the housing projects. Anyone who saw him with the duck might report him. Albert and his parents had waited too long to get into the projects to be kicked out because of a duck. When Albert finally found the duck's owner (a young, sad child named Julio), Julio's sister forced Albert to take the duck back. Still angry at Julio's sister, Albert took the duck to the project's day care center, where the teacher agreed to formally adopt the duck. Albert stayed at the center long enough to see Julio's happy surprise when he arrived and found the duck. Its appealing characters, the tension created by the writing style, and the book's humor make this a delightful story.

Interest Level: 2-5. Reading Level 2.2. Further Search Topics: Humorous Fiction, City Life-Fiction, Housing Projects-Fiction, Detectives-Fiction, Pets-Fiction, Ducks-Fiction, Read Aloud.

Blume, Judy. Freckle juice; illus by Sonia O. Lisker. Four Winds 1971, 40 pp.

A very funny story that should appeal to almost everyone. Andrew wanted freckles so that the dirt on his skin wouldn't show as much and he wouldn't have to wash as often. As luck would have it, Sharon, the most obnoxious girl in class, had a freckle juice recipe that she was willing to sell for 50 cents. Even after drinking the brew of grape juice, vinegar, mustard, olive oil, and more, Andrew didn't see any freckles, but, he certainly was sick. Although the protagonists are younger, this book will hold even a fifth grade reader's interest.

Interest Level: 2-5. Reading Level 3.1. Further Search Topics: Humorous Fiction, Group 2, Read Aloud, Everyday Stories, Beauty-Fiction, School Stories, Magic-Fiction, Best Sellers.

Bulla, Clyde Robert. The ghost of windy hill; illus by Don Bolognese. Har-Row 168, 84 pp.

If the reader doesn't expect a high adventure ghost story, he or she will not be disappointed by this low-keyed tale of a family who goes to live in a house that is supposedly haunted. Mr. Giddings asked the Carver family to move into his country home while he and his wife stayed in Boston. His intent was that the Carvers should either prove to his wife that the house was not haunted or drive the ghost out. The Carvers found no ghosts—at first—only an interesting group of neighbors. There was shy Miss Miggie who drifted around in a long, white dress and wore a flower-covered hat. Bruno was the gruff beggar boy who couldn't walk and had no friends but a goat, until the Carver children came along. Near the end of their stay Lorna Carver mentioned that because they had seen no ghosts the family would soon leave and the Giddings would return. Strange occurrences began almost immediately after Lorna's statement and ended only when the Carvers caught Bruno trying to convince them that he was the ghost. Lorna and Jamie were his only friends, so he had risked his guardians wrath and given up the pretense of being lame to trick the Carvers into staying. All ends well as Bruno's cruel guardian is run off, the Carvers take responsibility for Bruno's care, and Mrs. Giddings admits she made up the ghost story because she hated living in the country and had wanted to return to the city. Another serviceable book in the very successful Bulla style.

Interest Level: 2-5. Reading Level: 2.1. Further Search Topics: Ghosts-Fiction, Brothers and Sisters-Fiction, Orphans-Fiction, Country Life-Fiction, Courage-Fiction, Challenges-Fiction, Friendship-Fiction.

Bulla, Clyde Robert. Shoeshine girl; illus by Leigh Grant. Har-Row 1975, 84 pp.

A well-written, realistic story of 10-year-old Sarah who was sent to spend the summer with her Aunt Claudia. Sarah's parents felt that Sarah put too much importance on money and so insisted that Aunt Claudia give her no allowance for the summer. Sure that Aunt Claudia would call her bluff, Sarah threatened to get a job. Instead, Aunt Claudia thought it was a good idea. Sarah's experience as a shoeshine girl forced her to grow, to learn to like working, and finally to take responsibility for the stand when her boss was hit by a car. Told with quiet humor. For the reader who enjoys Judy Blume's books.

Interest Level: 2-5. Reading Level: 2.2. Further Search Topics: Children-Growth-Fiction, Family Problems-Fiction, Vacation-Fiction, Occupations-Fiction, Everyday Stories.

Bulla, Clyde Robert. Ghost town treasure; illus by Don Freeman. Har-Row 1957, 87 pp.

A very simple story whose title is somewhat misleading. Instead of a mystery or an exciting story of buried treasure, Bulla has written a very pleasant story of a family whose fortunes are reversed by the accidental discovery of a nearby cave. Young Ty Jackson and his family were the last people living in Gold Rock, California. Everyone else had moved out when the new highway had bypassed the town. The Jacksons had been able to stay on only because some of the nearby ranchers had continued to buy food and supplies from the Jacksons' store. Just as they, too, were preparing to move out, Ty's pen pals wrote that they were coming to visit the town. Their grandfather had died there, years earlier, during his search for gold. When Paul and Nora arrived, they brought with them their grandfather's diary. The last entry in the journal seemed to indicate that their grandfather had found gold in an isolated cave in the nearby canyon. After a long search, the children discovered the cave, but no gold. Ty's disappointment changed to joy when tourists started arriving to see the new natural attraction. Once again his parents could sell their groceries, the hotel could be reopened and Gold Rock would flourish.

Interest Level: 2-5. Reading Level: 2.2. Further Search Topics: Treasure-Fiction, Family Problems-Fiction, West-Fiction, California-Fiction, Family-Fiction, Pen Pals-Fiction.

Bulla, Clyde Robert. John Billington, friend of Squanto; illus by Peter Burchard. Har-Row 1956, 88 pp.

This historical novel about the Mayflower voyage and the Pilgrims' first year at Plymouth centers on young John Billington. John was considered the troublemaker of the children. His problems are woven around the events of the year, including the Pilgrims' first meetings with the Wampanoag Indians. It was finally John, however, who was responsible for bringing peace between the Pilgrims and the Wampanoag tribe who lived further down Cape Cod. The book is not as exciting or convincing as Bulla's books are generally. It also contains a few minor historical inaccuracies; yet it remains useful as both an introduction to American history and historical fiction.

Interest Level: 2-5. Reading Level: 2.1. Further Search Topics: Pilgrims-Fiction, Historical Fiction, United States-History-Fiction, Thanksgiving-Fiction, Troublemakers-Fiction, Indians of North America-Fiction.

Bulla, Clyde Robert. Riding the pony express; illus by Grace Paull. Har-Row 1948, 95 pp.

Although somewhat marred by the stereotyped speech of a young Indian boy, this is otherwise an exciting piece of historical fiction set in the 1860s. Dick was sent from New York City to join his father in St. Joseph, Missouri, only to find his father had moved to Nebraska to become a pony express rider. When

Dick finally found his father, after a long stagecoach ride, he thought his father didn't want him. Dick stayed at the way station and helped with the chores because he didn't know what else to do. Then one day the house was burned, his father was shot, and the horses were almost stolen. There was no one around who could carry the mail, except Dick. Despite a wolf pack at his heels, Dick rode to the next way station. On his way home he realized his father really did want him and he no longer wanted to leave his father. Chapters are short with separate episodes that tie them together. A few simple songs appear between the chapters.

Interest Level: 2-5. Reading Level: 2.1. Further Search Topics: Horses-Fiction, West-Fiction, United States-History-Fiction, Historical Fiction, Voyages and Travels-Fiction, Courage-Fiction, Frontier and Pioneer Life-Fiction.

Bulla, Clyde Robert. Indian hill; illus by James J. Spanfeller. T Y Crowell 1963, 74 pp.

A very low-key story of a Navajo family who moved from the reservation to a city because they could no longer support themselves on the reservation. The move was necessary, but it was not appreciated by young Kee and his mother. They hated their ugly apartment and the crowded city, and wanted to go home. When an excuse to return to the reservation arose, Kee and his mother left the city. However, by the time Kee's father arrived to tell them he had been wrong to force them to move, Kee and his mother had realized they never gave their new home a chance. They were ready to try again. No excitement here, only an understanding look at the difficulties of moving.

Interest Level: 2-5. Reading Level: 2.1. Further Search Topics: Indians of North America-Fiction, Navajo Indians-Fiction, City Life-Fiction, Moving, Household-Fiction.

Chew, Ruth. Witch's broom. Dodd 1977, 128 pp.

Amy's mother was the one who found the blue broom, but Amy and her friend Jean were the ones who learned it was magical. One night the broom flew Amy into a mountain cave where a coven of witches was meeting. It even forced Amy to answer the roll call for someone named Beryl. But it wasn't until it took both Amy and Jean back to the cave that they discovered the broom's connection to the strange bluejay that had been following them. The bluejay was really Beryl, a young and headstrong witch who had turned herself into the bluejay and then couldn't turn herself back. With the girls' unwitting help, Beryl found the charm to turn herself back into a witch and flew off on a scrawny old broom, leaving the blue broom for Amy and Jean.

What youngster wouldn't want a flying broomstick and the misadventures that go with owning one? Wish fulfillment can never be overrated as an appeal of Ruth Chew's books.

Interest Level: 2-5. Reading Level: 3.1. Further Search Topics: Witches-Fiction, Magic-Fiction, Fantasy, Birds-Fiction, Group 2, Transformations-Fiction.

Chew, Ruth. No such thing as a witch. Hastings 1971, 112 pp.

Despite the fact that their mother said there was no such thing as a witch, Tad and Nora were convinced that their neighbor Maggie Brown was indeed a witch. And they were right! Maggie Brown knew how to make a special kind of fudge that could make anyone into an animal-lover, enable people to talk with animals, or actually transform someone into an animal. All you had to do was to eat one, two, or three pieces of fudge respectively. But Maggie's overzealous love of animals and her disenchantment with housework eventually attracted the attention of her neighbors and the city health department. Only Tad and Nora's frantic efforts to help her saved Maggie from losing all of her animal friends.

A fairly detailed plot, the fascination of being able to change size and appearance and the intrigue involved in fooling the adults around Maggie make this one of Chew's best books.

Interest Level: 2-5. Reading Level: 2.2. Further Search Topics: Individualists-Fiction, Witches-Fiction, Animals-Fiction, Fantasy, Magic-Fiction, Brothers and Sisters-Fiction, Transformations-Fiction.

Chew, Ruth. The witch's garden. Hastings 1978, 112 pp.

Although its elements seem to promise an exciting adventure story, this is a disappointing book. The witch who moved into the dark, old home next door to Josh and Susan, was trying to improve her overgrown garden when Susan and Josh offered to help. The children accidentally splashed themselves with the witch's newest brew and found they suddenly became very tiny inhabitants of a dense and threatening jungle (the garden). After they regained their normal size, they dug into other areas of the garden. One hole they dug opened into an underground tunnel that they found was inhabited by a fire-breathing dragon. When the dragon cornered Mrs. Muldoon, Susan and Josh ran out of the tunnel, found the brew and splashed it onto the dragon. The dragon shrank away, Mrs. Muldoon was safe and the tunnel closed over.

Because there is little more suspense than in this description, the book fails to live up to its promise. In addition, the children's first sudden size change is just subtle enough to be confusing. Despite its problems the book is popular with Ruth Chew fans and therefore useful.

Interest Level: 2-5. Reading Level: 2.2. Further Search Topics: Witches-Fiction, Brothers and Sisters-Fiction, Magic-Fiction, Fantasy, Dragons-Fiction, Transformations-Fiction.

Chew, Ruth. The would-be witch. Hastings 1976, 112 pp.

Robin and her brother Andy took a liking to the clumsy white cat they saw in Zelda's Antique Shop. The cat apparently liked them, too, for it followed them home. Not having enough money to offer to buy Pearl from Zelda, the children tried to polish up an old pair of silver birds to trade for the cat. The polish turned out to be magical and made the birds real. When they tried the polish on a broom in Zelda's store, the broom began to fly. Upon discovering that Zelda wanted to be a witch but had failed the coven entrance exam, Rob helped her learn to fly and told her of the witches' meeting place that she and Andy had discovered. But the 12 witches who had been turned into cats were wicked enough to want to use Zelda to regain their human form and turn *her* into a cat. In attempting to prevent such a fate, Rob, Andy and Zelda set fire to the abandoned building being used as a meeting place. The 12 witches were rescued from the fire but charged with arson, which meant probable jail sentences for all of them. Zelda, finally a happy and capable witch, gave Pearl to Rob and Andy to thank them for their help.

A better-crafted story than many of the others, this also has a more evil cast of characters to provide additional interest.

Interest Level: 2-5. Reading Level: 2.2. Further Search Topics: Witches-Fiction, Brothers and Sisters-Fiction, Magic-Fiction, Fantasy, Transformations-Fiction, Cats-Fiction.

Chew, Ruth. Earthstar magic. Hastings 1979, 128 pp.

This is one of a series of similar stories by Ruth Chew. Each story involves two children and an old woman they usually suspect is a witch. As their suspicions become convictions they also find that, contrary to their expectation, the witch is very nice and often in need of help.

The children in this tale are brother and sister. Ben and Elizabeth first saw and then didn't see Trudy as she searched for a magical mushroom called an earthstar. Accidentally thrown together again, Ben and Elizabeth took a liking to Trudy, especially when she explained that she had been thrown out of her coven because she was so inept. In fact, she wasn't even able to control the earthstar. The earthstar manages to get all three in and out of adventures (including becoming tiny, flying and almost being eaten) before they learn to control its power. As the story ends, Trudy, finally respected by the other witches, flies off with a promise that Ben and Elizabeth will see her again.

Very lightweight but also very popular with young lovers of witch stories. There seems to be just the right amount of adventure to make up for the very benign witch.

Interest Level: 2-5. Reading Level: 2.2. Further Search Topics: Witches-Fiction, Magic-Fiction, Fantasy, Vacation-Fiction, Brothers and Sisters-Fiction, Transformations-Fiction.

Chew, Ruth. The wishing tree. Hastings 1980, 142 pp.

Peggy and Brian's discovery of a talking cat, a bird with a beautiful song, and a strange and frightening tree led them to a shopping bag lady, a giant named Fred, a gold key and a magical tablecloth. In a rather complicated series of events, the children and the cat finally succeeded in retrieving the tablecloth from Annie (the old woman to whom Puss had loaned it) and giving it back to Fred, who needed it to help satisfy his gigantic appetite. In addition, they returned Fred to normal human size, rescued Annie from a fall on the ice, introduced the two characters and encouraged them to live together in Fred's castle.

Complicated enough already, the story's lengthy adventure that leads up to the discovery of the key (climbing into the magical tree and swimming in a pond) makes the plot even more complex. If a reader doesn't expect more than benign fantasy and fun this is an adequate choice.

Interest Level: 2-5. Reading Level: 2.2. Further Search Topics: Magic-Fiction, Fantasy, Brothers and Sisters-Fiction, Giants-Fiction, Cats-Fiction.

Cleary, Beverly. Henry and Beezus; illus by Louis Darling. Morrow 1952, 192 pp.

When Henry's dog Ribsy stole the meat from a neighbor's barbecue, a friend rode after Ribsy on his bike and saved the meat. Henry was so embarrassed and jealous that he boasted about an even nicer bike that he was going to get. At first Henry thought he'd be able to earn money to buy a bike in a very short time (he found 49 boxes of bubble gum that he could sell). When that scheme fell through, Henry tried taking over a friend's paper route, but Ribsy kept retrieving the newspapers Henry delivered. Eventually Henry decided to buy a used bike at the police department auction. Beezus, who made a bid for Henry, ended up buying him a beaten-up girl's bike that was hardly worth fixing. The money finally appeared when Henry least expected it; he won $50.00 worth of work at a beauty salon.

Although all seven chapters continue the same story, Chapters 1, 2, 3 and 7, can each stand alone. Henry is definitely old-fashioned, but children still enjoy his humorous escapades and empathize with his desire for a bicycle. The revised paperback cover makes the book's physical appearance less dated. Reading level is somewhat inconsistent: from 2.2 to 3.2.

Interest Level: 2-5. Reading Level: 3.1. Further Search Topics: Humorous Fiction, Occupations-Fiction, Everyday Stories, Bicycles and Bicycling-Fiction, Read Aloud, Group 2.

Clifford, Eth. Help, I'm a prisoner in the library; illus by George Hughes. HM 1979, 103 pp.

When their car stopped, Mary Rose and Jo-Beth were left alone in a strange city while their father went to find some gas. Jo-Beth needed to use the bathroom, so the sisters headed for the closest public building they could see, the library. No one saw them go in, so no one knew that they were locked inside when the librarian secured the building for the night. With the lights out and a blizzard outside, the library was a very spooky place. The girls tried calling the police, but the police wouldn't take them seriously. Then they heard groans and eerie moans from the second floor. Gathering all their courage, the girls went to investigate, only to discover the librarian lying hurt and unconscious. Their ingenuity and imagination helped the sisters through the difficult hours before they were all rescued.

Don't read it too carefully or the book's implausibilities will become very evident. Most young readers, however, will enjoy this story for its suspense, spooky atmosphere and adventurous girls, and they will ignore its weaknesses.

Interest Level: 2-5. Reading Level: 3.1. Further Search Topics: Disasters-Fiction, Snow-Fiction, Brothers and Sisters-Fiction, Libraries-Fiction, Survival-Fiction, Courage-Fiction, Group 2.

Clifford, Eth. The dastardly murder of Dirty Pete; illus by George Hughes. HM 1981, 120 pp.

Although this is a sequel to *Help, I'm a Prisoner in the Library*, it does not depend on the previous title, and in fact, is likely to be the more successful introduction to Mary Rose and Jo-Beth Onetree. Given the choice, most young readers will take a mystery set in a ghost town over a mystery set in a library.

Mary Rose, Jo-Beth and their father were on their way across country when they became lost. As night grew closer, the only place they could find to stay was an old hotel in the ghost town where Sorehead Jones had allegedly killed Dirty Pete. It was Sorehead's ghost who was supposed to haunt the town, and indeed there was someone or something who was in the town with the Onetrees. To their surprise, that someone turned out to be Sourdough Sam, an aging actor who had become senile and spent his days acting out all the parts in the Dirty Pete story. The town was only a movie set and the story was only a movie script. The Onetrees discovered the truth bit by bit after a frightening venture into an abandoned gold mine, a harrowing night in the haunted hotel and a jail sentence for Mr. Onetree.

Beware of the rare, very difficult descriptive passage that may cause trouble for some readers.

Interest Level: 2-5. Reading Level: 3.1. Further Search Topics: Mystery and Detective Stories, West-Fiction, Brothers and Sisters-Fiction, Motion Pictures-Fiction, Ghosts-Fiction, Treasure-Fiction, Group 2, Acting-Fiction, Aging-Fiction, Mental Illness-Fiction.

Cohen, Barbara. The carp in the bathtub; illus by Joan Halpern. Lothrop 1972, 48 pp.

Leah and Harry couldn't face the prospect of seeing Joe, their pet carp, made into gefilte fish, even for such a special occasion as the Seder on the first night of Passover. The large, friendly carp had lived in the family's bathtub for over a week. It even swam right over to Leah and Harry to be fed everytime they went into the bathroom. At a time when most children in New York didn't have pets, Joe was as close to being a pet as possible. So, Leah and Harry hid Joe in a neighbor's apartment until their father discovered what they had done. When Joe's destiny was fulfilled, the children had to face a difficult fact of life. A week later, however, their despair became delight, when their father brought home a pet cat.

A short, warm and satisfying story.

Interest Level: 2-5. Reading Level: 3.1. Further Search Topics: Group 2, Jews-Fiction, Religion-Fiction, Pets-Fiction, Passover-Fiction, Family-Fiction, Holidays-Fiction, Read Aloud, Brothers and Sisters-Fiction.

Conklin, Gladys. Little apes; illus by Joseph Cellini. Holiday 1970, unp (32pp).

An informative as well as interesting look at gorillas, chimpanzees, orangutans and gibbons. Their habits and behavior patterns are described by following a young one of each species through a full day in its natural surroundings. The text is simple without being condescending and the illustrations are so life-like that they almost walk off the pages. An excellent treatment of a popular subject makes this a very useful book.

Interest Level: 2-5. Reading Level: 2.2. Further Search Topics: Apes, Gorillas, Nature Study, Infants, Group 2.

Davidson, Margaret. Nine true dolphin stories: illus by Roger Wilson. Hastings 1974, 67 pp.

Nine short stories about dolphins preceded by a brief description of their physical characteristics, their habits and their behavior. Each story is true, although some are more anecdotes than stories. Most are amusing; all are interesting. Satisfying to the dolphin enthusiast from grades two through five.

Interest Level: 2-5. Reading Level: 3.1. Further Search Topics: Dolphins, Group 2.

Dolch, Edward W. Andersen stories; illus by Carmen Mowry. Garrard 1956, 165 pp.

The best way to be introduced to Andersen's fairy tales is to hear them told or read aloud. Because they are beautifully written literary tales they suffer tremendously when the language is simplified enough so that the stories can be included in a reader. Furthermore, episodes have been cut out of some tales ("Big Klaus and Little Klaus") and others have been divided into chapters ("The Ugly Duckling"). But, where there is a need for such an easy version of Hans Christian Andersen, this selection will do. The 18 chapters tell only 11 stories. Most of the included stories are familiar ("The Emperor's New Clothes," "The Little Mermaid," "Thumbelina" etc.); all are enjoyable. Illustrations, however, are unattractive and uninspiring. One further caution: the reading level jumps from 2.1 to 3.2. Dolch Pleasure Reading Book series.

Interest Level: 2-5. Reading Level: 3.1. Further Search Topics: Folklore, Fantasy, Group 2, Fairy Tales, Andersen, Hans Christian.

Dolch, Edward W. Irish stories; illus by Carmen Mowry. Garrard 1958, 165 pp.

Besides controlling the vocabulary used in the stories, the Dolchs seem to include only stories with very uncomplicated plots. Once again they split the longer stories into two chapters. Thus, from 17 chapters there come only 12 stories. Most of the stories will be unfamiliar to readers (except perhaps those about Finn McCool), but all are pleasurable. See *Andersen Stories* for more information. Dolch Basic Vocabulary Book series.

Interest Level: 2-5. Reading Level: 2.2. Further Search Topics: Folklore, Fantasy, Ireland-Fiction, Giants-Fiction.

Harris, Robie H. Rosie's double dare; illus by Tony DeLuna. Knopf 1980, 112 pp.

Rosie wanted to play baseball with the Willard Street Gang, but she couldn't play well enough to play by their rules. She needed what her older brother called "shrimp rules." She couldn't hit a pitched ball, only a grounder; but grounders were "shrimp rules." In desperation Rosie agreed to take a dare that the gang made up. If she actually performed the dare, the gang would let her play with them by her rules.

The gang dared Rosie to sneak into cranky Mr. Quirk's apartment and borrow a set of his false teeth. Because Rosie couldn't find any extra false teeth, she borrowed his wig instead but that didn't satisfy the gang. They only laughed and made up another dare for Rosie. She was to untie Mrs. Samuels' dog and let it run loose. As Rosie untied him, Elmer ran away, Rosie ran off after him. One rainstorm later, Rosie caught up with him in the middle of a Red Sox game at Fenway Park. Rosie's attempt to catch Elmer stopped the game, brought her an interview on TV, and secured her a place on the Willard Street baseball team.

This very light story, made up almost entirely of action and examples of sibling rivalry, should have wide appeal through fifth grade. Beyond that, Rosie's age (almost nine) and childish behavior won't ring true. Capers series.

Interest Level: 2-5. Reading Level: 2.2. Further Search Topics: Baseball-Fiction, Humorous Fiction, Brothers and Sisters-Fiction, Challenges-Fiction, Courage-Fiction, Gangs-Fiction, Everyday Stories.

Krementz, Jill. A very young dancer. Knopf 1976, unp (121 pp).

This was the first of the five *Very Young* books to be written. Like the others, it is large in format and lavishly photographed. Unlike *A Very Young Circus Flyer*, this and the remaining books in the series are written about 10-year-old girls from obviously privileged backgrounds. All the girls are high achievers in their chosen areas but they seem very determined to work still harder until they attain whatever goals they have set for themselves. The books all follow the same formula. The girls introduce themselves, tell about their start in dancing, riding etc., describe their goals, and tell the reader how close they are to those goals. The girls go on to describe their daily routines, the practice, the chores, the hours, and the fun. Then the reader is ushered through approximately a year's worth of the young star's challenges, achievements, and defeats (the latter are only lightly touched upon). Through it all, the child shows enthusiasm, pride, dedication, hard work, and finally, hopes for the future.

Young readers love this series. Despite heavy use of jargon that makes the reading levels somewhat unstable, those already interested in the subject area pour over every word and picture in the books. Perhaps it's partly hero worship, or romance. Maybe it's the inspiration the books provide, but certainly one of the reasons the books are so popular is the vicarious thrill that they provide young enthusiasts.

A Very Young Dancer differs slightly from the formula. Instead of following Stephanie through a year of dance classes at the School of American Ballet, the book concentrates on New York City Ballet Company's production of the Nutcracker, in which Stephanie has a lead role.

Interest Level: 2-5. Reading Level: 3.1. Further Search Topics: Dancing, Ballet, Talent, Best Sellers, Group 2.

Malone, Mary. Annie Sullivan; illus by Lydia Rosier. Putnam 1971, 61 pp.

This is a very brief sketch of both Annie Sullivan's life and Helen Keller's life. Their lives were so intertwined that they cannot be separated. But because they are combined in such a short book, neither woman can be treated in much depth. That fact is not as harmful here as it might otherwise be, because even a bare bones description of the life of this extraordinary deaf, blind and mute woman or her near-blind, dedicated teacher, is interesting.

Interest Level: 2-5. Reading Level: 2.2. Further Search Topics: Sullivan, Annie, Keller, Helen, Vision, Biography, Physically Handicapped, Sound, Courage.

Newfield, Marcia. A book for Jodan; illus by Diane DeGroot. Atheneum 1975, unp (41 pp).

Jodan found her parents' separation very hard to understand and accept. She and her mother had moved 3,000 miles away from her father and she missed him very much. When Jodan visited her father for the first time, he gave her a very special present that lessened her loneliness. He created a book just for Jodan that was filled with his thoughts and memories.

The book is a sensitive portrayal of a very common experience. Only Jodan's age (nine-years-old) and consequent actions and reactions, limit the book's probable usefulness beyond fifth grade. Print is somewhat small.

Interest Level: 2-5. Reading Level: 3.2. Further Search Topics: Group 2, Divorce and Separation-Fiction, Family Problems-Fiction, Loneliness-Fiction.

Parish, Peggy. Hermit Dan; illus by Paul Frame. Macmillan 1977, 151 pp.

When the Roberts children tried to prove that Pirate Island really had been used by pirates, they encountered more action and intrigue than they had found in any of their earlier adventures. Liza, Bill and Jed suspected that Hermit Dan knew whether or not there had been pirates on the island, but he was so gruff and apparently mean that they didn't dare ask him any questions. Instead, they trailed and spied on him and asked questions of anyone who had known Hermit Dan as a child. It was rumored that his ancestors had actually been pirates. Until a terrible fire that had destroyed all they owned, Hermit Dan's family had been very wealthy. However, no one knew how they had become so rich.

In an attempt to see what the summer residents knew about Hermit Dan, the children introduced themselves to the vacationing youngsters. Among the visitors the Roberts met Hank and Ted, brothers bent on bullying Hermit Dan. When the children were rescued from a severe sandstorm by Hermit Dan, they were surprised to find that he wasn't nearly as gruff as he appeared. In fact they began to feel quite protective of the old man. Thus when Hank and Ted stole a secret box that held all of Hermit Dan's valuables, it was the Roberts children who fought (literally) to get the box back. It was after Liza, Bill and Jed returned the box to Hermit Dan, however, that the real surprises began: these included a surprise party for Hermit Dan, his wish to be friendly, and his gift to the children of three pieces of eight that proved his family members were pirates.

This title's more interesting and involved plot makes the book more likely to be a success with older readers than the other stories about the Roberts children. Otherwise it shares the same format, faults and strengths as the other series titles.

Interest Level: 2-5. Reading Level: 2.1. Further Search Topics: Mystery and Detective Stories, Pirates-Fiction, Vacation-Fiction, Loners-Fiction, Treasure-Fiction, Bullies-Fiction, Brothers and Sisters-Fiction, Grandparents-Fiction.

Silman, Roberta. Somebody else's child; illus by Chris Conover. Warne 1976, 64 pp.

Peter was adopted, but he had never questioned his family's love for him until Puddin' Paint, the school bus driver, made a thoughtless remark. Peter's affection for the older man was strong enough to help him understand Puddin' Paint's feelings. When Puddin' Paint's two dogs disappeared and the bus driver was almost heartbroken, it was Peter who helped the old man search for the dogs. That experience helped both Peter and Puddin' Paint understand that love doesn't only extend to natural born children, but can be just as strong and deep for others.

A simple telling of a moving story. It is as useful for readers who love dogs as for those interested in adoption. Rather inconsistent reading level, tests between 1.2 and 3.1.

Interest Level: 2-5. Reading Level: 2.2. Further Search Topics: Adoption-Fiction, Dogs-Fiction, Friendship-Fiction, Love-Fiction.

Slote, Alfred. My robot buddy; illus by Joel Schick. Lippincott 1975, 92 pp.

For Jack's tenth birthday he was given a robot—a robot so real it did everything but run like a human. The robot appeared so human that a thief, thinking he was stealing the robot, almost kidnapped Jack by mistake.

The few points at which the text becomes more difficult than the reading level indicates should not prove too intimidating to the reader. The suspense and humor of the story and the book's high interest subject matter should carry the reader through the rough spots. A satisfying read-aloud for second and third grades.

Interest Level: 2-5. Reading Level: 3.1. Further Search Topics: Science Fiction, Robots-Fiction, Friendship-Fiction, Kidnapping-Fiction, Read Aloud.

Tobias, Tobi. Marian Anderson; illus by Symeon Shimin. Har-Row 1972, 40 pp.

Marian Anderson's beautiful, strong voice and her great range set her apart from other singers even as a child. By the time she was in high school, she was being paid to sing. However, when she tried to apply to a well-known music school, because she was black she was turned away without even being heard. Anderson's determination as well as her own and others' faith in her kept her singing and seeking better and better coaches until she met Giuseppi Boghetti. He was one of the best voice coaches in the country. With him Marian trained and traveled until she finally won the chance to sing with the New York Philharmonic Orchestra. Anderson thought that at that point she would be invited to sing in famous theaters all across the United States, but because she was black she still received no invitations. She went to Europe where she studied and played to wildly enthusiastic audiences. Her European triumphs finally convinced American theater owners and audiences that she was a serious talent. For the next 30 years Marian Anderson sang all over the world, most of the time without incident, with one notable exception in 1939, when the D.A.R. prohibited her from singing in a hall they owned in Washington, D. C. She sang instead, in front of the Lincoln Memorial, at the invitation of the United States government. During the following years Marian married, bought a farm, sang opera and was made a delegate to the United Nations. In 1956, she retired from singing to help children, young singers, and world understanding.

Crowell Biographies make excellent school report sources for reluctant readers. They are short, interesting, and not overly juvenile looking, although the quasi-picture book format may be a problem for some older readers. This biography fits that description perfectly. The series is somewhat sentimental (as are many children's biographies), however, the sentimentality is not forbidding or condescending. A useful series. Crowell Biography series.

Interest Level: 2-5. Reading Level: 3.1. Further Search Topics: Biography, Music-Biography, Blacks-Biography, Talent, Women-Biography, Singers, Prejudice, Group 2.

Wolkoff, Judie. Wally. Bradbury 1977, 199 pp.

Michael Price agreed to take care of his friend Billy's chuckwalla for three weeks. But because his mother had declared a moratorium on any more reptiles in the house, Michael tried to hide Wally in his closet. With help from his brother Roger, Michael managed to keep Wally a secret until Wally was mistakenly left out of his box one night. Despite Michael and Roger's desperate searches, the chuckwalla did not reappear until Mr. and Mrs. Price were involved in the final negotiations for the sale of their house. Wally completely disrupted the proceedings, prevented the sale and thus made everyone happy. For as it turned out, none of the Prices had really wanted to move after all.

A fast-paced, funny book with much reader appeal.

Interest Level: 2-5. Reading Level: 2.2. Further Search Topics: Pets-Fiction, Humorous Fiction, Lizards-Fiction, Best Sellers, Reptiles-Fiction, Secrets-Fiction.

INTEREST LEVEL 2-6

Abisch, Roz. Mixed bag of magic tricks; illus by Boche Kaplan. Walker & Co. 1973, 64 pp.

The definition of magic is broadened here to include optical illusions, puzzles, age and date guessing formulae, as well as slight of hand and prearranged tricks. There are 25 "feats of magic" here, with especially good tips on performance, practice, costumes, and props. Although tricks in *Science Puzzles, It's Magic?, Funny Magic,* and *Magic Secrets* are showier, this is a more solid introduction to the subject. The Knot Magic Trick receives its best explanation here. See *It's Magic?* and *Science Puzzles* for others. Bonus: The book looks like a manual and not like a reader, therefore it should be useful even with sixth graders. It is now available in paperback version only; published by Grosset and Dunlap (Activity Books).

Interest Level: 2-6. Reading Level: 2.2. Further Search Topics: Magic, Optical Illusions, Puzzles.

Adler, Irving. Your eyes. John Day 1962, 48 pp.

Getting a young reader past this book's unattractive appearance may be difficult. Everything about the book's physical appearance screams "old." Some of the information and lack of information conveys the same message (e.g. no mention of contact lenses). For basic material about eyes and sight however, there is much here that is accessible and interesting to readers in grades two to six. Includes pronunciation guide, glossary, and detailed table of contents. No index. The Reason Why Series

Interest Level: 2-6. Reading Level: 3.1. Further Search Topics: Vision, Physically Handicapped, Group 2.

Aesop. Aesop's Fables; retold by Ann Terry White; illus by Helen Siegl. Random 1964, 77 pp.

An attractive, appealing-looking collection of forty of Aesop's fables. Children without a background in folklore are not likely to read these short tales without encouragement. Where there is such encouragement, or a curricular need, this is an excellent source. The use of many proper nouns in the text means the book tests artificially low at 2.2. It is probably more appropriate to consider it 3.1.

Interest Level: 2-6. Reading Level: 3.1. Further Search Topics: Fables, Folklore, Group 2.

Amon, Aline. Talking hands: Indian sign language. Doubleday 1968, 80 pp.

If you can ignore the author's patronizing tone and air of self-satisfaction, this is a book with great appeal. Children love ways of communicating privately, be it Pig Latin, codes and ciphers, or just whispering. This book appeals to that love by clearly, though unattractively, demonstrating over 200 words in American Indian sign language. By the time the young reader finishes the book, he/she will not only have had the fun of learning another method of communication, but will have learned a few simple generalities about North American Indians. The index is detailed enough that any word can be quickly checked. The book is useful for history, social studies, or language arts units, as well as for fun.

Interest Level: 2-6. Reading Level: 2.2. Further Search Topics: Indians of North America-Sign Language, Communication, Nonverbal Communication, Ethnic Groups.

Arkhurst, Joyce. The adventures of Spider; West African folktales; illus by Jerry Pinkney. Little 1964, 58 pp.

A delightful collection of six West African folktales about Spider. Spider is mischievous, greedy, lazy and clever. He loves to eat and he hates to work. Four of the stories tell of Spider's ill-fated attempts to get food without having to work for it ("How Spider Got a Thin Waist," "How Spider Got a Bald Head," "How Spider Helped a Fisherman," and "Why Spiders Live in Dark Corners"). One story tells of his greed ("How the World Got Wisdom"), and only one story is complimentary ("Why Spider Lives in Ceilings"). All are short, gentle, humorous, and adapt well to dramatization or retelling.

Interest Level: 2-6. Reading Level 3.1. Further Search Topics: Humorous Fiction, Spiders-Fiction, Folklore, Tricksters-Fiction, Africa-Folklore, Group 2, Read Aloud, Creation-Fiction, Drama.

Baylor, Byrd. Sometimes I dance mountains; illus by Ken Longtemps and Bill Sears. Scribner 1973, 42 pp.

The author feels strongly that dance is a creative personal statement. That feeling becomes very clear in this combination of photographs and drawings. The photographs record a young girl's dance interpretation of the author's prose. The background drawings enlarge upon the poetic mood of the sparse text. For the dance enthusiast.

Interest Level: 2-6. Reading Level: 2.2. Further Search Topics: Dancing.

Baylor, Byrd. And it is still that way: legends told by Arizona Indian children. Scribner 1976, 85 pp.

Byrd Baylor has collected and written notes for forty-one short American Indian legends from seven Arizona tribes whose school children were asked to write down or illustrate their favorite legend. The result is a collection that reflects the concerns, the history, religion, humor and pride of the children and their ancestors. This excellent collection is not only interesting reading, but it also fits well into social studies and language arts units.

Interest Level: 2-6. Reading Level: 3.1. Further Search Topics: Legends, Arizona-Fiction, Navajo Indians, Hopi Indians, Papago Indians, Pima Indians, Apache Indians, Quechan Indians, Cocopah Indians, Indians of North America-Legends, Mythology, Group 2.

Beame, Rona. Ladder company 108. Messner 1973, 63 pp.

The reader of this book will literally live through several days with a New York City fire company. The author's "Dragnet"-like writing style, her use of photographs, and actual people, all make the firefighters' experiences very real. It is an exciting, engrossing and satisfying book. The heavily-used jargon will be quickly understood, thus should pose no real obstacle to most readers.

Interest Level 2-6. Reading Level: 3.1. Further Search Topics: Firefighters, Occupations, City Life, New York City, Group 2, Best Sellers.

Bulla, Clyde Robert. The sword in the tree; illus by Paul Galdone. Har-Row 1956, 113 pp.

Shan didn't like or trust his Uncle Lionel, who had suddenly appeared at the castle gates after being away many years. Just as suddenly, Shan's father disappeared or died. Shan and his mother soon realized that Lionel wanted to take over the castle, even if it meant killing them. To save themselves, Shan and his mother fled. After walking many miles, they found a poor goat herder and his family who gave them a place to live. Sometime later Shan decided to travel to see King Arthur and ask for help in reclaiming the castle from Lionel. It wasn't until Shan was able to prove the castle was his, and Lionel lost a duel to one of Arthur's knights, that Shan was given back his home. Deep in the castle dungeon Shan found his father, still alive but imprisoned by Lionel.

This book, with its short chapters, short sentences, and steadily progressing plot should interest even the most reluctant reader from grade two through six.

Interest Level: 2-6. Reading Level: 2.2. Further Search Topics: Knights and Knighthood-Fiction, Survival-Fiction, Royalty-Fiction, Best Sellers, Courage-Fiction.

Bulla, Clyde Robert. Viking adventure; illus by Douglas Gorsline. T Y Crowell 1963, 117 pp.

An exciting story of a young Norwegian boy named Sigurd. Sigurd realized his dream when he finally set sail on a Viking ship in search of Wineland (Vinland). Leif Eriksson had told of his North American findings over 100 years earlier. Sigurd and his father's friend Grom, the captain of the ship, were sure they could find that land again. Their determination finally brought Grom's death at the hands of the ship's owner, Sigurd's near death, and the destruction of the ship.

This book, too, is true to Bulla's style of short chapters, short sentences, much action and high appeal. Although it is a little higher reading level than many of Bulla's others, it is still a good choice. Recently out of print, but worth a search.

Interest Level: 2-6. Reading Level: 3.1. Further Search Topics: Norway-Fiction, Historical Fiction, Seafaring Life-Fiction, Voyages and Travels-Fiction, Shipwrecks-Fiction, Explorers-Fiction, Vikings-Fiction, Courage-Fiction, Best Sellers, Group 2.

Burchard, Marshall. Sports hero: Joe Morgan. Putnam 1978, 93 pp.

Joe Morgan has been described as one of baseball's most complete players. He could field, hit, run and steal bases with the best. See *Sports Hero: Bill Walton* for more details about the book. Sports Hero series.

Interest Level: 2-6. Reading Level: 3.2. Further Search Topics: Biography, Morgan, Joe, Baseball-Biography, Blacks-Biography, Group 2.

Burchard, Marshall. Sports hero: Reggie Jackson. Putnam 1975, 93 pp.

Reggie Jackson was one of the big reasons why the Oakland A's won baseball's World Series three years in a row. *Sports Hero: Bill Walton* gives more information about the books in the series. Sports Hero series.

Interest Level: 2-6. Reading Level: 3.2. Further Search Topics: Biography, Jackson, Reggie, Baseball-Biography, Blacks-Biography, Group 2.

Burchard, Marshall. Sports hero: Bill Walton. Putnam 1978, 94 pp.

Burchard's series of *Sports Hero* biographies is better than many other sports biography series. Although heavy emphasis is placed on the subject's playing time, each person's life is capsulized from childhood to just before the book's publication date. Marshall and Sue Burchard (with whom he has collaborated and who writes an almost identical series called *Sports Stars*) treat each figure favorably and with enthusiasm. But, contrary to many children's writers, particularly sports biographers, these writers at least touch on those personal foibles that make players human (i.e. Joe Namath's tendency to break training is briefly described). Each book is abundantly illustrated with photographs, avoids patronizing the reader and is consistently interesting. Each is reliable, very useful and can be depended on to appeal to the sports enthusiast. Problems arise, however, with inconsistent and/or artificially inflated reading levels. The reading level of a title may vary from 2.2 to 4.2. The same passage tested on both a Spache and a Dale-Chall scale may show a similar two-year spread. The problem seems to be with jargon. Most sports jargon does not appear on either Spache's or Chall's list of familiar words and thus raises a book's reading level. But, the words may well be known to the reader (or quickly recognized after one introduction and so not truly unfamiliar). Keep in mind, therefore, that the true sports fan will often be able to read a title that tests well above his/her actual reading level.

Bill Walton's career is covered only through the end of the 1976-1977 season when the Portland Trailblazers won the NBA title. The reading level of this title is one of the most inconsistent of the series (from 2.2 to 4.2).

Interest Level: 2-6. Reading Level: 3.2. Further Search Topics: Biography, Walton, Bill, Basketball-Biography, Group 2.

Burchard, Marshall. Sports hero: Fred Lynn. Putnam 1976, 95 pp.

Fred Lynn was baseball's first rookie to be named Most Valuable Player. Consistent reading level. See *Sports Hero: Bill Walton*. Sports Hero series.

Interest Level: 2-6. Reading Level: 3.2. Further Search Topics: Biography, Lynn, Fred, Baseball-Biography, Group 2.

Burchard, Marshall. Sports hero: Joe Namath. Putnam 1971, 95 pp.

One of football's best and flashiest quarterbacks. See *Sports Hero: Bill Walton* entry. Sports Hero series.

Interest Level: 2-6. Reading Level: 2.2. Further Search Topics: Biography, Namath, Joe, Football-Biography.

Burchard, Marshall. Sports hero: Johnny Bench. Putnam 1973, 95 pp.

The youngest baseball player to receive the National League's Most Valuable Player award. See *Sports Hero: Bill Walton* for information about the book. Sports Hero series.

Interest Level: 2-6. Reading Level: 3.1. Further Search Topics: Biography, Bench, Johnny, Baseball-Biography, Group 2.

Burchard, Marshall. Sports hero: Larry Csonka. Putnam 1975, 95 pp.

Larry Csonka was almost the stereotype of a football player; big, fearless and driving. For more information about the books in the series see *Sports Hero: Bill Walton*. Sports Hero series.

Interest Level: 2-6. Reading Level: 3.1. Further Search Topics: Biography, Csonka, Larry, Football-Biography, Group 2.

Burchard, Marshall. Sports Hero: O.J. Simpson. Putnam 1975, 95 pp.

O.J. Simpson, who now flies through airports, still holds at least three NFL records, including most yards gained in a single season. See *Sports Hero: Bill Walton* for series information. Sports Hero series.

Interest Level: 2-6. Reading Level: 3.2. Further Search Topics: Biography, Simpson, O.J., Football-Biography, Blacks-Biography, Group 2.

Burchard, Marshall. Sports hero: Rick Barry. Putnam 1977, 95 pp.

Rick Barry, now a color commentator for televised basketball games, was once one of the best forwards in basketball. Details about the series with *Sports Hero: Bill Walton* entry. Sports Hero series.

Interest Level: 2-6. Reading Level: 3.1. Further Search Topics: Biography, Barry, Rick, Basketball-Biography, Group 2.

Burchard, Marshall. Sports hero: Henry Aaron. Putnam 1974, 96 pp.

Baseball's homerun king. See entry under *Sports Hero: Bill Walton* for more information. Sports Hero series.

Interest Level: 2-6. Reading Level: 3.1. Further Search Topics: Biography, Aaron, Henry, Baseball-Biography, Blacks-Biography.

Burchard, Susan H. Sports star: Pele. HarBrace J 1976, 64 pp.

At age 35, when many people thought he might be "past his prime," Pele proved he could still play superior soccer. More details about the series in *Sports Hero: Bill Walton* entry, by Marshall Burchard. Sports Star series.

Interest Level: 2-6. Reading Level: 3.1. Further Search Topics: Biography, Soccer-Biography, Pele, Group 2.

Burchard, Susan H. Sports star: Dorothy Hamill. HarBraceJ 1978, 63 pp.

Although written by Susan Burchard, this and most of the following listings are true to Marshall Burchard's *Sports Hero* format. For more explanation see *Sports Hero: Bill Walton*.

Dorothy Hamill was the darling of ice skating in 1976 and is now a top professional figure skater. This makes her rise to stardom sound romantic and glamorous. Skating jargon pushes the reading level from 3.1 to 3.2. Sports Star series.

Interest Level: 2-6. Reading Level: 3.2. Further Search Topics: Hamill, Dorothy, Ice Skating-Biography, Women-Biography, Biography, Group 2.

Burchard, Susan H. Sports star: Franco Harris. HarBraceJ 1976, 64 pp.

Franco is the talented son of a black Army man and his Italian wife. He became a hero to thousands of Pittsburgh Steeler fans, who called themselves Franco's Italian Army. See *Sports Hero: Bill Walton*, by Marshall Burchard for series details. Sports Star series.

Interest Level: 2-6. Reading Level: 3.1. Further Search Topics: Biography, Group 2, Harris, Franco, Football-Biography, Blacks-Biography.

Burchard, Susan H. Sports star: Jim "Catfish" Hunter. HarBraceJ 1976, 64 pp.

The pitcher who, because of contract violations by his club's owner, became the first free agent in baseball. See Marshall Burchard's *Sports Hero: Bill Walton* for information about the series. Sports Star series.

Interest Level: 2-6. Reading Level: 3.1. Further Search Topics: Biography, Baseball-Biography, Hunter, Jim "Catfish", Group 2.

Burchard, Susan H. Sports star: Mark "The Bird" Fidrych. HarBraceJ 1977, 64 pp.

Although his major league career was short, it was also notable. Mark Fidrych's way of concentrating on his pitching was by talking to the baseball. Entry for *Sports Hero: Bill Walton*, by Marshall Burchard, provides more information about the book. Sports Star series.

Interest Level: 2-6. Reading Level: 2.2. Further Search Topics: Biography, Baseball-Biography, Fidrych, Mark "The Bird."

Burchard, Susan H. Sports star: "Mean" Joe Greene. HarBraceJ 1976, 64 pp.

"Mean" Joe Greene's nickname is appropriate. He is big, "mean" on the playing field, and likes to win. He usually does. More details about the book under *Sports Hero: Bill Walton*, by Marshall Burchard. Sports Star series.

Interest Level: 2-6. Reading Level: 3.2. Further Search Topics: Biography, Football-Biography, Greene, "Mean" Joe, Blacks-Biography, Group 2.

Burchard, Susan H. Sports star: Tony Dorsett. HarBraceJ 1978, 64 pp.

One year after he set the college rushing record and won the Heisman Trophy, Tony Dorsett was named the NFL's Rookie of the Year and found himself playing in the Super Bowl. Reading level of this title varies from 2.2 to 3.2. For more information about the series see the entry for Marshall Burchard's *Sports Hero: Bill Walton*. Sports Star series.

Interest Level: 2-6. Reading Level: 3.2. Further Search Topics: Biography, Football-Biography, Dorsett, Tony, Blacks-Biography, Group 2.

Burchard, Susan H. Sports star: Walt Frazier. HarBraceJ 1975, 64 pp.

Walt Frazier earned his nickname Clyde (from *Bonnie and Clyde*) because of his style both on and off the basketball court. He could steal the ball from almost anyone on the court and he enjoyed high living and fancy dressing off the court. Entry for *Sports Hero: Bill Walton* gives more information about the series. Sports Star series.

Interest Level: 2-6. Reading Level: 3.1. Further Search Topics: Biography, Basketball-Biography, Frazier, Walt, Blacks-Biography.

Charlip, Remy. Handtalk; an ABC of finger spelling and sign language; photos by George Ancona. Schol. Bk. Serv. 1974, 42 pp.

This is not a book to be read and put away. It is a challenge to learn finger spelling (forming words letter by letter with the fingers) and signing (forming whole words or ideas by making a picture using one or both hands). It is a challenge that appeals to almost any child, reader and non-reader. One letter of the manual alphabet is shown at the top of each page. At the bottom of the page is a series of pictures that spell out a word which begins with the letter for that page. In the center of the page a model signs that same word. Only the first few words are explained, although there are hints for some of the more difficult words. The rest must be deciphered by the reader. In addition, the book includes over 25 more signs and a sentence about a very ugly vampire. The entire manual alphabet is also shown on a quick-reference, double page spread. The book provides an enjoyable and successful experience with language, especially if two or more children work with the book together. Although its picture book format would ordinarily turn older children away, interest in the book remains high through sixth grade. Because there are so few words that a child needs to read to enjoy this book, its reading level is an estimate.

Interest Level: 2-6. Reading Level: 2.1. Further Search Topics: Nonverbal Communication, Physically Handicapped, Communication.

Christopher, Matt. The year mom won the pennant; illus by Foster Caddell. Little 1968, 147 pp.

When no one's father had the time to coach the Thunderballs it began to look like the team would be disbanded. They just didn't seem to be able to work together without a coach. Then Nick Vassey's mother volunteered to coach for the season. After all, she knew baseball as well as anyone else and had watched her husband coach for several years. Nick wasn't at all pleased, but had to accept the idea when his teammates voted to make his mother their coach. Nick's embarrassment was almost as great as the rival coach's skepticism, but before the season was over Nick was proud of his mother. She coached the team to first place and forced even the rival coach to admit she was a good coach. Much baseball action. See note about (*No Arm In Left Field*).

Interest Level: 2-6. Reading Level: 3.1. Further Search Topics: Group 2, Baseball-Fiction, Friendship-Fiction, Prejudice-Fiction, Sex Role-Fiction, Women-Fiction.

Cleary, Beverly. Otis Spofford; illus by Louis Darling. Morrow 1953, 191 pp.

Here are six separate humorous adventures that link together, but can be read separately and out of order. Otis' favorite activity was "stirring up a little excitement," but his definition of excitement usually meant trouble. The school fiesta turned into a disaster when Otis decided to rechoreograph the bullfight and make the bull win. His attempt to liven up the reading lesson about Indians meant he almost scalped a classmate. However, a wild day at the skating pond finally gave everyone a chance to take revenge for all the things Otis had done to them. The remaining three chapters (2, 3 and 4) are slightly less exciting, but useful if a reader has enjoyed the others. There is much humor in Otis' antics and his tendency to act on every thought that comes to mind is one many readers can appreciate.

Interest Level: 2-6. Reading Level: 5.1. Further Search Topics: Troublemakers-Fiction, Group 2, Read Aloud, Everyday Stories, Humorous Fiction, School Stories.

Dolch, Edward W. Robin Hood stories; illus by Carmen Mowry. Garrard 1957, 162 pp.

The illustrations are still drab, but the stories in this volume are exciting. Here we find straight-forward adventure and familiar characters: Robin Hood, Little John, Will Scarlet, Sheriff of Nottingham, Allan-a-dale and Sir Richard of Lea. The book makes a good choice for adventure lovers. Dolch Pleasure Reading Book series.

Interest Level: 2-6. Reading Level: 2.2. Further Search Topics: Robin Hood, Knights and Knighthood-Fiction, Folklore, Crime-Fiction.

Dolch, Edward W. Stories from France; illus by Gordon Laite. Garrard 1963, 167 pp.

It is very difficult to simplify a story and not lose at least some of its original flavor. Such is the case here and in all the Dolch retellings. Nevertheless, this collection of folktales is quite useful for the French flavor it does maintain. The stories, as they are retold, are good; not great, but good. There are 14 stories related in the 19 chapters. This is a result of splitting the longer, more complicated stories into episodes. Some frustration may arise for readers because there is no indication that a story may involve more than one chapter. The much-improved illustrations that introduce each chapter and adorn the cover help make this more attractive than the earlier books. The book ends with a list of the provinces from which the stories came as well as a pronunciation key to French names. Folklore of the World series.

Interest Level: 2-6. Reading Level: 3.1. Further Search Topics: Folklore, Fantasy, France-Fiction, Royalty-Fiction, Group 2, Knights and Knighthood-Fiction.

Dolch, Edward W. Stories from Old Russia; illus by James Lewicki. Garrard 1964, 168 pp.

There are 21 chapters and only nine stories in this volume. These are more robust and exciting adventure stories than many of the other Dolch collections listed here, although once again the simplified vocabulary is somewhat restrictive. A guide to pronounciation of some Russian names is included at the end of the book. More colorful illustrations than some of the other titles. Very consistent reading level. See *Stories From France* for more information. Folklore of the World series.

Interest Level: 2-6. Reading Level: 2.1. Further Search Topics: Folklore, Fantasy, Russia-Fiction, Witches-Fiction.

Kalb, Jonah. The easy hockey book; illus by Bill Morrison. HM 1977, 64 pp.

This book is exactly what the title indicates; an easy-read introduction to the sport of hockey. It does not teach one how to skate, but in a logical non-sexist manner it does carefully and thoroughly teach the rules, techniques, and skills of hockey. Common mistakes are anticipated in each section. Chapter summaries make an already serviceable text even more useful. It could have been even better with an index.

Interest Level: 2-6. Reading Level: 2.2. Further Search Topics: Hockey.

Krementz, Jill. A very young circus flyer. Knopf 1979, unp (112 pp).

One of a series of five oversized, abundantly photographed views of unusual children. Tato Farfan is part of the Flying Farfans of Ringling Brothers and Barnum and Bailey Circus. He lives in a railroad car on a circus train with his mother, father, and older brother. The whole family performs as trapeze artists and flyers for the circus. Told as if Tato were speaking, this is the story of a fairly normal boy who also happens to be a circus flyer. Practice sessions are difficult, costumes must be readied, and time must be spent helping each other, but there is also time for Tato to watch TV, play with the clowns, play soccer, and just have fun.

In addition to Tato's story, the reader is given a behind-the-scenes tour of the circus right up to and including the performance itself (color photos used for the performance). It is an exciting world that should appeal to almost anyone who has enjoyed the circus.

Interest Level: 2-6. Reading Level: 3.2. Further Search Topics: Circus, Acrobats and Acrobatics, Best Sellers, Talent, Group 2, Gymnastics.

Krementz, Jill. A very young skater. Knopf 1979, unp (103 pp).

Katherine Healy started ice skating because her parents liked to skate and because it was easier for them to take her with them than it was to find a babysitter. From such beginnings, at age three, Katherine progressed to skating in Superskates at Madison Square Garden and ballet lessons at George Balanchine's School of American Ballet. See *A Very Young Dancer* for further explanation.

Interest Level: 2-6. Reading Level: 4.1. Further Search Topics: Ice Skating, Dancing, Ballet, Talent, Group 2, Best Sellers.

Krementz, Jill. A very young gymnast. Knopf 1978, unp (128 pp).

This is Torrence York's story. It includes a team trip to Germany for competition. See notes for *A Very Young Dancer* for more information.

Interest Level: 2-6. Reading Level: 3.2. Further Search Topics: Gymnastics, Talent, Acrobats and Acrobatics, Group 2, Best Sellers.

Krementz, Jill. A very young rider. Knopf 1977, unp (128 pp).

Vivi Malloy is the youngest rider in a family of several other riders. Her greatest dream is to make the Olympic equestrian team. She is progressing towards her goal with daily workouts and about fifteen major horse shows each year. See *A Very Young Dancer* for more extensive notes.

Interest Level: 2-6. Reading Level: 3.2. Further Search Topics: Horses, Riding, Talent, Group 2.

Montgomery, Raymond A. Space and beyond; illus by Paul Granger. Bantam 1980, 117 pp.

See entry for *Sugarcane Island*, by Edward Packard for full annotation. Available in paperback only. Choose Your Own Adventure series

Interest Level: 2-6. Reading Level: 4.1. Further Search Topics: Science Fiction, Outer Space-Fiction, Group 2, Best Sellers.

Montgomery, Raymond A. The lost jewels of Nabooti; illus by Paul Granger. Bantam 1981, 121 pp.

See entry for *Sugarcane Island*, by Edward Packard for series information. Only available in paperback edition. Choose Your Own Adventure series.

Interest Level: 2-6. Reading Level: 3.2. Further Search Topics: Mystery and Detective Stories, Detectives-Fiction, Treasure-Fiction, Best Sellers, Group 2.

Packard, Edward. Sugarcane Island; illus by Barbara Carter. Archway 1976, 105 pp.

The warning on the first page, that the book should *not* be read straight through, tells you that this book is different. And different it is. It is the first of what is now a new type of book; the "Choose Your Own Adventure" story. The formula is simple and highly successful, especially with reluctant readers. The reader is made the central character of the book. After a very brief series of events that set the stage, the reader is given choices to make. Upon making a decision, the reader is instructed to proceed to another page of the book. More action is described before the reader must make another choice. The sequence of action, choice, action and choice continues until the reader has finally completed an entire story. The books can be read over and over and the reader may never repeat exactly the same story unless he/she makes all of the same choices. What distinguishes one book from another is the setting, genre, and/or author (there are three: Edward Packard, R. A. Montgomery, and D. Terman). Don't expect quality writing or consistent reading levels because you won't find either. (Reading levels vary from 2.2 to 3.2 for most titles). What you will find is dependable, action-filled, enticing, light reading. Some are available only in paperback editions where the print size is fairly small. Choose Your Own Adventure series.

Interest Level: 2-6. Reading Level: 3.1. Further Search Topics: Shipwrecks-Fiction, Best Sellers, Survival-Fiction, Group 2.

Packard, Edward. Your code name is Jonah; illus by Paul Granger. Bantam 1980, 114 pp.

See *Sugarcane Island* for information about books in this series. Paperback only. Choose Your Own Adventure series.

Interest Level: 2-6. Reading Level: 3.2. Further Search Topics: Nonverbal Communication-Fiction, Best Sellers, Spies-Fiction, Group 2.

Packard, Edward. The cave of time; illus by Paul Granger. Bantam 1979, 115 pp.

Beware of the greater than usual inconsistency of reading levels within this book. Its difficulty level ranges from 2.2 to 4.2. See notes for *Sugarcane Island* for more information about the series. In paperback only. Choose Your Own Adventure series.

Interest Level: 2-6. Reading Level: 4.1. Further Search Topics: Time-Fiction, Science Fiction, Fantasy, Group 2.

Packard, Edward. The mystery of Chimney Rock; illus by Paul Granger. Bantam 1979, 121 pp.

See notes for *Sugarcane Island* for information about the series. Paperback only. Choose Your Own Adventure series.

Interest Level: 2-6. Reading Level: 3.2. Further Search Topics: Mystery and Detective Stories, Cats-Fiction, Witches-Fiction, Ghosts-Fiction, Detectives-Fiction, Best Sellers, Group 2.

Packard, Edward. Deadwood City; illus by Barbara Carter. Bantam 1978, 96 pp.

See *Sugarcane Island* for full series notes. Paperback edition only. Choose Your Own Adventure series.

Interest Level: 2-6. Reading Level: 3.1. Further Search Topics: West-Fiction, Cowboys-Fiction, Crime-Fiction, Best Sellers, Group 2.

Rudeen, Kenneth. Wilt Chamberlain; illus by Frank Mullins. Har-Row 1972, 33 pp.

A short and somewhat adoring version of Wilt Chamberlain's childhood, schooling, and professional career. Very little of Chamberlain's personality comes through in this book, but his superior talents and skills as well as his importance to the sport of basketball will be enough to prompt many basketball fans to read it. Although simplistic in style, the book is not condescending. It is, however, out of date, a fact most notable when Chamberlain's salary is quoted. Beware of juvenile format when using with older readers. Crowell Biography series.

Interest Level: 2-6. Reading Level: 3.2. Further Search Topics: Biography, Chamberlain, Wilt, Basketball-Biography, Blacks-Biography, Group 2.

Silverstein, Shel. Where the sidewalk ends. Har-Row 1974, 166 pp.

There is something here for almost everyone. It isn't always easy reading, but there are enough short, easier poems to pique almost any child's interest. Once caught, children will find the book hard to put down. The best way to encourage the use of this book is to read selections aloud so that potential readers may hear the rhythm and enjoy the humor. This method almost guarantees that they will then want to try reading the book themselves. Readers may struggle with a poem but once it is mastered, they will usually want more.

Interest Level: 2-6. Reading Level: 3.1. Further Search Topics: Poetry, Wit and Humor, Read Aloud, Group 2, Best Sellers.

Silverstein, Shel. A light in the attic. Har-Row 1981, 169 pp.

This is the second and most recent collection of Shel Silverstein's wonderfully wry poetry. No young person who has read and enjoyed *Where the Sidewalk Ends* will be disappointed in this effort. For those readers new to Silverstein or to poetry in general, this is as good a place as any to start enjoying both. Hearing a few of these poems read aloud is guaranteed to provoke loud cries of "May I read some?" from almost all listeners.

Interest Level: 2-6. Reading Level: 3.2. Further Search Topics: Poetry, Wit and Humor, Best Sellers, Group 2, Read Aloud.

Sobol, Donald J. Encyclopedia Brown, boy detective; illus by Leonard Shortall. Elsevier-Nelson 1963, 88 pp.

The first of a large number of books that challenge the reader to solve the same mysteries Encyclopedia Brown deciphers. See *Encyclopedia Brown and the Case of the Dead Eagles* for more information.

Interest Level: 2-6. Reading Level: 2.2. Further Search Topics: Mystery and Detective Stories, Puzzles, Best Sellers, Detectives-Fiction.

Sobol, Donald J. Encyclopedia Brown and the case of the dead eagles; illus by Leonard Shortall. Elsevier-Nelson 1975, 96 pp.

By all rights Idaville should be declared a disaster area and Mr. Brown, the chief of police, should be fired from his job. Idaville looks like an ordinary small town, but behind its sleepy exterior there exists a crime wave that would challenge the best police departments in the country. It is true that the crimes are always solved and the criminals always caught, but not by Chief Brown. Chief Brown is frequently so stumped by his police cases that he talks about them at home, usually at dinner time. Almost always, his son, Leroy "Encyclopedia" Brown, solves the case before dinner is even over. A clear case of superior intelligence and skill.

Encyclopedia (so nicknamed because of his intellect) not only solves his father's cases, but serves as a detective for his friends, too. He is kept so busy that each slim volume in this series contains 10 short mysteries. Needless to say Encyclopedia solves them all. The question is can the reader? All necessary clues are there and specialized knowledge is rarely required. Should the reader fail to solve a mystery (they are not always as easy as one would expect), a full explanation and solution for each case is provided at the back of the book. Each title follows exactly the same formula. Although a teacher or parent may grow bored hearing of Encyclopedia's accomplishments, most young readers thoroughly enjoy them.

The books actively challenge and thus involve the reader in a way most books do not. A very popular series that does not have to be read in sequence. Reading level is consistently 2.2 to 3.1. Encyclopedia Brown series.

Interest Level: 2-6. Reading Level: 3.1. Further Search Topics: Mystery and Detective Stories, Puzzles, Best Sellers, Group 2, Detectives-Fiction.

Sobol, Donald J. Encyclopedia Brown and the case of the midnight visitor; illus by Lillian Brandi. Elsevier-Nelson 1977, 96 pp.

See *Encyclopedia Brown and the Case of the Dead Eagles* for full annotation.

Interest Level: 2-6. Reading Level: 2.2. Further Search Topics: Mystery and Detective Stories, Puzzles, Detectives-Fiction, Best Sellers.

Sobol, Donald J. Encyclopedia Brown and the case of the secret pitch; illus by Leonard Shortall. Elsevier-Nelson 1965, 96 pp.

See *Encyclopedia Brown and the Case of the Dead Eagles* for full annotation.

Interest Level: 2-6. Reading Level: 3.1. Further Search Topics: Group 2, Mystery and Detective Stories, Puzzles, Best Sellers, Detectives-Fiction.

Sobol, Donald J. Encyclopedia Brown finds the clues; illus by Leonard Shortall. Elsevier-Nelson 1966, 96 pp.

See *Encyclopedia Brown and the Case of the Dead Eagles* for full annotation.

Interest Level 2-6. Reading Level: 3.1. Further Search Topics: Mystery and Detective Stories, Puzzles, Detectives-Fiction, Best Sellers, Group 2.

Sobol, Donald J. Encyclopedia Brown gets his man; illus by Leonard Shortall. Elsevier-Nelson 1967, 96 pp.

See *Encyclopedia Brown and the Case of the Dead Eagles* for full annotation.

Interest Level: 2-6. Reading Level: 3.1. Further Search Topics: Mystery and Detective Stories, Puzzles, Best Sellers, Group 2, Detectives-Fiction.

Sobol, Donald J. Encyclopedia Brown keeps the peace; illus by Leonard Shortall. Elsevier-Nelson 1969, 96 pp.

See *Encyclopedia Brown and the Case of the Dead Eagles* for full annotation.

Interest Level: 2-6. Reading Level: 2.2. Further Search Topics: Mystery and Detective Stories, Puzzles, Best Sellers, Detectives-Fiction.

Sobol, Donald J. Encyclopedia Brown lends a hand; illus by Leonard Shortall. Elsevier-Nelson 1974, 96 pp.

See *Encyclopedia Brown and the Case of the Dead Eagles* for full annotation.

Interest Level: 2-6. Reading Level: 3.1. Further Search Topics: Mystery and Detective Stories, Puzzles, Detectives-Fiction, Best Sellers, Group 2.

Sobol, Donald J. Encyclopedia Brown saves the day; illus by Leonard Shortall. Elsevier-Nelson 1970, 96 pp.

See *Encyclopedia Brown and the Case of the Dead Eagles* for full annotation.

Interest Level: 2-6. Reading Level: 2.2. Further Search Topics: Mystery and Detective Stories, Puzzles, Detectives-Fiction, Best Sellers.

Sobol, Donald J. Encyclopedia Brown shows the way; illus by Leonard Shortall. Elsevier-Nelson 1972, 96 pp.

See *Encyclopedia Brown and the Case of the Dead Eagles* for full annotation.

Interest Level: 2-6. Reading Level: 2.2. Further Search Topics: Mystery and Detective Stories, Puzzles, Detectives-Fiction, Best Sellers.

Sobol, Donald J. Encyclopedia Brown solves them all; illus by Leonard Shortall. Elsevier-Nelson 1968, 96 pp.

See *Encyclopedia Brown and the Case of the Dead Eagles* for full annotation.

Interest Level: 2-6. Reading Level: 3.1. Further Search Topics: Mystery and Detective Stories, Puzzles, Detectives-Fiction, Group 2, Best Sellers.

Sobol, Donald J. Encyclopedia Brown sets the pace; illus by Ib Ohlsson. Four Winds Pr 1982, 89 pp.

See *Encyclopedia Brown and the Case of the Dead Eagles* for full annotation.

Interest Level: 2-6. Reading Level: 3.1. Further Search Topics: Mystery and Detective Stories, Detectives-Fiction, Puzzles, Group 2, Best Sellers.

Sobol, Donald J. Encyclopedia Brown carries on; illus by Ib Ohlsson. Schol Bk Serv 1980, 72 pp.

See *Encyclopedia Brown and the Case of the Dead Eagle* for full annotation.

Interest Level: 2-6. Reading Level: 3.1. Further Search Topics: Mystery and Detective Stories, Puzzles, Detectives-Fiction, Group 2, Best Sellers.

Terman, Douglas. By balloons to the Sahara; illus by Paul Granger. Bantam 1979, 117 pp.

See the entry for *Sugarcane Island*, by Edward Packard for detailed information about the series. Available in paperback edition only. Choose Your Own Adventure series.

Interest Level: 2-6. Reading Level: 3.2. Further Search Topics: Voyages and Travels-Fiction, Flight-Fiction, Best Sellers, Group 2.

INTEREST LEVEL 3-4

Charosh, Mannis. Mathematical games for one or two; illus by Lois Ehlert. T Y Crowell 1975, 33 pp.

It will take a very special reader to appreciate this book, one who is excited by math puzzles and games and who is also willing to overlook the book's picture book format. Starting with a very simple, one-player game, the book progresses through six types of games, each progressively more taxing mentally. Each type of game is introduced by a very simple example that is thoroughly explained. For the up-and-coming Einstein.

Interest Level: 3-4. Reading Level: 2.2. Further Search Topics: Mathematics, Puzzles, Games.

Hurwitz, Johanna. Aldo Ice Cream; illus by John Wallner. Morrow 1981, 124 pp.

Aldo got his newest nickname (Ice Cream) from his friend DeDe when she heard that Aldo not only wanted to try every flavor of ice cream at the local store, but wanted to buy an ice cream freezer for his sister's birthday as well. Aldo decided his summer project would be to earn enough money for the freezer, but he soon found out that there were very few ways a nine-year-old boy could earn $49.95. In the meantime, he helped his mother deliver food for a Meals-On-Wheels project, learned to swim, found out about fish from Mr. Puccini, and shared his cat with Mrs. Nardo. As the summer came to an end he saw one last opportunity to earn enough money for the ice cream maker. A local shoe store offered a new pair of sneakers to the child who owned the most worn out pair. Aldo convinced his mother that if he won the sneakers, she should pay him the money she would otherwise have had to spend on his new sneakers. Aldo set about making sure that his already well-worn sneakers were the most dilapidated in town. A few days before the sneaker contest the hardware store lowered the price on the ice cream freezer to a point where Aldo could afford it if he won the sneakers. When Aldo did win, just as he knew he would, he and his mother bought the very last freezer in the store.

It is not as well-constructed a story as *Aldo Applesauce*, but for established Aldo fans, or those who want quiet, reassuring fiction, this is a usable title.

Interest Level: 3-4. Reading Level: 3.1. Further Search Topics: Humorous Fiction, Brothers and Sisters-Fiction, Vacation-Fiction, Occupations-Fiction, Everyday Stories, Aging-Fiction, Family-Fiction, Contests-Fiction.

INTEREST LEVEL 3-5

Adoff, Arnold. Malcolm X; illus by John Wilson. Har-Row 1970, 41 pp.

This is a simple, intellectually honest biography of a very controversial man. Taught a strong sense of self-respect by his father, Malcolm X could not accept the second-class status that white society tried to impose upon him. Instead he turned away from whites and all they stood for. He hated high school, the detention home he lived in after his father's death, and his mother's placement in a state hospital. He didn't feel comfortable until he moved to Harlem. There he found friends, but he also found crime. While he was in prison, Malcolm X began to read of great, black societies and people. His brother told him about the Nation of Islam, the Black Muslims, and Elijah Muhammad, the leader of the religion. He began corresponding with Mr. Muhammad. Shortly after he was released from prison, Malcolm X met Elijah Muhammad and eventually became a minister of the religion. There was even talk that he would be Elijah Muhammad's successor. But, as the years went on, Malcolm X began to think that black Christians as well as Muslims should be united in the fight for black rights. Despite threats against his life Malcolm X formed the Organization of Afro-American Unity. Both blacks and whites were angry with him. The threats continued until his house was firebombed; and, only a week later, at a public meeting, Malcolm X was assassinated.

An excellent overview of a complex man. The book may well prompt readers to learn more about the man and his beliefs. At the very least it will expose readers, in an interesting manner, to someone they should know. The book shares the same semi-picture book format of the others in Harper and Row/Crowell's biography series, therefore it will need a careful introduction to potential readers.

Interest Level: 3-5. Reading Level: 3.1. Further Search Topics: Blacks-Biography, Civil Rights, Biography, Crime, Religion, Assassinations, Prejudice, Poverty, Foster Homes,

Bulla, Clyde Robert. A lion to guard us; illus by Michele Chessare. Har-Row 1981, 117 pp.

Bulla's writing isn't quite as successful here as elsewhere. This story of three London children's attempt to go to their father in Jamestown, Virginia, has danger, adventure, daring and promise. It also has too many characters to allow the reader to get to know any of them well. There are also too many very short chapters to allow plot development (23 chapters and 117 pages). The short sentences help to keep the reading level low, but a glossary would have been useful to fully explain the many unfamiliar terms.

Despite its problems, the book is still useful. The story is based on the 1609 voyage of the Sea Adventure. Blown far off course and badly damaged by a storm, the ship landed at Bermuda rather than Jamestown. The survivors were unable to sail again for over nine months. When they reached Jamestown, they found that few people had survived the very harsh year.

The three Freebold children are the focus of this story. When their mother died they left London to find their father in the New World. Having no money of their own, they were lucky to find a doctor friend to pay their ship's passage and to go with them. Halfway across the ocean, the doctor was swept overboard and drowned. From that time until they found their father barely alive, the children were on their own, even though they were still with the ship's passengers.

Although not the best of Bulla, this is still serviceable as a piece of historical fiction (hard to get children to read), or as a choice for the lover of survival and/or sea stories.

Interest Level: 3-5. Reading Level: 2.1. Further Search Topics: United States-History-Fiction, Historical Fiction, Courage-Fiction, Survival-Fiction, Shipwrecks-Fiction, Voyages and Travels-Fiction, Seafaring Life-Fiction.

Chaikin, Miriam. I should worry, I should care; illus by Richard Egielski. Har-Row 1979, 103 pp.

A warm, well-written story about life in a Jewish family in Brooklyn just before World War II. This is the story of young Molly's adjustment to moving, to leaving old friends, to making and losing new friends (one by death) and to the small happenings that make up her life. In the background, but always there, is Hitler's ever-increasing threat to the world.

A comfortable, truthful look at a close-knit family. Also useful for its picture of the times and the place. An occasional Yiddish expression may slow the reader but adds to the book's authenticity. Print is slightly lighter and smaller than *Finders Weepers*.

Interest Level: 3-5. Reading Level: 2.2. Further Search Topics: Moving, Household-Fiction, Friendship-Fiction, City Life-Fiction, Jews-Fiction, Family-Fiction.

Chaikin, Miriam. Finders weepers; illus Richard Egielski. Har-Row 1980, 120 pp.

The children most likely to read this are those who have enjoyed *I Should Worry, I Should Care*. On her way home from school one day, Molly found a ring. Rather than try to find its owner, she made up excuses to keep the ring. Molly knew it was a sin to keep something that belonged to someone else, she even knew who *did* own the ring. When she finally decided to return it, the ring had become stuck on Molly's finger and wouldn't come off. With Yom Kippur just a few days away, Molly became convinced that all the unpleasant things happening around her were punishments for her sin. She finally had to have the ring cut off her finger. After she prayed for forgiveness life immediately went back to normal.

There's enough guilt here to satisfy even the most demanding reader. There is also the same solid family group that appeared in the first book. But this book probably lacks enough excitement and/or empathy to interest a reader new to Molly and her family. Print is dark but spacing between lines could have been wider.

Interest Level: 3-5. Reading Level: 3.1. Further Search Topics: Family-Fiction, Jews-Fiction, Honesty-Fiction, Holidays-Fiction, Religion-Fiction.

Chew, Ruth. What the witch left. Hastings 1973, 128 pp.

One afternoon Katy and Louise decided to search through the locked drawer of an old dresser. Inside they found strange-looking gloves, an old robe, boots, a mirror and a tin box. The girls quickly learned that each item was magical. With the gloves on, the girls could draw, play piano, weave or write. They thought their new talents were wonderful until they each wrote identical school compositions. When she wore the robe for the school play, Louise found out that it made people invisible. The boots, which travelled 21 miles with each step, took the girls to Mexico, but made them late for lunch at home. The mirror showed them anything they wanted to see, and the box "found"

everything that was lost. A very light story for children who don't need high adventure but like a mixture of humor and magic.

Interest Level: 3-5. Reading Level: 3.1. Further Search Topics: Magic-Fiction, Mexico-Fiction, Witches-Fiction, Fantasy, Humorous Fiction.

Clymer, Eleanor. Santiago's silver mine; illus by Ingrid Fetz. Atheneum 1973, 74 pp.

Although somewhat complicated by a large number of background incidents, especially early in the book, the story is both interesting and informative. Santiago and his friend Andreas wanted to be rich. The year's harvest had been very poor, so there was little food to eat. Both of their fathers had gone to Mexico City to find jobs and their mothers worked for very few pesos near home. Andreas wanted to search the old mine in the hills outside of town for silver, but the mining company had left a guard named Jose to prevent people from getting into the mines. While up on a hill, tending a cow, Andreas found an old piece of pottery and a back entrance to the mine. As they started to enter the mine, Andreas and Santiago found a basket full of old pottery pieces that Jose had apparently dug from the hill. Not knowing what the pottery pieces were, the boys took them to the local school teacher who identified them as ancient archeological treasures that by law belonged to the government. As soon as he realized others had found out that he had been selling the pottery, Jose disappeared. Shortly afterwards, the government paved the road through town and opened the hill as an official archaeological site. The extra jobs meant that the boys' fathers could once again find work at home. Although they hadn't become exactly rich, Santiago and Andreas had certainly found treasure.

Local flavor abounds, along with some history. Useful for Social Studies units. Print size fairly small, but spaces between lines are good sized. Recently out-of-print, but still worth looking for.

Interest Level: 3-5. Reading Level: 3.1. Further Search Topics: Archaeology-Fiction, Poverty-Fiction, Mexico-Fiction, Country Life-Fiction, Treasure-Fiction, Miners-Fiction.

Davidson, Carson. Fast-talking dolphin; illus by Sylvia Stone. Dodd 1978, 127 pp.

After a rather slow start, this story develops into a well-paced adventure-fantasy with touches of warmth and humor. Eric wasn't just surprised when he found a dolphin in the 10-foot fish pond, he was astonished. Not only had there never been a dolphin there before, but this dolphin spoke in poetry. His name was Wallingford Ullingham Lowell III; Wallingford for short. He was elegant, proud and cultured; but as Eric soon found out, he was very impractical. He didn't seem to realize that he needed salt water and more fish than those in the pond in order to live. It was Eric who figured out a way to keep salt flowing into the pond and a supply of fresh fish. He also kept Wallingford's presence a secret, just as Wallingford requested. The day that Wallingford was discovered was the day that Eric had to break his promise. In order to find out who else had found out about Wallingford, Eric talked with his brother. Together they scouted the town before they realized that Herbert Benson was the only other person who had seen Wallingford.

Herbert reluctantly admitted that he had told his father about the dolphin. Eric knew enough about Mr. Benson to realize that he was just crazy enough to want to harm the dolphin. Eric and his brother gathered all the local children together to shield Wallingford from Mr. Benson. Even Herbert dared to defy his father for the first time. As Mr. Benson struggled with Eric and his brother, he fell, hit his head and rolled into the pond. Wallingford dove to save him, but his leg was caught between two rocks. With the others' help, Wallingford, Eric and his brother Karl were able to save Mr. Benson from drowning.

A few days later Eric, with new-found skills, spontaneously recited a poem about friendship to Wallingford. Wallingford answered with a rare compliment and for the first time used Eric's name (a show of respect). They were such true friends that when Wallingford was helicopter-lifted out of the pond and taken back to his research project, Eric couldn't understand why his father didn't tell him of Wallingford's departure. Eventually he realized that his father had been right; he would rather remember Wallingford swimming in the pond than in a helicopter's sling. Also, Wallingford would have been embarrassed to be seen making so undignified a departure. Wallingford's final message to Eric was a note that Eric found scratched in the dirt thanking him for the salt and the fish and saying that they would one day meet again.

Don't take the plot too seriously or peruse it too carefully for it won't stand up to scrutiny. This is merely a pleasant story with enough humor, action and originality to intrigue many readers. The book's major drawback is the poetry Wallingford spouts: the poetic form and somewhat difficult language will throw some readers. On the other hand, the book could be very useful in a classroom unit about poetry.

Interest Level: 3-5. Reading Level: 3.1. Further Search Topics: Poetry, Dolphins-Fiction, Pets-Fiction, Fantasy, Friendship-Fiction, Humorous Fiction.

Fall, Thomas. Jim Thorpe; illus by John Gretzer. Har-Row 1970, 33 pp.

Jim Thorpe was an Indian from the Oklahoma territory who became one of the United State's greatest athletes. He and his twin brother were trained by their father to run and jump faster and farther than anyone else. When Charles died, Jim couldn't face returning to school without his twin, so his family kept him home for a few months before sending him away to school again. Jim ran home once more when his father and mother both became ill. Months later he went to still another school where he was noticed by Pop Warner. Pop advised Joe to concentrate on track until he was big enough to play football. His father's death left Jim so despondent he quit school to play professional baseball for a while. By the time he went back to school, Jim was big enough to play spectacular football and then to win the 1912 Olympic decathlon competition. Unfortunately, his short time as a paid baseball player made him ineligible for the Olympic honor and Jim's medal was taken away. Public sentiment was with Jim, but the rules were against him. He went on, however, to play both professional baseball and football. In 1982, 29 years after his death, Thorpe's medal was finally returned to him.

A short, meaty and readable biography of a person who should be interesting to many sports fans. Follows the usual format of Crowell biographies, but looks less like a picture book than many. Crowell Biography series.

Interest Level: 3-5. Reading Level: 3.1. Further Search Topics: Football-Biography, Indians of North America-Biography, Baseball-Biography, Olympic Games, Biography, Running-Biography, Twins-Biography.

Hall, Lynn. The mystery of Pony Hollow; illus by Ruth Sanderson. Garrard 1978, 64 pp.

Sarah investigated strange voices only to find the skeleton of a horse that had died 40 years earlier. She was determined to find out what it was that had killed the horse and why its ghost was uneasy.

The mystery element isn't as strong here as most mystery fans would like, but the book will not disappoint many true horse story enthusiasts.

Interest Level: 3-5. Reading Level: 3.2. Further Search Topics: Horses-Fiction, Ghosts-Fiction, Mystery and Detective Stories.

Heide, Florence Parry. Mystery of the mummy's mask; illus by Seymour Fleishman. A. Whitman 1979, 127 pp.

The Spotlight Club published a neighborhood newspaper. Just as the club was about to take the fourth issue to the printer, Jay discovered an ancient mummy mask hidden near Mr. Pruitt's house. Mr. Pruitt was intrigued by the discovery (he worked at the nearby museum) and he took the mask from Jay, but agreed that Jay could write about the mask for the paper. At about the same time, Dexter discovered that an old, abandoned house was being used. When the printer's office was broken into that night and only their newspaper was stolen, the three children began to suspect that something strange was going on at the abandoned house.

Dexter rode back to the house alone and was captured by Hank, one of three thieves hiding out there. Figuring that they never would have missed one item, Hank had taken the mask from the cache of goods that the other two had stolen. When he overheard Jay's conversation with Mr. Pruitt, Hank realized that his partners would find out what he had done if they ever read the newspaper article. To avoid being discovered, Hank broke into the printer's and stole the paste-up of the paper. In order to keep Dexter from escaping, Hank tied him up and placed him in a shipping crate. When he didn't return as soon as expected, Jay and Cindy realized that Dexter was in trouble, so they went out to the house to search for him. As the three escaped, Dexter and Cindy slashed the thieves' truck's tires, and Jay ran to phone for the police. After several nervous moments in which Cindy and Dexter thought Jay might not get back before they were caught, Jay finally brought the police, who captured all three thieves.

See *Mystery at Southport Cinema* for more information. Spotlight Club Mystery series.

Interest Level: 3-5. Reading Level: 3.1. Further Search Topics: Mystery and Detective Stories, Crime-Fiction, Egypt-Fiction, Archaeology-Fiction, Antiquities-Fiction, Journalism-Fiction, Gangs-Fiction, Brothers and Sisters-Fiction, Detectives-Fiction.

Heide, Florence Parry. The mystery of the silver tag; illus by Seymour Fleishman. A. Whitman 1972, 127 pp.

Jay's paper route took him to one house that he wished he could avoid. It was grumpy, old Mr. Pendleton's house that Jay hated. One rainy day he spotted what he later realized was a prize Angora cat hiding on Mr. Pendleton's porch. When the cat was reported lost in that night's paper, Jay and the other members of the Spotlight Club decided to try to return the cat to its owner, Miss Horton. Their attempts to get the cat back from Mr. Pendleton meant that they had to spy on him, to sneak into his garage, and to spend the night in a treehouse overlooking his house. They were afraid that they had failed when they saw Mr. Pendleton leave with the cat. Determined to be the ones to tell Miss Horton of their failure, they went to her apartment and found Mr. Pendleton already there. Mr. Pendleton was a famous animal photographer who, upon finding the cat, had asked Miss Horton if he could photograph him. The children, thinking only that Mr. Pendleton was a mad scientist who kidnapped cats, had jumped to all the wrong conclusions, but ended with a mystery solved, new friends, and their first lesson in being detectives.

See entry with *Mystery at Southport Cinema* for series information. Spotlight Club Mystery series.

Interest Level: 3-5. Reading Level: 2.2. Further Search Topics: Mystery and Detective Stories, Brothers and Sisters-Fiction, Gangs-Fiction, Cats-Fiction, Loners-Fiction, Detectives-Fiction, Photography-Fiction, Kidnapping-Fiction.

Heide, Florence Parry. Mystery at Southport Cinema; illus by Seymour Fleishman. A. Whitman 1978, 128 pp.

The Spotlight Club was the name Jay, his sister Cindy, and his friend Dexter gave themselves. Their main interest was solving mysteries and just as in Sobol's Encyclopedia Brown series, Hildick's McGurk Mysteries, and Warner books about the Alden children, mysteries seem to follow them around. Their cases are more intricate and lengthy than Encyclopedia Brown's. They involve more danger than most of McGurk's, and they center on more common themes than the Alden's. The series serves much the same audience, however, as the others. It serves those children who want action, intrigue, and the challenge of a mystery, and who don't care about character development or in-depth motivation. The chapters are 8 to 12 pages long, print size is adequate, and the children are normal enough to make this a very popular series. As an added attraction, reading levels here are fairly consistent.

Thorne prided himself on doing his job well, so when the grocery store he ran for Callie (the owner) was robbed by a bearded stranger, Thorne felt responsible. Thorne ran after the thief but lost him in the darkened Southport Cinema. The Spotlight Club members also tried to track the thief. They figured that he had hidden the bag with the stolen money somewhere in the movie house because no one had been seen leaving with such a bag.

In the janitor's lost and found basket Jay found a wig the thief must have used as a disguise. The children called the wig maker to find out who had ordered it and were directed to a local post office box. Jay and Dexter were surprised to find belonged to the grocery store. Because Thorne picked up the mail each day, he became a prime suspect. In the meantime, Cindy had gone back to the cinema to look for the money. In the dark she had scuffled with someone else looking for the money and had given the person a deep scratch on the face.

At the same time that Thorne decided to pay Callie back for the stolen money, the Club members decided to tell Callie their suspicions about him. As Thorne handed his veterinary school savings to Callie, Cindy took a close enough look at Callie's face to see a new scratch and accused her of being the thief. Callie had so wanted Thorne to run the store instead of going to school, and had needed money so intensely, that she had stolen from her own business. The ending is weak but the rest of the book will hold reader interest. Spotlight Club Mystery series.

Interest Level: 3-5. Reading Level: 3.1. Further Search Topics: Mystery and Detective Stories, Gangs-Fiction, Crime-Fiction, Detectives-Fiction, Brothers and Sisters-Fiction.

Heide, Florence Parry. Mystery of the melting snowman; illus by Seymour Fleishman. A. Whitman 1974, 128 pp.

Hidden inside of a snowman, the Spotlight Club found what they believed was a stolen iron statue of a dog. In order to try to catch the thief, the children hid the statue again and watched to see who came to look for it. Eventually they determined that the thief or thieves was either Tom and Jenny, the amenable young couple who were helping Mrs. Wellington sell her house or Alex, the man who seemed to be a detective. After a frightening episode in which Alex almost captured Cindy, the dog, and a cache of Mrs. Wellington's diamonds (hidden in a secret compartment to which the dog held the key), Cindy managed to lock Alex in a closet long enough to enable Jay and Dexter to alert Mrs. Wellington to what was happening. The case was closed as Mrs. Wellington revealed Alex to be her greedy, young nephew, whom she had indulged once too often, but would not indulge again.

See *Mystery at Southport Cinema* for series information. Spotlight Club Mystery series.

Interest Level: 3-5. Reading Level: 2.2. Further Search Topics: Mystery and Detective Stories, Gangs-Fiction, Crime-Fiction, Brothers and Sisters-Fiction, Detectives-Fiction, Inheritance-Fiction.

Heide, Florence Parry. Mystery of the midnight message; illus by Seymour Fleishman. A. Whitman 1977, 128 pp.

The challenge to the Spotlight Club this time was to stop a crime before it happened. Jay and his sister Cindy were on a bus trip home when a blizzard forced the bus to stop at a motel for the night. Jay answered the room telephone late that night and heard a woman's strange and stern instructions. The instructions were to say nothing, to look in the desk drawer for directions, to expect that Bee had the other half of the instructions, and to be at the place at 8:00 the next evening. The envelope, which Jay and Cindy found, showed the location of and half the combination to someone's bedroom safe.

Early the next morning, the children found themselves fleeing in terror from the evil Scull, the man who was supposed to have received the message. Scull pursued them as they escaped in a friendly salesman's car, caught them and locked them into a cold barn without jackets. When the two were finally back on the road and reunited with Dexter and his sister Anne, they had only a few hours and fewer clues to help them find Woodvale and Jeremiah Gibbon, the intended victim.

Despite difficult driving conditions in the snow, Anne managed to get the children to their destination a few minutes before the thieves arrived. Anne and Jeremiah's secretary left the house together to get the police while the Spotlight Club members and Mr. Gibbon hid near the safe. A few tense minutes later, the case was closed; Mr. Gibbons' money was safe, the ringleader had been named (Mr. Gibbon's doctor), and the thieves had been caught.

See *Mystery at Southport Cinema* for series information. Spotlight Club Mystery series.

Interest Level: 3-5. Reading Level: 3.1. Further Search Topics: Mystery and Detective Stories,

Crime-Fiction, Snow-Fiction, Disasters-Fiction, Gangs-Fiction, Brothers and Sisters-Fiction, Detectives-Fiction.

Heide, Florence Parry. Mystery of the vanishing visitor; illus by Seymour Fleishman. A. Whitman 1975, 128 pp.

Cindy was hired to take care of Mrs. Widget's house, animals, and plants for a weekend. That same weekend, someone tried to find and steal something from Mrs. Widget's overcrowded house. She had very few empty spaces in her house, so it was not a surprise that the thief wasn't able to find the object of his or her search. The three Spotlight Club members were determined to figure out not only who was the thief, but also what it was that the thief, wanted. Their prime suspects included the very nasty Bertha Beaker and the charming Charley Capp.

After spending a night in Mrs. Widget's house trying to, and almost succeeding in catching the thief, the children were surprised by an early morning visit from Mr. Capp. Mr. Capp was nearly able to steal away with a painting that hid a great deal of money before Cindy figured out that he was the thief. Even after Mr. Capp had been caught, he charmed his way out of any punishment and left before anyone had second thoughts.

See entry for *Mystery at Southport Cinema* for series information. Spotlight Club Mystery series.

Interest Level: 3-5. Reading Level: 2.2. Further Search Topics: Mystery and Detective Stories, Brothers and Sisters-Fiction, Gangs-Fiction, Crime-Fiction, Antiquities-Fiction, Detectives-Fiction.

Hildick, Edmund W. The great rabbit rip-off; illus by Lisl Weil. Macmillan 1976, 101 pp.

Why would anyone want to put red paint on all of the clay lawn rabbits in town? That was the first and easier of the mysteries the McGurk Organization had to solve. The bigger mystery was who would then steal them all and why? Almost everyone in town had purchased a rabbit to help a charity drive. Donny Towers a local social worker had thought of the idea. Donny, his fiancee, Joanne, and two reformed thieves, Sam and Ferdie, had made enough rabbits for everyone. When the rabbits disappeared, the Organization began to suspect, among others, Sam and Ferdie. Then when Donny replaced each one almost immediately with rabbits smelling of paint remover, the group began to think Donny might have been involved. It was Wanda's sharp eyes that revealed Donny's motive. Joanne's engagement ring had been accidentally molded into one of the rabbits and Donny had retrieved the rabbits to find the ring. Knowing he couldn't return the paint stained rabbits without raising suspicion, Donny had removed the red paint and told everyone that he was simply replacing the stolen rabbits with new ones.

See *Case of the Bashful Bank Robber* for series information. McGurk Mystery series.

Interest Level: 3-5. Reading Level: 2.2. Further Search Topics: Mystery and Detective Stories, Detectives-Fiction, Gangs-Fiction, Rabbits-Fiction, Crime-Fiction, Humorous Fiction.

Hildick, Edmund W. Deadline for McGurk; illus by Lisl Weil. Macmillan 1975, 104 pp.

When many of the dolls in the neighborhood began disappearing, their owners went to the McGurk Organization for help. At first McGurk was reluctant to take on such a silly task as recovering lost dolls. But when a ransom note appeared and the Organization

was linked to the dolls' safety, McGurk's reluctance vanished. The note stated that if, in a written public notice, the members of the Organization did not admit that they were no good, the dolls were doomed. McGurk's pride would never have allowed him to write such a notice. As the deadline approached, the group plotted a daring move designed to uncover the doll thief. The plan depended on Willie's super-sensitive nose, a particular perfume dabbed on a stolen doll, and the curiosity of the thief. Success came only minutes before the hour of doom. Once again Sandra Ennis was the culprit.

See *The Case of the Bashful Bank Robber* for series information. McGurk Mystery series.

Interest Level: 3-5. Reading Level: 2.2. Further Search Topics: Dolls-Fiction, Mystery and Detective Stories, Detectives-Fiction, Humorous Fiction, Gangs-Fiction, Jealousy-Fiction.

Hildick, Edmund W. The case of the phantom frog; illus by Lisl Weil. Macmillan 1979, 121 pp.

The McGurk Organization would not, under ordinary circumstances, have agreed to babysit for seven-year-old Bela, but there was an unusual twist to Bela's case. Bela's aunt, who asked them to babysit while she worked in her sculpture studio, had heard the eerie sounds of a VERY large frog coming from Bela's room. At first it appeared to the group that Bela actually turned into a frog at night, a werefrog. But, upon investigation they found a very clever, very lonely, and very unhappy young boy who had invented the phantom because he was afraid that his aunt would make him give up his pet frog.

See *The Case of the Bashful Bank Robber* for series information. McGurk Mystery series.

Interest Level: 3-5. Reading Level: 3.1. Further Search Topics: Mystery and Detective Stories, Gangs-Fiction, Frogs-Fiction, Supernatural-Fiction, Transformations-Fiction, Detectives-Fiction, Babysitting-Fiction, Humorous Fiction, Occupations-Fiction.

Hildick, Edmund W. The case of the treetop treasure; illus by Lisl Weil. Macmillan 1980, 121 pp.

As Wanda rescued a cat she discovered a stash of odd items tucked into a hollow high up in a tree. On top of the assortment was a sign that said simply "Beware!" The McGurk Organization suspected a thief was using the tree as a place to hide stolen goods, but until an antique silver bowl was added nothing that had been placed there was worth stealing. Shortly afterwards Wanda found out from the police that she was the prime suspect in the theft of the bowl. Brains devised a complicated system for determining the real thief while McGurk worked more from intuition. Nevertheless, it wasn't long before they both arrived at the same conclusion. The culprit was the gang's long-time enemy Sandra Ennis. Then it was just a simple matter of finding the right way to persuade Sandra to confess and apologize to her victims.

See *The Case of the Bashful Bank Robber* for series information. McGurk Mystery series.

Interest Level: 3-5. Reading Level: 3.1. Further Search Topics: Mystery and Detective Stories, Crime-Fiction, Gangs-Fiction, Detectives-Fiction, Humorous Fiction.

Hurwitz, Johanna. Aldo Applesauce; illus by John Wallner. Morrow 1979, 127 pp.

Aldo Sossi, vegetarian and new kid at school, was immediately dubbed Applesauce for obvious reasons. Aldo didn't like his new name. He didn't like being teased either—not the way he was teased at school.

Nothing went right for Aldo. His attempts at making friends only ended in disasters (once at a bowling alley and another time at a birthday party). He had been able to start a friendship only with a strange girl who wore a heavy, black fake moustache most of the time. After accidentally nearly ruining that friendship too, Aldo not only learned why DeDe wore the moustache, but helped her learn to live without it. DeDe, in turn, helped Aldo take himself less seriously and find more friends.

This is a comfortable, humorous story of two fourth grade children learning to be themselves. The vocabulary is occasionally difficult, but sentence length is almost always short.

Interest Level: 3-5. Reading Level: 3.1. Further Search Topics: Moving, Household-Fiction, Humorous Fiction, School Stories, Friendship-Fiction, Divorce and Separation-Fiction, Vegetarians-Fiction, Individualists-Fiction, Everyday Stories.

Hurwitz, Johanna. Once I was a plum tree; illus by Ingrid Fetz. Morrow 1980, 160 pp.

Ten-year-old Gerry Flam knew nothing about her religion except that she was Jewish. Her parents didn't practice their religion and only superficially observed some of the holidays. As they told Gerry, their reason was that they were assimilated Americans. In fact, they seemed to practice as many Christian as Jewish holidays. All Gerry's friends and neighbors were Catholic, so Gerry had very little chance to learn about Judaism or the prejudice to which Jews were still being subjected in 1947 in the Bronx. A Jewish family moved into the apartment building next door, and Gerry's quiet curiosity was stimulated. From the Wulfs, Gerry began to learn about Judaism, World War II, and Hitler. As her pride in her heritage grew, Gerry also felt prejudice for the first time. After celebrating her first Passover Seder, Gerry found that despite the problems, she was truly happy to be Jewish.

Much like Chaikin's *I Should Worry, I Should Care* in tone and mood. Will be useful where there is already an interest in Judaism.

Interest Level: 3-5. Reading Level: 3.1. Further Search Topics: Religion-Fiction, Family-Fiction, Jews-Fiction, City Life-Fiction, Children-Growth-Fiction, Prejudice-Fiction.

Jordan, June. Fannie Lou Hamer; illus by Albert Williams. Har-Row 1972, 41 pp.

In 1917, Fannie Lou Hamer was the last of 20 children born to a fearless black woman. Fannie and her family grew up working on a white man's cotton plantation. Although they were kept poor and hungry by the plantation owner and the field boss, Fannie Lou grew up in her mother's image—unafraid of white people and unhappy with the poor treatment of blacks that she saw all around her. In 1962, when most other blacks in Mississippi where afraid of the consequences, Fannie registered to vote. After both she and her husband lost their jobs and their home, and after she was beaten in a Mississippi jail, Fannie Lou Hamer drew national attention to her fight for blacks' civil rights. She spoke all over the country, helped to form a new political party, and raised money to help poor people. That money was what started the 640 acre Freedom Farm Cooperative that provided work and food for more than 5,000 people. It was Mrs. Hamer's dream to see poor people work together to feed themselves rather than to accept food from others. She made her dream come true.

Another competent entry in the Crowell Biography series. Only its picture book format keeps this book from being useful through sixth grade.

Interest Level: 3-5. Reading Level: 3.2. Further Search Topics: Biography, Blacks-Biography, Civil Rights, Poverty, Women-Biography.

Levy, Elizabeth. Lizzie lies a lot; illus by John Wallner. Delacorte 1976, 102 pp.

Almost any child can identify with Lizzie. She had found that it was sometimes easier to lie than to tell the truth. Her problem was that she had lost control. It seemed as if almost everything she said was a lie. She told so many lies it became difficult to keep track of them all. Lizzie wasn't even really sure why she lied so much. She knew that she sometimes lied because she thought people would be more apt to like her. Other times she lied to get herself out of trouble or to cover up her feelings when she was hurt or angry. But that didn't explain why she lied all the time. Maybe, as her grandmother said, she was a born liar.

It wasn't until Lizzie got herself caught in the middle of so many lies that she lost her only friend, that she could admit her problem to herself and to her family. After their initial shock had passed, everyone agreed to help Lizzie stop lying. Lizzie took the next step by admitting her lies to her friend Sue.

Levy has brought such an appropriately light touch to a fairly common problem that many children find this story enjoyable. Overlook the book's faults (Lizzie's grandmother is overdrawn and her mother's guilt feelings are unsupported by the story) for the fun and the message young readers get from it.

Interest Level: 3-5. Reading Level: 4.2. Further Search Topics: Honesty-Fiction, Group 2, Friendship-Fiction, Best Sellers, Everyday Stories, Family Problems-Fiction, Grandparents-Fiction, Humorous Fiction.

Miles, Betty. The secret life of the underwear champ; illus by Dan Jones. Knopf 1981, 117 pp.

Larry hadn't planned it; in fact, he hadn't even really wanted it to happen. But suddenly he found himself about to make a television commercial for ChampWin Knitting Mills, makers of sports clothing and underwear. He knew his family could use the money he would make, but he certainly didn't want the whole school seeing him in his underwear. Nevertheless, Larry went ahead and made the commercial, hoping that it would never be used. He even had to skip baseball practice to make the taping. Much to his horror, the commercial appeared the night before the team's first game. Not only did the entire opposing team tease him, but so did all his own teammates. By the time he got up to bat, Larry was mad enough to slam the ball out of the park. He didn't hit the ball quite that hard, but he did make a winning home run and end the others' giggles forever. He became the true underwear champ.

This is a funny look at the embarrassments of growing up. It also deals lightly with a boy's pride, his peer relationship, and his growing awareness of girls. An appealing and broadly usable title. Capers series.

Interest Level: 3-5. Reading Level: 2.2. Further Search Topics: Baseball-Fiction, Television-Fiction, Occupations-Fiction, School Stories, Humorous Fiction, Advertising-Fiction, Beauty-Fiction, Motion Pictures-Fiction, Best Sellers, Everyday Stories.

Morressy, John. The drought on Ziax II, illus by Stanley Skardinsky. Walker & Co 1978, 77 pp.

Ziax II, the planet that Toren, his father, and other Earth Pioneers were helping to colonize, was suffering a severe drought. It took both cooperation with the inhabitants of Ziax II and courage to seek out the frightening creature that could save the planet.

The importance of maintaining the balance of nature is the strongest message here. Respect for the ways of others is the secondary message.

Interest Level: 3-5. Reading Level: 3.1. Further Search Topics: Science Fiction, Ecology-Fiction, Outer Space-Fiction.

Pinkwater, Daniel Manus. Fat men from space. Dodd 1977, 57 pp.

The evening after his trip to the dentist William found that he could still hear radio programs when his radio was turned off. He was even more surprised to find that when he wired himself to a fence he could hear spacemen talking. When the spacemen discovered that William could hear them, they landed and captured him. They were on a top secret mission and couldn't risk any human knowing about their existence. The spacemen were about to invade Earth to consume all the junk food they could find. As mass panic set in on Earth, William could do nothing to save his fellow humans. He was held captive and helpless until the invaders' interest was captured by a giant potato pancake floating in outer space.

A tongue-in-check, slapstick spoof of science fiction, food fads, and junk food. Do not expect anything more.

Interest Level: 3-5. Reading Level: 3.2. Further Search Topics: Science Fiction, Humorous Fiction, Food-Fiction, Flying Saucers-Fiction, Aliens-Fiction, Best Sellers, Kidnapping-Fiction, Teeth-Fiction.

Robinson, Nancy K. Wendy and the bullies; illus by Ingrid Fetz. Hastings 1980, 128 pp.

Wendy and her best friend Karen had a very carefully mapped out route to and from school—a route that allowed them to meet up with the fewest number of bullies possible. But when Karen became sick enough to stay home from school, Wendy had to face the bullies alone. Wendy's fears escalated to panic so intense that she avoided walking to school by hiding in her basement. She finally realized that she was letting fear and anger control her life when she found herself bullying Karen. Only her new friendship with Monica, making up with Karen, and her involvement in a school project helped Wendy overcome her fears.

This is a humorous, episodic tale of a feeling and circumstances common to many children. The illustrations sometimes make Wendy and her classmates appear much younger than her actual nine years, but fortunately that doesn't happen often enough to spoil the book's appeal.

Interest Level: 3-5. Reading Level: 3.1. Further Search Topics: School Stories, Bullies-Fiction, Courage-Fiction, Best Sellers, Humorous Fiction, Friendship-Fiction, Everyday Stories.

Slote, Alfred. C.O.L.A.R.; illus by Anthony Kramer. Lippincott 1981, 146 pp.

Jack, his robot twin Danny, and Jack's mother and father were forced to make an emergency landing on an uncharted planet. There they were attacked by creatures who looked like rocks and who wanted to destroy all humans. They captured Danny, led him into an underground living complex, and revealed their true identities. The creatures were robots who had escaped from their owners and the slavery in which they had lived. They kept their planet secret from all

humans for fear of what would happen to them should they be discovered. Their main purpose was to free as many robots as possible and to allow robots the same pleasures humans enjoyed. Because Danny had been happy with his humans and claimed to have been treated as one of the family, the inhabitants of the planet C.O.L.A.R. felt he had to be reprogrammed to see the truth. Jack looked and acted so much like Danny that he was able to prevent Danny from being brainwashed, to save his parents from death, and to convince the other robots that some humans treated their robots quite well. In fact, he and Danny, together, were able to persuade the robot manufacturer that a great program of robot-owner re-education was needed.

This is a good adventure story which could also be useful as a lead into discussions of slavery, intelligence, and interpersonal relationships. It is a sequel to *My Robot Buddy*, but one which can be read without having read its predecessor.

Interest Level: 3-5. Reading Level: 3.1. Robots-Fiction, Science Fiction, Outer Space-Fiction, Kidnapping-Fiction, Brainwashing-Fiction, Slavery-Fiction.

Thomas, Kathleen. Out of the bug jar; illus by Tom O'Sullivan. Dodd 1981, 125 pp.

Even though 10-year-old Tom Jenkins didn't believe in the tooth fairy, when one of his teeth fell out, he placed it under his pillow just in case he was wrong. In the middle of that night he was awakened by a small creature crawling under his pillow and grumbling. Tom quickly scooped him into a bug jar he kept nearby and thus began two years of life with Marvin, a tooth fairy. Marvin was a delightful dictator; he ruled Tom's life. He put Tom into a terrible predicament when Tom tried to charge others to see him and Marvin became invisible. Marvin insisted on being fed just what he demanded, despite the difficulties he made for Tom. He badgered Tom to do his homework, to brush his teeth, and to tell the truth. He even managed to follow Tom to school. The only other person Marvin would allow to see or hear him was Tom's friend Sammy. Tom couldn't get rid of Marvin either. Because Tom had captured him, Marvin, should he ever have been able to escape, was entitled to take *all* of Tom's teeth as compensation for being held prisoner.

Actually Marvin didn't really want to escape. He had grown tired of having to race around and collect teeth. For a while then, everyone was fairly content. Tom had all his teeth and Marvin had a rather nice home. Then quite by accident, Marvin got loose. Both Tom and Marvin wanted Tom to catch Marvin again. Tom wanted to keep his teeth and Marvin wanted to keep his comfortable lifestyle, but Marvin played by the rules and wouldn't give Tom any help at all. After more than seven days of valient but fruitless efforts and nights of sleeping with tape over his mouth, Tom finally caught Marvin and all were happy again.

An amusing story told in short sentences and short chapters. The book should be popular with those who enjoy either fantasy or humor.

Interest Level: 3-5. Reading Level: 2.2. Further Search Topics: Fantasy, Fairies-Fiction, Humorous Fiction, Teeth-Fiction.

Waldorf, Mary. Jake McGee and his feet; illus by Leonard Shortall. HM 1980, 82 pp.

His severe reading difficulties made school the worst place in the world for Jake McGee. On the day that his reading tutor became so impatient with him that she sent Jake to the principal, Jake decided that he couldn't stand school any longer and ran away. He didn't actually run away, he just let his feet finally do what they wanted. His feet were always getting Jake in trouble. They walked too slowly to get him to school on time; they wouldn't stay still once he was in school; and they were always trying to trip someone.

Jake knew that in addition to having problems with his feet he had reading problems, but no one at his old school in the country had noticed. When he and his family moved to the city everything had changed. Jake's mother was always at work or tired. Jake hadn't made any friends and so was always alone. But Jake thought the biggest of all his immediate problems was his feet. The day he ran away, Jake's feet led him to a lost baby, an eccentric old woman, and a neighbor boy, all of whom helped Jake recognize and deal with his real problem.

The book is not high literary quality. The characterization is somewhat flat and the plot is fairly predictable. However, the sentences and chapters are short, the vocabulary is manageable, and Jake's feelings will be shared by many non-readers.

Interest Level: 3-5. Reading Level: 2.2. Further Search Topics: School Stories, Moving, Household-Fiction, Runaways-Fiction, Academic Problems-Fiction, Working Parents-Fiction, Loneliness-Fiction, Feet-Fiction.

Walker, Alice. Langston Hughes, American poet; illus by Don Miller. Har-Row 1974, 33 pp.

Langston Hughes is one of the world's most famous black poets. He spent most of his childhood in poverty and yet he shunned and was shunned by his wealthy father because his father disliked blacks. To Hughes the two most important things in the world were his heritage and his writing. His love of black history stemmed from the stories his grandmother told him. His love of language and writing grew out of the lonely hours he spent reading as a child. Hughes began to write poetry even before he was in high school and continued to write for many years. He wrote not only poems, but children's books, novels, plays and short stories. He wrote about and for blacks around the world. He was a proud and honest man who chose to share his pride in his race and his honesty through his writing.

This book is more of an inspirational tribute to a black hero than a fact-filled biography. That isn't to say that there are no facts included in the book. There are facts, but the book will not do as the sole source for a report about Langston Hughes. The book is, however, a good introduction to the man and his writing.

Interest Level: 3-5. Reading Level: 2.2. Further Search Topics: Biography, Blacks-Biography, Writing, Poverty, Divorce and Separation, Poetry.

Warner, Gertrude Chandler. Schoolhouse mystery; illus by David Cunningham. A. Whitman 1965, 128 pp.

On a dare, the Aldens went to a quiet fishing village to see what excitement they could find there. They found an isolated town filled with poor and unfriendly people. In their attempt to get to know the townspeople, the Aldens learned of the children's desire for schooling and the adults' anticipation of the Money Man's arrival. The Alden children took on the task of teaching school for the summer in an abandoned schoolhouse owned by Miss Gray, a recluse. The Money Man intrigued them more with each new bit of information they learned about him. They finally decided that the Money Man was a swindler who was practically stealing valuable antiques away from the villagers. By spying on the Money Man when he used the schoolhouse to store the antiques, the Aldens and an ex-FBI man were able to capture him. When the vacation was over, the Aldens had once more found excitement, Miss Gray had agreed to teach the local school, the Money Man was on his way to jail, and the townspeople knew the value of their old household items.

See the entry for *The Boxcar Children* for more information.

Interest Level: 3-5. Reading Level: 2.2. Further Search Topics: Mystery and Detective Stories, Vacation-Fiction, School Stories, Antiquities-Fiction, Crime-Fiction, Brothers and Sisters-Fiction, Challenges-Fiction.

Warner, Gertrude Chandler. The woodshed mystery; illus by David Cunningham. A. Whitman 1960, 159 pp.

The four Alden children have grown since their first appearance in *The Boxcar Children* but they are still as close a family as ever. Aunt Jane's telephone message that she wanted to move near them started this adventure. Grandfather proceeded to buy and refurbish his childhood home as a surprise for Aunt Jane. It was an easy house to buy because it had been abandoned and was thought to be haunted. Even though the children and Aunt Jane weren't really worried by the stories of odd occurrences that no one quite remembered, they began to be aware of strange noises and things missing. Upon investigation they discovered Aunt Jane's old boyfriend living in the woodshed in the forest. There beneath the floor of the woodshed, they also found a store of Revolutionary War supplies and a letter from the original owners of the house. The supplies and the letter helped to explain some of the stories. Andrew, Jane's long-lost boyfriend, explained the rest.

It is not necessary to have read any of the series in order to read this story, but those children who enjoyed *The Boxcar Children* are most likely to enjoy the Alden's further adventures. See the entry for *The Boxcar Children* for more information.

Interest Level: 3-5. Reading Level: 2.1. Further Search Topics: Mystery and Detective Stories, United States-History-War-Fiction, Brothers and Sisters-Fiction, Ghosts-Fiction, Vacation-Fiction.

Yolen, Jane. Shirlick Holmes and the case of the wandering wardrobe; illus by Anthony Rao. Coward 1981, 80 pp.

This is a light, fast-paced story of Shirli and her four friends' attempt to solve a local mystery. Its more fully developed characters and plot make this a better literary piece than any of the *Encyclopedia Brown* stories, but it resembles them in other ways. The children live in a small, secure town. The police chief, Shirli's neighbor and George's father, is working on the same case that interests the children but the children solve it first. The mystery is real and involves danger, as opposed to many of Hildick's McGurk mysteries, the other series this book resembles.

Shirli is a fiesty figure who took up George's challenge to solve the town's latest mystery. Thieves had been systematically robbing some of the wealthy summer homes of antiques. Shirli's plan, to search each of the houses for clues, only succeeded in angering the police chief when he caught Shirli and her friends. Being intrepid detectives, however, they did not give up. Instead, they staked out a likely house and waited for the thieves. When the robbers finally arrived Shirli and George hid. Only Gloria was able to escape and go for help. The oak wardrobe in which Shirli took refuge was one of the first pieces the thieves took out of the house. When Shirli tried to get out of it, she found the wardrobe had been placed on a truck with its door against the truck's side; she was caught. Very frightened, she stayed silent until she found herself in the middle of an antiques auction and recognized one of the voices making bids as George's father! As Shirli tumbled out of the wardrobe some of the police chief's men arrested the auctioneer for burglary and selling stolen goods. After she escaped, Gloria had told the police about the thieves, their truck, Shirli, and George, whom they found locked inside a closet still at the summer house.

A serviceable book that will be enjoyed by a wide range of readers.

Interest Level: 3-5. Reading Level: 3.1. Further Search Topics: Mystery and Detective Stories, Humorous Fiction, Friendship-Fiction, Crime-Fiction, Antiquities-Fiction, Detectives-Fiction, Challenges-Fiction.

INTEREST LEVEL 3-6

Avi. No more magic. Pantheon 1975, 138 pp.

Avi has woven a mixture of mystery and magic to produce an excellent story. Chris' belief in magic is bolstered when his new bicycle disappears on Halloween night. Chris, his best friend Eddie, and a new friend, Muffin, eventually decide that strange Mr. Bullen, the junk dealer, has magical powers. In order to keep his powers a secret, Mr. Bullen had to steal back the magical bike he sold Chris. With plenty of intriguing complications along the way, the three children attempt to prove their theory correct but only prove themselves wrong. The age of the protagonists (fourth grade) is touched on so lightly and the plot is interesting enough that even sixth grade readers should find the book enjoyable.

Interest Level: 3-6. Reading Level: 4.2. Further Search Topics: Divorce and Separation-Fiction, Mystery and Detective Stories, Magic-Fiction, Halloween-Fiction, Witches-Fiction, Group 2, Read Aloud, Bicycles and Bicycling-Fiction.

Bales, Carol Ann. Chinatown Sunday; the story of Lillian Der. Contemp Bks. 1973, 32 pp.

A short, personal visit with a fifth grade Chinese-American girl who lives in a Chicago suburb. The author transcribed taped interviews with Lillian Der to produce a first-person description of Lillian's daily life. The uniquely Chinese-American features of Lillian's life are casually intertwined with experiences common to most American children. Month-old parties, the celebration of Chinese New Year, lucky money, old-age birthday parties, Girl Scout meetings, homework, and being a tomboy are all important to Lillian. Not only is this an interesting portrait of Lillian, but it can be a useful part of a multi-ethnic unit or an introduction to autobiography. The book's usefulness is further extended by its introduction to Chinese immigration and by the glossary, which explains terms such as "abacus," "Chinese calendar," and "sea cucumber." The author saves the over-sized book from looking like a picture book by using photographs instead of drawings, thus she makes the book comfortable even for a sixth grade reader.

Interest Level: 3-6. Reading Level: 3.1. Further Search Topics: Ethnic Groups, Chinese-Americans, Biography, Chicago, Immigration and Emigration.

Blume, Judy. Tales of a fourth grade nothing; illus by Roy Doty. Dutton 1972, 120 pp.

Another humorous Blume book that can be counted on to appeal to third and fourth grade readers. If fifth and sixth graders can ignore the title's reference to fourth grade, they too will love it. The story is an exaggeration of a common theme—an older child whose life is in continual turmoil because of a somewhat spoiled younger sibling. Peter's problems with three-year-old Fudge become worse with each chapter until the final disaster when Fudge swallows Peter's pet turtle. Each approximately 15-page chapter is a complete, very funny episode.

Interest Level: 3-6. Reading Level 3.1. Further Search Topics: Humorous Fiction, Turtles-Fiction, Brothers and Sisters-Fiction, Pets-Fiction, Family-Fiction, Read Aloud, Best Sellers, Everyday Stories, Troublemakers-Fiction.

Blume, Judy. Otherwise known as Sheila the great. Dutton 1972, 128 pp.

Sheila first appears in *Tales of a Fourth Grade Nothing* as Peter Thatcher's neighbor. Sheila was a bundle of fears. She was afraid of dogs, thunderstorms, spiders, horses, putting her face in water, and strange noises at night. The summer she and her family rented a house in Tarrytown, New York, she confronted each one of her fears, even mastered one (putting her face in the water) and learned how to swim. That gave her the self-confidence to face a dog without running away. Sheila's progress was aided by her friend Mouse's steadfast belief that a person should always be honest about herself. Sheila's problems are treated realistically and with dignity, yet humorously. Reading level varies greatly from 1.2 - 4.1, therefore, the book is *most* suitable to grades four through six.

Interest Level: 3-6. Reading Level: 3.1. Further Search Topics: Humorous Fiction, Courage-Fiction, Camp-Fiction, Group 2, Vacation-Fiction, Swimming-Fiction, Brothers and Sisters-Fiction, Friendship-Fiction, Everyday Stories.

Blume, Judy. Superfudge. Dutton 1980, 166 pp.

On Fudge's first day in school his older brother Peter had to rescue him from the top of the kindergarten storage cabinets. Later in the school year Fudge's eagerness to join a school guest speaker on stage almost spelled disaster. Then when Fudge unexpectedly disappeared one day everyone, including Peter, thought he had drowned. In addition to Peter's problems with Fudge, Peter had to cope with a baby sister, moving to Princeton, New Jersey, a new job for his mother, and his father's attempts to write a book. Although the book is a sequel and is best enjoyed as such, it can be read alone. It is not as amusing or well-written as it's predecessor, *Tales of a Fourth Grade Nothing*, but will still be popular with young readers.

Interest Level: 3-6. Reading Level 3.1. Further Search Topics: Brothers and Sisters-Fiction, Moving, Household-Fiction, Infants-Fiction, Working Parents-Fiction, School Stories, Family-Fiction, Best Sellers, Humorous Fiction, Everyday Stories.

Bryant, Bernice. George Gershwin: young composer; illus by Nathan Goldstein. Bobbs 1965, 200 pp.

Even when George Gershwin was very young he loved music, showed signs of musical talent, and longed to play the piano. However, any boy who played the piano in George's neighborhood was called a sissy and George didn't like being teased in that way. When he was no longer able to keep his music lessons a secret, he stopped them for fear of the teasing. But each time George quit playing the piano, he always went back to it, even when his parents pressured him not to waste his time at the piano. A young teacher told George that he would never be a musician. One of George's teachers actually taught him to play poorly, instead of well. In time, however, George learned to play well and to compose his own music. Then came the hard work of determining his own style. Gradually, more and more people heard and appreciated his American jazz, until George Gershwin's music was heard all around the world.

Another adequate entry in the *Childhood of Famous Americans* series. Includes the usual glossary, bibliography, time line, and follow-up questions. It is most likely to appeal to the reader already interested in music. Childhood of Famous Americans series.

Interest Level: 3-6. Reading Level: 3.1. Further Search Topics: Biography, Composers, Immigration and Emigration-Biography, Jazz Music, Bullies, Music-Biography, Pianists.

Bulla, Clyde Robert. Dexter; illus by Glo Coalson. Har-Row 1973, 69 pp.

This is not as simple a story as it first appears. Dave, 12 years old and lonely, had hoped his new neighbors would be friends. But, the Arvin family kept very much to themselves until Dave accidentally discovered Alex, the Arvin's son, doing tricks on a trapeze in the barn. Because Dave kept the secret and shared Alex's love for Dexter, his circus pony, the boys soon became friends. Then in one horrible night, the Arvins were forced to leave the town and Dexter was so badly hurt he was believed to be dead. A week later Dave found Dexter alive, but crippled for life and so frightened that no one could get near him. The horse surprised everyone and managed to live through a very harsh winter as well as the townspeople's determination to kill him. When Alex and his father returned, almost a year later, they found Dexter and took the old and feeble horse back to a ranch with them. The story is told with sympathy, with an understanding of how it feels to be lonely, and with tension and suspense. It's appeal should last from third through sixth grade. Print size is smaller than Bulla's usual.

Interest Level: 3-6. Reading Level: 3.1. Further Search Topics: Survival-Fiction, Acrobats and Acrobatics-Fiction, Horses-Fiction, Read Aloud, Circus-Fiction, Loneliness-Fiction, Friendship-Fiction.

Bulla, Clyde Robert. Pirate's promise; illus by Peter Burchard. Har-Row 1958, 87 pp.

After their mother and father died, Tom and Dinah Pippin had nowhere to go but to their Uncle John's house. Uncle John had no place for them, so he sold Tom into bondage but kept Dinah to help his wife with housework. Tom was to be taken by ship to America where the ship's captain would sell him to the highest bidder. After several years, Tom would be free. But, Tom couldn't accept the idea of one person being another's property, so he spoke out at every opportunity. Tom spoke up to the seaman who dragged him aboard ship, to the captain, to the others who had been bonded, even to the pirate captain who captured their ship. Captain Land was so impressed by Tom's bravery that although he set everyone else he had captured adrift on a small boat, he kept Tom with him. He and Tom became good friends. He never asked Tom to become a pirate and Tom never did. Instead, they enjoyed each other's company. When the pirate ship needed work, they stopped at a safe island where Tom met and impressed Captain Red, a fierce enemy of Captain Land. Captain Red's insistence that Tom join his pirate ship led to another clash between the enemies. Although he was ill, Captain Land fought a duel with Captain Red and lost. Land's last requests were that Benjy, a freed slave

who loved him, take all his gold, and that Tom go to Charlestown, South Carolina to find Land's family. Benjy led their flight from Captain Red and arranged a way for Tom to sail to Charlestown before putting Tom on his own. When Tom reached Charlestown he found Land's parents were so angry with Land that at first they didn't even want to hear about him. But, eventually, they not only asked all about their son, but also asked Tom if he and Dinah would like to live with them as their family.

There is enough excitement, danger, and warmth here to satisfy almost any arm-chair adventurer. Usual format of short, episodic chapters.

Interest Level: 3-6. Reading Level 2.1. Further Search Topics: Pirates-Fiction, Seafaring Life-Fiction, Orphans-Fiction, Slavery-Fiction, Brothers and Sisters-Fiction, Best Sellers, Courage-Fiction.

Bulla, Clyde Robert. Marco Moonlight; illus by Julia Noonan. T Y Crowell 1976, 104 pp.

No one could explain Marco's strange, recurring dream. The dream seemed to be about a brother, but Marco had no brother. He had no family but his wealthy grandparents with whom he lived. Marco loved his grandparents very much, but he couldn't help wondering about his own past. He knew only what he and his grandparents could figure out from a few clues. His mother had run away to marry and for three years Marco's grandparents had heard nothing. Then, suddenly, they received a note that she was dying, had parted from her husband, and needed them. By the time they arrived, she was dead and two-year-old Marco could tell them no more. About the time of his thirteenth birthday Marco made friends with a strange man named Flint, who later became the gardener on Marco's grandparents' estate. Rather than live in the room provided for him with the other servants, Flint chose a bleak and isolated beach cottage. Being very careful that no one should suspect, Flint locked Marco into the cottage and forced Marco to change clothes with Matt, who was Marco's long-lost identical twin. Flint and Matt planned that Matt would steal all the money he could from the estate before killing Marco and fleeing. But when Matt began to realize how nice his grandparents were, how much he liked Marco, and how evil Flint was, he decided to thwart Flint's plan. In Matt and Marco's desperate attempt to flee from Flint, Flint was accidentally killed, leaving Marco free to return home and Matt free to find a way to feel he also had the right to claim his heritage before joining Marco.

The tense and dramatic plot immediately involves the reader and the short, fast-paced chapters sustain interest to the end of the book. Readers should also appreciate the small, paperback-size format. A good choice.

Interest Level: 3-6. Reading Level: 2.1. Further Search Topics: Dreams-Fiction, Mystery and Detective Stories, Kidnapping-Fiction, Twins-Fiction, Orphans-Fiction, Grandparents-Fiction, Best Sellers, Brothers and Sisters-Fiction, Jealousy-Fiction, Courage-Fiction.

Burchard, Marshall. Sports hero: Dr. J. Putnam 1976, 89 pp.

Julius Erving can jump higher and stay in the air longer than almost any other basketball player. He can also move around the court with the most agile of players. All in all he is a very exciting player to watch. This book includes his college and pro records (through 1975). See *Sports Hero: Bill Walton* for more information. Sports Hero series.

Interest Level: 3-6. Reading Level: 4.1. Further Search Topics: Biography, Blacks-Biography, Basketball-Biography, Erving, Julius, Group 2.

Burchard, Marshall. Sports hero: Mario Andretti. Putnam 1977, 90 pp.
Auto racing's all-around superstar. See *Sports Hero: Bill Walton* for details about the series. Sports Hero series.
Interest Level: 3-6. Reading Level: 3.2. Further Search Topics: Biography, Andretti, Mario, Auto Racing-Biography.

Burchard, Marshall. Sports hero: Billie Jean King. Putnam 1975, 95 pp.
Winner of every major women's tennis title and a very important person to women's professional sports. Consistent reading level. Book includes glossary of tennis terms. See entry under *Sports Hero: Bill Walton* Sports Hero series.
Interest Level: 3-6. Reading Level: 3.2. Further Search Topics: Biography, King, Billie Jean, Tennis-Biography, Women-Biography.

Burchard, Marshall. Sports hero: Fran Tarkenton. Putnam 1977, 95 pp.
From a strict religious background where athletics were not encouraged, Fran went on to set every NFL passing record possible See *Sports Hero: Bill Walton.* Sports Hero series.
Interest Level: 3-6. Reading Level: 3.2. Further Search Topics: Biography, Tarkenton, Fran, Football-Biography, Religion-Biography.

Burchard, Marshall. Sports hero: Muhammad Ali. Putnam 1975, 95 pp.
The man who brought a quick tongue as well as fast feet and flying fists to the sport of boxing. Entry for *Sports Hero: Bill Walton* gives series notes. Ring record included here. Sports Hero series.
Interest Level: 3-6. Reading Level: 4.1. Further Search Topics: Boxing-Biography, Blacks-Biography, Ali, Muhammad, Group 2.

Burchard, Marshall. Sports hero: Ron Guidry. Putnam 1981, 95 pp.
The Cajun, left-handed pitcher who led the Yankees to two World Championships. See *Sports Hero: Bill Walton* for series details. Sports Hero series.
Interest Level: 3-6. Reading Level: 3.2. Further Search Topics: Baseball-Biography, Biography, Guidry, Ron.

Burchard, Marshall. Sports hero: Terry Bradshaw. Putnam 1980, 95 pp.
Once labeled a "dumb hick," Terry Bradshaw went on to prove he was a talented and thinking quarterback, good enough to be named NFL Player of the Year. He is also a deeply religious man. Reading level of this title varies from 3.1 to 4.1. For more details about the series, see *Sports Hero: Bill Walton.* Sports Hero series.
Interest Level: 3-6. Reading Level: 3.2. Further Search Topics: Biography, Bradshaw, Terry, Football-Biography, Religion-Biography.

Burchard, Susan H. Sports star: Earl Campbell. HarBraceJ 1980, 63 pp.
The Houston Oiler's star running back, probably the best in football, has only been out of college a few years. He should have a long career ahead of him. *Sports Star: Elvin Hayes* includes series notes. Sports Star series.

Interest Level: 3-6. Reading Level: 3.1. Further Search Topics: Football-Biography, Blacks-Biography, Campbell, Earl, Biography.

Burchard, Susan H. Sports star: Elvin Hayes. HarBraceJ 1980, 63 pp.
Only this and three other Sue Burchard titles listed here differ much from the format described for the *Sports Hero* series (see *Sports Hero: Bill Walton*). It appears that in 1979 Ms. Burchard's books took on a slick new look. The covers began to sport color photos rather than black and white. The print size became noticeably smaller, although still of adequate size. More emphasis was placed on the players early life and background, in an apparent attempt to make him or her understandable as an individual rather than just as a star. A short career summary was added at the end of each book. All-in-all, the new, flashier approach should make the books more appealing than ever to older students.
Elvin Hayes came from a very poor family who lived in a town where blacks were badly treated. He went on to become one of the best college basketball players of his time. His deep religious convictions helped him through some rough times in his early years as a pro. Now he is happy, not just when he wins, but when he knows he has played his best. Sports Star series.
Interest Level: 3-6. Reading Level: 3.1. Further Search Topics: Biography, Hayes, Elvin, Basketball-Biography, Blacks-Biography, Religion-Biography.

Burchard, Susan H. Sports star: John McEnroe. HarBraceJ 1979, 63 pp.
In 1977, feisty John McEnroe became the youngest semi-finalist ever to play at Wimbledon. Both before and since then, he has been noted almost as often for his temper as his talent. The level of difficulty of this book varies from 3.1 to 4.1. See *Sports Star: Elvin Hayes* for more details about the book. Sports Star series.
Interest Level: 3-6. Reading Level: 3.2. Further Search Topics: Biography, Tennis-Biography, McEnroe, John.

Burchard, Susan H. Sports star: Tommy John. HarBraceJ 1981, 63 pp.
Tommy John's elbow injury was severe enough that no one thought he would be able to pitch again. He proved that the skeptics were wrong. For series notes see *Sports Star: Elvin Hayes.* Sports Star series.
Interest Level: 3-6. Reading Level: 4.1. Further Search Topics: Baseball-Biography, John, Tommy, Biography, Group 2, Physically Handicapped.

Butterworth, William E. Next stop, Earth; illus by Paul Frame. Walker 1978, 80 pp.
After two years on a desolate planet, 12-year-old Charley and his family were anticipating their return to Earth. But when Charley was awakened from sleep by a spaceship robot, he learned that an asteroid disturbance had caused several key systems on the ship to malfunction. Of 24 passengers on board the spaceship, only 10 were still alive and only Charley and his sister were able to be awakened. It was up to Charley to pilot the ship to its landing on Earth. The controls were all in an adjacent room which a faulty robot kept Charley from entering. Without someone at the controls the ship would burn up when re-entering Earth's atmosphere. By tricking the robot and commanding the ship's main computer, Charley was able to get to the control panel just in time to wake his father, help with reentry and save the ship.

Though the story tends to be heavy with conversations between Charley and various computers and robots, it is also that dialogue that helps maintain suspense. It is a story for the confirmed science fiction fan, not for the inductee.

Interest Level: 3-6. Reading Level: 2.2. Further Search Topics: Science Fiction, Outer Space-Fiction, Voyages and Travels-Fiction, Robots-Fiction, Computers-Fiction.

Byars, Betsy. Trouble River; illus by Rocco Negri. Viking Pr. 1969, 158 pp.

A gripping adventure story of survival. After being attacked by an Indian in the middle of the night, Dewey and his grandmother rushed to Trouble River to board a small raft which Dewey had just finished making. They thought they would only need to navigate a few miles down the river to safety at a neighbor's home, but found instead that the neighbor's cabin had been burned down. For almost 40 miles they fought against the unknown river, wolves and rapids.

This is a book that should satisfy many reluctant readers. It's frequent dialogue, fast action and high interest are only occasionally marred by an overly long sentence.

Interest Level: 3-6. Reading Level: 3.1. Further Search Topics: Courage-Fiction, Frontier and Pioneer Life-Fiction, Survival-Fiction, Grandparents-Fiction, Voyages and Travels-Fiction, Best Sellers, Read Aloud.

Christopher, Matt. Devil pony; illus by Lorence Bjorkland. Little 1977, 103 pp.

This book is a bit of a change from the usual Matt Christopher story line. There is no sports interest here; instead there is a good suspense story about a boy, his cousin and a horse. Stu had watched the black Morgan named Midnight being born and had fallen in love with him. A year later he returned to his aunt and uncle's ranch to claim the horse, as he had been promised he could, but strange things began to happen around him. His cousin Wilbur warned him that he had probably annoyed the ranch poltergeist by deciding to take Midnight away. The bizarre occurrences escalated until Stu was almost tempted to leave Midnight at the ranch. Then Stu discovered Wilbur had been orchestrating everything that had happened because he had wanted to keep the horse himself. Although Stu decided to take Midnight home as he had planned, their new honesty led Stu to believe that he and Wilbur could be friends after all. A surprisingly good story with strong reader appeal.

Interest Level: 3-6. Reading Level: 3.1. Further Search Topics: Horses-Fiction, Supernatural-Fiction, Ghosts-Fiction, Jealousy-Fiction, Relatives-Fiction.

Christopher, Matt. Football fugitive; illus by Larry Johnson. Little 1976, 119 pp.

Larry had been writing to the great football player Yancey Roote for about two years when his letters suddenly went unanswered. Because his relationship with his father was cool and distant, Larry's friendship with Yancey had meant a great deal to him. Shortly after Larry learned that Yancey was in legal trouble, Yancey showed up in town to ask Larry's father, a famous lawyer, to defend him in court. The court case and Yancey helped to bring Larry and his father closer together and to provide each one with new respect for the other. Lots of football action plus a realistic and somewhat common problem (though an unrealistic solution) make this a useful selection.

Interest Level: 3-6. Reading Level: 3.1. Further Search Topics: Football-Fiction, Lawyers-Fiction, Family Problems-Fiction.

Christopher, Matt. Face-off; illus by Harvey Kidder. Little 1972, 131 pp.

Christopher sticks strictly to the sports story formula here. The characters seem to have no time or thoughts for anything but sports. They epitomize the macho image, and once their problems with sports are solved everything in life seems to fall into place. But, for the young sports enthusiast who doesn't really like to read, this formula of much sports action and very little else is successful.

Scott had never played hockey but he was an extremely fast skater. When Del and Skinny asked him to join their hockey team and to be one of the Three Icekateers, Scott was thrilled. But Scott's performance was less than inspiring and Del's patience with his failures was short. The two almost came to blows when Scott discovered that he was puck-shy and would duck every time someone took a shot near him. Their coach's advice to both of them helped clear up Scott's problem and Del's impatience. All ends happily as Scott played well and he and Del became friends once more.

Interest Level: 3-6. Reading Level: 3.1. Further Search Topics: Hockey-Fiction, Ice Skating-Fiction, Courage-Fiction, Friendship-Fiction.

Christopher, Matt. No arm in left field; illus by Byron Goto. Little 1974, 131 pp.

Matt Christopher's books are just the thing for sports junkies. The play-by-play accounts of several sports events (here it is baseball games) are loosely tied together by secondary plot developments. Usually the plot revolves around the main character's successful attempt to overcome a difficulty of some sort.

Terry was a good baseball player so, when he was invited to join a local team shortly after he moved to Pennsylvania, he was very pleased. Almost immediately, he learned that a teammate was not at all happy about playing with Terry. Terry was black and his teammate, Tony, was very prejudiced. Terry had dealt with people like Tony before, so he was able to ignore most, but not all, of Tony's unkind comments and actions. But the day finally came when Tony realized that to play well as a team, they had to work together instead of against each other.

Interest Level: 3-6. Reading Level: 3.2. Further Search Topics: Prejudice-Fiction, Baseball-Fiction, Friendship-Fiction, Challenges-Fiction.

Clark, Margaret Goff. Barney and the UFO; illus by Ted Lewin. Dodd 1979, 159 pp.

Barney felt a strange prickly sensation several times before he discovered that it was caused by Tibbo, a Gark from the planet Ornam. Tibbo had selected Barney as a friend who would accompany him back to Ornam. Barney was to learn the peaceful ways of Gark and then return to Earth to help persuade the world to accept the aliens. At first the idea of visiting Ornam appealed to Barney because he liked Tibbo and felt very lonely and unsure of his adoptive family's love. Those were the very reasons that Tibbo had chosen Barney: he wanted someone without strong ties to Earth and Barney's only tie when he was first contacted by Tibbo was his little brother Scott. As the time to go grew closer, Barney found a new and strong friendship with Dave, a science whiz-kid, and great love for his new parents. Tibbo, however, was determined to hold Barney to his promise. Only a last minute confrontation between Tibbo and Barney,

David, Scott and Mr. and Mrs. Crandall prevented Tibbo from succeeding. But even as Tibbo left, he and Barney acknowledged their new friendship and agreed to keep in touch.

Because of its fairly slow beginning, readers must be well-introduced to this book. If they can be persuaded to be patient while the author sets the stage for about 18 pages they will be rewarded with a decent, if somewhat wordy, story of friendship, UFO's, space travel and family affection.

Interest Level: 3-6. Reading Level: 3.2. Further Search Topics: Science Fiction, Flying Saucers-Fiction, Kidnapping-Fiction, Foster Homes-Fiction, Family-Fiction, Adoption-Fiction, Aliens-Fiction, Loneliness-Fiction, Orphans-Fiction.

Clymer, Eleanor. Me and the Eggman; illus by David K. Stone. Dutton 1972, 57 pp.

As Donald's life became more and more miserable and as his chores and responsibilities around his small, overcrowded, urban apartment increased, he began to look for a way to escape. Thinking that if he could just get to the country, life would be better, Donald sneaked into a truck owned by a farmer who delivered eggs to the city. Not surprisingly the farmer, a sharp speaking, independent old man, was not at all happy to find Donald. Reluctantly, the Eggman, as the farmer was called, agreed to let Donald stay a week and help to work his rundown farm. The week stretched into a summer in which Donald learned to face and accept reality, to love the Eggman and to like himself.

This book is a surprisingly consistent success with reluctant readers, especially boys. Watch for the lack of quotation marks around the dialogue and the somewhat small print.

Interest Level: 3-6. Reading Level: 3.2. Further Search Topics: Family Problems-Fiction, Poverty-Fiction, Vacation-Fiction, Runaways-Fiction, Farm Life-Fiction, Best Sellers.

Clymer, Eleanor. Luke was there; illus by Diane de Groat. HR & W 1973, 74 pp.

Julius' father, uncle and finally his step-father had all walked out on him. Even his mother had left him, although she hadn't wanted to go. When his mother had been taken to the hospital, Julius and his younger brother Danny were sent to a children's home. Julius felt alone and cheated until he met a young, black, social worker named Luke. Luke liked and respected Julius and helped Julius learn to feel the same way about himself. When Luke, too, left Julius, Julius was so angry at the world that he stole food and then money. Afraid to go back to the children's home because he thought he'd be caught and punished, Julius ran away. It wasn't until he found an abandoned child, about Danny's age, who needed care, that Julius returned to the home. Luke was there when he arrived, just when Julius needed him most. Luke listened to Julius' unhappy feelings, arranged for him to see his mother and helped him begin to accept the fact that life is not always fair.

Julius tells his own story in a realistic, straight-forward book that will touch most readers. Only the lack of quotation marks and inadequate spacing between the lines may slow the reader.

Interest Level: 3-6. Reading Level: 2.2. Further Search Topics: Runaways-Fiction, Orphans-Fiction, Juvenile Delinquency-Fiction, Divorce and Separation-Fiction, Friendship-Fiction, Courage-Fiction, Survival-Fiction, Loneliness-Fiction, Best Sellers, Read Aloud.

Cohen, Daniel. Creatures from UFOs. Dodd 1978, 112 pp.

A series of reports about close encounters of the third kind. The author offers both sides of each story, then allows the reader to draw his or her own conclusions. Stories will intrigue even those readers not already interested in UFOs. Index. Photographs. A natural. Parts can even be read aloud.

Interest Level: 3-6. Reading Level: 3.1. Further Search Topics: Best Sellers, Flying Saucers.

Cone, Molly. The amazing memory of Harvey Bean; illus by Robert MacLean. HM 1980, 83 pp.

It had been a long time since Harvey had been happy. His memory was so bad that he was always in trouble at school. And now that his parents were separating, he had trouble at home, too. Because he thought that neither one of his parents wanted him he told each one that he was going to stay with the other and instead decided to spend the summer alone. A few hours after he left home, Harry ran into Mr. and Mrs. Katz and before he completely realized it, he was living with them.

Mr. Katz couldn't stand to see anything go to waste. He collected the usable food thrown out behind grocery stores, old furniture, tools, windows and more. Mrs. Katz, whose memory was just as bad as Harvey's, loved to cook, so she could always find a way to use the food. Everything else bulged from the house and garage into the driveway and yard. Harvey spent a happy summer learning to scavenge, eating well, learning not to worry about what others thought of him and even improving his memory. When his parents finally found him, Harvey realized that they really did want him, even if they were separated. He decided to live with his mother on weekdays, his father on weekends, and the Katzs during the summers.

The plot problems that are obvious to adult readers are ones that most young readers will be able to ignore (i.e. neither parent checks on Harvey for over two months). Young readers will enjoy the humor and realism of Harvey's pain, happiness and eventual feeling of self-confidence and triumph. The ten short chapters, good-sized print and adequate space between the lines help lower the book's reading level to late fourth grade.

Interest Level: 3-6. Reading Level: 5.1. Further Search Topics: Loners-Fiction, Vacation-Fiction, Divorce and Separation-Fiction, Humorous Fiction, Group 2, Memory-Fiction, Runaways-Fiction, Academic Problems-Fiction, Individualists-Fiction.

Corbett, Scott. The lemonade trick; illus by Paul Galdone. Little 1960, 103 pp.

This is the first book in a series of quite enjoyable stories (most of which are, unfortunately, too difficult to recommend here). Kerby was given an odd chemistry set by a strange old woman whom he helped one day. When he used the set to put together a brew, Kerby found himself completely under its spell. The sweet-smelling liquid he had concocted forced him to be good, so good that his parents began to worry about him. Luckily the spell wore off in a short time. But, Kerby kept experimenting with it: on himself, on his dog, on his friend, on his enemy and finally in desperation, on the entire boy's choir at church.

A succession of innocently humorous incidents are woven together into a satisfying story. Print size is on the small side.

Interest Level: 3-6. Reading Level: 3.1. Further Search Topics: Humorous Fiction, Bullies-Fiction, Magic-Fiction, Magicians-Fiction, Chemistry-Fiction, Read Aloud.

Curtis, Philip. The invasion of the Brain Sharpeners; illus by Tony Ross. Knopf 1979, 117 pp.

This book is one of a number of books published by Albert Knopf under the series title Capers. They are meant to be (and with few exceptions are) light, easy-to-read fiction, published simultaneously in hardcover and paperback editions. Each book is about 120 pages long with chapter length varying from 9 to 14 pages. Print is plenty large and spacing between lines is always adequate. Plots are built around an idea of guaranteed appeal, descriptive passages are kept to a minimum and action (often suspenseful) abounds. This should, on the whole, be a very useful series. Some entries (i.e., *Man From the Sky* and *Who Stole the Wizard of Oz*, both by Avi) are either too difficult or too obscure to be widely appealing, but they are by far the exceptions to the rule.

Invasion of the Brain Sharpeners is the catchy science fiction story of Michael's successful, but risky, attempt to rid his fifth grade classroom of the overpowering influence of the Brain Sharpeners. The Brain Sharpeners came from another galaxy to search for humans to help them colonize their Planet Five. Humans were so lacking in brain power that the Brain Sharpeners' plan was to periodically expose each child to brain-developing rays, then put them through intensive courses of study guided by their also-exposed teacher. When the children had all learned enough to be beneficial to the Brain Sharpeners, they were to be taken from Earth to Planet Five. Michael was the only one to see the danger they were in and to attempt to stop the plot. He managed to chase the aliens away and to prevent his classmates and teacher from receiving their second dose of rays, but in doing so, he sent the principal to the spaceship. Michael's classmates were thus saved, but his principal was never heard from again. Capers series.

Interest Level: 3-6. Reading Level: 3.1. Further Search Topics: Science Fiction, Flying Saucers-Fiction, Aliens-Fiction, School Stories, Kidnapping-Fiction, Best Sellers, Academic Problems-Fiction, Brainwashing-Fiction.

Dolan, Edward F., Jr. Let's make magic; photos by Jay Irving. Doubleday 1981, 96 pp.

With playing cards, coins, paper, a few commonly available odds and ends and some practice, the reader can perform most of the tricks in this book. The book is not a step-by-step description of how to put together a magic show (as some of the other titles are), but is more like a casual chat with a friend who wants to teach you to perform a few tricks. Some are simply optical illusions; some are brain teasers that involve mathematical calculations; some are card tricks; and others are much more traditional magic tricks.

Very little is said about how to use conversation as audience distraction or how to link the tricks together into a show. Instead, it is the kind of book that allows the reader to pick and choose any tricks he or she may want to learn without feeling pressured to do more than entertain a friend or two for a few moments. The tricks, with the possible exception of the mathematical brain teasers, are all easily manageable by third through sixth grade readers and yet are impressive to their peers. The use of photographs, rather than cartoon illustrations, helps to

make the book a probable success, especially with older readers who like to entertain, enjoy the spotlight, or are interested in magic.

Interest Level: 3-6. Reading Level: 3.1. Further Search Topics: Magic, Optical illusions, Best Sellers.

Eyerly, Jeannette. The seeing summer; illus by Emily Arnold McCully. Lippincott 1981, 153 pp.

That it attempts to be two books at the same time is the one flaw in this book that may be noticed by young readers. The first half of the book is an interesting story of the growing friendship between a sighted girl and a blind girl. Carey's delight at the idea of a new friend next door turned to disbelief and discomfort when she learned that Jenny was blind. Jenny too wanted to be friends, but not if she was to be pitied or patronized. Gradually she was able to show Carey that being blind was a nuisance, but nothing she was ashamed of or embarrassed about. The second half of the book presents the contrived and somewhat unnecessary story of Jenny's kidnapping. When Carey's attempt to rescue Jenny resulted in her capture too, it was, of course, Jenny's independence and ingenuity that led the way to their eventual rescue.

To the reader looking for a rousing story of a kidnapping the book may be a disappointment. Half of the book is a long time to wait for the slight adventure. But, for those readers interested in a good story of physical differences and friendship, this will be more satisfying.

Interest Level: 3-6. Reading Level: 3.1. Further Search Topics: Vision-Fiction, Friendship-Fiction, Kidnapping-Fiction, Single Parent Family-Fiction, Physically Handicapped-Fiction.

Ginsburg, Mirra. The lazies; illus by Marian Parry. Macmillan 1973, 70 pp.

A good collection of 15 short Russian folktales all having to do with laziness. Most are humorous tales; few are well-known. In just under a third of the stories the humor may be too subtle even for older elementary school children; however, the rest of the stories can be enjoyed by almost any child between third and sixth grade. ("Who Will Wash the Pot," "Easy Bread," "Who Will Row Next," and "The Princess Who Learned to Work" are the questionable stories). Print somewhat small.

Interest Level: 3-6. Reading Level: 3.1. Further Search Topics: Folklore, Humorous Fiction, Laziness-Fiction, Russia-Fiction.

Greene, Constance C. A girl called Al; illus by Byron Barton. Viking Pr. 1969, 127 pp.

Told in the first person, this is the story of two seventh grade girls. The girls' warm friendship began the moment Al introduced herself to the narrator as a non-conformist. Al was very independent, mostly because she was on her own so much of the time. Her parents were divorced and she seldom saw either one of them. Her father only wrote her postcards and her mother was rarely home. The narrator's family and Mr. Richards, their building superintendent, became Al's family. They cooked, ate, played, fought, talked and even made bookcases together. When Mr. Richards had a heart attack, they found help for him and later went to see him in the hospital. It was his death that helped Al and her mother grow closer, just as Mr. Richards' life had helped her understand why her father never came to see her.

A satisfying, low-key story of friendship and maturation. The girls are Judy Blume-style characters with much greater innocence. Their ages are not discernible by their actions or dialogue, only by the author's statement.

Interest Level: 3-6. Reading Level: 3.1. Further Search Topics: Children-Growth-Fiction, Single Parent Family-Fiction, Friendship-Fiction, Weight-Fiction, Aging-Fiction, Death-Fiction, Divorce and Separation-Fiction, Family Problems-Fiction, Everyday Stories, Humorous Fiction.

Greenfield, Eloise. Talk about a family; illus by James Calvin. Lippincott 1978, 60 pp.

Genny, Kim, and Mac knew something was wrong between their parents, and fully expected that their older brother Larry would be able to fix everything when he came home from the army. But even Larry's welcome home party was almost ruined by their parents' fighting and Kim's reaction. That night, as she listened to Larry and her parents' low voices, Genny was certain that Larry was bringing her parents back together. When her father announced the next morning that he was going to move out, Genny's anger and hurt was directed at Larry. With her friend Mr. Parker's help, Genny finally realized that they were still a family; a family with a new shape, but one that would be able to adjust. A one-theme, realistic and reassuring, short book with good-sized print. Very useful

Interest Level: 3-6. Reading Level: 3.1. Further Search Topics: Divorce and Separation-Fiction, Family Problems-Fiction, Brothers and Sisters-Fiction, Best Sellers.

Hildick, Edmund W. The case of the invisible dog; illus by Lisl Weil. Macmillan 1977, 101 pp.

Brains Bellingham, a nine-year-old scientific genius, interrupted the McGurk Organization's Annual Picnic with an invisible dog. It was only a short time before McGurk and his friends were convinced that Brains' discovery of how to make things invisible was the greatest event since putting a man on the moon. Although they had always scorned the idea of including anyone else in the Organization, they decided to persuade Brains to join. But, before the day was over, they discovered not only that they had been duped, but exactly how Brains had made the impossible seem real. The Organization took its revenge by using Brain's own trick to make him confess. When Brains began laughing at how well his trick had been used in reverse, McGurk admitted how impressed they all had been by Brain's clever thinking. The outcome of their discussion was that Brains was invited, a second time, to become a member of the McGurk Organization.

See *The Case of the Bashful Bank Robber* for series information. McGurk Mystery series.

Interest Level: 3-6. Reading Level: 3.1. Further Search Topics: Mystery and Detective Stories, Detectives-Fiction, Gangs-Fiction, Dogs-Fiction, Supernatural-Fiction, Humorous Fiction, Jealousy-Fiction.

Hildick, Edmund W. The case of the condemned cat; illus by Lisl Weil. Macmillan 1975, 106 pp.

Ray Williams had a terrible problem when he begged the McGurk Organization for help. His cat Whiskers had been accused of killing a neighbor's pet dove. Ray's mother decided that they couldn't risk upsetting the neighbors anymore and threatened to take Whiskers to the pound unless it could be proven that he was innocent. The Organization, needing time, hid Whiskers and told Mrs. Williams that he had run away. While Whiskers was safely hidden, the group interviewed all the neighbors, surveyed the scene of the crime, and tried to decide upon the real murderer. When the remains of another bird were found while Whiskers was safely locked away, it looked as if the cat was surely innocent. But then McGurk and his detectives found out that the cat had been sprung. It wasn't until they went back over all the information they had gathered that McGurk realized who was the real culprit. The only step left was to trick old Gramp Martin (the neighborhood grouch) into confessing.

See *The Case of the Bashful Bank Robber* for series information. McGurk Mystery series.

Interest Level: 3-6. Reading Level: 2.2. Further Search Topics: Mystery and Detective Stories, Cats-Fiction, Detectives-Fiction, Humorous Fiction, Gangs-Fiction, Pets-Fiction.

Hildick, Edmund W. The case of the secret scribbler; illus by Lisl Weil. Macmillan 1978, 106 pp.

Joey's discovery in a library book of a scrap of paper with part of a letter and a strange diagram on it led the McGurk Organization on a lively chase. Brains identified the diagram as that of a widely-used security system. The part of the letter that they could read told the group that there was a burglary being planned for the approaching weekend, but the youngsters knew the police would never take them seriously until they had much more evidence. By researching local alarm systems, determining who bought the unusual paper, and comparing handwriting samples, the detectives were able to convince the police of what was about to happen. In gratitude, the police loaned the Organization a police monitor so that they could listen as the thieves were caught. To all but McGurk it seemed like the perfect way to end the case: he tried to sneak into the midst of the capture, but only succeeded in getting himself in real trouble.

See *The Case of the Bashful Bank Robber* for series information. McGurk Mystery series.

Interest Level: 3-6. Reading Level: 2.2. Further Search Topics: Mystery and Detective Stories, Crime-Fiction, Gangs-Fiction, Nonverbal Communication-Fiction, Humorous Fiction, Detectives-Fiction.

Hildick, Edmund W. The case of the snowbound spy; illus by Lisl Weil. Macmillan 1980, 132 pp.

One snowy morning McGurk called the five members of his organization together to decipher a code. The code was part of a message from someone who wanted to hire them and would pay $5.00 a day. When they broke the code and met their employer, Mr. Fitch, he gave the group another code as part of their assignment. The second code told them where to deliver a small package that Mr. Fitch gave them. They were to pick up another coded message at the same place. After three pick-ups and drops they would be finished and Mr. Fitch, an ex-government spy, would have proved he was still a trustworthy and capable person to an ex-colleague with whom he wanted to work on a book. It seemed like just the challenging kind of assignment the McGurk Organization looked for. As they worked, however, it began to look more and more as if they were being used for illegal business. While Joey and McGurk staked out the next drop-off spot, Willie, Brains and Wanda pretended to Mr. Fitch to be unsuspecting. By working quickly and cleverly and by alerting the police, the McGurk gang uncovered and stopped two industrial spies who were stealing secret information about a new copying machine.

See *The Case of the Bashful Bank Robber* for series information. McGurk Mystery series.

Interest Level: 3-6. Reading Level: 3.1. Further Search Topics: Mystery and Detective Stories, Spies-Fiction, Detectives-Fiction, Gangs-Fiction, Humorous Fiction, Nonverbal Communication-Fiction, Crime-Fiction.

Hildick, Edmund W. The case of the bashful bank robber; illus by Lisl Weil. Macmillan 1981, 138 pp.
The McGurk Organization is a crime fighting detective agency. Led by Jack McGurk's strong ego, they had taken on many a seemingly impossible task and had always been successful. Never before, however, had they tried to protect the seven banks in town from being robbed. The five children's first idea was to regularly patrol each bank and watch for likely looking get-away cars. When that plan only led to a nasty confrontation with their new junior high school principal, they decided to try something else. Their second plan, to photograph all suspicious looking people near the banks, didn't fare much better than their first idea. Then, without knowing it, they found themselves holding the key to solving a real bank robbery. Before they realized its importance, they had literally given away the vital clue. Using only their own memories, powers of observation, and cleverness, they were still able to solve the crime with only a little help from the FBI.
The "McGurk mysteries" are light, fast-moving, and often humorous. Clues for solving the mysteries are sometimes subtle, but always there in the plot and illustrations for the reader to find. The characters are somewhat flat but still appealing. Joey, who is handy with words and a typewriter, is the narrator of each book. Jack McGurk, dedicated mastermind of all the group's activities is shrewd, a natural leader, and egotistical. Willie has the world's most sensitive nose and an excellent memory for odors. Wanda is the best tree-climber in town and a rational influence on the group. Brains, the newest and youngest member of the group, is a scientific genius, so he runs their crime lab. The books need not be read in chronological order although most have a brief reference to an earlier story. Reading level varies within each book from 2.1 to 3.1. A few books include enough more difficult passages that their average reading level is pushed from 2.2 to 3.1. Interest level in the series, once a reader has started on it, is high. McGurk Mystery series.
Interest Level: 3-6. Reading Level: 2.2. Further Search Topics: Mystery and Detective Stories, Crime-Fiction, Detectives-Fiction, Humorous Fiction, Gangs-Fiction.

Hildick, Edmund W. The case of the four flying fingers; illus by Lisl Weil. Macmillan 1981, 138 pp.
At first the four young strangers who were knocking over garbage cans had been merely a neighborhood nuisance. Later McGurk and his fellow detectives began to suspect that they were involved in the rash of break-ins and burglaries in the city. The Organization didn't think the "garbage gang" was actually committing the robberies, but rather that they were fingering houses for someone else to burglarize (thus their nickname: The Four Flying Fingers). It could be safely assumed by a would-be burglar that where no one picked up the spilled garbage, no one was home. It was the Organization's job to find the Thumb who was the mastermind behind the plot. When they caught up with the Fingers, McGurk and crew found out that the Flying Fingers hadn't realized what they were doing; only that a blonde lady in a camper was paying them a nickel for every driveway they left strewn with garbage. It didn't take long for the

Organization to track down the woman and her accomplice. But, in one of their less intelligent moves, they played right into her hands and soon found themselves being transported out of town in her camper. When they tried to call to passing cars for help, no one took them seriously. It wasn't until Brains, bound and gagged to appear authentic, used a flashlight and Morse code to signal for help that anyone paid any attention to them. A police car finally stopped the camper for speeding and after some clever arguments McGurk and his friends were able to convince the police that Lady Thumb was a thief.
This title is just as enjoyable as the best of the other books in the series, more exciting and universal in appeal than most, and equally humorous. It's only drawback is a very inconsistent reading level (from 2.1 to 4.1) that will discourage a reader new to McGurk. Established fans will be able to tolerate the range. McGurk Mystery series.
Interest Level: 3-6. Reading Level: 3.1. Further Search Topics: Mystery and Detective Stories, Detectives-Fiction, Humorous Fiction, Crime-Fiction, Gangs-Fiction.

Hurwitz, Johanna. Baseball fever; illus by Ray Cruz. Morrow 1981, 128 pp.
Only baseball nuts need even consider this title, but for the die-hard baseball fan this is perfect. Much to his father's disgust, Ezra had only one interest in life. Baseball was almost all Ezra ever thought of. His father was a German-born intellectual who couldn't understand how anyone could waste so much time watching men hit a ball with a stick. He wanted Ezra to become interested in history and chess. Ezra had no interest in history except baseball history. He hated chess, not just because he always lost, but because his father continually told him how badly he played. Predictably they reach a compromise; each learns to appreciate the other's passion, but not before everyone in the family and a few people outside the family have become involved in a series of warmly humorous incidents. Includes much baseball information.
Interest Level: 3-6. Reading Level: 3.1. Further Search Topics: Baseball-Fiction, Family Problems-Fiction, Humorous Fiction.

Law, Carol Russell. The case of the Weird Street firebug; illus by Bill Morrison. Knopf 1980, 119 pp.
This is the humorous story of a Nancy Drew-type character who gets involved in a mystery before she is even half finished with her mail-order detective lessons. Steffi wanted very much to be a detective. When she saw an ad for a local correspondence course, she tracked down the shabby office in a run-down building on Weir Street, and went to visit Jeff Dangerfield of Dangerfield Detective School. Steffi's first lesson, trailing suspects, was a disaster. She tried to pick out suspicious characters at a fire on Weir Street on her way home. The only really suspicious character (Beady Eyes) didn't go anywhere, so Steffi couldn't follow him. Her next attempts were very obvious and only resulted in her own anger and embarrassment. On her way back to seek advice from Dangerfield, Steffi literally ran into Beady Eyes again. She didn't think anything more about him until she saw him a short time later at another fire just down the street from Dangerfield's office. As the fire moved closer to Dangerfield's building, Steffi took desperate measures to try and save her friend. Steffi's efforts were interpreted by Beady Eyes as attempts to indicate that he was an arsonist. By the time Steffi figured out that Beady

Eyes really was an arsonist, he had her cornered. A timely entry by the police saved both Steffi and Dangerfield. Steffi's reward for the capture of Beady Eyes was a medal from the police and a partnership with Dangerfield.

A fast-paced story, as well as slightly more original characters than most stories of this genre, make this a likely success with third through sixth grade readers. Capers series.

Interest Level: 3-6. Reading Level: 3.1. Further Search Topics: Mystery and Detective Stories, Humorous Fiction, Fire-Fiction, Detectives-Fiction, Crime-Fiction.

Madian, Jon. Beautiful junk: a story of the Watts Towers; photos by Barbara Jacobs, Jr. and Lou Jacobs, Jr. Little 1968, 44 pp.

Although this book is now out of print; it is well worth trying to find. It is a fictionalized account of a young, angry black boy's encounter with the creator of Los Angeles' unusual Watts Towers. Simon Rodia, a poor tile setter, worked on the towers for 33 years until he was 75 years old. He used only his imagination, discarded materials he found around him, seashells, and sand to build three tall, fantasy-like towers in the middle of a ghetto. He created beauty where others saw only junk.

The book is illustrated with photography that makes the story more vivid and the towers and Rodia's accomplishment more impressive than they would have seemed with drawings. The print is good-sized, spacing is totally adequate. Rodia's life is quickly submarized and an update on the Towers is included at the book's end.

Interest Level: 3-6. Reading Level: 3.1. Further Search Topics: Blacks-Fiction, Read Aloud, Best Sellers, Poverty-Fiction, Rodia, Simon, Architecture, Biography, Aging-Fiction, Watts Towers, California, Poverty.

Miles, Miska. Annie and the old one; illus by Peter Parnall. Little 1971, 44 pp.

A quietly beautiful story that will not appeal to all readers. Annie, a young Navajo girl, had a very close relationship with her grandmother. Her grandmother announced that she would "go to Mother Earth" at the time when the new rug Annie's mother was weaving was "taken from the loom." Annie tried all she could think of to keep the rug from being finished in order to keep her grandmother alive. When her grandmother solemnly explained that Annie could not stop time, Annie listened and "understood many things" for the first time.

It will be a thoughtful, sensitive child or a child trying to understand death who will best appreciate this special book.

Interest Level: 3-6. Reading Level: 3.2. Further Search Topics: Grandparents-Fiction, Death-Fiction, Indians of North America-Fiction, Navajo Indians-Fiction.

Norton, Andre. Star Ka'at; illus by Bernard Colonna. Walker & Co 1976, 122 pp.

Jim Evans and Elly Mae Brown, both orphaned and alone, met each other and two strange cats at the same time. As the children became more unhappy with their lives, they began to realize that Tiro and Mer were not usual cats. They were highly intelligent Ka'ats from another planet who had come to Earth in search of new strong stock to add to their breed. Both Ka'ats became as fond of the children as the children became of them. When the time came for the transport ship to leave, Jim and Elly contrived to go with them. However, the only way they could go was if they were accepted by the other Ka'ats and adopted by Tiro and Mer.

This is the first book in a series. Unfortunately the second book *Star Ka'at World*, has a much more difficult reading level (sixth grade) and the third title, *Star Ka'at and the Plant People*, varies from 2.1 to 4.1. Reading level of this entry varies between 4.1 and 5.1 but children seem to like the book enough to put up with the variability.

Interest Level: 3-6. Reading Level: 4.2. Further Search Topics: Science Fiction, Friendship-Fiction, Cats-Fiction, Group 2, Outer Space-Fiction, Orphans-Fiction.

Pinkwater, Daniel Manus. The Hoboken chicken emergency. P-H 1977, 83 pp.

Arthur's mother sent him out with $16 to buy a Thanksgiving turkey. He returned with a live 266 pound chicken on a leash. It seemed that their turkey reservation had been lost at the meat market and, because it was Thanksgiving morning, there were no other turkeys available. Arthur searched everywhere but found nothing, until a strange old professor tricked him into buying the chicken. No one could bear to kill and eat such a large and friendly chicken, so Arthur and his family named it Henrietta and kept it as a pet. Henrietta was a difficult pet to keep hidden from the neighbors When the neighbors, and later the city, saw Henrietta running loose there was general hysteria. But all ended well when Henrietta and the city calmed down and Henrietta became a kind of neighborhood mascot.

A purely absurd plot but presented with enough energy and humor that most readers thoroughly enjoy the book. Some brief introduction may be necessary to get readers beyond the first few pages.

Interest Level: 3-6. Reading Level: 2.2. Further Search Topics: Humorous Fiction, Chickens-Fiction, Pets-Fiction, Thanksgiving-Fiction, Holidays-Fiction, Read Aloud, Best Sellers.

Place, Marian T. The boy who saw Bigfoot. Dodd 1979, 96 pp.

Joey and his foster mother searched for and found Bigfoot. But, when Joey told his classmates, no one would believe him. Joey's next idea was to take the entire class on a field trip to track Bigfoot.

Joey's rapid change from a difficult to a very well-adjusted child is not well supported. But interest in Bigfoot is so great that the book's flaws will be overlooked by its readers.

Interest Level: 3-6. Reading Level: 2.2. Further Search Topics: Bigfoot-Fiction, Foster Homes-Fiction, Monsters-Fiction, Troublemakers-Fiction, School Stories.

Platt, Kin. Dracula, go home; illus by Frank Mayo. Watts 1979, 87 pp.

From the chapter numbers that drip blood, and the humorously grotesque illustrations, to the short sentences and chapters, this is a book designed and almost guaranteed to appeal to the reluctant reader. A sense of immediacy and involvement is created by the first person narration. Tension is created on the opening page when Larry sees a man in the cemetery who looked exactly like Dracula. When that man registered at the hotel where Larry was working, Larry decided to find out more about him. It began to look as if Mr. A. R. Claude (the letters spell Dracula) was not only a vampire, but a thief and a murderer as well. The trouble was that Larry couldn't prove anything. Even when he found the stolen jewels for which Mr.

Claude had been searching, Larry still couldn't convince anyone of Claude's true identify. No one ever did believe Larry, thus Claude went free.

The author uses a light touch to treat an eerie subject. His inconclusive ending may disappoint some, but should delight many. Beware of the variability of the reading level however; it swings from high first grade to low third grade.

Interest Level: 3-6. Reading Level: 2.2. Further Search Topics: Monsters-Fiction, Horror-Fiction, Mystery and Detective Stories, Best Sellers, Murder-Fiction, Crime-Fiction, Transformations-Fiction.

Robinson, Barbara. The best Christmas pageant ever; illus by Judith Gwyn Brown. Har-Row 1972, 80 pp.

A truly delightful story of what happens when the meanest kids in town (they are all in one family) take over all the lead roles in the Sunday school Christmas pageant. The Herdmans (all six of them), having heard that the church was giving away free food, showed up to take some. While they were there, they heard about the Christmas pageant and decided it presented them with another perfect opportunity for food and mischief. With a little behind-the-scenes arm-twisting (literally), they managed to dissuade everyone else from showing interest in the major roles. Theirs was a completely original interpretation of the Christmas story that left nothing and no one around them untouched.

That the book's reading level will prove too high for many people is unfortunate. The story is well worth the struggle. A wonderful choice for reading aloud.

Interest Level: 3-6. Reading Level: 5.1 Further Search Topics: Christmas-Fiction, Bullies-Fiction, Troublemakers-Fiction, Humorous Fiction, Religion-Fiction, Group 2, Read Aloud, Acting-Fiction, Holidays-Fiction.

Robinson, Jean. The strange but wonderful cosmic awareness of Duffy Moon; illus by Lawrence Di Fiori. HM 1974, 142 pp.

Duffy was tired of being small, of always being on the losing side of fights, and of being unappreciated at home (by his ex-football star uncle). When he sent away for Mr. Flamel's Cosmic Awareness Kit, Duffy was sure he would then be able to take control over anything he wanted and direct his own life. His friend Peter, the narrator, wasn't quite so sure. Peter turned out to be right. Duffy almost made himself sick trying to build a stone wall. Babysitting two small boys and trying to bathe a Great Dane proved to be disastrous. But Duffy's biggest problem came from Boots McAfee's gang. A series of events finally brought Duffy and Peter face-to-face with the dreaded Boots. Luckily, she turned out to be a very smart girl who appreciated Duffy's true talents.

From the first to the last page this is a funny, very enjoyable book. A delightful book with a very palatable message.

Interest Level: 3-6. Reading Level: 3.2. Further Search Topics: Humorous Fiction, Bullies-Fiction, Magic-Fiction, Read Aloud, Occupations-Fiction, Sex Role-Fiction, Orphans-Fiction, Best Sellers, Gangs-Fiction, Courage-Fiction, Babysitting-Fiction.

Rockwell, Thomas. How to eat fried worms; illus by Emily McCully. Watts 1973, 116 pp.

It started more as a joke than anything else, but it escalated into a strange commitment. Alan bet Billy $50 that Billy couldn't eat a worm a day for fifteen days. Billy had always been willing to take almost any dare offered and he was stubborn enough to carry them out, but when he actually faced the first worm (an enormous night crawler), he almost backed down. He and his friend Tom had to keep repeating the word "minibike" (the prize he planned to buy with the money) and smother the worm in everything imaginable in order to eat it all. After the first worm, however, the next few were easier to face. That was when Alan and his ally Joe, began using psychological warfare and almost won. In 41 very short, grotesquely funny chapters Billy becomes the proud owner of a minibike and is the first person to become hooked on worm sandwiches.

Once this book is started, it is hard to resist its gruesome fascination. Although the print is somewhat small, and there are occasionally very difficult or babytalk words, the interest is strong enough to sustain almost all readers.

Interest Level: 3-6. Reading Level: 3.1. Further Search Topics: Humorous Fiction, Worms-Fiction, Read Aloud, Best Sellers, Challenges-Fiction, Food-Fiction, Bicycles and Bicycling-Fiction.

Roy, Ron. Nightmare Island; illus by Robert MacLean. Dutton 1981, 69 pp.

Harley didn't want to take his younger brother camping, but because he had promised his father he would, the boys packed a tent, sleeping bags, and plenty of food into a small boat and set off to nearby Little Island. Hidden in his pocket, Harley had matches and marshmallows for a midnight marshmallow roast. After they had finished the bag of marshmallows, Harley threw the last log of the fire into the water. The water erupted into flames that quickly spread around the island. As the boys fought desperately to save themselves and to find shelter, they realized that the large shape they had seen in the distance must have been an oil tanker that had spread an oil slick all around the island. With time running out Harley gave his brother the only truly secure shelter from the fire, curled up on top of a tall rock and went to sleep. When he awoke the fire had burned itself out and help was on the way.

Most young readers will be able to suspend disbelief long enough to enjoy this as an exciting adventure and survival story, but it is hard to believe that two young boys could not only survive such a holocaust, but that they could sleep through part of it, too. It is also difficult to believe that there would not be more of a fuss made about the oil tanker blowing up. Plot problems aside, young readers seem to love the story.

Interest Level: 3-6. Reading Level: 3.2. Further Search Topics: Brothers and Sisters-Fiction, Survival-Fiction, Camping-Fiction, Disasters-Fiction, Best Sellers.

Sharmat, Marjorie W. Getting something on Maggie Marmelstein; illus by Ben Shecter. Har-Row 1971, 101 pp.

A curious love-hate relationship existed between Thad and Maggie. It all began when Maggie overheard Thad say she squeaked like a mouse. Then Maggie caught Thad wearing an apron and cooking. Thad was so uncomfortable with the thought that Maggie might tell his friends, that he was determined to find out Maggie's deepest secret. That meant that Thad had to take a lead role as a frog opposite Maggie as the princess in the school play. While at Maggie's apartment for a costume fitting, Thad found a love letter Maggie had written to Cary Grant. Thad decided he would read the letter to the class right after the play was over. But during the play Maggie saved Thad from what could have been one of the most embarrassing moments of his life. By the time he finally had the chance to make Maggie appear foolish, Thad had changed his mind.

Written as Thad's story, the book is funny, warm, and realistic. A good, short, story that continues to be popular. Print is of moderate size.

Interest Level: 3-6. Reading Level: 3.1. Further Search Topics: Humorous Fiction, Everyday Stories, School Stories, Best Sellers, Friendship-Fiction, Sex Role-Fiction, Acting-Fiction.

Sharmat, Marjorie W. Maggie Marmelstein for President; illus by Ben Shecter. Har-Row 1975, 122 pp.

Maggie and Thad Smith are at it again. When Thad decided to run for sixth grade president, Maggie decided to become his campaign manager. However, because Thad thought Maggie was too strong and would end up managing him much more than he wanted to be managed, he turned down her offer. Thad's refusal made Maggie so angry that she not only decided to run against Thad, but she also enlisted Noah, the smartest kid in the class, as her manager. With Noah's expert guidance Maggie's campaign went rather well, despite attempts at sabotage by a spy for Thad. But as election day drew closer, both Thad and Maggie lost track of the campaign issues and concentrated only on beating each other. Consequently the pre-election debate turned into a disastrous shouting match. The next day Noah was elected class president by write-in votes.

Not very subtle, but funny. A satisfying sequel for those who enjoyed *Getting Something on Maggie Marmelstein*.

Interest Level: 3-6. Reading Level: 3.1. Further Search Topics: Humorous Fiction, Politics-Fiction, School Stories, Friendship-Fiction, Sex Role-Fiction.

Simon, Seymour. The paper airplane book; illus by Byron Barton. Viking Pr 1971, 48 pp.

For the theory as well as the practice behind successful paper airplanes, this is the book. This is as much a book about the principles of flight as it is about how to make a paper airplane. The reader is introduced to thrust, drag, lift and gravity through explanation, examples, diagrams and experiments. The effects of vertical and horizontal stabilizers, elevators, rudders, flaps, and ailerons on both paper and real airplanes, is explained and illustrated. Instructions are given for building and modifying a basic plane as each new idea is introduced. The book ends with plans for four more sophisticated planes and encouragement to try further experiments. An excellent resource for the enthusiast. Print is small.

Interest Level: 3-6. Reading Level: 3.2. Further Search Topics: Airplanes, Handicrafts, Flight.

Simon, Seymour. Einstein Anderson makes up for lost time; illus by Fred Winkowski. Viking Pr 1981, 73 pp.

Adam (nicknamed Einstein) Anderson loves science. He also loves bad puns and correcting wrongs. What he does best, however, is to figure out science puzzles. Each book in this series (this is the third) presents 10 science puzzles which challenge Einstein and the reader. Clues and background are established in several pages of scene setting. Einstein regularly solves the puzzle and then the reader is asked how he did it. The answer follows on the next page. Areas of science that are drawn upon vary widely and range from animal behavior through chemistry and space science to zoology. Very palatable science reading. Print is on the small side in all four books.

Interest Level: 3-6. Reading Level: 2.2. Further Search Topics: Science, Puzzles, Mystery and Detective Stories.

Simon, Seymour. Einstein Anderson, science sleuth; illus by Fred Winkowski. Viking Pr 1980, 73 pp.

Einstein Anderson is the scientific equivalent of Encyclopedia Brown. Einstein was the nickname that Adam Anderson earned at the age of six. Even at that early age he was a scientific genius. He seems to especially love solving scientific puzzles and mysteries and that is just what Einstein does throughout this and the other books. There are ten very brief, somewhat plotless cases that are presented to Einstein. The clues are all included in each story. The solutions are supplied at the end of each case after the reader has had a chance to try to figure out the answers. None of the cases or solutions are terribly technical. Some of the cases can be solved simply by paying careful attention to the text. The rest require a moderate knowledge of scientific principles. It is a satisfying series to the science sleuth. Print is somewhat small.

Interest Level: 3-6. Reading Level: 3.1. Further Search Topics: Mystery and Detective Stories, Science, Puzzles.

Simon, Seymour. Einstein Anderson shocks his friends; illus by Fred Winkowski. Viking Pr 1980, 73 pp.

Using the identical formula as that in *Einstein Anderson, Science Sleuth* the author presents 10 more science puzzles to be solved by the reader. Einstein (nee Adam) outwits a bully, discovers who broke the window on the school bus, helps the sixth grade win contests against both the seventh and the eighth grades and more. This book, as well as the others in the series, is both fun and instructive.

Interest Level: 3-6. Reading Level: 3.1. Further Search Topics: Science, Puzzles, Mystery and Detective Stories.

Simon, Seymour. Einstein Anderson tells a comet's tale; illus by Fred Winkowski. Viking Pr 1981, 73 pp.

Adam earned his nickname Einstein by proving over and over again that he could solve any science puzzle put to him. Ten more challenges are presented here, none of which prove to be too much for our scientific whiz kid. Like its predecessors, this book is for science sleuths who enjoy matching wits with a cocky punster.

Interest Level: 3-6. Reading Level: 3.1. Further Search Topics: Science, Puzzles, Mystery and Detective Stories.

Warner, Gertrude Chandler. The lighthouse mystery; illus by David Cunningham. A. Whitman 1963, 128 pp.

What better place for a mystery than a lighthouse late at night? Add the excitement of a storm at sea and a young man alone in a boat and the story should be unbeatable. Unfortunately this, as well as some of the other books in the series, does not quite live up to its potential. It will not attract many new readers but it will satisfy those who crave more adventures of the Alden family. The main problem with the book is its lack of definition. It isn't quite a mystery or an adventure story, it's a little of both. It is also part homespun family story, part science lesson, and part "problem story."

The Aldens rented a lighthouse in a very small fishing village one summer. Late each night their dog awoke them as he barked at a stranger who walked into or away from a closed-up building nearby. When the children investigated, they found that the surly son of a local fisherman was using the building to experiment on plankton as a food source. Harry was a brilliant young man who wanted to go to college, but whose father stubbornly refused to let him study. One night when Larry was at sea gathering samples, a terrible storm blew up. Only the Coast Guard and an improvised light in the lighthouse saved Larry from drowning. Larry's brush with death forced his father to acknowledge Larry's abilities and allow him to continue studying at college.

The sketchy illustrations in this and the following books in the series are an improvement over the silhouettes of *The Boxcar Children*. See the annotation for *The Boxcar Children* for further series information.

Interest Level: 3-6. Reading Level: 2.1. Further Search Topics: Mystery and Detective Stories, Lighthouses-Fiction, Food-Fiction, Disasters-Fiction, Vacation-Fiction.

Warner, Gertrude Chandler. Mountain top mystery; illus by David Cunningham. A. Whitman 1964, 128 pp.

A day's climb up and down Old Flat Top was all the Alden family had wanted. Instead, when a portion of the trail collapsed into a cave, they found themselves stranded on top of the mountain. From their vantage point that night they could see a shadowy light which they investigated the next day. They found a 90-year-old Indian woman who had a strange story to tell of treasure hidden in a cave somewhere on Old Flat Top. The treasure was rightfully hers as the last of her tribe, but she had never been able to find it. The collapse of the trail and the reopening of the cave attracted more attention than just the Alden's though. Both an expert on caves and a young Indian boy wanted to find out more about the cave. David, the Indian boy, turned out to be the old woman's grandnephew. The treasure was indeed unearthed; David and Lovan were reunited; the treasure was given to Lovan, and both David's and Lovan's futures were secured.

What in the other books is mild stereotyping becomes more noticeable here (the books are all around 20 years old). The print is smaller here than before but the spacing between the lines is adequate. See entry for *The Boxcar Children* for more information.

Interest Level: 3-6. Reading Level: 2.2. Further Search Topics: Mystery and Detective Stories, Treasure-Fiction, Survival-Fiction, Indians of North America-Fiction, Mountain Climbing-Fiction, Brothers and Sisters-Fiction.

Yolen, Jane. The boy who spoke chimp illus by David Wiesner. Knopf 1981, 120 pp.

Kriss was determined to prove to his father that, at 12 years old, he was perfectly capable of camping out by himself. To do so, he left home and headed up the coast of California with a sleeping bag, some food, a map and compass, and water. His plan was to camp, ride, and hike his way to his grandmother's house. On the way, the coast line was torn apart by the second great earthquake to strike California. The first had already destroyed great portions of the state. The second was even stronger. The truck he had been riding in was destroyed and everyone around Kriss was killed by the quake except for two chimpanzees. The chimps, in transit from one lab to another, were research animals who had been taught to use sign language. Kriss took the animals with him as he tried to get farther inland and finally home to Los Angeles. His trip not only confirmed his father's fears about Kriss' inadequacies but taught him how to overcome them. Kriss learned to communicate with the chimps,

to find food and to live on his own until Old Chris, a hermit, happened along. Together they continued to brave the chaos brought about by the earthquake even when Old Chris' heart troubled him. When a helicopter finally spotted them, Kriss decided to let the chimps go wild and promised Old Chris that he would be back in the woods very soon. It was a mature, capable Kriss who returned home.

This is typical of the Capers series—much action, few background details, little characterization. The books, however, are on appealing topics; they move quickly and they create intriguing (if sometimes implausible) situations. They are light, enjoyable and very useful. Capers series.

Interest Level: 3-6. Reading Level: 3.1. Further Search Topics: California-Fiction, Disasters-Fiction, Survival-Fiction, Apes-Fiction, Nonverbal Communication-Fiction, Camping-Fiction, Runaways-Fiction, Best Sellers.

Zim, Herbert S. Hoists, cranes and derricks; illus by Gary Ruse. Morrow 1969, 64 pp.

This is a very thorough treatment of lifting machinery. It is a straight-forward explanation that is technical, but not so technical that it can't be understood by young enthusiasts. The text is well-supplemented by a good number of clear illustrations and diagrams including drawings of the attachments to mobile cranes, motions used by signalmen, kinds of quay cranes, types of derricks, and even charts of the capacities of cranes and derricks and load-bearing materials. A fair index helps to make the book useful for reference or report writing.

Interest Level: 3-6. Reading Level: 3.2. Further Search Topics: Construction.

INTEREST LEVEL 4-6

Allen, Linda. Lionel and the spy next door; illus by Margot Apple. Morrow 1980, 94 pp.

No one in Lionel's family understood why he wanted to be a spy; but then, he couldn't understand why they were anthropologists and motorcycle freaks. Even though he wasn't supposed to do any more spying (especially while his parents were away) Lionel couldn't resist watching the man who moved into Miss Bannister's house, next-door. Mark Shakespeare was his name. His name was suspicious enough, but his actions firmly convinced Lionel that Mark was a spy. Lionel's attempts to trail Shakespeare only succeeded in angering others in the neighborhood. He interrupted a bird watcher and irritated a woman walking a large dog. She was already angry with Lionel's grandfather for disturbing the quiet neighborhood with his motorcycles. The closer Lionel got to finding proof that Mark was a spy, the friendlier Mark became. Mark even gave Lionel the old clock which Lionel and Miss Bannister had carefully wound each week until the old woman's death. When Lionel's grandfather finally convinced Lionel that Mark should be left alone, Mark enlisted Lionel's help in a project that left Lionel wondering again. Much to Lionel's surprise, he learned that the papers and secret documents he and Mark had burned had all belonged to Miss Bannister, Mark's great-aunt. Forty years earlier she, not Mark, had been a spy. Lionel had been wrong about who it was, but right about a spy living next-door.

Here we find a slightly anti-climactic ending to an otherwise enjoyable book. A grandfather who rides with motorcycle gangs and the intrigue of spying should be of interest to many readers. Readers may need a little help with the few British phrases that dot the book, but otherwise, the book has an impressively consistent reading level.

Interest Level: 4-6. Reading Level: 3.1. Further Search Topics: Spies-Fiction, Family-Fiction, Mystery and Detective Stories, Individualists-Fiction, Motorcycles-Fiction, Occupations-Fiction.

Anderson, C. S. The blind Connemara. Macmillan 1971, 80 pp.

Rhonda, not wealthy enough to own a horse of her own, was given a beautiful Connemara pony. Unfortunately, it had begun to go blind. A blind pony is usually put away, but Rhonda loved this pony too much to let that happen. Against all odds, Rhonda not only taught Pony to trot, canter, and even jump with confidence, but went on to win a ribbon at an important horse show. Though sentimental and predictable, this book is an almost insured success with lovers of horses and champions of the underdog. Be alert to the occasional descriptive passage that is both longer and more difficult than the rest of the text.

Interest Level: 4-6. Reading Level: 3.2. Further Search Topics: Vision-Fiction, Physically Handicapped-Fiction, Horses-Fiction.

Angell, Judie. Dear Lola; or how to build your own family. Bradbury 1980, 166 pp.

Arthur (age 18), James (13), Annie and Al-Willie (twins, age 10), Edmund (9), and Ben (5) wanted to run away from the orphanage and find a place where they could be a real family. After waiting months, their chance arrived one night. They escaped in a van and began living on the road. It was weeks before they found a house in which they thought they could live. They didn't want trouble with local authorities, so most of the children enrolled in school and pretended to be living with their widowed grandfather. Only James (who never left his room) and Arthur stayed home. Arthur was the anonymous author of a nationally syndicated newspaper advice column. It was with the income from his "Dear Lola" column that Arthur was able to support the "family." When the townspeople eventually began to wonder about the "strange" behavior of the children, they investigated and found no adult in charge of the household. Arthur went to court to be appointed the childrens' guardian, but the judge ruled against him. Rather than be sent to foster homes again, Arthur and the children raced from the courtroom. The book ends as the family is once more together and on their own. An unusual cast of characters in a surprisingly warm and humorous book.

Interest Level: 4-6. Reading Level 3.1. Further Search Topics: Loners-Fiction, Runaways-Fiction, Orphans-Fiction, Survival-Fiction, Family Problems-Fiction, Family-Fiction, Read Aloud, Foster Homes-Fiction, Individualists-Fiction, Humorous Fiction.

Bendick, Jeanne. The first book of airplanes. Watts 1975, revised edition, 65 pp.

It will take a determined reader to get much technical information from this overview of airplanes. The first sections (thrust, lift gravity, drag, and parts of a plane) promise simple, understandable explanations of complicated topics. The next portion of the book fails to live up to that promise. The descriptions of airplane engines will be intelligible only to the reader who already knows how an engine works. The history of flight is little more than an outline. The two-page chapter on air maps and distances will do more to confuse than instruct most readers. On the other hand, the information about airports, control towers, and types and uses of aircrafts is better. The book is well-indexed and includes a four-page glossary. It is perhaps best used as a general introduction to airplanes (skip the three areas mentioned above). For technical information about flight, look elsewhere. Print size is adequate but spacing between lines could have been more generous.

Interest Level: 4-6. Reading Level: 3.2. Further Search Topics: Airports, Engines, Flight, Airplanes.

Blume, Judy. Are you there God? It's me, Margaret. Bradbury 1970, 149 pp.

Sixth grade was a year of growth for Margaret and her friends. They all wondered when they would start growing breasts and when they would begin menstruating. Each was kissed for the first time. It was also a year in which Margaret tried to decide whether to be Jewish or Christian and ended up neither. She simply remained friends with God, just as she was when the year began. The book is a reassuring, very open, and humorous treatment of the pains and promise of maturation. It is exceptionally popular with older elementary school readers, so the book's slightly small print and narrow lines should not impede an interested reader's progress.

Interest Level: 4-6. Reading Level: 3.2. Further Search Topics: School Stories, Family-Fiction, Children-Growth-Fiction, Religion-Fiction, Humorous Fiction, Love-Fiction, Best Sellers, Grandparents-Fiction, Everyday Stories.

Blume, Judy. Blubber. Bradbury 1974, 153 pp.

Jill, like all the other fifth graders in her class, did exactly as Wendy directed her. When Wendy nicknamed one of the class members Blubber and launched a campaign against her, Jill joined right in. It wasn't until the tables were turned and Jill became Wendy's next victim that Jill realized how much it hurt to be the target of such nastiness. It was only then that Jill could stand up to Wendy. Wendy's meanness is extreme and her classmates, without exception, actively follow her lead, yet all adult characters in the book are blind to what happens. Despite those drawbacks, the book deals with a problem very real to children and thus it has guaranteed audience appeal.

Interest Level: 4-6. Reading Level: 3.1. School Stories, Bullies-Fiction, Weight-Fiction, Loners-Fiction, Gangs-Fiction, Read Aloud, Cruelty-Fiction, Best Sellers, Troublemakers-Fiction, Friendship-Fiction.

Blume, Judy. It's not the end of the world. Bradbury 1972, 169 pp.

This is a one theme book (as are many of Judy Blume's titles). It is the story of 11-year-old Karen's attempt to prevent her parents' divorce and then to accept it. In this first-person story she tells of her disappointment, anger, fear, and lack of understanding. She describes her parents' fights and her brother's and sister's reactions, too. It is a book with an obvious and mostly reassuring message to its readers, but it is not just for readers whose families may be in similar situations. It is also a book that will be enjoyed by any Judy Blume enthusiast.

Interest Level: 4-6. Reading Level: 3.1. Further Search Topics: Divorce and Separation-Fiction, Family Problems-Fiction, Everyday Stories.

Bulla, Clyde Robert. White bird; illus by Leonard Weisgard. T Y Crowell 1966, 79 pp.

This book is meant for a special reader. It will not appeal to the reader who wants only action and excitement from a book. It is a story of complex human relationships and differing definitions of love. John Thomas lost his parents in a river accident when he was just a baby. His cradle had been pulled from the river and he had been raised by reclusive Luke Vail. Luke placed no trust in the world or in people outside his tiny valley home and so forbade John Thomas to have anything to do with either one. Luke didn't allow John Thomas a pet either because he thought that John Thomas would only be hurt when he no longer had the animal. Despite Luke's argument, when he found an injured white crow, John Thomas kept it and tended it until the crow was stolen by three strangers as Luke stood by. Angry at Luke as much as at the strangers, John Thomas ran away to search for the bird, but found that it had been shot. Far from being fruitless, however, John Thomas's trip out of the valley gave him an entirely different view of people than the one Luke had shown him. Upon a friend's encouragement, John Thomas returned to Luke to share that view.

Subtle and unusual, this book needs a mature, sensitive reader and/or discussion in order to be fully appreciated.

Interest Level: 4-6. Reading Level 2.1. Further Search Topics: Pets-Fiction, Orphans-Fiction, Runaways-Fiction, Birds-Fiction, Love-Fiction, Loners-Fiction, Courage-Fiction.

Byars, Betsy. After the goat man; illus by Ronald Himler. Viking Pr. 1974, 126 pp.

Harold was fat and over-sensitive. Ada was serious and independent. Figgy was lonely, poor and in need of help. Figgy and his grandfather, the Goat Man, had been forced to move from their cabin to make room for a highway. The Goat Man had returned to the cabin with a shotgun, vowing to defend his right to live there. Figgy knew he had to persuade his grandfather to leave or someone would be hurt. But, in the children's hurry to reach the Goat Man, it was Figgy who was hurt and Harold who rescued both Figgy and the Goat Man. Harold grew up that day. He stopped dreaming about the way he wanted things to be and faced life realistically for the first time.

The book is very much a character study. Realistic characters are treated with sympathy and dignity and given a chance to grow. Introspective readers will understand and enjoy the book more than those looking for adventure. Print size is fairly large, but lines are separated by only average width.

Interest Level: 4-6. Reading Level: 3.2. Further Search Topics: Loneliness-Fiction, Weight-Fiction, Moving, Household-Fiction, Courage-Fiction, Grandparents-Fiction, Orphans-Fiction.

Byars, Betsy. The 18th emergency; illus by Robert Grossman. Viking Pr. 1973, 126 pp.

When your best friend knows how to escape from the world's 17 worst emergencies and you're faced with the eighteenth, you're in trouble. That was the spot in which Mouse found himself one day. He had drawn an arrow towards a large picture of the Neanderthal man and written Marv Hammerman's name. Hammerman had seen him do it and was out to kill, maim, or at least beat up Mouse. Mouse finally ran out of ways to avoid Hammerman and had to face the fight. When it was over and he was once again able to stand up, Mouse realized he felt better for having allowed Hammerman to regain his honor and for having taken responsibility for his own actions.

A funny, fast-moving look at real feelings of fear, honor and responsibility. Very popular. Print is dark and of good size but lines could have been spaced farther apart.

Interest Level: 4-6. Reading Level: 3.2. Further Search Topics: Bullies-Fiction, Humorous Fiction, Courage-Fiction, Best Sellers, Challenges-Fiction, Read Aloud.

Clark, Margaret Goff. Barney in space; illus by Ted Lewin. Dodd 1981, 155 pp.

This is a sequel to *Barney and the UFO*, but it stands by itself quite well. It's title is a misnomer, however, for it isn't until the last third of the book that Barney goes into space. In the previous book Barney made friends with Tibbo, a Gark from the planet Ornam. In this book Tibbo tries to save Barney from an evil Gark named Rokell. Because Barney knew about Garks, Rokell was afraid Barney would betray them and turn humans against Garks. To prevent that from happening, Rokell was determined to kidnap Barney. Tibbo was too far from Earth to do more than warn Barney of Rokell's intentions and tell him not to be alone at any time. Barney's friends Dick and Kara tried to protect Barney but only succeeded in endangering their own lives. When Kara was almost killed by Rokell, Barney decided to face Rokell alone and try to defeat him, but Rokell's powers were too strong for Barney. Against their wills both Barney and David were taken aboard a spaceship. They discovered later, to their relief, that the spaceship belonged to a friend of Tibbo's who was commanding the ship from the moon. Barney and Dick were to be taken to the moon for safety until Rokell could be controlled. Rokell didn't give up easily. He attacked the ship twice before he captured it and set it down on a remote portion of the moon. Only Barney's quick thinking stopped Rokell permanently and saved both Barney and Dick.

The preliminary sequences are more suspenseful and exciting than the space travel; however, the book will not disappoint young science fiction fans.

Interest Level: 4-6. Reading Level: 4.2. Further Search Topics: Science Fiction, Flying Saucers-Fiction, Outer Space-Fiction, Orphans-Fiction, Kidnapping-Fiction, Aliens-Fiction, Adoption-Fiction.

Coerr, Eleanor. Sadako and the thousand paper cranes; illus by Ronand Himler. Putnam 1977, 64 pp.

This is a beautiful and very sad story of a young girl who was only two years old when the atomic bomb was dropped on Hiroshima. Ten years later she contracted leukemia and died a slow, painful death. A fast and enthusiastic runner, she had been full of life and energy before her illness. Soon after she became sick Sadako's best friend folded a paper crane for her and reminded her of an old story: If someone folded 1000 paper cranes, the gods would give that person good health again. Sadako was able to fold only 644 before she died. After her death her classmates made 356 more in order that she could be buried with all 1000 paper cranes. About three years later, a statue, erected in Peace Park in Hiroshima, was dedicated to Sadako and to a hope for world peace.

Because of the theme and its straight-forward handling, this book needs a fairly mature reader.

Interest Level: 4-6. Reading Level: 3.1. Further Search Topics: Japan-Fiction, Historical Fiction, World War II-Fiction, Death-Fiction, Illness-Fiction, War-Fiction, Running-Fiction, Origami-Fiction, Read Aloud.

Cohen, Barbara. Thank you, Jackie Robinson; illus by Richard Cuffari. Lothrop 1974, 125 pp.

This story is not for everyone, but for the right reader it is perfect. The book is a catalog of baseball facts, thus it is likely to appeal primarily to baseball fans. But it is not the typical story of a child overcoming a problem through practice and perserverance, as are most sports books. This is a sensitive story of a fatherless boy whose life centered around the New York Dodgers.

Sam could repeat the starting line-up and details of any game the Dodgers had played within the last three years; however, no one cared. In fact, most people were bored when Sam began reciting. Only Davey, the old, black cook at the inn where Sam and his family lived, took any interest. Davey was as much a fan as Sam. They began spending hours together talking and then watching baseball as Davey and his daughter took Sam to the games with them. It was Sam and Davey's dream to catch a fly ball and have it autograped by all the Dodgers, especially Jackie Robinson, the first black major league player. When Davey had a severe heart attack, Sam gathered all his courage to make that dream come true. He bought a baseball, took the subway to a game, and argued with the ushers until he was finally able to get Jackie Robinson's and the team's autographs. Just a few days before Davey died Sam took the baseball to the hospital and gave it to Davey. Sam's feelings about Davey's death are real and painful. He felt sorry for himself, lonely, angry, sad and confused. But a remark by his mother and one more Jackie Robinson hit helped Sam accept Davey's death.

Because the story is told as a first-person flashback set in the late 1940s, it may need a little introduction. It also alludes to racial problems and practices that young readers may not understand without explanation (i.e., why Davey had some hesitation about taking a white child with him to the ballpark or on a trip).

Interest Level: 4-6. Reading Level: 4.2. Further Search Topics: Baseball-Fiction, Blacks-Fiction, Aging-Fiction, Single Parent Family-Fiction, Friendship-Fiction, Death-Fiction, Robinson, Jackie.

Conford, Ellen. The luck of Pokey Bloom; illus by Bernice Loewenstein. Little 1975, 135 pp.

Pokey Bloom's passion was entering contests. She entered every contest she heard of and always thought she would win. Unfortunately, she never won anything. She even went so far as to practice concentrating three times each day on winning every contest she had entered. Someone who had been interviewed on the radio had *guaranteed* she would win that way. She didn't! It only made more trouble for her at school and at home. Pokey had enough trouble getting along with her older brother and didn't need any more problems at home.

There isn't much plot or direction to this story, but it does have some amusing moments. It is an extra book for the reader who enjoys Judy Blume-type books and wants another story about "regular kids."

Interest Level: 4-6. Reading Level: 3.1. Further Search Topics: Family-Fiction, Contests-Fiction, Brothers and Sisters-Fiction, Humorous Fiction, Everyday Stories.

Conford, Ellen. And this is Laura. Little 1977, 179 pp.

As a member of a family of high-achievers, Laura was convinced that she was unloved and worthless because she had no talents. Then, suddenly Laura discovered she had very special psychic powers; powers she began to exploit. At first it was fun to give readings after school each day. Gradually, however, as Laura foresaw her friend hurt and her brother missing, she realized that having ESP was also a frightening responsibility. Finally, her ESP became the

vehicle that made it possible for Laura to tell her parents her true feelings and to understand that they loved her for herself, not for her achievements.

The author treats a common concern with sensitivity and humor. An especially good choice for Judy Blume lovers. Print somewhat small.

Interest Level: 4-6. Reading Level: 4.2. Further Search Topics: Occult-Fiction, Courage-Fiction, Extra Sensory Perception-Fiction, Family-Fiction, Humorous Fiction, Everyday Stories, Talent-Fiction.

Coombs, Charles. Be a winner in baseball. Morrow 1973, 127 pp.

A solid, though chauvanistic discussion of baseball basics. After a very short summary of baseball's history, the author spends a chapter emphasizing the importance of practice and physical training. From there he goes on to cover techniques of pitching, catching, hitting, running bases, playing the infield and playing the outfield. Directions are clear and often well-illustrated. There is great emphasis placed on playing correctly to avoid injury and on out-smarting the opponent. The book concludes with a reminder that the game is, above all, meant to be fun.

Although the book's reading level tests at 5.2, the jargon that influences the tests will be familiar to most baseball fans. For enthusiasts, therefore, the reading level is probably 4.2 to 5.1. Includes glossary and index.

Interest Level: 4-6. Reading Level: 5.1. Further Search Topics: Baseball.

Giff, Patricia Reilly. Have you seen Hyacinth Macaw?; illus by Anthony Kramer. Delacorte 1981, 135 pp.

Abby Jones was trying very hard to be a detective, but it was difficult without any mysteries to solve. So to keep in practice, Abby filled a memo book with her notes about anything that seemed at all unusual. At the same time, Abby kept in touch with two local police detectives who gave her hints about detective work. Because of her police friends and her observations, Abby found herself involved in what seemed to be four or more mysteries. Who had moved into the apartment next door and what were the screams that came from there? What was the theft that the police were worried about? Who was Hyacinth Macaw and why had she disappeared? And why was Abby's older brother Dan acting so strangely? Was he involved in the theft?

Abby and her friend Potsie ended up trailing a suspect through the New York subway system, breaking into the next-door apartment, suspecting Abby's brother of the theft, capturing an unusual bird, releasing the bird into a pet shop and recapturing it, before they realized that all the mysteries were linked together. Hyacinth Macaw was a valuable bird stolen from Justine's Junktique Shop. The daughter of Abby's landland had taken the bird and placed it in the empty apartment next to Abby's, so that she could paint the bird's portrait. The picture was to be entered in Justine's Junktique contest. Dan and his friend Holly Monk had been secretly constructing a Purple Pigeon Purifier to enter in the contest. They needed the prize money to repair a window they had accidentally broken. By the time the mysteries were all sorted out, Dan and Holly had won a special prize; Kiki, the portrait painter, had not only been forgiven, but had also been awarded first prize; and Abby had received the reward for finding and returning the bird.

The action in this mystery is both abundant and humorous enough to make the book enjoyable to many readers. There are also some problems that need to be noted. Some readers may find the action too swift and the characters too numerous to be easily followed. Abby's memo notes are sometimes written without vowels and are almost always in incomplete sentences. The reader who is highly motivated or has help from another person will still be able to enjoy the story; however, for the others another choice may be more appropriate.

Interest Level: 4-6. Reading Level: 3.1. Further Search Topics: Mystery and Detective Stories, Humorous Fiction, Writing-Fiction, Detectives-Fiction, Birds-Fiction.

Greene, Constance C. Isabelle the itch; illus by Emily A. McCully. Viking Pr. 1973, 126 pp.

This is a loosely plotted story about a spunky, original fifth grade girl who could drive everyone around her crazy without ever tiring. Isabelle's dearest dream was to win the 50-yard dash at her school's field day. Even though she took over her brother's paper route to earn money for the Adidas track shoes she needed, Isabelle still didn't win. However, she did meet some new people, make new friends and keep those around her on their toes. A very amusing story told mostly in dialogue.

Interest Level: 4-6. Reading Level: 3.2. Further Search Topics: School Stories, Occupations-Fiction, Humorous Fiction, Everyday Stories, Running-Fiction, Individualists-Fiction, Sex Role-Fiction, Read Aloud.

Greene, Constance C. I and Sproggy; illus by Emily A. McCully. Viking Pr. 1978, 155 pp.

Ten-year-old Adam had adjusted to his parents' divorce and had even grown to like living alone with his mother. When his father came back from London with his new wife and stepdaughter Sproggy and announced that they were moving into an apartment nearby, Adam was a little worried. But when his father asked him to take care of Sproggy, Adam was furious. First of all, he didn't know Sproggy and he didn't want to know her. Secondly, she was two months older than he, taller too, and she embarrassed him in public. And finally, she didn't need his help. She got along quite well by herself; so well that she even saved Adam from a mugger and became good friends with Adam's friends behind his back. It wasn't until Sproggy proved to be vulnerable that Adam and she became friends.

A warm, realistic and humorous story whose interesting characters (even the minor ones) heighten the book's appeal.

Interest Level: 4-6. Reading Level: 3.2. Further Search Topics: Brothers and Sisters-Fiction, Divorce and Separation-Fiction, City Life-Fiction, New York City-Fiction, Humorous Fiction, Friendship-Fiction, Everyday Stories.

Greenwald, Sheila. Give us a great big smile, Rosy Cole. Little 1981, 76 pp.

It was Rosy's turn to be the subject of her uncle's book. He needed to earn money again and Rosy had just turned 10, the age each of her sisters had been when Uncle Ralph wrote *Anitra Dances* and *Pippa Prances* about them. However, Rosy couldn't dance like Anitra or ride horses like Pippa. In fact, Rosy had no talent that was appropriate for a book. She drew well but Uncle Ralph said that wasn't visual enough. Then Rosy's mother and uncle decided that Rosy could be *A Very Little Fiddler*.

Rosy had been taking violin lessons for two years, but only Rosy and her music teacher knew how truly untalented she was. Rosy hated the whole idea of the book at first. But as people began to treat her like a

star, she found herself acting like one, until the day she heard her tape of the piece she was to play at the recital. Once again she realized that she could not play the violin and didn't want to go on with the charade. When everyone ignored her wishes, Rosy started to run away. Her route took her through the park where she thought of a brilliant idea. She ran home, changed clothes, picked up her violin, created a sign, and raced back to the park. There, with all the other street musicians Rosy set up her sign and began to play her violin. Her sign asked people to sign a petition if they felt that she should not be encouraged to play the violin anymore. Right away Rosy drew a large crowd. Before long, even her mother was one of the listeners and one of the signers. That was the end of Rosy's musical career and her uncle's book, but both were happier. Rosy went back to being normal and Uncle Ralph found another topic for his next book.

Chapters are long, but should not be a problem. Print is large. Some of the story is actually told in the illustrations, so the reader should be aware of them. Younger children may take the book more seriously than children whose sense of humor includes irony or children who were not as fond of Krementz's *Very Young* series.

Interest Level: 4-6. Reading Level: 3.1. Further Search Topics: Occupations-Fiction, Humorous Fiction, Family-Fiction, Relatives-Fiction, Talent-Fiction, Photography-Fiction, Everyday Stories.

Heide, Florence Parry. Body in the Brillstone garage. A. Whitman 1980, 127 pp.

Liza's trip into the apartment house garage late one night made her even more frightened of that dark area than she had been. As she bent to pick up an envelope she thought someone had dropped, she saw a body lying on the floor of the garage. Because of a jacket he wore, Liza was certain the dead man was Mr. Greening, a neighbor. But when she returned to the garage with the police, the body was gone. The next day Mr. Greening was very much alive. Then Liza began to suspect that Mr. Greening was a murderer, but she didn't know who or where the victim was. It could have been Mr. Feeney, another neighbor, or it might have been a stranger. When Mr. Greening's stolen car was later discovered with the body of the car thief inside, Liza began to suspect that the thief's body was the one she had discovered. When she was told that the thief's name was Sharkey, she was certain Mr. Greening had engineered Sharkey's death. Sharkey was the name used by an angry man who had said he was looking for someone at the Brillstone who owed him something.

About then Liza remembered to look in the envelope she had found in the garage. The envelope revealed a note from Sharkey to Greening stating that Sharkey had proof that Greening was a car thief and that he would keep quiet only if Greening paid him twice the money he was owed. Knowing that without proof, she couldn't convince the police that Greening was a crook, Liza went to get the proof from Sharkey's hiding place in the about-to-be-junked car. Greening followed Liza to see what she knew and made a desperate attempt to kill her when he realized that she knew enough to put him in prison. At the last minute, Logan appeared, accidentally knocked Greening out, and helped Liza prove Greening's guilt to the police.

This is a fast-paced book that should be useful with mystery readers who can handle the jump from 4.1 to an occasional 5.1 reading level. See notes included with *Black Magic at Brillstone* for more information. Brillstone Mystery series.

Interest Level: 4-6. Reading Level: 4.2. Further Search Topics: Mystery and Detective Stories, Murder-Fiction, Running-Fiction, Crime-Fiction, Detectives-Fiction.

Heide, Florence Parry. Mystery of the forgotten island; illus by Seymour Fleishman. A. Whitman 1980, 127 pp.

On a small island, unmarked on the map, the Spotlight Club members found old Mr. Whitson, who claimed that he was being kept prisoner by his granddaughter Lorrie and her husband John. Lorrie and John had told him he was being kept in the yard for his own good, so that he wouldn't wander off and get hurt or lost. They had also told him that he should will the island to them so that his daughter Cassie couldn't sell the island to a resort company for development. He was going to be forced to sign such a will unless he could get the children to help him smuggle a new will to his lawyer. Mr. Whitson wasn't convinced that Cassie wanted to sell the island, but he couldn't get in touch with her and he hadn'd had a letter from her in many months.

As the children went to secretly meet Mr. Whitson and mail his new will, they discovered that their trusted friend Guy was attempting to blackmail Lorrie and John into giving him some of the money from the sale of the island. He had evidence that Lorrie and John, not Cassie, wanted to sell the island and were tricking Mr. Whitson into signing a will in their favor. In a daring move, the children were able to free Mr. Whitson and isolate all three of the thieves so that the police could capture them.

This book involves a somewhat more complicated plot and slightly less familiar ingredients than most other Spotlight Club mysteries. One should progress to rather than begin the series with this title. Spotlight Club Mystery series.

Interest Level: 4-6. Reading Level: 3.1. Further Search Topics: Mystery and Detective Stories, Inheritance-Fiction, Gangs-Fiction, Kidnapping-Fiction, Brothers and Sisters-Fiction, Aging-Fiction, Detectives-Fiction.

Heide, Florence Parry. Face at the Brillstone window. A. Whitman 1979, 128 pp.

As Liza drove out of the garage one evening she heard a thump at the side of the car. She jumped out and found that she had accidentally hit Peter Pritchard, an insurance man and a new tenant of the apartment building. Pritchard seemed to be a very nice person who took some interest in Liza, her friends, and the criminal cases Liza's father (a journalist) was investigating. Liza was particularly interested in the case of the one-armed bandit who had been convicted of robbing and shooting a security guard. Against her father's research assistant's wishes she continued to search for evidence that would prove Robin Keck was innocent of the charges. As she interviewed the security guard, Keck's fiancee, his best friend, and the grandmother of a young girl who had had a strong crush on Keck, Liza found hints of his innocence. Young Bridgette's diary, however, held the proof she needed: an alibi. But someone else knew she had the information; someone who didn't want the information made public. Diary in hand, Liza began walking to her father's assistant's house (her father was out of town) when Pritchard offered her a ride. When Pritchard drove off in the wrong direction and then handed her a piece of incriminating evidence (gum), Liza realized she had played right into the real criminal's hands. Liza made a risky escape attempt that ended successfully with Pritchard's capture.

See *Black Magic at Brillstone* for more information about the series. Brillstone Mystery series.

Interest Level: 4-6. Reading Level: 3.2. Further Search Topics: Mystery and Detective Stories, Crime-Fiction, Detectives-Fiction.

Holland, John. The way it is. HarBraceJ 1969, 87 pp.

For 15 boys living in a run-down area of Brooklyn, school became interesting when they were assigned to photograph whatever was meaningful to them in their neighborhood. The results, described in their own words, were developed into this fascinating documentary which is at the same time a spontaneous glimpse of the boys themselves. The book should be of particular interest to older urban children. Print slightly on the small side. Has recently gone out of print, but is worth looking for.

Interest Level: 4-6. Reading Level: 3.2. Further Search Topics: Best Sellers, City Life, Photography, Poverty, Academic Problems.

Hurwitz, Johanna. The law of gravity; illus by Ingrid Fetz. Morrow 1978, 192 pp.

The summer between fifth and sixth grades looked very unexciting to Margot. Her best friends were both going away for the whole summer and her father, a musician, was going to be on tour for most of the summer. Margot's very overweight mother had sworn never to go downstairs from their fifth floor walk-up apartment. Unless Margot chose to stay upstairs too, she was sure she would have a very lonely vacation. In addition, she had to work on a summer project for school. The project she finally chose was to get her mother downstairs after nine years of staying upstairs. In search of help she went to the local library where she met Bernie. Bernie was only a year older than Margot, but he seemed to know the most interesting things about the city. He showed her places Margot had never heard of before, he taught her to play chess, backgammon, and even to ride a bicycle. He was so full of fascinating ideas and information that Margot had no chance to be bored or lonely. Best of all, he even tried to help Margot with her project. None of their ideas worked, however, until Margot pretended to run away and scared her mother into going downstairs. Only then did Margot realize that she loved her mother whether or not she stayed on the fifth floor and that she couldn't simply force her mother or anyone else to change to suit her own fancy.

The book is a warm, understanding, slightly humorous treatment of the fairly common wish to change someone else. Although not many readers are likely to share Margot's exact problem, most will recognize her feelings. The book is also a virtual Chamber of Commerce advertisement for urban living. One of its other charms is its picture of a non-competitive, open, real friendship between an 11-year-old girl and a 12-year-old boy. The only drawback to the book is its inconsistent reading level which varies from 4.1 to 5.1 with a rare leap to 5.2.

Interest Level: 4-6. Reading Level: 4.2. Further Search Topics: Vacation-Fiction, Friendship-Fiction, Loners-Fiction, City Life-Fiction, Individualists-Fiction, Courage-Fiction, New York City-Fiction, Humorous Fiction, Family-Fiction, Challenges-Fiction, Weight-Fiction, Everyday Stories, Best Sellers.

Kelley, Sally. Trouble with explosives. Bradbury 1976, 117 pp.

Polly Banks stuttered very badly. She wanted to stop but she couldn't. Moving, entering a new school, and facing a mean teacher who seemed in need of psychiatric help, all made Polly's stuttering worse. When Sis, Polly's new friend, rose to Polly's defense in one confrontation too many with Miss Patterson, the teacher took cruel revenge. Polly's desire to help Sis, her need to do something about her stuttering, and an understanding psychiatrist, all helped Polly learn to help herself with her speech problem. At the same time, she began to understand and have confidence in herself and her family.

Another "problem book" that older elementary school readers seem to crave. Polly and Sis are both very sympathetic characters who bring to life many of the uncertainties of growing up. Print and line spacing of only average size but otherwise a good choice.

Interest Level: 4-6. Reading Level: 3.2. Further Search Topics: Academic Problems-Fiction, Stuttering-Fiction, Psychiatrists-Fiction, School Stories, Mental Illness-Fiction, Troublemakers-Fiction, Courage-Fiction, Physically Handicapped-Fiction, Children-Growth-Fiction, Moving, Household-Fiction.

Kibbe, Pat. The hocus-pocus dilemma; illus by Dan Jones. Knopf 1979, 125 pp.

Each chapter of this book is a separate episode in B.J.'s attempt to cultivate her newly-discovered ESP talents (more invented than discovered). The episodes, each of which involves a different member of B.J.'s family, are slightly outlandish, but very funny. Even the dog and the cat become involved. The dog becomes the unwitting target for a skunk. The cat accidentally starts a tape recording of speech habits that sounds like burglars breaking into the house. After nine disasters, B.J. finally concludes that she was being ridiculous to think that she had ESP, but that everyone is allowed to be ridiculous sometimes.

The nine, reasonably short episodes, the moderate size print, the sympathetic characters, and the book's humor, make this a very useful and popular title.

Interest Level: 4-6. Reading Level: 3.1. Further Search Topics: Extra Sensory Perception-Fiction, Humorous Fiction, Family-Fiction, Everyday Stories, Best Sellers, Read Aloud.

Lowry, Lois. Anastasia Krupnik. HM 1979, 113 pp.

Anastasia Krupnik led a comfortable, relatively happy life until her parents announced that she was not going to be an only child for much longer. After 10 years of enjoying that luxury, Anastasia wasn't at all pleased with the change. Babies immediately went to a prominent, and as far as Anastasia was concerned, permanent place on her list of hates. Anastasia kept two lists: one for things and people she particularly liked, and one list for what she did not like. What went on and off the lists tells much about Anastasia. Anastasia tells the rest in this perceptive, sensitive, and humorous story of growing up and adjusting to a new sibling.

Spacing between lines is slightly too narrow for the rather large print.

Interest Level: 4-6. Reading Level: 3.1. Further Search Topics: Humorous Fiction, Brothers and Sisters-Fiction, Everyday Stories, Jealousy-Fiction, Infants-Fiction, Best Sellers, Children-Growth-Fiction.

Lowry, Lois. Anastasia again! HM 1981, 145 pp.

This is a sequel that is as funny and well-written as its predecessor. Because its plot involves less common experiences, this book may not enjoy quite the wide-spread success of *Anastasia Krupnik*. However, among those readers who liked their first meeting with Anastasia, this book will find many fans.

Anastasia's parents astounded her when they announced that the family was going to move from their Cambridge, Massachusetts apartment to a house in the suburbs. She didn't like the idea of leaving the apartment, but she *hated* the idea of the suburbs. The only thing that made the move bearable was the house itself. Anastasia had said she would move only if they could find a house with a tower—and they had. After she got over the shock of moving, Anastasia began to enjoy her new home. She met a neighborhood boy who became a special friend, she tried to help her cranky elderly neighbor Mrs. Stein make friends, and she even wrote a short mystery book.

Anastasia is as spunky and original as before. She is a bit precocious, but her precocity is nothing compared to that of her brother. At two-and-a-half years old, he speaks as well as many adults. As we mentioned above, the book will be most appealing to readers who want second helpings of Anastasia's adventures. The print is slightly smaller here than in the first title.

Interest Level: 4-6. Reading Level: 2.2. Further Search Topics: Moving, Household-Fiction, City Life-Fiction, Suburbia-Fiction, Humorous Fiction, Aging-Fiction, Writing-Fiction, Family-Fiction, Everyday Stories.

MacLachlan, Patricia. Arthur, for the very first time; illus by Lloyd Bloom. Har-Row 1980, 117 pp.

A beautifully written, sensitive yet humorous story of a boy's maturation and growing awareness of the world around him. When Arthur's unhappiness at home is made more intense by the advent of a new baby, he is sent to spend the summer with his older aunt and uncle. Their eccentricities and those of their friends are at first only material for Arthur to write about in his journal. But as the summer progresses he not only learns from them, but also grows from an observer of life to a participant. His final step is helping a large and beloved pig bear her litter in a driving rain storm aided only by his independent, totally untamed young friend Moira.

The print is somewhat small, but spacing between lines is generous.

Interest Level: 4-6. Reading Level: 4.2. Further Search Topics: Read Aloud, Children-Growth-Fiction, Humorous Fiction, Friendship-Fiction, Vacation-Fiction, Relatives-Fiction, Infants-Fiction, Individualists-Fiction, Writing-Fiction, Loners-Fiction, Group 2.

Park, Barbara. Don't make me smile. Knopf 1981, 114 pp.

As far as Charlie Hickle was concerned his parents' divorce was the worst thing in the world. His parents had ruined his life and he hadn't done anything to deserve such a fate. At first he didn't say very much. Then he ran away to live in a tree. Finally he cried a lot. That was all just in the first week after his parents announced their decision. After that, both his grades at school and his behavior began to deteriorate. It wasn't until Charlie had had several talks with a helpful children's psychologist and made a disastrous attempt to reunite his parents on his birthday, that he began to realize that he didn't like the divorce, but he could live with it.

The author's use of amusing anecdotes, Charlie's very strong feelings, and the frequency of divorce make this book very popular. Its major drawbacks are its superficiality and the overdrawn portrait of Charlie's mother. The book's faults will not deter many young readers from enjoying it, however.

Interest Level: 4-6. Reading Level: 3.1. Further Search Topics: Divorce and Separation-Fiction, Family Problems-Fiction, Psychiatrists-Fiction, Everyday Stories.

Peck, Robert Newton. Mr. Little; illus by Ben Stahl. Doubleday 1979, 87 pp.

All summer long Drag and Finley had looked forward to having Miss Kellogg as their teacher, so they were extremely disappointed to find ordinary-looking Mr. Little in her place on the first day of school. Used to playing tricks on their teachers anyway, Drag and Finley decided to go all out to get even with Mr. Little for spoiling their year. But try as they might, they couldn't get an advantage over Mr. Little; he seemed to be unflappable. Finally, in their riskiest prank ever, they stole Mr. Little's underwear to dress a statue in the town square. That attempt to embarrass Mr. Little only served to get Finley and Drag in serious trouble from which Mr. Little saved them. It was his later rescue of Miss Kellogg, however, that added respect to the boys' growing feeling of friendship for Mr. Little.

Because the author's adult viewpoint is never quite lost, even though he writes in the first person, and because the rural and historic time settings are not familiar to many readers, the book may need some introduction and encouragement. It is a prime candidate for reading aloud until the young reader's interest takes over. Print is of adequate size, but spacing between lines could have been more generous.

Interest Level: 4-6. Reading Level: 5.1. Further Search Topics: Humorous Fiction, School Stories, Troublemakers-Fiction, Group 2, Read Aloud, Country Life-Fiction, Best Sellers.

Pfeffer, Susan Beth. Just between us; illus by Lorna Tomei. Delacorte 1980, 116 pp.

Cass's inability to keep secrets finally became such a problem that Cass asked her mother to help her learn how to keep them. Cass's mother, a psychology student, devised a behavior modification experiment. Every day that Cass was able to figure out which bit of information she had been told was a secret and keep it, she received a dollar. After a poor start Cass did well for a while, until the day she told three secrets and made her entire family angry at her.

More determined than ever, Cass tried again. This time she found herself caught between two friends. Only Cass knew that Robin was adopted and Robin wanted it kept a secret. Jenny was so mad at Robin that she decided to spread an untrue story to hurt Robin. She told Cass not to tell anyone what she was going to do. The story Jenny was going to spread was that Robin was adopted. After hours of mental anguish Cass finally devised a way to stop Jenny and help Jenny return to being the nice person she had been before her parents' divorce.

The reading level of this book varies greatly from second grade to mid-fourth grade. Otherwise, it is good fare for Judy Blume fans. Print size just a slight bit on the small side.

Interest Level: 4-6. Reading Level: 3.2. Further Search Topics: Humorous Fiction, Everyday Stories, Friendship-Fiction, School Stories, Divorce and Separation-Fiction, Psychiatrists-Fiction, Secrets-Fiction.

Pfeffer, Susan Beth. Kid power; illus by Leigh Grant. Watts 1977, 121 pp.

When Janie's mother lost her job, her father's salary wouldn't stretch to provide any more money for the new bicycle fund. There was enough money already set aside to pay for one new bike, but both Janie and her older sister Carol wanted a bicycle. Carol, who had saved money of her own, suggested that they each pay for half a bike and their parents contribute the money for the other half. Then Janie's only problem was how to earn money, since she had none saved. Her solution was to create a business: Kid Power. Before long, Janie's business had blossomed and she was becoming rich, but she had lost her best friend and was ruining a client's roses. When Janie finally realized that getting rich wasn't the only thing that mattered in life, she relaxed, delegated jobs to friends better able to handle them, and became their agent.

A genuinely funny book that, as a bonus, takes a realistic look at the interworkings of a family. Consistent reading level.

Interest Level: 4-6. Reading Level: 3.1. Further Search Topics: Occupations-Fiction, Everyday Stories, Vacation-Fiction, Family-Fiction, Humorous Fiction, Best Sellers, Bicycles and Bicycling-Fiction, Friendship-Fiction.

Renner, Beverly. The Hideaway summer; illus by Ruth Sanderson. Har-Row 1978, 134 pp.

On their way to summer camp, Addie suddenly got off the bus and took her younger brother Clay to see the place where Addie had spent prior summer vacations. It was their grandmother's house and a small cabin called the Hideaway. The house had been sold after their grandmother had died that year, but Addie's father had decided to keep the Hideaway. Much to Addie's surprise she found the Hideaway beautifully fixed-up, just as Gram had promised she would do one day.

When they missed the last bus out of the tiny town and realized that they had enough money to buy the food they would need, Addie and Clay decided to make the Hideaway their summer home. One phone call to the camp and weekly calls to their father kept people from worrying about them. Their discovery of two small raccoons meant that their days were filled with caring for and training the animals. In addition, they had to build a warning system so that no one would discover them and they had to get their food and provisions from town about every two weeks without being too noticeable. They even had to figure out a way to survive a wild summer storm, a flood, and poachers who hunted raccoons. By summer's end Addie and Clay had grown independent, resourceful, and very close to each other.

An exciting story whose short chapters and fairly short sentences keep the reading level reasonably low. Print is dark and of adequate size, but space between the lines is somewhat narrow.

Interest Level: 4-6. Reading Level: 3.1. Further Search Topics: Brothers and Sisters-Fiction, Runaways-Fiction, Pets-Fiction, Survival-Fiction, Vacation-Fiction, Raccoons-Fiction, Read Aloud.

St. John, Wylly Folk. The ghost next door; illus by Trina Schart Hyman. Har-Row 1971, 178 pp.

Told by 13-year-old Lindsay, this is the story of her neighbor Miss Judith and Miss Judith's two nieces. Her niece Miranda had drowned years earlier in Miss Judith's backyard fish pond and Miss Judith had never fully recovered from her death. As the story begins, Miss Judith is about to welcome another niece

(Sherry) for a summer stay. Sherry, without ever being told about Miranda, seems to sense Miranda's presence all around. Her mother laughs and says that Sherry has an imaginary friend. Miss Judith, who is a strong believer in ESP, thinks that Sherry is communicating with Miranda. As the days go on Sherry learns more and more of Miranda' secrets. When Miss Judith is scared by Sherry, Lindsay and her friend, Tammy, decide to see what sort of tricks Sherry is playing.

A believable suspense story, made even more so by the illustrations.

Interest Level: 4-6. Reading Level: 5.1. Further Search Topics: Mystery and Detective Stories, Relatives-Fiction, Group 2, Extra Sensory Perception-Fiction, Best Sellers, Ghosts-Fiction.

Sharmat, Marjorie W. The Lancelot closes at five; illus by Lisl Weil. Macmillan 1976, 120 pp.

Despite a somewhat slow beginning, this is an amusing, almost sensitive story of two friends who decided to spend the night in the model home of the new housing development in which they both lived. Hutch, a health food fanatic whose mother pronounced judgment on everything Hutch did, conceived of the idea as her way of breaking away. Abby went along for the fun of it. When the local newspaper wrote of unusual vandalism at the model home, the townspeople became engrossed in finding the culprits. As the adults became enraged about the crime wave, their children began to admire the clever idea. Soon, almost every youngster in town had confessed to spending the night in the model home. By the time Abby and Hutch got around to admitting they had slept there, no one believed them. Only a sock with Abby's name in it could tie Abby and Hutch to the scene of the crime. As the book ends, the police have begun a thorough search of the house, after a real robbery, and the sock's discovery is imminent.

Interest Level: 4-6. Reading Level: 3.2. Further Search Topics: Humorous Fiction, Suburbia-Fiction, Runaways-Fiction, Crime-Fiction, Individualists-Fiction, Family Problems-Fiction.

Shura, Mary Francis. The Barkley Street six-pack: illus by Gene Sparkman. Dodd 1979, 159 pp.

Jane's best friend Natalie was everything Jane wanted to be. She was self-assured, pretty, vibrant, and even possessed magical talents. Jane didn't realize at first, and she later resisted seeing, that Natalie ran Jane's life and cleverly made sure that Jane had no other friends. Natalie's move left Jane with no friends among those people she had once enjoyed. Little by little, with the help of a stray dog and the new boy on the block, Jane bagan to see how destructive Natalie had been. She finally realized that a true friendship is one in which neither party tries to control the other.

With its enticements of ESP, magic, stray dogs, and problems with peers, this is a very appealing book to many young readers. As a bonus it is a thoughtful, sympathetic, fairly well-written story.

Interest Level: 4-6. Reading Level: 4.2. Further Search Topics: Gangs-Fiction, Pets-Fiction, Dogs-Fiction, Friendship-Fiction, Honesty-Fiction, Courage-Fiction, Loneliness-Fiction, Extra Sensory Perception-Fiction, Everyday Stories.

Singer, Marilyn. It can't hurt forever; illus by Leigh Grant. Har-Row 1978, 186 pp.

When she was 11 years old, it was discovered that Ellie had a heart valve that hadn't closed by itself.

Although her mother had promised her that she wouldn't die, Ellie was scared of the hospital and the operation she had to face. Her parents were kind and open about all that was to happen to her, but there was still much that Ellie had to learn from friends she made while she was in the hospital. There were times when she was frightened and only Sonia, a young open-heart surgery patient, could calm her. When Ellie, a special nurse, and a few other patients became close friends, Ellie learned enough from them to allow her to help another patient.

This is not a story of sweetness and light, but it is told with warmth, humor, and real understanding of a young person's fears. Thus it is not only an excellent candidate for bibliotherapy, but it is a truly satisfying story for the general reader as well.

Interest Level: 4-6. Reading Level: 2.2. Further Search Topics: Illness-Fiction, Physicians-Fiction, Medicine-Fiction, Courage-Fiction, Death-Fiction.

Smith, Alison. Help! There's a cat washing in here!; illus by Amy Rowen. Dutton 1981, 152 pp.

Henry Walker agreed to care for his younger brother and sister for two weeks so that his mother could spend her time preparing a portfolio of her art work in the hopes of getting a much-needed job. It was a desperate move for Henry, but it was the only way he could prevent his bossy Aunt Wilhemina from moving in to run the household. Despite Henry's best efforts, almost everything seemed to go wrong. He burned the food, couldn't keep his brother and sister from misbehaving, seemed to have poisoned his sister's friend, and was faced with making a costume in one night for a school play. The worst of it all was that his mother wasn't pleased with what she was drawing, and Henry only seemed to make her feel more discouraged and unhappy. After what appeared to be certain defeat, however, Henry's efforts were rewarded. His mother was given the job, the family proved they could take care of themselves, and all ended happily.

A light, humorous tale of a young boy's growing independence and maturation under stress and increased responsibility.

Interest Level: 4-6. Reading Level: 3.1. Further Search Topics: Brothers and Sisters-Fiction, Working Parents-Fiction, Single Parent Family-Fiction, Humorous Fiction, Family-Fiction, Challenges-Fiction, Children-Growth-Fiction.

Smith, Doris Buchanan. A taste of blackberries; illus by Charles Robinson. T Y Crowell 1973, 58 pp.

A beautifully written, sensitive tale of a boy whose best friend dies suddenly. Jamie was always joking, so, when he fell to the ground after being stung by a bee everyone thought he was playing. A short time later Jamie was dead. His friend, the story's narrator, tried to will Jamie back again until the funeral was over and he finally realized there would be no such miracle. The next day he accepted his feelings and picked the newly ripened blackberries, just as he and Jamie had planned to do. A basket full of the best blackberries he gave to Jamie's mother and promised her that he would "slam her door" daily just as he and Jamie had done.

Eight short chapters, small print but short sentences, and a child's point of view perfectly maintained. For the lovers of sad stories and stories of friendship. Very useful when discussing death.

Interest Level: 4-6. Reading Level: 3.2. Further Search Topics: Death-Fiction, Friendship-Fiction, Read Aloud.

Stoddard, Edward. The first book of magic; illus by Rod Slater. Watts 1977, 65 pp.

This is a good choice for readers who have already enjoyed reading and mastering an easier book of magic tricks (such as *Let's Make Magic*, by Edward Dolan, Jr.). The tricks the author includes are often too difficult for the casual beginner. They require both a good deal of practice, and the staging and poise that accompany experience. But for the magic enthusiast there are plenty of flashy tricks, hints for performing and detailed instructions. A few, but not many, are tricks found in other books. Most use easily found household objects. Print and illustrations are fairly small however.

Interest Level: 4-6. Reading Level: 3.1. Further Search Topics: Magic.

Talbot, Charlene Joy. The Great Rat Island adventure; illus by Ruth Sanderson. Atheneum 1977, 164 pp.

Joel dreaded spending the summer with his father. His parents were divorced and Joel was sure his father didn't want him. His father only wanted to study birds. Great Rat Island, where Joel and his father were to spend the summer, was of no interest to Joel. It had no television, no one his own age, only terns. Even the assignment Joel was given (to make sure that no more tern eggs were stolen) sounded dull. It led to an adventure and a friend, however, that were anything but dull.

Joel discovered that a girl his own age was the thief of the tern eggs. Her name was Vicky Owens. She had run away from camp and was spending the summer alone on Little Rat Island. Joel kept her secret until the day of hurricane warnings. As the storm approached Joel realized that Vicky wouldn't be safe on Little Rat Island. Without telling anyone else he took the only boat around and went to look for Vicky to bring her back to Great Rat Island. He found her with her leg stuck between two rocks, unable to move. By the time Joel got her loose, it was too late to get back to the big island. Not knowing what else to do, Joel and Vicky dragged the boat inside an abandoned building where Vicky had been living. As the water rose around them and Vicky grew delirious with fever, Joel set up camp in the boat. While the building filled with water they stayed dry in the boat. Rescue and medical care for Vicky finally came the next day.

A solid, steadily-paced survival story for the reader who wants a little more than just an adventure story. Print is small.

Interest Level: 4-6. Reading Level: 3.1. Further Search Topics: Vacation-Fiction, Family Problems-Fiction, Birds-Fiction, Divorce and Separation-Fiction, Disasters-Fiction, Survival-Fiction, Runaways-Fiction.

INTEREST LEVEL 5-6

Blume, Judy. Deenie. Bradbury 1973, 159 pp.

Deenie's mother wanted Deenie to be a model. Deenie didn't know what she wanted until she learned that she had scoliosis (curvature of the spine) and would have to wear a brace for four years. Then she knew she only wanted to be normal. She was repulsed by deformities of any kind. She couldn't stand the idea of a brace. Her mother's attitude made Deenie's adjustment even more difficult. It was her father, her doctor, her sister, and a new friend with excema who finally helped Deenie accept her brace and the idea of physical differences. Subplots include Deenie's budding romance with an eighth grade boy, her strained relationship with her mother, and her

growing awareness of sex (masturbation and intercourse). Print and line spacing are similar to *Are You There God? It's Me, Margaret.*

Interest Level: 5-6. Reading Level: 3.1. Further Search Topics: Models, Fashion-Fiction, Beauty-Fiction, Scoliosis-Fiction, Physically Handicapped-Fiction, Children-Growth-Fiction, Sex-Fiction, Love-Fiction, Family Problems-Fiction, Illness-Fiction, Adolescence-Fiction.

Buckley, Peter. I am from Puerto Rico. S ËAN S 1971, 127 pp.

Federico Ramirez had enjoyed his two years in New York City and didn't like the idea of moving back to Puerto Rico. When he arrived, he had no friends, no T.V., and nothing to do. Then Neri taught Federico the local games, showed him the sights and introduced him to Narcisco, a special fisherman. Narcisco took Federico through the wonders of the coral reefs. He taught him how to dive and fish. Within several months Federico was thoroughly at home in the water and loved Puerto Rico.

There is so much information about Puerto Rico and marine life that the book is never dry. Federico tells his own story as a series of fascinating experiences (meeting up with a shark, playing pinball, scuba diving at night, keeping a large turtle as a pet, etc.). There are abundant black and white photographs. An excellent choice for research (no index) or recreational reading. The print size is slightly on the small side, but the space between lines is good. Recently out of print, but worth looking for.

Interest Level: 5-6. Reading Level: 5.1. Further Search Topics: Puerto Rico, Fishing, Moving, Household-Fiction, Marine Biology, Scuba Diving, Ethnic Groups.

Burch, Robert. Queenie Peavy; illus by Jerry Lazare. Viking Pr. 1966, 159 pp.

Queenie was always in trouble. She could be mean, really mean, but, she was also bright, talented, independent and resilient. Queenie blamed her problems on the fact that people teased her because her father was in jail and because she was poor. She thought that she had to defend herself against the world. Queenie was proud of her poor reputation until she accidentally-on-purpose caused a classmate to break his leg. Then, when her father returned home and wasn't the person she'd hoped he'd be, Queenie realized that only she could make her life better. Being the strong person she was, she set out to do just that.

Queenie is a wonderfully alive and sympathetic character, one well worth introducing to older readers despite the book's reading level. Print somewhat small. Line spacing average width.

Interest Level: 5-6. Reading Level: 5.1. Further Search Topics: Family Problems-Fiction, Crime-Fiction, Loners-Fiction, Poverty-Fiction, Humorous Fiction, Bullies-Fiction, Troublemakers-Fiction, Academic Problems-Fiction, Read Aloud.

Byars, Betsy. The Cybil war; illus by Gail Owens. Viking Pr. 1981, 126 pp.

Simon and Tony both had a crush on Cybil, but according to Tony, Cybil liked Tony better than she liked Simon. Simon was unhappily willing to accept Tony's word even though he knew Tony was a chronic liar. After all, Cybil had been the one to talk their teacher out of giving the lead in the class play about nutrition to Simon. Consequently Simon was being forced to impersonate a jar of peanut butter. In an elaborate attempt to win Cybil's affection Tony began telling Cybil lies about Simon and then set up a double date with Cybil and Harriet. On their walk home, Simon learned from Harriet that Cybil had only agreed to the date because Simon was going along. Happy at last, Simon realized he wanted no more lies and tricks; that he wanted to be truthful with Cybil and with himself. In the name of truth, he was even willing to accept the fact that his father, who had deserted the family, would not be returning.

A good story with just enough humor and romance to make it widely appealing as either a shared book (read aloud) or a personal pick. Print is fairly small.

Interest Level: 5-6. Reading Level: 4.2. Further Search Topics: Humorous Fiction, Love-Fiction, School Stories, Honesty-Fiction, Friendship-Fiction, Single Parent Family-Fiction, Read Aloud, Everyday Stories, Adolescence-Fiction.

Byars, Betsy. The house of wings; illus by Daniel Schwarts. Viking Pr. 1972, 142 pp.

Sammy was the youngest of eight children. His parents were tired of raising children when Sammy was born, so they almost let Sammy raise himself. That meant that he grew up to be independent. It didn't mean it was any easier for Sammy to accept being left behind unexpectedly with his strange grandfather when his parents moved to Detroit. His reaction when his grandfather told him that his parents had gone was to deny it and to run away. He ran until he could run no more. When he stopped running, the old man stopped chasing him and they found a wild but blind crane in desperate need of help. Helping the crane heal and find the desire to live again taught Sammy and his grandfather respect and, most of all, love for each other.

The parallels between Sammy and the crane are strong but subtle. The story is a compelling one, but may need a brief introductory note to alleviate confusion in the first two chapters.

Interest Level: 5-6. Reading Level: 4.2. Further Search Topics: Grandparents-Fiction, Birds-Fiction, Family Problems-Fiction, Poverty-Fiction, Physically Handicapped-Fiction, Runaways-Fiction.

Conford, Ellen. The revenge of the incredible Dr. Rancid and his youthful assistant, Jeffrey. Little 1980, 119 pp.

There were two people Jeff hated and feared: Dewey Belasco, the sixth grade bully and Lana McCabe, Dewey's female counterpart. Only in his imagination could Jeff stand up to them. In the stories Jeff wrote in a notebook, he and his friend Dr. Rancid were superheroes who rid the world of such scum as Lana and Dewey. In real life, Jeff ran from bullies rather than face them; even if it meant that an eight-year-old boy and a girl Jeff's age were left to stand up to Dewey by themselves. Although the way Jeff took care of an injured child soon had most everyone thinking of Jeff as a hero, he saw that, too, as an indication of his failings at first. Finally, something inside Jeff snapped and he answered Dewey back when Dewey insulted him. Before long Jeff found himself flat on his back with a bloody nose and so many pains he couldn't count them. But, he had finally faced Dewey and showed Dewey that he was no longer afraid. Jeff felt good.

Similar to *The 18th Emergency* but a higher reading level. The notebook stories will appeal to fans of superheroes, but because they are stories within a story, they may also cause difficulties. Spacing between lines is somewhat narrow.

Interest Level: 5-6. Reading Level: 4.2. Further Search Topics: Courage-Fiction, Bullies-Fiction, Writing-Fiction, School Stories, Superheroes-Fiction, Humorous Fiction.

Danziger, Paula. The cat ate my gymsuit. Delacorte 1974, 147 pp.

Another book for fans of Judy Blume. Marcy was shy and insecure, unhappy at school and unhappy at home. She was self-conscious about being heavy and sure she would never have a date. Only Ms. Finney (a new teacher), her English class and Smedley (a communications group) meant anything to Marcy. When Ms. Finney was fired because of her refusal to recite the pledge of allegiance and her unorthodox teaching methods, Marcy began to organize a protest movement. Marcy's commitment brought more problems at school and at home, but eventually resulted in Ms. Finney's vindication and Marcy's and her mother's growth and understanding.

Don't expect much depth of characterization. Most of the characters are flat and stereotypical, but the book will have great appeal in spite of its faults, for Marcy's insecurities are ones with which many young readers can identify.

Interest Level: 5-6. Reading Level: 5.1. Further Search Topics: School Stories, Everyday Stories, Family Problems-Fiction, Challenges-Fiction, Weight-Fiction, Courage-Fiction, Individualists-Fiction, Sex Role-Fiction.

Danziger, Paula. There's a bat in bunk five. Delacorte 1980, 150 pp.

Although this is a sequel to *The Cat Ate My Gymsuit,* it can be read alone. Marcy accepted an offer to become a junior counselor at an arts camp run by her ex-English teacher Ms. Finney and Ms. Finney's husband. After a nervous beginning, Marcy found herself enjoying the other counselors and the campers, but most of all, her first romance. Marcy's only difficulty was dealing with Ginger, a very troubled 10-year-old in Marcy's cabin. Marcy couldn't seem to get through to Ginger. When Ginger ran away, Marcy was forced to consider whether she should have spent more time with the campers and not quite so much time with Ted.

Marcy is a normal teenager whose problems, questions and activities are appealing to many teen and pre-teen readers. The characters who surround Marcy here are less stereotyped and flat than those in The Cat Ate My Gymsuit. Even Marcy's parents are more human. The author's light touch is just right for Marcy's story.

Interest Level: 5-6. Reading Level: 3.2. Further Search Topics: Humorous Fiction, Camp-Fiction, Everyday Stories, Love-Fiction, Vacation-Fiction, Occupations-Fiction, Adolescence-Fiction.

Hamilton, Virginia. Zeely; illus by Symeon Shimin. Macmillan 1967, 122 pp.

A beautiful, almost mystical story of a black girl who learns about self-identity and pride from a statuesque neighbor whom Geeder is convinced must be a Watutsi princess. At first by chance and later at an arranged meeting, Zeely (Geeder's neighbor) gently and symbolically speaks to Geeder of her racial origins. She also tells Geeder of a young girl (Zeely as a child), too ignorant of the world around her to be able to recognize reality. It is a quietly moving story that is most likely to find an appreciative audience in the thoughtful, more mature reader.

Interest Level: 5-6. Reading Level: 5.1. Further Search Topics: Africa-Fiction, Royalty-Fiction,

Blacks-Fiction, Courage-Fiction, Vacation-Fiction, Country Life-Fiction, Read Aloud.

Heide, Florence Parry. Black magic at Brillstone. A. Whitman 1981, 126 pp.

Liza is a little older, her romance with Logan has progressed to a kiss, and the book's plot is more complex than earlier Brillstone adventures. Other than those differences, the book follows Heide's standard format. The Brillstone books all center on Liza Webster and Logan Forrest, teenage partners in crime detection, who live in the Brillstone Apartments. The stories are similar enough that one could almost substitute the names Nancy Drew and Ned for Liza and Logan. Both young women are only children who live with their fathers. They are both independent, resourceful, and very concerned that justice be done. The men in their lives play approximately the same roles; their fathers are proud and supportive, but distantly preoccupied with their own business; Logan and Ned are gallant, boyish, and devoted. Liza and Logan, like Nancy and Ned, are not distinctive characters. Instead, they are shells into which readers who want excitement and adventure can pour themselves. There is no parental interference to worry about. There is plenty of action, some suspense, and real world crime (for Liza: murder, bank robberies, etc.) rather than childish escapades. The books' success is practically guaranteed. Beware, however, of inconsistent reading levels that wander over a year's range.

Logan was first aware of strange occurrences at the Brillstone Apartments when someone entered his apartment late at night. While the person had searched the apartment, he or she had unconsciously whistled a nursery tune. Logan's neighbor, Miss Violet, said the tune reminded her of her deceased nephew. Slowly Logan and Liza realized that someone was trying to trick Miss Violet out of a substantial amount of money she had just inherited. They suspected that Bella Vine, a spiritualist, and an accomplice were trying to convince Miss Violet that her nephew was communicating from the dead and wanted Miss Violet to give her money to Bella. Not until it was almost too late did Liza and Logan realize that Bella was also posing as another possible recipient of the money and was really Miss Violet's nephew's wife. Miss Violet's nephew had only pretended to die in order to collect insurance money. When he and his wife had heard about Miss Violet's large inheritance, they had decided to reappear in order to bilk her out of the money. Brillstone Mystery series.

Interest Level: 5-6. Reading Level: 3.1. Further Search Topics: Mystery and Detective Stories, Occult-Fiction, Crime-Fiction, Ghosts-Fiction, Cats-Fiction, Detectives-Fiction, Inheritance-Fiction.

Kibbe, Pat. My mother the mayor, maybe; illus by Charles Robinson. Knopf 1981, 165 pp.

The Pinkertons first appeared in *The Hocus-Pocus Dilemma*, a better introduction to the family than this book. Although this is a satisfactory story, its appeal is somewhat limited by its subject matter. B.J.'s mother's decision to run for town mayor meant that the whole family became involved in the political process. B.J. became her mother's unofficial public relations coordinator, a position Sam Jessup (Mrs. Pinkerton's campaign manager) didn't want to see anyone fill but himself. But because Jessup's ideas seemed suspiciously designed to insure that Mrs. Pinkerton would lose the election, B.J. continued working on her mother's behalf. Almost every day she managed to get her mother's campaign on the front page of the newspaper, although not always in a flattering light. Once B.J. was arrested for breaking into her mother's campaign headquarters. Another day she inadvertently circulated a picture of her mother in a bikini all over town. B.J. and her brothers and sisters illegally campaigned on the high school campus during Homecoming. B.J. even accidentally succeeded in blowing her mother's opponent's wig off in the middle of a campaign appearance. Mrs. Pinkerton finally lost the election, but managed to bring an important issue to light and to stage the closest and most exciting election the town had known in a long time.

Election campaigns and political issues won't lure many new reluctant readers to this book, but those youngsters who have enjoyed the Pinkerton's previous adventures and can understand a simplified version of politics at work will enjoy this humorous tale.

Interest Level: 5-6. Reading Level: 3.1. Further Search Topics: Politics-Fiction, Humorous Fiction, Sex Role-Fiction, Family-Fiction.

Mazer, Harry. The war on Villa Street. Delacorte 1978, 182 pp.

Willis was a loner and a runner. He was a loner because he didn't want anyone to find out about his alcoholic father. He wasn't quite sure why he ran; perhaps because it was the only time he felt good. When Rabbit Slavin and his friends asked Willis to become part of their gang, he refused. He was flattered and wanted to join, but the gang wanted to meet at his house and Willis couldn't risk that. Then when he agreed to coach the local "retard" for the school's field day, Willis gave the gang the opportunity they wanted to take their revenge on him for turning them down. The gang's hatred for Willis increased still more when he beat their best runner and athlete. In payment, the gang jumped Willis and beat him badly. After he picked himself up, Willis realized that he had at least faced the worst of his fears and survived. Days later when his drunken father humiliated him, Willis realized he had to face that, too. He made peace with himself and the world by deciding he could neither continue to run away from, nor apologize for his father anymore. He was independent and strong.

There is much in this fast-paced book besides the obvious violence and action. It is written with an intuitive feel for a teenager's problems and emotions and is a sensitive portrayal of mature concepts. The print is large, but spacing between the lines should have been slightly increased.

Interest Level: 5-6. Reading Level: 5.1. Further Search Topics: Running-Fiction, Loneliness-Fiction, Alcoholism-Fiction, Loners-Fiction, Mental Retardation-Fiction, Gangs-Fiction, Child Abuse-Fiction, Bullies-Fiction, Family Problems-Fiction, Courage-Fiction.

Pevsner, Stella. And you give me a pain, Elaine. HM 1978, 182 pp.

Andrea was the youngest of three children. She was very close to her brother, Joe, but he was away at college. There was only Elaine at home, but Andrea and Elaine didn't get along at all. Elaine was a troubled young woman who took so much of her parents' attention that there was none left for Andrea. This is the story of Andrea's year in eighth grade, a year in which she discovered that she was a steady and strong person. It was the year in which Andrea worked on the school play, had her first boyfriend, weathered the storms when her sister ran away, and began to understand her sister more and resent her less. It was also the year that she had to learn to live with her brother's accidental death.

The author's Judy Blume style (but with less humor) guarantees readers among older children.

Interest Level: 5-6. Reading Level: 4.1. Further Search Topics: Family Problems-Fiction, Brothers and Sisters-Fiction, Love-Fiction, Death-Fiction, Runaways-Fiction, Troublemakers-Fiction, Adolescence-Fiction.

Platt, Kin. Brogg's brain. Lippincott 1981, 123 pp.

According to everyone else, Monty Davis should have been one of the fastest milers in the city. He had, after all, run a four minute and ten second mile in practice one day. He had run well enough that day to beat his high school's two best milers. That was a good enough performance to make the coach push him, his teacher talk about winning, and his father puff up with pride. Even the marathon runner he saw occasionally in the park and his girl friend Cindy seemed to think that he could be the best. Monty really didn't care, or he thought he didn't. Maybe he was just afraid to see how good or bad he really was. For whatever reason, he didn't want to run in the meet against Culver High School. He talked so much about not doing well, that by the time he was supposed to run, he even had his coach convinced he couldn't win. But as he ran, Monty heard a voice inside his head that sounded like the voice in a strange science fiction film that he and Cindy had just seen. The voice seemed to say that he could win, and suddenly that was what Monty wanted. The voice and his new-found determination were what pulled Monty through and gave him first place.

This book is for the track fan or the runner. Few others are likely to care about the difference between a four-twenty and a four-ten high school mile. For those who do care, this is a good choice.

Interest Level: 5-6. Reading Level: 3.1. Further Search Topics: Family Problems-Fiction, Love-Fiction, Running-Fiction, Courage-Fiction.

Platt, Kin. Run for your life; photos by Chuck Freedman. Watts 1977, 95 pp.

Lee almost lost his newspaper delivery job when someone began to regularly steal money and papers from the newspaper boxes along his route. Lee saw a chance for revenge if he could beat the thief in the mile race at the next track meet.

Most of the abundant dialogue is slang. The romantic interest is innocent and low keyed. The story has enough running to make that a strong appeal, but not so much that no one but a track or running enthusiast can enjoy it.

Interest Level: 5-6. Reading Level: 2.2. Further Search Topics: Running-Fiction, Love-Fiction, Occupations-Fiction, Crime-Fiction.

Sachs, Marily. The bears' house; illus by Louis Glanzman. Doubleday 1971, 81 pp.

Don't let the benign appearance of this book fool you. This is a disturbing, almost brutal story. It is the story of Fran Ellen, a fourth grader with more problems than anyone should have to shoulder at one time. Her father had left the family and her mother had had a mental breakdown. Fran Ellen and her older brother were left with responsibility for themselves, their mother, and three other children (including a baby). They were all ill-fed, poorly dressed, and unwashed. Neither the social worker nor Fran Ellen's teacher knew the extent of the family's problems. Fran Ellen's only happiness came from her baby sister and from a schoolroom model (of

Goldilocks and the Three Bears and their house) into which she mentally retreated whenever she had the chance.

As the school year closed, Fran Ellen's teacher visited her home to deliver the bears' house and discovered Fran Ellen's mother and very sick baby sister. Although she hated the idea that the family might have to split up, Fran Ellen had matured enough to realize that when her teacher insisted that she would get help for the family, her teacher was taking the proper action.

The book is inappropriately illustrated to make it appear cute and even humorous. The story is far from either. It is so stark that it probably shouldn't have been illustrated at all. And because the hope that is present in the book's ending is very subtle, a review and a discussion may be necessary to help relieve some young readers' anxieties.

Interest Level: 5-6. Reading Level: 3.1. Further Search Topics: Divorce and Separation-Fiction, Challenges-Fiction, Poverty-Fiction, Family Problems-Fiction, Loners-Fiction, Survival-Fiction, Mental Illness-Fiction, Brothers and Sisters-Fiction.

Shreve, Susan. The Nightmares of Geranium Street. Knopf 1977, 127 pp.

The Nightmares, a small neighborhood gang, had very little to do until beautiful Tess moved on the block. Tess dressed in satins, furs, and rhinestones, and sang in nightclubs. She was even more of a fascination to the gang because they had been told to stay away from her. When Amanda moved in with Tess, the Nightmares invited her to join the gang so that they would have a way of spying on Tess. Gradually her strange behavior, her moods, her bruises and shaking spells, the strangers she let in the house, and the fights she had, led the gang members to suspect that Tess dealt in drugs. When Amanda failed to show up for a picnic and the Nightmares learned the police were searching for Tess, the gang became worried enough to look for Amanda themselves. In doing so, they uncovered proof of Tess' drug dealings, put themselves in great danger, and were protected by Tess as they escaped only moments before Tess was arrested.

Despite its low reading level, the book's confusing sequence of final events, and its subject matter make it best suited to older readers. It is not great literature, but its subject has strong appeal.

Interest Level: 5-6. Reading Level: 3.1. Further Search Topics: Family Problems-Fiction, Gangs-Fiction, Drugs-Fiction, Mystery and Detective Stories, City Life-Fiction, Crime-Fiction, Philadelphia-Fiction.

Sleator, William. Into the dream; illus by Ruth Sanderson. Dutton 1979, 137 pp.

Paul and Francine each started having what, at first, seemed like nightmares. As the dreams became more detailed and forboding, they discovered that they were sharing the same nightmare. They dreamed of a four-year-old boy, swirling lights, and a large dog. After awhile they figured out that the dog was trying to save the little boy from some unknown danger. As the pieces of the puzzle began to increase in number, Paul and Francine decided that the dream was in some way connected to a night over four years earlier when they had both been staying at the same motel. They, a pregnant woman, and a pregnant dog had all been affected by the telepathic power given off by a spaceship. The progeny of the woman and the dog had been given extraordinary mental powers; powers that a secret government agency wanted to mold and then put to their own use. The danger Paul and Francine felt came from two government agents sent to take the young boy Noah from his mother. Their attempt ended in a bizarre scene at an amusement park, where Noah levitated a broken ferris wheel chair to safety. By thus exposing his talent in public, Noah unconsciously insured against its secret and unsupervised use by the government.

A terrifying and suspense-filled psychological thriller whose main problems are a slightly overdrawn ending and a variable reading level. Reading level drops as low as 2.1 and climbs occasionally to 4.1.

Interest Level: 5-6. Reading Level: 3.2. Further Search Topics: Best Sellers, Supernatural-Fiction, Occult-Fiction, Flying Saucers-Fiction, Nonverbal Communication-Fiction, Dreams-Fiction, Survival-Fiction, Extra Sensory Perception-Fiction, Horror-Fiction.

Smith, Doris Buchanan. Tough Chauncey. Morrow 1974, 222 pp.

Chauncey Childs had taught himself to be tough— very tough. Even though he was small for his age (13 years old), the only person who gave him any trouble was his sometimes-friend, Black Jack Levitt. Everyone else was scared of Chauncey. Chauncey felt that he had to be tough or he wouldn't be able to survive. He had to be tough to stand the beatings his grandfather gave him "for his own good," to put up with his mother's drinking and disappearances, and to stand the sight of his grandfather shooting the stray kittens born in their garage.

Chauncey's greatest wish was to be able to live with his mother, instead of with his grandparents. In a desperate attempt to achieve that end he accidentally fell from a moving train and badly hurt his leg. Instead of being returned to his mother he was once more taken back to his grandparents. Chauncey's unhappiness grew until he finally decided to take the one surviving stray kitten and run away. Jack helped him find an empty garage where he could hide while he figured out what to do with his future. After talking with Jack and doing more deep soul searching, Chauncey decided to reshape himself and his life. His first step was to curb his temper and his tongue when his hiding place was discovered. His second step was to see about finding a foster home where he would be treated well, and where he could get a new start.

Ugly as the story is in places, its ending is hopeful. Although it is not always realistic, Chauncey's story is compelling enough to appeal to many readers, especially those who have enjoyed *The War on Villa Street*, by Henry Mazer, *The Outsiders*, by Susan Hinton, or *Mystery of the Fat Cat*, by Frank Bonham. The book's length and its artificially low reading level (vocabulary is often difficult but sentences are very short) make this book most appropriate for an older reader whose reading level is 4.1 or higher.

Interest Level: 5-6. Reading Level: 3.2. Further Search Topics: Child Abuse-Fiction, Family Problems-Fiction, Grandparents-Fiction, Runaways-Fiction, Bullies-Fiction, Single Parent Family-Fiction, Loners-Fiction, Friendship-Fiction, Troublemakers-Fiction, Foster Homes-Fiction.

Thompson, Jean. Brother of the wolves; illus by Steve Marchesi. Morrow 1978, 159 pp.

Shadow Fox, a Sioux medicine man, went into a wolves' den looking for special items he needed for healing, but found much more. He found a baby boy who had apparently lost his parents in an accident and then been adopted by the wolves. Winter was approaching and Shadow Fox knew the baby would not be able to survive the cold, so he took the child back to his people. The people were reluctant to accept Wolf Brother, saying that he was an evil omen, that he was unnatural, and that he would bring them trouble. But Shadow Fox's will prevailed and Wolf Brother was allowed to stay and grow up with the Sioux.

As he grew Wolf Brother continued to communicate with the wolves and thus fueled the rumors that grew about him. A very jealous young man, Looks-Away, told the people that a vision had shown him that Wolf Brother and his wolves would one day destroy the village and all its people. The people grew so suspicious of Wolf Brother that, when their horses were stolen and they faced a drought, they blamed him and drove him from the village.

For a while Wolf Brother tried to live as a wolf but found that he could not be totally happy. He wandered away to look for a tribe by whom he might be accepted. On his way, he too had a vision—a vision that told him he would find horses and buffalo for the Sioux and be welcomed home again. It was weeks later before he accidentally found his tribe's horses. In a daring move and with help from the wolves, Wolf Brother not only rescued the horses from the raiders, but also found buffalo just as his vision had predicted. He was then, for the first time, fully welcomed by his people.

This is a taut, suspenseful and mature story about a strong and unusual character. Older readers are most likely to respond positively to the Indian culture and lore.

Interest Level: 5-6. Reading Level: 3.1. Further Search Topics: Survival-Fiction, Wolves-Fiction, Orphans-Fiction, Loners-Fiction, Indians of North America-Fiction, Sioux Indians-Fiction, Jealousy-Fiction, Best Sellers.

Wallace, Bill. A dog named Kitty. Holiday 1980, 153 pp.

Ricky's fear of dogs was extreme but also understandable. He had been attacked by a rabid dog when he was very young. Remembering the fear, the stitches and the painful rabies shots was enough to bring tears to Ricky's eyes even years later. When a local bully told his dog to attack Ricky, Ricky's fear was discovered. About that time, a stray puppy showed up at Ricky's farm. Not quite knowing why, Ricky began to warm to the puppy, to feed it, and finally to love it. When the dog was attacked by a pack of wild dogs (a brutal scene vividly described), Ricky fully overcame his fear of dogs, went to Kitty's defense, and was barely able to save her life. When Kitty was later tragically and accidentally killed, Ricky swore that he would never have anything to do with a dog again. He almost kept his promise to himself, but eventually a second stray dog wandered into the farm and Ricky decided to try again.

This is an emotional story that should appeal to many readers. However, because of the violence and the dog's two-stage death, the book is probably best suited to fifth and sixth grade children.

Interest Level: 5-6. Reading Level: 3.1. Further Search Topics: Dogs-Fiction, Pets-Fiction, Bullies-Fiction, Death-Fiction, Oklahoma-Fiction, Courage-Fiction, Country Life-Fiction.

Young, Carol Beach. Remember me when I am dead. Elsevier-Nelson 1980, 94 pp.

This is a short but taut story about the effect of their mother's death upon two young girls. For a long time Jenny, the younger and more vivacious of the sisters, refused to believe her mother had really died. Sara, quiet and serious, mourned and missed her mother, but eventually accepted her mother's sudden death as a fact. Jenny's continuing denial prompted her father and stepmother to talk of sending her away to a school where memories wouldn't be so vivid. That talk inspired Sara to develop a devious and calculated plan to insure that Jenny would indeed be sent away. All her life Sara had been given less attention than Jenny. With Jenny gone, Sara would finally have her father and stepmother's love and attention all to herself. With a Hitchcock-like twist Sara's plan proved too successful. Jenny was sent away to school, but because she didn't want to go alone and because her parents could deny Jenny nothing, Sara was to go too.

This suspenseful psychological thriller is almost guaranteed success with older readers.

Interest Level: 5-6. Reading Level: 4.2. Further Search Topics: Mystery and Detective Stories, Brothers and Sisters-Fiction, Death-Fiction, Horror-Fiction, Best Sellers, Jealousy-Fiction.

INTEREST LEVEL 5-6+

Slote, Alfred. Hang tough, Paul Mather. Lippincott 1973, 156 pp.

Paul Mather went against his doctor's and his parents' orders when he accepted his new neighbors' challenge to show his pitching skill. He had been told not to play baseball until he had been given permission, but Paul not only loved to pitch, he was also the best pitcher his new friends had ever seen. Knowing full well the medical problems he could be precipitating, Paul went ahead and pitched a spectacular game for the Wilson Dairy team against the Ace Appliance team. But by the end of the game, Paul was in the hospital again, and Wilson Dairy had been forced to forfeit the game because Paul had played illegally. As Paul's leukemia worsened, his determination to play baseball again grew. When the day came that his team was to play a second game against Ace Appliance, Paul made sure he was there. He was in a wheelchair and weak, but he was there. He couldn't actually play, but Paul's psychological support insured that Wilson Dairy won the game. He went back to the hospital proud, happy, and still determined to fight his disease.

This is more than the usual sports story. This is a very sensitive story of a young boy's determination to fight leukemia. The reader looking for only a baseball story may find this book more than he/she wants. However, the reader who is open to a story of human strength and courage will be well rewarded. The book neither dwells on nor minimizes the disease. Instead it uses both the disease and the sport to portray a character much more completely than in most sport stories, especially at this low a reading level. This is an excellent book for those special readers who respond well to thought-provoking material. Although chapters are short and reading level is low, the print is somewhat small. In addition, the first person style, told as if dictated into a tape recorder (complete with occasional interruptions), may be confusing to readers unless it is explained.

Interest Level: 5-6+Reading Level: 3.1. Further Search Topics: Baseball-Fiction, Death-Fiction, Illness-Fiction, Moving, Household-Fiction, Medicine-Fiction, Physicians-Fiction, Challenges-Fiction, Courage-Fiction.

Smith, Doris Buchanan. Last was Lloyd. Viking Pr 1981, 124 pp.

Lloyd had several problems: he was overweight, his mother was overprotective, he had no school friends, and there was a chance he might be taken away from home and put into foster care because he had missed so much school. Lloyd's mother, very young and very defensive when she had Lloyd, had done her best to be a "good mother," but in doing so, had made Lloyd fearful of the world. He had become the subject of his classmates' mockery so many times that the only way he could respond to his peers was with nastiness. The one skill he possessed was hitting a baseball. He kept this skill well hidden for fear of exposing himself to further mockery. When one of his classmates accidentally discovered how well Lloyd hit, he took the first step to becoming Lloyd's friend. Lloyd's reaction was to back away, but Kirby kept trying. Eventually Kirby's attempts and those of an understanding truant officer, helped Lloyd begin to make friends, to treat others decently, and to pull away from his mother; in short, he began to mature.

Because Lloyd's problems can be oversimplified too easily, this book requires a fairly mature reader and perhaps even discussion in order to fully understand its subtleties.

Interest Level: 5-6+Reading Level: 4.2. Further Search Topics: Weight-Fiction, Single Parent Family-Fiction, Courage-Fiction, School Stories, Loners-Fiction, Friendship-Fiction, Baseball-Fiction, Family Problems-Fiction, Foster Homes-Fiction, Children-Growth-Fiction.

INTEREST LEVEL 6

Bennett, Jay. The pigeon. Methuen 1980, 147 pp.

Despite a low testing score, this is not a truly easy book to read. The author assumes his readers are fairly sophisticated and worldly, thus he does not explain the meaning of the Iron Cross symbol or the word Aryan. The book's language varies from simple to difficult, making the reading level inconsistent (2.1 - 4.1). The setting is dark and forbidding; an underground world of fugitives and terrorists. And yet, the book will be popular with many readers in sixth grade; it will be even more popular with older readers. The tension in this story of a teenage boy, blamed for the murder of his ex-girlfriend, is almost palpable. Brian's flight from the police and his desire to find Donna's murderer take him directly into the midst of a ring of terrorists, for whom life has no meaning. In Brian's attempt to prove his innocence, two more lives are lost, but hundreds more are saved as Brian discovers and stops a bomb threat. The author has used riveting action, short, clipped sentences, and terse dialogue to create a very successful, highly suspenseful book. Print size is only moderate.

Interest Level: 6 . Reading Level: 3.2. Further Search Topics: Mystery and Detective Stories, Terrorism-Fiction, Murder-Fiction, Best Sellers, Crime-Fiction, Courage-Fiction, Survival-Fiction, Runaways-Fiction.

INTEREST LEVEL 6+

Blume, Judy. Tiger eyes. Bradbury 1981, 206 pp.

Davey's father's death was a shock that for awhile separated Davey from her mother. They occupied the same space, but Davey felt herself unable to communicate with her mother or with her aunt and uncle with whom they were living. The horror of the night her father was shot in a robbery attempt was too great for Davey to confront. It was too much for Davey's mother too, and so instead of growing closer, they draw apart. They let Davey's aunt and uncle direct their lives for almost a year before each was able to accept Mr. Wexler's death. During that time

Davey's closest, most helpful friend was a loner named only Wolf. With him Davey lost enough fear and hatred that she was finally able to begin to talk about her father.

The setting (New Mexico) is much more important than in most of Blume's stories, the book's reading level is considerably more difficult, and the plot is about experiences more unique than usual. It will not fail to draw crowds of older readers however, for in most other respects the book follows Blume's successful formula.

Interest Level: 6+. Reading Level 5.1. Further Search Topics: Death-Fiction, Moving, Household-Fiction, Love-Fiction, Single Parent Family-Fiction, Family Problems-Fiction.

Bonham, Frank. The mystery of the fat cat; illus by Alvin Smith. Dutton 1968, 160 pp.

Although noticeably dated at times, this is still an exciting story of an inner city neighborhood. Buddy, Little Pie, Rich, and Cool were among the many who used the local Boys' Club as their hangout. It was a place to stay out of trouble and off the streets, but it was also a haven for rats. The rats were big and brazen; so brazen that one attacked Buddy in the swimming pool. The club needed a new building desperately. The money was there; they just weren't able to use it. Fifteen years earlier an eccentric old woman willed the Boys' Club over $600,000, but stated that the money was first to be used to support her cat until it died. A caretaker, a lawyer, and a veterinarian all benefited as long as the cat lived. Buddy and his friends took on the job of discovering if the cat really was alive or if the Boys' Club was being cheated out of half a million dollars. It was a job that nearly killed them before they set things right. Plenty of action, some violence, a cast of street-smart characters, realistic trouble with the police, as well as a slight mystery almost insure the book's success with older readers. Moderate sized print. Line spacing somewhat narrow.

Interest Level: 6+. Reading Level: 5.1. Further Search Topics: Humorous Fiction, Cats-Fiction, Gangs-Fiction, City Life-Fiction, Mystery and Detective Stories, Poverty-Fiction, Friendship-Fiction, Juvenile Delinquency-Fiction, Crime-Fiction, Best Sellers.

Christopher, Matt. Wild pitch. Little 1980, 137 pp.

This is one of Christopher's better written books but it is also one that will find a smaller audience than usual. Here he has drawn interesting characters of flesh and bone rather than his normal stereotypes. The sports action is still detailed, but it is no longer the core around which a purely skeletal plot is stretched. Christopher has produced an intriguing story line here.

Eddie was a good strong pitcher who sometimes threw wild pitches. One of his wild pitches hit Phyl Monahan, the only girl playing in his league. It was well known that Eddie didn't like the idea of girls playing in the same league as the boys, so people accused him of purposely hitting Phyl. Eddie knew he hadn't meant to hit her, but he still felt very guilty that his pitch had put her into the hospital. He went to the hospital many times before he was finally able to see Phyl and apologize. When he did, he found that she was very likeable and reasonable. When she confessed that she wasn't sure she wanted to play baseball again, Eddie decided he owed it to her to help her regain her confidence. As they worked together each one gained respect for the other until theirs became a very solid friendship. The test for both was when Phyl had to hit against Eddie again.

For many baseball fans there may be too much plot here and not enough baseball. Because the problem of how to control wild pitches is never addressed, other readers may also find the book disappointing. But, for those baseball fans who are open to more than box scores and replays, this is a good story.

Interest Level: 6+. Reading Level: 4.2. Further Search Topics: Baseball-Fiction, Sex Role-Fiction, Friendship-Fiction, Courage-Fiction.

Danziger, Paula. The pistachio prescription. Delacorte 1978 154 pp.

Just as Cassie entered her freshman year in high school, the old stand-by that had helped her deal with all her problems (eating pistachio nuts) began to fail. To be sure, she did get through the class elections and was elected president. She met and started dating Bernie. She gained self-confidence. She even managed to stand up to a particularly mean teacher. But, eating pistachios didn't help at all at home where Cassie really needed them. She could hardly stand to be in the same room with her older sister. She hated the importance her mother placed on looking right and dressing well. Most of all, she hated the way her parents were constantly fighting. The only person with whom she was really confortable was her brother. But, before the year was over, Cassie's parents decided to get a divorce, she and her sister became friends and Cassie learned to accept her family.

Another Judy Blume-style author, but Danziger's portraits of adults tend to be even more one-dimensional and exaggerated than Blume's. Very popular anyway.

Interest Level: 6+. Reading Level: 5.1. Further Search Topics: Divorce and Separation-Fiction, Family Problems-Fiction, Beauty-Fiction, School Stories, Adolescence-Fiction, Love-Fiction, Brothers and Sisters-Fiction, Everyday Stories.

Hinton, Susan E. The outsiders. Viking Pr. 1967, 188 pp.

When she wrote this book Susan Hinton was only 17 years old, but she had the sensitivity of someone much older. She wrote a taut story of the rivalry between two city gangs; the Socs (the rich socialites) and the Greasers (poor kids from the wrong side of town) that is more than anything a plea for understanding and tolerance. Seen through the eyes of Ponyboy (a very bright, 14-year-old Greaser), the rivalry brought on violence and an accidental killing that forced Pony and his friend Johnny to flee for their lives. Dallas, the meanest and most dangerous of the Greasers, provided them with shelter, food for a week, and a gun. At the end of that week, Johnny decided that they should turn themselves in to the police. But before they could do that, their hideout (an old church) burned in a fire which threatened the lives of four children who had been playing there. In trying to rescue the children, Johnny, Pony, and Dallas were injured; Johnny was severely burned and probably permanently crippled. A vengeance rumble was held while Johnny lay in the hospital, but the Greasers' victory was empty when Johnny died. He had been the one member of the gang whom they all loved and who had most needed them. Dallas went to pieces: he robbed a store and set himself up to be killed by the police. He had nothing left to live for after Johnny's death. Pony found support and security with his brothers (their parents were dead) and, in a note from Johnny, some hope for the future.

Hinton speaks most often through Pony (his depth of understanding of the people around him is very impressive), but through Johnny and two of the Socs as well, Randy and Cherry. Her message is clear, but at no time does she fail to maintain believable characters in a compelling plot.

Although the book looks forbidding with its 188 pages of unrelenting small print, it is an exciting story, full of adventure, realism, and room for thought. Perhaps the best way to introduce this book is to read a fair portion of it aloud. Now a motion picture too.

Interest Level: 6+. Reading Level: 5.1. Further Search Topics: Crime-Fiction, Gangs-Fiction, Murder-Fiction, Read Aloud, Friendship-Fiction, Juvenile Delinquency-Fiction, Best Sellers, City Life-Fiction, Brothers and Sisters-Fiction, Orphans-Fiction, Runaways-Fiction, Troublemakers-Fiction, Poverty-Fiction.

Kluger, Ruth. The secret ship. Doubleday 1978, 136 pp.

A tense, true story about the secret transportation of hundreds of European Jews to Palestine early in World War II. The transport ship became ice-bound in a Rumanian harbor, the crew mutinied and the passengers threatened to expose their plight to the world. In complete charge of the operation was a 25-year-old woman. The book closes with a summary of the Jews' continuing fight for Israel.

The historical understanding that is necessary in order to really appreciate this excellent book make it best suited to readers no younger than sixth grade.

The paper on which this book is printed is so thin that the print shows through from one page to another and the print at the beginning and the end of the book is italicized. Both factors may distract the reader.

Interest Level: 6+. Reading Level: 3.1. Further Search Topics: World War II, Jews, Women, Sex Role, Israel, Survival, Courage.

IRELAND-FICTION
Dolch, Edward W. Irish stories; illus by Carmen Mowry. Garrard 1958, 165 pp.

Besides controlling the vocabulary used in the stories, the Dolchs seem to include only stories with very uncomplicated plots. Once again they split the longer stories into two chapters. Thus, from 17 chapters there come only 12 stories. Most of the stories will be unfamiliar to readers (except perhaps those about Finn McCool), but all are pleasurable. See *Andersen Stories* for more information. Dolch Basic Vocabulary Book series.

Interest Level: 2-5. Reading Level: 2.2. Further Search Topics: Folklore, Fantasy, Ireland-Fiction, Giants-Fiction.

ISRAEL
Kluger, Ruth. The secret ship. Doubleday 1978, 136 pp.

A tense, true story about the secret transportation of hundreds of European Jews to Palestine early in World War II. The transport ship became ice-bound in a Rumanian harbor, the crew mutinied and the passengers threatened to expose their plight to the world. In complete charge of the operation was a 25-year-old woman. The book closes with a summary of the Jews' continuing fight for Israel.

The historical understanding that is necessary in order to really appreciate this excellent book make it best suited to readers no younger than sixth grade.

The paper on which this book is printed is so thin that the print shows through from one page to another and the print at the beginning and the end of the book is italicized. Both factors may distract the reader.

Interest Level: 6+. Reading Level: 3.1. Further Search Topics: World War II, Jews, Women, Sex Role, Israel, Survival, Courage.

JACKSON, REGGIE
Burchard, Marshall. Sports hero: Reggie Jackson. Putnam 1975, 93 pp.

Reggie Jackson was one of the big reasons why the Oakland A's won baseball's World Series three years in a row. *Sports Hero: Bill Walton* gives more information about the books in the series. Sports Hero series.

Interest Level: 2-6. Reading Level: 3.2. Further Search Topics: Biography, Jackson, Reggie, Baseball-Biography, Blacks-Biography, Group 2.

JAPAN-FICTION
Coerr, Eleanor. Sadako and the thousand paper cranes; illus by Ronand Himler. Putnam 1977, 64 pp.

This is a beautiful and very sad story of a young girl who was only two years old when the atomic bomb was dropped on Hiroshima. Ten years later she contracted leukemia and died a slow, painful death. A fast and enthusiastic runner, she had been full of life and energy before her illness. Soon after she became sick Sadako's best friend folded a paper crane for her and reminded her of an old story: If someone folded 1000 paper cranes, the gods would give that person good health again. Sadako was able to fold only 644 before she died. After her death her classmates made 356 more in order that she could be buried with all 1000 paper cranes. About three years later, a statue, erected in Peace Park in Hiroshima, was dedicated to Sadako and to a hope for world peace.

Because of the theme and its straight-forward handling, this book needs a fairly mature reader.

Interest Level: 4-6. Reading Level: 3.1. Further Search Topics: Japan-Fiction, Historical Fiction, World War II-Fiction, Death-Fiction, Illness-Fiction, War-Fiction, Running-Fiction, Origami-Fiction, Read Aloud.

JAZZ MUSIC
Bryant, Bernice. George Gershwin: young composer; illus by Nathan Goldstein. Bobbs 1965, 200 pp.

Even when George Gershwin was very young he loved music, showed signs of musical talent, and longed to play the piano. However, any boy who played the piano in George's neighborhood was called a sissy and George didn't like being teased in that way. When he was no longer able to keep his music lessons a secret, he stopped them for fear of the teasing. But each time George quit playing the piano, he always went back to it, even when his parents pressured him not to waste his time at the piano. A young teacher told George that he would never be a musician. One of George's teachers actually taught him to play poorly, instead of well. In time, however, George learned to play well and to compose his own music. Then came the hard work of determining his own style. Gradually, more and more people heard and appreciated his American jazz, until George Gershwin's music was heard all around the world.

Another adequate entry in the *Childhood of Famous Americans* series. Includes the usual glossary, bibliography, time line, and follow-up questions. It is most likely to appeal to the reader already interested in music. Childhood of Famous Americans series.

Interest Level: 3-6. Reading Level: 3.1. Further Search Topics: Biography, Composers, Immigration and Emigration-Biography, Jazz Music, Bullies, Music-Biography, Pianists.

Mathis, Sharon Bell. Ray Charles; illus by George Ford. Har-Row 1973, 33 pp.

Dominent throughout this biography of Ray Charles is the theme of overcoming adversity. The book is not just a recounting of Ray Charles' music lessons, early schooling, family life, and talent. All of that is included, but it serves to illustrate the manner in which Charles met his troubles. His problems began when he was very young. His brother died, and Ray lost one eye and then the sight in his other eye. His family was poor, but close, and he missed them when he was sent away to a school for the blind. Music was his love, but even that was work, for Charles had to learn to read and write music in Braille. He worked hard at it and eventually could play and arrange music for every instrument in the band.

Determined to be independent, when Charles was orphaned at age 15, he left school and began playing music for a living. The first record he made resulted in a $16 fine because he made it during a musician's union strike. Charles took a series of sideman and nightclub jobs until he finally had enough money to hire seven other musicians to play his music. Today Charles is very wealthy, owns his own record company, has a family, and is considered a great jazz and blues musician. None of his success came easily; only through determination, will power, pride, and hard work.

The book, interesting and serviceable enough for music or biography units, is also designed to set an example for youngsters facing their own problems. It will, of course, be popular with Ray Charles fans, too. Crowell Biography series.

Interest Level: 2-4. Reading Level: 3.1. Further Search Topics: Jazz Music, Music-Biography, Vision, Physically Handicapped, Blacks-Biography, Group 2, Biography, Pianists, Orphans, Challenges, Courage.

JEALOUSY-FICTION

Bulla, Clyde Robert. Marco Moonlight; illus by Julia Noonan. T Y Crowell 1976, 104 pp.

No one could explain Marco's strange, recurring dream. The dream seemed to be about a brother, but Marco had no brother. He had no family but his wealthy grandparents with whom he lived. Marco loved his grandparents very much, but he couldn't help wondering about his own past. He knew only what he and his grandparents could figure out from a few clues. His mother had run away to marry and for three years Marco's grandparents had heard nothing. Then, suddenly, they received a note that she was dying, had parted from her husband, and needed them. By the time they arrived, she was dead and two-year-old Marco could tell them no more. About the time of his thirteenth birthday Marco made friends with a strange man named Flint, who later became the gardener on Marco's grandparents' estate. Rather than live in the room provided for him with the other servants, Flint chose a bleak and isolated beach cottage. Being very careful that no one should suspect, Flint locked Marco into the cottage and forced Marco to change clothes with Matt, who was Marco's long-lost identical twin. Flint and Matt planned that Matt would steal all the money he could from the estate before killing Marco and fleeing. But when Matt began to realize how nice his grandparents were, how much he liked Marco, and how evil Flint was, he decided to thwart Flint's plan. In Matt and Marco's desperate attempt to flee from Flint, Flint was accidentally killed, leaving Marco free to return home and Matt free to find a way to feel he also had the right to claim his heritage before joining Marco.

The tense and dramatic plot immediately involves the reader and the short, fast-paced chapters sustain interest to the end of the book. Readers should also appreciate the small, paperback-size format. A good choice.

Interest Level: 3-6. Reading Level: 2.1. Further Search Topics: Dreams-Fiction, Mystery and Detective Stories, Kidnapping-Fiction, Twins-Fiction, Orphans-Fiction, Grandparents-Fiction, Best Sellers, Brothers and Sisters-Fiction, Jealousy-Fiction, Courage-Fiction.

Christopher, Matt. Devil pony; illus by Lorence Bjorkland. Little 1977, 103 pp.

This book is a bit of a change from the usual Matt Christopher story line. There is no sports interest here; instead there is a good suspense story about a boy, his cousin and a horse. Stu had watched the black Morgan named Midnight being born and had fallen in love with him. A year later he returned to his aunt and uncle's ranch to claim the horse, as he had been promised he could, but strange things began to happen around him. His cousin Wilbur warned him that he had probably annoyed the ranch poltergeist by deciding to take Midnight away. The bizarre occurrences escalated until Stu was almost tempted to leave Midnight at the ranch. Then Stu discovered Wilbur had been orchestrating everything that had happened because he had wanted to keep the horse himself. Although Stu decided to take Midnight home as he had planned, their new honesty led Stu to believe that he and Wilbur could be friends after all. A surprisingly good story with strong reader appeal.

Interest Level: 3-6. Reading Level: 3.1. Further Search Topics: Horses-Fiction, Supernatural-Fiction, Ghosts-Fiction, Jealousy-Fiction, Relatives-Fiction.

Hildick, Edmund W. The case of the invisible dog; illus by Lisl Weil. Macmillan 1977, 101 pp.

Brains Bellingham, a nine-year-old scientific genius, interrupted the McGurk Organization's Annual Picnic with an invisible dog. It was only a short time before McGurk and his friends were convinced that Brains' discovery of how to make things invisible was the greatest event since putting a man on the moon. Although they had always scorned the idea of including anyone else in the Organization, they decided to persuade Brains to join. But, before the day was over, they discovered not only that they had been duped, but exactly how Brains had made the impossible seem real. The Organization took its revenge by using Brain's own trick to make him confess. When Brains began laughing at how well his trick had been used in reverse, McGurk admitted how impressed they all had been by Brain's clever thinking. The outcome of their discussion was that Brains was invited, a second time, to become a member of the McGurk Organization.

See *The Case of the Bashful Bank Robber* for series information. McGurk Mystery series.

Interest Level: 3-6. Reading Level: 3.1. Further Search Topics: Mystery and Detective Stories, Detectives-Fiction, Gangs-Fiction, Dogs-Fiction, Supernatural-Fiction, Humorous Fiction, Jealousy-Fiction.

Hildick, Edmund W. Deadline for McGurk; illus by Lisl Weil. Macmillan 1975, 104 pp.

When many of the dolls in the neighborhood began disappearing, their owners went to the McGurk

Organization for help. At first McGurk was reluctant to take on such a silly task as recovering lost dolls. But when a ransom note appeared and the Organization was linked to the dolls' safety, McGurk's reluctance vanished. The note stated that if, in a written public notice, the members of the Organization did not admit that they were no good, the dolls were doomed. McGurk's pride would never have allowed him to write such a notice. As the deadline approached, the group plotted a daring move designed to uncover the doll thief. The plan depended on Willie's super-sensitive nose, a particular perfume dabbed on a stolen doll, and the curiosity of the thief. Success came only minutes before the hour of doom. Once again Sandra Ennis was the culprit.

See *The Case of the Bashful Bank Robber* for series information. McGurk Mystery series.

Interest Level: 3-5. Reading Level: 2.2. Further Search Topics: Dolls-Fiction, Mystery and Detective Stories, Detectives-Fiction, Humorous Fiction, Gangs-Fiction, Jealousy-Fiction.

Lowry, Lois. Anastasia Krupnik. HM 1979, 113 pp.

Anastasia Krupnik led a comfortable, relatively happy life until her parents announced that she was not going to be an only child for much longer. After 10 years of enjoying that luxury, Anastasia wasn't at all pleased with the change. Babies immediately went to a prominent, and as far as Anastasia was concerned, permanent place on her list of hates. Anastasia kept two lists: one for things and people she particularly liked, and one list for what she did not like. What went on and off the lists tells much about Anastasia. Anastasia tells the rest in this perceptive, sensitive, and humorous story of growing up and adjusting to a new sibling.

Spacing between lines is slightly too narrow for the rather large print.

Interest Level: 4-6. Reading Level: 3.1. Further Search Topics: Humorous Fiction, Brothers and Sisters-Fiction, Everyday Stories, Jealousy-Fiction, Infants-Fiction, Best Sellers, Children-Growth-Fiction.

Thompson, Jean. Brother of the wolves; illus by Steve Marchesi. Morrow 1978, 159 pp.

Shadow Fox, a Sioux medicine man, went into a wolves' den looking for special items he needed for healing, but found much more. He found a baby boy who had apparently lost his parents in an accident and then been adopted by the wolves. Winter was approaching and Shadow Fox knew the baby would not be able to survive the cold, so he took the child back to his people. The people were reluctant to accept Wolf Brother, saying that he was an evil omen, that he was unnatural, and that he would bring them trouble. But Shadow Fox's will prevailed and Wolf Brother was allowed to stay and grow up with the Sioux.

As he grew Wolf Brother continued to communicate with the wolves and thus fueled the rumors that grew about him. A very jealous young man, Looks-Away, told the people that a vision had shown him that Wolf Brother and his wolves would one day destroy the village and all its people. The people grew so suspicious of Wolf Brother that, when their horses were stolen and they faced a drought, they blamed him and drove him from the village.

For a while Wolf Brother tried to live as a wolf but found that he could not be totally happy. He wandered away to look for a tribe by whom he might be accepted. On his way, he too had a vision—a vision that told him he would find horses and buffalo for the Sioux and be welcomed home again. It was weeks later before he accidentally found his tribe's horses. In a daring move and with help from the wolves, Wolf Brother not only rescued the horses from the raiders, but also found buffalo just as his vision had predicted. He was then, for the first time, fully welcomed by his people.

This is a taut, suspenseful and mature story about a strong and unusual character. Older readers are most likely to respond positively to the Indian culture and lore.

Interest Level: 5-6. Reading Level: 3.1. Further Search Topics: Survival-Fiction, Wolves-Fiction, Orphans-Fiction, Loners-Fiction, Indians of North America-Fiction, Sioux Indians-Fiction, Jealousy-Fiction, Best Sellers.

Young, Carol Beach. Remember me when I am dead. Elsevier-Nelson 1980, 94 pp.

This is a short but taut story about the effect of their mother's death upon two young girls. For a long time Jenny, the younger and more vivacious of the sisters, refused to believe her mother had really died. Sara, quiet and serious, mourned and missed her mother, but eventually accepted her mother's sudden death as a fact. Jenny's continuing denial prompted her father and stepmother to talk of sending her away to a school where memories wouldn't be so vivid. That talk inspired Sara to develop a devious and calculated plan to insure that Jenny would indeed be sent away. All her life Sara had been given less attention than Jenny. With Jenny gone, Sara would finally have her father and stepmother's love and attention all to herself. With a Hitchcock-like twist Sara's plan proved too successful. Jenny was sent away to school, but because she didn't want to go alone and because her parents could deny Jenny nothing, Sara was to go too.

This suspenseful psychological thriller is almost guaranteed success with older readers.

Interest Level: 5-6. Reading Level: 4.2. Further Search Topics: Mystery and Detective Stories, Brothers and Sisters-Fiction, Death-Fiction, Horror-Fiction, Best Sellers, Jealousy-Fiction.

JEWS

Kluger, Ruth. The secret ship. Doubleday 1978, 136 pp.

A tense, true story about the secret transportation of hundreds of European Jews to Palestine early in World War II. The transport ship became ice-bound in a Rumanian harbor, the crew mutinied and the passengers threatened to expose their plight to the world. In complete charge of the operation was a 25-year-old woman. The book closes with a summary of the Jews' continuing fight for Israel.

The historical understanding that is necessary in order to really appreciate this excellent book make it best suited to readers no younger than sixth grade.

The paper on which this book is printed is so thin that the print shows through from one page to another and the print at the beginning and the end of the book is italicized. Both factors may distract the reader.

Interest Level: 6+ Reading Level: 3.1. Further Search Topics: World War II, Jews, Women, Sex Role, Israel, Survival, Courage.

JEWS-FICTION

Chaikin, Miriam. I should worry, I should care; illus by Richard Egielski. Har-Row 1979, 103 pp.

A warm, well-written story about life in a Jewish family in Brooklyn just before World War II. This is the story of young Molly's adjustment to moving, to leaving old friends, to making and losing new friends (one by death) and to the small happenings that make up her life. In the background, but always there, is Hitler's ever-increasing threat to the world.

A comfortable, truthful look at a close-knit family. Also useful for its picture of the times and the place. An occasional Yiddish expression may slow the reader but adds to the book's authenticity. Print is slightly lighter and smaller than *Finders Weepers*.

Interest Level: 3-5. Reading Level: 2.2. Further Search Topics: Moving, Household-Fiction, Friendship-Fiction, City Life-Fiction, Jews-Fiction, Family-Fiction.

Chaikin, Miriam. Finders weepers; illus Richard Egielski. Har-Row 1980, 120 pp.

The children most likely to read this are those who have enjoyed *I Should Worry, I Should Care*. On her way home from school one day, Molly found a ring. Rather than try to find its owner, she made up excuses to keep the ring. Molly knew it was a sin to keep something that belonged to someone else, she even knew who *did* own the ring. When she finally decided to return it, the ring had become stuck on Molly's finger and wouldn't come off. With Yom Kippur just a few days away, Molly became convinced that all the unpleasant things happening around her were punishments for her sin. She finally had to have the ring cut off her finger. After she prayed for forgiveness life immediately went back to normal.

There's enough guilt here to satisfy even the most demanding reader. There is also the same solid family group that appeared in the first book. But this book probably lacks enough excitement and/or empathy to interest a reader new to Molly and her family. Print is dark but spacing between lines could have been wider.

Interest Level: 3-5. Reading Level: 3.1. Further Search Topics: Family-Fiction, Jews-Fiction, Honesty-Fiction, Holidays-Fiction, Religion-Fiction.

Cohen, Barbara. The carp in the bathtub; illus by Joan Halpern. Lothrop 1972, 48 pp.

Leah and Harry couldn't face the prospect of seeing Joe, their pet carp, made into gefilte fish, even for such a special occasion as the Seder on the first night of Passover. The large, friendly carp had lived in the family's bathtub for over a week. It even swam right over to Leah and Harry to be fed everytime they went into the bathroom. At a time when most children in New York didn't have pets, Joe was as close to being a pet as possible. So, Leah and Harry hid Joe in a neighbor's apartment until their father discovered what they had done. When Joe's destiny was fulfilled, the children had to face a difficult fact of life. A week later, however, their despair became delight, when their father brought home a pet cat.

A short, warm and satisfying story.

Interest Level: 2-5. Reading Level: 3.1. Further Search Topics: Group 2, Jews-Fiction, Religion-Fiction, Pets-Fiction, Passover-Fiction, Family-Fiction, Holidays-Fiction, Read Aloud, Brothers and Sisters-Fiction.

Hurwitz, Johanna. Once I was a plum tree; illus by Ingrid Fetz. Morrow 1980, 160 pp.

Ten-year-old Gerry Flam knew nothing about her religion except that she was Jewish. Her parents didn't practice their religion and only superficially observed some of the holidays. As they told Gerry, their reason was that they were assimilated Americans. In fact, they seemed to practice as many Christian as Jewish holidays. All Gerry's friends and neighbors were Catholic, so Gerry had very little chance to learn

about Judaism or the prejudice to which Jews were still being subjected in 1947 in the Bronx. A Jewish family moved into the apartment building next door, and Gerry's quiet curiosity was stimulated. From the Wulfs, Gerry began to learn about Judaism, World War II, and Hitler. As her pride in her heritage grew, Gerry also felt prejudice for the first time. After celebrating her first Passover Seder, Gerry found that despite the problems, she was truly happy to be Jewish.

Much like Chaikin's *I Should Worry, I Should Care* in tone and mood. Will be useful where there is already an interest in Judaism.

Interest Level: 3-5. Reading Level: 3.1. Further Search Topics: Religion-Fiction, Family-Fiction, Jews-Fiction, City Life-Fiction, Children-Growth-Fiction, Prejudice-Fiction.

JOHN, TOMMY

Burchard, Susan H. Sports star: Tommy John. HarBraceJ 1981, 63 pp.

Tommy John's elbow injury was severe enough that no one thought he would be able to pitch again. He proved that the skeptics were wrong. For series notes see *Sports Star: Elvin Hayes*. Sports Star series.

Interest Level: 3-6. Reading Level: 4.1. Further Search Topics: Baseball-Biography, John, Tommy, Biography, Group 2, Physically Handicapped.

JOURNALISM-FICTION

Heide, Florence Parry. Mystery of the mummy's mask; illus by Seymour Fleishman. A. Whitman 1979, 127 pp.

The Spotlight Club published a neighborhood newspaper. Just as the club was about to take the fourth issue to the printer, Jay discovered an ancient mummy mask hidden near Mr. Pruitt's house. Mr. Pruitt was intrigued by the discovery (he worked at the nearby museum) and he took the mask from Jay, but agreed that Jay could write about the mask for the paper. At about the same time, Dexter discovered that an old, abandoned house was being used. When the printer's office was broken into that night and only their newspaper was stolen, the three children began to suspect that something strange was going on at the abandoned house.

Dexter rode back to the house alone and was captured by Hank, one of three thieves hiding out there. Figuring that they never would have missed one item, Hank had taken the mask from the cache of goods that the other two had stolen. When he overheard Jay's conversation with Mr. Pruitt, Hank realized that his partners would find out what he had done if they ever read the newspaper article. To avoid being discovered, Hank broke into the printer's and stole the paste-up of the paper. In order to keep Dexter from escaping, Hank tied him up and placed him in a shipping crate. When he didn't return as soon as expected, Jay and Cindy realized that Dexter was in trouble, so they went out to the house to search for him. As the three escaped, Dexter and Cindy slashed the thieves' truck's tires, and Jay ran to phone for the police. After several nervous moments in which Cindy and Dexter thought Jay might not get back before they were caught, Jay finally brought the police, who captured all three thieves.

See *Mystery at Southport Cinema* for more information. Spotlight Club Mystery series.

Interest Level: 3-5. Reading Level: 3.1. Further Search Topics: Mystery and Detective Stories, Crime-Fiction, Egypt-Fiction, Archaeology-Fiction, Antiquities-Fiction, Journalism-Fiction, Gangs-Fiction, Brothers and Sisters-Fiction, Detectives-Fiction.

JUVENILE DELINQUENCY-FICTION

Bonham, Frank. The mystery of the fat cat; illus by Alvin Smith. Dutton 1968, 160 pp.

Although noticeably dated at times, this is still an exciting story of an inner city neighborhood. Buddy, Little Pie, Rich, and Cool were among the many who used the local Boys' Club as their hangout. It was a place to stay out of trouble and off the streets, but it was also a haven for rats. The rats were big and brazen; so brazen that one attacked Buddy in the swimming pool. The club needed a new building desperately. The money was there; they just weren't able to use it. Fifteen years earlier an eccentric old woman willed the Boys' Club over $600,000, but stated that the money was first to be used to support her cat until it died. A caretaker, a lawyer, and a veterinarian all benefited as long as the cat lived. Buddy and his friends took on the job of discovering if the cat really was alive or if the Boys' Club was being cheated out of half a million dollars. It was a job that nearly killed them before they set things right. Plenty of action, some violence, a cast of street-smart characters, realistic trouble with the police, as well as a slight mystery almost insure the book's success with older readers. Moderate sized print. Line spacing somewhat narrow.

Interest Level: 6+. Reading Level: 5.1. Further Search Topics: Humorous Fiction, Cats-Fiction, Gangs-Fiction, City Life-Fiction, Mystery and Detective Stories, Poverty-Fiction, Friendship-Fiction, Juvenile' Delinquency-Fiction, Crime-Fiction, Best Sellers.

Clymer, Eleanor. Luke was there; illus by Diane de Groat. HR & W 1973, 74 pp.

Julius' father, uncle and finally his step-father had all walked out on him. Even his mother had left him, although she hadn't wanted to go. When his mother had been taken to the hospital, Julius and his younger brother Danny were sent to a children's home. Julius felt alone and cheated until he met a young, black, social worker named Luke. Luke liked and respected Julius and helped Julius learn to feel the same way about himself. When Luke, too, left Julius, Julius was so angry at the world that he stole food and then money. Afraid to go back to the children's home because he thought he'd be caught and punished, 'ulius ran away. It wasn't until he found an abandoned child, about Danny's age, who needed care, that Julius returned to the home. Luke was there when he arrived, just when Julius needed him most. Luke listened to Julius' unhappy feelings, arranged for him to see his mother and helped him begin to accept the fact that life is not always fair.

Julius tells his own story in a realistic, straight-forward book that will touch most readers. Only the lack of quotation marks and inadequate spacing between the lines may slow the reader.

Interest Level: 3-6. Reading Level: 2.2. Further Search Topics: Runaways-Fiction, Orphans-Fiction, Juvenile Delinquency-Fiction, Divorce and Separation-Fiction, Friendship-Fiction, Courage-Fiction, Survival-Fiction, Loneliness-Fiction, Best Sellers, Read Aloud.

Hinton, Susan E. The outsiders. Viking Pr. 1967, 188 pp.

When she wrote this book Susan Hinton was only 17 years old, but she had the sensitivity of someone much older. She wrote a taut story of the rivalry between two city gangs; the Socs (the rich socialites) and the Greasers (poor kids from the wrong side of town) that is more than anything a plea for understanding and tolerance. Seen through the eyes of Ponyboy (a very bright, 14-year-old Greaser), the rivalry brought on violence and an accidental killing that forced Pony and his friend Johnny to flee for their lives. Dallas, the meanest and most dangerous of the Greasers, provided them with shelter, food for a week, and a gun. At the end of that week, Johnny decided that they should turn themselves in to the police. But before they could do that, their hideout (an old church) burned in a fire which threatened the lives of four children who had been playing there. In trying to rescue the children, Johnny, Pony, and Dallas were injured; Johnny was severely burned and probably permanently crippled. A vengeance rumble was held while Johnny lay in the hospital, but the Greasers' victory was empty when Johnny died. He had been the one member of the gang whom they all loved and who had most needed them. Dallas went to pieces: he robbed a store and set himself up to be killed by the police. He had nothing left to live for after Johnny's death. Pony found support and security with his brothers (their parents were dead) and, in a note from Johnny, some hope for the future.

Hinton speaks most often through Pony (his depth of understanding of the people around him is very impressive), but through Johnny and two of the Socs as well, Randy and Cherry. Her message is clear, but at no time does she fail to maintain believable characters in a compelling plot.

Although the book looks forbidding with its 188 pages of unrelenting small print, it is an exciting story, full of adventure, realism, and room for thought. Perhaps the best way to introduce this book is to read a fair portion of it aloud. Now a motion picture too.

Interest Level: 6+. Reading Level: 5.1. Further Search Topics: Crime-Fiction, Gangs-Fiction, Murder-Fiction, Read Aloud, Friendship-Fiction, Juvenile Delinquency-Fiction, Best Sellers, City Life-Fiction, Brothers and Sisters-Fiction, Orphans-Fiction, Runaways-Fiction, Troublemakers-Fiction, Poverty-Fiction.

KELLER, HELEN

Malone, Mary. Annie Sullivan; illus by Lydia Rosier. Putnam 1971, 61 pp.

This is a very brief sketch of both Annie Sullivan's life and Helen Keller's life. Their lives were so intertwined that they cannot be separated. But because they are combined in such a short book, neither woman can be treated in much depth. That fact is not as harmful here as it might otherwise be, because even a bare bones description of the life of this extraordinary deaf, blind and mute woman or her near-blind, dedicated teacher, is interesting.

Interest Level: 2-5. Reading Level: 2.2. Further Search Topics: Sullivan, Annie, Keller, Helen, Vision, Biography, Physically Handicapped, Sound, Courage.

KIDNAPPING-FICTION

Bulla, Clyde Robert. Marco Moonlight; illus by Julia Noonan. T Y Crowell 1976, 104 pp.

No one could explain Marco's strange, recurring dream. The dream seemed to be about a brother, but Marco had no brother. He had no family but his wealthy grandparents with whom he lived. Marco loved his grandparents very much, but he couldn't help wondering about his own past. He knew only what he and his grandparents could figure out from a few clues. His mother had run away to marry and for three years Marco's grandparents had heard nothing. Then, suddenly, they received a note that she was dying, had parted from her husband, and needed them. By the time they arrived, she was dead and two-year-old Marco could tell them no more. About the time of his thirteenth birthday Marco made friends with a strange man named Flint, who later became the gardener on Marco's grandparents' estate. Rather than live in the room provided for him with the other servants, Flint chose a bleak and isolated beach cottage. Being very careful that no one should suspect, Flint locked Marco into the cottage and forced Marco to change clothes with Matt, who was Marco's long-lost identical twin. Flint and Matt planned that Matt would steal all the money he could from the estate before killing Marco and fleeing. But when Matt began to realize how nice his grandparents were, how much he liked Marco, and how evil Flint was, he decided to thwart Flint's plan. In Matt and Marco's desperate attempt to flee from Flint, Flint was accidentally killed, leaving Marco free to return home and Matt free to find a way to feel he also had the right to claim his heritage before joining Marco.

The tense and dramatic plot immediately involves the reader and the short, fast-paced chapters sustain interest to the end of the book. Readers should also appreciate the small, paperback-size format. A good choice.

Interest Level: 3-6. Reading Level: 2.1. Further Search Topics: Dreams-Fiction, Mystery and Detective Stories, Kidnapping-Fiction, Twins-Fiction, Orphans-Fiction, Grandparents-Fiction, Best Sellers, Brothers and Sisters-Fiction, Jealousy-Fiction, Courage-Fiction.

Clark, Margaret Goff. Barney in space; illus by Ted Lewin. Dodd 1981, 155 pp.

This is a sequel to *Barney and the UFO*, but it stands by itself quite well. It's title is a misnomer, however, for it isn't until the last third of the book that Barney goes into space. In the previous book Barney made friends with Tibbo, a Gark from the planet Ornam. In this book Tibbo tries to save Barney from an evil Gark named Rokell. Because Barney knew about Garks, Rokell was afraid Barney would betray them and turn humans against Garks. To prevent that from happening, Rokell was determined to kidnap Barney. Tibbo was too far from Earth to do more than warn Barney of Rokell's intentions and tell him not to be alone at any time. Barney's friends Dick and Kara tried to protect Barney but only succeeded in endangering their own lives. When Kara was almost killed by Rokell, Barney decided to face Rokell alone and try to defeat him, but Rokell's powers were too strong for Barney. Against their wills both Barney and David were taken aboard a spaceship. They discovered later, to their relief, that the spaceship belonged to a friend of Tibbo's who was commanding the ship from the moon. Barney and Dick were to be taken to the moon for safety until Rokell could be controlled. Rokell didn't give up easily. He attacked the ship twice before he captured it and set it down on a remote portion of the moon. Only Barney's quick thinking stopped Rokell permanently and saved both Barney and Dick.

The preliminary sequences are more suspenseful and exciting than the space travel; however, the book will not disappoint young science fiction fans.

Interest Level: 4-6. Reading Level: 4.2. Further Search Topics: Science Fiction, Flying Saucers-Fiction, Outer Space-Fiction, Orphans-Fiction, Kidnapping-Fiction, Aliens-Fiction, Adoption-Fiction.

Clark, Margaret Goff. Barney and the UFO; illus by Ted Lewin. Dodd 1979, 159 pp.

Barney felt a strange prickly sensation several times before he discovered that it was caused by Tibbo, a Gark from the planet Ornam. Tibbo had selected Barney as a friend who would accompany him back to Ornam. Barney was to learn the peaceful ways of Gark and then return to Earth to help persuade the world to accept the aliens. At first the idea of visiting Ornam appealed to Barney because he liked Tibbo and felt very lonely and unsure of his adoptive family's love. Those were the very reasons that Tibbo had chosen Barney: he wanted someone without strong ties to Earth and Barney's only tie when he was first contacted by Tibbo was his little brother Scott. As the time to go grew closer, Barney found a new and strong friendship with Dave, a science whiz-kid, and great love for his new parents. Tibbo, however, was determined to hold Barney to his promise. Only a last minute confrontation between Tibbo and Barney, David, Scott and Mr. and Mrs. Crandall prevented Tibbo from succeeding. But even as Tibbo left, he and Barney acknowledged their new friendship and agreed to keep in touch.

Because of its fairly slow beginning, readers must be well-introduced to this book. If they can be persuaded to be patient while the author sets the stage for about 18 pages they will be rewarded with a decent, if somewhat wordy, story of friendship, UFO's, space travel and family affection.

Interest Level: 3-6. Reading Level: 3.2. Further Search Topics: Science Fiction, Flying Saucers-Fiction, Kidnapping-Fiction, Foster Homes-Fiction, Family-Fiction, Adoption-Fiction, Aliens-Fiction, Loneliness-Fiction, Orphans-Fiction.

Curtis, Philip. The invasion of the Brain Sharpeners; illus by Tony Ross. Knopf 1979, 117 pp.

This book is one of a number of books published by Albert Knopf under the series title Capers. They are meant to be (and with few exceptions are) light, easy-to-read fiction, published simultaneously in hardcover and paperback editions. Each book is about 120 pages long with chapter length varying from 9 to 14 pages. Print is plenty large and spacing between lines is always adequate. Plots are built around an idea of guaranteed appeal, descriptive passages are kept to a minimum and action (often suspenseful) abounds. This should, on the whole, be a very useful series. Some entries (i.e., *Man From the Sky* and *Who Stole the Wizard of Oz*, both by Avi) are either too difficult or too obscure to be widely appealing, but they are by far the exceptions to the rule.

Invasion of the Brain Sharpeners is the catchy science fiction story of Michael's successful, but risky, attempt to rid his fifth grade classroom of the overpowering influence of the Brain Sharpeners. The Brain Sharpeners came from another galaxy to search for humans to help them colonize their Planet Five. Humans were so lacking in brain power that the Brain Sharpeners' plan was to periodically expose each child to brain-developing rays, then put them through intensive courses of study guided by their also-exposed teacher. When the children had all learned enough to be beneficial to the Brain Sharpeners, they were to be taken from Earth to Planet Five. Michael was the only one to see the danger they were in and to attempt to stop the plot. He managed to chase the aliens away and to prevent his classmates and teacher from receiving their second dose of rays, but in doing so, he sent the principal to the spaceship. Michael's classmates were thus saved, but his principal was never heard from again. Capers series.

Interest Level: 3-6. Reading Level: 3.1. Further Search Topics: Science Fiction, Flying Saucers-Fiction, Aliens-Fiction, School Stories,

Kidnapping-Fiction, Best Sellers, Academic Problems-Fiction, Brainwashing-Fiction.

Eyerly, Jeannette. The seeing summer; illus by Emily Arnold McCully. Lippincott 1981, 153 pp.

That it attempts to be two books at the same time is the one flaw in this book that may be noticed by young readers. The first half of the book is an interesting story of the growing friendship between a sighted girl and a blind girl. Carey's delight at the idea of a new friend next door turned to disbelief and discomfort when she learned that Jenny was blind. Jenny too wanted to be friends, but not if she was to be pitied or patronized. Gradually she was able to show Carey that being blind was a nuisance, but nothing she was ashamed of or embarrassed about. The second half of the book presents the contrived and somewhat unnecessary story of Jenny's kidnapping. When Carey's attempt to rescue Jenny resulted in her capture too, it was, of course, Jenny's independence and ingenuity that led the way to their eventual rescue.

To the reader looking for a rousing story of a kidnapping the book may be a disappointment. Half of the book is a long time to wait for the slight adventure. But, for those readers interested in a good story of physical differences and friendship, this will be more satisfying.

Interest Level: 3-6. Reading Level: 3.1. Further Search Topics: Vision-Fiction, Friendship-Fiction, Kidnapping-Fiction, Single Parent Family-Fiction, Physically Handicapped-Fiction.

Heide, Florence Parry. Mystery of the forgotten island; illus by Seymour Fleishman. A. Whitman 1980, 127 pp.

On a small island, unmarked on the map, the Spotlight Club members found old Mr. Whitson, who claimed that he was being kept prisoner by his granddaughter Lorrie and her husband John. Lorrie and John had told him he was being kept in the yard for his own good, so that he wouldn't wander off and get hurt or lost. They had also told him that he should will the island to them so that his daughter Cassie couldn't sell the island to a resort company for development. He was going to be forced to sign such a will unless he could get the children to help him smuggle a new will to his lawyer. Mr. Whitson wasn't convinced that Cassie wanted to sell the island, but he couldn't get in touch with her and he hadn'd had a letter from her in many months.

As the children went to secretly meet Mr. Whitson and mail his new will, they discovered that their trusted friend Guy was attempting to blackmail Lorrie and John into giving him some of the money from the sale of the island. He had evidence that Lorrie and John, not Cassie, wanted to sell the island and were tricking Mr. Whitson into signing a will in their favor. In a daring move, the children were able to free Mr. Whitson and isolate all three of the thieves so that the police could capture them.

This book involves a somewhat more complicated plot and slightly less familiar ingredients than most other Spotlight Club mysteries. One should progress to rather than begin the series with this title. Spotlight Club Mystery series.

Interest Level: 4-6. Reading Level: 3.1. Further Search Topics: Mystery and Detective Stories, Inheritance-Fiction, Gangs-Fiction, Kidnapping-Fiction, Brothers and Sisters-Fiction, Aging-Fiction, Detectives-Fiction.

Heide, Florence Parry. The mystery of the silver tag; illus by Seymour Fleishman. A. Whitman 1972, 127 pp.

Jay's paper route took him to one house that he wished he could avoid. It was grumpy, old Mr. Pendleton's house that Jay hated. One rainy day he spotted what he later realized was a prize Angora cat hiding on Mr. Pendleton's porch. When the cat was reported lost in that night's paper, Jay and the other members of the Spotlight Club decided to try to return the cat to its owner, Miss Horton. Their attempts to get the cat back from Mr. Pendleton meant that they had to spy on him, to sneak into his garage, and to spend the night in a treehouse overlooking his house. They were afraid that they had failed when they saw Mr. Pendleton leave with the cat. Determined to be the ones to tell Miss Horton of their failure, they went to her apartment and found Mr. Pendleton already there. Mr. Pendleton was a famous animal photographer who, upon finding the cat, had asked Miss Horton if he could photograph him. The children, thinking only that Mr. Pendleton was a mad scientist who kidnapped cats, had jumped to all the wrong conclusions, but ended with a mystery solved, new friends, and their first lesson in being detectives.

See entry with *Mystery at Southport Cinema* for series information. Spotlight Club Mystery series.

Interest Level: 3-5. Reading Level: 2.2. Further Search Topics: Mystery and Detective Stories, Brothers and Sisters-Fiction, Gangs-Fiction, Cats-Fiction, Loners-Fiction, Detectives-Fiction, Photography-Fiction, Kidnapping-Fiction.

Pinkwater, Daniel Manus. Fat men from space. Dodd 1977, 57 pp.

The evening after his trip to the dentist William found that he could still hear radio programs when his radio was turned off. He was even more surprised to find that when he wired himself to a fence he could hear spacemen talking. When the spacemen discovered that William could hear them, they landed and captured him. They were on a top secret mission and couldn't risk any human knowing about their existence. The spacemen were about to invade Earth to consume all the junk food they could find. As mass panic set in on Earth, William could do nothing to save his fellow humans. He was held captive and helpless until the invaders' interest was captured by a giant potato pancake floating in outer space.

A tongue-in-check, slapstick spoof of science fiction, food fads, and junk food. Do not expect anything more.

Interest Level: 3-5. Reading Level: 3.2. Further Search Topics: Science Fiction, Humorous Fiction, Food-Fiction, Flying Saucers-Fiction, Aliens-Fiction, Best Sellers, Kidnapping-Fiction, Teeth-Fiction.

Slote, Alfred. C.O.L.A.R.; illus by Anthony Kramer. Lippincott 1981, 146 pp.

Jack, his robot twin Danny, and Jack's mother and father were forced to make an emergency landing on an uncharted planet. There they were attacked by creatures who looked like rocks and who wanted to destroy all humans. They captured Danny, led him into an underground living complex, and revealed their true identities. The creatures were robots who had escaped from their owners and the slavery in which they had lived. They kept their planet secret from all humans for fear of what would happen to them should they be discovered. Their main purpose was to free as many robots as possible and to allow robots the same pleasures humans enjoyed. Because Danny had been happy with his humans and claimed to have been treated as one of the family, the inhabitants of the planet C.O.L.A.R. felt he had to be reprogrammed to see the truth. Jack looked and acted so much like Danny that he was able to prevent Danny from being brainwashed, to save his parents from death, and to convince the other robots that some humans treated their robots quite well. In fact, he and Danny, together, were able to persuade the robot manufacturer that a great program of robot-owner re-education was needed.

This is a good adventure story which could also be useful as a lead into discussions of slavery, intelligence, and interpersonal relationships. It is a sequel to *My Robot Buddy*, but one which can be read without having read its predecessor.

Interest Level: 3-5. Reading Level: 3.1. Robots-Fiction, Science Fiction, Outer Space-Fiction, Kidnapping-Fiction, Brainwashing-Fiction, Slavery-Fiction.

Slote, Alfred. My robot buddy; illus by Joel Schick. Lippincott 1975, 92 pp.

For Jack's tenth birthday he was given a robot—a robot so real it did everything but run like a human. The robot appeared so human that a thief, thinking he was stealing the robot, almost kidnapped Jack by mistake.

The few points at which the text becomes more difficult than the reading level indicates should not prove too intimidating to the reader. The suspense and humor of the story and the book's high interest subject matter should carry the reader through the rough spots. A satisfying read-aloud for second and third grades.

Interest Level: 2-5. Reading Level: 3.1. Further Search Topics: Science Fiction, Robots-Fiction, Friendship-Fiction, Kidnapping-Fiction, Read Aloud.

KING, BILLIE JEAN

Burchard, Marshall. Sports hero: Billie Jean King. Putnam 1975, 95 pp.

Winner of every major women's tennis title and a very important person to women's professional sports. Consistent reading level. Book includes glossary of tennis terms. See entry under *Sports Hero: Bill Walton* Sports Hero series.

Interest Level: 3-6. Reading Level: 3.2. Further Search Topics: Biography, King, Billie Jean, Tennis-Biography, Women-Biography.

KNIGHTS AND KNIGHTHOOD-FICTION

Bulla, Clyde Robert. The sword in the tree; illus by Paul Galdone. Har-Row 1956, 113 pp.

Shan didn't like or trust his Uncle Lionel, who had suddenly appeared at the castle gates after being away many years. Just as suddenly, Shan's father disappeared or died. Shan and his mother soon realized that Lionel wanted to take over the castle, even if it meant killing them. To save themselves, Shan and his mother fled. After walking many miles, they found a poor goat herder and his family who gave them a place to live. Sometime later Shan decided to travel to see King Arthur and ask for help in reclaiming the castle from Lionel. It wasn't until Shan was able to prove the castle was his, and Lionel lost a duel to one of Arthur's knights, that Shan was given back his home. Deep in the castle dungeon Shan found his father, still alive but imprisoned by Lionel.

This book, with its short chapters, short sentences, and steadily progressing plot should interest even the most reluctant reader from grade two through six.

Interest Level: 2-6. Reading Level: 2.2. Further Search Topics: Knights and Knighthood-Fiction, Survival-Fiction, Royalty-Fiction, Best Sellers, Courage-Fiction.

Dolch, Edward W. Robin Hood stories; illus by Carmen Mowry. Garrard 1957, 162 pp.

The illustrations are still drab, but the stories in this volume are exciting. Here we find straight-forward adventure and familiar characters: Robin Hood, Little John, Will Scarlet, Sheriff of Nottingham, Allan-a-dale and Sir Richard of Lea. The book makes a good choice for adventure lovers. Dolch Pleasure Reading Book series.

Interest Level: 2-6. Reading Level: 2.2. Further Search Topics: Robin Hood, Knights and Knighthood-Fiction, Folklore, Crime-Fiction.

Dolch, Edward W. Stories from France; illus by Gordon Laite. Garrard 1963, 167 pp.

It is very difficult to simplify a story and not lose at least some of its original flavor. Such is the case here and in all the Dolch retellings. Nevertheless, this collection of folktales is quite useful for the French flavor it does maintain. The stories, as they are retold, are good; not great, but good. There are 14 stories related in the 19 chapters. This is a result of splitting the longer, more complicated stories into episodes. Some frustration may arise for readers because there is no indication that a story may involve more than one chapter. The much-improved illustrations that introduce each chapter and adorn the cover help make this more attractive than the earlier books. The book ends with a list of the provinces from which the stories came as well as a pronounciation key to French names. Folklore of the World series.

Interest Level: 2-6. Reading Level: 3.1. Further Search Topics: Folklore, Fantasy, France-Fiction, Royalty-Fiction, Group 2, Knights and Knighthood-Fiction.

LAWYERS-FICTION

Christopher, Matt. Football fugitive; illus by Larry Johnson. Little 1976, 119 pp.

Larry had been writing to the great football player Yancey Roote for about two years when his letters suddenly went unanswered. Because his relationship with his father was cool and distant, Larry's friendship with Yancey had meant a great deal to him. Shortly after Larry learned that Yancey was in legal trouble, Yancey showed up in town to ask Larry's father, a famous lawyer, to defend him in court. The court case and Yancey helped to bring Larry and his father closer together and to provide each one with new respect for the other. Lots of football action plus a realistic and somewhat common problem (though an unrealistic solution) make this a useful selection.

Interest Level: 3-6. Reading Level: 3.1. Further Search Topics: Football-Fiction, Lawyers-Fiction, Family Problems-Fiction.

LAZINESS-FICTION

Ginsburg, Mirra. The lazies; illus by Marian Parry. Macmillan 1973, 70 pp.

A good collection of 15 short Russian folktales all having to do with laziness. Most are humorous tales; few are well-known. In just under a third of the stories the humor may be too subtle even for older elementary school children; however, the rest of the stories can be enjoyed by almost any child between third and sixth grade. ("Who Will Wash the Pot," "Easy Bread," "Who Will Row Next," and "The Princess Who Learned to Work" are the questionable stories). Print somewhat small.

Interest Level: 3-6. Reading Level: 3.1. Further Search Topics: Folklore, Humorous Fiction, Laziness-Fiction, Russia-Fiction.

Pene du Bois, William. Lazy Tommy Pumpkinhead. Har-Row 1966, 32 pp.

Tommy lived a solitary life in an all-electric house. An electric bed woke Tommy and slid him into a tub full of warm water. The tub then tipped him out and into a harness that held Tommy upright while other machines dried him, combed his hair, brushed his teeth, dressed him, and fed him. But one day Tommy's life was literally turned upside down with disastrous results. His feet were cleaned and combed and his clothes were all put on upside down, but the worst part of all was that Tommy almost starved; the machine fed his feet instead of his mouth.

A tongue-in-cheek warning against laziness. The lesson is obvious but the treatment (both text and illustrations) is so enjoyable that the book is appealing to almost any reader who wants a short, funny book. Print is somewhat small but spacing between lines is more than adequate.

Interest Level: 1-6. Reading Level: 3.2. Further Search Topics: Electricity-Fiction, Robots-Fiction, Laziness-Fiction, Humorous Fiction, Group 2, Read Aloud.

LEGENDS

Baylor, Byrd. And it is still that way: legends told by Arizona Indian children. Scribner 1976, 85 pp.

Byrd Baylor has collected and written notes for forty-one short American Indian legends from seven Arizona tribes whose school children were asked to write down or illustrate their favorite legend. The result is a collection that reflects the concerns, the history, religion, humor and pride of the children and their ancestors. This excellent collection is not only interesting reading, but it also fits well into social studies and language arts units.

Interest Level: 2-6. Reading Level: 3.1. Further Search Topics: Legends, Arizona-Fiction, Navajo Indians, Hopi Indians, Papago Indians, Pima Indians, Apache Indians, Quechan Indians, Cocopah Indians, Indians of North America-Legends, Mythology, Group 2.

Bernstein, Margery. Coyote goes hunting for fire; illus by Ed Heffernan. Scribner 1974, 40 pp.

A delightful story that can be read for fun or used as part of a unit on North American Indians. A long time ago when there was no fire, all the animals but Coyote banded together to find it. The animals left Coyote behind because he was always spoiling their plans. Coyote saw them leave, chased after them and once more tried to direct everything, but only ended up losing fire. Cartoon-like illustrations add to the humor of the story. This book should make a simple, but effective play.

Interest Level: 1-4. Reading Level 2.1. Further Search Topics: Animals-Fiction, Legends, Mythology, Fire-Fiction, Indians of North America-Legends, Coyotes-Fiction, Group 2, Creation-Fiction, Drama.

LIBRARIES-FICTION

Clifford, Eth. Help, I'm a prisoner in the library; illus by George Hughes. HM 1979, 103 pp.

When their car stopped, Mary Rose and Jo-Beth were left alone in a strange city while their father went to find some gas. Jo-Beth needed to use the bathroom, so the sisters headed for the closest public building they could see, the library. No one saw them go in, so no one knew that they were locked inside when the librarian secured the building for the night.

With the lights out and a blizzard outside, the library was a very spooky place. The girls tried calling the police, but the police wouldn't take them seriously. Then they heard groans and eerie moans from the second floor. Gathering all their courage, the girls went to investigate, only to discover the librarian lying hurt and unconscious. Their ingenuity and imagination helped the sisters through the difficult hours before they were all rescued.

Don't read it too carefully or the book's implausibilities will become very evident. Most young readers, however, will enjoy this story for its suspense, spooky atmosphere and adventurous girls, and they will ignore its weaknesses.

Interest Level: 2-5. Reading Level: 3.1. Further Search Topics: Disasters-Fiction, Snow-Fiction, Brothers and Sisters-Fiction, Libraries-Fiction, Survival-Fiction, Courage-Fiction, Group 2.

LIGHT-FICTION

Bernstein, Margery. The first morning; illus by Enid Warner Romanek. Scribner 1976, 44 pp.

Spider, Mouse, and Fly volunteered to ask the king of the sky for light to take back to earth because the animals on earth were tired of living in darkness. The king didn't want to give away any light and so he set what he thought was an impossible task for the three animals. They were able to outwit the king three times and finally return to earth with a box Mouse was sure contained light. When they opened the box all they found was a rooster. Poor Mouse was ashamed at having been so badly tricked. But then Rooster crowed up the first morning and has done so ever since. A competent retelling of an African myth, nicely complemented by bold illustrations. Good candidate for dramatization.

Interest Level: 1-3. Reading Level: 2.1. Further Search Topics: Animals-Fiction, Group 2, Mythology, Light-Fiction, Drama, Time-Fiction, Calendars-Fiction, Creation-Fiction, Africa-Folklore.

LIGHTHOUSES-FICTION

Warner, Gertrude Chandler. The lighthouse mystery; illus by David Cunningham. A. Whitman 1963, 128 pp.

What better place for a mystery than a lighthouse late at night? Add the excitement of a storm at sea and a young man alone in a boat and the story should be unbeatable. Unfortunately this, as well as some of the other books in the series, does not quite live up to its potential. It will not attract many new readers but it will satisfy those who crave more adventures of the Alden family. The main problem with the book is its lack of definition. It isn't quite a mystery or an adventure story, it's a little of both. It is also part homespun family story, part science lesson, and part "problem story."

The Aldens rented a lighthouse in a very small fishing village one summer. Late each night their dog awoke them as he barked at a stranger who walked into or away from a closed-up building nearby. When the children investigated, they found that the surly son of a local fisherman was using the building to experiment on plankton as a food source. Harry was a brilliant young man who wanted to go to college, but whose father stubbornly refused to let him study. One night when Larry was at sea gathering samples, a terrible storm blew up. Only the Coast Guard and an improvised light in the lighthouse saved Larry from drowning. Larry's brush with death forced his father to acknowledge Larry's abilities and allow him to continue studying at college.

The sketchy illustrations in this and the following
books in the series are an improvement over the
silhouettes of *The Boxcar Children*. See the
annotation for *The Boxcar Children* for further series
information.

Interest Level: 3-6. Reading Level: 2.1. Further
Search Topics: Mystery and Detective Stories,
Lighthouses-Fiction, Food-Fiction, Disasters-Fiction,
Vacation-Fiction.

LIZARDS

Allen, Gertrude. Everyday turtles, toads and their
kin. HM 1970, 48 pp.

Straight-forward, short, chapter discussions of
turtles, lizards, snakes, salamanders, toads, frogs and
tree toads. Black and white drawings done by the
author amplify the text. The major part of the book is
simple enough to be understood at second grade, but
should still be interesting to fourth and fifth graders. A
few terms may need explanation: i.e., venomous,
prey. The chapters on the turtle, lizard, frog and tree
frog are the easiest. No index, but still useful for
reports.

Interest Level: 2-5. Reading Level: 2.2. Further
Search Topics: Turtles, Reptiles, Lizards, Toads,
Frogs, Snakes, Salamanders.

LIZARDS-FICTION

Wolkoff, Judie. Wally. Bradbury 1977, 199 pp.

Michael Price agreed to take care of his friend Billy's
chuckwalla for three weeks. But because his mother
had declared a moratorium on any more reptiles in the
house, Michael tried to hide Wally in his closet. With
help from his brother Roger, Michael managed to
keep Wally a secret until Wally was mistakenly left out
of his box one night. Despite Michael and Roger's
desperate searches, the chuckwalla did not reappear
until Mr. and Mrs. Price were involved in the final
negotiations for the sale of their house. Wally
completely disrupted the proceedings, prevented the
sale and thus made everyone happy. For as it turned
out, none of the Prices had really wanted to move
after all.

A fast-paced, funny book with much reader appeal.

Interest Level: 2-5. Reading Level: 2.2. Further
Search Topics: Pets-Fiction, Humorous Fiction,
Lizards-Fiction, Best Sellers, Reptiles-Fiction,
Secrets-Fiction.

LONELINESS-FICTION

Bulla, Clyde Robert. Dexter; illus by Glo Coalson.
Har-Row 1973, 69 pp.

This is not as simple a story as it first appears.
Dave, 12 years old and lonely, had hoped his new
neighbors would be friends. But, the Arvin family kept
very much to themselves until Dave accidentally
discovered Alex, the Arvin's son, doing tricks on a
trapeze in the barn. Because Dave kept the secret
and shared Alex's love for Dexter, his circus pony, the
boys soon became friends. Then in one horrible night,
the Arvins were forced to leave the town and Dexter
was so badly hurt he was believed to be dead. A
week later Dave found Dexter alive, but crippled for
life and so frightened that no one could get near him.
The horse surprised everyone and managed to live
through a very harsh winter as well as the
townspeople's determination to kill him. When Alex
and his father returned, almost a year later, they
found Dexter and took the old and feeble horse back
to a ranch with them. The story is told with sympathy,
with an understanding of how it feels to be lonely, and

with tension and suspense. It's appeal should last
from third through sixth grade. Print size is smaller
than Bulla's usual.

Interest Level: 3-6. Reading Level: 3.1. Further
Search Topics: Survival-Fiction, Acrobats and
Acrobatics-Fiction, Horses-Fiction, Read Aloud,
Circus-Fiction, Loneliness-Fiction, Friendship-Fiction.

Byars, Betsy. After the goat man; illus by Ronald
Himler. Viking Pr. 1974, 126 pp.

Harold was fat and over-sensitive. Ada was serious
and independent. Figgy was lonely, poor and in need
of help. Figgy and his grandfather, the Goat Man, had
been forced to move from their cabin to make room
for a highway. The Goat Man had returned to the
cabin with a shotgun, vowing to defend his right to live
there. Figgy knew he had to persuade his grandfather
to leave or someone would be hurt. But, in the
children's hurry to reach the Goat Man, it was Figgy
who was hurt and Harold who rescued both Figgy and
the Goat Man. Harold grew up that day. He stopped
dreaming about the way he wanted things to be and
faced life realistically for the first time.

The book is very much a character study. Realistic
characters are treated with sympathy and dignity and
given a chance to grow. Introspective readers will
understand and enjoy the book more than those
looking for adventure. Print size is fairly large, but
lines are separated by only average width.

Interest Level: 4-6. Reading Level: 3.2. Further
Search Topics: Loneliness-Fiction, Weight-Fiction,
Moving, Household-Fiction, Courage-Fiction,
Grandparents-Fiction, Orphans-Fiction.

Clark, Margaret Goff. Barney and the UFO; illus by
Ted Lewin. Dodd 1979, 159 pp.

Barney felt a strange prickly sensation several times
before he discovered that it was caused by Tibbo, a
Gark from the planet Ornam. Tibbo had selected
Barney as a friend who would accompany him back to
Ornam. Barney was to learn the peaceful ways of
Gark and then return to Earth to help persuade the
world to accept the aliens. At first the idea of visiting
Ornam appealed to Barney because he liked Tibbo
and felt very lonely and unsure of his adoptive family's
love. Those were the very reasons that Tibbo had
chosen Barney: he wanted someone without strong
ties to Earth and Barney's only tie when he was first
contacted by Tibbo was his little brother Scott. As the
time to go grew closer, Barney found a new and
strong friendship with Dave, a science whiz-kid, and
great love for his new parents. Tibbo, however, was
determined to hold Barney to his promise. Only a last
minute confrontation between Tibbo and Barney,
David, Scott and Mr. and Mrs. Crandall prevented
Tibbo from succeeding. But even as Tibbo left, he and
Barney acknowledged their new friendship and agreed
to keep in touch.

Because of its fairly slow beginning, readers must
be well-introduced to this book. If they can be
persuaded to be patient while the author sets the
stage for about 18 pages they will be rewarded with a
decent, if somewhat wordy, story of friendship, UFO's,
space travel and family affection.

Interest Level: 3-6. Reading Level: 3.2. Further
Search Topics: Science Fiction, Flying
Saucers-Fiction, Kidnapping-Fiction, Foster
Homes-Fiction, Family-Fiction, Adoption-Fiction,
Aliens-Fiction, Loneliness-Fiction, Orphans-Fiction.

Clymer, Eleanor. Luke was there; illus by Diane de
Groat. HR & W 1973, 74 pp.

Julius' father, uncle and finally his step-father had all walked out on him. Even his mother had left him, although she hadn't wanted to go. When his mother had been taken to the hospital, Julius and his younger brother Danny were sent to a children's home. Julius felt alone and cheated until he met a young, black, social worker named Luke. Luke liked and respected Julius and helped Julius learn to feel the same way about himself. When Luke, too, left Julius, Julius was so angry at the world that he stole food and then money. Afraid to go back to the children's home because he thought he'd be caught and punished, Julius ran away. It wasn't until he found an abandoned child, about Danny's age, who needed care, that Julius returned to the home. Luke was there when he arrived, just when Julius needed him most. Luke listened to Julius' unhappy feelings, arranged for him to see his mother and helped him begin to accept the fact that life is not always fair.

Julius tells his own story in a realistic, straight-forward book that will touch most readers. Only the lack of quotation marks and inadequate spacing between the lines may slow the reader.

Interest Level: 3-6. Reading Level: 2.2. Further Search Topics: Runaways-Fiction, Orphans-Fiction, Juvenile Delinquency-Fiction, Divorce and Separation-Fiction, Friendship-Fiction, Courage-Fiction, Survival-Fiction, Loneliness-Fiction, Best Sellers, Read Aloud.

Mazer, Harry. The war on Villa Street. Delacorte 1978, 182 pp.

Willis was a loner and a runner. He was a loner because he didn't want anyone to find out about his alcoholic father. He wasn't quite sure why he ran; perhaps because it was the only time he felt good. When Rabbit Slavin and his friends asked Willis to become part of their gang, he refused. He was flattered and wanted to join, but the gang wanted to meet at his house and Willis couldn't risk that. Then when he agreed to coach the local "retard" for the school's field day, Willis gave the gang the opportunity they wanted to take their revenge on him for turning them down. The gang's hatred for Willis increased still more when he beat their best runner and athlete. In payment, the gang jumped Willis and beat him badly. After he picked himself up, Willis realized that he had at least faced the worst of his fears and survived. Days later when his drunken father humiliated him, Willis realized he had to face that, too. He made peace with himself and the world by deciding he could neither continue to run away from, nor apologize for his father anymore. He was independent and strong.

There is much in this fast-paced book besides the obvious violence and action. It is written with an intuitive feel for a teenager's problems and emotions and is a sensitive portrayal of mature concepts. The print is large, but spacing between the lines should have been slightly increased.

Interest Level: 5-6. Reading Level: 5.1. Further Search Topics: Running-Fiction, Loneliness-Fiction, Alcoholism-Fiction, Loners-Fiction, Mental Retardation-Fiction, Gangs-Fiction, Child Abuse-Fiction, Bullies-Fiction, Family Problems-Fiction, Courage-Fiction.

Newfield, Marcia. A book for Jodan; illus by Diane DeGroot. Atheneum 1975, unp (41 pp).

Jodan found her parents' separation very hard to understand and accept. She and her mother had moved 3,000 miles away from her father and she missed him very much. When Jodan visited her father for the first time, he gave her a very special present that lessened her loneliness. He created a book just for Jodan that was filled with his thoughts and memories.

The book is a sensitive portrayal of a very common experience. Only Jodan's age (nine-years-old) and consequent actions and reactions, limit the book's probable usefulness beyond fifth grade. Print is somewhat small.

Interest Level: 2-5. Reading Level: 3.2. Further Search Topics: Group 2, Divorce and Separation-Fiction, Family Problems-Fiction, Loneliness-Fiction.

Shura, Mary Francis. The Barkley Street six-pack; illus by Gene Sparkman. Dodd 1979, 159 pp.

Jane's best friend Natalie was everything Jane wanted to be. She was self-assured, pretty, vibrant, and even possessed magical talents. Jane didn't realize at first, and she later resisted seeing, that Natalie ran Jane's life and cleverly made sure that Jane had no other friends. Natalie's move left Jane with no friends among those people she had once enjoyed. Little by little, with the help of a stray dog and the new boy on the block, Jane bagan to see how destructive Natalie had been. She finally realized that a true friendship is one in which neither party tries to control the other.

With its enticements of ESP, magic, stray dogs, and problems with peers, this is a very appealing book to many young readers. As a bonus it is a thoughtful, sympathetic, fairly well-written story.

Interest Level: 4-6. Reading Level: 4.2. Further Search Topics: Gangs-Fiction, Pets-Fiction, Dogs-Fiction, Friendship-Fiction, Honesty-Fiction, Courage-Fiction, Loneliness-Fiction, Extra Sensory Perception-Fiction, Everyday Stories.

Waldorf, Mary. Jake McGee and his feet; illus by Leonard Shortall. HM 1980, 82 pp.

His severe reading difficulties made school the worst place in the world for Jake McGee. On the day that his reading tutor became so impatient with him that she sent Jake to the principal, Jake decided that he couldn't stand school any longer and ran away. He didn't actually run away, he just let his feet finally do what they wanted. His feet were always getting Jake in trouble. They walked too slowly to get him to school on time; they wouldn't stay still once he was in school; and they were always trying to trip someone.

Jake knew that in addition to having problems with his feet he had reading problems, but no one at his old school in the country had noticed. When he and his family moved to the city everything had changed. Jake's mother was always at work or tired. Jake hadn't made any friends and so was always alone. But Jake thought the biggest of all his immediate problems was his feet. The day he ran away, Jake's feet led him to a lost baby, an eccentric old woman, and a neighbor boy, all of whom helped Jake recognize and deal with his real problem.

The book is not high literary quality. The characterization is somewhat flat and the plot is fairly predictable. However, the sentences and chapters are short, the vocabulary is manageable, and Jake's feelings will be shared by many non-readers.

Interest Level: 3-5. Reading Level: 2.2. Further Search Topics: School Stories, Moving, Household-Fiction, Runaways-Fiction, Academic Problems-Fiction, Working Parents-Fiction, Loneliness-Fiction, Feet-Fiction.

LONERS-FICTION

Angell, Judie. Dear Lola; or how to build your own family. Bradbury 1980, 166 pp.

Arthur (age 18), James (13), Annie and Al-Willie (twins, age 10), Edmund (9), and Ben (5) wanted to run away from the orphanage and find a place where they could be a real family. After waiting months, their chance arrived one night. They escaped in a van and began living on the road. It was weeks before they found a house in which they thought they could live. They didn't want trouble with local authorities, so most of the children enrolled in school and pretended to be living with their widowed grandfather. Only James (who never left his room) and Arthur stayed home. Arthur was the anonymous author of a nationally syndicated newspaper advice column. It was with the income from his "Dear Lola" column that Arthur was able to support the "family." When the townspeople eventually began to wonder about the "strange" behavior of the children, they investigated and found no adult in charge of the household. Arthur went to court to be appointed the childrens' guardian, but the judge ruled against him. Rather than be sent to foster homes again, Arthur and the children raced from the courtroom. The book ends as the family is once more together and on their own. An unusual cast of characters in a surprisingly warm and humorous book.

Interest Level: 4-6. Reading Level 3.1. Further Search Topics: Loners-Fiction, Runaways-Fiction, Orphans-Fiction, Survival-Fiction, Family Problems-Fiction, Family-Fiction, Read Aloud, Foster Homes-Fiction, Individualists-Fiction, Humorous Fiction.

Blume, Judy. Blubber. Bradbury 1974, 153 pp.

Jill, like all the other fifth graders in her class, did exactly as Wendy directed her. When Wendy nicknamed one of the class members Blubber and launched a campaign against her, Jill joined right in. It wasn't until the tables were turned and Jill became Wendy's next victim that Jill realized how much it hurt to be the target of such nastiness. It was only then that Jill could stand up to Wendy. Wendy's meanness is extreme and her classmates, without exception, actively follow her lead, yet all adult characters in the book are blind to what happens. Despite those drawbacks, the book deals with a problem very real to children and thus it has guaranteed audience appeal.

Interest Level: 4-6. Reading Level: 3.1. School Stories, Bullies-Fiction, Weight-Fiction, Loners-Fiction, Gangs-Fiction, Read Aloud, Cruelty-Fiction, Best Sellers, Troublemakers-Fiction, Friendship-Fiction.

Bulla, Clyde Robert. White bird; illus by Leonard Weisgard. T Y Crowell 1966, 79 pp.

This book is meant for a special reader. It will not appeal to the reader who wants only action and excitement from a book. It is a story of complex human relationships and differing definitions of love. John Thomas lost his parents in a river accident when he was just a baby. His cradle had been pulled from the river and he had been raised by reclusive Luke Vail. Luke placed no trust in the world or in people outside his tiny valley home and so forbade John Thomas to have anything to do with either one. Luke didn't allow John Thomas a pet either because he thought that John Thomas would only be hurt when he no longer had the animal. Despite Luke's argument, when he found an injured white crow, John Thomas kept it and tended it until the crow was stolen by three strangers as Luke stood by. Angry at Luke as much as at the strangers, John Thomas ran away to search for the bird, but found that it had been shot.

Far from being fruitless, however, John Thomas's trip out of the valley gave him an entirely different view of people than the one Luke had shown him. Upon a friend's encouragement, John Thomas returned to Luke to share that view.

Subtle and unusual, this book needs a mature, sensitive reader and/or discussion in order to be fully appreciated.

Interest Level: 4-6. Reading Level 2.1. Further Search Topics: Pets-Fiction, Orphans-Fiction, Runaways-Fiction, Birds-Fiction, Love-Fiction, Loners-Fiction, Courage-Fiction.

Burch, Robert. Queenie Peavy; illus by Jerry Lazare. Viking Pr. 1966, 159 pp.

Queenie was always in trouble. She could be mean, really mean, but, she was also bright, talented, independent and resilient. Queenie blamed her problems on the fact that people teased her because her father was in jail and because she was poor. She thought that she had to defend herself against the world. Queenie was proud of her poor reputation until she accidentally-on-purpose caused a classmate to break his leg. Then, when her father returned home and wasn't the person she'd hoped he'd be, Queenie realized that only she could make her life better. Being the strong person she was, she set out to do just that.

Queenie is a wonderfully alive and sympathetic character, one well worth introducing to older readers despite the book's reading level. Print somewhat small. Line spacing average width.

Interest Level: 5-6. Reading Level: 5.1. Further Search Topics: Family Problems-Fiction, Crime-Fiction, Loners-Fiction, Poverty-Fiction, Humorous Fiction, Bullies-Fiction, Troublemakers-Fiction, Academic Problems-Fiction, Read Aloud.

Cone, Molly. The amazing memory of Harvey Bean; illus by Robert MacLean. HM 1980, 83 pp.

It had been a long time since Harvey had been happy. His memory was so bad that he was always in trouble at school. And now that his parents were separating, he had trouble at home, too. Because he thought that neither one of his parents wanted him he told each one that he was going to stay with the other and instead decided to spend the summer alone. A few hours after he left home, Harry ran into Mr. and Mrs. Katz and before he completely realized it, he was living with them.

Mr. Katz couldn't stand to see anything go to waste. He collected the usable food thrown out behind grocery stores, old furniture, tools, windows and more. Mrs. Katz, whose memory was just as bad as Harvey's, loved to cook, so she could always find a way to use the food. Everything else bulged from the house and garage into the driveway and yard. Harvey spent a happy summer learning to scavenge, eating well, learning not to worry about what others thought of him and even improving his memory. When his parents finally found him, Harvey realized that they really did want him, even if they were separated. He decided to live with his mother on weekdays, his father on weekends, and the Katzs during the summers.

The plot problems that are obvious to adult readers are ones that most young readers will be able to ignore (i.e. neither parent checks on Harvey for over two months). Young readers will enjoy the humor and realism of Harvey's pain, happiness and eventual feeling of self-confidence and triumph. The ten short chapters, good-sized print and adequate space between the lines help lower the book's reading level to late fourth grade.

Interest Level: 3-6. Reading Level: 5.1. Further Search Topics: Loners-Fiction, Vacation-Fiction, Divorce and Separation-Fiction, Humorous Fiction, Group 2, Memory-Fiction, Runaways-Fiction, Academic Problems-Fiction, Individualists-Fiction.

Heide, Florence Parry. The mystery of the silver tag; illus by Seymour Fleishman. A. Whitman 1972, 127 pp.

Jay's paper route took him to one house that he wished he could avoid. It was grumpy, old Mr. Pendleton's house that Jay hated. One rainy day he spotted what he later realized was a prize Angora cat hiding on Mr. Pendleton's porch. When the cat was reported lost in that night's paper, Jay and the other members of the Spotlight Club decided to try to return the cat to its owner, Miss Horton. Their attempts to get the cat back from Mr. Pendleton meant that they had to spy on him, to sneak into his garage, and to spend the night in a treehouse overlooking his house. They were afraid that they had failed when they saw Mr. Pendleton leave with the cat. Determined to be the ones to tell Miss Horton of their failure, they went to her apartment and found Mr. Pendleton already there. Mr. Pendleton was a famous animal photographer who, upon finding the cat, had asked Miss Horton if he could photograph him. The children, thinking only that Mr. Pendleton was a mad scientist who kidnapped cats, had jumped to all the wrong conclusions, but ended with a mystery solved, new friends, and their first lesson in being detectives.

See entry with *Mystery at Southport Cinema* for series information. Spotlight Club Mystery series.

Interest Level: 3-5. Reading Level: 2.2. Further Search Topics: Mystery and Detective Stories, Brothers and Sisters-Fiction, Gangs-Fiction, Cats-Fiction, Loners-Fiction, Detectives-Fiction, Photography-Fiction, Kidnapping-Fiction.

Hurwitz, Johanna. The law of gravity; illus by Ingrid Fetz. Morrow 1978, 192 pp.

The summer between fifth and sixth grades looked very unexciting to Margot. Her best friends were both going away for the whole summer and her father, a musician, was going to be on tour for most of the summer. Margot's very overweight mother had sworn never to go downstairs from their fifth floor walk-up apartment. Unless Margot chose to stay upstairs too, she was sure she would have a very lonely vacation. In addition, she had to work on a summer project for school. The project she finally chose was to get her mother downstairs after nine years of staying upstairs. In search of help she went to the local library where she met Bernie. Bernie was only a year older than Margot, but he seemed to know the most interesting things about the city. He showed her places Margot had never heard of before, he taught her to play chess, backgammon, and even to ride a bicycle. He was so full of fascinating ideas and information that Margot had no chance to be bored or lonely. Best of all, he even tried to help Margot with her project. None of their ideas worked, however, until Margot pretended to run away and scared her mother into going downstairs. Only then did Margot realize that she loved her mother whether or not she stayed on the fifth floor and that she couldn't simply force her mother or anyone else to change to suit her own fancy.

The book is a warm, understanding, slightly humorous treatment of the fairly common wish to change someone else. Although not many readers are

likely to share Margot's exact problem, most will recognize her feelings. The book is also a virtual Chamber of Commerce advertisement for urban living. One of its other charms is its picture of a non-competitive, open, real friendship between an 11-year-old girl and a 12-year-old boy. The only drawback to the book is its inconsistent reading level which varies from 4.1 to 5.1 with a rare leap to 5.2.

Interest Level: 4-6. Reading Level: 4.2. Further Search Topics: Vacation-Fiction, Friendship-Fiction, Loners-Fiction, City Life-Fiction, Individualists-Fiction, Courage-Fiction, New York City-Fiction, Humorous Fiction, Family-Fiction, Challenges-Fiction, Weight-Fiction, Everyday Stories, Best Sellers.

MacLachlan, Patricia. Arthur, for the very first time; illus by Lloyd Bloom. Har-Row 1980, 117 pp.

A beautifully written, sensitive yet humorous story of a boy's maturation and growing awareness of the world around him. When Arthur's unhappiness at home is made more intense by the advent of a new baby, he is sent to spend the summer with his older aunt and uncle. Their eccentricities and those of their friends are at first only material for Arthur to write about in his journal. But as the summer progresses he not only learns from them, but also grows from an observer of life to a participant. His final step is helping a large and beloved pig bear her litter in a driving rain storm aided only by his independent, totally untamed young friend Moira.

The print is somewhat small, but spacing between lines is generous.

Interest Level: 4-6. Reading Level: 4.2. Further Search Topics: Read Aloud, Children-Growth-Fiction, Humorous Fiction, Friendship-Fiction, Vacation-Fiction, Relatives-Fiction, Infants-Fiction, Individualists-Fiction, Writing-Fiction, Loners-Fiction, Group 2.

Mazer, Harry. The war on Villa Street. Delacorte 1978, 182 pp.

Willis was a loner and a runner. He was a loner because he didn't want anyone to find out about his alcoholic father. He wasn't quite sure why he ran; perhaps because it was the only time he felt good. When Rabbit Slavin and his friends asked Willis to become part of their gang, he refused. He was flattered and wanted to join, but the gang wanted to meet at his house and Willis couldn't risk that. Then when he agreed to coach the local "retard" for the school's field day, Willis gave the gang the opportunity they wanted to take their revenge on him for turning them down. The gang's hatred for Willis increased still more when he beat their best runner and athlete. In payment, the gang jumped Willis and beat him badly. After he picked himself up, Willis realized that he had at least faced the worst of his fears and survived. Days later when his drunken father humiliated him, Willis realized he had to face that, too. He made peace with himself and the world by deciding he could neither continue to run away from, nor apologize for his father anymore. He was independent and strong.

There is much in this fast-paced book besides the obvious violence and action. It is written with an intuitive feel for a teenager's problems and emotions and is a sensitive portrayal of mature concepts. The print is large, but spacing between the lines should have been slightly increased.

Interest Level: 5-6. Reading Level: 5.1. Further Search Topics: Running-Fiction, Loneliness-Fiction, Alcoholism-Fiction, Loners-Fiction, Mental Retardation-Fiction, Gangs-Fiction, Child Abuse-Fiction, Bullies-Fiction, Family Problems-Fiction, Courage-Fiction.

Parish, Peggy. Hermit Dan; illus by Paul Frame. Macmillan 1977, 151 pp.

When the Roberts children tried to prove that Pirate Island really had been used by pirates, they encountered more action and intrigue than they had found in any of their earlier adventures. Liza, Bill and Jed suspected that Hermit Dan knew whether or not there had been pirates on the island, but he was so gruff and apparently mean that they didn't dare ask him any questions. Instead, they trailed and spied on him and asked questions of anyone who had known Hermit Dan as a child. It was rumored that his ancestors had actually been pirates. Until a terrible fire that had destroyed all they owned, Hermit Dan's family had been very wealthy. However, no one knew how they had become so rich.

In an attempt to see what the summer residents knew about Hermit Dan, the children introduced themselves to the vacationing youngsters. Among the visitors the Roberts met Hank and Ted, brothers bent on bullying Hermit Dan. When the children were rescued from a severe sandstorm by Hermit Dan, they were surprised to find that he wasn't nearly as gruff as he appeared. In fact they began to feel quite protective of the old man. Thus when Hank and Ted stole a secret box that held all of Hermit Dan's valuables, it was the Roberts children who fought (literally) to get the box back. It was after Liza, Bill and Jed returned the box to Hermit Dan, however, that the real surprises began: these included a surprise party for Hermit Dan, his wish to be friendly, and his gift to the children of three pieces of eight that proved his family members were pirates.

This title's more interesting and involved plot makes the book more likely to be a success with older readers than the other stories about the Roberts children. Otherwise it shares the same format, faults and strengths as the other series titles.

Interest Level: 2-5. Reading Level: 2.1. Further Search Topics: Mystery and Detective Stories, Pirates-Fiction, Vacation-Fiction, Loners-Fiction, Treasure-Fiction, Bullies-Fiction, Brothers and Sisters-Fiction, Grandparents-Fiction.

Sachs, Marily. The bears' house; illus by Louis Glanzman. Doubleday 1971, 81 pp.

Don't let the benign appearance of this book fool you. This is a disturbing, almost brutal story. It is the story of Fran Ellen, a fourth grader with more problems than anyone should have to shoulder at one time. Her father had left the family and her mother had had a mental breakdown. Fran Ellen and her older brother were left with responsibility for themselves, their mother, and three other children (including a baby). They were all ill-fed, poorly dressed, and unwashed. Neither the social worker nor Fran Ellen's teacher knew the extent of the family's problems. Fran Ellen's only happiness came from her baby sister and from a schoolroom model (of *Goldilocks and the Three Bears* and their house) into which she mentally retreated whenever she had the chance.

As the school year closed, Fran Ellen's teacher visited her home to deliver the bears' house and discovered Fran Ellen's mother and very sick baby sister. Although she hated the idea that the family might have to split up, Fran Ellen had matured enough to realize that when her teacher insisted that she would get help for the family, her teacher was taking the proper action.

The book is inappropriately illustrated to make it appear cute and even humorous. The story is far from either. It is so stark that it probably shouldn't have been illustrated at all. And because the hope that is present in the book's ending is very subtle, a review and a discussion may be necessary to help relieve some young readers' anxieties.

Interest Level: 5-6. Reading Level: 3.1. Further Search Topics: Divorce and Separation-Fiction, Challenges-Fiction, Poverty-Fiction, Family Problems-Fiction, Loners-Fiction, Survival-Fiction, Mental Illness-Fiction, Brothers and Sisters-Fiction.

Smith, Doris Buchanan. Tough Chauncey. Morrow 1974, 222 pp.

Chauncey Childs had taught himself to be tough— very tough. Even though he was small for his age (13 years old), the only person who gave him any trouble was his sometimes-friend, Black Jack Levitt. Everyone else was scared of Chauncey. Chauncey felt that he had to be tough or he wouldn't be able to survive. He had to be tough to stand the beatings his grandfather gave him "for his own good," to put up with his mother's drinking and disappearances, and to stand the sight of his grandfather shooting the stray kittens born in their garage.

Chauncey's greatest wish was to be able to live with his mother, instead of with his grandparents. In a desperate attempt to achieve that end he accidentally fell from a moving train and badly hurt his leg. Instead of being returned to his mother he was once more taken back to his grandparents. Chauncey's unhappiness grew until he finally decided to take the one surviving stray kitten and run away. Jack helped him find an empty garage where he could hide while he figured out what to do with his future. After talking with Jack and doing more deep soul searching, Chauncey decided to reshape himself and his life. His first step was to curb his temper and his tongue when his hiding place was discovered. His second step was to see about finding a foster home where he would be treated well, and where he could get a new start.

Ugly as the story is in places, its ending is hopeful. Although it is not always realistic, Chauncey's story is compelling enough to appeal to many readers, especially those who have enjoyed *The War on Villa Street*, by Henry Mazer, *The Outsiders*, by Susan Hinton, or *Mystery of the Fat Cat*, by Frank Bonham. The book's length and its artificially low reading level (vocabulary is often difficult but sentences are very short) make this book most appropriate for an older reader whose reading level is 4.1 or higher.

Interest Level: 5-6. Reading Level: 3.2. Further Search Topics: Child Abuse-Fiction, Family Problems-Fiction, Grandparents-Fiction, Runaways-Fiction, Bullies-Fiction, Single Parent Family-Fiction, Loners-Fiction, Friendship-Fiction, Troublemakers-Fiction, Foster Homes-Fiction.

Smith, Doris Buchanan. Last was Lloyd. Viking Pr 1981, 124 pp.

Lloyd had several problems: he was overweight, his mother was overprotective, he had no school friends, and there was a chance he might be taken away from home and put into foster care because he had missed so much school. Lloyd's mother, very young and very defensive when she had Lloyd, had done her best to be a "good mother," but in doing so, had made Lloyd fearful of the world. He had become the subject of his classmates' mockery so many times that the only way he could respond to his peers was with nastiness. The one skill he possessed was hitting a baseball. He kept this skill well hidden for fear of exposing himself to further mockery. When one of his classmates accidentally discovered how well Lloyd hit, he took the first step to becoming Lloyd's friend. Lloyd's reaction was to back away, but Kirby kept trying. Eventually Kirby's attempts and those of an understanding truant officer, helped Lloyd begin to make friends, to treat others decently, and to pull away from his mother; in short, he began to mature.

Because Lloyd's problems can be oversimplified too easily, this book requires a fairly mature reader and perhaps even discussion in order to fully understand its subtleties.

Interest Level: 5-6+ Reading Level: 4.2. Further Search Topics: Weight-Fiction, Single Parent Family-Fiction, Courage-Fiction, School Stories, Loners-Fiction, Friendship-Fiction, Baseball-Fiction, Family Problems-Fiction, Foster Homes-Fiction, Children-Growth-Fiction.

Thompson, Jean. Brother of the wolves; illus by Steve Marchesi. Morrow 1978, 159 pp.

Shadow Fox, a Sioux medicine man, went into a wolves' den looking for special items he needed for healing, but found much more. He found a baby boy who had apparently lost his parents in an accident and then been adopted by the wolves. Winter was approaching and Shadow Fox knew the baby would not be able to survive the cold, so he took the child back to his people. The people were reluctant to accept Wolf Brother, saying that he was an evil omen, that he was unnatural, and that he would bring them trouble. But Shadow Fox's will prevailed and Wolf Brother was allowed to stay and grow up with the Sioux.

As he grew Wolf Brother continued to communicate with the wolves and thus fueled the rumors that grew about him. A very jealous young man, Looks-Away, told the people that a vision had shown him that Wolf Brother and his wolves would one day destroy the village and all its people. The people grew so suspicious of Wolf Brother that, when their horses were stolen and they faced a drought, they blamed him and drove him from the village.

For a while Wolf Brother tried to live as a wolf but found that he could not be totally happy. He wandered away to look for a tribe by whom he might be accepted. On his way, he too had a vision—a vision that told him he would find horses and buffalo for the Sioux and be welcomed home again. It was weeks later before he accidentally found his tribe's horses. In a daring move and with help from the wolves, Wolf Brother not only rescued the horses from the raiders, but also found buffalo just as his vision had predicted. He was then, for the first time, fully welcomed by his people.

This is a taut, suspenseful and mature story about a strong and unusual character. Older readers are most likely to respond positively to the Indian culture and lore.

Interest Level: 5-6. Reading Level: 3.1. Further Search Topics: Survival-Fiction, Wolves-Fiction, Orphans-Fiction, Loners-Fiction, Indians of North America-Fiction, Sioux Indians-Fiction, Jealousy-Fiction, Best Sellers.

LOVE-FICTION

Blume, Judy. Are you there God? It's me, Margaret. Bradbury 1970, 149 pp.

Sixth grade was a year of growth for Margaret and her friends. They all wondered when they would start growing breasts and when they would begin menstruating. Each was kissed for the first time. It was also a year in which Margaret tried to decide whether to be Jewish or Christian and ended up neither. She simply remained friends with God, just as she was when the year began. The book is a reassuring, very open, and humorous treatment of the pains and promise of maturation. It is exceptionally popular with older elementary school readers, so the book's slightly small print and narrow lines should not impede an interested reader's progress.

Interest Level: 4-6. Reading Level: 3.2. Further Search Topics: School Stories, Family-Fiction, Children-Growth-Fiction, Religion-Fiction, Humorous Fiction, Love-Fiction, Best Sellers, Grandparents-Fiction, Everyday Stories.

Blume, Judy. Deenie. Bradbury 1973, 159 pp.

Deenie's mother wanted Deenie to be a model. Deenie didn't know what she wanted until she learned that she had scoliosis (curvature of the spine) and would have to wear a brace for four years. Then she knew she only wanted to be normal. She was repulsed by deformities of any kind. She couldn't stand the idea of a brace. Her mother's attitude made Deenie's adjustment even more difficult. It was her father, her doctor, her sister, and a new friend with excema who finally helped Deenie accept her brace and the idea of physical differences. Subplots include Deenie's budding romance with an eighth grade boy, her strained relationship with her mother, and her growing awareness of sex (masturbation and intercourse). Print and line spacing are similar to *Are You There God? It's Me, Margaret.*

Interest Level: 5-6. Reading Level: 3.1. Further Search Topics: Models, Fashion-Fiction, Beauty-Fiction, Scoliosis-Fiction, Physically Handicapped-Fiction, Children-Growth-Fiction, Sex-Fiction, Love-Fiction, Family Problems-Fiction, Illness-Fiction, Adolescence-Fiction.

Blume, Judy. Tiger eyes. Bradbury 1981, 206 pp.

Davey's father's death was a shock that for awhile separated Davey from her mother. They occupied the same space, but Davey felt herself unable to communicate with her mother or with her aunt and uncle with whom they were living. The horror of the night her father was shot in a robbery attempt was too great for Davey to confront. It was too much for Davey's mother too, and so instead of growing closer, they draw apart. They let Davey's aunt and uncle direct their lives for almost a year before each was able to accept Mr. Wexler's death. During that time Davey's closest, most helpful friend was a loner named only Wolf. With him Davey lost enough fear and hatred that she was finally able to begin to talk about her father.

The setting (New Mexico) is much more important than in most of Blume's stories, the book's reading level is considerably more difficult, and the plot is about experiences more unique than usual. It will not fail to draw crowds of older readers however, for in most other respects the book follows Blume's successful formula.

Interest Level: 6+ Reading Level 5.1. Further Search Topics: Death-Fiction, Moving, Household-Fiction, Love-Fiction, Single Parent Family-Fiction, Family Problems-Fiction.

Bulla, Clyde Robert. White bird; illus by Leonard Weisgard. T Y Crowell 1966, 79 pp.

This book is meant for a special reader. It will not appeal to the reader who wants only action and excitement from a book. It is a story of complex human relationships and differing definitions of love. John Thomas lost his parents in a river accident when he was just a baby. His cradle had been pulled from the river and he had been raised by reclusive Luke

Vail. Luke placed no trust in the world or in people outside his tiny valley home and so forbade John Thomas to have anything to do with either one. Luke didn't allow John Thomas a pet either because he thought that John Thomas would only be hurt when he no longer had the animal. Despite Luke's argument, when he found an injured white crow, John Thomas kept it and tended it until the crow was stolen by three strangers as Luke stood by. Angry at Luke as much as at the strangers, John Thomas ran away to search for the bird, but found that it had been shot. Far from being fruitless, however, John Thomas's trip out of the valley gave him an entirely different view of people than the one Luke had shown him. Upon a friend's encouragement, John Thomas returned to Luke to share that view.

Subtle and unusual, this book needs a mature, sensitive reader and/or discussion in order to be fully appreciated.

Interest Level: 4-6. Reading Level 2.1. Further Search Topics: Pets-Fiction, Orphans-Fiction, Runaways-Fiction, Birds-Fiction, Love-Fiction, Loners-Fiction, Courage-Fiction.

Byars, Betsy. The Cybil war; illus by Gail Owens. Viking Pr. 1981, 126 pp.

Simon and Tony both had a crush on Cybil, but according to Tony, Cybil liked Tony better than she liked Simon. Simon was unhappily willing to accept Tony's word even though he knew Tony was a chronic liar. After all, Cybil had been the one to talk their teacher out of giving the lead in the class play about nutrition to Simon. Consequently Simon was being forced to impersonate a jar of peanut butter. In an elaborate attempt to win Cybil's affection Tony began telling Cybil lies about Simon and then set up a double date with Cybil and Harriet. On their walk home, Simon learned from Harriet that Cybil had only agreed to the date because Simon was going along. Happy at last, Simon realized he wanted no more lies and tricks; that he wanted to be truthful with Cybil and with himself. In the name of truth, he was even willing to accept the fact that his father, who had deserted the family, would not be returning.

A good story with just enough humor and romance to make it widely appealing as either a shared book (read aloud) or a personal pick. Print is fairly small.

Interest Level: 5-6. Reading Level: 4.2. Further Search Topics: Humorous Fiction, Love-Fiction, School Stories, Honesty-Fiction, Friendship-Fiction, Single Parent Family-Fiction, Read Aloud, Everyday Stories, Adolescence-Fiction.

Danziger, Paula. There's a bat in bunk five. Delacorte 1980, 150 pp.

Although this is a sequel to *The Cat Ate My Gymsuit,* it can be read alone. Marcy accepted an offer to become a junior counselor at an arts camp run by her ex-English teacher Ms. Finney and Ms. Finney's husband. After a nervous beginning, Marcy found herself enjoying the other counselors and the campers, but most of all, her first romance. Marcy's only difficulty was dealing with Ginger, a very troubled 10-year-old in Marcy's cabin. Marcy couldn't seem to get through to Ginger. When Ginger ran away, Marcy was forced to consider whether she should have spent more time with the campers and not quite so much time with Ted.

Marcy is a normal teenager whose problems, questions and activities are appealing to many teen and pre-teen readers. The characters who surround Marcy here are less stereotyped and flat than those in The Cat Ate My Gymsuit. Even Marcy's parents are more human. The author's light touch is just right for Marcy's story.

Interest Level: 5-6. Reading Level: 3.2. Further Search Topics: Humorous Fiction, Camp-Fiction, Everyday Stories, Love-Fiction, Vacation-Fiction, Occupations-Fiction, Adolescence-Fiction.

Danziger, Paula. The pistachio prescription. Delacorte 1978 154 pp.

Just as Cassie entered her freshman year in high school, the old stand-by that had helped her deal with all her problems (eating pistachio nuts) began to fail. To be sure, she did get through the class elections and was elected president. She met and started dating Bernie. She gained self-confidence. She even managed to stand up to a particularly mean teacher. But, eating pistachios didn't help at all at home where Cassie really needed them. She could hardly stand to be in the same room with her older sister. She hated the importance her mother placed on looking right and dressing well. Most of all, she hated the way her parents were constantly fighting. The only person with whom she was really confortable was her brother. But, before the year was over, Cassie's parents decided to get a divorce, she and her sister became friends and Cassie learned to accept her family.

Another Judy Blume-style author, but Danziger's portraits of adults tend to be even more one-dimensional and exaggerated than Blume's. Very popular anyway.

Interest Level: 6+. Reading Level: 5.1. Further Search Topics: Divorce and Separation-Fiction, Family Problems-Fiction, Beauty-Fiction, School Stories, Adolescence-Fiction, Love-Fiction, Brothers and Sisters-Fiction, Everyday Stories.

Pevsner, Stella. And you give me a pain, Elaine. HM 1978, 182 pp.

Andrea was the youngest of three children. She was very close to her brother, Joe, but he was away at college. There was only Elaine at home, but Andrea and Elaine didn't get along at all. Elaine was a troubled young woman who took so much of her parents' attention that there was none left for Andrea. This is the story of Andrea's year in eighth grade, a year in which she discovered that she was a steady and strong person. It was the year in which Andrea worked on the school play, had her first boyfriend, weathered the storms when her sister ran away, and began to understand her sister more and resent her less. It was also the year that she had to learn to live with her brother's accidental death.

The author's Judy Blume style (but with less humor) guarantees readers among older children.

Interest Level: 5-6. Reading Level: 4.1. Further Search Topics: Family Problems-Fiction, Brothers and Sisters-Fiction, Love-Fiction, Death-Fiction, Runaways-Fiction, Troublemakers-Fiction, Adolescence-Fiction.

Platt, Kin. Brogg's brain. Lippincott 1981, 123 pp.

According to everyone else, Monty Davis should have been one of the fastest milers in the city. He had, after all, run a four minute and ten second mile in practice one day. He had run well enough that day to beat his high school's two best milers. That was a good enough performance to make the coach push him, his teacher talk about winning, and his father puff up with pride. Even the marathon runner he saw occasionally in the park and his girl friend Cindy seemed to think that he could be the best. Monty really didn't care, or he thought he didn't. Maybe he was just afraid to see how good or bad he really was.

For whatever reason, he didn't want to run in the meet against Culver High School. He talked so much about not doing well, that by the time he was supposed to run, he even had his coach convinced he couldn't win. But as he ran, Monty heard a voice inside his head that sounded like the voice in a strange science fiction film that he and Cindy had just seen. The voice seemed to say that he could win, and suddenly that was what Monty wanted. The voice and his new-found determination were what pulled Monty through and gave him first place.

This book is for the track fan or the runner. Few others are likely to care about the difference between a four-twenty and a four-ten high school mile. For those who do care, this is a good choice.

Interest Level: 5-6. Reading Level: 3.1. Further Search Topics: Family Problems-Fiction, Love-Fiction, Running-Fiction, Courage-Fiction.

Platt, Kin. Run for your life; photos by Chuck Freedman. Watts 1977, 95 pp.

Lee almost lost his newspaper delivery job when someone began to regularly steal money and papers from the newspaper boxes along his route. Lee saw a chance for revenge if he could beat the thief in the mile race at the next track meet.

Most of the abundant dialogue is slang. The romantic interest is innocent and low keyed. The story has enough running to make that a strong appeal, but not so much that no one but a track or running enthusiast can enjoy it.

Interest Level: 5-6. Reading Level: 2.2. Further Search Topics: Running-Fiction, Love-Fiction, Occupations-Fiction, Crime-Fiction.

Silman, Roberta. Somebody else's child; illus by Chris Conover. Warne 1976, 64 pp.

Peter was adopted, but he had never questioned his family's love for him until Puddin' Paint, the school bus driver, made a thoughtless remark. Peter's affection for the older man was strong enough to help him understand Puddin' Paint's feelings. When Puddin' Paint's two dogs disappeared and the bus driver was almost heartbroken, it was Peter who helped the old man search for the dogs. That experience helped both Peter and Puddin' Paint understand that love doesn't only extend to natural born children, but can be just as strong and deep for others.

A simple telling of a moving story. It is as useful for readers who love dogs as for those interested in adoption. Rather inconsistent reading level, tests between 1.2 and 3.1.

Interest Level: 2-5. Reading Level: 2.2. Further Search Topics: Adoption-Fiction, Dogs-Fiction, Friendship-Fiction, Love-Fiction.

LYNN, FRED

Burchard, Marshall. Sports hero: Fred Lynn. Putnam 1976, 95 pp.

Fred Lynn was baseball's first rookie to be named Most Valuable Player. Consistent reading level. See *Sports Hero: Bill Walton.* Sports Hero series.

Interest Level: 2-6. Reading Level: 3.2. Further Search Topics: Biography, Lynn, Fred, Baseball-Biography, Group 2.

MCENROE, JOHN

Burchard, Susan H. Sports star: John McEnroe. HarBraceJ 1979, 63 pp.

In 1977, feisty John McEnroe became the youngest semi-finalist ever to play at Wimbledon. Both before and since then, he has been noted almost as often for his temper as his talent. The level of difficulty of this book varies from 3.1 to 4.1. See *Sports Star: Elvin Hayes* for more details about the book. Sports Star series.

Interest Level: 3-6. Reading Level: 3.2. Further Search Topics: Biography, Tennis-Biography, McEnroe, John.

MAGIC

Abisch, Roz. Mixed bag of magic tricks; illus by Boche Kaplan. Walker & Co. 1973, 64 pp.

The definition of magic is broadened here to include optical illusions, puzzles, age and date guessing formulae, as well as slight of hand and prearranged tricks. There are 25 "feats of magic" here, with especially good tips on performance, practice, costumes, and props. Although tricks in *Science Puzzles, It's Magic?, Funny Magic,* and *Magic Secrets* are showier, this is a more solid introduction to the subject. The Knot Magic Trick receives its best explanation here. See *It's Magic?* and *Science Puzzles* for others. Bonus: The book looks like a manual and not like a reader, therefore it should be useful even with sixth graders. It is now available in paperback version only; published by Grosset and Dunlap (Activity Books).

Interest Level: 2-6. Reading Level: 2.2. Further Search Topics: Magic, Optical Illusions, Puzzles.

Dolan, Edward F., Jr. Let's make magic; photos by Jay Irving. Doubleday 1981, 96 pp.

With playing cards, coins, paper, a few commonly available odds and ends and some practice, the reader can perform most of the tricks in this book. The book is not a step-by-step description of how to put together a magic show (as some of the other titles are), but is more like a casual chat with a friend who wants to teach you to perform a few tricks. Some are simply optical illusions; some are brain teasers that involve mathematical calculations; some are card tricks; and others are much more traditional magic tricks.

Very little is said about how to use conversation as audience distraction or how to link the tricks together into a show. Instead, it is the kind of book that allows the reader to pick and choose any tricks he or she may want to learn without feeling pressured to do more than entertain a friend or two for a few moments. The tricks, with the possible exception of the mathematical brain teasers, are all easily manageable by third through sixth grade readers and yet are impressive to their peers. The use of photographs, rather than cartoon illustrations, helps to make the book a probable success, especially with older readers who like to entertain, enjoy the spotlight, or are interested in magic.

Interest Level: 3-6. Reading Level: 3.1. Further Search Topics: Magic, Optical illusions, Best Sellers.

Stoddard, Edward. The first book of magic; illus by Rod Slater. Watts 1977, 65 pp.

This is a good choice for readers who have already enjoyed reading and mastering an easier book of magic tricks (such as *Let's Make Magic,* by Edward Dolan, Jr.). The tricks the author includes are often too difficult for the casual beginner. They require both a good deal of practice, and the staging and poise that accompany experience. But for the magic enthusiast there are plenty of flashy tricks, hints for performing and detailed instructions. A few, but not many, are tricks found in other books. Most use easily found household objects. Print and illustrations are fairly small however.

Interest Level: 4-6. Reading Level: 3.1. Further Search Topics: Magic.

White, Laurence B., Jr. Science puzzles; illus by Marc Tolon Brown. A-W 1975, unp (46 pp).

There are twenty four very short experiments designed to illustrate the simplest of scientific principles clearly presented here. For all but a few experiments there is not only an explanation of what happens but also an explanation of why it happened. What makes the book even more useful, is that it can also be used as a book of easy magic tricks. Any child who enjoys it as science will, with a little help, be able to see its possibilities as magic. In fact it provides a better explanation of the Knot Magic trick than can be found in *It's Magic*.

Interest Level: 1-3. Reading Level: 1.2. Further Search Topics: Science, Magic, Puzzles, Experiments, Scientific.

White, Laurence B., Jr. Science toys; illus by Marc Tolon Brown. A-W 1975, unp (46 pp).

This book presents 23 toys that a young child can easily make and learn from at the same time. A sundial, a drinking straw that flies, a balloon that rolls over, a ghost that sticks to the wall by itself, a water-go-round, and a paper cup that roars are a few examples of what is to be found here. The construction and use of each toy is explained and illustrated in enough detail to enable the child to work alone. And as in *Science Puzzles*, some of the toys will double as magic tricks (i.e. can you balance the rim of a paper plate on your nose?).

Interest Level: 1-3. Reading Level: 2.1. Further Search Topics: Handicrafts, Science, Magic, Toys, Games, Group 2, Puzzles.

Wyler, Rose. Magic secrets; illus by Talivaldis Stubis. Har-Row 1967, 64 pp.

Another good selection of easily performed but impressive looking magic tricks. After a short section defining magic, 13 tricks are described. Another 11 tricks are included as the authors describe how to put on a magic show. Just what differentiates the first group of tricks from the second is not clear. With a little imagination any of the tricks shown in the book could be used in a magic show. Use of the book beyond fourth grade is not likely due to its "early-reader" appearance. An I-Can-Read-Book.

Interest Level: 1-4. Reading Level: 2.1. Further Search Topics: Magic, Group 2.

Wyler, Rose. Funny Magic; illus by Talivaldis Stubis. Schol Bk Serv 1972, 52 pp.

A collection of 20 simple but effective magic tricks that require some advance preparation and practice but which are well-suited to the third through fifth grade child's coordination. Because all tricks are meant to be performed in front of an audience, there are performance hints throughout the book. Most of the tricks are impressive enough to interest even sixth grade magicians, but the book's reader format and cute tone make it difficult to use beyond grade four.

Interest Level: 2-4. Reading Level: 2.1. Further Search Topics: Magic.

MAGIC-FICTION

Avi. No more magic. Pantheon 1975, 138 pp.

Avi has woven a mixture of mystery and magic to produce an excellent story. Chris' belief in magic is bolstered when his new bicycle disappears on Halloween night. Chris, his best friend Eddie, and a new friend, Muffin, eventually decide that strange Mr. Bullen, the junk dealer, has magical powers. In order to keep his powers a secret, Mr. Bullen had to steal back the magical bike he sold Chris. With plenty of intriguing complications along the way, the three children attempt to prove their theory correct but only prove themselves wrong. The age of the protagonists (fourth grade) is touched on so lightly and the plot is interesting enough that even sixth grade readers should find the book enjoyable.

Interest Level: 3-6. Reading Level: 4.2. Further Search Topics: Divorce and Separation-Fiction, Mystery and Detective Stories, Magic-Fiction, Halloween-Fiction, Witches-Fiction, Group 2, Read Aloud, Bicycles and Bicycling-Fiction.

Blume, Judy. Freckle juice; illus by Sonia O. Lisker. Four Winds 1971, 40 pp.

A very funny story that should appeal to almost everyone. Andrew wanted freckles so that the dirt on his skin wouldn't show as much and he wouldn't have to wash as often. As luck would have it, Sharon, the most obnoxious girl in class, had a freckle juice recipe that she was willing to sell for 50 cents. Even after drinking the brew of grape juice, vinegar, mustard, olive oil, and more, Andrew didn't see any freckles, but, he certainly was sick. Although the protagonists are younger, this book will hold even a fifth grade reader's interest.

Interest Level: 2-5. Reading Level 3.1. Further Search Topics: Humorous Fiction, Group 2, Read Aloud, Everyday Stories, Beauty-Fiction, School Stories, Magic-Fiction, Best Sellers.

Chew, Ruth. Witch's broom. Dodd 1977, 128 pp.

Amy's mother was the one who found the blue broom, but Amy and her friend Jean were the ones who learned it was magical. One night the broom flew Amy into a mountain cave where a coven of witches was meeting. It even forced Amy to answer the roll call for someone named Beryl. But it wasn't until it took both Amy and Jean back to the cave that they discovered the broom's connection to the strange bluejay that had been following them. The bluejay was really Beryl, a young and headstrong witch who had turned herself into the bluejay and then couldn't turn herself back. With the girls' unwitting help, Beryl found the charm to turn herself back into a witch and flew off on a scrawny old broom, leaving the blue broom for Amy and Jean.

What youngster wouldn't want a flying broomstick and the misadventures that go with owning one? Wish fulfillment can never be overrated as an appeal of Ruth Chew's books.

Interest Level: 2-5. Reading Level: 3.1. Further Search Topics: Witches-Fiction, Magic-Fiction, Fantasy, Birds-Fiction, Group 2, Transformations-Fiction.

Chew, Ruth. No such thing as a witch. Hastings 1971, 112 pp.

Despite the fact that their mother said there was no such thing as a witch, Tad and Nora were convinced that their neighbor Maggie Brown was indeed a witch. And they were right! Maggie Brown knew how to make a special kind of fudge that could make anyone into an animal-lover, enable people to talk with animals, or actually transform someone into an animal. All you had to do was to eat one, two, or three pieces of fudge respectively. But Maggie's overzealous love of animals and her disenchantment with housework eventually attracted the attention of her neighbors and the city health department. Only Tad and Nora's frantic efforts to help her saved Maggie from losing all of her animal friends.

A fairly detailed plot, the fascination of being able to change size and appearance and the intrigue involved in fooling the adults around Maggie make this one of Chew's best books.

Interest Level: 2-5. Reading Level: 2.2. Further Search Topics: Individualists-Fiction, Witches-Fiction, Animals-Fiction, Fantasy, Magic-Fiction, Brothers and Sisters-Fiction, Transformations-Fiction.

Chew, Ruth. The witch's garden. Hastings 1978, 112 pp.

Although its elements seem to promise an exciting adventure story, this is a disappointing book. The witch who moved into the dark, old home next door to Josh and Susan, was trying to improve her overgrown garden when Susan and Josh offered to help. The children accidentally splashed themselves with the witch's newest brew and found they suddenly became very tiny inhabitants of a dense and threatening jungle (the garden). After they regained their normal size, they dug into other areas of the garden. One hole they dug opened into an underground tunnel that they found was inhabited by a fire-breathing dragon. When the dragon cornered Mrs. Muldoon, Susan and Josh ran out of the tunnel, found the brew and splashed it onto the dragon. The dragon shrank away, Mrs. Muldoon was safe and the tunnel closed over.

Because there is little more suspense than in this description, the book fails to live up to its promise. In addition, the children's first sudden size change is just subtle enough to be confusing. Despite its problems the book is popular with Ruth Chew fans and therefore useful.

Interest Level: 2-5. Reading Level: 2.2. Further Search Topics: Witches-Fiction, Brothers and Sisters-Fiction, Magic-Fiction, Fantasy, Dragons-Fiction, Transformations-Fiction.

Chew, Ruth. The would-be witch. Hastings 1976, 112 pp.

Robin and her brother Andy took a liking to the clumsy white cat they saw in Zelda's Antique Shop. The cat apparently liked them, too, for it followed them home. Not having enough money to offer to buy Pearl from Zelda, the children tried to polish up an old pair of silver birds to trade for the cat. The polish turned out to be magical and made the birds real. When they tried the polish on a broom in Zelda's store, the broom began to fly. Upon discovering that Zelda wanted to be a witch but had failed the coven entrance exam, Rob helped her learn to fly and told her of the witches' meeting place that she and Andy had discovered. But the 12 witches who had been turned into cats were wicked enough to want to use Zelda to regain their human form and turn *her* into a cat. In attempting to prevent such a fate, Rob, Andy and Zelda set fire to the abandoned building being used as a meeting place. The 12 witches were rescued from the fire but charged with arson, which meant probable jail sentences for all of them. Zelda, finally a happy and capable witch, gave Pearl to Rob and Andy to thank them for their help.

A better-crafted story than many of the others, this also has a more evil cast of characters to provide additional interest.

Interest Level: 2-5. Reading Level: 2.2. Further Search Topics: Witches-Fiction, Brothers and Sisters-Fiction, Magic-Fiction, Fantasy, Transformations-Fiction, Cats-Fiction.

Chew, Ruth. Earthstar magic. Hastings 1979, 128 pp.

This is one of a series of similar stories by Ruth Chew. Each story involves two children and an old woman they usually suspect is a witch. As their suspicions become convictions they also find that, contrary to their expectation, the witch is very nice and often in need of help.

The children in this tale are brother and sister. Ben and Elizabeth first saw and then didn't see Trudy as she searched for a magical mushroom called an earthstar. Accidentally thrown together again, Ben and Elizabeth took a liking to Trudy, especially when she explained that she had been thrown out of her coven because she was so inept. In fact, she wasn't even able to control the earthstar. The earthstar manages to get all three in and out of adventures (including becoming tiny, flying and almost being eaten) before they learn to control its power. As the story ends, Trudy, finally respected by the other witches, flies off with a promise that Ben and Elizabeth will see her again.

Very lightweight but also very popular with young lovers of witch stories. There seems to be just the right amount of adventure to make up for the very benign witch.

Interest Level: 2-5. Reading Level: 2.2. Further Search Topics: Witches-Fiction, Magic-Fiction, Fantasy, Vacation-Fiction, Brothers and Sisters-Fiction, Transformations-Fiction.

Chew, Ruth. What the witch left. Hastings 1973, 128 pp.

One afternoon Katy and Louise decided to search through the locked drawer of an old dresser. Inside they found strange-looking gloves, an old robe, boots, a mirror and a tin box. The girls quickly learned that each item was magical. With the gloves on, the girls could draw, play piano, weave or write. They thought their new talents were wonderful until they each wrote identical school compositions. When she wore the robe for the school play, Louise found out that it made people invisible. The boots, which travelled 21 miles with each step, took the girls to Mexico, but made them late for lunch at home. The mirror showed them anything they wanted to see, and the box "found" everything that was lost. A very light story for children who don't need high adventure but like a mixture of humor and magic.

Interest Level: 3-5. Reading Level: 3.1. Further Search Topics: Magic-Fiction, Mexico-Fiction, Witches-Fiction, Fantasy, Humorous Fiction.

Chew, Ruth. The wishing tree. Hastings 1980, 142 pp.

Peggy and Brian's discovery of a talking cat, a bird with a beautiful song, and a strange and frightening tree led them to a shopping bag lady, a giant named Fred, a gold key and a magical tablecloth. In a rather complicated series of events, the children and the cat finally succeeded in retrieving the tablecloth from Annie (the old woman to whom Puss had loaned it) and giving it back to Fred, who needed it to help satisfy his gigantic appetite. In addition, they returned Fred to normal human size, rescued Annie from a fall on the ice, introduced the two characters and encouraged them to live together in Fred's castle.

Complicated enough already, the story's lengthy adventure that leads up to the discovery of the key (climbing into the magical tree and swimming in a pond) makes the plot even more complex. If a reader doesn't expect more than benign fantasy and fun this is an adequate choice.

Interest Level: 2-5. Reading Level: 2.2. Further Search Topics: Magic-Fiction, Fantasy, Brothers and Sisters-Fiction, Giants-Fiction, Cats-Fiction.

Corbett, Scott. The lemonade trick; illus by Paul Galdone. Little 1960, 103 pp.

This is the first book in a series of quite enjoyable stories (most of which are, unfortunately, too difficult to recommend here). Kerby was given an odd chemistry set by a strange old woman whom he helped one day. When he used the set to put together a brew, Kerby found himself completely under its spell. The sweet-smelling liquid he had concocted forced him to be good, so good that his parents began to worry about him. Luckily the spell wore off in a short time. But, Kerby kept experimenting with it: on himself, on his dog, on his friend, on his enemy and finally in desperation, on the entire boy's choir at church.

A succession of innocently humorous incidents are woven together into a satisfying story. Print size is on the small side.

Interest Level: 3-6. Reading Level: 3.1. Further Search Topics: Humorous Fiction, Bullies-Fiction, Magic-Fiction, Magicians-Fiction, Chemistry-Fiction, Read Aloud.

Robinson, Jean. The strange but wonderful cosmic awareness of Duffy Moon; illus by Lawrence Di Fiori. HM 1974, 142 pp.

Duffy was tired of being small, of always being on the losing side of fights, and of being unappreciated at home (by his ex-football star uncle). When he sent away for Mr. Flamel's Cosmic Awareness Kit, Duffy was sure he would then be able to take control over anything he wanted and direct his own life. His friend Peter, the narrator, wasn't quite so sure. Peter turned out to be right. Duffy almost made himself sick trying to build a stone wall. Babysitting two small boys and trying to bathe a Great Dane proved to be disastrous. But Duffy's biggest problem came from Boots McAfee's gang. A series of events finally brought Duffy and Peter face-to-face with the dreaded Boots. Luckily, she turned out to be a very smart girl who appreciated Duffy's true talents.

From the first to the last page this is a funny, very enjoyable book. A delightful book with a very palatable message.

Interest Level: 3-6. Reading Level: 3.2. Further Search Topics: Humorous Fiction, Bullies-Fiction, Magic-Fiction, Read Aloud, Occupations-Fiction, Sex Role-Fiction, Orphans-Fiction, Best Sellers, Gangs-Fiction, Courage-Fiction, Babysitting-Fiction.

Scism, Carol K. The wizard of Walnut Street; illus by Martha Alexander. Dial 1973, 54 pp.

John and his friends had no room in their Wizard Club for Ford Owens, the new kid. John thought Ford was a conceited show-off who only wanted to make John look like a coward. It was true that John was afraid of some things, such as going down the giant slide into the lake, but he didn't want anyone else to know it. So he excluded Ford from all the club's activities until Ford pushed his way into their magic wishing-well project.

It had been John's idea to charge everyone a dime who wanted to make a wish. They could use the money to buy the few simple things that they would need to make the wishes come true. But it was Ford's eerie volcano and his large dog that had added just the right atmosphere to the trick to make people believe. Even John and Ford found themselves making wishes. John wished to be able to go down

the giant slide. He didn't know what Ford wished. Much to John's initial surprise, people's wishes began to be fulfilled. Even Arthur, who had wished he could learn to dive, found he could. Then because John began to realize that the magic was in believing in himself and not in the wishing well, he tried the slide and succeeded. Once John's reason to avoid Ford was gone, he relaxed and asked Ford to join the club. At that point, even Ford's wish was granted.

Interest Level: 2-4. Reading Level: 2.1. Further Search Topics: Friendship-Fiction, Gangs-Fiction, Courage-Fiction, Magic-Fiction, Vacation-Fiction, Best Sellers.

MAGICIANS-FICTION

Corbett, Scott. The lemonade trick; illus by Paul Galdone. Little 1960, 103 pp.

This is the first book in a series of quite enjoyable stories (most of which are, unfortunately, too difficult to recommend here). Kerby was given an odd chemistry set by a strange old woman whom he helped one day. When he used the set to put together a brew, Kerby found himself completely under its spell. The sweet-smelling liquid he had concocted forced him to be good, so good that his parents began to worry about him. Luckily the spell wore off in a short time. But, Kerby kept experimenting with it: on himself, on his dog, on his friend, on his enemy and finally in desperation, on the entire boy's choir at church.

A succession of innocently humorous incidents are woven together into a satisfying story. Print size is on the small side.

Interest Level: 3-6. Reading Level: 3.1. Further Search Topics: Humorous Fiction, Bullies-Fiction, Magic-Fiction, Magicians-Fiction, Chemistry-Fiction, Read Aloud.

MARINE BIOLOGY

Buckley, Peter. I am from Puerto Rico. S ËAN S 1971, 127 pp.

Federico Ramirez had enjoyed his two years in New York City and didn't like the idea of moving back to Puerto Rico. When he arrived, he had no friends, no T.V., and nothing to do. Then Neri taught Federico the local games, showed him the sights and introduced him to Narcisco, a special fisherman. Narcisco took Federico through the wonders of the coral reefs. He taught him how to dive and fish. Within several months Federico was thoroughly at home in the water and loved Puerto Rico.

There is so much information about Puerto Rico and marine life that the book is never dry. Federico tells his own story as a series of fascinating experiences (meeting up with a shark, playing pinball, scuba diving at night, keeping a large turtle as a pet, etc.). There are abundant black and white photographs. An excellent choice for research (no index) or recreational reading. The print size is slightly on the small side, but the space between lines is good. Recently out of print, but worth looking for.

Interest Level: 5-6. Reading Level: 5.1. Further Search Topics: Puerto Rico, Fishing, Moving, Household-Fiction, Marine Biology, Scuba Diving, Ethnic Groups.

MATHEMATICS

Charosh, Mannis. Mathematical games for one or two; illus by Lois Ehlert. T Y Crowell 1975, 33 pp.

It will take a very special reader to appreciate this book, one who is excited by math puzzles and games and who is also willing to overlook the book's picture book format. Starting with a very simple, one-player game, the book progresses through six types of games, each progressively more taxing mentally. Each type of game is introduced by a very simple example that is thoroughly explained. For the up-and-coming Einstein.

Interest Level: 3-4. Reading Level: 2.2. Further Search Topics: Mathematics, Puzzles, Games.

MEDICINE-FICTION

Singer, Marilyn. It can't hurt forever; illus by Leigh Grant. Har-Row 1978, 186 pp.

When she was 11 years old, it was discovered that Ellie had a heart valve that hadn't closed by itself. Although her mother had promised her that she wouldn't die, Ellie was scared of the hospital and the operation she had to face. Her parents were kind and open about all that was to happen to her, but there was still much that Ellie had to learn from friends she made while she was in the hospital. There were times when she was frightened and only Sonia, a young open-heart surgery patient, could calm her. When Ellie, a special nurse, and a few other patients became close friends, Ellie learned enough from them to allow her to help another patient.

This is not a story of sweetness and light, but it is told with warmth, humor, and real understanding of a young person's fears. Thus it is not only an excellent candidate for bibliotherapy, but it is a truly satisfying story for the general reader as well.

Interest Level: 4-6. Reading Level: 2.2. Further Search Topics: Illness-Fiction, Physicians-Fiction, Medicine-Fiction, Courage-Fiction, Death-Fiction.

Slote, Alfred. Hang tough, Paul Mather. Lippincott 1973, 156 pp.

Paul Mather went against his doctor's and his parents' orders when he accepted his new neighbors' challenge to show his pitching skill. He had been told not to play baseball until he had been given permission, but Paul not only loved to pitch, he was also the best pitcher his new friends had ever seen. Knowing full well the medical problems he could be precipitating, Paul went ahead and pitched a spectacular game for the Wilson Dairy team against the Ace Appliance team. But by the end of the game, Paul was in the hospital again, and Wilson Dairy had been forced to forfeit the game because Paul had played illegally. As Paul's leukemia worsened, his determination to play baseball again grew. When the day came that his team was to play a second game against Ace Appliance, Paul made sure he was there. He was in a wheelchair and weak, but he was there. He couldn't actually play, but Paul's psychological support insured that Wilson Dairy won the game. He went back to the hospital proud, happy, and still determined to fight his disease.

This is more than the usual sports story. This is a very sensitive story of a young boy's determination to fight leukemia. The reader looking for only a baseball story may find this book more than he/she wants. However, the reader who is open to a story of human strength and courage will be well rewarded. The book neither dwells on nor minimizes the disease. Instead it uses both the disease and the sport to portray a character much more completely than in most sport stories, especially at this low a reading level. This is an excellent book for those special readers who respond well to thought-provoking material. Although chapters are short and reading level is low, the print is somewhat small. In addition, the first person style, told as if dictated into a tape recorder (complete with occasional interruptions), may be confusing to readers unless it is explained.

Interest Level: 5-6+Reading Level: 3.1. Further Search Topics: Baseball-Fiction, Death-Fiction, Illness-Fiction, Moving, Household-Fiction, Medicine-Fiction, Physicians-Fiction, Challenges-Fiction, Courage-Fiction.

MEMORY-FICTION

Cone, Molly. The amazing memory of Harvey Bean; illus by Robert MacLean. HM 1980, 83 pp.

It had been a long time since Harvey had been happy. His memory was so bad that he was always in trouble at school. And now that his parents were separating, he had trouble at home, too. Because he thought that neither one of his parents wanted him he told each one that he was going to stay with the other and instead decided to spend the summer alone. A few hours after he left home, Harry ran into Mr. and Mrs. Katz and before he completely realized it, he was living with them.

Mr. Katz couldn't stand to see anything go to waste. He collected the usable food thrown out behind grocery stores, old furniture, tools, windows and more. Mrs. Katz, whose memory was just as bad as Harvey's, loved to cook, so she could always find a way to use the food. Everything else bulged from the house and garage into the driveway and yard. Harvey spent a happy summer learning to scavenge, eating well, learning not to worry about what others thought of him and even improving his memory. When his parents finally found him, Harvey realized that they really did want him, even if they were separated. He decided to live with his mother on weekdays, his father on weekends, and the Katzs during the summers.

The plot problems that are obvious to adult readers are ones that most young readers will be able to ignore (i.e. neither parent checks on Harvey for over two months). Young readers will enjoy the humor and realism of Harvey's pain, happiness and eventual feeling of self-confidence and triumph. The ten short chapters, good-sized print and adequate space between the lines help lower the book's reading level to late fourth grade.

Interest Level: 3-6. Reading Level: 5.1. Further Search Topics: Loners-Fiction, Vacation-Fiction, Divorce and Separation-Fiction, Humorous Fiction, Group 2, Memory-Fiction, Runaways-Fiction, Academic Problems-Fiction, Individualists-Fiction.

MENTAL ILLNESS-FICTION

Clifford, Eth. The dastardly murder of Dirty Pete; illus by George Hughes. HM 1981, 120 pp.

Although this is a sequel to *Help, I'm a Prisoner in the Library*, it does not depend on the previous title, and in fact, is likely to be the more successful introduction to Mary Rose and Jo-Beth Onetree. Given the choice, most young readers will take a mystery set in a ghost town over a mystery set in a library.

Mary Rose, Jo-Beth and their father were on their way across country when they became lost. As night grew closer, the only place they could find to stay was an old hotel in the ghost town where Sorehead Jones had allegedly killed Dirty Pete. It was Sorehead's ghost who was supposed to haunt the town, and indeed there was someone or something who was in the town with the Onetrees. To their surprise, that someone turned out to be Sourdough Sam, an aging actor who had become senile and spent his days acting out all the parts in the Dirty Pete story. The town was only a movie set and the story was only a movie script. The Onetrees discovered the truth bit by bit after a frightening venture into an abandoned gold mine, a harrowing night in the haunted hotel and a jail sentence for Mr. Onetree.

Beware of the rare, very difficult descriptive passage that may cause trouble for some readers.

Interest Level: 2-5. Reading Level: 3.1. Further Search Topics: Mystery and Detective Stories, West-Fiction, Brothers and Sisters-Fiction, Motion Pictures-Fiction, Ghosts-Fiction, Treasure-Fiction, Group 2, Acting-Fiction, Aging-Fiction, Mental Illness-Fiction.

Kelley, Sally. Trouble with explosives. Bradbury 1976, 117 pp.

Polly Banks stuttered very badly. She wanted to stop but she couldn't. Moving, entering a new school, and facing a mean teacher who seemed in need of psychiatric help, all made Polly's stuttering worse. When Sis, Polly's new friend, rose to Polly's defense in one confrontation too many with Miss Patterson, the teacher took cruel revenge. Polly's desire to help Sis, her need to do something about her stuttering, and an understanding psychiatrist, all helped Polly learn to help herself with her speech problem. At the same time, she began to understand and have confidence in herself and her family.

Another "problem book" that older elementary school readers seem to crave. Polly and Sis are both very sympathetic characters who bring to life many of the uncertainties of growing up. Print and line spacing of only average size but otherwise a good choice.

Interest Level: 4-6. Reading Level: 3.2. Further Search Topics: Academic Problems-Fiction, Stuttering-Fiction, Psychiatrists-Fiction, School Stories, Mental Illness-Fiction, Troublemakers-Fiction, Courage-Fiction, Physically Handicapped-Fiction, Children-Growth-Fiction, Moving, Household-Fiction.

Sachs, Marily. The bears' house; illus by Louis Glanzman. Doubleday 1971, 81 pp.

Don't let the benign appearance of this book fool you. This is a disturbing, almost brutal story. It is the story of Fran Ellen, a fourth grader with more problems than anyone should have to shoulder at one time. Her father had left the family and her mother had had a mental breakdown. Fran Ellen and her older brother were left with responsibility for themselves, their mother, and three other children (including a baby). They were all ill-fed, poorly dressed, and unwashed. Neither the social worker nor Fran Ellen's teacher knew the extent of the family's problems. Fran Ellen's only happiness came from her baby sister and from a schoolroom model (of *Goldilocks and the Three Bears* and their house) into which she mentally retreated whenever she had the chance.

As the school year closed, Fran Ellen's teacher visited her home to deliver the bears' house and discovered Fran Ellen's mother and very sick baby sister. Although she hated the idea that the family might have to split up, Fran Ellen had matured enough to realize that when her teacher insisted that she would get help for the family, her teacher was taking the proper action.

The book is inappropriately illustrated to make it appear cute and even humorous. The story is far from either. It is so stark that it probably shouldn't have been illustrated at all. And because the hope that is present in the book's ending is very subtle, a review and a discussion may be necessary to help relieve some young readers' anxieties.

Interest Level: 5-6. Reading Level: 3.1. Further Search Topics: Divorce and Separation-Fiction, Challenges-Fiction, Poverty-Fiction, Family Problems-Fiction, Loners-Fiction, Survival-Fiction, Mental Illness-Fiction, Brothers and Sisters-Fiction.

MENTAL RETARDATION-FICTION

Mazer, Harry. The war on Villa Street. Delacorte 1978, 182 pp.

Willis was a loner and a runner. He was a loner because he didn't want anyone to find out about his alcoholic father. He wasn't quite sure why he ran; perhaps because it was the only time he felt good. When Rabbit Slavin and his friends asked Willis to become part of their gang, he refused. He was flattered and wanted to join, but the gang wanted to meet at his house and Willis couldn't risk that. Then when he agreed to coach the local "retard" for the school's field day, Willis gave the gang the opportunity they wanted to take their revenge on him for turning them down. The gang's hatred for Willis increased still more when he beat their best runner and athlete. In payment, the gang jumped Willis and beat him badly. After he picked himself up, Willis realized that he had at least faced the worst of his fears and survived. Days later when his drunken father humiliated him, Willis realized he had to face that, too. He made peace with himself and the world by deciding he could neither continue to run away from, nor apologize for his father anymore. He was independent and strong.

There is much in this fast-paced book besides the obvious violence and action. It is written with an intuitive feel for a teenager's problems and emotions and is a sensitive portrayal of mature concepts. The print is large, but spacing between the lines should have been slightly increased.

Interest Level: 5-6. Reading Level: 5.1. Further Search Topics: Running-Fiction, Loneliness-Fiction, Alcoholism-Fiction, Loners-Fiction, Mental Retardation-Fiction, Gangs-Fiction, Child Abuse-Fiction, Bullies-Fiction, Family Problems-Fiction, Courage-Fiction.

MEXICO

Lewis, Thomas P. Hill of fire; illus by Joan Sandin. Har-Row 1971, 63 pp.

A personalized account of the volcano that suddenly erupted in the middle of a farmer's field in Mexico on February 20, 1943. Because the account is written as a story and because of its easy-reader format, the book is most useful only through third grade. An I-Can-Read-History-Book.

Interest Level: 1-3. Reading Level: 2.2. Further Search Topics: Volcanoes, Group 2, Mexico, Disasters, Historical Fiction.

MEXICO-FICTION

Chew, Ruth. What the witch left. Hastings 1973, 128 pp.

One afternoon Katy and Louise decided to search through the locked drawer of an old dresser. Inside they found strange-looking gloves, an old robe, boots, a mirror and a tin box. The girls quickly learned that each item was magical. With the gloves on, the girls could draw, play piano, weave or write. They thought their new talents were wonderful until they each wrote identical school compositions. When she wore the robe for the school play, Louise found out that it made people invisible. The boots, which travelled 21 miles with each step, took the girls to Mexico, but made them late for lunch at home. The mirror showed them anything they wanted to see, and the box "found" everything that was lost. A very light story for children who don't need high adventure but like a mixture of humor and magic.

Interest Level: 3-5. Reading Level: 3.1. Further Search Topics: Magic-Fiction, Mexico-Fiction, Witches-Fiction, Fantasy, Humorous Fiction.

Clymer, Eleanor. Santiago's silver mine; illus by Ingrid Fetz. Atheneum 1973, 74 pp.

Although somewhat complicated by a large number of background incidents, especially early in the book, the story is both interesting and informative. Santiago and his friend Andreas wanted to be rich. The year's harvest had been very poor, so there was little food to eat. Both of their fathers had gone to Mexico City to find jobs and their mothers worked for very few pesos near home. Andreas wanted to search the old mine in the hills outside of town for silver, but the mining company had left a guard named Jose to prevent people from getting into the mines. While up on a hill, tending a cow, Andreas found an old piece of pottery and a back entrance to the mine. As they started to enter the mine, Andreas and Santiago found a basket full of old pottery pieces that Jose had apparently dug from the hill. Not knowing what the pottery pieces were, the boys took them to the local school teacher who identified them as ancient archeological treasures that by law belonged to the government. As soon as he realized others had found out that he had been selling the pottery, Jose disappeared. Shortly afterwards, the government paved the road through town and opened the hill as an official archaeological site. The extra jobs meant that the boys' fathers could once again find work at home. Although they hadn't become exactly rich, Santiago and Andreas had certainly found treasure.

Local flavor abounds, along with some history. Useful for Social Studies units. Print size fairly small, but spaces between lines are good sized. Recently out-of-print, but still worth looking for.

Interest Level: 3-5. Reading Level: 3.1. Further Search Topics: Archaeology-Fiction, Poverty-Fiction, Mexico-Fiction, Country Life-Fiction, Treasure-Fiction, Miners-Fiction.

MINERS-FICTION

Clymer, Eleanor. Santiago's silver mine; illus by Ingrid Fetz. Atheneum 1973, 74 pp.

Although somewhat complicated by a large number of background incidents, especially early in the book, the story is both interesting and informative. Santiago and his friend Andreas wanted to be rich. The year's harvest had been very poor, so there was little food to eat. Both of their fathers had gone to Mexico City to find jobs and their mothers worked for very few pesos near home. Andreas wanted to search the old mine in the hills outside of town for silver, but the mining company had left a guard named Jose to prevent people from getting into the mines. While up on a hill, tending a cow, Andreas found an old piece of pottery and a back entrance to the mine. As they started to enter the mine, Andreas and Santiago found a basket full of old pottery pieces that Jose had apparently dug from the hill. Not knowing what the pottery pieces were, the boys took them to the local school teacher who identified them as ancient archeological treasures that by law belonged to the government. As soon as he realized others had found out that he had been selling the pottery, Jose disappeared. Shortly afterwards, the government paved the road through town and opened the hill as an official archaeological site. The extra jobs meant that the boys' fathers could

once again find work at home. Although they hadn't become exactly rich, Santiago and Andreas had certainly found treasure.

Local flavor abounds, along with some history. Useful for Social Studies units. Print size fairly small, but spaces between lines are good sized. Recently out-of-print, but still worth looking for.

Interest Level: 3-5. Reading Level: 3.1. Further Search Topics: Archaeology-Fiction, Poverty-Fiction, Mexico-Fiction, Country Life-Fiction, Treasure-Fiction, Miners-Fiction.

MODELS, FASHION-FICTION

Blume, Judy. Deenie. Bradbury 1973, 159 pp.

Deenie's mother wanted Deenie to be a model. Deenie didn't know what she wanted until she learned that she had scoliosis (curvature of the spine) and would have to wear a brace for four years. Then she knew she only wanted to be normal. She was repulsed by deformities of any kind. She couldn't stand the idea of a brace. Her mother's attitude made Deenie's adjustment even more difficult. It was her father, her doctor, her sister, and a new friend with excema who finally helped Deenie accept her brace and the idea of physical differences. Subplots include Deenie's budding romance with an eighth grade boy, her strained relationship with her mother, and her growing awareness of sex (masturbation and intercourse). Print and line spacing are similar to *Are You There God? It's Me, Margaret*.

Interest Level: 5-6. Reading Level: 3.1. Further Search Topics: Models, Fashion-Fiction, Beauty-Fiction, Scoliosis-Fiction, Physically Handicapped-Fiction, Children-Growth-Fiction, Sex-Fiction, Love-Fiction, Family Problems-Fiction, Illness-Fiction, Adolescence-Fiction.

MONSTERS

Aylesworth, Thomas G. Movie monsters. Lippincott 1975, 79 pp.

If you are looking for an example of fine writing, you won't find it here. What you will find is a collection of monster movie photographs and facts. This is a wealth of trivia about eleven famous monsters (including King Kong, Godzilla, the Fly, Frankenstein's monster, the Mummy, Dracula, Wolf Man and others), their films, sequels, historic backgrounds, identifying characteristics, and more. There is an extensive index, a list of monster movies and their credits, and even brief information about famous monster actors. The book is not great literature, but it is interesting and fun.

Interest Level: 1-6. Reading Level 3.1. Further Search Topics: Acting, Motion Pictures, Monsters, Horror-Fiction, Group 2, Best Sellers.

Hornblow, Leonora. Prehistoric monsters did the strangest things; illus by Michael K. Frith. Random 1974, 65 pp.

A basic survey of an era and its animal life forms. Animals from the earliest water creatures through Diplocaulus, Ichthyosaurs, dinosaurs (about 12 varieties) and early mammals (including the Beast of Baluchistan) to the appearance of man are introduced and illustrated. It is a brief but meaty treatment of a very popular subject that should be especially useful with second and third grade children. Reader format.

Interest Level: 1-3. Reading Level: 2.1. Further Search Topics: Prehistory, Dinosaurs, Evolution, Monsters, Group 2.

MONSTERS-FICTION

Bulla, Clyde Robert. My friend the monster; illus by Michele Chessare. Har-Row 1980, 75 pp.

Even though Hal was plain and not very clever, his disappointed parents knew that he was still a prince; thus he had to be raised as one. Hal didn't like his lonely, dull life until a new world was accidentally opened to him. A servant's child gave him an old book of monsters and told him that the monsters still lived under the distant mountains. Hal finally made a trip to the mountains, spent a day exploring, and by chance met Humbert, a young monster curious about the world. But, Hal's cruel cousin Archer captured Humbert and put him in a cage. Hal's daring rescue attempt almost resulted in disaster for both Humbert and Hal.

This is another example of Bulla's forte; a book with an action-filled plot, short chapters, large print, wide spaces between the lines, and a low reading level. A book about monsters has almost guaranteed appeal through third grade. Although the book is useful beyond third grade, readers in fourth and fifth grade may be more sensitive to Hal's apparent youth and the fantastic elements of the story.

Interest Level: 1-3. Reading Level: 2.1. Further Search Topics: Fantasy, Monsters-Fiction, Royalty-Fiction, Group 2, Read Aloud, Best Sellers.

Place, Marian T. The boy who saw Bigfoot. Dodd 1979, 96 pp.

Joey and his foster mother searched for and found Bigfoot. But, when Joey told his classmates, no one would believe him. Joey's next idea was to take the entire class on a field trip to track Bigfoot.

Joey's rapid change from a difficult to a very well-adjusted child is not well supported. But interest in Bigfoot is so great that the book's flaws will be overlooked by its readers.

Interest Level: 3-6. Reading Level: 2.2. Further Search Topics: Bigfoot-Fiction, Foster Homes-Fiction, Monsters-Fiction, Troublemakers-Fiction, School Stories.

Platt, Kin. Dracula, go home; illus by Frank Mayo. Watts 1979, 87 pp.

From the chapter numbers that drip blood, and the humorously grotesque illustrations, to the short sentences and chapters, this is a book designed and almost guaranteed to appeal to the reluctant reader. A sense of immediacy and involvement is created by the first person narration. Tension is created on the opening page when Larry sees a man in the cemetery who looked exactly like Dracula. When that man registered at the hotel where Larry was working, Larry decided to find out more about him. It began to look as if Mr. A. R. Claude (the letters spell Dracula) was not only a vampire, but a thief and a murderer as well. The trouble was that Larry couldn't prove anything. Even when he found the stolen jewels for which Mr. Claude had been searching, Larry still couldn't convince anyone of Claude's true identify. No one ever did believe Larry, thus Claude went free.

The author uses a light touch to treat an eerie subject. His inconclusive ending may disappoint some, but should delight many. Beware of the variability of the reading level however; it swings from high first grade to low third grade.

Interest Level: 3-6. Reading Level: 2.2. Further Search Topics: Monsters-Fiction, Horror-Fiction, Mystery and Detective Stories, Best Sellers, Murder-Fiction, Crime-Fiction, Transformations-Fiction.

MOON

Branley, Franklyn M. Eclipse: darkness in daytime; illus by Donald Crews. Har-Row 1973, 33 pp.

The subject is so well-explained and the book is so physically attractive, it's a shame that some older readers will be put off by this title's picture book appearance. Aside from an occasional jarring, condescending note, this is a fine introduction to an interesting subject. Use comfortably with third and fourth graders. Recommend to fifth graders with caution. No index or table of contents. Lets-Read-and-Find-Out-Science-Book series.

Interest Level: 2-4. Reading Level: 2.2. Further Search Topics: Sun, Astronomy, Eclipses, Moon.

MORGAN, JOE

Burchard, Marshall. Sports hero: Joe Morgan. Putnam 1978, 93 pp.

Joe Morgan has been described as one of baseball's most complete players. He could field, hit, run and steal bases with the best. See *Sports Hero: Bill Walton* for more details about the book. Sports Hero series.

Interest Level: 2-6. Reading Level: 3.2. Further Search Topics: Biography, Morgan, Joe, Baseball-Biography, Blacks-Biography, Group 2.

MOTION PICTURES

Aylesworth, Thomas G. Movie monsters. Lippincott 1975, 79 pp.

If you are looking for an example of fine writing, you won't find it here. What you will find is a collection of monster movie photographs and facts. This is a wealth of trivia about eleven famous monsters (including King Kong, Godzilla, the Fly, Frankenstein's monster, the Mummy, Dracula, Wolf Man and others), their films, sequels, historic backgrounds, identifying characteristics, and more. There is an extensive index, a list of monster movies and their credits, and even brief information about famous monster actors. The book is not great literature, but it is interesting and fun.

Interest Level: 1-6. Reading Level 3.1. Further Search Topics: Acting, Motion Pictures, Monsters, Horror-Fiction, Group 2, Best Sellers.

MOTION PICTURES-FICTION

Clifford, Eth. The dastardly murder of Dirty Pete; illus by George Hughes. HM 1981, 120 pp.

Although this is a sequel to *Help, I'm a Prisoner in the Library*, it does not depend on the previous title, and in fact, is likely to be the more successful introduction to Mary Rose and Jo-Beth Onetree. Given the choice, most young readers will take a mystery set in a ghost town over a mystery set in a library.

Mary Rose, Jo-Beth and their father were on their way across country when they became lost. As night grew closer, the only place they could find to stay was an old hotel in the ghost town where Sorehead Jones had allegedly killed Dirty Pete. It was Sorehead's ghost who was supposed to haunt the town, and indeed there was someone or something who was in the town with the Onetrees. To their surprise, that someone turned out to be Sourdough Sam, an aging actor who had become senile and spent his days acting out all the parts in the Dirty Pete story. The town was only a movie set and the story was only a movie script. The Onetrees discovered the truth bit by bit after a frightening venture into an abandoned gold mine, a harrowing night in the haunted hotel and a jail sentence for Mr. Onetree.

Beware of the rare, very difficult descriptive passage that may cause trouble for some readers.

Interest Level: 2-5. Reading Level: 3.1. Further Search Topics: Mystery and Detective Stories, West-Fiction, Brothers and Sisters-Fiction, Motion Pictures-Fiction, Ghosts-Fiction, Treasure-Fiction, Group 2, Acting-Fiction, Aging-Fiction, Mental Illness-Fiction.

Miles, Betty. The secret life of the underwear champ; illus by Dan Jones. Knopf 1981, 117 pp.

Larry hadn't planned it; in fact, he hadn't even really wanted it to happen. But suddenly he found himself about to make a television commercial for ChampWin Knitting Mills, makers of sports clothing and underwear. He knew his family could use the money he would make, but he certainly didn't want the whole school seeing him in his underwear. Nevertheless, Larry went ahead and made the commercial, hoping that it would never be used. He even had to skip baseball practice to make the taping. Much to his horror, the commercial appeared the night before the team's first game. Not only did the entire opposing team tease him, but so did all his own teammates. By the time he got up to bat, Larry was mad enough to slam the ball out of the park. He didn't hit the ball quite that hard, but he did make a winning home run and end the others' giggles forever. He became the true underwear champ.

This is a funny look at the embarrassments of growing up. It also deals lightly with a boy's pride, his peer relationship, and his growing awareness of girls. An appealing and broadly usable title. Capers series.

Interest Level: 3-5. Reading Level: 2.2. Further Search Topics: Baseball-Fiction, Television-Fiction, Occupations-Fiction, School Stories, Humorous Fiction, Advertising-Fiction, Beauty-Fiction, Motion Pictures-Fiction, Best Sellers, Everyday Stories.

MOTORCYCLES-FICTION
Allen, Linda. Lionel and the spy next door; illus by Margot Apple. Morrow 1980, 94 pp.

No one in Lionel's family understood why he wanted to be a spy; but then, he couldn't understand why they were anthropologists and motorcycle freaks. Even though he wasn't supposed to do any more spying (especially while his parents were away) Lionel couldn't resist watching the man who moved into Miss Bannister's house, next-door. Mark Shakespeare was his name. His name was suspicious enough, but his actions firmly convinced Lionel that Mark was a spy. Lionel's attempts to trail Shakespeare only succeeded in angering others in the neighborhood. He interrupted a bird watcher and irritated a woman walking a large dog. She was already angry with Lionel's grandfather for disturbing the quiet neighborhood with his motorcycles. The closer Lionel got to finding proof that Mark was a spy, the friendlier Mark became. Mark even gave Lionel the old clock which Lionel and Miss Bannister had carefully wound each week until the old woman's death. When Lionel's grandfather finally convinced Lionel that Mark should be left alone, Mark enlisted Lionel's help in a project that left Lionel wondering again. Much to Lionel's surprise, he learned that the papers and secret documents he and Mark had burned had all belonged to Miss Bannister, Mark's great-aunt. Forty years earlier she, not Mark, had been a spy. Lionel had been wrong about who it was, but right about a spy living next-door.

Here we find a slightly anti-climactic ending to an otherwise enjoyable book. A grandfather who rides with motorcycle gangs and the intrigue of spying should be of interest to many readers. Readers may need a little help with the few British phrases that dot the book, but otherwise, the book has an impressively consistent reading level.

Interest Level: 4-6. Reading Level: 3.1. Further Search Topics: Spies-Fiction, Family-Fiction, Mystery and Detective Stories, Individualists-Fiction, Motorcycles-Fiction, Occupations-Fiction.

MOUNTAIN CLIMBING-FICTION
Warner, Gertrude Chandler. Mountain top mystery; illus by David Cunningham. A. Whitman 1964, 128 pp.

A day's climb up and down Old Flat Top was all the Alden family had wanted. Instead, when a portion of the trail collapsed into a cave, they found themselves stranded on top of the mountain. From their vantage point that night they could see a shadowy light which they investigated the next day. They found a 90-year-old Indian woman who had a strange story to tell of treasure hidden in a cave somewhere on Old Flat Top. The treasure was rightfully hers as the last of her tribe, but she had never been able to find it. The collapse of the trail and the reopening of the cave attracted more attention than just the Alden's though. Both an expert on caves and a young Indian boy wanted to find out more about the cave. David, the Indian boy, turned out to be the old woman's grandnephew. The treasure was indeed unearthed; David and Lovan were reunited; the treasure was given to Lovan, and both David's and Lovan's futures were secured.

What in the other books is mild stereotyping becomes more noticeable here (the books are all around 20 years old). The print is smaller here than before but the spacing between the lines is adequate. See entry for *The Boxcar Children* for more information.

Interest Level: 3-6. Reading Level: 2.2. Further Search Topics: Mystery and Detective Stories, Treasure-Fiction, Survival-Fiction, Indians of North America-Fiction, Mountain Climbing-Fiction, Brothers and Sisters-Fiction.

MOVING, HOUSEHOLD-FICTION
Blume, Judy. Tiger eyes. Bradbury 1981, 206 pp.

Davey's father's death was a shock that for awhile separated Davey from her mother. They occupied the same space, but Davey felt herself unable to communicate with her mother or with her aunt and uncle with whom they were living. The horror of the night her father was shot in a robbery attempt was too great for Davey to confront. It was too much for Davey's mother too, and so instead of growing closer, they draw apart. They let Davey's aunt and uncle direct their lives for almost a year before each was able to accept Mr. Wexler's death. During that time Davey's closest, most helpful friend was a loner named only Wolf. With him Davey lost enough fear and hatred that she was finally able to begin to talk about her father.

The setting (New Mexico) is much more important than in most of Blume's stories, the book's reading level is considerably more difficult, and the plot is about experiences more unique than usual. It will not fail to draw crowds of older readers however, for in most other respects the book follows Blume's successful formula.

Interest Level: 6+. Reading Level 5.1. Further Search Topics: Death-Fiction, Moving, Household-Fiction, Love-Fiction, Single Parent Family-Fiction, Family Problems-Fiction.

Blume, Judy. Superfudge. Dutton 1980, 166 pp.

On Fudge's first day in school his older brother Peter had to rescue him from the top of the kindergarten storage cabinets. Later in the school year Fudge's eagerness to join a school guest speaker on stage almost spelled disaster. Then when Fudge unexpectedly disappeared one day everyone, including Peter, thought he had drowned. In addition to Peter's problems with Fudge, Peter had to cope with a baby sister, moving to Princeton, New Jersey, a new job for his mother, and his father's attempts to write a book. Although the book is a sequel and is best enjoyed as such, it can be read alone. It is not as amusing or well-written as it's predecessor, *Tales of a Fourth Grade Nothing*, but will still be popular with young readers.

Interest Level: 3-6. Reading Level 3.1. Further Search Topics: Brothers and Sisters-Fiction, Moving, Household-Fiction, Infants-Fiction, Working Parents-Fiction, School Stories, Family-Fiction, Best Sellers, Humorous Fiction, Everyday Stories.

Buckley, Peter. I am from Puerto Rico. S ËAN S 1971, 127 pp.

Federico Ramirez had enjoyed his two years in New York City and didn't like the idea of moving back to Puerto Rico. When he arrived, he had no friends, no T.V., and nothing to do. Then Neri taught Federico the local games, showed him the sights and introduced him to Narcisco, a special fisherman. Narcisco took Federico through the wonders of the coral reefs. He taught him how to dive and fish. Within several months Federico was thoroughly at home in the water and loved Puerto Rico.

There is so much information about Puerto Rico and marine life that the book is never dry. Federico tells his own story as a series of fascinating experiences (meeting up with a shark, playing pinball, scuba diving at night, keeping a large turtle as a pet, etc.). There are abundant black and white photographs. An excellent choice for research (no index) or recreational reading. The print size is slightly on the small side, but the space between lines is good. Recently out of print, but worth looking for.

Interest Level: 5-6. Reading Level: 5.1. Further Search Topics: Puerto Rico, Fishing, Moving, Household-Fiction, Marine Biology, Scuba Diving, Ethnic Groups.

Bulla, Clyde Robert. The sugar pear tree; illus by Taro Yashima. T Y Crowell 1960, 54 pp.

Lonnie lived with his mother and his grandfather in a house owned by the state. A new highway was to be built that would force the family to move, but Gramp refused to acknowledge that the state could force them out of their home. He chased away every state representative who came to warn the family that they should move. Lonnie's mother had always been at work when the representatives came and so knew nothing about the warnings until she came home to find their belongings on the sidewalk and their house on wheels. The only person they could turn to was their friend Nick. Nick owned a nursery in town and a small house with a large yard in the country. He had become a friend of Lonnie's when he gave Lonnie first prize in a school essay contest on the topic of "favorite trees." Lonnie's prize had been a sugar pear tree, his favorite. Nick had next become Lonnie's mother's friend. Nick arranged for them to stay in the greenhouse at his country place. The longer they stayed, the better friends Nick and Lonnie's mother became. Gramp was the only person who didn't adjust to the move. He stopped speaking the moment he

was carried out of his old home. In a final and successful attempt to make Gramp happy, Nick bought the old house and had it moved out to his country lot.

The idea of a state government being able to force a family to move may need some explaining. The story's warmth and very consistent early second grade reading level make this a particularly useful book with quiet readers.

Interest Level: 2-4. Reading Level: 2.1. Further Search Topics: Trees-Fiction, Moving, Household-Fiction, Family Problems-Fiction, Grandparents-Fiction, Poverty-Fiction.

Bulla, Clyde Robert. Open the door and see all the people; illus by Wendy Watson. T Y Crowell 1972, 69 pp.

A slight story that makes up for its lack of excitement with warmth. When Joann, Teeney and Mama were burned out of their house in the country, they decided it was time to move to the city. With the help of a friend, Mama was quickly able to find a job and an apartment. Only Teeney was noticeably unhappy. She missed her doll and resented anyone else who had one. Then the girls learned about the Toy House, a place to borrow or adopt toys. Both girls found dolls they wanted to adopt. Just before the end of the six week trial period Tenney lost her doll and almost lost her chance to adopt it. After the doll was found and repaired, the people at the Toy House realized how much she wanted the doll and let Teeney keep it.

Because of the ages of the characters, (six and eight), and the subject matter, the book's appeal is doubtful beyond third grade. Print size slightly smaller than usual for Bulla.

Interest Level: 1-3. Reading Level: 2.1. Further Search Topics: Dolls-Fiction, Brothers and Sisters-Fiction, Moving, Household-Fiction, Family-Fiction, Group 2.

Bulla, Clyde Robert. Indian hill; illus by James J. Spanfeller. T Y Crowell 1963, 74 pp.

A very low-key story of a Navajo family who moved from the reservation to a city because they could no longer support themselves on the reservation. The move was necessary, but it was not appreciated by young Kee and his mother. They hated their ugly apartment and the crowded city, and wanted to go home. When an excuse to return to the reservation arose, Kee and his mother left the city. However, by the time Kee's father arrived to tell them he had been wrong to force them to move, Kee and his mother had realized they never gave their new home a chance. They were ready to try again. No excitement here, only an understanding look at the difficulties of moving.

Interest Level: 2-5. Reading Level: 2.1. Further Search Topics: Indians of North America-Fiction, Navajo Indians-Fiction, City Life-Fiction, Moving, Household-Fiction.

Byars, Betsy. After the goat man; illus by Ronald Himler. Viking Pr. 1974, 126 pp.

Harold was fat and over-sensitive. Ada was serious and independent. Figgy was lonely, poor and in need of help. Figgy and his grandfather, the Goat Man, had been forced to move from their cabin to make room for a highway. The Goat Man had returned to the cabin with a shotgun, vowing to defend his right to live there. Figgy knew he had to persuade his grandfather to leave or someone would be hurt. But, in the children's hurry to reach the Goat Man, it was Figgy who was hurt and Harold who rescued both Figgy and the Goat Man. Harold grew up that day. He stopped dreaming about the way he wanted things to be and faced life realistically for the first time.

The book is very much a character study. Realistic characters are treated with sympathy and dignity and given a chance to grow. Introspective readers will understand and enjoy the book more than those looking for adventure. Print size is fairly large, but lines are separated by only average width.

Interest Level: 4-6. Reading Level: 3.2. Further Search Topics: Loneliness-Fiction, Weight-Fiction, Moving, Household-Fiction, Courage-Fiction, Grandparents-Fiction, Orphans-Fiction.

Chaikin, Miriam. I should worry, I should care; illus by Richard Egielski. Har-Row 1979, 103 pp.

A warm, well-written story about life in a Jewish family in Brooklyn just before World War II. This is the story of young Molly's adjustment to moving, to leaving old friends, to making and losing new friends (one by death) and to the small happenings that make up her life. In the background, but always there, is Hitler's ever-increasing threat to the world.

A comfortable, truthful look at a close-knit family. Also useful for its picture of the times and the place. An occasional Yiddish expression may slow the reader but adds to the book's authenticity. Print is slightly lighter and smaller than *Finders Weepers*.

Interest Level: 3-5. Reading Level: 2.2. Further Search Topics: Moving, Household-Fiction, Friendship-Fiction, City Life-Fiction, Jews-Fiction, Family-Fiction.

Hurwitz, Johanna. Aldo Applesauce; illus by John Wallner. Morrow 1979, 127 pp.

Aldo Sossi, vegetarian and new kid at school, was immediately dubbed Applesauce for obvious reasons. Aldo didn't like his new name. He didn't like being teased either—not the way he was teased at school. Nothing went right for Aldo. His attempts at making friends only ended in disasters (once at a bowling alley and another time at a birthday party). He had been able to start a friendship only with a strange girl who wore a heavy, black fake moustache most of the time. After accidentally nearly ruining that friendship too, Aldo not only learned why DeDe wore the moustache, but helped her learn to live without it. DeDe, in turn, helped Aldo take himself less seriously and find more friends.

This is a comfortable, humorous story of two fourth grade children learning to be themselves. The vocabulary is occasionally difficult, but sentence length is almost always short.

Interest Level: 3-5. Reading Level: 3.1. Further Search Topics: Moving, Household-Fiction, Humorous Fiction, School Stories, Friendship-Fiction, Divorce and Separation-Fiction, Vegetarians-Fiction, Individualists-Fiction, Everyday Stories.

Kelley, Sally. Trouble with explosives. Bradbury 1976, 117 pp.

Polly Banks stuttered very badly. She wanted to stop but she couldn't. Moving, entering a new school, and facing a mean teacher who seemed in need of psychiatric help, all made Polly's stuttering worse. When Sis, Polly's new friend, rose to Polly's defense in one confrontation too many with Miss Patterson, the teacher took cruel revenge. Polly's desire to help Sis, her need to do something about her stuttering, and an understanding psychiatrist, all helped Polly learn to

help herself with her speech problem. At the same time, she began to understand and have confidence in herself and her family.

Another "problem book" that older elementary school readers seem to crave. Polly and Sis are both very sympathetic characters who bring to life many of the uncertainties of growing up. Print and line spacing of only average size but otherwise a good choice.

Interest Level: 4-6. Reading Level: 3.2. Further Search Topics: Academic Problems-Fiction, Stuttering-Fiction, Psychiatrists-Fiction, School Stories, Mental Illness-Fiction, Troublemakers-Fiction, Courage-Fiction, Physically Handicapped-Fiction, Children-Growth-Fiction, Moving, Household-Fiction.

Lowry, Lois. Anastasia again! HM 1981, 145 pp.

This is a sequel that is as funny and well-written as its predecessor. Because its plot involves less common experiences, this book may not enjoy quite the wide-spread success of *Anastasia Krupnik*. However, among those readers who liked their first meeting with Anastasia, this book will find many fans.

Anastasia's parents astounded her when they announced that the family was going to move from their Cambridge, Massachusetts apartment to a house in the suburbs. She didn't like the idea of leaving the apartment, but she _IThated_ME the idea of the suburbs. The only thing that made the move bearable was the house itself. Anastasia had said she would move only if they could find a house with a tower— and they had. After she got over the shock of moving, Anastasia began to enjoy her new home. She met a neighborhood boy who became a special friend, she tried to help her cranky elderly neighbor Mrs. Stein make friends, and she even wrote a short mystery book.

Anastasia is as spunky and original as before. She is a bit precocious, but her precocity is nothing compared to that of her brother. At two-and-a-half years old, he speaks as well as many adults. As we mentioned above, the book will be most appealing to readers who want second helpings of Anastasia's adventures. The print is slightly smaller here than in the first title.

Interest Level: 4-6. Reading Level: 2.2. Further Search Topics: Moving, Household-Fiction, City Life-Fiction, Suburbia-Fiction, Humorous Fiction, Aging-Fiction, Writing-Fiction, Family-Fiction, Everyday Stories.

Parish, Peggy. Haunted house; illus by Paul Frame. Macmillan 1971, 151 pp.

Although this is the third book about Jed, Bill and Liza Roberts, it too can be read out of order. This time the family has moved into what was locally known as a haunted house. Very shortly after they moved into the house, a coded note appeared that led them to a series of messages and unusual occurrences. Lights that flashed into Liza's room turned out to be the headlights of cars, but the messages and a secret compartment in an old clock couldn't be as easily explained. Each day took them closer to the surprise that the messages hinted would be theirs. That surprise turned out to be three kittens and a treehouse. Two of the children's best friends had planned the whole mystery just to lead to the surprises.

This book has the same faults and strong points as the others about the Roberts children. Each chapter is short; the book is episodic; reading level is consistent; there is much dialogue and action and little description, and the plot has a comfortable familiarity about it. It can be very useful to the right readers.

Interest Level: 1-4. Reading Level: 2.1. Further Search Topics: Mystery and Detective Stories. Brothers and Sisters-Fiction, Ghosts-Fiction, Moving, Household-Fiction, Nonverbal Communication-Fiction, Group 2.

Slote, Alfred. Hang tough, Paul Mather. Lippincott 1973, 156 pp.

Paul Mather went against his doctor's and his parents' orders when he accepted his new neighbors' challenge to show his pitching skill. He had been told not to play baseball until he had been given permission, but Paul not only loved to pitch, he was also the best pitcher his new friends had ever seen. Knowing full well the medical problems he could be precipitating, Paul went ahead and pitched a spectacular game for the Wilson Dairy team against the Ace Appliance team. But by the end of the game, Paul was in the hospital again, and Wilson Dairy had been forced to forfeit the game because Paul had played illegally. As Paul's leukemia worsened, his determination to play baseball again grew. When the day came that his team was to play a second game against Ace Appliance, Paul made sure he was there. He was in a wheelchair and weak, but he was there. He couldn't actually play, but Paul's psychological support insured that Wilson Dairy won the game. He went back to the hospital proud, happy, and still determined to fight his disease.

This is more than the usual sports story. This is a very sensitive story of a young boy's determination to fight leukemia. The reader looking for only a baseball story may find this book more than he/she wants. However, the reader who is open to a story of human strength and courage will be well rewarded. The book neither dwells on nor minimizes the disease. Instead it uses both the disease and the sport to portray a character much more completely than in most sport stories, especially at this low a reading level. This is an excellent book for those special readers who respond well to thought-provoking material. Although chapters are short and reading level is low, the print is somewhat small. In addition, the first person style, told as if dictated into a tape recorder (complete with occasional interruptions), may be confusing to readers unless it is explained.

Interest Level: 5-6+Reading Level: 3.1. Further Search Topics: Baseball-Fiction, Death-Fiction, Illness-Fiction, Moving, Household-Fiction, Medicine-Fiction, Physicians-Fiction, Challenges-Fiction, Courage-Fiction.

Waldorf, Mary. Jake McGee and his feet; illus by Leonard Shortall. HM 1980, 82 pp.

His severe reading difficulties made school the worst place in the world for Jake McGee. On the day that his reading tutor became so impatient with him that she sent Jake to the principal, Jake decided that he couldn't stand school any longer and ran away. He didn't actually run away, he just let his feet finally do what they wanted. His feet were always getting Jake in trouble. They walked too slowly to get him to school on time; they wouldn't stay still once he was in school; and they were always trying to trip someone.

Jake knew that in addition to having problems with his feet he had reading problems, but no one at his old school in the country had noticed. When he and his family moved to the city everything had changed. Jake's mother was always at work or tired. Jake hadn't made any friends and so was always alone. But Jake thought the biggest of all his immediate problems was his feet. The day he ran away, Jake's feet led him to a lost baby, an eccentric old woman,

and a neighbor boy, all of whom helped Jake recognize and deal with his real problem.

The book is not high literary quality. The characterization is somewhat flat and the plot is fairly predictable. However, the sentences and chapters are short, the vocabulary is manageable, and Jake's feelings will be shared by many non-readers.

Interest Level: 3-5. Reading Level: 2.2. Further Search Topics: School Stories, Moving, Household-Fiction, Runaways-Fiction, Academic Problems-Fiction, Working Parents-Fiction, Loneliness-Fiction, Feet-Fiction.

MURDER-FICTION

Bennett, Jay. The pigeon. Methuen 1980, 147 pp.

Despite a low testing score, this is not a truly easy book to read. The author assumes his readers are fairly sophisticated and worldly, thus he does not explain the meaning of the Iron Cross symbol or the word Aryan. The book's language varies from simple to difficult, making the reading level inconsistent (2.1 - 4.1). The setting is dark and forbidding; an underground world of fugitives and terrorists. And yet, the book will be popular with many readers in sixth grade; it will be even more popular with older readers. The tension in this story of a teenage boy, blamed for the murder of his ex-girlfriend, is almost palpable. Brian's flight from the police and his desire to find Donna's murderer take him directly into the midst of a ring of terrorists, for whom life has no meaning. In Brian's attempt to prove his innocence, two more lives are lost, but hundreds more are saved as Brian discovers and stops a bomb threat. The author has used riveting action, short, clipped sentences, and terse dialogue to create a very successful, highly suspenseful book. Print size is only moderate.

Interest Level: 6 . Reading Level: 3.2. Further Search Topics: Mystery and Detective Stories, Terrorism-Fiction, Murder-Fiction, Best Sellers, Crime-Fiction, Courage-Fiction, Survival-Fiction, Runaways-Fiction.

Heide, Florence Parry. Body in the Brillstone garage. A. Whitman 1980, 127 pp.

Liza's trip into the apartment house garage late one night made her even more frightened of that dark area than she had been. As she bent to pick up an envelope she thought someone had dropped, she saw a body lying on the floor of the garage. Because of a jacket he wore, Liza was certain the dead man was Mr. Greening, a neighbor. But when she returned to the garage with the police, the body was gone. The next day Mr. Greening was very much alive. Then Liza began to suspect that Mr. Greening was a murderer, but she didn't know who or where the victim was. It could have been Mr. Feeney, another neighbor, or it might have been a stranger. When Mr. Greening's stolen car was later discovered with the body of the car thief inside, Liza began to suspect that the thief's body was the one she had discovered. When she was told that the thief's name was Sharkey, she was certain Mr. Greening had engineered Sharkey's death. Sharkey was the name used by an angry man who had said he was looking for someone at the Brillstone who owed him something.

About then Liza remembered to look in the envelope she had found in the garage. The envelope revealed a note from Sharkey to Greening stating that Sharkey had proof that Greening was a car thief and that he would keep quiet only if Greening paid him twice the money he was owed. Knowing that without proof, she couldn't convince the police that Greening was a crook, Liza went to get the proof from Sharkey's hiding place in the about-to-be-junked car. Greening followed Liza to see what she knew and made a desperate attempt to kill her when he realized that she knew enough to put him in prison. At the last minute, Logan appeared, accidentally knocked Greening out, and helped Liza prove Greening's guilt to the police.

This is a fast-paced book that should be useful with mystery readers who can handle the jump from 4.1 to an occasional 5.1 reading level. See notes included with *Black Magic at Brillstone* for more information. Brillstone Mystery series.

Interest Level: 4-6. Reading Level: 4.2. Further Search Topics: Mystery and Detective Stories, Murder-Fiction, Running-Fiction, Crime-Fiction, Detectives-Fiction.

Hinton, Susan E. The outsiders. Viking Pr. 1967, 188 pp.

When she wrote this book Susan Hinton was only 17 years old, but she had the sensitivity of someone much older. She wrote a taut story of the rivalry between two city gangs; the Socs (the rich socialites) and the Greasers (poor kids from the wrong side of town) that is more than anything a plea for understanding and tolerance. Seen through the eyes of Ponyboy (a very bright, 14-year-old Greaser), the rivalry brought on violence and an accidental killing that forced Pony and his friend Johnny to flee for their lives. Dallas, the meanest and most dangerous of the Greasers, provided them with shelter, food for a week, and a gun. At the end of that week, Johnny decided that they should turn themselves in to the police. But before they could do that, their hideout (an old church) burned in a fire which threatened the lives of four children who had been playing there. In trying to rescue the children, Johnny, Pony, and Dallas were injured; Johnny was severely burned and probably permanently crippled. A vengeance rumble was held while Johnny lay in the hospital, but the Greasers' victory was empty when Johnny died. He had been the one member of the gang whom they all loved and who had most needed them. Dallas went to pieces: he robbed a store and set himself up to be killed by the police. He had nothing left to live for after Johnny's death. Pony found support and security with his brothers (their parents were dead) and, in a note from Johnny, some hope for the future.

Hinton speaks most often through Pony (his depth of understanding of the people around him is very impressive), but through Johnny and two of the Socs as well, Randy and Cherry. Her message is clear, but at no time does she fail to maintain believable characters in a compelling plot.

Although the book looks forbidding with its 188 pages of unrelenting small print, it is an exciting story, full of adventure, realism, and room for thought. Perhaps the best way to introduce this book is to read a fair portion of it aloud. Now a motion picture too.

Interest Level: 6+. Reading Level: 5.1. Further Search Topics: Crime-Fiction, Gangs-Fiction, Murder-Fiction, Read Aloud, Friendship-Fiction, Juvenile Delinquency-Fiction, Best Sellers, City Life-Fiction, Brothers and Sisters-Fiction, Orphans-Fiction, Runaways-Fiction, Troublemakers-Fiction, Poverty-Fiction.

Platt, Kin. Dracula, go home; illus by Frank Mayo. Watts 1979, 87 pp.

From the chapter numbers that drip blood, and the humorously grotesque illustrations, to the short sentences and chapters, this is a book designed and almost guaranteed to appeal to the reluctant reader. A sense of immediacy and involvement is created by the first person narration. Tension is created on the opening page when Larry sees a man in the cemetery who looked exactly like Dracula. When that man registered at the hotel where Larry was working, Larry decided to find out more about him. It began to look as if Mr. A. R. Claude (the letters spell Dracula) was not only a vampire, but a thief and a murderer as well. The trouble was that Larry couldn't prove anything. Even when he found the stolen jewels for which Mr. Claude had been searching, Larry still couldn't convince anyone of Claude's true identify. No one ever did believe Larry, thus Claude went free.

The author uses a light touch to treat an eerie subject. His inconclusive ending may disappoint some, but should delight many. Beware of the variability of the reading level however; it swings from high first grade to low third grade.

Interest Level: 3-6. Reading Level: 2.2. Further Search Topics: Monsters-Fiction, Horror-Fiction, Mystery and Detective Stories, Best Sellers, Murder-Fiction, Crime-Fiction, Transformations-Fiction.

MUSIC-BIOGRAPHY

Bryant, Bernice. George Gershwin: young composer; illus by Nathan Goldstein. Bobbs 1965, 200 pp.

Even when George Gershwin was very young he loved music, showed signs of musical talent, and longed to play the piano. However, any boy who played the piano in George's neighborhood was called a sissy and George didn't like being teased in that way. When he was no longer able to keep his music lessons a secret, he stopped them for fear of the teasing. But each time George quit playing the piano, he always went back to it, even when his parents pressured him not to waste his time at the piano. A young teacher told George that he would never be a musician. One of George's teachers actually taught him to play poorly, instead of well. In time, however, George learned to play well and to compose his own music. Then came the hard work of determining his own style. Gradually, more and more people heard and appreciated his American jazz, until George Gershwin's music was heard all around the world.

Another adequate entry in the *Childhood of Famous Americans* series. Includes the usual glossary, bibliography, time line, and follow-up questions. It is most likely to appeal to the reader already interested in music. Childhood of Famous Americans series.

Interest Level: 3-6. Reading Level: 3.1. Further Search Topics: Biography, Composers, Immigration and Emigration-Biography, Jazz Music, Bullies, Music-Biography, Pianists.

Cone, Molly. Leonard Bernstein; illus by Robert Galster. Har-Row 1970, 33 pp.

This is a bare bones outline that will appeal to music enthusiasts but will not attract anyone else. The reader catches very little of Bernstein's personality, but *is* awed by an impressive list of his accomplishments. The few attempts made to recreate the real person may have to be explained (i.e., references to Bernstein forgetting to get his hair cut because he was so busy). Picture book format of the hardback may deter some readers. Now published in paperback edition only. Crowell Biography series.

Interest Level: 2-4. Reading Level: 2.2. Further Search Topics: Music-Biography, Biography, Conductors, Composers, Pianists, Group 2,

Mathis, Sharon Bell. Ray Charles; illus by George Ford. Har-Row 1973, 33 pp.

Dominent throughout this biography of Ray Charles is the theme of overcoming adversity. The book is not just a recounting of Ray Charles' music lessons, early schooling, family life, and talent. All of that is included, but it serves to illustrate the manner in which Charles met his troubles. His problems began when he was very young. His brother died, and Ray lost one eye and then the sight in his other eye. His family was poor, but close, and he missed them when he was sent away to a school for the blind. Music was his love, but even that was work, for Charles had to learn to read and write music in Braille. He worked hard at it and eventually could play and arrange music for every instrument in the band.

Determined to be independent, when Charles was orphaned at age 15, he left school and began playing music for a living. The first record he made resulted in a $16 fine because he made it during a musician's union strike. Charles took a series of sideman and nightclub jobs until he finally had enough money to hire seven other musicians to play his music. Today Charles is very wealthy, owns his own record company, has a family, and is considered a great jazz and blues musician. None of his success came easily; only through determination, will power, pride, and hard work.

The book, interesting and serviceable enough for music or biography units, is also designed to set an example for youngsters facing their own problems. It will, of course, be popular with Ray Charles fans, too. Crowell Biography series.

Interest Level: 2-4. Reading Level: 3.1. Further Search Topics: Jazz Music, Music-Biography, Vision, Physically Handicapped, Blacks-Biography, Group 2, Biography, Pianists, Orphans, Challenges, Courage.

Tobias, Tobi. Marian Anderson; illus by Symeon Shimin. Har-Row 1972, 40 pp.

Marian Anderson's beautiful, strong voice and her great range set her apart from other singers even as a child. By the time she was in high school, she was being paid to sing. However, when she tried to apply to a well-known music school, because she was black she was turned away without even being heard. Anderson's determination as well as her own and others' faith in her kept her singing and seeking better and better coaches until she met Giuseppi Boghetti. He was one of the best voice coaches in the country. With him Marian trained and traveled until she finally won the chance to sing with the New York Philharmonic Orchestra. Anderson thought that at that point she would be invited to sing in famous theaters all across the United States, but because she was black she still received no invitations. She went to Europe where she studied and played to wildly enthusiastic audiences. Her European triumphs finally convinced American theater owners and audiences that she was a serious talent. For the next 30 years Marian Anderson sang all over the world, most of the time without incident, with one notable exception in 1939, when the D.A.R. prohibited her from singing in a hall they owned in Washington, D. C. She sang instead, in front of the Lincoln Memorial, at the invitation of the United States government. During the following years Marian married, bought a farm, sang opera and was made a delegate to the United Nations. In 1956, she retired from singing to help children, young singers, and world understanding.

Crowell Biographies make excellent school report sources for reluctant readers. They are short, interesting, and not overly juvenile looking, although the quasi-picture book format may be a problem for some older readers. This biography fits that description perfectly. The series is somewhat sentimental (as are many children's biographies), however, the sentimentality is not forbidding or condescending. A useful series. Crowell Biography series.

Interest Level: 2-5. Reading Level: 3.1. Further Search Topics: Biography, Music-Biography, Blacks-Biography, Talent, Women-Biography, Singers, Prejudice, Group 2.

MYSTERY AND DETECTIVE STORIES

Adrian, Mary. The fireball mystery illus by Reisie Lonette. Hastings 1977, 118 pp.

While stargazing one night, Tim and Vicky and their friend Joey saw a meteor fall onto their private island. Before they were able to find it the children realized that someone else was trying to steal the meteorite from them. As much astronomy as mystery here. Beyond fourth grade, the reader may begin to find the astronomy lesson heavy-handed and the mystery light.

Interest Level: 2-4. Reading Level: 3.1. Further Search Topics: Mystery and Detective Stories, Astronomy, Flying Saucers-Fiction, Outer Space-Fiction, Group 2.

Allen, Linda. Lionel and the spy next door; illus by Margot Apple. Morrow 1980, 94 pp.

No one in Lionel's family understood why he wanted to be a spy; but then, he couldn't understand why they were anthropologists and motorcycle freaks. Even though he wasn't supposed to do any more spying (especially while his parents were away) Lionel couldn't resist watching the man who moved into Miss Bannister's house, next-door. Mark Shakespeare was his name. His name was suspicious enough, but his actions firmly convinced Lionel that Mark was a spy. Lionel's attempts to trail Shakespeare only succeeded in angering others in the neighborhood. He interrupted a bird watcher and irritated a woman walking a large dog. She was already angry with Lionel's grandfather for disturbing the quiet neighborhood with his motorcycles. The closer Lionel got to finding proof that Mark was a spy, the friendlier Mark became. Mark even gave Lionel the old clock which Lionel and Miss Bannister had carefully wound each week until the old woman's death. When Lionel's grandfather finally convinced Lionel that Mark should be left alone, Mark enlisted Lionel's help in a project that left Lionel wondering again. Much to Lionel's surprise, he learned that the papers and secret documents he and Mark had burned had all belonged to Miss Bannister, Mark's great-aunt. Forty years earlier she, not Mark, had been a spy. Lionel had been wrong about who it was, but right about a spy living next-door.

Here we find a slightly anti-climactic ending to an otherwise enjoyable book. A grandfather who rides with motorcycle gangs and the intrigue of spying should be of interest to many readers. Readers may need a little help with the few British phrases that dot the book, but otherwise, the book has an impressively consistent reading level.

Interest Level: 4-6. Reading Level: 3.1. Further Search Topics: Spies-Fiction, Family-Fiction, Mystery and Detective Stories, Individualists-Fiction, Motorcycles-Fiction, Occupations-Fiction.

Avi. No more magic. Pantheon 1975, 138 pp.

Avi has woven a mixture of mystery and magic to produce an excellent story. Chris' belief in magic is bolstered when his new bicycle disappears on Halloween night. Chris, his best friend Eddie, and a new friend, Muffin, eventually decide that strange Mr. Bullen, the junk dealer, has magical powers. In order to keep his powers a secret, Mr. Bullen had to steal back the magical bike he sold Chris. With plenty of intriguing complications along the way, the three children attempt to prove their theory correct but only prove themselves wrong. The age of the protagonists (fourth grade) is touched on so lightly and the plot is interesting enough that even sixth grade readers should find the book enjoyable.

Interest Level: 3-6. Reading Level: 4.2. Further Search Topics: Divorce and Separation-Fiction, Mystery and Detective Stories, Magic-Fiction, Halloween-Fiction, Witches-Fiction, Group 2, Read Aloud, Bicycles and Bicycling-Fiction.

Bennett, Jay. The pigeon. Methuen 1980, 147 pp.

Despite a low testing score, this is not a truly easy book to read. The author assumes his readers are fairly sophisticated and worldly, thus he does not explain the meaning of the Iron Cross symbol or the word Aryan. The book's language varies from simple to difficult, making the reading level inconsistent (2.1 - 4.1). The setting is dark and forbidding; an underground world of fugitives and terrorists. And yet, the book will be popular with many readers in sixth grade; it will be even more popular with older readers. The tension in this story of a teenage boy, blamed for the murder of his ex-girlfriend, is almost palpable. Brian's flight from the police and his desire to find Donna's murderer take him directly into the midst of a ring of terrorists, for whom life has no meaning. In Brian's attempt to prove his innocence, two more lives are lost, but hundreds more are saved as Brian discovers and stops a bomb threat. The author has used riveting action, short, clipped sentences, and terse dialogue to create a very successful, highly suspenseful book. Print size is only moderate.

Interest Level: 6 . Reading Level: 3.2. Further Search Topics: Mystery and Detective Stories, Terrorism-Fiction, Murder-Fiction, Best Sellers, Crime-Fiction, Courage-Fiction, Survival-Fiction, Runaways-Fiction.

Bonham, Frank. The mystery of the fat cat; illus by Alvin Smith. Dutton 1968, 160 pp.

Although noticeably dated at times, this is still an exciting story of an inner city neighborhood. Buddy, Little Pie, Rich, and Cool were among the many who used the local Boys' Club as their hangout. It was a place to stay out of trouble and off the streets, but it was also a haven for rats. The rats were big and brazen; so brazen that one attacked Buddy in the swimming pool. The club needed a new building desperately. The money was there; they just weren't able to use it. Fifteen years earlier an eccentric old woman willed the Boys' Club over $600,000, but stated that the money was first to be used to support her cat until it died. A caretaker, a lawyer, and a veterinarian all benefited as long as the cat lived. Buddy and his friends took on the job of discovering if the cat really was alive or if the Boys' Club was being cheated out of half a million dollars. It was a job that nearly killed them before they set things right. Plenty of action, some violence, a cast of street-smart characters, realistic trouble with the police, as well as

a slight mystery almost insure the book's success with older readers. Moderate sized print. Line spacing somewhat narrow.

Interest Level: 6+ Reading Level: 5.1. Further Search Topics: Humorous Fiction, Cats-Fiction, Gangs-Fiction, City Life-Fiction, Mystery and Detective Stories, Poverty-Fiction, Friendship-Fiction, Juvenile Delinquency-Fiction, Crime-Fiction, Best Sellers.

Bulla, Clyde Robert. Marco Moonlight; illus by Julia Noonan. T Y Crowell 1976, 104 pp.

No one could explain Marco's strange, recurring dream. The dream seemed to be about a brother, but Marco had no brother. He had no family but his wealthy grandparents with whom he lived. Marco loved his grandparents very much, but he couldn't help wondering about his own past. He knew only what he and his grandparents could figure out from a few clues. His mother had run away to marry and for three years Marco's grandparents had heard nothing. Then, suddenly, they received a note that she was dying, had parted from her husband, and needed them. By the time they arrived, she was dead and two-year-old Marco could tell them no more. About the time of his thirteenth birthday Marco made friends with a strange man named Flint, who later became the gardener on Marco's grandparents' estate. Rather than live in the room provided for him with the other servants, Flint chose a bleak and isolated beach cottage. Being very careful that no one should suspect, Flint locked Marco into the cottage and forced Marco to change clothes with Matt, who was Marco's long-lost identical twin. Flint and Matt planned that Matt would steal all the money he could from the estate before killing Marco and fleeing. But when Matt began to realize how nice his grandparents were, how much he liked Marco, and how evil Flint was, he decided to thwart Flint's plan. In Matt and Marco's desperate attempt to flee from Flint, Flint was accidentally killed, leaving Marco free to return home and Matt free to find a way to feel he also had the right to claim his heritage before joining Marco.

The tense and dramatic plot immediately involves the reader and the short, fast-paced chapters sustain interest to the end of the book. Readers should also appreciate the small, paperback-size format. A good choice.

Interest Level: 3-6. Reading Level: 2.1. Further Search Topics: Dreams-Fiction, Mystery and Detective Stories, Kidnapping-Fiction, Twins-Fiction, Orphans-Fiction, Grandparents-Fiction, Best Sellers, Brothers and Sisters-Fiction, Jealousy-Fiction, Courage-Fiction.

Bunting, Eve. The skate patrol; illus by Don Madden. Albert Whitman 1980, 40 pp.

The book is funny, clever, undemanding and short. The combination of those qualities plus its slight mystery and its consistent reading level make this a very appealing and useful book for young readers. The plot is simple: in the hopes that their neighbors would be so grateful that they would allow the boys to roller skate in the neighborhood again, two friends decided to capture a local thief. James and Milton even knew who the thief was. He was the "mysterious man" who sat in the park. They only had to capture him in the act of stealing to prove that they were correct. They watched him continuously and trailed him as he followed old ladies. Then came the day that they heard Mrs. Grump scream that her purse had been snatched. The boys sped after the "mysterious man" on their skates. They caught him and knocked him down. To their surprise he declared that he was an undercover policeman and they were letting the real thief get away. Off they went again. This time they caught the right person and were rewarded just the way that they had hoped: Mrs. Crump (not Grump) promised that the boys would be allowed to roller skate any time they wished. A light and lively entertainment.

Interest Level: 2-4. Reading Level: 2.2. Further Search Topics: Mystery and Detective Stories, Humorous Fiction, Spies-Fiction, Roller Skating-Fiction, Crime-Fiction, Best Sellers.

Clifford, Eth. The dastardly murder of Dirty Pete; illus by George Hughes. HM 1981, 120 pp.

Although this is a sequel to *Help, I'm a Prisoner in the Library*, it does not depend on the previous title, and in fact, is likely to be the more successful introduction to Mary Rose and Jo-Beth Onetree. Given the choice, most young readers will take a mystery set in a ghost town over a mystery set in a library.

Mary Rose, Jo-Beth and their father were on their way across country when they became lost. As night grew closer, the only place they could find to stay was an old hotel in the ghost town where Sorehead Jones had allegedly killed Dirty Pete. It was Sorehead's ghost who was supposed to haunt the town, and indeed there was someone or something who was in the town with the Onetrees. To their surprise, that someone turned out to be Sourdough Sam, an aging actor who had become senile and spent his days acting out all the parts in the Dirty Pete story. The town was only a movie set and the story was only a movie script. The Onetrees discovered the truth bit by bit after a frightening venture into an abandoned gold mine, a harrowing night in the haunted hotel and a jail sentence for Mr. Onetree.

Beware of the rare, very difficult descriptive passage that may cause trouble for some readers.

Interest Level: 2-5. Reading Level: 3.1. Further Search Topics: Mystery and Detective Stories, West-Fiction, Brothers and Sisters-Fiction, Motion Pictures-Fiction, Ghosts-Fiction, Treasure-Fiction, Group 2, Acting-Fiction, Aging-Fiction, Mental Illness-Fiction.

Fife, Dale. Follow that ghost!; illus by Joan Drescher. Dutton 1979, 58 pp.

In short sentences reminiscent of "Dragnet," Chuck tells a very simple story of Chuck and Jason's first detective case. He and Jason were practicing following people, when their next-door-neighbor caught them following her home. Instead of being angry at the two boys, Glory decided to hire them to find the ghost she and her mother were hearing at 5:00 every morning. Despite their best attempts to capture and bury the ghost, or a find a human cause for the ghostly sounds, Chuck and Jason couldn't rid Glory's apartment of its ghost. Their final effort nearly resulted in injury to a neighbor. Ultimately, Chuck discovered that the ghost was merely a displaced woodpecker looking for a new home.

Not a terribly ambitious mystery, but one whose consistent reading level, familiar urban setting and interesting characters will please many young readers.

Interest Level: 2-4. Reading Level: 2.1. Further Search Topics: Ghosts-Fiction, Mystery and Detective Stories, Spies-Fiction, Humorous Fiction.

Giff, Patricia Reilly. Have you seen Hyacinth Macaw?; illus by Anthony Kramer. Delacorte 1981, 135 pp.

Abby Jones was trying very hard to be a detective, but it was difficult without any mysteries to solve. So to keep in practice, Abby filled a memo book with her notes about anything that seemed at all unusual. At the same time, Abby kept in touch with two local police detectives who gave her hints about detective work. Because of her police friends and her observations, Abby found herself involved in what seemed to be four or more mysteries. Who had moved into the apartment next door and what were the screams that came from there? What was the theft that the police were worried about? Who was Hyacinth Macaw and why had she disappeared? And why was Abby's older brother Dan acting so strangely? Was he involved in the theft?

Abby and her friend Potsie ended up trailing a suspect through the New York subway system, breaking into the next-door apartment, suspecting Abby's brother of the theft, capturing an unusual bird, releasing the bird into a pet shop and recapturing it, before they realized that all the mysteries were linked together. Hyacinth Macaw was a valuable bird stolen from Justine's Junktique Shop. The daughter of Abby's landland had taken the bird and placed it in the empty apartment next to Abby's, so that she could paint the bird's portrait. The picture was to be entered in Justine's Junktique contest. Dan and his friend Holly Monk had been secretly constructing a Purple Pigeon Purifier to enter in the contest. They needed the prize money to repair a window they had accidentally broken. By the time the mysteries were all sorted out, Dan and Holly had won a special prize; Kiki, the portrait painter, had not only been forgiven, but had also been awarded first prize; and Abby had received the reward for finding and returning the bird.

The action in this mystery is both abundant and humorous enough to make the book enjoyable to many readers. There are also some problems that need to be noted. Some readers may find the action too swift and the characters too numerous to be easily followed. Abby's memo notes are sometimes written without vowels and are almost always in incomplete sentences. The reader who is highly motivated or has help from another person will still be able to enjoy the story; however, for the others another choice may be more appropriate.

Interest Level: 4-6. Reading Level: 3.1. Further Search Topics: Mystery and Detective Stories, Humorous Fiction, Writing-Fiction, Detectives-Fiction, Birds-Fiction.

Hall, Lynn. The mystery of Pony Hollow; illus by Ruth Sanderson. Garrard 1978, 64 pp.

Sarah investigated strange voices only to find the skeleton of a horse that had died 40 years earlier. She was determined to find out what it was that had killed the horse and why its ghost was uneasy.

The mystery element isn't as strong here as most mystery fans would like, but the book will not disappoint many true horse story enthusiasts.

Interest Level: 3-5. Reading Level: 3.2. Further Search Topics: Horses-Fiction, Ghosts-Fiction, Mystery and Detective Stories.

Heide, Florence Parry. Black magic at Brillstone. A. Whitman 1981, 126 pp.

Liza is a little older, her romance with Logan has progressed to a kiss, and the book's plot is more complex than earlier Brillstone adventures. Other than those differences, the book follows Heide's standard format. The Brillstone books all center on Liza Webster and Logan Forrest, teenage partners in crime detection, who live in the Brillstone Apartments. The stories are similar enough that one could almost substitute the names Nancy Drew and Ned for Liza and Logan. Both young women are only children who live with their fathers. They are both independent, resourceful, and very concerned that justice be done. The men in their lives play approximately the same roles; their fathers are proud and supportive, but distantly preoccupied with their own business; Logan and Ned are gallant, boyish, and devoted. Liza and Logan, like Nancy and Ned, are not distinctive characters. Instead, they are shells into which readers who want excitement and adventure can pour themselves. There is no parental interference to worry about. There is plenty of action, some suspense, and real world crime (for Liza: murder, bank robberies, etc.) rather than childish escapades. The books' success is practically guaranteed. Beware, however, of inconsistent reading levels that wander over a year's range.

Logan was first aware of strange occurrences at the Brillstone Apartments when someone entered his apartment late at night. While the person had searched the apartment, he or she had unconsciously whistled a nursery tune. Logan's neighbor, Miss Violet, said the tune reminded her of her deceased nephew. Slowly Logan and Liza realized that someone was trying to trick Miss Violet out of a substantial amount of money she had just inherited. They suspected that Bella Vine, a spiritualist, and an accomplice were trying to convince Miss Violet that her nephew was communicating from the dead and wanted Miss Violet to give her money to Bella. Not until it was almost too late did Liza and Logan realize that Bella was also posing as another possible recipient of the money and was really Miss Violet's nephew's wife. Miss Violet's nephew had only pretended to die in order to collect insurance money. When he and his wife had heard about Miss Violet's large inheritance, they had decided to reappear in order to bilk her out of the money. Brillstone Mystery series.

Interest Level: 5-6. Reading Level: 3.1. Further Search Topics: Mystery and Detective Stories, Occult-Fiction, Crime-Fiction, Ghosts-Fiction, Cats-Fiction, Detectives-Fiction, Inheritance-Fiction.

Heide, Florence Parry. Body in the Brillstone garage. A. Whitman 1980, 127 pp.

Liza's trip into the apartment house garage late one night made her even more frightened of that dark area than she had been. As she bent to pick up an envelope she thought someone had dropped, she saw a body lying on the floor of the garage. Because of a jacket he wore, Liza was certain the dead man was Mr. Greening, a neighbor. But when she returned to the garage with the police, the body was gone. The next day Mr. Greening was very much alive. Then Liza began to suspect that Mr. Greening was a murderer, but she didn't know who or where the victim was. It could have been Mr. Feeney, another neighbor, or it might have been a stranger. When Mr. Greening's stolen car was later discovered with the body of the car thief inside, Liza began to suspect that the thief's body was the one she had discovered. When she was told that the thief's name was Sharkey, she was certain Mr. Greening had engineered Sharkey's death. Sharkey was the name used by an angry man who had said he was looking for someone at the Brillstone who owed him something.

About then Liza remembered to look in the envelope she had found in the garage. The envelope revealed a note from Sharkey to Greening stating that Sharkey had proof that Greening was a car thief and that he would keep quiet only if Greening paid him twice the money he was owed. Knowing that without proof, she couldn't convince the police that Greening was a crook, Liza went to get the proof from Sharkey's hiding place in the about-to-be-junked car. Greening followed Liza to see what she knew and made a desperate attempt to kill her when he realized that she knew enough to put him in prison. At the last minute, Logan appeared, accidentally knocked Greening out, and helped Liza prove Greening's guilt to the police.

This is a fast-paced book that should be useful with mystery readers who can handle the jump from 4.1 to an occasional 5.1 reading level. See notes included with *Black Magic at Brillstone* for more information. Brillstone Mystery series.

Interest Level: 4-6. Reading Level: 4.2. Further Search Topics: Mystery and Detective Stories, Murder-Fiction, Running-Fiction, Crime-Fiction, Detectives-Fiction.

Heide, Florence Parry. Mystery of the forgotten island; illus by Seymour Fleishman. A. Whitman 1980, 127 pp.

On a small island, unmarked on the map, the Spotlight Club members found old Mr. Whitson, who claimed that he was being kept prisoner by his granddaughter Lorrie and her husband John. Lorrie and John had told him he was being kept in the yard for his own good, so that he wouldn't wander off and get hurt or lost. They had also told him that he should will the island to them so that his daughter Cassie couldn't sell the island to a resort company for development. He was going to be forced to sign such a will unless he could get the children to help him smuggle a new will to his lawyer. Mr. Whitson wasn't convinced that Cassie wanted to sell the island, but he couldn't get in touch with her and he hadn'd had a letter from her in many months.

As the children went to secretly meet Mr. Whitson and mail his new will, they discovered that their trusted friend Guy was attempting to blackmail Lorrie and John into giving him some of the money from the sale of the island. He had evidence that Lorrie and John, not Cassie, wanted to sell the island and were tricking Mr. Whitson into signing a will in their favor. In a daring move, the children were able to free Mr. Whitson and isolate all three of the thieves so that the police could capture them.

This book involves a somewhat more complicated plot and slightly less familiar ingredients than most other Spotlight Club mysteries. One should progress to rather than begin the series with this title. Spotlight Club Mystery series.

Interest Level: 4-6. Reading Level: 3.1. Further Search Topics: Mystery and Detective Stories, Inheritance-Fiction, Gangs-Fiction, Kidnapping-Fiction, Brothers and Sisters-Fiction, Aging-Fiction, Detectives-Fiction.

Heide, Florence Parry. Mystery of the mummy's mask; illus by Seymour Fleishman. A. Whitman 1979, 127 pp.

The Spotlight Club published a neighborhood newspaper. Just as the club was about to take the fourth issue to the printer, Jay discovered an ancient mummy mask hidden near Mr. Pruitt's house. Mr. Pruitt was intrigued by the discovery (he worked at the nearby museum) and he took the mask from Jay, but agreed that Jay could write about the mask for the paper. At about the same time, Dexter discovered that an old, abandoned house was being used. When the printer's office was broken into that night and only their newspaper was stolen, the three children began to suspect that something strange was going on at the abandoned house.

Dexter rode back to the house alone and was captured by Hank, one of three thieves hiding out there. Figuring that they never would have missed one item, Hank had taken the mask from the cache of goods that the other two had stolen. When he overheard Jay's conversation with Mr. Pruitt, Hank realized that his partners would find out what he had done if they ever read the newspaper article. To avoid being discovered, Hank broke into the printer's and stole the paste-up of the paper. In order to keep Dexter from escaping, Hank tied him up and placed him in a shipping crate. When he didn't return as soon as expected, Jay and Cindy realized that Dexter was in trouble, so they went out to the house to search for him. As the three escaped, Dexter and Cindy slashed the thieves' truck's tires, and Jay ran to phone for the police. After several nervous moments in which Cindy and Dexter thought Jay might not get back before they were caught, Jay finally brought the police, who captured all three thieves.

See *Mystery at Southport Cinema* for more information. Spotlight Club Mystery series.

Interest Level: 3-5. Reading Level: 3.1. Further Search Topics: Mystery and Detective Stories, Crime-Fiction, Egypt-Fiction, Archaeology-Fiction, Antiquities-Fiction, Journalism-Fiction, Gangs-Fiction, Brothers and Sisters-Fiction, Detectives-Fiction.

Heide, Florence Parry. The mystery of the silver tag; illus by Seymour Fleishman. A. Whitman 1972, 127 pp.

Jay's paper route took him to one house that he wished he could avoid. It was grumpy, old Mr. Pendleton's house that Jay hated. One rainy day he spotted what he later realized was a prize Angora cat hiding on Mr. Pendleton's porch. When the cat was reported lost in that night's paper, Jay and the other members of the Spotlight Club decided to try to return the cat to its owner, Miss Horton. Their attempts to get the cat back from Mr. Pendleton meant that they had to spy on him, to sneak into his garage, and to spend the night in a treehouse overlooking his house. They were afraid that they had failed when they saw Mr. Pendleton leave with the cat. Determined to be the ones to tell Miss Horton of their failure, they went to her apartment and found Mr. Pendleton already there. Mr. Pendleton was a famous animal photographer who, upon finding the cat, had asked Miss Horton if he could photograph him. The children, thinking only that Mr. Pendleton was a mad scientist who kidnapped cats, had jumped to all the wrong conclusions, but ended with a mystery solved, new friends, and their first lesson in being detectives.

See entry with *Mystery at Southport Cinema* for series information. Spotlight Club Mystery series.

Interest Level: 3-5. Reading Level: 2.2. Further Search Topics: Mystery and Detective Stories, Brothers and Sisters-Fiction, Gangs-Fiction, Cats-Fiction, Loners-Fiction, Detectives-Fiction, Photography-Fiction, Kidnapping-Fiction.

Heide, Florence Parry. Face at the Brillstone window. A. Whitman 1979, 128 pp.

As Liza drove out of the garage one evening she heard a thump at the side of the car. She jumped out and found that she had accidentally hit Peter Pritchard, an insurance man and a new tenant of the apartment building. Pritchard seemed to be a very nice person who took some interest in Liza, her friends, and the criminal cases Liza's father (a journalist) was investigating. Liza was particularly interested in the case of the one-armed bandit who had been convicted of robbing and shooting a security

guard. Against her father's research assistant's wishes she continued to search for evidence that would prove Robin Keck was innocent of the charges. As she interviewed the security guard, Keck's fiancee, his best friend, and the grandmother of a young girl who had had a strong crush on Keck, Liza found hints of his innocence. Young Bridgette's diary, however, held the proof she needed: an alibi. But someone else knew she had the information; someone who didn't want the information made public. Diary in hand, Liza began walking to her father's assistant's house (her father was out of town) when Pritchard offered her a ride. When Pritchard drove off in the wrong direction and then handed her a piece of incriminating evidence (gum), Liza realized she had played right into the real criminal's hands. Liza made a risky escape attempt that ended successfully with Pritchard's capture.

See *Black Magic at Brillstone* for more information about the series. Brillstone Mystery series.

Interest Level: 4-6. Reading Level: 3.2. Further Search Topics: Mystery and Detective Stories, Crime-Fiction, Detectives-Fiction.

Heide, Florence Parry. Mystery at Southport Cinema; illus by Seymour Fleishman. A. Whitman 1978, 128 pp.

The Spotlight Club was the name Jay, his sister Cindy, and his friend Dexter gave themselves. Their main interest was solving mysteries and just as in Sobol's Encyclopedia Brown series, Hildick's McGurk Mysteries, and Warner books about the Alden children, mysteries seem to follow them around. Their cases are more intricate and lengthy than Encyclopedia Brown's. They involve more danger than most of McGurk's, and they center on more common themes than the Alden's. The series serves much the same audience, however, as the others. It serves those children who want action, intrigue, and the challenge of a mystery, and who don't care about character development or in-depth motivation. The chapters are 8 to 12 pages long, print size is adequate, and the children are normal enough to make this a very popular series. As an added attraction, reading levels here are fairly consistent.

Thorne prided himself on doing his job well, so when the grocery store he ran for Callie (the owner) was robbed by a bearded stranger, Thorne felt responsible. Thorne ran after the thief but lost him in the darkened Southport Cinema. The Spotlight Club members also tried to track the thief. They figured that he had hidden the bag with the stolen money somewhere in the movie house because no one had been seen leaving with such a bag.

In the janitor's lost and found basket Jay found a wig the thief must have used as a disguise. The children called the wig maker to find out who had ordered it and were directed to a local post office box, Jay and Dexter were surprised to find belonged to the grocery store. Because Thorne picked up the mail each day, he became a prime suspect. In the meantime, Cindy had gone back to the cinema to look for the money. In the dark she had scuffled with someone else looking for the money and had given the person a deep scratch on the face.

At the same time that Thorne decided to pay Callie back for the stolen money, the Club members decided to tell Callie their suspicions about him. As Thorne handed his veterinary school savings to Callie, Cindy took a close enough look at Callie's face to see a new scratch and accused her of being the thief. Callie had so wanted Thorne to run the store instead of going to school, and had needed money so intensely, that she had stolen from her own business. The ending is weak but the rest of the book will hold reader interest. Spotlight Club Mystery series.

Interest Level: 3-5. Reading Level: 3.1. Further Search Topics: Mystery and Detective Stories, Gangs-Fiction, Crime-Fiction, Detectives-Fiction, Brothers and Sisters-Fiction.

Heide, Florence Parry. Mystery of the melting snowman; illus by Seymour Fleishman. A. Whitman 1974, 128 pp.

Hidden inside of a snowman, the Spotlight Club found what they believed was a stolen iron statue of a dog. In order to try to catch the thief, the children hid the statue again and watched to see who came to look for it. Eventually they determined that the thief or thieves was either Tom and Jenny, the amenable young couple who were helping Mrs. Wellington sell her house or Alex, the man who seemed to be a detective. After a frightening episode in which Alex almost captured Cindy, the dog, and a cache of Mrs. Wellington's diamonds (hidden in a secret compartment to which the dog held the key), Cindy managed to lock Alex in a closet long enough to enable Jay and Dexter to alert Mrs. Wellington to what was happening. The case was closed as Mrs. Wellington revealed Alex to be her greedy, young nephew, whom she had indulged once too often, but would not indulge again.

See *Mystery at Southport Cinema* for series information. Spotlight Club Mystery series.

Interest Level: 3-5. Reading Level: 2.2. Further Search Topics: Mystery and Detective Stories, Gangs-Fiction, Crime-Fiction, Brothers and Sisters-Fiction, Detectives-Fiction, Inheritance-Fiction.

Heide, Florence Parry. Mystery of the midnight message; illus by Seymour Fleishman. A. Whitman 1977, 128 pp.

The challenge to the Spotlight Club this time was to stop a crime before it happened. Jay and his sister Cindy were on a bus trip home when a blizzard forced the bus to stop at a motel for the night. Jay answered the room telephone late that night and heard a woman's strange and stern instructions. The instructions were to say nothing, to look in the desk drawer for directions, to expect that Bee had the other half of the instructions, and to be at the place at 8:00 the next evening. The envelope, which Jay and Cindy found, showed the location of and half the combination to someone's bedroom safe.

Early the next morning, the children found themselves fleeing in terror from the evil Scull, the man who was supposed to have received the message. Scull pursued them as they escaped in a friendly salesman's car, caught them and locked them into a cold barn without jackets. When the two were finally back on the road and reunited with Dexter and his sister Anne, they had only a few hours and fewer clues to help them find Woodvale and Jeremiah Gibbon, the intended victim.

Despite difficult driving conditions in the snow, Anne managed to get the children to their destination a few minutes before the thieves arrived. Anne and Jeremiah's secretary left the house together to get the police while the Spotlight Club members and Mr. Gibbon hid near the safe. A few tense minutes later, the case was closed; Mr. Gibbons' money was safe, the ringleader had been named (Mr. Gibbon's doctor), and the thieves had been caught.

See *Mystery at Southport Cinema* for series information. Spotlight Club Mystery series.

Interest Level: 3-5. Reading Level: 3.1. Further Search Topics: Mystery and Detective Stories, Crime-Fiction, Snow-Fiction, Disasters-Fiction, Gangs-Fiction, Brothers and Sisters-Fiction, Detectives-Fiction.

Heide, Florence Parry. Mystery of the vanishing visitor; illus by Seymour Fleishman. A. Whitman 1975, 128 pp.

Cindy was hired to take care of Mrs. Widget's house, animals, and plants for a weekend. That same weekend, someone tried to find and steal something from Mrs. Widget's overcrowded house. She had very few empty spaces in her house, so it was not a surprise that the thief wasn't able to find the object of his or her search. The three Spotlight Club members were determined to figure out not only who was the thief, but also what it was that the thief, wanted. Their prime suspects included the very nasty Bertha Beaker and the charming Charley Capp.

After spending a night in Mrs. Widget's house trying to, and almost succeeding in catching the thief, the children were surprised by an early morning visit from Mr. Capp. Mr. Capp was nearly able to steal away with a painting that hid a great deal of money before Cindy figured out that he was the thief. Even after Mr. Capp had been caught, he charmed his way out of any punishment and left before anyone had second thoughts.

See entry for *Mystery at Southport Cinema* for series information. Spotlight Club Mystery series.

Interest Level: 3-5. Reading Level: 2.2. Further Search Topics: Mystery and Detective Stories, Brothers and Sisters-Fiction, Gangs-Fiction, Crime-Fiction, Antiquities-Fiction, Detectives-Fiction.

Hildick, Edmund W. The case of the invisible dog; illus by Lisl Weil. Macmillan 1977, 101 pp.

Brains Bellingham, a nine-year-old scientific genius, interrupted the McGurk Organization's Annual Picnic with an invisible dog. It was only a short time before McGurk and his friends were convinced that Brains' discovery of how to make things invisible was the greatest event since putting a man on the moon. Although they had always scorned the idea of including anyone else in the Organization, they decided to persuade Brains to join. But, before the day was over, they discovered not only that they had been duped, but exactly how Brains had made the impossible seem real. The Organization took its revenge by using Brain's own trick to make him confess. When Brains began laughing at how well his trick had been used in reverse, McGurk admitted how impressed they all had been by Brain's clever thinking. The outcome of their discussion was that Brains was invited, a second time, to become a member of the McGurk Organization.

See *The Case of the Bashful Bank Robber* for series information. McGurk Mystery series.

Interest Level: 3-6. Reading Level: 3.1. Further Search Topics: Mystery and Detective Stories, Detectives-Fiction, Gangs-Fiction, Dogs-Fiction, Supernatural-Fiction, Humorous Fiction, Jealousy-Fiction.

Hildick, Edmund W. The great rabbit rip-off; illus by Lisl Weil. Macmillan 1976, 101 pp.

Why would anyone want to put red paint on all of the clay lawn rabbits in town? That was the first and easier of the mysteries the McGurk Organization had to solve. The bigger mystery was who would then steal them all and why? Almost everyone in town had purchased a rabbit to help a charity drive. Donny Towers a local social worker had thought of the idea. Donny, his fiancee, Joanne, and two reformed thieves, Sam and Ferdie, had made enough rabbits for everyone. When the rabbits disappeared, the Organization began to suspect, among others, Sam and Ferdie. Then when Donny replaced each one almost immediately with rabbits smelling of paint remover, the group began to think Donny might have been involved. It was Wanda's sharp eyes that revealed Donny's motive. Joanne's engagement ring had been accidentally molded into one of the rabbits and Donny had retrieved the rabbits to find the ring. Knowing he couldn't return the paint stained rabbits without raising suspicion, Donny had removed the red paint and told everyone that he was simply replacing the stolen rabbits with new ones.

See Case of the Bashful Bank Robber for series information. McGurk Mystery series.

Interest Level: 3-5. Reading Level: 2.2. Further Search Topics: Mystery and Detective Stories, Detectives-Fiction, Gangs-Fiction, Rabbits-Fiction, Crime-Fiction, Humorous Fiction.

Hildick, Edmund W. Deadline for McGurk; illus by Lisl Weil. Macmillan 1975, 104 pp.

When many of the dolls in the neighborhood began disappearing, their owners went to the McGurk Organization for help. At first McGurk was reluctant to take on such a silly task as recovering lost dolls. But when a ransom note appeared and the Organization was linked to the dolls' safety, McGurk's reluctance vanished. The note stated that if, in a written public notice, the members of the Organization did not admit that they were no good, the dolls were doomed. McGurk's pride would never have allowed him to write such a notice. As the deadline approached, the group plotted a daring move designed to uncover the doll thief. The plan depended on Willie's super-sensitive nose, a particular perfume dabbed on a stolen doll, and the curiosity of the thief. Success came only minutes before the hour of doom. Once again Sandra Ennis was the culprit.

See The Case of the Bashful Bank Robber for series information. McGurk Mystery series.

Interest Level: 3-5 Reading Level: 2.2. Further Search Topics: Dolls-Fiction, Mystery and Detective Stories, Detectives-Fiction, Humorous Fiction, Gangs-Fiction, Jealousy-Fiction.

Hildick, Edmund W. The case of the condemned cat; illus by Lisl Weil. Macmillan 1975, 106 pp.

Ray Williams had a terrible problem when he begged the McGurk Organization for help. His cat Whiskers had been accused of killing a neighbor's pet dove. Ray's mother decided that they couldn't risk upsetting the neighbors anymore and threatened to take Whiskers to the pound unless it could be proven that he was innocent. The Organization, needing time, hid Whiskers and told Mrs. Williams that he had run away. While Whiskers was safely hidden, the group interviewed all the neighbors, surveyed the scene of the crime, and tried to decide upon the real murderer. When the remains of another bird were found while Whiskers was safely locked away, it looked as if the cat was surely innocent. But then McGurk and his detectives found out that the cat had been sprung. It wasn't until they went back over all the information they had gathered that McGurk realized who was the real culprit. The only step left was to trick old Gramp Martin (the neighborhood grouch) into confessing.

See The Case of the Bashful Bank Robber for series information. McGurk Mystery series.
Interest Level: 3-6. Reading Level: 2.2. Further Search Topics: Mystery and Detective Stories, Cats-Fiction, Detectives-Fiction, Humorous Fiction, Gangs-Fiction, Pets-Fiction.

Hildick, Edmund W. The case of the secret scribbler; illus by Lisl Weil. Macmillan 1978, 106 pp.

Joey's discovery in a library book of a scrap of paper with part of a letter and a strange diagram on it led the McGurk Organization on a lively chase. Brains identified the diagram as that of a widely-used security system. The part of the letter that they could read told the group that there was a burglary being planned for the approaching weekend, but the youngsters knew the police would never take them seriously until they had much more evidence. By researching local alarm systems, determining who bought the unusual paper, and comparing handwriting samples, the detectives were able to convince the police of what was about to happen. In gratitude, the police loaned the Organization a police monitor so that they could listen as the thieves were caught. To all but McGurk it seemed like the perfect way to end the case: he tried to sneak into the midst of the capture, but only succeeded in getting himself in real trouble.

See The Case of the Bashful Bank Robber for series information. McGurk Mystery series.
Interest Level: 3-6. Reading Level: 2.2. Further Search Topics: Mystery and Detective Stories, Crime-Fiction, Gangs-Fiction, Nonverbal Communication-Fiction, Humorous Fiction, Detectives-Fiction.

Hildick, Edmund W. The case of the phantom frog; illus by Lisl Weil. Macmillan 1979, 121 pp.

The McGurk Organization would not, under ordinary circumstances, have agreed to babysit for seven-year-old Bela, but there was an unusual twist to Bela's case. Bela's aunt, who asked them to babysit while she worked in her sculpture studio, had heard the eerie sounds of a VERY large frog coming from Bela's room. At first it appeared to the group that Bela actually turned into a frog at night, a werefrog. But, upon investigation they found a very clever, very lonely, and very unhappy young boy who had invented the phantom because he was afraid that his aunt would make him give up his pet frog.

See The Case of the Bashful Bank Robber for series information. McGurk Mystery series.
Interest Level: 3-5. Reading Level: 3.1. Further Search Topics: Mystery and Detective Stories, Gangs-Fiction, Frogs-Fiction, Supernatural-Fiction, Transformations-Fiction, Detectives-Fiction, Babysitting-Fiction, Humorous Fiction, Occupations-Fiction.

Hildick, Edmund W. The case of the treetop treasure; illus by Lisl Weil. Macmillan 1980, 121 pp.

As Wanda rescued a cat she discovered a stash of odd items tucked into a hollow high up in a tree. On top of the assortment was a sign that said simply "Beware!" The McGurk Organization suspected a thief was using the tree as a place to hide stolen goods, but until an antique silver bowl was added nothing that had been placed there was worth stealing. Shortly afterwards Wanda found out from the police that she was the prime suspect in the theft of the bowl. Brains devised a complicated system for determining the real thief while McGurk worked more from intuition. Nevertheless, it wasn't long before they both arrived at the same conclusion. The culprit was the gang's long-time enemy Sandra Ennis. Then it was just a simple matter of finding the right way to persuade Sandra to confess and apologize to her victims.

See *The Case of the Bashful Bank Robber* for series information. McGurk Mystery series.

Interest Level: 3-5. Reading Level: 3.1. Further Search Topics: Mystery and Detective Stories, Crime-Fiction, Gangs-Fiction, Detectives-Fiction, Humorous Fiction.

Hildick, Edmund W. The case of the snowbound spy; illus by Lisl Weil. Macmillan 1980, 132 pp.

One snowy morning McGurk called the five members of his organization together to decipher a code. The code was part of a message from someone who wanted to hire them and would pay $5.00 a day. When they broke the code and met their employer, Mr. Fitch, he gave the group another code as part of their assignment. The second code told them where to deliver a small package that Mr. Fitch gave them. They were to pick up another coded message at the same place. After three pick-ups and drops they would be finished and Mr. Fitch, an ex-government spy, would have proved he was still a trustworthy and capable person to an ex-colleague with whom he wanted to work on a book. It seemed like just the challenging kind of assignment the McGurk Organization looked for. As they worked, however, it began to look more and more as if they were being used for illegal business. While Joey and McGurk staked out the next drop-off spot, Willie, Brains and Wanda pretended to Mr. Fitch to be unsuspecting. By working quickly and cleverly and by alerting the police, the McGurk gang uncovered and stopped two industrial spies who were stealing secret information about a new copying machine.

See *The Case of the Bashful Bank Robber* for series information. McGurk Mystery series.

Interest Level: 3-6. Reading Level: 3.1. Further Search Topics: Mystery and Detective Stories, Spies-Fiction, Detectives-Fiction, Gangs-Fiction, Humorous Fiction, Nonverbal Communication-Fiction, Crime-Fiction.

Hildick, Edmund W. The case of the bashful bank robber; illus by Lisl Weil. Macmillan 1981, 138 pp.

The McGurk Organization is a crime fighting detective agency. Led by Jack McGurk's strong ego, they had taken on many a seemingly impossible task and had always been successful. Never before, however, had they tried to protect the seven banks in town from being robbed. The five children's first idea was to regularly patrol each bank and watch for likely looking get-away cars. When that plan only led to a nasty confrontation with their new junior high school principal, they decided to try something else. Their second plan, to photograph all suspicious looking people near the banks, didn't fare much better than their first idea. Then, without knowing it, they found themselves holding the key to solving a real bank robbery. Before they realized its importance, they had literally given away the vital clue. Using only their own memories, powers of observation, and cleverness, they were still able to solve the crime with only a little help from the FBI.

The "McGurk mysteries" are light, fast-moving, and often humorous. Clues for solving the mysteries are sometimes subtle, but always there in the plot and illustrations for the reader to find. The characters are somewhat flat but still appealing. Joey, who is handy with words and a typewriter, is the narrator of each book. Jack McGurk, dedicated mastermind of all the group's activities is shrewd, a natural leader, and

egotistical. Willie has the world's most sensitive nose and an excellent memory for odors. Wanda is the best tree-climber in town and a rational influence on the group. Brains, the newest and youngest member of the group, is a scientific genius, so he runs their crime lab. The books need not be read in chronological order although most have a brief reference to an earlier story. Reading level varies within each book from 2.1 to 3.1. A few books include enough more difficult passages that their average reading level is pushed from 2.2 to 3.1. Interest level in the series, once a reader has started on it, is high. McGurk Mystery series.

Interest Level: 3-6. Reading Level: 2.2. Further Search Topics: Mystery and Detective Stories, Crime-Fiction, Detectives-Fiction, Humorous Fiction, Gangs-Fiction.

Hildick, Edmund W. The case of the four flying fingers; illus by Lisl Weil. Macmillan 1981, 138 pp.

At first the four young strangers who were knocking over garbage cans had been merely a neighborhood nuisance. Later McGurk and his fellow detectives began to suspect that they were involved in the rash of break-ins and burglaries in the city. The Organization didn't think the "garbage gang" was actually committing the robberies, but rather that they were fingering houses for someone else to burglarize (thus their nickname: The Four Flying Fingers). It could be safely assumed by a would-be burglar that where no one picked up the spilled garbage, no one was home. It was the Organization's job to find the Thumb who was the mastermind behind the plot. When they caught up with the Fingers, McGurk and crew found out that the Flying Fingers hadn't realized what they were doing; only that a blonde lady in a camper was paying them a nickel for every driveway they left strewn with garbage. It didn't take long for the Organization to track down the woman and her accomplice. But, in one of their less intelligent moves, they played right into her hands and soon found themselves being transported out of town in her camper. When they tried to call to passing cars for help, no one took them seriously. It wasn't until Brains, bound and gagged to appear authentic, used a flashlight and Morse code to signal for help that anyone paid any attention to them. A police car finally stopped the camper for speeding apd after some clever arguments McGurk and his friends were able to convince the police that Lady Thumb was a thief.

This title is just as enjoyable as the best of the other books in the series, more exciting and universal in appeal than most, and equally humorous. It's only drawback is a very inconsistent reading level (from 2.1 to 4.1) that will discourage a reader new to McGurk. Established fans will be able to tolerate the range. McGurk Mystery series.

Interest Level: 3-6. Reading Level: 3.1. Further Search Topics: Mystery and Detective Stories, Detectives-Fiction, Humorous Fiction, Crime-Fiction, Gangs-Fiction.

Law, Carol Russell. The case of the Weird Street firebug; illus by Bill Morrison. Knopf 1980, 119 pp.

This is the humorous story of a Nancy Drew-type character who gets involved in a mystery before she is even half finished with her mail-order detective lessons. Steffi wanted very much to be a detective. When she saw an ad for a local correspondence course, she tracked down the shabby office in a run-down building on Weir Street, and went to visit Jeff Dangerfield of Dangerfield Detective School. Steffi's first lesson, trailing suspects, was a disaster.

She tried to pick out suspicious characters at a fire on Weir Street on her way home. The only really suspicious character (Beady Eyes) didn't go anywhere, so Steffi couldn't follow him. Her next attempts were very obvious and only resulted in her own anger and embarrassment. On her way back to seek advice from Dangerfield, Steffi literally ran into Beady Eyes again. She didn't think anything more about him until she saw him a short time later at another fire just down the street from Dangerfield's office. As the fire moved closer to Dangerfield's building, Steffi took desperate measures to try and save her friend. Steffi's efforts were interpreted by Beady Eyes as attempts to indicate that he was an arsonist. By the time Steffi figured out that Beady Eyes really was an arsonist, he had her cornered. A timely entry by the police saved both Steffi and Dangerfield. Steffi's reward for the capture of Beady Eyes was a medal from the police and a partnership with Dangerfield.

A fast-paced story, as well as slightly more original characters than most stories of this genre, make this a likely success with third through sixth grade readers. Capers series.

Interest Level: 3-6. Reading Level: 3.1. Further Search Topics: Mystery and Detective Stories, Humorous Fiction, Fire-Fiction, Detectives-Fiction, Crime-Fiction.

Montgomery, Raymond A. The lost jewels of Nabooti; illus by Paul Granger. Bantam 1981, 121 pp.

See entry for *Sugarcane Island*, by Edward Packard for series information. Only available in paperback edition. Choose Your Own Adventure series.

Interest Level: 2-6. Reading Level: 3.2. Further Search Topics: Mystery and Detective Stories, Detectives-Fiction, Treasure-Fiction, Best Sellers, Group 2.

Packard, Edward. The mystery of Chimney Rock; illus by Paul Granger. Bantam 1979, 121 pp.

See notes for *Sugarcane Island* for information about the series. Paperback only. Choose Your Own Adventure series.

Interest Level: 2-6. Reading Level: 3.2. Further Search Topics: Mystery and Detective Stories, Cats-Fiction, Witches-Fiction, Ghosts-Fiction, Detectives-Fiction, Best Sellers, Group 2.

Parish, Peggy. Haunted house; illus by Paul Frame. Macmillan 1971, 151 pp.

Although this is the third book about Jed, Bill and Liza Roberts, it too can be read out of order. This time the family has moved into what was locally known as a haunted house. Very shortly after they moved into the house, a coded note appeared that led them to a series of messages and unusual occurrences. Lights that flashed into Liza's room turned out to be the headlights of cars, but the messages and a secret compartment in an old clock couldn't be as easily explained. Each day took them closer to the surprise that the messages hinted would be theirs. That surprise turned out to be three kittens and a treehouse. Two of the children's best friends had planned the whole mystery just to lead to the surprises.

This book has the same faults and strong points as the others about the Roberts children. Each chapter is short; the book is episodic; reading level is consistent; there is much dialogue and action and little description, and the plot has a comfortable familiarity about it. It can be very useful to the right readers.

Interest Level: 1-4. Reading Level: 2.1. Further Search Topics: Mystery and Detective Stories. Brothers and Sisters-Fiction, Ghosts-Fiction, Moving, Household-Fiction, Nonverbal Communication-Fiction, Group 2.

Parish, Peggy. Hermit Dan; illus by Paul Frame. Macmillan 1977, 151 pp.

When the Roberts children tried to prove that Pirate Island really had been used by pirates, they encountered more action and intrigue than they had found in any of their earlier adventures. Liza, Bill and Jed suspected that Hermit Dan knew whether or not there had been pirates on the island, but he was so gruff and apparently mean that they didn't dare ask him any questions. Instead, they trailed and spied on him and asked questions of anyone who had known Hermit Dan as a child. It was rumored that his ancestors had actually been pirates. Until a terrible fire that had destroyed all they owned, Hermit Dan's family had been very wealthy. However, no one knew how they had become so rich.

In an attempt to see what the summer residents knew about Hermit Dan, the children introduced themselves to the vacationing youngsters. Among the visitors the Roberts met Hank and Ted, brothers bent on bullying Hermit Dan. When the children were rescued from a severe sandstorm by Hermit Dan, they were surprised to find that he wasn't nearly as gruff as he appeared. In fact they began to feel quite protective of the old man. Thus when Hank and Ted stole a secret box that held all of Hermit Dan's valuables, it was the Roberts children who fought (literally) to get the box back. It was after Liza, Bill and Jed returned the box to Hermit Dan, however, that the real surprises began: these included a surprise party for Hermit Dan, his wish to be friendly, and his gift to the children of three pieces of eight that proved his family members were pirates.

This title's more interesting and involved plot makes the book more likely to be a success with older readers than the other stories about the Roberts children. Otherwise it shares the same format, faults and strengths as the other series titles.

Interest Level: 2-5. Reading Level: 2.1. Further Search Topics: Mystery and Detective Stories, Pirates-Fiction, Vacation-Fiction, Loners-Fiction, Treasure-Fiction, Bullies-Fiction, Brothers and Sisters-Fiction, Grandparents-Fiction.

Parish, Peggy. Clues in the woods; illus by Paul Frame. Macmillan 1968, 154 pp.

The books about the three Roberts children share problems that are obvious to adults and felt by some young readers as well, but they continue to be popular with undemanding young readers. The characters are very white and middle class and their actions often fit out-of-date stereotypes. The plots have few surprises or suspense, but the reading levels are consistent and the very predictability of the books makes them familiar and therefore comfortable.

This particular story takes place at the end of the same summer the children solved the mystery of *The Key to the Treasure*. The children were alerted by their grandmother to the disappearance of food scraps, left outside the house. Thinking that two runaway children, about whom they had read, had taken the food, Liza, Bill, and Jed tried to find the runaways. Their attempts eventually brought them new friends and thus the solution to their mystery. It had not been the runaways who had taken the food, it was their new friends' dog.

Interest Level: 1-4. Reading Level: 2.2. Further Search Topics: Mystery and Detective Stories, Brothers and Sisters-Fiction, Vacation-Fiction, Dogs-Fiction, Runaways-Fiction, Grandparents-Fiction, Group 2.

Parish, Peggy. Key to the treasure; illus by Paul Frame. Macmillan 1966, 154 pp.

This is the first of the stories about Jed, Bill and Liza Roberts. The three children are very middle-class, the book's plots are simple and often lack suspense, but the stories still enjoy widespread popularity among unsophisticated readers.

All three children went to spend the summer with their grandparents and decided to tackle a mystery left unsolved for over 75 years. An old drawing and an authentic war bonnet provided the only clues to finding three Indian artifacts. At each step along the way there were crumbled, brittle pieces of paper bearing coded messages that led to the next clue. The search ended when the children found that a storage area in a porch piller contained an Indian doll, mask, and leather shield that had belonged to their great-grandfather.

Interest Level: 1-4. Reading Level: 2.1. Further Search Topics: Vacation-Fiction, Brothers and Sisters-Fiction, Group 2, Mystery and Detective Stories, Grandparents-Fiction, Nonverbal Communication-Fiction.

Parish, Peggy. Pirate Island adventure; illus by Paul Frame. Macmillan 1975, 167 pp.

Although this is the fourth book in the series about the Roberts children, none of the titles must be read in chronological order. This time the three rather privileged children spent the summer with their grandparents on a resort island. They lived in a house that their family had owned for years, explored the island, and swam in their own private cove. But, most of their time was spent trying to solve an old mystery. Their great-uncle had hidden several very special items (one for each member of his family) years earlier, and had left only one clue with their grandfather. After he gave the children that clue it was only a matter of time before they found the hidden treasures.

This book is also lengthy, but is divided into 22 very manageable chapters. It is, like the others, almost entirely dialogue and action, which makes it especially appealing to young reluctant readers.

Interest Level: 1-4. Reading Level: 2.1. Further Search Topics: Mystery and Detective Stories, Vacation-Fiction, Treasure-Fiction, Brothers and Sisters-Fiction, Grandparents-Fiction, Group 2.

Platt, Kin. Dracula, go home; illus by Frank Mayo. Watts 1979, 87 pp.

From the chapter numbers that drip blood, and the humorously grotesque illustrations, to the short sentences and chapters, this is a book designed and almost guaranteed to appeal to the reluctant reader. A sense of immediacy and involvement is created by the first person narration. Tension is created on the opening page when Larry sees a man in the cemetery who looked exactly like Dracula. When that man registered at the hotel where Larry was working, Larry decided to find out more about him. It began to look as if Mr. A. R. Claude (the letters spell Dracula) was not only a vampire, but a thief and a murderer as well. The trouble was that Larry couldn't prove anything. Even when he found the stolen jewels for which Mr.

Claude had been searching, Larry still couldn't convince anyone of Claude's true identify. No one ever did believe Larry, thus Claude went free.

The author uses a light touch to treat an eerie subject. His inconclusive ending may disappoint some, but should delight many. Beware of the variability of the reading level however; it swings from high first grade to low third grade.

Interest Level: 3-6. Reading Level: 2.2. Further Search Topics: Monsters-Fiction, Horror-Fiction, Mystery and Detective Stories, Best Sellers, Murder-Fiction, Crime-Fiction, Transformations-Fiction.

St. John, Wylly Folk. The ghost next door; illus by Trina Schart Hyman. Har-Row 1971, 178 pp.

Told by 13-year-old Lindsay, this is the story of her neighbor Miss Judith and Miss Judith's two nieces. Her niece Miranda had drowned years earlier in Miss Judith's backyard fish pond and Miss Judith had never fully recovered from her death. As the story begins, Miss Judith is about to welcome another niece (Sherry) for a summer stay. Sherry, without ever being told about Miranda, seems to sense Miranda's presence all around. Her mother laughs and says that Sherry has an imaginary friend. Miss Judith, who is a strong believer in ESP, thinks that Sherry is communicating with Miranda. As the days go on Sherry learns more and more of Miranda' secrets. When Miss Judith is scared by Sherry, Lindsay and her friend, Tammy, decide to see what sort of tricks Sherry is playing.

A believable suspense story, made even more so by the illustrations.

Interest Level: 4-6. Reading Level: 5.1. Further Search Topics: Mystery and Detective Stories, Relatives-Fiction, Group 2, Extra Sensory Perception-Fiction, Best Sellers, Ghosts-Fiction.

Sharmat, Marjorie W. Nate the great goes undercover; illus by Marc Simont. Coward 1974, 47 pp.

Nate's next door neighbor Oliver was a pest, but Oliver had a mystery for Nate to solve. Oliver's garbage can was being burglarized at night. He wanted Nate to catch the garbage snatcher. Nate quickly drew up a list of human suspects and just as quickly eliminated them all. A night spent hiding in the garbage can proved the best way to catch the thief. Much to Nate's surprise, the thief turned out to be his new dog.

Very amusing and very useful. Reader format.

Interest Level: 1-3. Reading Level: 2.1. Further Search Topics: Humorous Fiction, Mystery and Detective Stories, Group 2, Detectives-Fiction, Best Sellers.

Sharmat, Marjorie W. Nate the great; illus by Marc Simont. Coward 1972, 62 pp.

This is a young imitation of Humphrey Bogart solving a *Dragnet* style mystery. Annie's recently finished painting of her dog had disappeared so she hired Nate to search for it. Nate gathered all the facts, investigated his suspects, and eventually solved the mystery, but not before he had consumed plenty of pancakes (his favorite food) and solved a second mystery by accident.

A simple plot, humorous telling, and a sympathetic, likeable protagonist make this one of a very popular series. Reader format.

Interest Level: 1-3. Reading Level: 2.1. Further Search Topics: Humorous Fiction, Detectives-Fiction, Mystery and Detective Stories, Group 2, Best Sellers.

Shearer, John. Billy Jo Jive and the case of the missing pigeons; illus by Ted Shearer. Delacorte 1978, 47 pp.

This is the third in a series of slight mysteries, always solved by Billy Jo Jive and his crime fighter partner, Susie Sunset. Jive and Sunset are street-wise, black youngsters who take their jobs as crime fighters very seriously, and are never detered for long from finding the criminals they seek. The crimes are always thefts, and the criminals vary from young children to neighborhood menaces. Suspense is created more by the manner in which Jive and Sunset catch the thieves, plus the determination and pace of the young detectives, than by guessing who the culprits might be. Jive, his street-slang manner of telling the first-person stories, and the urban setting will appeal to many readers. Jive and Sunset also appear on *Sesame Street*.

Jive accidentally photographed the fleeing pigeon thief as he was being chased by Flip, the victim. The photograph didn't show the thief's face, but did give Jive and Sunset a good look at what he was wearing. Jive and Sunset concluded that the thief was Snake Hips Robberts. They later realized that they had been wrong. When they looked carefully at the picture, they remembered that any dark color clothing photographs almost black in a black and white picture. Snake Hips had a black jacket, but he was innocent. The real thief was Sugar Brown. Then it was a simple matter of showing the evidence to both Flip and Sugar to get Sugar to confess.

Interest Level: 1-4. Reading Level: 2.2. Further Search Topics: Mystery and Detective Stories, Detectives-Fiction, Blacks-Fiction, City Life-Fiction, Group 2, Best Sellers.

Shearer, John. Billy Jo Jive and the walkie-talkie caper; illus by Ted Shearer. Delacorte 1981, 47 pp.

When Steam Boat Louis went to Jive and Sunset for help, he was desperate. Because Jive and Sunset had already solved three cases, they were the logical people to find the walkie-talkie that had been stolen from Steam Boat. The walkie-talkie was one of two that Steam Boat had been told to buy as part of a secret communication system for the Bugaloo Smackers. Even as Jive and Sunset hunted for the thief, the second walkie-talkie was stolen. Their only clue was a footprint found outside Steam Boat's fix-it shop. Eventually, after trial and error, Jive and Sunset uncovered the real thieves; Steam Boat's young twin cousins. Unhappy at being separated in school, they wanted to use the walkie-talkies to be able to talk with each other.

The high reading level of this book will make it most useful for those children who have read and enjoyed other books in the series and are willing to stretch to read one more.

Interest Level: 1-4. Reading Level: 3.2. Further Search Topics: Mystery and Detective Stories, Detectives-Fiction, Blacks-Fiction, City Life-Fiction, Group 2.

Shearer, John. Billy Jo Jive super private eye: the case of the missing ten speed bike; illus by Ted Shearer. Delacorte 1976, 47 pp.

Jive and Sunset began their friendship and their sleuthing career with this book. It all started when Sunset borrowed her older brother's 10-speed bicycle. Jive met Sunset while she sat at the side of the road crying, after her brother's bike had been stolen. Some careful joint detective work proved to Jive and Sunset that Dynamite Jones, jealous of Sunset's brother, had stolen the bike. The young crime fighters recovered the bicycle before Sunset's brother even knew it was missing.

This book sets the formula that all the others follow. A neighborhood person finds that something has been stolen and goes to Jive and Sunset for help. Jive and Sunset never have much trouble finding the thief even though they are sometimes misled for a short time. Often the culprit is quite obvious to the reader. After some attempts at clever detective work and an occasional bit of preaching, the crime is solved. It is the manner of the pursuit and the street-smart characters that give the stories their interest.

Interest Level: 1-4. Reading Level: 2.2. Further Search Topics: Mystery and Detective Stories, Blacks-Fiction, Detectives-Fiction, City Life-Fiction, Best Sellers, Group 2, Bicycles and Bicycling-Fiction.

Shreve, Susan. The Nightmares of Geranium Street. Knopf 1977, 127 pp.

The Nightmares, a small neighborhood gang, had very little to do until beautiful Tess moved on the block. Tess dressed in satins, furs, and rhinestones, and sang in nightclubs. She was even more of a fascination to the gang because they had been told to stay away from her. When Amanda moved in with Tess, the Nightmares invited her to join the gang so that they would have a way of spying on Tess. Gradually her strange behavior, her moods, her bruises and shaking spells, the strangers she let in the house, and the fights she had, led the gang members to suspect that Tess dealt in drugs. When Amanda failed to show up for a picnic and the Nightmares learned the police were searching for Tess, the gang became worried enough to look for Amanda themselves. In doing so, they uncovered proof of Tess' drug dealings, put themselves in great danger, and were protected by Tess as they escaped only moments before Tess was arrested.

Despite its low reading level, the book's confusing sequence of final events, and its subject matter make it best suited to older readers. It is not great literature, but its subject has strong appeal.

Interest Level: 5-6. Reading Level: 3.1. Further Search Topics: Family Problems-Fiction, Gangs-Fiction, Drugs-Fiction, Mystery and Detective Stories, City Life-Fiction, Crime-Fiction, Philadelphia-Fiction.

Simon, Seymour. Einstein Anderson makes up for lost time; illus by Fred Winkowski. Viking Pr 1981, 73 pp.

Adam (nicknamed Einstein) Anderson loves science. He also loves bad puns and correcting wrongs. What he does best, however, is to figure out science puzzles. Each book in this series (this is the third) presents 10 science puzzles which challenge Einstein and the reader. Clues and background are established in several pages of scene setting. Einstein regularly solves the puzzle and then the reader is asked how he did it. The answer follows on the next page. Areas of science that are drawn upon vary widely and range from animal behavior through chemistry and space science to zoology. Very palatable science reading. Print is on the small side in all four books.

Interest Level: 3-6. Reading Level: 2.2. Further Search Topics: Science, Puzzles, Mystery and Detective Stories.

Simon, Seymour. Einstein Anderson, science sleuth; illus by Fred Winkowski. Viking Pr 1980, 73 pp.

Einstein Anderson is the scientific equivalent of Encyclopedia Brown. Einstein was the nickname that Adam Anderson earned at the age of six. Even at that early age he was a scientific genius. He seems to especially love solving scientific puzzles and mysteries and that is just what Einstein does throughout this and the other books. There are ten very brief, somewhat plotless cases that are presented to Einstein. The clues are all included in each story. The solutions are supplied at the end of each case after the reader has had a chance to try to figure out the answers. None of the cases or solutions are terribly technical. Some of the cases can be solved simply by paying careful attention to the text. The rest require a moderate knowledge of scientific principles. It is a satisfying series to the science sleuth. Print is somewhat small.

Interest Level: 3-6. Reading Level: 3.1. Further Search Topics: Mystery and Detective Stories, Science, Puzzles.

Simon, Seymour. Einstein Anderson shocks his friends; illus by Fred Winkowski. Viking Pr 1980, 73 pp.

Using the identical formula as that in *Einstein Anderson, Science Sleuth* the author presents 10 more science puzzles to be solved by the reader. Einstein (nee Adam) outwits a bully, discovers who broke the window on the school bus, helps the sixth grade win contests against both the seventh and the eighth grades and more. This book, as well as the others in the series, is both fun and instructive.

Interest Level: 3-6. Reading Level: 3.1. Further Search Topics: Science, Puzzles, Mystery and Detective Stories.

Simon, Seymour. Einstein Anderson tells a comet's tale; illus by Fred Winkowski. Viking Pr 1981, 73 pp.

Adam earned his nickname Einstein by proving over and over again that he could solve any science puzzle put to him. Ten more challenges are presented here, none of which prove to be too much for our scientific whiz kid. Like its predecessors, this book is for science sleuths who enjoy matching wits with a cocky punster.

Interest Level: 3-6. Reading Level: 3.1. Further Search Topics: Science, Puzzles, Mystery and Detective Stories.

Sobol, Donald J. Encyclopedia Brown, boy detective; illus by Leonard Shortall. Elsevier-Nelson 1963, 88 pp.

The first of a large number of books that challenge the reader to solve the same mysteries Encyclopedia Brown deciphers. See *Encyclopedia Brown and the Case of the Dead Eagles* for more information.

Interest Level: 2-6. Reading Level: 2.2. Further Search Topics: Mystery and Detective Stories, Puzzles, Best Sellers, Detectives-Fiction.

Sobol, Donald J. Encyclopedia Brown and the case of the dead eagles; illus by Leonard Shortall. Elsevier-Nelson 1975, 96 pp.

By all rights Idaville should be declared a disaster area and Mr. Brown, the chief of police, should be fired from his job. Idaville looks like an ordinary small town, but behind its sleepy exterior there exists a crime wave that would challenge the best police departments in the country. It is true that the crimes are always solved and the criminals always caught, but not by Chief Brown. Chief Brown is frequently so stumped by his police cases that he talks about them at home, usually at dinner time. Almost always, his son, Leroy "Encyclopedia" Brown, solves the case before dinner is even over. A clear case of superior intelligence and skill.

Encyclopedia (so nicknamed because of his intellect) not only solves his father's cases, but serves as a detective for his friends, too. He is kept so busy that each slim volume in this series contains 10 short mysteries. Needless to say Encyclopedia solves them all. The question is can the reader? All necessary clues are there and specialized knowledge is rarely required. Should the reader fail to solve a mystery (they are not always as easy as one would expect), a full explanation and solution for each case is provided at the back of the book. Each title follows exactly the same formula. Although a teacher or parent may grow bored hearing of Encyclopedia's accomplishments, most young readers thoroughly enjoy them.

The books actively challenge and thus involve the reader in a way most books do not. A very popular series that does not have to be read in sequence. Reading level is consistently 2.2 to 3.1. Encyclopedia Brown series.

Interest Level: 2-6. Reading Level: 3.1. Further Search Topics: Mystery and Detective Stories, Puzzles, Best Sellers, Group 2, Detectives-Fiction.

Sobol, Donald J. Encyclopedia Brown and the case of the midnight visitor; illus by Lillian Brandi. Elsevier-Nelson 1977, 96 pp.

See *Encyclopedia Brown and the Case of the Dead Eagles* for full annotation.

Interest Level: 2-6. Reading Level: 2.2. Further Search Topics: Mystery and Detective Stories, Puzzles, Detectives-Fiction, Best Sellers.

Sobol, Donald J. Encyclopedia Brown and the case of the secret pitch; illus by Leonard Shortall. Elsevier-Nelson 1965, 96 pp.

See *Encyclopedia Brown and the Case of the Dead Eagles* for full annotation.

Interest Level: 2-6. Reading Level: 3.1. Further Search Topics: Group 2, Mystery and Detective Stories, Puzzles, Best Sellers, Detectives-Fiction.

Sobol, Donald J. Encyclopedia Brown finds the clues; illus by Leonard Shortall. Elsevier-Nelson 1966, 96 pp.

See *Encyclopedia Brown and the Case of the Dead Eagles* for full annotation.

Interest Level 2-6. Reading Level: 3.1. Further Search Topics: Mystery and Detective Stories, Puzzles, Detectives-Fiction, Best Sellers, Group 2.

Sobol, Donald J. Encyclopedia Brown gets his man; illus by Leonard Shortall. Elsevier-Nelson 1967, 96 pp.

See *Encyclopedia Brown and the Case of the Dead Eagles* for full annotation.

Interest Level: 2-6. Reading Level: 3.1. Further Search Topics: Mystery and Detective Stories, Puzzles, Best Sellers, Group 2, Detectives-Fiction.

Sobol, Donald J. Encyclopedia Brown keeps the peace; illus by Leonard Shortall. Elsevier-Nelson 1969, 96 pp.

See *Encyclopedia Brown and the Case of the Dead Eagles* for full annotation.

Interest Level: 2-6. Reading Level: 2.2. Further Search Topics: Mystery and Detective Stories, Puzzles, Best Sellers, Detectives-Fiction.

Sobol, Donald J. Encyclopedia Brown lends a hand; illus by Leonard Shortall. Elsevier-Nelson 1974, 96 pp.

See *Encyclopedia Brown and the Case of the Dead Eagles* for full annotation.

Interest Level: 2-6. Reading Level: 3.1. Further Search Topics: Mystery and Detective Stories, Puzzles, Detectives-Fiction, Best Sellers, Group 2.

Sobol, Donald J. Encyclopedia Brown saves the day; illus by Leonard Shortall. Elsevier-Nelson 1970, 96 pp.
See *Encyclopedia Brown and the Case of the Dead Eagles* for full annotation.
Interest Level: 2-6. Reading Level: 2.2. Further Search Topics: Mystery and Detective Stories, Puzzles, Detectives-Fiction, Best Sellers.

Sobol, Donald J. Encyclopedia Brown shows the way; illus by Leonard Shortall. Elsevier-Nelson 1972, 96 pp.
See *Encyclopedia Brown and the Case of the Dead Eagles* for full annotation.
Interest Level: 2-6. Reading Level: 2.2. Further Search Topics: Mystery and Detective Stories, Puzzles, Detectives-Fiction, Best Sellers.

Sobol, Donald J. Encyclopedia Brown solves them all; illus by Leonard Shortall. Elsevier-Nelson 1968, 96 pp.
See *Encyclopedia Brown and the Case of the Dead Eagles* for full annotation.
Interest Level: 2-6. Reading Level: 3.1. Further Search Topics: Mystery and Detective Stories, Puzzles, Detectives-Fiction, Group 2, Best Sellers.

Sobol, Donald J. Encyclopedia Brown sets the pace; illus by Ib Ohlsson. Four Winds Pr 1982, 89 pp.
See *Encyclopedia Brown and the Case of the Dead Eagles* for full annotation.
Interest Level: 2-6. Reading Level: 3.1. Further Search Topics: Mystery and Detective Stories, Detectives-Fiction, Puzzles, Group 2, Best Sellers.

Sobol, Donald J. Encyclopedia Brown carries on; illus by Ib Ohlsson. Schol Bk Serv 1980, 72 pp.
See *Encyclopedia Brown and the Case of the Dead Eagle* for full annotation.
Interest Level: 2-6. Reading Level: 3.1. Further Search Topics: Mystery and Detective Stories, Puzzles, Detectives-Fiction, Group 2, Best Sellers.

Warner, Gertrude Chandler. The lighthouse mystery; illus by David Cunningham. A. Whitman 1963, 128 pp.
What better place for a mystery than a lighthouse late at night? Add the excitement of a storm at sea and a young man alone in a boat and the story should be unbeatable. Unfortunately this, as well as some of the other books in the series, does not quite live up to its potential. It will not attract many new readers but it will satisfy those who crave more adventures of the Alden family. The main problem with the book is its lack of definition. It isn't quite a mystery or an adventure story, it's a little of both. It is also part homespun family story, part science lesson, and part "problem story."
The Aldens rented a lighthouse in a very small fishing village one summer. Late each night their dog awoke them as he barked at a stranger who walked into or away from a closed-up building nearby. When the children investigated, they found that the surly son of a local fisherman was using the building to experiment on plankton as a food source. Harry was a brilliant young man who wanted to go to college, but whose father stubbornly refused to let him study. One night when Larry was at sea gathering samples, a terrible storm blew up. Only the Coast Guard and an improvised light in the lighthouse saved Larry from

drowning. Larry's brush with death forced his father to acknowledge Larry's abilities and allow him to continue studying at college.
The sketchy illustrations in this and the following books in the series are an improvement over the siihouettes of *The Boxcar Children*. See the annotation for *The Boxcar Children* for further series information.
Interest Level: 3-6. Reading Level: 2.1. Further Search Topics: Mystery and Detective Stories, Lighthouses-Fiction, Food-Fiction, Disasters-Fiction, Vacation-Fiction.

Warner, Gertrude Chandler. Mountain top mystery; illus by David Cunningham. A. Whitman 1964, 128 pp.
A day's climb up and down Old Flat Top was all the Alden family had wanted. Instead, when a portion of the trail collapsed into a cave, they found themselves stranded on top of the mountain. From their vantage point that night they could see a shadowy light which they investigated the next day. They found a 90-year-old Indian woman who had a strange story to tell of treasure hidden in a cave somewhere on Old Flat Top. The treasure was rightfully hers as the last of her tribe, but she had never been able to find it. The collapse of the trail and the reopening of the cave attracted more attention than just the Alden's though. Both an expert on caves and a young Indian boy wanted to find out more about the cave. David, the Indian boy, turned out to be the old woman's grandnephew. The treasure was indeed unearthed; David and Lovan were reunited; the treasure was given to Lovan, and both David's and Lovan's futures were secured.
What in the other books is mild stereotyping becomes more noticeable here (the books are all around 20 years old). The print is smaller here than before but the spacing between the lines is adequate. See entry for *The Boxcar Children* for more information.
Interest Level: 3-6. Reading Level: 2.2. Further Search Topics: Mystery and Detective Stories, Treasure-Fiction, Survival-Fiction, Indians of North America-Fiction, Mountain Climbing-Fiction, Brothers and Sisters-Fiction.

Warner, Gertrude Chandler. Schoolhouse mystery; illus by David Cunningham. A. Whitman 1965, 128 pp.
On a dare, the Aldens went to a quiet fishing village to see what excitement they could find there. They found an isolated town filled with poor and unfriendly people. In their attempt to get to know the townspeople, the Aldens learned of the children's desire for schooling and the adults' anticipation of the Money Man's arrival. The Alden children took on the task of teaching school for the summer in an abandoned schoolhouse owned by Miss Gray, a recluse. The Money Man intrigued them more with each new bit of information they learned about him. They finally decided that the Money Man was a swindler who was practically stealing valuable antiques away from the villagers. By spying on the Money Man when he used the schoolhouse to store the antiques, the Aldens and an ex-FBI man were able to capture him. When the vacation was over, the Aldens had once more found excitement, Miss Gray had agreed to teach the local school, the Money Man was on his way to jail, and the townspeople knew the value of their old household items.
See the entry for *The Boxcar Children* for more information.

Interest Level: 3-5. Reading Level: 2.2. Further Search Topics: Mystery and Detective Stories, Vacation-Fiction, School Stories, Antiquities-Fiction, Crime-Fiction, Brothers and Sisters-Fiction, Challenges-Fiction.

Warner, Gertrude Chandler. The woodshed mystery; illus by David Cunningham. A. Whitman 1960, 159 pp.

The four Alden children have grown since their first appearance in *The Boxcar Children* but they are still as close a family as ever. Aunt Jane's telephone message that she wanted to move near them started this adventure. Grandfather proceeded to buy and refurbish his childhood home as a surprise for Aunt Jane. It was an easy house to buy because it had been abandoned and was thought to be haunted. Even though the children and Aunt Jane weren't really worried by the stories of odd occurrences that no one quite remembered, they began to be aware of strange noises and things missing. Upon investigation they discovered Aunt Jane's old boyfriend living in the woodshed in the forest. There beneath the floor of the woodshed, they also found a store of Revolutionary War supplies and a letter from the original owners of the house. The supplies and the letter helped to explain some of the stories. Andrew, Jane's long-lost boyfriend, explained the rest.

It is not necessary to have read any of the series in order to read this story, but those children who enjoyed *The Boxcar Children* are most likely to enjoy the Alden's further adventures. See the entry for *The Boxcar Children* for more information.

Interest Level: 3-5. Reading Level: 2.1. Further Search Topics: Mystery and Detective Stories, United States-History-War-Fiction, Brothers and Sisters-Fiction, Ghosts-Fiction, Vacation-Fiction.

Yolen, Jane. Shirlick Holmes and the case of the wandering wardrobe; illus by Anthony Rao. Coward 1981, 80 pp.

This is a light, fast-paced story of Shirli and her four friends' attempt to solve a local mystery. Its more fully developed characters and plot make this a better literary piece than any of the *Encyclopedia Brown* stories, but it resembles them in other ways. The children live in a small, secure town. The police chief, Shirli's neighbor and George's father, is working on the same case that interests the children but the children solve it first. The mystery is real and involves danger, as opposed to many of Hildick's McGurk mysteries, the other series this book resembles.

Shirli is a fiesty figure who took up George's challenge to solve the town's latest mystery. Thieves had been systematically robbing some of the wealthy summer homes of antiques. Shirli's plan, to search each of the houses for clues, only succeeded in angering the police chief when he caught Shirli and her friends. Being intrepid detectives, however, they did not give up. Instead, they staked out a likely house and waited for the thieves. When the robbers finally arrived Shirli and George hid. Only Gloria was able to escape and go for help. The oak wardrobe in which Shirli took refuge was one of the first pieces the thieves took out of the house. When Shirli tried to get out of it, she found the wardrobe had been placed on a truck with its door against the truck's side; she was caught. Very frightened, she stayed silent until she found herself in the middle of an antiques auction and recognized one of the voices making bids as George's father! As Shirli tumbled out of the wardrobe some of the police chief's men arrested the auctioneer for burglary and selling stolen goods. After she escaped, Gloria had told the police about the thieves, their

truck, Shirli, and George, whom they found locked inside a closet still at the summer house.

A serviceable book that will be enjoyed by a wide range of readers.

Interest Level: 3-5. Reading Level: 3.1. Further Search Topics: Mystery and Detective Stories, Humorous Fiction, Friendship-Fiction, Crime-Fiction, Antiquities-Fiction, Detectives-Fiction, Challenges-Fiction.

Young, Carol Beach. Remember me when I am dead. Elsevier-Nelson 1980, 94 pp.

This is a short but taut story about the effect of their mother's death upon two young girls. For a long time Jenny, the younger and more vivacious of the sisters, refused to believe her mother had really died. Sara, quiet and serious, mourned and missed her mother, but eventually accepted her mother's sudden death as a fact. Jenny's continuing denial prompted her father and stepmother to talk of sending her away to a school where memories wouldn't be so vivid. That talk inspired Sara to develop a devious and calculated plan to insure that Jenny would indeed be sent away. All her life Sara had been given less attention than Jenny. With Jenny gone, Sara would finally have her father and stepmother's love and attention all to herself. With a Hitchcock-like twist Sara's plan proved too successful. Jenny was sent away to school, but because she didn't want to go alone and because her parents could deny Jenny nothing, Sara was to go too.

This suspenseful psychological thriller is almost guaranteed success with older readers.

Interest Level: 5-6. Reading Level: 4.2. Further Search Topics: Mystery and Detective Stories, Brothers and Sisters-Fiction, Death-Fiction, Horror-Fiction, Best Sellers, Jealousy-Fiction.

MYTHOLOGY

Baylor, Byrd. And it is still that way: legends told by Arizona Indian children. Scribner 1976, 85 pp.

Byrd Baylor has collected and written notes for forty-one short American Indian legends from seven Arizona tribes whose school children were asked to write down or illustrate their favorite legend. The result is a collection that reflects the concerns, the history, religion, humor and pride of the children and their ancestors. This excellent collection is not only interesting reading, but it also fits well into social studies and language arts units.

Interest Level: 2-6. Reading Level: 3.1. Further Search Topics: Legends, Arizona-Fiction, Navajo Indians, Hopi Indians, Papago Indians, Pima Indians, Apache Indians, Quechan Indians, Cocopah Indians, Indians of North America-Legends, Mythology, Group 2.

Bernstein, Margery. Coyote goes hunting for fire; illus by Ed Heffernan. Scribner 1974, 40 pp.

A delightful story that can be read for fun or used as part of a unit on North American Indians. A long time ago when there was no fire, all the animals but Coyote banded together to find it. The animals left Coyote behind because he was always spoiling their plans. Coyote saw them leave, chased after them and once more tried to direct everything, but only ended up losing fire. Cartoon-like illustrations add to the humor of the story. This book should make a simple, but effective play.

Interest Level: 1-4. Reading Level 2.1. Further Search Topics: Animals-Fiction, Legends, Mythology, Fire-Fiction, Indians of North America-Legends, Coyotes-Fiction, Group 2, Creation-Fiction, Drama.

Bernstein, Margery. The first morning; illus by Enid Warner Romanek. Scribner 1976, 44 pp.

Spider, Mouse, and Fly volunteered to ask the king of the sky for light to take back to earth because the animals on earth were tired of living in darkness. The king didn't want to give away any light and so he set what he thought was an impossible task for the three animals. They were able to outwit the king three times and finally return to earth with a box Mouse was sure contained light. When they opened the box all they found was a rooster. Poor Mouse was ashamed at having been so badly tricked. But then Rooster crowed up the first morning and has done so ever since. A competent retelling of an African myth, nicely complemented by bold illustrations. Good candidate for dramatization.

Interest Level: 1-3. Reading Level: 2.1. Further Search Topics: Animals-Fiction, Group 2, Mythology, Light-Fiction, Drama, Time-Fiction, Calendars-Fiction, Creation-Fiction, Africa-Folklore.

NAMATH, JOE

Burchard, Marshall. Sports hero: Joe Namath. Putnam 1971, 95 pp.

One of football's best and flashiest quarterbacks. See *Sports Hero: Bill Walton* entry. Sports Hero series.

Interest Level: 2-6. Reading Level: 2.2. Further Search Topics: Biography, Namath, Joe, Football-Biography.

NATURE STUDY

Branley, Franklyn M. Roots are food finders; illus by Joseph Low. Har-Row 1975, 33 pp.

It really is a shame that the picture book format of this and other *Let's-Read-and-Find-Out-Science-Books* will prevent older children from using them. There is much good information here that is thoroughly and logically explained without patronizing the reader. Functions and types of roots are described. Experiments to show root growth, root hairs, and absorption are given. A very useful book through third grade and possibly fourth grade. Beyond fourth grade children will certainly balk at the book's "babyish" appearance. Let's-Read-and-Find-Out-Science-Book series.

Interest Level: 1-4. Reading Level: 2.2. Further Search Topics: Nature Study, Botany, Group 2, Experiments, Scientific.

Brenner, Barbara. Baltimore Orioles; illus by J. Winslow Higginbottom. Har-Row 1974, 62 pp.

An impressive combination of very easy, as well as interesting and informative reading. Within the barest skeleton of a story the author gives a great deal of information about young Baltimore Orioles and the mating and hatching cycle of the older birds. Unfortunately its easy reader format will discourage use beyond third grade. Use freely until that point. Science I Can Read Book series.

Interest Level: 1-3. Reading Level 1.2. Further Search Topics: Birds, Nature Study.

Chenery, Janet. Wolfie; illus by Marc Simont. Har-Row 1969, 64 pp.

This slight but satisfying story is the vehicle for much information about spiders. Harry caught a wolf spider. To keep his sister Polly out of the way, Harry and his friend George told her she could see the spider only after she caught 100 flies to feed it. In the meantime, they took the spider to the nature center where they were treated to a fascinating lesson about insects and spiders (especially wolf spiders). It's too bad that the book's cartoon style illustrations prevent this book from being very useful beyond grade three.

Interest Level: 1-3. Reading Level: 2.1. Further Search Topics: Spiders, Pets, Nature Study, Group 2.

Conklin, Gladys. Little apes; illus by Joseph Cellini. Holiday 1970, unp (32pp).

An informative as well as interesting look at gorillas, chimpanzees, orangutans and gibbons. Their habits and behavior patterns are described by following a young one of each species through a full day in its natural surroundings. The text is simple without being condescending and the illustrations are so life-like that they almost walk off the pages. An excellent treatment of a popular subject makes this a very useful book.

Interest Level: 2-5. Reading Level: 2.2. Further Search Topics: Apes, Gorillas, Nature Study, Infants, Group 2.

Goldin, Augusta. Spider silk; illus by Joseph Low. Har-Row 1964, unp (34 pp).

No gimmicks here, just straight-forward information about spider webs. Where are spider webs found? How are they formed? What are their shapes? For what are they used? How strong are they? And, what are the other uses of spider silk? In answering those questions the author also gives a bit of information about particular types of spiders. The book can easily be used through grade three. Its picture book format will turn many fourth and fifth graders away even though the book's information is still quite interesting and useful. Let's-Read- & -Find-Out Science Book series.

Interest Level: 1-5. Reading Level: 2.2. Further Search Topics: Spiders, Nature Study, Group 2.

McNulty, Faith. Woodchuck; illus by Joan Sandin. Har-Row 64 pp.

There's a great deal of information in this little book. It describes a woodchuck's physical appearance, its habits and behavior, and its life cycle. The treatment is very direct and very honest (two of four young woodchucks are killed before the first year is over). Only an overly repetitive, slightly condescending beginning, and the reader format hamper the book's usefulness beyond grade four. A Science-I-Can-Read-Book.

Interest Level: 1-4. Reading Level: 3.1. Further Search Topics: Nature Study, Groundhogs, Group 2, Woodchucks.

Shaw, Evelyn. Alligator; illus by Frances Zweifel. Har-Row 1972, 61 pp.

A straight-forward, respectful description of an alligator's life cycle. Emphasis is placed on the time between the mother's nest-building and the birth of the young alligators. The danger to alligators posed by man is expressed, but not stressed. Little physical description is included. An interesting and competent treatment of a narrow subject. Reader format. A Science-I-Can-Read Book series.

Interest Level: 1-4. Reading Level: 2.1. Further Search Topics: Alligators, Nature Study, Group 2.

NAVAJO INDIANS

Baylor, Byrd. And it is still that way: legends told by Arizona Indian children. Scribner 1976, 85 pp.

Byrd Baylor has collected and written notes for forty-one short American Indian legends from seven Arizona tribes whose school children were asked to write down or illustrate their favorite legend. The result is a collection that reflects the concerns, the history, religion, humor and pride of the children and their ancestors. This excellent collection is not only interesting reading, but it also fits well into social studies and language arts units.

Interest Level: 2-6. Reading Level: 3.1. Further Search Topics: Legends, Arizona-Fiction, Navajo Indians, Hopi Indians, Papago Indians, Pima Indians, Apache Indians, Quechan Indians, Cocopah Indians, Indians of North America-Legends, Mythology, Group 2.

NAVAJO INDIANS-FICTION

Bulla, Clyde Robert. Indian hill; illus by James J. Spanfeller. T Y Crowell 1963, 74 pp.

A very low-key story of a Navajo family who moved from the reservation to a city because they could no longer support themselves on the reservation. The move was necessary, but it was not appreciated by young Kee and his mother. They hated their ugly apartment and the crowded city, and wanted to go home. When an excuse to return to the reservation arose, Kee and his mother left the city. However, by the time Kee's father arrived to tell them he had been wrong to force them to move, Kee and his mother had realized they never gave their new home a chance. They were ready to try again. No excitement here, only an understanding look at the difficulties of moving.

Interest Level: 2-5. Reading Level: 2.1. Further Search Topics: Indians of North America-Fiction, Navajo Indians-Fiction, City Life-Fiction, Moving, Household-Fiction.

Miles, Miska. Annie and the old one; illus by Peter Parnall. Little 1971, 44 pp.

A quietly beautiful story that will not appeal to all readers. Annie, a young Navajo girl, had a very close relationship with her grandmother. Her grandmother announced that she would "go to Mother Earth" at the time when the new rug Annie's mother was weaving was "taken from the loom." Annie tried all she could think of to keep the rug from being finished in order to keep her grandmother alive. When her grandmother solemnly explained that Annie could not stop time, Annie listened and "understood many things" for the first time.

It will be a thoughtful, sensitive child or a child trying to understand death who will best appreciate this special book.

Interest Level: 3-6. Reading Level: 3.2. Further Search Topics: Grandparents-Fiction, Death-Fiction, Indians of North America-Fiction, Navajo Indians-Fiction.

NEW YORK CITY

Beame, Rona. Ladder company 108. Messner 1973, 63 pp.

The reader of this book will literally live through several days with a New York City fire company. The author's "Dragnet"-like writing style, her use of photographs, and actual people, all make the firefighters' experiences very real. It is an exciting, engrossing and satisfying book. The heavily-used jargon will be quickly understood, thus should pose no real obstacle to most readers.

Interest Level 2-6. Reading Level: 3.1. Further Search Topics: Firefighters, Occupations, City Life, New York City, Group 2, Best Sellers.

NEW YORK CITY-FICTION

Benchley, Nathaniel. Small Wolf; illus by Joan Sandin. Har-Row 1972, 64 pp.

A straight-forward telling of white man's purchase of Manhattan and the resulting displacement of the Indians. The text is simple. The tone is sympathetic to the plight of the Indians. The reader is neither lectured nor patronized, but the early-reader format will prevent using the book comfortably beyond fourth grade. An I Can Read History Book.

Interest Level: 1-4. Reading Level 2.2. Further Search Topics: Historical Fiction, New York City-Fiction, United States-History-Fiction, Indians of North America-Fiction, Group 2.

Greene, Constance C. I and Sproggy; illus by Emily A. McCully. Viking Pr. 1978, 155 pp.

Ten-year-old Adam had adjusted to his parents' divorce and had even grown to like living alone with his mother. When his father came back from London with his new wife and stepdaughter Sproggy and announced that they were moving into an apartment nearby, Adam was a little worried. But when his father asked him to take care of Sproggy, Adam was furious. First of all, he didn't know Sproggy and he didn't want to know her. Secondly, she was two months older than he, taller too, and she embarrassed him in public. And finally, she didn't need his help. She got along quite well by herself; so well that she even saved Adam from a mugger and became good friends with Adam's friends behind his back. It wasn't until Sproggy proved to be vulnerable that Adam and she became friends.

A warm, realistic and humorous story whose interesting characters (even the minor ones) heighten the book's appeal.

Interest Level: 4-6. Reading Level: 3.2. Further Search Topics: Brothers and Sisters-Fiction, Divorce and Separation-Fiction, City Life-Fiction, New York City-Fiction, Humorous Fiction, Friendship-Fiction, Everyday Stories.

Hurwitz, Johanna. The law of gravity; illus by Ingrid Fetz. Morrow 1978, 192 pp.

The summer between fifth and sixth grades looked very unexciting to Margot. Her best friends were both going away for the whole summer and her father, a musician, was going to be on tour for most of the summer. Margot's very overweight mother had sworn never to go downstairs from their fifth floor walk-up apartment. Unless Margot chose to stay upstairs too, she was sure she would have a very lonely vacation. In addition, she had to work on a summer project for school. The project she finally chose was to get her mother downstairs after nine years of staying upstairs. In search of help she went to the local library where she met Bernie. Bernie was only a year older than Margot, but he seemed to know the most interesting things about the city. He showed her places Margot had never heard of before, he taught her to play chess, backgammon, and even to ride a bicycle. He was so full of fascinating ideas and information that Margot had no chance to be bored or lonely. Best of all, he even tried to help Margot with her project. None of their ideas worked, however, until Margot pretended to run away and scared her mother into going downstairs. Only then did Margot realize that she loved her mother whether or not she stayed on the fifth floor and that she couldn't simply force her mother or anyone else to change to suit her own fancy.

The book is a warm, understanding, slightly humorous treatment of the fairly common wish to change someone else. Although not many readers are likely to share Margot's exact problem, most will recognize her feelings. The book is also a virtual Chamber of Commerce advertisement for urban living. One of its other charms is its picture of a non-competitive, open, real friendship between an

11-year-old girl and a 12-year-old boy. The only drawback to the book is its inconsistent reading level which varies from 4.1 to 5.1 with a rare leap to 5.2.

Interest Level: 4-6. Reading Level: 4.2. Further Search Topics: Vacation-Fiction, Friendship-Fiction, Loners-Fiction, City Life-Fiction, Individualists-Fiction, Courage-Fiction, New York City-Fiction, Humorous Fiction, Family-Fiction, Challenges-Fiction, Weight-Fiction, Everyday Stories, Best Sellers.

NONVERBAL COMMUNICATION

Amon, Aline. Talking hands: Indian sign language. Doubleday 1968, 80 pp.

If you can ignore the author's patronizing tone and air of self-satisfaction, this is a book with great appeal. Children love ways of communicating privately, be it Pig Latin, codes and ciphers, or just whispering. This book appeals to that love by clearly, though unattractively, demonstrating over 200 words in American Indian sign language. By the time the young reader finishes the book, he/she will not only have had the fun of learning another method of communication, but will have learned a few simple generalities about North American Indians. The index is detailed enough that any word can be quickly checked. The book is useful for history, social studies, or language arts units, as well as for fun.

Interest Level: 2-6. Reading Level: 2.2. Further Search Topics: Indians of North America-Sign Language, Communication, Nonverbal Communication, Ethnic Groups.

Charlip, Remy. Handtalk; an ABC of finger spelling and sign language; photos by George Ancona. Schol. Bk. Serv. 1974, 42 pp.

This is not a book to be read and put away. It is a challenge to learn finger spelling (forming words letter by letter with the fingers) and signing (forming whole words or ideas by making a picture using one or both hands). It is a challenge that appeals to almost any child, reader and non-reader. One letter of the manual alphabet is shown at the top of each page. At the bottom of the page is a series of pictures that spell out a word which begins with the letter for that page. In the center of the page a model signs that same word. Only the first few words are explained, although there are hints for some of the more difficult words. The rest must be deciphered by the reader. In addition, the book includes over 25 more signs and a sentence about a very ugly vampire. The entire manual alphabet is also shown on a quick-reference, double page spread. The book provides an enjoyable and successful experience with language, especially if two or more children work with the book together. Although its picture book format would ordinarily turn older children away, interest in the book remains high through sixth grade. Because there are so few words that a child needs to read to enjoy this book, its reading level is an estimate.

Interest Level: 2-6. Reading Level: 2.1. Further Search Topics: Nonverbal Communication, Physically Handicapped, Communication.

Sarnoff, Jane. What? A riddle book; illus by Reynold Ruffins. Scribner 1974, 62 pp.

A good, lengthy collection of both familiar and unfamiliar riddles. Every other page is brightened by bold and humorous illustrations. The first part of the book seems to have slightly more riddles for younger readers than the rest of the book. Some of the riddles in the collection involve rather sophisticated puns; thus they are more appealing to fifth and sixth grade readers. The final three pages of the book include 35 riddles whose answers are in code. The key to the code is given on the last page of the book. It is a picture book printed in two tones. The riddles sometimes slant diagonally across the page.

Interest Level: 1-6. Reading Level: 3.1. Further Search Topics: Riddles, Wit and Humor, Group 2, Nonverbal Communication.

NONVERBAL COMMUNICATION-FICTION

Hildick, Edmund W. The case of the secret scribbler; illus by Lisl Weil. Macmillan 1978, 106 pp.

Joey's discovery in a library book of a scrap of paper with part of a letter and a strange diagram on it led the McGurk Organization on a lively chase. Brains identified the diagram as that of a widely-used security system. The part of the letter that they could read told the group that there was a burglary being planned for the approaching weekend, but the youngsters knew the police would never take them seriously until they had much more evidence. By researching local alarm systems, determining who bought the unusual paper, and comparing handwriting samples, the detectives were able to convince the police of what was about to happen. In gratitude, the police loaned the Organization a police monitor so that they could listen as the thieves were caught. To all but McGurk it seemed like the perfect way to end the case: he tried to sneak into the midst of the capture, but only succeeded in getting himself in real trouble.

See *The Case of the Bashful Bank Robber* for series information. McGurk Mystery series.

Interest Level: 3-6. Reading Level: 2.2. Further Search Topics: Mystery and Detective Stories, Crime-Fiction, Gangs-Fiction, Nonverbal Communication-Fiction, Humorous Fiction, Detectives-Fiction.

Hildick, Edmund W. The case of the snowbound spy; illus by Lisl Weil. Macmillan 1980, 132 pp.

One snowy morning McGurk called the five members of his organization together to decipher a code. The code was part of a message from someone who wanted to hire them and would pay $5.00 a day. When they broke the code and met their employer, Mr. Fitch, he gave the group another code as part of their assignment. The second code told them where to deliver a small package that Mr. Fitch gave them. They were to pick up another coded message at the same place. After three pick-ups and drops they would be finished and Mr. Fitch, an ex-government spy, would have proved he was still a trustworthy and capable person to an ex-colleague with whom he wanted to work on a book. It seemed like just the challenging kind of assignment the McGurk Organization looked for. As they worked, however, it began to look more and more as if they were being used for illegal business. While Joey and McGurk staked out the next drop-off spot, Willie, Brains and Wanda pretended to Mr. Fitch to be unsuspecting. By working quickly and cleverly and by alerting the police, the McGurk gang uncovered and stopped two industrial spies who were stealing secret information about a new copying machine.

See *The Case of the Bashful Bank Robber* for series information. McGurk Mystery series.

Interest Level: 3-6. Reading Level: 3.1. Further Search Topics: Mystery and Detective Stories, Spies-Fiction, Detectives-Fiction, Gangs-Fiction, Humorous Fiction, Nonverbal Communication-Fiction, Crime-Fiction.

Packard, Edward. Your code name is Jonah; illus by Paul Granger. Bantam 1980, 114 pp.

See *Sugarcane Island* for information about books in this series. Paperback only. Choose Your Own Adventure series.

Interest Level: 2-6. Reading Level: 3.2. Further Search Topics: Nonverbal Communication-Fiction, Best Sellers, Spies-Fiction, Group 2.

Parish, Peggy. Haunted house; illus by Paul Frame. Macmillan 1971, 151 pp.

Although this is the third book about Jed, Bill and Liza Roberts, it too can be read out of order. This time the family has moved into what was locally known as a haunted house. Very shortly after they moved into the house, a coded note appeared that led them to a series of messages and unusual occurrences. Lights that flashed into Liza's room turned out to be the headlights of cars, but the messages and a secret compartment in an old clock couldn't be as easily explained. Each day took them closer to the surprise that the messages hinted would be theirs. That surprise turned out to be three kittens and a treehouse. Two of the children's best friends had planned the whole mystery just to lead to the surprises.

This book has the same faults and strong points as the others about the Roberts children. Each chapter is short; the book is episodic; reading level is consistent; there is much dialogue and action and little description, and the plot has a comfortable familiarity about it. It can be very useful to the right readers.

Interest Level: 1-4. Reading Level: 2.1. Further Search Topics: Mystery and Detective Stories. Brothers and Sisters-Fiction, Ghosts-Fiction, Moving, Household-Fiction, Nonverbal Communication-Fiction, Group 2.

Parish, Peggy. Key to the treasure; illus by Paul Frame. Macmillan 1966, 154 pp.

This is the first of the stories about Jed, Bill and Liza Roberts. The three children are very middle-class, the book's plots are simple and often lack suspense, but the stories still enjoy widespread popularity among unsophisticated readers.

All three children went to spend the summer with their grandparents and decided to tackle a mystery left unsolved for over 75 years. An old drawing and an authentic war bonnet provided the only clues to finding three Indian artifacts. At each step along the way there were crumbled, brittle pieces of paper bearing coded messages that led to the next clue. The search ended when the children found that a storage area in a porch piller contained an Indian doll, mask, and leather shield that had belonged to their great-grandfather.

Interest Level: 1-4. Reading Level: 2.1. Further Search Topics: Vacation-Fiction, Brothers and Sisters-Fiction, Group 2, Mystery and Detective Stories, Grandparents-Fiction, Nonverbal Communication-Fiction.

Sleator, William. Into the dream; illus by Ruth Sanderson. Dutton 1979, 137 pp.

Paul and Francine each started having what, at first, seemed like nightmares. As the dreams became more detailed and forboding, they discovered that they were sharing the same nightmare. They dreamed of a four-year-old boy, swirling lights, and a large dog. After awhile they figured out that the dog was trying to save the little boy from some unknown danger. As the pieces of the puzzle began to increase in number, Paul and Francine decided that the dream was in some way connected to a night over four years earlier when they had both been staying at the same motel. They, a pregnant woman, and a pregnant dog had all been affected by the telepathic power given off by a spaceship. The progeny of the woman and the dog had been given extraordinary mental powers; powers that a secret government agency wanted to mold and then put to their own use. The danger Paul and Francine felt came from two government agents sent to take the young boy Noah from his mother. Their attempt ended in a bizarre scene at an amusement park, where Noah levitated a broken ferris wheel chair to safety. By thus exposing his talent in public, Noah unconsciously insured against its secret and unsupervised use by the government.

A terrifying and suspense-filled psychological thriller whose main problems are a slightly overdrawn ending and a variable reading level. Reading level drops as low as 2.1 and climbs occasionally to 4.1.

Interest Level: 5-6. Reading Level: 3.2. Further Search Topics: Best Sellers, Supernatural-Fiction, Occult-Fiction, Flying Saucers-Fiction, Nonverbal Communication-Fiction, Dreams-Fiction, Survival-Fiction, Extra Sensory Perception-Fiction, Horror-Fiction.

Yolen, Jane. The boy who spoke chimp illus by David Wiesner. Knopf 1981, 120 pp.

Kriss was determined to prove to his father that, at 12 years old, he was perfectly capable of camping out by himself. To do so, he left home and headed up the coast of California with a sleeping bag, some food, a map and compass, and water. His plan was to camp, ride, and hike his way to his grandmother's house. On the way, the coast line was torn apart by the second great earthquake to strike California. The first had already destroyed great portions of the state. The second was even stronger. The truck he had been riding in was destroyed and everyone around Kriss was killed by the quake except for two chimpanzees. The chimps, in transit from one lab to another, were research animals who had been taught to use sign language. Kriss took the animals with him as he tried to get farther inland and finally home to Los Angeles. His trip not only confirmed his father's fears about Kriss' inadequacies but taught him how to overcome them. Kriss learned to communicate with the chimps, to find food and to live on his own until Old Chris, a hermit, happened along. Together they continued to brave the chaos brought about by the earthquake even when Old Chris' heart troubled him. When a helicopter finally spotted them, Kriss decided to let the chimps go wild and promised Old Chris that he would be back in the woods very soon. It was a mature, capable Kriss who returned home.

This is typical of the Capers series—much action, few background details, little characterization. The books, however, are on appealing topics; they move quickly and they create intriguing (if sometimes implausible) situations. They are light, enjoyable and very useful. Capers series.

Interest Level: 3-6. Reading Level: 3.1. Further Search Topics: California-Fiction, Disasters-Fiction, Survival-Fiction, Apes-Fiction, Nonverbal Communication-Fiction, Camping-Fiction, Runaways-Fiction, Best Sellers.

NORWAY-FICTION

Bulla, Clyde Robert. Viking adventure; illus by Douglas Gorsline. T Y Crowell 1963, 117 pp.

An exciting story of a young Norwegian boy named Sigurd. Sigurd realized his dream when he finally set sail on a Viking ship in search of Wineland (Vinland).

Leif Eriksson had told of his North American findings over 100 years earlier. Sigurd and his father's friend Grom, the captain of the ship, were sure they could find that land again. Their determination finally brought Grom's death at the hands of the ship's owner, Sigurd's near death, and the destruction of the ship.

This book, too, is true to Bulla's style of short chapters, short sentences, much action and high appeal. Although it is a little higher reading level than many of Bulla's others, it is still a good choice. Recently out of print, but worth a search.

Interest Level: 2-6. Reading Level: 3.1. Further Search Topics: Norway-Fiction, Historical Fiction, Seafaring Life-Fiction, Voyages and Travels-Fiction, Shipwrecks-Fiction, Explorers-Fiction, Vikings-Fiction, Courage-Fiction, Best Sellers, Group 2.

OCCULT-FICTION

Conford, Ellen. And this is Laura. Little 1977, 179 pp.

As a member of a family of high-achievers, Laura was convinced that she was unloved and worthless because she had no talents. Then, suddenly Laura discovered she had very special psychic powers; powers she began to exploit. At first it was fun to give readings after school each day. Gradually, however, as Laura foresaw her friend hurt and her brother missing, she realized that having ESP was also a frightening responsibility. Finally, her ESP became the vehicle that made it possible for Laura to tell her parents her true feelings and to understand that they loved her for herself, not for her achievements.

The author treats a common concern with sensitivity and humor. An especially good choice for Judy Blume lovers. Print somewhat small.

Interest Level: 4-6. Reading Level: 4.2. Further Search Topics: Occult-Fiction, Courage-Fiction, Extra Sensory Perception-Fiction, Family-Fiction, Humorous Fiction, Everyday Stories, Talent-Fiction.

Heide, Florence Parry. Black magic at Brillstone. A. Whitman 1981, 126 pp.

Liza is a little older, her romance with Logan has progressed to a kiss, and the book's plot is more complex than earlier Brillstone adventures. Other than those differences, the book follows Heide's standard format. The Brillstone books all center on Liza Webster and Logan Forrest, teenage partners in crime detection, who live in the Brillstone Apartments. The stories are similar enough that one could almost substitute the names Nancy Drew and Ned for Liza and Logan. Both young women are only children who live with their fathers. They are both independent, resourceful, and very concerned that justice be done. The men in their lives play approximately the same roles; their fathers are proud and supportive, but distantly preoccupied with their own business; Logan and Ned are gallant, boyish, and devoted. Liza and Logan, like Nancy and Ned, are not distinctive characters. Instead, they are shells into which readers who want excitement and adventure can pour themselves. There is no parental interference to worry about. There is plenty of action, some suspense, and real world crime (for Liza: murder, bank robberies, etc.) rather than childish escapades. The books' success is practically guaranteed. Beware, however, of inconsistent reading levels that wander over a year's range.

Logan was first aware of strange occurrences at the Brillstone Apartments when someone entered his apartment late at night. While the person had searched the apartment, he or she had unconsciously whistled a nursery tune. Logan's neighbor, Miss Violet, said the tune reminded her of her deceased nephew. Slowly Logan and Liza realized that someone was trying to trick Miss Violet out of a substantial amount of money she had just inherited. They suspected that Bella Vine, a spiritualist, and an accomplice were trying to convince Miss Violet that her nephew was communicating from the dead and wanted Miss Violet to give her money to Bella. Not until it was almost too late did Liza and Logan realize that Bella was also posing as another possible recipient of the money and was really Miss Violet's nephew's wife. Miss Violet's nephew had only pretended to die in order to collect insurance money. When he and his wife had heard about Miss Violet's large inheritance, they had decided to reappear in order to bilk her out of the money. Brillstone Mystery series.

Interest Level: 5-6. Reading Level: 3.1. Further Search Topics: Mystery and Detective Stories, Occult-Fiction, Crime-Fiction, Ghosts-Fiction, Cats-Fiction, Detectives-Fiction, Inheritance-Fiction.

Sleator, William. Into the dream; illus by Ruth Sanderson. Dutton 1979, 137 pp.

Paul and Francine each started having what, at first, seemed like nightmares. As the dreams became more detailed and forboding, they discovered that they were sharing the same nightmare. They dreamed of a four-year-old boy, swirling lights, and a large dog. After awhile they figured out that the dog was trying to save the little boy from some unknown danger. As the pieces of the puzzle began to increase in number, Paul and Francine decided that the dream was in some way connected to a night over four years earlier when they had both been staying at the same motel. They, a pregnant woman, and a pregnant dog had all been affected by the telepathic power given off by a spaceship. The progeny of the woman and the dog had been given extraordinary mental powers; powers that a secret government agency wanted to mold and then put to their own use. The danger Paul and Francine felt came from two government agents sent to take the young boy Noah from his mother. Their attempt ended in a bizarre scene at an amusement park, where Noah levitated a broken ferris wheel chair to safety. By thus exposing his talent in public, Noah unconsciously insured against its secret and unsupervised use by the government.

A terrifying and suspense-filled psychological thriller whose main problems are a slightly overdrawn ending and a variable reading level. Reading level drops as low as 2.1 and climbs occasionally to 4.1.

Interest Level: 5-6. Reading Level: 3.2. Further Search Topics: Best Sellers, Supernatural-Fiction, Occult-Fiction, Flying Saucers-Fiction, Nonverbal Communication-Fiction, Dreams-Fiction, Survival-Fiction, Extra Sensory Perception-Fiction, Horror-Fiction.

OCCUPATIONS

Beame, Rona. Ladder company 108. Messner 1973, 63 pp.

The reader of this book will literally live through several days with a New York City fire company. The author's "Dragnet"-like writing style, her use of photographs, and actual people, all make the firefighters' experiences very real. It is an exciting, engrossing and satisfying book. The heavily-used jargon will be quickly understood, thus should pose no real obstacle to most readers.

Interest Level 2-6. Reading Level: 3.1. Further Search Topics: Firefighters, Occupations, City Life, New York City, Group 2, Best Sellers.

OCCUPATIONS-FICTION

Allen, Linda. Lionel and the spy next door; illus by Margot Apple. Morrow 1980, 94 pp.

No one in Lionel's family understood why he wanted to be a spy; but then, he couldn't understand why they were anthropologists and motorcycle freaks. Even though he wasn't supposed to do any more spying (especially while his parents were away) Lionel couldn't resist watching the man who moved into Miss Bannister's house, next-door. Mark Shakespeare was his name. His name was suspicious enough, but his actions firmly convinced Lionel that Mark was a spy. Lionel's attempts to trail Shakespeare only succeeded in angering others in the neighborhood. He interrupted a bird watcher and irritated a woman walking a large dog. She was already angry with Lionel's grandfather for disturbing the quiet neighborhood with his motorcycles. The closer Lionel got to finding proof that Mark was a spy, the friendlier Mark became. Mark even gave Lionel the old clock which Lionel and Miss Bannister had carefully wound each week until the old woman's death. When Lionel's grandfather finally convinced Lionel that Mark should be left alone, Mark enlisted Lionel's help in a project that left Lionel wondering again. Much to Lionel's surprise, he learned that the papers and secret documents he and Mark had burned had all belonged to Miss Bannister, Mark's great-aunt. Forty years earlier she, not Mark, had been a spy. Lionel had been wrong about who it was, but right about a spy living next-door.

Here we find a slightly anti-climactic ending to an otherwise enjoyable book. A grandfather who rides with motorcycle gangs and the intrigue of spying should be of interest to many readers. Readers may need a little help with the few British phrases that dot the book, but otherwise, the book has an impressively consistent reading level.

Interest Level: 4-6. Reading Level: 3.1. Further Search Topics: Spies-Fiction, Family-Fiction, Mystery and Detective Stories, Individualists-Fiction, Motorcycles-Fiction, Occupations-Fiction.

Bulla, Clyde Robert. Shoeshine girl; illus by Leigh Grant. Har-Row 1975, 84 pp.

A well-written, realistic story of 10-year-old Sarah who was sent to spend the summer with her Aunt Claudia. Sarah's parents felt that Sarah put too much importance on money and so insisted that Aunt Claudia give her no allowance for the summer. Sure that Aunt Claudia would call her bluff, Sarah threatened to get a job. Instead, Aunt Claudia thought it was a good idea. Sarah's experience as a shoeshine girl forced her to grow, to learn to like working, and finally to take responsibility for the stand when her boss was hit by a car. Told with quiet humor. For the reader who enjoys Judy Blume's books.

Interest Level: 2-5. Reading Level: 2.2. Further Search Topics: Children-Growth-Fiction, Family Problems-Fiction, Vacation-Fiction, Occupations-Fiction, Everyday Stories.

Cleary, Beverly. Henry and Beezus; illus by Louis Darling. Morrow 1952, 192 pp.

When Henry's dog Ribsy stole the meat from a neighbor's barbecue, a friend rode after Ribsy on his bike and saved the meat. Henry was so embarrassed and jealous that he boasted about an even nicer bike that he was going to get. At first Henry thought he'd be able to earn money to buy a bike in a very short time (he found 49 boxes of bubble gum that he could sell). When that scheme fell through, Henry tried taking over a friend's paper route, but Ribsy kept retrieving the newspapers Henry delivered. Eventually Henry decided to buy a used bike at the police department auction. Beezus, who made a bid for Henry, ended up buying him a beaten-up girl's bike that was hardly worth fixing. The money finally appeared when Henry least expected it; he won $50.00 worth of work at a beauty salon.

Although all seven chapters continue the same story, Chapters 1, 2, 3 and 7, can each stand alone. Henry is definitely old-fashioned, but children still enjoy his humorous escapades and empathize with his desire for a bicycle. The revised paperback cover makes the book's physical appearance less dated. Reading level is somewhat inconsistent: from 2.2 to 3.2.

Interest Level: 2-5. Reading Level: 3.1. Further Search Topics: Humorous Fiction, Occupations-Fiction, Everyday Stories, Bicycles and Bicycling-Fiction, Read Aloud, Group 2.

Danziger, Paula. There's a bat in bunk five. Delacorte 1980, 150 pp.

Although this is a sequel to *The Cat Ate My Gymsuit,* it can be read alone. Marcy accepted an offer to become a junior counselor at an arts camp run by her ex-English teacher Ms. Finney and Ms. Finney's husband. After a nervous beginning, Marcy found herself enjoying the other counselors and the campers, but most of all, her first romance. Marcy's only difficulty was dealing with Ginger, a very troubled 10-year-old in Marcy's cabin. Marcy couldn't seem to get through to Ginger. When Ginger ran away, Marcy was forced to consider whether she should have spent more time with the campers and not quite so much time with Ted.

Marcy is a normal teenager whose problems, questions and activities are appealing to many teen and pre-teen readers. The characters who surround Marcy here are less stereotyped and flat than those in The Cat Ate My Gymsuit. Even Marcy's parents are more human. The author's light touch is just right for Marcy's story.

Interest Level: 5-6. Reading Level: 3.2. Further Search Topics: Humorous Fiction, Camp-Fiction, Everyday Stories, Love-Fiction, Vacation-Fiction, Occupations-Fiction, Adolescence-Fiction.

Greene, Constance C. Isabelle the itch; illus by Emily A. McCully. Viking Pr. 1973, 126 pp.

This is a loosely plotted story about a spunky, original fifth grade girl who could drive everyone around her crazy without ever tiring. Isabelle's dearest dream was to win the 50-yard dash at her school's field day. Even though she took over her brother's paper route to earn money for the Adidas track shoes she needed, Isabelle still didn't win. However, she did meet some new people, make new friends and keep those around her on their toes. A very amusing story told mostly in dialogue.

Interest Level: 4-6. Reading Level: 3.2. Further Search Topics: School Stories, Occupations-Fiction, Humorous Fiction, Everyday Stories, Running-Fiction, Individualists-Fiction, Sex Role-Fiction, Read Aloud.

Greenwald, Sheila. Give us a great big smile, Rosy Cole. Little 1981, 76 pp.

It was Rosy's turn to be the subject of her uncle's book. He needed to earn money again and Rosy had just turned 10, the age each of her sisters had been when Uncle Ralph wrote *Anitra Dances* and *Pippa Prances* about them. However, Rosy couldn't dance like Anitra or ride horses like Pippa. In fact, Rosy had no talent that was appropriate for a book. She drew well but Uncle Ralph said that wasn't visual enough. Then Rosy's mother and uncle decided that Rosy could be *A Very Little Fiddler.*

Rosy had been taking violin lessons for two years, but only Rosy and her music teacher knew how truly untalented she was. Rosy hated the whole idea of the book at first. But as people began to treat her like a star, she found herself acting like one, until the day she heard her tape of the piece she was to play at the recital. Once again she realized that she could not play the violin and didn't want to go on with the charade. When everyone ignored her wishes, Rosy started to run away. Her route took her through the park where she thought of a brilliant idea. She ran home, changed clothes, picked up her violin, created a sign, and raced back to the park. There, with all the other street musicians Rosy set up her sign and began to play her violin. Her sign asked people to sign a petition if they felt that she should not be encouraged to play the violin anymore. Right away Rosy drew a large crowd. Before long, even her mother was one of the listeners and one of the signers. That was the end of Rosy's musical career and her uncle's book, but both were happier. Rosy went back to being normal and Uncle Ralph found another topic for his next book.

Chapters are long, but should not be a problem. Print is large. Some of the story is actually told in the illustrations, so the reader should be aware of them. Younger children may take the book more seriously than children whose sense of humor includes irony or children who were not as fond of Krementz's *Very Young* series.

Interest Level: 4-6. Reading Level: 3.1. Further Search Topics: Occupations-Fiction, Humorous Fiction, Family-Fiction, Relatives-Fiction, Talent-Fiction, Photography-Fiction, Everyday Stories.

Hildick, Edmund W. The case of the phantom frog; illus by Lisl Weil. Macmillan 1979, 121 pp.

The McGurk Organization would not, under ordinary circumstances, have agreed to babysit for seven-year-old Bela, but there was an unusual twist to Bela's case. Bela's aunt, who asked them to babysit while she worked in her sculpture studio, had heard the eerie sounds of a VERY large frog coming from Bela's room. At first it appeared to the group that Bela actually turned into a frog at night, a werefrog. But, upon investigation they found a very clever, very lonely, and very unhappy young boy who had invented the phantom because he was afraid that his aunt would make him give up his pet frog.

See *The Case of the Bashful Bank Robber* for series information. McGurk Mystery series.

Interest Level: 3-5. Reading Level: 3.1. Further Search Topics: Mystery and Detective Stories, Gangs-Fiction, Frogs-Fiction, Supernatural-Fiction, Transformations-Fiction, Detectives-Fiction, Babysitting-Fiction, Humorous Fiction, Occupations-Fiction.

Hurwitz, Johanna. Aldo Ice Cream; illus by John Wallner. Morrow 1981, 124 pp.

Aldo got his newest nickname (Ice Cream) from his friend DeDe when she heard that Aldo not only wanted to try every flavor of ice cream at the local store, but wanted to buy an ice cream freezer for his sister's birthday as well. Aldo decided his summer project would be to earn enough money for the freezer, but he soon found out that there were very few ways a nine-year-old boy could earn $49.95. In the meantime, he helped his mother deliver food for a Meals-On-Wheels project, learned to swim, found out about fish from Mr. Puccini, and shared his cat with Mrs. Nardo. As the summer came to an end he saw one last opportunity to earn enough money for the ice cream maker. A local shoe store offered a new pair of sneakers to the child who owned the most worn out pair. Aldo convinced his mother that if he won the sneakers, she should pay him the money she would otherwise have had to spend on his new sneakers. Aldo set about making sure that his already well-worn sneakers were the most dilapidated in town. A few days before the sneaker contest the hardware store lowered the price on the ice cream freezer to a point where Aldo could afford it if he won the sneakers. When Aldo did win, just as he knew he would, he and his mother bought the very last freezer in the store.

It is not as well-constructed a story as *Aldo Applesauce,* but for established Aldo fans, or those who want quiet, reassuring fiction, this is a usable title.

Interest Level: 3-4. Reading Level: 3.1. Further Search Topics: Humorous Fiction, Brothers and Sisters-Fiction, Vacation-Fiction, Occupations-Fiction, Everyday Stories, Aging-Fiction, Family-Fiction, Contests-Fiction.

Miles, Betty. The secret life of the underwear champ; illus by Dan Jones. Knopf 1981, 117 pp.

Larry hadn't planned it; in fact, he hadn't even really wanted it to happen. But suddenly he found himself about to make a television commercial for ChampWin Knitting Mills, makers of sports clothing and underwear. He knew his family could use the money he would make, but he certainly didn't want the whole school seeing him in his underwear. Nevertheless, Larry went ahead and made the commercial, hoping that it would never be used. He even had to skip baseball practice to make the taping. Much to his horror, the commercial appeared the night before the team's first game. Not only did the entire opposing team tease him, but so did all his own teammates. By the time he got up to bat, Larry was mad enough to slam the ball out of the park. He didn't hit the ball quite that hard, but he did make a winning home run and end the others' giggles forever. He became the true underwear champ.

This is a funny look at the embarrassments of growing up. It also deals lightly with a boy's pride, his peer relationship, and his growing awareness of girls. An appealing and broadly usable title. Capers series.

Interest Level: 3-5. Reading Level: 2.2. Further Search Topics: Baseball-Fiction, Television-Fiction, Occupations-Fiction, School Stories, Humorous Fiction, Advertising-Fiction, Beauty-Fiction, Motion Pictures-Fiction, Best Sellers, Everyday Stories.

Pfeffer, Susan Beth. Kid power; illus by Leigh Grant. Watts 1977, 121 pp.

When Janie's mother lost her job, her father's salary wouldn't stretch to provide any more money for the new bicycle fund. There was enough money already set aside to pay for one new bike, but both Janie and her older sister Carol wanted a bicycle. Carol, who had saved money of her own, suggested that they each pay for half a bike and their parents contribute the money for the other half. Then Janie's only problem was how to earn money, since she had none saved. Her solution was to create a business: Kid Power. Before long, Janie's business had blossomed and she was becoming rich, but she had lost her best friend and was ruining a client's roses. When Janie finally realized that getting rich wasn't the only thing that mattered in life, she relaxed, delegated jobs to friends better able to handle them, and became their agent.

A genuinely funny book that, as a bonus, takes a realistic look at the interworkings of a family. Consistent reading level.

Interest Level: 4-6. Reading Level: 3.1. Further Search Topics: Occupations-Fiction, Everyday Stories, Vacation-Fiction, Family-Fiction, Humorous Fiction, Best Sellers, Bicycles and Bicycling-Fiction, Friendship-Fiction.

Platt, Kin. Run for your life; photos by Chuck Freedman. Watts 1977, 95 pp.

Lee almost lost his newspaper delivery job when someone began to regularly steal money and papers from the newspaper boxes along his route. Lee saw a chance for revenge if he could beat the thief in the mile race at the next track meet.

Most of the abundant dialogue is slang. The romantic interest is innocent and low keyed. The story has enough running to make that a strong appeal, but not so much that no one but a track or running enthusiast can enjoy it.

Interest Level: 5-6. Reading Level: 2.2. Further Search Topics: Running-Fiction, Love-Fiction, Occupations-Fiction, Crime-Fiction.

Robinson, Jean. The strange but wonderful cosmic awareness of Duffy Moon; illus by Lawrence Di Fiori. HM 1974, 142 pp.

Duffy was tired of being small, of always being on the losing side of fights, and of being unappreciated at home (by his ex-football star uncle). When he sent away for Mr. Flamel's Cosmic Awareness Kit, Duffy was sure he would then be able to take control over anything he wanted and direct his own life. His friend Peter, the narrator, wasn't quite so sure. Peter turned out to be right. Duffy almost made himself sick trying to build a stone wall. Babysitting two small boys and trying to bathe a Great Dane proved to be disastrous. But Duffy's biggest problem came from Boots McAfee's gang. A series of events finally brought Duffy and Peter face-to-face with the dreaded Boots. Luckily, she turned out to be a very smart girl who appreciated Duffy's true talents.

From the first to the last page this is a funny, very enjoyable book. A delightful book with a very palatable message.

Interest Level: 3-6. Reading Level: 3.2. Further Search Topics: Humorous Fiction, Bullies-Fiction, Magic-Fiction, Read Aloud, Occupations-Fiction, Sex Role-Fiction, Orphans-Fiction, Best Sellers, Gangs-Fiction, Courage-Fiction, Babysitting-Fiction.

OKLAHOMA-FICTION

Wallace, Bill. A dog named Kitty. Holiday 1980, 153 pp.

Ricky's fear of dogs was extreme but also understandable. He had been attacked by a rabid dog when he was very young. Remembering the fear, the stitches and the painful rabies shots was enough to bring tears to Ricky's eyes even years later. When a local bully told his dog to attack Ricky, Ricky's fear was discovered. About that time, a stray puppy showed up at Ricky's farm. Not quite knowing why, Ricky began to warm to the puppy, to feed it, and finally to love it. When the dog was attacked by a pack of wild dogs (a brutal scene vividly described), Ricky fully overcame his fear of dogs, went to Kitty's defense, and was barely able to save her life. When Kitty was later tragically and accidentally killed, Ricky swore that he would never have anything to do with a

dog again. He almost kept his promise to himself, but eventually a second stray dog wandered into the farm and Ricky decided to try again.

This is an emotional story that should appeal to many readers. However, because of the violence and the dog's two-stage death, the book is probably best suited to fifth and sixth grade children.

Interest Level: 5-6. Reading Level: 3.1. Further Search Topics: Dogs-Fiction, Pets-Fiction, Bullies-Fiction, Death-Fiction, Oklahoma-Fiction, Courage-Fiction, Country Life-Fiction.

OLYMPIC GAMES

Fall, Thomas. Jim Thorpe; illus by John Gretzer. Har-Row 1970, 33 pp.

Jim Thorpe was an Indian from the Oklahoma territory who became one of the United State's greatest athletes. He and his twin brother were trained by their father to run and jump faster and farther than anyone else. When Charles died, Jim couldn't face returning to school without his twin, so his family kept him home for a few months before sending him away to school again. Jim ran home once more when his father and mother both became ill. Months later he went to still another school where he was noticed by Pop Warner. Pop advised Joe to concentrate on track until he was big enough to play football. His father's death left Jim so despondent he quit school to play professional baseball for a while. By the time he went back to school, Jim was big enough to play spectacular football and then to win the 1912 Olympic decathlon competition. Unfortunately, his short time as a paid baseball player made him ineligible for the Olympic honor and Jim's medal was taken away. Public sentiment was with Jim, but the rules were against him. He went on, however, to play both professional baseball and football. In 1982, 29 years after his death, Thorpe's medal was finally returned to him.

A short, meaty and readable biography of a person who should be interesting to many sports fans. Follows the usual format of Crowell biographies, but looks less like a picture book than many. Crowell Biography series.

Interest Level: 3-5. Reading Level: 3.1. Further Search Topics: Football-Biography, Indians of North America-Biography, Baseball-Biography, Olympic Games, Biography, Running-Biography, Twins-Biography.

OPTICAL ILLUSIONS

Abisch, Roz. Mixed bag of magic tricks; illus by Boche Kaplan. Walker & Co. 1973, 64 pp.

The definition of magic is broadened here to include optical illusions, puzzles, age and date guessing formulae, as well as slight of hand and prearranged tricks. There are 25 "feats of magic" here, with especially good tips on performance, practice, costumes, and props. Although tricks in *Science Puzzles, It's Magic?, Funny Magic,* and *Magic Secrets* are showier, this is a more solid introduction to the subject. The Knot Magic Trick receives its best explanation here. See *It's Magic?* and *Science Puzzles* for others. Bonus: The book looks like a manual and not like a reader, therefore it should be useful even with sixth graders. It is now available in paperback version only; published by Grosset and Dunlap (Activity Books).

Interest Level: 2-6. Reading Level: 2.2. Further Search Topics: Magic, Optical Illusions, Puzzles.

Dolan, Edward F., Jr. Let's make magic; photos by Jay Irving. Doubleday 1981, 96 pp.

With playing cards, coins, paper, a few commonly available odds and ends and some practice, the reader can perform most of the tricks in this book. The book is not a step-by-step description of how to put together a magic show (as some of the other titles are), but is more like a casual chat with a friend who wants to teach you to perform a few tricks. Some are simply optical illusions; some are brain teasers that involve mathematical calculations; some are card tricks; and others are much more traditional magic tricks.

Very little is said about how to use conversation as audience distraction or how to link the tricks together into a show. Instead, it is the kind of book that allows the reader to pick and choose any tricks he or she may want to learn without feeling pressured to do more than entertain a friend or two for a few moments. The tricks, with the possible exception of the mathematical brain teasers, are all easily manageable by third through sixth grade readers and yet are impressive to their peers. The use of photographs, rather than cartoon illustrations, helps to make the book a probable success, especially with older readers who like to entertain, enjoy the spotlight, or are interested in magic.

Interest Level: 3-6. Reading Level: 3.1. Further Search Topics: Magic, Optical illusions, Best Sellers.

ORIGAMI-FICTION

Coerr, Eleanor. Sadako and the thousand paper cranes; illus by Ronand Himler. Putnam 1977, 64 pp.

This is a beautiful and very sad story of a young girl who was only two years old when the atomic bomb was dropped on Hiroshima. Ten years later she contracted leukemia and died a slow, painful death. A fast and enthusiastic runner, she had been full of life and energy before her illness. Soon after she became sick Sadako's best friend folded a paper crane for her and reminded her of an old story: If someone folded 1000 paper cranes, the gods would give that person good health again. Sadako was able to fold only 644 before she died. After her death her classmates made 356 more in order that she could be buried with all 1000 paper cranes. About three years later, a statue, erected in Peace Park in Hiroshima, was dedicated to Sadako and to a hope for world peace.

Because of the theme and its straight-forward handling, this book needs a fairly mature reader.

Interest Level: 4-6. Reading Level: 3.1. Further Search Topics: Japan-Fiction, Historical Fiction, World War II-Fiction, Death-Fiction, Illness-Fiction, War-Fiction, Running-Fiction, Origami-Fiction, Read Aloud.

ORPHANS

Mathis, Sharon Bell. Ray Charles; illus by George Ford. Har-Row 1973, 33 pp.

Dominent throughout this biography of Ray Charles is the theme of overcoming adversity. The book is not just a recounting of Ray Charles' music lessons, early schooling, family life, and talent. All of that is included, but it serves to illustrate the manner in which Charles met his troubles. His problems began when he was very young. His brother died, and Ray lost one eye and then the sight in his other eye. His family was poor, but close, and he missed them when he was sent away to a school for the blind. Music was his love, but even that was work, for Charles had to learn to read and write music in Braille. He worked hard at it and eventually could play and arrange music for every instrument in the band.

Determined to be independent, when Charles was orphaned at age 15, he left school and began playing music for a living. The first record he made resulted in a $16 fine because he made it during a musician's union strike. Charles took a series of sideman and nightclub jobs until he finally had enough money to hire seven other musicians to play his music. Today Charles is very wealthy, owns his own record company, has a family, and is considered a great jazz and blues musician. None of his success came easily; only through determination, will power, pride, and hard work.

The book, interesting and serviceable enough for music or biography units, is also designed to set an example for youngsters facing their own problems. It will, of course, be popular with Ray Charles fans, too. Crowell Biography series.

Interest Level: 2-4. Reading Level: 3.1. Further Search Topics: Jazz Music, Music-Biography, Vision, Physically Handicapped, Blacks-Biography, Group 2, Biography, Pianists, Orphans, Challenges, Courage.

ORPHANS-FICTION

Angell, Judie. Dear Lola; or how to build your own family. Bradbury 1980, 166 pp.

Arthur (age 18), James (13), Annie and Al-Willie (twins, age 10), Edmund (9), and Ben (5) wanted to run away from the orphanage and find a place where they could be a real family. After waiting months, their chance arrived one night. They escaped in a van and began living on the road. It was weeks before they found a house in which they thought they could live. They didn't want trouble with local authorities, so most of the children enrolled in school and pretended to be living with their widowed grandfather. Only James (who never left his room) and Arthur stayed home. Arthur was the anonymous author of a nationally syndicated newspaper advice column. It was with the income from his "Dear Lola" column that Arthur was able to support the "family." When the townspeople eventually began to wonder about the "strange" behavior of the children, they investigated and found no adult in charge of the household. Arthur went to court to be appointed the childrens' guardian, but the judge ruled against him. Rather than be sent to foster homes again, Arthur and the children raced from the courtroom. The book ends as the family is once more together and on their own. An unusual cast of characters in a surprisingly warm and humorous book.

Interest Level: 4-6. Reading Level 3.1. Further Search Topics: Loners-Fiction, Runaways-Fiction, Orphans-Fiction, Survival-Fiction, Family Problems-Fiction, Family-Fiction, Read Aloud, Foster Homes-Fiction, Individualists-Fiction, Humorous Fiction.

Bulla, Clyde Robert. The ghost of windy hill; illus by Don Bolognese. Har-Row 168, 84 pp.

If the reader doesn't expect a high adventure ghost story, he or she will not be disappointed by this low-keyed tale of a family who goes to live in a house that is supposedly haunted. Mr. Giddings asked the Carver family to move into his country home while he and his wife stayed in Boston. His intent was that the Carvers should either prove to his wife that the house was not haunted or drive the ghost out. The Carvers found no ghosts—at first—only an interesting group of neighbors. There was shy Miss Miggie who drifted around in a long, white dress and wore a flower-covered hat. Bruno was the gruff beggar boy who couldn't walk and had no friends but a goat, until the Carver children came along. Near the end of their stay Lorna Carver mentioned that because they had seen no ghosts the family would soon leave and the Giddings would return. Strange occurrences began almost immediately after Lorna's statement and ended only when the Carvers caught Bruno trying to convince them that he was the ghost. Lorna and Jamie were his only friends, so he had risked his guardians wrath and given up the pretense of being lame to trick the Carvers into staying. All ends well as Bruno's cruel guardian is run off, the Carvers take responsibility for Bruno's care, and Mrs. Giddings admits she made up the ghost story because she hated living in the country and had wanted to return to the city. Another serviceable book in the very successful Bulla style.

Interest Level: 2-5. Reading Level: 2.1. Further Search Topics: Ghosts-Fiction, Brothers and Sisters-Fiction, Orphans-Fiction, Country Life-Fiction, Courage-Fiction, Challenges-Fiction, Friendship-Fiction.

Bulla, Clyde Robert. Pirate's promise; illus by Peter Burchard. Har-Row 1958, 87 pp.

After their mother and father died, Tom and Dinah Pippin had nowhere to go but to their Uncle John's house. Uncle John had no place for them, so he sold Tom into bondage but kept Dinah to help his wife with housework. Tom was to be taken by ship to America where the ship's captain would sell him to the highest bidder. After several years, Tom would be free. But, Tom couldn't accept the idea of one person being another's property, so he spoke out at every opportunity. Tom spoke up to the seaman who dragged him aboard ship, to the captain, to the others who had been bonded, even to the pirate captain who captured their ship. Captain Land was so impressed by Tom's bravery that although he set everyone else he had captured adrift on a small boat, he kept Tom with him. He and Tom became good friends. He never asked Tom to become a pirate and Tom never did. Instead, they enjoyed each other's company. When the pirate ship needed work, they stopped at a safe island where Tom met and impressed Captain Red, a fierce enemy of Captain Land. Captain Red's insistence that Tom join his pirate ship led to another clash between the enemies. Although he was ill, Captain Land fought a duel with Captain Red and lost. Land's last requests were that Benjy, a freed slave who loved him, take all his gold, and that Tom go to Charlestown, South Carolina to find Land's family. Benjy led their flight from Captain Red and arranged a way for Tom to sail to Charlestown before putting Tom on his own. When Tom reached Charlestown he found Land's parents were so angry with Land that at first they didn't even want to hear about him. But, eventually, they not only asked all about their son, but also asked Tom if he and Dinah would like to live with them as their family.

There is enough excitement, danger, and warmth here to satisfy almost any arm-chair adventurer. Usual format of short, episodic chapters.

Interest Level: 3-6. Reading Level 2.1. Further Search Topics: Pirates-Fiction, Seafaring Life-Fiction, Orphans-Fiction, Slavery-Fiction, Brothers and Sisters-Fiction, Best Sellers, Courage-Fiction.

Bulla, Clyde Robert. Marco Moonlight; illus by Julia Noonan. T Y Crowell 1976, 104 pp.

No one could explain Marco's strange, recurring dream. The dream seemed to be about a brother, but Marco had no brother. He had no family but his wealthy grandparents with whom he lived. Marco loved his grandparents very much, but he couldn't help wondering about his own past. He knew only what he and his grandparents could figure out from a few clues. His mother had run away to marry and for three years Marco's grandparents had heard nothing. Then, suddenly, they received a note that she was dying, had parted from her husband, and needed them. By the time they arrived, she was dead and two-year-old Marco could tell them no more. About the time of his thirteenth birthday Marco made friends with a strange man named Flint, who later became the gardener on Marco's grandparents' estate. Rather than live in the room provided for him with the other servants, Flint chose a bleak and isolated beach cottage. Being very careful that no one should suspect, Flint locked Marco into the cottage and forced Marco to change clothes with Matt, who was Marco's long-lost identical twin. Flint and Matt planned that Matt would steal all the money he could from the estate before killing Marco and fleeing. But when Matt began to realize how nice his grandparents were, how much he liked Marco, and how evil Flint was, he decided to thwart Flint's plan. In Matt and Marco's desperate attempt to flee from Flint, Flint was accidentally killed, leaving Marco free to return home and Matt free to find a way to feel he also had the right to claim his heritage before joining Marco.

The tense and dramatic plot immediately involves the reader and the short, fast-paced chapters sustain interest to the end of the book. Readers should also appreciate the small, paperback-size format. A good choice.

Interest Level: 3-6. Reading Level: 2.1. Further Search Topics: Dreams-Fiction, Mystery and Detective Stories, Kidnapping-Fiction, Twins-Fiction, Orphans-Fiction, Grandparents-Fiction, Best Sellers, Brothers and Sisters-Fiction, Jealousy-Fiction, Courage-Fiction.

Bulla, Clyde Robert. White bird; illus by Leonard Weisgard. T Y Crowell 1966, 79 pp.

This book is meant for a special reader. It will not appeal to the reader who wants only action and excitement from a book. It is a story of complex human relationships and differing definitions of love. John Thomas lost his parents in a river accident when he was just a baby. His cradle had been pulled from the river and he had been raised by reclusive Luke Vail. Luke placed no trust in the world or in people outside his tiny valley home and so forbade John Thomas to have anything to do with either one. Luke didn't allow John Thomas a pet either because he thought that John Thomas would only be hurt when he no longer had the animal. Despite Luke's argument, when he found an injured white crow, John Thomas kept it and tended it until the crow was stolen by three strangers as Luke stood by. Angry at Luke as much as at the strangers, John Thomas ran away to search for the bird, but found that it had been shot. Far from being fruitless, however, John Thomas's trip out of the valley gave him an entirely different view of people than the one Luke had shown him. Upon a friend's encouragement, John Thomas returned to Luke to share that view.

Subtle and unusual, this book needs a mature, sensitive reader and/or discussion in order to be fully appreciated.

Interest Level: 4-6. Reading Level 2.1. Further Search Topics: Pets-Fiction, Orphans-Fiction, Runaways-Fiction, Birds-Fiction, Love-Fiction, Loners-Fiction, Courage-Fiction.

Byars, Betsy. After the goat man; illus by Ronald Himler. Viking Pr. 1974, 126 pp.

Harold was fat and over-sensitive. Ada was serious and independent. Figgy was lonely, poor and in need of help. Figgy and his grandfather, the Goat Man, had been forced to move from their cabin to make room for a highway. The Goat Man had returned to the cabin with a shotgun, vowing to defend his right to live there. Figgy knew he had to persuade his grandfather to leave or someone would be hurt. But, in the children's hurry to reach the Goat Man, it was Figgy who was hurt and Harold who rescued both Figgy and the Goat Man. Harold grew up that day. He stopped dreaming about the way he wanted things to be and faced life realistically for the first time.

The book is very much a character study. Realistic characters are treated with sympathy and dignity and given a chance to grow. Introspective readers will understand and enjoy the book more than those looking for adventure. Print size is fairly large, but lines are separated by only average width.

Interest Level: 4-6. Reading Level: 3.2. Further Search Topics: Loneliness-Fiction, Weight-Fiction, Moving, Household-Fiction, Courage-Fiction, Grandparents-Fiction, Orphans-Fiction.

Clark, Margaret Goff. Barney in space; illus by Ted Lewin. Dodd 1981, 155 pp.

This is a sequel to *Barney and the UFO*, but it stands by itself quite well. It's title is a misnomer, however, for it isn't until the last third of the book that Barney goes into space. In the previous book Barney made friends with Tibbo, a Gark from the planet Ornam. In this book Tibbo tries to save Barney from an evil Gark named Rokell. Because Barney knew about Garks, Rokell was afraid Barney would betray them and turn humans against Garks. To prevent that from happening, Rokell was determined to kidnap Barney. Tibbo was too far from Earth to do more than warn Barney of Rokell's intentions and tell him not to be alone at any time. Barney's friends Dick and Kara tried to protect Barney but only succeeded in endangering their own lives. When Kara was almost killed by Rokell, Barney decided to face Rokell alone and try to defeat him, but Rokell's powers were too strong for Barney. Against their wills both Barney and David were taken aboard a spaceship. They discovered later, to their relief, that the spaceship belonged to a friend of Tibbo's who was commanding the ship from the moon. Barney and Dick were to be taken to the moon for safety until Rokell could be controlled. Rokell didn't give up easily. He attacked the ship twice before he captured it and set it down on a remote portion of the moon. Only Barney's quick thinking stopped Rokell permanently and saved both Barney and Dick.

The preliminary sequences are more suspenseful and exciting than the space travel; however, the book will not disappoint young science fiction fans.

Interest Level: 4-6. Reading Level: 4.2. Further Search Topics: Science Fiction, Flying Saucers-Fiction, Outer Space-Fiction, Orphans-Fiction, Kidnapping-Fiction, Aliens-Fiction, Adoption-Fiction.

Clark, Margaret Goff. Barney and the UFO; illus by Ted Lewin. Dodd 1979, 159 pp.

Barney felt a strange prickly sensation several times before he discovered that it was caused by Tibbo, a Gark from the planet Ornam. Tibbo had selected Barney as a friend who would accompany him back to Ornam. Barney was to learn the peaceful ways of Gark and then return to Earth to help persuade the world to accept the aliens. At first the idea of visiting Ornam appealed to Barney because he liked Tibbo and felt very lonely and unsure of his adoptive family's love. Those were the very reasons that Tibbo had chosen Barney: he wanted someone without strong ties to Earth and Barney's only tie when he was first contacted by Tibbo was his little brother Scott. As the time to go grew closer, Barney found a new and strong friendship with Dave, a science whiz-kid, and great love for his new parents. Tibbo, however, was determined to hold Barney to his promise. Only a last minute confrontation between Tibbo and Barney, David, Scott and Mr. and Mrs. Crandall prevented Tibbo from succeeding. But even as Tibbo left, he and Barney acknowledged their new friendship and agreed to keep in touch.

Because of its fairly slow beginning, readers must be well-introduced to this book. If they can be persuaded to be patient while the author sets the stage for about 18 pages they will be rewarded with a decent, if somewhat wordy, story of friendship, UFO's, space travel and family affection.

Interest Level: 3-6. Reading Level: 3.2. Further Search Topics: Science Fiction, Flying Saucers-Fiction, Kidnapping-Fiction, Foster Homes-Fiction, Family-Fiction, Adoption-Fiction, Aliens-Fiction, Loneliness-Fiction, Orphans-Fiction.

Clymer, Eleanor. Luke was there; illus by Diane de Groat. HR & W 1973, 74 pp.

Julius' father, uncle and finally his step-father had all walked out on him. Even his mother had left him, although she hadn't wanted to go. When his mother had been taken to the hospital, Julius and his younger brother Danny were sent to a children's home. Julius felt alone and cheated until he met a young, black, social worker named Luke. Luke liked and respected Julius and helped Julius learn to feel the same way about himself. When Luke, too, left Julius, Julius was so angry at the world that he stole food and then money. Afraid to go back to the children's home because he thought he'd be caught and punished, Julius ran away. It wasn't until he found an abandoned child, about Danny's age, who needed care, that Julius returned to the home. Luke was there when he arrived, just when Julius needed him most. Luke listened to Julius' unhappy feelings, arranged for him to see his mother and helped him begin to accept the fact that life is not always fair.

Julius tells his own story in a realistic, straight-forward book that will touch most readers. Only the lack of quotation marks and inadequate spacing between the lines may slow the reader.

Interest Level: 3-6. Reading Level: 2.2. Further Search Topics: Runaways-Fiction, Orphans-Fiction, Juvenile Delinquency-Fiction, Divorce and Separation-Fiction, Friendship-Fiction, Courage-Fiction, Survival-Fiction, Loneliness-Fiction, Best Sellers, Read Aloud.

Hinton, Susan E. The outsiders. Viking Pr. 1967, 188 pp.

When she wrote this book Susan Hinton was only 17 years old, but she had the sensitivity of someone much older. She wrote a taut story of the rivalry between two city gangs; the Socs (the rich socialites) and the Greasers (poor kids from the wrong side of town) that is more than anything a plea for understanding and tolerance. Seen through the eyes of Ponyboy (a very bright, 14-year-old Greaser), the rivalry brought on violence and an accidental killing that forced Pony and his friend Johnny to flee for their lives. Dallas, the meanest and most dangerous of the Greasers, provided them with shelter, food for a week, and a gun. At the end of that week, Johnny decided that they should turn themselves in to the police. But before they could do that, their hideout (an old church) burned in a fire which threatened the lives of four children who had been playing there. In trying to rescue the children, Johnny, Pony, and Dallas were injured; Johnny was severely burned and probably permanently crippled. A vengeance rumble was held while Johnny lay in the hospital, but the Greasers' victory was empty when Johnny died. He had been the one member of the gang whom they all loved and who had most needed them. Dallas went to pieces: he robbed a store and set himself up to be killed by the police. He had nothing left to live for after Johnny's death. Pony found support and security with his brothers (their parents were dead) and, in a note from Johnny, some hope for the future.

Hinton speaks most often through Pony (his depth of understanding of the people around him is very impressive), but through Johnny and two of the Socs as well, Randy and Cherry. Her message is clear, but at no time does she fail to maintain believable characters in a compelling plot.

Although the book looks forbidding with its 188 pages of unrelenting small print, it is an exciting story, full of adventure, realism, and room for thought. Perhaps the best way to introduce this book is to read a fair portion of it aloud. Now a motion picture too.

Interest Level: 6+ Reading Level: 5.1. Further Search Topics: Crime-Fiction, Gangs-Fiction, Murder-Fiction, Read Aloud, Friendship-Fiction, Juvenile Delinquency-Fiction, Best Sellers, City Life-Fiction, Brothers and Sisters-Fiction, Orphans-Fiction, Runaways-Fiction, Troublemakers-Fiction, Poverty-Fiction.

Norton, Andre. Star Ka'at; illus by Bernard Colonna. Walker & Co 1976, 122 pp.

Jim Evans and Elly Mae Brown, both orphaned and alone, met each other and two strange cats at the same time. As the children became more unhappy with their lives, they began to realize that Tiro and Mer were not usual cats. They were highly intelligent Ka'ats from another planet who had come to Earth in search of new strong stock to add to their breed. Both Ka'ats became as fond of the children as the children became of them. When the time came for the transport ship to leave, Jim and Elly contrived to go with them. However, the only way they could go was if they were accepted by the other Ka'ats and adopted by Tiro and Mer.

This is the first book in a series. Unfortunately the second book Star Ka'at World, has a much more difficult reading level (sixth grade) and the third title, Star Ka'at and the Plant People, varies from 2.1 to 4.1. Reading level of this entry varies between 4.1 and 5.1 but children seem to like the book enough to put up with the variability.

Interest Level: 3-6. Reading Level: 4.2. Further Search Topics: Science Fiction, Friendship-Fiction, Cats-Fiction, Group 2, Outer Space-Fiction, Orphans-Fiction.

Robinson, Jean. The strange but wonderful cosmic awareness of Duffy Moon; illus by Lawrence Di Fiori. HM 1974, 142 pp.

Duffy was tired of being small, of always being on the losing side of fights, and of being unappreciated at home (by his ex-football star uncle). When he sent away for Mr. Flamel's Cosmic Awareness Kit, Duffy was sure he would then be able to take control over anything he wanted and direct his own life. His friend Peter, the narrator, wasn't quite so sure. Peter turned

out to be right. Duffy almost made himself sick trying to build a stone wall. Babysitting two small boys and trying to bathe a Great Dane proved to be disastrous. But Duffy's biggest problem came from Boots McAfee's gang. A series of events finally brought Duffy and Peter face-to-face with the dreaded Boots. Luckily, she turned out to be a very smart girl who appreciated Duffy's true talents.

From the first to the last page this is a funny, very enjoyable book. A delightful book with a very palatable message.

Interest Level: 3-6. Reading Level: 3.2. Further Search Topics: Humorous Fiction, Bullies-Fiction, Magic-Fiction, Read Aloud, Occupations-Fiction, Sex Role-Fiction, Orphans-Fiction, Best Sellers, Gangs-Fiction, Courage-Fiction, Babysitting-Fiction.

Thompson, Jean. Brother of the wolves; illus by Steve Marchesi. Morrow 1978, 159 pp.

Shadow Fox, a Sioux medicine man, went into a wolves' den looking for special items he needed for healing, but found much more. He found a baby boy who had apparently lost his parents in an accident and then been adopted by the wolves. Winter was approaching and Shadow Fox knew the baby would not be able to survive the cold, so he took the child back to his people. The people were reluctant to accept Wolf Brother, saying that he was an evil omen, that he was unnatural, and that he would bring them trouble. But Shadow Fox's will prevailed and Wolf Brother was allowed to stay and grow up with the Sioux.

As he grew Wolf Brother continued to communicate with the wolves and thus fueled the rumors that grew about him. A very jealous young man, Looks-Away, told the people that a vision had shown him that Wolf Brother and his wolves would one day destroy the village and all its people. The people grew so suspicious of Wolf Brother that, when their horses were stolen and they faced a drought, they blamed him and drove him from the village.

For a while Wolf Brother tried to live as a wolf but found that he could not be totally happy. He wandered away to look for a tribe by whom he might be accepted. On his way, he too had a vision—a vision that told him he would find horses and buffalo for the Sioux and be welcomed home again. It was weeks later before he accidentally found his tribe's horses. In a daring move and with help from the wolves, Wolf Brother not only rescued the horses from the raiders, but also found buffalo just as his vision had predicted. He was then, for the first time, fully welcomed by his people.

This is a taut, suspenseful and mature story about a strong and unusual character. Older readers are most likely to respond positively to the Indian culture and lore.

Interest Level: 5-6. Reading Level: 3.1. Further Search Topics: Survival-Fiction, Wolves-Fiction, Orphans-Fiction, Loners-Fiction, Indians of North America-Fiction, Sioux Indians-Fiction, Jealousy-Fiction, Best Sellers.

Warner, Gertrude Chandler. The boxcar children; illus by L. Kate Deal. A. Whitman 1950, 154 pp.

This is the first in a series of very early hi/lo books. Although they often bear signs of stilted "Dick and Jane"-style writing, occasionally preach to the reader, and are interrupted by frequent asides from the author, the stories are still popular with young readers. In each book the children are not simply manipulated, but control their own destiny. They fulfill many a child's dream of finding a loving home and family, becoming rich, having adventures, and solving mysteries. This is the simplest story of the series, most of the other entries assume interest in such advanced subjects as fossils, food sources, antiques, or the Revolutionary War.

The only place the four orphaned Alden children had to live was with a grandfather whom they had never met, but whom they had heard was mean. Rather than live with him, they decided to try and survive on their own. They found an abandoned railway boxcar and filled it was items that they found in a junkyard in order to make it their home. Henry, the oldest, went to work for a doctor who, in addition to money, gave him food and kept a silent but watchful eye over all the children without their knowledge. When Violet became ill, the children had no choice but to take her to Dr. Moore. He gave them all a temporary home and arranged for them to gradually get to know their grandfather. By the time Violet was almost well the children had grown to like the elderly stranger. It was a happy day when the children finally realized that the man to whom Dr. Moore had introduced them was really their grandfather.

Interest Level: 1-4. Reading Level: 2.1. Further Search Topics: Orphans-Fiction, Survival-Fiction, Runaways-Fiction, Brothers and Sisters-Fiction, Grandparents-Fiction.

OUTER SPACE-FICTION

Adrian, Mary. The fireball mystery illus by Reisie Lonette. Hastings 1977, 118 pp.

While stargazing one night, Tim and Vicky and their friend Joey saw a meteor fall onto their private island. Before they were able to find it the children realized that someone else was trying to steal the meteorite from them. As much astronomy as mystery here. Beyond fourth grade, the reader may begin to find the astronomy lesson heavy-handed and the mystery light.

Interest Level: 2-4. Reading Level: 3.1. Further Search Topics: Mystery and Detective Stories, Astronomy, Flying Saucers-Fiction, Outer Space-Fiction, Group 2.

Butterworth, William E. Next stop, Earth; illus by Paul Frame. Walker 1978, 80 pp.

After two years on a desolate planet, 12-year-old Charley and his family were anticipating their return to Earth. But when Charley was awakened from sleep by a spaceship robot, he learned that an asteroid disturbance had caused several key systems on the ship to malfunction. Of 24 passengers on board the spaceship, only 10 were still alive and only Charley and his sister were able to be awakened. It was up to Charley to pilot the ship to its landing on Earth. The controls were all in an adjacent room which a faulty robot kept Charley from entering. Without someone at the controls the ship would burn up when re-entering Earth's atmosphere. By tricking the robot and commanding the ship's main computer, Charley was able to get to the control panel just in time to wake his father, help with reentry and save the ship.

Though the story tends to be heavy with conversations between Charley and various computers and robots, it is also that dialogue that helps maintain suspense. It is a story for the confirmed science fiction fan, not for the inductee.

Interest Level: 3-6. Reading Level: 2.2. Further Search Topics: Science Fiction, Outer Space-Fiction, Voyages and Travels-Fiction, Robots-Fiction, Computers-Fiction.

Clark, Margaret Goff. Barney in space; illus by Ted Lewin. Dodd 1981, 155 pp.

This is a sequel to *Barney and the UFO*, but it stands by itself quite well. It's title is a misnomer, however, for it isn't until the last third of the book that Barney goes into space. In the previous book Barney made friends with Tibbo, a Gark from the planet Ornam. In this book Tibbo tries to save Barney from an evil Gark named Rokell. Because Barney knew about Garks, Rokell was afraid Barney would betray them and turn humans against Garks. To prevent that from happening, Rokell was determined to kidnap Barney. Tibbo was too far from Earth to do more than warn Barney of Rokell's intentions and tell him not to be alone at any time. Barney's friends Dick and Kara tried to protect Barney but only succeeded in endangering their own lives. When Kara was almost killed by Rokell, Barney decided to face Rokell alone and try to defeat him, but Rokell's powers were too strong for Barney. Against their wills both Barney and David were taken aboard a spaceship. They discovered later, to their relief, that the spaceship belonged to a friend of Tibbo's who was commanding the ship from the moon. Barney and Dick were to be taken to the moon for safety until Rokell could be controlled. Rokell didn't give up easily. He attacked the ship twice before he captured it and set it down on a remote portion of the moon. Only Barney's quick thinking stopped Rokell permanently and saved both Barney and Dick.

The preliminary sequences are more suspenseful and exciting than the space travel; however, the book will not disappoint young science fiction fans.

Interest Level: 4-6. Reading Level: 4.2. Further Search Topics: Science Fiction, Flying Saucers-Fiction, Outer Space-Fiction, Orphans-Fiction, Kidnapping-Fiction, Aliens-Fiction, Adoption-Fiction.

Montgomery, Raymond A. Space and beyond; illus by Paul Granger. Bantam 1980, 117 pp.

See entry for *Sugarcane Island*, by Edward Packard for full annotation. Available in paperback only. Choose Your Own Adventure series

Interest Level: 2-6. Reading Level: 4.1. Further Search Topics: Science Fiction, Outer Space-Fiction, Group 2, Best Sellers.

Morressy, John. The drought on Ziax II, illus by Stanley Skardinsky. Walker & Co 1978, 77 pp.

Ziax II, the planet that Toren, his father, and other Earth Pioneers were helping to colonize, was suffering a severe drought. It took both cooperation with the inhabitants of Ziax II and courage to seek out the frightening creature that could save the planet.

The importance of maintaining the balance of nature is the strongest message here. Respect for the ways of others is the secondary message.

Interest Level: 3-5. Reading Level: 3.1. Further Search Topics: Science Fiction, Ecology-Fiction, Outer Space-Fiction.

Norton, Andre. Star Ka'at; illus by Bernard Colonna. Walker & Co 1976, 122 pp.

Jim Evans and Elly Mae Brown, both orphaned and alone, met each other and two strange cats at the same time. As the children became more unhappy with their lives, they began to realize that Tiro and Mer were not usual cats. They were highly intelligent Ka'ats from another planet who had come to Earth in search of new strong stock to add to their breed. Both Ka'ats became as fond of the children as the children became of them. When the time came for the transport ship to leave, Jim and Elly contrived to go with them. However, the only way they could go was if they were accepted by the other Ka'ats and adopted by Tiro and Mer.

This is the first book in a series. Unfortunately the second book *Star Ka'at World*, has a much more difficult reading level (sixth grade) and the third title, *Star Ka'at and the Plant People*, varies from 2.1 to 4.1. Reading level of this entry varies between 4.1 and 5.1 but children seem to like the book enough to put up with the variability.

Interest Level: 3-6. Reading Level: 4.2. Further Search Topics: Science Fiction, Friendship-Fiction, Cats-Fiction, Group 2, Outer Space-Fiction, Orphans-Fiction.

Slote, Alfred. C.O.L.A.R.; illus by Anthony Kramer. Lippincott 1981, 146 pp.

Jack, his robot twin Danny, and Jack's mother and father were forced to make an emergency landing on an uncharted planet. There they were attacked by creatures who looked like rocks and who wanted to destroy all humans. They captured Danny, led him into an underground living complex, and revealed their true identities. The creatures were robots who had escaped from their owners and the slavery in which they had lived. They kept their planet secret from all humans for fear of what would happen to them should they be discovered. Their main purpose was to free as many robots as possible and to allow robots the same pleasures humans enjoyed. Because Danny had been happy with his humans and claimed to have been treated as one of the family, the inhabitants of the planet C.O.L.A.R. felt he had to be reprogrammed to see the truth. Jack looked and acted so much like Danny that he was able to prevent Danny from being brainwashed, to save his parents from death, and to convince the other robots that some humans treated their robots quite well. In fact, he and Danny, together, were able to persuade the robot manufacturer that a great program of robot-owner re-education was needed.

This is a good adventure story which could also be useful as a lead into discussions of slavery, intelligence, and interpersonal relationships. It is a sequel to *My Robot Buddy*, but one which can be read without having read its predecessor.

Interest Level: 3-5. Reading Level: 3.1. Robots-Fiction, Science Fiction, Outer Space-Fiction, Kidnapping-Fiction, Brainwashing-Fiction, Slavery-Fiction.

OWLS-FICTION

Eastman, Philip D. Sam and the firefly. Beginner 1958, 62 pp.

Sam, the owl, went looking for a playmate one night but found everyone was asleep except a mischievous firefly named Gus. When Sam showed Gus how to write words with his light in the dark sky, Gus went wild. First he tried to direct auto traffic, then airplane traffic, until finally the Hot Dog Man, an angry victim of Gus' tricks, captured him. However, when the Hot Dog Man tried to take Gus out of town, his truck became stuck on the railroad tracks in front of an oncoming train. Gus, freed from the jar in which he'd been caught, quickly wrote the word STOP in the sky and saved everyone. Gus' silliness, the catastrophies he caused and his final triumph should interest almost any young child who likes humor or excitement. Reader format.

Interest Level: 1-2. Reading Level: 1.2. Further Search Topics: Best Sellers, Fireflies-Fiction, Owls-Fiction, Humorous Fiction.

PAPAGO INDIANS

Baylor, Byrd. And it is still that way: legends told by Arizona Indian children. Scribner 1976, 85 pp.

Byrd Baylor has collected and written notes for forty-one short American Indian legends from seven Arizona tribes whose school children were asked to write down or illustrate their favorite legend. The result is a collection that reflects the concerns, the history, religion, humor and pride of the children and their ancestors. This excellent collection is not only interesting reading, but it also fits well into social studies and language arts units.

Interest Level: 2-6. Reading Level: 3.1. Further Search Topics: Legends, Arizona-Fiction, Navajo Indians, Hopi Indians, Papago Indians, Pima Indians, Apache Indians, Quechan Indians, Cocopah Indians, Indians of North America-Legends, Mythology, Group 2.

PASSOVER-FICTION

Cohen, Barbara. The carp in the bathtub; illus by Joan Halpern. Lothrop 1972, 48 pp.

Leah and Harry couldn't face the prospect of seeing Joe, their pet carp, made into gefilte fish, even for such a special occasion as the Seder on the first night of Passover. The large, friendly carp had lived in the family's bathtub for over a week. It even swam right over to Leah and Harry to be fed everytime they went into the bathroom. At a time when most children in New York didn't have pets, Joe was as close to being a pet as possible. So, Leah and Harry hid Joe in a neighbor's apartment until their father discovered what they had done. When Joe's destiny was fulfilled, the children had to face a difficult fact of life. A week later, however, their despair became delight, when their father brought home a pet cat.

A short, warm and satisfying story.

Interest Level: 2-5. Reading Level: 3.1. Further Search Topics: Group 2, Jews-Fiction, Religion-Fiction, Pets-Fiction, Passover-Fiction, Family-Fiction, Holidays-Fiction, Read Aloud, Brothers and Sisters-Fiction.

PELE

Burchard, Susan H. Sports star: Pele. HarBrace J 1976, 64 pp.

At age 35, when many people thought he might be "past his prime," Pele proved he could still play superior soccer. More details about the series in *Sports Hero: Bill Walton* entry, by Marshall Burchard. Sports Star series.

Interest Level: 2-6. Reading Level: 3.1. Further Search Topics: Biography, Soccer-Biography, Pele, Group 2.

PEN PALS-FICTION

Bulla, Clyde Robert. Ghost town treasure; illus by Don Freeman. Har-Row 1957, 87 pp.

A very simple story whose title is somewhat misleading. Instead of a mystery or an exciting story of buried treasure, Bulla has written a very pleasant story of a family whose fortunes are reversed by the accidental discovery of a nearby cave. Young Ty Jackson and his family were the last people living in Gold Rock, California. Everyone else had moved out when the new highway had bypassed the town. The Jacksons had been able to stay on only because some of the nearby ranchers had continued to buy food and supplies from the Jacksons' store. Just as they, too, were preparing to move out, Ty's pen pals wrote that they were coming to visit the town. Their grandfather had died there, years earlier, during his search for gold. When Paul and Nora arrived, they brought with them their grandfather's diary. The last entry in the journal seemed to indicate that their grandfather had found gold in an isolated cave in the nearby canyon. After a long search, the children discovered the cave, but no gold. Ty's disappointment changed to joy when tourists started arriving to see the new natural attraction. Once again his parents could sell their groceries, the hotel could be reopened and Gold Rock would flourish.

Interest Level: 2-5. Reading Level: 2.2. Further Search Topics: Treasure-Fiction, Family Problems-Fiction, West-Fiction, California-Fiction, Family-Fiction, Pen Pals-Fiction.

PETS

Chenery, Janet. Wolfie; illus by Marc Simont. Har-Row 1969, 64 pp.

This slight but satisfying story is the vehicle for much information about spiders. Harry caught a wolf spider. To keep his sister Polly out of the way, Harry and his friend George told her she could see the spider only after she caught 100 flies to feed it. In the meantime, they took the spider to the nature center where they were treated to a fascinating lesson about insects and spiders (especially wolf spiders). It's too bad that the book's cartoon style illustrations prevent this book from being very useful beyond grade three.

Interest Level: 1-3. Reading Level: 2.1. Further Search Topics: Spiders, Pets, Nature Study, Group 2.

Cole, Joanna. My puppy is born; photos by Jerome Wexler. Morrow 1973, unp (38 pp).

This is an unadorned description of a dachshund puppy's birth and first eight weeks of growth. The black and white photographs are large, sometimes graphic, and most often charming. The text is direct, carefully worded, concise and interesting. It is only the intrusion of an obviously young narrator that keeps this excellent book from being useful beyond third grade.

Interest Level: 1-3. Reading Level: 2.1. Further Search Topics: Group 2, Infants, Dogs, Pets, Birth.

Selsam, Millicent E. How kittens grow; photos by Esther Bubley. School Bk Serv 1973, unp (28 pp).

A warm picture essay that illustrates and briefly describes the first eight weeks in kittens' lives. Guaranteed to charm cat fanciers.

Interest Level: 1-3. Reading Level: 2.1. Further Search Topics: Cats, Pets, Infants, Group 2, Birth.

PETS-FICTION

Berends, Polly Berrien. The case of the elevator duck; illus by James K. Washburn. Random 1973, 54 pp.

Although it would be stretching the meaning of the word to call this a mystery, it is a story of an 11-year-old detective. Albert tells his own story in a clipped style that resembles adult detective novels. One morning Albert found a duck abandoned in the apartment house elevator. He was determined to find the owner of the duck and return it. He had to be very careful as he searched because pets were absolutely forbidden in the housing projects. Anyone who saw him with the duck might report him. Albert and his parents had waited too long to get into the projects to be kicked out because of a duck. When Albert finally found the duck's owner (a young, sad child named Julio), Julio's sister forced Albert to take the duck back. Still angry at Julio's sister, Albert took the duck to the project's day care center, where the teacher agreed to formally adopt the duck. Albert stayed at the center long enough to see Julio's happy surprise when he arrived and found the duck. Its appealing

characters, the tension created by the writing style, and the book's humor make this a delightful story.

Interest Level: 2-5. Reading Level 2.2. Further Search Topics: Humorous Fiction, City Life-Fiction, Housing Projects-Fiction, Detectives-Fiction, Pets-Fiction, Ducks-Fiction, Read Aloud.

Blegvad, Lenore. The great hamster hunt; illus by Erik Blegvad. HarBraceJ 1969, 32 pp.

Nicholas wanted a hamster; but, because his mother didn't like them, he couldn't have one. She did, however, agree to let Nicholas take care of his friend Tony's hamster for a week. It was a good and happy week for Nicholas until the evening before Tony was to return for his hamster. Nicholas accidentally broke the glass front of Harvey's cage and temporarily replaced it with cardboard. By morning Harvey had chewed through the cardbroad and was gone. Nicholas and his family searched all day but couldn't find Harvey. They finally bought another hamster and waited for Tony to arrive. As evening came Nicholas realized that hamsters are nocturnal and began to look for Harvey once more. This time Harvey was awake and active. The happy result was that Harvey was found and the new hampster became Nicholas' own pet. A simple, satisfying story even to fourth grade readers.

Interest Level: 1-4. Reading Level: 2.2. Further Search Topics: Pets-Fiction, Hamsters-Fiction, Group 2, Everyday Stories.

Blume, Judy. Tales of a fourth grade nothing; illus by Roy Doty. Dutton 1972, 120 pp.

Another humorous Blume book that can be counted on to appeal to third and fourth grade readers. If fifth and sixth graders can ignore the title's reference to fourth grade, they too will love it. The story is an exaggeration of a common theme—an older child whose life is in continual turmoil because of a somewhat spoiled younger sibling. Peter's problems with three-year-old Fudge become worse with each chapter until the final disaster when Fudge swallows Peter's pet turtle. Each approximately 15-page chapter is a complete, very funny episode.

Interest Level: 3-6. Reading Level 3.1. Further Search Topics: Humorous Fiction, Turtles-Fiction, Brothers and Sisters-Fiction, Pets-Fiction, Family-Fiction, Read Aloud, Best Sellers, Everyday Stories, Troublemakers-Fiction.

Bulla, Clyde Robert. White bird; illus by Leonard Weisgard. T Y Crowell 1966, 79 pp.

This book is meant for a special reader. It will not appeal to the reader who wants only action and excitement from a book. It is a story of complex human relationships and differing definitions of love. John Thomas lost his parents in a river accident when he was just a baby. His cradle had been pulled from the river and he had been raised by reclusive Luke Vail. Luke placed no trust in the world or in people outside his tiny valley home and so forbade John Thomas to have anything to do with either one. Luke didn't allow John Thomas a pet either because he thought that John Thomas would only be hurt when he no longer had the animal. Despite Luke's argument, when he found an injured white crow, John Thomas kept it and tended it until the crow was stolen by three strangers as Luke stood by. Angry at Luke as much as at the strangers, John Thomas ran away to search for the bird, but found that it had been shot. Far from being fruitless, however, John Thomas's trip out of the valley gave him an entirely different view of people than the one Luke had shown him. Upon a friend's encouragement, John Thomas returned to Luke to share that view.

Subtle and unusual, this book needs a mature, sensitive reader and/or discussion in order to be fully appreciated.

Interest Level: 4-6. Reading Level 2.1. Further Search Topics: Pets-Fiction, Orphans-Fiction, Runaways-Fiction, Birds-Fiction, Love-Fiction, Loners-Fiction, Courage-Fiction.

Cleary, Beverly. Henry Huggins; illus by Louis Darling. Morrow 1950, 155 pp.

Henry Huggins is over 30 years old now, so if he occasionally seems a little old-fashioned, it is not surprising. What is surprising is how well he has withstood the years. His antics are innocent, but humorous and realistic. The book's six chapters are six separate stories that follow the same cast of characters through an entire year.

In the first chapter, Henry finds a stray dog (Ribsy) whom he must then transport home on a bus. Ribsy was too large and too frisky not to get into trouble, so before Henry finally gets him home, they have been kicked off of three buses and have ridden in a police car. The second chapter describes what happens when Henry buys two guppies and ends up with millions. In the third chapter Henry accidentally throws his friend's football into the back seat of a speeding car and tries to earn the money to replace it by catching and selling 1,331 night crawlers. The fourth chapter involves Henry's attempts to get out of playing the lead in a school Christmas play. His last minute rescue comes in the form of a can of green paint that spills all over him. It is Ribsy's turn to change colors in Chapter 5. Henry tries to cover Ribsy's dirt spots with talcolm powder for a dog show, but only succeeds in turning Ribsy pink. And in Chapter 6, Ribsy's original owner finally finds him and wants him back, but Ribsy chooses to stay with Henry. Only the occasional extra cute expression and Henry's age (third grade) keep this from being enjoyed beyond fourth grade.

Interest Level: 1-4. Reading Level: 2.2. Further Search Topics: Humorous Fiction, Everyday Stories, Read Aloud Pets-Fiction, Dogs-Fiction, Group 2.

Cohen, Barbara. The carp in the bathtub; illus by Joan Halpern. Lothrop 1972, 48 pp.

Leah and Harry couldn't face the prospect of seeing Joe, their pet carp, made into gefilte fish, even for such a special occasion as the Seder on the first night of Passover. The large, friendly carp had lived in the family's bathtub for over a week. It even swam right over to Leah and Harry to be fed everytime they went into the bathroom. At a time when most children in New York didn't have pets, Joe was as close to being a pet as possible. So, Leah and Harry hid Joe in a neighbor's apartment until their father discovered what they had done. When Joe's destiny was fulfilled, the children had to face a difficult fact of life. A week later, however, their despair became delight, when their father brought home a pet cat.

A short, warm and satisfying story.

Interest Level: 2-5. Reading Level: 3.1. Further Search Topics: Group 2, Jews-Fiction, Religion-Fiction, Pets-Fiction, Passover-Fiction, Family-Fiction, Holidays-Fiction, Read Aloud, Brothers and Sisters-Fiction.

Davidson, Carson. Fast-talking dolphin; illus by Sylvia Stone. Dodd 1978, 127 pp.

After a rather slow start, this story develops into a well-paced adventure-fantasy with touches of warmth and humor. Eric wasn't just surprised when he found a dolphin in the 10-foot fish pond, he was astonished. Not only had there never been a dolphin there before, but this dolphin spoke in poetry. His name was Wallingford Ullingham Lowell III; Wallingford for short. He was elegant, proud and cultured; but as Eric soon found out, he was very impractical. He didn't seem to realize that he needed salt water and more fish than those in the pond in order to live. It was Eric who figured out a way to keep salt flowing into the pond and a supply of fresh fish. He also kept Wallingford's presence a secret, just as Wallingford requested. The day that Wallingford was discovered was the day that Eric had to break his promise. In order to find out who else had found out about Wallingford, Eric talked with his brother. Together they scouted the town before they realized that Herbert Benson was the only other person who had seen Wallingford.

Herbert reluctantly admitted that he had told his father about the dolphin. Eric knew enough about Mr. Benson to realize that he was just crazy enough to want to harm the dolphin. Eric and his brother gathered all the local children together to shield Wallingford from Mr. Benson. Even Herbert dared to defy his father for the first time. As Mr. Benson struggled with Eric and his brother, he fell, hit his head and rolled into the pond. Wallingford dove to save him, but his leg was caught between two rocks. With the others' help, Wallingford, Eric and his brother Karl were able to save Mr. Benson from drowning.

A few days later Eric, with new-found skills, spontaneously recited a poem about friendship to Wallingford. Wallingford answered with a rare compliment and for the first time used Eric's name (a show of respect). They were such true friends that when Wallingford was helicopter-lifted out of the pond and taken back to his research project, Eric couldn't understand why his father didn't tell him of Wallingford's departure. Eventually he realized that his father had been right; he would rather remember Wallingford swimming in the pond than in a helicopter's sling. Also, Wallingford would have been embarrassed to be seen making so undignified a departure. Wallingford's final message to Eric was a note that Eric found scratched in the dirt thanking him for the salt and the fish and saying that they would one day meet again.

Don't take the plot too seriously or peruse it too carefully for it won't stand up to scrutiny. This is merely a pleasant story with enough humor, action and originality to intrigue many readers. The book's major drawback is the poetry Wallingford spouts: the poetic form and somewhat difficult language will throw some readers. On the other hand, the book could be very useful in a classroom unit about poetry.

Interest Level: 3-5. Reading Level: 3.1. Further Search Topics: Poetry, Dolphins-Fiction, Pets-Fiction, Fantasy, Friendship-Fiction, Humorous Fiction.

Dobrin, Arnold. Jillions of gerbils. Lothrop 1973, 64 pp.

Right after his family moved into a big and very old house, David's gerbil disappeared. Before long, the replacement gerbil disappeared also. The house was very old and did have strange creakings. Could there also have been secret hiding places for ghosts, maybe? Determined to find out, David searched the entire house until he really did find a secret room. And in that room he found his two gerbils with their new family — the beginnings of David's millions and billions and jillions of gerbils.

A comfortable, somewhat old-fashioned book that is neatly divided into six short chapters. It includes a page of facts about gerbils at the end. A good choice to follow the very easy readers; it is easy, but not "too babyish."

Interest Level: 1-4. Reading Level: 2.1. Further Search Topics: Gerbils-Fiction, Pets-Fiction, Group 2, Humorous Fiction.

Dolch, Edward W. Dog stories; illus by Bernette Johnson and Robert S. Kerr. Garrard 1954, 169 pp.

Although overly sentimental for most adult tastes, this collection of true dog stories appeals to young dog lovers. Eighteen chapters tell 15 stories, ranging from the first story in which dog rescues boy, to the final story in which boy rescues dog. There is a dog who played baseball, a dog who went to live at a newspaper, a dog who saved a fireman from a fire, two dogs who were lost and several more dogs who became heroes. A consistent reading level, large print and a popular topic make this a good choice to offer reluctant readers despite the Dolch books' usual unattractive illustrations. Dolch Basic Vocabulary Book series.

Interest Level: 2-4. Reading Level: 2.1. Further Search Topics: Dogs-Fiction, Courage-Fiction, Pets-Fiction.

Hildick, Edmund W. The case of the condemned cat; illus by Lisl Weil. Macmillan 1975, 106 pp.

Ray Williams had a terrible problem when he begged the McGurk Organization for help. His cat Whiskers had been accused of killing a neighbor's pet dove. Ray's mother decided that they couldn't risk upsetting the neighbors anymore and threatened to take Whiskers to the pound unless it could be proven that he was innocent. The Organization, needing time, hid Whiskers and told Mrs. Williams that he had run away. While Whiskers was safely hidden, the group interviewed all the neighbors, surveyed the scene of the crime, and tried to decide upon the real murderer. When the remains of another bird were found while Whiskers was safely locked away, it looked as if the cat was surely innocent. But then McGurk and his detectives found out that the cat had been sprung. It wasn't until they went back over all the information they had gathered that McGurk realized who was the real culprit. The only step left was to trick old Gramp Martin (the neighborhood grouch) into confessing.

See *The Case of the Bashful Bank Robber* for series information. McGurk Mystery series.

Interest Level: 3-6. Reading Level: 2.2. Further Search Topics: Mystery and Detective Stories, Cats-Fiction, Detectives-Fiction, Humorous Fiction, Gangs-Fiction, Pets-Fiction.

Moore, Lilian. The snake that went to school; illus by Mary Stevens. Random 1957, 99 pp.

Hank's pet snake Puffy disappeared from the Science Room at school and his little brother, Benjy (in first grade) became ill on the same day. Hank was so worried about finding Puffy that he hardly thought about his pesky little brother, until Puffy was found two days later. Then Hank learned that Benjy had secretly gone to visit Puffy, after being rejected by Hank and had accidentally let the snake out of its cage. Benjy had been so worried about letting the snake out that he had actually made himself ill. Hank finally realized that Benjy wasn't the pest he had thought he was, and promised to be a better older brother.

A somewhat old-fashioned but satisfying story told in ten short chapters.

Interest Level: 2-4. Reading Level: 3.1. Further Search Topics: Pets-Fiction, Snakes-Fiction, Brothers and Sisters-Fiction, School Stories.

Nodset, Joan L. Go away dog; illus by Crosby Bonsall. Har-Row 1963, unp (29 pp).

A small boy who doesn't like dogs meets a shaggy, homeless dog who wants to play. The little boy, resisting all the way, gradually gives in to the dog's charms. Finally he tells the dog to follow him home. At home, he finds out that the dog was sent to him for his birthday by his Uncle George.

The dog, the boy, and the book are irresistible. You must, however, notice the illustrations on both the dedication and title pages to fully understand the story. Since much of the story is told by the illustrations and the text is repetitive as well as simple, it is an excellent beginning-to-read story.

Interest Level: 1-2. Reading Level: 1.1. Further Search Topics: Dogs-Fiction, Humorous Fiction, Best Sellers, Pets-Fiction, Birthdays-Fiction.

Pinkwater, Daniel Manus. The Hoboken chicken emergency. P-H 1977, 83 pp.

Arthur's mother sent him out with $16 to buy a Thanksgiving turkey. He returned with a live 266 pound chicken on a leash. It seemed that their turkey reservation had been lost at the meat market and, because it was Thanksgiving morning, there were no other turkeys available. Arthur searched everywhere but found nothing, until a strange old professor tricked him into buying the chicken. No one could bear to kill and eat such a large and friendly chicken, so Arthur and his family named it Henrietta and kept it as a pet. Henrietta was a difficult pet to keep hidden from the neighbors When the neighbors, and later the city, saw Henrietta running loose there was general hysteria. But all ended well when Henrietta and the city calmed down and Henrietta became a kind of neighborhood mascot.

A purely absurd plot but presented with enough energy and humor that most readers thoroughly enjoy the book. Some brief introduction may be necessary to get readers beyond the first few pages.

Interest Level: 3-6. Reading Level: 2.2. Further Search Topics: Humorous Fiction, Chickens-Fiction, Pets-Fiction, Thanksgiving-Fiction, Holidays-Fiction, Read Aloud, Best Sellers.

Renner, Beverly. The Hideaway summer; illus by Ruth Sanderson. Har-Row 1978, 134 pp.

On their way to summer camp, Addie suddenly got off the bus and took her younger brother Clay to see the place where Addie had spent prior summer vacations. It was their grandmother's house and a small cabin called the Hideaway. The house had been sold after their grandmother had died that year, but Addie's father had decided to keep the Hideaway. Much to Addie's surprise she found the Hideaway beautifully fixed-up, just as Gram had promised she would do one day.

When they missed the last bus out of the tiny town and realized that they had enough money to buy the food they would need, Addie and Clay decided to make the Hideaway their summer home. One phone call to the camp and weekly calls to their father kept people from worrying about them. Their discovery of two small raccoons meant that their days were filled with caring for and training the animals. In addition, they had to build a warning system so that no one would discover them and they had to get their food and provisions from town about every two weeks without being too noticeable. They even had to figure out a way to survive a wild summer storm, a flood, and poachers who hunted raccoons. By summer's end Addie and Clay had grown independent, resourceful, and very close to each other.

An exciting story whose short chapters and fairly short sentences keep the reading level reasonably low. Print is dark and of adequate size, but space between the lines is somewhat narrow.

Interest Level: 4-6. Reading Level: 3.1. Further Search Topics: Brothers and Sisters-Fiction, Runaways-Fiction, Pets-Fiction, Survival-Fiction, Vacation-Fiction, Raccoons-Fiction, Read Aloud.

Shura, Mary Francis. The Barkley Street six-pack: illus by Gene Sparkman. Dodd 1979, 159 pp.

Jane's best friend Natalie was everything Jane wanted to be. She was self-assured, pretty, vibrant, and even possessed magical talents. Jane didn't realize at first, and she later resisted seeing, that Natalie ran Jane's life and cleverly made sure that Jane had no other friends. Natalie's move left Jane with no friends among those people she had once enjoyed. Little by little, with the help of a stray dog and the new boy on the block, Jane bagan to see how destructive Natalie had been. She finally realized that a true friendship is one in which neither party tries to control the other.

With its enticements of ESP, magic, stray dogs, and problems with peers, this is a very appealing book to many young readers. As a bonus it is a thoughtful, sympathetic, fairly well-written story.

Interest Level: 4-6. Reading Level: 4.2. Further Search Topics: Gangs-Fiction, Pets-Fiction, Dogs-Fiction, Friendship-Fiction, Honesty-Fiction, Courage-Fiction, Loneliness-Fiction, Extra Sensory Perception-Fiction, Everyday Stories.

Viorst, Judith. The tenth good thing about Barney; illus by Erik Blegvad. Atheneum 1971, 25 pp.

A quiet, thoughtful book to help a child face the difficult experience of death. When a family's beloved cat Barney died, their little boy tried to find 10 good things to say about him at the funeral. Nine things came easily to mind, but it was not until he had worked in the garden with his father that the little boy realized the tenth good thing. Barney, buried in the ground, would help the flowers, trees, and grass grow. A special picture book, small in size, but large in impact. Print is somewhat small but well-spaced.

Interest Level: 1-4. Reading Level: 2.1. Further Search Topics: Pets-Fiction, Cats-Fiction, Death-Fiction, Group 2, Read Aloud.

Wagner, Jane. J.T; photos by Gordon Parks, Jr. Van Nostrand 1969, 64 pp.

This is a sentimental story that rarely fails to elicit a sympathetic response from young readers. J.T. is a poor black boy who saw a portable radio almost begging to be stolen and stole it. Two of the neighborhood bullies, Boomer and Claymore, saw J.T. take the radio. Though they threatened him, even poured soap in his eyes in the school bathrooms, J.T. wouldn't give them the radio as they demanded.

About the same time J.T. found a scrawny, scared little cat with only one eye. Because his mother wouldn't let him take the cat home, J.T. built it a warm but ramshackle little house in an abandoned building. He fed it by charging tuna to his mother's grocery store account without her knowledge. Bones became the only thing in J.T.'s life that he had cared about since his father had walked out.

When Boomer and Claymore found out about Bones, they taunted J.T. by throwing the cat back and forth between them until the frightened cat escaped, darted out into the street and was hit by a car. J.T.'s heart broke as he looked at Bones, but he spoke to no one to tell them of his sadness. Only time, his mother's and grandmother's love and a small kitten from Mr. Rosen, the grocer, helped him recover. On the morning that he decided to accept the kitten, J.T. returned the stolen radio, faced Boomer and Claymore without fear, and asked Mr. Rosen for a job in order to pay for cat food.

The book is oversized and illustrated with photographs from the television movie version. It is not only an excellent story to read aloud but one that will prompt listeners to want to finish it on their own or to reread it. It is now available only in paperback from Dell.

Interest Level: 3-6. Reading Level: 3.1. Further Search Topics: Read Aloud, Courage-Fiction, Best Sellers, Cats-Fiction, Single Parent Family-Fiction, Bullies-Fiction, Blacks-Fiction, Poverty-Fiction, City Life-Fiction, Christmas Stories, Crime-Fiction, Pets-Fiction, Holidays-Fiction.

Wallace, Bill. A dog named Kitty. Holiday 1980, 153 pp.

Ricky's fear of dogs was extreme but also understandable. He had been attacked by a rabid dog when he was very young. Remembering the fear, the stitches and the painful rabies shots was enough to bring tears to Ricky's eyes even years later. When a local bully told his dog to attack Ricky, Ricky's fear was discovered. About that time, a stray puppy showed up at Ricky's farm. Not quite knowing why, Ricky began to warm to the puppy, to feed it, and finally to love it. When the dog was attacked by a pack of wild dogs (a brutal scene vividly described), Ricky fully overcame his fear of dogs, went to Kitty's defense, and was barely able to save her life. When Kitty was later tragically and accidentally killed, Ricky swore that he would never have anything to do with a dog again. He almost kept his promise to himself, but eventually a second stray dog wandered into the farm and Ricky decided to try again.

This is an emotional story that should appeal to many readers. However, because of the violence and the dog's two-stage death, the book is probably best suited to fifth and sixth grade children.

Interest Level: 5-6. Reading Level: 3.1. Further Search Topics: Dogs-Fiction, Pets-Fiction, Bullies-Fiction, Death-Fiction, Oklahoma-Fiction, Courage-Fiction, Country Life-Fiction.

Wolkoff, Judie. Wally. Bradbury 1977, 199 pp.

Michael Price agreed to take care of his friend Billy's chuckwalla for three weeks. But because his mother had declared a moratorium on any more reptiles in the house, Michael tried to hide Wally in his closet. With help from his brother Roger, Michael managed to keep Wally a secret until Wally was mistakenly left out of his box one night. Despite Michael and Roger's desperate searches, the chuckwalla did not reappear until Mr. and Mrs. Price were involved in the final negotiations for the sale of their house. Wally completely disrupted the proceedings, prevented the sale and thus made everyone happy. For as it turned out, none of the Prices had really wanted to move after all.

A fast-paced, funny book with much reader appeal.

Interest Level: 2-5. Reading Level: 2.2. Further Search Topics: Pets-Fiction, Humorous Fiction, Lizards-Fiction, Best Sellers, Reptiles-Fiction, Secrets-Fiction.

PHILADELPHIA-FICTION

Shreve, Susan. The Nightmares of Geranium Street. Knopf 1977, 127 pp.

The Nightmares, a small neighborhood gang, had very little to do until beautiful Tess moved on the block. Tess dressed in satins, furs, and rhinestones, and sang in nightclubs. She was even more of a fascination to the gang because they had been told to stay away from her. When Amanda moved in with Tess, the Nightmares invited her to join the gang so that they would have a way of spying on Tess. Gradually her strange behavior, her moods, her bruises and shaking spells, the strangers she let in the house, and the fights she had, led the gang members to suspect that Tess dealt in drugs. When Amanda failed to show up for a picnic and the Nightmares learned the police were searching for Tess, the gang became worried enough to look for Amanda themselves. In doing so, they uncovered proof of Tess' drug dealings, put themselves in great danger, and were protected by Tess as they escaped only moments before Tess was arrested.

Despite its low reading level, the book's confusing sequence of final events, and its subject matter make it best suited to older readers. It is not great literature, but its subject has strong appeal.

Interest Level: 5-6. Reading Level: 3.1. Further Search Topics: Family Problems-Fiction, Gangs-Fiction, Drugs-Fiction, Mystery and Detective Stories, City Life-Fiction, Crime-Fiction, Philadelphia-Fiction.

PHOTOGRAPHY

Holland, John. The way it is. HarBraceJ 1969, 87 pp.

For 15 boys living in a run-down area of Brooklyn, school became interesting when they were assigned to photograph whatever was meaningful to them in their neighborhood. The results, described in their own words, were developed into this fascinating documentary which is at the same time a spontaneous glimpse of the boys themselves. The book should be of particular interest to older urban children. Print slightly on the small side. Has recently gone out of print, but is worth looking for.

Interest Level: 4-6. Reading Level: 3.2. Further Search Topics: Best Sellers, City Life, Photography, Poverty, Academic Problems.

PHOTOGRAPHY-FICTION

Greenwald, Sheila. Give us a great big smile, Rosy Cole. Little 1981, 76 pp.

It was Rosy's turn to be the subject of her uncle's book. He needed to earn money again and Rosy had just turned 10, the age each of her sisters had been when Uncle Ralph wrote *Anitra Dances* and *Pippa Prances* about them. However, Rosy couldn't dance like Anitra or ride horses like Pippa. In fact, Rosy had no talent that was appropriate for a book. She drew well but Uncle Ralph said that wasn't visual enough. Then Rosy's mother and uncle decided that Rosy could be *A Very Little Fiddler*.

Rosy had been taking violin lessons for two years, but only Rosy and her music teacher knew how truly untalented she was. Rosy hated the whole idea of the book at first. But as people began to treat her like a star, she found herself acting like one, until the day she heard her tape of the piece she was to play at the recital. Once again she realized that she could not play the violin and didn't want to go on with the charade. When everyone ignored her wishes, Rosy started to run away. Her route took her through the park where she thought of a brilliant idea. She ran

home, changed clothes, picked up her violin, created a sign, and raced back to the park. There, with all the other street musicians Rosy set up her sign and began to play her violin. Her sign asked people to sign a petition if they felt that she should not be encouraged to play the violin anymore. Right away Rosy drew a large crowd. Before long, even her mother was one of the listeners and one of the signers. That was the end of Rosy's musical career and her uncle's book, but both were happier. Rosy went back to being normal and Uncle Ralph found another topic for his next book.

Chapters are long, but should not be a problem. Print is large. Some of the story is actually told in the illustrations, so the reader should be aware of them. Younger children may take the book more seriously than children whose sense of humor includes irony or children who were not as fond of Krementz's *Very Young* series.

Interest Level: 4-6. Reading Level: 3.1. Further Search Topics: Occupations-Fiction, Humorous Fiction, Family-Fiction, Relatives-Fiction, Talent-Fiction, Photography-Fiction, Everyday Stories.

Heide, Florence Parry. The mystery of the silver tag; illus by Seymour Fleishman. A. Whitman 1972, 127 pp.

Jay's paper route took him to one house that he wished he could avoid. It was grumpy, old Mr. Pendleton's house that Jay hated. One rainy day he spotted what he later realized was a prize Angora cat hiding on Mr. Pendleton's porch. When the cat was reported lost in that night's paper, Jay and the other members of the Spotlight Club decided to try to return the cat to its owner, Miss Horton. Their attempts to get the cat back from Mr. Pendleton meant that they had to spy on him, to sneak into his garage, and to spend the night in a treehouse overlooking his house. They were afraid that they had failed when they saw Mr. Pendleton leave with the cat. Determined to be the ones to tell Miss Horton of their failure, they went to her apartment and found Mr. Pendleton already there. Mr. Pendleton was a famous animal photographer who, upon finding the cat, had asked Miss Horton if he could photograph him. The children, thinking only that Mr. Pendleton was a mad scientist who kidnapped cats, had jumped to all the wrong conclusions, but ended with a mystery solved, new friends, and their first lesson in being detectives.

See entry with *Mystery at Southport Cinema* for series information. Spotlight Club Mystery series.

Interest Level: 3-5. Reading Level: 2.2. Further Search Topics: Mystery and Detective Stories, Brothers and Sisters-Fiction, Gangs-Fiction, Cats-Fiction, Loners-Fiction, Detectives-Fiction, Photography-Fiction, Kidnapping-Fiction.

PHYSICALLY HANDICAPPED

Adler, Irving. Your eyes. John Day 1962, 48 pp.

Getting a young reader past this book's unattractive appearance may be difficult. Everything about the book's physical appearance screams "old." Some of the information and lack of information conveys the same message (e.g. no mention of contact lenses). For basic material about eyes and sight however, there is much here that is accessible and interesting to readers in grades two to six. Includes pronunciation guide, glossary, and detailed table of contents. No index. The Reason Why Series

Interest Level: 2-6. Reading Level: 3.1. Further Search Topics: Vision, Physically Handicapped, Group 2.

Burchard, Susan H. Sports star: Tommy John. HarBraceJ 1981, 63 pp.

Tommy John's elbow injury was severe enough that no one thought he would be able to pitch again. He proved that the skeptics were wrong. For series notes see *Sports Star: Elvin Hayes.* Sports Star series.

Interest Level: 3-6. Reading Level: 4.1. Further Search Topics: Baseball-Biography, John, Tommy, Biography, Group 2, Physically Handicapped.

Charlip, Remy. Handtalk; an ABC of finger spelling and sign language; photos by George Ancona. Schol. Bk. Serv. 1974, 42 pp.

This is not a book to be read and put away. It is a challenge to learn finger spelling (forming words letter by letter with the fingers) and signing (forming whole words or ideas by making a picture using one or both hands). It is a challenge that appeals to almost any child, reader and non-reader. One letter of the manual alphabet is shown at the top of each page. At the bottom of the page is a series of pictures that spell out a word which begins with the letter for that page. In the center of the page a model signs that same word. Only the first few words are explained, although there are hints for some of the more difficult words. The rest must be deciphered by the reader. In addition, the book includes over 25 more signs and a sentence about a very ugly vampire. The entire manual alphabet is also shown on a quick-reference, double page spread. The book provides an enjoyable and successful experience with language, especially if two or more children work with the book together. Although its picture book format would ordinarily turn older children away, interest in the book remains high through sixth grade. Because there are so few words that a child needs to read to enjoy this book, its reading level is an estimate.

Interest Level: 2-6. Reading Level: 2.1. Further Search Topics: Nonverbal Communication, Physically Handicapped, Communication.

Malone, Mary. Annie Sullivan; illus by Lydia Rosier. Putnam 1971, 61 pp.

This is a very brief sketch of both Annie Sullivan's life and Helen Keller's life. Their lives were so intertwined that they cannot be separated. But because they are combined in such a short book, neither woman can be treated in much depth. That fact is not as harmful here as it might otherwise be, because even a bare bones description of the life of this extraordinary deaf, blind and mute woman or her near-blind, dedicated teacher, is interesting.

Interest Level: 2-5. Reading Level: 2.2. Further Search Topics: Sullivan, Annie, Keller, Helen, Vision, Biography, Physically Handicapped, Sound, Courage.

Mathis, Sharon Bell. Ray Charles; illus by George Ford. Har-Row 1973, 33 pp.

Dominent throughout this biography of Ray Charles is the theme of overcoming adversity. The book is not just a recounting of Ray Charles' music lessons, early schooling, family life, and talent. All of that is included, but it serves to illustrate the manner in which Charles met his troubles. His problems began when he was very young. His brother died, and Ray lost one eye and then the sight in his other eye. His family was poor, but close, and he missed them when he was sent away to a school for the blind. Music was his love, but even that was work, for Charles had to learn to read and write music in Braille. He worked hard at it and eventually could play and arrange music for every instrument in the band.

Determined to be independent, when Charles was orphaned at age 15, he left school and began playing music for a living. The first record he made resulted in a $16 fine because he made it during a musician's union strike. Charles took a series of sideman and nightclub jobs until he finally had enough money to hire seven other musicians to play his music. Today Charles is very wealthy, owns his own record company, has a family, and is considered a great jazz and blues musician. None of his success came easily; only through determination, will power, pride, and hard work.

The book, interesting and serviceable enough for music or biography units, is also designed to set an example for youngsters facing their own problems. It will, of course, be popular with Ray Charles fans, too. Crowell Biography series.

Interest Level: 2-4. Reading Level: 3.1. Further Search Topics: Jazz Music, Music-Biography, Vision, Physically Handicapped, Blacks-Biography, Group 2, Biography, Pianists, Orphans, Challenges, Courage.

PHYSICALLY HANDICAPPED-FICTION

Anderson, C. S. The blind Connemara. Macmillan 1971, 80 pp.

Rhonda, not wealthy enough to own a horse of her own, was given a beautiful Connemara pony. Unfortunately, it had begun to go blind. A blind pony is usually put away, but Rhonda loved this pony too much to let that happen. Against all odds, Rhonda not only taught Pony to trot, canter, and even jump with confidence, but went on to win a ribbon at an important horse show. Though sentimental and predictable, this book is an almost insured success with lovers of horses and champions of the underdog. Be alert to the occasional descriptive passage that is both longer and more difficult than the rest of the text.

Interest Level: 4-6. Reading Level: 3.2. Further Search Topics: Vision-Fiction, Physically Handicapped-Fiction, Horses-Fiction.

Blume, Judy. Deenie. Bradbury 1973, 159 pp.

Deenie's mother wanted Deenie to be a model. Deenie didn't know what she wanted until she learned that she had scoliosis (curvature of the spine) and would have to wear a brace for four years. Then she knew she only wanted to be normal. She was repulsed by deformities of any kind. She couldn't stand the idea of a brace. Her mother's attitude made Deenie's adjustment even more difficult. It was her father, her doctor, her sister, and a new friend with excema who finally helped Deenie accept her brace and the idea of physical differences. Subplots include Deenie's budding romance with an eighth grade boy, her strained relationship with her mother, and her growing awareness of sex (masturbation and intercourse). Print and line spacing are similar to *Are You There God? It's Me, Margaret.*

Interest Level: 5-6. Reading Level: 3.1. Further Search Topics: Models, Fashion-Fiction, Beauty-Fiction, Scoliosis-Fiction, Physically Handicapped-Fiction, Children-Growth-Fiction, Sex-Fiction, Love-Fiction, Family Problems-Fiction, Illness-Fiction, Adolescence-Fiction.

Byars, Betsy. The house of wings; illus by Daniel Schwarts. Viking Pr. 1972, 142 pp.

Sammy was the youngest of eight children. His parents were tired of raising children when Sammy was born, so they almost let Sammy raise himself. That meant that he grew up to be independent. It didn't mean it was any easier for Sammy to accept being left behind unexpectedly with his strange grandfather when his parents moved to Detroit. His reaction when his grandfather told him that his parents had gone was to deny it and to run away. He ran until he could run no more. When he stopped running, the old man stopped chasing him and they found a wild but blind crane in desperate need of help. Helping the crane heal and find the desire to live again taught Sammy and his grandfather respect and, most of all, love for each other.

The parallels between Sammy and the crane are strong but subtle. The story is a compelling one, but may need a brief introductory note to alleviate confusion in the first two chapters.

Interest Level: 5-6. Reading Level: 4.2. Further Search Topics: Grandparents-Fiction, Birds-Fiction, Family Problems-Fiction, Poverty-Fiction, Physically Handicapped-Fiction, Runaways-Fiction.

Eyerly, Jeannette. The seeing summer; illus by Emily Arnold McCully. Lippincott 1981, 153 pp.

That it attempts to be two books at the same time is the one flaw in this book that may be noticed by young readers. The first half of the book is an interesting story of the growing friendship between a sighted girl and a blind girl. Carey's delight at the idea of a new friend next door turned to disbelief and discomfort when she learned that Jenny was blind. Jenny too wanted to be friends, but not if she was to be pitied or patronized. Gradually she was able to show Carey that being blind was a nuisance, but nothing she was ashamed of or embarrassed about. The second half of the book presents the contrived and somewhat unnecessary story of Jenny's kidnapping. When Carey's attempt to rescue Jenny resulted in her capture too, it was, of course, Jenny's independence and ingenuity that led the way to their eventual rescue.

To the reader looking for a rousing story of a kidnapping the book may be a disappointment. Half of the book is a long time to wait for the slight adventure. But, for those readers interested in a good story of physical differences and friendship, this will be more satisfying.

Interest Level: 3-6. Reading Level: 3.1. Further Search Topics: Vision-Fiction, Friendship-Fiction, Kidnapping-Fiction, Single Parent Family-Fiction, Physically Handicapped-Fiction.

Kelley, Sally. Trouble with explosives. Bradbury 1976, 117 pp.

Polly Banks stuttered very badly. She wanted to stop but she couldn't. Moving, entering a new school, and facing a mean teacher who seemed in need of psychiatric help, all made Polly's stuttering worse. When Sis, Polly's new friend, rose to Polly's defense in one confrontation too many with Miss Patterson, the teacher took cruel revenge. Polly's desire to help Sis, her need to do something about her stuttering, and an understanding psychiatrist, all helped Polly learn to help herself with her speech problem. At the same time, she began to understand and have confidence in herself and her family.

Another "problem book" that older elementary school readers seem to crave. Polly and Sis are both very sympathetic characters who bring to life many of the uncertainties of growing up. Print and line spacing of only average size but otherwise a good choice.

Interest Level: 4-6. Reading Level: 3.2. Further Search Topics: Academic Problems-Fiction, Stuttering-Fiction, Psychiatrists-Fiction, School Stories, Mental Illness-Fiction, Troublemakers-Fiction, Courage-Fiction, Physically Handicapped-Fiction, Children-Growth-Fiction, Moving, Household-Fiction.

PHYSICIANS-FICTION

Singer, Marilyn. It can't hurt forever; illus by Leigh Grant. Har-Row 1978, 186 pp.

When she was 11 years old, it was discovered that Ellie had a heart valve that hadn't closed by itself. Although her mother had promised her that she wouldn't die, Ellie was scared of the hospital and the operation she had to face. Her parents were kind and open about all that was to happen to her, but there was still much that Ellie had to learn from friends she made while she was in the hospital. There were times when she was frightened and only Sonia, a young open-heart surgery patient, could calm her. When Ellie, a special nurse, and a few other patients became close friends, Ellie learned enough from them to allow her to help another patient.

This is not a story of sweetness and light, but it is told with warmth, humor, and real understanding of a young person's fears. Thus it is not only an excellent candidate for bibliotherapy, but it is a truly satisfying story for the general reader as well.

Interest Level: 4-6. Reading Level: 2.2. Further Search Topics: Illness-Fiction, Physicians-Fiction, Medicine-Fiction, Courage-Fiction, Death-Fiction.

Slote, Alfred. Hang tough, Paul Mather. Lippincott 1973, 156 pp.

Paul Mather went against his doctor's and his parents' orders when he accepted his new neighbors' challenge to show his pitching skill. He had been told not to play baseball until he had been given permission, but Paul not only loved to pitch, he was also the best pitcher his new friends had ever seen. Knowing full well the medical problems he could be precipitating, Paul went ahead and pitched a spectacular game for the Wilson Dairy team against the Ace Appliance team. But by the end of the game, Paul was in the hospital again, and Wilson Dairy had been forced to forfeit the game because Paul had played illegally. As Paul's leukemia worsened, his determination to play baseball again grew. When the day came that his team was to play a second game against Ace Appliance, Paul made sure he was there. He was in a wheelchair and weak, but he was there. He couldn't actually play, but Paul's psychological support insured that Wilson Dairy won the game. He went back to the hospital proud, happy, and still determined to fight his disease.

This is more than the usual sports story. This is a very sensitive story of a young boy's determination to fight leukemia. The reader looking for only a baseball story may find this book more than he/she wants. However, the reader who is open to a story of human strength and courage will be well rewarded. The book neither dwells on nor minimizes the disease. Instead it uses both the disease and the sport to portray a character much more completely than in most sport stories, especially at this low a reading level. This is an excellent book for those special readers who respond well to thought-provoking material. Although chapters are short and reading level is low, the print is somewhat small. In addition, the first person style, told as if dictated into a tape recorder (complete with occasional interruptions), may be confusing to readers unless it is explained.

Interest Level: 5-6+Reading Level: 3.1. Further Search Topics: Baseball-Fiction, Death-Fiction,

Illness-Fiction, Moving, Household-Fiction,
Medicine-Fiction, Physicians-Fiction,
Challenges-Fiction, Courage-Fiction.

PIANISTS

Bryant, Bernice. George Gershwin: young composer;
illus by Nathan Goldstein. Bobbs 1965, 200 pp.

Even when George Gershwin was very young he
loved music, showed signs of musical talent, and
longed to play the piano. However, any boy who
played the piano in George's neighborhood was called
a sissy and George didn't like being teased in that
way. When he was no longer able to keep his music
lessons a secret, he stopped them for fear of the
teasing. But each time George quit playing the piano,
he always went back to it, even when his parents
pressured him not to waste his time at the piano. A
young teacher told George that he would never be a
musician. One of George's teachers actually taught
him to play poorly, instead of well. In time, however,
George learned to play well and to compose his own
music. Then came the hard work of determining his
own style. Gradually, more and more people heard
and appreciated his American jazz, until George
Gershwin's music was heard all around the world.

Another adequate entry in the *Childhood of Famous
Americans* series. Includes the usual glossary,
bibliography, time line, and follow-up questions. It is
most likely to appeal to the reader already interested
in music. Childhood of Famous Americans series.

Interest Level: 3-6. Reading Level: 3.1. Further
Search Topics: Biography, Composers, Immigration
and Emigration-Biography, Jazz Music, Bullies,
Music-Biography, Pianists.

Cone, Molly. Leonard Bernstein; illus by Robert
Galster. Har-Row 1970, 33 pp.

This is a bare bones outline that will appeal to music
enthusiasts but will not attract anyone else. The
reader catches very little of Bernstein's personality,
but *is* awed by an impressive list of his
accomplishments. The few attempts made to recreate
the real person may have to be explained (i.e.,
references to Bernstein forgetting to get his hair cut
because he was so busy). Picture book format of the
hardback may deter some readers. Now published in
paperback edition only. Crowell Biography series.

Interest Level: 2-4. Reading Level: 2.2. Further
Search Topics: Music-Biography, Biography,
Conductors, Composers, Pianists, Group 2.

Mathis, Sharon Bell. Ray Charles; illus by George
Ford. Har-Row 1973, 33 pp.

Dominent throughout this biography of Ray Charles
is the theme of overcoming adversity. The book is not
just a recounting of Ray Charles' music lessons, early
schooling, family life, and talent. All of that is included,
but it serves to illustrate the manner in which Charles
met his troubles. His problems began when he was
very young. His brother died, and Ray lost one eye
and then the sight in his other eye. His family was
poor, but close, and he missed them when he was
sent away to a school for the blind. Music was his
love, but even that was work, for Charles had to learn
to read and write music in Braille. He worked hard at
it and eventually could play and arrange music for
every instrument in the band.

Determined to be independent, when Charles was
orphaned at age 15, he left school and began playing
music for a living. The first record he made resulted in
a $16 fine because he made it during a musician's
union strike. Charles took a series of sideman and
nightclub jobs until he finally had enough money to
hire seven other musicians to play his music. Today
Charles is very wealthy, owns his own record
company, has a family, and is considered a great jazz
and blues musician. None of his success came easily;
only through determination, will power, pride, and hard
work.

The book, interesting and serviceable enough for
music or biography units, is also designed to set an
example for youngsters facing their own problems. It
will, of course, be popular with Ray Charles fans, too.
Crowell Biography series.

Interest Level: 2-4. Reading Level: 3.1. Further
Search Topics: Jazz Music, Music-Biography, Vision,
Physically Handicapped, Blacks-Biography, Group 2,
Biography, Pianists, Orphans,
Challenges, Courage.

PIGS-FICTION

Baker, Betty. The pig war; illus by Robert Lopshire.
Har-Row 1969, 64 pp.

A brief, fictionalized account of an 1859 land
squabble between the United States and Britain. The
incident, which took place in what is now the state of
Washington, became known as the Pig War.
Frightened British pigs destroyed the American
farmers' gardens. When the farmers shot one of the
pigs, the war began. Simply told and humorously
illustrated. Should appeal to history or military fans.
Early reader format.

Interest Level: 2-4. Reading Level: 2.1. Further
Search Topics: United States-History-War-Fiction,
Great Britain-History-Fiction, War-Fiction, Washington
(state)-Fiction, Historical Fiction, Pigs-Fiction.

Steven, Carla. Hooray for Pig!; illus by Rainey
Bennett. HM 1974, 48 pp.

Pig couldn't spend the day swimming with his friend
Raccoon because he didn't know how to swim.
Instead Pig took a picnic to the lake by himself. At the
lake, Pig met Otter, who encouraged Pig to at least try
getting in the water. After several days of Otter's
patient coaching, not only could Pig stay afloat, but he
liked it, too!

For much the same audience as Kessler's *Last One
In Is A Rotten Egg*, but because of a more interesting
plot it is a little more useful. Reader format.

Interest Level: 1-2. Reading Level: 1.2. Further
Search Topics: Pigs-Fiction, Courage-Fiction,
Swimming-Fiction, Humorous Fiction.

PILGRIMS-FICTION

Bulla, Clyde Robert. John Billington, friend of
Squanto; illus by Peter Burchard. Har-Row 1956, 88
pp.

This historical novel about the Mayflower voyage
and the Pilgrims' first year at Plymouth centers on
young John Billington. John was considered the
troublemaker of the children. His problems are woven
around the events of the year, including the Pilgrims'
first meetings with the Wampanoag Indians. It was
finally John, however, who was responsible for
bringing peace between the Pilgrims and the
Wampanoag tribe who lived further down Cape Cod.
The book is not as exciting or convincing as Bulla's
books are generally. It also contains a few minor
historical inaccuracies; yet it remains useful as both
an introduction to American history and historical
fiction.

Interest Level: 2-5. Reading Level: 2.1. Further
Search Topics: Pilgrims-Fiction, Historical Fiction,

United States-History-Fiction, Thanksgiving-Fiction, Troublemakers-Fiction, Indians of North America-Fiction.

PIMA INDIANS

Baylor, Byrd. And it is still that way: legends told by Arizona Indian children. Scribner 1976, 85 pp.

Byrd Baylor has collected and written notes for forty-one short American Indian legends from seven Arizona tribes whose school children were asked to write down or illustrate their favorite legend. The result is a collection that reflects the concerns, the history, religion, humor and pride of the children and their ancestors. This excellent collection is not only interesting reading, but it also fits well into social studies and language arts units.

Interest Level: 2-6. Reading Level: 3.1. Further Search Topics: Legends, Arizona-Fiction, Navajo Indians, Hopi Indians, Papago Indians, Pima Indians, Apache Indians, Quechan Indians, Cocopah Indians, Indians of North America-Legends, Mythology, Group 2.

PIRATES-FICTION

Bulla, Clyde Robert. Pirate's promise; illus by Peter Burchard. Har-Row 1958, 87 pp.

After their mother and father died, Tom and Dinah Pippin had nowhere to go but to their Uncle John's house. Uncle John had no place for them, so he sold Tom into bondage but kept Dinah to help his wife with housework. Tom was to be taken by ship to America where the ship's captain would sell him to the highest bidder. After several years, Tom would be free. But, Tom couldn't accept the idea of one person being another's property, so he spoke out at every opportunity. Tom spoke up to the seaman who dragged him aboard ship, to the captain, to the others who had been bonded, even to the pirate captain who captured their ship. Captain Land was so impressed by Tom's bravery that although he set everyone else he had captured adrift on a small boat, he kept Tom with him. He and Tom became good friends. He never asked Tom to become a pirate and Tom never did. Instead, they enjoyed each other's company. When the pirate ship needed work, they stopped at a safe island where Tom met and impressed Captain Red, a fierce enemy of Captain Land. Captain Red's insistence that Tom join his pirate ship led to another clash between the enemies. Although he was ill, Captain Land fought a duel with Captain Red and lost. Land's last requests were that Benjy, a freed slave who loved him, take all his gold, and that Tom go to Charlestown, South Carolina to find Land's family. Benjy led their flight from Captain Red and arranged a way for Tom to sail to Charlestown before putting Tom on his own. When Tom reached Charlestown he found Land's parents were so angry with Land that at first they didn't even want to hear about him. But, eventually, they not only asked all about their son, but also asked Tom if he and Dinah would like to live with them as their family.

There is enough excitement, danger, and warmth here to satisfy almost any arm-chair adventurer. Usual format of short, episodic chapters.

Interest Level: 3-6. Reading Level 2.1. Further Search Topics: Pirates-Fiction, Seafaring Life-Fiction, Orphans-Fiction, Slavery-Fiction, Brothers and Sisters-Fiction, Best Sellers, Courage-Fiction.

Parish, Peggy. Hermit Dan; illus by Paul Frame. Macmillan 1977, 151 pp.

When the Roberts children tried to prove that Pirate Island really had been used by pirates, they encountered more action and intrigue than they had found in any of their earlier adventures. Liza, Bill and Jed suspected that Hermit Dan knew whether or not there had been pirates on the island, but he was so gruff and apparently mean that they didn't dare ask him any questions. Instead, they trailed and spied on him and asked questions of anyone who had known Hermit Dan as a child. It was rumored that his ancestors had actually been pirates. Until a terrible fire that had destroyed all they owned, Hermit Dan's family had been very wealthy. However, no one knew how they had become so rich.

In an attempt to see what the summer residents knew about Hermit Dan, the children introduced themselves to the vacationing youngsters. Among the visitors the Roberts met Hank and Ted, brothers bent on bullying Hermit Dan. When the children were rescued from a severe sandstorm by Hermit Dan, they were surprised to find that he wasn't nearly as gruff as he appeared. In fact they began to feel quite protective of the old man. Thus when Hank and Ted stole a secret box that held all of Hermit Dan's valuables, it was the Roberts children who fought (literally) to get the box back. It was after Liza, Bill and Jed returned the box to Hermit Dan, however, that the real surprises began: these included a surprise party for Hermit Dan, his wish to be friendly, and his gift to the children of three pieces of eight that proved his family members were pirates.

This title's more interesting and involved plot makes the book more likely to be a success with older readers than the other stories about the Roberts children. Otherwise it shares the same format, faults and strengths as the other series titles.

Interest Level: 2-5. Reading Level: 2.1. Further Search Topics: Mystery and Detective Stories, Pirates-Fiction, Vacation-Fiction, Loners-Fiction, Treasure-Fiction, Bullies-Fiction, Brothers and Sisters-Fiction, Grandparents-Fiction.

POETRY

Ciardi, John. I met a man; illus by Robert Osborn. HM 1961, 74 pp.

Ciardi's poems are pure fun. About half are riddle poems (poems that describe something without naming it until the end) and the rest are humorous descriptions or nonsense poems. There is a problem, however, with the riddle poems: they are somewhat more difficult to read than the other poems, but of interest to younger rather than older readers. For that reason pages 1-21 (primarily nonsense verse) can be recommended for grades one through five. The remainder of the book, although enjoyable to the very young, needs to be read to them or needs a strong young reader.

Interest Level: 1-5. Reading Level: 2.2. Further Search Topics: Wit and Humor, Poetry, Riddles, Group 2.

Davidson, Carson. Fast-talking dolphin; illus by Sylvia Stone. Dodd 1978, 127 pp.

After a rather slow start, this story develops into a well-paced adventure-fantasy with touches of warmth and humor. Eric wasn't just surprised when he found a dolphin in the 10-foot fish pond, he was astonished. Not only had there never been a dolphin there before, but this dolphin spoke in poetry. His name was Wallingford Ullingham Lowell III; Wallingford for short. He was elegant, proud and cultured; but as Eric soon found out, he was very impractical. He didn't seem to realize that he needed salt water and more fish than those in the pond in order to live. It was Eric who figured out a way to keep salt flowing into the pond and a supply of fresh fish. He also kept Wallingford's presence a secret, just as Wallingford requested. The day that Wallingford was discovered was the day that Eric had to break his promise. In order to find out who else had found out about Wallingford, Eric talked with his brother. Together they scouted the town before they realized that Herbert Benson was the only other person who had seen Wallingford.

Herbert reluctantly admitted that he had told his father about the dolphin. Eric knew enough about Mr. Benson to realize that he was just crazy enough to want to harm the dolphin. Eric and his brother gathered all the local children together to shield Wallingford from Mr. Benson. Even Herbert dared to defy his father for the first time. As Mr. Benson struggled with Eric and his brother, he fell, hit his head and rolled into the pond. Wallingford dove to save him, but his leg was caught between two rocks. With the others' help, Wallingford, Eric and his brother Karl were able to save Mr. Benson from drowning.

A few days later Eric, with new-found skills, spontaneously recited a poem about friendship to Wallingford. Wallingford answered with a rare compliment and for the first time used Eric's name (a show of respect). They were such true friends that when Wallingford was helicopter-lifted out of the pond and taken back to his research project, Eric couldn't understand why his father didn't tell him of Wallingford's departure. Eventually he realized that his father had been right; he would rather remember Wallingford swimming in the pond than in a helicopter's sling. Also, Wallingford would have been embarrassed to be seen making so undignified a departure. Wallingford's final message to Eric was a note that Eric found scratched in the dirt thanking him for the salt and the fish and saying that they would one day meet again.

Don't take the plot too seriously or peruse it too carefully for it won't stand up to scrutiny. This is merely a pleasant story with enough humor, action and originality to intrigue many readers. The book's major drawback is the poetry Wallingford spouts: the poetic form and somewhat difficult language will throw some readers. On the other hand, the book could be very useful in a classroom unit about poetry. Interest Level: 3-5. Reading Level: 3.1. Further Search Topics: Poetry, Dolphins-Fiction, Pets-Fiction, Fantasy, Friendship-Fiction, Humorous Fiction.

LeSieg, Theo. Wacky Wednesday; illus by George Booth. Beginner 1974, unp. (36 pp).
A series of true picture puzzles. A little boy wakes up one Wednesday to find everything around him has gone "wacky." People are missing heads but have extra legs. Cars are being driven from the back seat. Doors are placed in the wrong places. Airplanes fly backwards. At the end of the day everything settles back to normal, but not before readers have had fun finding the numerous "wacky" things on each page.

The story is told in silly rhyme (LeSieg and Seuss are the same person). What is wrong with each picture is not always easily located, making this reader an excellent excerise in observation as well as great fun. Interest Level: 1-3. Reading Level: 1.2. Further Search Topics: Puzzles, Humorous Fiction, Wit and Humor, Poetry, Best Sellers.

O'Neill, Mary. Hailstones and halibut bones; illus by Leonard Weisgard. Doubleday 1961, 59 pp.
This is a classic collection of twelve poems about colors. The poems are rhymed mood pieces of two or three pages that should appeal to almost any age reader. The difficulty of the vocabulary within each poem can vary greatly; however, most stanzas are short, most of the vocabulary is at least familiar, and the rhyme scheme is consistent. Interest Level: 1-5. Reading Level: 3.2. Further Search Topics: Poetry, Colors, Group 2.

Seuss, Dr. One fish, two fish, red fish, blue fish. Beginner 1960, 63pp.
Beginning with one almost ordinary-looking fish, this is a humorous look at the "funny things that go by." When Dr. Seuss says "funny," he really means highly imaginative, whimsical, and totally nonsensical. Each of the more than 20 silly creatures are described and appropriately illustrated to appeal to a child's sense of the ridiculous. Reader. Interest Level: 1-2. Reading Level: 1.1. Further Search Topics: Fantasy, Wit and Humor, Poetry, Humorous Fiction, Stories in Rhyme.

Seuss, Dr. Hop on Pop. Beginner 1963, 64pp.
Between one and four rhyming words are introduced or reviewed and used in a silly sentence on each page. The sentence is interpreted with even more amusing illustrations. It is one of the simplest of books (no story at all) and yet it is usable through second grade because of Dr. Seuss' playful style and ridiculous illustrations. Reader format. Interest Level: 1-2. Reading Level: 1.1. Further Search Topics: Poetry, Best Sellers, Wit and Humor, Humorous Fiction, Stories in Rhyme.

Seuss, Dr. The cat in the hat. Beginner 1957, 61 pp.
When the Cat in the Hat visits two children, a dreary, boring afternoon becomes almost too exciting. The Cat's juggling act and the two "things" he brings with him almost destroy the house. But the Cat cleans up so well that when the children's mother comes home and asks what they did all afternoon, they can't decide if they should tell her.

A funny, rhyming tale of the destruction all children can create and the boredom all children can feel. Reader format. Interest Level: 1-3. Reading Level: 1.2. Further Search Topics: Humorous Fiction, Fantasy, Cats-Fiction, Poetry, Troublemakers-Fiction, Best Sellers, Stories in Rhyme.

Seuss, Dr. The cat in the hat comes back. Beginner 1958, 63 pp.
Sally and her brother were doing a good job of clearing the front walk of snow when the Cat in the Hat showed up. While they worked, the Cat created a pink mess in the house. The mess only became worse when he tried to clean it. The pink spot finally covered the snow all around the house until the Cat called upon his friends Little Cats A-Z. It was Little Cat Z and his magic zoom that eventually not only cleaned the snow, but cleared the front walk as well.

Another zany, rhymed adventure of the mischievious Cat whose ability to get into trouble endears him to most children from pre-school to early third grade. Reader format. Interest Level: 1-3. Reading Level: 1.2. Further Search Topics: Fantasy, Cats-Fiction, Troublemakers-Fiction, Humorous Fiction, Snow-Fiction, Poetry, Best Sellers, Stories in Rhyme.

Seuss, Dr. The foot book. Random 1968, unp (27 pp).

Left feet, right feet, big feet, small feet; with its rhyme, silly illustrations and rhythmic celebration of feet of all descriptions, this book is a sure winner with the very young. Reader format.

Interest Level 1-2. Reading Level: 1.1. Further Search Topics: Best Sellers, Feet-Fiction, Humorous Fiction, Poetry, Wit and Humor, Stories in Rhyme.

Silverstein, Shel. Where the sidewalk ends. Har-Row 1974, 166 pp.

There is something here for almost everyone. It isn't always easy reading, but there are enough short, easier poems to pique almost any child's interest. Once caught, children will find the book hard to put down. The best way to encourage the use of this book is to read selections aloud so that potential readers may hear the rhythm and enjoy the humor. This method almost guarantees that they will then want to try reading the book themselves. Readers may struggle with a poem but once it is mastered, they will usually want more.

Interest Level: 2-6. Reading Level: 3.1. Further Search Topics: Poetry, Wit and Humor, Read Aloud, Group 2, Best Sellers.

Silverstein, Shel. A light in the attic. Har-Row 1981, 169 pp.

This is the second and most recent collection of Shel Silverstein's wonderfully wry poetry. No young person who has read and enjoyed *Where the Sidewalk Ends* will be disappointed in this effort. For those readers new to Silverstein or to poetry in general, this is as good a place as any to start enjoying both. Hearing a few of these poems read aloud is guaranteed to provoke loud cries of ''May I read some?'' from almost all listeners.

Interest Level: 2-6. Reading Level: 3.2. Further Search Topics: Poetry, Wit and Humor, Best Sellers, Group 2, Read Aloud.

Walker, Alice. Langston Hughes, American poet; illus by Don Miller. Har-Row 1974, 33 pp.

Langston Hughes is one of the world's most famous black poets. He spent most of his childhood in poverty and yet he shunned and was shunned by his wealthy father because his father disliked blacks. To Hughes the two most important things in the world were his heritage and his writing. His love of black history stemmed from the stories his grandmother told him. His love of language and writing grew out of the lonely hours he spent reading as a child. Hughes began to write poetry even before he was in high school and continued to write for many years. He wrote not only poems, but children's books, novels, plays and short stories. He wrote about and for blacks around the world. He was a proud and honest man who chose to share his pride in his race and his honesty through his writing.

This book is more of an inspirational tribute to a black hero than a fact-filled biography. That isn't to say that there are no facts included in the book. There are facts, but the book will not do as the sole source for a report about Langston Hughes. The book is, however, a good introduction to the man and his writing.

Interest Level: 3-5. Reading Level: 2.2. Further Search Topics: Biography, Blacks-Biography, Writing, Poverty, Divorce and Separation, Poetry.

POLITICS-BIOGRAPHY

Meriwether, Louise. The freedom ship of Robert Smalls; illus by Lee Jack Morton. P-H 1971, unp (30 pp).

A brief, but very interesting biography of a black man whose dreams of freedom as a young slave during the Civil War, led to a daring plan of escape. Robert Smalls sailed 16 slaves to freedom and presented the Northern Navy with a valuable gunboat of which he was eventually named captain. Smalls later went on to serve five terms in Congress.

Although the picture book format of this book prevents its confortable use much beyond fourth grade, it is a compelling enough story to interest even sixth graders. Print is somewhat small.

Interest Level: 1-4. Reading Level: 3.1. Further Search Topics: Biography, United States-History-War, Blacks-Biography, Smalls, Robert, Group 2, Slavery, Politics-Biography.

POLITICS-FICTION

Kibbe, Pat. My mother the mayor, maybe; illus by Charles Robinson. Knopf 1981, 165 pp.

The Pinkertons first appeared in *The Hocus-Pocus Dilemma*, a better introduction to the family than this book. Although this is a satisfactory story, its appeal is somewhat limited by its subject matter. B.J.'s mother's decision to run for town mayor meant that the whole family became involved in the political process. B.J. became her mother's unofficial public relations coordinator, a position Sam Jessup (Mrs. Pinkerton's campaign manager) didn't want to see anyone fill but himself. But because Jessup's ideas seemed suspiciously designed to insure that Mrs. Pinkerton would lose the election, B.J. continued working on her mother's behalf. Almost every day she managed to get her mother's campaign on the front page of the newspaper, although not always in a flattering light. Once B.J. was arrested for breaking into her mother's campaign headquarters. Another day she inadvertently circulated a picture of her mother in a bikini all over town. B.J. and her brothers and sisters illegally campaigned on the high school campus during Homecoming. B.J. even accidentally succeeded in blowing her mother's opponent's wig off in the middle of a campaign appearance. Mrs. Pinkerton finally lost the election, but managed to bring an important issue to light and to stage the closest and most exciting election the town had known in a long time.

Election campaigns and political issues won't lure many new reluctant readers to this book, but those youngsters who have enjoyed the Pinkerton's previous adventures and can understand a simplified version of politics at work will enjoy this humorous tale.

Interest Level: 5-6. Reading Level: 3.1. Further Search Topics: Politics-Fiction, Humorous Fiction, Sex Role-Fiction, Family-Fiction.

Sharmat, Marjorie W. Maggie Marmelstein for President; illus by Ben Shecter. Har-Row 1975, 122 pp.

Maggie and Thad Smith are at it again. When Thad decided to run for sixth grade president, Maggie decided to become his campaign manager. However, because Thad thought Maggie was too strong and would end up managing him much more than he wanted to be managed, he turned down her offer. Thad's refusal made Maggie so angry that she not only decided to run against Thad, but she also enlisted Noah, the smartest kid in the class, as her manager. With Noah's expert guidance Maggie's campaign went rather well, despite attempts at sabotage by a spy for Thad. But as election day drew closer, both Thad and Maggie lost track of the campaign issues and concentrated only on beating each other. Consequently the pre-election debate turned into a disastrous shouting match. The next day Noah was elected class president by write-in votes.

Not very subtle, but funny. A satisfying sequel for those who enjoyed *Getting Something on Maggie Marmelstein.*

Interest Level: 3-6. Reading Level: 3.1. Further Search Topics: Humorous Fiction, Politics-Fiction, School Stories, Friendship-Fiction, Sex Role-Fiction.

POVERTY

Adoff, Arnold. Malcolm X; illus by John Wilson. Har-Row 1970, 41 pp.

This is a simple, intellectually honest biography of a very controversial man. Taught a strong sense of self-respect by his father, Malcolm X could not accept the second-class status that white society tried to impose upon him. Instead he turned away from whites and all they stood for. He hated high school, the detention home he lived in after his father's death, and his mother's placement in a state hospital. He didn't feel comfortable until he moved to Harlem. There he found friends, but he also found crime. While he was in prison, Malcolm X began to read of great, black societies and people. His brother told him about the Nation of Islam, the Black Muslims, and Elijah Muhammad, the leader of the religion. He began corresponding with Mr. Muhammad. Shortly after he was released from prison, Malcolm X met Elijah Muhammad and eventually became a minister of the religion. There was even talk that he would be Elijah Muhammad's successor. But, as the years went on, Malcolm X began to think that black Christians as well as Muslims should be united in the fight for black rights. Despite threats against his life Malcolm X formed the Organization of Afro-American Unity. Both blacks and whites were angry with him. The threats continued until his house was firebombed; and, only a week later, at a public meeting, Malcolm X was assassinated.

An excellent overview of a complex man. The book may well prompt readers to learn more about the man and his beliefs. At the very least it will expose readers, in an interesting manner, to someone they should know. The book shares the same semi-picture book format of the others in Harper and Row/Crowell's biography series, therefore it will need a careful introduction to potential readers.

Interest Level: 3-5. Reading Level: 3.1. Further Search Topics: Blacks-Biography, Civil Rights, Biography, Crime, Religion, Assassinations, Prejudice, Poverty, Foster Homes.

Holland, John. The way it is. HarBraceJ 1969, 87 pp.

For 15 boys living in a run-down area of Brooklyn, school became interesting when they were assigned to photograph whatever was meaningful to them in their neighborhood. The results, described in their own words, were developed into this fascinating documentary which is at the same time a spontaneous glimpse of the boys themselves. The book should be of particular interest to older urban children. Print slightly on the small side. Has recently gone out of print, but is worth looking for.

Interest Level: 4-6. Reading Level: 3.2. Further Search Topics: Best Sellers, City Life, Photography, Poverty, Academic Problems.

Jordan, June. Fannie Lou Hamer; illus by Albert Williams. Har-Row 1972, 41 pp.

In 1917, Fannie Lou Hamer was the last of 20 children born to a fearless black woman. Fannie and her family grew up working on a white man's cotton plantation. Although they were kept poor and hungry by the plantation owner and the field boss, Fannie Lou grew up in her mother's image—unafraid of white people and unhappy with the poor treatment of blacks that she saw all around her. In 1962, when most other blacks in Mississippi where afraid of the consequences, Fannie registered to vote. After both she and her husband lost their jobs and their home, and after she was beaten in a Mississippi jail, Fannie Lou Hamer drew national attention to her fight for blacks' civil rights. She spoke all over the country, helped to form a new political party, and raised money to help poor people. That money was what started the 640 acre Freedom Farm Cooperative that provided work and food for more than 5,000 people. It was Mrs. Hamer's dream to see poor people work together to feed themselves rather than to accept food from others. She made her dream come true.

Another competent entry in the Crowell Biography series. Only its picture book format keeps this book from being useful through sixth grade.

Interest Level: 3-5. Reading Level: 3.2. Further Search Topics: Biography, Blacks-Biography, Civil Rights, Poverty, Women-Biography.

Rudeen, Kenneth. Jackie Robinson; illus by Richard Cuffari. Har-Row 1971, 41 pp.

Jackie Robinson was the youngest child in a large, poor family. As early as high school it was Robinson's superior athletic talent that set him apart. He could run track or play baseball, football, or basketball. He was the first student at UCLA to win a letter in all four sports. But because he wasn't happy to see the way his mother still had to struggle to earn money to live, after a year and a half at UCLA, Robinson left college to take a job. Soon after that, the United States entered World War II and Robinson went into the Army. His refusal to ride in the back of a bus in Texas resulted in a courtmartial, but he was found innocent after an uproar was made by the newspapers.

After the Army, Robinson played baseball with a Negro League team. A short time later, he was asked by the Dodger manager Branch Rickey to become the first black man to play in the major leagues. Rickey warned Robinson that it would mean he not only had to play well, but that he would also have to take all the anger and bitterness that would be directed at him. Robinson agreed. For three long years, while there were no other black players in the major leagues, Robinson played well and took everything without fighting back. Robinson was then able to stop trying to be perfect because he had successfully broken a very important color barrier and no longer had to prove to white managers, players and fans that blacks belonged in baseball just as much as whites. Robinson played for the Dodgers for ten years. When he left baseball he was elected into the Baseball Hall of Fame. He continued to fight for civil rights throughout the rest of his life, although there is only a brief mention of his activities in the book. Since the book's publication Jackie Robinson has died.

This is an excellent choice for the child who thinks of nothing but sports. It may be helpful in opening up an interest in the civil rights movement, black history, or black heroes. It is unfortunate that the traditional Crowell biography format (semi-picture book), and the author's slight tendency to be condescending, prevents the book from being useful beyond fourth grade. Crowell Biography series.

Interest Level: 2-4. Reading Level: 2.2. Further Search Topics: Civil Rights, Robinson, Jackie, Baseball-Biography, Biography, Blacks-Biography, Prejudice, Poverty.

Walker, Alice. Langston Hughes, American poet; illus by Don Miller. Har-Row 1974, 33 pp.

Langston Hughes is one of the world's most famous black poets. He spent most of his childhood in poverty and yet he shunned and was shunned by his wealthy father because his father disliked blacks. To Hughes the two most important things in the world were his heritage and his writing. His love of black history stemmed from the stories his grandmother told him. His love of language and writing grew out of the lonely hours he spent reading as a child. Hughes began to write poetry even before he was in high school and continued to write for many years. He wrote not only poems, but children's books, novels, plays and short stories. He wrote about and for blacks around the world. He was a proud and honest man who chose to share his pride in his race and his honesty through his writing.

This book is more of an inspirational tribute to a black hero than a fact-filled biography. That isn't to say that there are no facts included in the book. There are facts, but the book will not do as the sole source for a report about Langston Hughes. The book is, however, a good introduction to the man and his writing.

Interest Level: 3-5. Reading Level: 2.2. Further Search Topics: Biography, Blacks-Biography, Writing, Poverty, Divorce and Separation, Poetry.

POVERTY-FICTION

Bonham, Frank. The mystery of the fat cat; illus by Alvin Smith. Dutton 1968, 160 pp.

Although noticeably dated at times, this is still an exciting story of an inner city neighborhood. Buddy, Little Pie, Rich, and Cool were among the many who used the local Boys' Club as their hangout. It was a place to stay out of trouble and off the streets, but it was also a haven for rats. The rats were big and brazen; so brazen that one attacked Buddy in the swimming pool. The club needed a new building desperately. The money was there; they just weren't able to use it. Fifteen years earlier an eccentric old woman willed the Boys' Club over $600,000, but stated that the money was first to be used to support her cat until it died. A caretaker, a lawyer, and a veterinarian all benefited as long as the cat lived. Buddy and his friends took on the job of discovering if the cat really was alive or if the Boys' Club was being cheated out of half a million dollars. It was a job that nearly killed them before they set things right. Plenty of action, some violence, a cast of street-smart characters, realistic trouble with the police, as well as a slight mystery almost insure the book's success with older readers. Moderate sized print. Line spacing somewhat narrow.

Interest Level: 6+ Reading Level: 5.1. Further Search Topics: Humorous Fiction, Cats-Fiction, Gangs-Fiction, City Life-Fiction, Mystery and Detective Stories, Poverty-Fiction, Friendship-Fiction, Juvenile Delinquency-Fiction, Crime-Fiction, Best Sellers.

Bulla, Clyde Robert. The sugar pear tree; illus by Taro Yashima. T Y Crowell 1960, 54 pp.

Lonnie lived with his mother and his grandfather in a house owned by the state. A new highway was to be built that would force the family to move, but Gramp refused to acknowledge that the state could force them out of their home. He chased away every state representative who came to warn the family that they should move. Lonnie's mother had always been at work when the representatives came and so knew nothing about the warnings until she came home to find their belongings on the sidewalk and their house on wheels. The only person they could turn to was their friend Nick. Nick owned a nursery in town and a small house with a large yard in the country. He had become a friend of Lonnie's when he gave Lonnie first prize in a school essay contest on the topic of "favorite trees." Lonnie's prize had been a sugar pear tree, his favorite. Nick had next become Lonnie's mother's friend. Nick arranged for them to stay in the greenhouse at his country place. The longer they stayed, the better friends Nick and Lonnie's mother became. Gramp was the only person who didn't adjust to the move. He stopped speaking the moment he was carried out of his old home. In a final and successful attempt to make Gramp happy, Nick bought the old house and had it moved out to his country lot.

The idea of a state government being able to force a family to move may need some explaining. The story's warmth and very consistent early second grade reading level make this a particularly useful book with quiet readers.

Interest Level: 2-4. Reading Level: 2.1. Further Search Topics: Trees-Fiction, Moving, Household-Fiction, Family Problems-Fiction, Grandparents-Fiction, Poverty-Fiction.

Burch, Robert. Queenie Peavy; illus by Jerry Lazare. Viking Pr. 1966, 159 pp.

Queenie was always in trouble. She could be mean, really mean, but, she was also bright, talented, independent and resilient. Queenie blamed her problems on the fact that people teased her because her father was in jail and because she was poor. She thought that she had to defend herself against the world. Queenie was proud of her poor reputation until she accidentally-on-purpose caused a classmate to break his leg. Then, when her father returned home and wasn't the person she'd hoped he'd be, Queenie realized that only she could make her life better. Being the strong person she was, she set out to do just that.

Queenie is a wonderfully alive and sympathetic character, one well worth introducing to older readers despite the book's reading level. Print somewhat small. Line spacing average width.

Interest Level: 5-6. Reading Level: 5.1. Further Search Topics: Family Problems-Fiction, Crime-Fiction, Loners-Fiction, Poverty-Fiction, Humorous Fiction, Bullies-Fiction, Troublemakers-Fiction, Academic Problems-Fiction, Read Aloud.

Byars, Betsy. The house of wings; illus by Daniel Schwarts. Viking Pr. 1972, 142 pp.

Sammy was the youngest of eight children. His parents were tired of raising children when Sammy was born, so they almost let Sammy raise himself. That meant that he grew up to be independent. It didn't mean it was any easier for Sammy to accept being left behind unexpectedly with his strange grandfather when his parents moved to Detroit. His reaction when his grandfather told him that his parents had gone was to deny it and to run away. He ran until he could run no more. When he stopped running, the old man stopped chasing him and they found a wild but blind crane in desperate need of help. Helping the crane heal and find the desire to live again taught

Sammy and his grandfather respect and, most of all, love for each other.

The parallels between Sammy and the crane are strong but subtle. The story is a compelling one, but may need a brief introductory note to alleviate confusion in the first two chapters.

Interest Level: 5-6. Reading Level: 4.2. Further Search Topics: Grandparents-Fiction, Birds-Fiction, Family Problems-Fiction, Poverty-Fiction, Physically Handicapped-Fiction, Runaways-Fiction.

Clymer, Eleanor. Santiago's silver mine; illus by Ingrid Fetz. Atheneum 1973, 74 pp.

Although somewhat complicated by a large number of background incidents, especially early in the book, the story is both interesting and informative. Santiago and his friend Andreas wanted to be rich. The year's harvest had been very poor, so there was little food to eat. Both of their fathers had gone to Mexico City to find jobs and their mothers worked for very few pesos near home. Andreas wanted to search the old mine in the hills outside of town for silver, but the mining company had left a guard named Jose to prevent people from getting into the mines. While up on a hill, tending a cow, Andreas found an old piece of pottery and a back entrance to the mine. As they started to enter the mine, Andreas and Santiago found a basket full of old pottery pieces that Jose had apparently dug from the hill. Not knowing what the pottery pieces were, the boys took them to the local school teacher who identified them as ancient archeological treasures that by law belonged to the government. As soon as he realized others had found out that he had been selling the pottery, Jose disappeared. Shortly afterwards, the government paved the road through town and opened the hill as an official archaeological site. The extra jobs meant that the boys' fathers could once again find work at home. Although they hadn't become exactly rich, Santiago and Andreas had certainly found treasure.

Local flavor abounds, along with some history. Useful for Social Studies units. Print size fairly small, but spaces between lines are good sized. Recently out-of-print, but still worth looking for.

Interest Level: 3-5. Reading Level: 3.1. Further Search Topics: Archaeology-Fiction, Poverty-Fiction, Mexico-Fiction, Country Life-Fiction, Treasure-Fiction, Miners-Fiction.

Clymer, Eleanor. Me and the Eggman; illus by David K. Stone. Dutton 1972, 57 pp.

As Donald's life became more and more miserable and as his chores and responsibilities around his small, overcrowded, urban apartment increased, he began to look for a way to escape. Thinking that if he could just get to the country, life would be better, Donald sneaked into a truck owned by a farmer who delivered eggs to the city. Not surprisingly the farmer, a sharp speaking, independent old man, was not at all happy to find Donald. Reluctantly, the Eggman, as the farmer was called, agreed to let Donald stay a week and help to work his rundown farm. The week stretched into a summer in which Donald learned to face and accept reality, to love the Eggman and to like himself.

This book is a surprisingly consistent success with reluctant readers, especially boys. Watch for the lack of quotation marks around the dialogue and the somewhat small print.

Interest Level: 3-6. Reading Level: 3.2. Further Search Topics: Family Problems-Fiction, Poverty-Fiction, Vacation-Fiction, Runaways-Fiction, Farm Life-Fiction, Best Sellers.

Hinton, Susan E. The outsiders. Viking Pr. 1967, 188 pp.

When she wrote this book Susan Hinton was only 17 years old, but she had the sensitivity of someone much older. She wrote a taut story of the rivalry between two city gangs; the Socs (the rich socialites) and the Greasers (poor kids from the wrong side of town) that is more than anything a plea for understanding and tolerance. Seen through the eyes of Ponyboy (a very bright, 14-year-old Greaser), the rivalry brought on violence and an accidental killing that forced Pony and his friend Johnny to flee for their lives. Dallas, the meanest and most dangerous of the Greasers, provided them with shelter, food for a week, and a gun. At the end of that week, Johnny decided that they should turn themselves in to the police. But before they could do that, their hideout (an old church) burned in a fire which threatened the lives of four children who had been playing there. In trying to rescue the children, Johnny, Pony, and Dallas were injured; Johnny was severely burned and probably permanently crippled. A vengeance rumble was held while Johnny lay in the hospital, but the Greasers' victory was empty when Johnny died. He had been the one member of the gang whom they all loved and who had most needed them. Dallas went to pieces: he robbed a store and set himself up to be killed by the police. He had nothing left to live for after Johnny's death. Pony found support and security with his brothers (their parents were dead) and, in a note from Johnny, some hope for the future.

Hinton speaks most often through Pony (his depth of understanding of the people around him is very impressive), but through Johnny and two of the Socs as well, Randy and Cherry. Her message is clear, but at no time does she fail to maintain believable characters in a compelling plot.

Although the book looks forbidding with its 188 pages of unrelenting small print, it is an exciting story, full of adventure, realism, and room for thought. Perhaps the best way to introduce this book is to read a fair portion of it aloud. Now a motion picture too.

Interest Level: 6+ Reading Level: 5.1. Further Search Topics: Crime-Fiction, Gangs-Fiction, Murder-Fiction, Read Aloud, Friendship-Fiction, Juvenile Delinquency-Fiction, Best Sellers, City Life-Fiction, Brothers and Sisters-Fiction, Orphans-Fiction, Runaways-Fiction, Troublemakers-Fiction, Poverty-Fiction.

Madian, Jon. Beautiful junk: a story of the Watts Towers; photos by Barbara Jacobs, Jr. and Lou Jacobs, Jr. Little 1968, 44 pp.

Although this book is now out of print; it is well worth trying to find. It is a fictionalized account of a young, angry black boy's encounter with the creator of Los Angeles' unusual Watts Towers. Simon Rodia, a poor tile setter, worked on the towers for 33 years until he was 75 years old. He used only his imagination, discarded materials he found around him, seashells, and sand to build three tall, fantasy-like towers in the middle of a ghetto. He created beauty where others saw only junk.

The book is illustrated with photography that makes the story more vivid and the towers and Rodia's accomplishment more impressive than they would have seemed with drawings. The print is good-sized, spacing is totally adequate. Rodia's life is quickly submarized and an update on the Towers is included at the book's end.

Interest Level: 3-6. Reading Level: 3.1. Further Search Topics: Blacks-Fiction, Read Aloud, Best

Sellers, Poverty-Fiction, Rodia, Simon, Architecture, Biography, Aging-Fiction, Watts Towers, California, Poverty.

Sachs, Marily. The bears' house; illus by Louis Glanzman. Doubleday 1971, 81 pp.

Don't let the benign appearance of this book fool you. This is a disturbing, almost brutal story. It is the story of Fran Ellen, a fourth grader with more problems than anyone should have to shoulder at one time. Her father had left the family and her mother had had a mental breakdown. Fran Ellen and her older brother were left with responsibility for themselves, their mother, and three other children (including a baby). They were all ill-fed, poorly dressed, and unwashed. Neither the social worker nor Fran Ellen's teacher knew the extent of the family's problems. Fran Ellen's only happiness came from her baby sister and from a schoolroom model (of *Goldilocks and the Three Bears* and their house) into which she mentally retreated whenever she had the chance.

As the school year closed, Fran Ellen's teacher visited her home to deliver the bears' house and discovered Fran Ellen's mother and very sick baby sister. Although she hated the idea that the family might have to split up, Fran Ellen had matured enough to realize that when her teacher insisted that she would get help for the family, her teacher was taking the proper action.

The book is inappropriately illustrated to make it appear cute and even humorous. The story is far from either. It is so stark that it probably shouldn't have been illustrated at all. And because the hope that is present in the book's ending is very subtle, a review and a discussion may be necessary to help relieve some young readers' anxieties.

Interest Level: 5-6. Reading Level: 3.1. Further Search Topics: Divorce and Separation-Fiction, Challenges-Fiction, Poverty-Fiction, Family Problems-Fiction, Loners-Fiction, Survival-Fiction, Mental Illness-Fiction, Brothers and Sisters-Fiction.

Wagner, Jane. J.T; photos by Gordon Parks, Jr. Van Nostrand 1969, 64 pp.

This is a sentimental story that rarely fails to elicit a sympathetic response from young readers. J.T. is a poor black boy who saw a portable radio almost begging to be stolen and stole it. Two of the neighborhood bullies, Boomer and Claymore, saw J.T. take the radio. Though they threatened him, even poured soap in his eyes in the school bathrooms, J.T. wouldn't give them the radio as they demanded.

About the same time J.T. found a scrawny, scared little cat with only one eye. Because his mother wouldn't let him take the cat home, J.T. built it a warm but ramshackle little house in an abandoned building. He fed it by charging tuna to his mother's grocery store account without her knowledge. Bones became the only thing in J.T.'s life that he had cared about since his father had walked out.

When Boomer and Claymore found out about Bones, they taunted J.T. by throwing the cat back and forth between them until the frightened cat escaped, darted out into the street and was hit by a car. J.T.'s heart broke as he looked at Bones, but he spoke to no one to tell them of his sadness. Only time, his mother's and grandmother's love and a small kitten from Mr. Rosen, the grocer, helped him recover. On the morning that he decided to accept the kitten, J.T. returned the stolen radio, faced Boomer and Claymore without fear, and asked Mr. Rosen for a job in order to pay for cat food.

The book is oversized and illustrated with photographs from the television movie version. It is not only an excellent story to read aloud but one that will prompt listeners to want to finish it on their own or to reread it. It is now available only in paperback from Dell.

Interest Level: 3-6. Reading Level: 3.1. Further Search Topics: Read Aloud, Courage-Fiction, Best Sellers, Cats-Fiction, Single Parent Family-Fiction, Bullies-Fiction, Blacks-Fiction, Poverty-Fiction, City Life-Fiction, Christmas Stories, Crime-Fiction, Pets-Fiction, Holidays-Fiction.

PREHISTORY

Cole, Joanna. Dinosaur story; illus by Mort Kunstler. Morrow 1974, unp (30 pp).

A general introduction to eight dinosaurs: Brontosaurus, Allosaurus, Stegosaurus, Ornitholestes, Protoceratops, Triceratops, Tyrannosaurus rex and Duckbills. Although not a wealth of information, there is more than enough interesting material here to attract a young dinosaur enthusiast. Because of the short sentences, the text is somewhat plodding. The subject matter's great appeal and the appropriately fierce-looking illustrations, however, make up for that problem.

Interest Level: 1-3. Reading Level: 2.1. Further Search Topics: Group 2, Dinosaurs, Prehistory.

Hornblow, Leonora. Prehistoric monsters did the strangest things; illus by Michael K. Frith. Random 1974, 65 pp.

A basic survey of an era and its animal life forms. Animals from the earliest water creatures through Diplocaulus, Ichthyosaurs, dinosaurs (about 12 varieties) and early mammals (including the Beast of Baluchistan) to the appearance of man are introduced and illustrated. It is a brief but meaty treatment of a very popular subject that should be especially useful with second and third grade children. Reader format.

Interest Level: 1-3. Reading Level: 2.1. Further Search Topics: Prehistory, Dinosaurs, Evolution, Monsters, Group 2.

PREJUDICE

Adoff, Arnold. Malcolm X; illus by John Wilson. Har-Row 1970, 41 pp.

This is a simple, intellectually honest biography of a very controversial man. Taught a strong sense of self-respect by his father, Malcolm X could not accept the second-class status that white society tried to impose upon him. Instead he turned away from whites and all they stood for. He hated high school, the detention home he lived in after his father's death, and his mother's placement in a state hospital. He didn't feel comfortable until he moved to Harlem. There he found friends, but he also found crime. While he was in prison, Malcolm X began to read of great, black societies and people. His brother told him about the Nation of Islam, the Black Muslims, and Elijah Muhammad, the leader of the religion. He began corresponding with Mr. Muhammad. Shortly after he was released from prison, Malcolm X met Elijah Muhammad and eventually became a minister of the religion. There was even talk that he would be Elijah Muhammad's successor. But, as the years went on, Malcolm X began to think that black Christians as well as Muslims should be united in the fight for black rights. Despite threats against his life Malcolm X formed the Organization of Afro-American Unity. Both blacks and whites were angry with him. The threats continued until his house was firebombed; and, only a week later, at a public meeting, Malcolm X was assassinated.

An excellent overview of a complex man. The book may well prompt readers to learn more about the man and his beliefs. At the very least it will expose readers, in an interesting manner, to someone they should know. The book shares the same semi-picture book format of the others in Harper and Row/Crowell's biography series, therefore it will need a careful introduction to potential readers.

Interest Level: 3-5. Reading Level: 3.1. Further Search Topics: Blacks-Biography, Civil Rights, Biography, Crime, Religion, Assassinations, Prejudice, Poverty, Foster Homes.

Greenfield, Eloise. Rosa Parks; illus by Eric Marlow. Har-Row 1973, 33 pp.

This book succumbs to the difficulty of writing for children about a subject that needs more explanation. The occasionally condescending tone combined with the Crowell Biography picture book format will keep this otherwise adequate introduction to the civil rights movement from being useful beyond fourth grade. The book should be very useful, however, for third and fourth grade social studies, history or biography units.

Rosa Parks' childhood and her feelings about the special rules for blacks make up the first half of the book. The second half is devoted to Rosa's act of defiance (refusing to give up her seat on a bus to a white man) and the repercussions of that act. Crowell Biography series.

Interest Level: 2-4. Reading Level 2.2. Further Search Topics: Blacks-Biography, Biography, Prejudice, Civil Rights, Women-Biography, Courage.

Rudeen, Kenneth. Jackie Robinson; illus by Richard Cuffari. Har-Row 1971, 41 pp.

Jackie Robinson was the youngest child in a large, poor family. As early as high school it was Robinson's superior athletic talent that set him apart. He could run track or play baseball, football, or basketball. He was the first student at UCLA to win a letter in all four sports. But because he wasn't happy to see the way his mother still had to struggle to earn money to live, after a year and a half at UCLA, Robinson left college to take a job. Soon after that, the United States entered World War II and Robinson went into the Army. His refusal to ride in the back of a bus in Texas resulted in a courtmartial, but he was found innocent after an uproar was made by the newspapers.

After the Army, Robinson played baseball with a Negro League team. A short time later, he was asked by the Dodger manager Branch Rickey to become the first black man to play in the major leagues. Rickey warned Robinson that it would mean he not only had to play well, but that he would also have to take all the anger and bitterness that would be directed at him. Robinson agreed. For three long years, while there were no other black players in the major leagues, Robinson played well and took everything without fighting back. Robinson was then able to stop trying to be perfect because he had successfully broken a very important color barrier and no longer had to prove to white managers, players and fans that blacks belonged in baseball just as much as whites. Robinson played for the Dodgers for ten years. When he left baseball he was elected into the Baseball Hall of Fame. He continued to fight for civil rights throughout the rest of his life, although there is only a brief mention of his activities in the book. Since the book's publication Jackie Robinson has died.

This is an excellent choice for the child who thinks of nothing but sports. It may be helpful in opening up an interest in the civil rights movement, black history, or black heroes. It is unfortunate that the traditional Crowell biography format (semi-picture book), and the author's slight tendency to be condescending, prevents the book from being useful beyond fourth grade. Crowell Biography series.

Interest Level: 2-4. Reading Level: 2.2. Further Search Topics: Civil Rights, Robinson, Jackie, Baseball-Biography, Biography, Blacks-Biography, Prejudice, Poverty.

Tobias, Tobi. Marian Anderson; illus by Symeon Shimin. Har-Row 1972, 40 pp.

Marian Anderson's beautiful, strong voice and her great range set her apart from other singers even as a child. By the time she was in high school, she was being paid to sing. However, when she tried to apply to a well-known music school, because she was black she was turned away without even being heard. Anderson's determination as well as her own and others' faith in her kept her singing and seeking better and better coaches until she met Giuseppi Boghetti. He was one of the best voice coaches in the country. With him Marian trained and traveled until she finally won the chance to sing with the New York Philharmonic Orchestra. Anderson thought that at that point she would be invited to sing in famous theaters all across the United States, but because she was black she still received no invitations. She went to Europe where she studied and played to wildly enthusiastic audiences. Her European triumphs finally convinced American theater owners and audiences that she was a serious talent. For the next 30 years Marian Anderson sang all over the world, most of the time without incident, with one notable exception in 1939, when the D.A.R. prohibited her from singing in a hall they owned in Washington, D. C. She sang instead, in front of the Lincoln Memorial, at the invitation of the United States government. During the following years Marian married, bought a farm, sang opera and was made a delegate to the United Nations. In 1956, she retired from singing to help children, young singers, and world understanding.

Crowell Biographies make excellent school report sources for reluctant readers. They are short, interesting, and not overly juvenile looking, although the quasi-picture book format may be a problem for some older readers. This biography fits that description perfectly. The series is somewhat sentimental (as are many children's biographies), however, the sentimentality is not forbidding or condescending. A useful series. Crowell Biography series.

Interest Level: 2-5. Reading Level: 3.1. Further Search Topics: Biography, Music-Biography, Blacks-Biography, Talent, Women-Biography, Singers, Prejudice, Group 2.

PREJUDICE-FICTION

Christopher, Matt. No arm in left field; illus by Byron Goto. Little 1974, 131 pp.

Matt Christopher's books are just the thing for sports junkies. The play-by-play accounts of several sports events (here it is baseball games) are loosely tied together by secondary plot developments. Usually the plot revolves around the main character's successful attempt to overcome a difficulty of some sort.

Terry was a good baseball player so, when he was invited to join a local team shortly after he moved to Pennsylvania, he was very pleased. Almost immediately, he learned that a teammate was not at all happy about playing with Terry. Terry was black and his teammate, Tony, was very prejudiced. Terry had dealt with people like Tony before, so he was able to ignore most, but not all, of Tony's unkind comments and actions. But the day finally came when Tony realized that to play well as a team, they had to work together instead of against each other.

Interest Level: 3-6. Reading Level: 3.2. Further Search Topics: Prejudice-Fiction, Baseball-Fiction, Friendship-Fiction, Challenges-Fiction.

Christopher, Matt. The year mom won the pennant; illus by Foster Caddell. Little 1968, 147 pp.

When no one's father had the time to coach the Thunderballs it began to look like the team would be disbanded. They just didn't seem to be able to work together without a coach. Then Nick Vassey's mother volunteered to coach for the season. After all, she knew baseball as well as anyone else and had watched her husband coach for several years. Nick wasn't at all pleased, but had to accept the idea when his teammates voted to make his mother their coach. Nick's embarrassment was almost as great as the rival coach's skepticism, but before the season was over Nick was proud of his mother. She coached the team to first place and forced even the rival coach to admit she was a good coach. Much baseball action. See note about (*No Arm In Left Field*).

Interest Level: 2-6. Reading Level: 3.1. Further Search Topics: Group 2, Baseball-Fiction, Friendship-Fiction, Prejudice-Fiction, Sex Role-Fiction, Women-Fiction.

Hurwitz, Johanna. Once I was a plum tree; illus by Ingrid Fetz. Morrow 1980, 160 pp.

Ten-year-old Gerry Flam knew nothing about her religion except that she was Jewish. Her parents didn't practice their religion and only superficially observed some of the holidays. As they told Gerry, their reason was that they were assimilated Americans. In fact, they seemed to practice as many Christian as Jewish holidays. All Gerry's friends and neighbors were Catholic, so Gerry had very little chance to learn about Judaism or the prejudice to which Jews were still being subjected in 1947 in the Bronx. A Jewish family moved into the apartment building next door, and Gerry's quiet curiosity was stimulated. From the Wulfs, Gerry began to learn about Judaism, World War II, and Hitler. As her pride in her heritage grew, Gerry also felt prejudice for the first time. After celebrating her first Passover Seder, Gerry found that despite the problems, she was truly happy to be Jewish.

Much like Chaikin's *I Should Worry, I Should Care* in tone and mood. Will be useful where there is already an interest in Judaism.

Interest Level: 3-5. Reading Level: 3.1. Further Search Topics: Religion-Fiction, Family-Fiction, Jews-Fiction, City Life-Fiction, Children-Growth-Fiction, Prejudice-Fiction.

PSYCHIATRISTS-FICTION

Kelley, Sally. Trouble with explosives. Bradbury 1976, 117 pp.

Polly Banks stuttered very badly. She wanted to stop but she couldn't. Moving, entering a new school, and facing a mean teacher who seemed in need of psychiatric help, all made Polly's stuttering worse. When Sis, Polly's new friend, rose to Polly's defense in one confrontation too many with Miss Patterson, the teacher took cruel revenge. Polly's desire to help Sis, her need to do something about her stuttering, and an understanding psychiatrist, all helped Polly learn to

help herself with her speech problem. At the same time, she began to understand and have confidence in herself and her family.

Another "problem book" that older elementary school readers seem to crave. Polly and Sis are both very sympathetic characters who bring to life many of the uncertainties of growing up. Print and line spacing of only average size but otherwise a good choice.

Interest Level: 4-6. Reading Level: 3.2. Further Search Topics: Academic Problems-Fiction, Stuttering-Fiction, Psychiatrists-Fiction, School Stories, Mental Illness-Fiction, Troublemakers-Fiction, Courage-Fiction, Physically Handicapped-Fiction, Children-Growth-Fiction, Moving, Household-Fiction.

Park, Barbara. Don't make me smile. Knopf 1981, 114 pp.

As far as Charlie Hickle was concerned his parents' divorce was the worst thing in the world. His parents had ruined his life and he hadn't done anything to deserve such a fate. At first he didn't say very much. Then he ran away to live in a tree. Finally he cried a lot. That was all just in the first week after his parents announced their decision. After that, both his grades at school and his behavior began to deteriorate. It wasn't until Charlie had had several talks with a helpful children's psychologist and made a disastrous attempt to reunite his parents on his birthday, that he began to realize that he didn't like the divorce, but he could live with it.

The author's use of amusing anecdotes, Charlie's very strong feelings, and the frequency of divorce make this book very popular. Its major drawbacks are its superficiality and the overdrawn portrait of Charlie's mother. The book's faults will not deter many young readers from enjoying it, however.

Interest Level: 4-6. Reading Level: 3.1. Further Search Topics: Divorce and Separation-Fiction, Family Problems-Fiction, Psychiatrists-Fiction, Everyday Stories.

Pfeffer, Susan Beth. Just between us; illus by Lorna Tomei. Delacorte 1980, 116 pp.

Cass's inability to keep secrets finally became such a problem that Cass asked her mother to help her learn how to keep them. Cass's mother, a psychology student, devised a behavior modification experiment. Every day that Cass was able to figure out which bit of information she had been told was a secret and keep it, she received a dollar. After a poor start Cass did well for a while, until the day she told three secrets and made her entire family angry at her.

More determined than ever, Cass tried again. This time she found herself caught between two friends. Only Cass knew that Robin was adopted and Robin wanted it kept a secret. Jenny was so mad at Robin that she decided to spread an untrue story to hurt Robin. She told Cass not to tell anyone what she was going to do. The story Jenny was going to spread was that Robin was adopted. After hours of mental anguish Cass finally devised a way to stop Jenny and help Jenny return to being the nice person she had been before her parents' divorce.

The reading level of this book varies greatly from second grade to mid-fourth grade. Otherwise, it is good fare for Judy Blume fans. Print size just a slight bit on the small side.

Interest Level: 4-6. Reading Level: 3.2. Further Search Topics: Humorous Fiction, Everyday Stories, Friendship-Fiction, School Stories, Divorce and Separation-Fiction, Psychiatrists-Fiction, Secrets-Fiction.

PUERTO RICO

Buckley, Peter. I am from Puerto Rico. S ËAN S 1971, 127 pp.

Federico Ramirez had enjoyed his two years in New York City and didn't like the idea of moving back to Puerto Rico. When he arrived, he had no friends, no T.V., and nothing to do. Then Neri taught Federico the local games, showed him the sights and introduced him to Narcisco, a special fisherman. Narcisco took Federico through the wonders of the coral reefs. He taught him how to dive and fish. Within several months Federico was thoroughly at home in the water and loved Puerto Rico.

There is so much information about Puerto Rico and marine life that the book is never dry. Federico tells his own story as a series of fascinating experiences (meeting up with a shark, playing pinball, scuba diving at night, keeping a large turtle as a pet, etc.). There are abundant black and white photographs. An excellent choice for research (no index) or recreational reading. The print size is slightly on the small side, but the space between lines is good. Recently out of print, but worth looking for.

Interest Level: 5-6. Reading Level: 5.1. Further Search Topics: Puerto Rico, Fishing, Moving, Household-Fiction, Marine Biology, Scuba Diving, Ethnic Groups.

Rudeen, Kenneth. Roberto Clemente; illus by Frank Mullins. Har-Row 1974, 33 pp.

A romanticized retelling of a great baseball player's life. Those already interested in baseball or in Clemente will probably not mind the romantic tone, but may notice the almost patronizing explanations of some of the basics of baseball. Crowell Biography series.

Interest Level: 2-4. Reading Level: 3.1. Further Search Topics: Baseball-Biography, Biography, Puerto Rico, Group 2, Clemente, Roberto.

PUZZLES

Abisch, Roz. Mixed bag of magic tricks; illus by Boche Kaplan. Walker & Co. 1973, 64 pp.

The definition of magic is broadened here to include optical illusions, puzzles, age and date guessing formulae, as well as slight of hand and prearranged tricks. There are 25 "feats of magic" here, with especially good tips on performance, practice, costumes, and props. Although tricks in *Science Puzzles, It's Magic?, Funny Magic*, and *Magic Secrets* are showier, this is a more solid introduction to the subject. The Knot Magic Trick receives its best explanation here. See *It's Magic?* and *Science Puzzles* for others. Bonus: The book looks like a manual and not like a reader, therefore it should be useful even with sixth graders. It is now available in paperback version only; published by Grosset and Dunlap (Activity Books).

Interest Level: 2-6. Reading Level: 2.2. Further Search Topics: Magic, Optical Illusions, Puzzles.

Charosh, Mannis. Mathematical games for one or two; illus by Lois Ehlert. T Y Crowell 1975, 33 pp.

It will take a very special reader to appreciate this book, one who is excited by math puzzles and games and who is also willing to overlook the book's picture book format. Starting with a very simple, one-player game, the book progresses through six types of games, each progressively more taxing mentally. Each type of game is introduced by a very simple example that is thoroughly explained. For the up-and-coming Einstein.

Interest Level: 3-4. Reading Level: 2.2. Further Search Topics: Mathematics, Puzzles, Games.

LeSieg, Theo. Wacky Wednesday; illus by George Booth. Beginner 1974, unp (36 pp).

A series of true picture puzzles. A little boy wakes up one Wednesday to find everything around him has gone "wacky." People are missing heads but have extra legs. Cars are being driven from the back seat. Doors are placed in the wrong places. Airplanes fly backwards. At the end of the day everything settles back to normal, but not before readers have had fun finding the numerous "wacky" things on each page.

The story is told in silly rhyme (LeSieg and Seuss are the same person). What is wrong with each picture is not always easily located, making this reader an excellent excerise in observation as well as great fun.

Interest Level: 1-3. Reading Level: 1.2. Further Search Topics: Puzzles, Humorous Fiction, Wit and Humor, Poetry, Best Sellers.

Simon, Seymour. Einstein Anderson makes up for lost time; illus by Fred Winkowski. Viking Pr 1981, 73 pp.

Adam (nicknamed Einstein) Anderson loves science. He also loves bad puns and correcting wrongs. What he does best, however, is to figure out science puzzles. Each book in this series (this is the third) presents 10 science puzzles which challenge Einstein and the reader. Clues and background are established in several pages of scene setting. Einstein regularly solves the puzzle and then the reader is asked how he did it. The answer follows on the next page. Areas of science that are drawn upon vary widely and range from animal behavior through chemistry and space science to zoology. Very palatable science reading. Print is on the small side in all four books.

Interest Level: 3-6. Reading Level: 2.2. Further Search Topics: Science, Puzzles, Mystery and Detective Stories.

Simon, Seymour. Einstein Anderson, science sleuth; illus by Fred Winkowski. Viking Pr 1980, 73 pp.

Einstein Anderson is the scientific equivalent of Encyclopedia Brown. Einstein was the nickname that Adam Anderson earned at the age of six. Even at that early age he was a scientific genius. He seems to especially love solving scientific puzzles and mysteries and that is just what Einstein does throughout this and the other books. There are ten very brief, somewhat plotless cases that are presented to Einstein. The clues are all included in each story. The solutions are supplied at the end of each case after the reader has had a chance to try to figure out the answers. None of the cases or solutions are terribly technical. Some of the cases can be solved simply by paying careful attention to the text. The rest require a moderate knowledge of scientific principles. It is a satisfying series to the science sleuth. Print is somewhat small.

Interest Level: 3-6. Reading Level: 3.1. Further Search Topics: Mystery and Detective Stories, Science, Puzzles.

Simon, Seymour. Einstein Anderson shocks his friends; illus by Fred Winkowski. Viking Pr 1980, 73 pp.

Using the identical formula as that in *Einstein Anderson, Science Sleuth* the author presents 10 more science puzzles to be solved by the reader. Einstein (nee Adam) outwits a bully, discovers who broke the window on the school bus, helps the sixth grade win contests against both the seventh and the eighth grades and more. This book, as well as the others in the series, is both fun and instructive.

Interest Level: 3-6. Reading Level: 3.1. Further Search Topics: Science, Puzzles, Mystery and Detective Stories.

Simon, Seymour. Einstein Anderson tells a comet's tale; illus by Fred Winkowski. Viking Pr 1981, 73 pp.

Adam earned his nickname Einstein by proving over and over again that he could solve any science puzzle put to him. Ten more challenges are presented here, none of which prove to be too much for our scientific whiz kid. Like its predecessors, this book is for science sleuths who enjoy matching wits with a cocky punster.

Interest Level: 3-6. Reading Level: 3.1. Further Search Topics: Science, Puzzles, Mystery and Detective Stories.

Sobol, Donald J. Encyclopedia Brown, boy detective; illus by Leonard Shortall. Elsevier-Nelson 1963, 88 pp.

The first of a large number of books that challenge the reader to solve the same mysteries Encyclopedia Brown deciphers. See *Encyclopedia Brown and the Case of the Dead Eagles* for more information.

Interest Level: 2-6. Reading Level: 2.2. Further Search Topics: Mystery and Detective Stories, Puzzles, Best Sellers, Detectives-Fiction.

Sobol, Donald J. Encyclopedia Brown and the case of the dead eagles; illus by Leonard Shortall. Elsevier-Nelson 1975, 96 pp.

By all rights Idaville should be declared a disaster area and Mr. Brown, the chief of police, should be fired from his job. Idaville looks like an ordinary small town, but behind its sleepy exterior there exists a crime wave that would challenge the best police departments in the country. It is true that the crimes are always solved and the criminals always caught, but not by Chief Brown. Chief Brown is frequently so stumped by his police cases that he talks about them at home, usually at dinner time. Almost always, his son, Leroy "Encyclopedia" Brown, solves the case before dinner is even over. A clear case of superior intelligence and skill.

Encyclopedia (so nicknamed because of his intellect) not only solves his father's cases, but serves as a detective for his friends, too. He is kept so busy that each slim volume in this series contains 10 short mysteries. Needless to say Encyclopedia solves them all. The question is can the reader? All necessary clues are there and specialized knowledge is rarely required. Should the reader fail to solve a mystery (they are not always as easy as one would expect), a full explanation and solution for each case is provided at the back of the book. Each title follows exactly the same formula. Although a teacher or parent may grow bored hearing of Encyclopedia's accomplishments, most young readers thoroughly enjoy them.

The books actively challenge and thus involve the reader in a way most books do not. A very popular series that does not have to be read in sequence. Reading level is consistently 2.2 to 3.1. Encyclopedia Brown series.

Interest Level: 2-6. Reading Level: 3.1. Further Search Topics: Mystery and Detective Stories, Puzzles, Best Sellers, Group 2, Detectives-Fiction.

Sobol, Donald J. Encyclopedia Brown and the case of the midnight visitor; illus by Lillian Brandi. Elsevier-Nelson 1977, 96 pp.

See *Encyclopedia Brown and the Case of the Dead Eagles* for full annotation.

Interest Level: 2-6. Reading Level: 2.2. Further Search Topics: Mystery and Detective Stories, Puzzles, Detectives-Fiction, Best Sellers.

Sobol, Donald J. Encyclopedia Brown and the case of the secret pitch; illus by Leonard Shortall. Elsevier-Nelson 1965, 96 pp.

See *Encyclopedia Brown and the Case of the Dead Eagles* for full annotation.

Interest Level: 2-6. Reading Level: 3.1. Further Search Topics: Group 2, Mystery and Detective Stories, Puzzles, Best Sellers, Detectives-Fiction.

Sobol, Donald J. Encyclopedia Brown finds the clues; illus by Leonard Shortall. Elsevier-Nelson 1966, 96 pp.

See *Encyclopedia Brown and the Case of the Dead Eagles* for full annotation.

Interest Level 2-6. Reading Level: 3.1. Further Search Topics: Mystery and Detective Stories, Puzzles, Detectives-Fiction, Best Sellers, Group 2.

Sobol, Donald J. Encyclopedia Brown gets his man; illus by Leonard Shortall. Elsevier-Nelson 1967, 96 pp.

See *Encyclopedia Brown and the Case of the Dead Eagles* for full annotation.

Interest Level: 2-6. Reading Level: 3.1. Further Search Topics: Mystery and Detective Stories, Puzzles, Best Sellers, Group 2, Detectives-Fiction.

Sobol, Donald J. Encyclopedia Brown keeps the peace; illus by Leonard Shortall. Elsevier-Nelson 1969, 96 pp.

See *Encyclopedia Brown and the Case of the Dead Eagles* for full annotation.

Interest Level: 2-6. Reading Level: 2.2. Further Search Topics: Mystery and Detective Stories, Puzzles, Best Sellers, Detectives-Fiction.

Sobol, Donald J. Encyclopedia Brown lends a hand; illus by Leonard Shortall. Elsevier-Nelson 1974, 96 pp.

See *Encyclopedia Brown and the Case of the Dead Eagles* for full annotation.

Interest Level: 2-6. Reading Level: 3.1. Further Search Topics: Mystery and Detective Stories, Puzzles, Detectives-Fiction, Best Sellers, Group 2.

Sobol, Donald J. Encyclopedia Brown saves the day; illus by Leonard Shortall. Elsevier-Nelson 1970, 96 pp.

See *Encyclopedia Brown and the Case of the Dead Eagles* for full annotation.

Interest Level: 2-6. Reading Level: 2.2. Further Search Topics: Mystery and Detective Stories, Puzzles, Detectives-Fiction, Best Sellers.

Sobol, Donald J. Encyclopedia Brown shows the way; illus by Leonard Shortall. Elsevier-Nelson 1972, 96 pp.

See *Encyclopedia Brown and the Case of the Dead Eagles* for full annotation.

Interest Level: 2-6. Reading Level: 2.2. Further Search Topics: Mystery and Detective Stories, Puzzles, Detectives-Fiction, Best Sellers.

Sobol, Donald J. Encyclopedia Brown solves them all; illus by Leonard Shortall. Elsevier-Nelson 1968, 96 pp.

See *Encyclopedia Brown and the Case of the Dead Eagles* for full annotation.

Interest Level: 2-6. Reading Level: 3.1. Further Search Topics: Mystery and Detective Stories, Puzzles, Detectives-Fiction, Group 2, Best Sellers.

Sobol, Donald J. Encyclopedia Brown sets the pace; illus by Ib Ohlsson. Four Winds Pr 1982, 89 pp.

See *Encyclopedia Brown and the Case of the Dead Eagles* for full annotation.

Interest Level: 2-6. Reading Level: 3.1. Further Search Topics: Mystery and Detective Stories, Detectives-Fiction, Puzzles, Group 2, Best Sellers.

Sobol, Donald J. Encyclopedia Brown carries on; illus by Ib Ohlsson. Schol Bk Serv 1980, 72 pp.

See *Encyclopedia Brown and the Case of the Dead Eagle* for full annotation.

Interest Level: 2-6. Reading Level: 3.1. Further Search Topics: Mystery and Detective Stories, Puzzles, Detectives-Fiction, Group 2, Best Sellers.

White, Laurence B., Jr. Science puzzles; illus by Marc Tolon Brown. A-W 1975, unp (46 pp).

There are twenty four very short experiments designed to illustrate the simplest of scientific principles clearly presented here. For all but a few experiments there is not only an explanation of what happens but also an explanation of why it happened. What makes the book even more useful, is that it can also be used as a book of easy magic tricks. Any child who enjoys it as science will, with a little help, be able to see its possibilities as magic. In fact it provides a better explanation of the Knot Magic trick than can be found in *It's Magic*.

Interest Level: 1-3. Reading Level: 1.2. Further Search Topics: Science, Magic, Puzzles, Experiments, Scientific.

White, Laurence B., Jr. Science toys; illus by Marc Tolon Brown. A-W 1975, unp (46 pp).

This book presents 23 toys that a young child can easily make and learn from at the same time. A sundial, a drinking straw that flies, a balloon that rolls over, a ghost that sticks to the wall by itself, a water-go-round, and a paper cup that roars are a few examples of what is to be found here. The construction and use of each toy is explained and illustrated in enough detail to enable the child to work alone. And as in *Science Puzzles*, some of the toys will double as magic tricks (i.e. can you balance the rim of a paper plate on your nose?).

Interest Level: 1-3. Reading Level: 2.1. Further Search Topics: Handicrafts, Science, Magic, Toys, Games, Group 2, Puzzles.

QUECHAN INDIANS

Baylor, Byrd. And it is still that way: legends told by Arizona Indian children. Scribner 1976, 85 pp.

Byrd Baylor has collected and written notes for forty-one short American Indian legends from seven Arizona tribes whose school children were asked to write down or illustrate their favorite legend. The result is a collection that reflects the concerns, the history, religion, humor and pride of the children and their ancestors. This excellent collection is not only interesting reading, but it also fits well into social studies and language arts units.

Interest Level: 2-6. Reading Level: 3.1. Further Search Topics: Legends, Arizona-Fiction, Navajo Indians, Hopi Indians, Papago Indians, Pima Indians, Apache Indians, Quechan Indians, Cocopah Indians, Indians of North America-Legends, Mythology, Group 2.

RABBITS-FICTION

Hildick, Edmund W. The great rabbit rip-off; illus by Lisl Weil. Macmillan 1976, 101 pp.

Why would anyone want to put red paint on all of the clay lawn rabbits in town? That was the first and easier of the mysteries the McGurk Organization had to solve. The bigger mystery was who would then steal them all and why? Almost everyone in town had purchased a rabbit to help a charity drive. Donny Towers a local social worker had thought of the idea. Donny, his fiancee, Joanne, and two reformed thieves, Sam and Ferdie, had made enough rabbits for everyone. When the rabbits disappeared, the Organization began to suspect, among others, Sam and Ferdie. Then when Donny replaced each one almost immediately with rabbits smelling of paint remover, the group began to think Donny might have been involved. It was Wanda's sharp eyes that revealed Donny's motive. Joanne's engagement ring had been accidentally molded into one of the rabbits and Donny had retrieved the rabbits to find the ring. Knowing he couldn't return the paint stained rabbits without raising suspicion, Donny had removed the red paint and told everyone that he was simply replacing the stolen rabbits with new ones.

See *Case of the Bashful Bank Robber* for series information. McGurk Mystery series.

Interest Level: 3-5. Reading Level: 2.2. Further Search Topics: Mystery and Detective Stories, Detectives-Fiction, Gangs-Fiction, Rabbits-Fiction, Crime-Fiction, Humorous Fiction.

Parish, Peggy. Too many rabbits; illus by Leonard Kessler. Macmillan 1974, 48 pp.

One day Miss Molly opened her front door to find a rabbit waiting to be invited inside. The next day Miss Molly discovered the rabbit had had baby rabbits, lots of baby rabbits. Because babies need care, Miss Molly couldn't just turn them out, so she kept them all. Before long she had more rabbits than she could handle. She tried giving them away, but all the children's mothers refused to keep them, the zoo didn't need any, and Miss Molly didn't want to sell them to the butcher. Finally a man who owned an island where they could live, asked to take all the rabbits. As Miss Molly was about to close the door after giving the rabbits to the man with an island, a cat walked right up to her and inside her house. The next day Miss Molly discovered she had kittens—lots of kittens. A very humorous story in a reader format.

Interest Level: 1-3. Reading Level: 1.2. Further Search Topics: Humorous Fiction, Rabbits-Fiction, Best Sellers.

RACCOONS-FICTION

Renner, Beverly. The Hideaway summer; illus by Ruth Sanderson. Har-Row 1978, 134 pp.

On their way to summer camp, Addie suddenly got off the bus and took her younger brother Clay to see the place where Addie had spent prior summer vacations. It was their grandmother's house and a small cabin called the Hideaway. The house had been sold after their grandmother had died that year, but Addie's father had decided to keep the Hideaway. Much to Addie's surprise she found the Hideaway beautifully fixed-up, just as Gram had promised she would do one day.

When they missed the last bus out of the tiny town and realized that they had enough money to buy the food they would need, Addie and Clay decided to make the Hideaway their summer home. One phone call to the camp and weekly calls to their father kept people from worrying about them. Their discovery of two small raccoons meant that their days were filled with caring for and training the animals. In addition, they had to build a warning system so that no one would discover them and they had to get their food and provisions from town about every two weeks without being too noticeable. They even had to figure out a way to survive a wild summer storm, a flood, and poachers who hunted raccoons. By summer's end Addie and Clay had grown independent, resourceful, and very close to each other.

An exciting story whose short chapters and fairly short sentences keep the reading level reasonably low. Print is dark and of adequate size, but space between the lines is somewhat narrow.

Interest Level: 4-6. Reading Level: 3.1. Further Search Topics: Brothers and Sisters-Fiction, Runaways-Fiction, Pets-Fiction, Survival-Fiction, Vacation-Fiction, Raccoons-Fiction, Read Aloud.

READ ALOUD

Angell, Judie. Dear Lola; or how to build your own family. Bradbury 1980, 166 pp.

Arthur (age 18), James (13), Annie and Al-Willie (twins, age 10), Edmund (9), and Ben (5) wanted to run away from the orphanage and find a place where they could be a real family. After waiting months, their chance arrived one night. They escaped in a van and began living on the road. It was weeks before they found a house in which they thought they could live. They didn't want trouble with local authorities, so most of the children enrolled in school and pretended to be living with their widowed grandfather. Only James (who never left his room) and Arthur stayed home. Arthur was the anonymous author of a nationally syndicated newspaper advice column. It was with the income from his "Dear Lola" column that Arthur was able to support the "family." When the townspeople eventually began to wonder about the "strange" behavior of the children, they investigated and found no adult in charge of the household. Arthur went to court to be appointed the childrens' guardian, but the judge ruled against him. Rather than be sent to foster homes again, Arthur and the children raced from the courtroom. The book ends as the family is once more together and on their own. An unusual cast of characters in a surprisingly warm and humorous book.

Interest Level: 4-6. Reading Level 3.1. Further Search Topics: Loners-Fiction, Runaways-Fiction, Orphans-Fiction, Survival-Fiction, Family Problems-Fiction, Family-Fiction, Read Aloud, Foster Homes-Fiction, Individualists-Fiction, Humorous Fiction.

Arkhurst, Joyce. The adventures of Spider; West African folktales; illus by Jerry Pinkney. Little 1964, 58 pp.

A delightful collection of six West African folktales about Spider. Spider is mischievous, greedy, lazy and clever. He loves to eat and he hates to work. Four of the stories tell of Spider's ill-fated attempts to get food without having to work for it ("How Spider Got a Thin Waist," "How Spider Got a Bald Head," "How Spider Helped a Fisherman," and "Why Spiders Live in Dark Corners"). One story tells of his greed ("How the World Got Wisdom"), and only one story is complimentary ("Why Spider Lives in Ceilings"). All are short, gentle, humorous, and adapt well to dramatization or retelling.

Interest Level: 2-6. Reading Level 3.1. Further Search Topics: Humorous Fiction, Spiders-Fiction, Folklore, Tricksters-Fiction, Africa-Folklore, Group 2, Read Aloud, Creation-Fiction, Drama.

Avi. No more magic. Pantheon 1975, 138 pp.

Avi has woven a mixture of mystery and magic to produce an excellent story. Chris' belief in magic is bolstered when his new bicycle disappears on Halloween night. Chris, his best friend Eddie, and a new friend, Muffin, eventually decide that strange Mr. Bullen, the junk dealer, has magical powers. In order to keep his powers a secret, Mr. Bullen had to steal back the magical bike he sold Chris. With plenty of intriguing complications along the way, the three children attempt to prove their theory correct but only prove themselves wrong. The age of the protagonists (fourth grade) is touched on so lightly and the plot is interesting enough that even sixth grade readers should find the book enjoyable.

Interest Level: 3-6. Reading Level: 4.2. Further Search Topics: Divorce and Separation-Fiction, Mystery and Detective Stories, Magic-Fiction, Halloween-Fiction, Witches-Fiction, Group 2, Read Aloud, Bicycles and Bicycling-Fiction.

Berends, Polly Berrien. The case of the elevator duck; illus by James K. Washburn. Random 1973, 54 pp.

Although it would be stretching the meaning of the word to call this a mystery, it is a story of an 11-year-old detective. Albert tells his own story in a clipped style that resembles adult detective novels. One morning Albert found a duck abandoned in the apartment house elevator. He was determined to find the owner of the duck and return it. He had to be very careful as he searched because pets were absolutely forbidden in the housing projects. Anyone who saw him with the duck might report him. Albert and his parents had waited too long to get into the projects to be kicked out because of a duck. When Albert finally found the duck's owner (a young, sad child named Julio), Julio's sister forced Albert to take the duck back. Still angry at Julio's sister, Albert took the duck to the project's day care center, where the teacher agreed to formally adopt the duck. Albert stayed at the center long enough to see Julio's happy surprise when he arrived and found the duck. Its appealing characters, the tension created by the writing style, and the book's humor make this a delightful story.

Interest Level: 2-5. Reading Level 2.2. Further Search Topics: Humorous Fiction, City Life-Fiction, Housing Projects-Fiction, Detectives-Fiction, Pets-Fiction, Ducks-Fiction, Read Aloud.

Blume, Judy. Blubber. Bradbury 1974, 153 pp.

Jill, like all the other fifth graders in her class, did exactly as Wendy directed her. When Wendy nicknamed one of the class members Blubber and launched a campaign against her, Jill joined right in. It wasn't until the tables were turned and Jill became Wendy's next victim that Jill realized how much it hurt to be the target of such nastiness. It was only then that Jill could stand up to Wendy. Wendy's meanness is extreme and her classmates, without exception, actively follow her lead, yet all adult characters in the book are blind to what happens. Despite those drawbacks, the book deals with a problem very real to children and thus it has guaranteed audience appeal.

Interest Level: 4-6. Reading Level: 3.1. School Stories, Bullies-Fiction, Weight-Fiction, Loners-Fiction, Gangs-Fiction, Read Aloud, Cruelty-Fiction, Best Sellers, Troublemakers-Fiction, Friendship-Fiction.

Blume, Judy. Tales of a fourth grade nothing; illus by Roy Doty. Dutton 1972, 120 pp.

Another humorous Blume book that can be counted on to appeal to third and fourth grade readers. If fifth and sixth graders can ignore the title's reference to fourth grade, they too will love it. The story is an exaggeration of a common theme—an older child whose life is in continual turmoil because of a somewhat spoiled younger sibling. Peter's problems with three-year-old Fudge become worse with each chapter until the final disaster when Fudge swallows Peter's pet turtle. Each approximately 15-page chapter is a complete, very funny episode.

Interest Level: 3-6. Reading Level 3.1. Further Search Topics: Humorous Fiction, Turtles-Fiction, Brothers and Sisters-Fiction, Pets-Fiction, Family-Fiction, Read Aloud, Best Sellers, Everyday Stories, Troublemakers-Fiction.

Blume, Judy. Freckle juice; illus by Sonia O. Lisker. Four Winds 1971, 40 pp.

A very funny story that should appeal to almost everyone. Andrew wanted freckles so that the dirt on his skin wouldn't show as much and he wouldn't have to wash as often. As luck would have it, Sharon, the most obnoxious girl in class, had a freckle juice recipe that she was willing to sell for 50 cents. Even after drinking the brew of grape juice, vinegar, mustard, olive oil, and more, Andrew didn't see any freckles, but, he certainly was sick. Although the protagonists are younger, this book will hold even a fifth grade reader's interest.

Interest Level: 2-5. Reading Level 3.1. Further Search Topics: Humorous Fiction, Group 2, Read Aloud, Everyday Stories, Beauty-Fiction, School Stories, Magic-Fiction, Best Sellers.

Bulla, Clyde Robert. Dexter; illus by Glo Coalson. Har-Row 1973, 69 pp.

This is not as simple a story as it first appears. Dave, 12 years old and lonely, had hoped his new neighbors would be friends. But, the Arvin family kept very much to themselves until Dave accidentally discovered Alex, the Arvin's son, doing tricks on a trapeze in the barn. Because Dave kept the secret and shared Alex's love for Dexter, his circus pony, the boys soon became friends. Then in one horrible night, the Arvins were forced to leave the town and Dexter was so badly hurt he was believed to be dead. A week later Dave found Dexter alive, but crippled for life and so frightened that no one could get near him. The horse surprised everyone and managed to live through a very harsh winter as well as the townspeople's determination to kill him. When Alex and his father returned, almost a year later, they found Dexter and took the old and feeble horse back to a ranch with them. The story is told with sympathy, with an understanding of how it feels to be lonely, and with tension and suspense. It's appeal should last from third through sixth grade. Print size is smaller than Bulla's usual.

Interest Level: 3-6. Reading Level: 3.1. Further Search Topics: Survival-Fiction, Acrobats and Acrobatics-Fiction, Horses-Fiction, Read Aloud, Circus-Fiction, Loneliness-Fiction, Friendship-Fiction.

Bulla, Clyde Robert. My friend the monster; illus by Michele Chessare. Har-Row 1980, 75 pp.

Even though Hal was plain and not very clever, his disappointed parents knew that he was still a prince; thus he had to be raised as one. Hal didn't like his lonely, dull life until a new world was accidentally opened to him. A servant's child gave him an old book of monsters and told him that the monsters still lived under the distant mountains. Hal finally made a trip to the mountains, spent a day exploring, and by chance met Humbert, a young monster curious about the world. But, Hal's cruel cousin Archer captured Humbert and put him in a cage. Hal's daring rescue attempt almost resulted in disaster for both Humbert and Hal.

This is another example of Bulla's forte; a book with an action-filled plot, short chapters, large print, wide spaces between the lines, and a low reading level. A book about monsters has almost guaranteed appeal through third grade. Although the book is useful beyond third grade, readers in fourth and fifth grade may be more sensitive to Hal's apparent youth and the fantastic elements of the story.

Interest Level: 1-3. Reading Level: 2.1. Further Search Topics: Fantasy, Monsters-Fiction, Royalty-Fiction, Group 2, Read Aloud, Best Sellers.

Burch, Robert. Queenie Peavy; illus by Jerry Lazare. Viking Pr. 1966, 159 pp.

Queenie was always in trouble. She could be mean, really mean, but, she was also bright, talented, independent and resilient. Queenie blamed her problems on the fact that people teased her because her father was in jail and because she was poor. She thought that she had to defend herself against the world. Queenie was proud of her poor reputation until she accidentally-on-purpose caused a classmate to break his leg. Then, when her father returned home and wasn't the person she'd hoped he'd be, Queenie realized that only she could make her life better. Being the strong person she was, she set out to do just that.

Queenie is a wonderfully alive and sympathetic character, one well worth introducing to older readers despite the book's reading level. Print somewhat small. Line spacing average width.

Interest Level: 5-6. Reading Level: 5.1. Further Search Topics: Family Problems-Fiction, Crime-Fiction, Loners-Fiction, Poverty-Fiction, Humorous Fiction, Bullies-Fiction, Troublemakers-Fiction, Academic Problems-Fiction, Read Aloud.

Byars, Betsy. The Cybil war; illus by Gail Owens. Viking Pr. 1981, 126 pp.

Simon and Tony both had a crush on Cybil, but according to Tony, Cybil liked Tony better than she liked Simon. Simon was unhappily willing to accept Tony's word even though he knew Tony was a chronic liar. After all, Cybil had been the one to talk their teacher out of giving the lead in the class play about nutrition to Simon. Consequently Simon was being forced to impersonate a jar of peanut butter. In an elaborate attempt to win Cybil's affection Tony began telling Cybil lies about Simon and then set up a double date with Cybil and Harriet. On their walk home, Simon learned from Harriet that Cybil had only agreed to the date because Simon was going along. Happy at last, Simon realized he wanted no more lies and tricks; that he wanted to be truthful with Cybil and with himself. In the name of truth, he was even willing to accept the fact that his father, who had deserted the family, would not be returning.

A good story with just enough humor and romance to make it widely appealing as either a shared book (read aloud) or a personal pick. Print is fairly small.

Interest Level: 5-6. Reading Level: 4.2. Further Search Topics: Humorous Fiction, Love-Fiction, School Stories, Honesty-Fiction, Friendship-Fiction, Single Parent Family-Fiction, Read Aloud, Everyday Stories, Adolescence-Fiction.

Byars, Betsy. The 18th emergency; illus by Robert Grossman. Viking Pr. 1973, 126 pp.

When your best friend knows how to escape from the world's 17 worst emergencies and you're faced with the eighteenth, you're in trouble. That was the spot in which Mouse found himself one day. He had drawn an arrow towards a large picture of the Neanderthal man and written Marv Hammerman's name. Hammerman had seen him do it and was out to kill, maim, or at least beat up Mouse. Mouse finally ran out of ways to avoid Hammerman and had to face the fight. When it was over and he was once again able to stand up, Mouse realized he felt better for having allowed Hammerman to regain his honor and for having taken responsibility for his own actions.

A funny, fast-moving look at real feelings of fear, honor and responsibility. Very popular. Print is dark and of good size but lines could have been spaced farther apart.

Interest Level: 4-6. Reading Level: 3.2. Further Search Topics: Bullies-Fiction, Humorous Fiction, Courage-Fiction, Best Sellers, Challenges-Fiction, Read Aloud.

Byars, Betsy. Trouble River; illus by Rocco Negri. Viking Pr. 1969, 158 pp.

A gripping adventure story of survival. After being attacked by an Indian in the middle of the night, Dewey and his grandmother rushed to Trouble River to board a small raft which Dewey had just finished making. They thought they would only need to navigate a few miles down the river to safety at a neighbor's home, but found instead that the neighbor's cabin had been burned down. For almost 40 miles they fought against the unknown river, wolves and rapids.

This is a book that should satisfy many reluctant readers. It's frequent dialogue, fast action and high interest are only occasionally marred by an overly long sentence.

Interest Level: 3-6. Reading Level: 3.1. Further Search Topics: Courage-Fiction, Frontier and Pioneer Life-Fiction, Survival-Fiction, Grandparents-Fiction, Voyages and Travels-Fiction, Best Sellers, Read Aloud.

Cleary, Beverly. Henry Huggins; illus by Louis Darling. Morrow 1950, 155 pp.

Henry Huggins is over 30 years old now, so if he occasionally seems a little old-fashioned, it is not surprising. What is surprising is how well he has withstood the years. His antics are innocent, but humorous and realistic. The book's six chapters are six separate stories that follow the same cast of characters through an entire year.

In the first chapter, Henry finds a stray dog (Ribsy) whom he must then transport home on a bus. Ribsy was too large and too frisky not to get into trouble, so before Henry finally gets him home, they have been kicked off of three buses and have ridden in a police car. The second chapter describes what happens when Henry buys two guppies and ends up with millions. In the third chapter Henry accidentally throws his friend's football into the back seat of a speeding car and tries to earn the money to replace it by catching and selling 1,331 night crawlers. The fourth chapter involves Henry's attempts to get out of playing the lead in a school Christmas play. His last minute rescue comes in the form of a can of green paint that spills all over him. It is Ribsy's turn to change colors in Chapter 5. Henry tries to cover Ribsy's dirt spots with talcolm powder for a dog show, but only succeeds in turning Ribsy pink. And in Chapter 6, Ribsy's original

owner finally finds him and wants him back, but Ribsy chooses to stay with Henry. Only the occasional extra cute expression and Henry's age (third grade) keep this from being enjoyed beyond fourth grade.

Interest Level: 1-4. Reading Level: 2.2. Further Search Topics: Humorous Fiction, Everyday Stories, Read Aloud Pets-Fiction, Dogs-Fiction, Group 2.

Cleary, Beverly. Otis Spofford; illus by Louis Darling. Morrow 1953, 191 pp.

Here are six separate humorous adventures that link together, but can be read separately and out of order. Otis' favorite activity was "stirring up a little excitement," but his definition of excitement usually meant trouble. The school fiesta turned into a disaster when Otis decided to rechoreograph the bullfight and make the bull win. His attempt to liven up the reading lesson about Indians meant he almost scalped a classmate. However, a wild day at the skating pond finally gave everyone a chance to take revenge for all the things Otis had done to them. The remaining three chapters (2, 3 and 4) are slightly less exciting, but useful if a reader has enjoyed the others. There is much humor in Otis' antics and his tendency to act on every thought that comes to mind is one many readers can appreciate.

Interest Level: 2-6. Reading Level: 5.1. Further Search Topics: Troublemakers-Fiction, Group 2, Read Aloud, Everyday Stories, Humorous Fiction, School Stories.

Cleary, Beverly. Henry and Beezus; illus by Louis Darling. Morrow 1952, 192 pp.

When Henry's dog Ribsy stole the meat from a neighbor's barbecue, a friend rode after Ribsy on his bike and saved the meat. Henry was so embarrassed and jealous that he boasted about an even nicer bike that he was going to get. At first Henry thought he'd be able to earn money to buy a bike in a very short time (he found 49 boxes of bubble gum that he could sell). When that scheme fell through, Henry tried taking over a friend's paper route, but Ribsy kept retrieving the newspapers Henry delivered. Eventually Henry decided to buy a used bike at the police department auction. Beezus, who made a bid for Henry, ended up buying him a beaten-up girl's bike that was hardly worth fixing. The money finally appeared when Henry least expected it; he won $50.00 worth of work at a beauty salon.

Although all seven chapters continue the same story, Chapters 1, 2, 3 and 7, can each stand alone. Henry is definitely old-fashioned, but children still enjoy his humorous escapades and empathize with his desire for a bicycle. The revised paperback cover makes the book's physical appearance less dated. Reading level is somewhat inconsistent: from 2.2 to 3.2.

Interest Level: 2-5. Reading Level: 3.1. Further Search Topics: Humorous Fiction, Occupations-Fiction, Everyday Stories, Bicycles and Bicycling-Fiction, Read Aloud, Group 2.

Clymer, Eleanor. Luke was there; illus by Diane de Groat. HR & W 1973, 74 pp.

Julius' father, uncle and finally his step-father had all walked out on him. Even his mother had left him, although she hadn't wanted to go. When his mother had been taken to the hospital, Julius and his younger brother Danny were sent to a children's home. Julius felt alone and cheated until he met a young, black, social worker named Luke. Luke liked and respected Julius and helped Julius learn to feel the same way about himself. When Luke, too, left Julius, Julius was so angry at the world that he stole food and then money. Afraid to go back to the children's home because he thought he'd be caught and punished, Julius ran away. It wasn't until he found an abandoned child, about Danny's age, who needed care, that Julius returned to the home. Luke was there when he arrived, just when Julius needed him most. Luke listened to Julius' unhappy feelings, arranged for him to see his mother and helped him begin to accept the fact that life is not always fair.

Julius tells his own story in a realistic, straight-forward book that will touch most readers. Only the lack of quotation marks and inadequate spacing between the lines may slow the reader.

Interest Level: 3-6. Reading Level: 2.2. Further Search Topics: Runaways-Fiction, Orphans-Fiction, Juvenile Delinquency-Fiction, Divorce and Separation-Fiction, Friendship-Fiction, Courage-Fiction, Survival-Fiction, Loneliness-Fiction, Best Sellers, Read Aloud.

Coerr, Eleanor. Sadako and the thousand paper cranes; illus by Ronand Himler. Putnam 1977, 64 pp.

This is a beautiful and very sad story of a young girl who was only two years old when the atomic bomb was dropped on Hiroshima. Ten years later she contracted leukemia and died a slow, painful death. A fast and enthusiastic runner, she had been full of life and energy before her illness. Soon after she became sick Sadako's best friend folded a paper crane for her and reminded her of an old story: If someone folded 1000 paper cranes, the gods would give that person good health again. Sadako was able to fold only 644 before she died. After her death her classmates made 356 more in order that she could be buried with all 1000 paper cranes. About three years later, a statue, erected in Peace Park in Hiroshima, was dedicated to Sadako and to a hope for world peace.

Because of the theme and its straight-forward handling, this book needs a fairly mature reader.

Interest Level: 4-6. Reading Level: 3.1. Further Search Topics: Japan-Fiction, Historical Fiction, World War II-Fiction, Death-Fiction, Illness-Fiction, War-Fiction, Running-Fiction, Origami-Fiction, Read Aloud.

Cohen, Barbara. The carp in the bathtub; illus by Joan Halpern. Lothrop 1972, 48 pp.

Leah and Harry couldn't face the prospect of seeing Joe, their pet carp, made into gefilte fish, even for such a special occasion as the Seder on the first night of Passover. The large, friendly carp had lived in the family's bathtub for over a week. It even swam right over to Leah and Harry to be fed everytime they went into the bathroom. At a time when most children in New York didn't have pets, Joe was as close to being a pet as possible. So, Leah and Harry hid Joe in a neighbor's apartment until their father discovered what they had done. When Joe's destiny was fulfilled, the children had to face a difficult fact of life. A week later, however, their despair became delight, when their father brought home a pet cat.

A short, warm and satisfying story.

Interest Level: 2-5. Reading Level: 3.1. Further Search Topics: Group 2, Jews-Fiction, Religion-Fiction, Pets-Fiction, Passover-Fiction, Family-Fiction, Holidays-Fiction, Read Aloud, Brothers and Sisters-Fiction.

Corbett, Scott. The lemonade trick; illus by Paul Galdone. Little 1960, 103 pp.

This is the first book in a series of quite enjoyable stories (most of which are, unfortunately, too difficult to recommend here). Kerby was given an odd chemistry set by a strange old woman whom he helped one day. When he used the set to put together a brew, Kerby found himself completely under its spell. The sweet-smelling liquid he had concocted forced him to be good, so good that his parents began to worry about him. Luckily the spell wore off in a short time. But, Kerby kept experimenting with it: on himself, on his dog, on his friend, on his enemy and finally in desperation, on the entire boy's choir at church.

A succession of innocently humorous incidents are woven together into a satisfying story. Print size is on the small side.

Interest Level: 3-6. Reading Level: 3.1. Further Search Topics: Humorous Fiction, Bullies-Fiction, Magic-Fiction, Magicians-Fiction, Chemistry-Fiction, Read Aloud.

Greene, Constance C. Isabelle the itch; illus by Emily A. McCully. Viking Pr. 1973, 126 pp.

This is a loosely plotted story about a spunky, original fifth grade girl who could drive everyone around her crazy without ever tiring. Isabelle's dearest dream was to win the 50-yard dash at her school's field day. Even though she took over her brother's paper route to earn money for the Adidas track shoes she needed, Isabelle still didn't win. However, she did meet some new people, make new friends and keep those around her on their toes. A very amusing story told mostly in dialogue.

Interest Level: 4-6. Reading Level: 3.2. Further Search Topics: School Stories, Occupations-Fiction, Humorous Fiction, Everyday Stories, Running-Fiction, Individualists-Fiction, Sex Role-Fiction, Read Aloud.

Hamilton, Virginia. Zeely; illus by Symeon Shimin. Macmillan 1967, 122 pp.

A beautiful, almost mystical story of a black girl who learns about self-identity and pride from a statuesque neighbor whom Geeder is convinced must be a Watutsi princess. At first by chance and later at an arranged meeting, Zeely (Geeder's neighbor) gently and symbolically speaks to Geeder of her racial origins. She also tells Geeder of a young girl (Zeely as a child), too ignorant of the world around her to be able to recognize reality. It is a quietly moving story that is most likely to find an appreciative audience in the thoughtful, more mature reader.

Interest Level: 5-6. Reading Level: 5.1. Further Search Topics: Africa-Fiction, Royalty-Fiction, Blacks-Fiction, Courage-Fiction, Vacation-Fiction, Country Life-Fiction, Read Aloud.

Hinton, Susan E. The outsiders. Viking Pr. 1967, 188 pp.

When she wrote this book Susan Hinton was only 17 years old, but she had the sensitivity of someone much older. She wrote a taut story of the rivalry between two city gangs; the Socs (the rich socialites) and the Greasers (poor kids from the wrong side of town) that is more than anything a plea for understanding and tolerance. Seen through the eyes of Ponyboy (a very bright, 14-year-old Greaser), the rivalry brought on violence and an accidental killing that forced Pony and his friend Johnny to flee for their lives. Dallas, the meanest and most dangerous of the Greasers, provided them with shelter, food for a week, and a gun. At the end of that week, Johnny decided that they should turn themselves in to the police. But before they could do that, their hideout (an old church) burned in a fire which threatened the lives of four children who had been playing there. In trying to rescue the children, Johnny, Pony, and Dallas were injured; Johnny was severely burned and probably permanently crippled. A vengeance rumble was held while Johnny lay in the hospital, but the Greasers' victory was empty when Johnny died. He had been the one member of the gang whom they all loved and who had most needed them. Dallas went to pieces: he robbed a store and set himself up to be killed by the police. He had nothing left to live for after Johnny's death. Pony found support and security with his brothers (their parents were dead) and, in a note from Johnny, some hope for the future.

Hinton speaks most often through Pony (his depth of understanding of the people around him is very impressive), but through Johnny and two of the Socs as well, Randy and Cherry. Her message is clear, but at no time does she fail to maintain believable characters in a compelling plot.

Although the book looks forbidding with its 188 pages of unrelenting small print, it is an exciting story, full of adventure, realism, and room for thought. Perhaps the best way to introduce this book is to read a fair portion of it aloud. Now a motion picture too.

Interest Level: 6+. Reading Level: 5.1. Further Search Topics: Crime-Fiction, Gangs-Fiction, Murder-Fiction, Read Aloud, Friendship-Fiction, Juvenile Delinquency-Fiction, Best Sellers, City Life-Fiction, Brothers and Sisters-Fiction, Orphans-Fiction, Runaways-Fiction, Troublemakers-Fiction, Poverty-Fiction.

Kibbe, Pat. The hocus-pocus dilemma; illus by Dan Jones. Knopf 1979, 125 pp.

Each chapter of this book is a separate episode in B.J.'s attempt to cultivate her newly-discovered ESP talents (more invented than discovered). The episodes, each of which involves a different member of B.J.'s family, are slightly outlandish, but very funny. Even the dog and the cat become involved. The dog becomes the unwitting target for a skunk. The cat accidentally starts a tape recording of speech habits that sounds like burglars breaking into the house. After nine disasters, B.J. finally concludes that she was being ridiculous to think that she had ESP, but that everyone is allowed to be ridiculous sometimes.

The nine, reasonably short episodes, the moderate size print, the sympathetic characters, and the book's humor, make this a very useful and popular title.

Interest Level: 4-6. Reading Level: 3.1. Further Search Topics: Extra Sensory Perception-Fiction, Humorous Fiction, Family-Fiction, Everyday Stories, Best Sellers, Read Aloud.

MacLachlan, Patricia. Arthur, for the very first time; illus by Lloyd Bloom. Har-Row 1980, 117 pp.

A beautifully written, sensitive yet humorous story of a boy's maturation and growing awareness of the world around him. When Arthur's unhappiness at home is made more intense by the advent of a new baby, he is sent to spend the summer with his older aunt and uncle. Their eccentricities and those of their friends are at first only material for Arthur to write about in his journal. But as the summer progresses he not only learns from them, but also grows from an observer of life to a participant. His final step is helping a large and beloved pig bear her litter in a driving rain storm aided only by his independent, totally untamed young friend Moira.

The print is somewhat small, but spacing between lines is generous.

Interest Level: 4-6. Reading Level: 4.2. Further Search Topics: Read Aloud, Children-Growth-Fiction, Humorous Fiction, Friendship-Fiction, Vacation-Fiction, Relatives-Fiction, Infants-Fiction, Individualists-Fiction, Writing-Fiction, Loners-Fiction, Group 2.

Madian, Jon. Beautiful junk: a story of the Watts Towers; photos by Barbara Jacobs, Jr. and Lou Jacobs, Jr. Little 1968, 44 pp.

Although this book is now out of print; it is well worth trying to find. It is a fictionalized account of a young, angry black boy's encounter with the creator of Los Angeles' unusual Watts Towers. Simon Rodia, a poor tile setter, worked on the towers for 33 years until he was 75 years old. He used only his imagination, discarded materials he found around him, seashells, and sand to build three tall, fantasy-like towers in the middle of a ghetto. He created beauty where others saw only junk.

The book is illustrated with photography that makes the story more vivid and the towers and Rodia's accomplishment more impressive than they would have seemed with drawings. The print is good-sized, spacing is totally adequate. Rodia's life is quickly submarized and an update on the Towers is included at the book's end.

Interest Level: 3-6. Reading Level: 3.1. Further Search Topics: Blacks-Fiction, Read Aloud, Best Sellers, Poverty-Fiction, Rodia, Simon, Architecture, Biography, Aging-Fiction, Watts Towers, California, Poverty.

Peck, Robert Newton. Mr. Little; illus by Ben Stahl. Doubleday 1979, 87 pp.

All summer long Drag and Finley had looked forward to having Miss Kellogg as their teacher, so they were extremely disappointed to find ordinary-looking Mr. Little in her place on the first day of school. Used to playing tricks on their teachers anyway, Drag and Finley decided to go all out to get even with Mr. Little for spoiling their year. But try as they might, they couldn't get an advantage over Mr. Little; he seemed to be unflappable. Finally, in their riskiest prank ever, they stole Mr. Little's underwear to dress a statue in the town square. That attempt to embarrass Mr. Little only served to get Finley and Drag in serious trouble from which Mr. Little saved them. It was his later rescue of Miss Kellogg, however, that added respect to the boys' growing feeling of friendship for Mr. Little.

Because the author's adult viewpoint is never quite lost, even though he writes in the first person, and because the rural and historic time settings are not familiar to many readers, the book may need some introduction and encouragement. It is a prime candidate for reading aloud until the young reader's interest takes over. Print is of adequate size, but spacing between lines could have been more generous.

Interest Level: 4-6. Reading Level: 5.1. Further Search Topics: Humorous Fiction, School Stories, Troublemakers-Fiction, Group 2, Read Aloud, Country Life-Fiction, Best Sellers.

Pene du Bois, William. Lazy Tommy Pumpkinhead. Har-Row 1966, 32 pp.

Tommy lived a solitary life in an all-electric house. An electric bed woke Tommy and slid him into a tub full of warm water. The tub then tipped him out and into a harness that held Tommy upright while other machines dried him, combed his hair, brushed his teeth, dressed him, and fed him. But one day Tommy's life was literally turned upside down with disastrous results. His feet were cleaned and combed and his clothes were all put on upside down, but the worst part of all was that Tommy almost starved; the machine fed his feet instead of his mouth.

A tongue-in-cheek warning against laziness. The lesson is obvious but the treatment (both text and illustrations) is so enjoyable that the book is appealing to almost any reader who wants a short, funny book. Print is somewhat small but spacing between lines is more than adequate.

Interest Level: 1-6. Reading Level: 3.2. Further Search Topics: Electricity-Fiction, Robots-Fiction, Laziness-Fiction, Humorous Fiction, Group 2, Read Aloud.

Pinkwater, Daniel Manus. The Hoboken chicken emergency. P-H 1977, 83 pp.

Arthur's mother sent him out with $16 to buy a Thanksgiving turkey. He returned with a live 266 pound chicken on a leash. It seemed that their turkey reservation had been lost at the meat market and, because it was Thanksgiving morning, there were no other turkeys available. Arthur searched everywhere but found nothing, until a strange old professor tricked him into buying the chicken. No one could bear to kill and eat such a large and friendly chicken, so Arthur and his family named it Henrietta and kept it as a pet. Henrietta was a difficult pet to keep hidden from the neighbors When the neighbors, and later the city, saw Henrietta running loose there was general hysteria. But all ended well when Henrietta and the city calmed down and Henrietta became a kind of neighborhood mascot.

A purely absurd plot but presented with enough energy and humor that most readers thoroughly enjoy the book. Some brief introduction may be necessary to get readers beyond the first few pages.

Interest Level: 3-6. Reading Level: 2.2. Further Search Topics: Humorous Fiction, Chickens-Fiction, Pets-Fiction, Thanksgiving-Fiction, Holidays-Fiction, Read Aloud, Best Sellers.

Renner, Beverly. The Hideaway summer; illus by Ruth Sanderson. Har-Row 1978, 134 pp.

On their way to summer camp, Addie suddenly got off the bus and took her younger brother Clay to see the place where Addie had spent prior summer vacations. It was their grandmother's house and a small cabin called the Hideaway. The house had been sold after their grandmother had died that year, but Addie's father had decided to keep the Hideaway. Much to Addie's surprise she found the Hideaway beautifully fixed-up, just as Gram had promised she would do one day.

When they missed the last bus out of the tiny town and realized that they had enough money to buy the food they would need, Addie and Clay decided to make the Hideaway their summer home. One phone call to the camp and weekly calls to their father kept people from worrying about them. Their discovery of two small raccoons meant that their days were filled with caring for and training the animals. In addition, they had to build a warning system so that no one would discover them and they had to get their food and provisions from town about every two weeks without being too noticeable. They even had to figure out a way to survive a wild summer storm, a flood, and poachers who hunted raccoons. By summer's end Addie and Clay had grown independent, resourceful, and very close to each other.

An exciting story whose short chapters and fairly short sentences keep the reading level reasonably low. Print is dark and of adequate size, but space between the lines is somewhat narrow.

Interest Level: 4-6. Reading Level: 3.1. Further Search Topics: Brothers and Sisters-Fiction, Runaways-Fiction, Pets-Fiction, Survival-Fiction, Vacation-Fiction, Raccoons-Fiction, Read Aloud.

Robinson, Barbara. The best Christmas pageant ever; illus by Judith Gwyn Brown. Har-Row 1972, 80 pp.

A truly delightful story of what happens when the meanest kids in town (they are all in one family) take over all the lead roles in the Sunday school Christmas pageant. The Herdmans (all six of them), having heard that the church was giving away free food, showed up to take some. While they were there, they heard about the Christmas pageant and decided it presented them with another perfect opportunity for food and mischief. With a little behind-the-scenes arm-twisting (literally), they managed to dissuade everyone else from showing interest in the major roles. Theirs was a completely original interpretation of the Christmas story that left nothing and no one around them untouched.

That the book's reading level will prove too high for many people is unfortunate. The story is well worth the struggle. A wonderful choice for reading aloud.

Interest Level: 3-6. Reading Level: 5.1 Further Search Topics: Christmas-Fiction, Bullies-Fiction, Troublemakers-Fiction, Humorous Fiction, Religion-Fiction, Group 2, Read Aloud, Acting-Fiction, Holidays-Fiction.

Robinson, Jean. The strange but wonderful cosmic awareness of Duffy Moon; illus by Lawrence Di Fiori. HM 1974, 142 pp.

Duffy was tired of being small, of always being on the losing side of fights, and of being unappreciated at home (by his ex-football star uncle). When he sent away for Mr. Flamel's Cosmic Awareness Kit, Duffy was sure he would then be able to take control over anything he wanted and direct his own life. His friend Peter, the narrator, wasn't quite so sure. Peter turned out to be right. Duffy almost made himself sick trying to build a stone wall. Babysitting two small boys and trying to bathe a Great Dane proved to be disastrous. But Duffy's biggest problem came from Boots McAfee's gang. A series of events finally brought Duffy and Peter face-to-face with the dreaded Boots. Luckily, she turned out to be a very smart girl who appreciated Duffy's true talents.

From the first to the last page this is a funny, very enjoyable book. A delightful book with a very palatable message.

Interest Level: 3-6. Reading Level: 3.2. Further Search Topics: Humorous Fiction, Bullies-Fiction, Magic-Fiction, Read Aloud, Occupations-Fiction, Sex Role-Fiction, Orphans-Fiction, Best Sellers, Gangs-Fiction, Courage-Fiction, Babysitting-Fiction.

Rockwell, Thomas. How to eat fried worms; illus by Emily McCully. Watts 1973, 116 pp.

It started more as a joke than anything else, but it escalated into a strange commitment. Alan bet Billy $50 that Billy couldn't eat a worm a day for fifteen days. Billy had always been willing to take almost any dare offered and he was stubborn enough to carry them out, but when he actually faced the first worm (an enormous night crawler), he almost backed down. He and his friend Tom had to keep repeating the word "minibike" (the prize he planned to buy with the money) and smother the worm in everything imaginable in order to eat it all. After the first worm, however, the next few were easier to face. That was when Alan and his ally Joe, began using psychological warfare and almost won. In 41 very short, grotesquely funny chapters Billy becomes the proud owner of a minibike and is the first person to become hooked on worm sandwiches.

Once this book is started, it is hard to resist its gruesome fascination. Although the print is somewhat small, and there are occasionally very difficult or babytalk words, the interest is strong enough to sustain almost all readers.

Interest Level: 3-6. Reading Level: 3.1. Further Search Topics: Humorous Fiction, Worms-Fiction, Read Aloud, Best Sellers, Challenges-Fiction, Food-Fiction, Bicycles and Bicycling-Fiction.

Silverstein, Shel. Where the sidewalk ends. Har-Row 1974, 166 pp.

There is something here for almost everyone. It isn't always easy reading, but there are enough short, easier poems to pique almost any child's interest. Once caught, children will find the book hard to put down. The best way to encourage the use of this book is to read selections aloud so that potential readers may hear the rhythm and enjoy the humor. This method almost guarantees that they will then want to try reading the book themselves. Readers may struggle with a poem but once it is mastered, they will usually want more.

Interest Level: 2-6. Reading Level: 3.1. Further Search Topics: Poetry, Wit and Humor, Read Aloud, Group 2, Best Sellers.

Silverstein, Shel. A light in the attic. Har-Row 1981, 169 pp.

This is the second and most recent collection of Shel Silverstein's wonderfully wry poetry. No young person who has read and enjoyed *Where the Sidewalk Ends* will be disappointed in this effort. For those readers new to Silverstein or to poetry in general, this is as good a place as any to start enjoying both. Hearing a few of these poems read aloud is guaranteed to provoke loud cries of "May I read some?" from almost all listeners.

Interest Level: 2-6. Reading Level: 3.2. Further Search Topics: Poetry, Wit and Humor, Best Sellers, Group 2, Read Aloud.

Slote, Alfred. My robot buddy; illus by Joel Schick. Lippincott 1975, 92 pp.

For Jack's tenth birthday he was given a robot—a robot so real it did everything but run like a human. The robot appeared so human that a thief, thinking he was stealing the robot, almost kidnapped Jack by mistake.

The few points at which the text becomes more difficult than the reading level indicates should not prove too intimidating to the reader. The suspense and humor of the story and the book's high interest subject matter should carry the reader through the rough spots. A satisfying read-aloud for second and third grades.

Interest Level: 2-5. Reading Level: 3.1. Further Search Topics: Science Fiction, Robots-Fiction, Friendship-Fiction, Kidnapping-Fiction, Read Aloud.

Smith, Doris Buchanan. A taste of blackberries; illus by Charles Robinson. T Y Crowell 1973, 58 pp.

A beautifully written, sensitive tale of a boy whose best friend dies suddenly. Jamie was always joking, so, when he fell to the ground after being stung by a bee everyone thought he was playing. A short time later Jamie was dead. His friend, the story's narrator, tried to will Jamie back again until the funeral was over and he finally realized there would be no such miracle. The next day he accepted his feelings and picked the newly ripened blackberries, just as he and Jamie had planned to do. A basket full of the best blackberries he gave to Jamie's mother and promised her that he would "slam her door" daily just as he and Jamie had done.

Eight short chapters, small print but short sentences, and a child's point of view perfectly maintained. For the lovers of sad stories and stories of friendship. Very useful when discussing death.

Interest Level: 4-6. Reading Level: 3.2. Further Search Topics: Death-Fiction, Friendship-Fiction, Read Aloud.

Viorst, Judith. The tenth good thing about Barney; illus by Erik Blegvad. Atheneum 1971, 25 pp.

A quiet, thoughtful book to help a child face the difficult experience of death. When a family's beloved cat Barney died, their little boy tried to find 10 good things to say about him at the funeral. Nine things came easily to mind, but it was not until he had worked in the garden with his father that the little boy realized the tenth good thing. Barney, buried in the ground, would help the flowers, trees, and grass grow. A special picture book, small in size, but large in impact. Print is somewhat small but well-spaced.

Interest Level: 1-4. Reading Level: 2.1. Further Search Topics: Pets-Fiction, Cats-Fiction, Death-Fiction, Group 2, Read Aloud.

READING LEVEL 1.1

Berenstain, Stan. Bears in the night. Random 1971, 30 pp.

This is for the very beginning reader. Only 24 words plus illustrations are used to tell the story of a bedtime adventure for seven small bears. Bravely they sneak out of the house, through the woods, and up Spook Hill. Frightened by an owl's hoot, they run back over the same route until they are safely back in bed again.

Interest Level: K-2. Reading Level: 1.1. Further Search Topics: Bears-Fiction, Group 2, Courage-Fiction, Humorous Fiction.

Bonsall, Crosby. The day I had to play with my sister. Har-Row 1972, 32 pp.

A very easy reader, only slightly less universally appealing and humorous than *And I Mean It, Stanley*. This time a little boy tries very hard to teach his younger sister to play hide-and-seek. He is totally unsuccessful and thoroughly frustrated. Again the story is told as much with pictures as with words. Useful through second grade. Reader format. An Early I Can Read Book.

Interest Level: 1-2. Reading Level: 1.1. Further Search Topics: Humorous Fiction, Games-Fiction, Brothers and Sisters-Fiction, Everyday Stories.

Nodset, Joan L. Go away dog; illus by Crosby Bonsall. Har-Row 1963, unp (29 pp).

A small boy who doesn't like dogs meets a shaggy, homeless dog who wants to play. The little boy, resisting all the way, gradually gives in to the dog's charms. Finally he tells the dog to follow him home. At home, he finds out that the dog was sent to him for his birthday by his Uncle George.

The dog, the boy, and the book are irresistible. You must, however, notice the illustrations on both the dedication and title pages to fully understand the story. Since much of the story is told by the illustrations and the text is repetitive as well as simple, it is an excellent beginning-to-read story.

Interest Level: 1-2. Reading Level: 1.1. Further Search Topics: Dogs-Fiction, Humorous Fiction, Best Sellers, Pets-Fiction, Birthdays-Fiction.

Seuss, Dr. One fish, two fish, red fish, blue fish. Beginner 1960, 63pp.

Beginning with one almost ordinary-looking fish, this is a humorous look at the "funny things that go by." When Dr. Seuss says "funny," he really means highly imaginative, whimsical, and totally nonsensical. Each of the more than 20 silly creatures are described and appropriately illustrated to appeal to a child's sense of the ridiculous. Reader.

Interest Level: 1-2. Reading Level: 1.1. Further Search Topics: Fantasy, Wit and Humor, Poetry, Humorous Fiction, Stories in Rhyme.

Seuss, Dr. Hop on Pop. Beginner 1963, 64pp.

Between one and four rhyming words are introduced or reviewed and used in a silly sentence on each page. The sentence is interpreted with even more amusing illustrations. It is one of the simplest of books (no story at all) and yet it is usable through second grade because of Dr. Seuss' playful style and ridiculous illustrations. Reader format.

Interest Level: 1-2. Reading Level: 1.1. Further Search Topics: Poetry, Best Sellers, Wit and Humor, Humorous Fiction, Stories in Rhyme.

Seuss, Dr. The foot book. Random 1968, unp (27 pp).

Left feet, right feet, big feet, small feet; with its rhyme, silly illustrations and rhythmic celebration of feet of all descriptions, this book is a sure winner with the very young. Reader format.

Interest Level 1-2. Reading Level: 1.1. Further Search Topics: Best Sellers, Feet-Fiction, Humorous Fiction, Poetry, Wit and Humor, Stories in Rhyme.

READING LEVEL 1.2

Berenstain, Stan. The bike lesson. Beginner 1964, 61 pp.

This story of a bumbling father trying to teach his eager son how to ride a bike is pure silliness. Much of the action is shown in the humorous illustrations. The rhymed text adds dialogue and description. Good fun.

Interest Level: K-3. Reading Level: 1.2. Further Search Topics: Humorous Fiction, Bicycles and Bicycling-Fiction, Stories in Rhyme, Group 2.

Bonsall, Crosby. And I mean it, Stanley. Har-Row 1974, 32 pp.

A little girl builds "the very best thing I ever made," but all the while calls to Stanley to tell him not to look and to stay on the other side of the fence. Stanley pays attention only long enough for the "thing" to be completed - then crashes through the fence and bounds into the "thing." He draws no anger from the little girl, though, for Stanley is an enormous, loveable mutt. Told as much through pictures as words, this very easy reader will draw smiles from most first and second graders - especially dog lovers. An Early I Can Read Book.

Interest Level: 1-2. Reading Level: 1.2. Further Search Topics: Dogs-Fiction, Humorous Fiction, Best Sellers.

Brenner, Barbara. Baltimore Orioles; illus by J. Winslow Higginbottom. Har-Row 1974, 62 pp.

An impressive combination of very easy, as well as interesting and informative reading. Within the barest skeleton of a story the author gives a great deal of information about young Baltimore Orioles and the mating and hatching cycle of the older birds. Unfortunately its easy reader format will discourage use beyond third grade. Use freely until that point. Science I Can Read Book series.

Interest Level: 1-3. Reading Level 1.2. Further Search Topics: Birds, Nature Study.

Eastman, Philip D. Sam and the firefly. Beginner 1958, 62 pp.

Sam, the owl, went looking for a playmate one night but found everyone was asleep except a mischievous firefly named Gus. When Sam showed Gus how to write words with his light in the dark sky, Gus went wild. First he tried to direct auto traffic, then airplane traffic, until finally the Hot Dog Man, an angry victim of Gus' tricks, captured him. However, when the Hot Dog Man tried to take Gus out of town, his truck became stuck on the railroad tracks in front of an oncoming train. Gus, freed from the jar in which he'd been caught, quickly wrote the word STOP in the sky and saved everyone. Gus' silliness, the catastrophies he caused and his final triumph should interest almost any young child who likes humor or excitement. Reader format.

Interest Level: 1-2. Reading Level: 1.2. Further Search Topics: Best Sellers, Fireflies-Fiction, Owls-Fiction, Humorous Fiction.

Kessler, Leonard. Last one in is a rotten egg. Har-Row 1969, 64 pp.

Willie and Bobby could swim, but Freddy could not. After all three went to the local swimming pool and Freddy was pushed into the water by two older bullies, he was scared to try swimming again. Finally, a sympathetic lifeguard gave Freddy lessons. After much practice, Freddy became competent and confident enough to swim in the deep water and to stand up to the bullies.

A very slight plot designed to reassure new swimmers and provide a few basic rules of swimming. Reader format. A Sports-I-Can-Read-Book.

Interest Level: 1-2. Reading Level: 1.2. Further Search Topics: Courage-Fiction, Swimming-Fiction, Challenges-Fiction, Bullies-Fiction.

LeSieg, Theo. Wacky Wednesday; illus by George Booth. Beginner 1974, unp (36 pp).

A series of true picture puzzles. A little boy wakes up one Wednesday to find everything around him has gone "wacky." People are missing heads but have extra legs. Cars are being driven from the back seat. Doors are placed in the wrong places. Airplanes fly backwards. At the end of the day everything settles back to normal, but not before readers have had fun finding the numerous "wacky" things on each page.

The story is told in silly rhyme (LeSieg and Seuss are the same person). What is wrong with each picture is not always easily located, making this reader an excellent excerise in observation as well as great fun.

Interest Level: 1-3. Reading Level: 1.2. Further Search Topics: Puzzles, Humorous Fiction, Wit and Humor, Poetry, Best Sellers.

Parish, Peggy. Too many rabbits; illus by Leonard Kessler. Macmillan 1974, 48 pp.

One day Miss Molly opened her front door to find a rabbit waiting to be invited inside. The next day Miss Molly discovered the rabbit had had baby rabbits, lots of baby rabbits. Because babies need care, Miss Molly couldn't just turn them out, so she kept them all. Before long she had more rabbits than she could handle. She tried giving them away, but all the children's mothers refused to keep them, the zoo didn't need any, and Miss Molly didn't want to sell them to the butcher. Finally a man who owned an island where they could live, asked to take all the rabbits. As Miss Molly was about to close the door after giving the rabbits to the man with an island, a cat walked right up to her and inside her house. The next day Miss Molly discovered she had kittens—lots of kittens. A very humorous story in a reader format.

Interest Level: 1-3. Reading Level: 1.2. Further Search Topics: Humorous Fiction, Rabbits-Fiction, Best Sellers.

Seuss, Dr. The cat in the hat. Beginner 1957, 61 pp.

When the Cat in the Hat visits two children, a dreary, boring afternoon becomes almost too exciting. The Cat's juggling act and the two "things" he brings with him almost destroy the house. But the Cat cleans up so well that when the children's mother comes home and asks what they did all afternoon, they can't decide if they should tell her.

A funny, rhyming tale of the destruction all children can create and the boredom all children can feel. Reader format.

Interest Level: 1-3. Reading Level: 1.2. Further Search Topics: Humorous Fiction, Fantasy, Cats-Fiction, Poetry, Troublemakers-Fiction, Best Sellers, Stories in Rhyme.

Seuss, Dr. The cat in the hat comes back. Beginner 1958, 63 pp.

Sally and her brother were doing a good job of clearing the front walk of snow when the Cat in the Hat showed up. While they worked, the Cat created a pink mess in the house. The mess only became worse when he tried to clean it. The pink spot finally covered the snow all around the house until the Cat called upon his friends Little Cats A-Z. It was Little Cat Z and his magic zoom that eventually not only cleaned the snow, but cleared the front walk as well.

Another zany, rhymed adventure of the mischievious Cat whose ability to get into trouble endears him to most children from pre-school to early third grade. Reader format.

Interest Level: 1-3. Reading Level: 1.2. Further Search Topics: Fantasy, Cats-Fiction, Troublemakers-Fiction, Humorous Fiction, Snow-Fiction, Poetry, Best Sellers, Stories in Rhyme.

Steven, Carla. Hooray for Pig!; illus by Rainey Bennett. HM 1974, 48 pp.

Pig couldn't spend the day swimming with his friend Raccoon because he didn't know how to swim. Instead Pig took a picnic to the lake by himself. At the lake, Pig met Otter, who encouraged Pig to at least try getting in the water. After several days of Otter's patient coaching, not only could Pig stay afloat, but he liked it, too!

For much the same audience as Kessler's *Last One In Is A Rotten Egg*, but because of a more interesting plot it is a little more useful. Reader format.

Interest Level: 1-2. Reading Level: 1.2. Further Search Topics: Pigs-Fiction, Courage-Fiction, Swimming-Fiction, Humorous Fiction.

White, Laurence B., Jr. Science puzzles; illus by Marc Tolon Brown. A-W 1975, unp (46 pp).

There are twenty four very short experiments designed to illustrate the simplest of scientific principles clearly presented here. For all but a few experiments there is not only an explanation of what happens but also an explanation of why it happened. What makes the book even more useful, is that it can also be used as a book of easy magic tricks. Any child who enjoys it as science will, with a little help, be able to see its possibilities as magic. In fact it provides a better explanation of the Knot Magic trick than can be found in *It's Magic*.

Interest Level: 1-3. Reading Level: 1.2. Further Search Topics: Science, Magic, Puzzles, Experiments, Scientific.

Wiseman, Bernard. Morris and Boris. Dodd 1974, 64 pp.

This is a compilation of three silly stories about Morris the Moose and Boris the Bear. When Boris tries to interest Morris in telling riddles, Morris frustrates Boris so completely that Boris runs off angrily. Later Boris tries to teach Morris a tongue twister, but ends up running off in total confusion. Finally Boris tries to teach Morris to play hide-and-seek and that, too, is a disaster. Boris tells Morris that Morris just cannot do anything. A bird who has seen everything reminds Boris that Morris can make him very angry and that is something. When Boris agrees they all laugh happily.

Broad, slapstick humor makes this appealing to children well into third grade. Reader format.

Interest Level: 1-3. Reading Level: 1.2. Further Search Topics: Wit and Humor, Riddles, Tongue Twisters, Games, Humorous Fiction.

READING LEVEL 2.1

Alexander, Sue. Small plays for you and a friend; illus by Olivia H. Cole. Seabury 1974, 48 pp.

Five very short and very simple plays for two actors that will be of more interest to the players than the audience. However, because the reading level is low, and because children's love of acting is strong and their tolerance of weak plot is high, this can be used through grade three. A companion volume *Small Plays for Special Days* presents seven more short plays for two characters.

Interest Level: 1-3. Reading Level: 2.1. Further Search Topics: Acting, Drama, Group 2.

Baker, Betty. The pig war; illus by Robert Lopshire. Har-Row 1969, 64 pp.

A brief, fictionalized account of an 1859 land squabble between the United States and Britain. The incident, which took place in what is now the state of Washington, became known as the Pig War. Frightened British pigs destroyed the American farmers' gardens. When the farmers shot one of the pigs, the war began. Simply told and humorously illustrated. Should appeal to history or military fans. Early reader format.

Interest Level: 2-4. Reading Level: 2.1. Further Search Topics: United States-History-War-Fiction, Great Britain-History-Fiction, War-Fiction, Washington (state)-Fiction, Historical Fiction, Pigs-Fiction.

Bernstein, Margery. Coyote goes hunting for fire; illus by Ed Heffernan. Scribner 1974, 40 pp.

A delightful story that can be read for fun or used as part of a unit on North American Indians. A long time ago when there was no fire, all the animals but Coyote banded together to find it. The animals left Coyote behind because he was always spoiling their plans. Coyote saw them leave, chased after them and once more tried to direct everything, but only ended up losing fire. Cartoon-like illustrations add to the humor of the story. This book should make a simple, but effective play.

Interest Level: 1-4. Reading Level 2.1. Further Search Topics: Animals-Fiction, Legends, Mythology, Fire-Fiction, Indians of North America-Legends, Coyotes-Fiction, Group 2, Creation-Fiction, Drama.

Bernstein, Margery. The first morning; illus by Enid Warner Romanek. Scribner 1976, 44 pp.

Spider, Mouse, and Fly volunteered to ask the king of the sky for light to take back to earth because the animals on earth were tired of living in darkness. The king didn't want to give away any light and so he set what he thought was an impossible task for the three animals. They were able to outwit the king three times and finally return to earth with a box Mouse was sure contained light. When they opened the box all they found was a rooster. Poor Mouse was ashamed at having been so badly tricked. But then Rooster crowed up the first morning and has done so ever since. A competent retelling of an African myth, nicely complemented by bold illustrations. Good candidate for dramatization.

Interest Level: 1-3. Reading Level: 2.1. Further Search Topics: Animals-Fiction, Group 2, Mythology, Light-Fiction, Drama, Time-Fiction, Calendars-Fiction, Creation-Fiction, Africa-Folklore.

Bulla, Clyde Robert. A lion to guard us; illus by Michele Chessare. Har-Row 1981, 117 pp.

Bulla's writing isn't quite as successful here as elsewhere. This story of three London children's attempt to go to their father in Jamestown, Virginia, has danger, adventure, daring and promise. It also has too many characters to allow the reader to get to know any of them well. There are also too many very short chapters to allow plot development (23 chapters and 117 pages). The short sentences help to keep the reading level low, but a glossary would have been useful to fully explain the many unfamiliar terms.

Despite its problems, the book is still useful. The story is based on the 1609 voyage of the Sea Adventure. Blown far off course and badly damaged by a storm, the ship landed at Bermuda rather than Jamestown. The survivors were unable to sail again for over nine months. When they reached Jamestown, they found that few people had survived the very harsh year.

The three Freebold children are the focus of this story. When their mother died they left London to find their father in the New World. Having no money of their own, they were lucky to find a doctor friend to pay their ship's passage and to go with them. Halfway across the ocean, the doctor was swept overboard and drowned. From that time until they found their father barely alive, the children were on their own, even though they were still with the ship's passengers.

Although not the best of Bulla, this is still serviceable as a piece of historical fiction (hard to get children to read), or as a choice for the lover of survival and/or sea stories.

Interest Level: 3-5. Reading Level: 2.1. Further Search Topics: United States-History-Fiction, Historical Fiction, Courage-Fiction, Survival-Fiction, Shipwrecks-Fiction, Voyages and Travels-Fiction, Seafaring Life-Fiction.

Bulla, Clyde Robert. My friend the monster; illus by Michele Chessare. Har-Row 1980, 75 pp.

Even though Hal was plain and not very clever, his disappointed parents knew that he was still a prince; thus he had to be raised as one. Hal didn't like his lonely, dull life until a new world was accidentally opened to him. A servant's child gave him an old book of monsters and told him that the monsters still lived under the distant mountains. Hal finally made a trip to the mountains, spent a day exploring, and by chance met Humbert, a young monster curious about the world. But, Hal's cruel cousin Archer captured Humbert and put him in a cage. Hal's daring rescue attempt almost resulted in disaster for both Humbert and Hal.

This is another example of Bulla's forte; a book with an action-filled plot, short chapters, large print, wide spaces between the lines, and a low reading level. A book about monsters has almost guaranteed appeal through third grade. Although the book is useful beyond third grade, readers in fourth and fifth grade may be more sensitive to Hal's apparent youth and the fantastic elements of the story.

Interest Level: 1-3. Reading Level: 2.1. Further Search Topics: Fantasy, Monsters-Fiction, Royalty-Fiction, Group 2, Read Aloud, Best Sellers.

Bulla, Clyde Robert. The ghost of windy hill; illus by Don Bolognese. Har-Row 168, 84 pp.

If the reader doesn't expect a high adventure ghost story, he or she will not be disappointed by this low-keyed tale of a family who goes to live in a house that is supposedly haunted. Mr. Giddings asked the Carver family to move into his country home while he and his wife stayed in Boston. His intent was that the Carvers should either prove to his wife that the house was not haunted or drive the ghost out. The Carvers found no ghosts—at first—only an interesting group of neighbors. There was shy Miss Miggie who drifted around in a long, white dress and wore a flower-covered hat. Bruno was the gruff beggar boy who couldn't walk and had no friends but a goat, until the Carver children came along. Near the end of their stay Lorna Carver mentioned that because they had seen no ghosts the family would soon leave and the Giddings would return. Strange occurrences began almost immediately after Lorna's statement and ended only when the Carvers caught Bruno trying to convince them that he was the ghost. Lorna and Jamie were his only friends, so he had risked his guardians wrath and given up the pretense of being lame to trick the Carvers into staying. All ends well as Bruno's cruel guardian is run off, the Carvers take responsibility for Bruno's care, and Mrs. Giddings admits she made up the ghost story because she hated living in the country and had wanted to return to the city. Another serviceable book in the very successful Bulla style.

Interest Level: 2-5. Reading Level: 2.1. Further Search Topics: Ghosts-Fiction, Brothers and Sisters-Fiction, Orphans-Fiction, Country Life-Fiction, Courage-Fiction, Challenges-Fiction, Friendship-Fiction.

Bulla, Clyde Robert. Pirate's promise; illus by Peter Burchard. Har-Row 1958, 87 pp.

After their mother and father died, Tom and Dinah Pippin had nowhere to go but to their Uncle John's house. Uncle John had no place for them, so he sold Tom into bondage but kept Dinah to help his wife with housework. Tom was to be taken by ship to America where the ship's captain would sell him to the highest bidder. After several years, Tom would be free. But, Tom couldn't accept the idea of one person being another's property, so he spoke out at every opportunity. Tom spoke up to the seaman who dragged him aboard ship, to the captain, to the others who had been bonded, even to the pirate captain who captured their ship. Captain Land was so impressed by Tom's bravery that although he set everyone else he had captured adrift on a small boat, he kept Tom with him. He and Tom became good friends. He never asked Tom to become a pirate and Tom never did. Instead, they enjoyed each other's company. When the pirate ship needed work, they stopped at a safe island where Tom met and impressed Captain Red, a fierce enemy of Captain Land. Captain Red's insistence that Tom join his pirate ship led to another clash between the enemies. Although he was ill, Captain Land fought a duel with Captain Red and lost. Land's last requests were that Benjy, a freed slave who loved him, take all his gold, and that Tom go to Charlestown, South Carolina to find Land's family. Benjy led their flight from Captain Red and arranged a way for Tom to sail to Charlestown before putting Tom on his own. When Tom reached Charlestown he found Land's parents were so angry with Land that at first they didn't even want to hear about him. But, eventually, they not only asked all about their son, but also asked Tom if he and Dinah would like to live with them as their family.

There is enough excitement, danger, and warmth here to satisfy almost any arm-chair adventurer. Usual format of short, episodic chapters.

Interest Level: 3-6. Reading Level 2.1. Further Search Topics: Pirates-Fiction, Seafaring Life-Fiction, Orphans-Fiction, Slavery-Fiction, Brothers and Sisters-Fiction, Best Sellers, Courage-Fiction.

Bulla, Clyde Robert. John Billington, friend of Squanto; illus by Peter Burchard. Har-Row 1956, 88 pp.

This historical novel about the Mayflower voyage and the Pilgrims' first year at Plymouth centers on young John Billington. John was considered the troublemaker of the children. His problems are woven around the events of the year, including the Pilgrims' first meetings with the Wampanoag Indians. It was finally John, however, who was responsible for bringing peace between the Pilgrims and the Wampanoag tribe who lived further down Cape Cod. The book is not as exciting or convincing as Bulla's books are generally. It also contains a few minor historical inaccuracies; yet it remains useful as both an introduction to American history and historical fiction.

Interest Level: 2-5. Reading Level: 2.1. Further Search Topics: Pilgrims-Fiction, Historical Fiction, United States-History-Fiction, Thanksgiving-Fiction, Troublemakers-Fiction, Indians of North America-Fiction.

Bulla, Clyde Robert. Riding the pony express; illus by Grace Paull. Har-Row 1948, 95 pp.

Although somewhat marred by the stereotyped speech of a young Indian boy, this is otherwise an exciting piece of historical fiction set in the 1860s. Dick was sent from New York City to join his father in St. Joseph, Missouri, only to find his father had moved to Nebraska to become a pony express rider. When Dick finally found his father, after a long stagecoach ride, he thought his father didn't want him. Dick stayed at the way station and helped with the chores because he didn't know what else to do. Then one day the house was burned, his father was shot, and the horses were almost stolen. There was no one around who could carry the mail, except Dick. Despite

a wolf pack at his heels, Dick rode to the next way station. On his way home he realized his father really did want him and he no longer wanted to leave his father. Chapters are short with separate episodes that tie them together. A few simple songs appear between the chapters.

Interest Level: 2-5. Reading Level: 2.1. Further Search Topics: Horses-Fiction, West-Fiction, United States-History-Fiction, Historical Fiction, Voyages and Travels-Fiction, Courage-Fiction, Frontier and Pioneer Life-Fiction.

Bulla, Clyde Robert. Marco Moonlight; illus by Julia Noonan. T Y Crowell 1976, 104 pp.

No one could explain Marco's strange, recurring dream. The dream seemed to be about a brother, but Marco had no brother. He had no family but his wealthy grandparents with whom he lived. Marco loved his grandparents very much, but he couldn't help wondering about his own past. He knew only what he and his grandparents could figure out from a few clues. His mother had run away to marry and for three years Marco's grandparents had heard nothing. Then, suddenly, they received a note that she was dying, had parted from her husband, and needed them. By the time they arrived, she was dead and two-year-old Marco could tell them no more. About the time of his thirteenth birthday Marco made friends with a strange man named Flint, who later became the gardener on Marco's grandparents' estate. Rather than live in the room provided for him with the other servants, Flint chose a bleak and isolated beach cottage. Being very careful that no one should suspect, Flint locked Marco into the cottage and forced Marco to change clothes with Matt, who was Marco's long-lost identical twin. Flint and Matt planned that Matt would steal all the money he could from the estate before killing Marco and fleeing. But when Matt began to realize how nice his grandparents were, how much he liked Marco, and how evil Flint was, he decided to thwart Flint's plan. In Matt and Marco's desperate attempt to flee from Flint, Flint was accidentally killed, leaving Marco free to return home and Matt free to find a way to feel he also had the right to claim his heritage before joining Marco.

The tense and dramatic plot immediately involves the reader and the short, fast-paced chapters sustain interest to the end of the book. Readers should also appreciate the small, paperback-size format. A good choice.

Interest Level: 3-6. Reading Level: 2.1. Further Search Topics: Dreams-Fiction, Mystery and Detective Stories, Kidnapping-Fiction, Twins-Fiction, Orphans-Fiction, Grandparents-Fiction, Best Sellers, Brothers and Sisters-Fiction, Jealousy-Fiction, Courage-Fiction.

Bulla, Clyde Robert. The sugar pear tree; illus by Taro Yashima. T Y Crowell 1960, 54 pp.

Lonnie lived with his mother and his grandfather in a house owned by the state. A new highway was to be built that would force the family to move, but Gramp refused to acknowledge that the state could force them out of their home. He chased away every state representative who came to warn the family that they should move. Lonnie's mother had always been at work when the representatives came and so knew nothing about the warnings until she came home to find their belongings on the sidewalk and their house on wheels. The only person they could turn to was their friend Nick. Nick owned a nursery in town and a small house with a large yard in the country. He had become a friend of Lonnie's when he gave Lonnie first prize in a school essay contest on the topic of "favorite trees." Lonnie's prize had been a sugar pear tree, his favorite. Nick had next become Lonnie's mother's friend. Nick arranged for them to stay in the greenhouse at his country place. The longer they stayed, the better friends Nick and Lonnie's mother became. Gramp was the only person who didn't adjust to the move. He stopped speaking the moment he was carried out of his old home. In a final and successful attempt to make Gramp happy, Nick bought the old house and had it moved out to his country lot.

The idea of a state government being able to force a family to move may need some explaining. The story's warmth and very consistent early second grade reading level make this a particularly useful book with quiet readers.

Interest Level: 2-4. Reading Level: 2.1. Further Search Topics: Trees-Fiction, Moving, Household-Fiction, Family Problems-Fiction, Grandparents-Fiction, Poverty-Fiction.

Bulla, Clyde Robert. Open the door and see all the people; illus by Wendy Watson. T Y Crowell 1972, 69 pp.

A slight story that makes up for its lack of excitement with warmth. When Joann, Teeney and Mama were burned out of their house in the country, they decided it was time to move to the city. With the help of a friend, Mama was quickly able to find a job and an apartment. Only Teeney was noticeably unhappy. She missed her doll and resented anyone else who had one. Then the girls learned about the Toy House, a place to borrow or adopt toys. Both girls found dolls they wanted to adopt. Just before the end of the six week trial period Tenney lost her doll and almost lost her chance to adopt it. After the doll was found and repaired, the people at the Toy House realized how much she wanted the doll and let Teeney keep it.

Because of the ages of the characters, (six and eight), and the subject matter, the book's appeal is doubtful beyond third grade. Print size slightly smaller than usual for Bulla.

Interest Level: 1-3. Reading Level: 2.1. Further Search Topics: Dolls-Fiction, Brothers and Sisters-Fiction, Moving, Household-Fiction, Family-Fiction, Group 2.

Bulla, Clyde Robert. Indian hill; illus by James J. Spanfeller. T Y Crowell 1963, 74 pp.

A very low-key story of a Navajo family who moved from the reservation to a city because they could no longer support themselves on the reservation. The move was necessary, but it was not appreciated by young Kee and his mother. They hated their ugly apartment and the crowded city, and wanted to go home. When an excuse to return to the reservation arose, Kee and his mother left the city. However, by the time Kee's father arrived to tell them he had been wrong to force them to move, Kee and his mother had realized they never gave their new home a chance. They were ready to try again. No excitement here, only an understanding look at the difficulties of moving.

Interest Level: 2-5. Reading Level: 2.1. Further Search Topics: Indians of North America-Fiction, Navajo Indians-Fiction, City Life-Fiction, Moving, Household-Fiction.

Bulla, Clyde Robert. White bird; illus by Leonard Weisgard. T Y Crowell 1966, 79 pp.

This book is meant for a special reader. It will not appeal to the reader who wants only action and excitement from a book. It is a story of complex human relationships and differing definitions of love. John Thomas lost his parents in a river accident when he was just a baby. His cradle had been pulled from the river and he had been raised by reclusive Luke Vail. Luke placed no trust in the world or in people outside his tiny valley home and so forbade John Thomas to have anything to do with either one. Luke didn't allow John Thomas a pet either because he thought that John Thomas would only be hurt when he no longer had the animal. Despite Luke's argument, when he found an injured white crow, John Thomas kept it and tended it until the crow was stolen by three strangers as Luke stood by. Angry at Luke as much as at the strangers, John Thomas ran away to search for the bird, but found that it had been shot. Far from being fruitless, however, John Thomas's trip out of the valley gave him an entirely different view of people than the one Luke had shown him. Upon a friend's encouragement, John Thomas returned to Luke to share that view.

Subtle and unusual, this book needs a mature, sensitive reader and/or discussion in order to be fully appreciated.

Interest Level: 4-6. Reading Level 2.1. Further Search Topics: Pets-Fiction, Orphans-Fiction, Runaways-Fiction, Birds-Fiction, Love-Fiction, Loners-Fiction, Courage-Fiction.

Cerf, Bennett. Bennett Cerf's book of animal riddles; illus by Roy McKie. Beginner 1964, 62 pp.

A slightly more difficult selection of riddles than the following listing. The riddles are longer and less familiar, but still very useful. See *Bennett Cerf's Book of Riddles* for more explanation. Reader format.

Interest Level: 1-3. Reading Level: 2.1. Further Search Topics: Riddles, Wit and Humor, Group 2.

Cerf, Bennett. Bennett Cerf's book of riddles; illus by Roy McKie. Beginner 1960, 64 pp.

Simple, well-known riddles that are always popular with children. The riddle is introduced on one page and answered on the reverse side of the page. Silly drawings illustrate each riddle and answer. Because each riddle and answer stands alone, even the most problematic of readers can have the satisfaction of completing a unit in a short time. That satisfaction, plus the universal appeal of humor make this book and the preceding listing useful through grade four, despite the book's reader format.

Interest Level: 1-4. Reading Level: 2.1. Further Search Topics: Riddles, Wit and Humor, Group 2.

Charlip, Remy. Handtalk; an ABC of finger spelling and sign language; photos by George Ancona. Schol. Bk. Serv. 1974, 42 pp.

This is not a book to be read and put away. It is a challenge to learn finger spelling (forming words letter by letter with the fingers) and signing (forming whole words or ideas by making a picture using one or both hands). It is a challenge that appeals to almost any child, reader and non-reader. One letter of the manual alphabet is shown at the top of each page. At the bottom of the page is a series of pictures that spell out a word which begins with the letter for that page. In the center of the page a model signs that same word. Only the first few words are explained, although there are hints for some of the more difficult words. The rest must be deciphered by the reader. In addition, the book includes over 25 more signs and a sentence about a very ugly vampire. The entire manual alphabet is also shown on a quick-reference, double page spread. The book provides an enjoyable and successful experience with language, especially if two or more children work with the book together. Although its picture book format would ordinarily turn older children away, interest in the book remains high through sixth grade. Because there are so few words that a child needs to read to enjoy this book, its reading level is an estimate.

Interest Level: 2-6. Reading Level: 2.1. Further Search Topics: Nonverbal Communication, Physically Handicapped, Communication.

Chenery, Janet. Wolfie; illus by Marc Simont. Har-Row 1969, 64 pp.

This slight but satisfying story is the vehicle for much information about spiders. Harry caught a wolf spider. To keep his sister Polly out of the way, Harry and his friend George told her she could see the spider only after she caught 100 flies to feed it. In the meantime, they took the spider to the nature center where they were treated to a fascinating lesson about insects and spiders (especially wolf spiders). It's too bad that the book's cartoon style illustrations prevent this book from being very useful beyond grade three.

Interest Level: 1-3. Reading Level: 2.1. Further Search Topics: Spiders, Pets, Nature Study, Group 2.

Clymer, Eleanor. Chipmunk in the forest; illus by Ingrid Fetz. Atheneum 1965, 56 pp.

A simple story of an Indian boy who learned the meaning of the word "courage". Chipmunk had never admitted to anyone that he was afraid of the forest. But when his uncle tried to teach him to hunt, Chipmunk was too frightened to be quiet, and thus he scared away all the animals. He returned to the village in disgrace to do "women's work." One of his jobs was to watch Little Brother. When Little Brother disappeared, Chipmunk went in search of him. It began to snow as Chipmunk went farther and farther into the forest, but even though he was frightened, Chipmunk kept on looking. By the time he found Little Brother, the snow had covered their tracks. Chipmunk had to use all that he had learned from his uncle to get them safely home. When he arrived back at the village, Chipmunk had finally proven that he was brave.

Interest Level: 2-4. Reading Level: 2.1. Further Search Topics: Indians of North America-Fiction, Courage-Fiction, Snow-Fiction, Hunting-Fiction, Survival-Fiction.

Cole, Joanna. Dinosaur story; illus by Mort Kunstler. Morrow 1974, unp (30 pp).

A general introduction to eight dinosaurs: Brontosaurus, Allosaurus, Stegosaurus, Ornitholestes, Protoceratops, Triceratops, Tyrannosaurus rex and Duckbills. Although not a wealth of information, there is more than enough interesting material here to attract a young dinosaur enthusiast. Because of the short sentences, the text is somewhat plodding. The subject matter's great appeal and the appropriately fierce-looking illustrations, however, make up for that problem.

Interest Level: 1-3. Reading Level: 2.1. Further Search Topics: Group 2, Dinosaurs, Prehistory.

Cole, Joanna. My puppy is born; photos by Jerome Wexler. Morrow 1973, unp (38 pp).

This is an unadorned description of a dachshund puppy's birth and first eight weeks of growth. The black and white photographs are large, sometimes graphic, and most often charming. The text is direct, carefully worded, concise and interesting. It is only the intrusion of an obviously young narrator that keeps this excellent book from being useful beyond third grade.

Interest Level: 1-3. Reading Level: 2.1. Further Search Topics: Group 2, Infants, Dogs, Pets, Birth.

Dobrin, Arnold. Jillions of gerbils. Lothrop 1973, 64 pp.

Right after his family moved into a big and very old house, David's gerbil disappeared. Before long, the replacement gerbil disappeared also. The house was very old and did have strange creakings. Could there also have been secret hiding places for ghosts, maybe? Determined to find out, David searched the entire house until he really did find a secret room. And in that room he found his two gerbils with their new family — the beginnings of David's millions and billions and jillions of gerbils.

A comfortable, somewhat old-fashioned book that is neatly divided into six short chapters. It includes a page of facts about gerbils at the end. A good choice to follow the very easy readers; it is easy, but not "too babyish."

Interest Level: 1-4. Reading Level: 2.1. Further Search Topics: Gerbils-Fiction, Pets-Fiction, Group 2, Humorous Fiction.

Dolch, Edward W. Stories from Old Russia; illus by James Lewicki. Garrard 1964, 168 pp.

There are 21 chapters and only nine stories in this volume. These are more robust and exciting adventure stories than many of the other Dolch collections listed here, although once again the simplified vocabulary is somewhat restrictive. A guide to pronounciation of some Russian names is included at the end of the book. More colorful illustrations than some of the other titles. Very consistent reading level. See *Stories From France* for more information. Folklore of the World series.

Interest Level: 2-6. Reading Level: 2.1. Further Search Topics: Folklore, Fantasy, Russia-Fiction, Witches-Fiction.

Dolch, Edward W. Dog stories; illus by Bernette Johnson and Robert S. Kerr. Garrard 1954, 169 pp.

Although overly sentimental for most adult tastes, this collection of true dog stories appeals to young dog lovers. Eighteen chapters tell 15 stories, ranging from the first story in which dog rescues boy, to the final story in which boy rescues dog. There is a dog who played baseball, a dog who went to live at a newspaper, a dog who saved a fireman from a fire, two dogs who were lost and several more dogs who became heroes. A consistent reading level, large print and a popular topic make this a good choice to offer reluctant readers despite the Dolch books' usual unattractive illustrations. Dolch Basic Vocabulary Book series.

Interest Level: 2-4. Reading Level: 2.1. Further Search Topics: Dogs-Fiction, Courage-Fiction, Pets-Fiction.

Fife, Dale. Follow that ghost!; illus by Joan Drescher. Dutton 1979, 58 pp.

In short sentences reminiscent of "Dragnet," Chuck tells a very simple story of Chuck and Jason's first detective case. He and Jason were practicing following people, when their next-door-neighbor caught them following her home. Instead of being angry at the two boys, Glory decided to hire them to find the ghost she and her mother were hearing at 5:00 every morning. Despite their best attempts to capture and bury the ghost, or a find a human cause for the ghostly sounds, Chuck and Jason couldn't rid Glory's apartment of its ghost. Their final effort nearly resulted in injury to a neighbor. Ultimately, Chuck discovered that the ghost was merely a displaced woodpecker looking for a new home.

Not a terribly ambitious mystery, but one whose consistent reading level, familiar urban setting and interesting characters will please many young readers.

Interest Level: 2-4. Reading Level: 2.1. Further Search Topics: Ghosts-Fiction, Mystery and Detective Stories, Spies-Fiction, Humorous Fiction.

Foley, Louise Munro. Tackle 22; illus by John Heinly. Delacorte 1978, unp (43 pp).

When their quarterback came down with the mumps, it looked like the Wildcats would have to forfeit the big football game to the Spacemen. But Chub's little brother Herb surprised everyone and saved the game.

Brief and somewhat predictable, the book maintains a light touch that many young readers will like. Heavily illustrated.

Interest Level: 1-4. Reading Level: 2.1. Further Search Topics: Football-Fiction, Brothers and Sisters-Fiction, Humorous Fiction, Group 2.

Hornblow, Leonora. Prehistoric monsters did the strangest things; illus by Michael K. Frith. Random 1974, 65 pp.

A basic survey of an era and its animal life forms. Animals from the earliest water creatures through Diplocaulus, Ichthyosaurs, dinosaurs (about 12 varieties) and early mammals (including the Beast of Baluchistan) to the appearance of man are introduced and illustrated. It is a brief but meaty treatment of a very popular subject that should be especially useful with second and third grade children. Reader format.

Interest Level: 1-3. Reading Level: 2.1. Further Search Topics: Prehistory, Dinosaurs, Evolution, Monsters, Group 2.

Low, Joseph. Five men under one umbrella. Macmillan 1975, 64 pp.

Twenty-nine riddles, most of which are fairly familiar. Nothing special in this collection, just an additional choice for the young comedian.

Interest Level: 1-3. Reading Level: 2.1. Further Search Topics: Riddles, Wit and Humor, Group 2.

Parish, Peggy. Haunted house; illus by Paul Frame. Macmillan 1971, 151 pp.

Although this is the third book about Jed, Bill and Liza Roberts, it too can be read out of order. This time the family has moved into what was locally known as a haunted house. Very shortly after they moved into the house, a coded note appeared that led them to a series of messages and unusual occurrences. Lights that flashed into Liza's room turned out to be the headlights of cars, but the messages and a secret compartment in an old clock couldn't be as easily

explained. Each day took them closer to the surprise that the messages hinted would be theirs. That surprise turned out to be three kittens and a treehouse. Two of the children's best friends had planned the whole mystery just to lead to the surprises.

This book has the same faults and strong points as the others about the Roberts children. Each chapter is short; the book is episodic; reading level is consistent; there is much dialogue and action and little description, and the plot has a comfortable familiarity about it. It can be very useful to the right readers.

Interest Level: 1-4. Reading Level: 2.1. Further Search Topics: Mystery and Detective Stories, Brothers and Sisters-Fiction, Ghosts-Fiction, Moving, Household-Fiction, Nonverbal Communication-Fiction, Group 2.

Parish, Peggy. Hermit Dan; illus by Paul Frame. Macmillan 1977, 151 pp.

When the Roberts children tried to prove that Pirate Island really had been used by pirates, they encountered more action and intrigue than they had found in any of their earlier adventures. Liza, Bill and Jed suspected that Hermit Dan knew whether or not there had been pirates on the island, but he was so gruff and apparently mean that they didn't dare ask him any questions. Instead, they trailed and spied on him and asked questions of anyone who had known Hermit Dan as a child. It was rumored that his ancestors had actually been pirates. Until a terrible fire that had destroyed all they owned, Hermit Dan's family had been very wealthy. However, no one knew how they had become so rich.

In an attempt to see what the summer residents knew about Hermit Dan, the children introduced themselves to the vacationing youngsters. Among the visitors the Roberts met Hank and Ted, brothers bent on bullying Hermit Dan. When the children were rescued from a severe sandstorm by Hermit Dan, they were surprised to find that he wasn't nearly as gruff as he appeared. In fact they began to feel quite protective of the old man. Thus when Hank and Ted stole a secret box that held all of Hermit Dan's valuables, it was the Roberts children who fought (literally) to get the box back. It was after Liza, Bill and Jed returned the box to Hermit Dan, however, that the real surprises began: these included a surprise party for Hermit Dan, his wish to be friendly, and his gift to the children of three pieces of eight that proved his family members were pirates.

This title's more interesting and involved plot makes the book more likely to be a success with older readers than the other stories about the Roberts children. Otherwise it shares the same format, faults and strengths as the other series titles.

Interest Level: 2-5. Reading Level: 2.1. Further Search Topics: Mystery and Detective Stories, Pirates-Fiction, Vacation-Fiction, Loners-Fiction, Treasure-Fiction, Bullies-Fiction, Brothers and Sisters-Fiction, Grandparents-Fiction.

Parish, Peggy. Key to the treasure; illus by Paul Frame. Macmillan 1966, 154 pp.

This is the first of the stories about Jed, Bill and Liza Roberts. The three children are very middle-class, the book's plots are simple and often lack suspense, but the stories still enjoy widespread popularity among unsophisticated readers.

All three children went to spend the summer with their grandparents and decided to tackle a mystery left unsolved for over 75 years. An old drawing and an authentic war bonnet provided the only clues to finding three Indian artifacts. At each step along the way there were crumbled, brittle pieces of paper bearing coded messages that led to the next clue. The search ended when the children found that a storage area in a porch piller contained an Indian doll, mask, and leather shield that had belonged to their great-grandfather.

Interest Level: 1-4. Reading Level: 2.1. Further Search Topics: Vacation-Fiction, Brothers and Sisters-Fiction, Group 2, Mystery and Detective Stories, Grandparents-Fiction, Nonverbal Communication-Fiction.

Parish, Peggy. Pirate Island adventure; illus by Paul Frame. Macmillan 1975, 167 pp.

Although this is the fourth book in the series about the Roberts children, none of the titles must be read in chronological order. This time the three rather privileged children spent the summer with their grandparents on a resort island. They lived in a house that their family had owned for years, explored the island, and swam in their own private cove. But, most of their time was spent trying to solve an old mystery. Their great-uncle had hidden several very special items (one for each member of his family) years earlier, and had left only one clue with their grandfather. After he gave the children that clue it was only a matter of time before they found the hidden treasures.

This book is also lengthy, but is divided into 22 very manageable chapters. It is, like the others, almost entirely dialogue and action, which makes it especially appealing to young reluctant readers.

Interest Level: 1-4. Reading Level: 2.1. Further Search Topics: Mystery and Detective Stories, Vacation-Fiction, Treasure-Fiction, Brothers and Sisters-Fiction, Grandparents-Fiction, Group 2.

Scism, Carol K. The wizard of Walnut Street; illus by Martha Alexander. Dial 1973, 54 pp.

John and his friends had no room in their Wizard Club for Ford Owens, the new kid. John thought Ford was a conceited show-off who only wanted to make John look like a coward. It was true that John was afraid of some things, such as going down the giant slide into the lake, but he didn't want anyone else to know it. So he excluded Ford from all the club's activities until Ford pushed his way into their magic wishing-well project.

It had been John's idea to charge everyone a dime who wanted to make a wish. They could use the money to buy the few simple things that they would need to make the wishes come true. But it was Ford's eerie volcano and his large dog that had added just the right atmosphere to the trick to make people believe. Even John and Ford found themselves making wishes. John wished to be able to go down the giant slide. He didn't know what Ford wished. Much to John's initial surprise, people's wishes began to be fulfilled. Even Arthur, who had wished he could learn to dive, found he could. Then because John began to realize that the magic was in believing in himself and not in the wishing well, he tried the slide and succeeded. Once John's reason to avoid Ford was gone, he relaxed and asked Ford to join the club. At that point, even Ford's wish was granted.

Interest Level: 2-4. Reading Level: 2.1. Further Search Topics: Friendship-Fiction, Gangs-Fiction, Courage-Fiction, Magic-Fiction, Vacation-Fiction, Best Sellers.

Selsam, Millicent E. How kittens grow; photos by Esther Bubley. School Bk Serv 1973, unp (28 pp).

A warm picture essay that illustrates and briefly describes the first eight weeks in kittens' lives. Guaranteed to charm cat fanciers.

Interest Level: 1-3. Reading Level: 2.1. Further Search Topics: Cats, Pets, Infants, Group 2, Birth.

Sharmat, Marjorie W. Nate the great goes undercover; illus by Marc Simont. Coward 1974, 47 pp.

Nate's next door neighbor Oliver was a pest, but Oliver had a mystery for Nate to solve. Oliver's garbage can was being burglarized at night. He wanted Nate to catch the garbage snatcher. Nate quickly drew up a list of human suspects and just as quickly eliminated them all. A night spent hiding in the garbage can proved the best way to catch the thief. Much to Nate's surprise, the thief turned out to be his new dog.

Very amusing and very useful. Reader format.

Interest Level: 1-3. Reading Level: 2.1. Further Search Topics: Humorous Fiction, Mystery and Detective Stories, Group 2, Detectives-Fiction, Best Sellers.

Sharmat, Marjorie W. Nate the great; illus by Marc Simont. Coward 1972, 62 pp.

This is a young imitation of Humphrey Bogart solving a *Dragnet* style mystery. Annie's recently finished painting of her dog had disappeared so she hired Nate to search for it. Nate gathered all the facts, investigated his suspects, and eventually solved the mystery, but not before he had consumed plenty of pancakes (his favorite food) and solved a second mystery by accident.

A simple plot, humorous telling, and a sympathetic, likeable protagonist make this one of a very popular series. Reader format.

Interest Level: 1-3. Reading Level: 2.1. Further Search Topics: Humorous Fiction, Detectives-Fiction, Mystery and Detective Stories, Group 2, Best Sellers.

Shaw, Evelyn. Alligator; illus by Frances Zweifel. Har-Row 1972, 61 pp.

A straight-forward, respectful description of an alligator's life cycle. Emphasis is placed on the time between the mother's nest-building and the birth of the young alligators. The danger to alligators posed by man is expressed, but not stressed. Little physical description is included. An interesting and competent treatment of a narrow subject. Reader format. A Science-I-Can-Read Book series.

Interest Level: 1-4. Reading Level: 2.1. Further Search Topics: Alligators, Nature Study, Group 2.

Viorst, Judith. The tenth good thing about Barney; illus by Erik Blegvad. Atheneum 1971, 25 pp.

A quiet, thoughtful book to help a child face the difficult experience of death. When a family's beloved cat Barney died, their little boy tried to find 10 good things to say about him at the funeral. Nine things came easily to mind, but it was not until he had worked in the garden with his father that the little boy realized the tenth good thing. Barney, buried in the ground, would help the flowers, trees, and grass grow. A special picture book, small in size, but large in impact. Print is somewhat small but well-spaced.

Interest Level: 1-4. Reading Level: 2.1. Further Search Topics: Pets-Fiction, Cats-Fiction, Death-Fiction, Group 2, Read Aloud.

Warner, Gertrude Chandler. The lighthouse mystery; illus by David Cunningham. A. Whitman 1963, 128 pp.

What better place for a mystery than a lighthouse late at night? Add the excitement of a storm at sea and a young man alone in a boat and the story should be unbeatable. Unfortunately this, as well as some of the other books in the series, does not quite live up to its potential. It will not attract many new readers but it will satisfy those who crave more adventures of the Alden family. The main problem with the book is its lack of definition. It isn't quite a mystery or an adventure story, it's a little of both. It is also part homespun family story, part science lesson, and part "problem story."

The Aldens rented a lighthouse in a very small fishing village one summer. Late each night their dog awoke them as he barked at a stranger who walked into or away from a closed-up building nearby. When the children investigated, they found that the surly son of a local fisherman was using the building to experiment on plankton as a food source. Harry was a brilliant young man who wanted to go to college, but whose father stubbornly refused to let him study. One night when Larry was at sea gathering samples, a terrible storm blew up. Only the Coast Guard and an improvised light in the lighthouse saved Larry from drowning. Larry's brush with death forced his father to acknowledge Larry's abilities and allow him to continue studying at college.

The sketchy illustrations in this and the following books in the series are an improvement over the silhouettes of *The Boxcar Children*. See the annotation for *The Boxcar Children* for further series information.

Interest Level: 3-6. Reading Level: 2.1. Further Search Topics: Mystery and Detective Stories, Lighthouses-Fiction, Food-Fiction, Disasters-Fiction, Vacation-Fiction.

Warner, Gertrude Chandler. The boxcar children; illus by L. Kate Deal. A. Whitman 1950, 154 pp.

This is the first in a series of very early hi/lo books. Although they often bear signs of stilted "Dick and Jane"-style writing, occasionally preach to the reader, and are interrupted by frequent asides from the author, the stories are still popular with young readers. In each book the children are not simply manipulated, but control their own destiny. They fulfill many a child's dream of finding a loving home and family, becoming rich, having adventures, and solving mysteries. This is the simplest story of the series, most of the other entries assume interest in such advanced subjects as fossils, food sources, antiques, or the Revolutionary War.

The only place the four orphaned Alden children had to live was with a grandfather whom they had never met, but whom they had heard was mean. Rather than live with him, they decided to try and survive on their own. They found an abandoned railway boxcar and filled it was items that they found in a junkyard in order to make it their home. Henry, the oldest, went to work for a doctor who, in addition to money, gave him food and kept a silent but watchful eye over all the children without their knowledge. When Violet became ill, the children had no choice but to take her to Dr. Moore. He gave them all a temporary home and arranged for them to gradually get to know their grandfather. By the time Violet was almost well the children had grown to like the elderly stranger. It was a happy day when the children finally realized that the man to whom Dr. Moore had introduced them was really their grandfather.

Interest Level: 1-4. Reading Level: 2.1. Further Search Topics: Orphans-Fiction, Survival-Fiction, Runaways-Fiction, Brothers and Sisters-Fiction, Grandparents-Fiction.

Warner, Gertrude Chandler. The woodshed mystery; illus by David Cunningham. A. Whitman 1960, 159 pp.

The four Alden children have grown since their first appearance in *The Boxcar Children* but they are still as close a family as ever. Aunt Jane's telephone message that she wanted to move near them started this adventure. Grandfather proceeded to buy and refurbish his childhood home as a surprise for Aunt Jane. It was an easy house to buy because it had been abandoned and was thought to be haunted. Even though the children and Aunt Jane weren't really worried by the stories of odd occurrences that no one quite remembered, they began to be aware of strange noises and things missing. Upon investigation they discovered Aunt Jane's old boyfriend living in the woodshed in the forest. There beneath the floor of the woodshed, they also found a store of Revolutionary War supplies and a letter from the original owners of the house. The supplies and the letter helped to explain some of the stories. Andrew, Jane's long-lost boyfriend, explained the rest.

It is not necessary to have read any of the series in order to read this story, but those children who enjoyed *The Boxcar Children* are most likely to enjoy the Alden's further adventures. See the entry for *The Boxcar Children* for more information.

Interest Level: 3-5. Reading Level: 2.1. Further Search Topics: Mystery and Detective Stories, United States-History-War-Fiction, Brothers and Sisters-Fiction, Ghosts-Fiction, Vacation-Fiction.

White, Laurence B., Jr. Science toys; illus by Marc Tolon Brown. A-W 1975, unp (46 pp).

This book presents 23 toys that a young child can easily make and learn from at the same time. A sundial, a drinking straw that flies, a balloon that rolls over, a ghost that sticks to the wall by itself, a water-go-round, and a paper cup that roars are a few examples of what is to be found here. The construction and use of each toy is explained and illustrated in enough detail to enable the child to work alone. And as in *Science Puzzles*, some of the toys will double as magic tricks (i.e. can you balance the rim of a paper plate on your nose?).

Interest Level: 1-3. Reading Level: 2.1. Further Search Topics: Handicrafts, Science, Magic, Toys, Games, Group 2, Puzzles.

Wyler, Rose. Magic secrets; illus by Talivaldis Stubis. Har-Row 1967, 64 pp.

Another good selection of easily performed but impressive looking magic tricks. After a short section defining magic, 13 tricks are described. Another 11 tricks are included as the authors describe how to put on a magic show. Just what differentiates the first group of tricks from the second is not clear. With a little imagination any of the tricks shown in the book could be used in a magic show. Use of the book beyond fourth grade is not likely due to its "early-reader" appearance. An I-Can-Read-Book.

Interest Level: 1-4. Reading Level: 2.1. Further Search Topics: Magic, Group 2.

Wyler, Rose. Funny Magic; illus by Talivaldis Stubis. Schol Bk Serv 1972, 52 pp.

A collection of 20 simple but effective magic tricks that require some advance preparation and practice but which are well-suited to the third through fifth grade child's coordination. Because all tricks are meant to be performed in front of an audience, there are performance hints throughout the book. Most of the tricks are impressive enough to interest even sixth grade magicians, but the book's reader format and cute tone make it difficult to use beyond grade four.

Interest Level: 2-4. Reading Level: 2.1. Further Search Topics: Magic.

READING LEVEL 2.2

Abisch, Roz. Mixed bag of magic tricks; illus by Boche Kaplan. Walker & Co. 1973, 64 pp.

The definition of magic is broadened here to include optical illusions, puzzles, age and date guessing formulae, as well as slight of hand and prearranged tricks. There are 25 "feats of magic" here, with especially good tips on performance, practice, costumes, and props. Although tricks in *Science Puzzles, It's Magic?, Funny Magic,* and *Magic Secrets* are showier, this is a more solid introduction to the subject. The Knot Magic Trick receives its best explanation here. See *It's Magic?* and *Science Puzzles* for others. Bonus: The book looks like a manual and not like a reader, therefore it should be useful even with sixth graders. It is now available in paperback version only; published by Grosset and Dunlap (Activity Books).

Interest Level: 2-6. Reading Level: 2.2. Further Search Topics: Magic, Optical Illusions, Puzzles.

Allen, Gertrude. Everyday turtles, toads and their kin. HM 1970, 48 pp.

Straight-forward, short, chapter discussions of turtles, lizards, snakes, salamanders, toads, frogs and tree toads. Black and white drawings done by the author amplify the text. The major part of the book is simple enough to be understood at second grade, but should still be interesting to fourth and fifth graders. A few terms may need explanation: i.e., venomous, prey. The chapters on the turtle, lizard, frog and tree frog are the easiest. No index, but still useful for reports.

Interest Level: 2-5. Reading Level: 2.2. Further Search Topics: Turtles, Reptiles, Lizards, Toads, Frogs, Snakes, Salamanders.

Amon, Aline. Talking hands: Indian sign language. Doubleday 1968, 80 pp.

If you can ignore the author's patronizing tone and air of self-satisfaction, this is a book with great appeal. Children love ways of communicating privately, be it Pig Latin, codes and ciphers, or just whispering. This book appeals to that love by clearly, though unattractively, demonstrating over 200 words in American Indian sign language. By the time the young reader finishes the book, he/she will not only have had the fun of learning another method of communication, but will have learned a few simple generalities about North American Indians. The index is detailed enough that any word can be quickly checked. The book is useful for history, social studies, or language arts units, as well as for fun.

Interest Level: 2-6. Reading Level: 2.2. Further Search Topics: Indians of North America-Sign Language, Communication, Nonverbal Communication, Ethnic Groups.

Baylor, Byrd. Sometimes I dance mountains; illus by Ken Longtemps and Bill Sears. Scribner 1973, 42 pp.

The author feels strongly that dance is a creative personal statement. That feeling becomes very clear in this combination of photographs and drawings. The photographs record a young girl's dance interpretation of the author's prose. The background drawings enlarge upon the poetic mood of the sparse text. For the dance enthusiast.

Interest Level: 2-6. Reading Level: 2.2. Further Search Topics: Dancing.

Benchley, Nathaniel. Sam the Minutemen; illus by Arnold Lobel. Har-Row 1969, 62 pp.

A good but limited book. It is a simple, personalized account of the beginning of the Revolutionary War as seen by the young son of a Minuteman. The book is a fairly exciting, uncomplicated and enjoyable story. Its limitations rest in its format (it's designed as a reader), the apparent young age of the main character, and the fact that it is told as a story. Its usefulness extends no further than grade three. An I Can Read History Book

Interest Level: 1-3. Reading Level: 2.2. Further Search Topics: United States-History-War-Fiction, Historical Fiction, War-Fiction, Group 2, Courage-Fiction.

Benchley, Nathaniel. Small Wolf; illus by Joan Sandin. Har-Row 1972, 64 pp.

A straight-forward telling of white man's purchase of Manhattan and the resulting displacement of the Indians. The text is simple. The tone is sympathetic to the plight of the Indians. The reader is neither lectured nor patronized, but the early-reader format will prevent using the book comfortably beyond fourth grade. An I Can Read History Book.

Interest Level: 1-4. Reading Level 2.2. Further Search Topics: Historical Fiction, New York City-Fiction, United States-History-Fiction, Indians of North America-Fiction, Group 2.

Berends, Polly Berrien. The case of the elevator duck; illus by James K. Washburn. Random 1973, 54 pp.

Although it would be stretching the meaning of the word to call this a mystery, it is a story of an 11-year-old detective. Albert tells his own story in a clipped style that resembles adult detective novels. One morning Albert found a duck abandoned in the apartment house elevator. He was determined to find the owner of the duck and return it. He had to be very careful as he searched because pets were absolutely forbidden in the housing projects. Anyone who saw him with the duck might report him. Albert and his parents had waited too long to get into the projects to be kicked out because of a duck. When Albert finally found the duck's owner (a young, sad child named Julio), Julio's sister forced Albert to take the duck back. Still angry at Julio's sister, Albert took the duck to the project's day care center, where the teacher agreed to formally adopt the duck. Albert stayed at the center long enough to see Julio's happy surprise when he arrived and found the duck. Its appealing characters, the tension created by the writing style, and the book's humor make this a delightful story.

Interest Level: 2-5. Reading Level 2.2. Further Search Topics: Humorous Fiction, City Life-Fiction, Housing Projects-Fiction, Detectives-Fiction, Pets-Fiction, Ducks-Fiction, Read Aloud.

Berger, Melvin. Time after time; illus by Richard Cuffari. Coward 1975, 45 pp.

The book begins with a description of inner clocks, proceeds into measurement of time, the seasons, and finally demonstrates the making of a simple clock. The explanations are simple but interesting. One point logically follows from another. It is a solid, serviceable tool limited only somewhat by the fact that it looks like a cross between a picture book and a reader. A brief index is included.

Interest Level: 1-4. Reading Level: 2.2. Further Search Topics: Time, Clocks and Watches, Seasons, Group 2.

Blegvad, Lenore. The great hamster hunt; illus by Erik Blegvad. HarBraceJ 1969, 32 pp.

Nicholas wanted a hamster; but, because his mother didn't like them, he couldn't have one. She did, however, agree to let Nicholas take care of his friend Tony's hamster for a week. It was a good and happy week for Nicholas until the evening before Tony was to return for his hamster. Nicholas accidentally broke the glass front of Harvey's cage and temporarily replaced it with cardboard. By morning Harvey had chewed through the cardbroad and was gone. Nicholas and his family searched all day but couldn't find Harvey. They finally bought another hamster and waited for Tony to arrive. As evening came Nicholas realized that hamsters are nocturnal and began to look for Harvey once more. This time Harvey was awake and active. The happy result was that Harvey was found and the new hampster became Nicholas' own pet. A simple, satisfying story even to fourth grade readers.

Interest Level: 1-4. Reading Level: 2.2. Further Search Topics: Pets-Fiction, Hamsters-Fiction, Group 2, Everyday Stories.

Branley, Franklyn M. Eclipse: darkness in daytime; illus by Donald Crews. Har-Row 1973, 33 pp.

The subject is so well-explained and the book is so physically attractive, it's a shame that some older readers will be put off by this title's picture book appearance. Aside from an occasional jarring, condescending note, this is a fine introduction to an interesting subject. Use comfortably with third and fourth graders. Recommend to fifth graders with caution. No index or table of contents. Lets-Read-and-Find-Out-Science-Book series.

Interest Level: 2-4. Reading Level: 2.2. Further Search Topics: Sun, Astronomy, Eclipses, Moon.

Branley, Franklyn M. Oxygen keeps you alive; illus by Don Madden. Har-Row 1971, 33 pp.

A well-explained, beginning treatment of the functions, importance, and uses of oxygen. The explanation is not limited to humans, but extends to plants and animals as well. Although the book can be stretched to use with fifth graders, its picture book format and sometimes condescending tone indicate it is most easily used through fourth grade. No index or table to contents. Let's-Read-and-Find-Out-Science-Book series.

Interest Level: 2-4. Reading Level: 2.2. Further Search Topics: Air, Respiration, Scuba Diving, Astronauts.

Branley, Franklyn M. Roots are food finders; illus by Joseph Low. Har-Row 1975, 33 pp.

It really is a shame that the picture book format of this and other *Let's-Read-and-Find-Out-Science-Books* will prevent older children from using them. There is much good information here that is thoroughly and logically explained without patronizing the reader. Functions and types of roots are described. Experiments to show root growth, root hairs, and absorption are given. A very useful book through third grade and possibly fourth grade. Beyond fourth grade children will certainly balk at the book's "babyish" appearance. Let's-Read-and-Find-Out-Science-Book series.

Interest Level: 1-4. Reading Level: 2.2. Further Search Topics: Nature Study, Botany, Group 2, Experiments, Scientific.

Branley, Franklyn M. High sounds, low sounds; illus by Paul Galdone. Har-Row 1967, 35 pp.

A no-nonsense, informative, thorough introduction to sound, sound waves, and hearing. Includes a couple of simple, illustrative experiments. Useful through third and fourth grade with no problems. The picture book format and opening and closing questions to the reader may turn away fifth and sixth grade users. Worth trying anyway. No index or table of contents. Let's-Read-and-Find-Out-Science-Book series.

Interest Level: 2-4. Reading Level: 2.2. Further Search Topics: Sound, Experiments, Scientific.

Bulla, Clyde Robert. The sword in the tree; illus by Paul Galdone. Har-Row 1956, 113 pp.

Shan didn't like or trust his Uncle Lionel, who had suddenly appeared at the castle gates after being away many years. Just as suddenly, Shan's father disappeared or died. Shan and his mother soon realized that Lionel wanted to take over the castle, even if it meant killing them. To save themselves, Shan and his mother fled. After walking many miles, they found a poor goat herder and his family who gave them a place to live. Sometime later Shan decided to travel to see King Arthur and ask for help in reclaiming the castle from Lionel. It wasn't until Shan was able to prove the castle was his, and Lionel lost a duel to one of Arthur's knights, that Shan was given back his home. Deep in the castle dungeon Shan found his father, still alive but imprisoned by Lionel.

This book, with its short chapters, short sentences, and steadily progressing plot should interest even the most reluctant reader from grade two through six.

Interest Level: 2-6. Reading Level: 2.2. Further Search Topics: Knights and Knighthood-Fiction, Survival-Fiction, Royalty-Fiction, Best Sellers, Courage-Fiction.

Bulla, Clyde Robert. Shoeshine girl; illus by Leigh Grant. Har-Row 1975, 84 pp.

A well-written, realistic story of 10-year-old Sarah who was sent to spend the summer with her Aunt Claudia. Sarah's parents felt that Sarah put too much importance on money and so insisted that Aunt Claudia give her no allowance for the summer. Sure that Aunt Claudia would call her bluff, Sarah threatened to get a job. Instead, Aunt Claudia thought it was a good idea. Sarah's experience as a shoeshine girl forced her to grow, to learn to like working, and finally to take responsibility for the stand when her boss was hit by a car. Told with quiet humor. For the reader who enjoys Judy Blume's books.

Interest Level: 2-5. Reading Level: 2.2. Further Search Topics: Children-Growth-Fiction, Family Problems-Fiction, Vacation-Fiction, Occupations-Fiction, Everyday Stories.

Bulla, Clyde Robert. Ghost town treasure; illus by Don Freeman. Har-Row 1957, 87 pp.

A very simple story whose title is somewhat misleading. Instead of a mystery or an exciting story of buried treasure, Bulla has written a very pleasant story of a family whose fortunes are reversed by the accidental discovery of a nearby cave. Young Ty Jackson and his family were the last people living in Gold Rock, California. Everyone else had moved out when the new highway had bypassed the town. The Jacksons had been able to stay on only because some of the nearby ranchers had continued to buy food and supplies from the Jacksons' store. Just as they, too, were preparing to move out, Ty's pen pals wrote that they were coming to visit the town. Their grandfather had died there, years earlier, during his search for gold. When Paul and Nora arrived, they brought with them their grandfather's diary. The last entry in the journal seemed to indicate that their grandfather had found gold in an isolated cave in the nearby canyon. After a long search, the children discovered the cave, but no gold. Ty's disappointment changed to joy when tourists started arriving to see the new natural attraction. Once again his parents could sell their groceries, the hotel could be reopened and Gold Rock would flourish.

Interest Level: 2-5. Reading Level: 2.2. Further Search Topics: Treasure-Fiction, Family Problems-Fiction, West-Fiction, California-Fiction, Family-Fiction, Pen Pals-Fiction.

Bunting, Eve. The skate patrol; illus by Don Madden. Albert Whitman 1980, 40 pp.

The book is funny, clever, undemanding and short. The combination of those qualities plus its slight mystery and its consistent reading level make this a very appealing and useful book for young readers. The plot is simple: in the hopes that their neighbors would be so grateful that they would allow the boys to roller skate in the neighborhood again, two friends decided to capture a local thief. James and Milton even knew who the thief was. He was the "mysterious man" who sat in the park. They only had to capture him in the act of stealing to prove that they were correct. They watched him continuously and trailed him as he followed old ladies. Then came the day that they heard Mrs. Grump scream that her purse had been snatched. The boys sped after the "mysterious man" on their skates. They caught him and knocked him down. To their surprise he declared that he was an undercover policeman and they were letting the real thief get away. Off they went again. This time they caught the right person and were rewarded just the way that they had hoped: Mrs. Crump (not Grump) promised that the boys would be allowed to roller skate any time they wished. A light and lively entertainment.

Interest Level: 2-4. Reading Level: 2.2. Further Search Topics: Mystery and Detective Stories, Humorous Fiction, Spies-Fiction, Roller Skating-Fiction, Crime-Fiction, Best Sellers.

Burchard, Marshall. Sports hero: Joe Namath. Putnam 1971, 95 pp.

One of football's best and flashiest quarterbacks. See Sports Hero: Bill Walton entry. Sports Hero series.

Interest Level: 2-6. Reading Level: 2.2. Further Search Topics: Biography, Namath, Joe, Football-Biography.

Burchard, Susan H. Sports star: Mark "The Bird" Fidrych. HarBraceJ 1977, 64 pp.

Although his major league career was short, it was also notable. Mark Fidrych's way of concentrating on his pitching was by talking to the baseball. Entry for Sports Hero: Bill Walton, by Marshall Burchard, provides more information about the book. Sports Star series.

Interest Level: 2-6. Reading Level: 2.2. Further Search Topics: Biography, Baseball-Biography, Fidrych, Mark "The Bird."

Butterworth, William E. Next stop, Earth; illus by Paul Frame. Walker 1978, 80 pp.

After two years on a desolate planet, 12-year-old Charley and his family were anticipating their return to Earth. But when Charley was awakened from sleep by a spaceship robot, he learned that an asteroid disturbance had caused several key systems on the ship to malfunction. Of 24 passengers on board the spaceship, only 10 were still alive and only Charley and his sister were able to be awakened. It was up to Charley to pilot the ship to its landing on Earth. The controls were all in an adjacent room which a faulty robot kept Charley from entering. Without someone at the controls the ship would burn up when re-entering Earth's atmosphere. By tricking the robot and commanding the ship's main computer, Charley was able to get to the control panel just in time to wake his father, help with reentry and save the ship.

Though the story tends to be heavy with conversations between Charley and various computers and robots, it is also that dialogue that helps maintain suspense. It is a story for the confirmed science fiction fan, not for the inductee.

Interest Level: 3-6. Reading Level: 2.2. Further Search Topics: Science Fiction, Outer Space-Fiction, Voyages and Travels-Fiction, Robots-Fiction, Computers-Fiction.

Chaikin, Miriam. I should worry, I should care; illus by Richard Egielski. Har-Row 1979, 103 pp.

A warm, well-written story about life in a Jewish family in Brooklyn just before World War II. This is the story of young Molly's adjustment to moving, to leaving old friends, to making and losing new friends (one by death) and to the small happenings that make up her life. In the background, but always there, is Hitler's ever-increasing threat to the world.

A comfortable, truthful look at a close-knit family. Also useful for its picture of the times and the place. An occasional Yiddish expression may slow the reader but adds to the book's authenticity. Print is slightly lighter and smaller than *Finders Weepers*.

Interest Level: 3-5. Reading Level: 2.2. Further Search Topics: Moving, Household-Fiction, Friendship-Fiction, City Life-Fiction, Jews-Fiction, Family-Fiction.

Charosh, Mannis. Mathematical games for one or two; illus by Lois Ehlert. T Y Crowell 1975, 33 pp.

It will take a very special reader to appreciate this book, one who is excited by math puzzles and games and who is also willing to overlook the book's picture book format. Starting with a very simple, one-player game, the book progresses through six types of games, each progressively more taxing mentally. Each type of game is introduced by a very simple example that is thoroughly explained. For the up-and-coming Einstein.

Interest Level: 3-4. Reading Level: 2.2. Further Search Topics: Mathematics, Puzzles, Games.

Chew, Ruth. No such thing as a witch. Hastings 1971, 112 pp.

Despite the fact that their mother said there was no such thing as a witch, Tad and Nora were convinced that their neighbor Maggie Brown was indeed a witch. And they were right! Maggie Brown knew how to make a special kind of fudge that could make anyone into an animal-lover, enable people to talk with animals, or actually transform someone into an animal. All you had to do was to eat one, two, or three pieces of fudge respectively. But Maggie's overzealous love of animals and her disenchantment with housework eventually attracted the attention of her neighbors and the city health department. Only Tad and Nora's frantic efforts to help her saved Maggie from losing all of her animal friends.

A fairly detailed plot, the fascination of being able to change size and appearance and the intrigue involved in fooling the adults around Maggie make this one of Chew's best books.

Interest Level: 2-5. Reading Level: 2.2. Further Search Topics: Individualists-Fiction, Witches-Fiction, Animals-Fiction, Fantasy, Magic-Fiction, Brothers and Sisters-Fiction, Transformations-Fiction.

Chew, Ruth. The witch's garden. Hastings 1978, 112 pp.

Although its elements seem to promise an exciting adventure story, this is a disappointing book. The witch who moved into the dark, old home next door to Josh and Susan, was trying to improve her overgrown garden when Susan and Josh offered to help. The children accidentally splashed themselves with the witch's newest brew and found they suddenly became very tiny inhabitants of a dense and threatening jungle (the garden). After they regained their normal size, they dug into other areas of the garden. One hole they dug opened into an underground tunnel that they found was inhabited by a fire-breathing dragon. When the dragon cornered Mrs. Muldoon, Susan and Josh ran out of the tunnel, found the brew and splashed it onto the dragon. The dragon shrank away, Mrs. Muldoon was safe and the tunnel closed over.

Because there is little more suspense than in this description, the book fails to live up to its promise. In addition, the children's first sudden size change is just subtle enough to be confusing. Despite its problems the book is popular with Ruth Chew fans and therefore useful.

Interest Level: 2-5. Reading Level: 2.2. Further Search Topics: Witches-Fiction, Brothers and Sisters-Fiction, Magic-Fiction, Fantasy, Dragons-Fiction, Transformations-Fiction.

Chew, Ruth. The would-be witch. Hastings 1976, 112 pp.

Robin and her brother Andy took a liking to the clumsy white cat they saw in Zelda's Antique Shop. The cat apparently liked them, too, for it followed them home. Not having enough money to offer to buy Pearl from Zelda, the children tried to polish up an old pair of silver birds to trade for the cat. The polish turned out to be magical and made the birds real. When they tried the polish on a broom in Zelda's store, the broom began to fly. Upon discovering that Zelda wanted to be a witch but had failed the coven entrance exam, Rob helped her learn to fly and told her of the witches' meeting place that she and Andy had discovered. But the 12 witches who had been turned into cats were wicked enough to want to use Zelda to regain their human form and turn *her* into a cat. In attempting to prevent such a fate, Rob, Andy and Zelda set fire to the abandoned building being used as a meeting place. The 12 witches were rescued from the fire but charged with arson, which meant probable jail sentences for all of them. Zelda, finally a happy and capable witch, gave Pearl to Rob and Andy to thank them for their help.

A better-crafted story than many of the others, this also has a more evil cast of characters to provide additional interest.

Interest Level: 2-5. Reading Level: 2.2. Further Search Topics: Witches-Fiction, Brothers and Sisters-Fiction, Magic-Fiction, Fantasy, Transformations-Fiction, Cats-Fiction.

Chew, Ruth. Earthstar magic. Hastings 1979, 128 pp.

This is one of a series of similar stories by Ruth Chew. Each story involves two children and an old woman they usually suspect is a witch. As their suspicions become convictions they also find that, contrary to their expectation, the witch is very nice and often in need of help.

The children in this tale are brother and sister. Ben and Elizabeth first saw and then didn't see Trudy as she searched for a magical mushroom called an earthstar. Accidentally thrown together again, Ben and Elizabeth took a liking to Trudy, especially when she explained that she had been thrown out of her coven because she was so inept. In fact, she wasn't even able to control the earthstar. The earthstar manages to get all three in and out of adventures (including becoming tiny, flying and almost being eaten) before they learn to control its power. As the story ends, Trudy, finally respected by the other witches, flies off with a promise that Ben and Elizabeth will see her again.

Very lightweight but also very popular with young lovers of witch stories. There seems to be just the right amount of adventure to make up for the very benign witch.

Interest Level: 2-5. Reading Level: 2.2. Further Search Topics: Witches-Fiction, Magic-Fiction, Fantasy, Vacation-Fiction, Brothers and Sisters-Fiction, Transformations-Fiction.

Chew, Ruth. The wishing tree. Hastings 1980, 142 pp.

Peggy and Brian's discovery of a talking cat, a bird with a beautiful song, and a strange and frightening tree led them to a shopping bag lady, a giant named Fred, a gold key and a magical tablecloth. In a rather complicated series of events, the children and the cat finally succeeded in retrieving the tablecloth from Annie (the old woman to whom Puss had loaned it) and giving it back to Fred, who needed it to help satisfy his gigantic appetite. In addition, they returned Fred to normal human size, rescued Annie from a fall on the ice, introduced the two characters and encouraged them to live together in Fred's castle.

Complicated enough already, the story's lengthy adventure that leads up to the discovery of the key (climbing into the magical tree and swimming in a pond) makes the plot even more complex. If a reader doesn't expect more than benign fantasy and fun this is an adequate choice.

Interest Level: 2-5. Reading Level: 2.2. Further Search Topics: Magic-Fiction, Fantasy, Brothers and Sisters-Fiction, Giants-Fiction, Cats-Fiction.

Ciardi, John. I met a man; illus by Robert Osborn. HM 1961, 74 pp.

Ciardi's poems are pure fun. About half are riddle poems (poems that describe something without naming it until the end) and the rest are humorous descriptions or nonsense poems. There is a problem, however, with the riddle poems: they are somewhat more difficult to read than the other poems, but of interest to younger rather than older readers. For that reason pages 1-21 (primarily nonsense verse) can be recommended for grades one through five. The remainder of the book, although enjoyable to the very young, needs to be read to them or needs a strong young reader.

Interest Level: 1-5. Reading Level: 2.2. Further Search Topics: Wit and Humor, Poetry, Riddles, Group 2.

Cleary, Beverly. Henry Huggins; illus by Louis Darling. Morrow 1950, 155 pp.

Henry Huggins is over 30 years old now, so if he occasionally seems a little old-fashioned, it is not surprising. What is surprising is how well he has withstood the years. His antics are innocent, but humorous and realistic. The book's six chapters are six separate stories that follow the same cast of characters through an entire year.

In the first chapter, Henry finds a stray dog (Ribsy) whom he must then transport home on a bus. Ribsy was too large and too frisky not to get into trouble, so before Henry finally gets him home, they have been kicked off of three buses and have ridden in a police car. The second chapter describes what happens when Henry buys two guppies and ends up with millions. In the third chapter Henry accidentally throws his friend's football into the back seat of a speeding car and tries to earn the money to replace it by catching and selling 1,331 night crawlers. The fourth chapter involves Henry's attempts to get out of playing the lead in a school Christmas play. His last minute rescue comes in the form of a can of green paint that spills all over him. It is Ribsy's turn to change colors in Chapter 5. Henry tries to cover Ribsy's dirt spots with talcolm powder for a dog show, but only succeeds in turning Ribsy pink. And in Chapter 6, Ribsy's original owner finally finds him and wants him back, but Ribsy chooses to stay with Henry. Only the occasional extra cute expression and Henry's age (third grade) keep this from being enjoyed beyond fourth grade.

Interest Level: 1-4. Reading Level: 2.2. Further Search Topics: Humorous Fiction, Everyday Stories, Read Aloud Pets-Fiction, Dogs-Fiction, Group 2.

Clymer, Eleanor. Luke was there; illus by Diane de Groat. HR & W 1973, 74 pp.

Julius' father, uncle and finally his step-father had all walked out on him. Even his mother had left him, although she hadn't wanted to go. When his mother had been taken to the hospital, Julius and his younger brother Danny were sent to a children's home. Julius felt alone and cheated until he met a young, black, social worker named Luke. Luke liked and respected Julius and helped Julius learn to feel the same way about himself. When Luke, too, left Julius, Julius was so angry at the world that he stole food and then money. Afraid to go back to the children's home because he thought he'd be caught and punished, Julius ran away. It wasn't until he found an abandoned child, about Danny's age, who needed care, that Julius returned to the home. Luke was there when he arrived, just when Julius needed him most. Luke listened to Julius' unhappy feelings, arranged for him to see his mother and helped him begin to accept the fact that life is not always fair.

Julius tells his own story in a realistic, straight-forward book that will touch most readers. Only the lack of quotation marks and inadequate spacing between the lines may slow the reader.

Interest Level: 3-6. Reading Level: 2.2. Further Search Topics: Runaways-Fiction, Orphans-Fiction, Juvenile Delinquency-Fiction, Divorce and Separation-Fiction, Friendship-Fiction, Courage-Fiction, Survival-Fiction, Loneliness-Fiction, Best Sellers, Read Aloud.

Cone, Molly. Leonard Bernstein; illus by Robert Galster. Har-Row 1970, 33 pp.

This is a bare bones outline that will appeal to music enthusiasts but will not attract anyone else. The reader catches very little of Bernstein's personality, but *is* awed by an impressive list of his accomplishments. The few attempts made to recreate the real person may have to be explained (i.e., references to Bernstein forgetting to get his hair cut because he was so busy). Picture book format of the hardback may deter some readers. Now published in paperback edition only. Crowell Biography series.

Interest Level: 2-4. Reading Level: 2.2. Further Search Topics: Music-Biography, Biography, Conductors, Composers, Pianists, Group 2.

Conklin, Gladys. Little apes; illus by Joseph Cellini. Holiday 1970, unp (32pp).

An informative as well as interesting look at gorillas, chimpanzees, orangutans and gibbons. Their habits and behavior patterns are described by fol'owing a young one of each species through a full day in its natural surroundings. The text is simple without being condescending and the illustrations are so life-like that they almost walk off the pages. An excellent treatment of a popular subject makes this a very useful book.

Interest Level: 2-5. Reading Level: 2.2. Further Search Topics: Apes, Gorillas, Nature Study, Infants, Group 2.

Dolch, Edward W. "Why" stories; illus by Marguerite Dolch. Garrard 1952, 160 pp.

"Why the Bear Has a Little Tail," "Why Turkeys Have Red Eyes," and "How the Tiger Got His Stripes" are three titles that illustrate the type of stories found in this collection. Seventeen short, simple folktales explain why the world and creatures in it operate and appear as they do. All of the tales can be found elsewhere. However, few if any stories are likely to be familiar to readers. This type of story is one children often find very appealing. The stories are understandable, logical within their own framework and simple enough to be retold to others. The reading level varies from 1.2 to 2.2. Dolch Basic Vocabulary Book series.

Interest Level: 1-4. Reading Level: 2.2. Further Search Topics: Folklore, Why Stories, Animals-Fiction, Group 2, Creation-Fiction.

Dolch, Edward W. Robin Hood stories; illus by Carmen Mowry. Garrard 1957, 162 pp.

The illustrations are still drab, but the stories in this volume are exciting. Here we find straight-forward adventure and familiar characters: Robin Hood, Little John, Will Scarlet, Sheriff of Nottingham, Allan-a-dale and Sir Richard of Lea. The book makes a good choice for adventure lovers. Dolch Pleasure Reading Book series.

Interest Level: 2-6. Reading Level: 2.2. Further Search Topics: Robin Hood, Knights and Knighthood-Fiction, Folklore, Crime-Fiction.

Dolch, Edward W. Fairy stories; illus by Marguerite Dolch and Yolande Cuypers-Fransen. Garrard 1950, 165 pp.

A collection of mostly familiar fairy tales told in the Dolchs' very simplified manner. Because the book's purpose is not to provide the most literate version of favorite fairy tales, better versions of any of the stories can be found elsewhere. It provides instead, very accessible versions of tales young readers have enjoyed for years. Includes "Cinderella," "Hansel and Gretel," "Jack and the Bean Stalk," "Snow White," "Sleeping Beauty," and "The Elves and the Shoemaker," among others. Dolch Pleasure Reading Book series.

Interest Level: 1-4. Reading Level: 2.2. Further Search Topics: Folklore, Fairy Tales, Fantasy, Group 2.

Dolch, Edward W. Irish stories; illus by Carmen Mowry. Garrard 1958, 165 pp.

Besides controlling the vocabulary used in the stories, the Dolchs seem to include only stories with very uncomplicated plots. Once again they split the longer stories into two chapters. Thus, from 17 chapters there come only 12 stories. Most of the stories will be unfamiliar to readers (except perhaps those about Finn McCool), but all are pleasurable. See *Andersen Stories* for more information. Dolch Basic Vocabulary Book series.

Interest Level: 2-5. Reading Level: 2.2. Further Search Topics: Folklore, Fantasy, Ireland-Fiction, Giants-Fiction.

Dolch, Edward W. Circus stories; illus by Dee Wallace. Garrard 1956, 166 pp.

A collection of 18 chapters that tell 15 true stories about the circus. Some are descriptions of activities (trapeze flying) or people (Emmett Kelly, a circus doctor, the Ringling Brothers). Other chapters tell of unusual occurrences; i.e., the bareback rider who was thrown off her horse into the lap of a spectator whom she later married. Some stories, such as the story of the horse trainer whose life was saved by an elephant, are exciting. Others are sad ("Blinky," the dog who was killed by an angry lion).

The authors' tone becomes condescending off and on through this collection, thus hampering its usefulness somewhat. Otherwise, it is very similar to the other Dolch books; it is a decent collection of very simplified stories. Dolch Basic Vocabulary Book series.

Interest Level: 1-4. Reading Level: 2.2. Further Search Topics: Circus-Fiction, Clowns-Fiction, Acrobats and Acrobatics-Fiction, Group 2.

Goldin, Augusta. Spider silk; illus by Joseph Low. Har-Row 1964, unp (34 pp).

No gimmicks here, just straight-forward information about spider webs. Where are spider webs found? How are they formed? What are their shapes? For what are they used? How strong are they? And, what are the other uses of spider silk? In answering those questions the author also gives a bit of information about particular types of spiders. The book can easily be used through grade three. Its picture book format will turn many fourth and fifth graders away even though the book's information is still quite interesting and useful. Let's-Read- & -Find-Out Science Book series.

Interest Level: 1-5. Reading Level: 2.2. Further Search Topics: Spiders, Nature Study, Group 2.

Greenfield, Eloise. Rosa Parks; illus by Eric Marlow. Har-Row 1973, 33 pp.

This book succumbs to the difficulty of writing for children about a subject that needs more explanation. The occasionally condescending tone combined with the Crowell Biography picture book format will keep this otherwise adequate introduction to the civil rights movement from being useful beyond fourth grade. The book should be very useful, however, for third and fourth grade social studies, history or biography units.

Rosa Parks' childhood and her feelings about the special rules for blacks make up the first half of the book. The second half is devoted to Rosa's act of defiance (refusing to give up her seat on a bus to a white man) and the repercussions of that act. Crowell Biography series.

Interest Level: 2-4. Reading Level 2.2. Further Search Topics: Blacks-Biography, Biography, Prejudice, Civil Rights, Women-Biography, Courage.

Harris, Robie H. Rosie's double dare; illus by Tony DeLuna. Knopf 1980, 112 pp.

Rosie wanted to play baseball with the Willard Street Gang, but she couldn't play well enough to play by their rules. She needed what her older brother called "shrimp rules." She couldn't hit a pitched ball, only a grounder; but grounders were "shrimp rules." In desperation Rosie agreed to take a dare that the gang made up. If she actually performed the dare, the gang would let her play with them by her rules.

The gang dared Rosie to sneak into cranky Mr. Quirk's apartment and borrow a set of his false teeth. Because Rosie couldn't find any extra false teeth, she borrowed his wig instead but that didn't satisfy the gang. They only laughed and made up another dare for Rosie. She was to untie Mrs. Samuels' dog and let it run loose. As Rosie untied him, Elmer ran away, Rosie ran off after him. One rainstorm later, Rosie caught up with him in the middle of a Red Sox game at Fenway Park. Rosie's attempt to catch Elmer stopped the game, brought her an interview on TV, and secured her a place on the Willard Street baseball team.

This very light story, made up almost entirely of action and examples of sibling rivalry, should have wide appeal through fifth grade. Beyond that, Rosie's age (almost nine) and childish behavior won't ring true. Capers series.

Interest Level: 2-5. Reading Level: 2.2. Further Search Topics: Baseball-Fiction, Humorous Fiction, Brothers and Sisters-Fiction, Challenges-Fiction, Courage-Fiction, Gangs-Fiction, Everyday Stories.

Heide, Florence Parry. The mystery of the silver tag; illus by Seymour Fleishman. A. Whitman 1972, 127 pp.

Jay's paper route took him to one house that he wished he could avoid. It was grumpy, old Mr. Pendleton's house that Jay hated. One rainy day he spotted what he later realized was a prize Angora cat hiding on Mr. Pendleton's porch. When the cat was reported lost in that night's paper, Jay and the other members of the Spotlight Club decided to try to return the cat to its owner, Miss Horton. Their attempts to get the cat back from Mr. Pendleton meant that they had to spy on him, to sneak into his garage, and to spend the night in a treehouse overlooking his house. They were afraid that they had failed when they saw Mr. Pendleton leave with the cat. Determined to be the ones to tell Miss Horton of their failure, they went to her apartment and found Mr. Pendleton already there. Mr. Pendleton was a famous animal photographer who, upon finding the cat, had asked Miss Horton if he could photograph him. The children, thinking only that Mr. Pendleton was a mad scientist who kidnapped cats, had jumped to all the wrong conclusions, but ended with a mystery solved, new friends, and their first lesson in being detectives.

See entry with *Mystery at Southport Cinema* for series information. Spotlight Club Mystery series.

Interest Level: 3-5. Reading Level: 2.2. Further Search Topics: Mystery and Detective Stories, Brothers and Sisters-Fiction, Gangs-Fiction, Cats-Fiction, Loners-Fiction, Detectives-Fiction, Photography-Fiction, Kidnapping-Fiction.

Heide, Florence Parry. Mystery of the melting snowman; illus by Seymour Fleishman. A. Whitman 1974, 128 pp.

Hidden inside of a snowman, the Spotlight Club found what they believed was a stolen iron statue of a dog. In order to try to catch the thief, the children hid the statue again and watched to see who came to look for it. Eventually they determined that the thief or thieves was either Tom and Jenny, the amenable young couple who were helping Mrs. Wellington sell her house or Alex, the man who seemed to be a detective. After a frightening episode in which Alex almost captured Cindy, the dog, and a cache of Mrs. Wellington's diamonds (hidden in a secret compartment to which the dog held the key), Cindy managed to lock Alex in a closet long enough to enable Jay and Dexter to alert Mrs. Wellington to what was happening. The case was closed as Mrs. Wellington revealed Alex to be her greedy, young nephew, whom she had indulged once too often, but would not indulge again.

See *Mystery at Southport Cinema* for series information. Spotlight Club Mystery series.

Interest Level: 3-5. Reading Level: 2.2. Further Search Topics: Mystery and Detective Stories, Gangs-Fiction, Crime-Fiction, Brothers and Sisters-Fiction, Detectives-Fiction, Inheritance-Fiction.

Heide, Florence Parry. Mystery of the vanishing visitor; illus by Seymour Fleishman. A. Whitman 1975, 128 pp.

Cindy was hired to take care of Mrs. Widget's house, animals, and plants for a weekend. That same weekend, someone tried to find and steal something from Mrs. Widget's overcrowded house. She had very few empty spaces in her house, so it was not a surprise that the thief wasn't able to find the object of his or her search. The three Spotlight Club members were determined to figure out not only who was the thief, but also what it was that the thief, wanted. Their prime suspects included the very nasty Bertha Beaker and the charming Charley Capp.

After spending a night in Mrs. Widget's house trying to, and almost succeeding in catching the thief, the children were surprised by an early morning visit from Mr. Capp. Mr. Capp was nearly able to steal away with a painting that hid a great deal of money before Cindy figured out that he was the thief. Even after Mr. Capp had been caught, he charmed his way out of any punishment and left before anyone had second thoughts.

See entry for *Mystery at Southport Cinema* for series information. Spotlight Club Mystery series.

Interest Level: 3-5. Reading Level: 2.2. Further Search Topics: Mystery and Detective Stories, Brothers and Sisters-Fiction, Gangs-Fiction, Crime-Fiction, Antiquities-Fiction, Detectives-Fiction.

Hildick, Edmund W. The great rabbit rip-off; illus by Lisl Weil. Macmillan 1976, 101 pp.

Why would anyone want to put red paint on all of the clay lawn rabbits in town? That was the first and easier of the mysteries the McGurk Organization had to solve. The bigger mystery was who would then steal them all and why? Almost everyone in town had purchased a rabbit to help a charity drive. Donny Towers a local social worker had thought of the idea. Donny, his fiancee, Joanne, and two reformed thieves, Sam and Ferdie, had made enough rabbits for everyone. When the rabbits disappeared, the Organization began to suspect, among others, Sam and Ferdie. Then when Donny replaced each one

almost immediately with rabbits smelling of paint remover, the group began to think Donny might have been involved. It was Wanda's sharp eyes that revealed Donny's motive. Joanne's engagement ring had been accidentally molded into one of the rabbits and Donny had retrieved the rabbits to find the ring. Knowing he couldn't return the paint stained rabbits without raising suspicion, Donny had removed the red paint and told everyone that he was simply replacing the stolen rabbits with new ones.

See *Case of the Bashful Bank Robber* for series information. McGurk Mystery series.

Interest Level: 3-5. Reading Level: 2.2. Further Search Topics: Mystery and Detective Stories, Detectives-Fiction, Gangs-Fiction, Rabbits-Fiction, Crime-Fiction, Humorous Fiction.

Hildick, Edmund W. Deadline for McGurk; illus by Lisl Weil. Macmillan 1975, 104 pp.

When many of the dolls in the neighborhood began disappearing, their owners went to the McGurk Organization for help. At first McGurk was reluctant to take on such a silly task as recovering lost dolls. But when a ransom note appeared and the Organization was linked to the dolls' safety, McGurk's reluctance vanished. The note stated that if, in a written public notice, the members of the Organization did not admit that they were no good, the dolls were doomed. McGurk's pride would never have allowed him to write such a notice. As the deadline approached, the group plotted a daring move designed to uncover the doll thief. The plan depended on Willie's super-sensitive nose, a particular perfume dabbed on a stolen doll, and the curiosity of the thief. Success came only minutes before the hour of doom. Once again Sandra Ennis was the culprit.

See *The Case of the Bashful Bank Robber* for series information. McGurk Mystery series.

Interest Level: 3-5. Reading Level: 2.2. Further Search Topics: Dolls-Fiction, Mystery and Detective Stories, Detectives-Fiction, Humorous Fiction, Gangs-Fiction, Jealousy-Fiction.

Hildick, Edmund W. The case of the condemned cat; illus by Lisl Weil. Macmillan 1975, 106 pp.

Ray Williams had a terrible problem when he begged the McGurk Organization for help. His cat Whiskers had been accused of killing a neighbor's pet dove. Ray's mother decided that they couldn't risk upsetting the neighbors anymore and threatened to take Whiskers to the pound unless it could be proven that he was innocent. The Organization, needing time, hid Whiskers and told Mrs. Williams that he had run away. While Whiskers was safely hidden, the group interviewed all the neighbors, surveyed the scene of the crime, and tried to decide upon the real murderer. When the remains of another bird were found while Whiskers was safely locked away, it looked as if the cat was surely innocent. But then McGurk and his detectives found out that the cat had been sprung. It wasn't until they went back over all the information they had gathered that McGurk realized who was the real culprit. The only step left was to trick old Gramp Martin (the neighborhood grouch) into confessing.

See *The Case of the Bashful Bank Robber* for series information. McGurk Mystery series.

Interest Level: 3-6. Reading Level: 2.2. Further Search Topics: Mystery and Detective Stories, Cats-Fiction, Detectives-Fiction, Humorous Fiction, Gangs-Fiction, Pets-Fiction.

Hildick, Edmund W. The case of the secret scribbler; illus by Lisl Weil. Macmillan 1978, 106 pp.

Joey's discovery in a library book of a scrap of paper with part of a letter and a strange diagram on it led the McGurk Organization on a lively chase. Brains identified the diagram as that of a widely-used security system. The part of the letter that they could read told the group that there was a burglary being planned for the approaching weekend, but the youngsters knew the police would never take them seriously until they had much more evidence. By researching local alarm systems, determining who bought the unusual paper, and comparing handwriting samples, the detectives were able to convince the police of what was about to happen. In gratitude, the police loaned the Organization a police monitor so that they could listen as the thieves were caught. To all but McGurk it seemed like the perfect way to end the case: he tried to sneak into the midst of the capture, but only succeeded in getting himself in real trouble.

See *The Case of the Bashful Bank Robber* for series information. McGurk Mystery series.

Interest Level: 3-6. Reading Level: 2.2. Further Search Topics: Mystery and Detective Stories, Crime-Fiction, Gangs-Fiction, Nonverbal Communication-Fiction, Humorous Fiction, Detectives-Fiction.

Hildick, Edmund W. The case of the bashful bank robber; illus by Lisl Weil. Macmillan 1981, 138 pp.

The McGurk Organization is a crime fighting detective agency. Led by Jack McGurk's strong ego, they had taken on many a seemingly impossible task and had always been successful. Never before, however, had they tried to protect the seven banks in town from being robbed. The five children's first idea was to regularly patrol each bank and watch for likely looking get-away cars. When that plan only led to a nasty confrontation with their new junior high school principal, they decided to try something else. Their second plan, to photograph all suspicious looking people near the banks, didn't fare much better than their first idea. Then, without knowing it, they found themselves holding the key to solving a real bank robbery. Before they realized its importance, they had literally given away the vital clue. Using only their own memories, powers of observation, and cleverness, they were still able to solve the crime with only a little help from the FBI.

The "McGurk mysteries" are light, fast-moving, and often humorous. Clues for solving the mysteries are sometimes subtle, but always there in the plot and illustrations for the reader to find. The characters are somewhat flat but still appealing. Joey, who is handy with words and a typewriter, is the narrator of each book. Jack McGurk, dedicated mastermind of all the group's activities is shrewd, a natural leader, and egotistical. Willie has the world's most sensitive nose and an excellent memory for odors. Wanda is the best tree-climber in town and a rational influence on the group. Brains, the newest and youngest member of the group, is a scientific genius, so he runs their crime lab. The books need not be read in chronological order although most have a brief reference to an earlier story. Reading level varies within each book from 2.1 to 3.1. A few books include enough more difficult passages that their average reading level is pushed from 2.2 to 3.1. Interest level in the series, once a reader has started on it, is high. McGurk Mystery series.

Interest Level: 3-6. Reading Level: 2.2. Further Search Topics: Mystery and Detective Stories, Crime-Fiction, Detectives-Fiction, Humorous Fiction, Gangs-Fiction.

Kalb, Jonah. The easy hockey book; illus by Bill Morrison. HM 1977, 64 pp.

This book is exactly what the title indicates; an easy-read introduction to the sport of hockey. It does not teach one how to skate, but in a logical non-sexist manner it does carefully and thoroughly teach the rules, techniques, and skills of hockey. Common mistakes are anticipated in each section. Chapter summaries make an already serviceable text even more useful. It could have been even better with an index.

Interest Level: 2-6. Reading Level: 2.2. Further Search Topics: Hockey.

Lewis, Thomas P. Hill of fire; illus by Joan Sandin. Har-Row 1971, 63 pp.

A personalized account of the volcano that suddenly erupted in the middle of a farmer's field in Mexico on February 20, 1943. Because the account is written as a story and because of its easy-reader format, the book is most useful only through third grade. An I-Can-Read-History-Book.

Interest Level: 1-3. Reading Level: 2.2. Further Search Topics: Volcanoes, Group 2, Mexico, Disasters, Historical Fiction.

Lowry, Lois. Anastasia again! HM 1981, 145 pp.

This is a sequel that is as funny and well-written as its predecessor. Because its plot involves less common experiences, this book may not enjoy quite the wide-spread success of *Anastasia Krupnik*. However, among those readers who liked their first meeting with Anastasia, this book will find many fans.

Anastasia's parents astounded her when they announced that the family was going to move from their Cambridge, Massachusetts apartment to a house in the suburbs. She didn't like the idea of leaving the apartment, but she *hated* the idea of the suburbs. The only thing that made the move bearable was the house itself. Anastasia had said she would move only if they could find a house with a tower—and they had. After she got over the shock of moving, Anastasia began to enjoy her new home. She met a neighborhood boy who became a special friend, she tried to help her cranky elderly neighbor Mrs. Stein make friends, and she even wrote a short mystery book.

Anastasia is as spunky and original as before. She is a bit precocious, but her precocity is nothing compared to that of her brother. At two-and-a-half years old, he speaks as well as many adults. As we mentioned above, the book will be most appealing to readers who want second helpings of Anastasia's adventures. The print is slightly smaller here than in the first title.

Interest Level: 4-6. Reading Level: 2.2. Further Search Topics: Moving, Household-Fiction, City Life-Fiction, Suburbia-Fiction, Humorous Fiction, Aging-Fiction, Writing-Fiction, Family-Fiction, Everyday Stories.

Malone, Mary. Annie Sullivan; illus by Lydia Rosier. Putnam 1971, 61 pp.

This is a very brief sketch of both Annie Sullivan's life and Helen Keller's life. Their lives were so intertwined that they cannot be separated. But because they are combined in such a short book, neither woman can be treated in much depth. That fact is not as harmful here as it might otherwise be, because even a bare bones description of the life of this extraordinary deaf, blind and mute woman or her near-blind, dedicated teacher, is interesting.

Interest Level: 2-5. Reading Level: 2.2. Further Search Topics: Sullivan, Annie, Keller, Helen, Vision, Biography, Physically Handicapped, Sound, Courage.

Miles, Betty. The secret life of the underwear champ; illus by Dan Jones. Knopf 1981, 117 pp.

Larry hadn't planned it; in fact, he hadn't even really wanted it to happen. But suddenly he found himself about to make a television commercial for ChampWin Knitting Mills, makers of sports clothing and underwear. He knew his family could use the money he would make, but he certainly didn't want the whole school seeing him in his underwear. Nevertheless, Larry went ahead and made the commercial, hoping that it would never be used. He even had to skip baseball practice to make the taping. Much to his horror, the commercial appeared the night before the team's first game. Not only did the entire opposing team tease him, but so did all his own teammates. By the time he got up to bat, Larry was mad enough to slam the ball out of the park. He didn't hit the ball quite that hard, but he did make a winning home run and end the others' giggles forever. He became the true underwear champ.

This is a funny look at the embarrassments of growing up. It also deals lightly with a boy's pride, his peer relationship, and his growing awareness of girls. An appealing and broadly usable title. Capers series.

Interest Level: 3-5. Reading Level: 2.2. Further Search Topics: Baseball-Fiction, Television-Fiction, Occupations-Fiction, School Stories, Humorous Fiction, Advertising-Fiction, Beauty-Fiction, Motion Pictures-Fiction, Best Sellers, Everyday Stories.

Parish, Peggy. Clues in the woods; illus by Paul Frame. Macmillan 1968, 154 pp.

The books about the three Roberts children share problems that are obvious to adults and felt by some young readers as well, but they continue to be popular with undemanding young readers. The characters are very white and middle class and their actions often fit out-of-date stereotypes. The plots have few surprises or suspense, but the reading levels are consistent and the very predictability of the books makes them familiar and therefore comfortable.

This particular story takes place at the end of the same summer the children solved the mystery of *The Key to the Treasure*. The children were alerted by their grandmother to the disappearance of food scraps, left outside the house. Thinking that two runaway children, about whom they had read, had taken the food, Liza, Bill, and Jed tried to find the runaways. Their attempts eventually brought them new friends and thus the solution to their mystery. It had not been the runaways who had taken the food, it was their new friends' dog.

Interest Level: 1-4. Reading Level: 2.2. Further Search Topics: Mystery and Detective Stories, Brothers and Sisters-Fiction, Vacation-Fiction, Dogs-Fiction, Runaways-Fiction, Grandparents-Fiction, Group 2.

Pinkwater, Daniel Manus. The Hoboken chicken emergency. P-H 1977, 83 pp.

Arthur's mother sent him out with $16 to buy a Thanksgiving turkey. He returned with a live 266 pound chicken on a leash. It seemed that their turkey reservation had been lost at the meat market and, because it was Thanksgiving morning, there were no other turkeys available. Arthur searched everywhere

but found nothing, until a strange old professor tricked him into buying the chicken. No one could bear to kill and eat such a large and friendly chicken, so Arthur and his family named it Henrietta and kept it as a pet. Henrietta was a difficult pet to keep hidden from the neighbors When the neighbors, and later the city, saw Henrietta running loose there was general hysteria. But all ended well when Henrietta and the city calmed down and Henrietta became a kind of neighborhood mascot.

A purely absurd plot but presented with enough energy and humor that most readers thoroughly enjoy the book. Some brief introduction may be necessary to get readers beyond the first few pages.

Interest Level: 3-6. Reading Level: 2.2. Further Search Topics: Humorous Fiction, Chickens-Fiction, Pets-Fiction, Thanksgiving-Fiction, Holidays-Fiction, Read Aloud, Best Sellers.

Place, Marian T. The boy who saw Bigfoot. Dodd 1979, 96 pp.

Joey and his foster mother searched for and found Bigfoot. But, when Joey told his classmates, no one would believe him. Joey's next idea was to take the entire class on a field trip to track Bigfoot.

Joey's rapid change from a difficult to a very well-adjusted child is not well supported. But interest in Bigfoot is so great that the book's flaws will be overlooked by its readers.

Interest Level: 3-6. Reading Level: 2.2. Further Search Topics: Bigfoot-Fiction, Foster Homes-Fiction, Monsters-Fiction, Troublemakers-Fiction, School Stories.

Platt, Kin. Dracula, go home; illus by Frank Mayo. Watts 1979, 87 pp.

From the chapter numbers that drip blood, and the humorously grotesque illustrations, to the short sentences and chapters, this is a book designed and almost guaranteed to appeal to the reluctant reader. A sense of immediacy and involvement is created by the first person narration. Tension is created on the opening page when Larry sees a man in the cemetery who looked exactly like Dracula. When that man registered at the hotel where Larry was working, Larry decided to find out more about him. It began to look as if Mr. A. R. Claude (the letters spell Dracula) was not only a vampire, but a thief and a murderer as well. The trouble was that Larry couldn't prove anything. Even when he found the stolen jewels for which Mr. Claude had been searching, Larry still couldn't convince anyone of Claude's true identify. No one ever did believe Larry, thus Claude went free.

The author uses a light touch to treat an eerie subject. His inconclusive ending may disappoint some, but should delight many. Beware of the variability of the reading level however; it swings from high first grade to low third grade.

Interest Level: 3-6. Reading Level: 2.2. Further Search Topics: Monsters-Fiction, Horror-Fiction, Mystery and Detective Stories, Best Sellers, Murder-Fiction, Crime-Fiction, Transformations-Fiction.

Platt, Kin. Run for your life; photos by Chuck Freedman. Watts 1977, 95 pp.

Lee almost lost his newspaper delivery job when someone began to regularly steal money and papers from the newspaper boxes along his route. Lee saw a chance for revenge if he could beat the thief in the mile race at the next track meet.

Most of the abundant dialogue is slang. The romantic interest is innocent and low keyed. The story has enough running to make that a strong appeal, but not so much that no one but a track or running enthusiast can enjoy it.

Interest Level: 5-6. Reading Level: 2.2. Further Search Topics: Running-Fiction, Love-Fiction, Occupations-Fiction, Crime-Fiction.

Rudeen, Kenneth. Jackie Robinson; illus by Richard Cuffari. Har-Row 1971, 41 pp.

Jackie Robinson was the youngest child in a large, poor family. As early as high school it was Robinson's superior athletic talent that set him apart. He could run track or play baseball, football, or basketball. He was the first student at UCLA to win a letter in all four sports. But because he wasn't happy to see the way his mother still had to struggle to earn money to live, after a year and a half at UCLA, Robinson left college to take a job. Soon after that, the United States entered World War II and Robinson went into the Army. His refusal to ride in the back of a bus in Texas resulted in a courtmartial, but he was found innocent after an uproar was made by the newspapers.

After the Army, Robinson played baseball with a Negro League team. A short time later, he was asked by the Dodger manager Branch Rickey to become the first black man to play in the major leagues. Rickey warned Robinson that it would mean he not only had to play well, but that he would also have to take all the anger and bitterness that would be directed at him. Robinson agreed. For three long years, while there were no other black players in the major leagues, Robinson played well and took everything without fighting back. Robinson was then able to stop trying to be perfect because he had successfully broken a very important color barrier and no longer had to prove to white managers, players and fans that blacks belonged in baseball just as much as whites. Robinson played for the Dodgers for ten years. When he left baseball he was elected into the Baseball Hall of Fame. He continued to fight for civil rights throughout the rest of his life, although there is only a brief mention of his activities in the book. Since the book's publication Jackie Robinson has died.

This is an excellent choice for the child who thinks of nothing but sports. It may be helpful in opening up an interest in the civil rights movement, black history, or black heroes. It is unfortunate that the traditional Crowell biography format (semi-picture book), and the author's slight tendency to be condescending, prevents the book from being useful beyond fourth grade. Crowell Biography series.

Interest Level: 2-4. Reading Level: 2.2. Further Search Topics: Civil Rights, Robinson, Jackie, Baseball-Biography, Biography, Blacks-Biography, Prejudice, Poverty.

Shearer, John. Billy Jo Jive and the case of the missing pigeons; illus by Ted Shearer. Delacorte 1978, 47 pp.

This is the third in a series of slight mysteries, always solved by Billy Jo Jive and his crime fighter partner, Susie Sunset. Jive and Sunset are street-wise, black youngsters who take their jobs as crime fighters very seriously, and are never detered for long from finding the criminals they seek. The crimes are always thefts, and the criminals vary from young children to neighborhood menaces. Suspense is created more by the manner in which Jive and Sunset catch the thieves, plus the determination and pace of the young detectives, than by guessing who the culprits might be. Jive, his street-slang manner of telling the first-person stories, and the urban setting will appeal to many readers. Jive and Sunset also appear on *Sesame Street*.

Jive accidentally photographed the fleeing pigeon thief as he was being chased by Flip, the victim. The photograph didn't show the thief's face, but did give Jive and Sunset a good look at what he was wearing. Jive and Sunset concluded that the thief was Snake Hips Robberts. They later realized that they had been wrong. When they looked carefully at the picture, they remembered that any dark color clothing photographs almost black in a black and white picture. Snake Hips had a black jacket, but he was innocent. The real thief was Sugar Brown. Then it was a simple matter of showing the evidence to both Flip and Sugar to get Sugar to confess.

Interest Level: 1-4. Reading Level: 2.2. Further Search Topics: Mystery and Detective Stories, Detectives-Fiction, Blacks-Fiction, City Life-Fiction, Group 2, Best Sellers.

Shearer, John. Billy Jo Jive super private eye: the case of the missing ten speed bike; illus by Ted Shearer. Delacorte 1976, 47 pp.

Jive and Sunset began their friendship and their sleuthing career with this book. It all started when Sunset borrowed her older brother's 10-speed bicycle. Jive met Sunset while she sat at the side of the road crying, after her brother's bike had been stolen. Some careful joint detective work proved to Jive and Sunset that Dynamite Jones, jealous of Sunset's brother, had stolen the bike. The young crime fighters recovered the bicycle before Sunset's brother even knew it was missing.

This book sets the formula that all the others follow. A neighborhood person finds that something has been stolen and goes to Jive and Sunset for help. Jive and Sunset never have much trouble finding the thief even though they are sometimes misled for a short time. Often the culprit is quite obvious to the reader. After some attempts at clever detective work and an occasional bit of preaching, the crime is solved. It is the manner of the pursuit and the street-smart characters that give the stories their interest.

Interest Level: 1-4. Reading Level: 2.2. Further Search Topics: Mystery and Detective Stories, Blacks-Fiction, Detectives-Fiction, City Life-Fiction, Best Sellers, Group 2, Bicycles and Bicycling-Fiction.

Silman, Roberta. Somebody else's child; illus by Chris Conover. Warne 1976, 64 pp.

Peter was adopted, but he had never questioned his family's love for him until Puddin' Paint, the school bus driver, made a thoughtless remark. Peter's affection for the older man was strong enough to help him understand Puddin' Paint's feelings. When Puddin' Paint's two dogs disappeared and the bus driver was almost heartbroken, it was Peter who helped the old man search for the dogs. That experience helped both Peter and Puddin' Paint understand that love doesn't only extend to natural born children, but can be just as strong and deep for others.

A simple telling of a moving story. It is as useful for readers who love dogs as for those interested in adoption. Rather inconsistent reading level, tests between 1.2 and 3.1.

Interest Level: 2-5. Reading Level: 2.2. Further Search Topics: Adoption-Fiction, Dogs-Fiction, Friendship-Fiction, Love-Fiction.

Simon, Seymour. Einstein Anderson makes up for lost time; illus by Fred Winkowski. Viking Pr 1981, 73 pp.

Adam (nicknamed Einstein) Anderson loves science. He also loves bad puns and correcting wrongs. What he does best, however, is to figure out science puzzles. Each book in this series (this is the third) presents 10 science puzzles which challenge Einstein and the reader. Clues and background are established in several pages of scene setting. Einstein regularly solves the puzzle and then the reader is asked how he did it. The answer follows on the next page. Areas of science that are drawn upon vary widely and range from animal behavior through chemistry and space science to zoology. Very palatable science reading. Print is on the small side in all four books.

Interest Level: 3-6. Reading Level: 2.2. Further Search Topics: Science, Puzzles, Mystery and Detective Stories.

Singer, Marilyn. It can't hurt forever; illus by Leigh Grant. Har-Row 1978, 186 pp.

When she was 11 years old, it was discovered that Ellie had a heart valve that hadn't closed by itself. Although her mother had promised her that she wouldn't die, Ellie was scared of the hospital and the operation she had to face. Her parents were kind and open about all that was to happen to her, but there was still much that Ellie had to learn from friends she made while she was in the hospital. There were times when she was frightened and only Sonia, a young open-heart surgery patient, could calm her. When Ellie, a special nurse, and a few other patients became close friends, Ellie learned enough from them to allow her to help another patient.

This is not a story of sweetness and light, but it is told with warmth, humor, and real understanding of a young person's fears. Thus it is not only an excellent candidate for bibliotherapy, but it is a truly satisfying story for the general reader as well.

Interest Level: 4-6. Reading Level: 2.2. Further Search Topics: Illness-Fiction, Physicians-Fiction, Medicine-Fiction, Courage-Fiction, Death-Fiction.

Sobol, Donald J. Encyclopedia Brown, boy detective; illus by Leonard Shortall. Elsevier-Nelson 1963, 88 pp.

The first of a large number of books that challenge the reader to solve the same mysteries Encyclopedia Brown deciphers. See *Encyclopedia Brown and the Case of the Dead Eagles* for more information.

Interest Level: 2-6. Reading Level: 2.2. Further Search Topics: Mystery and Detective Stories, Puzzles, Best Sellers, Detectives-Fiction.

Sobol, Donald J. Encyclopedia Brown and the case of the midnight visitor; illus by Lillian Brandi. Elsevier-Nelson 1977, 96 pp.

See *Encyclopedia Brown and the Case of the Dead Eagles* for full annotation.

Interest Level: 2-6. Reading Level: 2.2. Further Search Topics: Mystery and Detective Stories, Puzzles, Detectives-Fiction, Best Sellers.

Sobol, Donald J. Encyclopedia Brown keeps the peace; illus by Leonard Shortall. Elsevier-Nelson 1969, 96 pp.

See *Encyclopedia Brown and the Case of the Dead Eagles* for full annotation.

Interest Level: 2-6. Reading Level: 2.2. Further Search Topics: Mystery and Detective Stories, Puzzles, Best Sellers, Detectives-Fiction.

Sobol, Donald J. Encyclopedia Brown saves the day; illus by Leonard Shortall. Elsevier-Nelson 1970, 96 pp.

See *Encyclopedia Brown and the Case of the Dead Eagles* for full annotation.

Interest Level: 2-6. Reading Level: 2.2. Further Search Topics: Mystery and Detective Stories, Puzzles, Detectives-Fiction, Best Sellers.

Sobol, Donald J. Encyclopedia Brown shows the way; illus by Leonard Shortall. Elsevier-Nelson 1972, 96 pp.

See *Encyclopedia Brown and the Case of the Dead Eagles* for full annotation.

Interest Level: 2-6. Reading Level: 2.2. Further Search Topics: Mystery and Detective Stories, Puzzles, Detectives-Fiction, Best Sellers.

Thomas, Kathleen. Out of the bug jar; illus by Tom O'Sullivan. Dodd 1981, 125 pp.

Even though 10-year-old Tom Jenkins didn't believe in the tooth fairy, when one of his teeth fell out, he placed it under his pillow just in case he was wrong. In the middle of that night he was awakened by a small creature crawling under his pillow and grumbling. Tom quickly scooped him into a bug jar he kept nearby and thus began two years of life with Marvin, a tooth fairy. Marvin was a delightful dictator; he ruled Tom's life. He put Tom into a terrible predicament when Tom tried to charge others to see him and Marvin became invisible. Marvin insisted on being fed just what he demanded, despite the difficulties he made for Tom. He badgered Tom to do his homework, to brush his teeth, and to tell the truth. He even managed to follow Tom to school. The only other person Marvin would allow to see or hear him was Tom's friend Sammy. Tom couldn't get rid of Marvin either. Because Tom had captured him, Marvin, should he ever have been able to escape, was entitled to take *all* of Tom's teeth as compensation for being held prisoner.

Actually Marvin didn't really want to escape. He had grown tired of having to race around and collect teeth. For a while then, everyone was fairly content. Tom had all his teeth and Marvin had a rather nice home. Then quite by accident, Marvin got loose. Both Tom and Marvin wanted Tom to catch Marvin again. Tom wanted to keep his teeth and Marvin wanted to keep his comfortable lifestyle, but Marvin played by the rules and wouldn't give Tom any help at all. After more than seven days of valient but fruitless efforts and nights of sleeping with tape over his mouth, Tom finally caught Marvin and all were happy again.

An amusing story told in short sentences and short chapters. The book should be popular with those who enjoy either fantasy or humor.

Interest Level: 3-5. Reading Level: 2.2. Further Search Topics: Fantasy, Fairies-Fiction, Humorous Fiction, Teeth-Fiction.

Waldorf, Mary. Jake McGee and his feet; illus by Leonard Shortall. HM 1980, 82 pp.

His severe reading difficulties made school the worst place in the world for Jake McGee. On the day that his reading tutor became so impatient with him that she sent Jake to the principal, Jake decided that he couldn't stand school any longer and ran away. He didn't actually run away, he just let his feet finally do what they wanted. His feet were always getting Jake in trouble. They walked too slowly to get him to school on time; they wouldn't stay still once he was in school; and they were always trying to trip someone.

Jake knew that in addition to having problems with his feet he had reading problems, but no one at his old school in the country had noticed. When he and his family moved to the city everything had changed. Jake's mother was always at work or tired. Jake hadn't made any friends and so was always alone.

But Jake thought the biggest of all his immediate problems was his feet. The day he ran away, Jake's feet led him to a lost baby, an eccentric old woman, and a neighbor boy, all of whom helped Jake recognize and deal with his real problem.

The book is not high literary quality. The characterization is somewhat flat and the plot is fairly predictable. However, the sentences and chapters are short, the vocabulary is manageable, and Jake's feelings will be shared by many non-readers.

Interest Level: 3-5. Reading Level: 2.2. Further Search Topics: School Stories, Moving, Household-Fiction, Runaways-Fiction, Academic Problems-Fiction, Working Parents-Fiction, Loneliness-Fiction, Feet-Fiction.

Walker, Alice. Langston Hughes, American poet; illus by Don Miller. Har-Row 1974, 33 pp.

Langston Hughes is one of the world's most famous black poets. He spent most of his childhood in poverty and yet he shunned and was shunned by his wealthy father because his father disliked blacks. To Hughes the two most important things in the world were his heritage and his writing. His love of black history stemmed from the stories his grandmother told him. His love of language and writing grew out of the lonely hours he spent reading as a child. Hughes began to write poetry even before he was in high school and continued to write for many years. He wrote not only poems, but children's books, novels, plays and short stories. He wrote about and for blacks around the world. He was a proud and honest man who chose to share his pride in his race and his honesty through his writing.

This book is more of an inspirational tribute to a black hero than a fact-filled biography. That isn't to say that there are no facts included in the book. There are facts, but the book will not do as the sole source for a report about Langston Hughes. The book is, however, a good introduction to the man and his writing.

Interest Level: 3-5. Reading Level: 2.2. Further Search Topics: Biography, Blacks-Biography, Writing, Poverty, Divorce and Separation, Poetry.

Warner, Gertrude Chandler. Mountain top mystery; illus by David Cunningham. A. Whitman 1964, 128 pp.

A day's climb up and down Old Flat Top was all the Alden family had wanted. Instead, when a portion of the trail collapsed into a cave, they found themselves stranded on top of the mountain. From their vantage point that night they could see a shadowy light which they investigated the next day. They found a 90-year-old Indian woman who had a strange story to tell of treasure hidden in a cave somewhere on Old Flat Top. The treasure was rightfully hers as the last of her tribe, but she had never been able to find it. The collapse of the trail and the reopening of the cave attracted more attention than just the Alden's though. Both an expert on caves and a young Indian boy wanted to find out more about the cave. David, the Indian boy, turned out to be the old woman's grandnephew. The treasure was indeed unearthed; David and Lovan were reunited; the treasure was given to Lovan, and both David's and Lovan's futures were secured.

What in the other books is mild stereotyping becomes more noticeable here (the books are all around 20 years old). The print is smaller here than before but the spacing between the lines is adequate. See entry for *The Boxcar Children* for more information.

Interest Level: 3-6. Reading Level: 2.2. Further Search Topics: Mystery and Detective Stories, Treasure-Fiction, Survival-Fiction, Indians of North America-Fiction, Mountain Climbing-Fiction, Brothers and Sisters-Fiction.

Warner, Gertrude Chandler. Schoolhouse mystery; illus by David Cunningham. A. Whitman 1965, 128 pp.

On a dare, the Aldens went to a quiet fishing village to see what excitement they could find there. They found an isolated town filled with poor and unfriendly people. In their attempt to get to know the townspeople, the Aldens learned of the children's desire for schooling and the adults' anticipation of the Money Man's arrival. The Alden children took on the task of teaching school for the summer in an abandoned schoolhouse owned by Miss Gray, a recluse. The Money Man intrigued them more with each new bit of information they learned about him. They finally decided that the Money Man was a swindler who was practically stealing valuable antiques away from the villagers. By spying on the Money Man when he used the schoolhouse to store the antiques, the Aldens and an ex-FBI man were able to capture him. When the vacation was over, the Aldens had once more found excitement, Miss Gray had agreed to teach the local school, the Money Man was on his way to jail, and the townspeople knew the value of their old household items.

See the entry for *The Boxcar Children* for more information.

Interest Level: 3-5. Reading Level: 2.2. Further Search Topics: Mystery and Detective Stories, Vacation-Fiction, School Stories, Antiquities-Fiction, Crime-Fiction, Brothers and Sisters-Fiction, Challenges-Fiction.

Wolkoff, Judie. Wally. Bradbury 1977, 199 pp.

Michael Price agreed to take care of his friend Billy's chuckwalla for three weeks. But because his mother had declared a moratorium on any more reptiles in the house, Michael tried to hide Wally in his closet. With help from his brother Roger, Michael managed to keep Wally a secret until Wally was mistakenly left out of his box one night. Despite Michael and Roger's desperate searches, the chuckwalla did not reappear until Mr. and Mrs. Price were involved in the final negotiations for the sale of their house. Wally completely disrupted the proceedings, prevented the sale and thus made everyone happy. For as it turned out, none of the Prices had really wanted to move after all.

A fast-paced, funny book with much reader appeal.

Interest Level: 2-5. Reading Level: 2.2. Further Search Topics: Pets-Fiction, Humorous Fiction, Lizards-Fiction, Best Sellers, Reptiles-Fiction, Secrets-Fiction.

READING LEVEL 3.1

Adoff, Arnold. Malcolm X; illus by John Wilson. Har-Row 1970, 41 pp.

This is a simple, intellectually honest biography of a very controversial man. Taught a strong sense of self-respect by his father, Malcolm X could not accept the second-class status that white society tried to impose upon him. Instead he turned away from whites and all they stood for. He hated high school, the detention home he lived in after his father's death, and his mother's placement in a state hospital. He didn't feel comfortable until he moved to Harlem. There he found friends, but he also found crime. While he was in prison, Malcolm X began to read of great, black societies and people. His brother told him about the Nation of Islam, the Black Muslims, and Elijah Muhammad, the leader of the religion. He began corresponding with Mr. Muhammad. Shortly after he was released from prison, Malcolm X met Elijah Muhammad and eventually became a minister of the religion. There was even talk that he would be Elijah Muhammad's successor. But, as the years went on, Malcolm X began to think that black Christians as well as Muslims should be united in the fight for black rights. Despite threats against his life Malcolm X formed the Organization of Afro-American Unity. Both blacks and whites were angry with him. The threats continued until his house was firebombed; and, only a week later, at a public meeting, Malcolm X was assassinated.

An excellent overview of a complex man. The book may well prompt readers to learn more about the man and his beliefs. At the very least it will expose readers, in an interesting manner, to someone they should know. The book shares the same semi-picture book format of the others in Harper and Row/Crowell's biography series, therefore it will need a careful introduction to potential readers.

Interest Level: 3-5. Reading Level: 3.1. Further Search Topics: Blacks-Biography, Civil Rights, Biography, Crime, Religion, Assassinations, Prejudice, Poverty, Foster Homes.

Adrian, Mary. The fireball mystery illus by Reisie Lonette. Hastings 1977, 118 pp.

While stargazing one night, Tim and Vicky and their friend Joey saw a meteor fall onto their private island. Before they were able to find it the children realized that someone else was trying to steal the meteorite from them. As much astronomy as mystery here. Beyond fourth grade, the reader may begin to find the astronomy lesson heavy-handed and the mystery light.

Interest Level: 2-4. Reading Level: 3.1. Further Search Topics: Mystery and Detective Stories, Astronomy, Flying Saucers-Fiction, Outer Space-Fiction, Group 2.

Aesop. Aesop's Fables; retold by Ann Terry White; illus by Helen Siegl. Random 1964, 77 pp.

An attractive, appealing-looking collection of forty of Aesop's fables. Children without a background in folklore are not likely to read these short tales without encouragement. Where there is such encouragement, or a curricular need, this is an excellent source. The use of many proper nouns in the text means the book tests artificially low at 2.2. It is probably more appropriate to consider it 3.1.

Interest Level: 2-6. Reading Level: 3.1. Further Search Topics: Fables, Folklore, Group 2.

Allen, Linda. Lionel and the spy next door; illus by Margot Apple. Morrow 1980, 94 pp.

No one in Lionel's family understood why he wanted to be a spy; but then, he couldn't understand why they were anthropologists and motorcycle freaks. Even though he wasn't supposed to do any more spying (especially while his parents were away) Lionel couldn't resist watching the man who moved into Miss Bannister's house, next-door. Mark Shakespeare was his name. His name was suspicious enough, but his actions firmly convinced Lionel that Mark was a spy. Lionel's attempts to trail Shakespeare only succeeded in angering others in the neighborhood. He interrupted a bird watcher and irritated a woman walking a large dog. She was already angry with Lionel's grandfather for disturbing the quiet neighborhood with his motorcycles. The closer Lionel got to finding proof that Mark was a spy, the friendlier Mark became. Mark

even gave Lionel the old clock which Lionel and Miss Bannister had carefully wound each week until the old woman's death. When Lionel's grandfather finally convinced Lionel that Mark should be left alone, Mark enlisted Lionel's help in a project that left Lionel wondering again. Much to Lionel's surprise, he learned that the papers and secret documents he and Mark had burned had all belonged to Miss Bannister, Mark's great-aunt. Forty years earlier she, not Mark, had been a spy. Lionel had been wrong about who it was, but right about a spy living next-door.

Here we find a slightly anti-climactic ending to an otherwise enjoyable book. A grandfather who rides with motorcycle gangs and the intrigue of spying should be of interest to many readers. Readers may need a little help with the few British phrases that dot the book, but otherwise, the book has an impressively consistent reading level.

Interest Level: 4-6. Reading Level: 3.1. Further Search Topics: Spies-Fiction, Family-Fiction, Mystery and Detective Stories, Individualists-Fiction, Motorcycles-Fiction, Occupations-Fiction.

Angell, Judie. Dear Lola; or how to build your own family. Bradbury 1980, 166 pp.

Arthur (age 18), James (13), Annie and Al-Willie (twins, age 10), Edmund (9), and Ben (5) wanted to run away from the orphanage and find a place where they could be a real family. After waiting months, their chance arrived one night. They escaped in a van and began living on the road. It was weeks before they found a house in which they thought they could live. They didn't want trouble with local authorities, so most of the children enrolled in school and pretended to be living with their widowed grandfather. Only James (who never left his room) and Arthur stayed home. Arthur was the anonymous author of a nationally syndicated newspaper advice column. It was with the income from his "Dear Lola" column that Arthur was able to support the "family." When the townspeople eventually began to wonder about the "strange" behavior of the children, they investigated and found no adult in charge of the household. Arthur went to court to be appointed the childrens' guardian, but the judge ruled against him. Rather than be sent to foster homes again, Arthur and the children raced from the courtroom. The book ends as the family is once more together and on their own. An unusual cast of characters in a surprisingly warm and humorous book.

Interest Level: 4-6. Reading Level 3.1. Further Search Topics: Loners-Fiction, Runaways-Fiction, Orphans-Fiction, Survival-Fiction, Family Problems-Fiction, Family-Fiction, Read Aloud, Foster Homes-Fiction, Individualists-Fiction, Humorous Fiction.

Arkhurst, Joyce. The adventures of Spider; West African folktales; illus by Jerry Pinkney. Little 1964, 58 pp.

A delightful collection of six West African folktales about Spider. Spider is mischievous, greedy, lazy and clever. He loves to eat and he hates to work. Four of the stories tell of Spider's ill-fated attempts to get food without having to work for it ("How Spider Got a Thin Waist," "How Spider Got a Bald Head," "How Spider Helped a Fisherman," and "Why Spiders Live in Dark Corners"). One story tells of his greed ("How the World Got Wisdom"), and only one story is complimentary ("Why Spider Lives in Ceilings"). All are short, gentle, humorous, and adapt well to dramatization or retelling.

Interest Level: 2-6. Reading Level 3.1. Further Search Topics: Humorous Fiction, Spiders-Fiction, Folklore, Tricksters-Fiction, Africa-Folklore, Group 2, Read Aloud, Creation-Fiction, Drama.

Aylesworth, Thomas G. Movie monsters. Lippincott 1975, 79 pp.

If you are looking for an example of fine writing, you won't find it here. What you will find is a collection of monster movie photographs and facts. This is a wealth of trivia about eleven famous monsters (including King Kong, Godzilla, the Fly, Frankenstein's monster, the Mummy, Dracula, Wolf Man and others), their films, sequels, historic backgrounds, identifying characteristics, and more. There is an extensive index, a list of monster movies and their credits, and even brief information about famous monster actors. The book is not great literature, but it is interesting and fun.

Interest Level: 1-6. Reading Level 3.1. Further Search Topics: Acting, Motion Pictures, Monsters, Horror-Fiction, Group 2, Best Sellers.

Bales, Carol Ann. Chinatown Sunday; the story of Lillian Der. Contemp Bks. 1973, 32 pp.

A short, personal visit with a fifth grade Chinese-American girl who lives in a Chicago suburb. The author transcribed taped interviews with Lillian Der to produce a first-person description of Lillian's daily life. The uniquely Chinese-American features of Lillian's life are casually intertwined with experiences common to most American children. Month-old parties, the celebration of Chinese New Year, lucky money, old-age birthday parties, Girl Scout meetings, homework, and being a tomboy are all important to Lillian. Not only is this an interesting portrait of Lillian, but it can be a useful part of a multi-ethnic unit or an introduction to autobiography. The book's usefulness is further extended by its introduction to Chinese immigration and by the glossary, which explains terms such as "abacus," "Chinese calendar," and "sea cucumber." The author saves the over-sized book from looking like a picture book by using photographs instead of drawings, thus she makes the book comfortable even for a sixth grade reader.

Interest Level: 3-6. Reading Level: 3.1. Further Search Topics: Ethnic Groups, Chinese-Americans, Biography, Chicago, Immigration and Emigration.

Baylor, Byrd. And it is still that way: legends told by Arizona Indian children. Scribner 1976, 85 pp.

Byrd Baylor has collected and written notes for forty-one short American Indian legends from seven Arizona tribes whose school children were asked to write down or illustrate their favorite legend. The result is a collection that reflects the concerns, the history, religion, humor and pride of the children and their ancestors. This excellent collection is not only interesting reading, but it also fits well into social studies and language arts units.

Interest Level: 2-6. Reading Level: 3.1. Further Search Topics: Legends, Arizona-Fiction, Navajo Indians, Hopi Indians, Papago Indians, Pima Indians, Apache Indians, Quechan Indians, Cocopah Indians, Indians of North America-Legends, Mythology, Group 2.

Beame, Rona. Ladder company 108. Messner 1973, 63 pp.

The reader of this book will literally live through several days with a New York City fire company. The author's "Dragnet"-like writing style, her use of photographs, and actual people, all make the firefighters' experiences very real. It is an exciting,

engrossing and satisfying book. The heavily-used jargon will be quickly understood, thus should pose no real obstacle to most readers.

Interest Level 2-6. Reading Level: 3.1. Further Search Topics: Firefighters, Occupations, City Life, New York City, Group 2, Best Sellers.

Blume, Judy. Blubber. Bradbury 1974, 153 pp.

Jill, like all the other fifth graders in her class, did exactly as Wendy directed her. When Wendy nicknamed one of the class members Blubber and launched a campaign against her, Jill joined right in. It wasn't until the tables were turned and Jill became Wendy's next victim that Jill realized how much it hurt to be the target of such nastiness. It was only then that Jill could stand up to Wendy. Wendy's meanness is extreme and her classmates, without exception, actively follow her lead, yet all adult characters in the book are blind to what happens. Despite those drawbacks, the book deals with a problem very real to children and thus it has guaranteed audience appeal.

Interest Level: 4-6. Reading Level: 3.1. School Stories, Bullies-Fiction, Weight-Fiction, Loners-Fiction, Gangs-Fiction, Read Aloud, Cruelty-Fiction, Best Sellers, Troublemakers-Fiction, Friendship-Fiction.

Blume, Judy. Deenie. Bradbury 1973, 159 pp.

Deenie's mother wanted Deenie to be a model. Deenie didn't know what she wanted until she learned that she had scoliosis (curvature of the spine) and would have to wear a brace for four years. Then she knew she only wanted to be normal. She was repulsed by deformities of any kind. She couldn't stand the idea of a brace. Her mother's attitude made Deenie's adjustment even more difficult. It was her father, her doctor, her sister, and a new friend with excema who finally helped Deenie accept her brace and the idea of physical differences. Subplots include Deenie's budding romance with an eighth grade boy, her strained relationship with her mother, and her growing awareness of sex (masturbation and intercourse). Print and line spacing are similar to *Are You There God? It's Me, Margaret.*

Interest Level: 5-6. Reading Level: 3.1. Further Search Topics: Models, Fashion-Fiction, Beauty-Fiction, Scoliosis-Fiction, Physically Handicapped-Fiction, Children-Growth-Fiction, Sex-Fiction, Love-Fiction, Family Problems-Fiction, Illness-Fiction, Adolescence-Fiction.

Blume, Judy. It's not the end of the world. Bradbury 1972, 169 pp.

This is a one theme book (as are many of Judy Blume's titles). It is the story of 11-year-old Karen's attempt to prevent her parents' divorce and then to accept it. In this first-person story she tells of her disappointment, anger, fear, and lack of understanding. She describes her parents' fights and her brother's and sister's reactions, too. It is a book with an obvious and mostly reassuring message to its readers, but it is not just for readers whose families may be in similar situations. It is also a book that will be enjoyed by any Judy Blume enthusiast.

Interest Level: 4-6. Reading Level: 3.1. Further Search Topics: Divorce and Separation-Fiction, Family Problems-Fiction, Everyday Stories.

Blume, Judy. Tales of a fourth grade nothing; illus by Roy Doty. Dutton 1972, 120 pp.

Another humorous Blume book that can be counted on to appeal to third and fourth grade readers. If fifth and sixth graders can ignore the title's reference to fourth grade, they too will love it. The story is an exaggeration of a common theme—an older child whose life is in continual turmoil because of a somewhat spoiled younger sibling. Peter's problems with three-year-old Fudge become worse with each chapter until the final disaster when Fudge swallows Peter's pet turtle. Each approximately 15-page chapter is a complete, very funny episode.

Interest Level: 3-6. Reading Level 3.1. Further Search Topics: Humorous Fiction, Turtles-Fiction, Brothers and Sisters-Fiction, Pets-Fiction, Family-Fiction, Read Aloud, Best Sellers, Everyday Stories, Troublemakers-Fiction.

Blume, Judy. Otherwise known as Sheila the great. Dutton 1972, 128 pp.

Sheila first appears in *Tales of a Fourth Grade Nothing* as Peter Thatcher's neighbor. Sheila was a bundle of fears. She was afraid of dogs, thunderstorms, spiders, horses, putting her face in water, and strange noises at night. The summer she and her family rented a house in Tarrytown, New York, she confronted each one of her fears, even mastered one (putting her face in the water) and learned how to swim. That gave her the self-confidence to face a dog without running away. Sheila's progress was aided by her friend Mouse's steadfast belief that a person should always be honest about herself. Sheila's problems are treated realistically and with dignity, yet humorously. Reading level varies greatly from 1.2 - 4.1, therefore, the book is *most* suitable to grades four through six.

Interest Level: 3-6. Reading Level: 3.1. Further Search Topics: Humorous Fiction, Courage-Fiction, Camp-Fiction, Group 2, Vacation-Fiction, Swimming-Fiction, Brothers and Sisters-Fiction, Friendship-Fiction, Everyday Stories.

Blume, Judy. Superfudge. Dutton 1980, 166 pp.

On Fudge's first day in school his older brother Peter had to rescue him from the top of the kindergarten storage cabinets. Later in the school year Fudge's eagerness to join a school guest speaker on stage almost spelled disaster. Then when Fudge unexpectedly disappeared one day everyone, including Peter, thought he had drowned. In addition to Peter's problems with Fudge, Peter had to cope with a baby sister, moving to Princeton, New Jersey, a new job for his mother, and his father's attempts to write a book. Although the book is a sequel and is best enjoyed as such, it can be read alone. It is not as amusing or well-written as it's predecessor, *Tales of a Fourth Grade Nothing*, but will still be popular with young readers.

Interest Level: 3-6. Reading Level 3.1. Further Search Topics: Brothers and Sisters-Fiction, Moving, Household-Fiction, Infants-Fiction, Working Parents-Fiction, School Stories, Family-Fiction, Best Sellers, Humorous Fiction, Everyday Stories.

Blume, Judy. Freckle juice; illus by Sonia O. Lisker. Four Winds 1971, 40 pp.

A very funny story that should appeal to almost everyone. Andrew wanted freckles so that the dirt on his skin wouldn't show as much and he wouldn't have to wash as often. As luck would have it, Sharon, the most obnoxious girl in class, had a freckle juice recipe that she was willing to sell for 50 cents. Even after drinking the brew of grape juice, vinegar, mustard, olive oil, and more, Andrew didn't see any freckles, but, he certainly was sick. Although the protagonists are younger, this book will hold even a fifth grade reader's interest.

Interest Level: 2-5. Reading Level 3.1. Further Search Topics: Humorous Fiction, Group 2, Read

Aloud, Everyday Stories, Beauty-Fiction, School Stories, Magic-Fiction, Best Sellers.

Bryant, Bernice. George Gershwin: young composer; illus by Nathan Goldstein. Bobbs 1965, 200 pp.

Even when George Gershwin was very young he loved music, showed signs of musical talent, and longed to play the piano. However, any boy who played the piano in George's neighborhood was called a sissy and George didn't like being teased in that way. When he was no longer able to keep his music lessons a secret, he stopped them for fear of the teasing. But each time George quit playing the piano, he always went back to it, even when his parents pressured him not to waste his time at the piano. A young teacher told George that he would never be a musician. One of George's teachers actually taught him to play poorly, instead of well. In time, however, George learned to play well and to compose his own music. Then came the hard work of determining his own style. Gradually, more and more people heard and appreciated his American jazz, until George Gershwin's music was heard all around the world.

Another adequate entry in the *Childhood of Famous Americans* series. Includes the usual glossary, bibliography, time line, and follow-up questions. It is most likely to appeal to the reader already interested in music. Childhood of Famous Americans series.

Interest Level: 3-6. Reading Level: 3.1. Further Search Topics: Biography, Composers, Immigration and Emigration-Biography, Jazz Music, Bullies, Music-Biography, Pianists.

Bulla, Clyde Robert. Dexter; illus by Glo Coalson. Har-Row 1973, 69 pp.

This is not as simple a story as it first appears. Dave, 12 years old and lonely, had hoped his new neighbors would be friends. But, the Arvin family kept very much to themselves until Dave accidentally discovered Alex, the Arvin's son, doing tricks on a trapeze in the barn. Because Dave kept the secret and shared Alex's love for Dexter, his circus pony, the boys soon became friends. Then in one horrible night, the Arvins were forced to leave the town and Dexter was so badly hurt he was believed to be dead. A week later Dave found Dexter alive, but crippled for life and so frightened that no one could get near him. The horse surprised everyone and managed to live through a very harsh winter as well as the townspeople's determination to kill him. When Alex and his father returned, almost a year later, they found Dexter and took the old and feeble horse back to a ranch with them. The story is told with sympathy, with an understanding of how it feels to be lonely, and with tension and suspense. It's appeal should last from third through sixth grade. Print size is smaller than Bulla's usual.

Interest Level: 3-6. Reading Level: 3.1. Further Search Topics: Survival-Fiction, Acrobats and Acrobatics-Fiction, Horses-Fiction, Read Aloud, Circus-Fiction, Loneliness-Fiction, Friendship-Fiction.

Bulla, Clyde Robert. Viking adventure; illus by Douglas Gorsline. T Y Crowell 1963, 117 pp.

An exciting story of a young Norwegian boy named Sigurd. Sigurd realized his dream when he finally set sail on a Viking ship in search of Wineland (Vinland). Leif Eriksson had told of his North American findings over 100 years earlier. Sigurd and his father's friend Grom, the captain of the ship, were sure they could find that land again. Their determination finally brought Grom's death at the hands of the ship's owner, Sigurd's near death, and the destruction of the ship.

This book, too, is true to Bulla's style of short chapters, short sentences, much action and high appeal. Although it is a little higher reading level than many of Bulla's others, it is still a good choice. Recently out of print, but worth a search.

Interest Level: 2-6. Reading Level: 3.1. Further Search Topics: Norway-Fiction, Historical Fiction, Seafaring Life-Fiction, Voyages and Travels-Fiction, Shipwrecks-Fiction, Explorers-Fiction, Vikings-Fiction, Courage-Fiction, Best Sellers, Group 2.

Burchard, Marshall. Sports hero: Johnny Bench. Putnam 1973, 95 pp.

The youngest baseball player to receive the National League's Most Valuable Player award. See *Sports Hero: Bill Walton* for information about the book. Sports Hero series.

Interest Level: 2-6. Reading Level: 3.1. Further Search Topics: Biography, Bench, Johnny, Baseball-Biography, Group 2.

Burchard, Marshall. Sports hero: Larry Csonka. Putnam 1975, 95 pp.

Larry Csonka was almost the stereotype of a football player; big, fearless and driving. For more information about the books in the series see *Sports Hero: Bill Walton.* Sports Hero series.

Interest Level: 2-6. Reading Level: 3.1. Further Search Topics: Biography, Csonka, Larry, Football-Biography, Group 2.

Burchard, Marshall. Sports hero: Rick Barry. Putnam 1977, 95 pp.

Rick Barry, now a color commentator for televised basketball games, was once one of the best forwards in basketball. Details about the series with *Sports Hero: Bill Walton* entry. Sports Hero series.

Interest Level: 2-6. Reading Level: 3.1. Further Search Topics: Biography, Barry, Rick, Basketball-Biography, Group 2.

Burchard, Marshall. Sports hero: Henry Aaron. Putnam 1974, 96 pp.

Baseball's homerun king. See entry under *Sports Hero: Bill Walton* for more information. Sports Hero series.

Interest Level: 2-6. Reading Level: 3.1. Further Search Topics: Biography, Aaron, Henry, Baseball-Biography, Blacks-Biography.

Burchard, Susan H. Sports star: Pele. HarBrace J 1976, 64 pp.

At age 35, when many people thought he might be "past his prime," Pele proved he could still play superior soccer. More details about the series in *Sports Hero: Bill Walton* entry, by Marshall Burchard. Sports Star series.

Interest Level: 2-6. Reading Level: 3.1. Further Search Topics: Biography, Soccer-Biography, Pele, Group 2.

Burchard, Susan H. Sports star: Earl Campbell. HarBraceJ 1980, 63 pp.

The Houston Oiler's star running back, probably the best in football, has only been out of college a few years. He should have a long career ahead of him. *Sports Star: Elvin Hayes* includes series notes. Sports Star series.

Interest Level: 3-6. Reading Level: 3.1. Further Search Topics: Football-Biography, Blacks-Biography, Campbell, Earl, Biography.

Burchard, Susan H. Sports star: Elvin Hayes. HarBraceJ 1980, 63 pp.

Only this and three other Sue Burchard titles listed here differ much from the format described for the *Sports Hero* series (see *Sports Hero: Bill Walton*). It appears that in 1979 Ms. Burchard's books took on a slick new look. The covers began to sport color photos rather than black and white. The print size became noticeably smaller, although still of adequate size. More emphasis was placed on the players early life and background, in an apparent attempt to make him or her understandable as an individual rather than just as a star. A short career summary was added at the end of each book. All-in-all, the new, flashier approach should make the books more appealing than ever to older students.

Elvin Hayes came from a very poor family who lived in a town where blacks were badly treated. He went on to become one of the best college basketball players of his time. His deep religious convictions helped him through some rough times in his early years as a pro. Now he is happy, not just when he wins, but when he knows he has played his best. Sports Star series.

Interest Level: 3-6. Reading Level: 3.1. Further Search Topics: Biography, Hayes, Elvin, Basketball-Biography, Blacks-Biography, Religion-Biography.

Burchard, Susan H. Sports star: Franco Harris. HarBraceJ 1976, 64 pp.

Franco is the talented son of a black Army man and his Italian wife. He became a hero to thousands of Pittsburgh Steeler fans, who called themselves Franco's Italian Army. See *Sports Hero: Bill Walton,* by Marshall Burchard for series details. Sports Star series.

Interest Level: 2-6. Reading Level: 3.1. Further Search Topics: Biography, Group 2, Harris, Franco, Football-Biography, Blacks-Biography.

Burchard, Susan H. Sports star: Jim "Catfish" Hunter. HarBraceJ 1976, 64 pp.

The pitcher who, because of contract violations by his club's owner, became the first free agent in baseball. See Marshall Burchard's *Sports Hero: Bill Walton* for information about the series. Sports Star series.

Interest Level: 2-6. Reading Level: 3.1. Further Search Topics: Biography, Baseball-Biography, Hunter, Jim "Catfish", Group 2.

Burchard, Susan H. Sports star: Walt Frazier. HarBraceJ 1975, 64 pp.

Walt Frazier earned his nickname Clyde (from *Bonnie and Clyde*) because of his style both on and off the basketball court. He could steal the ball from almost anyone on the court and he enjoyed high living and fancy dressing off the court. Entry for *Sports Hero: Bill Walton* gives more information about the series. Sports Star series.

Interest Level: 2-6. Reading Level: 3.1. Further Search Topics: Biography, Basketball-Biography, Frazier, Walt, Blacks-Biography.

Byars, Betsy. Trouble River; illus by Rocco Negri. Viking Pr. 1969, 158 pp.

A gripping adventure story of survival. After being attacked by an Indian in the middle of the night, Dewey and his grandmother rushed to Trouble River to board a small raft which Dewey had just finished making. They thought they would only need to navigate a few miles down the river to safety at a neighbor's home, but found instead that the neighbor's cabin had been burned down. For almost 40 miles they fought against the unknown river, wolves and rapids.

This is a book that should satisfy many reluctant readers. It's frequent dialogue, fast action and high interest are only occasionally marred by an overly long sentence.

Interest Level: 3-6. Reading Level: 3.1. Further Search Topics: Courage-Fiction, Frontier and Pioneer Life-Fiction, Survival-Fiction, Grandparents-Fiction, Voyages and Travels-Fiction, Best Sellers, Read Aloud.

Chaikin, Miriam. Finders weepers; illus Richard Egielski. Har-Row 1980, 120 pp.

The children most likely to read this are those who have enjoyed *I Should Worry, I Should Care.* On her way home from school one day, Molly found a ring. Rather than try to find its owner, she made up excuses to keep the ring. Molly knew it was a sin to keep something that belonged to someone else, she even knew who *did* own the ring. When she finally decided to return it, the ring had become stuck on Molly's finger and wouldn't come off. With Yom Kippur just a few days away, Molly became convinced that all the unpleasant things happening around her were punishments for her sin. She finally had to have the ring cut off her finger. After she prayed for forgiveness life immediately went back to normal.

There's enough guilt here to satisfy even the most demanding reader. There is also the same solid family group that appeared in the first book. But this book probably lacks enough excitement and/or empathy to interest a reader new to Molly and her family. Print is dark but spacing between lines could have been wider.

Interest Level: 3-5. Reading Level: 3.1. Further Search Topics: Family-Fiction, Jews-Fiction, Honesty-Fiction, Holidays-Fiction, Religion-Fiction.

Chew, Ruth. Witch's broom. Dodd 1977, 128 pp.

Amy's mother was the one who found the blue broom, but Amy and her friend Jean were the ones who learned it was magical. One night the broom flew Amy into a mountain cave where a coven of witches was meeting. It even forced Amy to answer the roll call for someone named Beryl. But it wasn't until it took both Amy and Jean back to the cave that they discovered the broom's connection to the strange bluejay that had been following them. The bluejay was really Beryl, a young and headstrong witch who had turned herself into the bluejay and then couldn't turn herself back. With the girls' unwitting help, Beryl found the charm to turn herself back into a witch and flew off on a scrawny old broom, leaving the blue broom for Amy and Jean.

What youngster wouldn't want a flying broomstick and the misadventures that go with owning one? Wish fulfillment can never be overrated as an appeal of Ruth Chew's books.

Interest Level: 2-5. Reading Level: 3.1. Further Search Topics: Witches-Fiction, Magic-Fiction, Fantasy, Birds-Fiction, Group 2, Transformations-Fiction.

Chew, Ruth. What the witch left. Hastings 1973, 128 pp.

One afternoon Katy and Louise decided to search through the locked drawer of an old dresser. Inside they found strange-looking gloves, an old robe, boots, a mirror and a tin box. The girls quickly learned that each item was magical. With the gloves on, the girls could draw, play piano, weave or write. They thought their new talents were wonderful until they each wrote identical school compositions. When she wore the robe for the school play, Louise found out that it made people invisible. The boots, which travelled 21 miles with each step, took the girls to Mexico, but made them late for lunch at home. The mirror showed them anything they wanted to see, and the box "found" everything that was lost. A very light story for children who don't need high adventure but like a mixture of humor and magic.

Interest Level: 3-5. Reading Level: 3.1. Further Search Topics: Magic-Fiction, Mexico-Fiction, Witches-Fiction, Fantasy, Humorous Fiction.

Christopher, Matt. Devil pony; illus by Lorence Bjorkland. Little 1977, 103 pp.

This book is a bit of a change from the usual Matt Christopher story line. There is no sports interest here; instead there is a good suspense story about a boy, his cousin and a horse. Stu had watched the black Morgan named Midnight being born and had fallen in love with him. A year later he returned to his aunt and uncle's ranch to claim the horse, as he had been promised he could, but strange things began to happen around him. His cousin Wilbur warned him that he had probably annoyed the ranch poltergeist by deciding to take Midnight away. The bizarre occurrences escalated until Stu was almost tempted to leave Midnight at the ranch. Then Stu discovered Wilbur had been orchestrating everything that had happened because he had wanted to keep the horse himself. Although Stu decided to take Midnight home as he had planned, their new honesty led Stu to believe that he and Wilbur could be friends after all. A surprisingly good story with strong reader appeal.

Interest Level: 3-6. Reading Level: 3.1. Further Search Topics: Horses-Fiction, Supernatural-Fiction, Ghosts-Fiction, Jealousy-Fiction, Relatives-Fiction.

Christopher, Matt. Football fugitive; illus by Larry Johnson. Little 1976, 119 pp.

Larry had been writing to the great football player Yancey Roote for about two years when his letters suddenly went unanswered. Because his relationship with his father was cool and distant, Larry's friendship with Yancey had meant a great deal to him. Shortly after Larry learned that Yancey was in legal trouble, Yancey showed up in town to ask Larry's father, a famous lawyer, to defend him in court. The court case and Yancey helped to bring Larry and his father closer together and to provide each one with new respect for the other. Lots of football action plus a realistic and somewhat common problem (though an unrealistic solution) make this a useful selection.

Interest Level: 3-6. Reading Level: 3.1. Further Search Topics: Football-Fiction, Lawyers-Fiction, Family Problems-Fiction.

Christopher, Matt. Face-off; illus by Harvey Kidder. Little 1972, 131 pp.

Christopher sticks strictly to the sports story formula here. The characters seem to have no time or thoughts for anything but sports. They epitomize the macho image, and once their problems with sports are solved everything in life seems to fall into place. But, for the young sports enthusiast who doesn't really like to read, this formula of much sports action and very little else is successful.

Scott had never played hockey but he was an extremely fast skater. When Del and Skinny asked him to join their hockey team and to be one of the Three Icekateers, Scott was thrilled. But Scott's performance was less than inspiring and Del's patience with his failures was short. The two almost came to blows when Scott discovered that he was puck-shy and would duck every time someone took a shot near him. Their coach's advice to both of them helped clear up Scott's problem and Del's impatience. All ends happily as Scott played well and he and Del became friends once more.

Interest Level: 3-6. Reading Level: 3.1. Further Search Topics: Hockey-Fiction, Ice Skating-Fiction, Courage-Fiction, Friendship-Fiction.

Christopher, Matt. The year mom won the pennant; illus by Foster Caddell. Little 1968, 147 pp.

When no one's father had the time to coach the Thunderballs it began to look like the team would be disbanded. They just didn't seem to be able to work together without a coach. Then Nick Vassey's mother volunteered to coach for the season. After all, she knew baseball as well as anyone else and had watched her husband coach for several years. Nick wasn't at all pleased, but had to accept the idea when his teammates voted to make his mother their coach. Nick's embarrassment was almost as great as the rival coach's skepticism, but before the season was over Nick was proud of his mother. She coached the team to first place and forced even the rival coach to admit she was a good coach. Much baseball action. See note about (*No Arm In Left Field*).

Interest Level: 2-6. Reading Level: 3.1. Further Search Topics: Group 2, Baseball-Fiction, Friendship-Fiction, Prejudice-Fiction, Sex Role-Fiction, Women-Fiction.

Cleary, Beverly. Henry and Beezus; illus by Louis Darling. Morrow 1952, 192 pp.

When Henry's dog Ribsy stole the meat from a neighbor's barbecue, a friend rode after Ribsy on his bike and saved the meat. Henry was so embarrassed and jealous that he boasted about an even nicer bike that he was going to get. At first Henry thought he'd be able to earn money to buy a bike in a very short time (he found 49 boxes of bubble gum that he could sell). When that scheme fell through, Henry tried taking over a friend's paper route, but Ribsy kept retrieving the newspapers Henry delivered. Eventually Henry decided to buy a used bike at the police department auction. Beezus, who made a bid for Henry, ended up buying him a beaten-up girl's bike that was hardly worth fixing. The money finally appeared when Henry least expected it; he won $50.00 worth of work at a beauty salon.

Although all seven chapters continue the same story, Chapters 1, 2, 3 and 7, can each stand alone. Henry is definitely old-fashioned, but children still enjoy his humorous escapades and empathize with his desire for a bicycle. The revised paperback cover makes the book's physical appearance less dated. Reading level is somewhat inconsistent: from 2.2 to 3.2.

Interest Level: 2-5. Reading Level: 3.1. Further Search Topics: Humorous Fiction, Occupations-Fiction, Everyday Stories, Bicycles and Bicycling-Fiction, Read Aloud, Group 2.

Clifford, Eth. Help, I'm a prisoner in the library; illus by George Hughes. HM 1979, 103 pp.

When their car stopped, Mary Rose and Jo-Beth were left alone in a strange city while their father went to find some gas. Jo-Beth needed to use the bathroom, so the sisters headed for the closest public building they could see, the library. No one saw them go in, so no one knew that they were locked inside when the librarian secured the building for the night. With the lights out and a blizzard outside, the library was a very spooky place. The girls tried calling the police, but the police wouldn't take them seriously. Then they heard groans and eerie moans from the second floor. Gathering all their courage, the girls went to investigate, only to discover the librarian lying hurt and unconscious. Their ingenuity and imagination helped the sisters through the difficult hours before they were all rescued.

Don't read it too carefully or the book's implausibilities will become very evident. Most young readers, however, will enjoy this story for its suspense, spooky atmosphere and adventurous girls, and they will ignore its weaknesses.

Interest Level: 2-5. Reading Level: 3.1. Further Search Topics: Disasters-Fiction, Snow-Fiction, Brothers and Sisters-Fiction, Libraries-Fiction, Survival-Fiction, Courage-Fiction, Group 2.

Clifford, Eth. The dastardly murder of Dirty Pete; illus by George Hughes. HM 1981, 120 pp.

Although this is a sequel to *Help, I'm a Prisoner in the Library*, it does not depend on the previous title, and in fact, is likely to be the more successful introduction to Mary Rose and Jo-Beth Onetree. Given the choice, most young readers will take a mystery set in a ghost town over a mystery set in a library.

Mary Rose, Jo-Beth and their father were on their way across country when they became lost. As night grew closer, the only place they could find to stay was an old hotel in the ghost town where Sorehead Jones had allegedly killed Dirty Pete. It was Sorehead's ghost who was supposed to haunt the town, and indeed there was someone or something who was in the town with the Onetrees. To their surprise, that someone turned out to be Sourdough Sam, an aging actor who had become senile and spent his days acting out all the parts in the Dirty Pete story. The town was only a movie set and the story was only a movie script. The Onetrees discovered the truth bit by bit after a frightening venture into an abandoned gold mine, a harrowing night in the haunted hotel and a jail sentence for Mr. Onetree.

Beware of the rare, very difficult descriptive passage that may cause trouble for some readers.

Interest Level: 2-5. Reading Level: 3.1. Further Search Topics: Mystery and Detective Stories, West-Fiction, Brothers and Sisters-Fiction, Motion Pictures-Fiction, Ghosts-Fiction, Treasure-Fiction, Group 2, Acting-Fiction, Aging-Fiction, Mental Illness-Fiction.

Clymer, Eleanor. Santiago's silver mine; illus by Ingrid Fetz. Atheneum 1973, 74 pp.

Although somewhat complicated by a large number of background incidents, especially early in the book, the story is both interesting and informative. Santiago and his friend Andreas wanted to be rich. The year's harvest had been very poor, so there was little food to eat. Both of their fathers had gone to Mexico City to find jobs and their mothers worked for very few pesos near home. Andreas wanted to search the old mine in the hills outside of town for silver, but the mining company had left a guard named Jose to prevent people from getting into the mines. While up on a hill, tending a cow, Andreas found an old piece of pottery and a back entrance to the mine. As they started to enter the mine, Andreas and Santiago found a basket full of old pottery pieces that Jose had apparently dug from the hill. Not knowing what the pottery pieces were, the boys took them to the local school teacher who identified them as ancient archeological treasures that by law belonged to the government. As soon as he realized others had found out that he had been selling the pottery, Jose disappeared. Shortly afterwards, the government paved the road through town and opened the hill as an official archaeological site. The extra jobs meant that the boys' fathers could once again find work at home. Although they hadn't become exactly rich, Santiago and Andreas had certainly found treasure.

Local flavor abounds, along with some history. Useful for Social Studies units. Print size fairly small, but spaces between lines are good sized. Recently out-of-print, but still worth looking for.

Interest Level: 3-5. Reading Level: 3.1. Further Search Topics: Archaeology-Fiction, Poverty-Fiction, Mexico-Fiction, Country Life-Fiction, Treasure-Fiction, Miners-Fiction.

Coerr, Eleanor. Sadako and the thousand paper cranes; illus by Ronand Himler. Putnam 1977, 64 pp.

This is a beautiful and very sad story of a young girl who was only two years old when the atomic bomb was dropped on Hiroshima. Ten years later she contracted leukemia and died a slow, painful death. A fast and enthusiastic runner, she had been full of life and energy before her illness. Soon after she became sick Sadako's best friend folded a paper crane for her and reminded her of an old story: If someone folded 1000 paper cranes, the gods would give that person good health again. Sadako was able to fold only 644 before she died. After her death her classmates made 356 more in order that she could be buried with all 1000 paper cranes. About three years later, a statue, erected in Peace Park in Hiroshima, was dedicated to Sadako and to a hope for world peace.

Because of the theme and its straight-forward handling, this book needs a fairly mature reader.

Interest Level: 4-6. Reading Level: 3.1. Further Search Topics: Japan-Fiction, Historical Fiction, World War II-Fiction, Death-Fiction, Illness-Fiction, War-Fiction, Running-Fiction, Origami-Fiction, Read Aloud.

Cohen, Barbara. The carp in the bathtub; illus by Joan Halpern. Lothrop 1972, 48 pp.

Leah and Harry couldn't face the prospect of seeing Joe, their pet carp, made into gefilte fish, even for such a special occasion as the Seder on the first night of Passover. The large, friendly carp had lived in the family's bathtub for over a week. It even swam right over to Leah and Harry to be fed everytime they went into the bathroom. At a time when most children in New York didn't have pets, Joe was as close to being a pet as possible. So, Leah and Harry hid Joe in a neighbor's apartment until their father discovered what they had done. When Joe's destiny was fulfilled, the children had to face a difficult fact of life. A week later, however, their despair became delight, when their father brought home a pet cat.

A short, warm and satisfying story.

Interest Level: 2-5. Reading Level: 3.1. Further Search Topics: Group 2, Jews-Fiction, Religion-Fiction, Pets-Fiction, Passover-Fiction, Family-Fiction, Holidays-Fiction, Read Aloud, Brothers and Sisters-Fiction.

Cohen, Daniel. Creatures from UFOs. Dodd 1978, 112 pp.

A series of reports about close encounters of the third kind. The author offers both sides of each story, then allows the reader to draw his or her own conclusions. Stories will intrigue even those readers not already interested in UFOs. Index. Photographs. A natural. Parts can even be read aloud.

Interest Level: 3-6. Reading Level: 3.1. Further Search Topics: Best Sellers, Flying Saucers.

Conford, Ellen. The luck of Pokey Bloom; illus by Bernice Loewenstein. Little 1975, 135 pp.

Pokey Bloom's passion was entering contests. She entered every contest she heard of and always thought she would win. Unfortunately, she never won anything. She even went so far as to practice concentrating three times each day on winning every contest she had entered. Someone who had been interviewed on the radio had *guaranteed* she would win that way. She didn't! It only made more trouble for her at school and at home. Pokey had enough trouble getting along with her older brother and didn't need any more problems at home.

There isn't much plot or direction to this story, but it does have some amusing moments. It is an extra book for the reader who enjoys Judy Blume-type books and wants another story about "regular kids."

Interest Level: 4-6. Reading Level: 3.1. Further Search Topics: Family-Fiction, Contests-Fiction, Brothers and Sisters-Fiction, Humorous Fiction, Everyday Stories.

Corbett, Scott. The lemonade trick; illus by Paul Galdone. Little 1960, 103 pp.

This is the first book in a series of quite enjoyable stories (most of which are, unfortunately, too difficult to recommend here). Kerby was given an odd chemistry set by a strange old woman whom he helped one day. When he used the set to put together a brew, Kerby found himself completely under its spell. The sweet-smelling liquid he had concocted forced him to be good, so good that his parents began to worry about him. Luckily the spell wore off in a short time. But, Kerby kept experimenting with it: on himself, on his dog, on his friend, on his enemy and finally in desperation, on the entire boy's choir at church.

A succession of innocently humorous incidents are woven together into a satisfying story. Print size is on the small side.

Interest Level: 3-6. Reading Level: 3.1. Further Search Topics: Humorous Fiction, Bullies-Fiction, Magic-Fiction, Magicians-Fiction, Chemistry-Fiction, Read Aloud.

Curtis, Philip. The invasion of the Brain Sharpeners; illus by Tony Ross. Knopf 1979, 117 pp.

This book is one of a number of books published by Albert Knopf under the series title Capers. They are meant to be (and with few exceptions are) light, easy-to-read fiction, published simultaneously in hardcover and paperback editions. Each book is about 120 pages long with chapter length varying from 9 to 14 pages. Print is plenty large and spacing between lines is always adequate. Plots are built around an idea of guaranteed appeal, descriptive passages are kept to a minimum and action (often suspenseful) abounds. This should, on the whole, be a very useful series. Some entries (i.e., *Man From the Sky* and *Who Stole the Wizard of Oz*, both by Avi) are either too difficult or too obscure to be widely appealing, but they are by far the exceptions to the rule.

Invasion of the Brain Sharpeners is the catchy science fiction story of Michael's successful, but risky, attempt to rid his fifth grade classroom of the overpowering influence of the Brain Sharpeners. The Brain Sharpeners came from another galaxy to search for humans to help them colonize their Planet Five. Humans were so lacking in brain power that the Brain Sharpeners' plan was to periodically expose each child to brain-developing rays, then put them through intensive courses of study guided by their also-exposed teacher. When the children had all learned enough to be beneficial to the Brain Sharpeners, they were to be taken from Earth to Planet Five. Michael was the only one to see the danger they were in and to attempt to stop the plot. He managed to chase the aliens away and to prevent his classmates and teacher from receiving their second dose of rays, but in doing so, he sent the principal to the spaceship. Michael's classmates were thus saved, but his principal was never heard from again. Capers series.

Interest Level: 3-6. Reading Level: 3.1. Further Search Topics: Science Fiction, Flying Saucers-Fiction, Aliens-Fiction, School Stories, Kidnapping-Fiction, Best Sellers, Academic Problems-Fiction, Brainwashing-Fiction.

Davidson, Carson. Fast-talking dolphin; illus by Sylvia Stone. Dodd 1978, 127 pp.

After a rather slow start, this story develops into a well-paced adventure-fantasy with touches of warmth and humor. Eric wasn't just surprised when he found a dolphin in the 10-foot fish pond, he was astonished. Not only had there never been a dolphin there before, but this dolphin spoke in poetry. His name was Wallingford Ullingham Lowell III; Wallingford for short. He was elegant, proud and cultured; but as Eric soon found out, he was very impractical. He didn't seem to realize that he needed salt water and more fish than those in the pond in order to live. It was Eric who figured out a way to keep salt flowing into the pond and a supply of fresh fish. He also kept Wallingford's presence a secret, just as Wallingford requested. The day that Wallingford was discovered was the day that Eric had to break his promise. In order to find out who else had found out about Wallingford, Eric talked with his brother. Together they scouted the town before they realized that Herbert Benson was the only other person who had seen Wallingford.

Herbert reluctantly admitted that he had told his father about the dolphin. Eric knew enough about Mr. Benson to realize that he was just crazy enough to want to harm the dolphin. Eric and his brother gathered all the local children together to shield Wallingford from Mr. Benson. Even Herbert dared to defy his father for the first time. As Mr. Benson struggled with Eric and his brother, he fell, hit his head and rolled into the pond. Wallingford dove to save him, but his leg was caught between two rocks. With the others' help, Wallingford, Eric and his brother Karl were able to save Mr. Benson from drowning.

A few days later Eric, with new-found skills, spontaneously recited a poem about friendship to Wallingford. Wallingford answered with a rare compliment and for the first time used Eric's name (a show of respect). They were such true friends that when Wallingford was helicopter-lifted out of the pond and taken back to his research project, Eric couldn't understand why his father didn't tell him of Wallingford's departure. Eventually he realized that his father had been right; he would rather remember Wallingford swimming in the pond than in a helicopter's sling. Also, Wallingford would have been embarrassed to be seen making so undignified a departure. Wallingford's final message to Eric was a note that Eric found scratched in the dirt thanking him for the salt and the fish and saying that they would one day meet again.

Don't take the plot too seriously or peruse it too carefully for it won't stand up to scrutiny. This is merely a pleasant story with enough humor, action and originality to intrigue many readers. The book's major drawback is the poetry Wallingford spouts: the poetic form and somewhat difficult language will throw some readers. On the other hand, the book could be very useful in a classroom unit about poetry.

Interest Level: 3-5. Reading Level: 3.1. Further Search Topics: Poetry, Dolphins-Fiction, Pets-Fiction, Fantasy, Friendship-Fiction, Humorous Fiction.

Davidson, Margaret. Nine true dolphin stories: illus by Roger Wilson. Hastings 1974, 67 pp.

Nine short stories about dolphins preceded by a brief description of their physical characteristics, their habits and their behavior. Each story is true, although some are more anecdotes than stories. Most are amusing; all are interesting. Satisfying to the dolphin enthusiast from grades two through five.

Interest Level: 2-5. Reading Level: 3.1. Further Search Topics: Dolphins, Group 2.

Dolan, Edward F., Jr. Let's make magic; photos by Jay Irving. Doubleday 1981, 96 pp.

With playing cards, coins, paper, a few commonly available odds and ends and some practice, the reader can perform most of the tricks in this book. The book is not a step-by-step description of how to put together a magic show (as some of the other titles are), but is more like a casual chat with a friend who wants to teach you to perform a few tricks. Some are simply optical illusions; some are brain teasers that involve mathematical calculations; some are card tricks; and others are much more traditional magic tricks.

Very little is said about how to use conversation as audience distraction or how to link the tricks together into a show. Instead, it is the kind of book that allows the reader to pick and choose any tricks he or she may want to learn without feeling pressured to do more than entertain a friend or two for a few moments. The tricks, with the possible exception of the mathematical brain teasers, are all easily manageable by third through sixth grade readers and yet are impressive to their peers. The use of photographs, rather than cartoon illustrations, helps to make the book a probable success, especially with older readers who like to entertain, enjoy the spotlight, or are interested in magic.

Interest Level: 3-6. Reading Level: 3.1. Further Search Topics: Magic, Optical illusions, Best Sellers.

Dolch, Edward W. Andersen stories; illus by Carmen Mowry. Garrard 1956, 165 pp.

The best way to be introduced to Andersen's fairy tales is to hear them told or read aloud. Because they are beautifully written literary tales they suffer tremendously when the language is simplified enough so that the stories can be included in a reader. Furthermore, episodes have been cut out of some tales ("Big Klaus and Little Klaus") and others have been divided into chapters ("The Ugly Duckling"). But, where there is a need for such an easy version of Hans Christian Andersen, this selection will do. The 18 chapters tell only 11 stories. Most of the included stories are familiar ("The Emperor's New Clothes," "The Little Mermaid," "Thumbelina" etc.); all are enjoyable. Illustrations, however, are unattractive and uninspiring. One further caution: the reading level jumps from 2.1 to 3.2. Dolch Pleasure Reading Book series.

Interest Level: 2-5. Reading Level: 3.1. Further Search Topics: Folklore, Fantasy, Group 2, Fairy Tales, Andersen, Hans Christian.

Dolch, Edward W. Stories from France; illus by Gordon Laite. Garrard 1963, 167 pp.

It is very difficult to simplify a story and not lose at least some of its original flavor. Such is the case here and in all the Dolch retellings. Nevertheless, this collection of folktales is quite useful for the French flavor it does maintain. The stories, as they are retold, are good; not great, but good. There are 14 stories related in the 19 chapters. This is a result of splitting the longer, more complicated stories into episodes. Some frustration may arise for readers because there is no indication that a story may involve more than one chapter. The much-improved illustrations that introduce each chapter and adorn the cover help make this more attractive than the earlier books. The book ends with a list of the provinces from which the stories came as well as a pronounciation key to French names. Folklore of the World series.

Interest Level: 2-6. Reading Level: 3.1. Further Search Topics: Folklore, Fantasy, France-Fiction, Royalty-Fiction, Group 2, Knights and Knighthood-Fiction.

Eyerly, Jeannette. The seeing summer; illus by Emily Arnold McCully. Lippincott 1981, 153 pp.

That it attempts to be two books at the same time is the one flaw in this book that may be noticed by young readers. The first half of the book is an interesting story of the growing friendship between a sighted girl and a blind girl. Carey's delight at the idea of a new friend next door turned to disbelief and discomfort when she learned that Jenny was blind. Jenny too wanted to be friends, but not if she was to be pitied or patronized. Gradually she was able to show Carey that being blind was a nuisance, but nothing she was ashamed of or embarrassed about. The second half of the book presents the contrived and somewhat unnecessary story of Jenny's kidnapping. When Carey's attempt to rescue Jenny resulted in her capture too, it was, of course, Jenny's independence and ingenuity that led the way to their eventual rescue.

To the reader looking for a rousing story of a kidnapping the book may be a disappointment. Half of the book is a long time to wait for the slight adventure. But, for those readers interested in a good story of physical differences and friendship, this will be more satisfying.

Interest Level: 3-6. Reading Level: 3.1. Further Search Topics: Vision-Fiction, Friendship-Fiction, Kidnapping-Fiction, Single Parent Family-Fiction, Physically Handicapped-Fiction.

Fall, Thomas. Jim Thorpe; illus by John Gretzer. Har-Row 1970, 33 pp.

Jim Thorpe was an Indian from the Oklahoma territory who became one of the United State's greatest athletes. He and his twin brother were trained by their father to run and jump faster and farther than anyone else. When Charles died, Jim couldn't face returning to school without his twin, so his family kept him home for a few months before sending him away to school again. Jim ran home once more when his father and mother both became ill. Months later he went to still another school where he was noticed by Pop Warner. Pop advised Joe to concentrate on track until he was big enough to play football. His father's death left Jim so despondent he quit school to play professional baseball for a while. By the time he went back to school, Jim was big enough to play spectacular football and then to win the 1912 Olympic decathlon competition. Unfortunately, his short time as a paid baseball player made him ineligible for the Olympic honor and Jim's medal was taken away. Public sentiment was with Jim, but the rules were against him. He went on, however, to play both professional baseball and football. In 1982, 29 years after his death, Thorpe's medal was finally returned to him.

A short, meaty and readable biography of a person who should be interesting to many sports fans. Follows the usual format of Crowell biographies, but looks less like a picture book than many. Crowell Biography series.

Interest Level: 3-5. Reading Level: 3.1. Further Search Topics: Football-Biography, Indians of North America-Biography, Baseball-Biography, Olympic Games, Biography, Running-Biography, Twins-Biography.

Giff, Patricia Reilly. Have you seen Hyacinth Macaw?; illus by Anthony Kramer. Delacorte 1981, 135 pp.

Abby Jones was trying very hard to be a detective, but it was difficult without any mysteries to solve. So to keep in practice, Abby filled a memo book with her notes about anything that seemed at all unusual. At the same time, Abby kept in touch with two local police detectives who gave her hints about detective work. Because of her police friends and her observations, Abby found herself involved in what seemed to be four or more mysteries. Who had moved into the apartment next door and what were the screams that came from there? What was the theft that the police were worried about? Who was Hyacinth Macaw and why had she disappeared? And why was Abby's older brother Dan acting so strangely? Was he involved in the theft?

Abby and her friend Potsie ended up trailing a suspect through the New York subway system, breaking into the next-door apartment, suspecting Abby's brother of the theft, capturing an unusual bird, releasing the bird into a pet shop and recapturing it, before they realized that all the mysteries were linked together. Hyacinth Macaw was a valuable bird stolen from Justine's Junktique Shop. The daughter of Abby's landland had taken the bird and placed it in the empty apartment next to Abby's, so that she could paint the bird's portrait. The picture was to be entered in Justine's Junktique contest. Dan and his friend Holly Monk had been secretly constructing a Purple Pigeon Purifier to enter in the contest. They needed the prize money to repair a window they had accidentally broken. By the time the mysteries were all sorted out, Dan and Holly had won a special prize; Kiki, the portrait painter, had not only been forgiven, but had also been awarded first prize; and Abby had received the reward for finding and returning the bird.

The action in this mystery is both abundant and humorous enough to make the book enjoyable to many readers. There are also some problems that need to be noted. Some readers may find the action too swift and the characters too numerous to be easily followed. Abby's memo notes are sometimes written without vowels and are almost always in incomplete sentences. The reader who is highly motivated or has help from another person will still be able to enjoy the story; however, for the others another choice may be more appropriate.

Interest Level: 4-6. Reading Level: 3.1. Further Search Topics: Mystery and Detective Stories, Humorous Fiction, Writing-Fiction, Detectives-Fiction, Birds-Fiction.

Ginsburg, Mirra. The lazies; illus by Marian Parry. Macmillan 1973, 70 pp.

A good collection of 15 short Russian folktales all having to do with laziness. Most are humorous tales; few are well-known. In just under a third of the stories the humor may be too subtle even for older elementary school children; however, the rest of the stories can be enjoyed by almost any child between third and sixth grade. ("Who Will Wash the Pot," "Easy Bread," "Who Will Row Next," and "The Princess Who Learned to Work" are the questionable stories). Print somewhat small.

Interest Level: 3-6. Reading Level: 3.1. Further Search Topics: Folklore, Humorous Fiction, Laziness-Fiction, Russia-Fiction.

Green, Phyllis. The fastest quitter in town; illus by Lorenzo Lynch. A-W 1972, 62 pp.

Whenever Johnny played baseball and things went wrong for him, he would quit. Johnny's teammates finally grew so angry with him that they told him to leave the team. That same day, Johnny's 90-year-old great-grandfather lost a very special ring his wife had given him. Johnny's love for this great-grandfather pushed him to keep looking for the ring until days later, when everyone else had quit searching, Johnny found the ring. Having learned a hard lesson, Johnny returned to his team for one more chance. That evening Johnny went to see his great-grandfather to tell him, with legitimate pride, that he had played the entire game.

Although the lesson is pointed, the story is very satisfying. Johnny's relationship with this great-grandfather is close and supportive. His problem is one shared by many children, especially those with a weak self-image.

Interest Level: 1-4. Reading Level: 3.1. Further Search Topics: Blacks-Fiction, Challenges-Fiction, Courage-Fiction, Group 2, Baseball-Fiction, Grandparents-Fiction, Friendship-Fiction.

Greene, Constance C. A girl called Al; illus by Byron Barton. Viking Pr. 1969, 127 pp.

Told in the first person, this is the story of two seventh grade girls. The girls' warm friendship began the moment Al introduced herself to the narrator as a non-conformist. Al was very independent, mostly because she was on her own so much of the time. Her parents were divorced and she seldom saw either one of them. Her father only wrote her postcards and her mother was rarely home. The narrator's family and Mr. Richards, their building superintendent, became Al's family. They cooked, ate, played, fought, talked and even made bookcases together. When Mr. Richards had a heart attack, they found help for him and later went to see him in the hospital. It was his death that helped Al and her mother grow closer, just as Mr. Richards' life had helped her understand why her father never came to see her.

A satisfying, low-key story of friendship and maturation. The girls are Judy Blume-style characters with much greater innocence. Their ages are not discernible by their actions or dialogue, only by the author's statement.

Interest Level: 3-6. Reading Level: 3.1. Further Search Topics: Children-Growth-Fiction, Single Parent Family-Fiction, Friendship-Fiction, Weight-Fiction, Aging-Fiction, Death-Fiction, Divorce and Separation-Fiction, Family Problems-Fiction, Everyday Stories, Humorous Fiction.

Greenfield, Eloise. Talk about a family; illus by James Calvin. Lippincott 1978, 60 pp.

Genny, Kim, and Mac knew something was wrong between their parents, and fully expected that their older brother Larry would be able to fix everything when he came home from the army. But even Larry's welcome home party was almost ruined by their parents' fighting and Kim's reaction. That night, as she listened to Larry and her parents' low voices, Genny was certain that Larry was bringing her parents back together. When her father announced the next morning that he was going to move out, Genny's anger and hurt was directed at Larry. With her friend Mr. Parker's help, Genny finally realized that they were still a family; a family with a new shape, but one that would be able to adjust. A one-theme, realistic and reassuring, short book with good-sized print. Very useful

Interest Level: 3-6. Reading Level: 3.1. Further Search Topics: Divorce and Separation-Fiction, Family Problems-Fiction, Brothers and Sisters-Fiction, Best Sellers.

Greenwald, Sheila. Give us a great big smile, Rosy Cole. Little 1981, 76 pp.

It was Rosy's turn to be the subject of her uncle's book. He needed to earn money again and Rosy had just turned 10, the age each of her sisters had been when Uncle Ralph wrote *Anitra Dances* and *Pippa Prances* about them. However, Rosy couldn't dance like Anitra or ride horses like Pippa. In fact, Rosy had no talent that was appropriate for a book. She drew well but Uncle Ralph said that wasn't visual enough. Then Rosy's mother and uncle decided that Rosy could be *A Very Little Fiddler*.

Rosy had been taking violin lessons for two years, but only Rosy and her music teacher knew how truly untalented she was. Rosy hated the whole idea of the book at first. But as people began to treat her like a star, she found herself acting like one, until the day she heard her tape of the piece she was to play at the recital. Once again she realized that she could not play the violin and didn't want to go on with the charade. When everyone ignored her wishes, Rosy started to run away. Her route took her through the park where she thought of a brilliant idea. She ran home, changed clothes, picked up her violin, created a sign, and raced back to the park. There, with all the other street musicians Rosy set up her sign and began to play her violin. Her sign asked people to sign a petition if they felt that she should not be encouraged to play the violin anymore. Right away Rosy drew a large crowd. Before long, even her mother was one of the listeners and one of the signers. That was the end of Rosy's musical career and her uncle's book, but both were happier. Rosy went back to being normal and Uncle Ralph found another topic for his next book.

Chapters are long, but should not be a problem. Print is large. Some of the story is actually told in the illustrations, so the reader should be aware of them. Younger children may take the book more seriously than children whose sense of humor includes irony or children who were not as fond of Krementz's *Very Young* series.

Interest Level: 4-6. Reading Level: 3.1. Further Search Topics: Occupations-Fiction, Humorous Fiction, Family-Fiction, Relatives-Fiction, Talent-Fiction, Photography-Fiction, Everyday Stories.

Heide, Florence Parry. Black magic at Brillstone. A. Whitman 1981, 126 pp.

Liza is a little older, her romance with Logan has progressed to a kiss, and the book's plot is more complex than earlier Brillstone adventures. Other than those differences, the book follows Heide's standard format. The Brillstone books all center on Liza Webster and Logan Forrest, teenage partners in crime detection, who live in the Brillstone Apartments. The stories are similar enough that one could almost substitute the names Nancy Drew and Ned for Liza and Logan. Both young women are only children who live with their fathers. They are both independent, resourceful, and very concerned that justice be done. The men in their lives play approximately the same roles; their fathers are proud and supportive, but distantly preoccupied with their own business; Logan and Ned are gallant, boyish, and devoted. Liza and Logan, like Nancy and Ned, are not distinctive characters. Instead, they are shells into which readers who want excitement and adventure can pour themselves. There is no parental interference to worry about. There is plenty of action, some suspense, and real world crime (for Liza: murder, bank robberies, etc.) rather than childish escapades. The books' success is practically guaranteed. Beware, however, of inconsistent reading levels that wander over a year's range.

Logan was first aware of strange occurrences at the Brillstone Apartments when someone entered his apartment late at night. While the person had searched the apartment, he or she had unconsciously whistled a nursery tune. Logan's neighbor, Miss Violet, said the tune reminded her of her deceased nephew. Slowly Logan and Liza realized that someone was trying to trick Miss Violet out of a substantial amount of money she had just inherited. They suspected that Bella Vine, a spiritualist, and an accomplice were trying to convince Miss Violet that her nephew was communicating from the dead and wanted Miss Violet to give her money to Bella. Not until it was almost too late did Liza and Logan realize that Bella was also posing as another possible recipient of the money and was really Miss Violet's nephew's wife. Miss Violet's nephew had only pretended to die in order to collect insurance money. When he and his wife had heard about Miss Violet's large inheritance, they had decided to reappear in order to bilk her out of the money. Brillstone Mystery series.

Interest Level: 5-6. Reading Level: 3.1. Further Search Topics: Mystery and Detective Stories, Occult-Fiction, Crime-Fiction, Ghosts-Fiction, Cats-Fiction, Detectives-Fiction, Inheritance-Fiction.

Heide, Florence Parry. Mystery of the forgotten island; illus by Seymour Fleishman. A. Whitman 1980, 127 pp.

On a small island, unmarked on the map, the Spotlight Club members found old Mr. Whitson, who claimed that he was being kept prisoner by his granddaughter Lorrie and her husband John. Lorrie and John had told him he was being kept in the yard for his own good, so that he wouldn't wander off and get hurt or lost. They had also told him that he should will the island to them so that his daughter Cassie couldn't sell the island to a resort company for development. He was going to be forced to sign such a will unless he could get the children to help him smuggle a new will to his lawyer. Mr. Whitson wasn't convinced that Cassie wanted to sell the island, but he couldn't get in touch with her and he hadn'd had a letter from her in many months.

As the children went to secretly meet Mr. Whitson and mail his new will, they discovered that their trusted friend Guy was attempting to blackmail Lorrie and John into giving him some of the money from the sale of the island. He had evidence that Lorrie and John, not Cassie, wanted to sell the island and were tricking Mr. Whitson into signing a will in their favor. In a daring move, the children were able to free Mr. Whitson and isolate all three of the thieves so that the police could capture them.

This book involves a somewhat more complicated plot and slightly less familiar ingredients than most other Spotlight Club mysteries. One should progress to rather than begin the series with this title. Spotlight Club Mystery series.

Interest Level: 4-6. Reading Level: 3.1. Further Search Topics: Mystery and Detective Stories, Inheritance-Fiction, Gangs-Fiction, Kidnapping-Fiction, Brothers and Sisters-Fiction, Aging-Fiction, Detectives-Fiction.

Heide, Florence Parry. Mystery of the mummy's mask; illus by Seymour Fleishman. A. Whitman 1979, 127 pp.

The Spotlight Club published a neighborhood newspaper. Just as the club was about to take the fourth issue to the printer, Jay discovered an ancient mummy mask hidden near Mr. Pruitt's house. Mr. Pruitt was intrigued by the discovery (he worked at the nearby museum) and he took the mask from Jay, but agreed that Jay could write about the mask for the paper. At about the same time, Dexter discovered that an old, abandoned house was being used. When the printer's office was broken into that night and only their newspaper was stolen, the three children began to suspect that something strange was going on at the abandoned house.

Dexter rode back to the house alone and was captured by Hank, one of three thieves hiding out there. Figuring that they never would have missed one item, Hank had taken the mask from the cache of goods that the other two had stolen. When he overheard Jay's conversation with Mr. Pruitt, Hank realized that his partners would find out what he had done if they ever read the newspaper article. To avoid being discovered, Hank broke into the printer's and stole the paste-up of the paper. In order to keep Dexter from escaping, Hank tied him up and placed him in a shipping crate. When he didn't return as soon as expected, Jay and Cindy realized that Dexter was in trouble, so they went out to the house to search for him. As the three escaped, Dexter and Cindy slashed the thieves' truck's tires, and Jay ran to phone for the police. After several nervous moments in which Cindy and Dexter thought Jay might not get back before they were caught, Jay finally brought the police, who captured all three thieves.

See *Mystery at Southport Cinema* for more information. Spotlight Club Mystery series.

Interest Level: 3-5. Reading Level: 3.1. Further Search Topics: Mystery and Detective Stories, Crime-Fiction, Egypt-Fiction, Archaeology-Fiction, Antiquities-Fiction, Journalism-Fiction, Gangs-Fiction, Brothers and Sisters-Fiction, Detectives-Fiction.

Heide, Florence Parry. Mystery at Southport Cinema; illus by Seymour Fleishman. A. Whitman 1978, 128 pp.

The Spotlight Club was the name Jay, his sister Cindy, and his friend Dexter gave themselves. Their main interest was solving mysteries and just as in Sobol's Encyclopedia Brown series, Hildick's McGurk Mysteries, and Warner books about the Alden children, mysteries seem to follow them around. Their cases are more intricate and lengthy than Encyclopedia Brown's. They involve more danger than most of McGurk's, and they center on more common themes than the Alden's. The series serves much the same audience, however, as the others. It serves those children who want action, intrigue, and the challenge of a mystery, and who don't care about character development or in-depth motivation. The chapters are 8 to 12 pages long, print size is adequate, and the children are normal enough to make this a very popular series. As an added attraction, reading levels here are fairly consistent.

Thorne prided himself on doing his job well, so when the grocery store he ran for Callie (the owner) was robbed by a bearded stranger, Thorne felt responsible. Thorne ran after the thief but lost him in the darkened Southport Cinema. The Spotlight Club members also tried to track the thief. They figured that he had hidden the bag with the stolen money somewhere in the movie house because no one had been seen leaving with such a bag.

In the janitor's lost and found basket Jay found a wig the thief must have used as a disguise. The children called the wig maker to find out who had ordered it and were directed to a local post office box, Jay and Dexter were surprised to find belonged to the grocery store. Because Thorne picked up the mail each day, he became a prime suspect. In the meantime, Cindy had gone back to the cinema to look for the money. In the dark she had scuffled with someone else looking for the money and had given the person a deep scratch on the face.

At the same time that Thorne decided to pay Callie back for the stolen money, the Club members decided to tell Callie their suspicions about him. As Thorne handed his veterinary school savings to Callie, Cindy took a close enough look at Callie's face to see a new scratch and accused her of being the thief. Callie had so wanted Thorne to run the store instead of going to school, and had needed money so intensely, that she had stolen from her own business. The ending is weak but the rest of the book will hold reader interest. Spotlight Club Mystery series.

Interest Level: 3-5. Reading Level: 3.1. Further Search Topics: Mystery and Detective Stories, Gangs-Fiction, Crime-Fiction, Detectives-Fiction, Brothers and Sisters-Fiction.

Heide, Florence Parry. Mystery of the midnight message; illus by Seymour Fleishman. A. Whitman 1977, 128 pp.

The challenge to the Spotlight Club this time was to stop a crime before it happened. Jay and his sister Cindy were on a bus trip home when a blizzard forced the bus to stop at a motel for the night. Jay answered the room telephone late that night and heard a woman's strange and stern instructions. The instructions were to say nothing, to look in the desk drawer for directions, to expect that Bee had the other half of the instructions, and to be at the place at 8:00 the next evening. The envelope, which Jay and Cindy found, showed the location of and half the combination to someone's bedroom safe.

Early the next morning, the children found themselves fleeing in terror from the evil Scull; the man who was supposed to have received the message. Scull pursued them as they escaped in a friendly salesman's car, caught them and locked them into a cold barn without jackets. When the two were finally back on the road and reunited with Dexter and his sister Anne, they had only a few hours and fewer

clues to help them find Woodvale and Jeremiah Gibbon, the intended victim.

Despite difficult driving conditions in the snow, Anne managed to get the children to their destination a few minutes before the thieves arrived. Anne and Jeremiah's secretary left the house together to get the police while the Spotlight Club members and Mr. Gibbon hid near the safe. A few tense minutes later, the case was closed; Mr. Gibbons' money was safe, the ringleader had been named (Mr. Gibbon's doctor), and the thieves had been caught.

See *Mystery at Southport Cinema* for series information. Spotlight Club Mystery series.

Interest Level: 3-5. Reading Level: 3.1. Further Search Topics: Mystery and Detective Stories, Crime-Fiction, Snow-Fiction, Disasters-Fiction, Gangs-Fiction, Brothers and Sisters-Fiction, Detectives-Fiction.

Hildick, Edmund W. The case of the invisible dog; illus by Lisl Weil. Macmillan 1977, 101 pp.

Brains Bellingham, a nine-year-old scientific genius, interrupted the McGurk Organization's Annual Picnic with an invisible dog. It was only a short time before McGurk and his friends were convinced that Brains' discovery of how to make things invisible was the greatest event since putting a man on the moon. Although they had always scorned the idea of including anyone else in the Organization, they decided to persuade Brains to join. But, before the day was over, they discovered not only that they had been duped, but exactly how Brains had made the impossible seem real. The Organization took its revenge by using Brain's own trick to make him confess. When Brains began laughing at how well his trick had been used in reverse, McGurk admitted how impressed they all had been by Brain's clever thinking. The outcome of their discussion was that Brains was invited, a second time, to become a member of the McGurk Organization.

See *The Case of the Bashful Bank Robber* for series information. McGurk Mystery series.

Interest Level: 3-6. Reading Level: 3.1. Further Search Topics: Mystery and Detective Stories, Detectives-Fiction, Gangs-Fiction, Dogs-Fiction, Supernatural-Fiction, Humorous Fiction, Jealousy-Fiction.

Hildick, Edmund W. The case of the phantom frog; illus by Lisl Weil. Macmillan 1979, 121 pp.

The McGurk Organization would not, under ordinary circumstances, have agreed to babysit for seven-year-old Bela, but there was an unusual twist to Bela's case. Bela's aunt, who asked them to babysit while she worked in her sculpture studio, had heard the eerie sounds of a VERY large frog coming from Bela's room. At first it appeared to the group that Bela actually turned into a frog at night, a werefrog. But, upon investigation they found a very clever, very lonely, and very unhappy young boy who had invented the phantom because he was afraid that his aunt would make him give up his pet frog.

See *The Case of the Bashful Bank Robber* for series information. McGurk Mystery series.

Interest Level: 3-5. Reading Level: 3.1. Further Search Topics: Mystery and Detective Stories, Gangs-Fiction, Frogs-Fiction, Supernatural-Fiction, Transformations-Fiction, Detectives-Fiction, Babysitting-Fiction, Humorous Fiction, Occupations-Fiction.

Hildick, Edmund W. The case of the treetop treasure; illus by Lisl Weil. Macmillan 1980, 121 pp.

As Wanda rescued a cat she discovered a stash of odd items tucked into a hollow high up in a tree. On top of the assortment was a sign that said simply "Beware!" The McGurk Organization suspected a thief was using the tree as a place to hide stolen goods, but until an antique silver bowl was added nothing that had been placed there was worth stealing. Shortly afterwards Wanda found out from the police that she was the prime suspect in the theft of the bowl. Brains devised a complicated system for determining the real thief while McGurk worked more from intuition. Nevertheless, it wasn't long before they both arrived at the same conclusion. The culprit was the gang's long-time enemy Sandra Ennis. Then it was just a simple matter of finding the right way to persuade Sandra to confess and apologize to her victims.

See *The Case of the Bashful Bank Robber* for series information. McGurk Mystery series.

Interest Level: 3-5. Reading Level: 3.1. Further Search Topics: Mystery and Detective Stories, Crime-Fiction, Gangs-Fiction, Detectives-Fiction, Humorous Fiction.

Hildick, Edmund W. The case of the snowbound spy; illus by Lisl Weil. Macmillan 1980, 132 pp.

One snowy morning McGurk called the five members of his organization together to decipher a code. The code was part of a message from someone who wanted to hire them and would pay $5.00 a day. When they broke the code and met their employer, Mr. Fitch, he gave the group another code as part of their assignment. The second code told them where to deliver a small package that Mr. Fitch gave them. They were to pick up another coded message at the same place. After three pick-ups and drops they would be finished and Mr. Fitch, an ex-government spy, would have proved he was still a trustworthy and capable person to an ex-colleague with whom he wanted to work on a book. It seemed like just the challenging kind of assignment the McGurk Organization looked for. As they worked, however, it began to look more and more as if they were being used for illegal business. While Joey and McGurk staked out the next drop-off spot, Willie, Brains and Wanda pretended to Mr. Fitch to be unsuspecting. By working quickly and cleverly and by alerting the police, the McGurk gang uncovered and stopped two industrial spies who were stealing secret information about a new copying machine.

See *The Case of the Bashful Bank Robber* for series information. McGurk Mystery series.

Interest Level: 3-6. Reading Level: 3.1. Further Search Topics: Mystery and Detective Stories, Spies-Fiction, Detectives-Fiction, Gangs-Fiction, Humorous Fiction, Nonverbal Communication-Fiction, Crime-Fiction.

Hildick, Edmund W. The case of the four flying fingers; illus by Lisl Weil. Macmillan 1981, 138 pp.

At first the four young strangers who were knocking over garbage cans had been merely a neighborhood nuisance. Later McGurk and his fellow detectives began to suspect that they were involved in the rash of break-ins and burglaries in the city. The Organization didn't think the "garbage gang" was actually committing the robberies, but rather that they were fingering houses for someone else to burglarize (thus their nickname: The Four Flying Fingers). It could be safely assumed by a would-be burglar that where no one picked up the spilled garbage, no one was home. It was the Organization's job to find the

Thumb who was the mastermind behind the plot. When they caught up with the Fingers, McGurk and crew found out that the Flying Fingers hadn't realized what they were doing; only that a blonde lady in a camper was paying them a nickel for every driveway they left strewn with garbage. It didn't take long for the Organization to track down the woman and her accomplice. But, in one of their less intelligent moves, they played right into her hands and soon found themselves being transported out of town in her camper. When they tried to call to passing cars for help, no one took them seriously. It wasn't until Brains, bound and gagged to appear authentic, used a flashlight and Morse code to signal for help that anyone paid any attention to them. A police car finally stopped the camper for speeding apd after some clever arguments McGurk and his friends were able to convince the police that Lady Thumb was a thief.

This title is just as enjoyable as the best of the other books in the series, more exciting and universal in appeal than most, and equally humorous. It's only drawback is a very inconsistent reading level (from 2.1 to 4.1) that will discourage a reader new to McGurk. Established fans will be able to tolerate the range. McGurk Mystery series.

Interest Level: 3-6. Reading Level: 3.1. Further Search Topics: Mystery and Detective Stories, Detectives-Fiction, Humorous Fiction, Crime-Fiction, Gangs-Fiction.

Hurwitz, Johanna. Aldo Ice Cream; illus by John Wallner. Morrow 1981, 124 pp.

Aldo got his newest nickname (Ice Cream) from his friend DeDe when she heard that Aldo not only wanted to try every flavor of ice cream at the local store, but wanted to buy an ice cream freezer for his sister's birthday as well. Aldo decided his summer project would be to earn enough money for the freezer, but he soon found out that there were very few ways a nine-year-old boy could earn $49.95. In the meantime, he helped his mother deliver food for a Meals-On-Wheels project, learned to swim, found out about fish from Mr. Puccini, and shared his cat with Mrs. Nardo. As the summer came to an end he saw one last opportunity to earn enough money for the ice cream maker. A local shoe store offered a new pair of sneakers to the child who owned the most worn out pair. Aldo convinced his mother that if he won the sneakers, she should pay him the money she would otherwise have had to spend on his new sneakers. Aldo set about making sure that his already well-worn sneakers were the most dilapidated in town. A few days before the sneaker contest the hardware store lowered the price on the ice cream freezer to a point where Aldo could afford it if he won the sneakers. When Aldo did win, just as he knew he would, he and his mother bought the very last freezer in the store.

It is not as well-constructed a story as *Aldo Applesauce*, but for established Aldo fans, or those who want quiet, reassuring fiction, this is a usable title.

Interest Level: 3-4. Reading Level: 3.1. Further Search Topics: Humorous Fiction, Brothers and Sisters-Fiction, Vacation-Fiction, Occupations-Fiction, Everyday Stories, Aging-Fiction, Family-Fiction, Contests-Fiction.

Hurwitz, Johanna. Aldo Applesauce; illus by John Wallner. Morrow 1979, 127 pp.

Aldo Sossi, vegetarian and new kid at school, was immediately dubbed Applesauce for obvious reasons. Aldo didn't like his new name. He didn't like being teased either—not the way he was teased at school.

Nothing went right for Aldo. His attempts at making friends only ended in disasters (once at a bowling alley and another time at a birthday party). He had been able to start a friendship only with a strange girl who wore a heavy, black fake moustache most of the time. After accidentally nearly ruining that friendship too, Aldo not only learned why DeDe wore the moustache, but helped her learn to live without it. DeDe, in turn, helped Aldo take himself less seriously and find more friends.

This is a comfortable, humorous story of two fourth grade children learning to be themselves. The vocabulary is occasionally difficult, but sentence length is almost always short.

Interest Level: 3-5. Reading Level: 3.1. Further Search Topics: Moving, Household-Fiction, Humorous Fiction, School Stories, Friendship-Fiction, Divorce and Separation-Fiction, Vegetarians-Fiction, Individualists-Fiction, Everyday Stories.

Hurwitz, Johanna. Baseball fever; illus by Ray Cruz. Morrow 1981, 128 pp.

Only baseball nuts need even consider this title, but for the die-hard baseball fan this is perfect. Much to his father's disgust, Ezra had only one interest in life. Baseball was almost all Ezra ever thought of. His father was a German-born intellectual who couldn't understand how anyone could waste so much time watching men hit a ball with a stick. He wanted Ezra to become interested in history and chess. Ezra had no interest in history except baseball history. He hated chess, not just because he always lost, but because his father continually told him how badly he played. Predictably they reach a compromise; each learns to appreciate the other's passion, but not before everyone in the family and a few people outside the family have become involved in a series of warmly humorous incidents. Includes much baseball information.

Interest Level: 3-6. Reading Level: 3.1. Further Search Topics: Baseball-Fiction, Family Problems-Fiction, Humorous Fiction.

Hurwitz, Johanna. Once I was a plum tree; illus by Ingrid Fetz. Morrow 1980, 160 pp.

Ten-year-old Gerry Flam knew nothing about her religion except that she was Jewish. Her parents didn't practice their religion and only superficially observed some of the holidays. As they told Gerry, their reason was that they were assimilated Americans. In fact, they seemed to practice as many Christian as Jewish holidays. All Gerry's friends and neighbors were Catholic, so Gerry had very little chance to learn about Judaism or the prejudice to which Jews were still being subjected in 1947 in the Bronx. A Jewish family moved into the apartment building next door, and Gerry's quiet curiosity was stimulated. From the Wulfs, Gerry began to learn about Judaism, World War II, and Hitler. As her pride in her heritage grew, Gerry also felt prejudice for the first time. After celebrating her first Passover Seder, Gerry found that despite the problems, she was truly happy to be Jewish.

Much like Chaikin's *I Should Worry, I Should Care* in tone and mood. Will be useful where there is already an interest in Judaism.

Interest Level: 3-5. Reading Level: 3.1. Further Search Topics: Religion-Fiction, Family-Fiction, Jews-Fiction, City Life-Fiction, Children-Growth-Fiction, Prejudice-Fiction.

Kibbe, Pat. The hocus-pocus dilemma; illus by Dan Jones. Knopf 1979, 125 pp.

Each chapter of this book is a separate episode in B.J.'s attempt to cultivate her newly-discovered ESP talents (more invented than discovered). The episodes, each of which involves a different member of B.J.'s family, are slightly outlandish, but very funny. Even the dog and the cat become involved. The dog becomes the unwitting target for a skunk. The cat accidentally starts a tape recording of speech habits that sounds like burglars breaking into the house. After nine disasters, B.J. finally concludes that she was being ridiculous to think that she had ESP, but that everyone is allowed to be ridiculous sometimes.

The nine, reasonably short episodes, the moderate size print, the sympathetic characters, and the book's humor, make this a very useful and popular title.

Interest Level: 4-6. Reading Level: 3.1. Further Search Topics: Extra Sensory Perception-Fiction, Humorous Fiction, Family-Fiction, Everyday Stories, Best Sellers, Read Aloud.

Kibbe, Pat. My mother the mayor, maybe; illus by Charles Robinson. Knopf 1981, 165 pp.

The Pinkertons first appeared in *The Hocus-Pocus Dilemma*, a better introduction to the family than this book. Although this is a satisfactory story, its appeal is somewhat limited by its subject matter. B.J.'s mother's decision to run for town mayor meant that the whole family became involved in the political process. B.J. became her mother's unofficial public relations coordinator, a position Sam Jessup (Mrs. Pinkerton's campaign manager) didn't want to see anyone fill but himself. But because Jessup's ideas seemed suspiciously designed to insure that Mrs. Pinkerton would lose the election, B.J. continued working on her mother's behalf. Almost every day she managed to get her mother's campaign on the front page of the newspaper, although not always in a flattering light. Once B.J. was arrested for breaking into her mother's campaign headquarters. Another day she inadvertently circulated a picture of her mother in a bikini all over town. B.J. and her brothers and sisters illegally campaigned on the high school campus during Homecoming. B.J. even accidentally succeeded in blowing her mother's opponent's wig off in the middle of a campaign appearance. Mrs. Pinkerton finally lost the election, but managed to bring an important issue to light and to stage the closest and most exciting election the town had known in a long time.

Election campaigns and political issues won't lure many new reluctant readers to this book, but those youngsters who have enjoyed the Pinkerton's previous adventures and can understand a simplified version of politics at work will enjoy this humorous tale.

Interest Level: 5-6. Reading Level: 3.1. Further Search Topics: Politics-Fiction, Humorous Fiction, Sex Role-Fiction, Family-Fiction.

Kluger, Ruth. The secret ship. Doubleday 1978, 136 pp.

A tense, true story about the secret transportation of hundreds of European Jews to Palestine early in World War II. The transport ship became ice-bound in a Rumanian harbor, the crew mutinied and the passengers threatened to expose their plight to the world. In complete charge of the operation was a 25-year-old woman. The book closes with a summary of the Jews' continuing fight for Israel.

The historical understanding that is necessary in order to really appreciate this excellent book make it best suited to readers no younger than sixth grade.

The paper on which this book is printed is so thin that the print shows through from one page to another and the print at the beginning and the end of the book is italicized. Both factors may distract the reader.

Interest Level: 6+ Reading Level: 3.1. Further Search Topics: World War II, Jews, Women, Sex Role, Israel, Survival, Courage.

Krementz, Jill. A very young dancer. Knopf 1976, unp (121 pp).

This was the first of the five *Very Young* books to be written. Like the others, it is large in format and lavishly photographed. Unlike *A Very Young Circus Flyer*, this and the remaining books in the series are written about 10-year-old girls from obviously privileged backgrounds. All the girls are high achievers in their chosen areas but they seem very determined to work still harder until they attain whatever goals they have set for themselves. The books all follow the same formula. The girls introduce themselves, tell about their start in dancing, riding etc., describe their goals, and tell the reader how close they are to those goals. The girls go on to describe their daily routines, the practice, the chores, the hours, and the fun. Then the reader is ushered through approximately a year's worth of the young star's challenges, achievements, and defeats (the latter are only lightly touched upon). Through it all, the child shows enthusiasm, pride, dedication, hard work, and finally, hopes for the future.

Young readers love this series. Despite heavy use of jargon that makes the reading levels somewhat unstable, those already interested in the subject area pour over every word and picture in the books. Perhaps it's partly hero worship, or romance. Maybe it's the inspiration the books provide, but certainly one of the reasons the books are so popular is the vicarious thrill that they provide young enthusiasts.

A Very Young Dancer differs slightly from the formula. Instead of following Stephanie through a year of dance classes at the School of American Ballet, the book concentrates on New York City Ballet Company's production of the Nutcracker, in which Stephanie has a lead role.

Interest Level: 2-5. Reading Level: 3.1. Further Search Topics: Dancing, Ballet, Talent, Best Sellers, Group 2.

Law, Carol Russell. The case of the Weird Street firebug; illus by Bill Morrison. Knopf 1980, 119 pp.

This is the humorous story of a Nancy Drew-type character who gets involved in a mystery before she is even half finished with her mail-order detective lessons. Steffi wanted very much to be a detective. When she saw an ad for a local correspondence course, she tracked down the shabby office in a run-down building on Weir Street, and went to visit Jeff Dangerfield of Dangerfield Detective School. Steffi's first lesson, trailing suspects, was a disaster. She tried to pick out suspicious characters at a fire on Weir Street on her way home. The only really suspicious character (Beady Eyes) didn't go anywhere, so Steffi couldn't follow him. Her next attempts were very obvious and only resulted in her own anger and embarrassment. On her way back to seek advice from Dangerfield, Steffi literally ran into Beady Eyes again. She didn't think anything more about him until she saw him a short time later at another fire just down the street from Dangerfield's office. As the fire moved closer to Dangerfield's building, Steffi took desperate measures to try and save her friend. Steffi's efforts were interpreted by Beady Eyes as attempts to indicate that he was an

arsonist. By the time Steffi figured out that Beady Eyes really was an arsonist, he had her cornered. A timely entry by the police saved both Steffi and Dangerfield. Steffi's reward for the capture of Beady Eyes was a medal from the police and a partnership with Dangerfield.

A fast-paced story, as well as slightly more original characters than most stories of this genre, make this a likely success with third through sixth grade readers. Capers series.

Interest Level: 3-6. Reading Level: 3.1. Further Search Topics: Mystery and Detective Stories, Humorous Fiction, Fire-Fiction, Detectives-Fiction, Crime-Fiction.

Lowry, Lois. Anastasia Krupnik. HM 1979, 113 pp.

Anastasia Krupnik led a comfortable, relatively happy life until her parents announced that she was not going to be an only child for much longer. After 10 years of enjoying that luxury, Anastasia wasn't at all pleased with the change. Babies immediately went to a prominent, and as far as Anastasia was concerned, permanent place on her list of hates. Anastasia kept two lists: one for things and people she particularly liked, and one list for what she did not like. What went on and off the lists tells much about Anastasia. Anastasia tells the rest in this perceptive, sensitive, and humorous story of growing up and adjusting to a new sibling.

Spacing between lines is slightly too narrow for the rather large print.

Interest Level: 4-6. Reading Level: 3.1. Further Search Topics: Humorous Fiction, Brothers and Sisters-Fiction, Everyday Stories, Jealousy-Fiction, Infants-Fiction, Best Sellers, Children-Growth-Fiction.

McNulty, Faith. Woodchuck; illus by Joan Sandin. Har-Row 64 pp.

There's a great deal of information in this little book. It describes a woodchuck's physical appearance, its habits and behavior, and its life cycle. The treatment is very direct and very honest (two of four young woodchucks are killed before the first year is over). Only an overly repetitive, slightly condescending beginning, and the reader format hamper the book's usefulness beyond grade four. A Science-I-Can-Read-Book.

Interest Level: 1-4. Reading Level: 3.1. Further Search Topics: Nature Study, Groundhogs, Group 2, Woodchucks.

Madian, Jon. Beautiful junk: a story of the Watts Towers; photos by Barbara Jacobs, Jr. and Lou Jacobs, Jr. Little 1968, 44 pp.

Although this book is now out of print; it is well worth trying to find. It is a fictionalized account of a young, angry black boy's encounter with the creator of Los Angeles' unusual Watts Towers. Simon Rodia, a poor tile setter, worked on the towers for 33 years until he was 75 years old. He used only his imagination, discarded materials he found around him, seashells, and sand to build three tall, fantasy-like towers in the middle of a ghetto. He created beauty where others saw only junk.

The book is illustrated with photography that makes the story more vivid and the towers and Rodia's accomplishment more impressive than they would have seemed with drawings. The print is good-sized, spacing is totally adequate. Rodia's life is quickly submarized and an update on the Towers is included at the book's end.

Interest Level: 3-6. Reading Level: 3.1. Further Search Topics: Blacks-Fiction, Read Aloud, Best

Sellers, Poverty-Fiction, Rodia, Simon, Architecture, Biography, Aging-Fiction, Watts Towers, California, Poverty.

Mathis, Sharon Bell. Ray Charles; illus by George Ford. Har-Row 1973, 33 pp.

Dominent throughout this biography of Ray Charles is the theme of overcoming adversity. The book is not just a recounting of Ray Charles' music lessons, early schooling, family life, and talent. All of that is included, but it serves to illustrate the manner in which Charles met his troubles. His problems began when he was very young. His brother died, and Ray lost one eye and then the sight in his other eye. His family was poor, but close, and he missed them when he was sent away to a school for the blind. Music was his love, but even that was work, for Charles had to learn to read and write music in Braille. He worked hard at it and eventually could play and arrange music for every instrument in the band.

Determined to be independent, when Charles was orphaned at age 15, he left school and began playing music for a living. The first record he made resulted in a $16 fine because he made it during a musician's union strike. Charles took a series of sideman and nightclub jobs until he finally had enough money to hire seven other musicians to play his music. Today Charles is very wealthy, owns his own record company, has a family, and is considered a great jazz and blues musician. None of his success came easily; only through determination, will power, pride, and hard work.

The book, interesting and serviceable enough for music or biography units, is also designed to set an example for youngsters facing their own problems. It will, of course, be popular with Ray Charles fans, too. Crowell Biography series.

Interest Level: 2-4. Reading Level: 3.1. Further Search Topics: Jazz Music, Music-Biography, Vision, Physically Handicapped, Blacks-Biography, Group 2, Biography, Pianists, Orphans, Challenges, Courage.

Meriwether, Louise. The freedom ship of Robert Smalls; illus by Lee Jack Morton. P-H 1971, unp (30 pp).

A brief, but very interesting biography of a black man whose dreams of freedom as a young slave during the Civil War, led to a daring plan of escape. Robert Smalls sailed 16 slaves to freedom and presented the Northern Navy with a valuable gunboat of which he was eventually named captain. Smalls later went on to serve five terms in Congress.

Although the picture book format of this book prevents its confortable use much beyond fourth grade, it is a compelling enough story to interest even sixth graders. Print is somewhat small.

Interest Level: 1-4. Reading Level: 3.1. Further Search Topics: Biography, United States-History-War, Blacks-Biography, Smalls, Robert, Group 2, Slavery, Politics-Biography.

Moore, Lilian. The snake that went to school; illus by Mary Stevens. Random 1957, 99 pp.

Hank's pet snake Puffy disappeared from the Science Room at school and his little brother, Benjy (in first grade) became ill on the same day. Hank was so worried about finding Puffy that he hardly thought about his pesky little brother, until Puffy was found two days later. Then Hank learned that Benjy had secretly gone to visit Puffy, after being rejected by Hank and had accidentally let the snake out of its cage. Benjy had been so worried about letting the snake out that he had actually made himself ill. Hank finally realized that Benjy wasn't the pest he had thought he was, and promised to be a better older brother.

A somewhat old-fashioned but satisfying story told in ten short chapters.

Interest Level: 2-4. Reading Level: 3.1. Further Search Topics: Pets-Fiction, Snakes-Fiction, Brothers and Sisters-Fiction, School Stories.

Morressy, John. The drought on Ziax II, illus by Stanley Skardinsky. Walker & Co 1978, 77 pp.

Ziax II, the planet that Toren, his father, and other Earth Pioneers were helping to colonize, was suffering a severe drought. It took both cooperation with the inhabitants of Ziax II and courage to seek out the frightening creature that could save the planet.

The importance of maintaining the balance of nature is the strongest message here. Respect for the ways of others is the secondary message.

Interest Level: 3-5. Reading Level: 3.1. Further Search Topics: Science Fiction, Ecology-Fiction, Outer Space-Fiction.

Packard, Edward. Sugarcane Island; illus by Barbara Carter. Archway 1976, 105 pp.

The warning on the first page, that the book should *not* be read straight through, tells you that this book is different. And different it is. It is the first of what is now a new type of book; the "Choose Your Own Adventure" story. The formula is simple and highly successful, especially with reluctant readers. The reader is made the central character of the book. After a very brief series of events that set the stage, the reader is given choices to make. Upon making a decision, the reader is instructed to proceed to another page of the book. More action is described before the reader must make another choice. The sequence of action, choice, action and choice continues until the reader has finally completed an entire story. The books can be read over and over and the reader may never repeat exactly the same story unless he/she makes all of the same choices. What distinguishes one book from another is the setting, genre, and/or author (there are three: Edward Packard, R. A. Montgomery, and D. Terman). Don't expect quality writing or consistent reading levels because you won't find either. (Reading levels vary from 2.2 to 3.2 for most titles). What you will find is dependable, action-filled, enticing, light reading. Some are available only in paperback editions where the print size is fairly small. Choose Your Own Adventure series.

Interest Level: 2-6. Reading Level: 3.1. Further Search Topics: Shipwrecks-Fiction, Best Sellers, Survival-Fiction, Group 2.

Packard, Edward. Deadwood City; illus by Barbara Carter. Bantam 1978, 96 pp.

See *Sugarcane Island* for full series notes. Paperback edition only. Choose Your Own Adventure series.

Interest Level: 2-6. Reading Level: 3.1. Further Search Topics: West-Fiction, Cowboys-Fiction, Crime-Fiction, Best Sellers, Group 2.

Park, Barbara. Don't make me smile. Knopf 1981, 114 pp.

As far as Charlie Hickle was concerned his parents' divorce was the worst thing in the world. His parents had ruined his life and he hadn't done anything to deserve such a fate. At first he didn't say very much. Then he ran away to live in a tree. Finally he cried a lot. That was all just in the first week after his parents announced their decision. After that, both his grades at school and his behavior began to deteriorate. It wasn't until Charlie had had several talks with a helpful children's psychologist and made a disastrous attempt to reunite his parents on his birthday, that he began to realize that he didn't like the divorce, but he could live with it.

The author's use of amusing anecdotes, Charlie's very strong feelings, and the frequency of divorce make this book very popular. Its major drawbacks are its superficiality and the overdrawn portrait of Charlie's mother. The book's faults will not deter many young readers from enjoying it, however.

Interest Level: 4-6. Reading Level: 3.1. Further Search Topics: Divorce and Separation-Fiction, Family Problems-Fiction, Psychiatrists-Fiction, Everyday Stories.

Pfeffer, Susan Beth. Kid power; illus by Leigh Grant. Watts 1977, 121 pp.

When Janie's mother lost her job, her father's salary wouldn't stretch to provide any more money for the new bicycle fund. There was enough money already set aside to pay for one new bike, but both Janie and her older sister Carol wanted a bicycle. Carol, who had saved money of her own, suggested that they each pay for half a bike and their parents contribute the money for the other half. Then Janie's only problem was how to earn money, since she had none saved. Her solution was to create a business: Kid Power. Before long, Janie's business had blossomed and she was becoming rich, but she had lost her best friend and was ruining a client's roses. When Janie finally realized that getting rich wasn't the only thing that mattered in life, she relaxed, delegated jobs to friends better able to handle them, and became their agent.

A genuinely funny book that, as a bonus, takes a realistic look at the interworkings of a family. Consistent reading level.

Interest Level: 4-6. Reading Level: 3.1. Further Search Topics: Occupations-Fiction, Everyday Stories, Vacation-Fiction, Family-Fiction, Humorous Fiction, Best Sellers, Bicycles and Bicycling-Fiction, Friendship-Fiction.

Platt, Kin. Brogg's brain. Lippincott 1981, 123 pp.

According to everyone else, Monty Davis should have been one of the fastest milers in the city. He had, after all, run a four minute and ten second mile in practice one day. He had run well enough that day to beat his high school's two best milers. That was a good enough performance to make the coach push him, his teacher talk about winning, and his father puff up with pride. Even the marathon runner he saw occasionally in the park and his girl friend Cindy seemed to think that he could be the best. Monty really didn't care, or he thought he didn't. Maybe he was just afraid to see how good or bad he really was. For whatever reason, he didn't want to run in the meet against Culver High School. He talked so much about not doing well, that by the time he was supposed to run, he even had his coach convinced he couldn't win. But as he ran, Monty heard a voice inside his head that sounded like the voice in a strange science fiction film that he and Cindy had just seen. The voice seemed to say that he could win, and suddenly that was what Monty wanted. The voice and his new-found determination were what pulled Monty through and gave him first place.

This book is for the track fan or the runner. Few others are likely to care about the difference between a four-twenty and a four-ten high school mile. For those who do care, this is a good choice.

Interest Level: 5-6. Reading Level: 3.1. Further Search Topics: Family Problems-Fiction, Love-Fiction, Running-Fiction, Courage-Fiction.

Renner, Beverly. The Hideaway summer; illus by Ruth Sanderson. Har-Row 1978, 134 pp.

On their way to summer camp, Addie suddenly got off the bus and took her younger brother Clay to see the place where Addie had spent prior summer vacations. It was their grandmother's house and a small cabin called the Hideaway. The house had been sold after their grandmother had died that year, but Addie's father had decided to keep the Hideaway. Much to Addie's surprise she found the Hideaway beautifully fixed-up, just as Gram had promised she would do one day.

When they missed the last bus out of the tiny town and realized that they had enough money to buy the food they would need, Addie and Clay decided to make the Hideaway their summer home. One phone call to the camp and weekly calls to their father kept people from worrying about them. Their discovery of two small raccoons meant that their days were filled with caring for and training the animals. In addition, they had to build a warning system so that no one would discover them and they had to get their food and provisions from town about every two weeks without being too noticeable. They even had to figure out a way to survive a wild summer storm, a flood, and poachers who hunted raccoons. By summer's end Addie and Clay had grown independent, resourceful, and very close to each other.

An exciting story whose short chapters and fairly short sentences keep the reading level reasonably low. Print is dark and of adequate size, but space between the lines is somewhat narrow.

Interest Level: 4-6. Reading Level: 3.1. Further Search Topics: Brothers and Sisters-Fiction, Runaways-Fiction, Pets-Fiction, Survival-Fiction, Vacation-Fiction, Raccoons-Fiction, Read Aloud.

Robinson, Nancy K. Wendy and the bullies; illus by Ingrid Fetz. Hastings 1980, 128 pp.

Wendy and her best friend Karen had a very carefully mapped out route to and from school—a route that allowed them to meet up with the fewest number of bullies possible. But when Karen became sick enough to stay home from school, Wendy had to face the bullies alone. Wendy's fears escalated to panic so intense that she avoided walking to school by hiding in her basement. She finally realized that she was letting fear and anger control her life when she found herself bullying Karen. Only her new friendship with Monica, making up with Karen, and her involvement in a school project helped Wendy overcome her fears.

This is a humorous, episodic tale of a feeling and circumstances common to many children. The illustrations sometimes make Wendy and her classmates appear much younger than her actual nine years, but fortunately that doesn't happen often enough to spoil the book's appeal.

Interest Level: 3-5. Reading Level: 3.1. Further Search Topics: School Stories, Bullies-Fiction, Courage-Fiction, Best Sellers, Humorous Fiction, Friendship-Fiction, Everyday Stories.

Rockwell, Thomas. How to eat fried worms; illus by Emily McCully. Watts 1973, 116 pp.

It started more as a joke than anything else, but it escalated into a strange commitment. Alan bet Billy $50 that Billy couldn't eat a worm a day for fifteen days. Billy had always been willing to take almost any dare offered and he was stubborn enough to carry them out, but when he actually faced the first worm (an enormous night crawler), he almost backed down. He and his friend Tom had to keep repeating the word "minibike" (the prize he planned to buy with the money) and smother the worm in everything imaginable in order to eat it all. After the first worm, however, the next few were easier to face. That was when Alan and his ally Joe, began using psychological warfare and almost won. In 41 very short, grotesquely funny chapters Billy becomes the proud owner of a minibike and is the first person to become hooked on worm sandwiches.

Once this book is started, it is hard to resist its gruesome fascination. Although the print is somewhat small, and there are occasionally very difficult or babytalk words, the interest is strong enough to sustain almost all readers.

Interest Level: 3-6. Reading Level: 3.1. Further Search Topics: Humorous Fiction, Worms-Fiction, Read Aloud, Best Sellers, Challenges-Fiction, Food-Fiction, Bicycles and Bicycling-Fiction.

Rudeen, Kenneth. Roberto Clemente; illus by Frank Mullins. Har-Row 1974, 33 pp.

A romanticized retelling of a great baseball player's life. Those already interested in baseball or in Clemente will probably not mind the romantic tone, but may notice the almost patronizing explanations of some of the basics of baseball. Crowell Biography series.

Interest Level: 2-4. Reading Level: 3.1. Further Search Topics: Baseball-Biography, Biography, Puerto Rico, Group 2, Clemente, Roberto.

Sachs, Marily. The bears' house; illus by Louis Glanzman. Doubleday 1971, 81 pp.

Don't let the benign appearance of this book fool you. This is a disturbing, almost brutal story. It is the story of Fran Ellen, a fourth grader with more problems than anyone should have to shoulder at one time. Her father had left the family and her mother had had a mental breakdown. Fran Ellen and her older brother were left with responsibility for themselves, their mother, and three other children (including a baby). They were all ill-fed, poorly dressed, and unwashed. Neither the social worker nor Fran Ellen's teacher knew the extent of the family's problems. Fran Ellen's only happiness came from her baby sister and from a schoolroom model (of *Goldilocks and the Three Bears* and their house) into which she mentally retreated whenever she had the chance.

As the school year closed, Fran Ellen's teacher visited her home to deliver the bears' house and discovered Fran Ellen's mother and very sick baby sister. Although she hated the idea that the family might have to split up, Fran Ellen had matured enough to realize that when her teacher insisted that she would get help for the family, her teacher was taking the proper action.

The book is inappropriately illustrated to make it appear cute and even humorous. The story is far from either. It is so stark that it probably shouldn't have been illustrated at all. And because the hope that is present in the book's ending is very subtle, a review and a discussion may be necessary to help relieve some young readers' anxieties.

Interest Level: 5-6. Reading Level: 3.1. Further Search Topics: Divorce and Separation-Fiction, Challenges-Fiction, Poverty-Fiction, Family Problems-Fiction, Loners-Fiction, Survival-Fiction, Mental Illness-Fiction, Brothers and Sisters-Fiction.

Sarnoff, Jane. What? A riddle book; illus by Reynold Ruffins. Scribner 1974, 62 pp.

A good, lengthy collection of both familiar and unfamiliar riddles. Every other page is brightened by bold and humorous illustrations. The first part of the book seems to have slightly more riddles for younger readers than the rest of the book. Some of the riddles in the collection involve rather sophisticated puns; thus they are more appealing to fifth and sixth grade readers. The final three pages of the book include 35 riddles whose answers are in code. The key to the code is given on the last page of the book. It is a picture book printed in two tones. The riddles sometimes slant diagonally across the page.

Interest Level: 1-6. Reading Level: 3.1. Further Search Topics: Riddles, Wit and Humor, Group 2, Nonverbal Communication.

Sharmat, Marjorie W. Getting something on Maggie Marmelstein; illus by Ben Shecter. Har-Row 1971, 101 pp.

A curious love-hate relationship existed between Thad and Maggie. It all began when Maggie overheard Thad say she squeaked like a mouse. Then Maggie caught Thad wearing an apron and cooking. Thad was so uncomfortable with the thought that Maggie might tell his friends, that he was determined to find out Maggie's deepest secret. That meant that Thad had to take a lead role as a frog opposite Maggie as the princess in the school play. While at Maggie's apartment for a costume fitting, Thad found a love letter Maggie had written to Cary Grant. Thad decided he would read the letter to the class right after the play was over. But during the play Maggie saved Thad from what could have been one of the most embarrassing moments of his life. By the time he finally had the chance to make Maggie appear foolish, Thad had changed his mind.

Written as Thad's story, the book is funny, warm, and realistic. A good, short, story that continues to be popular. Print is of moderate size.

Interest Level: 3-6. Reading Level: 3.1. Further Search Topics: Humorous Fiction, Everyday Stories, School Stories, Best Sellers, Friendship-Fiction, Sex Role-Fiction, Acting-Fiction.

Sharmat, Marjorie W. Maggie Marmelstein for President; illus by Ben Shecter. Har-Row 1975, 122 pp.

Maggie and Thad Smith are at it again. When Thad decided to run for sixth grade president, Maggie decided to become his campaign manager. However, because Thad thought Maggie was too strong and would end up managing him much more than he wanted to be managed, he turned down her offer. Thad's refusal made Maggie so angry that she not only decided to run against Thad, but she also enlisted Noah, the smartest kid in the class, as her manager. With Noah's expert guidance Maggie's campaign went rather well, despite attempts at sabotage by a spy for Thad. But as election day drew closer, both Thad and Maggie lost track of the campaign issues and concentrated only on beating each other. Consequently the pre-election debate turned into a disastrous shouting match. The next day Noah was elected class president by write-in votes.

Not very subtle, but funny. A satisfying sequel for those who enjoyed *Getting Something on Maggie Marmelstein.*

Interest Level: 3-6. Reading Level: 3.1. Further Search Topics: Humorous Fiction, Politics-Fiction, School Stories, Friendship-Fiction, Sex Role-Fiction.

Shreve, Susan. The Nightmares of Geranium Street. Knopf 1977, 127 pp.

The Nightmares, a small neighborhood gang, had very little to do until beautiful Tess moved on the block. Tess dressed in satins, furs, and rhinestones, and sang in nightclubs. She was even more of a fascination to the gang because they had been told to stay away from her. When Amanda moved in with Tess, the Nightmares invited her to join the gang so that they would have a way of spying on Tess. Gradually her strange behavior, her moods, her bruises and shaking spells, the strangers she let in the house, and the fights she had, led the gang members to suspect that Tess dealt in drugs. When Amanda failed to show up for a picnic and the Nightmares learned the police were searching for Tess, the gang became worried enough to look for Amanda themselves. In doing so, they uncovered proof of Tess' drug dealings, put themselves in great danger, and were protected by Tess as they escaped only moments before Tess was arrested.

Despite its low reading level, the book's confusing sequence of final events, and its subject matter make it best suited to older readers. It is not great literature, but its subject has strong appeal.

Interest Level: 5-6. Reading Level: 3.1. Further Search Topics: Family Problems-Fiction, Gangs-Fiction, Drugs-Fiction, Mystery and Detective Stories, City Life-Fiction, Crime-Fiction, Philadelphia-Fiction.

Silverstein, Shel. Where the sidewalk ends. Har-Row 1974, 166 pp.

There is something here for almost everyone. It isn't always easy reading, but there are enough short, easier poems to pique almost any child's interest. Once caught, children will find the book hard to put down. The best way to encourage the use of this book is to read selections aloud so that potential readers may hear the rhythm and enjoy the humor. This method almost guarantees that they will then want to try reading the book themselves. Readers may struggle with a poem but once it is mastered, they will usually want more.

Interest Level: 2-6. Reading Level: 3.1. Further Search Topics: Poetry, Wit and Humor, Read Aloud, Group 2, Best Sellers.

Simon, Seymour. Einstein Anderson, science sleuth; illus by Fred Winkowski. Viking Pr 1980, 73 pp.

Einstein Anderson is the scientific equivalent of Encyclopedia Brown. Einstein was the nickname that Adam Anderson earned at the age of six. Even at that early age he was a scientific genius. He seems to especially love solving scientific puzzles and mysteries and that is just what Einstein does throughout this and the other books. There are ten very brief, somewhat plotless cases that are presented to Einstein. The clues are all included in each story. The solutions are supplied at the end of each case after the reader has had a chance to try to figure out the answers. None of the cases or solutions are terribly technical. Some of the cases can be solved simply by paying careful attention to the text. The rest require a moderate knowledge of scientific principles. It is a satisfying series to the science sleuth. Print is somewhat small.

Interest Level: 3-6. Reading Level: 3.1. Further Search Topics: Mystery and Detective Stories, Science, Puzzles.

Simon, Seymour. Einstein Anderson shocks his friends; illus by Fred Winkowski. Viking Pr 1980, 73 pp.

Using the identical formula as that in *Einstein Anderson, Science Sleuth* the author presents 10 more science puzzles to be solved by the reader. Einstein (nee Adam) outwits a bully, discovers who broke the window on the school bus, helps the sixth grade win contests against both the seventh and the eighth grades and more. This book, as well as the others in the series, is both fun and instructive.

Interest Level: 3-6. Reading Level: 3.1. Further Search Topics: Science, Puzzles, Mystery and Detective Stories.

Simon, Seymour. Einstein Anderson tells a comet's tale; illus by Fred Winkowski. Viking Pr 1981, 73 pp.

Adam earned his nickname Einstein by proving over and over again that he could solve any science puzzle put to him. Ten more challenges are presented here, none of which prove to be too much for our scientific whiz kid. Like its predecessors, this book is for science sleuths who enjoy matching wits with a cocky punster.

Interest Level: 3-6. Reading Level: 3.1. Further Search Topics: Science, Puzzles, Mystery and Detective Stories.

Slote, Alfred. C.O.L.A.R.; illus by Anthony Kramer. Lippincott 1981, 146 pp.

Jack, his robot twin Danny, and Jack's mother and father were forced to make an emergency landing on an uncharted planet. There they were attacked by creatures who looked like rocks and who wanted to destroy all humans. They captured Danny, led him into an underground living complex, and revealed their true identities. The creatures were robots who had escaped from their owners and the slavery in which they had lived. They kept their planet secret from all humans for fear of what would happen to them should they be discovered. Their main purpose was to free as many robots as possible and to allow robots the same pleasures humans enjoyed. Because Danny had been happy with his humans and claimed to have been treated as one of the family, the inhabitants of the planet C.O.L.A.R. felt he had to be reprogrammed to see the truth. Jack looked and acted so much like Danny that he was able to prevent Danny from being brainwashed, to save his parents from death, and to convince the other robots that some humans treated their robots quite well. In fact, he and Danny, together, were able to persuade the robot manufacturer that a great program of robot-owner re-education was needed.

This is a good adventure story which could also be useful as a lead into discussions of slavery, intelligence, and interpersonal relationships. It is a sequel to *My Robot Buddy*, but one which can be read without having read its predecessor.

Interest Level: 3-5. Reading Level: 3.1. Robots-Fiction, Science Fiction, Outer Space-Fiction, Kidnapping-Fiction, Brainwashing-Fiction, Slavery-Fiction.

Slote, Alfred. Hang tough, Paul Mather. Lippincott 1973, 156 pp.

Paul Mather went against his doctor's and his parents' orders when he accepted his new neighbors' challenge to show his pitching skill. He had been told not to play baseball until he had been given permission, but Paul not only loved to pitch, he was also the best pitcher his new friends had ever seen. Knowing full well the medical problems he could be precipitating, Paul went ahead and pitched a spectacular game for the Wilson Dairy team against the Ace Appliance team. But by the end of the game, Paul was in the hospital again, and Wilson Dairy had been forced to forfeit the game because Paul had played illegally. As Paul's leukemia worsened, his determination to play baseball again grew. When the day came that his team was to play a second game against Ace Appliance, Paul made sure he was there. He was in a wheelchair and weak, but he was there. He couldn't actually play, but Paul's psychological support insured that Wilson Dairy won the game. He went back to the hospital proud, happy, and still determined to fight his disease.

This is more than the usual sports story. This is a very sensitive story of a young boy's determination to fight leukemia. The reader looking for only a baseball story may find this book more than he/she wants. However, the reader who is open to a story of human strength and courage will be well rewarded. The book neither dwells on nor minimizes the disease. Instead it uses both the disease and the sport to portray a character much more completely than in most sport stories, especially at this low a reading level. This is an excellent book for those special readers who respond well to thought-provoking material. Although chapters are short and reading level is low, the print is somewhat small. In addition, the first person style, told as if dictated into a tape recorder (complete with occasional interruptions), may be confusing to readers unless it is explained.

Interest Level: 5-6+Reading Level: 3.1. Further Search Topics: Baseball-Fiction, Death-Fiction, Illness-Fiction, Moving, Household-Fiction, Medicine-Fiction, Physicians-Fiction, Challenges-Fiction, Courage-Fiction.

Slote, Alfred. My robot buddy; illus by Joel Schick. Lippincott 1975, 92 pp.

For Jack's tenth birthday he was given a robot—a robot so real it did everything but run like a human. The robot appeared so human that a thief, thinking he was stealing the robot, almost kidnapped Jack by mistake.

The few points at which the text becomes more difficult than the reading level indicates should not prove too intimidating to the reader. The suspense and humor of the story and the book's high interest subject matter should carry the reader through the rough spots. A satisfying read-aloud for second and third grades.

Interest Level: 2-5. Reading Level: 3.1. Further Search Topics: Science Fiction, Robots-Fiction, Friendship-Fiction, Kidnapping-Fiction, Read Aloud.

Smith, Alison. Help! There's a cat washing in here!; illus by Amy Rowen. Dutton 1981, 152 pp.

Henry Walker agreed to care for his younger brother and sister for two weeks so that his mother could spend her time preparing a portfolio of her art work in the hopes of getting a much-needed job. It was a desperate move for Henry, but it was the only way he could prevent his bossy Aunt Wilhemina from moving in to run the household. Despite Henry's best efforts, almost everything seemed to go wrong. He burned the food, couldn't keep his brother and sister from

misbehaving, seemed to have poisoned his sister's friend, and was faced with making a costume in one night for a school play. The worst of it all was that his mother wasn't pleased with what she was drawing, and Henry only seemed to make her feel more discouraged and unhappy. After what appeared to be certain defeat, however, Henry's efforts were rewarded. His mother was given the job, the family proved they could take care of themselves, and all ended happily.

A light, humorous tale of a young boy's growing independence and maturation under stress and increased responsibility.

Interest Level: 4-6. Reading Level: 3.1. Further Search Topics: Brothers and Sisters-Fiction, Working Parents-Fiction, Single Parent Family-Fiction, Humorous Fiction, Family-Fiction, Challenges-Fiction, Children-Growth-Fiction.

Sobol, Donald J. Encyclopedia Brown and the case of the dead eagles; illus by Leonard Shortall. Elsevier-Nelson 1975, 96 pp.

By all rights Idaville should be declared a disaster area and Mr. Brown, the chief of police, should be fired from his job. Idaville looks like an ordinary small town, but behind its sleepy exterior there exists a crime wave that would challenge the best police departments in the country. It is true that the crimes are always solved and the criminals always caught, but not by Chief Brown. Chief Brown is frequently so stumped by his police cases that he talks about them at home, usually at dinner time. Almost always, his son, Leroy "Encyclopedia" Brown, solves the case before dinner is even over. A clear case of superior intelligence and skill.

Encyclopedia (so nicknamed because of his intellect) not only solves his father's cases, but serves as a detective for his friends, too. He is kept so busy that each slim volume in this series contains 10 short mysteries. Needless to say Encyclopedia solves them all. The question is can the reader? All necessary clues are there and specialized knowledge is rarely required. Should the reader fail to solve a mystery (they are not always as easy as one would expect), a full explanation and solution for each case is provided at the back of the book. Each title follows exactly the same formula. Although a teacher or parent may grow bored hearing of Encyclopedia's accomplishments, most young readers thoroughly enjoy them.

The books actively challenge and thus involve the reader in a way most books do not. A very popular series that does not have to be read in sequence. Reading level is consistently 2.2 to 3.1. Encyclopedia Brown series.

Interest Level: 2-6. Reading Level: 3.1. Further Search Topics: Mystery and Detective Stories, Puzzles, Best Sellers, Group 2, Detectives-Fiction.

Sobol, Donald J. Encyclopedia Brown and the case of the secret pitch; illus by Leonard Shortall. Elsevier-Nelson 1965, 96 pp.

See *Encyclopedia Brown and the Case of the Dead Eagles* for full annotation.

Interest Level: 2-6. Reading Level: 3.1. Further Search Topics: Group 2, Mystery and Detective Stories, Puzzles, Best Sellers, Detectives-Fiction.

Sobol, Donald J. Encyclopedia Brown finds the clues; illus by Leonard Shortall. Elsevier-Nelson 1966, 96 pp.

See *Encyclopedia Brown and the Case of the Dead Eagles* for full annotation.

Interest Level 2-6. Reading Level: 3.1. Further Search Topics: Mystery and Detective Stories, Puzzles, Detectives-Fiction, Best Sellers, Group 2.

Sobol, Donald J. Encyclopedia Brown gets his man; illus by Leonard Shortall. Elsevier-Nelson 1967, 96 pp.
See *Encyclopedia Brown and the Case of the Dead Eagles* for full annotation.
Interest Level: 2-6. Reading Level: 3.1. Further Search Topics: Mystery and Detective Stories, Puzzles, Best Sellers, Group 2, Detectives-Fiction.

Sobol, Donald J. Encyclopedia Brown lends a hand; illus by Leonard Shortall. Elsevier-Nelson 1974, 96 pp.
See *Encyclopedia Brown and the Case of the Dead Eagles* for full annotation.
Interest Level: 2-6. Reading Level: 3.1. Further Search Topics: Mystery and Detective Stories, Puzzles, Detectives-Fiction, Best Sellers, Group 2.

Sobol, Donald J. Encyclopedia Brown solves them all; illus by Leonard Shortall. Elsevier-Nelson 1968, 96 pp.
See *Encyclopedia Brown and the Case of the Dead Eagles* for full annotation.
Interest Level: 2-6. Reading Level: 3.1. Further Search Topics: Mystery and Detective Stories, Puzzles, Detectives-Fiction, Group 2, Best Sellers.

Sobol, Donald J. Encyclopedia Brown sets the pace; illus by Ib Ohlsson. Four Winds Pr 1982, 89 pp.
See *Encyclopedia Brown and the Case of the Dead Eagles* for full annotation.
Interest Level: 2-6. Reading Level: 3.1. Further Search Topics: Mystery and Detective Stories, Detectives-Fiction, Puzzles, Group 2, Best Sellers.

Sobol, Donald J. Encyclopedia Brown carries on; illus by Ib Ohlsson. Schol Bk Serv 1980, 72 pp.
See *Encyclopedia Brown and the Case of the Dead Eagle* for full annotation.
Interest Level: 2-6. Reading Level: 3.1. Further Search Topics: Mystery and Detective Stories, Puzzles, Detectives-Fiction, Group 2, Best Sellers.

Stoddard, Edward. The first book of magic; illus by Rod Slater. Watts 1977, 65 pp.
This is a good choice for readers who have already enjoyed reading and mastering an easier book of magic tricks (such as *Let's Make Magic*, by Edward Dolan, Jr.). The tricks the author includes are often too difficult for the casual beginner. They require both a good deal of practice, and the staging and poise that accompany experience. But for the magic enthusiast there are plenty of flashy tricks, hints for performing and detailed instructions. A few, but not many, are tricks found in other books. Most use easily found household objects. Print and illustrations are fairly small however.
Interest Level: 4-6. Reading Level: 3.1. Further Search Topics: Magic.

Talbot, Charlene Joy. The Great Rat Island adventure; illus by Ruth Sanderson. Atheneum 1977, 164 pp.
Joel dreaded spending the summer with his father. His parents were divorced and Joel was sure his father didn't want him. His father only wanted to study birds. Great Rat Island, where Joel and his father were to spend the summer, was of no interest to Joel. It had no television, no one his own age, only terns. Even the assignment Joel was given (to make sure that no more tern eggs were stolen) sounded dull. It

led to an adventure and a friend, however, that were anything but dull.
Joel discovered that a girl his own age was the thief of the tern eggs. Her name was Vicky Owens. She had run away from camp and was spending the summer alone on Little Rat Island. Joel kept her secret until the day of hurricane warnings. As the storm approached Joel realized that Vicky wouldn't be safe on Little Rat Island. Without telling anyone else he took the only boat around and went to look for Vicky to bring her back to Great Rat Island. He found her with her leg stuck between two rocks, unable to move. By the time Joel got her loose, it was too late to get back to the big island. Not knowing what else to do, Joel and Vicky dragged the boat inside an abandoned building where Vicky had been living. As the water rose around them and Vicky grew delirious with fever, Joel set up camp in the boat. While the building filled with water they stayed dry in the boat. Rescue and medical care for Vicky finally came the next day.
A solid, steadily-paced survival story for the reader who wants a little more than just an adventure story. Print is small.
Interest Level: 4-6. Reading Level: 3.1. Further Search Topics: Vacation-Fiction, Family Problems-Fiction, Birds-Fiction, Divorce and Separation-Fiction, Disasters-Fiction, Survival-Fiction, Runaways-Fiction.

Thompson, Jean. Brother of the wolves; illus by Steve Marchesi. Morrow 1978, 159 pp.
Shadow Fox, a Sioux medicine man, went into a wolves' den looking for special items he needed for healing, but found much more. He found a baby boy who had apparently lost his parents in an accident and then been adopted by the wolves. Winter was approaching and Shadow Fox knew the baby would not be able to survive the cold, so he took the child back to his people. The people were reluctant to accept Wolf Brother, saying that he was an evil omen, that he was unnatural, and that he would bring them trouble. But Shadow Fox's will prevailed and Wolf Brother was allowed to stay and grow up with the Sioux.
As he grew Wolf Brother continued to communicate with the wolves and thus fueled the rumors that grew about him. A very jealous young man, Looks-Away, told the people that a vision had shown him that Wolf Brother and his wolves would one day destroy the village and all its people. The people grew so suspicious of Wolf Brother that, when their horses were stolen and they faced a drought, they blamed him and drove him from the village.
For a while Wolf Brother tried to live as a wolf but found that he could not be totally happy. He wandered away to look for a tribe by whom he might be accepted. On his way, he too had a vision—a vision that told him he would find horses and buffalo for the Sioux and be welcomed home again. It was weeks later before he accidentally found his tribe's horses. In a daring move and with help from the wolves, Wolf Brother not only rescued the horses from the raiders, but also found buffalo just as his vision had predicted. He was then, for the first time, fully welcomed by his people.
This is a taut, suspenseful and mature story about a strong and unusual character. Older readers are most likely to respond positively to the Indian culture and lore.
Interest Level: 5-6. Reading Level: 3.1. Further Search Topics: Survival-Fiction, Wolves-Fiction,

Orphans-Fiction, Loners-Fiction, Indians of North America-Fiction, Sioux Indians-Fiction, Jealousy-Fiction, Best Sellers.

Tobias, Tobi. Marian Anderson; illus by Symeon Shimin. Har-Row 1972, 40 pp.

Marian Anderson's beautiful, strong voice and her great range set her apart from other singers even as a child. By the time she was in high school, she was being paid to sing. However, when she tried to apply to a well-known music school, because she was black she was turned away without even being heard. Anderson's determination as well as her own and others' faith in her kept her singing and seeking better and better coaches until she met Giuseppi Boghetti. He was one of the best voice coaches in the country. With him Marian trained and traveled until she finally won the chance to sing with the New York Philharmonic Orchestra. Anderson thought that at that point she would be invited to sing in famous theaters all across the United States, but because she was black she still received no invitations. She went to Europe where she studied and played to wildly enthusiastic audiences. Her European triumphs finally convinced American theater owners and audiences that she was a serious talent. For the next 30 years Marian Anderson sang all over the world, most of the time without incident, with one notable exception in 1939, when the D.A.R. prohibited her from singing in a hall they owned in Washington, D. C. She sang instead, in front of the Lincoln Memorial, at the invitation of the United States government. During the following years Marian married, bought a farm, sang opera and was made a delegate to the United Nations. In 1956, she retired from singing to help children, young singers, and world understanding.

Crowell Biographies make excellent school report sources for reluctant readers. They are short, interesting, and not overly juvenile looking, although the quasi-picture book format may be a problem for some older readers. This biography fits that description perfectly. The series is somewhat sentimental (as are many children's biographies), however, the sentimentality is not forbidding or condescending. A useful series. Crowell Biography series.

Interest Level: 2-5. Reading Level: 3.1. Further Search Topics: Biography, Music-Biography, Blacks-Biography, Talent, Women-Biography, Singers, Prejudice, Group 2.

Wallace, Bill. A dog named Kitty. Holiday 1980, 153 pp.

Ricky's fear of dogs was extreme but also understandable. He had been attacked by a rabid dog when he was very young. Remembering the fear, the stitches and the painful rabies shots was enough to bring tears to Ricky's eyes even years later. When a local bully told his dog to attack Ricky, Ricky's fear was discovered. About that time, a stray puppy showed up at Ricky's farm. Not quite knowing why, Ricky began to warm to the puppy, to feed it, and finally to love it. When the dog was attacked by a pack of wild dogs (a brutal scene vividly described), Ricky fully overcame his fear of dogs, went to Kitty's defense, and was barely able to save her life. When Kitty was later tragically and accidentally killed, Ricky swore that he would never have anything to do with a dog again. He almost kept his promise to himself, but eventually a second stray dog wandered into the farm and Ricky decided to try again.

This is an emotional story that should appeal to many readers. However, because of the violence and the dog's two-stage death, the book is probably best suited to fifth and sixth grade children.

Interest Level: 5-6. Reading Level: 3.1. Further Search Topics: Dogs-Fiction, Pets-Fiction, Bullies-Fiction, Death-Fiction, Oklahoma-Fiction, Courage-Fiction, Country Life-Fiction.

Yolen, Jane. Shirlick Holmes and the case of the wandering wardrobe; illus by Anthony Rao. Coward 1981, 80 pp.

This is a light, fast-paced story of Shirli and her four friends' attempt to solve a local mystery. Its more fully developed characters and plot make this a better literary piece than any of the *Encyclopedia Brown* stories, but it resembles them in other ways. The children live in a small, secure town. The police chief, Shirli's neighbor and George's father, is working on the same case that interests the children but the children solve it first. The mystery is real and involves danger, as opposed to many of Hildick's McGurk mysteries, the other series this book resembles.

Shirli is a fiesty figure who took up George's challenge to solve the town's latest mystery. Thieves had been systematically robbing some of the wealthy summer homes of antiques. Shirli's plan, to search each of the houses for clues, only succeeded in angering the police chief when he caught Shirli and her friends. Being intrepid detectives, however, they did not give up. Instead, they staked out a likely house and waited for the thieves. When the robbers finally arrived Shirli and George hid. Only Gloria was able to escape and go for help. The oak wardrobe in which Shirli took refuge was one of the first pieces the thieves took out of the house. When Shirli tried to get out of it, she found the wardrobe had been placed on a truck with its door against the truck's side; she was caught. Very frightened, she stayed silent until she found herself in the middle of an antiques auction and recognized one of the voices making bids as George's father! As Shirli tumbled out of the wardrobe some of the police chief's men arrested the auctioneer for burglary and selling stolen goods. After she escaped, Gloria had told the police about the thieves, their truck, Shirli, and George, whom they found locked inside a closet still at the summer house.

A serviceable book that will be enjoyed by a wide range of readers.

Interest Level: 3-5. Reading Level: 3.1. Further Search Topics: Mystery and Detective Stories, Humorous Fiction, Friendship-Fiction, Crime-Fiction, Antiquities-Fiction, Detectives-Fiction, Challenges-Fiction.

Yolen, Jane. The boy who spoke chimp illus by David Wiesner. Knopf 1981, 120 pp.

Kriss was determined to prove to his father that, at 12 years old, he was perfectly capable of camping out by himself. To do so, he left home and headed up the coast of California with a sleeping bag, some food, a map and compass, and water. His plan was to camp, ride, and hike his way to his grandmother's house. On the way, the coast line was torn apart by the second great earthquake to strike California. The first had already destroyed great portions of the state. The second was even stronger. The truck he had been riding in was destroyed and everyone around Kriss was killed by the quake except for two chimpanzees. The chimps, in transit from one lab to another, were research animals who had been taught to use sign language. Kriss took the animals with him as he tried to get farther inland and finally home to Los Angeles.

His trip not only confirmed his father's fears about Kriss' inadequacies but taught him how to overcome them. Kriss learned to communicate with the chimps, to find food and to live on his own until Old Chris, a hermit, happened along. Together they continued to brave the chaos brought about by the earthquake even when Old Chris' heart troubled him. When a helicopter finally spotted them, Kriss decided to let the chimps go wild and promised Old Chris that he would be back in the woods very soon. It was a mature, capable Kriss who returned home.

This is typical of the Capers series—much action, few background details, little characterization. The books, however, are on appealing topics; they move quickly and they create intriguing (if sometimes implausible) situations. They are light, enjoyable and very useful. Capers series.

Interest Level: 3-6. Reading Level: 3.1. Further Search Topics: California-Fiction, Disasters-Fiction, Survival-Fiction, Apes-Fiction, Nonverbal Communication-Fiction, Camping-Fiction, Runaways-Fiction, Best Sellers.

READING LEVEL 3.2

Adler, Irving. Your eyes. John Day 1962, 48 pp.

Getting a young reader past this book's unattractive appearance may be difficult. Everything about the book's physical appearance screams "old." Some of the information and lack of information conveys the same message (e.g. no mention of contact lenses). For basic material about eyes and sight however, there is much here that is accessible and interesting to readers in grades two to six. Includes pronunciation guide, glossary, and detailed table of contents. No index. The Reason Why Series

Interest Level: 2-6. Reading Level: 3.1. Further Search Topics: Vision, Physically Handicapped, Group 2.

Anderson, C. S. The blind Connemara. Macmillan 1971, 80 pp.

Rhonda, not wealthy enough to own a horse of her own, was given a beautiful Connemara pony. Unfortunately, it had begun to go blind. A blind pony is usually put away, but Rhonda loved this pony too much to let that happen. Against all odds, Rhonda not only taught Pony to trot, canter, and even jump with confidence, but went on to win a ribbon at an important horse show. Though sentimental and predictable, this book is an almost insured success with lovers of horses and champions of the underdog. Be alert to the occasional descriptive passage that is both longer and more difficult than the rest of the text.

Interest Level: 4-6. Reading Level: 3.2. Further Search Topics: Vision-Fiction, Physically Handicapped-Fiction, Horses-Fiction.

Bendick, Jeanne. The first book of airplanes. Watts 1975, revised edition, 65 pp.

It will take a determined reader to get much technical information from this overview of airplanes. The first sections (thrust, lift gravity, drag, and parts of a plane) promise simple, understandable explanations of complicated topics. The next portion of the book fails to live up to that promise. The descriptions of airplane engines will be intelligible only to the reader who already knows how an engine works. The history of flight is little more than an outline. The two-page chapter on air maps and distances will do more to confuse than instruct most readers. On the other hand, the information about airports, control towers, and types and uses of aircrafts is better. The book is well-indexed and includes a four-page glossary. It is perhaps best used as a general introduction to airplanes (skip the three areas mentioned above). For technical information about flight, look elsewhere. Print size is adequate but spacing between lines could have been more generous.

Interest Level: 4-6. Reading Level: 3.2. Further Search Topics: Airports, Engines, Flight, Airplanes.

Bennett, Jay. The pigeon. Methuen 1980, 147 pp.

Despite a low testing score, this is not a truly easy book to read. The author assumes his readers are fairly sophisticated and worldly, thus he does not explain the meaning of the Iron Cross symbol or the word Aryan. The book's language varies from simple to difficult, making the reading level inconsistent (2.1 - 4.1). The setting is dark and forbidding; an underground world of fugitives and terrorists. And yet, the book will be popular with many readers in sixth grade; it will be even more popular with older readers. The tension in this story of a teenage boy, blamed for the murder of his ex-girlfriend, is almost palpable. Brian's flight from the police and his desire to find Donna's murderer take him directly into the midst of a ring of terrorists, for whom life has no meaning. In Brian's attempt to prove his innocence, two more lives are lost, but hundreds more are saved as Brian discovers and stops a bomb threat. The author has used riveting action, short, clipped sentences, and terse dialogue to create a very successful, highly suspenseful book. Print size is only moderate.

Interest Level: 6 . Reading Level: 3.2. Further Search Topics: Mystery and Detective Stories, Terrorism-Fiction, Murder-Fiction, Best Sellers, Crime-Fiction, Courage-Fiction, Survival-Fiction, Runaways-Fiction.

Blume, Judy. Are you there God? It's me, Margaret. Bradbury 1970, 149 pp.

Sixth grade was a year of growth for Margaret and her friends. They all wondered when they would start growing breasts and when they would begin menstruating. Each was kissed for the first time. It was also a year in which Margaret tried to decide whether to be Jewish or Christian and ended up neither. She simply remained friends with God, just as she was when the year began. The book is a reassuring, very open, and humorous treatment of the pains and promise of maturation. It is exceptionally popular with older elementary school readers, so the book's slightly small print and narrow lines should not impede an interested reader's progress.

Interest Level: 4-6. Reading Level: 3.2. Further Search Topics: School Stories, Family-Fiction, Children-Growth-Fiction, Religion-Fiction, Humorous Fiction, Love-Fiction, Best Sellers, Grandparents-Fiction, Everyday Stories.

Burchard, Marshall. Sports hero: Mario Andretti. Putnam 1977, 90 pp.

Auto racing's all-around superstar. See *Sports Hero: Bill Walton* for details about the series. Sports Hero series.

Interest Level: 3-6. Reading Level: 3.2. Further Search Topics: Biography, Andretti, Mario, Auto Racing-Biography.

Burchard, Marshall. Sports hero: Joe Morgan. Putnam 1978, 93 pp.

Joe Morgan has been described as one of baseball's most complete players. He could field, hit, run and steal bases with the best. See *Sports Hero: Bill Walton* for more details about the book. Sports Hero series.

Interest Level: 2-6. Reading Level: 3.2. Further Search Topics: Biography, Morgan, Joe, Baseball-Biography, Blacks-Biography, Group 2.

Burchard, Marshall. Sports hero: Reggie Jackson. Putnam 1975, 93 pp.

Reggie Jackson was one of the big reasons why the Oakland A's won baseball's World Series three years in a row. *Sports Hero: Bill Walton* gives more information about the books in the series. Sports Hero series.

Interest Level: 2-6. Reading Level: 3.2. Further Search Topics: Biography, Jackson, Reggie, Baseball-Biography, Blacks-Biography, Group 2.

Burchard, Marshall. Sports hero: Bill Walton. Putnam 1978, 94 pp.

Burchard's series of *Sports Hero* biographies is better than many other sports biography series. Although heavy emphasis is placed on the subject's playing time, each person's life is capsulized from childhood to just before the book's publication date. Marshall and Sue Burchard (with whom he has collaborated and who writes an almost identical series called *Sports Stars*) treat each figure favorably and with enthusiasm. But, contrary to many children's writers, particularly sports biographers, these writers at least touch on those personal foibles that make players human (i.e. Joe Namath's tendency to break training is briefly described). Each book is abundantly illustrated with photographs, avoids patronizing the reader and is consistently interesting. Each is reliable, very useful and can be depended on to appeal to the sports enthusiast. Problems arise, however, with inconsistent and/or artificially inflated reading levels. The reading level of a title may vary from 2.2 to 4.2. The same passage tested on both a Spache and a Dale-Chall scale may show a similar two-year spread. The problem seems to be with jargon. Most sports jargon does not appear on either Spache's or Chall's list of familiar words and thus raises a book's reading level. But, the words may well be known to the reader (or quickly recognized after one introduction and so not truly unfamiliar). Keep in mind, therefore, that the true sports fan will often be able to read a title that tests well above his/her actual reading level.

Bill Walton's career is covered only through the end of the 1976-1977 season when the Portland Trailblazers won the NBA title. The reading level of this title is one of the most inconsistent of the series (from 2.2 to 4.2).

Interest Level: 2-6. Reading Level: 3.2. Further Search Topics: Biography, Walton, Bill, Basketball-Biography, Group 2.

Burchard, Marshall. Sports hero: Billie Jean King. Putnam 1975, 95 pp.

Winner of every major women's tennis title and a very important person to women's professional sports. Consistent reading level. Book includes glossary of tennis terms. See entry under *Sports Hero: Bill Walton* Sports Hero series.

Interest Level: 3-6. Reading Level: 3.2. Further Search Topics: Biography, King, Billie Jean, Tennis-Biography, Women-Biography.

Burchard, Marshall. Sports hero: Fran Tarkenton. Putnam 1977, 95 pp.

From a strict religious background where athletics were not encouraged, Fran went on to set every NFL passing record possible See *Sports Hero: Bill Walton*. Sports Hero series.

Interest Level: 3-6. Reading Level: 3.2. Further Search Topics: Biography, Tarkenton, Fran, Football-Biography, Religion-Biography.

Burchard, Marshall. Sports hero: Fred Lynn. Putnam 1976, 95 pp.

Fred Lynn was baseball's first rookie to be named Most Valuable Player. Consistent reading level. See *Sports Hero: Bill Walton*. Sports Hero series.

Interest Level: 2-6. Reading Level: 3.2. Further Search Topics: Biography, Lynn, Fred, Baseball-Biography, Group 2.

Burchard, Marshall. Sports Hero: O.J. Simpson. Putnam 1975, 95 pp.

O.J. Simpson, who now flies through airports, still holds at least three NFL records, including most yards gained in a single season. See *Sports Hero: Bill Walton* for series information. Sports Hero series.

Interest Level: 2-6. Reading Level: 3.2. Further Search Topics: Biography, Simpson, O.J., Football-Biography, Blacks-Biography, Group 2.

Burchard, Marshall. Sports hero: Ron Guidry. Putnam 1981, 95 pp.

The Cajun, left-handed pitcher who led the Yankees to two World Championships. See *Sports Hero: Bill Walton* for series details. Sports Hero series.

Interest Level: 3-6. Reading Level: 3.2. Further Search Topics: Baseball-Biography, Biography, Guidry, Ron.

Burchard, Marshall. Sports hero: Terry Bradshaw. Putnam 1980, 95 pp.

Once labeled a "dumb hick," Terry Bradshaw went on to prove he was a talented and thinking quarterback, good enough to be named NFL Player of the Year. He is also a deeply religious man. Reading level of this title varies from 3.1 to 4.1. For more details about the series, see *Sports Hero: Bill Walton*. Sports Hero series.

Interest Level: 3-6. Reading Level: 3.2. Further Search Topics: Biography, Bradshaw, Terry, Football-Biography, Religion-Biography.

Burchard, Susan H. Sports star: Dorothy Hamill. HarBraceJ 1978, 63 pp.

Although written by Susan Burchard, this and most of the following listings are true to Marshall Burchard's *Sports Hero* format. For more explanation see *Sports Hero: Bill Walton*.

Dorothy Hamill was the darling of ice skating in 1976 and is now a top professional figure skater. This makes her rise to stardom sound romantic and glamorous. Skating jargon pushes the reading level from 3.1 to 3.2. Sports Star series.

Interest Level: 2-6. Reading Level: 3.2. Further Search Topics: Hamill, Dorothy, Ice Skating-Biography, Women-Biography, Biography, Group 2.

Burchard, Susan H. Sports star: John McEnroe. HarBraceJ 1979, 63 pp.

In 1977, feisty John McEnroe became the youngest semi-finalist ever to play at Wimbledon. Both before and since then, he has been noted almost as often for his temper as his talent. The level of difficulty of this book varies from 3.1 to 4.1. See *Sports Star: Elvin Hayes* for more details about the book. Sports Star series.

Interest Level: 3-6. Reading Level: 3.2. Further Search Topics: Biography, Tennis-Biography, McEnroe, John.

Burchard, Susan H. Sports star: "Mean" Joe Greene. HarBraceJ 1976, 64 pp.

"Mean" Joe Greene's nickname is appropriate. He is big, "mean" on the playing field, and likes to win. He usually does. More details about the book under *Sports Hero: Bill Walton*, by Marshall Burchard. Sports Star series.

Interest Level: 2-6. Reading Level: 3.2. Further Search Topics: Biography, Football-Biography, Greene, "Mean" Joe, Blacks-Biography, Group 2.

Burchard, Susan H. Sports star: Tony Dorsett. HarBraceJ 1978, 64 pp.

One year after he set the college rushing record and won the Heisman Trophy, Tony Dorsett was named the NFL's Rookie of the Year and found himself playing in the Super Bowl. Reading level of this title varies from 2.2 to 3.2. For more information about the series see the entry for Marshall Burchard's *Sports Hero: Bill Walton*. Sports Star series.

Interest Level: 2-6. Reading Level: 3.2. Further Search Topics: Biography, Football-Biography, Dorsett, Tony, Blacks-Biography, Group 2.

Byars, Betsy. After the goat man; illus by Ronald Himler. Viking Pr. 1974, 126 pp.

Harold was fat and over-sensitive. Ada was serious and independent. Figgy was lonely, poor and in need of help. Figgy and his grandfather, the Goat Man, had been forced to move from their cabin to make room for a highway. The Goat Man had returned to the cabin with a shotgun, vowing to defend his right to live there. Figgy knew he had to persuade his grandfather to leave or someone would be hurt. But, in the children's hurry to reach the Goat Man, it was Figgy who was hurt and Harold who rescued both Figgy and the Goat Man. Harold grew up that day. He stopped dreaming about the way he wanted things to be and faced life realistically for the first time.

The book is very much a character study. Realistic characters are treated with sympathy and dignity and given a chance to grow. Introspective readers will understand and enjoy the book more than those looking for adventure. Print size is fairly large, but lines are separated by only average width.

Interest Level: 4-6. Reading Level: 3.2. Further Search Topics: Loneliness-Fiction, Weight-Fiction, Moving, Household-Fiction, Courage-Fiction, Grandparents-Fiction, Orphans-Fiction.

Byars, Betsy. The 18th emergency; illus by Robert Grossman. Viking Pr. 1973, 126 pp.

When your best friend knows how to escape from the world's 17 worst emergencies and you're faced with the eighteenth, you're in trouble. That was the spot in which Mouse found himself one day. He had drawn an arrow towards a large picture of the Neanderthal man and written Marv Hammerman's name. Hammerman had seen him do it and was out to kill, maim, or at least beat up Mouse. Mouse finally ran out of ways to avoid Hammerman and had to face the fight. When it was over and he was once again able to stand up, Mouse realized he felt better for having allowed Hammerman to regain his honor and for having taken responsibility for his own actions.

A funny, fast-moving look at real feelings of fear, honor and responsibility. Very popular. Print is dark and of good size but lines could have been spaced farther apart.

Interest Level: 4-6. Reading Level: 3.2. Further Search Topics: Bullies-Fiction, Humorous Fiction, Courage-Fiction, Best Sellers, Challenges-Fiction, Read Aloud.

Christopher, Matt. No arm in left field; illus by Byron Goto. Little 1974, 131 pp.

Matt Christopher's books are just the thing for sports junkies. The play-by-play accounts of several sports events (here it is baseball games) are loosely tied together by secondary plot developments. Usually the plot revolves around the main character's successful attempt to overcome a difficulty of some sort.

Terry was a good baseball player so, when he was invited to join a local team shortly after he moved to Pennsylvania, he was very pleased. Almost immediately, he learned that a teammate was not at all happy about playing with Terry. Terry was black and his teammate, Tony, was very prejudiced. Terry had dealt with people like Tony before, so he was able to ignore most, but not all, of Tony's unkind comments and actions. But the day finally came when Tony realized that to play well as a team, they had to work together instead of against each other.

Interest Level: 3-6. Reading Level: 3.2. Further Search Topics: Prejudice-Fiction, Baseball-Fiction, Friendship-Fiction, Challenges-Fiction.

Clark, Margaret Goff. Barney and the UFO; illus by Ted Lewin. Dodd 1979, 159 pp.

Barney felt a strange prickly sensation several times before he discovered that it was caused by Tibbo, a Gark from the planet Ornam. Tibbo had selected Barney as a friend who would accompany him back to Ornam. Barney was to learn the peaceful ways of Gark and then return to Earth to help persuade the world to accept the aliens. At first the idea of visiting Ornam appealed to Barney because he liked Tibbo and felt very lonely and unsure of his adoptive family's love. Those were the very reasons that Tibbo had chosen Barney: he wanted someone without strong ties to Earth and Barney's only tie when he was first contacted by Tibbo was his little brother Scott. As the time to go grew closer, Barney found a new and strong friendship with Dave, a science whiz-kid, and great love for his new parents. Tibbo, however, was determined to hold Barney to his promise. Only a last minute confrontation between Tibbo and Barney, David, Scott and Mr. and Mrs. Crandall prevented Tibbo from succeeding. But even as Tibbo left, he and Barney acknowledged their new friendship and agreed to keep in touch.

Because of its fairly slow beginning, readers must be well-introduced to this book. If they can be persuaded to be patient while the author sets the stage for about 18 pages they will be rewarded with a decent, if somewhat wordy, story of friendship, UFO's, space travel and family affection.

Interest Level: 3-6. Reading Level: 3.2. Further Search Topics: Science Fiction, Flying Saucers-Fiction, Kidnapping-Fiction, Foster Homes-Fiction, Family-Fiction, Adoption-Fiction, Aliens-Fiction, Loneliness-Fiction, Orphans-Fiction.

Clymer, Eleanor. Me and the Eggman; illus by David K. Stone. Dutton 1972, 57 pp.

As Donald's life became more and more miserable and as his chores and responsibilities around his small, overcrowded, urban apartment increased, he began to look for a way to escape. Thinking that if he could just get to the country, life would be better, Donald sneaked into a truck owned by a farmer who delivered eggs to the city. Not surprisingly the farmer, a sharp speaking, independent old man, was not at all happy to find Donald. Reluctantly, the Eggman, as the farmer was called, agreed to let Donald stay a week and help to work his rundown farm. The week stretched into a summer in which Donald learned to face and accept reality, to love the Eggman and to like himself.

This book is a surprisingly consistent success with reluctant readers, especially boys. Watch for the lack of quotation marks around the dialogue and the somewhat small print.

Interest Level: 3-6. Reading Level: 3.2. Further Search Topics: Family Problems-Fiction, Poverty-Fiction, Vacation-Fiction, Runaways-Fiction, Farm Life-Fiction, Best Sellers.

Danziger, Paula. There's a bat in bunk five. Delacorte 1980, 150 pp.

Although this is a sequel to *The Cat Ate My Gymsuit,* it can be read alone. Marcy accepted an offer to become a junior counselor at an arts camp run by her ex-English teacher Ms. Finney and Ms. Finney's husband. After a nervous beginning, Marcy found herself enjoying the other counselors and the campers, but most of all, her first romance. Marcy's only difficulty was dealing with Ginger, a very troubled 10-year-old in Marcy's cabin. Marcy couldn't seem to get through to Ginger. When Ginger ran away, Marcy was forced to consider whether she should have spent more time with the campers and not quite so much time with Ted.

Marcy is a normal teenager whose problems, questions and activities are appealing to many teen and pre-teen readers. The characters who surround Marcy here are less stereotyped and flat than those in The Cat Ate My Gymsuit. Even Marcy's parents are more human. The author's light touch is just right for Marcy's story.

Interest Level: 5-6. Reading Level: 3.2. Further Search Topics: Humorous Fiction, Camp-Fiction, Everyday Stories, Love-Fiction, Vacation-Fiction, Occupations-Fiction, Adolescence-Fiction.

Greene, Constance C. Isabelle the itch; illus by Emily A. McCully. Viking Pr. 1973, 126 pp.

This is a loosely plotted story about a spunky, original fifth grade girl who could drive everyone around her crazy without ever tiring. Isabelle's dearest dream was to win the 50-yard dash at her school's field day. Even though she took over her brother's paper route to earn money for the Adidas track shoes she needed, Isabelle still didn't win. However, she did meet some new people, make new friends and keep those around her on their toes. A very amusing story told mostly in dialogue.

Interest Level: 4-6. Reading Level: 3.2. Further Search Topics: School Stories, Occupations-Fiction, Humorous Fiction, Everyday Stories, Running-Fiction, Individualists-Fiction, Sex Role-Fiction, Read Aloud.

Greene, Constance C. I and Sproggy; illus by Emily A. McCully. Viking Pr. 1978, 155 pp.

Ten-year-old Adam had adjusted to his parents' divorce and had even grown to like living alone with his mother. When his father came back from London with his new wife and stepdaughter Sproggy and announced that they were moving into an apartment nearby, Adam was a little worried. But when his father asked him to take care of Sproggy, Adam was furious. First of all, he didn't know Sproggy and he didn't want to know her. Secondly, she was two months older than he, taller too, and she embarrassed him in public. And finally, she didn't need his help. She got along quite well by herself; so well that she even saved Adam from a mugger and became good friends with Adam's friends behind his back. It wasn't until Sproggy proved to be vulnerable that Adam and she became friends.

A warm, realistic and humorous story whose interesting characters (even the minor ones) heighten the book's appeal.

Interest Level: 4-6. Reading Level: 3.2. Further Search Topics: Brothers and Sisters-Fiction, Divorce and Separation-Fiction, City Life-Fiction, New York City-Fiction, Humorous Fiction, Friendship-Fiction, Everyday Stories.

Hall, Lynn. The mystery of Pony Hollow; illus by Ruth Sanderson. Garrard 1978, 64 pp.

Sarah investigated strange voices only to find the skeleton of a horse that had died 40 years earlier. She was determined to find out what it was that had killed the horse and why its ghost was uneasy.

The mystery element isn't as strong here as most mystery fans would like, but the book will not disappoint many true horse story enthusiasts.

Interest Level: 3-5. Reading Level: 3.2. Further Search Topics: Horses-Fiction, Ghosts-Fiction, Mystery and Detective Stories.

Heide, Florence Parry. Face at the Brillstone window. A. Whitman 1979, 128 pp.

As Liza drove out of the garage one evening she heard a thump at the side of the car. She jumped out and found that she had accidentally hit Peter Pritchard, an insurance man and a new tenant of the apartment building. Pritchard seemed to be a very nice person who took some interest in Liza, her friends, and the criminal cases Liza's father (a journalist) was investigating. Liza was particularly interested in the case of the one-armed bandit who had been convicted of robbing and shooting a security guard. Against her father's research assistant's wishes she continued to search for evidence that would prove Robin Keck was innocent of the charges. As she interviewed the security guard, Keck's fiancee, his best friend, and the grandmother of a young girl who had had a strong crush on Keck, Liza found hints of his innocence. Young Bridgette's diary, however, held the proof she needed: an alibi. But someone else knew she had the information; someone who didn't want the information made public. Diary in hand, Liza began walking to her father's assistant's house (her father was out of town) when Pritchard offered her a ride. When Pritchard drove off in the wrong direction and then handed her a piece of incriminating evidence (gum), Liza realized she had played right into the real criminal's hands. Liza made a risky escape attempt that ended successfully with Pritchard's capture.

See *Black Magic at Brillstone* for more information about the series. Brillstone Mystery series.

Interest Level: 4-6. Reading Level: 3.2. Further Search Topics: Mystery and Detective Stories, Crime-Fiction, Detectives-Fiction.

Holland, John. The way it is. HarBraceJ 1969, 87 pp.

For 15 boys living in a run-down area of Brooklyn, school became interesting when they were assigned to photograph whatever was meaningful to them in their neighborhood. The results, described in their own words, were developed into this fascinating documentary which is at the same time a spontaneous glimpse of the boys themselves. The book should be of particular interest to older urban children. Print slightly on the small side. Has recently gone out of print, but is worth looking for.

Interest Level: 4-6. Reading Level: 3.2. Further Search Topics: Best Sellers, City Life, Photography, Poverty, Academic Problems.

Jordan, June. Fannie Lou Hamer; illus by Albert Williams. Har-Row 1972, 41 pp.

In 1917, Fannie Lou Hamer was the last of 20 children born to a fearless black woman. Fannie and her family grew up working on a white man's cotton plantation. Although they were kept poor and hungry by the plantation owner and the field boss, Fannie Lou grew up in her mother's image—unafraid of white people and unhappy with the poor treatment of blacks that she saw all around her. In 1962, when most other blacks in Mississippi where afraid of the consequences, Fannie registered to vote. After both she and her husband lost their jobs and their home, and after she was beaten in a Mississippi jail, Fannie Lou Hamer drew national attention to her fight for blacks' civil rights. She spoke all over the country, helped to form a new political party, and raised money to help poor people. That money was what started the 640 acre Freedom Farm Cooperative that provided work and food for more than 5,000 people. It was Mrs. Hamer's dream to see poor people work together to feed themselves rather than to accept food from others. She made her dream come true.

Another competent entry in the Crowell Biography series. Only its picture book format keeps this book from being useful through sixth grade.

Interest Level: 3-5. Reading Level: 3.2. Further Search Topics: Biography, Blacks-Biography, Civil Rights, Poverty, Women-Biography.

Kelley, Sally. Trouble with explosives. Bradbury 1976, 117 pp.

Polly Banks stuttered very badly. She wanted to stop but she couldn't. Moving, entering a new school, and facing a mean teacher who seemed in need of psychiatric help, all made Polly's stuttering worse. When Sis, Polly's new friend, rose to Polly's defense in one confrontation too many with Miss Patterson, the teacher took cruel revenge. Polly's desire to help Sis, her need to do something about her stuttering, and an understanding psychiatrist, all helped Polly learn to help herself with her speech problem. At the same time, she began to understand and have confidence in herself and her family.

Another "problem book" that older elementary school readers seem to crave. Polly and Sis are both very sympathetic characters who bring to life many of the uncertainties of growing up. Print and line spacing of only average size but otherwise a good choice.

Interest Level: 4-6. Reading Level: 3.2. Further Search Topics: Academic Problems-Fiction, Stuttering-Fiction, Psychiatrists-Fiction, School Stories, Mental Illness-Fiction, Troublemakers-Fiction, Courage-Fiction, Physically Handicapped-Fiction, Children-Growth-Fiction, Moving, Household-Fiction.

Krementz, Jill. A very young circus flyer. Knopf 1979, unp (112 pp).

One of a series of five oversized, abundantly photographed views of unusual children. Tato Farfan is part of the Flying Farfans of Ringling Brothers and Barnum and Bailey Circus. He lives in a railroad car on a circus train with his mother, father, and older brother. The whole family performs as trapeze artists and flyers for the circus. Told as if Tato were speaking, this is the story of a fairly normal boy who also happens to be a circus flyer. Practice sessions are difficult, costumes must be readied, and time must be spent helping each other, but there is also time for Tato to watch TV, play with the clowns, play soccer, and just have fun.

In addition to Tato's story, the reader is given a behind-the-scenes tour of the circus right up to and including the performance itself (color photos used for the performance). It is an exciting world that should appeal to almost anyone who has enjoyed the circus.

Interest Level: 2-6. Reading Level: 3.2. Further Search Topics: Circus, Acrobats and Acrobatics, Best Sellers, Talent, Group 2, Gymnastics.

Krementz, Jill. A very young gymnast. Knopf 1978, unp. (128 pp).

This is Torrence York's story. It includes a team trip to Germany for competition. See notes for *A Very Young Dancer* for more information.

Interest Level: 2-6. Reading Level: 3.2. Further Search Topics: Gymnastics, Talent, Acrobats and Acrobatics, Group 2, Best Sellers.

Krementz, Jill. A very young rider. Knopf 1977, unp (128 pp).

Vivi Malloy is the youngest rider in a family of several other riders. Her greatest dream is to make the Olympic equestrian team. She is progressing towards her goal with daily workouts and about fifteen major horse shows each year. See *A Very Young Dancer* for more extensive notes.

Interest Level: 2-6. Reading Level: 3.2. Further Search Topics: Horses, Riding, Talent, Group 2.

Miles, Miska. Annie and the old one; illus by Peter Parnall. Little 1971, 44 pp.

A quietly beautiful story that will not appeal to all readers. Annie, a young Navajo girl, had a very close relationship with her grandmother. Her grandmother announced that she would "go to Mother Earth" at the time when the new rug Annie's mother was weaving was "taken from the loom." Annie tried all she could think of to keep the rug from being finished in order to keep her grandmother alive. When her grandmother solemnly explained that Annie could not stop time, Annie listened and "understood many things" for the first time.

It will be a thoughtful, sensitive child or a child trying to understand death who will best appreciate this special book.

Interest Level: 3-6. Reading Level: 3.2. Further Search Topics: Grandparents-Fiction, Death-Fiction, Indians of North America-Fiction, Navajo Indians-Fiction.

Montgomery, Raymond A. The lost jewels of Nabooti; illus by Paul Granger. Bantam 1981, 121 pp.

See entry for *Sugarcane Island*, by Edward Packard for series information. Only available in paperback edition. Choose Your Own Adventure series.

Interest Level: 2-6. Reading Level: 3.2. Further Search Topics: Mystery and Detective Stories, Detectives-Fiction, Treasure-Fiction, Best Sellers, Group 2.

Newfield, Marcia. A book for Jodan; illus by Diane DeGroot. Atheneum 1975, unp (41 pp).

Jodan found her parents' separation very hard to understand and accept. She and her mother had moved 3,000 miles away from her father and she missed him very much. When Jodan visited her father for the first time, he gave her a very special present that lessened her loneliness. He created a book just for Jodan that was filled with his thoughts and memories.

The book is a sensitive portrayal of a very common experience. Only Jodan's age (nine-years-old) and consequent actions and reactions, limit the book's probable usefulness beyond fifth grade. Print is somewhat small.

Interest Level: 2-5. Reading Level: 3.2. Further Search Topics: Group 2, Divorce and Separation-Fiction, Family Problems-Fiction, Loneliness-Fiction.

O'Neill, Mary. Hailstones and halibut bones; illus by Leonard Weisgard. Doubleday 1961, 59 pp.

This is a classic collection of twelve poems about colors. The poems are rhymed mood pieces of two or three pages that should appeal to almost any age reader. The difficulty of the vocabulary within each poem can vary greatly; however, most stanzas are short, most of the vocabulary is at least familiar, and the rhyme scheme is consistent.

Interest Level: 1-5. Reading Level: 3.2. Further Search Topics: Poetry, Colors, Group 2.

Packard, Edward. Your code name is Jonah; illus by Paul Granger. Bantam 1980, 114 pp.

See *Sugarcane Island* for information about books in this series. Paperback only. Choose Your Own Adventure series.

Interest Level: 2-6. Reading Level: 3.2. Further Search Topics: Nonverbal Communication-Fiction, Best Sellers, Spies-Fiction, Group 2.

Packard, Edward. The mystery of Chimney Rock; illus by Paul Granger. Bantam 1979, 121 pp.

See notes for *Sugarcane Island* for information about the series. Paperback only. Choose Your Own Adventure series.

Interest Level: 2-6. Reading Level: 3.2. Further Search Topics: Mystery and Detective Stories, Cats-Fiction, Witches-Fiction, Ghosts-Fiction, Detectives-Fiction, Best Sellers, Group 2.

Pene du Bois, William. Lazy Tommy Pumpkinhead. Har-Row 1966, 32 pp.

Tommy lived a solitary life in an all-electric house. An electric bed woke Tommy and slid him into a tub full of warm water. The tub then tipped him out and into a harness that held Tommy upright while other machines dried him, combed his hair, brushed his teeth, dressed him, and fed him. But one day Tommy's life was literally turned upside down with disastrous results. His feet were cleaned and combed and his clothes were all put on upside down, but the worst part of all was that Tommy almost starved; the machine fed his feet instead of his mouth.

A tongue-in-cheek warning against laziness. The lesson is obvious but the treatment (both text and illustrations) is so enjoyable that the book is appealing to almost any reader who wants a short, funny book. Print is somewhat small but spacing between lines is more than adequate.

Interest Level: 1-6. Reading Level: 3.2. Further Search Topics: Electricity-Fiction, Robots-Fiction, Laziness-Fiction, Humorous Fiction, Group 2, Read Aloud.

Pfeffer, Susan Beth. Just between us; illus by Lorna Tomei. Delacorte 1980, 116 pp.

Cass's inability to keep secrets finally became such a problem that Cass asked her mother to help her learn how to keep them. Cass's mother, a psychology student, devised a behavior modification experiment. Every day that Cass was able to figure out which bit of information she had been told was a secret and keep it, she received a dollar. After a poor start Cass did well for a while, until the day she told three secrets and made her entire family angry at her.

More determined than ever, Cass tried again. This time she found herself caught between two friends. Only Cass knew that Robin was adopted and Robin wanted it kept a secret. Jenny was so mad at Robin that she decided to spread an untrue story to hurt Robin. She told Cass not to tell anyone what she was going to do. The story Jenny was going to spread was that Robin was adopted. After hours of mental anguish Cass finally devised a way to stop Jenny and help Jenny return to being the nice person she had been before her parents' divorce.

The reading level of this book varies greatly from second grade to mid-fourth grade. Otherwise, it is good fare for Judy Blume fans. Print size just a slight bit on the small side.

Interest Level: 4-6. Reading Level: 3.2. Further Search Topics: Humorous Fiction, Everyday Stories, Friendship-Fiction, School Stories, Divorce and Separation-Fiction, Psychiatrists-Fiction, Secrets-Fiction.

Pinkwater, Daniel Manus. Fat men from space. Dodd 1977, 57 pp.

The evening after his trip to the dentist William found that he could still hear radio programs when his radio was turned off. He was even more surprised to find that when he wired himself to a fence he could hear spacemen talking. When the spacemen discovered that William could hear them, they landed and captured him. They were on a top secret mission and couldn't risk any human knowing about their existence. The spacemen were about to invade Earth to consume all the junk food they could find. As mass panic set in on Earth, William could do nothing to save his fellow humans. He was held captive and helpless until the invaders' interest was captured by a giant potato pancake floating in outer space.

A tongue-in-check, slapstick spoof of science fiction, food fads, and junk food. Do not expect anything more.

Interest Level: 3-5. Reading Level: 3.2. Further Search Topics: Science Fiction, Humorous Fiction, Food-Fiction, Flying Saucers-Fiction, Aliens-Fiction, Best Sellers, Kidnapping-Fiction, Teeth-Fiction.

Robinson, Jean. The strange but wonderful cosmic awareness of Duffy Moon; illus by Lawrence Di Fiori. HM 1974, 142 pp.

Duffy was tired of being small, of always being on the losing side of fights, and of being unappreciated at home (by his ex-football star uncle). When he sent away for Mr. Flamel's Cosmic Awareness Kit, Duffy was sure he would then be able to take control over anything he wanted and direct his own life. His friend Peter, the narrator, wasn't quite so sure. Peter turned out to be right. Duffy almost made himself sick trying to build a stone wall. Babysitting two small boys and trying to bathe a Great Dane proved to be disastrous. But Duffy's biggest problem came from Boots McAfee's gang. A series of events finally brought Duffy and Peter face-to-face with the dreaded Boots. Luckily, she turned out to be a very smart girl who appreciated Duffy's true talents.

From the first to the last page this is a funny, very enjoyable book. A delightful book with a very palatable message.

Interest Level: 3-6. Reading Level: 3.2. Further Search Topics: Humorous Fiction, Bullies-Fiction, Magic-Fiction, Read Aloud, Occupations-Fiction, Sex Role-Fiction, Orphans-Fiction, Best Sellers, Gangs-Fiction, Courage-Fiction, Babysitting-Fiction.

Roy, Ron. Nightmare Island; illus by Robert MacLean. Dutton 1981, 69 pp.

Harley didn't want to take his younger brother camping, but because he had promised his father he would, the boys packed a tent, sleeping bags, and plenty of food into a small boat and set off to nearby Little Island. Hidden in his pocket, Harley had matches and marshmallows for a midnight marshmallow roast. After they had finished the bag of marshmallows, Harley threw the last log of the fire into the water. The water erupted into flames that quickly spread around the island. As the boys fought desperately to save themselves and to find shelter, they realized that the large shape they had seen in the distance must have been an oil tanker that had spread an oil slick all around the island. With time running out Harley gave his brother the only truly secure shelter from the fire, curled up on top of a tall rock and went to sleep. When he awoke the fire had burned itself out and help was on the way.

Most young readers will be able to suspend disbelief long enough to enjoy this as an exciting adventure and survival story, but it is hard to believe that two young boys could not only survive such a holocaust, but that they could sleep through part of it, too. It is also difficult to believe that there would not be more of a fuss made about the oil tanker blowing up. Plot problems aside, young readers seem to love the story.

Interest Level: 3-6. Reading Level: 3.2. Further Search Topics: Brothers and Sisters-Fiction, Survival-Fiction, Camping-Fiction, Disasters-Fiction, Best Sellers.

Rudeen, Kenneth. Wilt Chamberlain; illus by Frank Mullins. Har-Row 1972, 33 pp.

A short and somewhat adoring version of Wilt Chamberlain's childhood, schooling, and professional career. Very little of Chamberlain's personality comes through in this book, but his superior talents and skills as well as his importance to the sport of basketball will be enough to prompt many basketball fans to read it. Although simplistic in style, the book is not condescending. It is, however, out of date, a fact most notable when Chamberlain's salary is quoted. Beware of juvenile format when using with older readers. Crowell Biography series.

Interest Level: 2-6. Reading Level: 3.2. Further Search Topics: Biography, Chamberlain, Wilt, Basketball-Biography, Blacks-Biography, Group 2.

Sharmat, Marjorie W. The Lancelot closes at five; illus by Lisl Weil. Macmillan 1976, 120 pp.

Despite a somewhat slow beginning, this is an amusing, almost sensitive story of two friends who decided to spend the night in the model home of the new housing development in which they both lived. Hutch, a health food fanatic whose mother pronounced judgment on everything Hutch did, conceived of the idea as her way of breaking away. Abby went along for the fun of it. When the local newspaper wrote of unusual vandalism at the model home, the townspeople became engrossed in finding the culprits. As the adults became enraged about the crime wave, their children began to admire the clever idea. Soon, almost every youngster in town had confessed to spending the night in the model home. By the time Abby and Hutch got around to admitting they had slept there, no one believed them. Only a sock with Abby's name in it could tie Abby and Hutch to the scene of the crime. As the book ends, the police have begun a thorough search of the house, after a real robbery, and the sock's discovery is imminent.

Interest Level: 4-6. Reading Level: 3.2. Further Search Topics: Humorous Fiction, Suburbia-Fiction, Runaways-Fiction, Crime-Fiction, Individualists-Fiction, Family Problems-Fiction.

Shearer, John. Billy Jo Jive and the walkie-talkie caper; illus by Ted Shearer. Delacorte 1981, 47 pp.

When Steam Boat Louis went to Jive and Sunset for help, he was desperate. Because Jive and Sunset had already solved three cases, they were the logical people to find the walkie-talkie that had been stolen from Steam Boat. The walkie-talkie was one of two that Steam Boat had been told to buy as part of a secret communication system for the Bugaloo Smackers. Even as Jive and Sunset hunted for the thief, the second walkie-talkie was stolen. Their only clue was a footprint found outside Steam Boat's fix-it shop. Eventually, after trial and error, Jive and Sunset uncovered the real thieves; Steam Boat's young twin cousins. Unhappy at being separated in school, they wanted to use the walkie-talkies to be able to talk with each other.

The high reading level of this book will make it most useful for those children who have read and enjoyed other books in the series and are willing to stretch to read one more.

Interest Level: 1-4. Reading Level: 3.2. Further Search Topics: Mystery and Detective Stories, Detectives-Fiction, Blacks-Fiction, City Life-Fiction, Group 2.

Silverstein, Shel. A light in the attic. Har-Row 1981, 169 pp.

This is the second and most recent collection of Shel Silverstein's wonderfully wry poetry. No young person who has read and enjoyed *Where the Sidewalk Ends* will be disappointed in this effort. For those readers new to Silverstein or to poetry in general, this is as good a place as any to start enjoying both. Hearing a few of these poems read aloud is guaranteed to provoke loud cries of "May I read some?" from almost all listeners.

Interest Level: 2-6. Reading Level: 3.2. Further Search Topics: Poetry, Wit and Humor, Best Sellers, Group 2, Read Aloud.

Simon, Seymour. The paper airplane book; illus by Byron Barton. Viking Pr 1971, 48 pp.

For the theory as well as the practice behind successful paper airplanes, this is the book. This is as much a book about the principles of flight as it is about how to make a paper airplane. The reader is introduced to thrust, drag, lift and gravity through explanation, examples, diagrams and experiments. The effects of vertical and horizontal stabilizers, elevators, rudders, flaps, and ailerons on both paper and real airplanes, is explained and illustrated. Instructions are given for building and modifying a basic plane as each new idea is introduced. The book ends with plans for four more sophisticated planes and encouragement to try further experiments. An excellent resource for the enthusiast. Print is small.

Interest Level: 3-6. Reading Level: 3.2. Further Search Topics: Airplanes, Handicrafts, Flight.

Sleator, William. Into the dream; illus by Ruth Sanderson. Dutton 1979, 137 pp.

Paul and Francine each started having what, at first, seemed like nightmares. As the dreams became more detailed and forboding, they discovered that they were sharing the same nightmare. They dreamed of a four-year-old boy, swirling lights, and a large dog. After awhile they figured out that the dog was trying to save the little boy from some unknown danger. As the pieces of the puzzle began to increase in number, Paul and Francine decided that the dream was in some way connected to a night over four years earlier when they had both been staying at the same motel. They, a pregnant woman, and a pregnant dog had all been affected by the telepathic power given off by a spaceship. The progeny of the woman and the dog had been given extraordinary mental powers; powers that a secret government agency wanted to mold and then put to their own use. The danger Paul and Francine felt came from two government agents sent to take the young boy Noah from his mother. Their attempt ended in a bizarre scene at an amusement park, where Noah levitated a broken ferris wheel chair to safety. By thus exposing his talent in public, Noah unconsciously insured against its secret and unsupervised use by the government.

A terrifying and suspense-filled psychological thriller whose main problems are a slightly overdrawn ending and a variable reading level. Reading level drops as low as 2.1 and climbs occasionally to 4.1.

Interest Level: 5-6. Reading Level: 3.2. Further Search Topics: Best Sellers, Supernatural-Fiction, Occult-Fiction, Flying Saucers-Fiction, Nonverbal Communication-Fiction, Dreams-Fiction, Survival-Fiction, Extra Sensory Perception-Fiction, Horror-Fiction.

Smith, Doris Buchanan. Tough Chauncey. Morrow 1974, 222 pp.

Chauncey Childs had taught himself to be tough— very tough. Even though he was small for his age (13 years old), the only person who gave him any trouble was his sometimes-friend, Black Jack Levitt. Everyone else was scared of Chauncey. Chauncey felt that he had to be tough or he wouldn't be able to survive. He had to be tough to stand the beatings his grandfather gave him "for his own good," to put up with his mother's drinking and disappearances, and to stand the sight of his grandfather shooting the stray kittens born in their garage.

Chauncey's greatest wish was to be able to live with his mother, instead of with his grandparents. In a desperate attempt to achieve that end he accidentally fell from a moving train and badly hurt his leg. Instead of being returned to his mother he was once more taken back to his grandparents. Chauncey's unhappiness grew until he finally decided to take the one surviving stray kitten and run away. Jack helped him find an empty garage where he could hide while he figured out what to do with his future. After talking with Jack and doing more deep soul searching, Chauncey decided to reshape himself and his life. His first step was to curb his temper and his tongue when his hiding place was discovered. His second step was to see about finding a foster home where he would be treated well, and where he could get a new start.

Ugly as the story is in places, its ending is hopeful. Although it is not always realistic, Chauncey's story is compelling enough to appeal to many readers, especially those who have enjoyed *The War on Villa Street*, by Henry Mazer, *The Outsiders*, by Susan Hinton, or *Mystery of the Fat Cat*, by Frank Bonham. The book's length and its artificially low reading level (vocabulary is often difficult but sentences are very short) make this book most appropriate for an older reader whose reading level is 4.1 or higher.

Interest Level: 5-6. Reading Level: 3.2. Further Search Topics: Child Abuse-Fiction, Family Problems-Fiction, Grandparents-Fiction, Runaways-Fiction, Bullies-Fiction, Single Parent Family-Fiction, Loners-Fiction, Friendship-Fiction, Troublemakers-Fiction, Foster Homes-Fiction.

Smith, Doris Buchanan. A taste of blackberries; illus by Charles Robinson. T Y Crowell 1973, 58 pp.

A beautifully written, sensitive tale of a boy whose best friend dies suddenly. Jamie was always joking, so, when he fell to the ground after being stung by a bee everyone thought he was playing. A short time later Jamie was dead. His friend, the story's narrator, tried to will Jamie back again until the funeral was over and he finally realized there would be no such miracle. The next day he accepted his feelings and picked the newly ripened blackberries, just as he and Jamie had planned to do. A basket full of the best blackberries he gave to Jamie's mother and promised her that he would "slam her door" daily just as he and Jamie had done.

Eight short chapters, small print but short sentences, and a child's point of view perfectly maintained. For the lovers of sad stories and stories of friendship. Very useful when discussing death.

Interest Level: 4-6. Reading Level: 3.2. Further Search Topics: Death-Fiction, Friendship-Fiction, Read Aloud.

Terman, Douglas. By balloons to the Sahara; illus by Paul Granger. Bantam 1979, 117 pp.

See the entry for *Sugarcane Island*, by Edward Packard for detailed information about the series. Available in paperback edition only. Choose Your Own Adventure series.

Interest Level: 2-6. Reading Level: 3.2. Further Search Topics: Voyages and Travels-Fiction, Flight-Fiction, Best Sellers, Group 2.

Zim, Herbert S. Hoists, cranes and derricks; illus by Gary Ruse. Morrow 1969, 64 pp.

This is a very thorough treatment of lifting machinery. It is a straight-forward explanation that is technical, but not so technical that it can't be understood by young enthusiasts. The text is well-supplemented by a good number of clear illustrations and diagrams including drawings of the attachments to mobile cranes, motions used by signalmen, kinds of quay cranes, types of derricks, and even charts of the capacities of cranes and derricks and load-bearing materials. A fair index helps to make the book useful for reference or report writing.

Interest Level: 3-6. Reading Level: 3.2. Further Search Topics: Construction.

READING LEVEL 4.1

Burchard, Marshall. Sports hero: Dr. J. Putnam 1976, 89 pp.

Julius Erving can jump higher and stay in the air longer than almost any other basketball player. He can also move around the court with the most agile of players. All in all he is a very exciting player to watch. This book includes his college and pro records (through 1975). See *Sports Hero: Bill Walton* for more information. Sports Hero series.

Interest Level: 3-6. Reading Level: 4.1. Further Search Topics: Biography, Blacks-Biography, Basketball-Biography, Erving, Julius, Group 2.

Burchard, Marshall. Sports hero: Muhammad Ali. Putnam 1975, 95 pp.

The man who brought a quick tongue as well as fast feet and flying fists to the sport of boxing. Entry for *Sports Hero: Bill Walton* gives series notes. Ring record included here. Sports Hero series.

Interest Level: 3-6. Reading Level: 4.1. Further Search Topics: Boxing-Biography, Blacks-Biography, Ali, Muhammad, Group 2.

Burchard, Susan H. Sports star: Tommy John. HarBraceJ 1981, 63 pp.

Tommy John's elbow injury was severe enough that no one thought he would be able to pitch again. He proved that the skeptics were wrong. For series notes see *Sports Star: Elvin Hayes*. Sports Star series.

Interest Level: 3-6. Reading Level: 4.1. Further Search Topics: Baseball-Biography, John, Tommy, Biography, Group 2, Physically Handicapped.

Krementz, Jill. A very young skater. Knopf 1979, unp (103 pp).

Katherine Healy started ice skating because her parents liked to skate and because it was easier for them to take her with them than it was to find a babysitter. From such beginnings, at age three, Katherine progressed to skating in Superskates at Madison Square Garden and ballet lessons at George Balanchine's School of American Ballet. See *A Very Young Dancer* for further explanation.

Interest Level: 2-6. Reading Level: 4.1. Further Search Topics: Ice Skating, Dancing, Ballet, Talent, Group 2, Best Sellers.

Montgomery, Raymond A. Space and beyond; illus by Paul Granger. Bantam 1980, 117 pp.

See entry for *Sugarcane Island*, by Edward Packard for full annotation. Available in paperback only. Choose Your Own Adventure series

Interest Level: 2-6. Reading Level: 4.1. Further Search Topics: Science Fiction, Outer Space-Fiction, Group 2, Best Sellers.

Packard, Edward. The cave of time; illus by Paul Granger. Bantam 1979, 115 pp.

Beware of the greater than usual inconsistency of reading levels within this book. Its difficulty level ranges from 2.2 to 4.2. See notes for *Sugarcane Island* for more information about the series. In paperback only. Choose Your Own Adventure series.

Interest Level: 2-6. Reading Level: 4.1. Further Search Topics: Time-Fiction, Science Fiction, Fantasy, Group 2.

Pevsner, Stella. And you give me a pain, Elaine. HM 1978, 182 pp.

Andrea was the youngest of three children. She was very close to her brother, Joe, but he was away at college. There was only Elaine at home, but Andrea and Elaine didn't get along at all. Elaine was a troubled young woman who took so much of her parents' attention that there was none left for Andrea. This is the story of Andrea's year in eighth grade, a year in which she discovered that she was a steady and strong person. It was the year in which Andrea worked on the school play, had her first boyfriend, weathered the storms when her sister ran away, and began to understand her sister more and resent her less. It was also the year that she had to learn to live with her brother's accidental death.

The author's Judy Blume style (but with less humor) guarantees readers among older children.

Interest Level: 5-6. Reading Level: 4.1. Further Search Topics: Family Problems-Fiction, Brothers and Sisters-Fiction, Love-Fiction, Death-Fiction, Runaways-Fiction, Troublemakers-Fiction, Adolescence-Fiction.

READING LEVEL 4.2

Avi. No more magic. Pantheon 1975, 138 pp.

Avi has woven a mixture of mystery and magic to produce an excellent story. Chris' belief in magic is bolstered when his new bicycle disappears on Halloween night. Chris, his best friend Eddie, and a new friend, Muffin, eventually decide that strange Mr. Bullen, the junk dealer, has magical powers. In order to keep his powers a secret, Mr. Bullen had to steal back the magical bike he sold Chris. With plenty of intriguing complications along the way, the three children attempt to prove their theory correct but only prove themselves wrong. The age of the protagonists (fourth grade) is touched on so lightly and the plot is interesting enough that even sixth grade readers should find the book enjoyable.

Interest Level: 3-6. Reading Level: 4.2. Further Search Topics: Divorce and Separation-Fiction, Mystery and Detective Stories, Magic-Fiction, Halloween-Fiction, Witches-Fiction, Group 2, Read Aloud, Bicycles and Bicycling-Fiction.

Byars, Betsy. The Cybil war; illus by Gail Owens. Viking Pr. 1981, 126 pp.

Simon and Tony both had a crush on Cybil, but according to Tony, Cybil liked Tony better than she liked Simon. Simon was unhappily willing to accept Tony's word even though he knew Tony was a chronic liar. After all, Cybil had been the one to talk their teacher out of giving the lead in the class play about nutrition to Simon. Consequently Simon was being forced to impersonate a jar of peanut butter. In an elaborate attempt to win Cybil's affection Tony began telling Cybil lies about Simon and then set up a double date with Cybil and Harriet. On their walk home, Simon learned from Harriet that Cybil had only agreed to the date because Simon was going along. Happy at last, Simon realized he wanted no more lies and tricks; that he wanted to be truthful with Cybil and with himself. In the name of truth, he was even willing to accept the fact that his father, who had deserted the family, would not be returning.

A good story with just enough humor and romance to make it widely appealing as either a shared book (read aloud) or a personal pick. Print is fairly small.

Interest Level: 5-6. Reading Level: 4.2. Further Search Topics: Humorous Fiction, Love-Fiction, School Stories, Honesty-Fiction, Friendship-Fiction, Single Parent Family-Fiction, Read Aloud, Everyday Stories, Adolescence-Fiction.

Byars, Betsy. The house of wings; illus by Daniel Schwarts. Viking Pr. 1972, 142 pp.

Sammy was the youngest of eight children. His parents were tired of raising children when Sammy was born, so they almost let Sammy raise himself. That meant that he grew up to be independent. It didn't mean it was any easier for Sammy to accept being left behind unexpectedly with his strange grandfather when his parents moved to Detroit. His reaction when his grandfather told him that his parents had gone was to deny it and to run away. He ran until he could run no more. When he stopped running, the old man stopped chasing him and they found a wild but blind crane in desperate need of help. Helping the crane heal and find the desire to live again taught Sammy and his grandfather respect and, most of all, love for each other.

The parallels between Sammy and the crane are strong but subtle. The story is a compelling one, but may need a brief introductory note to alleviate confusion in the first two chapters.

Interest Level: 5-6. Reading Level: 4.2. Further Search Topics: Grandparents-Fiction, Birds-Fiction, Family Problems-Fiction, Poverty-Fiction, Physically Handicapped-Fiction, Runaways-Fiction.

Christopher, Matt. Wild pitch. Little 1980, 137 pp.

This is one of Christopher's better written books but it is also one that will find a smaller audience than usual. Here he has drawn interesting characters of flesh and bone rather than his normal stereotypes. The sports action is still detailed, but it is no longer the core around which a purely skeletal plot is stretched. Christopher has produced an intriguing story line here.

Eddie was a good strong pitcher who sometimes threw wild pitches. One of his wild pitches hit Phyl Monahan, the only girl playing in his league. It was well known that Eddie didn't like the idea of girls playing in the same league as the boys, so people accused him of purposely hitting Phyl. Eddie knew he hadn't meant to hit her, but he still felt very guilty that his pitch had put her into the hospital. He went to the hospital many times before he was finally able to see Phyl and apologize. When he did, he found that she was very likeable and reasonable. When she confessed that she wasn't sure she wanted to play baseball again, Eddie decided he owed it to her to help her regain her confidence. As they worked together each one gained respect for the other until theirs became a very solid friendship. The test for both was when Phyl had to hit against Eddie again.

For many baseball fans there may be too much plot here and not enough baseball. Because the problem of how to control wild pitches is never addressed, other readers may also find the book disappointing. But, for those baseball fans who are open to more than box scores and replays, this is a good story.

Interest Level: 6+ Reading Level: 4.2. Further Search Topics: Baseball-Fiction, Sex Role-Fiction, Friendship-Fiction, Courage-Fiction.

Clark, Margaret Goff. Barney in space; illus by Ted Lewin. Dodd 1981, 155 pp.

This is a sequel to *Barney and the UFO,* but it stands by itself quite well. It's title is a misnomer, however, for it isn't until the last third of the book that Barney goes into space. In the previous book Barney made friends with Tibbo, a Gark from the planet Ornam. In this book Tibbo tries to save Barney from an evil Gark named Rokell. Because Barney knew about Garks, Rokell was afraid Barney would betray them and turn humans against Garks. To prevent that from happening, Rokell was determined to kidnap Barney. Tibbo was too far from Earth to do more than warn Barney of Rokell's intentions and tell him not to be alone at any time. Barney's friends Dick and Kara tried to protect Barney but only succeeded in endangering their own lives. When Kara was almost killed by Rokell, Barney decided to face Rokell alone and try to defeat him, but Rokell's powers were too strong for Barney. Against their wills both Barney and David were taken aboard a spaceship. They discovered later, to their relief, that the spaceship belonged to a friend of Tibbo's who was commanding the ship from the moon. Barney and Dick were to be taken to the moon for safety until Rokell could be controlled. Rokell didn't give up easily. He attacked the ship twice before he captured it and set it down on a remote portion of the moon. Only Barney's quick thinking stopped Rokell permanently and saved both Barney and Dick.

The preliminary sequences are more suspenseful and exciting than the space travel; however, the book will not disappoint young science fiction fans.

Interest Level: 4-6. Reading Level: 4.2. Further Search Topics: Science Fiction, Flying Saucers-Fiction, Outer Space-Fiction, Orphans-Fiction, Kidnapping-Fiction, Aliens-Fiction, Adoption-Fiction.

Cohen, Barbara. Thank you, Jackie Robinson; illus by Richard Cuffari. Lothrop 1974, 125 pp.

This story is not for everyone, but for the right reader it is perfect. The book is a catalog of baseball facts, thus it is likely to appeal primarily to baseball fans. But it is not the typical story of a child overcoming a problem through practice and perserverance, as are most sports books. This is a sensitive story of a fatherless boy whose life centered around the New York Dodgers.

Sam could repeat the starting line-up and details of any game the Dodgers had played within the last three years; however, no one cared. In fact, most people were bored when Sam began reciting. Only Davey, the old, black cook at the inn where Sam and his family lived, took any interest. Davey was as much a fan as Sam. They began spending hours together talking and then watching baseball as Davey and his daughter took Sam to the games with them. It was Sam and Davey's dream to catch a fly ball and have it autograped by all the Dodgers, especially Jackie Robinson, the first black major league player. When Davey had a severe heart attack, Sam gathered all his courage to make that dream come true. He bought a baseball, took the subway to a game, and argued with the ushers until he was finally able to get Jackie Robinson's and the team's autographs. Just a few days before Davey died Sam took the baseball to the hospital and gave it to Davey. Sam's feelings about Davey's death are real and painful. He felt sorry for himself, lonely, angry, sad and confused. But a remark by his mother and one more Jackie Robinson hit helped Sam accept Davey's death.

Because the story is told as a first-person flashback set in the late 1940s, it may need a little introduction. It also alludes to racial problems and practices that young readers may not understand without explanation (i.e., why Davey had some hesitation about taking a white child with him to the ballpark or on a trip).

Interest Level: 4-6. Reading Level: 4.2. Further Search Topics: Baseball-Fiction, Blacks-Fiction, Aging-Fiction, Single Parent Family-Fiction, Friendship-Fiction, Death-Fiction, Robinson, Jackie.

Conford, Ellen. The revenge of the incredible Dr. Rancid and his youthful assistant, Jeffrey. Little 1980, 119 pp.

There were two people Jeff hated and feared: Dewey Belasco, the sixth grade bully and Lana McCabe, Dewey's female counterpart. Only in his imagination could Jeff stand up to them. In the stories Jeff wrote in a notebook, he and his friend Dr. Rancid were superheroes who rid the world of such scum as Lana and Dewey. In real life, Jeff ran from bullies rather than face them; even if it meant that an eight-year-old boy and a girl Jeff's age were left to stand up to Dewey by themselves. Although the way Jeff took care of an injured child soon had most everyone thinking of Jeff as a hero, he saw that, too, as an indication of his failings at first. Finally, something inside Jeff snapped and he answered Dewey back when Dewey insulted him. Before long Jeff found himself flat on his back with a bloody nose and so many pains he couldn't count them. But, he had finally faced Dewey and showed Dewey that he was no longer afraid. Jeff felt good.

Similar to *The 18th Emergency* but a higher reading level. The notebook stories will appeal to fans of superheroes, but because they are stories within a story, they may also cause difficulties. Spacing between lines is somewhat narrow.

Interest Level: 5-6. Reading Level: 4.2. Further Search Topics: Courage-Fiction, Bullies-Fiction, Writing-Fiction, School Stories, Superheroes-Fiction, Humorous Fiction.

Conford, Ellen. And this is Laura. Little 1977, 179 pp.

As a member of a family of high-achievers, Laura was convinced that she was unloved and worthless because she had no talents. Then, suddenly Laura discovered she had very special psychic powers; powers she began to exploit. At first it was fun to give readings after school each day. Gradually, however, as Laura foresaw her friend hurt and her brother missing, she realized that having ESP was also a frightening responsibility. Finally, her ESP became the vehicle that made it possible for Laura to tell her parents her true feelings and to understand that they loved her for herself, not for her achievements.

The author treats a common concern with sensitivity and humor. An especially good choice for Judy Blume lovers. Print somewhat small.

Interest Level: 4-6. Reading Level: 4.2. Further Search Topics: Occult-Fiction, Courage-Fiction, Extra Sensory Perception-Fiction, Family-Fiction, Humorous Fiction, Everyday Stories, Talent-Fiction.

Heide, Florence Parry. Body in the Brillstone garage. A. Whitman 1980, 127 pp.

Liza's trip into the apartment house garage late one night made her even more frightened of that dark area than she had been. As she bent to pick up an envelope she thought someone had dropped, she saw a body lying on the floor of the garage. Because of a jacket he wore, Liza was certain the dead man was Mr. Greening, a neighbor. But when she returned to the garage with the police, the body was gone. The next day Mr. Greening was very much alive. Then Liza began to suspect that Mr. Greening was a murderer, but she didn't know who or where the victim was. It could have been Mr. Feeney, another neighbor, or it might have been a stranger. When Mr. Greening's stolen car was later discovered with the body of the car thief inside, Liza began to suspect that the thief's body was the one she had discovered. When she was told that the thief's name was Sharkey, she was certain Mr. Greening had engineered Sharkey's death. Sharkey was the name used by an angry man who had said he was looking for someone at the Brillstone who owed him something.

About then Liza remembered to look in the envelope she had found in the garage. The envelope revealed a note from Sharkey to Greening stating that Sharkey had proof that Greening was a car thief and that he would keep quiet only if Greening paid him twice the money he was owed. Knowing that without proof, she couldn't convince the police that Greening was a crook, Liza went to get the proof from Sharkey's hiding place in the about-to-be-junked car. Greening followed Liza to see what she knew and made a desperate attempt to kill her when he realized that she knew enough to put him in prison. At the last minute, Logan appeared, accidentally knocked Greening out, and helped Liza prove Greening's guilt to the police.

This is a fast-paced book that should be useful with mystery readers who can handle the jump from 4.1 to an occasional 5.1 reading level. See notes included with *Black Magic at Brillstone* for more information. Brillstone Mystery series.

Interest Level: 4-6. Reading Level: 4.2. Further Search Topics: Mystery and Detective Stories, Murder-Fiction, Running-Fiction, Crime-Fiction, Detectives-Fiction.

Hurwitz, Johanna. The law of gravity; illus by Ingrid Fetz. Morrow 1978, 192 pp.

The summer between fifth and sixth grades looked very unexciting to Margot. Her best friends were both going away for the whole summer and her father, a musician, was going to be on tour for most of the summer. Margot's very overweight mother had sworn never to go downstairs from their fifth floor walk-up apartment. Unless Margot chose to stay upstairs too, she was sure she would have a very lonely vacation. In addition, she had to work on a summer project for school. The project she finally chose was to get her mother downstairs after nine years of staying upstairs. In search of help she went to the local library where she met Bernie. Bernie was only a year older than Margot, but he seemed to know the most interesting things about the city. He showed her places Margot had never heard of before, he taught her to play chess, backgammon, and even to ride a bicycle. He was so full of fascinating ideas and information that Margot had no chance to be bored or lonely. Best of all, he even tried to help Margot with her project. None of their ideas worked, however, until Margot pretended to run away and scared her mother into going downstairs. Only then did Margot realize that she loved her mother whether or not she stayed on the fifth floor and that she couldn't simply force her mother or anyone else to change to suit her own fancy.

The book is a warm, understanding, slightly humorous treatment of the fairly common wish to change someone else. Although not many readers are likely to share Margot's exact problem, most will recognize her feelings. The book is also a virtual Chamber of Commerce advertisement for urban living. One of its other charms is its picture of a non-competitive, open, real friendship between an 11-year-old girl and a 12-year-old boy. The only drawback to the book is its inconsistent reading level which varies from 4.1 to 5.1 with a rare leap to 5.2.

Interest Level: 4-6. Reading Level: 4.2. Further Search Topics: Vacation-Fiction, Friendship-Fiction, Loners-Fiction, City Life-Fiction, Individualists-Fiction, Courage-Fiction, New York City-Fiction, Humorous Fiction, Family-Fiction, Challenges-Fiction, Weight-Fiction, Everyday Stories, Best Sellers.

Levy, Elizabeth. Lizzie lies a lot; illus by John Wallner. Delacorte 1976, 102 pp.

Almost any child can identify with Lizzie. She had found that it was sometimes easier to lie than to tell the truth. Her problem was that she had lost control. It seemed as if almost everything she said was a lie. She told so many lies it became difficult to keep track of them all. Lizzie wasn't even really sure why she lied so much. She knew that she sometimes lied because she thought people would be more apt to like her. Other times she lied to get herself out of trouble or to cover up her feelings when she was hurt or angry. But that didn't explain why she lied all the time. Maybe, as her grandmother said, she was a born liar.

It wasn't until Lizzie got herself caught in the middle of so many lies that she lost her only friend, that she could admit her problem to herself and to her family. After their initial shock had passed, everyone agreed to help Lizzie stop lying. Lizzie took the next step by admitting her lies to her friend Sue.

Levy has brought such an appropriately light touch to a fairly common problem that many children find this story enjoyable. Overlook the book's faults (Lizzie's grandmother is overdrawn and her mother's guilt feelings are unsupported by the story) for the fun and the message young readers get from it.

Interest Level: 3-5. Reading Level: 4.2. Further Search Topics: Honesty-Fiction, Group 2, Friendship-Fiction, Best Sellers, Everyday Stories, Family Problems-Fiction, Grandparents-Fiction, Humorous Fiction.

MacLachlan, Patricia. Arthur, for the very first time; illus by Lloyd Bloom. Har-Row 1980, 117 pp.

A beautifully written, sensitive yet humorous story of a boy's maturation and growing awareness of the world around him. When Arthur's unhappiness at home is made more intense by the advent of a new baby, he is sent to spend the summer with his older aunt and uncle. Their eccentricities and those of their friends are at first only material for Arthur to write about in his journal. But as the summer progresses he not only learns from them, but also grows from an observer of life to a participant. His final step is helping a large and beloved pig bear her litter in a driving rain storm aided only by his independent, totally untamed young friend Moira.

The print is somewhat small, but spacing between lines is generous.

Interest Level: 4-6. Reading Level: 4.2. Further Search Topics: Read Aloud, Children-Growth-Fiction, Humorous Fiction, Friendship-Fiction, Vacation-Fiction, Relatives-Fiction, Infants-Fiction, Individualists-Fiction, Writing-Fiction, Loners-Fiction, Group 2.

Norton, Andre. Star Ka'at; illus by Bernard Colonna. Walker & Co 1976, 122 pp.

Jim Evans and Elly Mae Brown, both orphaned and alone, met each other and two strange cats at the same time. As the children became more unhappy with their lives, they began to realize that Tiro and Mer were not usual cats. They were highly intelligent Ka'ats from another planet who had come to Earth in search of new strong stock to add to their breed. Both Ka'ats became as fond of the children as the children became of them. When the time came for the transport ship to leave, Jim and Elly contrived to go with them. However, the only way they could go was if they were accepted by the other Ka'ats and adopted by Tiro and Mer.

This is the first book in a series. Unfortunately the second book Star Ka'at World, has a much more difficult reading level (sixth grade) and the third title, Star Ka'at and the Plant People, varies from 2.1 to 4.1. Reading level of this entry varies between 4.1 and 5.1 but children seem to like the book enough to put up with the variability.

Interest Level: 3-6. Reading Level: 4.2. Further Search Topics: Science Fiction, Friendship-Fiction, Cats-Fiction, Group 2, Outer Space-Fiction, Orphans-Fiction.

Shura, Mary Francis. The Barkley Street six-pack; illus by Gene Sparkman. Dodd 1979, 159 pp.

Jane's best friend Natalie was everything Jane wanted to be. She was self-assured, pretty, vibrant, and even possessed magical talents. Jane didn't realize at first, and she later resisted seeing, that Natalie ran Jane's life and cleverly made sure that Jane had no other friends. Natalie's move left Jane with no friends among those people she had once enjoyed. Little by little, with the help of a stray dog and the new boy on the block, Jane bagan to see how destructive Natalie had been. She finally realized that a true friendship is one in which neither party tries to control the other.

With its enticements of ESP, magic, stray dogs, and problems with peers, this is a very appealing book to many young readers. As a bonus it is a thoughtful, sympathetic, fairly well-written story.

Interest Level: 4-6. Reading Level: 4.2. Further Search Topics: Gangs-Fiction, Pets-Fiction, Dogs-Fiction, Friendship-Fiction, Honesty-Fiction, Courage-Fiction, Loneliness-Fiction, Extra Sensory Perception-Fiction, Everyday Stories.

Smith, Doris Buchanan. Last was Lloyd. Viking Pr 1981, 124 pp.

Lloyd had several problems: he was overweight, his mother was overprotective, he had no school friends, and there was a chance he might be taken away from home and put into foster care because he had missed so much school. Lloyd's mother, very young and very defensive when she had Lloyd, had done her best to be a "good mother," but in doing so, had made Lloyd fearful of the world. He had become the subject of his classmates' mockery so many times that the only way he could respond to his peers was with nastiness. The one skill he possessed was hitting a baseball. He kept this skill well hidden for fear of exposing himself to further mockery. When one of his classmates accidentally discovered how well Lloyd hit, he took the first step to becoming Lloyd's friend. Lloyd's reaction was to back away, but Kirby kept trying. Eventually Kirby's attempts and those of an understanding truant officer, helped Lloyd begin to make friends, to treat others decently, and to pull away from his mother; in short, he began to mature.

Because Lloyd's problems can be oversimplified too easily, this book requires a fairly mature reader and perhaps even discussion in order to fully understand its subtleties.

Interest Level: 5-6+ Reading Level: 4.2. Further Search Topics: Weight-Fiction, Single Parent Family-Fiction, Courage-Fiction, School Stories, Loners-Fiction, Friendship-Fiction, Baseball-Fiction, Family Problems-Fiction, Foster Homes-Fiction, Children-Growth-Fiction.

Young, Carol Beach. Remember me when I am dead. Elsevier-Nelson 1980, 94 pp.

This is a short but taut story about the effect of their mother's death upon two young girls. For a long time Jenny, the younger and more vivacious of the sisters, refused to believe her mother had really died. Sara, quiet and serious, mourned and missed her mother, but eventually accepted her mother's sudden death as a fact. Jenny's continuing denial prompted her father and stepmother to talk of sending her away to a school where memories wouldn't be so vivid. That talk inspired Sara to develop a devious and calculated plan to insure that Jenny would indeed be sent away. All her life Sara had been given less attention than Jenny. With Jenny gone, Sara would finally have her father and stepmother's love and attention all to herself. With a Hitchcock-like twist Sara's plan proved too successful. Jenny was sent away to school, but because she didn't want to go alone and because her parents could deny Jenny nothing, Sara was to go too.

This suspenseful psychological thriller is almost guaranteed success with older readers.

Interest Level: 5-6. Reading Level: 4.2. Further Search Topics: Mystery and Detective Stories, Brothers and Sisters-Fiction, Death-Fiction, Horror-Fiction, Best Sellers, Jealousy-Fiction.

READING LEVEL 5.1

Blume, Judy. Tiger eyes. Bradbury 1981, 206 pp.

Davey's father's death was a shock that for awhile separated Davey from her mother. They occupied the same space, but Davey felt herself unable to communicate with her mother or with her aunt and uncle with whom they were living. The horror of the night her father was shot in a robbery attempt was too great for Davey to confront. It was too much for Davey's mother too, and so instead of growing closer, they draw apart. They let Davey's aunt and uncle direct their lives for almost a year before each was able to accept Mr. Wexler's death. During that time Davey's closest, most helpful friend was a loner named only Wolf. With him Davey lost enough fear and hatred that she was finally able to begin to talk about her father.

The setting (New Mexico) is much more important than in most of Blume's stories, the book's reading level is considerably more difficult, and the plot is about experiences more unique than usual. It will not fail to draw crowds of older readers however, for in most other respects the book follows Blume's successful formula.

Interest Level: 6+ Reading Level 5.1. Further Search Topics: Death-Fiction, Moving, Household-Fiction, Love-Fiction, Single Parent Family-Fiction, Family Problems-Fiction.

Bonham, Frank. The mystery of the fat cat; illus by Alvin Smith. Dutton 1968, 160 pp.

Although noticeably dated at times, this is still an exciting story of an inner city neighborhood. Buddy, Little Pie, Rich, and Cool were among the many who used the local Boys' Club as their hangout. It was a place to stay out of trouble and off the streets, but it was also a haven for rats. The rats were big and brazen; so brazen that one attacked Buddy in the swimming pool. The club needed a new building desperately. The money was there; they just weren't able to use it. Fifteen years earlier an eccentric old woman willed the Boys' Club over $600,000, but stated that the money was first to be used to support her cat until it died. A caretaker, a lawyer, and a veterinarian all benefited as long as the cat lived. Buddy and his friends took on the job of discovering if the cat really was alive or if the Boys' Club was being cheated out of half a million dollars. It was a job that nearly killed them before they set things right. Plenty of action, some violence, a cast of street-smart characters, realistic trouble with the police, as well as a slight mystery almost insure the book's success with older readers. Moderate sized print. Line spacing somewhat narrow.

Interest Level: 6+ Reading Level: 5.1. Further Search Topics: Humorous Fiction, Cats-Fiction, Gangs-Fiction, City Life-Fiction, Mystery and Detective Stories, Poverty-Fiction, Friendship-Fiction, Juvenile Delinquency-Fiction, Crime-Fiction, Best Sellers.

Buckley, Peter. I am from Puerto Rico. S ËAN S 1971, 127 pp.

Federico Ramirez had enjoyed his two years in New York City and didn't like the idea of moving back to Puerto Rico. When he arrived, he had no friends, no T.V., and nothing to do. Then Neri taught Federico the local games, showed him the sights and introduced him to Narcisco, a special fisherman. Narcisco took Federico through the wonders of the coral reefs. He taught him how to dive and fish. Within several months Federico was thoroughly at home in the water and loved Puerto Rico.

There is so much information about Puerto Rico and marine life that the book is never dry. Federico tells his own story as a series of fascinating experiences (meeting up with a shark, playing pinball, scuba diving at night, keeping a large turtle as a pet, etc.). There are abundant black and white photographs. An excellent choice for research (no index) or recreational reading. The print size is slightly on the small side, but the space between lines is good. Recently out of print, but worth looking for.

Interest Level: 5-6. Reading Level: 5.1. Further Search Topics: Puerto Rico, Fishing, Moving, Household-Fiction, Marine Biology, Scuba Diving, Ethnic Groups.

Burch, Robert. Queenie Peavy; illus by Jerry Lazare. Viking Pr. 1966, 159 pp.

Queenie was always in trouble. She could be mean, really mean, but, she was also bright, talented, independent and resilient. Queenie blamed her problems on the fact that people teased her because her father was in jail and because she was poor. She thought that she had to defend herself against the world. Queenie was proud of her poor reputation until she accidentally-on-purpose caused a classmate to break his leg. Then, when her father returned home and wasn't the person she'd hoped he'd be, Queenie realized that only she could make her life better. Being the strong person she was, she set out to do just that.

Queenie is a wonderfully alive and sympathetic character, one well worth introducing to older readers despite the book's reading level. Print somewhat small. Line spacing average width.

Interest Level: 5-6. Reading Level: 5.1. Further Search Topics: Family Problems-Fiction, Crime-Fiction, Loners-Fiction, Poverty-Fiction, Humorous Fiction, Bullies-Fiction, Troublemakers-Fiction, Academic Problems-Fiction, Read Aloud.

Cleary, Beverly. Otis Spofford; illus by Louis Darling. Morrow 1953, 191 pp.

Here are six separate humorous adventures that link together, but can be read separately and out of order. Otis' favorite activity was "stirring up a little excitement," but his definition of excitement usually meant trouble. The school fiesta turned into a disaster when Otis decided to rechoreograph the bullfight and make the bull win. His attempt to liven up the reading lesson about Indians meant he almost scalped a classmate. However, a wild day at the skating pond finally gave everyone a chance to take revenge for all the things Otis had done to them. The remaining three chapters (2, 3 and 4) are slightly less exciting, but useful if a reader has enjoyed the others. There is much humor in Otis' antics and his tendency to act on every thought that comes to mind is one many readers can appreciate.

Interest Level: 2-6. Reading Level: 5.1. Further Search Topics: Troublemakers-Fiction, Group 2, Read Aloud, Everyday Stories, Humorous Fiction, School Stories.

Cone, Molly. The amazing memory of Harvey Bean; illus by Robert MacLean. HM 1980, 83 pp.

It had been a long time since Harvey had been happy. His memory was so bad that he was always in trouble at school. And now that his parents were separating, he had trouble at home, too. Because he thought that neither one of his parents wanted him he told each one that he was going to stay with the other and instead decided to spend the summer alone. A few hours after he left home, Harry ran into Mr. and Mrs. Katz and before he completely realized it, he was living with them.

Mr. Katz couldn't stand to see anything go to waste. He collected the usable food thrown out behind grocery stores, old furniture, tools, windows and more. Mrs. Katz, whose memory was just as bad as Harvey's, loved to cook, so she could always find a way to use the food. Everything else bulged from the house and garage into the driveway and yard. Harvey spent a happy summer learning to scavenge, eating well, learning not to worry about what others thought of him and even improving his memory. When his parents finally found him, Harvey realized that they really did want him, even if they were separated. He decided to live with his mother on weekdays, his father on weekends, and the Katzs during the summers.

The plot problems that are obvious to adult readers are ones that most young readers will be able to ignore (i.e. neither parent checks on Harvey for over two months). Young readers will enjoy the humor and realism of Harvey's pain, happiness and eventual feeling of self-confidence and triumph. The ten short chapters, good-sized print and adequate space between the lines help lower the book's reading level to late fourth grade.

Interest Level: 3-6. Reading Level: 5.1. Further Search Topics: Loners-Fiction, Vacation-Fiction, Divorce and Separation-Fiction, Humorous Fiction, Group 2, Memory-Fiction, Runaways-Fiction, Academic Problems-Fiction, Individualists-Fiction.

Coombs, Charles. Be a winner in baseball. Morrow 1973, 127 pp.

A solid, though chauvanistic discussion of baseball basics. After a very short summary of baseball's history, the author spends a chapter emphasizing the importance of practice and physical training. From there he goes on to cover techniques of pitching, catching, hitting, running bases, playing the infield and playing the outfield. Directions are clear and often well-illustrated. There is great emphasis placed on playing correctly to avoid injury and on out-smarting the opponent. The book concludes with a reminder that the game is, above all, meant to be fun.

Although the book's reading level tests at 5.2, the jargon that influences the tests will be familiar to most baseball fans. For enthusiasts, therefore, the reading level is probably 4.2 to 5.1. Includes glossary and index.

Interest Level: 4-6. Reading Level: 5.1. Further Search Topics: Baseball.

Danziger, Paula. The cat ate my gymsuit. Delacorte 1974, 147 pp.

Another book for fans of Judy Blume. Marcy was shy and insecure, unhappy at school and unhappy at home. She was self-conscious about being heavy and sure she would never have a date. Only Ms. Finney (a new teacher), her English class and Smedley (a communications group) meant anything to Marcy. When Ms. Finney was fired because of her refusal to recite the pledge of allegiance and her unorthodox teaching methods, Marcy began to organize a protest movement. Marcy's commitment brought more problems at school and at home, but eventually resulted in Ms. Finney's vindication and Marcy's and her mother's growth and understanding.

Don't expect much depth of characterization. Most of the characters are flat and stereotypical, but the book will have great appeal in spite of its faults, for Marcy's insecurities are ones with which many young readers can identify.

Interest Level: 5-6. Reading Level: 5.1. Further Search Topics: School Stories, Everyday Stories, Family Problems-Fiction, Challenges-Fiction, Weight-Fiction, Courage-Fiction, Individualists-Fiction, Sex Role-Fiction.

Danziger, Paula. The pistachio prescription. Delacorte 1978 154 pp.

Just as Cassie entered her freshman year in high school, the old stand-by that had helped her deal with all her problems (eating pistachio nuts) began to fail. To be sure, she did get through the class elections and was elected president. She met and started dating Bernie. She gained self-confidence. She even managed to stand up to a particularly mean teacher. But, eating pistachios didn't help at all at home where Cassie really needed them. She could hardly stand to be in the same room with her older sister. She hated the importance her mother placed on looking right and dressing well. Most of all, she hated the way her parents were constantly fighting. The only person with whom she was really confortable was her brother. But, before the year was over, Cassie's parents decided to get a divorce, she and her sister became friends and Cassie learned to accept her family.

Another Judy Blume-style author, but Danziger's portraits of adults tend to be even more one-dimensional and exaggerated than Blume's. Very popular anyway.

Interest Level: 6+ Reading Level: 5.1. Further Search Topics: Divorce and Separation-Fiction, Family Problems-Fiction, Beauty-Fiction, School Stories, Adolescence-Fiction, Love-Fiction, Brothers and Sisters-Fiction, Everyday Stories.

Hamilton, Virginia. Zeely; illus by Symeon Shimin. Macmillan 1967, 122 pp.

A beautiful, almost mystical story of a black girl who learns about self-identity and pride from a statuesque neighbor whom Geeder is convinced must be a Watutsi princess. At first by chance and later at an arranged meeting, Zeely (Geeder's neighbor) gently and symbolically speaks to Geeder of her racial origins. She also tells Geeder of a young girl (Zeely as a child), too ignorant of the world around her to be able to recognize reality. It is a quietly moving story that is most likely to find an appreciative audience in the thoughtful, more mature reader.

Interest Level: 5-6. Reading Level: 5.1. Further Search Topics: Africa-Fiction, Royalty-Fiction, Blacks-Fiction, Courage-Fiction, Vacation-Fiction, Country Life-Fiction, Read Aloud.

Hinton, Susan E. The outsiders. Viking Pr. 1967, 188 pp.

When she wrote this book Susan Hinton was only 17 years old, but she had the sensitivity of someone much older. She wrote a taut story of the rivalry between two city gangs; the Socs (the rich socialites) and the Greasers (poor kids from the wrong side of town) that is more than anything a plea for understanding and tolerance. Seen through the eyes of Ponyboy (a very bright, 14-year-old Greaser), the rivalry brought on violence and an accidental killing that forced Pony and his friend Johnny to flee for their lives. Dallas, the meanest and most dangerous of the Greasers, provided them with shelter, food for a week, and a gun. At the end of that week, Johnny decided that they should turn themselves in to the police. But before they could do that, their hideout (an old church) burned in a fire which threatened the lives of four children who had been playing there. In trying to rescue the children, Johnny, Pony, and Dallas were injured; Johnny was severely burned and probably permanently crippled. A vengeance rumble was held while Johnny lay in the hospital, but the Greasers' victory was empty when Johnny died. He had been the one member of the gang whom they all loved and who had most needed them. Dallas went to pieces: he robbed a store and set himself up to be killed by the police. He had nothing left to live for after Johnny's death. Pony found support and security with his brothers (their parents were dead) and, in a note from Johnny, some hope for the future.

Hinton speaks most often through Pony (his depth of understanding of the people around him is very impressive), but through Johnny and two of the Socs as well, Randy and Cherry. Her message is clear, but at no time does she fail to maintain believable characters in a compelling plot.

Although the book looks forbidding with its 188 pages of unrelenting small print, it is an exciting story, full of adventure, realism, and room for thought. Perhaps the best way to introduce this book is to read a fair portion of it aloud. Now a motion picture too.

Interest Level: 6+ Reading Level: 5.1. Further Search Topics: Crime-Fiction, Gangs-Fiction, Murder-Fiction, Read Aloud, Friendship-Fiction, Juvenile Delinquency-Fiction, Best Sellers, City Life-Fiction, Brothers and Sisters-Fiction, Orphans-Fiction, Runaways-Fiction, Troublemakers-Fiction, Poverty-Fiction.

Mazer, Harry. The war on Villa Street. Delacorte 1978, 182 pp.

Willis was a loner and a runner. He was a loner because he didn't want anyone to find out about his alcoholic father. He wasn't quite sure why he ran; perhaps because it was the only time he felt good. When Rabbit Slavin and his friends asked Willis to become part of their gang, he refused. He was flattered and wanted to join, but the gang wanted to meet at his house and Willis couldn't risk that. Then when he agreed to coach the local "retard" for the school's field day, Willis gave the gang the opportunity they wanted to take their revenge on him for turning them down. The gang's hatred for Willis increased still more when he beat their best runner and athlete. In payment, the gang jumped Willis and beat him badly. After he picked himself up, Willis realized that he had at least faced the worst of his fears and survived. Days later when his drunken father humiliated him, Willis realized he had to face that, too. He made peace with himself and the world by deciding he could neither continue to run away from, nor apologize for his father anymore. He was independent and strong.

There is much in this fast-paced book besides the obvious violence and action. It is written with an intuitive feel for a teenager's problems and emotions and is a sensitive portrayal of mature concepts. The print is large, but spacing between the lines should have been slightly increased.

Interest Level: 5-6. Reading Level: 5.1. Further Search Topics: Running-Fiction, Loneliness-Fiction, Alcoholism-Fiction, Loners-Fiction, Mental Retardation-Fiction, Gangs-Fiction, Child Abuse-Fiction, Bullies-Fiction, Family Problems-Fiction, Courage-Fiction.

Peck, Robert Newton. Mr. Little; illus by Ben Stahl. Doubleday 1979, 87 pp.

All summer long Drag and Finley had looked forward to having Miss Kellogg as their teacher, so they were extremely disappointed to find ordinary-looking Mr. Little in her place on the first day of school. Used to playing tricks on their teachers anyway, Drag and Finley decided to go all out to get even with Mr. Little for spoiling their year. But try as they might, they couldn't get an advantage over Mr. Little; he seemed to be unflappable. Finally, in their riskiest prank ever, they stole Mr. Little's underwear to dress a statue in the town square. That attempt to embarrass Mr. Little only served to get Finley and Drag in serious trouble from which Mr. Little saved them. It was his later rescue of Miss Kellogg, however, that added respect to the boys' growing feeling of friendship for Mr. Little.

Because the author's adult viewpoint is never quite lost, even though he writes in the first person, and because the rural and historic time settings are not familiar to many readers, the book may need some introduction and encouragement. It is a prime candidate for reading aloud until the young reader's interest takes over. Print is of adequate size, but spacing between lines could have been more generous.

Interest Level: 4-6. Reading Level: 5.1. Further Search Topics: Humorous Fiction, School Stories, Troublemakers-Fiction, Group 2, Read Aloud, Country Life-Fiction, Best Sellers.

Robinson, Barbara. The best Christmas pageant ever; illus by Judith Gwyn Brown. Har-Row 1972, 80 pp.

A truly delightful story of what happens when the meanest kids in town (they are all in one family) take over all the lead roles in the Sunday school Christmas pageant. The Herdmans (all six of them), having heard that the church was giving away free food, showed up to take some. While they were there, they heard about the Christmas pageant and decided it presented them with another perfect opportunity for food and mischief. With a little behind-the-scenes arm-twisting (literally), they managed to dissuade everyone else from showing interest in the major roles. Theirs was a completely original interpretation of the Christmas story that left nothing and no one around them untouched.

That the book's reading level will prove too high for many people is unfortunate. The story is well worth the struggle. A wonderful choice for reading aloud.

Interest Level: 3-6. Reading Level: 5.1 Further Search Topics: Christmas-Fiction, Bullies-Fiction, Troublemakers-Fiction, Humorous Fiction, Religion-Fiction, Group 2, Read Aloud, Acting-Fiction, Holidays-Fiction.

St. John, Wylly Folk. The ghost next door; illus by Trina Schart Hyman. Har-Row 1971, 178 pp.

Told by 13-year-old Lindsay, this is the story of her neighbor Miss Judith and Miss Judith's two nieces. Her niece Miranda had drowned years earlier in Miss Judith's backyard fish pond and Miss Judith had never fully recovered from her death. As the story begins, Miss Judith is about to welcome another niece (Sherry) for a summer stay. Sherry, without ever being told about Miranda, seems to sense Miranda's presence all around. Her mother laughs and says that

Sherry has an imaginary friend. Miss Judith, who is a strong believer in ESP, thinks that Sherry is communicating with Miranda. As the days go on Sherry learns more and more of Miranda' secrets. When Miss Judith is scared by Sherry, Lindsay and her friend, Tammy, decide to see what sort of tricks Sherry is playing.

A believable suspense story, made even more so by the illustrations.

Interest Level: 4-6. Reading Level: 5.1. Further Search Topics: Mystery and Detective Stories, Relatives-Fiction, Group 2, Extra Sensory Perception-Fiction, Best Sellers, Ghosts-Fiction.

RELATIVES-FICTION

Christopher, Matt. Devil pony; illus by Lorence Bjorkland. Little 1977, 103 pp.

This book is a bit of a change from the usual Matt Christopher story line. There is no sports interest here; instead there is a good suspense story about a boy, his cousin and a horse. Stu had watched the black Morgan named Midnight being born and had fallen in love with him. A year later he returned to his aunt and uncle's ranch to claim the horse, as he had been promised he could, but strange things began to happen around him. His cousin Wilbur warned him that he had probably annoyed the ranch poltergeist by deciding to take Midnight away. The bizarre occurrences escalated until Stu was almost tempted to leave Midnight at the ranch. Then Stu discovered Wilbur had been orchestrating everything that had happened because he had wanted to keep the horse himself. Although Stu decided to take Midnight home as he had planned, their new honesty led Stu to believe that he and Wilbur could be friends after all. A surprisingly good story with strong reader appeal.

Interest Level: 3-6. Reading Level: 3.1. Further Search Topics: Horses-Fiction, Supernatural-Fiction, Ghosts-Fiction, Jealousy-Fiction, Relatives-Fiction.

Greenwald, Sheila. Give us a great big smile, Rosy Cole. Little 1981, 76 pp.

It was Rosy's turn to be the subject of her uncle's book. He needed to earn money again and Rosy had just turned 10, the age each of her sisters had been when Uncle Ralph wrote *Anitra Dances* and *Pippa Prances* about them. However, Rosy couldn't dance like Anitra or ride horses like Pippa. In fact, Rosy had no talent that was appropriate for a book. She drew well but Uncle Ralph said that wasn't visual enough. Then Rosy's mother and uncle decided that Rosy could be *A Very Little Fiddler*.

Rosy had been taking violin lessons for two years, but only Rosy and her music teacher knew how truly untalented she was. Rosy hated the whole idea of the book at first. But as people began to treat her like a star, she found herself acting like one, until the day she heard her tape of the piece she was to play at the recital. Once again she realized that she could not play the violin and didn't want to go on with the charade. When everyone ignored her wishes, Rosy started to run away. Her route took her through the park where she thought of a brilliant idea. She ran home, changed clothes, picked up her violin, created a sign, and raced back to the park. There, with all the other street musicians Rosy set up her sign and began to play her violin. Her sign asked people to sign a petition if they felt that she should not be encouraged to play the violin anymore. Right away Rosy drew a large crowd. Before long, even her mother was one of the listeners and one of the signers. That was the end of Rosy's musical career and her uncle's book, but both were happier. Rosy

went back to being normal and Uncle Ralph found another topic for his next book.

Chapters are long, but should not be a problem. Print is large. Some of the story is actually told in the illustrations, so the reader should be aware of them. Younger children may take the book more seriously than children whose sense of humor includes irony or children who were not as fond of Krementz's *Very Young* series.

Interest Level: 4-6. Reading Level: 3.1. Further Search Topics: Occupations-Fiction, Humorous Fiction, Family-Fiction, Relatives-Fiction, Talent-Fiction, Photography-Fiction, Everyday Stories.

MacLachlan, Patricia. Arthur, for the very first time; illus by Lloyd Bloom. Har-Row 1980, 117 pp.

A beautifully written, sensitive yet humorous story of a boy's maturation and growing awareness of the world around him. When Arthur's unhappiness at home is made more intense by the advent of a new baby, he is sent to spend the summer with his older aunt and uncle. Their eccentricities and those of their friends are at first only material for Arthur to write about in his journal. But as the summer progresses he not only learns from them, but also grows from an observer of life to a participant. His final step is helping a large and beloved pig bear her litter in a driving rain storm aided only by his independent, totally untamed young friend Moira.

The print is somewhat small, but spacing between lines is generous.

Interest Level: 4-6. Reading Level: 4.2. Further Search Topics: Read Aloud, Children-Growth-Fiction, Humorous Fiction, Friendship-Fiction, Vacation-Fiction, Relatives-Fiction, Infants-Fiction, Individualists-Fiction, Writing-Fiction, Loners-Fiction, Group 2.

St. John, Wylly Folk. The ghost next door; illus by Trina Schart Hyman. Har-Row 1971, 178 pp.

Told by 13-year-old Lindsay, this is the story of her neighbor Miss Judith and Miss Judith's two nieces. Her niece Miranda had drowned years earlier in Miss Judith's backyard fish pond and Miss Judith had never fully recovered from her death. As the story begins, Miss Judith is about to welcome another niece (Sherry) for a summer stay. Sherry, without ever being told about Miranda, seems to sense Miranda's presence all around. Her mother laughs and says that Sherry has an imaginary friend. Miss Judith, who is a strong believer in ESP, thinks that Sherry is communicating with Miranda. As the days go on Sherry learns more and more of Miranda' secrets. When Miss Judith is scared by Sherry, Lindsay and her friend, Tammy, decide to see what sort of tricks Sherry is playing.

A believable suspense story, made even more so by the illustrations.

Interest Level: 4-6. Reading Level: 5.1. Further Search Topics: Mystery and Detective Stories, Relatives-Fiction, Group 2, Extra Sensory Perception-Fiction, Best Sellers, Ghosts-Fiction.

RELIGION

Adoff, Arnold. Malcolm X; illus by John Wilson. Har-Row 1970, 41 pp.

This is a simple, intellectually honest biography of a very controversial man. Taught a strong sense of self-respect by his father, Malcolm X could not accept the second-class status that white society tried to impose upon him. Instead he turned away from whites and all they stood for. He hated high school, the detention home he lived in after his father's death, and his mother's placement in a state hospital. He didn't feel comfortable until he moved to Harlem. There he found friends, but he also found crime. While he was in prison, Malcolm X began to read of great, black societies and people. His brother told him about the Nation of Islam, the Black Muslims, and Elijah Muhammad, the leader of the religion. He began corresponding with Mr. Muhammad. Shortly after he was released from prison, Malcolm X met Elijah Muhammad and eventually became a minister of the religion. There was even talk that he would be Elijah Muhammad's successor. But, as the years went on, Malcolm X began to think that black Christians as well as Muslims should be united in the fight for black rights. Despite threats against his life Malcolm X formed the Organization of Afro-American Unity. Both blacks and whites were angry with him. The threats continued until his house was firebombed; and, only a week later, at a public meeting, Malcolm X was assassinated.

An excellent overview of a complex man. The book may well prompt readers to learn more about the man and his beliefs. At the very least it will expose readers, in an interesting manner, to someone they should know. The book shares the same semi-picture book format of the others in Harper and Row/Crowell's biography series, therefore it will need a careful introduction to potential readers.

Interest Level: 3-5. Reading Level: 3.1. Further Search Topics: Blacks-Biography, Civil Rights, Biography, Crime, Religion, Assassinations, Prejudice, Poverty, Foster Homes.

RELIGION-BIOGRAPHY

Burchard, Marshall. Sports hero: Fran Tarkenton. Putnam 1977, 95 pp.

From a strict religious background where athletics were not encouraged, Fran went on to set every NFL passing record possible See *Sports Hero: Bill Walton.* Sports Hero series.

Interest Level: 3-6. Reading Level: 3.2. Further Search Topics: Biography, Tarkenton, Fran, Football-Biography, Religion-Biography.

Burchard, Marshall. Sports hero: Terry Bradshaw. Putnam 1980, 95 pp.

Once labeled a "dumb hick," Terry Bradshaw went on to prove he was a talented and thinking quarterback, good enough to be named NFL Player of the Year. He is also a deeply religious man. Reading level of this title varies from 3.1 to 4.1. For more details about the series, see *Sports Hero: Bill Walton.* Sports Hero series.

Interest Level: 3-6. Reading Level: 3.2. Further Search Topics: Biography, Bradshaw, Terry, Football-Biography, Religion-Biography.

Burchard, Susan H. Sports star: Elvin Hayes. HarBraceJ 1980, 63 pp.

Only this and three other Sue Burchard titles listed here differ much from the format described for the *Sports Hero* series (see *Sports Hero: Bill Walton*). It appears that in 1979 Ms. Burchard's books took on a slick new look. The covers began to sport color photos rather than black and white. The print size became noticeably smaller, although still of adequate size. More emphasis was placed on the players early life and background, in an apparent attempt to make him or her understandable as an individual rather than just as a star. A short career summary was added at the end of each book. All-in-all, the new, flashier approach should make the books more appealing than ever to older students.

Elvin Hayes came from a very poor family who lived in a town where blacks were badly treated. He went on to become one of the best college basketball players of his time. His deep religious convictions helped him through some rough times in his early years as a pro. Now he is happy, not just when he wins, but when he knows he has played his best. Sports Star series.

Interest Level: 3-6. Reading Level: 3.1. Further Search Topics: Biography, Hayes, Elvin, Basketball-Biography, Blacks-Biography, Religion-Biography.

RELIGION-FICTION

Blume, Judy. Are you there God? It's me, Margaret. Bradbury 1970, 149 pp.

Sixth grade was a year of growth for Margaret and her friends. They all wondered when they would start growing breasts and when they would begin menstruating. Each was kissed for the first time. It was also a year in which Margaret tried to decide whether to be Jewish or Christian and ended up neither. She simply remained friends with God, just as she was when the year began. The book is a reassuring, very open, and humorous treatment of the pains and promise of maturation. It is exceptionally popular with older elementary school readers, so the book's slightly small print and narrow lines should not impede an interested reader's progress.

Interest Level: 4-6. Reading Level: 3.2. Further Search Topics: School Stories, Family-Fiction, Children-Growth-Fiction, Religion-Fiction, Humorous Fiction, Love-Fiction, Best Sellers, Grandparents-Fiction, Everyday Stories.

Chaikin, Miriam. Finders weepers; illus Richard Egielski. Har-Row 1980, 120 pp.

The children most likely to read this are those who have enjoyed *I Should Worry, I Should Care.* On her way home from school one day, Molly found a ring. Rather than try to find its owner, she made up excuses to keep the ring. Molly knew it was a sin to keep something that belonged to someone else, she even knew who *did* own the ring. When she finally decided to return it, the ring had become stuck on Molly's finger and wouldn't come off. With Yom Kippur just a few days away, Molly became convinced that all the unpleasant things happening around her were punishments for her sin. She finally had to have the ring cut off her finger. After she prayed for forgiveness life immediately went back to normal.

There's enough guilt here to satisfy even the most demanding reader. There is also the same solid family group that appeared in the first book. But this book probably lacks enough excitement and/or empathy to interest a reader new to Molly and her family. Print is dark but spacing between lines could have been wider.

Interest Level: 3-5. Reading Level: 3.1. Further Search Topics: Family-Fiction, Jews-Fiction, Honesty-Fiction, Holidays-Fiction, Religion-Fiction.

Cohen, Barbara. The carp in the bathtub; illus by Joan Halpern. Lothrop 1972, 48 pp.

Leah and Harry couldn't face the prospect of seeing Joe, their pet carp, made into gefilte fish, even for such a special occasion as the Seder on the first night of Passover. The large, friendly carp had lived in the family's bathtub for over a week. It even swam right over to Leah and Harry to be fed everytime they went into the bathroom. At a time when most children in New York didn't have pets, Joe was as close to being a pet as possible. So, Leah and Harry hid Joe in a neighbor's apartment until their father discovered what they had done. When Joe's destiny was fulfilled, the children had to face a difficult fact of life. A week later, however, their despair became delight, when their father brought home a pet cat.

A short, warm and satisfying story.

Interest Level: 2-5. Reading Level: 3.1. Further Search Topics: Group 2, Jews-Fiction, Religion-Fiction, Pets-Fiction, Passover-Fiction, Family-Fiction, Holidays-Fiction, Read Aloud, Brothers and Sisters-Fiction.

Hurwitz, Johanna. Once I was a plum tree; illus by Ingrid Fetz. Morrow 1980, 160 pp.

Ten-year-old Gerry Flam knew nothing about her religion except that she was Jewish. Her parents didn't practice their religion and only superficially observed some of the holidays. As they told Gerry, their reason was that they were assimilated Americans. In fact, they seemed to practice as many Christian as Jewish holidays. All Gerry's friends and neighbors were Catholic, so Gerry had very little chance to learn about Judaism or the prejudice to which Jews were still being subjected in 1947 in the Bronx. A Jewish family moved into the apartment building next door, and Gerry's quiet curiosity was stimulated. From the Wulfs, Gerry began to learn about Judaism, World War II, and Hitler. As her pride in her heritage grew, Gerry also felt prejudice for the first time. After celebrating her first Passover Seder, Gerry found that despite the problems, she was truly happy to be Jewish.

Much like Chaikin's *I Should Worry, I Should Care* in tone and mood. Will be useful where there is already an interest in Judaism.

Interest Level: 3-5. Reading Level: 3.1. Further Search Topics: Religion-Fiction, Family-Fiction, Jews-Fiction, City Life-Fiction, Children-Growth-Fiction, Prejudice-Fiction.

Robinson, Barbara. The best Christmas pageant ever; illus by Judith Gwyn Brown. Har-Row 1972, 80 pp.

A truly delightful story of what happens when the meanest kids in town (they are all in one family) take over all the lead roles in the Sunday school Christmas pageant. The Herdmans (all six of them), having heard that the church was giving away free food, showed up to take some. While they were there, they heard about the Christmas pageant and decided it presented them with another perfect opportunity for food and mischief. With a little behind-the-scenes arm-twisting (literally), they managed to dissuade everyone else from showing interest in the major roles. Theirs was a completely original interpretation of the Christmas story that left nothing and no one around them untouched.

That the book's reading level will prove too high for many people is unfortunate. The story is well worth the struggle. A wonderful choice for reading aloud.

Interest Level: 3-6. Reading Level: 5.1 Further Search Topics: Christmas-Fiction, Bullies-Fiction, Troublemakers-Fiction, Humorous Fiction, Religion-Fiction, Group 2, Read Aloud, Acting-Fiction, Holidays-Fiction.

REPTILES

Allen, Gertrude. Everyday turtles, toads and their kin. HM 1970, 48 pp.

Straight-forward, short, chapter discussions of turtles, lizards, snakes, salamanders, toads, frogs and tree toads. Black and white drawings done by the author amplify the text. The major part of the book is simple enough to be understood at second grade, but should still be interesting to fourth and fifth graders. A few terms may need explanation: i.e., venomous, prey. The chapters on the turtle, lizard, frog and tree frog are the easiest. No index, but still useful for reports.

Interest Level: 2-5. Reading Level: 2.2. Further Search Topics: Turtles, Reptiles, Lizards, Toads, Frogs, Snakes, Salamanders.

REPTILES-FICTION

Wolkoff, Judie. Wally. Bradbury 1977, 199 pp.

Michael Price agreed to take care of his friend Billy's chuckwalla for three weeks. But because his mother had declared a moratorium on any more reptiles in the house, Michael tried to hide Wally in his closet. With help from his brother Roger, Michael managed to keep Wally a secret until Wally was mistakenly left out of his box one night. Despite Michael and Roger's desperate searches, the chuckwalla did not reappear until Mr. and Mrs. Price were involved in the final negotiations for the sale of their house. Wally completely disrupted the proceedings, prevented the sale and thus made everyone happy. For as it turned out, none of the Prices had really wanted to move after all.

A fast-paced, funny book with much reader appeal.

Interest Level: 2-5. Reading Level: 2.2. Further Search Topics: Pets-Fiction, Humorous Fiction, Lizards-Fiction, Best Sellers, Reptiles-Fiction, Secrets-Fiction.

RESPIRATION

Branley, Franklyn M. Oxygen keeps you alive; illus by Don Madden. Har-Row 1971, 33 pp.

A well-explained, beginning treatment of the functions, importance, and uses of oxygen. The explanation is not limited to humans, but extends to plants and animals as well. Although the book can be stretched to use with fifth graders, its picture book format and sometimes condescending tone indicate it is most easily used through fourth grade. No index or table to contents.

Let's-Read-and-Find-Out-Science-Book series.

Interest Level: 2-4. Reading Level: 2.2. Further Search Topics: Air, Respiration, Scuba Diving, Astronauts.

RIDDLES

Cerf, Bennett. Bennett Cerf's book of animal riddles; illus by Roy McKie. Beginner 1964, 62 pp.

A slightly more difficult selection of riddles than the following listing. The riddles are longer and less familiar, but still very useful. See *Bennett Cerf's Book of Riddles* for more explanation. Reader format.

Interest Level: 1-3. Reading Level: 2.1. Further Search Topics: Riddles, Wit and Humor, Group 2.

Cerf, Bennett. Bennett Cerf's book of riddles; illus by Roy McKie. Beginner 1960, 64 pp.

Simple, well-known riddles that are always popular with children. The riddle is introduced on one page and answered on the reverse side of the page. Silly drawings illustrate each riddle and answer. Because each riddle and answer stands alone, even the most problematic of readers can have the satisfaction of completing a unit in a short time. That satisfaction, plus the universal appeal of humor make this book and the preceding listing useful through grade four, despite the book's reader format.

Interest Level: 1-4. Reading Level: 2.1. Further Search Topics: Riddles, Wit and Humor, Group 2.

Ciardi, John. I met a man; illus by Robert Osborn. HM 1961, 74 pp.

Ciardi's poems are pure fun. About half are riddle poems (poems that describe something without naming it until the end) and the rest are humorous descriptions or nonsense poems. There is a problem, however, with the riddle poems: they are somewhat more difficult to read than the other poems, but of interest to younger rather than older readers. For that reason pages 1-21 (primarily nonsense verse) can be recommended for grades one through five. The remainder of the book, although enjoyable to the very young, needs to be read to them or needs a strong young reader.

Interest Level: 1-5. Reading Level: 2.2. Further Search Topics: Wit and Humor, Poetry, Riddles, Group 2.

Low, Joseph. Five men under one umbrella. Macmillan 1975, 64 pp.

Twenty-nine riddles, most of which are fairly familiar. Nothing special in this collection, just an additional choice for the young comedian.

Interest Level: 1-3. Reading Level: 2.1. Further Search Topics: Riddles, Wit and Humor, Group 2.

Sarnoff, Jane. What? A riddle book; illus by Reynold Ruffins. Scribner 1974, 62 pp.

A good, lengthy collection of both familiar and unfamiliar riddles. Every other page is brightened by bold and humorous illustrations. The first part of the book seems to have slightly more riddles for younger readers than the rest of the book. Some of the riddles in the collection involve rather sophisticated puns; thus they are more appealing to fifth and sixth grade readers. The final three pages of the book include 35 riddles whose answers are in code. The key to the code is given on the last page of the book. It is a picture book printed in two tones. The riddles sometimes slant diagonally across the page.

Interest Level: 1-6. Reading Level: 3.1. Further Search Topics: Riddles, Wit and Humor, Group 2, Nonverbal Communication.

Wiseman, Bernard. Morris and Boris. Dodd 1974, 64 pp.

This is a compilation of three silly stories about Morris the Moose and Boris the Bear. When Boris tries to interest Morris in telling riddles, Morris frustrates Boris so completely that Boris runs off angrily. Later Boris tries to teach Morris a tongue twister, but ends up running off in total confusion. Finally Boris tries to teach Morris to play hide-and-seek and that, too, is a disaster. Boris tells Morris that Morris just cannot do anything. A bird who has seen everything reminds Boris that Morris can make him very angry and that is something. When Boris agrees they all laugh happily.

Broad, slapstick humor makes this appealing to children well into third grade. Reader format.

Interest Level: 1-3. Reading Level: 1.2. Further Search Topics: Wit and Humor, Riddles, Tongue Twisters, Games, Humorous Fiction.

RIDING

Krementz, Jill. A very young rider. Knopf 1977, unp (128 pp).

Vivi Malloy is the youngest rider in a family of several other riders. Her greatest dream is to make the Olympic equestrian team. She is progressing towards her goal with daily workouts and about fifteen major horse shows each year. See *A Very Young Dancer* for more extensive notes.

Interest Level: 2-6. Reading Level: 3.2. Further Search Topics: Horses, Riding, Talent, Group 2.

ROBIN HOOD

Dolch, Edward W. Robin Hood stories; illus by Carmen Mowry. Garrard 1957, 162 pp.

The illustrations are still drab, but the stories in this volume are exciting. Here we find straight-forward adventure and familiar characters: Robin Hood, Little John, Will Scarlet, Sheriff of Nottingham, Allan-a-dale and Sir Richard of Lea. The book makes a good choice for adventure lovers. Dolch Pleasure Reading Book series.

Interest Level: 2-6. Reading Level: 2.2. Further Search Topics: Robin Hood, Knights and Knighthood-Fiction, Folklore, Crime-Fiction.

ROBINSON, JACKIE

Cohen, Barbara. Thank you, Jackie Robinson; illus by Richard Cuffari. Lothrop 1974, 125 pp.

This story is not for everyone, but for the right reader it is perfect. The book is a catalog of baseball facts, thus it is likely to appeal primarily to baseball fans. But it is not the typical story of a child overcoming a problem through practice and perserverance, as are most sports books. This is a sensitive story of a fatherless boy whose life centered around the New York Dodgers.

Sam could repeat the starting line-up and details of any game the Dodgers had played within the last three years; however, no one cared. In fact, most people were bored when Sam began reciting. Only Davey, the old, black cook at the inn where Sam and his family lived, took any interest. Davey was as much a fan as Sam. They began spending hours together talking and then watching baseball as Davey and his daughter took Sam to the games with them. It was Sam and Davey's dream to catch a fly ball and have it autograped by all the Dodgers, especially Jackie Robinson, the first black major league player. When Davey had a severe heart attack, Sam gathered all his courage to make that dream come true. He bought a baseball, took the subway to a game, and argued with the ushers until he was finally able to get Jackie Robinson's and the team's autographs. Just a few days before Davey died Sam took the baseball to the hospital and gave it to Davey. Sam's feelings about Davey's death are real and painful. He felt sorry for himself, lonely, angry, sad and confused. But a remark by his mother and one more Jackie Robinson hit helped Sam accept Davey's death.

Because the story is told as a first-person flashback set in the late 1940s, it may need a little introduction. It also alludes to racial problems and practices that young readers may not understand without explanation (i.e., why Davey had some hesitation about taking a white child with him to the ballpark or on a trip).

Interest Level: 4-6. Reading Level: 4.2. Further Search Topics: Baseball-Fiction, Blacks-Fiction, Aging-Fiction, Single Parent Family-Fiction, Friendship-Fiction, Death-Fiction, Robinson, Jackie.

Rudeen, Kenneth. Jackie Robinson; illus by Richard Cuffari. Har-Row 1971, 41 pp.

Jackie Robinson was the youngest child in a large, poor family. As early as high school it was Robinson's superior athletic talent that set him apart. He could run track or play baseball, football, or basketball. He was the first student at UCLA to win a letter in all four sports. But because he wasn't happy to see the way his mother still had to struggle to earn money to live, after a year and a half at UCLA, Robinson left college to take a job. Soon after that, the United States entered World War II and Robinson went into the Army. His refusal to ride in the back of a bus in Texas resulted in a courtmartial, but he was found innocent after an uproar was made by the newspapers.

After the Army, Robinson played baseball with a Negro League team. A short time later, he was asked by the Dodger manager Branch Rickey to become the first black man to play in the major leagues. Rickey warned Robinson that it would mean he not only had to play well, but that he would also have to take all the anger and bitterness that would be directed at him. Robinson agreed. For three long years, while there were no other black players in the major leagues, Robinson played well and took everything without fighting back. Robinson was then able to stop trying to be perfect because he had successfully broken a very important color barrier and no longer had to prove to white managers, players and fans that blacks belonged in baseball just as much as whites. Robinson played for the Dodgers for ten years. When he left baseball he was elected into the Baseball Hall of Fame. He continued to fight for civil rights throughout the rest of his life, although there is only a brief mention of his activities in the book. Since the book's publication Jackie Robinson has died.

This is an excellent choice for the child who thinks of nothing but sports. It may be helpful in opening up an interest in the civil rights movement, black history, or black heroes. It is unfortunate that the traditional Crowell biography format (semi-picture book), and the author's slight tendency to be condescending, prevents the book from being useful beyond fourth grade. Crowell Biography series.

Interest Level: 2-4. Reading Level: 2.2. Further Search Topics: Civil Rights, Robinson, Jackie, Baseball-Biography, Biography, Blacks-Biography, Prejudice, Poverty.

ROBOTS-FICTION
Butterworth, William E. Next stop, Earth; illus by Paul Frame. Walker 1978, 80 pp.

After two years on a desolate planet, 12-year-old Charley and his family were anticipating their return to Earth. But when Charley was awakened from sleep by a spaceship robot, he learned that an asteroid disturbance had caused several key systems on the ship to malfunction. Of 24 passengers on board the spaceship, only 10 were still alive and only Charley and his sister were able to be awakened. It was up to Charley to pilot the ship to its landing on Earth. The controls were all in an adjacent room which a faulty robot kept Charley from entering. Without someone at the controls the ship would burn up when re-entering Earth's atmosphere. By tricking the robot and commanding the ship's main computer, Charley was able to get to the control panel just in time to wake his father, help with reentry and save the ship.

Though the story tends to be heavy with conversations between Charley and various computers and robots, it is also that dialogue that helps maintain suspense. It is a story for the confirmed science fiction fan, not for the inductee.

Interest Level: 3-6. Reading Level: 2.2. Further Search Topics: Science Fiction, Outer Space-Fiction, Voyages and Travels-Fiction, Robots-Fiction, Computers-Fiction.

Pene du Bois, William. Lazy Tommy Pumpkinhead. Har-Row 1966, 32 pp.

Tommy lived a solitary life in an all-electric house. An electric bed woke Tommy and slid him into a tub full of warm water. The tub then tipped him out and

into a harness that held Tommy upright while other machines dried him, combed his hair, brushed his teeth, dressed him, and fed him. But one day Tommy's life was literally turned upside down with disastrous results. His feet were cleaned and combed and his clothes were all put on upside down, but the worst part of all was that Tommy almost starved; the machine fed his feet instead of his mouth.

A tongue-in-cheek warning against laziness. The lesson is obvious but the treatment (both text and illustrations) is so enjoyable that the book is appealing to almost any reader who wants a short, funny book. Print is somewhat small but spacing between lines is more than adequate.

Interest Level: 1-6. Reading Level: 3.2. Further Search Topics: Electricity-Fiction, Robots-Fiction, Laziness-Fiction, Humorous Fiction, Group 2, Read Aloud.

Slote, Alfred. C.O.L.A.R.; illus by Anthony Kramer. Lippincott 1981, 146 pp.

Jack, his robot twin Danny, and Jack's mother and father were forced to make an emergency landing on an uncharted planet. There they were attacked by creatures who looked like rocks and who wanted to destroy all humans. They captured Danny, led him into an underground living complex, and revealed their true identities. The creatures were robots who had escaped from their owners and the slavery in which they had lived. They kept their planet secret from all humans for fear of what would happen to them should they be discovered. Their main purpose was to free as many robots as possible and to allow robots the same pleasures humans enjoyed. Because Danny had been happy with his humans and claimed to have been treated as one of the family, the inhabitants of the planet C.O.L.A.R. felt he had to be reprogrammed to see the truth. Jack looked and acted so much like Danny that he was able to prevent Danny from being brainwashed, to save his parents from death, and to convince the other robots that some humans treated their robots quite well. In fact, he and Danny, together, were able to persuade the robot manufacturer that a great program of robot-owner re-education was needed.

This is a good adventure story which could also be useful as a lead into discussions of slavery, intelligence, and interpersonal relationships. It is a sequel to *My Robot Buddy*, but one which can be read without having read its predecessor.

Interest Level: 3-5. Reading Level: 3.1. Robots-Fiction, Science Fiction, Outer Space-Fiction, Kidnapping-Fiction, Brainwashing-Fiction, Slavery-Fiction.

Slote, Alfred. My robot buddy; illus by Joel Schick. Lippincott 1975, 92 pp.

For Jack's tenth birthday he was given a robot—a robot so real it did everything but run like a human. The robot appeared so human that a thief, thinking he was stealing the robot, almost kidnapped Jack by mistake.

The few points at which the text becomes more difficult than the reading level indicates should not prove too intimidating to the reader. The suspense and humor of the story and the book's high interest subject matter should carry the reader through the rough spots. A satisfying read-aloud for second and third grades.

Interest Level: 2-5. Reading Level: 3.1. Further Search Topics: Science Fiction, Robots-Fiction, Friendship-Fiction, Kidnapping-Fiction, Read Aloud.

RODIA, SIMON

Madian, Jon. Beautiful junk: a story of the Watts Towers; photos by Barbara Jacobs, Jr. and Lou Jacobs, Jr. Little 1968, 44 pp.

Although this book is now out of print; it is well worth trying to find. It is a fictionalized account of a young, angry black boy's encounter with the creator of Los Angeles' unusual Watts Towers. Simon Rodia, a poor tile setter, worked on the towers for 33 years until he was 75 years old. He used only his imagination, discarded materials he found around him, seashells, and sand to build three tall, fantasy-like towers in the middle of a ghetto. He created beauty where others saw only junk.

The book is illustrated with photography that makes the story more vivid and the towers and Rodia's accomplishment more impressive than they would have seemed with drawings. The print is good-sized, spacing is totally adequate. Rodia's life is quickly submarized and an update on the Towers is included at the book's end.

Interest Level: 3-6. Reading Level: 3.1. Further Search Topics: Blacks-Fiction, Read Aloud, Best Sellers, Poverty-Fiction, Rodia, Simon, Architecture, Biography, Aging-Fiction, Watts Towers, California, Poverty.

ROLLER SKATING-FICTION

Bunting, Eve. The skate patrol; illus by Don Madden. Albert Whitman 1980, 40 pp.

The book is funny, clever, undemanding and short. The combination of those qualities plus its slight mystery and its consistent reading level make this a very appealing and useful book for young readers. The plot is simple: in the hopes that their neighbors would be so grateful that they would allow the boys to roller skate in the neighborhood again, two friends decided to capture a local thief. James and Milton even knew who the thief was. He was the "mysterious man" who sat in the park. They only had to capture him in the act of stealing to prove that they were correct. They watched him continuously and trailed him as he followed old ladies. Then came the day that they heard Mrs. Grump scream that her purse had been snatched. The boys sped after the "mysterious man" on their skates. They caught him and knocked him down. To their surprise he declared that he was an undercover policeman and they were letting the real thief get away. Off they went again. This time they caught the right person and were rewarded just the way that they had hoped: Mrs. Crump (not Grump) promised that the boys would be allowed to roller skate any time they wished. A light and lively entertainment.

Interest Level: 2-4. Reading Level: 2.2. Further Search Topics: Mystery and Detective Stories, Humorous Fiction, Spies-Fiction, Roller Skating-Fiction, Crime-Fiction, Best Sellers.

ROYALTY-FICTION

Bulla, Clyde Robert. The sword in the tree; illus by Paul Galdone. Har-Row 1956, 113 pp.

Shan didn't like or trust his Uncle Lionel, who had suddenly appeared at the castle gates after being away many years. Just as suddenly, Shan's father disappeared or died. Shan and his mother soon realized that Lionel wanted to take over the castle, even if it meant killing them. To save themselves, Shan and his mother fled. After walking many miles, they found a poor goat herder and his family who gave them a place to live. Sometime later Shan decided to travel to see King Arthur and ask for help in reclaiming the castle from Lionel. It wasn't until Shan was able to prove the castle was his, and Lionel lost a duel to one of Arthur's knights, that Shan was given back his home. Deep in the castle dungeon Shan found his father, still alive but imprisoned by Lionel.

This book, with its short chapters, short sentences, and steadily progressing plot should interest even the most reluctant reader from grade two through six.

Interest Level: 2-6. Reading Level: 2.2. Further Search Topics: Knights and Knighthood-Fiction, Survival-Fiction, Royalty-Fiction, Best Sellers, Courage-Fiction.

Bulla, Clyde Robert. My friend the monster; illus by Michele Chessare. Har-Row 1980, 75 pp.

Even though Hal was plain and not very clever, his disappointed parents knew that he was still a prince; thus he had to be raised as one. Hal didn't like his lonely, dull life until a new world was accidentally opened to him. A servant's child gave him an old book of monsters and told him that the monsters still lived under the distant mountains. Hal finally made a trip to the mountains, spent a day exploring, and by chance met Humbert, a young monster curious about the world. But, Hal's cruel cousin Archer captured Humbert and put him in a cage. Hal's daring rescue attempt almost resulted in disaster for both Humbert and Hal.

This is another example of Bulla's forte; a book with an action-filled plot, short chapters, large print, wide spaces between the lines, and a low reading level. A book about monsters has almost guaranteed appeal through third grade. Although the book is useful beyond third grade, readers in fourth and fifth grade may be more sensitive to Hal's apparent youth and the fantastic elements of the story.

Interest Level: 1-3. Reading Level: 2.1. Further Search Topics: Fantasy, Monsters-Fiction, Royalty-Fiction, Group 2, Read Aloud, Best Sellers.

Dolch, Edward W. Stories from France; illus by Gordon Laite. Garrard 1963, 167 pp.

It is very difficult to simplify a story and not lose at least some of its original flavor. Such is the case here and in all the Dolch retellings. Nevertheless, this collection of folktales is quite useful for the French flavor it does maintain. The stories, as they are retold, are good; not great, but good. There are 14 stories related in the 19 chapters. This is a result of splitting the longer, more complicated stories into episodes. Some frustration may arise for readers because there is no indication that a story may involve more than one chapter. The much-improved illustrations that introduce each chapter and adorn the cover help make this more attractive than the earlier books. The book ends with a list of the provinces from which the stories came as well as a pronounciation key to French names. Folklore of the World series.

Interest Level: 2-6. Reading Level: 3.1. Further Search Topics: Folklore, Fantasy, France-Fiction, Royalty-Fiction, Group 2, Knights and Knighthood-Fiction.

Hamilton, Virginia. Zeely; illus by Symeon Shimin. Macmillan 1967, 122 pp.

A beautiful, almost mystical story of a black girl who learns about self-identity and pride from a statuesque neighbor whom Geeder is convinced must be a Watutsi princess. At first by chance and later at an arranged meeting, Zeely (Geeder's neighbor) gently and symbolically speaks to Geeder of her racial origins. She also tells Geeder of a young girl (Zeely as a child), too ignorant of the world around her to be able to recognize reality. It is a quietly moving story that is most likely to find an appreciative audience in the thoughtful, more mature reader.

Interest Level: 5-6. Reading Level: 5.1. Further Search Topics: Africa-Fiction, Royalty-Fiction, Blacks-Fiction, Courage-Fiction, Vacation-Fiction, Country Life-Fiction, Read Aloud.

RUNAWAYS-FICTION

Angell, Judie. Dear Lola; or how to build your own family. Bradbury 1980, 166 pp.

Arthur (age 18), James (13), Annie and Al-Willie (twins, age 10), Edmund (9), and Ben (5) wanted to run away from the orphanage and find a place where they could be a real family. After waiting months, their chance arrived one night. They escaped in a van and began living on the road. It was weeks before they found a house in which they thought they could live. They didn't want trouble with local authorities, so most of the children enrolled in school and pretended to be living with their widowed grandfather. Only James (who never left his room) and Arthur stayed home. Arthur was the anonymous author of a nationally syndicated newspaper advice column. It was with the income from his "Dear Lola" column that Arthur was able to support the "family." When the townspeople eventually began to wonder about the "strange" behavior of the children, they investigated and found no adult in charge of the household. Arthur went to court to be appointed the childrens' guardian, but the judge ruled against him. Rather than be sent to foster homes again, Arthur and the children raced from the courtroom. The book ends as the family is once more together and on their own. An unusual cast of characters in a surprisingly warm and humorous book.

Interest Level: 4-6. Reading Level 3.1. Further Search Topics: Loners-Fiction, Runaways-Fiction, Orphans-Fiction, Survival-Fiction, Family Problems-Fiction, Family-Fiction, Read Aloud, Foster Homes-Fiction, Individualists-Fiction, Humorous Fiction.

Bennett, Jay. The pigeon. Methuen 1980, 147 pp.

Despite a low testing score, this is not a truly easy book to read. The author assumes his readers are fairly sophisticated and worldly, thus he does not explain the meaning of the Iron Cross symbol or the word Aryan. The book's language varies from simple to difficult, making the reading level inconsistent (2.1 - 4.1). The setting is dark and forbidding; an underground world of fugitives and terrorists. And yet, the book will be popular with many readers in sixth grade; it will be even more popular with older readers. The tension in this story of a teenage boy, blamed for the murder of his ex-girlfriend, is almost palpable. Brian's flight from the police and his desire to find Donna's murderer take him directly into the midst of a ring of terrorists, for whom life has no meaning. In Brian's attempt to prove his innocence, two more lives are lost, but hundreds more are saved as Brian discovers and stops a bomb threat. The author has used riveting action, short, clipped sentences, and terse dialogue to create a very successful, highly suspenseful book. Print size is only moderate.

Interest Level: 6 . Reading Level: 3.2. Further Search Topics: Mystery and Detective Stories, Terrorism-Fiction, Murder-Fiction, Best Sellers, Crime-Fiction, Courage-Fiction, Survival-Fiction, Runaways-Fiction.

Bulla, Clyde Robert. White bird; illus by Leonard Weisgard. T Y Crowell 1966, 79 pp.

This book is meant for a special reader. It will not appeal to the reader who wants only action and excitement from a book. It is a story of complex human relationships and differing definitions of love. John Thomas lost his parents in a river accident when he was just a baby. His cradle had been pulled from the river and he had been raised by reclusive Luke Vail. Luke placed no trust in the world or in people outside his tiny valley home and so forbade John Thomas to have anything to do with either one. Luke didn't allow John Thomas a pet either because he thought that John Thomas would only be hurt when he no longer had the animal. Despite Luke's argument, when he found an injured white crow, John Thomas kept it and tended it until the crow was stolen by three strangers as Luke stood by. Angry at Luke as much as at the strangers, John Thomas ran away to search for the bird, but found that it had been shot. Far from being fruitless, however, John Thomas's trip out of the valley gave him an entirely different view of people than the one Luke had shown him. Upon a friend's encouragement, John Thomas returned to Luke to share that view.

Subtle and unusual, this book needs a mature, sensitive reader and/or discussion in order to be fully appreciated.

Interest Level: 4-6. Reading Level 2.1. Further Search Topics: Pets-Fiction, Orphans-Fiction, Runaways-Fiction, Birds-Fiction, Love-Fiction, Loners-Fiction, Courage-Fiction.

Byars, Betsy. The house of wings; illus by Daniel Schwarts. Viking Pr. 1972, 142 pp.

Sammy was the youngest of eight children. His parents were tired of raising children when Sammy was born, so they almost let Sammy raise himself. That meant that he grew up to be independent. It didn't mean it was any easier for Sammy to accept being left behind unexpectedly with his strange grandfather when his parents moved to Detroit. His reaction when his grandfather told him that his parents had gone was to deny it and to run away. He ran until he could run no more. When he stopped running, the old man stopped chasing him and they found a wild but blind crane in desperate need of help. Helping the crane heal and find the desire to live again taught Sammy and his grandfather respect and, most of all, love for each other.

The parallels between Sammy and the crane are strong but subtle. The story is a compelling one, but may need a brief introductory note to alleviate confusion in the first two chapters.

Interest Level: 5-6. Reading Level: 4.2. Further Search Topics: Grandparents-Fiction, Birds-Fiction, Family Problems-Fiction, Poverty-Fiction, Physically Handicapped-Fiction, Runaways-Fiction.

Clymer, Eleanor. Me and the Eggman; illus by David K. Stone. Dutton 1972, 57 pp.

As Donald's life became more and more miserable and as his chores and responsibilities around his small, overcrowded, urban apartment increased, he began to look for a way to escape. Thinking that if he could just get to the country, life would be better, Donald sneaked into a truck owned by a farmer who delivered eggs to the city. Not surprisingly the farmer, a sharp speaking, independent old man, was not at all happy to find Donald. Reluctantly, the Eggman, as the farmer was called, agreed to let Donald stay a week and help to work his rundown farm. The week stretched into a summer in which Donald learned to face and accept reality, to love the Eggman and to like himself.

This book is a surprisingly consistent success with reluctant readers, especially boys. Watch for the lack of quotation marks around the dialogue and the somewhat small print.

Interest Level: 3-6. Reading Level: 3.2. Further Search Topics: Family Problems-Fiction, Poverty-Fiction, Vacation-Fiction, Runaways-Fiction, Farm Life-Fiction, Best Sellers.

Clymer, Eleanor. Luke was there; illus by Diane de Groat. HR & W 1973, 74 pp.

Julius' father, uncle and finally his step-father had all walked out on him. Even his mother had left him, although she hadn't wanted to go. When his mother had been taken to the hospital, Julius and his younger brother Danny were sent to a children's home. Julius felt alone and cheated until he met a young, black, social worker named Luke. Luke liked and respected Julius and helped Julius learn to feel the same way about himself. When Luke, too, left Julius, Julius was so angry at the world that he stole food and then money. Afraid to go back to the children's home because he thought he'd be caught and punished, Julius ran away. It wasn't until he found an abandoned child, about Danny's age, who needed care, that Julius returned to the home. Luke was there when he arrived, just when Julius needed him most. Luke listened to Julius' unhappy feelings, arranged for him to see his mother and helped him begin to accept the fact that life is not always fair.

Julius tells his own story in a realistic, straight-forward book that will touch most readers. Only the lack of quotation marks and inadequate spacing between the lines may slow the reader.

Interest Level: 3-6. Reading Level: 2.2. Further Search Topics: Runaways-Fiction, Orphans-Fiction, Juvenile Delinquency-Fiction, Divorce and Separation-Fiction, Friendship-Fiction, Courage-Fiction, Survival-Fiction, Loneliness-Fiction, Best Sellers, Read Aloud.

Cone, Molly. The amazing memory of Harvey Bean; illus by Robert MacLean. HM 1980, 83 pp.

It had been a long time since Harvey had been happy. His memory was so bad that he was always in trouble at school. And now that his parents were separating, he had trouble at home, too. Because he thought that neither one of his parents wanted him he told each one that he was going to stay with the other and instead decided to spend the summer alone. A few hours after he left home, Harry ran into Mr. and Mrs. Katz and before he completely realized it, he was living with them.

Mr. Katz couldn't stand to see anything go to waste. He collected the usable food thrown out behind grocery stores, old furniture, tools, windows and more. Mrs. Katz, whose memory was just as bad as Harvey's, loved to cook, so she could always find a way to use the food. Everything else bulged from the house and garage into the driveway and yard. Harvey spent a happy summer learning to scavenge, eating well, learning not to worry about what others thought of him and even improving his memory. When his parents finally found him, Harvey realized that they really did want him, even if they were separated. He decided to live with his mother on weekdays, his father on weekends, and the Katzs during the summers.

The plot problems that are obvious to adult readers are ones that most young readers will be able to ignore (i.e. neither parent checks on Harvey for over two months). Young readers will enjoy the humor and realism of Harvey's pain, happiness and eventual

feeling of self-confidence and triumph. The ten short chapters, good-sized print and adequate space between the lines help lower the book's reading level to late fourth grade.

Interest Level: 3-6. Reading Level: 5.1. Further Search Topics: Loners-Fiction, Vacation-Fiction, Divorce and Separation-Fiction, Humorous Fiction, Group 2, Memory-Fiction, Runaways-Fiction, Academic Problems-Fiction, Individualists-Fiction.

Hinton, Susan E. The outsiders. Viking Pr. 1967, 188 pp.

When she wrote this book Susan Hinton was only 17 years old, but she had the sensitivity of someone much older. She wrote a taut story of the rivalry between two city gangs; the Socs (the rich socialites) and the Greasers (poor kids from the wrong side of town) that is more than anything a plea for understanding and tolerance. Seen through the eyes of Ponyboy (a very bright, 14-year-old Greaser), the rivalry brought on violence and an accidental killing that forced Pony and his friend Johnny to flee for their lives. Dallas, the meanest and most dangerous of the Greasers, provided them with shelter, food for a week, and a gun. At the end of that week, Johnny decided that they should turn themselves in to the police. But before they could do that, their hideout (an old church) burned in a fire which threatened the lives of four children who had been playing there. In trying to rescue the children, Johnny, Pony, and Dallas were injured; Johnny was severely burned and probably permanently crippled. A vengeance rumble was held while Johnny lay in the hospital, but the Greasers' victory was empty when Johnny died. He had been the one member of the gang whom they all loved and who had most needed them. Dallas went to pieces: he robbed a store and set himself up to be killed by the police. He had nothing left to live for after Johnny's death. Pony found support and security with his brothers (their parents were dead) and, in a note from Johnny, some hope for the future.

Hinton speaks most often through Pony (his depth of understanding of the people around him is very impressive), but through Johnny and two of the Socs as well, Randy and Cherry. Her message is clear, but at no time does she fail to maintain believable characters in a compelling plot.

Although the book looks forbidding with its 188 pages of unrelenting small print, it is an exciting story, full of adventure, realism, and room for thought. Perhaps the best way to introduce this book is to read a fair portion of it aloud. Now a motion picture too.

Interest Level: 6+ Reading Level: 5.1. Further Search Topics: Crime-Fiction, Gangs-Fiction, Murder-Fiction, Read Aloud, Friendship-Fiction, Juvenile Delinquency-Fiction, Best Sellers, City Life-Fiction, Brothers and Sisters-Fiction, Orphans-Fiction, Runaways-Fiction, Troublemakers-Fiction, Poverty-Fiction.

Parish, Peggy. Clues in the woods; illus by Paul Frame. Macmillan 1968, 154 pp.

The books about the three Roberts children share problems that are obvious to adults and felt by some young readers as well, but they continue to be popular with undemanding young readers. The characters are very white and middle class and their actions often fit out-of-date stereotypes. The plots have few surprises or suspense, but the reading levels are consistent and the very predictability of the books makes them familiar and therefore comfortable.

This particular story takes place at the end of the same summer the children solved the mystery of *The Key to the Treasure*. The children were alerted by their grandmother to the disappearance of food scraps, left outside the house. Thinking that two runaway children, about whom they had read, had taken the food, Liza, Bill, and Jed tried to find the runaways. Their attempts eventually brought them new friends and thus the solution to their mystery. It had not been the runaways who had taken the food, it was their new friends' dog.

Interest Level: 1-4. Reading Level: 2.2. Further Search Topics: Mystery and Detective Stories, Brothers and Sisters-Fiction, Vacation-Fiction, Dogs-Fiction, Runaways-Fiction, Grandparents-Fiction, Group 2.

Pevsner, Stella. And you give me a pain, Elaine. HM 1978, 182 pp.

Andrea was the youngest of three children. She was very close to her brother, Joe, but he was away at college. There was only Elaine at home, but Andrea and Elaine didn't get along at all. Elaine was a troubled young woman who took so much of her parents' attention that there was none left for Andrea. This is the story of Andrea's year in eighth grade, a year in which she discovered that she was a steady and strong person. It was the year in which Andrea worked on the school play, had her first boyfriend, weathered the storms when her sister ran away, and began to understand her sister more and resent her less. It was also the year that she had to learn to live with her brother's accidental death.

The author's Judy Blume style (but with less humor) guarantees readers among older children.

Interest Level: 5-6. Reading Level: 4.1. Further Search Topics: Family Problems-Fiction, Brothers and Sisters-Fiction, Love-Fiction, Death-Fiction, Runaways-Fiction, Troublemakers-Fiction, Adolescence-Fiction.

Renner, Beverly. The Hideaway summer; illus by Ruth Sanderson. Har-Row 1978, 134 pp.

On their way to summer camp, Addie suddenly got off the bus and took her younger brother Clay to see the place where Addie had spent prior summer vacations. It was their grandmother's house and a small cabin called the Hideaway. The house had been sold after their grandmother had died that year, but Addie's father had decided to keep the Hideaway. Much to Addie's surprise she found the Hideaway beautifully fixed-up, just as Gram had promised she would do one day.

When they missed the last bus out of the tiny town and realized that they had enough money to buy the food they would need, Addie and Clay decided to make the Hideaway their summer home. One phone call to the camp and weekly calls to their father kept people from worrying about them. Their discovery of two small raccoons meant that their days were filled with caring for and training the animals. In addition, they had to build a warning system so that no one would discover them and they had to get their food and provisions from town about every two weeks without being too noticeable. They even had to figure out a way to survive a wild summer storm, a flood, and poachers who hunted raccoons. By summer's end Addie and Clay had grown independent, resourceful, and very close to each other.

An exciting story whose short chapters and fairly short sentences keep the reading level reasonably low. Print is dark and of adequate size, but space between the lines is somewhat narrow.

Interest Level: 4-6. Reading Level: 3.1. Further Search Topics: Brothers and Sisters-Fiction, Runaways-Fiction, Pets-Fiction, Survival-Fiction, Vacation-Fiction, Raccoons-Fiction, Read Aloud.

Sharmat, Marjorie W. The Lancelot closes at five; illus by Lisl Weil. Macmillan 1976, 120 pp.

Despite a somewhat slow beginning, this is an amusing, almost sensitive story of two friends who decided to spend the night in the model home of the new housing development in which they both lived. Hutch, a health food fanatic whose mother pronounced judgment on everything Hutch did, conceived of the idea as her way of breaking away. Abby went along for the fun of it. When the local newspaper wrote of unusual vandalism at the model home, the townspeople became engrossed in finding the culprits. As the adults became enraged about the crime wave, their children began to admire the clever idea. Soon, almost every youngster in town had confessed to spending the night in the model home. By the time Abby and Hutch got around to admitting they had slept there, no one believed them. Only a sock with Abby's name in it could tie Abby and Hutch to the scene of the crime. As the book ends, the police have begun a thorough search of the house, after a real robbery, and the sock's discovery is imminent.

Interest Level: 4-6. Reading Level: 3.2. Further Search Topics: Humorous Fiction, Suburbia-Fiction, Runaways-Fiction, Crime-Fiction, Individualists-Fiction, Family Problems-Fiction.

Smith, Doris Buchanan. Tough Chauncey. Morrow 1974, 222 pp.

Chauncey Childs had taught himself to be tough— very tough. Even though he was small for his age (13 years old), the only person who gave him any trouble was his sometimes-friend, Black Jack Levitt. Everyone else was scared of Chauncey. Chauncey felt that he had to be tough or he wouldn't be able to survive. He had to be tough to stand the beatings his grandfather gave him "for his own good," to put up with his mother's drinking and disappearances, and to stand the sight of his grandfather shooting the stray kittens born in their garage.

Chauncey's greatest wish was to be able to live with his mother, instead of with his grandparents. In a desperate attempt to achieve that end he accidentally fell from a moving train and badly hurt his leg. Instead of being returned to his mother he was once more taken back to his grandparents. Chauncey's unhappiness grew until he finally decided to take the one surviving stray kitten and run away. Jack helped him find an empty garage where he could hide while he figured out what to do with his future. After talking with Jack and doing more deep soul searching, Chauncey decided to reshape himself and his life. His first step was to curb his temper and his tongue when his hiding place was discovered. His second step was to see about finding a foster home where he would be treated well, and where he could get a new start.

Ugly as the story is in places, its ending is hopeful. Although it is not always realistic, Chauncey's story is compelling enough to appeal to many readers, especially those who have enjoyed *The War on Villa Street*, by Henry Mazer, *The Outsiders*, by Susan Hinton, or *Mystery of the Fat Cat*, by Frank Bonham. The book's length and its artificially low reading level (vocabulary is often difficult but sentences are very short) make this book most appropriate for an older reader whose reading level is 4.1 or higher.

Interest Level: 5-6. Reading Level: 3.2. Further Search Topics: Child Abuse-Fiction, Family Problems-Fiction, Grandparents-Fiction, Runaways-Fiction, Bullies-Fiction, Single Parent Family-Fiction, Loners-Fiction, Friendship-Fiction, Troublemakers-Fiction, Foster Homes-Fiction.

Talbot, Charlene Joy. The Great Rat Island adventure; illus by Ruth Sanderson. Atheneum 1977, 164 pp.

Joel dreaded spending the summer with his father. His parents were divorced and Joel was sure his father didn't want him. His father only wanted to study birds. Great Rat Island, where Joel and his father were to spend the summer, was of no interest to Joel. It had no television, no one his own age, only terns. Even the assignment Joel was given (to make sure that no more tern eggs were stolen) sounded dull. It led to an adventure and a friend, however, that were anything but dull.

Joel discovered that a girl his own age was the thief of the tern eggs. Her name was Vicky Owens. She had run away from camp and was spending the summer alone on Little Rat Island. Joel kept her secret until the day of hurricane warnings. As the storm approached Joel realized that Vicky wouldn't be safe on Little Rat Island. Without telling anyone else he took the only boat around and went to look for Vicky to bring her back to Great Rat Island. He found her with her leg stuck between two rocks, unable to move. By the time Joel got her loose, it was too late to get back to the big island. Not knowing what else to do, Joel and Vicky dragged the boat inside an abandoned building where Vicky had been living. As the water rose around them and Vicky grew delirious with fever, Joel set up camp in the boat. While the building filled with water they stayed dry in the boat. Rescue and medical care for Vicky finally came the next day.

A solid, steadily-paced survival story for the reader who wants a little more than just an adventure story. Print is small.

Interest Level: 4-6. Reading Level: 3.1. Further Search Topics: Vacation-Fiction, Family Problems-Fiction, Birds-Fiction, Divorce and Separation-Fiction, Disasters-Fiction, Survival-Fiction, Runaways-Fiction.

Waldorf, Mary. Jake McGee and his feet; illus by Leonard Shortall. HM 1980, 82 pp.

His severe reading difficulties made school the worst place in the world for Jake McGee. On the day that his reading tutor became so impatient with him that she sent Jake to the principal, Jake decided that he couldn't stand school any longer and ran away. He didn't actually run away, he just let his feet finally do what they wanted. His feet were always getting Jake in trouble. They walked too slowly to get him to school on time; they wouldn't stay still once he was in school; and they were always trying to trip someone.

Jake knew that in addition to having problems with his feet he had reading problems, but no one at his old school in the country had noticed. When he and his family moved to the city everything had changed. Jake's mother was always at work or tired. Jake hadn't made any friends and so was always alone. But Jake thought the biggest of all his immediate problems was his feet. The day he ran away, Jake's feet led him to a lost baby, an eccentric old woman, and a neighbor boy, all of whom helped Jake recognize and deal with his real problem.

The book is not high literary quality. The characterization is somewhat flat and the plot is fairly predictable. However, the sentences and chapters are short, the vocabulary is manageable, and Jake's feelings will be shared by many non-readers.

Interest Level: 3-5. Reading Level: 2.2. Further Search Topics: School Stories, Moving, Household-Fiction, Runaways-Fiction, Academic Problems-Fiction, Working Parents-Fiction, Loneliness-Fiction, Feet-Fiction.

Warner, Gertrude Chandler. The boxcar children; illus by L. Kate Deal. A. Whitman 1950, 154 pp.

This is the first in a series of very early hi/lo books. Although they often bear signs of stilted "Dick and Jane"-style writing, occasionally preach to the reader, and are interrupted by frequent asides from the author, the stories are still popular with young readers. In each book the children are not simply manipulated, but control their own destiny. They fulfill many a child's dream of finding a loving home and family, becoming rich, having adventures, and solving mysteries. This is the simplest story of the series, most of the other entries assume interest in such advanced subjects as fossils, food sources, antiques, or the Revolutionary War.

The only place the four orphaned Alden children had to live was with a grandfather whom they had never met, but whom they had heard was mean. Rather than live with him, they decided to try and survive on their own. They found an abandoned railway boxcar and filled it was items that they found in a junkyard in order to make it their home. Henry, the oldest, went to work for a doctor who, in addition to money, gave him food and kept a silent but watchful eye over all the children without their knowledge. When Violet became ill, the children had no choice but to take her to Dr. Moore. He gave them all a temporary home and arranged for them to gradually get to know their grandfather. By the time Violet was almost well the children had grown to like the elderly stranger. It was a happy day when the children finally realized that the man to whom Dr. Moore had introduced them was really their grandfather.

Interest Level: 1-4. Reading Level: 2.1. Further Search Topics: Orphans-Fiction, Survival-Fiction, Runaways-Fiction, Brothers and Sisters-Fiction, Grandparents-Fiction.

Yolen, Jane. The boy who spoke chimp illus by David Wiesner. Knopf 1981, 120 pp.

Kriss was determined to prove to his father that, at 12 years old, he was perfectly capable of camping out by himself. To do so, he left home and headed up the coast of California with a sleeping bag, some food, a map and compass, and water. His plan was to camp, ride, and hike his way to his grandmother's house. On the way, the coast line was torn apart by the second great earthquake to strike California. The first had already destroyed great portions of the state. The second was even stronger. The truck he had been riding in was destroyed and everyone around Kriss was killed by the quake except for two chimpanzees. The chimps, in transit from one lab to another, were research animals who had been taught to use sign language. Kriss took the animals with him as he tried to get farther inland and finally home to Los Angeles. His trip not only confirmed his father's fears about Kriss' inadequacies but taught him how to overcome them. Kriss learned to communicate with the chimps, to find food and to live on his own until Old Chris, a hermit, happened along. Together they continued to brave the chaos brought about by the earthquake even when Old Chris' heart troubled him. When a helicopter finally spotted them, Kriss decided to let the chimps go wild and promised Old Chris that he would be back in the woods very soon. It was a mature, capable Kriss who returned home.

This is typical of the Capers series—much action, few background details, little characterization. The books, however, are on appealing topics; they move quickly and they create intriguing (if sometimes implausible) situations. They are light, enjoyable and very useful. Capers series.

Interest Level: 3-6. Reading Level: 3.1. Further Search Topics: California-Fiction, Disasters-Fiction, Survival-Fiction, Apes-Fiction, Nonverbal Communication-Fiction, Camping-Fiction, Runaways-Fiction, Best Sellers.

RUNNING-BIOGRAPHY

Fall, Thomas. Jim Thorpe; illus by John Gretzer. Har-Row 1970, 33 pp.

Jim Thorpe was an Indian from the Oklahoma territory who became one of the United State's greatest athletes. He and his twin brother were trained by their father to run and jump faster and farther than anyone else. When Charles died, Jim couldn't face returning to school without his twin, so his family kept him home for a few months before sending him away to school again. Jim ran home once more when his father and mother both became ill. Months later he went to still another school where he was noticed by Pop Warner. Pop advised Joe to concentrate on track until he was big enough to play football. His father's death left Jim so despondent he quit school to play professional baseball for a while. By the time he went back to school, Jim was big enough to play spectacular football and then to win the 1912 Olympic decathlon competition. Unfortunately, his short time as a paid baseball player made him ineligible for the Olympic honor and Jim's medal was taken away. Public sentiment was with Jim, but the rules were against him. He went on, however, to play both professional baseball and football. In 1982, 29 years after his death, Thorpe's medal was finally returned to him.

A short, meaty and readable biography of a person who should be interesting to many sports fans. Follows the usual format of Crowell biographies, but looks less like a picture book than many. Crowell Biography series.

Interest Level: 3-5. Reading Level: 3.1. Further Search Topics: Football-Biography, Indians of North America-Biography, Baseball-Biography, Olympic Games, Biography, Running-Biography, Twins-Biography.

RUNNING-FICTION

Coerr, Eleanor. Sadako and the thousand paper cranes; illus by Ronand Himler. Putnam 1977, 64 pp.

This is a beautiful and very sad story of a young girl who was only two years old when the atomic bomb was dropped on Hiroshima. Ten years later she contracted leukemia and died a slow, painful death. A fast and enthusiastic runner, she had been full of life and energy before her illness. Soon after she became sick Sadako's best friend folded a paper crane for her and reminded her of an old story: If someone folded 1000 paper cranes, the gods would give that person good health again. Sadako was able to fold only 644 before she died. After her death her classmates made 356 more in order that she could be buried with all 1000 paper cranes. About three years later, a statue, erected in Peace Park in Hiroshima, was dedicated to Sadako and to a hope for world peace.

Because of the theme and its straight-forward handling, this book needs a fairly mature reader.

Interest Level: 4-6. Reading Level: 3.1. Further Search Topics: Japan-Fiction, Historical Fiction, World War II-Fiction, Death-Fiction, Illness-Fiction, War-Fiction, Running-Fiction, Origami-Fiction, Read Aloud.

Greene, Constance C. Isabelle the itch; illus by Emily A. McCully. Viking Pr. 1973, 126 pp.

This is a loosely plotted story about a spunky, original fifth grade girl who could drive everyone around her crazy without ever tiring. Isabelle's dearest dream was to win the 50-yard dash at her school's field day. Even though she took over her brother's paper route to earn money for the Adidas track shoes she needed, Isabelle still didn't win. However, she did meet some new people, make new friends and keep those around her on their toes. A very amusing story told mostly in dialogue.

Interest Level: 4-6. Reading Level: 3.2. Further Search Topics: School Stories, Occupations-Fiction, Humorous Fiction, Everyday Stories, Running-Fiction, Individualists-Fiction, Sex Role-Fiction, Read Aloud.

Heide, Florence Parry. Body in the Brillstone garage. A. Whitman 1980, 127 pp.

Liza's trip into the apartment house garage late one night made her even more frightened of that dark area than she had been. As she bent to pick up an envelope she thought someone had dropped, she saw a body lying on the floor of the garage. Because of a jacket he wore, Liza was certain the dead man was Mr. Greening, a neighbor. But when she returned to the garage with the police, the body was gone. The next day Mr. Greening was very much alive. Then Liza began to suspect that Mr. Greening was a murderer, but she didn't know who or where the victim was. It could have been Mr. Feeney, another neighbor, or it might have been a stranger. When Mr. Greening's stolen car was later discovered with the body of the car thief inside, Liza began to suspect that the thief's body was the one she had discovered. When she was told that the thief's name was Sharkey, she was certain Mr. Greening had engineered Sharkey's death. Sharkey was the name used by an angry man who had said he was looking for someone at the Brillstone who owed him something.

About then Liza remembered to look in the envelope she had found in the garage. The envelope revealed a note from Sharkey to Greening stating that Sharkey had proof that Greening was a car thief and that he would keep quiet only if Greening paid him twice the money he was owed. Knowing that without proof, she couldn't convince the police that Greening was a crook, Liza went to get the proof from Sharkey's hiding place in the about-to-be-junked car. Greening followed Liza to see what she knew and made a desperate attempt to kill her when he realized that she knew enough to put him in prison. At the last minute, Logan appeared, accidentally knocked Greening out, and helped Liza prove Greening's guilt to the police.

This is a fast-paced book that should be useful with mystery readers who can handle the jump from 4.1 to an occasional 5.1 reading level. See notes included with *Black Magic at Brillstone* for more information. Brillstone Mystery series.

Interest Level: 4-6. Reading Level: 4.2. Further Search Topics: Mystery and Detective Stories, Murder-Fiction, Running-Fiction, Crime-Fiction, Detectives-Fiction.

Mazer, Harry. The war on Villa Street. Delacorte 1978, 182 pp.

Willis was a loner and a runner. He was a loner because he didn't want anyone to find out about his alcoholic father. He wasn't quite sure why he ran; perhaps because it was the only time he felt good. When Rabbit Slavin and his friends asked Willis to become part of their gang, he refused. He was flattered and wanted to join, but the gang wanted to meet at his house and Willis couldn't risk that. Then when he agreed to coach the local "retard" for the school's field day, Willis gave the gang the opportunity they wanted to take their revenge on him for turning them down. The gang's hatred for Willis increased still more when he beat their best runner and athlete. In payment, the gang jumped Willis and beat him badly. After he picked himself up, Willis realized that he had at least faced the worst of his fears and survived. Days later when his drunken father humiliated him, Willis realized he had to face that, too. He made peace with himself and the world by deciding he could neither continue to run away from, nor apologize for his father anymore. He was independent and strong.

There is much in this fast-paced book besides the obvious violence and action. It is written with an intuitive feel for a teenager's problems and emotions and is a sensitive portrayal of mature concepts. The print is large, but spacing between the lines should have been slightly increased.

Interest Level: 5-6. Reading Level: 5.1. Further Search Topics: Running-Fiction, Loneliness-Fiction, Alcoholism-Fiction, Loners-Fiction, Mental Retardation-Fiction, Gangs-Fiction, Child Abuse-Fiction, Bullies-Fiction, Family Problems-Fiction, Courage-Fiction.

Platt, Kin. Brogg's brain. Lippincott 1981, 123 pp.

According to everyone else, Monty Davis should have been one of the fastest milers in the city. He had, after all, run a four minute and ten second mile in practice one day. He had run well enough that day to beat his high school's two best milers. That was a good enough performance to make the coach push him, his teacher talk about winning, and his father puff up with pride. Even the marathon runner he saw occasionally in the park and his girl friend Cindy seemed to think that he could be the best. Monty really didn't care, or he thought he didn't. Maybe he was just afraid to see how good or bad he really was. For whatever reason, he didn't want to run in the meet against Culver High School. He talked so much about not doing well, that by the time he was supposed to run, he even had his coach convinced he couldn't win. But as he ran, Monty heard a voice inside his head that sounded like the voice in a strange science fiction film that he and Cindy had just seen. The voice seemed to say that he could win, and suddenly that was what Monty wanted. The voice and his new-found determination were what pulled Monty through and gave him first place.

This book is for the track fan or the runner. Few others are likely to care about the difference between a four-twenty and a four-ten high school mile. For those who do care, this is a good choice.

Interest Level: 5-6. Reading Level: 3.1. Further Search Topics: Family Problems-Fiction, Love-Fiction, Running-Fiction, Courage-Fiction.

Platt, Kin. Run for your life; photos by Chuck Freedman. Watts 1977, 95 pp.

Lee almost lost his newspaper delivery job when someone began to regularly steal money and papers from the newspaper boxes along his route. Lee saw a chance for revenge if he could beat the thief in the mile race at the next track meet.

Most of the abundant dialogue is slang. The romantic interest is innocent and low keyed. The story has enough running to make that a strong appeal, but not so much that no one but a track or running enthusiast can enjoy it.

Interest Level: 5-6. Reading Level: 2.2. Further Search Topics: Running-Fiction, Love-Fiction, Occupations-Fiction, Crime-Fiction.

RUSSIA-FICTION

Dolch, Edward W. Stories from Old Russia; illus by James Lewicki. Garrard 1964, 168 pp.

There are 21 chapters and only nine stories in this volume. These are more robust and exciting adventure stories than many of the other Dolch collections listed here, although once again the simplified vocabulary is somewhat restrictive. A guide to pronounciation of some Russian names is included at the end of the book. More colorful illustrations than some of the other titles. Very consistent reading level. See Stories From France for more information. Folklore of the World series.

Interest Level: 2-6. Reading Level: 2.1. Further Search Topics: Folklore, Fantasy, Russia-Fiction, Witches-Fiction.

Ginsburg, Mirra. The lazies; illus by Marian Parry. Macmillan 1973, 70 pp.

A good collection of 15 short Russian folktales all having to do with laziness. Most are humorous tales; few are well-known. In just under a third of the stories the humor may be too subtle even for older elementary school children; however, the rest of the stories can be enjoyed by almost any child between third and sixth grade. ("Who Will Wash the Pot," "Easy Bread," "Who Will Row Next," and "The Princess Who Learned to Work" are the questionable stories). Print somewhat small.

Interest Level: 3-6. Reading Level: 3.1. Further Search Topics: Folklore, Humorous Fiction, Laziness-Fiction, Russia-Fiction.

SALAMANDERS

Allen, Gertrude. Everyday turtles, toads and their kin. HM 1970, 48 pp.

Straight-forward, short, chapter discussions of turtles, lizards, snakes, salamanders, toads, frogs and tree toads. Black and white drawings done by the author amplify the text. The major part of the book is simple enough to be understood at second grade, but should still be interesting to fourth and fifth graders. A few terms may need explanation: i.e., venomous, prey. The chapters on the turtle, lizard, frog and tree frog are the easiest. No index, but still useful for reports.

Interest Level: 2-5. Reading Level: 2.2. Further Search Topics: Turtles, Reptiles, Lizards, Toads, Frogs, Snakes, Salamanders.

SCHOOL STORIES

Blume, Judy. Are you there God? It's me, Margaret. Bradbury 1970, 149 pp.

Sixth grade was a year of growth for Margaret and her friends. They all wondered when they would start growing breasts and when they would begin menstruating. Each was kissed for the first time. It was also a year in which Margaret tried to decide whether to be Jewish or Christian and ended up neither. She simply remained friends with God, just as she was when the year began. The book is a reassuring, very open, and humorous treatment of the pains and promise of maturation. It is exceptionally popular with older elementary school readers, so the book's slightly small print and narrow lines should not impede an interested reader's progress.

Interest Level: 4-6. Reading Level: 3.2. Further Search Topics: School Stories, Family-Fiction, Children-Growth-Fiction, Religion-Fiction, Humorous Fiction, Love-Fiction, Best Sellers, Grandparents-Fiction, Everyday Stories.

Blume, Judy. Blubber. Bradbury 1974, 153 pp.

Jill, like all the other fifth graders in her class, did exactly as Wendy directed her. When Wendy nicknamed one of the class members Blubber and launched a campaign against her, Jill joined right in. It wasn't until the tables were turned and Jill became Wendy's next victim that Jill realized how much it hurt to be the target of such nastiness. It was only then that Jill could stand up to Wendy. Wendy's meanness is extreme and her classmates, without exception, actively follow her lead, yet all adult characters in the book are blind to what happens. Despite those drawbacks, the book deals with a problem very real to children and thus it has guaranteed audience appeal.

Interest Level: 4-6. Reading Level: 3.1. School Stories, Bullies-Fiction, Weight-Fiction, Loners-Fiction, Gangs-Fiction, Read Aloud, Cruelty-Fiction, Best Sellers, Troublemakers-Fiction, Friendship-Fiction.

Blume, Judy. Superfudge. Dutton 1980, 166 pp.

On Fudge's first day in school his older brother Peter had to rescue him from the top of the kindergarten storage cabinets. Later in the school year Fudge's eagerness to join a school guest speaker on stage almost spelled disaster. Then when Fudge unexpectedly disappeared one day everyone, including Peter, thought he had drowned. In addition to Peter's problems with Fudge, Peter had to cope with a baby sister, moving to Princeton, New Jersey, a new job for his mother, and his father's attempts to write a book. Although the book is a sequel and is best enjoyed as such, it can be read alone. It is not as amusing or well-written as it's predecessor, *Tales of a Fourth Grade Nothing*, but will still be popular with young readers.

Interest Level: 3-6. Reading Level 3.1. Further Search Topics: Brothers and Sisters-Fiction, Moving, Household-Fiction, Infants-Fiction, Working Parents-Fiction, School Stories, Family-Fiction, Best Sellers, Humorous Fiction, Everyday Stories.

Blume, Judy. Freckle juice; illus by Sonia O. Lisker. Four Winds 1971, 40 pp.

A very funny story that should appeal to almost everyone. Andrew wanted freckles so that the dirt on his skin wouldn't show as much and he wouldn't have to wash as often. As luck would have it, Sharon, the most obnoxious girl in class, had a freckle juice recipe that she was willing to sell for 50 cents. Even after drinking the brew of grape juice, vinegar, mustard, olive oil, and more, Andrew didn't see any freckles, but, he certainly was sick. Although the protagonists are younger, this book will hold even a fifth grade reader's interest.

Interest Level: 2-5. Reading Level 3.1. Further Search Topics: Humorous Fiction, Group 2, Read Aloud, Everyday Stories, Beauty-Fiction, School Stories, Magic-Fiction, Best Sellers.

Byars, Betsy. The Cybil war; illus by Gail Owens. Viking Pr. 1981, 126 pp.

Simon and Tony both had a crush on Cybil, but according to Tony, Cybil liked Tony better than she liked Simon. Simon was unhappily willing to accept Tony's word even though he knew Tony was a chronic liar. After all, Cybil had been the one to talk their teacher out of giving the lead in the class play about nutrition to Simon. Consequently Simon was being forced to impersonate a jar of peanut butter. In an elaborate attempt to win Cybil's affection Tony began telling Cybil lies about Simon and then set up a double date with Cybil and Harriet. On their walk home, Simon learned from Harriet that Cybil had only agreed to the date because Simon was going along. Happy at last, Simon realized he wanted no more lies and tricks; that he wanted to be truthful with Cybil and with himself. In the name of truth, he was even willing to accept the fact that his father, who had deserted the family, would not be returning.

A good story with just enough humor and romance to make it widely appealing as either a shared book (read aloud) or a personal pick. Print is fairly small.

Interest Level: 5-6. Reading Level: 4.2. Further Search Topics: Humorous Fiction, Love-Fiction, School Stories, Honesty-Fiction, Friendship-Fiction, Single Parent Family-Fiction, Read Aloud, Everyday Stories, Adolescence-Fiction.

Cleary, Beverly. Otis Spofford; illus by Louis Darling. Morrow 1953, 191 pp.

Here are six separate humorous adventures that link together, but can be read separately and out of order. Otis' favorite activity was "stirring up a little excitement," but his definition of excitement usually meant trouble. The school fiesta turned into a disaster when Otis decided to rechoreograph the bullfight and make the bull win. His attempt to liven up the reading lesson about Indians meant he almost scalped a classmate. However, a wild day at the skating pond finally gave everyone a chance to take revenge for all the things Otis had done to them. The remaining three chapters (2, 3 and 4) are slightly less exciting, but useful if a reader has enjoyed the others. There is much humor in Otis' antics and his tendency to act on every thought that comes to mind is one many readers can appreciate.

Interest Level: 2-6. Reading Level: 5.1. Further Search Topics: Troublemakers-Fiction, Group 2, Read Aloud, Everyday Stories, Humorous Fiction, School Stories.

Conford, Ellen. The revenge of the incredible Dr. Rancid and his youthful assistant, Jeffrey. Little 1980, 119 pp.

There were two people Jeff hated and feared: Dewey Belasco, the sixth grade bully and Lana McCabe, Dewey's female counterpart. Only in his imagination could Jeff stand up to them. In the stories Jeff wrote in a notebook, he and his friend Dr. Rancid were superheroes who rid the world of such scum as Lana and Dewey. In real life, Jeff ran from bullies rather than face them; even if it meant that an eight-year-old boy and a girl Jeff's age were left to stand up to Dewey by themselves. Although the way Jeff took care of an injured child soon had most everyone thinking of Jeff as a hero, he saw that, too, as an indication of his failings at first. Finally, something inside Jeff snapped and he answered Dewey back when Dewey insulted him. Before long Jeff found himself flat on his back with a bloody nose and so many pains he couldn't count them. But, he had finally faced Dewey and showed Dewey that he was no longer afraid. Jeff felt good.

Similar to *The 18th Emergency* but a higher reading level. The notebook stories will appeal to fans of superheroes, but because they are stories within a story, they may also cause difficulties. Spacing between lines is somewhat narrow.

Interest Level: 5-6. Reading Level: 4.2. Further Search Topics: Courage-Fiction, Bullies-Fiction, Writing-Fiction, School Stories, Superheroes-Fiction, Humorous Fiction.

Curtis, Philip. The invasion of the Brain Sharpeners; illus by Tony Ross. Knopf 1979, 117 pp.

This book is one of a number of books published by Albert Knopf under the series title Capers. They are meant to be (and with few exceptions are) light, easy-to-read fiction, published simultaneously in hardcover and paperback editions. Each book is about 120 pages long with chapter length varying from 9 to 14 pages. Print is plenty large and spacing between lines is always adequate. Plots are built around an idea of guaranteed appeal, descriptive passages are kept to a minimum and action (often suspenseful) abounds. This should, on the whole, be a very useful series. Some entries (i.e., *Man From the Sky* and *Who Stole the Wizard of Oz*, both by Avi) are either too difficult or too obscure to be widely appealing, but they are by far the exceptions to the rule.

Invasion of the Brain Sharpeners is the catchy science fiction story of Michael's successful, but risky, attempt to rid his fifth grade classroom of the overpowering influence of the Brain Sharpeners. The Brain Sharpeners came from another galaxy to search for humans to help them colonize their Planet Five. Humans were so lacking in brain power that the Brain Sharpeners' plan was to periodically expose each child to brain-developing rays, then put them through intensive courses of study guided by their also-exposed teacher. When the children had all learned enough to be beneficial to the Brain Sharpeners, they were to be taken from Earth to Planet Five. Michael was the only one to see the danger they were in and to attempt to stop the plot. He managed to chase the aliens away and to prevent his classmates and teacher from receiving their second dose of rays, but in doing so, he sent the principal to the spaceship. Michael's classmates were thus saved, but his principal was never heard from again. Capers series.

Interest Level: 3-6. Reading Level: 3.1. Further Search Topics: Science Fiction, Flying Saucers-Fiction, Aliens-Fiction, School Stories, Kidnapping-Fiction, Best Sellers, Academic Problems-Fiction, Brainwashing-Fiction.

Danziger, Paula. The cat ate my gymsuit. Delacorte 1974, 147 pp.

Another book for fans of Judy Blume. Marcy was shy and insecure, unhappy at school and unhappy at home. She was self-conscious about being heavy and sure she would never have a date. Only Ms. Finney (a new teacher), her English class and Smedley (a communications group) meant anything to Marcy. When Ms. Finney was fired because of her refusal to recite the pledge of allegiance and her unorthodox teaching methods, Marcy began to organize a protest movement. Marcy's commitment brought more problems at school and at home, but eventually resulted in Ms. Finney's vindication and Marcy's and her mother's growth and understanding.

Don't expect much depth of characterization. Most of the characters are flat and stereotypical, but the book will have great appeal in spite of its faults, for Marcy's insecurities are ones with which many young readers can identify.

Interest Level: 5-6. Reading Level: 5.1. Further Search Topics: School Stories, Everyday Stories, Family Problems-Fiction, Challenges-Fiction, Weight-Fiction, Courage-Fiction, Individualists-Fiction, Sex Role-Fiction.

Danziger, Paula. The pistachio prescription. Delacorte 1978 154 pp.

Just as Cassie entered her freshman year in high school, the old stand-by that had helped her deal with all her problems (eating pistachio nuts) began to fail. To be sure, she did get through the class elections and was elected president. She met and started dating Bernie. She gained self-confidence. She even managed to stand up to a particularly mean teacher. But, eating pistachios didn't help at all at home where Cassie really needed them. She could hardly stand to be in the same room with her older sister. She hated the importance her mother placed on looking right and dressing well. Most of all, she hated the way her parents were constantly fighting. The only person with whom she was really confortable was her brother. But, before the year was over, Cassie's parents decided to get a divorce, she and her sister became friends and Cassie learned to accept her family.

Another Judy Blume-style author, but Danziger's portraits of adults tend to be even more one-dimensional and exaggerated than Blume's. Very popular anyway.

Interest Level: 6+ Reading Level: 5.1. Further Search Topics: Divorce and Separation-Fiction, Family Problems-Fiction, Beauty-Fiction, School Stories, Adolescence-Fiction, Love-Fiction, Brothers and Sisters-Fiction, Everyday Stories.

Greene, Constance C. Isabelle the itch; illus by Emily A. McCully. Viking Pr. 1973, 126 pp.

This is a loosely plotted story about a spunky, original fifth grade girl who could drive everyone around her crazy without ever tiring. Isabelle's dearest dream was to win the 50-yard dash at her school's field day. Even though she took over her brother's paper route to earn money for the Adidas track shoes she needed, Isabelle still didn't win. However, she did meet some new people, make new friends and keep those around her on their toes. A very amusing story told mostly in dialogue.

Interest Level: 4-6. Reading Level: 3.2. Further Search Topics: School Stories, Occupations-Fiction, Humorous Fiction, Everyday Stories, Running-Fiction, Individualists-Fiction, Sex Role-Fiction. Read Aloud.

Hurwitz, Johanna. Aldo Applesauce; illus by John Wallner. Morrow 1979, 127 pp.

Aldo Sossi, vegetarian and new kid at school, was immediately dubbed Applesauce for obvious reasons. Aldo didn't like his new name. He didn't like being teased either—not the way he was teased at school. Nothing went right for Aldo. His attempts at making friends only ended in disasters (once at a bowling alley and another time at a birthday party). He had been able to start a friendship only with a strange girl who wore a heavy, black fake moustache most of the time. After accidentally nearly ruining that friendship too, Aldo not only learned why DeDe wore the moustache, but helped her learn to live without it. DeDe, in turn, helped Aldo take himself less seriously and find more friends.

This is a comfortable, humorous story of two fourth grade children learning to be themselves. The vocabulary is occasionally difficult, but sentence length is almost always short.

Interest Level: 3-5. Reading Level: 3.1. Further Search Topics: Moving, Household-Fiction, Humorous Fiction, School Stories, Friendship-Fiction, Divorce and Separation-Fiction, Vegetarians-Fiction, Individualists-Fiction, Everyday Stories.

Kelley, Sally. Trouble with explosives. Bradbury 1976, 117 pp.

Polly Banks stuttered very badly. She wanted to stop but she couldn't. Moving, entering a new school, and facing a mean teacher who seemed in need of psychiatric help, all made Polly's stuttering worse. When Sis, Polly's new friend, rose to Polly's defense in one confrontation too many with Miss Patterson, the teacher took cruel revenge. Polly's desire to help Sis, her need to do something about her stuttering, and an understanding psychiatrist, all helped Polly learn to help herself with her speech problem. At the same time, she began to understand and have confidence in herself and her family.

Another "problem book" that older elementary school readers seem to crave. Polly and Sis are both very sympathetic characters who bring to life many of the uncertainties of growing up. Print and line spacing of only average size but otherwise a good choice.

Interest Level: 4-6. Reading Level: 3.2. Further Search Topics: Academic Problems-Fiction, Stuttering-Fiction, Psychiatrists-Fiction, School Stories, Mental Illness-Fiction, Troublemakers-Fiction, Courage-Fiction, Physically Handicapped-Fiction, Children-Growth-Fiction, Moving, Household-Fiction.

Miles, Betty. The secret life of the underwear champ; illus by Dan Jones. Knopf 1981, 117 pp.

Larry hadn't planned it; in fact, he hadn't even really wanted it to happen. But suddenly he found himself about to make a television commercial for ChampWin Knitting Mills, makers of sports clothing and underwear. He knew his family could use the money he would make, but he certainly didn't want the whole school seeing him in his underwear. Nevertheless, Larry went ahead and made the commercial, hoping that it would never be used. He even had to skip baseball practice to make the taping. Much to his horror, the commercial appeared the night before the team's first game. Not only did the entire opposing team tease him, but so did all his own teammates. By the time he got up to bat, Larry was mad enough to slam the ball out of the park. He didn't hit the ball quite that hard, but he did make a winning home run and end the others' giggles forever. He became the true underwear champ.

This is a funny look at the embarrassments of growing up. It also deals lightly with a boy's pride, his peer relationship, and his growing awareness of girls. An appealing and broadly usable title. Capers series.

Interest Level: 3-5. Reading Level: 2.2. Further Search Topics: Baseball-Fiction, Television-Fiction, Occupations-Fiction, School Stories, Humorous Fiction, Advertising-Fiction, Beauty-Fiction, Motion Pictures-Fiction, Best Sellers, Everyday Stories.

Moore, Lilian. The snake that went to school; illus by Mary Stevens. Random 1957, 99 pp.

Hank's pet snake Puffy disappeared from the Science Room at school and his little brother, Benjy (in first grade) became ill on the same day. Hank was so worried about finding Puffy that he hardly thought about his pesky little brother, until Puffy was found two days later. Then Hank learned that Benjy had secretly gone to visit Puffy, after being rejected by Hank and had accidentally let the snake out of its cage. Benjy had been so worried about letting the

snake out that he had actually made himself ill. Hank finally realized that Benjy wasn't the pest he had thought he was, and promised to be a better older brother.

A somewhat old-fashioned but satisfying story told in ten short chapters.

Interest Level: 2-4. Reading Level: 3.1. Further Search Topics: Pets-Fiction, Snakes-Fiction, Brothers and Sisters-Fiction, School Stories.

Peck, Robert Newton. Mr. Little; illus by Ben Stahl. Doubleday 1979, 87 pp.

All summer long Drag and Finley had looked forward to having Miss Kellogg as their teacher, so they were extremely disappointed to find ordinary-looking Mr. Little in her place on the first day of school. Used to playing tricks on their teachers anyway, Drag and Finley decided to go all out to get even with Mr. Little for spoiling their year. But try as they might, they couldn't get an advantage over Mr. Little; he seemed to be unflappable. Finally, in their riskiest prank ever, they stole Mr. Little's underwear to dress a statue in the town square. That attempt to embarrass Mr. Little only served to get Finley and Drag in serious trouble from which Mr. Little saved them. It was his later rescue of Miss Kellogg, however, that added respect to the boys' growing feeling of friendship for Mr. Little.

Because the author's adult viewpoint is never quite lost, even though he writes in the first person, and because the rural and historic time settings are not familiar to many readers, the book may need some introduction and encouragement. It is a prime candidate for reading aloud until the young reader's interest takes over. Print is of adequate size, but spacing between lines could have been more generous.

Interest Level: 4-6. Reading Level: 5.1. Further Search Topics: Humorous Fiction, School Stories, Troublemakers-Fiction, Group 2, Read Aloud, Country Life-Fiction, Best Sellers.

Pfeffer, Susan Beth. Just between us; illus by Lorna Tomei. Delacorte 1980, 116 pp.

Cass's inability to keep secrets finally became such a problem that Cass asked her mother to help her learn how to keep them. Cass's mother, a psychology student, devised a behavior modification experiment. Every day that Cass was able to figure out which bit of information she had been told was a secret and keep it, she received a dollar. After a poor start Cass did well for a while, until the day she told three secrets and made her entire family angry at her.

More determined than ever, Cass tried again. This time she found herself caught between two friends. Only Cass knew that Robin was adopted and Robin wanted it kept a secret. Jenny was so mad at Robin that she decided to spread an untrue story to hurt Robin. She told Cass not to tell anyone what she was going to do. The story Jenny was going to spread was that Robin was adopted. After hours of mental anguish Cass finally devised a way to stop Jenny and help Jenny return to being the nice person she had been before her parents' divorce.

The reading level of this book varies greatly from second grade to mid-fourth grade. Otherwise, it is good fare for Judy Blume fans. Print size just a slight bit on the small side.

Interest Level: 4-6. Reading Level: 3.2. Further Search Topics: Humorous Fiction, Everyday Stories, Friendship-Fiction, School Stories, Divorce and Separation-Fiction, Psychiatrists-Fiction, Secrets-Fiction.

Place, Marian T. The boy who saw Bigfoot. Dodd 1979, 96 pp.

Joey and his foster mother searched for and found Bigfoot. But, when Joey told his classmates, no one would believe him. Joey's next idea was to take the entire class on a field trip to track Bigfoot.

Joey's rapid change from a difficult to a very well-adjusted child is not well supported. But interest in Bigfoot is so great that the book's flaws will be overlooked by its readers.

Interest Level: 3-6. Reading Level: 2.2. Further Search Topics: Bigfoot-Fiction, Foster Homes-Fiction, Monsters-Fiction, Troublemakers-Fiction, School Stories.

Robinson, Nancy K. Wendy and the bullies; illus by Ingrid Fetz. Hastings 1980, 128 pp.

Wendy and her best friend Karen had a very carefully mapped out route to and from school—a route that allowed them to meet up with the fewest number of bullies possible. But when Karen became sick enough to stay home from school, Wendy had to face the bullies alone. Wendy's fears escalated to panic so intense that she avoided walking to school by hiding in her basement. She finally realized that she was letting fear and anger control her life when she found herself bullying Karen. Only her new friendship with Monica, making up with Karen, and her involvement in a school project helped Wendy overcome her fears.

This is a humorous, episodic tale of a feeling and circumstances common to many children. The illustrations sometimes make Wendy and her classmates appear much younger than her actual nine years, but fortunately that doesn't happen often enough to spoil the book's appeal.

Interest Level: 3-5. Reading Level: 3.1. Further Search Topics: School Stories, Bullies-Fiction, Courage-Fiction, Best Sellers, Humorous Fiction, Friendship-Fiction, Everyday Stories.

Sharmat, Marjorie W. Getting something on Maggie Marmelstein; illus by Ben Shecter. Har-Row 1971, 101 pp.

A curious love-hate relationship existed between Thad and Maggie. It all began when Maggie overheard Thad say she squeaked like a mouse. Then Maggie caught Thad wearing an apron and cooking. Thad was so uncomfortable with the thought that Maggie might tell his friends, that he was determined to find out Maggie's deepest secret. That meant that Thad had to take a lead role as a frog opposite Maggie as the princess in the school play. While at Maggie's apartment for a costume fitting, Thad found a love letter Maggie had written to Cary Grant. Thad decided he would read the letter to the class right after the play was over. But during the play Maggie saved Thad from what could have been one of the most embarrassing moments of his life. By the time he finally had the chance to make Maggie appear foolish, Thad had changed his mind.

Written as Thad's story, the book is funny, warm, and realistic. A good, short, story that continues to be popular. Print is of moderate size.

Interest Level: 3-6. Reading Level: 3.1. Further Search Topics: Humorous Fiction, Everyday Stories, School Stories, Best Sellers, Friendship-Fiction, Sex Role-Fiction, Acting-Fiction.

Sharmat, Marjorie W. Maggie Marmelstein for President; illus by Ben Shecter. Har-Row 1975, 122 pp.

Maggie and Thad Smith are at it again. When Thad decided to run for sixth grade president, Maggie decided to become his campaign manager. However, because Thad thought Maggie was too strong and would end up managing him much more than he wanted to be managed, he turned down her offer. Thad's refusal made Maggie so angry that she not only decided to run against Thad, but she also enlisted Noah, the smartest kid in the class, as her manager. With Noah's expert guidance Maggie's campaign went rather well, despite attempts at sabotage by a spy for Thad. But as election day drew closer, both Thad and Maggie lost track of the campaign issues and concentrated only on beating each other. Consequently the pre-election debate turned into a disastrous shouting match. The next day Noah was elected class president by write-in votes.

Not very subtle, but funny. A satisfying sequel for those who enjoyed *Getting Something on Maggie Marmelstein*.

Interest Level: 3-6. Reading Level: 3.1. Further Search Topics: Humorous Fiction, Politics-Fiction, School Stories, Friendship-Fiction, Sex Role-Fiction.

Smith, Doris Buchanan. Last was Lloyd. Viking Pr 1981, 124 pp.

Lloyd had several problems: he was overweight, his mother was overprotective, he had no school friends, and there was a chance he might be taken away from home and put into foster care because he had missed so much school. Lloyd's mother, very young and very defensive when she had Lloyd, had done her best to be a "good mother," but in doing so, had made Lloyd fearful of the world. He had become the subject of his classmates' mockery so many times that the only way he could respond to his peers was with nastiness. The one skill he possessed was hitting a baseball. He kept this skill well hidden for fear of exposing himself to further mockery. When one of his classmates accidentally discovered how well Lloyd hit, he took the first step to becoming Lloyd's friend. Lloyd's reaction was to back away, but Kirby kept trying. Eventually Kirby's attempts and those of an understanding truant officer, helped Lloyd begin to make friends, to treat others decently, and to pull away from his mother; in short, he began to mature.

Because Lloyd's problems can be oversimplified too easily, this book requires a fairly mature reader and perhaps even discussion in order to fully understand its subtleties.

Interest Level: 5-6+Reading Level: 4.2. Further Search Topics: Weight-Fiction, Single Parent Family-Fiction, Courage-Fiction, School Stories, Loners-Fiction, Friendship-Fiction, Baseball-Fiction, Family Problems-Fiction, Foster Homes-Fiction, Children-Growth-Fiction.

Waldorf, Mary. Jake McGee and his feet; illus by Leonard Shortall. HM 1980, 82 pp.

His severe reading difficulties made school the worst place in the world for Jake McGee. On the day that his reading tutor became so impatient with him that she sent Jake to the principal, Jake decided that he couldn't stand school any longer and ran away. He didn't actually run away, he just let his feet finally do what they wanted. His feet were always getting Jake in trouble. They walked too slowly to get him to school on time; they wouldn't stay still once he was in school; and they were always trying to trip someone.

Jake knew that in addition to having problems with his feet he had reading problems, but no one at his old school in the country had noticed. When he and his family moved to the city everything had changed.

Jake's mother was always at work or tired. Jake hadn't made any friends and so was always alone. But Jake thought the biggest of all his immediate problems was his feet. The day he ran away, Jake's feet led him to a lost baby, an eccentric old woman, and a neighbor boy, all of whom helped Jake recognize and deal with his real problem.

The book is not high literary quality. The characterization is somewhat flat and the plot is fairly predictable. However, the sentences and chapters are short, the vocabulary is manageable, and Jake's feelings will be shared by many non-readers.

Interest Level: 3-5. Reading Level: 2.2. Further Search Topics: School Stories, Moving, Household-Fiction, Runaways-Fiction, Academic Problems-Fiction, Working Parents-Fiction, Loneliness-Fiction, Feet-Fiction.

Warner, Gertrude Chandler. Schoolhouse mystery; illus by David Cunningham. A. Whitman 1965, 128 pp.

On a dare, the Aldens went to a quiet fishing village to see what excitement they could find there. They found an isolated town filled with poor and unfriendly people. In their attempt to get to know the townspeople, the Aldens learned of the children's desire for schooling and the adults' anticipation of the Money Man's arrival. The Alden children took on the task of teaching school for the summer in an abandoned schoolhouse owned by Miss Gray, a recluse. The Money Man intrigued them more with each new bit of information they learned about him. They finally decided that the Money Man was a swindler who was practically stealing valuable antiques away from the villagers. By spying on the Money Man when he used the schoolhouse to store the antiques, the Aldens and an ex-FBI man were able to capture him. When the vacation was over, the Aldens had once more found excitement, Miss Gray had agreed to teach the local school, the Money Man was on his way to jail, and the townspeople knew the value of their old household items.

See the entry for *The Boxcar Children* for more information.

Interest Level: 3-5. Reading Level: 2.2. Further Search Topics: Mystery and Detective Stories, Vacation-Fiction, School Stories, Antiquities-Fiction, Crime-Fiction, Brothers and Sisters-Fiction, Challenges-Fiction.

SCIENCE

Simon, Seymour. Einstein Anderson makes up for lost time; illus by Fred Winkowski. Viking Pr 1981, 73 pp.

Adam (nicknamed Einstein) Anderson loves science. He also loves bad puns and correcting wrongs. What he does best, however, is to figure out science puzzles. Each book in this series (this is the third) presents 10 science puzzles which challenge Einstein and the reader. Clues and background are established in several pages of scene setting. Einstein regularly solves the puzzle and then the reader is asked how he did it. The answer follows on the next page. Areas of science that are drawn upon vary widely and range from animal behavior through chemistry and space science to zoology. Very palatable science reading. Print is on the small side in all four books.

Interest Level: 3-6. Reading Level: 2.2. Further Search Topics: Science, Puzzles, Mystery and Detective Stories.

Simon, Seymour. Einstein Anderson, science sleuth; illus by Fred Winkowski. Viking Pr 1980, 73 pp.

Einstein Anderson is the scientific equivalent of Encyclopedia Brown. Einstein was the nickname that Adam Anderson earned at the age of six. Even at that early age he was a scientific genius. He seems to especially love solving scientific puzzles and mysteries and that is just what Einstein does throughout this and the other books. There are ten very brief, somewhat plotless cases that are presented to Einstein. The clues are all included in each story. The solutions are supplied at the end of each case after the reader has had a chance to try to figure out the answers. None of the cases or solutions are terribly technical. Some of the cases can be solved simply by paying careful attention to the text. The rest require a moderate knowledge of scientific principles. It is a satisfying series to the science sleuth. Print is somewhat small.

Interest Level: 3-6. Reading Level: 3.1. Further Search Topics: Mystery and Detective Stories, Science, Puzzles.

Simon, Seymour. Einstein Anderson shocks his friends; illus by Fred Winkowski. Viking Pr 1980, 73 pp.

Using the identical formula as that in *Einstein Anderson, Science Sleuth* the author presents 10 more science puzzles to be solved by the reader. Einstein (nee Adam) outwits a bully, discovers who broke the window on the school bus, helps the sixth grade win contests against both the seventh and the eighth grades and more. This book, as well as the others in the series, is both fun and instructive.

Interest Level: 3-6. Reading Level: 3.1. Further Search Topics: Science, Puzzles, Mystery and Detective Stories.

Simon, Seymour. Einstein Anderson tells a comet's tale; illus by Fred Winkowski. Viking Pr 1981, 73 pp.

Adam earned his nickname Einstein by proving over and over again that he could solve any science puzzle put to him. Ten more challenges are presented here, none of which prove to be too much for our scientific whiz kid. Like its predecessors, this book is for science sleuths who enjoy matching wits with a cocky punster.

Interest Level: 3-6. Reading Level: 3.1. Further Search Topics: Science, Puzzles, Mystery and Detective Stories.

White, Laurence B., Jr. Science puzzles; illus by Marc Tolon Brown. A-W 1975, unp (46 pp).

There are twenty four very short experiments designed to illustrate the simplest of scientific principles clearly presented here. For all but a few experiments there is not only an explanation of what happens but also an explanation of why it happened. What makes the book even more useful, is that it can also be used as a book of easy magic tricks. Any child who enjoys it as science will, with a little help, be able to see its possibilities as magic. In fact it provides a better explanation of the Knot Magic trick than can be found in *It's Magic*.

Interest Level: 1-3. Reading Level: 1.2. Further Search Topics: Science, Magic, Puzzles, Experiments, Scientific.

White, Laurence B., Jr. Science toys; illus by Marc Tolon Brown. A-W 1975, unp (46 pp).

This book presents 23 toys that a young child can easily make and learn from at the same time. A sundial, a drinking straw that flies, a balloon that rolls over, a ghost that sticks to the wall by itself, a water-go-round, and a paper cup that roars are a few examples of what is to be found here. The construction and use of each toy is explained and illustrated in enough detail to enable the child to work alone. And as in *Science Puzzles*, some of the toys will double as magic tricks (i.e. can you balance the rim of a paper plate on your nose?).

Interest Level: 1-3. Reading Level: 2.1. Further Search Topics: Handicrafts, Science, Magic, Toys, Games, Group 2, Puzzles.

SCIENCE FICTION

Butterworth, William E. Next stop, Earth; illus by Paul Frame. Walker 1978, 80 pp.

After two years on a desolate planet, 12-year-old Charley and his family were anticipating their return to Earth. But when Charley was awakened from sleep by a spaceship robot, he learned that an asteroid disturbance had caused several key systems on the ship to malfunction. Of 24 passengers on board the spaceship, only 10 were still alive and only Charley and his sister were able to be awakened. It was up to Charley to pilot the ship to its landing on Earth. The controls were all in an adjacent room which a faulty robot kept Charley from entering. Without someone at the controls the ship would burn up when re-entering Earth's atmosphere. By tricking the robot and commanding the ship's main computer, Charley was able to get to the control panel just in time to wake his father, help with reentry and save the ship.

Though the story tends to be heavy with conversations between Charley and various computers and robots, it is also that dialogue that helps maintain suspense. It is a story for the confirmed science fiction fan, not for the inductee.

Interest Level: 3-6. Reading Level: 2.2. Further Search Topics: Science Fiction, Outer Space-Fiction, Voyages and Travels-Fiction, Robots-Fiction, Computers-Fiction.

Clark, Margaret Goff. Barney in space; illus by Ted Lewin. Dodd 1981, 155 pp.

This is a sequel to *Barney and the UFO*, but it stands by itself quite well. It's title is a misnomer, however, for it isn't until the last third of the book that Barney goes into space. In the previous book Barney made friends with Tibbo, a Gark from the planet Ornam. In this book Tibbo tries to save Barney from an evil Gark named Rokell. Because Barney knew about Garks, Rokell was afraid Barney would betray them and turn humans against Garks. To prevent that from happening, Rokell was determined to kidnap Barney. Tibbo was too far from Earth to do more than warn Barney of Rokell's intentions and tell him not to be alone at any time. Barney's friends Dick and Kara tried to protect Barney but only succeeded in endangering their own lives. When Kara was almost killed by Rokell, Barney decided to face Rokell alone and try to defeat him, but Rokell's powers were too strong for Barney. Against their wills both Barney and David were taken aboard a spaceship. They discovered later, to their relief, that the spaceship belonged to a friend of Tibbo's who was commanding the ship from the moon. Barney and Dick were to be taken to the moon for safety until Rokell could be controlled. Rokell didn't give up easily. He attacked the ship twice before he captured it and set it down on a remote portion of the moon. Only Barney's quick thinking stopped Rokell permanently and saved both Barney and Dick.

The preliminary sequences are more suspenseful and exciting than the space travel; however, the book will not disappoint young science fiction fans.

Interest Level: 4-6. Reading Level: 4.2. Further Search Topics: Science Fiction, Flying Saucers-Fiction, Outer Space-Fiction, Orphans-Fiction, Kidnapping-Fiction, Aliens-Fiction, Adoption-Fiction.

Clark, Margaret Goff. Barney and the UFO; illus by Ted Lewin. Dodd 1979, 159 pp.

Barney felt a strange prickly sensation several times before he discovered that it was caused by Tibbo, a Gark from the planet Ornam. Tibbo had selected Barney as a friend who would accompany him back to Ornam. Barney was to learn the peaceful ways of Gark and then return to Earth to help persuade the world to accept the aliens. At first the idea of visiting Ornam appealed to Barney because he liked Tibbo and felt very lonely and unsure of his adoptive family's love. Those were the very reasons that Tibbo had chosen Barney: he wanted someone without strong ties to Earth and Barney's only tie when he was first contacted by Tibbo was his little brother Scott. As the time to go grew closer, Barney found a new and strong friendship with Dave, a science whiz-kid, and great love for his new parents. Tibbo, however, was determined to hold Barney to his promise. Only a last minute confrontation between Tibbo and Barney, David, Scott and Mr. and Mrs. Crandall prevented Tibbo from succeeding. But even as Tibbo left, he and Barney acknowledged their new friendship and agreed to keep in touch.

Because of its fairly slow beginning, readers must be well-introduced to this book. If they can be persuaded to be patient while the author sets the stage for about 18 pages they will be rewarded with a decent, if somewhat wordy, story of friendship, UFO's, space travel and family affection.

Interest Level: 3-6. Reading Level: 3.2. Further Search Topics: Science Fiction, Flying Saucers-Fiction, Kidnapping-Fiction, Foster Homes-Fiction, Family-Fiction, Adoption-Fiction, Aliens-Fiction, Loneliness-Fiction, Orphans-Fiction.

Curtis, Philip. The invasion of the Brain Sharpeners; illus by Tony Ross. Knopf 1979, 117 pp.

This book is one of a number of books published by Albert Knopf under the series title Capers. They are meant to be (and with few exceptions are) light, easy-to-read fiction, published simultaneously in hardcover and paperback editions. Each book is about 120 pages long with chapter length varying from 9 to 14 pages. Print is plenty large and spacing between lines is always adequate. Plots are built around an idea of guaranteed appeal, descriptive passages are kept to a minimum and action (often suspenseful) abounds. This should, on the whole, be a very useful series. Some entries (i.e., *Man From the Sky* and *Who Stole the Wizard of Oz*, both by Avi) are either too difficult or too obscure to be widely appealing, but they are by far the exceptions to the rule.

Invasion of the Brain Sharpeners is the catchy science fiction story of Michael's successful, but risky, attempt to rid his fifth grade classroom of the overpowering influence of the Brain Sharpeners. The Brain Sharpeners came from another galaxy to search for humans to help them colonize their Planet Five. Humans were so lacking in brain power that the Brain Sharpeners' plan was to periodically expose each child to brain-developing rays, then put them through intensive courses of study guided by their also-exposed teacher. When the children had all learned enough to be beneficial to the Brain Sharpeners, they were to be taken from Earth to Planet Five. Michael was the only one to see the danger they were in and to attempt to stop the plot.

He managed to chase the aliens away and to prevent his classmates and teacher from receiving their second dose of rays, but in doing so, he sent the principal to the spaceship. Michael's classmates were thus saved, but his principal was never heard from again. Capers series.

Interest Level: 3-6. Reading Level: 3.1. Further Search Topics: Science Fiction, Flying Saucers-Fiction, Aliens-Fiction, School Stories, Kidnapping-Fiction, Best Sellers, Academic Problems-Fiction, Brainwashing-Fiction.

Montgomery, Raymond A. Space and beyond; illus by Paul Granger. Bantam 1980, 117 pp.

See entry for *Sugarcane Island*, by Edward Packard for full annotation. Available in paperback only. Choose Your Own Adventure series

Interest Level: 2-6. Reading Level: 4.1. Further Search Topics: Science Fiction, Outer Space-Fiction, Group 2, Best Sellers.

Morressy, John. The drought on Ziax II, illus by Stanley Skardinsky. Walker & Co 1978, 77 pp.

Ziax II, the planet that Toren, his father, and other Earth Pioneers were helping to colonize, was suffering a severe drought. It took both cooperation with the inhabitants of Ziax II and courage to seek out the frightening creature that could save the planet.

The importance of maintaining the balance of nature is the strongest message here. Respect for the ways of others is the secondary message.

Interest Level: 3-5. Reading Level: 3.1. Further Search Topics: Science Fiction, Ecology-Fiction, Outer Space-Fiction.

Norton, Andre. Star Ka'at; illus by Bernard Colonna. Walker & Co 1976, 122 pp.

Jim Evans and Elly Mae Brown, both orphaned and alone, met each other and two strange cats at the same time. As the children became more unhappy with their lives, they began to realize that Tiro and Mer were not usual cats. They were highly intelligent Ka'ats from another planet who had come to Earth in search of new strong stock to add to their breed. Both Ka'ats became as fond of the children as the children became of them. When the time came for the transport ship to leave, Jim and Elly contrived to go with them. However, the only way they could go was if they were accepted by the other Ka'ats and adopted by Tiro and Mer.

This is the first book in a series. Unfortunately the second book *Star Ka'at World*, has a much more difficult reading level (sixth grade) and the third title, *Star Ka'at and the Plant People*, varies from 2.1 to 4.1. Reading level of this entry varies between 4.1 and 5.1 but children seem to like the book enough to put up with the variability.

Interest Level: 3-6. Reading Level: 4.2. Further Search Topics: Science Fiction, Friendship-Fiction, Cats-Fiction, Group 2, Outer Space-Fiction, Orphans-Fiction.

Packard, Edward. The cave of time; illus by Paul Granger. Bantam 1979, 115 pp.

Beware of the greater than usual inconsistency of reading levels within this book. Its difficulty level ranges from 2.2 to 4.2. See notes for *Sugarcane Island* for more information about the series. In paperback only. Choose Your Own Adventure series.

Interest Level: 2-6. Reading Level: 4.1. Further Search Topics: Time-Fiction, Science Fiction, Fantasy, Group 2.

Pinkwater, Daniel Manus. Fat men from space. Dodd 1977, 57 pp.

The evening after his trip to the dentist William found that he could still hear radio programs when his radio was turned off. He was even more surprised to find that when he wired himself to a fence he could hear spacemen talking. When the spacemen discovered that William could hear them, they landed and captured him. They were on a top secret mission and couldn't risk any human knowing about their existence. The spacemen were about to invade Earth to consume all the junk food they could find. As mass panic set in on Earth, William could do nothing to save his fellow humans. He was held captive and helpless until the invaders' interest was captured by a giant potato pancake floating in outer space.

A tongue-in-check, slapstick spoof of science fiction, food fads, and junk food. Do not expect anything more.

Interest Level: 3-5. Reading Level: 3.2. Further Search Topics: Science Fiction, Humorous Fiction, Food-Fiction, Flying Saucers-Fiction, Aliens-Fiction, Best Sellers, Kidnapping-Fiction, Teeth-Fiction.

Slote, Alfred. C.O.L.A.R.; illus by Anthony Kramer. Lippincott 1981, 146 pp.

Jack, his robot twin Danny, and Jack's mother and father were forced to make an emergency landing on an uncharted planet. There they were attacked by creatures who looked like rocks and who wanted to destroy all humans. They captured Danny, led him into an underground living complex, and revealed their true identities. The creatures were robots who had escaped from their owners and the slavery in which they had lived. They kept their planet secret from all humans for fear of what would happen to them should they be discovered. Their main purpose was to free as many robots as possible and to allow robots the same pleasures humans enjoyed. Because Danny had been happy with his humans and claimed to have been treated as one of the family, the inhabitants of the planet C.O.L.A.R. felt he had to be reprogrammed to see the truth. Jack looked and acted so much like Danny that he was able to prevent Danny from being brainwashed, to save his parents from death, and to convince the other robots that some humans treated their robots quite well. In fact, he and Danny, together, were able to persuade the robot manufacturer that a great program of robot-owner re-education was needed.

This is a good adventure story which could also be useful as a lead into discussions of slavery, intelligence, and interpersonal relationships. It is a sequel to *My Robot Buddy*, but one which can be read without having read its predecessor.

Interest Level: 3-5. Reading Level: 3.1. Robots-Fiction, Science Fiction, Outer Space-Fiction, Kidnapping-Fiction, Brainwashing-Fiction, Slavery-Fiction.

Slote, Alfred. My robot buddy; illus by Joel Schick. Lippincott 1975, 92 pp.

For Jack's tenth birthday he was given a robot—a robot so real it did everything but run like a human. The robot appeared so human that a thief, thinking he was stealing the robot, almost kidnapped Jack by mistake.

The few points at which the text becomes more difficult than the reading level indicates should not prove too intimidating to the reader. The suspense and humor of the story and the book's high interest subject matter should carry the reader through the rough spots. A satisfying read-aloud for second and third grades.

Interest Level: 2-5. Reading Level: 3.1. Further Search Topics: Science Fiction, Robots-Fiction, Friendship-Fiction, Kidnapping-Fiction, Read Aloud.

SCOLIOSIS-FICTION

Blume, Judy. Deenie. Bradbury 1973, 159 pp.

Deenie's mother wanted Deenie to be a model. Deenie didn't know what she wanted until she learned that she had scoliosis (curvature of the spine) and would have to wear a brace for four years. Then she knew she only wanted to be normal. She was repulsed by deformities of any kind. She couldn't stand the idea of a brace. Her mother's attitude made Deenie's adjustment even more difficult. It was her father, her doctor, her sister, and a new friend with excema who finally helped Deenie accept her brace and the idea of physical differences. Subplots include Deenie's budding romance with an eighth grade boy, her strained relationship with her mother, and her growing awareness of sex (masturbation and intercourse). Print and line spacing are similar to *Are You There God? It's Me, Margaret.*

Interest Level: 5-6. Reading Level: 3.1. Further Search Topics: Models, Fashion-Fiction, Beauty-Fiction, Scoliosis-Fiction, Physically Handicapped-Fiction, Children-Growth-Fiction, Sex-Fiction, Love-Fiction, Family Problems-Fiction, Illness-Fiction, Adolescence-Fiction.

SCUBA DIVING

Branley, Franklyn M. Oxygen keeps you alive; illus by Don Madden. Har-Row 1971, 33 pp.

A well-explained, beginning treatment of the functions, importance, and uses of oxygen. The explanation is not limited to humans, but extends to plants and animals as well. Although the book can be stretched to use with fifth graders, its picture book format and sometimes condescending tone indicate it is most easily used through fourth grade. No index or table to contents.
Let's-Read-and-Find-Out-Science-Book series.

Interest Level: 2-4. Reading Level: 2.2. Further Search Topics: Air, Respiration, Scuba Diving, Astronauts.

Buckley, Peter. I am from Puerto Rico. S ËAN S 1971, 127 pp.

Federico Ramirez had enjoyed his two years in New York City and didn't like the idea of moving back to Puerto Rico. When he arrived, he had no friends, no T.V., and nothing to do. Then Neri taught Federico the local games, showed him the sights and introduced him to Narcisco, a special fisherman. Narcisco took Federico through the wonders of the coral reefs. He taught him how to dive and fish. Within several months Federico was thoroughly at home in the water and loved Puerto Rico.

There is so much information about Puerto Rico and marine life that the book is never dry. Federico tells his own story as a series of fascinating experiences (meeting up with a shark, playing pinball, scuba diving at night, keeping a large turtle as a pet, etc.). There are abundant black and white photographs. An excellent choice for research (no index) or recreational reading. The print size is slightly on the small side, but the space between lines is good. Recently out of print, but worth looking for.

Interest Level: 5-6. Reading Level: 5.1. Further Search Topics: Puerto Rico, Fishing, Moving, Household-Fiction, Marine Biology, Scuba Diving, Ethnic Groups.

SEAFARING LIFE-FICTION

Bulla, Clyde Robert. A lion to guard us; illus by Michele Chessare. Har-Row 1981, 117 pp.

Bulla's writing isn't quite as successful here as elsewhere. This story of three London children's attempt to go to their father in Jamestown, Virginia, has danger, adventure, daring and promise. It also has too many characters to allow the reader to get to know any of them well. There are also too many very short chapters to allow plot development (23 chapters and 117 pages). The short sentences help to keep the reading level low, but a glossary would have been useful to fully explain the many unfamiliar terms.

Despite its problems, the book is still useful. The story is based on the 1609 voyage of the Sea Adventure. Blown far off course and badly damaged by a storm, the ship landed at Bermuda rather than Jamestown. The survivors were unable to sail again for over nine months. When they reached Jamestown, they found that few people had survived the very harsh year.

The three Freebold children are the focus of this story. When their mother died they left London to find their father in the New World. Having no money of their own, they were lucky to find a doctor friend to pay their ship's passage and to go with them. Halfway across the ocean, the doctor was swept overboard and drowned. From that time until they found their father barely alive, the children were on their own, even though they were still with the ship's passengers.

Although not the best of Bulla, this is still serviceable as a piece of historical fiction (hard to get children to read), or as a choice for the lover of survival and/or sea stories.

Interest Level: 3-5. Reading Level: 2.1. Further Search Topics: United States-History-Fiction, Historical Fiction, Courage-Fiction, Survival-Fiction, Shipwrecks-Fiction, Voyages and Travels-Fiction, Seafaring Life-Fiction.

Bulla, Clyde Robert. Pirate's promise; illus by Peter Burchard. Har-Row 1958, 87 pp.

After their mother and father died, Tom and Dinah Pippin had nowhere to go but to their Uncle John's house. Uncle John had no place for them, so he sold Tom into bondage but kept Dinah to help his wife with housework. Tom was to be taken by ship to America where the ship's captain would sell him to the highest bidder. After several years, Tom would be free. But, Tom couldn't accept the idea of one person being another's property, so he spoke out at every opportunity. Tom spoke up to the seaman who dragged him aboard ship, to the captain, to the others who had been bonded, even to the pirate captain who captured their ship. Captain Land was so impressed by Tom's bravery that although he set everyone else he had captured adrift on a small boat, he kept Tom with him. He and Tom became good friends. He never asked Tom to become a pirate and Tom never did. Instead, they enjoyed each other's company. When the pirate ship needed work, they stopped at a safe island where Tom met and impressed Captain Red, a fierce enemy of Captain Land. Captain Red's insistence that Tom join his pirate ship led to another clash between the enemies. Although he was ill, Captain Land fought a duel with Captain Red and lost. Land's last requests were that Benjy, a freed slave who loved him, take all his gold, and that Tom go to

Charlestown, South Carolina to find Land's family. Benjy led their flight from Captain Red and arranged a way for Tom to sail to Charlestown before putting Tom on his own. When Tom reached Charlestown he found Land's parents were so angry with Land that at first they didn't even want to hear about him. But, eventually, they not only asked all about their son, but also asked Tom if he and Dinah would like to live with them as their family.

There is enough excitement, danger, and warmth here to satisfy almost any arm-chair adventurer. Usual format of short, episodic chapters.

Interest Level: 3-6. Reading Level 2.1. Further Search Topics: Pirates-Fiction, Seafaring Life-Fiction, Orphans-Fiction, Slavery-Fiction, Brothers and Sisters-Fiction, Best Sellers, Courage-Fiction.

Bulla, Clyde Robert. Viking adventure; illus by Douglas Gorsline. T Y Crowell 1963, 117 pp.

An exciting story of a young Norwegian boy named Sigurd. Sigurd realized his dream when he finally set sail on a Viking ship in search of Wineland (Vinland). Leif Eriksson had told of his North American findings over 100 years earlier. Sigurd and his father's friend Grom, the captain of the ship, were sure they could find that land again. Their determination finally brought Grom's death at the hands of the ship's owner, Sigurd's near death, and the destruction of the ship.

This book, too, is true to Bulla's style of short chapters, short sentences, much action and high appeal. Although it is a little higher reading level than many of Bulla's others, it is still a good choice. Recently out of print, but worth a search.

Interest Level: 2-6. Reading Level: 3.1. Further Search Topics: Norway-Fiction, Historical Fiction, Seafaring Life-Fiction, Voyages and Travels-Fiction, Shipwrecks-Fiction, Explorers-Fiction, Vikings-Fiction, Courage-Fiction, Best Sellers, Group 2.

SEASONS
Berger, Melvin. Time after time; illus by Richard Cuffari. Coward 1975, 45 pp.

The book begins with a description of inner clocks, proceeds into measurement of time, the seasons, and finally demonstrates the making of a simple clock. The explanations are simple but interesting. One point logically follows from another. It is a solid, serviceable tool limited only somewhat by the fact that it looks like a cross between a picture book and a reader. A brief index is included.

Interest Level: 1-4. Reading Level: 2.2. Further Search Topics: Time, Clocks and Watches, Seasons, Group 2.

SECRETS-FICTION
Pfeffer, Susan Beth. Just between us; illus by Lorna Tomei. Delacorte 1980, 116 pp.

Cass's inability to keep secrets finally became such a problem that Cass asked her mother to help her learn how to keep them. Cass's mother, a psychology student, devised a behavior modification experiment. Every day that Cass was able to figure out which bit of information she had been told was a secret and keep it, she received a dollar. After a poor start Cass did well for a while, until the day she told three secrets and made her entire family angry at her.

More determined than ever, Cass tried again. This time she found herself caught between two friends. Only Cass knew that Robin was adopted and Robin wanted it kept a secret. Jenny was so mad at Robin that she decided to spread an untrue story to hurt Robin. She told Cass not to tell anyone what she was going to do. The story Jenny was going to spread was that Robin was adopted. After hours of mental anguish Cass finally devised a way to stop Jenny and help Jenny return to being the nice person she had been before her parents' divorce.

The reading level of this book varies greatly from second grade to mid-fourth grade. Otherwise, it is good fare for Judy Blume fans. Print size just a slight bit on the small side.

Interest Level: 4-6. Reading Level: 3.2. Further Search Topics: Humorous Fiction, Everyday Stories, Friendship-Fiction, School Stories, Divorce and Separation-Fiction, Psychiatrists-Fiction, Secrets-Fiction.

Wolkoff, Judie. Wally. Bradbury 1977, 199 pp.

Michael Price agreed to take care of his friend Billy's chuckwalla for three weeks. But because his mother had declared a moratorium on any more reptiles in the house, Michael tried to hide Wally in his closet. With help from his brother Roger, Michael managed to keep Wally a secret until Wally was mistakenly left out of his box one night. Despite Michael and Roger's desperate searches, the chuckwalla did not reappear until Mr. and Mrs. Price were involved in the final negotiations for the sale of their house. Wally completely disrupted the proceedings, prevented the sale and thus made everyone happy. For as it turned out, none of the Prices had really wanted to move after all.

A fast-paced, funny book with much reader appeal.

Interest Level: 2-5. Reading Level: 2.2. Further Search Topics: Pets-Fiction, Humorous Fiction, Lizards-Fiction, Best Sellers, Reptiles-Fiction, Secrets-Fiction.

SEX-FICTION
Blume, Judy. Deenie. Bradbury 1973, 159 pp.

Deenie's mother wanted Deenie to be a model. Deenie didn't know what she wanted until she learned that she had scoliosis (curvature of the spine) and would have to wear a brace for four years. Then she knew she only wanted to be normal. She was repulsed by deformities of any kind. She couldn't stand the idea of a brace. Her mother's attitude made Deenie's adjustment even more difficult. It was her father, her doctor, her sister, and a new friend with excema who finally helped Deenie accept her brace and the idea of physical differences. Subplots include Deenie's budding romance with an eighth grade boy, her strained relationship with her mother, and her growing awareness of sex (masturbation and intercourse). Print and line spacing are similar to *Are You There God? It's Me, Margaret.*

Interest Level: 5-6. Reading Level: 3.1. Further Search Topics: Models, Fashion-Fiction, Beauty-Fiction, Scoliosis-Fiction, Physically Handicapped-Fiction, Children-Growth-Fiction, Sex-Fiction, Love-Fiction, Family Problems-Fiction, Illness-Fiction, Adolescence-Fiction.

SEX ROLE
Kluger, Ruth. The secret ship. Doubleday 1978, 136 pp.

A tense, true story about the secret transportation of hundreds of European Jews to Palestine early in World War II. The transport ship became ice-bound in a Rumanian harbor, the crew mutinied and the passengers threatened to expose their plight to the world. In complete charge of the operation was a 25-year-old woman. The book closes with a summary of the Jews' continuing fight for Israel.

The historical understanding that is necessary in order to really appreciate this excellent book make it best suited to readers no younger than sixth grade.

The paper on which this book is printed is so thin that the print shows through from one page to another and the print at the beginning and the end of the book is italicized. Both factors may distract the reader.

Interest Level: 6+. Reading Level: 3.1. Further Search Topics: World War II, Jews, Women, Sex Role, Israel, Survival, Courage.

SEX ROLE-FICTION

Christopher, Matt. Wild pitch. Little 1980, 137 pp.

This is one of Christopher's better written books but it is also one that will find a smaller audience than usual. Here he has drawn interesting characters of flesh and bone rather than his normal stereotypes. The sports action is still detailed, but it is no longer the core around which a purely skeletal plot is stretched. Christopher has produced an intriguing story line here.

Eddie was a good strong pitcher who sometimes threw wild pitches. One of his wild pitches hit Phyl Monahan, the only girl playing in his league. It was well known that Eddie didn't like the idea of girls playing in the same league as the boys, so people accused him of purposely hitting Phyl. Eddie knew he hadn't meant to hit her, but he still felt very guilty that his pitch had put her into the hospital. He went to the hospital many times before he was finally able to see Phyl and apologize. When he did, he found that she was very likeable and reasonable. When she confessed that she wasn't sure she wanted to play baseball again, Eddie decided he owed it to her to help her regain her confidence. As they worked together each one gained respect for the other until theirs became a very solid friendship. The test for both was when Phyl had to hit against Eddie again.

For many baseball fans there may be too much plot here and not enough baseball. Because the problem of how to control wild pitches is never addressed, other readers may also find the book disappointing. But, for those baseball fans who are open to more than box scores and replays, this is a good story.

Interest Level: 6+. Reading Level: 4.2. Further Search Topics: Baseball-Fiction, Sex Role-Fiction, Friendship-Fiction, Courage-Fiction.

Christopher, Matt. The year mom won the pennant; illus by Foster Caddell. Little 1968, 147 pp.

When no one's father had the time to coach the Thunderballs it began to look like the team would be disbanded. They just didn't seem to be able to work together without a coach. Then Nick Vassey's mother volunteered to coach for the season. After all, she knew baseball as well as anyone else and had watched her husband coach for several years. Nick wasn't at all pleased, but had to accept the idea when his teammates voted to make his mother their coach. Nick's embarrassment was almost as great as the rival coach's skepticism, but before the season was over Nick was proud of his mother. She coached the team to first place and forced even the rival coach to admit she was a good coach. Much baseball action. See note about (*No Arm In Left Field*).

Interest Level: 2-6. Reading Level: 3.1. Further Search Topics: Group 2, Baseball-Fiction, Friendship-Fiction, Prejudice-Fiction, Sex Role-Fiction, Women-Fiction.

Danziger, Paula. The cat ate my gymsuit. Delacorte 1974, 147 pp.

Another book for fans of Judy Blume. Marcy was shy and insecure, unhappy at school and unhappy at home. She was self-conscious about being heavy and sure she would never have a date. Only Ms. Finney (a new teacher), her English class and Smedley (a communications group) meant anything to Marcy. When Ms. Finney was fired because of her refusal to recite the pledge of allegiance and her unorthodox teaching methods, Marcy began to organize a protest movement. Marcy's commitment brought more problems at school and at home, but eventually resulted in Ms. Finney's vindication and Marcy's and her mother's growth and understanding.

Don't expect much depth of characterization. Most of the characters are flat and stereotypical, but the book will have great appeal in spite of its faults, for Marcy's insecurities are ones with which many young readers can identify.

Interest Level: 5-6. Reading Level: 5.1. Further Search Topics: School Stories, Everyday Stories, Family Problems-Fiction, Challenges-Fiction, Weight-Fiction, Courage-Fiction, Individualists-Fiction, Sex Role-Fiction.

Greene, Constance C. Isabelle the itch; illus by Emily A. McCully. Viking Pr. 1973, 126 pp.

This is a loosely plotted story about a spunky, original fifth grade girl who could drive everyone around her crazy without ever tiring. Isabelle's dearest dream was to win the 50-yard dash at her school's field day. Even though she took over her brother's paper route to earn money for the Adidas track shoes she needed, Isabelle still didn't win. However, she did meet some new people, make new friends and keep those around her on their toes. A very amusing story told mostly in dialogue.

Interest Level: 4-6. Reading Level: 3.2. Further Search Topics: School Stories, Occupations-Fiction, Humorous Fiction, Everyday Stories, Running-Fiction, Individualists-Fiction, Sex Role-Fiction, Read Aloud.

Kibbe, Pat. My mother the mayor, maybe; illus by Charles Robinson. Knopf 1981, 165 pp.

The Pinkertons first appeared in *The Hocus-Pocus Dilemma*, a better introduction to the family than this book. Although this is a satisfactory story, its appeal is somewhat limited by its subject matter. B.J.'s mother's decision to run for town mayor meant that the whole family became involved in the political process. B.J. became her mother's unofficial public relations coordinator, a position Sam Jessup (Mrs. Pinkerton's campaign manager) didn't want to see anyone fill but himself. But because Jessup's ideas seemed suspiciously designed to insure that Mrs. Pinkerton would lose the election, B.J. continued working on her mother's behalf. Almost every day she managed to get her mother's campaign on the front page of the newspaper, although not always in a flattering light. Once B.J. was arrested for breaking into her mother's campaign headquarters. Another day she inadvertently circulated a picture of her mother in a bikini all over town. B.J. and her brothers and sisters illegally campaigned on the high school campus during Homecoming. B.J. even accidentally succeeded in blowing her mother's opponent's wig off in the middle of a campaign appearance. Mrs. Pinkerton finally lost the election, but managed to bring an important issue to light and to stage the closest and most exciting election the town had known in a long time.

Election campaigns and political issues won't lure many new reluctant readers to this book, but those youngsters who have enjoyed the Pinkerton's previous adventures and can understand a simplified version of politics at work will enjoy this humorous tale.

Interest Level: 5-6. Reading Level: 3.1. Further Search Topics: Politics-Fiction, Humorous Fiction, Sex Role-Fiction, Family-Fiction.

Robinson, Jean. The strange but wonderful cosmic awareness of Duffy Moon; illus by Lawrence Di Fiori. HM 1974, 142 pp.

Duffy was tired of being small, of always being on the losing side of fights, and of being unappreciated at home (by his ex-football star uncle). When he sent away for Mr. Flamel's Cosmic Awareness Kit, Duffy was sure he would then be able to take control over anything he wanted and direct his own life. His friend Peter, the narrator, wasn't quite so sure. Peter turned out to be right. Duffy almost made himself sick trying to build a stone wall. Babysitting two small boys and trying to bathe a Great Dane proved to be disastrous. But Duffy's biggest problem came from Boots McAfee's gang. A series of events finally brought Duffy and Peter face-to-face with the dreaded Boots. Luckily, she turned out to be a very smart girl who appreciated Duffy's true talents.

From the first to the last page this is a funny, very enjoyable book. A delightful book with a very palatable message.

Interest Level: 3-6. Reading Level: 3.2. Further Search Topics: Humorous Fiction, Bullies-Fiction, Magic-Fiction, Read Aloud, Occupations-Fiction, Sex Role-Fiction, Orphans-Fiction, Best Sellers, Gangs-Fiction, Courage-Fiction, Babysitting-Fiction.

Sharmat, Marjorie W. Getting something on Maggie Marmelstein; illus by Ben Shecter. Har-Row 1971, 101 pp.

A curious love-hate relationship existed between Thad and Maggie. It all began when Maggie overheard Thad say she squeaked like a mouse. Then Maggie caught Thad wearing an apron and cooking. Thad was so uncomfortable with the thought that Maggie might tell his friends, that he was determined to find out Maggie's deepest secret. That meant that Thad had to take a lead role as a frog opposite Maggie as the princess in the school play. While at Maggie's apartment for a costume fitting, Thad found a love letter Maggie had written to Cary Grant. Thad decided he would read the letter to the class right after the play was over. But during the play Maggie saved Thad from what could have been one of the most embarrassing moments of his life. By the time he finally had the chance to make Maggie appear foolish, Thad had changed his mind.

Written as Thad's story, the book is funny, warm, and realistic. A good, short, story that continues to be popular. Print is of moderate size.

Interest Level: 3-6. Reading Level: 3.1. Further Search Topics: Humorous Fiction, Everyday Stories, School Stories, Best Sellers, Friendship-Fiction, Sex Role-Fiction, Acting-Fiction.

Sharmat, Marjorie W. Maggie Marmelstein for President; illus by Ben Shecter. Har-Row 1975, 122 pp.

Maggie and Thad Smith are at it again. When Thad decided to run for sixth grade president, Maggie decided to become his campaign manager. However, because Thad thought Maggie was too strong and would end up managing him much more than he wanted to be managed, he turned down her offer. Thad's refusal made Maggie so angry that she not only decided to run against Thad, but she also enlisted Noah, the smartest kid in the class, as her manager. With Noah's expert guidance Maggie's campaign went rather well, despite attempts at sabotage by a spy for Thad. But as election day drew closer, both Thad and Maggie lost track of the campaign issues and concentrated only on beating each other. Consequently the pre-election debate turned into a disastrous shouting match. The next day Noah was elected class president by write-in votes.

Not very subtle, but funny. A satisfying sequel for those who enjoyed *Getting Something on Maggie Marmelstein*.

Interest Level: 3-6. Reading Level: 3.1. Further Search Topics: Humorous Fiction, Politics-Fiction, School Stories, Friendship-Fiction, Sex Role-Fiction.

SHIPWRECKS-FICTION

Bulla, Clyde Robert. A lion to guard us; illus by Michele Chessare. Har-Row 1981, 117 pp.

Bulla's writing isn't quite as successful here as elsewhere. This story of three London children's attempt to go to their father in Jamestown, Virginia, has danger, adventure, daring and promise. It also has too many characters to allow the reader to get to know any of them well. There are also too many very short chapters to allow plot development (23 chapters and 117 pages). The short sentences help to keep the reading level low, but a glossary would have been useful to fully explain the many unfamiliar terms.

Despite its problems, the book is still useful. The story is based on the 1609 voyage of the Sea Adventure. Blown far off course and badly damaged by a storm, the ship landed at Bermuda rather than Jamestown. The survivors were unable to sail again for over nine months. When they reached Jamestown, they found that few people had survived the very harsh year.

The three Freebold children are the focus of this story. When their mother died they left London to find their father in the New World. Having no money of their own, they were lucky to find a doctor friend to pay their ship's passage and to go with them. Halfway across the ocean, the doctor was swept overboard and drowned. From that time until they found their father barely alive, the children were on their own, even though they were still with the ship's passengers.

Although not the best of Bulla, this is still serviceable as a piece of historical fiction (hard to get children to read), or as a choice for the lover of survival and/or sea stories.

Interest Level: 3-5. Reading Level: 2.1. Further Search Topics: United States-History-Fiction, Historical Fiction, Courage-Fiction, Survival-Fiction, Shipwrecks-Fiction, Voyages and Travels-Fiction, Seafaring Life-Fiction.

Bulla, Clyde Robert. Viking adventure; illus by Douglas Gorsline. T Y Crowell 1963, 117 pp.

An exciting story of a young Norwegian boy named Sigurd. Sigurd realized his dream when he finally set sail on a Viking ship in search of Wineland (Vinland). Leif Eriksson had told of his North American findings over 100 years earlier. Sigurd and his father's friend Grom, the captain of the ship, were sure they could find that land again. Their determination finally brought Grom's death at the hands of the ship's owner, Sigurd's near death, and the destruction of the ship.

This book, too, is true to Bulla's style of short chapters, short sentences, much action and high appeal. Although it is a little higher reading level than many of Bulla's others, it is still a good choice. Recently out of print, but worth a search.

Interest Level: 2-6. Reading Level: 3.1. Further Search Topics: Norway-Fiction, Historical Fiction, Seafaring Life-Fiction, Voyages and Travels-Fiction, Shipwrecks-Fiction, Explorers-Fiction, Vikings-Fiction, Courage-Fiction, Best Sellers, Group 2.

Packard, Edward. Sugarcane Island; illus by Barbara Carter. Archway 1976, 105 pp.

The warning on the first page, that the book should *not* be read straight through, tells you that this book is different. And different it is. It is the first of what is now a new type of book; the "Choose Your Own Adventure" story. The formula is simple and highly successful, especially with reluctant readers. The reader is made the central character of the book. After a very brief series of events that set the stage, the reader is given choices to make. Upon making a decision, the reader is instructed to proceed to another page of the book. More action is described before the reader must make another choice. The sequence of action, choice, action and choice continues until the reader has finally completed an entire story. The books can be read over and over and the reader may never repeat exactly the same story unless he/she makes all of the same choices. What distinguishes one book from another is the setting, genre, and/or author (there are three: Edward Packard, R. A. Montgomery, and D. Terman). Don't expect quality writing or consistent reading levels because you won't find either. (Reading levels vary from 2.2 to 3.2 for most titles). What you will find is dependable, action-filled, enticing, light reading. Some are available only in paperback editions where the print size is fairly small. Choose Your Own Adventure series.

Interest Level: 2-6. Reading Level: 3.1. Further Search Topics: Shipwrecks-Fiction, Best Sellers, Survival-Fiction, Group 2.

SIMPSON, O.J.

Burchard, Marshall. Sports Hero: O.J. Simpson. Putnam 1975, 95 pp.

O.J. Simpson, who now flies through airports, still holds at least three NFL records, including most yards gained in a single season. See *Sports Hero: Bill Walton* for series information. Sports Hero series.

Interest Level: 2-6. Reading Level: 3.2. Further Search Topics: Biography, Simpson, O.J., Football-Biography, Blacks-Biography, Group 2.

SINGERS

Tobias, Tobi. Marian Anderson; illus by Symeon Shimin. Har-Row 1972, 40 pp.

Marian Anderson's beautiful, strong voice and her great range set her apart from other singers even as a child. By the time she was in high school, she was being paid to sing. However, when she tried to apply to a well-known music school, because she was black she was turned away without even being heard. Anderson's determination as well as her own and others' faith in her kept her singing and seeking better and better coaches until she met Giuseppi Boghetti. He was one of the best voice coaches in the country. With him Marian trained and traveled until she finally won the chance to sing with the New York Philharmonic Orchestra. Anderson thought that at that point she would be invited to sing in famous theaters all across the United States, but because she was black she still received no invitations. She went to Europe where she studied and played to wildly enthusiastic audiences. Her European triumphs finally convinced American theater owners and audiences that she was a serious talent. For the next 30 years

Marian Anderson sang all over the world, most of the time without incident, with one notable exception in 1939, when the D.A.R. prohibited her from singing in a hall they owned in Washington, D. C. She sang instead, in front of the Lincoln Memorial, at the invitation of the United States government. During the following years Marian married, bought a farm, sang opera and was made a delegate to the United Nations. In 1956, she retired from singing to help children, young singers, and world understanding.

Crowell Biographies make excellent school report sources for reluctant readers. They are short, interesting, and not overly juvenile looking, although the quasi-picture book format may be a problem for some older readers. This biography fits that description perfectly. The series is somewhat sentimental (as are many children's biographies), however, the sentimentality is not forbidding or condescending. A useful series. Crowell Biography series.

Interest Level: 2-5. Reading Level: 3.1. Further Search Topics: Biography, Music-Biography, Blacks-Biography, Talent, Women-Biography, Singers, Prejudice, Group 2.

SINGLE PARENT FAMILY-FICTION

Blume, Judy. Tiger eyes. Bradbury 1981, 206 pp.

Davey's father's death was a shock that for awhile separated Davey from her mother. They occupied the same space, but Davey felt herself unable to communicate with her mother or with her aunt and uncle with whom they were living. The horror of the night her father was shot in a robbery attempt was too great for Davey to confront. It was too much for Davey's mother too, and so instead of growing closer, they draw apart. They let Davey's aunt and uncle direct their lives for almost a year before each was able to accept Mr. Wexler's death. During that time Davey's closest, most helpful friend was a loner named only Wolf. With him Davey lost enough fear and hatred that she was finally able to begin to talk about her father.

The setting (New Mexico) is much more important than in most of Blume's stories, the book's reading level is considerably more difficult, and the plot is about experiences more unique than usual. It will not fail to draw crowds of older readers however, for in most other respects the book follows Blume's successful formula.

Interest Level: 6+ Reading Level 5.1. Further Search Topics: Death-Fiction, Moving, Household-Fiction, Love-Fiction, Single Parent Family-Fiction, Family Problems-Fiction.

Byars, Betsy. The Cybil war; illus by Gail Owens. Viking Pr. 1981, 126 pp.

Simon and Tony both had a crush on Cybil, but according to Tony, Cybil liked Tony better than she liked Simon. Simon was unhappily willing to accept Tony's word even though he knew Tony was a chronic liar. After all, Cybil had been the one to talk their teacher out of giving the lead in the class play about nutrition to Simon. Consequently Simon was being forced to impersonate a jar of peanut butter. In an elaborate attempt to win Cybil's affection Tony began telling Cybil lies about Simon and then set up a double date with Cybil and Harriet. On their walk home, Simon learned from Harriet that Cybil had only agreed to the date because Simon was going along. Happy at last, Simon realized he wanted no more lies and tricks; that he wanted to be truthful with Cybil and with himself. In the name of truth, he was even willing to accept the fact that his father, who had deserted the family, would not be returning.

A good story with just enough humor and romance to make it widely appealing as either a shared book (read aloud) or a personal pick. Print is fairly small.

Interest Level: 5-6. Reading Level: 4.2. Further Search Topics: Humorous Fiction, Love-Fiction, School Stories, Honesty-Fiction, Friendship-Fiction, Single Parent Family-Fiction, Read Aloud, Everyday Stories, Adolescence-Fiction.

Cohen, Barbara. Thank you, Jackie Robinson; illus by Richard Cuffari. Lothrop 1974, 125 pp.

This story is not for everyone, but for the right reader it is perfect. The book is a catalog of baseball facts, thus it is likely to appeal primarily to baseball fans. But it is not the typical story of a child overcoming a problem through practice and perserverance, as are most sports books. This is a sensitive story of a fatherless boy whose life centered around the New York Dodgers.

Sam could repeat the starting line-up and details of any game the Dodgers had played within the last three years; however, no one cared. In fact, most people were bored when Sam began reciting. Only Davey, the old, black cook at the inn where Sam and his family lived, took any interest. Davey was as much a fan as Sam. They began spending hours together talking and then watching baseball as Davey and his daughter took Sam to the games with them. It was Sam and Davey's dream to catch a fly ball and have it autograped by all the Dodgers, especially Jackie Robinson, the first black major league player. When Davey had a severe heart attack, Sam gathered all his courage to make that dream come true. He bought a baseball, took the subway to a game, and argued with the ushers until he was finally able to get Jackie Robinson's and the team's autographs. Just a few days before Davey died Sam took the baseball to the hospital and gave it to Davey. Sam's feelings about Davey's death are real and painful. He felt sorry for himself, lonely, angry, sad and confused. But a remark by his mother and one more Jackie Robinson hit helped Sam accept Davey's death.

Because the story is told as a first-person flashback set in the late 1940s, it may need a little introduction. It also alludes to racial problems and practices that young readers may not understand without explanation (i.e., why Davey had some hesitation about taking a white child with him to the ballpark or on a trip).

Interest Level: 4-6. Reading Level: 4.2. Further Search Topics: Baseball-Fiction, Blacks-Fiction, Aging-Fiction, Single Parent Family-Fiction, Friendship-Fiction, Death-Fiction, Robinson, Jackie.

Eyerly, Jeannette. The seeing summer; illus by Emily Arnold McCully. Lippincott 1981, 153 pp.

That it attempts to be two books at the same time is the one flaw in this book that may be noticed by young readers. The first half of the book is an interesting story of the growing friendship between a sighted girl and a blind girl. Carey's delight at the idea of a new friend next door turned to disbelief and discomfort when she learned that Jenny was blind. Jenny too wanted to be friends, but not if she was to be pitied or patronized. Gradually she was able to show Carey that being blind was a nuisance, but nothing she was ashamed of or embarrassed about. The second half of the book presents the contrived and somewhat unnecessary story of Jenny's kidnapping. When Carey's attempt to rescue Jenny

resulted in her capture too, it was, of course, Jenny's independence and ingenuity that led the way to their eventual rescue.

To the reader looking for a rousing story of a kidnapping the book may be a disappointment. Half of the book is a long time to wait for the slight adventure. But, for those readers interested in a good story of physical differences and friendship, this will be more satisfying.

Interest Level: 3-6. Reading Level: 3.1. Further Search Topics: Vision-Fiction, Friendship-Fiction, Kidnapping-Fiction, Single Parent Family-Fiction, Physically Handicapped-Fiction.

Greene, Constance C. A girl called Al; illus by Byron Barton. Viking Pr. 1969, 127 pp.

Told in the first person, this is the story of two seventh grade girls. The girls' warm friendship began the moment Al introduced herself to the narrator as a non-conformist. Al was very independent, mostly because she was on her own so much of the time. Her parents were divorced and she seldom saw either one of them. Her father only wrote her postcards and her mother was rarely home. The narrator's family and Mr. Richards, their building superintendent, became Al's family. They cooked, ate, played, fought, talked and even made bookcases together. When Mr. Richards had a heart attack, they found help for him and later went to see him in the hospital. It was his death that helped Al and her mother grow closer, just as Mr. Richards' life had helped her understand why her father never came to see her.

A satisfying, low-key story of friendship and maturation. The girls are Judy Blume-style characters with much greater innocence. Their ages are not discernible by their actions or dialogue, only by the author's statement.

Interest Level: 3-6. Reading Level: 3.1. Further Search Topics: Children-Growth-Fiction, Single Parent Family-Fiction, Friendship-Fiction, Weight-Fiction, Aging-Fiction, Death-Fiction, Divorce and Separation-Fiction, Family Problems-Fiction, Everyday Stories, Humorous Fiction.

Smith, Alison. Help! There's a cat washing in here!; illus by Amy Rowen. Dutton 1981, 152 pp.

Henry Walker agreed to care for his younger brother and sister for two weeks so that his mother could spend her time preparing a portfolio of her art work in the hopes of getting a much-needed job. It was a desperate move for Henry, but it was the only way he could prevent his bossy Aunt Wilhemina from moving in to run the household. Despite Henry's best efforts, almost everything seemed to go wrong. He burned the food, couldn't keep his brother and sister from misbehaving, seemed to have poisoned his sister's friend, and was faced with making a costume in one night for a school play. The worst of it all was that his mother wasn't pleased with what she was drawing, and Henry only seemed to make her feel more discouraged and unhappy. After what appeared to be certain defeat, however, Henry's efforts were rewarded. His mother was given the job, the family proved they could take care of themselves, and all ended happily.

A light, humorous tale of a young boy's growing independence and maturation under stress and increased responsibility.

Interest Level: 4-6. Reading Level: 3.1. Further Search Topics: Brothers and Sisters-Fiction, Working Parents-Fiction, Single Parent Family-Fiction, Humorous Fiction, Family-Fiction, Challenges-Fiction, Children-Growth-Fiction.

Smith, Doris Buchanan. Tough Chauncey. Morrow 1974, 222 pp.

Chauncey Childs had taught himself to be tough—very tough. Even though he was small for his age (13 years old), the only person who gave him any trouble was his sometimes-friend, Black Jack Levitt. Everyone else was scared of Chauncey. Chauncey felt that he had to be tough or he wouldn't be able to survive. He had to be tough to stand the beatings his grandfather gave him "for his own good," to put up with his mother's drinking and disappearances, and to stand the sight of his grandfather shooting the stray kittens born in their garage.

Chauncey's greatest wish was to be able to live with his mother, instead of with his grandparents. In a desperate attempt to achieve that end he accidentally fell from a moving train and badly hurt his leg. Instead of being returned to his mother he was once more taken back to his grandparents. Chauncey's unhappiness grew until he finally decided to take the one surviving stray kitten and run away. Jack helped him find an empty garage where he could hide while he figured out what to do with his future. After talking with Jack and doing more deep soul searching, Chauncey decided to reshape himself and his life. His first step was to curb his temper and his tongue when his hiding place was discovered. His second step was to see about finding a foster home where he would be treated well, and where he could get a new start.

Ugly as the story is in places, its ending is hopeful. Although it is not always realistic, Chauncey's story is compelling enough to appeal to many readers, especially those who have enjoyed *The War on Villa Street*, by Henry Mazer, *The Outsiders*, by Susan Hinton, or *Mystery of the Fat Cat*, by Frank Bonham. The book's length and its artificially low reading level (vocabulary is often difficult but sentences are very short) make this book most appropriate for an older reader whose reading level is 4.1 or higher.

Interest Level: 5-6. Reading Level: 3.2. Further Search Topics: Child Abuse-Fiction, Family Problems-Fiction, Grandparents-Fiction, Runaways-Fiction, Bullies-Fiction, Single Parent Family-Fiction, Loners-Fiction, Friendship-Fiction, Troublemakers-Fiction, Foster Homes-Fiction.

Smith, Doris Buchanan. Last was Lloyd. Viking Pr 1981, 124 pp.

Lloyd had several problems: he was overweight, his mother was overprotective, he had no school friends, and there was a chance he might be taken away from home and put into foster care because he had missed so much school. Lloyd's mother, very young and very defensive when she had Lloyd, had done her best to be a "good mother," but in doing so, had made Lloyd fearful of the world. He had become the subject of his classmates' mockery so many times that the only way he could respond to his peers was with nastiness. The one skill he possessed was hitting a baseball. He kept this skill well hidden for fear of exposing himself to further mockery. When one of his classmates accidentally discovered how well Lloyd hit, he took the first step to becoming Lloyd's friend. Lloyd's reaction was to back away, but Kirby kept trying. Eventually Kirby's attempts and those of an understanding truant officer, helped Lloyd begin to make friends, to treat others decently, and to pull away from his mother; in short, he began to mature.

Because Lloyd's problems can be oversimplified too easily, this book requires a fairly mature reader and perhaps even discussion in order to fully understand its subtleties.

Interest Level: 5-6. Reading Level: 4.2. Further Search Topics: Weight-Fiction, Single Parent Family-Fiction, Courage-Fiction, School Stories, Loners-Fiction, Friendship-Fiction, Baseball-Fiction, Family Problems-Fiction, Foster Homes-Fiction, Children-Growth-Fiction.

Wagner, Jane. J.T; photos by Gordon Parks, Jr. Van Nostrand 1969, 64 pp.

This is a sentimental story that rarely fails to elicit a sympathetic response from young readers. J.T. is a poor black boy who saw a portable radio almost begging to be stolen and stole it. Two of the neighborhood bullies, Boomer and Claymore, saw J.T. take the radio. Though they threatened him, even poured soap in his eyes in the school bathrooms, J.T. wouldn't give them the radio as they demanded.

About the same time J.T. found a scrawny, scared little cat with only one eye. Because his mother wouldn't let him take the cat home, J.T. built it a warm but ramshackle little house in an abandoned building. He fed it by charging tuna to his mother's grocery store account without her knowledge. Bones became the only thing in J.T.'s life that he had cared about since his father had walked out.

When Boomer and Claymore found out about Bones, they taunted J.T. by throwing the cat back and forth between them until the frightened cat escaped, darted out into the street and was hit by a car. J.T.'s heart broke as he looked at Bones, but he spoke to no one to tell them of his sadness. Only time, his mother's and grandmother's love and a small kitten from Mr. Rosen, the grocer, helped him recover. On the morning that he decided to accept the kitten, J.T. returned the stolen radio, faced Boomer and Claymore without fear, and asked Mr. Rosen for a job in order to pay for cat food.

The book is oversized and illustrated with photographs from the television movie version. It is not only an excellent story to read aloud but one that will prompt listeners to want to finish it on their own or to reread it. It is now available only in paperback from Dell.

Interest Level: 3-6. Reading Level: 3.1. Further Search Topics: Read Aloud, Courage-Fiction, Best Sellers, Cats-Fiction, Single Parent Family-Fiction, Bullies-Fiction, Blacks-Fiction, Poverty-Fiction, City Life-Fiction, Christmas Stories, Crime-Fiction, Pets-Fiction, Holidays-Fiction.

SIOUX INDIANS-FICTION

Thompson, Jean. Brother of the wolves; illus by Steve Marchesi. Morrow 1978, 159 pp.

Shadow Fox, a Sioux medicine man, went into a wolves' den looking for special items he needed for healing, but found much more. He found a baby boy who had apparently lost his parents in an accident and then been adopted by the wolves. Winter was approaching and Shadow Fox knew the baby would not be able to survive the cold, so he took the child back to his people. The people were reluctant to accept Wolf Brother, saying that he was an evil omen, that he was unnatural, and that he would bring them trouble. But Shadow Fox's will prevailed and Wolf Brother was allowed to stay and grow up with the Sioux.

As he grew Wolf Brother continued to communicate with the wolves and thus fueled the rumors that grew about him. A very jealous young man, Looks-Away, told the people that a vision had shown him that Wolf Brother and his wolves would one day destroy the village and all its people. The people grew so suspicious of Wolf Brother that, when their horses were stolen and they faced a drought, they blamed him and drove him from the village.

For a while Wolf Brother tried to live as a wolf but found that he could not be totally happy. He wandered away to look for a tribe by whom he might be accepted. On his way, he too had a vision—a vision that told him he would find horses and buffalo for the Sioux and be welcomed home again. It was weeks later before he accidentally found his tribe's horses. In a daring move and with help from the wolves, Wolf Brother not only rescued the horses from the raiders, but also found buffalo just as his vision had predicted. He was then, for the first time, fully welcomed by his people.

This is a taut, suspenseful and mature story about a strong and unusual character. Older readers are most likely to respond positively to the Indian culture and lore.

Interest Level: 5-6. Reading Level: 3.1. Further Search Topics: Survival-Fiction, Wolves-Fiction, Orphans-Fiction, Loners-Fiction, Indians of North America-Fiction, Sioux Indians-Fiction, Jealousy-Fiction, Best Sellers.

SLAVERY

Meriwether, Louise. The freedom ship of Robert Smalls; illus by Lee Jack Morton. P-H 1971, unp (30 pp).

A brief, but very interesting biography of a black man whose dreams of freedom as a young slave during the Civil War, led to a daring plan of escape. Robert Smalls sailed 16 slaves to freedom and presented the Northern Navy with a valuable gunboat of which he was eventually named captain. Smalls later went on to serve five terms in Congress.

Although the picture book format of this book prevents its confortable use much beyond fourth grade, it is a compelling enough story to interest even sixth graders. Print is somewhat small.

Interest Level: 1-4. Reading Level: 3.1. Further Search Topics: Biography, United States-History-War, Blacks-Biography, Smalls, Robert, Group 2, Slavery, Politics-Biography.

SLAVERY-FICTION

Bulla, Clyde Robert. Pirate's promise; illus by Peter Burchard. Har-Row 1958, 87 pp.

After their mother and father died, Tom and Dinah Pippin had nowhere to go but to their Uncle John's house. Uncle John had no place for them, so he sold Tom into bondage but kept Dinah to help his wife with housework. Tom was to be taken by ship to America where the ship's captain would sell him to the highest bidder. After several years, Tom would be free. But, Tom couldn't accept the idea of one person being another's property, so he spoke out at every opportunity. Tom spoke up to the seaman who dragged him aboard ship, to the captain, to the others who had been bonded, even to the pirate captain who captured their ship. Captain Land was so impressed by Tom's bravery that although he set everyone else he had captured adrift on a small boat, he kept Tom with him. He and Tom became good friends. He never asked Tom to become a pirate and Tom never did. Instead, they enjoyed each other's company. When the pirate ship needed work, they stopped at a safe island where Tom met and impressed Captain Red, a fierce enemy of Captain Land. Captain Red's insistence that Tom join his pirate ship led to another clash between the enemies. Although he was ill, Captain Land fought a duel with Captain Red and lost. Land's last requests were that Benjy, a freed slave who loved him, take all his gold, and that Tom go to

Charlestown, South Carolina to find Land's family. Benjy led their flight from Captain Red and arranged a way for Tom to sail to Charlestown before putting Tom on his own. When Tom reached Charlestown he found Land's parents were so angry with Land that at first they didn't even want to hear about him. But, eventually, they not only asked all about their son, but also asked Tom if he and Dinah would like to live with them as their family.

There is enough excitement, danger, and warmth here to satisfy almost any arm-chair adventurer. Usual format of short, episodic chapters.

Interest Level: 3-6. Reading Level 2.1. Further Search Topics: Pirates-Fiction, Seafaring Life-Fiction, Orphans-Fiction, Slavery-Fiction, Brothers and Sisters-Fiction, Best Sellers, Courage-Fiction.

Slote, Alfred. C.O.L.A.R.; illus by Anthony Kramer. Lippincott 1981, 146 pp.

Jack, his robot twin Danny, and Jack's mother and father were forced to make an emergency landing on an uncharted planet. There they were attacked by creatures who looked like rocks and who wanted to destroy all humans. They captured Danny, led him into an underground living complex, and revealed their true identities. The creatures were robots who had escaped from their owners and the slavery in which they had lived. They kept their planet secret from all humans for fear of what would happen to them should they be discovered. Their main purpose was to free as many robots as possible and to allow robots the same pleasures humans enjoyed. Because Danny had been happy with his humans and claimed to have been treated as one of the family, the inhabitants of the planet C.O.L.A.R. felt he had to be reprogrammed to see the truth. Jack looked and acted so much like Danny that he was able to prevent Danny from being brainwashed, to save his parents from death, and to convince the other robots that some humans treated their robots quite well. In fact, he and Danny, together, were able to persuade the robot manufacturer that a great program of robot-owner re-education was needed.

This is a good adventure story which could also be useful as a lead into discussions of slavery, intelligence, and interpersonal relationships. It is a sequel to *My Robot Buddy*, but one which can be read without having read its predecessor.

Interest Level: 3-5. Reading Level: 3.1. Robots-Fiction, Science Fiction, Outer Space-Fiction, Kidnapping-Fiction, Brainwashing-Fiction, Slavery-Fiction.

SMALLS, ROBERT

Meriwether, Louise. The freedom ship of Robert Smalls; illus by Lee Jack Morton. P-H 1971, unp (30 pp).

A brief, but very interesting biography of a black man whose dreams of freedom as a young slave during the Civil War, led to a daring plan of escape. Robert Smalls sailed 16 slaves to freedom and presented the Northern Navy with a valuable gunboat of which he was eventually named captain. Smalls later went on to serve five terms in Congress.

Although the picture book format of this book prevents its confortable use much beyond fourth grade, it is a compelling enough story to interest even sixth graders. Print is somewhat small.

Interest Level: 1-4. Reading Level: 3.1. Further Search Topics: Biography, United States-History-War, Blacks-Biography, Smalls, Robert, Group 2, Slavery, Politics-Biography.

SNAKES

Allen, Gertrude. Everyday turtles, toads and their kin. HM 1970, 48 pp.

Straight-forward, short, chapter discussions of turtles, lizards, snakes, salamanders, toads, frogs and tree toads. Black and white drawings done by the author amplify the text. The major part of the book is simple enough to be understood at second grade, but should still be interesting to fourth and fifth graders. A few terms may need explanation: i.e., venomous, prey. The chapters on the turtle, lizard, frog and tree frog are the easiest. No index, but still useful for reports.

Interest Level: 2-5. Reading Level: 2.2. Further Search Topics: Turtles, Reptiles, Lizards, Toads, Frogs, Snakes, Salamanders.

SNAKES-FICTION

Moore, Lilian. The snake that went to school; illus by Mary Stevens. Random 1957, 99 pp.

Hank's pet snake Puffy disappeared from the Science Room at school and his little brother, Benjy (in first grade) became ill on the same day. Hank was so worried about finding Puffy that he hardly thought about his pesky little brother, until Puffy was found two days later. Then Hank learned that Benjy had secretly gone to visit Puffy, after being rejected by Hank and had accidentally let the snake out of its cage. Benjy had been so worried about letting the snake out that he had actually made himself ill. Hank finally realized that Benjy wasn't the pest he had thought he was, and promised to be a better older brother.

A somewhat old-fashioned but satisfying story told in ten short chapters.

Interest Level: 2-4. Reading Level: 3.1. Further Search Topics: Pets-Fiction, Snakes-Fiction, Brothers and Sisters-Fiction, School Stories.

SNOW-FICTION

Clifford, Eth. Help, I'm a prisoner in the library; illus by George Hughes. HM 1979, 103 pp.

When their car stopped, Mary Rose and Jo-Beth were left alone in a strange city while their father went to find some gas. Jo-Beth needed to use the bathroom, so the sisters headed for the closest public building they could see, the library. No one saw them go in, so no one knew that they were locked inside when the librarian secured the building for the night. With the lights out and a blizzard outside, the library was a very spooky place. The girls tried calling the police, but the police wouldn't take them seriously. Then they heard groans and eerie moans from the second floor. Gathering all their courage, the girls went to investigate, only to discover the librarian lying hurt and unconscious. Their ingenuity and imagination helped the sisters through the difficult hours before they were all rescued.

Don't read it too carefully or the book's implausibilities will become very evident. Most young readers, however, will enjoy this story for its suspense, spooky atmosphere and adventurous girls, and they will ignore its weaknesses.

Interest Level: 2-5. Reading Level: 3.1. Further Search Topics: Disasters-Fiction, Snow-Fiction, Brothers and Sisters-Fiction, Libraries-Fiction, Survival-Fiction, Courage-Fiction, Group 2.

Clymer, Eleanor. Chipmunk in the forest; illus by Ingrid Fetz. Atheneum 1965, 56 pp.

A simple story of an Indian boy who learned the meaning of the word "courage". Chipmunk had never admitted to anyone that he was afraid of the forest. But when his uncle tried to teach him to hunt, Chipmunk was too frightened to be quiet, and thus he scared away all the animals. He returned to the village in disgrace to do "women's work." One of his jobs was to watch Little Brother. When Little Brother disappeared, Chipmunk went in search of him. It began to snow as Chipmunk went farther and farther into the forest, but even though he was frightened, Chipmunk kept on looking. By the time he found Little Brother, the snow had covered their tracks. Chipmunk had to use all that he had learned from his uncle to get them safely home. When he arrived back at the village, Chipmunk had finally proven that he was brave.

Interest Level: 2-4. Reading Level: 2.1. Further Search Topics: Indians of North America-Fiction, Courage-Fiction, Snow-Fiction, Hunting-Fiction, Survival-Fiction.

Heide, Florence Parry. Mystery of the midnight message; illus by Seymour Fleishman. A. Whitman 1977, 128 pp.

The challenge to the Spotlight Club this time was to stop a crime before it happened. Jay and his sister Cindy were on a bus trip home when a blizzard forced the bus to stop at a motel for the night. Jay answered the room telephone late that night and heard a woman's strange and stern instructions. The instructions were to say nothing, to look in the desk drawer for directions, to expect that Bee had the other half of the instructions, and to be at the place at 8:00 the next evening. The envelope, which Jay and Cindy found, showed the location of and half the combination to someone's bedroom safe.

Early the next morning, the children found themselves fleeing in terror from the evil Scull, the man who was supposed to have received the message. Scull pursued them as they escaped in a friendly salesman's car, caught them and locked them into a cold barn without jackets. When the two were finally back on the road and reunited with Dexter and his sister Anne, they had only a few hours and fewer clues to help them find Woodvale and Jeremiah Gibbon, the intended victim.

Despite difficult driving conditions in the snow, Anne managed to get the children to their destination a few minutes before the thieves arrived. Anne and Jeremiah's secretary left the house together to get the police while the Spotlight Club members and Mr. Gibbon hid near the safe. A few tense minutes later, the case was closed; Mr. Gibbons' money was safe, the ringleader had been named (Mr. Gibbon's doctor), and the thieves had been caught.

See *Mystery at Southport Cinema* for series information. Spotlight Club Mystery series.

Interest Level: 3-5. Reading Level: 3.1. Further Search Topics: Mystery and Detective Stories, Crime-Fiction, Snow-Fiction, Disasters-Fiction, Gangs-Fiction, Brothers and Sisters-Fiction, Detectives-Fiction.

Seuss, Dr. The cat in the hat comes back. Beginner 1958, 63 pp.

Sally and her brother were doing a good job of clearing the front walk of snow when the Cat in the Hat showed up. While they worked, the Cat created a pink mess in the house. The mess only became worse when he tried to clean it. The pink spot finally covered the snow all around the house until the Cat called upon his friends Little Cats A-Z. It was Little Cat Z and his magic zoom that eventually not only cleaned the snow, but cleared the front walk as well.

Another zany, rhymed adventure of the mischievious Cat whose ability to get into trouble endears him to most children from pre-school to early third grade. Reader format.

Interest Level: 1-3. Reading Level: 1.2. Further Search Topics: Fantasy, Cats-Fiction, Troublemakers-Fiction, Humorous Fiction, Snow-Fiction, Poetry, Best Sellers, Stories in Rhyme.

SOCCER-BIOGRAPHY

Burchard, Susan H. Sports star: Pele. HarBrace J 1976, 64 pp.

At age 35, when many people thought he might be "past his prime," Pele proved he could still play superior soccer. More details about the series in *Sports Hero: Bill Walton* entry, by Marshall Burchard. Sports Star series.

Interest Level: 2-6. Reading Level: 3.1. Further Search Topics: Biography, Soccer-Biography, Pele, Group 2.

SOUND

Branley, Franklyn M. High sounds, low sounds; illus by Paul Galdone. Har-Row 1967, 35 pp.

A no-nonsense, informative, thorough introduction to sound, sound waves, and hearing. Includes a couple of simple, illustrative experiments. Useful through third and fourth grade with no problems. The picture book format and opening and closing questions to the reader may turn away fifth and sixth grade users. Worth trying anyway. No index or table of contents. Let's-Read-and-Find-Out-Science-Book series.

Interest Level: 2-4. Reading Level: 2.2. Further Search Topics: Sound, Experiments, Scientific.

Malone, Mary. Annie Sullivan; illus by Lydia Rosier. Putnam 1971, 61 pp.

This is a very brief sketch of both Annie Sullivan's life and Helen Keller's life. Their lives were so intertwined that they cannot be separated. But because they are combined in such a short book, neither woman can be treated in much depth. That fact is not as harmful here as it might otherwise be, because even a bare bones description of the life of this extraordinary deaf, blind and mute woman or her near-blind, dedicated teacher, is interesting.

Interest Level: 2-5. Reading Level: 2.2. Further Search Topics: Sullivan, Annie, Keller, Helen, Vision, Biography, Physically Handicapped, Sound, Courage.

SPIDERS

Chenery, Janet. Wolfie; illus by Marc Simont. Har-Row 1969, 64 pp.

This slight but satisfying story is the vehicle for much information about spiders. Harry caught a wolf spider. To keep his sister Polly out of the way, Harry and his friend George told her she could see the spider only after she caught 100 flies to feed it. In the meantime, they took the spider to the nature center where they were treated to a fascinating lesson about insects and spiders (especially wolf spiders). It's too bad that the book's cartoon style illustrations prevent this book from being very useful beyond grade three.

Interest Level: 1-3. Reading Level: 2.1. Further Search Topics: Spiders, Pets, Nature Study, Group 2.

Goldin, Augusta. Spider silk; illus by Joseph Low. Har-Row 1964, unp (34 pp).

No gimmicks here, just straight-forward information about spider webs. Where are spider webs found? How are they formed? What are their shapes? For what are they used? How strong are they? And, what are the other uses of spider silk? In answering those questions the author also gives a bit of information about particular types of spiders. The book can easily be used through grade three. Its picture book format will turn many fourth and fifth graders away even though the book's information is still quite interesting and useful. Let's-Read- & -Find-Out Science Book series.

Interest Level: 1-5. Reading Level: 2.2. Further Search Topics: Spiders, Nature Study, Group 2.

SPIDERS-FICTION

Arkhurst, Joyce. The adventures of Spider; West African folktales; illus by Jerry Pinkney. Little 1964, 58 pp.

A delightful collection of six West African folktales about Spider. Spider is mischievous, greedy, lazy and clever. He loves to eat and he hates to work. Four of the stories tell of Spider's ill-fated attempts to get food without having to work for it ("How Spider Got a Thin Waist," "How Spider Got a Bald Head," "How Spider Helped a Fisherman," and "Why Spiders Live in Dark Corners"). One story tells of his greed ("How the World Got Wisdom"), and only one story is complimentary ("Why Spider Lives in Ceilings"). All are short, gentle, humorous, and adapt well to dramatization or retelling.

Interest Level: 2-6. Reading Level 3.1. Further Search Topics: Humorous Fiction, Spiders-Fiction, Folklore, Tricksters-Fiction, Africa-Folklore, Group 2, Read Aloud, Creation-Fiction, Drama.

SPIES-FICTION

Allen, Linda. Lionel and the spy next door; illus by Margot Apple. Morrow 1980, 94 pp.

No one in Lionel's family understood why he wanted to be a spy; but then, he couldn't understand why they were anthropologists and motorcycle freaks. Even though he wasn't supposed to do any more spying (especially while his parents were away) Lionel couldn't resist watching the man who moved into Miss Bannister's house, next-door. Mark Shakespeare was his name. His name was suspicious enough, but his actions firmly convinced Lionel that Mark was a spy. Lionel's attempts to trail Shakespeare only succeeded in angering others in the neighborhood. He interrupted a bird watcher and irritated a woman walking a large dog. She was already angry with Lionel's grandfather for disturbing the quiet neighborhood with his motorcycles. The closer Lionel got to finding proof that Mark was a spy, the friendlier Mark became. Mark even gave Lionel the old clock which Lionel and Miss Bannister had carefully wound each week until the old woman's death. When Lionel's grandfather finally convinced Lionel that Mark should be left alone, Mark enlisted Lionel's help in a project that left Lionel wondering again. Much to Lionel's surprise, he learned that the papers and secret documents he and Mark had burned had all belonged to Miss Bannister, Mark's great-aunt. Forty years earlier she, not Mark, had been a spy. Lionel had been wrong about who it was, but right about a spy living next-door.

Here we find a slightly anti-climactic ending to an otherwise enjoyable book. A grandfather who rides with motorcycle gangs and the intrigue of spying should be of interest to many readers. Readers may need a little help with the few British phrases that dot the book, but otherwise, the book has an impressively consistent reading level.

Interest Level: 4-6. Reading Level: 3.1. Further Search Topics: Spies-Fiction, Family-Fiction, Mystery and Detective Stories, Individualists-Fiction, Motorcycles-Fiction, Occupations-Fiction.

Bunting, Eve. The skate patrol; illus by Don Madden. Albert Whitman 1980, 40 pp.

The book is funny, clever, undemanding and short. The combination of those qualities plus its slight mystery and its consistent reading level make this a very appealing and useful book for young readers. The plot is simple: in the hopes that their neighbors would be so grateful that they would allow the boys to roller skate in the neighborhood again, two friends decided to capture a local thief. James and Milton even knew who the thief was. He was the "mysterious man" who sat in the park. They only had to capture him in the act of stealing to prove that they were correct. They watched him continuously and trailed him as he followed old ladies. Then came the day that they heard Mrs. Grump scream that her purse had been snatched. The boys sped after the "mysterious man" on their skates. They caught him and knocked him down. To their surprise he declared that he was an undercover policeman and they were letting the real thief get away. Off they went again. This time they caught the right person and were rewarded just the way that they had hoped: Mrs. Crump (not Grump) promised that the boys would be allowed to roller skate any time they wished. A light and lively entertainment.

Interest Level: 2-4. Reading Level: 2.2. Further Search Topics: Mystery and Detective Stories, Humorous Fiction, Spies-Fiction, Roller Skating-Fiction, Crime-Fiction, Best Sellers.

Fife, Dale. Follow that ghost!; illus by Joan Drescher. Dutton 1979, 58 pp.

In short sentences reminiscent of "Dragnet," Chuck tells a very simple story of Chuck and Jason's first detective case. He and Jason were practicing following people, when their next-door-neighbor caught them following her home. Instead of being angry at the two boys, Glory decided to hire them to find the ghost she and her mother were hearing at 5:00 every morning. Despite their best attempts to capture and bury the ghost, or a find a human cause for the ghostly sounds, Chuck and Jason couldn't rid Glory's apartment of its ghost. Their final effort nearly resulted in injury to a neighbor. Ultimately, Chuck discovered that the ghost was merely a displaced woodpecker looking for a new home.

Not a terribly ambitious mystery, but one whose consistent reading level, familiar urban setting and interesting characters will please many young readers.

Interest Level: 2-4. Reading Level: 2.1. Further Search Topics: Ghosts-Fiction, Mystery and Detective Stories, Spies-Fiction, Humorous Fiction.

Hildick, Edmund W. The case of the snowbound spy; illus by Lisl Weil. Macmillan 1980, 132 pp.

One snowy morning McGurk called the five members of his organization together to decipher a code. The code was part of a message from someone who wanted to hire them and would pay $5.00 a day. When they broke the code and met their employer, Mr. Fitch, he gave the group another code as part of their assignment. The second code told them where to deliver a small package that Mr. Fitch gave them. They were to pick up another coded message at the same place. After three pick-ups and drops they would be finished and Mr. Fitch, an ex-government spy, would have proved he was still a trustworthy and capable person to an ex-colleague with whom he wanted to work on a book. It seemed like just the challenging kind of assignment the McGurk Organization looked for. As they worked, however, it began to look more and more as if they were being

used for illegal business. While Joey and McGurk staked out the next drop-off spot, Willie, Brains and Wanda pretended to Mr. Fitch to be unsuspecting. By working quickly and cleverly and by alerting the police, the McGurk gang uncovered and stopped two industrial spies who were stealing secret information about a new copying machine.

See *The Case of the Bashful Bank Robber* for series information. McGurk Mystery series.

Interest Level: 3-6. Reading Level: 3.1. Further Search Topics: Mystery and Detective Stories, Spies-Fiction, Detectives-Fiction, Gangs-Fiction, Humorous Fiction, Nonverbal Communication-Fiction, Crime-Fiction.

Packard, Edward. Your code name is Jonah; illus by Paul Granger. Bantam 1980, 114 pp.

See *Sugarcane Island* for information about books in this series. Paperback only. Choose Your Own Adventure series.

Interest Level: 2-6. Reading Level: 3.2. Further Search Topics: Nonverbal Communication-Fiction, Best Sellers, Spies-Fiction, Group 2.

STORIES IN RHYME

Berenstain, Stan. The bike lesson. Beginner 1964, 61 pp.

This story of a bumbling father trying to teach his eager son how to ride a bike is pure silliness. Much of the action is shown in the humorous illustrations. The rhymed text adds dialogue and description. Good fun.

Interest Level: K-3. Reading Level: 1.2. Further Search Topics: Humorous Fiction, Bicycles and Bicycling-Fiction, Stories in Rhyme, Group 2.

Seuss, Dr. One fish, two fish, red fish, blue fish. Beginner 1960, 63pp.

Beginning with one almost ordinary-looking fish, this is a humorous look at the "funny things that go by." When Dr. Seuss says "funny," he really means highly imaginative, whimsical, and totally nonsensical. Each of the more than 20 silly creatures are described and appropriately illustrated to appeal to a child's sense of the ridiculous. Reader.

Interest Level: 1-2. Reading Level: 1.1. Further Search Topics: Fantasy, Wit and Humor, Poetry, Humorous Fiction, Stories in Rhyme.

Seuss, Dr. Hop on Pop. Beginner 1963, 64pp.

Between one and four rhyming words are introduced or reviewed and used in a silly sentence on each page. The sentence is interpreted with even more amusing illustrations. It is one of the simplest of books (no story at all) and yet it is usable through second grade because of Dr. Seuss' playful style and ridiculous illustrations. Reader format.

Interest Level: 1-2. Reading Level: 1.1. Further Search Topics: Poetry, Best Sellers, Wit and Humor, Humorous Fiction, Stories in Rhyme.

Seuss, Dr. The foot book. Random 1968, unp (27 pp).

Left feet, right feet, big feet, small feet; with its rhyme, silly illustrations and rhythmic celebration of feet of all descriptions, this book is a sure winner with the very young. Reader format.

Interest Level 1-2. Reading Level: 1.1. Further Search Topics: Best Sellers, Feet-Fiction, Humorous Fiction, Poetry, Wit and Humor, Stories in Rhyme.

STUTTERING-FICTION

Kelley, Sally. Trouble with explosives. Bradbury 1976, 117 pp.

Polly Banks stuttered very badly. She wanted to stop but she couldn't. Moving, entering a new school, and facing a mean teacher who seemed in need of psychiatric help, all made Polly's stuttering worse. When Sis, Polly's new friend, rose to Polly's defense in one confrontation too many with Miss Patterson, the teacher took cruel revenge. Polly's desire to help Sis, her need to do something about her stuttering, and an understanding psychiatrist, all helped Polly learn to help herself with her speech problem. At the same time, she began to understand and have confidence in herself and her family.

Another "problem book" that older elementary school readers seem to crave. Polly and Sis are both very sympathetic characters who bring to life many of the uncertainties of growing up. Print and line spacing of only average size but otherwise a good choice.

Interest Level: 4-6. Reading Level: 3.2. Further Search Topics: Academic Problems-Fiction, Stuttering-Fiction, Psychiatrists-Fiction, School Stories, Mental Illness-Fiction, Troublemakers-Fiction, Courage-Fiction, Physically Handicapped-Fiction, Children-Growth-Fiction, Moving, Household-Fiction.

SUBURBIA-FICTION

Lowry, Lois. Anastasia again! HM 1981, 145 pp.

This is a sequel that is as funny and well-written as its predecessor. Because its plot involves less common experiences, this book may not enjoy quite the wide-spread success of *Anastasia Krupnik*. However, among those readers who liked their first meeting with Anastasia, this book will find many fans.

Anastasia's parents astounded her when they announced that the family was going to move from their Cambridge, Massachusetts apartment to a house in the suburbs. She didn't like the idea of leaving the apartment, but she *hated* the idea of the suburbs. The only thing that made the move bearable was the house itself. Anastasia had said she would move only if they could find a house with a tower—and they had. After she got over the shock of moving, Anastasia began to enjoy her new home. She met a neighborhood boy who became a special friend, she tried to help her cranky elderly neighbor Mrs. Stein make friends, and she even wrote a short mystery book.

Anastasia is as spunky and original as before. She is a bit precocious, but her precocity is nothing compared to that of her brother. At two-and-a-half years old, he speaks as well as many adults. As we mentioned above, the book will be most appealing to readers who want second helpings of Anastasia's adventures. The print is slightly smaller here than in the first title.

Interest Level: 4-6. Reading Level: 2.2. Further Search Topics: Moving, Household-Fiction, City Life-Fiction, Suburbia-Fiction, Humorous Fiction, Aging-Fiction, Writing-Fiction, Family-Fiction, Everyday Stories.

Sharmat, Marjorie W. The Lancelot closes at five; illus by Lisl Weil. Macmillan 1976, 120 pp.

Despite a somewhat slow beginning, this is an amusing, almost sensitive story of two friends who decided to spend the night in the model home of the new housing development in which they both lived. Hutch, a health food fanatic whose mother pronounced judgment on everything Hutch did, conceived of the idea as her way of breaking away. Abby went along for the fun of it. When the local newspaper wrote of unusual vandalism at the model home, the townspeople became engrossed in finding the culprits. As the adults became enraged about the crime wave, their children began to admire the clever idea. Soon, almost every youngster in town had confessed to spending the night in the model home. By the time Abby and Hutch got around to admitting they had slept there, no one believed them. Only a sock with Abby's name in it could tie Abby and Hutch to the scene of the crime. As the book ends, the police have begun a thorough search of the house, after a real robbery, and the sock's discovery is imminent.

Interest Level: 4-6. Reading Level: 3.2. Further Search Topics: Humorous Fiction, Suburbia-Fiction, Runaways-Fiction, Crime-Fiction, Individualists-Fiction, Family Problems-Fiction.

SULLIVAN, ANNIE

Malone, Mary. Annie Sullivan; illus by Lydia Rosier. Putnam 1971, 61 pp.

This is a very brief sketch of both Annie Sullivan's life and Helen Keller's life. Their lives were so intertwined that they cannot be separated. But because they are combined in such a short book, neither woman can be treated in much depth. That fact is not as harmful here as it might otherwise be, because even a bare bones description of the life of this extraordinary deaf, blind and mute woman or her near-blind, dedicated teacher, is interesting.

Interest Level: 2-5. Reading Level: 2.2. Further Search Topics: Sullivan, Annie, Keller, Helen, Vision, Biography, Physically Handicapped, Sound, Courage.

SUN

Branley, Franklyn M. Eclipse: darkness in daytime; illus by Donald Crews. Har-Row 1973, 33 pp.

The subject is so well-explained and the book is so physically attractive, it's a shame that some older readers will be put off by this title's picture book appearance. Aside from an occasional jarring, condescending note, this is a fine introduction to an interesting subject. Use comfortably with third and fourth graders. Recommend to fifth graders with caution. No index or table of contents. Lets-Read-and-Find-Out-Science-Book series.

Interest Level: 2-4. Reading Level: 2.2. Further Search Topics: Sun, Astronomy, Eclipses, Moon.

SUPERHEROES-FICTION

Conford, Ellen. The revenge of the incredible Dr. Rancid and his youthful assistant, Jeffrey. Little 1980, 119 pp.

There were two people Jeff hated and feared: Dewey Belasco, the sixth grade bully and Lana McCabe, Dewey's female counterpart. Only in his imagination could Jeff stand up to them. In the stories Jeff wrote in a notebook, he and his friend Dr. Rancid were superheroes who rid the world of such scum as Lana and Dewey. In real life, Jeff ran from bullies rather than face them; even if it meant that an eight-year-old boy and a girl Jeff's age were left to stand up to Dewey by themselves. Although the way Jeff took care of an injured child soon had most everyone thinking of Jeff as a hero, he saw that, too, as an indication of his failings at first. Finally, something inside Jeff snapped and he answered Dewey back when Dewey insulted him. Before long Jeff found himself flat on his back with a bloody nose and so many pains he couldn't count them. But, he had finally faced Dewey and showed Dewey that he was no longer afraid. Jeff felt good.

Similar to *The 18th Emergency* but a higher reading level. The notebook stories will appeal to fans of superheroes, but because they are stories within a story, they may also cause difficulties. Spacing between lines is somewhat narrow.

Interest Level: 5-6. Reading Level: 4.2. Further Search Topics: Courage-Fiction, Bullies-Fiction, Writing-Fiction, School Stories, Superheroes-Fiction, Humorous Fiction.

SUPERNATURAL-FICTION

Christopher, Matt. Devil pony; illus by Lorence Bjorkland. Little 1977, 103 pp.

This book is a bit of a change from the usual Matt Christopher story line. There is no sports interest here; instead there is a good suspense story about a boy, his cousin and a horse. Stu had watched the black Morgan named Midnight being born and had fallen in love with him. A year later he returned to his aunt and uncle's ranch to claim the horse, as he had been promised he could, but strange things began to happen around him. His cousin Wilbur warned him that he had probably annoyed the ranch poltergeist by deciding to take Midnight away. The bizarre occurrences escalated until Stu was almost tempted to leave Midnight at the ranch. Then Stu discovered Wilbur had been orchestrating everything that had happened because he had wanted to keep the horse himself. Although Stu decided to take Midnight home as he had planned, their new honesty led Stu to believe that he and Wilbur could be friends after all. A surprisingly good story with strong reader appeal.

Interest Level: 3-6. Reading Level: 3.1. Further Search Topics: Horses-Fiction, Supernatural-Fiction, Ghosts-Fiction, Jealousy-Fiction, Relatives-Fiction.

Hildick, Edmund W. The case of the invisible dog; illus by Lisl Weil. Macmillan 1977, 101 pp.

Brains Bellingham, a nine-year-old scientific genius, interrupted the McGurk Organization's Annual Picnic with an invisible dog. It was only a short time before McGurk and his friends were convinced that Brains' discovery of how to make things invisible was the greatest event since putting a man on the moon. Although they had always scorned the idea of including anyone else in the Organization, they decided to persuade Brains to join. But, before the day was over, they discovered not only that they had been duped, but exactly how Brains had made the impossible seem real. The Organization took its revenge by using Brain's own trick to make him confess. When Brains began laughing at how well his trick had been used in reverse, McGurk admitted how impressed they all had been by Brain's clever thinking. The outcome of their discussion was that Brains was invited, a second time, to become a member of the McGurk Organization.

See *The Case of the Bashful Bank Robber* for series information. McGurk Mystery series.

Interest Level: 3-6. Reading Level: 3.1. Further Search Topics: Mystery and Detective Stories, Detectives-Fiction, Gangs-Fiction, Dogs-Fiction, Supernatural-Fiction, Humorous Fiction, Jealousy-Fiction.

Hildick, Edmund W. The case of the phantom frog; illus by Lisl Weil. Macmillan 1979, 121 pp.

The McGurk Organization would not, under ordinary circumstances, have agreed to babysit for seven-year-old Bela, but there was an unusual twist to Bela's case. Bela's aunt, who asked them to babysit while she worked in her sculpture studio, had heard the eerie sounds of a VERY large frog coming from Bela's room. At first it appeared to the group that Bela actually turned into a frog at night, a werefrog. But,

upon investigation they found a very clever, very lonely, and very unhappy young boy who had invented the phantom because he was afraid that his aunt would make him give up his pet frog.

See *The Case of the Bashful Bank Robber* for series information. McGurk Mystery series.

Interest Level: 3-5. Reading Level: 3.1. Further Search Topics: Mystery and Detective Stories, Gangs-Fiction, Frogs-Fiction, Supernatural-Fiction, Transformations-Fiction, Detectives-Fiction, Babysitting-Fiction, Humorous Fiction, Occupations-Fiction.

Sleator, William. Into the dream; illus by Ruth Sanderson. Dutton 1979, 137 pp.

Paul and Francine each started having what, at first, seemed like nightmares. As the dreams became more detailed and forboding, they discovered that they were sharing the same nightmare. They dreamed of a four-year-old boy, swirling lights, and a large dog. After awhile they figured out that the dog was trying to save the little boy from some unknown danger. As the pieces of the puzzle began to increase in number, Paul and Francine decided that the dream was in some way connected to a night over four years earlier when they had both been staying at the same motel. They, a pregnant woman, and a pregnant dog had all been affected by the telepathic power given off by a spaceship. The progeny of the woman and the dog had been given extraordinary mental powers; powers that a secret government agency wanted to mold and then put to their own use. The danger Paul and Francine felt came from two government agents sent to take the young boy Noah from his mother. Their attempt ended in a bizarre scene at an amusement park, where Noah levitated a broken ferris wheel chair to safety. By thus exposing his talent in public, Noah unconsciously insured against its secret and unsupervised use by the government.

A terrifying and suspense-filled psychological thriller whose main problems are a slightly overdrawn ending and a variable reading level. Reading level drops as low as 2.1 and climbs occasionally to 4.1.

Interest Level: 5-6. Reading Level: 3.2. Further Search Topics: Best Sellers, Supernatural-Fiction, Occult-Fiction, Flying Saucers-Fiction, Nonverbal Communication-Fiction, Dreams-Fiction, Survival-Fiction, Extra Sensory Perception-Fiction, Horror-Fiction.

SURVIVAL

Kluger, Ruth. The secret ship. Doubleday 1978, 136 pp.

A tense, true story about the secret transportation of hundreds of European Jews to Palestine early in World War II. The transport ship became ice-bound in a Rumanian harbor, the crew mutinied and the passengers threatened to expose their plight to the world. In complete charge of the operation was a 25-year-old woman. The book closes with a summary of the Jews' continuing fight for Israel.

The historical understanding that is necessary in order to really appreciate this excellent book make it best suited to readers no younger than sixth grade.

The paper on which this book is printed is so thin that the print shows through from one page to another and the print at the beginning and the end of the book is italicized. Both factors may distract the reader.

Interest Level: 6+ Reading Level: 3.1. Further Search Topics: World War II, Jews, Women, Sex Role, Israel, Survival, Courage.

SURVIVAL-FICTION

Angell, Judie. Dear Lola; or how to build your own family. Bradbury 1980, 166 pp.

Arthur (age 18), James (13), Annie and Al-Willie (twins, age 10), Edmund (9), and Ben (5) wanted to run away from the orphanage and find a place where they could be a real family. After waiting months, their chance arrived one night. They escaped in a van and began living on the road. It was weeks before they found a house in which they thought they could live. They didn't want trouble with local authorities, so most of the children enrolled in school and pretended to be living with their widowed grandfather. Only James (who never left his room) and Arthur stayed home. Arthur was the anonymous author of a nationally syndicated newspaper advice column. It was with the income from his "Dear Lola" column that Arthur was able to support the "family." When the townspeople eventually began to wonder about the "strange" behavior of the children, they investigated and found no adult in charge of the household. Arthur went to court to be appointed the childrens' guardian, but the judge ruled against him. Rather than be sent to foster homes again, Arthur and the children raced from the courtroom. The book ends as the family is once more together and on their own. An unusual cast of characters in a surprisingly warm and humorous book.

Interest Level: 4-6. Reading Level 3.1. Further Search Topics: Loners-Fiction, Runaways-Fiction, Orphans-Fiction, Survival-Fiction, Family Problems-Fiction, Family-Fiction, Read Aloud, Foster Homes-Fiction, Individualists-Fiction, Humorous Fiction.

Bennett, Jay. The pigeon. Methuen 1980, 147 pp.

Despite a low testing score, this is not a truly easy book to read. The author assumes his readers are fairly sophisticated and worldly, thus he does not explain the meaning of the Iron Cross symbol or the word Aryan. The book's language varies from simple to difficult, making the reading level inconsistent (2.1 - 4.1). The setting is dark and forbidding; an underground world of fugitives and terrorists. And yet, the book will be popular with many readers in sixth grade; it will be even more popular with older readers. The tension in this story of a teenage boy, blamed for the murder of his ex-girlfriend, is almost palpable. Brian's flight from the police and his desire to find Donna's murderer take him directly into the midst of a ring of terrorists, for whom life has no meaning. In Brian's attempt to prove his innocence, two more lives are lost, but hundreds more are saved as Brian discovers and stops a bomb threat. The author has used riveting action, short, clipped sentences, and terse dialogue to create a very successful, highly suspenseful book. Print size is only moderate.

Interest Level: 6 . Reading Level: 3.2. Further Search Topics: Mystery and Detective Stories, Terrorism-Fiction, Murder-Fiction, Best Sellers, Crime-Fiction, Courage-Fiction, Survival-Fiction, Runaways-Fiction.

Bulla, Clyde Robert. Dexter; illus by Glo Coalson. Har-Row 1973, 69 pp.

This is not as simple a story as it first appears. Dave, 12 years old and lonely, had hoped his new neighbors would be friends. But, the Arvin family kept very much to themselves until Dave accidentally discovered Alex, the Arvin's son, doing tricks on a trapeze in the barn. Because Dave kept the secret and shared Alex's love for Dexter, his circus pony, the boys soon became friends. Then in one horrible night, the Arvins were forced to leave the town and Dexter

was so badly hurt he was believed to be dead. A week later Dave found Dexter alive, but crippled for life and so frightened that no one could get near him. The horse surprised everyone and managed to live through a very harsh winter as well as the townspeople's determination to kill him. When Alex and his father returned, almost a year later, they found Dexter and took the old and feeble horse back to a ranch with them. The story is told with sympathy, with an understanding of how it feels to be lonely, and with tension and suspense. It's appeal should last from third through sixth grade. Print size is smaller than Bulla's usual.

Interest Level: 3-6. Reading Level: 3.1. Further Search Topics: Survival-Fiction, Acrobats and Acrobatics-Fiction, Horses-Fiction, Read Aloud, Circus-Fiction, Loneliness-Fiction, Friendship-Fiction.

Bulla, Clyde Robert. The sword in the tree; illus by Paul Galdone. Har-Row 1956, 113 pp.

Shan didn't like or trust his Uncle Lionel, who had suddenly appeared at the castle gates after being away many years. Just as suddenly, Shan's father disappeared or died. Shan and his mother soon realized that Lionel wanted to take over the castle, even if it meant killing them. To save themselves, Shan and his mother fled. After walking many miles, they found a poor goat herder and his family who gave them a place to live. Sometime later Shan decided to travel to see King Arthur and ask for help in reclaiming the castle from Lionel. It wasn't until Shan was able to prove the castle was his, and Lionel lost a duel to one of Arthur's knights, that Shan was given back his home. Deep in the castle dungeon Shan found his father, still alive but imprisoned by Lionel.

This book, with its short chapters, short sentences, and steadily progressing plot should interest even the most reluctant reader from grade two through six.

Interest Level: 2-6. Reading Level: 2.2. Further Search Topics: Knights and Knighthood-Fiction, Survival-Fiction, Royalty-Fiction, Best Sellers, Courage-Fiction.

Bulla, Clyde Robert. A lion to guard us; illus by Michele Chessare. Har-Row 1981, 117 pp.

Bulla's writing isn't quite as successful here as elsewhere. This story of three London children's attempt to go to their father in Jamestown, Virginia, has danger, adventure, daring and promise. It also has too many characters to allow the reader to get to know any of them well. There are also too many very short chapters to allow plot development (23 chapters and 117 pages). The short sentences help to keep the reading level low, but a glossary would have been useful to fully explain the many unfamiliar terms.

Despite its problems, the book is still useful. The story is based on the 1609 voyage of the Sea Adventure. Blown far off course and badly damaged by a storm, the ship landed at Bermuda rather than Jamestown. The survivors were unable to sail again for over nine months. When they reached Jamestown, they found that few people had survived the very harsh year.

The three Freebold children are the focus of this story. When their mother died they left London to find their father in the New World. Having no money of their own, they were lucky to find a doctor friend to pay their ship's passage and to go with them. Halfway across the ocean, the doctor was swept overboard and drowned. From that time until they found their father barely alive, the children were on their own, even though they were still with the ship's passengers.

Although not the best of Bulla, this is still serviceable as a piece of historical fiction (hard to get children to read), or as a choice for the lover of survival and/or sea stories.

Interest Level: 3-5. Reading Level: 2.1. Further Search Topics: United States-History-Fiction, Historical Fiction, Courage-Fiction, Survival-Fiction, Shipwrecks-Fiction, Voyages and Travels-Fiction, Seafaring Life-Fiction.

Byars, Betsy. Trouble River; illus by Rocco Negri. Viking Pr. 1969, 158 pp.

A gripping adventure story of survival. After being attacked by an Indian in the middle of the night, Dewey and his grandmother rushed to Trouble River to board a small raft which Dewey had just finished making. They thought they would only need to navigate a few miles down the river to safety at a neighbor's home, but found instead that the neighbor's cabin had been burned down. For almost 40 miles they fought against the unknown river, wolves and rapids.

This is a book that should satisfy many reluctant readers. It's frequent dialogue, fast action and high interest are only occasionally marred by an overly long sentence.

Interest Level: 3-6. Reading Level: 3.1. Further Search Topics: Courage-Fiction, Frontier and Pioneer Life-Fiction, Survival-Fiction, Grandparents-Fiction, Voyages and Travels-Fiction, Best Sellers, Read Aloud.

Clifford, Eth. Help, I'm a prisoner in the library; illus by George Hughes. HM 1979, 103 pp.

When their car stopped, Mary Rose and Jo-Beth were left alone in a strange city while their father went to find some gas. Jo-Beth needed to use the bathroom, so the sisters headed for the closest public building they could see, the library. No one saw them go in, so no one knew that they were locked inside when the librarian secured the building for the night. With the lights out and a blizzard outside, the library was a very spooky place. The girls tried calling the police, but the police wouldn't take them seriously. Then they heard groans and eerie moans from the second floor. Gathering all their courage, the girls went to investigate, only to discover the librarian lying hurt and unconscious. Their ingenuity and imagination helped the sisters through the difficult hours before they were all rescued.

Don't read it too carefully or the book's implausibilities will become very evident. Most young readers, however, will enjoy this story for its suspense, spooky atmosphere and adventurous girls, and they will ignore its weaknesses.

Interest Level: 2-5. Reading Level: 3.1. Further Search Topics: Disasters-Fiction, Snow-Fiction, Brothers and Sisters-Fiction, Libraries-Fiction, Survival-Fiction, Courage-Fiction, Group 2.

Clymer, Eleanor. Chipmunk in the forest; illus by Ingrid Fetz. Atheneum 1965, 56 pp.

A simple story of an Indian boy who learned the meaning of the word "courage". Chipmunk had never admitted to anyone that he was afraid of the forest. But when his uncle tried to teach him to hunt, Chipmunk was too frightened to be quiet, and thus he scared away all the animals. He returned to the village in disgrace to do "women's work." One of his jobs was to watch Little Brother. When Little Brother disappeared, Chipmunk went in search of him. It began to snow as Chipmunk went farther and farther into the forest, but even though he was frightened, Chipmunk kept on looking. By the time he found Little Brother, the snow had covered their tracks. Chipmunk had to use all that he had learned from his uncle to get them safely home. When he arrived back at the village, Chipmunk had finally proven that he was brave.

Interest Level: 2-4. Reading Level: 2.1. Further Search Topics: Indians of North America-Fiction, Courage-Fiction, Snow-Fiction, Hunting-Fiction, Survival-Fiction.

Clymer, Eleanor. Luke was there; illus by Diane de Groat. HR & W 1973, 74 pp.

Julius' father, uncle and finally his step-father had all walked out on him. Even his mother had left him, although she hadn't wanted to go. When his mother had been taken to the hospital, Julius and his younger brother Danny were sent to a children's home. Julius felt alone and cheated until he met a young, black, social worker named Luke. Luke liked and respected Julius and helped Julius learn to feel the same way about himself. When Luke, too, left Julius, Julius was so angry at the world that he stole food and then money. Afraid to go back to the children's home because he thought he'd be caught and punished, Julius ran away. It wasn't until he found an abandoned child, about Danny's age, who needed care, that Julius returned to the home. Luke was there when he arrived, just when Julius needed him most. Luke listened to Julius' unhappy feelings, arranged for him to see his mother and helped him begin to accept the fact that life is not always fair.

Julius tells his own story in a realistic, straight-forward book that will touch most readers. Only the lack of quotation marks and inadequate spacing between the lines may slow the reader.

Interest Level: 3-6. Reading Level: 2.2. Further Search Topics: Runaways-Fiction, Orphans-Fiction, Juvenile Delinquency-Fiction, Divorce and Separation-Fiction, Friendship-Fiction, Courage-Fiction, Survival-Fiction, Loneliness-Fiction, Best Sellers, Read Aloud.

Packard, Edward. Sugarcane Island; illus by Barbara Carter. Archway 1976, 105 pp.

The warning on the first page, that the book should *not* be read straight through, tells you that this book is different. And different it is. It is the first of what is now a new type of book; the "Choose Your Own Adventure" story. The formula is simple and highly successful, especially with reluctant readers. The reader is made the central character of the book. After a very brief series of events that set the stage, the reader is given choices to make. Upon making a decision, the reader is instructed to proceed to another page of the book. More action is described before the reader must make another choice. The sequence of action, choice, action and choice continues until the reader has finally completed an entire story. The books can be read over and over and the reader may never repeat exactly the same story unless he/she makes all of the same choices. What distinguishes one book from another is the setting, genre, and/or author (there are three: Edward Packard, R. A. Montgomery, and D. Terman). Don't expect quality writing or consistent reading levels because you won't find either. (Reading levels vary from 2.2 to 3.2 for most titles). What you will find is dependable, action-filled, enticing, light reading. Some are available only in paperback editions where the print size is fairly small. Choose Your Own Adventure series.

Interest Level: 2-6. Reading Level: 3.1. Further Search Topics: Shipwrecks-Fiction, Best Sellers, Survival-Fiction, Group 2.

Renner, Beverly. The Hideaway summer; illus by Ruth Sanderson. Har-Row 1978, 134 pp.

On their way to summer camp, Addie suddenly got off the bus and took her younger brother Clay to see the place where Addie had spent prior summer vacations. It was their grandmother's house and a small cabin called the Hideaway. The house had been sold after their grandmother had died that year, but Addie's father had decided to keep the Hideaway. Much to Addie's surprise she found the Hideaway beautifully fixed-up, just as Gram had promised she would do one day.

When they missed the last bus out of the tiny town and realized that they had enough money to buy the food they would need, Addie and Clay decided to make the Hideaway their summer home. One phone call to the camp and weekly calls to their father kept people from worrying about them. Their discovery of two small raccoons meant that their days were filled with caring for and training the animals. In addition, they had to build a warning system so that no one would discover them and they had to get their food and provisions from town about every two weeks without being too noticeable. They even had to figure out a way to survive a wild summer storm, a flood, and poachers who hunted raccoons. By summer's end Addie and Clay had grown independent, resourceful, and very close to each other.

An exciting story whose short chapters and fairly short sentences keep the reading level reasonably low. Print is dark and of adequate size, but space between the lines is somewhat narrow.

Interest Level: 4-6. Reading Level: 3.1. Further Search Topics: Brothers and Sisters-Fiction, Runaways-Fiction, Pets-Fiction, Survival-Fiction, Vacation-Fiction, Raccoons-Fiction, Read Aloud.

Roy, Ron. Nightmare Island; illus by Robert MacLean. Dutton 1981, 69 pp.

Harley didn't want to take his younger brother camping, but because he had promised his father he would, the boys packed a tent, sleeping bags, and plenty of food into a small boat and set off to nearby Little Island. Hidden in his pocket, Harley had matches and marshmallows for a midnight marshmallow roast. After they had finished the bag of marshmallows, Harley threw the last log of the fire into the water. The water erupted into flames that quickly spread around the island. As the boys fought desperately to save themselves and to find shelter, they realized that the large shape they had seen in the distance must have been an oil tanker that had spread an oil slick all around the island. With time running out Harley gave his brother the only truly secure shelter from the fire, curled up on top of a tall rock and went to sleep. When he awoke the fire had burned itself out and help was on the way.

Most young readers will be able to suspend disbelief long enough to enjoy this as an exciting adventure and survival story, but it is hard to believe that two young boys could not only survive such a holocaust, but that they could sleep through part of it, too. It is also difficult to believe that there would not be more of a fuss made about the oil tanker blowing up. Plot problems aside, young readers seem to love the story.

Interest Level: 3-6. Reading Level: 3.2. Further Search Topics: Brothers and Sisters-Fiction, Survival-Fiction, Camping-Fiction, Disasters-Fiction, Best Sellers.

Sachs, Marily. The bears' house; illus by Louis Glanzman. Doubleday 1971, 81 pp.

Don't let the benign appearance of this book fool you. This is a disturbing, almost brutal story. It is the story of Fran Ellen, a fourth grader with more problems than anyone should have to shoulder at one time. Her father had left the family and her mother had had a mental breakdown. Fran Ellen and her older brother were left with responsibility for themselves, their mother, and three other children (including a baby). They were all ill-fed, poorly dressed, and unwashed. Neither the social worker nor Fran Ellen's teacher knew the extent of the family's problems. Fran Ellen's only happiness came from her baby sister and from a schoolroom model (of *Goldilocks and the Three Bears* and their house) into which she mentally retreated whenever she had the chance.

As the school year closed, Fran Ellen's teacher visited her home to deliver the bears' house and discovered Fran Ellen's mother and very sick baby sister. Although she hated the idea that the family might have to split up, Fran Ellen had matured enough to realize that when her teacher insisted that she would get help for the family, her teacher was taking the proper action.

The book is inappropriately illustrated to make it appear cute and even humorous. The story is far from either. It is so stark that it probably shouldn't have been illustrated at all. And because the hope that is present in the book's ending is very subtle, a review and a discussion may be necessary to help relieve some young readers' anxieties.

Interest Level: 5-6. Reading Level: 3.1. Further Search Topics: Divorce and Separation-Fiction, Challenges-Fiction, Poverty-Fiction, Family Problems-Fiction, Loners-Fiction, Survival-Fiction, Mental Illness-Fiction, Brothers and Sisters-Fiction.

Sleator, William. Into the dream; illus by Ruth Sanderson. Dutton 1979, 137 pp.

Paul and Francine each started having what, at first, seemed like nightmares. As the dreams became more detailed and forboding, they discovered that they were sharing the same nightmare. They dreamed of a four-year-old boy, swirling lights, and a large dog. After awhile they figured out that the dog was trying to save the little boy from some unknown danger. As the pieces of the puzzle began to increase in number, Paul and Francine decided that the dream was in some way connected to a night over four years earlier when they had both been staying at the same motel. They, a pregnant woman, and a pregnant dog had all been affected by the telepathic power given off by a spaceship. The progeny of the woman and the dog had been given extraordinary mental powers; powers that a secret government agency wanted to mold and then put to their own use. The danger Paul and Francine felt came from two government agents sent to take the young boy Noah from his mother. Their attempt ended in a bizarre scene at an amusement park, where Noah levitated a broken ferris wheel chair to safety. By thus exposing his talent in public, Noah unconsciously insured against its secret and unsupervised use by the government.

A terrifying and suspense-filled psychological thriller whose main problems are a slightly overdrawn ending and a variable reading level. Reading level drops as low as 2.1 and climbs occasionally to 4.1.

Interest Level: 5-6. Reading Level: 3.2. Further Search Topics: Best Sellers, Supernatural-Fiction, Occult-Fiction, Flying Saucers-Fiction, Nonverbal

Communication-Fiction, Dreams-Fiction,
Survival-Fiction, Extra Sensory Perception-Fiction,
Horror-Fiction.

Talbot, Charlene Joy. The Great Rat Island
adventure; illus by Ruth Sanderson. Atheneum
1977, 164 pp.

Joel dreaded spending the summer with his father.
His parents were divorced and Joel was sure his
father didn't want him. His father only wanted to study
birds. Great Rat Island, where Joel and his father
were to spend the summer, was of no interest to Joel.
It had no television, no one his own age, only terns.
Even the assignment Joel was given (to make sure
that no more tern eggs were stolen) sounded dull. It
led to an adventure and a friend, however, that were
anything but dull.

Joel discovered that a girl his own age was the thief
of the tern eggs. Her name was Vicky Owens. She
had run away from camp and was spending the
summer alone on Little Rat Island. Joel kept her
secret until the day of hurricane warnings. As the
storm approached Joel realized that Vicky wouldn't be
safe on Little Rat Island. Without telling anyone else
he took the only boat around and went to look for
Vicky to bring her back to Great Rat Island. He found
her with her leg stuck between two rocks, unable to
move. By the time Joel got her loose, it was too late
to get back to the big island. Not knowing what else to
do, Joel and Vicky dragged the boat inside an
abandoned building where Vicky had been living. As
the water rose around them and Vicky grew delirious
with fever, Joel set up camp in the boat. While the
building filled with water they stayed dry in the boat.
Rescue and medical care for Vicky finally came the
next day.

A solid, steadily-paced survival story for the reader
who wants a little more than just an adventure story.
Print is small.

Interest Level: 4-6. Reading Level: 3.1. Further
Search Topics: Vacation-Fiction, Family
Problems-Fiction, Birds-Fiction, Divorce and
Separation-Fiction, Disasters-Fiction, Survival-Fiction,
Runaways-Fiction.

Thompson, Jean. Brother of the wolves; illus by
Steve Marchesi. Morrow 1978, 159 pp.

Shadow Fox, a Sioux medicine man, went into a
wolves' den looking for special items he needed for
healing, but found much more. He found a baby boy
who had apparently lost his parents in an accident
and then been adopted by the wolves. Winter was
approaching and Shadow Fox knew the baby would
not be able to survive the cold, so he took the child
back to his people. The people were reluctant to
accept Wolf Brother, saying that he was an evil omen,
that he was unnatural, and that he would bring them
trouble. But Shadow Fox's will prevailed and Wolf
Brother was allowed to stay and grow up with the
Sioux.

As he grew Wolf Brother continued to communicate
with the wolves and thus fueled the rumors that grew
about him. A very jealous young man, Looks-Away,
told the people that a vision had shown him that Wolf
Brother and his wolves would one day destroy the
village and all its people. The people grew so
suspicious of Wolf Brother that, when their horses
were stolen and they faced a drought, they blamed
him and drove him from the village.

For a while Wolf Brother tried to live as a wolf but
found that he could not be totally happy. He wandered
away to look for a tribe by whom he might be
accepted. On his way, he too had a vision—a vision

that told him he would find horses and buffalo for the
Sioux and be welcomed home again. It was weeks
later before he accidentally found his tribe's horses. In
a daring move and with help from the wolves, Wolf
Brother not only rescued the horses from the raiders,
but also found buffalo just as his vision had predicted.
He was then, for the first time, fully welcomed by his
people.

This is a taut, suspenseful and mature story about a
strong and unusual character. Older readers are most
likely to respond positively to the Indian culture and
lore.

Interest Level: 5-6. Reading Level: 3.1. Further
Search Topics: Survival-Fiction, Wolves-Fiction,
Orphans-Fiction, Loners-Fiction, Indians of North
America-Fiction, Sioux Indians-Fiction,
Jealousy-Fiction, Best Sellers.

Warner, Gertrude Chandler. Mountain top mystery;
illus by David Cunningham. A. Whitman 1964, 128 pp.

A day's climb up and down Old Flat Top was all the
Alden family had wanted. Instead, when a portion of
the trail collapsed into a cave, they found themselves
stranded on top of the mountain. From their vantage
point that night they could see a shadowy light which
they investigated the next day. They found a
90-year-old Indian woman who had a strange story to
tell of treasure hidden in a cave somewhere on Old
Flat Top. The treasure was rightfully hers as the last
of her tribe, but she had never been able to find it.
The collapse of the trail and the reopening of the cave
attracted more attention than just the Alden's though.
Both an expert on caves and a young Indian boy
wanted to find out more about the cave. David, the
Indian boy, turned out to be the old woman's
grandnephew. The treasure was indeed unearthed;
David and Lovan were reunited; the treasure was
given to Lovan, and both David's and Lovan's futures
were secured.

What in the other books is mild stereotyping
becomes more noticeable here (the books are all
around 20 years old). The print is smaller here than
before but the spacing between the lines is adequate.
See entry for *The Boxcar Children* for more
information.

Interest Level: 3-6. Reading Level: 2.2. Further
Search Topics: Mystery and Detective Stories,
Treasure-Fiction, Survival-Fiction, Indians of North
America-Fiction, Mountain Climbing-Fiction, Brothers
and Sisters-Fiction.

Warner, Gertrude Chandler. The boxcar children;
illus by L. Kate Deal. A. Whitman 1950, 154 pp.

This is the first in a series of very early hi/lo books.
Although they often bear signs of stilted ''Dick and
Jane''-style writing, occasionally preach to the reader,
and are interrupted by frequent asides from the
author, the stories are still popular with young readers.
In each book the children are not simply manipulated,
but control their own destiny. They fulfill many a
child's dream of finding a loving home and family,
becoming rich, having adventures, and solving
mysteries. This is the simplest story of the series,
most of the other entries assume interest in such
advanced subjects as fossils, food sources, antiques,
or the Revolutionary War.

The only place the four orphaned Alden children had
to live was with a grandfather whom they had never
met, but whom they had heard was mean. Rather
than live with him, they decided to try and survive on
their own. They found an abandoned railway boxcar
and filled it was items that they found in a junkyard in
order to make it their home. Henry, the oldest, went to

work for a doctor who, in addition to money, gave him food and kept a silent but watchful eye over all the children without their knowledge. When Violet became ill, the children had no choice but to take her to Dr. Moore. He gave them all a temporary home and arranged for them to gradually get to know their grandfather. By the time Violet was almost well the children had grown to like the elderly stranger. It was a happy day when the children finally realized that the man to whom Dr. Moore had introduced them was really their grandfather.

Interest Level: 1-4. Reading Level: 2.1. Further Search Topics: Orphans-Fiction, Survival-Fiction, Runaways-Fiction, Brothers and Sisters-Fiction, Grandparents-Fiction.

Yolen, Jane. The boy who spoke chimp illus by David Wiesner. Knopf 1981, 120 pp.

Kriss was determined to prove to his father that, at 12 years old, he was perfectly capable of camping out by himself. To do so, he left home and headed up the coast of California with a sleeping bag, some food, a map and compass, and water. His plan was to camp, ride, and hike his way to his grandmother's house. On the way, the coast line was torn apart by the second great earthquake to strike California. The first had already destroyed great portions of the state. The second was even stronger. The truck he had been riding in was destroyed and everyone around Kriss was killed by the quake except for two chimpanzees. The chimps, in transit from one lab to another, were research animals who had been taught to use sign language. Kriss took the animals with him as he tried to get farther inland and finally home to Los Angeles. His trip not only confirmed his father's fears about Kriss' inadequacies but taught him how to overcome them. Kriss learned to communicate with the chimps, to find food and to live on his own until Old Chris, a hermit, happened along. Together they continued to brave the chaos brought about by the earthquake even when Old Chris' heart troubled him. When a helicopter finally spotted them, Kriss decided to let the chimps go wild and promised Old Chris that he would be back in the woods very soon. It was a mature, capable Kriss who returned home.

This is typical of the Capers series—much action, few background details, little characterization. The books, however, are on appealing topics; they move quickly and they create intriguing (if sometimes implausible) situations. They are light, enjoyable and very useful. Capers series.

Interest Level: 3-6. Reading Level: 3.1. Further Search Topics: California-Fiction, Disasters-Fiction, Survival-Fiction, Apes-Fiction, Nonverbal Communication-Fiction, Camping-Fiction, Runaways-Fiction, Best Sellers.

SWIMMING-FICTION

Blume, Judy. Otherwise known as Sheila the great. Dutton 1972, 128 pp.

Sheila first appears in *Tales of a Fourth Grade Nothing* as Peter Thatcher's neighbor. Sheila was a bundle of fears. She was afraid of dogs, thunderstorms, spiders, horses, putting her face in water, and strange noises at night. The summer she and her family rented a house in Tarrytown, New York, she confronted each one of her fears, even mastered one (putting her face in the water) and learned how to swim. That gave her the self-confidence to face a dog without running away. Sheila's progress was aided by her friend Mouse's steadfast belief that a person should always be honest about herself. Sheila's problems are treated

realistically and with dignity, yet humorously. Reading level varies greatly from 1.2 - 4.1, therefore, the book is *most* suitable to grades four through six.

Interest Level: 3-6. Reading Level: 3.1. Further Search Topics: Humorous Fiction, Courage-Fiction, Camp-Fiction, Group 2, Vacation-Fiction, Swimming-Fiction, Brothers and Sisters-Fiction, Friendship-Fiction, Everyday Stories.

Kessler, Leonard. Last one in is a rotten egg. Har-Row 1969, 64 pp.

Willie and Bobby could swim, but Freddy could not. After all three went to the local swimming pool and Freddy was pushed into the water by two older bullies, he was scared to try swimming again. Finally, a sympathetic lifeguard gave Freddy lessons. After much practice, Freddy became competent and confident enough to swim in the deep water and to stand up to the bullies.

A very slight plot designed to reassure new swimmers and provide a few basic rules of swimming. Reader format. A Sports-I-Can-Read-Book.

Interest Level: 1-2. Reading Level: 1.2. Further Search Topics: Courage-Fiction, Swimming-Fiction, Challenges-Fiction, Bullies-Fiction.

Steven, Carla. Hooray for Pig!; illus by Rainey Bennett. HM 1974, 48 pp.

Pig couldn't spend the day swimming with his friend Raccoon because he didn't know how to swim. Instead Pig took a picnic to the lake by himself. At the lake, Pig met Otter, who encouraged Pig to at least try getting in the water. After several days of Otter's patient coaching, not only could Pig stay afloat, but he liked it, too!

For much the same audience as Kessler's *Last One In Is A Rotten Egg*, but because of a more interesting plot it is a little more useful. Reader format.

Interest Level: 1-2. Reading Level: 1.2. Further Search Topics: Pigs-Fiction, Courage-Fiction, Swimming-Fiction, Humorous Fiction.

TALENT

Krementz, Jill. A very young circus flyer. Knopf 1979, unp (112 pp).

One of a series of five oversized, abundantly photographed views of unusual children. Tato Farfan is part of the Flying Farfans of Ringling Brothers and Barnum and Bailey Circus. He lives in a railroad car on a circus train with his mother, father, and older brother. The whole family performs as trapeze artists and flyers for the circus. Told as if Tato were speaking, this is the story of a fairly normal boy who also happens to be a circus flyer. Practice sessions are difficult, costumes must be readied, and time must be spent helping each other, but there is also time for Tato to watch TV, play with the clowns, play soccer, and just have fun.

In addition to Tato's story, the reader is given a behind-the-scenes tour of the circus right up to and including the performance itself (color photos used for the performance). It is an exciting world that should appeal to almost anyone who has enjoyed the circus.

Interest Level: 2-6. Reading Level: 3.2. Further Search Topics: Circus, Acrobats and Acrobatics, Best Sellers, Talent, Group 2, Gymnastics.

Krementz, Jill. A very young dancer. Knopf 1976, unp (121 pp).

This was the first of the five *Very Young* books to be written. Like the others, it is large in format and lavishly photographed. Unlike *A Very Young Circus Flyer*, this and the remaining books in the series are written about 10-year-old girls from obviously privileged backgrounds. All the girls are high achievers in their chosen areas but they seem very determined to work still harder until they attain whatever goals they have set for themselves. The books all follow the same formula. The girls introduce themselves, tell about their start in dancing, riding etc., describe their goals, and tell the reader how close they are to those goals. The girls go on to describe their daily routines, the practice, the chores, the hours, and the fun. Then the reader is ushered through approximately a year's worth of the young star's challenges, achievements, and defeats (the latter are only lightly touched upon). Through it all, the child shows enthusiasm, pride, dedication, hard work, and finally, hopes for the future.

Young readers love this series. Despite heavy use of jargon that makes the reading levels somewhat unstable, those already interested in the subject area pour over every word and picture in the books. Perhaps it's partly hero worship, or romance. Maybe it's the inspiration the books provide, but certainly one of the reasons the books are so popular is the vicarious thrill that they provide young enthusiasts.

A Very Young Dancer differs slightly from the formula. Instead of following Stephanie through a year of dance classes at the School of American Ballet, the book concentrates on New York City Ballet Company's production of the Nutcracker, in which Stephanie has a lead role.

Interest Level: 2-5. Reading Level: 3.1. Further Search Topics: Dancing, Ballet, Talent, Best Sellers, Group 2.

Krementz, Jill. A very young skater. Knopf 1979, unp (103 pp).

Katherine Healy started ice skating because her parents liked to skate and because it was easier for them to take her with them than it was to find a babysitter. From such beginnings, at age three, Katherine progressed to skating in Superskates at Madison Square Garden and ballet lessons at George Balanchine's School of American Ballet. See *A Very Young Dancer* for further explanation.

Interest Level: 2-6. Reading Level: 4.1. Further Search Topics: Ice Skating, Dancing, Ballet, Talent, Group 2, Best Sellers.

Krementz, Jill. A very young gymnast. Knopf 1978, unp (128 pp).

This is Torrence York's story. It includes a team trip to Germany for competition. See notes for *A Very Young Dancer* for more information.

Interest Level: 2-6. Reading Level: 3.2. Further Search Topics: Gymnastics, Talent, Acrobats and Acrobatics, Group 2, Best Sellers.

Krementz, Jill. A very young rider. Knopf 1977, unp (128 pp).

Vivi Malloy is the youngest rider in a family of several other riders. Her greatest dream is to make the Olympic equestrian team. She is progressing towards her goal with daily workouts and about fifteen major horse shows each year. See *A Very Young Dancer* for more extensive notes.

Interest Level: 2-6. Reading Level: 3.2. Further Search Topics: Horses, Riding, Talent, Group 2.

Tobias, Tobi. Marian Anderson; illus by Symeon Shimin. Har-Row 1972, 40 pp.

Marian Anderson's beautiful, strong voice and her great range set her apart from other singers even as a child. By the time she was in high school, she was being paid to sing. However, when she tried to apply to a well-known music school, because she was black she was turned away without even being heard. Anderson's determination as well as her own and others' faith in her kept her singing and seeking better and better coaches until she met Giuseppi Boghetti. He was one of the best voice coaches in the country. With him Marian trained and traveled until she finally won the chance to sing with the New York Philharmonic Orchestra. Anderson thought that at that point she would be invited to sing in famous theaters all across the United States, but because she was black she still received no invitations. She went to Europe where she studied and played to wildly enthusiastic audiences. Her European triumphs finally convinced American theater owners and audiences that she was a serious talent. For the next 30 years Marian Anderson sang all over the world, most of the time without incident, with one notable exception in 1939, when the D.A.R. prohibited her from singing in a hall they owned in Washington, D. C. She sang instead, in front of the Lincoln Memorial, at the invitation of the United States government. During the following years Marian married, bought a farm, sang opera and was made a delegate to the United Nations. In 1956, she retired from singing to help children, young singers, and world understanding.

Crowell Biographies make excellent school report sources for reluctant readers. They are short, interesting, and not overly juvenile looking, although the quasi-picture book format may be a problem for some older readers. This biography fits that description perfectly. The series is somewhat sentimental (as are many children's biographies), however, the sentimentality is not forbidding or condescending. A useful series. Crowell Biography series.

Interest Level: 2-5. Reading Level: 3.1. Further Search Topics: Biography, Music-Biography, Blacks-Biography, Talent, Women-Biography, Singers, Prejudice, Group 2.

TALENT-FICTION

Conford, Ellen. And this is Laura. Little 1977, 179 pp.

As a member of a family of high-achievers, Laura was convinced that she was unloved and worthless because she had no talents. Then, suddenly Laura discovered she had very special psychic powers; powers she began to exploit. At first it was fun to give readings after school each day. Gradually, however, as Laura foresaw her friend hurt and her brother missing, she realized that having ESP was also a frightening responsibility. Finally, her ESP became the vehicle that made it possible for Laura to tell her parents her true feelings and to understand that they loved her for herself, not for her achievements.

The author treats a common concern with sensitivity and humor. An especially good choice for Judy Blume lovers. Print somewhat small.

Interest Level: 4-6. Reading Level: 4.2. Further Search Topics: Occult-Fiction, Courage-Fiction, Extra Sensory Perception-Fiction, Family-Fiction, Humorous Fiction, Everyday Stories, Talent-Fiction.

Greenwald, Sheila. Give us a great big smile, Rosy Cole. Little 1981, 76 pp.

It was Rosy's turn to be the subject of her uncle's book. He needed to earn money again and Rosy had just turned 10, the age each of her sisters had been when Uncle Ralph wrote *Anitra Dances* and *Pippa Prances* about them. However, Rosy couldn't dance like Anitra or ride horses like Pippa. In fact, Rosy had no talent that was appropriate for a book. She drew well but Uncle Ralph said that wasn't visual enough.

Then Rosy's mother and uncle decided that Rosy could be *A Very Little Fiddler.*

Rosy had been taking violin lessons for two years, but only Rosy and her music teacher knew how truly untalented she was. Rosy hated the whole idea of the book at first. But as people began to treat her like a star, she found herself acting like one, until the day she heard her tape of the piece she was to play at the recital. Once again she realized that she could not play the violin and didn't want to go on with the charade. When everyone ignored her wishes, Rosy started to run away. Her route took her through the park where she thought of a brilliant idea. She ran home, changed clothes, picked up her violin, created a sign, and raced back to the park. There, with all the other street musicians Rosy set up her sign and began to play her violin. Her sign asked people to sign a petition if they felt that she should not be encouraged to play the violin anymore. Right away Rosy drew a large crowd. Before long, even her mother was one of the listeners and one of the signers. That was the end of Rosy's musical career and her uncle's book, but both were happier. Rosy went back to being normal and Uncle Ralph found another topic for his next book.

Chapters are long, but should not be a problem. Print is large. Some of the story is actually told in the illustrations, so the reader should be aware of them. Younger children may take the book more seriously than children whose sense of humor includes irony or children who were not as fond of Krementz's *Very Young* series.

Interest Level: 4-6. Reading Level: 3.1. Further Search Topics: Occupations-Fiction, Humorous Fiction, Family-Fiction, Relatives-Fiction, Talent-Fiction, Photography-Fiction, Everyday Stories.

TARKENTON, FRAN

Burchard, Marshall. Sports hero: Fran Tarkenton. Putnam 1977, 95 pp.

From a strict religious background where athletics were not encouraged, Fran went on to set every NFL passing record possible See *Sports Hero: Bill Walton.* Sports Hero series.

Interest Level: 3-6. Reading Level: 3.2. Further Search Topics: Biography, Tarkenton, Fran, Football-Biography, Religion-Biography.

TEETH-FICTION

Pinkwater, Daniel Manus. Fat men from space. Dodd 1977, 57 pp.

The evening after his trip to the dentist William found that he could still hear radio programs when his radio was turned off. He was even more surprised to find that when he wired himself to a fence he could hear spacemen talking. When the spacemen discovered that William could hear them, they landed and captured him. They were on a top secret mission and couldn't risk any human knowing about their existence. The spacemen were about to invade Earth to consume all the junk food they could find. As mass panic set in on Earth, William could do nothing to save his fellow humans. He was held captive and helpless until the invaders' interest was captured by a giant potato pancake floating in outer space.

A tongue-in-check, slapstick spoof of science fiction, food fads, and junk food. Do not expect anything more.

Interest Level: 3-5. Reading Level: 3.2. Further Search Topics: Science Fiction, Humorous Fiction, Food-Fiction, Flying Saucers-Fiction, Aliens-Fiction, Best Sellers, Kidnapping-Fiction, Teeth-Fiction.

Thomas, Kathleen. Out of the bug jar; illus by Tom O'Sullivan. Dodd 1981, 125 pp.

Even though 10-year-old Tom Jenkins didn't believe in the tooth fairy, when one of his teeth fell out, he placed it under his pillow just in case he was wrong. In the middle of that night he was awakened by a small creature crawling under his pillow and grumbling. Tom quickly scooped him into a bug jar he kept nearby and thus began two years of life with Marvin, a tooth fairy. Marvin was a delightful dictator; he ruled Tom's life. He put Tom into a terrible predicament when Tom tried to charge others to see him and Marvin became invisible. Marvin insisted on being fed just what he demanded, despite the difficulties he made for Tom. He badgered Tom to do his homework, to brush his teeth, and to tell the truth. He even managed to follow Tom to school. The only other person Marvin would allow to see or hear him was Tom's friend Sammy. Tom couldn't get rid of Marvin either. Because Tom had captured him, Marvin, should he ever have been able to escape, was entitled to take *all* of Tom's teeth as compensation for being held prisoner.

Actually Marvin didn't really want to escape. He had grown tired of having to race around and collect teeth. For a while then, everyone was fairly content. Tom had all his teeth and Marvin had a rather nice home. Then quite by accident, Marvin got loose. Both Tom and Marvin wanted Tom to catch Marvin again. Tom wanted to keep his teeth and Marvin wanted to keep his comfortable lifestyle, but Marvin played by the rules and wouldn't give Tom any help at all. After more than seven days of valient but fruitless efforts and nights of sleeping with tape over his mouth, Tom finally caught Marvin and all were happy again.

An amusing story told in short sentences and short chapters. The book should be popular with those who enjoy either fantasy or humor.

Interest Level: 3-5. Reading Level: 2.2. Further Search Topics: Fantasy, Fairies-Fiction, Humorous Fiction, Teeth-Fiction.

TELEVISION-FICTION

Miles, Betty. The secret life of the underwear champ; illus by Dan Jones. Knopf 1981, 117 pp.

Larry hadn't planned it; in fact, he hadn't even really wanted it to happen. But suddenly he found himself about to make a television commercial for ChampWin Knitting Mills, makers of sports clothing and underwear. He knew his family could use the money he would make, but he certainly didn't want the whole school seeing him in his underwear. Nevertheless, Larry went ahead and made the commercial, hoping that it would never be used. He even had to skip baseball practice to make the taping. Much to his horror, the commercial appeared the night before the team's first game. Not only did the entire opposing team tease him, but so did all his own teammates. By the time he got up to bat, Larry was mad enough to slam the ball out of the park. He didn't hit the ball quite that hard, but he did make a winning home run and end the others' giggles forever. He became the true underwear champ.

This is a funny look at the embarrassments of growing up. It also deals lightly with a boy's pride, his peer relationship, and his growing awareness of girls. An appealing and broadly usable title. Capers series.

Interest Level: 3-5. Reading Level: 2.2. Further Search Topics: Baseball-Fiction, Television-Fiction, Occupations-Fiction, School Stories, Humorous Fiction, Advertising-Fiction, Beauty-Fiction, Motion Pictures-Fiction, Best Sellers, Everyday Stories.

TENNIS-BIOGRAPHY

Burchard, Marshall. Sports hero: Billie Jean King. Putnam 1975, 95 pp.

Winner of every major women's tennis title and a very important person to women's professional sports. Consistent reading level. Book includes glossary of tennis terms. See entry under *Sports Hero: Bill Walton* Sports Hero series.

Interest Level: 3-6. Reading Level: 3.2. Further Search Topics: Biography, King, Billie Jean, Tennis-Biography, Women-Biography.

Burchard, Susan H. Sports star: John McEnroe. HarBraceJ 1979, 63 pp.

In 1977, feisty John McEnroe became the youngest semi-finalist ever to play at Wimbledon. Both before and since then, he has been noted almost as often for his temper as his talent. The level of difficulty of this book varies from 3.1 to 4.1. See *Sports Star: Elvin Hayes* for more details about the book. Sports Star series.

Interest Level: 3-6. Reading Level: 3.2. Further Search Topics: Biography, Tennis-Biography, McEnroe, John.

TERRORISM-FICTION

Bennett, Jay. The pigeon. Methuen 1980, 147 pp.

Despite a low testing score, this is not a truly easy book to read. The author assumes his readers are fairly sophisticated and worldly, thus he does not explain the meaning of the Iron Cross symbol or the word Aryan. The book's language varies from simple to difficult, making the reading level inconsistent (2.1 - 4.1). The setting is dark and forbidding; an underground world of fugitives and terrorists. And yet, the book will be popular with many readers in sixth grade; it will be even more popular with older readers. The tension in this story of a teenage boy, blamed for the murder of his ex-girlfriend, is almost palpable. Brian's flight from the police and his desire to find Donna's murderer take him directly into the midst of a ring of terrorists, for whom life has no meaning. In Brian's attempt to prove his innocence, two more lives are lost, but hundreds more are saved as Brian discovers and stops a bomb threat. The author has used riveting action, short, clipped sentences, and terse dialogue to create a very successful, highly suspenseful book. Print size is only moderate.

Interest Level: 6 . Reading Level: 3.2. Further Search Topics: Mystery and Detective Stories, Terrorism-Fiction, Murder-Fiction, Best Sellers, Crime-Fiction, Courage-Fiction, Survival-Fiction, Runaways-Fiction.

THANKSGIVING-FICTION

Bulla, Clyde Robert. John Billington, friend of Squanto; illus by Peter Burchard. Har-Row 1956, 88 pp.

This historical novel about the Mayflower voyage and the Pilgrims' first year at Plymouth centers on young John Billington. John was considered the troublemaker of the children. His problems are woven around the events of the year, including the Pilgrims' first meetings with the Wampanoag Indians. It was finally John, however, who was responsible for bringing peace between the Pilgrims and the Wampanoag tribe who lived further down Cape Cod. The book is not as exciting or convincing as Bulla's books are generally. It also contains a few minor historical inaccuracies; yet it remains useful as both an introduction to American history and historical fiction.

Interest Level: 2-5. Reading Level: 2.1. Further Search Topics: Pilgrims-Fiction, Historical Fiction, United States-History-Fiction, Thanksgiving-Fiction, Troublemakers-Fiction, Indians of North America-Fiction.

Pinkwater, Daniel Manus. The Hoboken chicken emergency. P-H 1977, 83 pp.

Arthur's mother sent him out with $16 to buy a Thanksgiving turkey. He returned with a live 266 pound chicken on a leash. It seemed that their turkey reservation had been lost at the meat market and, because it was Thanksgiving morning, there were no other turkeys available. Arthur searched everywhere but found nothing, until a strange old professor tricked him into buying the chicken. No one could bear to kill and eat such a large and friendly chicken, so Arthur and his family named it Henrietta and kept it as a pet. Henrietta was a difficult pet to keep hidden from the neighbors When the neighbors, and later the city, saw Henrietta running loose there was general hysteria. But all ended well when Henrietta and the city calmed down and Henrietta became a kind of neighborhood mascot.

A purely absurd plot but presented with enough energy and humor that most readers thoroughly enjoy the book. Some brief introduction may be necessary to get readers beyond the first few pages.

Interest Level: 3-6. Reading Level: 2.2. Further Search Topics: Humorous Fiction, Chickens-Fiction, Pets-Fiction, Thanksgiving-Fiction, Holidays-Fiction, Read Aloud, Best Sellers.

TIME

Berger, Melvin. Time after time; illus by Richard Cuffari. Coward 1975, 45 pp.

The book begins with a description of inner clocks, proceeds into measurement of time, the seasons, and finally demonstrates the making of a simple clock. The explanations are simple but interesting. One point logically follows from another. It is a solid, serviceable tool limited only somewhat by the fact that it looks like a cross between a picture book and a reader. A brief index is included.

Interest Level: 1-4. Reading Level: 2.2. Further Search Topics: Time, Clocks and Watches, Seasons, Group 2.

TIME-FICTION

Bernstein, Margery. The first morning; illus by Enid Warner Romanek. Scribner 1976, 44 pp.

Spider, Mouse, and Fly volunteered to ask the king of the sky for light to take back to earth because the animals on earth were tired of living in darkness. The king didn't want to give away any light and so he set what he thought was an impossible task for the three animals. They were able to outwit the king three times and finally return to earth with a box Mouse was sure contained light. When they opened the box all they found was a rooster. Poor Mouse was ashamed at having been so badly tricked. But then Rooster crowed up the first morning and has done so ever since. A competent retelling of an African myth, nicely complemented by bold illustrations. Good candidate for dramatization.

Interest Level: 1-3. Reading Level: 2.1. Further Search Topics: Animals-Fiction, Group 2, Mythology, Light-Fiction, Drama, Time-Fiction, Calendars-Fiction, Creation-Fiction, Africa-Folklore.

Packard, Edward. The cave of time; illus by Paul Granger. Bantam 1979, 115 pp.

Beware of the greater than usual inconsistency of reading levels within this book. Its difficulty level ranges from 2.2 to 4.2. See notes for *Sugarcane Island* for more information about the series. In paperback only. Choose Your Own Adventure series.

Interest Level: 2-6. Reading Level: 4.1. Further Search Topics: Time-Fiction, Science Fiction, Fantasy, Group 2.

TOADS

Allen, Gertrude. Everyday turtles, toads and their kin. HM 1970, 48 pp.

Straight-forward, short, chapter discussions of turtles, lizards, snakes, salamanders, toads, frogs and tree toads. Black and white drawings done by the author amplify the text. The major part of the book is simple enough to be understood at second grade, but should still be interesting to fourth and fifth graders. A few terms may need explanation: i.e., venomous, prey. The chapters on the turtle, lizard, frog and tree frog are the easiest. No index, but still useful for reports.

Interest Level: 2-5. Reading Level: 2.2. Further Search Topics: Turtles, Reptiles, Lizards, Toads, Frogs, Snakes, Salamanders.

TONGUE TWISTERS

Wiseman, Bernard. Morris and Boris. Dodd 1974, 64 pp.

This is a compilation of three silly stories about Morris the Moose and Boris the Bear. When Boris tries to interest Morris in telling riddles, Morris frustrates Boris so completely that Boris runs off angrily. Later Boris tries to teach Morris a tongue twister, but ends up running off in total confusion. Finally Boris tries to teach Morris to play hide-and-seek and that, too, is a disaster. Boris tells Morris that Morris just cannot do anything. A bird who has seen everything reminds Boris that Morris can make him very angry and that is something. When Boris agrees they all laugh happily.

Broad, slapstick humor makes this appealing to children well into third grade. Reader format.

Interest Level: 1-3. Reading Level: 1.2. Further Search Topics: Wit and Humor, Riddles, Tongue Twisters, Games, Humorous Fiction.

TOYS

White, Laurence B., Jr. Science toys; illus by Marc Tolon Brown. A-W 1975, unp (46 pp).

This book presents 23 toys that a young child can easily make and learn from at the same time. A sundial, a drinking straw that flies, a balloon that rolls over, a ghost that sticks to the wall by itself, a water-go-round, and a paper cup that roars are a few examples of what is to be found here. The construction and use of each toy is explained and illustrated in enough detail to enable the child to work alone. And as in *Science Puzzles*, some of the toys will double as magic tricks (i.e. can you balance the rim of a paper plate on your nose?).

Interest Level: 1-3. Reading Level: 2.1. Further Search Topics: Handicrafts, Science, Magic, Toys, Games, Group 2, Puzzles.

TRANSFORMATIONS-FICTION

Chew, Ruth. Witch's broom. Dodd 1977, 128 pp.

Amy's mother was the one who found the blue broom, but Amy and her friend Jean were the ones who learned it was magical. One night the broom flew Amy into a mountain cave where a coven of witches was meeting. It even forced Amy to answer the roll call for someone named Beryl. But it wasn't until it took both Amy and Jean back to the cave that they discovered the broom's connection to the strange bluejay that had been following them. The bluejay was really Beryl, a young and headstrong witch who had turned herself into the bluejay and then couldn't turn herself back. With the girls' unwitting help, Beryl found the charm to turn herself back into a witch and flew off on a scrawny old broom, leaving the blue broom for Amy and Jean.

What youngster wouldn't want a flying broomstick and the misadventures that go with owning one? Wish fulfillment can never be overrated as an appeal of Ruth Chew's books.

Interest Level: 2-5. Reading Level: 3.1. Further Search Topics: Witches-Fiction, Magic-Fiction, Fantasy, Birds-Fiction, Group 2, Transformations-Fiction.

Chew, Ruth. No such thing as a witch. Hastings 1971, 112 pp.

Despite the fact that their mother said there was no such thing as a witch, Tad and Nora were convinced that their neighbor Maggie Brown was indeed a witch. And they were right! Maggie Brown knew how to make a special kind of fudge that could make anyone into an animal-lover, enable people to talk with animals, or actually transform someone into an animal. All you had to do was to eat one, two, or three pieces of fudge respectively. But Maggie's overzealous love of animals and her disenchantment with housework eventually attracted the attention of her neighbors and the city health department. Only Tad and Nora's frantic efforts to help her saved Maggie from losing all of her animal friends.

A fairly detailed plot, the fascination of being able to change size and appearance and the intrigue involved in fooling the adults around Maggie make this one of Chew's best books.

Interest Level: 2-5. Reading Level: 2.2. Further Search Topics: Individualists-Fiction, Witches-Fiction, Animals-Fiction, Fantasy, Magic-Fiction, Brothers and Sisters-Fiction, Transformations-Fiction.

Chew, Ruth. The witch's garden. Hastings 1978, 112 pp.

Although its elements seem to promise an exciting adventure story, this is a disappointing book. The witch who moved into the dark, old home next door to Josh and Susan, was trying to improve her overgrown garden when Susan and Josh offered to help. The children accidentally splashed themselves with the witch's newest brew and found they suddenly became very tiny inhabitants of a dense and threatening jungle (the garden). After they regained their normal size, they dug into other areas of the garden. One hole they dug opened into an underground tunnel that they found was inhabited by a fire-breathing dragon. When the dragon cornered Mrs. Muldoon, Susan and Josh ran out of the tunnel, found the brew and splashed it onto the dragon. The dragon shrank away, Mrs. Muldoon was safe and the tunnel closed over.

Because there is little more suspense than in this description, the book fails to live up to its promise. In addition, the children's first sudden size change is just subtle enough to be confusing. Despite its problems the book is popular with Ruth Chew fans and therefore useful.

Interest Level: 2-5. Reading Level: 2.2. Further Search Topics: Witches-Fiction, Brothers and Sisters-Fiction, Magic-Fiction, Fantasy, Dragons-Fiction, Transformations-Fiction.

Chew, Ruth. The would-be witch. Hastings 1976, 112 pp.

Robin and her brother Andy took a liking to the clumsy white cat they saw in Zelda's Antique Shop. The cat apparently liked them, too, for it followed them home. Not having enough money to offer to buy Pearl from Zelda, the children tried to polish up an old pair of silver birds to trade for the cat. The polish turned out to be magical and made the birds real. When they tried the polish on a broom in Zelda's store, the broom began to fly. Upon discovering that Zelda wanted to be a witch but had failed the coven entrance exam, Rob helped her learn to fly and told her of the witches' meeting place that she and Andy had discovered. But the 12 witches who had been turned into cats were wicked enough to want to use Zelda to regain their human form and turn *her* into a cat. In attempting to prevent such a fate, Rob, Andy and Zelda set fire to the abandoned building being used as a meeting place. The 12 witches were rescued from the fire but charged with arson, which meant probable jail sentences for all of them. Zelda, finally a happy and capable witch, gave Pearl to Rob and Andy to thank them for their help.

A better-crafted story than many of the others, this also has a more evil cast of characters to provide additional interest.

Interest Level: 2-5. Reading Level: 2.2. Further Search Topics: Witches-Fiction, Brothers and Sisters-Fiction, Magic-Fiction, Fantasy, Transformations-Fiction, Cats-Fiction.

Chew, Ruth. Earthstar magic. Hastings 1979, 128 pp.

This is one of a series of similar stories by Ruth Chew. Each story involves two children and an old woman they usually suspect is a witch. As their suspicions become convictions they also find that, contrary to their expectation, the witch is very nice and often in need of help.

The children in this tale are brother and sister. Ben and Elizabeth first saw and then didn't see Trudy as she searched for a magical mushroom called an earthstar. Accidentally thrown together again, Ben and Elizabeth took a liking to Trudy, especially when she explained that she had been thrown out of her coven because she was so inept. In fact, she wasn't even able to control the earthstar. The earthstar manages to get all three in and out of adventures (including becoming tiny, flying and almost being eaten) before they learn to control its power. As the story ends, Trudy, finally respected by the other witches, flies off with a promise that Ben and Elizabeth will see her again.

Very lightweight but also very popular with young lovers of witch stories. There seems to be just the right amount of adventure to make up for the very benign witch.

Interest Level: 2-5. Reading Level: 2.2. Further Search Topics: Witches-Fiction, Magic-Fiction, Fantasy, Vacation-Fiction, Brothers and Sisters-Fiction, Transformations-Fiction.

Hildick, Edmund W. The case of the phantom frog; illus by Lisl Weil. Macmillan 1979, 121 pp.

The McGurk Organization would not, under ordinary circumstances, have agreed to babysit for seven-year-old Bela, but there was an unusual twist to Bela's case. Bela's aunt, who asked them to babysit while she worked in her sculpture studio, had heard the eerie sounds of a VERY large frog coming from Bela's room. At first it appeared to the group that Bela actually turned into a frog at night, a werefrog. But, upon investigation they found a very clever, very lonely, and very unhappy young boy who had invented the phantom because he was afraid that his aunt would make him give up his pet frog.

See *The Case of the Bashful Bank Robber* for series information. McGurk Mystery series.

Interest Level: 3-5. Reading Level: 3.1. Further Search Topics: Mystery and Detective Stories, Gangs-Fiction, Frogs-Fiction, Supernatural-Fiction, Transformations-Fiction, Detectives-Fiction, Babysitting-Fiction, Humorous Fiction, Occupations-Fiction.

Platt, Kin. Dracula, go home; illus by Frank Mayo. Watts 1979, 87 pp.

From the chapter numbers that drip blood, and the humorously grotesque illustrations, to the short sentences and chapters, this is a book designed and almost guaranteed to appeal to the reluctant reader. A sense of immediacy and involvement is created by the first person narration. Tension is created on the opening page when Larry sees a man in the cemetery who looked exactly like Dracula. When that man registered at the hotel where Larry was working, Larry decided to find out more about him. It began to look as if Mr. A. R. Claude (the letters spell Dracula) was not only a vampire, but a thief and a murderer as well. The trouble was that Larry couldn't prove anything. Even when he found the stolen jewels for which Mr. Claude had been searching, Larry still couldn't convince anyone of Claude's true identify. No one ever did believe Larry, thus Claude went free.

The author uses a light touch to treat an eerie subject. His inconclusive ending may disappoint some, but should delight many. Beware of the variability of the reading level however; it swings from high first grade to low third grade.

Interest Level: 3-6. Reading Level: 2.2. Further Search Topics: Monsters-Fiction, Horror-Fiction, Mystery and Detective Stories, Best Sellers, Murder-Fiction, Crime-Fiction, Transformations-Fiction.

TREASURE-FICTION

Bulla, Clyde Robert. Ghost town treasure; illus by Don Freeman. Har-Row 1957, 87 pp.

A very simple story whose title is somewhat misleading. Instead of a mystery or an exciting story of buried treasure, Bulla has written a very pleasant story of a family whose fortunes are reversed by the accidental discovery of a nearby cave. Young Ty Jackson and his family were the last people living in Gold Rock, California. Everyone else had moved out when the new highway had bypassed the town. The Jacksons had been able to stay on only because some of the nearby ranchers had continued to buy food and supplies from the Jacksons' store. Just as they, too, were preparing to move out, Ty's pen pals wrote that they were coming to visit the town. Their grandfather had died there, years earlier, during his search for gold. When Paul and Nora arrived, they brought with them their grandfather's diary. The last entry in the journal seemed to indicate that their grandfather had found gold in an isolated cave in the nearby canyon. After a long search, the children discovered the cave, but no gold. Ty's disappointment changed to joy when tourists started arriving to see the new natural attraction. Once again his parents could sell their groceries, the hotel could be reopened and Gold Rock would flourish.

Interest Level: 2-5. Reading Level: 2.2. Further Search Topics: Treasure-Fiction, Family Problems-Fiction, West-Fiction, California-Fiction, Family-Fiction, Pen Pals-Fiction.

Clifford, Eth. The dastardly murder of Dirty Pete; illus by George Hughes. HM 1981, 120 pp.

Although this is a sequel to *Help, I'm a Prisoner in the Library*, it does not depend on the previous title, and in fact, is likely to be the more successful introduction to Mary Rose and Jo-Beth Onetree. Given the choice, most young readers will take a mystery set in a ghost town over a mystery set in a library.

Mary Rose, Jo-Beth and their father were on their way across country when they became lost. As night grew closer, the only place they could find to stay was an old hotel in the ghost town where Sorehead Jones had allegedly killed Dirty Pete. It was Sorehead's ghost who was supposed to haunt the town, and indeed there was someone or something who was in the town with the Onetrees. To their surprise, that someone turned out to be Sourdough Sam, an aging actor who had become senile and spent his days acting out all the parts in the Dirty Pete story. The town was only a movie set and the story was only a movie script. The Onetrees discovered the truth bit by bit after a frightening venture into an abandoned gold mine, a harrowing night in the haunted hotel and a jail sentence for Mr. Onetree.

Beware of the rare, very difficult descriptive passage that may cause trouble for some readers.

Interest Level: 2-5. Reading Level: 3.1. Further Search Topics: Mystery and Detective Stories, West-Fiction, Brothers and Sisters-Fiction, Motion Pictures-Fiction, Ghosts-Fiction, Treasure-Fiction, Group 2, Acting-Fiction, Aging-Fiction, Mental Illness-Fiction.

Clymer, Eleanor. Santiago's silver mine; illus by Ingrid Fetz. Atheneum 1973, 74 pp.

Although somewhat complicated by a large number of background incidents, especially early in the book, the story is both interesting and informative. Santiago and his friend Andreas wanted to be rich. The year's harvest had been very poor, so there was little food to eat. Both of their fathers had gone to Mexico City to find jobs and their mothers worked for very few pesos near home. Andreas wanted to search the old mine in the hills outside of town for silver, but the mining company had left a guard named Jose to prevent people from getting into the mines. While up on a hill, tending a cow, Andreas found an old piece of pottery and a back entrance to the mine. As they started to enter the mine, Andreas and Santiago found a basket full of old pottery pieces that Jose had apparently dug from the hill. Not knowing what the pottery pieces were, the boys took them to the local school teacher who identified them as ancient archeological treasures that by law belonged to the government. As soon as he realized others had found out that he had been selling the pottery, Jose disappeared. Shortly afterwards, the government paved the road through town and opened the hill as an official archaeological site. The extra jobs meant that the boys' fathers could once again find work at home. Although they hadn't become exactly rich, Santiago and Andreas had certainly found treasure.

Local flavor abounds, along with some history. Useful for Social Studies units. Print size fairly small, but spaces between lines are good sized. Recently out-of-print, but still worth looking for.

Interest Level: 3-5. Reading Level: 3.1. Further Search Topics: Archaeology-Fiction, Poverty-Fiction, Mexico-Fiction, Country Life-Fiction, Treasure-Fiction, Miners-Fiction.

Montgomery, Raymond A. The lost jewels of Nabooti; illus by Paul Granger. Bantam 1981, 121 pp.

See entry for *Sugarcane Island*, by Edward Packard for series information. Only available in paperback edition. Choose Your Own Adventure series.

Interest Level: 2-6. Reading Level: 3.2. Further Search Topics: Mystery and Detective Stories, Detectives-Fiction, Treasure-Fiction, Best Sellers, Group 2.

Parish, Peggy. Hermit Dan; illus by Paul Frame. Macmillan 1977, 151 pp.

When the Roberts children tried to prove that Pirate Island really had been used by pirates, they encountered more action and intrigue than they had found in any of their earlier adventures. Liza, Bill and Jed suspected that Hermit Dan knew whether or not there had been pirates on the island, but he was so gruff and apparently mean that they didn't dare ask him any questions. Instead, they trailed and spied on him and asked questions of anyone who had known Hermit Dan as a child. It was rumored that his ancestors had actually been pirates. Until a terrible fire that had destroyed all they owned, Hermit Dan's family had been very wealthy. However, no one knew how they had become so rich.

In an attempt to see what the summer residents knew about Hermit Dan, the children introduced themselves to the vacationing youngsters. Among the visitors the Roberts met Hank and Ted, brothers bent on bullying Hermit Dan. When the children were rescued from a severe sandstorm by Hermit Dan, they were surprised to find that he wasn't nearly as gruff as he appeared. In fact they began to feel quite protective of the old man. Thus when Hank and Ted stole a secret box that held all of Hermit Dan's valuables, it was the Roberts children who fought (literally) to get the box back. It was after Liza, Bill and Jed returned the box to Hermit Dan, however, that the real surprises began: these included a surprise party for Hermit Dan, his wish to be friendly, and his gift to the children of three pieces of eight that proved his family members were pirates.

This title's more interesting and involved plot makes the book more likely to be a success with older readers than the other stories about the Roberts children. Otherwise it shares the same format, faults and strengths as the other series titles.

Interest Level: 2-5. Reading Level: 2.1. Further Search Topics: Mystery and Detective Stories, Pirates-Fiction, Vacation-Fiction, Loners-Fiction, Treasure-Fiction, Bullies-Fiction, Brothers and Sisters-Fiction, Grandparents-Fiction.

Parish, Peggy. Pirate Island adventure; illus by Paul Frame. Macmillan 1975, 167 pp.

Although this is the fourth book in the series about the Roberts children, none of the titles must be read in chronological order. This time the three rather privileged children spent the summer with their grandparents on a resort island. They lived in a house that their family had owned for years, explored the island, and swam in their own private cove. But, most of their time was spent trying to solve an old mystery. Their great-uncle had hidden several very special items (one for each member of his family) years earlier, and had left only one clue with their grandfather. After he gave the children that clue it was only a matter of time before they found the hidden treasures.

This book is also lengthy, but is divided into 22 very manageable chapters. It is, like the others, almost entirely dialogue and action, which makes it especially appealing to young reluctant readers.

Interest Level: 1-4. Reading Level: 2.1. Further Search Topics: Mystery and Detective Stories, Vacation-Fiction, Treasure-Fiction, Brothers and Sisters-Fiction, Grandparents-Fiction, Group 2.

Warner, Gertrude Chandler. Mountain top mystery; illus by David Cunningham. A. Whitman 1964, 128 pp.

A day's climb up and down Old Flat Top was all the Alden family had wanted. Instead, when a portion of the trail collapsed into a cave, they found themselves stranded on top of the mountain. From their vantage point that night they could see a shadowy light which they investigated the next day. They found a 90-year-old Indian woman who had a strange story to tell of treasure hidden in a cave somewhere on Old Flat Top. The treasure was rightfully hers as the last of her tribe, but she had never been able to find it. The collapse of the trail and the reopening of the cave attracted more attention than just the Alden's though. Both an expert on caves and a young Indian boy wanted to find out more about the cave. David, the Indian boy, turned out to be the old woman's grandnephew. The treasure was indeed unearthed; David and Lovan were reunited; the treasure was given to Lovan, and both David's and Lovan's futures were secured.

What in the other books is mild stereotyping becomes more noticeable here (the books are all around 20 years old). The print is smaller here than before but the spacing between the lines is adequate. See entry for *The Boxcar Children* for more information.

Interest Level: 3-6. Reading Level: 2.2. Further Search Topics: Mystery and Detective Stories, Treasure-Fiction, Survival-Fiction, Indians of North America-Fiction, Mountain Climbing-Fiction, Brothers and Sisters-Fiction.

TREES-FICTION

Bulla, Clyde Robert. The sugar pear tree; illus by Taro Yashima. T Y Crowell 1960, 54 pp.

Lonnie lived with his mother and his grandfather in a house owned by the state. A new highway was to be built that would force the family to move, but Gramp refused to acknowledge that the state could force them out of their home. He chased away every state representative who came to warn the family that they should move. Lonnie's mother had always been at work when the representatives came and so knew nothing about the warnings until she came home to find their belongings on the sidewalk and their house on wheels. The only person they could turn to was their friend Nick. Nick owned a nursery in town and a small house with a large yard in the country. He had become a friend of Lonnie's when he gave Lonnie first prize in a school essay contest on the topic of "favorite trees." Lonnie's prize had been a sugar pear tree, his favorite. Nick had next become Lonnie's mother's friend. Nick arranged for them to stay in the greenhouse at his country place. The longer they stayed, the better friends Nick and Lonnie's mother became. Gramp was the only person who didn't adjust to the move. He stopped speaking the moment he was carried out of his old home. In a final and successful attempt to make Gramp happy, Nick bought the old house and had it moved out to his country lot.

The idea of a state government being able to force a family to move may need some explaining. The story's warmth and very consistent early second grade reading level make this a particularly useful book with quiet readers.

Interest Level: 2-4. Reading Level: 2.1. Further Search Topics: Trees-Fiction, Moving, Household-Fiction, Family Problems-Fiction, Grandparents-Fiction, Poverty-Fiction.

TRICKSTERS-FICTION

Arkhurst, Joyce. The adventures of Spider; West African folktales; illus by Jerry Pinkney. Little 1964, 58 pp.

A delightful collection of six West African folktales about Spider. Spider is mischievous, greedy, lazy and clever. He loves to eat and he hates to work. Four of the stories tell of Spider's ill-fated attempts to get food without having to work for it ("How Spider Got a Thin Waist," "How Spider Got a Bald Head," "How Spider Helped a Fisherman," and "Why Spiders Live in Dark Corners"). One story tells of his greed ("How the World Got Wisdom"), and only one story is complimentary ("Why Spider Lives in Ceilings"). All are short, gentle, humorous, and adapt well to dramatization or retelling.

Interest Level: 2-6. Reading Level 3.1. Further Search Topics: Humorous Fiction, Spiders-Fiction, Folklore, Tricksters-Fiction, Africa-Folklore, Group 2, Read Aloud, Creation-Fiction, Drama.

TROUBLEMAKERS-FICTION

Blume, Judy. Blubber. Bradbury 1974, 153 pp.

Jill, like all the other fifth graders in her class, did exactly as Wendy directed her. When Wendy nicknamed one of the class members Blubber and launched a campaign against her, Jill joined right in. It wasn't until the tables were turned and Jill became Wendy's next victim that Jill realized how much it hurt to be the target of such nastiness. It was only then that Jill could stand up to Wendy. Wendy's meanness is extreme and her classmates, without exception, actively follow her lead, yet all adult characters in the book are blind to what happens. Despite those drawbacks, the book deals with a problem very real to children and thus it has guaranteed audience appeal.

Interest Level: 4-6. Reading Level: 3.1. School Stories, Bullies-Fiction, Weight-Fiction, Loners-Fiction, Gangs-Fiction, Read Aloud, Cruelty-Fiction, Best Sellers, Troublemakers-Fiction, Friendship-Fiction.

Blume, Judy. Tales of a fourth grade nothing; illus by Roy Doty. Dutton 1972, 120 pp.

Another humorous Blume book that can be counted on to appeal to third and fourth grade readers. If fifth and sixth graders can ignore the title's reference to fourth grade, they too will love it. The story is an exaggeration of a common theme—an older child whose life is in continual turmoil because of a somewhat spoiled younger sibling. Peter's problems with three-year-old Fudge become worse with each chapter until the final disaster when Fudge swallows Peter's pet turtle. Each approximately 15-page chapter is a complete, very funny episode.

Interest Level: 3-6. Reading Level 3.1. Further Search Topics: Humorous Fiction, Turtles-Fiction, Brothers and Sisters-Fiction, Pets-Fiction, Family-Fiction, Read Aloud, Best Sellers, Everyday Stories, Troublemakers-Fiction.

Bulla, Clyde Robert. John Billington, friend of Squanto; illus by Peter Burchard. Har-Row 1956, 88 pp.

This historical novel about the Mayflower voyage and the Pilgrims' first year at Plymouth centers on young John Billington. John was considered the troublemaker of the children. His problems are woven around the events of the year, including the Pilgrims' first meetings with the Wampanoag Indians. It was finally John, however, who was responsible for bringing peace between the Pilgrims and the Wampanoag tribe who lived further down Cape Cod. The book is not as exciting or convincing as Bulla's books are generally. It also contains a few minor historical inaccuracies; yet it remains useful as both an introduction to American history and historical fiction.

Interest Level: 2-5. Reading Level: 2.1. Further Search Topics: Pilgrims-Fiction, Historical Fiction, United States-History-Fiction, Thanksgiving-Fiction, Troublemakers-Fiction, Indians of North America-Fiction.

Burch, Robert. Queenie Peavy; illus by Jerry Lazare. Viking Pr. 1966, 159 pp.

Queenie was always in trouble. She could be mean, really mean, but, she was also bright, talented, independent and resilient. Queenie blamed her problems on the fact that people teased her because her father was in jail and because she was poor. She thought that she had to defend herself against the world. Queenie was proud of her poor reputation until she accidentally-on-purpose caused a classmate to break his leg. Then, when her father returned home and wasn't the person she'd hoped he'd be, Queenie realized that only she could make her life better. Being the strong person she was, she set out to do just that.

Queenie is a wonderfully alive and sympathetic character, one well worth introducing to older readers despite the book's reading level. Print somewhat small. Line spacing average width.

Interest Level: 5-6. Reading Level: 5.1. Further Search Topics: Family Problems-Fiction, Crime-Fiction, Loners-Fiction, Poverty-Fiction, Humorous Fiction, Bullies-Fiction, Troublemakers-Fiction, Academic Problems-Fiction, Read Aloud.

Cleary, Beverly. Otis Spofford; illus by Louis Darling. Morrow 1953, 191 pp.

Here are six separate humorous adventures that link together, but can be read separately and out of order. Otis' favorite activity was "stirring up a little excitement," but his definition of excitement usually meant trouble. The school fiesta turned into a disaster when Otis decided to rechoreograph the bullfight and make the bull win. His attempt to liven up the reading lesson about Indians meant he almost scalped a classmate. However, a wild day at the skating pond finally gave everyone a chance to take revenge for all the things Otis had done to them. The remaining three chapters (2, 3 and 4) are slightly less exciting, but useful if a reader has enjoyed the others. There is much humor in Otis' antics and his tendency to act on every thought that comes to mind is one many readers can appreciate.

Interest Level: 2-6. Reading Level: 5.1. Further Search Topics: Troublemakers-Fiction, Group 2, Read Aloud, Everyday Stories, Humorous Fiction, School Stories.

Hinton, Susan E. The outsiders. Viking Pr. 1967, 188 pp.

When she wrote this book Susan Hinton was only 17 years old, but she had the sensitivity of someone much older. She wrote a taut story of the rivalry between two city gangs; the Socs (the rich socialites) and the Greasers (poor kids from the wrong side of town) that is more than anything a plea for understanding and tolerance. Seen through the eyes of Ponyboy (a very bright, 14-year-old Greaser), the rivalry brought on violence and an accidental killing that forced Pony and his friend Johnny to flee for their lives. Dallas, the meanest and most dangerous of the Greasers, provided them with shelter, food for a week, and a gun. At the end of that week, Johnny decided that they should turn themselves in to the police. But before they could do that, their hideout (an old church) burned in a fire which threatened the lives of four children who had been playing there. In trying to rescue the children, Johnny, Pony, and Dallas were injured; Johnny was severely burned and probably permanently crippled. A vengeance rumble was held while Johnny lay in the hospital, but the Greasers' victory was empty when Johnny died. He had been the one member of the gang whom they all loved and who had most needed them. Dallas went to pieces: he robbed a store and set himself up to be killed by the police. He had nothing left to live for after Johnny's death. Pony found support and security with his brothers (their parents were dead) and, in a note from Johnny, some hope for the future.

Hinton speaks most often through Pony (his depth of understanding of the people around him is very impressive), but through Johnny and two of the Socs as well, Randy and Cherry. Her message is clear, but at no time does she fail to maintain believable characters in a compelling plot.

Although the book looks forbidding with its 188 pages of unrelenting small print, it is an exciting story, full of adventure, realism, and room for thought. Perhaps the best way to introduce this book is to read a fair portion of it aloud. Now a motion picture too.

Interest Level: 6+. Reading Level: 5.1. Further Search Topics: Crime-Fiction, Gangs-Fiction, Murder-Fiction, Read Aloud, Friendship-Fiction, Juvenile Delinquency-Fiction, Best Sellers, City Life-Fiction, Brothers and Sisters-Fiction, Orphans-Fiction, Runaways-Fiction, Troublemakers-Fiction, Poverty-Fiction.

Kelley, Sally. Trouble with explosives. Bradbury 1976, 117 pp.

Polly Banks stuttered very badly. She wanted to stop but she couldn't. Moving, entering a new school, and facing a mean teacher who seemed in need of psychiatric help, all made Polly's stuttering worse. When Sis, Polly's new friend, rose to Polly's defense in one confrontation too many with Miss Patterson, the teacher took cruel revenge. Polly's desire to help Sis, her need to do something about her stuttering, and an understanding psychiatrist, all helped Polly learn to help herself with her speech problem. At the same time, she began to understand and have confidence in herself and her family.

Another "problem book" that older elementary school readers seem to crave. Polly and Sis are both very sympathetic characters who bring to life many of the uncertainties of growing up. Print and line spacing of only average size but otherwise a good choice.

Interest Level: 4-6. Reading Level: 3.2. Further Search Topics: Academic Problems-Fiction, Stuttering-Fiction, Psychiatrists-Fiction, School Stories, Mental Illness-Fiction, Troublemakers-Fiction, Courage-Fiction, Physically Handicapped-Fiction, Children-Growth-Fiction, Moving, Household-Fiction.

Peck, Robert Newton. Mr. Little; illus by Ben Stahl. Doubleday 1979, 87 pp.

All summer long Drag and Finley had looked forward to having Miss Kellogg as their teacher, so they were extremely disappointed to find ordinary-looking Mr. Little in her place on the first day of school. Used to playing tricks on their teachers anyway, Drag and Finley decided to go all out to get even with Mr. Little for spoiling their year. But try as they might, they couldn't get an advantage over Mr. Little; he seemed to be unflappable. Finally, in their riskiest prank ever, they stole Mr. Little's underwear to dress a statue in the town square. That attempt to embarrass Mr. Little only served to get Finley and Drag in serious trouble from which Mr. Little saved them. It was his later rescue of Miss Kellogg, however, that added respect to the boys' growing feeling of friendship for Mr. Little.

Because the author's adult viewpoint is never quite lost, even though he writes in the first person, and because the rural and historic time settings are not familiar to many readers, the book may need some introduction and encouragement. It is a prime candidate for reading aloud until the young reader's interest takes over. Print is of adequate size, but spacing between lines could have been more generous.

Interest Level: 4-6. Reading Level: 5.1. Further Search Topics: Humorous Fiction, School Stories, Troublemakers-Fiction, Group 2, Read Aloud, Country Life-Fiction, Best Sellers.

Pevsner, Stella. And you give me a pain, Elaine. HM 1978, 182 pp.

Andrea was the youngest of three children. She was very close to her brother, Joe, but he was away at college. There was only Elaine at home, but Andrea and Elaine didn't get along at all. Elaine was a troubled young woman who took so much of her parents' attention that there was none left for Andrea. This is the story of Andrea's year in eighth grade, a year in which she discovered that she was a steady and strong person. It was the year in which Andrea worked on the school play, had her first boyfriend, weathered the storms when her sister ran away, and began to understand her sister more and resent her less. It was also the year that she had to learn to live with her brother's accidental death.

The author's Judy Blume style (but with less humor) guarantees readers among older children.

Interest Level: 5-6. Reading Level: 4.1. Further Search Topics: Family Problems-Fiction, Brothers and Sisters-Fiction, Love-Fiction, Death-Fiction, Runaways-Fiction, Troublemakers-Fiction, Adolescence-Fiction.

Place, Marian T. The boy who saw Bigfoot. Dodd 1979, 96 pp.

Joey and his foster mother searched for and found Bigfoot. But, when Joey told his classmates, no one would believe him. Joey's next idea was to take the entire class on a field trip to track Bigfoot.

Joey's rapid change from a difficult to a very well-adjusted child is not well supported. But interest in Bigfoot is so great that the book's flaws will be overlooked by its readers.

Interest Level: 3-6. Reading Level: 2.2. Further Search Topics: Bigfoot-Fiction, Foster Homes-Fiction, Monsters-Fiction, Troublemakers-Fiction, School Stories.

Robinson, Barbara. The best Christmas pageant ever; illus by Judith Gwyn Brown. Har-Row 1972, 80 pp.

A truly delightful story of what happens when the meanest kids in town (they are all in one family) take over all the lead roles in the Sunday school Christmas pageant. The Herdmans (all six of them), having heard that the church was giving away free food, showed up to take some. While they were there, they heard about the Christmas pageant and decided it presented them with another perfect opportunity for food and mischief. With a little behind-the-scenes arm-twisting (literally), they managed to dissuade everyone else from showing interest in the major roles. Theirs was a completely original interpretation of the Christmas story that left nothing and no one around them untouched.

That the book's reading level will prove too high for many people is unfortunate. The story is well worth the struggle. A wonderful choice for reading aloud.

Interest Level: 3-6. Reading Level: 5.1 Further Search Topics: Christmas-Fiction, Bullies-Fiction, Troublemakers-Fiction, Humorous Fiction, Religion-Fiction, Group 2, Read Aloud, Acting-Fiction, Holidays-Fiction.

Seuss, Dr. The cat in the hat. Beginner 1957, 61 pp.

When the Cat in the Hat visits two children, a dreary, boring afternoon becomes almost too exciting. The Cat's juggling act and the two "things" he brings with him almost destroy the house. But the Cat cleans up so well that when the children's mother comes home and asks what they did all afternoon, they can't decide if they should tell her.

A funny, rhyming tale of the destruction all children can create and the boredom all children can feel. Reader format.

Interest Level: 1-3. Reading Level: 1.2. Further Search Topics: Humorous Fiction, Fantasy, Cats-Fiction, Poetry, Troublemakers-Fiction, Best Sellers, Stories in Rhyme.

Seuss, Dr. The cat in the hat comes back. Beginner 1958, 63 pp.

Sally and her brother were doing a good job of clearing the front walk of snow when the Cat in the Hat showed up. While they worked, the Cat created a pink mess in the house. The mess only became worse when he tried to clean it. The pink spot finally covered the snow all around the house until the Cat called upon his friends Little Cats A-Z. It was Little Cat Z and his magic zoom that eventually not only cleaned the snow, but cleared the front walk as well.

Another zany, rhymed adventure of the mischievious Cat whose ability to get into trouble endears him to most children from pre-school to early third grade. Reader format.

Interest Level: 1-3. Reading Level: 1.2. Further Search Topics: Fantasy, Cats-Fiction, Troublemakers-Fiction, Humorous Fiction, Snow-Fiction, Poetry, Best Sellers, Stories in Rhyme.

Smith, Doris Buchanan. Tough Chauncey. Morrow 1974, 222 pp.

Chauncey Childs had taught himself to be tough— very tough. Even though he was small for his age (13 years old), the only person who gave him any trouble was his sometimes-friend, Black Jack Levitt. Everyone else was scared of Chauncey. Chauncey felt that he had to be tough or he wouldn't be able to survive. He had to be tough to stand the beatings his grandfather gave him "for his own good," to put up with his mother's drinking and disappearances, and to stand the sight of his grandfather shooting the stray kittens born in their garage.

Chauncey's greatest wish was to be able to live with his mother, instead of with his grandparents. In a desperate attempt to achieve that end he accidentally fell from a moving train and badly hurt his leg. Instead of being returned to his mother he was once more taken back to his grandparents. Chauncey's unhappiness grew until he finally decided to take the one surviving stray kitten and run away. Jack helped him find an empty garage where he could hide while he figured out what to do with his future. After talking with Jack and doing more deep soul searching, Chauncey decided to reshape himself and his life. His first step was to curb his temper and his tongue when his hiding place was discovered. His second step was to see about finding a foster home where he would be treated well, and where he could get a new start.

Ugly as the story is in places, its ending is hopeful. Although it is not always realistic, Chauncey's story is compelling enough to appeal to many readers, especially those who have enjoyed *The War on Villa Street*, by Henry Mazer, *The Outsiders*, by Susan Hinton, or *Mystery of the Fat Cat*, by Frank Bonham. The book's length and its artificially low reading level (vocabulary is often difficult but sentences are very short) make this book most appropriate for an older reader whose reading level is 4.1 or higher.

Interest Level: 5-6. Reading Level: 3.2. Further Search Topics: Child Abuse-Fiction, Family Problems-Fiction, Grandparents-Fiction, Runaways-Fiction, Bullies-Fiction, Single Parent Family-Fiction, Loners-Fiction, Friendship-Fiction, Troublemakers-Fiction, Foster Homes-Fiction.

TURTLES

Allen, Gertrude. Everyday turtles, toads and their kin. HM 1970, 48 pp.

Straight-forward, short, chapter discussions of turtles, lizards, snakes, salamanders, toads, frogs and tree toads. Black and white drawings done by the author amplify the text. The major part of the book is simple enough to be understood at second grade, but should still be interesting to fourth and fifth graders. A few terms may need explanation: i.e., venomous, prey. The chapters on the turtle, lizard, frog and tree frog are the easiest. No index, but still useful for reports.

Interest Level: 2-5. Reading Level: 2.2. Further Search Topics: Turtles, Reptiles, Lizards, Toads, Frogs, Snakes, Salamanders.

TURTLES-FICTION

Blume, Judy. Tales of a fourth grade nothing; illus by Roy Doty. Dutton 1972, 120 pp.

Another humorous Blume book that can be counted on to appeal to third and fourth grade readers. If fifth and sixth graders can ignore the title's reference to fourth grade, they too will love it. The story is an exaggeration of a common theme—an older child whose life is in continual turmoil because of a somewhat spoiled younger sibling. Peter's problems with three-year-old Fudge become worse with each chapter until the final disaster when Fudge swallows Peter's pet turtle. Each approximately 15-page chapter is a complete, very funny episode.

Interest Level: 3-6. Reading Level 3.1. Further Search Topics: Humorous Fiction, Turtles-Fiction, Brothers and Sisters-Fiction, Pets-Fiction, Family-Fiction, Read Aloud, Best Sellers, Everyday Stories, Troublemakers-Fiction.

TWINS-BIOGRAPHY

Fall, Thomas. Jim Thorpe; illus by John Gretzer. Har-Row 1970, 33 pp.

Jim Thorpe was an Indian from the Oklahoma territory who became one of the United State's greatest athletes. He and his twin brother were trained by their father to run and jump faster and farther than anyone else. When Charles died, Jim couldn't face returning to school without his twin, so his family kept him home for a few months before sending him away to school again. Jim ran home once more when his father and mother both became ill. Months later he went to still another school where he was noticed by Pop Warner. Pop advised Joe to concentrate on track until he was big enough to play football. His father's death left Jim so despondent he quit school to play professional baseball for a while. By the time he went back to school, Jim was big enough to play spectacular football and then to win the 1912 Olympic decathlon competition. Unfortunately, his short time as a paid baseball player made him ineligible for the Olympic honor and Jim's medal was taken away. Public sentiment was with Jim, but the rules were against him. He went on, however, to play both professional baseball and football. In 1982, 29 years after his death, Thorpe's medal was finally returned to him.

A short, meaty and readable biography of a person who should be interesting to many sports fans. Follows the usual format of Crowell biographies, but looks less like a picture book than many. Crowell Biography series.

Interest Level: 3-5. Reading Level: 3.1. Further Search Topics: Football-Biography, Indians of North America-Biography, Baseball-Biography, Olympic Games, Biography, Running-Biography, Twins-Biography.

TWINS-FICTION

Bulla, Clyde Robert. Marco Moonlight; illus by Julia Noonan. T Y Crowell 1976, 104 pp.

No one could explain Marco's strange, recurring dream. The dream seemed to be about a brother, but Marco had no brother. He had no family but his wealthy grandparents with whom he lived. Marco loved his grandparents very much, but he couldn't help wondering about his own past. He knew only what he and his grandparents could figure out from a few clues. His mother had run away to marry and for three years Marco's grandparents had heard nothing. Then, suddenly, they received a note that she was dying, had parted from her husband, and needed them. By the time they arrived, she was dead and two-year-old Marco could tell them no more. About the time of his thirteenth birthday Marco made friends with a strange man named Flint, who later became the gardener on Marco's grandparents' estate. Rather than live in the room provided for him with the other servants, Flint chose a bleak and isolated beach cottage. Being very careful that no one should suspect, Flint locked Marco into the cottage and forced Marco to change clothes with Matt, who was Marco's long-lost identical twin. Flint and Matt planned that Matt would steal all the money he could from the estate before killing Marco and fleeing. But when Matt began to realize how nice his grandparents were, how much he liked Marco, and how evil Flint was, he decided to thwart Flint's plan. In Matt and Marco's desperate attempt to flee from Flint, Flint was accidentally killed, leaving Marco free to return home and Matt free to find a way to feel he also had the right to claim his heritage before joining Marco.

The tense and dramatic plot immediately involves the reader and the short, fast-paced chapters sustain interest to the end of the book. Readers should also appreciate the small, paperback-size format. A good choice.

Interest Level: 3-6. Reading Level: 2.1. Further Search Topics: Dreams-Fiction, Mystery and Detective Stories, Kidnapping-Fiction, Twins-Fiction, Orphans-Fiction, Grandparents-Fiction, Best Sellers, Brothers and Sisters-Fiction, Jealousy-Fiction, Courage-Fiction.

UNITED STATES-HISTORY-FICTION

Benchley, Nathaniel. Small Wolf; illus by Joan Sandin. Har-Row 1972, 64 pp.

A straight-forward telling of white man's purchase of Manhattan and the resulting displacement of the Indians. The text is simple. The tone is sympathetic to the plight of the Indians. The reader is neither lectured nor patronized, but the early-reader format will prevent using the book comfortably beyond fourth grade. An I Can Read History Book.

Interest Level: 1-4. Reading Level 2.2. Further Search Topics: Historical Fiction, New York City-Fiction, United States-History-Fiction, Indians of North America-Fiction, Group 2.

Bulla, Clyde Robert. A lion to guard us; illus by Michele Chessare. Har-Row 1981, 117 pp.

Bulla's writing isn't quite as successful here as elsewhere. This story of three London children's attempt to go to their father in Jamestown, Virginia, has danger, adventure, daring and promise. It also has too many characters to allow the reader to get to know any of them well. There are also too many very short chapters to allow plot development (23 chapters and 117 pages). The short sentences help to keep the reading level low, but a glossary would have been useful to fully explain the many unfamiliar terms.

Despite its problems, the book is still useful. The story is based on the 1609 voyage of the Sea Adventure. Blown far off course and badly damaged by a storm, the ship landed at Bermuda rather than Jamestown. The survivors were unable to sail again for over nine months. When they reached Jamestown, they found that few people had survived the very harsh year.

The three Freebold children are the focus of this story. When their mother died they left London to find their father in the New World. Having no money of their own, they were lucky to find a doctor friend to pay their ship's passage and to go with them. Halfway across the ocean, the doctor was swept overboard and drowned. From that time until they found their father barely alive, the children were on their own, even though they were still with the ship's passengers.

Although not the best of Bulla, this is still serviceable as a piece of historical fiction (hard to get children to read), or as a choice for the lover of survival and/or sea stories.

Interest Level: 3-5. Reading Level: 2.1. Further Search Topics: United States-History-Fiction, Historical Fiction, Courage-Fiction, Survival-Fiction, Shipwrecks-Fiction, Voyages and Travels-Fiction, Seafaring Life-Fiction.

Bulla, Clyde Robert. John Billington, friend of Squanto; illus by Peter Burchard. Har-Row 1956, 88 pp.

This historical novel about the Mayflower voyage and the Pilgrims' first year at Plymouth centers on young John Billington. John was considered the troublemaker of the children. His problems are woven around the events of the year, including the Pilgrims' first meetings with the Wampanoag Indians. It was finally John, however, who was responsible for bringing peace between the Pilgrims and the Wampanoag tribe who lived further down Cape Cod. The book is not as exciting or convincing as Bulla's books are generally. It also contains a few minor historical inaccuracies; yet it remains useful as both an introduction to American history and historical fiction.

Interest Level: 2-5. Reading Level: 2.1. Further Search Topics: Pilgrims-Fiction, Historical Fiction, United States-History-Fiction, Thanksgiving-Fiction, Troublemakers-Fiction, Indians of North America-Fiction.

Bulla, Clyde Robert. Riding the pony express; illus by Grace Paull. Har-Row 1948, 95 pp.

Although somewhat marred by the stereotyped speech of a young Indian boy, this is otherwise an exciting piece of historical fiction set in the 1860s. Dick was sent from New York City to join his father in St. Joseph, Missouri, only to find his father had moved to Nebraska to become a pony express rider. When Dick finally found his father, after a long stagecoach ride, he thought his father didn't want him. Dick stayed at the way station and helped with the chores because he didn't know what else to do. Then one day the house was burned, his father was shot, and the horses were almost stolen. There was no one around who could carry the mail, except Dick. Despite a wolf pack at his heels, Dick rode to the next way station. On his way home he realized his father really did want him and he no longer wanted to leave his father. Chapters are short with separate episodes that tie them together. A few simple songs appear between the chapters.

Interest Level: 2-5. Reading Level: 2.1. Further Search Topics: Horses-Fiction, West-Fiction, United States-History-Fiction, Historical Fiction, Voyages and Travels-Fiction, Courage-Fiction, Frontier and Pioneer Life-Fiction.

UNITED STATES-HISTORY-WAR

Meriwether, Louise. The freedom ship of Robert Smalls; illus by Lee Jack Morton. P-H 1971, unp (30 pp).

A brief, but very interesting biography of a black man whose dreams of freedom as a young slave during the Civil War, led to a daring plan of escape. Robert Smalls sailed 16 slaves to freedom and presented the Northern Navy with a valuable gunboat of which he was eventually named captain. Smalls later went on to serve five terms in Congress.

Although the picture book format of this book prevents its confortable use much beyond fourth grade, it is a compelling enough story to interest even sixth graders. Print is somewhat small.

Interest Level: 1-4. Reading Level: 3.1. Further Search Topics: Biography, United States-History-War, Blacks-Biography, Smalls, Robert, Group 2, Slavery, Politics-Biography.

UNITED STATES-HISTORY-WAR-FICTION

Baker, Betty. The pig war; illus by Robert Lopshire. Har-Row 1969, 64 pp.

A brief, fictionalized account of an 1859 land squabble between the United States and Britain. The incident, which took place in what is now the state of Washington, became known as the Pig War. Frightened British pigs destroyed the American farmers' gardens. When the farmers shot one of the pigs, the war began. Simply told and humorously illustrated. Should appeal to history or military fans. Early reader format.

Interest Level: 2-4. Reading Level: 2.1. Further Search Topics: United States-History-War-Fiction, Great Britain-History-Fiction, War-Fiction, Washington (state)-Fiction, Historical Fiction, Pigs-Fiction.

Benchley, Nathaniel. Sam the Minutemen; illus by Arnold Lobel. Har-Row 1969, 62 pp.

A good but limited book. It is a simple, personalized account of the beginning of the Revolutionary War as seen by the young son of a Minuteman. The book is a fairly exciting, uncomplicated and enjoyable story. Its limitations rest in its format (it's designed as a reader), the apparent young age of the main character, and the fact that it is told as a story. Its usefulness extends no further than grade three. An I Can Read History Book

Interest Level: 1-3. Reading Level: 2.2. Further Search Topics: United States-History-War-Fiction, Historical Fiction, War-Fiction, Group 2, Courage-Fiction.

Warner, Gertrude Chandler. The woodshed mystery; illus by David Cunningham. A. Whitman 1960, 159 pp.

The four Alden children have grown since their first appearance in *The Boxcar Children* but they are still as close a family as ever. Aunt Jane's telephone message that she wanted to move near them started this adventure. Grandfather proceeded to buy and refurbish his childhood home as a surprise for Aunt Jane. It was an easy house to buy because it had been abandoned and was thought to be haunted. Even though the children and Aunt Jane weren't really worried by the stories of odd occurrences that no one quite remembered, they began to be aware of strange noises and things missing. Upon investigation they discovered Aunt Jane's old boyfriend living in the woodshed in the forest. There beneath the floor of the woodshed, they also found a store of Revolutionary War supplies and a letter from the original owners of the house. The supplies and the letter helped to explain some of the stories. Andrew, Jane's long-lost boyfriend, explained the rest.

It is not necessary to have read any of the series in order to read this story, but those children who enjoyed *The Boxcar Children* are most likely to enjoy the Alden's further adventures. See the entry for *The Boxcar Children* for more information.

Interest Level: 3-5. Reading Level: 2.1. Further Search Topics: Mystery and Detective Stories, United States-History-War-Fiction, Brothers and Sisters-Fiction, Ghosts-Fiction, Vacation-Fiction.

VACATION-FICTION

Blume, Judy. Otherwise known as Sheila the great. Dutton 1972, 128 pp.

Sheila first appears in *Tales of a Fourth Grade Nothing* as Peter Thatcher's neighbor. Sheila was a bundle of fears. She was afraid of dogs, thunderstorms, spiders, horses, putting her face in water, and strange noises at night. The summer she and her family rented a house in Tarrytown, New York, she confronted each one of her fears, even mastered one (putting her face in the water) and learned how to swim. That gave her the self-confidence to face a dog without running away. Sheila's progress was aided by her friend Mouse's steadfast belief that a person should always be honest about herself. Sheila's problems are treated realistically and with dignity, yet humorously. Reading level varies greatly from 1.2 - 4.1, therefore, the book is *most* suitable to grades four through six.

Interest Level: 3-6. Reading Level: 3.1. Further Search Topics: Humorous Fiction, Courage-Fiction, Camp-Fiction, Group 2, Vacation-Fiction, Swimming-Fiction, Brothers and Sisters-Fiction, Friendship-Fiction, Everyday Stories.

Bulla, Clyde Robert. Shoeshine girl; illus by Leigh Grant. Har-Row 1975, 84 pp.

A well-written, realistic story of 10-year-old Sarah who was sent to spend the summer with her Aunt Claudia. Sarah's parents felt that Sarah put too much importance on money and so insisted that Aunt Claudia give her no allowance for the summer. Sure that Aunt Claudia would call her bluff, Sarah threatened to get a job. Instead, Aunt Claudia thought it was a good idea. Sarah's experience as a shoeshine girl forced her to grow, to learn to like working, and finally to take responsibility for the stand when her boss was hit by a car. Told with quiet humor. For the reader who enjoys Judy Blume's books.

Interest Level: 2-5. Reading Level: 2.2. Further Search Topics: Children-Growth-Fiction, Family Problems-Fiction, Vacation-Fiction, Occupations-Fiction, Everyday Stories.

Chew, Ruth. Earthstar magic. Hastings 1979, 128 pp.

This is one of a series of similar stories by Ruth Chew. Each story involves two children and an old woman they usually suspect is a witch. As their suspicions become convictions they also find that, contrary to their expectation, the witch is very nice and often in need of help.

The children in this tale are brother and sister. Ben and Elizabeth first saw and then didn't see Trudy as she searched for a magical mushroom called an earthstar. Accidentally thrown together again, Ben and Elizabeth took a liking to Trudy, especially when she explained that she had been thrown out of her coven because she was so inept. In fact, she wasn't even able to control the earthstar. The earthstar manages to get all three in and out of adventures (including becoming tiny, flying and almost being eaten) before they learn to control its power. As the story ends, Trudy, finally respected by the other witches, flies off with a promise that Ben and Elizabeth will see her again.

Very lightweight but also very popular with young lovers of witch stories. There seems to be just the right amount of adventure to make up for the very benign witch.

Interest Level: 2-5. Reading Level: 2.2. Further Search Topics: Witches-Fiction, Magic-Fiction, Fantasy, Vacation-Fiction, Brothers and Sisters-Fiction, Transformations-Fiction.

Clymer, Eleanor. Me and the Eggman; illus by David K. Stone. Dutton 1972, 57 pp.

As Donald's life became more and more miserable and as his chores and responsibilities around his small, overcrowded, urban apartment increased, he began to look for a way to escape. Thinking that if he could just get to the country, life would be better, Donald sneaked into a truck owned by a farmer who delivered eggs to the city. Not surprisingly the farmer, a sharp speaking, independent old man, was not at all happy to find Donald. Reluctantly, the Eggman, as the farmer was called, agreed to let Donald stay a week and help to work his rundown farm. The week stretched into a summer in which Donald learned to face and accept reality, to love the Eggman and to like himself.

This book is a surprisingly consistent success with reluctant readers, especially boys. Watch for the lack of quotation marks around the dialogue and the somewhat small print.

Interest Level: 3-6. Reading Level: 3.2. Further Search Topics: Family Problems-Fiction, Poverty-Fiction, Vacation-Fiction, Runaways-Fiction, Farm Life-Fiction, Best Sellers.

Cone, Molly. The amazing memory of Harvey Bean; illus by Robert MacLean. HM 1980, 83 pp.

It had been a long time since Harvey had been happy. His memory was so bad that he was always in trouble at school. And now that his parents were separating, he had trouble at home, too. Because he thought that neither one of his parents wanted him he told each one that he was going to stay with the other and instead decided to spend the summer alone. A few hours after he left home, Harry ran into Mr. and Mrs. Katz and before he completely realized it, he was living with them.

Mr. Katz couldn't stand to see anything go to waste. He collected the usable food thrown out behind grocery stores, old furniture, tools, windows and more. Mrs. Katz, whose memory was just as bad as Harvey's, loved to cook, so she could always find a way to use the food. Everything else bulged from the house and garage into the driveway and yard. Harvey spent a happy summer learning to scavenge, eating well, learning not to worry about what others thought of him and even improving his memory. When his parents finally found him, Harvey realized that they really did want him, even if they were separated. He decided to live with his mother on weekdays, his father on weekends, and the Katzs during the summers.

The plot problems that are obvious to adult readers are ones that most young readers will be able to ignore (i.e. neither parent checks on Harvey for over two months). Young readers will enjoy the humor and realism of Harvey's pain, happiness and eventual feeling of self-confidence and triumph. The ten short chapters, good-sized print and adequate space between the lines help lower the book's reading level to late fourth grade.

Interest Level: 3-6. Reading Level: 5.1. Further Search Topics: Loners-Fiction, Vacation-Fiction, Divorce and Separation-Fiction, Humorous Fiction, Group 2, Memory-Fiction, Runaways-Fiction, Academic Problems-Fiction, Individualists-Fiction.

Danziger, Paula. There's a bat in bunk five. Delacorte 1980, 150 pp.

Although this is a sequel to *The Cat Ate My Gymsuit,* it can be read alone. Marcy accepted an offer to become a junior counselor at an arts camp run by her ex-English teacher Ms. Finney and Ms. Finney's husband. After a nervous beginning, Marcy found herself enjoying the other counselors and the campers, but most of all, her first romance. Marcy's only difficulty was dealing with Ginger, a very troubled 10-year-old in Marcy's cabin. Marcy couldn't seem to get through to Ginger. When Ginger ran away, Marcy was forced to consider whether she should have spent more time with the campers and not quite so much time with Ted.

Marcy is a normal teenager whose problems, questions and activities are appealing to many teen and pre-teen readers. The characters who surround Marcy here are less stereotyped and flat than those in The Cat Ate My Gymsuit. Even Marcy's parents are more human. The author's light touch is just right for Marcy's story.

Interest Level: 5-6. Reading Level: 3.2. Further Search Topics: Humorous Fiction, Camp-Fiction, Everyday Stories, Love-Fiction, Vacation-Fiction, Occupations-Fiction, Adolescence-Fiction.

Hamilton, Virginia. Zeely; illus by Symeon Shimin. Macmillan 1967, 122 pp.

A beautiful, almost mystical story of a black girl who learns about self-identity and pride from a statuesque neighbor whom Geeder is convinced must be a Watutsi princess. At first by chance and later at an arranged meeting, Zeely (Geeder's neighbor) gently and symbolically speaks to Geeder of her racial origins. She also tells Geeder of a young girl (Zeely as a child), too ignorant of the world around her to be able to recognize reality. It is a quietly moving story that is most likely to find an appreciative audience in the thoughtful, more mature reader.

Interest Level: 5-6. Reading Level: 5.1. Further Search Topics: Africa-Fiction, Royalty-Fiction, Blacks-Fiction, Courage-Fiction, Vacation-Fiction, Country Life-Fiction, Read Aloud.

Hurwitz, Johanna. Aldo Ice Cream; illus by John Wallner. Morrow 1981, 124 pp.

Aldo got his newest nickname (Ice Cream) from his friend DeDe when she heard that Aldo not only wanted to try every flavor of ice cream at the local store, but wanted to buy an ice cream freezer for his sister's birthday as well. Aldo decided his summer project would be to earn enough money for the freezer, but he soon found out that there were very few ways a nine-year-old boy could earn $49.95. In the meantime, he helped his mother deliver food for a Meals-On-Wheels project, learned to swim, found out about fish from Mr. Puccini, and shared his cat with Mrs. Nardo. As the summer came to an end he saw one last opportunity to earn enough money for the ice cream maker. A local shoe store offered a new pair of sneakers to the child who owned the most worn out pair. Aldo convinced his mother that if he won the sneakers, she should pay him the money she would otherwise have had to spend on his new sneakers. Aldo set about making sure that his already well-worn sneakers were the most dilapidated in town. A few days before the sneaker contest the hardware store lowered the price on the ice cream freezer to a point where Aldo could afford it if he won the sneakers. When Aldo did win, just as he knew he would, he and his mother bought the very last freezer in the store.

It is not as well-constructed a story as *Aldo Applesauce,* but for established Aldo fans, or those who want quiet, reassuring fiction, this is a usable title.

Interest Level: 3-4. Reading Level: 3.1. Further Search Topics: Humorous Fiction, Brothers and Sisters-Fiction, Vacation-Fiction, Occupations-Fiction, Everyday Stories, Aging-Fiction, Family-Fiction, Contests-Fiction.

Hurwitz, Johanna. The law of gravity; illus by Ingrid Fetz. Morrow 1978, 192 pp.

The summer between fifth and sixth grades looked very unexciting to Margot. Her best friends were both going away for the whole summer and her father, a musician, was going to be on tour for most of the summer. Margot's very overweight mother had sworn never to go downstairs from their fifth floor walk-up apartment. Unless Margot chose to stay upstairs too, she was sure she would have a very lonely vacation. In addition, she had to work on a summer project for school. The project she finally chose was to get her mother downstairs after nine years of staying upstairs.

In search of help she went to the local library where she met Bernie. Bernie was only a year older than Margot, but he seemed to know the most interesting things about the city. He showed her places Margot had never heard of before, he taught her to play chess, backgammon, and even to ride a bicycle. He was so full of fascinating ideas and information that Margot had no chance to be bored or lonely. Best of all, he even tried to help Margot with her project. None of their ideas worked, however, until Margot pretended to run away and scared her mother into going downstairs. Only then did Margot realize that she loved her mother whether or not she stayed on the fifth floor and that she couldn't simply force her mother or anyone else to change to suit her own fancy.

The book is a warm, understanding, slightly humorous treatment of the fairly common wish to change someone else. Although not many readers are likely to share Margot's exact problem, most will recognize her feelings. The book is also a virtual Chamber of Commerce advertisement for urban living. One of its other charms is its picture of a non-competitive, open, real friendship between an 11-year-old girl and a 12-year-old boy. The only drawback to the book is its inconsistent reading level which varies from 4.1 to 5.1 with a rare leap to 5.2.

Interest Level: 4-6. Reading Level: 4.2. Further Search Topics: Vacation-Fiction, Friendship-Fiction, Loners-Fiction, City Life-Fiction, Individualists-Fiction, Courage-Fiction, New York City-Fiction, Humorous Fiction, Family-Fiction, Challenges-Fiction, Weight-Fiction, Everyday Stories, Best Sellers.

MacLachlan, Patricia. Arthur, for the very first time; illus by Lloyd Bloom. Har-Row 1980, 117 pp.

A beautifully written, sensitive yet humorous story of a boy's maturation and growing awareness of the world around him. When Arthur's unhappiness at home is made more intense by the advent of a new baby, he is sent to spend the summer with his older aunt and uncle. Their eccentricities and those of their friends are at first only material for Arthur to write about in his journal. But as the summer progresses he not only learns from them, but also grows from an observer of life to a participant. His final step is helping a large and beloved pig bear her litter in a driving rain storm aided only by his independent, totally untamed young friend Moira.

The print is somewhat small, but spacing between lines is generous.

Interest Level: 4-6. Reading Level: 4.2. Further Search Topics: Read Aloud, Children-Growth-Fiction, Humorous Fiction, Friendship-Fiction, Vacation-Fiction, Relatives-Fiction, Infants-Fiction, Individualists-Fiction, Writing-Fiction, Loners-Fiction, Group 2.

Parish, Peggy. Hermit Dan; illus by Paul Frame. Macmillan 1977, 151 pp.

When the Roberts children tried to prove that Pirate Island really had been used by pirates, they encountered more action and intrigue than they had found in any of their earlier adventures. Liza, Bill and Jed suspected that Hermit Dan knew whether or not there had been pirates on the island, but he was so gruff and apparently mean that they didn't dare ask him any questions. Instead, they trailed and spied on him and asked questions of anyone who had known Hermit Dan as a child. It was rumored that his ancestors had actually been pirates. Until a terrible fire that had destroyed all they owned, Hermit Dan's family had been very wealthy. However, no one knew how they had become so rich.

In an attempt to see what the summer residents knew about Hermit Dan, the children introduced themselves to the vacationing youngsters. Among the visitors the Roberts met Hank and Ted, brothers bent on bullying Hermit Dan. When the children were rescued from a severe sandstorm by Hermit Dan, they were surprised to find that he wasn't nearly as gruff as he appeared. In fact they began to feel quite protective of the old man. Thus when Hank and Ted stole a secret box that held all of Hermit Dan's valuables, it was the Roberts children who fought (literally) to get the box back. It was after Liza, Bill and Jed returned the box to Hermit Dan, however, that the real surprises began: these included a surprise party for Hermit Dan, his wish to be friendly, and his gift to the children of three pieces of eight that proved his family members were pirates.

This title's more interesting and involved plot makes the book more likely to be a success with older readers than the other stories about the Roberts children. Otherwise it shares the same format, faults and strengths as the other series titles.

Interest Level: 2-5. Reading Level: 2.1. Further Search Topics: Mystery and Detective Stories, Pirates-Fiction, Vacation-Fiction, Loners-Fiction, Treasure-Fiction, Bullies-Fiction, Brothers and Sisters-Fiction, Grandparents-Fiction.

Parish, Peggy. Clues in the woods; illus by Paul Frame. Macmillan 1968, 154 pp.

The books about the three Roberts children share problems that are obvious to adults and felt by some young readers as well, but they continue to be popular with undemanding young readers. The characters are very white and middle class and their actions often fit out-of-date stereotypes. The plots have few surprises or suspense, but the reading levels are consistent and the very predictability of the books makes them familiar and therefore comfortable.

This particular story takes place at the end of the same summer the children solved the mystery of *The Key to the Treasure*. The children were alerted by their grandmother to the disappearance of food scraps, left outside the house. Thinking that two runaway children, about whom they had read, had taken the food, Liza, Bill, and Jed tried to find the runaways. Their attempts eventually brought them new friends and thus the solution to their mystery. It had not been the runaways who had taken the food, it was their new friends' dog.

Interest Level: 1-4. Reading Level: 2.2. Further Search Topics: Mystery and Detective Stories, Brothers and Sisters-Fiction, Vacation-Fiction, Dogs-Fiction, Runaways-Fiction, Grandparents-Fiction, Group 2.

Parish, Peggy. Key to the treasure; illus by Paul Frame. Macmillan 1966, 154 pp.

This is the first of the stories about Jed, Bill and Liza Roberts. The three children are very middle-class, the book's plots are simple and often lack suspense, but the stories still enjoy widespread popularity among unsophisticated readers.

All three children went to spend the summer with their grandparents and decided to tackle a mystery left unsolved for over 75 years. An old drawing and an authentic war bonnet provided the only clues to finding three Indian artifacts. At each step along the way there were crumbled, brittle pieces of paper bearing coded messages that led to the next clue. The search ended when the children found that a storage area in a porch piller contained an Indian doll, mask, and leather shield that had belonged to their great-grandfather.

Interest Level: 1-4. Reading Level: 2.1. Further Search Topics: Vacation-Fiction, Brothers and Sisters-Fiction, Group 2, Mystery and Detective Stories, Grandparents-Fiction, Nonverbal Communication-Fiction.

Parish, Peggy. Pirate Island adventure; illus by Paul Frame. Macmillan 1975, 167 pp.

Although this is the fourth book in the series about the Roberts children, none of the titles must be read in chronological order. This time the three rather privileged children spent the summer with their grandparents on a resort island. They lived in a house that their family had owned for years, explored the island, and swam in their own private cove. But, most of their time was spent trying to solve an old mystery. Their great-uncle had hidden several very special items (one for each member of his family) years earlier, and had left only one clue with their grandfather. After he gave the children that clue it was only a matter of time before they found the hidden treasures.

This book is also lengthy, but is divided into 22 very manageable chapters. It is, like the others, almost entirely dialogue and action, which makes it especially appealing to young reluctant readers.

Interest Level: 1-4. Reading Level: 2.1. Further Search Topics: Mystery and Detective Stories, Vacation-Fiction, Treasure-Fiction, Brothers and Sisters-Fiction, Grandparents-Fiction, Group 2.

Pfeffer, Susan Beth. Kid power; illus by Leigh Grant. Watts 1977, 121 pp.

When Janie's mother lost her job, her father's salary wouldn't stretch to provide any more money for the new bicycle fund. There was enough money already set aside to pay for one new bike, but both Janie and her older sister Carol wanted a bicycle. Carol, who had saved money of her own, suggested that they each pay for half a bike and their parents contribute the money for the other half. Then Janie's only problem was how to earn money, since she had none saved. Her solution was to create a business: Kid Power. Before long, Janie's business had blossomed and she was becoming rich, but she had lost her best friend and was ruining a client's roses. When Janie finally realized that getting rich wasn't the only thing that mattered in life, she relaxed, delegated jobs to friends better able to handle them, and became their agent.

A genuinely funny book that, as a bonus, takes a realistic look at the interworkings of a family. Consistent reading level.

Interest Level: 4-6. Reading Level: 3.1. Further Search Topics: Occupations-Fiction, Everyday Stories, Vacation-Fiction, Family-Fiction, Humorous Fiction, Best Sellers, Bicycles and Bicycling-Fiction, Friendship-Fiction.

Renner, Beverly. The Hideaway summer; illus by Ruth Sanderson. Har-Row 1978, 134 pp.

On their way to summer camp, Addie suddenly got off the bus and took her younger brother Clay to see the place where Addie had spent prior summer vacations. It was their grandmother's house and a small cabin called the Hideaway. The house had been sold after their grandmother had died that year, but Addie's father had decided to keep the Hideaway.

Much to Addie's surprise she found the Hideaway beautifully fixed-up, just as Gram had promised she would do one day.

When they missed the last bus out of the tiny town and realized that they had enough money to buy the food they would need, Addie and Clay decided to make the Hideaway their summer home. One phone call to the camp and weekly calls to their father kept people from worrying about them. Their discovery of two small raccoons meant that their days were filled with caring for and training the animals. In addition, they had to build a warning system so that no one would discover them and they had to get their food and provisions from town about every two weeks without being too noticeable. They even had to figure out a way to survive a wild summer storm, a flood, and poachers who hunted raccoons. By summer's end Addie and Clay had grown independent, resourceful, and very close to each other.

An exciting story whose short chapters and fairly short sentences keep the reading level reasonably low. Print is dark and of adequate size, but space between the lines is somewhat narrow.

Interest Level: 4-6. Reading Level: 3.1. Further Search Topics: Brothers and Sisters-Fiction, Runaways-Fiction, Pets-Fiction, Survival-Fiction, Vacation-Fiction, Raccoons-Fiction, Read Aloud.

Scism, Carol K. The wizard of Walnut Street; illus by Martha Alexander. Dial 1973, 54 pp.

John and his friends had no room in their Wizard Club for Ford Owens, the new kid. John thought Ford was a conceited show-off who only wanted to make John look like a coward. It was true that John was afraid of some things, such as going down the giant slide into the lake, but he didn't want anyone else to know it. So he excluded Ford from all the club's activities until Ford pushed his way into their magic wishing-well project.

It had been John's idea to charge everyone a dime who wanted to make a wish. They could use the money to buy the few simple things that they would need to make the wishes come true. But it was Ford's eerie volcano and his large dog that had added just the right atmosphere to the trick to make people believe. Even John and Ford found themselves making wishes. John wished to be able to go down the giant slide. He didn't know what Ford wished. Much to John's initial surprise, people's wishes began to be fulfilled. Even Arthur, who had wished he could learn to dive, found he could. Then because John began to realize that the magic was in believing in himself and not in the wishing well, he tried the slide and succeeded. Once John's reason to avoid Ford was gone, he relaxed and asked Ford to join the club. At that point, even Ford's wish was granted.

Interest Level: 2-4. Reading Level: 2.1. Further Search Topics: Friendship-Fiction, Gangs-Fiction, Courage-Fiction, Magic-Fiction, Vacation-Fiction, Best Sellers.

Talbot, Charlene Joy. The Great Rat Island adventure; illus by Ruth Sanderson. Atheneum 1977, 164 pp.

Joel dreaded spending the summer with his father. His parents were divorced and Joel was sure his father didn't want him. His father only wanted to study birds. Great Rat Island, where Joel and his father were to spend the summer, was of no interest to Joel. It had no television, no one his own age, only terns. Even the assignment Joel was given (to make sure that no more tern eggs were stolen) sounded dull. It led to an adventure and a friend, however, that were anything but dull.

Joel discovered that a girl his own age was the thief of the tern eggs. Her name was Vicky Owens. She had run away from camp and was spending the summer alone on Little Rat Island. Joel kept her secret until the day of hurricane warnings. As the storm approached Joel realized that Vicky wouldn't be safe on Little Rat Island. Without telling anyone else he took the only boat around and went to look for Vicky to bring her back to Great Rat Island. He found her with her leg stuck between two rocks, unable to move. By the time Joel got her loose, it was too late to get back to the big island. Not knowing what else to do, Joel and Vicky dragged the boat inside an abandoned building where Vicky had been living. As the water rose around them and Vicky grew delirious with fever, Joel set up camp in the boat. While the building filled with water they stayed dry in the boat. Rescue and medical care for Vicky finally came the next day.

A solid, steadily-paced survival story for the reader who wants a little more than just an adventure story. Print is small.

Interest Level: 4-6. Reading Level: 3.1. Further Search Topics: Vacation-Fiction, Family Problems-Fiction, Birds-Fiction, Divorce and Separation-Fiction, Disasters-Fiction, Survival-Fiction, Runaways-Fiction.

Warner, Gertrude Chandler. The lighthouse mystery; illus by David Cunningham. A. Whitman 1963, 128 pp.

What better place for a mystery than a lighthouse late at night? Add the excitement of a storm at sea and a young man alone in a boat and the story should be unbeatable. Unfortunately this, as well as some of the other books in the series, does not quite live up to its potential. It will not attract many new readers but it will satisfy those who crave more adventures of the Alden family. The main problem with the book is its lack of definition. It isn't quite a mystery or an adventure story, it's a little of both. It is also part homespun family story, part science lesson, and part "problem story."

The Aldens rented a lighthouse in a very small fishing village one summer. Late each night their dog awoke them as he barked at a stranger who walked into or away from a closed-up building nearby. When the children investigated, they found that the surly son of a local fisherman was using the building to experiment on plankton as a food source. Harry was a brilliant young man who wanted to go to college, but whose father stubbornly refused to let him study. One night when Larry was at sea gathering samples, a terrible storm blew up. Only the Coast Guard and an improvised light in the lighthouse saved Larry from drowning. Larry's brush with death forced his father to acknowledge Larry's abilities and allow him to continue studying at college.

The sketchy illustrations in this and the following books in the series are an improvement over the silhouettes of *The Boxcar Children*. See the annotation for *The Boxcar Children* for further series information.

Interest Level: 3-6. Reading Level: 2.1. Further Search Topics: Mystery and Detective Stories, Lighthouses-Fiction, Food-Fiction, Disasters-Fiction, Vacation-Fiction.

Warner, Gertrude Chandler. Schoolhouse mystery; illus by David Cunningham. A. Whitman 1965, 128 pp.

On a dare, the Aldens went to a quiet fishing village to see what excitement they could find there. They found an isolated town filled with poor and unfriendly people. In their attempt to get to know the townspeople, the Aldens learned of the children's desire for schooling and the adults' anticipation of the Money Man's arrival. The Alden children took on the task of teaching school for the summer in an abandoned schoolhouse owned by Miss Gray, a recluse. The Money Man intrigued them more with each new bit of information they learned about him. They finally decided that the Money Man was a swindler who was practically stealing valuable antiques away from the villagers. By spying on the Money Man when he used the schoolhouse to store the antiques, the Aldens and an ex-FBI man were able to capture him. When the vacation was over, the Aldens had once more found excitement, Miss Gray had agreed to teach the local school, the Money Man was on his way to jail, and the townspeople knew the value of their old household items.

See the entry for *The Boxcar Children* for more information.

Interest Level: 3-5. Reading Level: 2.2. Further Search Topics: Mystery and Detective Stories, Vacation-Fiction, School Stories, Antiquities-Fiction, Crime-Fiction, Brothers and Sisters-Fiction, Challenges-Fiction.

Warner, Gertrude Chandler. The woodshed mystery; illus by David Cunningham. A. Whitman 1960, 159 pp.

The four Alden children have grown since their first appearance in *The Boxcar Children* but they are still as close a family as ever. Aunt Jane's telephone message that she wanted to move near them started this adventure. Grandfather proceeded to buy and refurbish his childhood home as a surprise for Aunt Jane. It was an easy house to buy because it had been abandoned and was thought to be haunted. Even though the children and Aunt Jane weren't really worried by the stories of odd occurrences that no one quite remembered, they began to be aware of strange noises and things missing. Upon investigation they discovered Aunt Jane's old boyfriend living in the woodshed in the forest. There beneath the floor of the woodshed, they also found a store of Revolutionary War supplies and a letter from the original owners of the house. The supplies and the letter helped to explain some of the stories. Andrew, Jane's long-lost boyfriend, explained the rest.

It is not necessary to have read any of the series in order to read this story, but those children who enjoyed *The Boxcar Children* are most likely to enjoy the Alden's further adventures. See the entry for *The Boxcar Children* for more information.

Interest Level: 3-5. Reading Level: 2.1. Further Search Topics: Mystery and Detective Stories, United States-History-War-Fiction, Brothers and Sisters-Fiction, Ghosts-Fiction, Vacation-Fiction.

VEGETARIANS-FICTION

Hurwitz, Johanna. Aldo Applesauce; illus by John Wallner. Morrow 1979, 127 pp.

Aldo Sossi, vegetarian and new kid at school, was immediately dubbed Applesauce for obvious reasons. Aldo didn't like his new name. He didn't like being teased either—not the way he was teased at school. Nothing went right for Aldo. His attempts at making friends only ended in disasters (once at a bowling alley and another time at a birthday party). He had been able to start a friendship only with a strange girl who wore a heavy, black fake moustache most of the time. After accidentally nearly ruining that friendship too, Aldo not only learned why DeDe wore the moustache, but helped her learn to live without it. DeDe, in turn, helped Aldo take himself less seriously and find more friends.

This is a comfortable, humorous story of two fourth grade children learning to be themselves. The vocabulary is occasionally difficult, but sentence length is almost always short.

Interest Level: 3-5. Reading Level: 3.1. Further Search Topics: Moving, Household-Fiction, Humorous Fiction, School Stories, Friendship-Fiction, Divorce and Separation-Fiction, Vegetarians-Fiction, Individualists-Fiction, Everyday Stories.

VIKINGS-FICTION

Bulla, Clyde Robert. Viking adventure; illus by Douglas Gorsline. T Y Crowell 1963, 117 pp.

An exciting story of a young Norwegian boy named Sigurd. Sigurd realized his dream when he finally set sail on a Viking ship in search of Wineland (Vinland). Leif Eriksson had told of his North American findings over 100 years earlier. Sigurd and his father's friend Grom, the captain of the ship, were sure they could find that land again. Their determination finally brought Grom's death at the hands of the ship's owner, Sigurd's near death, and the destruction of the ship.

This book, too, is true to Bulla's style of short chapters, short sentences, much action and high appeal. Although it is a little higher reading level than many of Bulla's others, it is still a good choice. Recently out of print, but worth a search.

Interest Level: 2-6. Reading Level: 3.1. Further Search Topics: Norway-Fiction, Historical Fiction, Seafaring Life-Fiction, Voyages and Travels-Fiction, Shipwrecks-Fiction, Explorers-Fiction, Vikings-Fiction, Courage-Fiction, Best Sellers, Group 2.

VISION

Adler, Irving. Your eyes. John Day 1962, 48 pp.

Getting a young reader past this book's unattractive appearance may be difficult. Everything about the book's physical appearance screams "old." Some of the information and lack of information conveys the same message (e.g. no mention of contact lenses). For basic material about eyes and sight however, there is much here that is accessible and interesting to readers in grades two to six. Includes pronunciation guide, glossary, and detailed table of contents. No index. The Reason Why Series

Interest Level: 2-6. Reading Level: 3.1. Further Search Topics: Vision, Physically Handicapped, Group 2.

Malone, Mary. Annie Sullivan; illus by Lydia Rosier. Putnam 1971, 61 pp.

This is a very brief sketch of both Annie Sullivan's life and Helen Keller's life. Their lives were so intertwined that they cannot be separated. But because they are combined in such a short book, neither woman can be treated in much depth. That fact is not as harmful here as it might otherwise be, because even a bare bones description of the life of this extraordinary deaf, blind and mute woman or her near-blind, dedicated teacher, is interesting.

Interest Level: 2-5. Reading Level: 2.2. Further Search Topics: Sullivan, Annie, Keller, Helen, Vision, Biography, Physically Handicapped, Sound, Courage.

Mathis, Sharon Bell. Ray Charles; illus by George Ford. Har-Row 1973, 33 pp.

Dominent throughout this biography of Ray Charles is the theme of overcoming adversity. The book is not just a recounting of Ray Charles' music lessons, early schooling, family life, and talent. All of that is included, but it serves to illustrate the manner in which Charles met his troubles. His problems began when he was very young. His brother died, and Ray lost one eye and then the sight in his other eye. His family was poor, but close, and he missed them when he was sent away to a school for the blind. Music was his love, but even that was work, for Charles had to learn to read and write music in Braille. He worked hard at it and eventually could play and arrange music for every instrument in the band.

Determined to be independent, when Charles was orphaned at age 15, he left school and began playing music for a living. The first record he made resulted in a $16 fine because he made it during a musician's union strike. Charles took a series of sideman and nightclub jobs until he finally had enough money to hire seven other musicians to play his music. Today Charles is very wealthy, owns his own record company, has a family, and is considered a great jazz and blues musician. None of his success came easily; only through determination, will power, pride, and hard work.

The book, interesting and serviceable enough for music or biography units, is also designed to set an example for youngsters facing their own problems. It will, of course, be popular with Ray Charles fans, too. Crowell Biography series.

Interest Level: 2-4. Reading Level: 3.1. Further Search Topics: Jazz Music, Music-Biography, Vision, Physically Handicapped, Blacks-Biography, Group 2, Biography, Pianists, Orphans, Challenges, Courage.

VISION-FICTION

Anderson, C. S. The blind Connemara. Macmillan 1971, 80 pp.

Rhonda, not wealthy enough to own a horse of her own, was given a beautiful Connemara pony. Unfortunately, it had begun to go blind. A blind pony is usually put away, but Rhonda loved this pony too much to let that happen. Against all odds, Rhonda not only taught Pony to trot, canter, and even jump with confidence, but went on to win a ribbon at an important horse show. Though sentimental and predictable, this book is an almost insured success with lovers of horses and champions of the underdog. Be alert to the occasional descriptive passage that is both longer and more difficult than the rest of the text.

Interest Level: 4-6. Reading Level: 3.2. Further Search Topics: Vision-Fiction, Physically Handicapped-Fiction, Horses-Fiction.

Eyerly, Jeannette. The seeing summer; illus by Emily Arnold McCully. Lippincott 1981, 153 pp.

That it attempts to be two books at the same time is the one flaw in this book that may be noticed by young readers. The first half of the book is an interesting story of the growing friendship between a sighted girl and a blind girl. Carey's delight at the idea of a new friend next door turned to disbelief and discomfort when she learned that Jenny was blind. Jenny too wanted to be friends, but not if she was to be pitied or patronized. Gradually she was able to show Carey that being blind was a nuisance, but nothing she was ashamed of or embarrassed about. The second half of the book presents the contrived and somewhat unnecessary story of Jenny's kidnapping. When Carey's attempt to rescue Jenny resulted in her capture too, it was, of course, Jenny's independence and ingenuity that led the way to their eventual rescue.

To the reader looking for a rousing story of a kidnapping the book may be a disappointment. Half of the book is a long time to wait for the slight adventure. But, for those readers interested in a good story of physical differences and friendship, this will be more satisfying.

Interest Level: 3-6. Reading Level: 3.1. Further Search Topics: Vision-Fiction, Friendship-Fiction, Kidnapping-Fiction, Single Parent Family-Fiction, Physically Handicapped-Fiction.

VOLCANOES

Lewis, Thomas P. Hill of fire; illus by Joan Sandin. Har-Row 1971, 63 pp.

A personalized account of the volcano that suddenly erupted in the middle of a farmer's field in Mexico on February 20, 1943. Because the account is written as a story and because of its easy-reader format, the book is most useful only through third grade. An I-Can-Read-History-Book.

Interest Level: 1-3. Reading Level: 2.2. Further Search Topics: Volcanoes, Group 2, Mexico, Disasters, Historical Fiction.

VOYAGES AND TRAVELS-FICTION

Bulla, Clyde Robert. A lion to guard us; illus by Michele Chessare. Har-Row 1981, 117 pp.

Bulla's writing isn't quite as successful here as elsewhere. This story of three London children's attempt to go to their father in Jamestown, Virginia, has danger, adventure, daring and promise. It also has too many characters to allow the reader to get to know any of them well. There are also too many very short chapters to allow plot development (23 chapters and 117 pages). The short sentences help to keep the reading level low, but a glossary would have been useful to fully explain the many unfamiliar terms.

Despite its problems, the book is still useful. The story is based on the 1609 voyage of the Sea Adventure. Blown far off course and badly damaged by a storm, the ship landed at Bermuda rather than Jamestown. The survivors were unable to sail again for over nine months. When they reached Jamestown, they found that few people had survived the very harsh year.

The three Freebold children are the focus of this story. When their mother died they left London to find their father in the New World. Having no money of their own, they were lucky to find a doctor friend to pay their ship's passage and to go with them. Halfway across the ocean, the doctor was swept overboard and drowned. From that time until they found their father barely alive, the children were on their own, even though they were still with the ship's passengers.

Although not the best of Bulla, this is still serviceable as a piece of historical fiction (hard to get children to read), or as a choice for the lover of survival and/or sea stories.

Interest Level: 3-5. Reading Level: 2.1. Further Search Topics: United States-History-Fiction, Historical Fiction, Courage-Fiction, Survival-Fiction, Shipwrecks-Fiction, Voyages and Travels-Fiction, Seafaring Life-Fiction.

Bulla, Clyde Robert. Riding the pony express; illus by Grace Paull. Har-Row 1948, 95 pp.

Although somewhat marred by the stereotyped speech of a young Indian boy, this is otherwise an exciting piece of historical fiction set in the 1860s. Dick was sent from New York City to join his father in St. Joseph, Missouri, only to find his father had moved to Nebraska to become a pony express rider. When Dick finally found his father, after a long stagecoach ride, he thought his father didn't want him. Dick stayed at the way station and helped with the chores because he didn't know what else to do. Then one day the house was burned, his father was shot, and the horses were almost stolen. There was no one around who could carry the mail, except Dick. Despite a wolf pack at his heels, Dick rode to the next way station. On his way home he realized his father really did want him and he no longer wanted to leave his father. Chapters are short with separate episodes that tie them together. A few simple songs appear between the chapters.

Interest Level: 2-5. Reading Level: 2.1. Further Search Topics: Horses-Fiction, West-Fiction, United States-History-Fiction, Historical Fiction, Voyages and Travels-Fiction, Courage-Fiction, Frontier and Pioneer Life-Fiction.

Bulla, Clyde Robert. Viking adventure; illus by Douglas Gorsline. T Y Crowell 1963, 117 pp.

An exciting story of a young Norwegian boy named Sigurd. Sigurd realized his dream when he finally set sail on a Viking ship in search of Wineland (Vinland). Leif Eriksson had told of his North American findings over 100 years earlier. Sigurd and his father's friend Grom, the captain of the ship, were sure they could find that land again. Their determination finally brought Grom's death at the hands of the ship's owner, Sigurd's near death, and the destruction of the ship.

This book, too, is true to Bulla's style of short chapters, short sentences, much action and high appeal. Although it is a little higher reading level than many of Bulla's others, it is still a good choice. Recently out of print, but worth a search.

Interest Level: 2-6. Reading Level: 3.1. Further Search Topics: Norway-Fiction, Historical Fiction, Seafaring Life-Fiction, Voyages and Travels-Fiction, Shipwrecks-Fiction, Explorers-Fiction, Vikings-Fiction, Courage-Fiction, Best Sellers, Group 2.

Butterworth, William E. Next stop, Earth; illus by Paul Frame. Walker 1978, 80 pp.

After two years on a desolate planet, 12-year-old Charley and his family were anticipating their return to Earth. But when Charley was awakened from sleep by a spaceship robot, he learned that an asteroid disturbance had caused several key systems on the ship to malfunction. Of 24 passengers on board the spaceship, only 10 were still alive and only Charley and his sister were able to be awakened. It was up to Charley to pilot the ship to its landing on Earth. The controls were all in an adjacent room which a faulty robot kept Charley from entering. Without someone at the controls the ship would burn up when re-entering Earth's atmosphere. By tricking the robot and commanding the ship's main computer, Charley was able to get to the control panel just in time to wake his father, help with reentry and save the ship.

Though the story tends to be heavy with conversations between Charley and various computers and robots, it is also that dialogue that helps maintain suspense. It is a story for the confirmed science fiction fan, not for the inductee.

Interest Level: 3-6. Reading Level: 2.2. Further Search Topics: Science Fiction, Outer Space-Fiction, Voyages and Travels-Fiction, Robots-Fiction, Computers-Fiction.

Byars, Betsy. Trouble River; illus by Rocco Negri. Viking Pr. 1969, 158 pp.

A gripping adventure story of survival. After being attacked by an Indian in the middle of the night, Dewey and his grandmother rushed to Trouble River to board a small raft which Dewey had just finished making. They thought they would only need to navigate a few miles down the river to safety at a neighbor's home, but found instead that the neighbor's cabin had been burned down. For almost 40 miles they fought against the unknown river, wolves and rapids.

This is a book that should satisfy many reluctant readers. It's frequent dialogue, fast action and high interest are only occasionally marred by an overly long sentence.

Interest Level: 3-6. Reading Level: 3.1. Further Search Topics: Courage-Fiction, Frontier and Pioneer Life-Fiction, Survival-Fiction, Grandparents-Fiction, Voyages and Travels-Fiction, Best Sellers, Read Aloud.

Terman, Douglas. By balloons to the Sahara; illus by Paul Granger. Bantam 1979, 117 pp.

See the entry for *Sugarcane Island*, by Edward Packard for detailed information about the series. Available in paperback edition only. Choose Your Own Adventure series.

Interest Level: 2-6. Reading Level: 3.2. Further Search Topics: Voyages and Travels-Fiction, Flight-Fiction, Best Sellers, Group 2.

WALTON, BILL

Burchard, Marshall. Sports hero: Bill Walton. Putnam 1978, 94 pp.

Burchard's series of *Sports Hero* biographies is better than many other sports biography series. Although heavy emphasis is placed on the subject's playing time, each person's life is capsulized from childhood to just before the book's publication date. Marshall and Sue Burchard (with whom he has collaborated and who writes an almost identical series called *Sports Stars*) treat each figure favorably and with enthusiasm. But, contrary to many children's writers, particularly sports biographers, these writers at least touch on those personal foibles that make players human (i.e. Joe Namath's tendency to break training is briefly described). Each book is abundantly illustrated with photographs, avoids patronizing the reader and is consistently interesting. Each is reliable, very useful and can be depended on to appeal to the sports enthusiast. Problems arise, however, with inconsistent and/or artificially inflated reading levels. The reading level of a title may vary from 2.2 to 4.2. The same passage tested on both a Spache and a Dale-Chall scale may show a similar two-year spread. The problem seems to be with jargon. Most sports jargon does not appear on either Spache's or Chall's list of familiar words and thus raises a book's reading level. But, the words may well be known to the reader (or quickly recognized after one introduction and so not truly unfamiliar). Keep in mind, therefore, that the true sports fan will often be able to read a title that tests well above his/her actual reading level.

Bill Walton's career is covered only through the end of the 1976-1977 season when the Portland Trailblazers won the NBA title. The reading level of this title is one of the most inconsistent of the series (from 2.2 to 4.2).

Interest Level: 2-6. Reading Level: 3.2. Further Search Topics: Biography, Walton, Bill, Basketball-Biography, Group 2.

WAR-FICTION

Baker, Betty. The pig war; illus by Robert Lopshire. Har-Row 1969, 64 pp.

A brief, fictionalized account of an 1859 land squabble between the United States and Britain. The incident, which took place in what is now the state of Washington, became known as the Pig War. Frightened British pigs destroyed the American farmers' gardens. When the farmers shot one of the pigs, the war began. Simply told and humorously illustrated. Should appeal to history or military fans. Early reader format.

Interest Level: 2-4. Reading Level: 2.1. Further Search Topics: United States-History-War-Fiction, Great Britain-History-Fiction, War-Fiction, Washington (state)-Fiction, Historical Fiction, Pigs-Fiction.

Benchley, Nathaniel. Sam the Minutemen; illus by Arnold Lobel. Har-Row 1969, 62 pp.

A good but limited book. It is a simple, personalized account of the beginning of the Revolutionary War as seen by the young son of a Minuteman. The book is a fairly exciting, uncomplicated and enjoyable story. Its limitations rest in its format (it's designed as a reader), the apparent young age of the main character, and the fact that it is told as a story. Its usefulness extends no further than grade three. An I Can Read History Book

Interest Level: 1-3. Reading Level: 2.2. Further Search Topics: United States-History-War-Fiction, Historical Fiction, War-Fiction, Group 2, Courage-Fiction.

Coerr, Eleanor. Sadako and the thousand paper cranes; illus by Ronand Himler. Putnam 1977, 64 pp.

This is a beautiful and very sad story of a young girl who was only two years old when the atomic bomb was dropped on Hiroshima. Ten years later she contracted leukemia and died a slow, painful death. A fast and enthusiastic runner, she had been full of life and energy before her illness. Soon after she became sick Sadako's best friend folded a paper crane for her and reminded her of an old story: If someone folded 1000 paper cranes, the gods would give that person good health again. Sadako was able to fold only 644 before she died. After her death her classmates made 356 more in order that she could be buried with all 1000 paper cranes. About three years later, a statue, erected in Peace Park in Hiroshima, was dedicated to Sadako and to a hope for world peace.

Because of the theme and its straight-forward handling, this book needs a fairly mature reader.

Interest Level: 4-6. Reading Level: 3.1. Further Search Topics: Japan-Fiction, Historical Fiction, World War II-Fiction, Death-Fiction, Illness-Fiction, War-Fiction, Running-Fiction, Origami-Fiction, Read Aloud.

WASHINGTON (STATE)-FICTION

Baker, Betty. The pig war; illus by Robert Lopshire. Har-Row 1969, 64 pp.

A brief, fictionalized account of an 1859 land squabble between the United States and Britain. The incident, which took place in what is now the state of Washington, became known as the Pig War. Frightened British pigs destroyed the American farmers' gardens. When the farmers shot one of the pigs, the war began. Simply told and humorously illustrated. Should appeal to history or military fans. Early reader format.

Interest Level: 2-4. Reading Level: 2.1. Further Search Topics: United States-History-War-Fiction, Great Britain-History-Fiction, War-Fiction, Washington (state)-Fiction, Historical Fiction, Pigs-Fiction.

WATTS TOWERS

Madian, Jon. Beautiful junk: a story of the Watts Towers; photos by Barbara Jacobs, Jr. and Lou Jacobs, Jr. Little 1968, 44 pp.

Although this book is now out of print; it is well worth trying to find. It is a fictionalized account of a young, angry black boy's encounter with the creator of Los Angeles' unusual Watts Towers. Simon Rodia, a poor tile setter, worked on the towers for 33 years until he was 75 years old. He used only his imagination, discarded materials he found around him, seashells, and sand to build three tall, fantasy-like towers in the middle of a ghetto. He created beauty where others saw only junk.

The book is illustrated with photography that makes the story more vivid and the towers and Rodia's accomplishment more impressive than they would have seemed with drawings. The print is good-sized, spacing is totally adequate. Rodia's life is quickly submarized and an update on the Towers is included at the book's end.

Interest Level: 3-6. Reading Level: 3.1. Further Search Topics: Blacks-Fiction, Read Aloud, Best Sellers, Poverty-Fiction, Rodia, Simon, Architecture, Biography, Aging-Fiction, Watts Towers, California, Poverty.

WEIGHT-FICTION

Blume, Judy. Blubber. Bradbury 1974, 153 pp.

Jill, like all the other fifth graders in her class, did exactly as Wendy directed her. When Wendy nicknamed one of the class members Blubber and launched a campaign against her, Jill joined right in. It wasn't until the tables were turned and Jill became Wendy's next victim that Jill realized how much it hurt to be the target of such nastiness. It was only then that Jill could stand up to Wendy. Wendy's meanness is extreme and her classmates, without exception, actively follow her lead, yet all adult characters in the book are blind to what happens. Despite those drawbacks, the book deals with a problem very real to children and thus it has guaranteed audience appeal.

Interest Level: 4-6. Reading Level: 3.1. School Stories, Bullies-Fiction, Weight-Fiction, Loners-Fiction, Gangs-Fiction, Read Aloud, Cruelty-Fiction, Best Sellers, Troublemakers-Fiction, Friendship-Fiction.

Byars, Betsy. After the goat man; illus by Ronald Himler. Viking Pr. 1974, 126 pp.

Harold was fat and over-sensitive. Ada was serious and independent. Figgy was lonely, poor and in need of help. Figgy and his grandfather, the Goat Man, had been forced to move from their cabin to make room for a highway. The Goat Man had returned to the cabin with a shotgun, vowing to defend his right to live there. Figgy knew he had to persuade his grandfather to leave or someone would be hurt. But, in the children's hurry to reach the Goat Man, it was Figgy who was hurt and Harold who rescued both Figgy and the Goat Man. Harold grew up that day. He stopped dreaming about the way he wanted things to be and faced life realistically for the first time.

The book is very much a character study. Realistic characters are treated with sympathy and dignity and given a chance to grow. Introspective readers will understand and enjoy the book more than those looking for adventure. Print size is fairly large, but lines are separated by only average width.

Interest Level: 4-6. Reading Level: 3.2. Further Search Topics: Loneliness-Fiction, Weight-Fiction, Moving, Household-Fiction, Courage-Fiction, Grandparents-Fiction, Orphans-Fiction.

Danziger, Paula. The cat ate my gymsuit. Delacorte 1974, 147 pp.

Another book for fans of Judy Blume. Marcy was shy and insecure, unhappy at school and unhappy at home. She was self-conscious about being heavy and sure she would never have a date. Only Ms. Finney (a new teacher), her English class and Smedley (a communications group) meant anything to Marcy. When Ms. Finney was fired because of her refusal to recite the pledge of allegiance and her unorthodox teaching methods, Marcy began to organize a protest movement. Marcy's commitment brought more problems at school and at home, but eventually resulted in Ms. Finney's vindication and Marcy's and her mother's growth and understanding.

Don't expect much depth of characterization. Most of the characters are flat and stereotypical, but the book will have great appeal in spite of its faults, for Marcy's insecurities are ones with which many young readers can identify.

Interest Level: 5-6. Reading Level: 5.1. Further Search Topics: School Stories, Everyday Stories, Family Problems-Fiction, Challenges-Fiction, Weight-Fiction, Courage-Fiction, Individualists-Fiction, Sex Role-Fiction.

Greene, Constance C. A girl called Al; illus by Byron Barton. Viking Pr. 1969, 127 pp.

Told in the first person, this is the story of two seventh grade girls. The girls' warm friendship began the moment Al introduced herself to the narrator as a non-conformist. Al was very independent, mostly because she was on her own so much of the time. Her parents were divorced and she seldom saw either one of them. Her father only wrote her postcards and her mother was rarely home. The narrator's family and Mr. Richards, their building superintendent, became Al's family. They cooked, ate, played, fought, talked and even made bookcases together. When Mr. Richards had a heart attack, they found help for him and later went to see him in the hospital. It was his death that helped Al and her mother grow closer, just as Mr. Richards' life had helped her understand why her father never came to see her.

A satisfying, low-key story of friendship and maturation. The girls are Judy Blume-style characters with much greater innocence. Their ages are not discernible by their actions or dialogue, only by the author's statement.

Interest Level: 3-6. Reading Level: 3.1. Further Search Topics: Children-Growth-Fiction, Single Parent Family-Fiction, Friendship-Fiction, Weight-Fiction, Aging-Fiction, Death-Fiction, Divorce and Separation-Fiction, Family Problems-Fiction, Everyday Stories, Humorous Fiction.

Hurwitz, Johanna. The law of gravity; illus by Ingrid Fetz. Morrow 1978, 192 pp.

The summer between fifth and sixth grades looked very unexciting to Margot. Her best friends were both going away for the whole summer and her father, a musician, was going to be on tour for most of the summer. Margot's very overweight mother had sworn never to go downstairs from their fifth floor walk-up apartment. Unless Margot chose to stay upstairs too, she was sure she would have a very lonely vacation. In addition, she had to work on a summer project for school. The project she finally chose was to get her mother downstairs after nine years of staying upstairs. In search of help she went to the local library where she met Bernie. Bernie was only a year older than Margot, but he seemed to know the most interesting things about the city. He showed her places Margot had never heard of before, he taught her to play chess, backgammon, and even to ride a bicycle. He was so full of fascinating ideas and information that Margot had no chance to be bored or lonely. Best of all, he even tried to help Margot with her project. None of their ideas worked, however, until Margot pretended to run away and scared her mother into going downstairs. Only then did Margot realize that she loved her mother whether or not she stayed on the fifth floor and that she couldn't simply force her mother or anyone else to change to suit her own fancy.

The book is a warm, understanding, slightly humorous treatment of the fairly common wish to change someone else. Although not many readers are likely to share Margot's exact problem, most will recognize her feelings. The book is also a virtual Chamber of Commerce advertisement for urban living. One of its other charms is its picture of a non-competitive, open, real friendship between an 11-year-old girl and a 12-year-old boy. The only drawback to the book is its inconsistent reading level which varies from 4.1 to 5.1 with a rare leap to 5.2.

Interest Level: 4-6. Reading Level: 4.2. Further Search Topics: Vacation-Fiction, Friendship-Fiction, Loners-Fiction, City Life-Fiction, Individualists-Fiction, Courage-Fiction, New York City-Fiction, Humorous Fiction, Family-Fiction, Challenges-Fiction, Weight-Fiction, Everyday Stories, Best Sellers.

Smith, Doris Buchanan. Last was Lloyd. Viking Pr 1981, 124 pp.

Lloyd had several problems: he was overweight, his mother was overprotective, he had no school friends, and there was a chance he might be taken away from home and put into foster care because he had missed so much school. Lloyd's mother, very young and very defensive when she had Lloyd, had done her best to be a "good mother," but in doing so, had made Lloyd fearful of the world. He had become the subject of his classmates' mockery so many times that the only way he could respond to his peers was with nastiness. The one skill he possessed was hitting a baseball. He kept this skill well hidden for fear of exposing himself to further mockery. When one of his classmates accidentally discovered how well Lloyd hit, he took the first step to becoming Lloyd's friend. Lloyd's reaction was to back away, but Kirby kept trying. Eventually Kirby's attempts and those of an understanding truant officer, helped Lloyd begin to make friends, to treat others decently, and to pull away from his mother; in short, he began to mature.

Because Lloyd's problems can be oversimplified too easily, this book requires a fairly mature reader and perhaps even discussion in order to fully understand its subtleties.

Interest Level: 5-6+Reading Level: 4.2. Further Search Topics: Weight-Fiction, Single Parent Family-Fiction, Courage-Fiction, School Stories, Loners-Fiction, Friendship-Fiction, Baseball-Fiction, Family Problems-Fiction, Foster Homes-Fiction, Children-Growth-Fiction.

WEST-FICTION

Bulla, Clyde Robert. Ghost town treasure; illus by Don Freeman. Har-Row 1957, 87 pp.

A very simple story whose title is somewhat misleading. Instead of a mystery or an exciting story of buried treasure, Bulla has written a very pleasant story of a family whose fortunes are reversed by the accidental discovery of a nearby cave. Young Ty Jackson and his family were the last people living in Gold Rock, California. Everyone else had moved out when the new highway had bypassed the town. The Jacksons had been able to stay on only because some of the nearby ranchers had continued to buy food and supplies from the Jacksons' store. Just as they, too, were preparing to move out, Ty's pen pals wrote that they were coming to visit the town. Their grandfather had died there, years earlier, during his search for gold. When Paul and Nora arrived, they brought with them their grandfather's diary. The last entry in the journal seemed to indicate that their grandfather had found gold in an isolated cave in the nearby canyon. After a long search, the children discovered the cave, but no gold. Ty's disappointment changed to joy when tourists started arriving to see the new natural attraction. Once again his parents could sell their groceries, the hotel could be reopened and Gold Rock would flourish.

Interest Level: 2-5. Reading Level: 2.2. Further Search Topics: Treasure-Fiction, Family Problems-Fiction, West-Fiction, California-Fiction, Family-Fiction, Pen Pals-Fiction.

Bulla, Clyde Robert. Riding the pony express; illus by Grace Paull. Har-Row 1948, 95 pp.

Although somewhat marred by the stereotyped speech of a young Indian boy, this is otherwise an exciting piece of historical fiction set in the 1860s. Dick was sent from New York City to join his father in St. Joseph, Missouri, only to find his father had moved to Nebraska to become a pony express rider. When Dick finally found his father, after a long stagecoach ride, he thought his father didn't want him. Dick stayed at the way station and helped with the chores because he didn't know what else to do. Then one day the house was burned, his father was shot, and the horses were almost stolen. There was no one around who could carry the mail, except Dick. Despite a wolf pack at his heels, Dick rode to the next way station. On his way home he realized his father really did want him and he no longer wanted to leave his father. Chapters are short with separate episodes that tie them together. A few simple songs appear between the chapters.

Interest Level: 2-5. Reading Level: 2.1. Further Search Topics: Horses-Fiction, West-Fiction, United States-History-Fiction, Historical Fiction, Voyages and Travels-Fiction, Courage-Fiction, Frontier and Pioneer Life-Fiction.

Clifford, Eth. The dastardly murder of Dirty Pete; illus by George Hughes. HM 1981, 120 pp.

Although this is a sequel to *Help, I'm a Prisoner in the Library*, it does not depend on the previous title, and in fact, is likely to be the more successful introduction to Mary Rose and Jo-Beth Onetree. Given the choice, most young readers will take a mystery set in a ghost town over a mystery set in a library.

Mary Rose, Jo-Beth and their father were on their way across country when they became lost. As night grew closer, the only place they could find to stay was an old hotel in the ghost town where Sorehead Jones had allegedly killed Dirty Pete. It was Sorehead's ghost who was supposed to haunt the town, and indeed there was someone or something who was in the town with the Onetrees. To their surprise, that someone turned out to be Sourdough Sam, an aging actor who had become senile and spent his days acting out all the parts in the Dirty Pete story. The town was only a movie set and the story was only a movie script. The Onetrees discovered the truth bit by bit after a frightening venture into an abandoned gold mine, a harrowing night in the haunted hotel and a jail sentence for Mr. Onetree.

Beware of the rare, very difficult descriptive passage that may cause trouble for some readers.

Interest Level: 2-5. Reading Level: 3.1. Further Search Topics: Mystery and Detective Stories, West-Fiction, Brothers and Sisters-Fiction, Motion Pictures-Fiction, Ghosts-Fiction, Treasure-Fiction, Group 2, Acting-Fiction, Aging-Fiction, Mental Illness-Fiction.

Packard, Edward. Deadwood City; illus by Barbara Carter. Bantam 1978, 96 pp.

See *Sugarcane Island* for full series notes. Paperback edition only. Choose Your Own Adventure series.

Interest Level: 2-6. Reading Level: 3.1. Further Search Topics: West-Fiction, Cowboys-Fiction, Crime-Fiction, Best Sellers, Group 2.

WHY STORIES

Dolch, Edward W. "Why" stories; illus by Marguerite Dolch. Garrard 1952, 160 pp.

"Why the Bear Has a Little Tail," "Why Turkeys Have Red Eyes," and "How the Tiger Got His Stripes" are three titles that illustrate the type of stories found in this collection. Seventeen short, simple folktales explain why the world and creatures in it operate and appear as they do. All of the tales can be found elsewhere. However, few if any stories are likely to be familiar to readers. This type of story is one children often find very appealing. The stories are understandable, logical within their own framework and simple enough to be retold to others. The reading level varies from 1.2 to 2.2. Dolch Basic Vocabulary Book series.

Interest Level: 1-4. Reading Level: 2.2. Further Search Topics: Folklore, Why Stories, Animals-Fiction, Group 2, Creation-Fiction.

WIT AND HUMOR

Cerf, Bennett. Bennett Cerf's book of animal riddles; illus by Roy McKie. Beginner 1964, 62 pp.

A slightly more difficult selection of riddles than the following listing. The riddles are longer and less familiar, but still very useful. See *Bennett Cerf's Book of Riddles* for more explanation. Reader format.

Interest Level: 1-3. Reading Level: 2.1. Further Search Topics: Riddles, Wit and Humor, Group 2.

Cerf, Bennett. Bennett Cerf's book of riddles; illus by Roy McKie. Beginner 1960, 64 pp.

Simple, well-known riddles that are always popular with children. The riddle is introduced on one page and answered on the reverse side of the page. Silly drawings illustrate each riddle and answer. Because each riddle and answer stands alone, even the most problematic of readers can have the satisfaction of completing a unit in a short time. That satisfaction, plus the universal appeal of humor make this book and the preceding listing useful through grade four, despite the book's reader format.

Interest Level: 1-4. Reading Level: 2.1. Further Search Topics: Riddles, Wit and Humor, Group 2.

Ciardi, John. I met a man; illus by Robert Osborn. HM 1961, 74 pp.

Ciardi's poems are pure fun. About half are riddle poems (poems that describe something without naming it until the end) and the rest are humorous descriptions or nonsense poems. There is a problem, however, with the riddle poems: they are somewhat more difficult to read than the other poems, but of interest to younger rather than older readers. For that reason pages 1-21 (primarily nonsense verse) can be recommended for grades one through five. The remainder of the book, although enjoyable to the very young, needs to be read to them or needs a strong young reader.

Interest Level: 1-5. Reading Level: 2.2. Further Search Topics: Wit and Humor, Poetry, Riddles, Group 2.

LeSieg, Theo. Wacky Wednesday; illus by George Booth. Beginner 1974, unp. (36 pp).

A series of true picture puzzles. A little boy wakes up one Wednesday to find everything around him has gone "wacky." People are missing heads but have extra legs. Cars are being driven from the back seat. Doors are placed in the wrong places. Airplanes fly backwards. At the end of the day everything settles back to normal, but not before readers have had fun finding the numerous "wacky" things on each page.

The story is told in silly rhyme (LeSieg and Seuss are the same person). What is wrong with each picture is not always easily located, making this reader an excellent excerise in observation as well as great fun.

Interest Level: 1-3. Reading Level: 1.2. Further Search Topics: Puzzles, Humorous Fiction, Wit and Humor, Poetry, Best Sellers.

Low, Joseph. Five men under one umbrella. Macmillan 1975, 64 pp.

Twenty-nine riddles, most of which are fairly familiar. Nothing special in this collection, just an additional choice for the young comedian.

Interest Level: 1-3. Reading Level: 2.1. Further Search Topics: Riddles, Wit and Humor, Group 2.

Sarnoff, Jane. What? A riddle book; illus by Reynold Ruffins. Scribner 1974, 62 pp.

A good, lengthy collection of both familiar and unfamiliar riddles. Every other page is brightened by bold and humorous illustrations. The first part of the book seems to have slightly more riddles for younger readers than the rest of the book. Some of the riddles in the collection involve rather sophisticated puns; thus they are more appealing to fifth and sixth grade readers. The final three pages of the book include 35 riddles whose answers are in code. The key to the code is given on the last page of the book. It is a picture book printed in two tones. The riddles sometimes slant diagonally across the page.

Interest Level: 1-6. Reading Level: 3.1. Further Search Topics: Riddles, Wit and Humor, Group 2, Nonverbal Communication.

Seuss, Dr. One fish, two fish, red fish, blue fish. Beginner 1960, 63pp.

Beginning with one almost ordinary-looking fish, this is a humorous look at the "funny things that go by." When Dr. Seuss says "funny," he really means highly imaginative, whimsical, and totally nonsensical. Each of the more than 20 silly creatures are described and appropriately illustrated to appeal to a child's sense of the ridiculous. Reader.

Interest Level: 1-2. Reading Level: 1.1. Further Search Topics: Fantasy, Wit and Humor, Poetry, Humorous Fiction, Stories in Rhyme.

Seuss, Dr. Hop on Pop. Beginner 1963, 64pp.

Between one and four rhyming words are introduced or reviewed and used in a silly sentence on each page. The sentence is interpreted with even more amusing illustrations. It is one of the simplest of books (no story at all) and yet it is usable through second grade because of Dr. Seuss' playful style and ridiculous illustrations. Reader format.

Interest Level: 1-2. Reading Level: 1.1. Further Search Topics: Poetry, Best Sellers, Wit and Humor, Humorous Fiction, Stories in Rhyme.

Seuss, Dr. The foot book. Random 1968, unp (27 pp).

Left feet, right feet, big feet, small feet; with its rhyme, silly illustrations and rhythmic celebration of feet of all descriptions, this book is a sure winner with the very young. Reader format.

Interest Level 1-2. Reading Level: 1.1. Further Search Topics: Best Sellers, Feet-Fiction, Humorous Fiction, Poetry, Wit and Humor, Stories in Rhyme.

Silverstein, Shel. Where the sidewalk ends. Har-Row 1974, 166 pp.

There is something here for almost everyone. It isn't always easy reading, but there are enough short, easier poems to pique almost any child's interest. Once caught, children will find the book hard to put down. The best way to encourage the use of this book is to read selections aloud so that potential readers may hear the rhythm and enjoy the humor. This method almost guarantees that they will then want to try reading the book themselves. Readers may struggle with a poem but once it is mastered, they will usually want more.

Interest Level: 2-6. Reading Level: 3.1. Further Search Topics: Poetry, Wit and Humor, Read Aloud, Group 2, Best Sellers.

Silverstein, Shel. A light in the attic. Har-Row 1981, 169 pp.

This is the second and most recent collection of Shel Silverstein's wonderfully wry poetry. No young person who has read and enjoyed *Where the Sidewalk Ends* will be disappointed in this effort. For those readers new to Silverstein or to poetry in general, this is as good a place as any to start enjoying both. Hearing a few of these poems read aloud is guaranteed to provoke loud cries of "May I read some?" from almost all listeners.

Interest Level: 2-6. Reading Level: 3.2. Further Search Topics: Poetry, Wit and Humor, Best Sellers, Group 2, Read Aloud.

Wiseman, Bernard. Morris and Boris. Dodd 1974, 64 pp.

This is a compilation of three silly stories about Morris the Moose and Boris the Bear. When Boris tries to interest Morris in telling riddles, Morris frustrates Boris so completely that Boris runs off angrily. Later Boris tries to teach Morris a tongue twister, but ends up running off in total confusion. Finally Boris tries to teach Morris to play hide-and-seek and that, too, is a disaster. Boris tells Morris that Morris just cannot do anything. A bird who has seen everything reminds Boris that Morris can make him very angry and that is something. When Boris agrees they all laugh happily.

Broad, slapstick humor makes this appealing to children well into third grade. Reader format.

Interest Level: 1-3. Reading Level: 1.2. Further Search Topics: Wit and Humor, Riddles, Tongue Twisters, Games, Humorous Fiction.

WITCHES-FICTION

Avi. No more magic. Pantheon 1975, 138 pp.

Avi has woven a mixture of mystery and magic to produce an excellent story. Chris' belief in magic is bolstered when his new bicycle disappears on Halloween night. Chris, his best friend Eddie, and a new friend, Muffin, eventually decide that strange Mr. Bullen, the junk dealer, has magical powers. In order to keep his powers a secret, Mr. Bullen had to steal back the magical bike he sold Chris. With plenty of intriguing complications along the way, the three children attempt to prove their theory correct but only prove themselves wrong. The age of the protagonists (fourth grade) is touched on so lightly and the plot is interesting enough that even sixth grade readers should find the book enjoyable.

Interest Level: 3-6. Reading Level: 4.2. Further Search Topics: Divorce and Separation-Fiction, Mystery and Detective Stories, Magic-Fiction, Halloween-Fiction, Witches-Fiction, Group 2, Read Aloud, Bicycles and Bicycling-Fiction.

Chew, Ruth. Witch's broom. Dodd 1977, 128 pp.

Amy's mother was the one who found the blue broom, but Amy and her friend Jean were the ones who learned it was magical. One night the broom flew Amy into a mountain cave where a coven of witches was meeting. It even forced Amy to answer the roll call for someone named Beryl. But it wasn't until it took both Amy and Jean back to the cave that they discovered the broom's connection to the strange bluejay that had been following them. The bluejay was really Beryl, a young and headstrong witch who had turned herself into the bluejay and then couldn't turn herself back. With the girls' unwitting help, Beryl found the charm to turn herself back into a witch and flew off on a scrawny old broom, leaving the blue broom for Amy and Jean.

What youngster wouldn't want a flying broomstick and the misadventures that go with owning one? Wish fulfillment can never be overrated as an appeal of Ruth Chew's books.

Interest Level: 2-5. Reading Level: 3.1. Further Search Topics: Witches-Fiction, Magic-Fiction, Fantasy, Birds-Fiction, Group 2, Transformations-Fiction.

Chew, Ruth. No such thing as a witch. Hastings 1971, 112 pp.

Despite the fact that their mother said there was no such thing as a witch, Tad and Nora were convinced that their neighbor Maggie Brown was indeed a witch. And they were right! Maggie Brown knew how to make a special kind of fudge that could make anyone into an animal-lover, enable people to talk with animals, or actually transform someone into an animal. All you had to do was to eat one, two, or three pieces of fudge respectively. But Maggie's overzealous love of animals and her disenchantment with housework eventually attracted the attention of her neighbors and the city health department. Only Tad and Nora's frantic efforts to help her saved Maggie from losing all of her animal friends.

A fairly detailed plot, the fascination of being able to change size and appearance and the intrigue involved in fooling the adults around Maggie make this one of Chew's best books.

Interest Level: 2-5. Reading Level: 2.2. Further Search Topics: Individualists-Fiction, Witches-Fiction, Animals-Fiction, Fantasy, Magic-Fiction, Brothers and Sisters-Fiction, Transformations-Fiction.

Chew, Ruth. The witch's garden. Hastings 1978, 112 pp.

Although its elements seem to promise an exciting adventure story, this is a disappointing book. The witch who moved into the dark, old home next door to Josh and Susan, was trying to improve her overgrown garden when Susan and Josh offered to help. The children accidentally splashed themselves with the witch's newest brew and found they suddenly became very tiny inhabitants of a dense and threatening jungle (the garden). After they regained their normal size, they dug into other areas of the garden. One hole they dug opened into an underground tunnel that they found was inhabited by a fire-breathing dragon. When the dragon cornered Mrs. Muldoon, Susan and Josh ran out of the tunnel, found the brew and splashed it onto the dragon. The dragon shrank away, Mrs. Muldoon was safe and the tunnel closed over.

Because there is little more suspense than in this description, the book fails to live up to its promise. In addition, the children's first sudden size change is just subtle enough to be confusing. Despite its problems the book is popular with Ruth Chew fans and therefore useful.

Interest Level: 2-5. Reading Level: 2.2. Further Search Topics: Witches-Fiction, Brothers and Sisters-Fiction, Magic-Fiction, Fantasy, Dragons-Fiction, Transformations-Fiction.

Chew, Ruth. The would-be witch. Hastings 1976, 112 pp.

Robin and her brother Andy took a liking to the clumsy white cat they saw in Zelda's Antique Shop. The cat apparently liked them, too, for it followed them home. Not having enough money to offer to buy Pearl from Zelda, the children tried to polish up an old pair of silver birds to trade for the cat. The polish turned out to be magical and made the birds real. When they tried the polish on a broom in Zelda's store, the broom began to fly. Upon discovering that Zelda wanted to be a witch but had failed the coven entrance exam, Rob helped her learn to fly and told her of the witches' meeting place that she and Andy had discovered. But the 12 witches who had been turned into cats were wicked enough to want to use Zelda to regain their human form and turn *her* into a cat. In attempting to prevent such a fate, Rob, Andy and Zelda set fire to the abandoned building being used as a meeting place. The 12 witches were rescued from the fire but charged with arson, which meant probable jail sentences for all of them. Zelda, finally a happy and capable witch, gave Pearl to Rob and Andy to thank them for their help.

A better-crafted story than many of the others, this also has a more evil cast of characters to provide additional interest.

Interest Level: 2-5. Reading Level: 2.2. Further Search Topics: Witches-Fiction, Brothers and Sisters-Fiction, Magic-Fiction, Fantasy, Transformations-Fiction, Cats-Fiction.

Chew, Ruth. Earthstar magic. Hastings 1979, 128 pp.

This is one of a series of similar stories by Ruth Chew. Each story involves two children and an old woman they usually suspect is a witch. As their suspicions become convictions they also find that, contrary to their expectation, the witch is very nice and often in need of help.

The children in this tale are brother and sister. Ben and Elizabeth first saw and then didn't see Trudy as she searched for a magical mushroom called an earthstar. Accidentally thrown together again, Ben and Elizabeth took a liking to Trudy, especially when she explained that she had been thrown out of her coven because she was so inept. In fact, she wasn't even able to control the earthstar. The earthstar manages to get all three in and out of adventures (including becoming tiny, flying and almost being eaten) before they learn to control its power. As the story ends, Trudy, finally respected by the other witches, flies off with a promise that Ben and Elizabeth will see her again.

Very lightweight but also very popular with young lovers of witch stories. There seems to be just the right amount of adventure to make up for the very benign witch.

Interest Level: 2-5. Reading Level: 2.2. Further Search Topics: Witches-Fiction, Magic-Fiction, Fantasy, Vacation-Fiction, Brothers and Sisters-Fiction, Transformations-Fiction.

Chew, Ruth. What the witch left. Hastings 1973, 128 pp.

One afternoon Katy and Louise decided to search through the locked drawer of an old dresser. Inside they found strange-looking gloves, an old robe, boots, a mirror and a tin box. The girls quickly learned that each item was magical. With the gloves on, the girls could draw, play piano, weave or write. They thought their new talents were wonderful until they each wrote identical school compositions. When she wore the robe for the school play, Louise found out that it made people invisible. The boots, which travelled 21 miles with each step, took the girls to Mexico, but made them late for lunch at home. The mirror showed them anything they wanted to see, and the box "found" everything that was lost. A very light story for children who don't need high adventure but like a mixture of humor and magic.

Interest Level: 3-5. Reading Level: 3.1. Further Search Topics: Magic-Fiction, Mexico-Fiction, Witches-Fiction, Fantasy, Humorous Fiction.

Dolch, Edward W. Stories from Old Russia; illus by James Lewicki. Garrard 1964, 168 pp.

There are 21 chapters and only nine stories in this volume. These are more robust and exciting adventure stories than many of the other Dolch collections listed here, although once again the simplified vocabulary is somewhat restrictive. A guide to pronounciation of some Russian names is included at the end of the book. More colorful illustrations than some of the other titles. Very consistent reading level. See *Stories From France* for more information. Folklore of the World series.

Interest Level: 2-6. Reading Level: 2.1. Further Search Topics: Folklore, Fantasy, Russia-Fiction, Witches-Fiction.

Packard, Edward. The mystery of Chimney Rock; illus by Paul Granger. Bantam 1979, 121 pp.

See notes for *Sugarcane Island* for information about the series. Paperback only. Choose Your Own Adventure series.

Interest Level: 2-6. Reading Level: 3.2. Further Search Topics: Mystery and Detective Stories, Cats-Fiction, Witches-Fiction, Ghosts-Fiction, Detectives-Fiction, Best Sellers, Group 2.

WOLVES-FICTION

Thompson, Jean. Brother of the wolves; illus by Steve Marchesi. Morrow 1978, 159 pp.

Shadow Fox, a Sioux medicine man, went into a wolves' den looking for special items he needed for healing, but found much more. He found a baby boy who had apparently lost his parents in an accident and then been adopted by the wolves. Winter was approaching and Shadow Fox knew the baby would not be able to survive the cold, so he took the child back to his people. The people were reluctant to accept Wolf Brother, saying that he was an evil omen, that he was unnatural, and that he would bring them trouble. But Shadow Fox's will prevailed and Wolf Brother was allowed to stay and grow up with the Sioux.

As he grew Wolf Brother continued to communicate with the wolves and thus fueled the rumors that grew about him. A very jealous young man, Looks-Away, told the people that a vision had shown him that Wolf Brother and his wolves would one day destroy the village and all its people. The people grew so suspicious of Wolf Brother that, when their horses were stolen and they faced a drought, they blamed him and drove him from the village.

For a while Wolf Brother tried to live as a wolf but found that he could not be totally happy. He wandered away to look for a tribe by whom he might be accepted. On his way, he too had a vision—a vision that told him he would find horses and buffalo for the Sioux and be welcomed home again. It was weeks later before he accidentally found his tribe's horses. In a daring move and with help from the wolves, Wolf Brother not only rescued the horses from the raiders, but also found buffalo just as his vision had predicted. He was then, for the first time, fully welcomed by his people.

This is a taut, suspenseful and mature story about a strong and unusual character. Older readers are most likely to respond positively to the Indian culture and lore.

Interest Level: 5-6. Reading Level: 3.1. Further Search Topics: Survival-Fiction, Wolves-Fiction, Orphans-Fiction, Loners-Fiction, Indians of North America-Fiction, Sioux Indians-Fiction, Jealousy-Fiction, Best Sellers.

WOMEN

Kluger, Ruth. The secret ship. Doubleday 1978, 136 pp.

A tense, true story about the secret transportation of hundreds of European Jews to Palestine early in World War II. The transport ship became ice-bound in a Rumanian harbor, the crew mutinied and the passengers threatened to expose their plight to the world. In complete charge of the operation was a 25-year-old woman. The book closes with a summary of the Jews' continuing fight for Israel.

The historical understanding that is necessary in order to really appreciate this excellent book make it best suited to readers no younger than sixth grade.

The paper on which this book is printed is so thin that the print shows through from one page to another and the print at the beginning and the end of the book is italicized. Both factors may distract the reader.

Interest Level: 6+. Reading Level: 3.1. Further Search Topics: World War II, Jews, Women, Sex Role, Israel, Survival, Courage.

WOMEN-BIOGRAPHY

Burchard, Marshall. Sports hero: Billie Jean King. Putnam 1975, 95 pp.

Winner of every major women's tennis title and a very important person to women's professional sports. Consistent reading level. Book includes glossary of tennis terms. See entry under *Sports Hero: Bill Walton* Sports Hero series.

Interest Level: 3-6. Reading Level: 3.2. Further Search Topics: Biography, King, Billie Jean, Tennis-Biography, Women-Biography.

Burchard, Susan H. Sports star: Dorothy Hamill. HarBraceJ 1978, 63 pp.

Although written by Susan Burchard, this and most of the following listings are true to Marshall Burchard's *Sports Hero* format. For more explanation see *Sports Hero: Bill Walton.*

Dorothy Hamill was the darling of ice skating in 1976 and is now a top professional figure skater. This makes her rise to stardom sound romantic and glamorous. Skating jargon pushes the reading level from 3.1 to 3.2. Sports Star series.

Interest Level: 2-6. Reading Level: 3.2. Further Search Topics: Hamill, Dorothy, Ice Skating-Biography, Women-Biography, Biography, Group 2.

Greenfield, Eloise. Rosa Parks; illus by Eric Marlow. Har-Row 1973, 33 pp.

This book succumbs to the difficulty of writing for children about a subject that needs more explanation. The occasionally condescending tone combined with the Crowell Biography picture book format will keep this otherwise adequate introduction to the civil rights movement from being useful beyond fourth grade. The book should be very useful, however, for third and fourth grade social studies, history or biography units.

Rosa Parks' childhood and her feelings about the special rules for blacks make up the first half of the book. The second half is devoted to Rosa's act of defiance (refusing to give up her seat on a bus to a white man) and the repercussions of that act. Crowell Biography series.

Interest Level: 2-4. Reading Level 2.2. Further Search Topics: Blacks-Biography, Biography, Prejudice, Civil Rights, Women-Biography, Courage.

Jordan, June. Fannie Lou Hamer; illus by Albert Williams. Har-Row 1972, 41 pp.

In 1917, Fannie Lou Hamer was the last of 20 children born to a fearless black woman. Fannie and her family grew up working on a white man's cotton plantation. Although they were kept poor and hungry by the plantation owner and the field boss, Fannie Lou grew up in her mother's image—unafraid of white people and unhappy with the poor treatment of blacks that she saw all around her. In 1962, when most other blacks in Mississippi where afraid of the consequences, Fannie registered to vote. After both she and her husband lost their jobs and their home, and after she was beaten in a Mississippi jail, Fannie Lou Hamer drew national attention to her fight for blacks' civil rights. She spoke all over the country, helped to form a new political party, and raised money to help poor people. That money was what started the 640 acre Freedom Farm Cooperative that provided work and food for more than 5,000 people. It was Mrs. Hamer's dream to see poor people work together to feed themselves rather than to accept food from others. She made her dream come true.

Another competent entry in the Crowell Biography series. Only its picture book format keeps this book from being useful through sixth grade.

Interest Level: 3-5. Reading Level: 3.2. Further Search Topics: Biography, Blacks-Biography, Civil Rights, Poverty, Women-Biography.

Tobias, Tobi. Marian Anderson; illus by Symeon Shimin. Har-Row 1972, 40 pp.

Marian Anderson's beautiful, strong voice and her great range set her apart from other singers even as a child. By the time she was in high school, she was being paid to sing. However, when she tried to apply to a well-known music school, because she was black she was turned away without even being heard. Anderson's determination as well as her own and others' faith in her kept her singing and seeking better and better coaches until she met Giuseppi Boghetti. He was one of the best voice coaches in the country. With him Marian trained and traveled until she finally won the chance to sing with the New York Philharmonic Orchestra. Anderson thought that at that point she would be invited to sing in famous theaters all across the United States, but because she was black she still received no invitations. She went to Europe where she studied and played to wildly enthusiastic audiences. Her European triumphs finally convinced American theater owners and audiences that she was a serious talent. For the next 30 years Marian Anderson sang all over the world, most of the time without incident, with one notable exception in 1939, when the D.A.R. prohibited her from singing in a hall they owned in Washington, D. C. She sang instead, in front of the Lincoln Memorial, at the invitation of the United States government. During the following years Marian married, bought a farm, sang opera and was made a delegate to the United Nations. In 1956, she retired from singing to help children, young singers, and world understanding.

Crowell Biographies make excellent school report sources for reluctant readers. They are short, interesting, and not overly juvenile looking, although the quasi-picture book format may be a problem for some older readers. This biography fits that description perfectly. The series is somewhat sentimental (as are many children's biographies), however, the sentimentality is not forbidding or condescending. A useful series. Crowell Biography series.

Interest Level: 2-5. Reading Level: 3.1. Further Search Topics: Biography, Music-Biography, Blacks-Biography, Talent, Women-Biography, Singers, Prejudice, Group 2.

WOMEN-FICTION

Christopher, Matt. The year mom won the pennant; illus by Foster Caddell. Little 1968, 147 pp.

When no one's father had the time to coach the Thunderballs it began to look like the team would be disbanded. They just didn't seem to be able to work together without a coach. Then Nick Vassey's mother volunteered to coach for the season. After all, she knew baseball as well as anyone else and had watched her husband coach for several years. Nick wasn't at all pleased, but had to accept the idea when his teammates voted to make his mother their coach. Nick's embarrassment was almost as great as the rival coach's skepticism, but before the season was over Nick was proud of his mother. She coached the team to first place and forced even the rival coach to admit she was a good coach. Much baseball action. See note about (*No Arm In Left Field*).

Interest Level: 2-6. Reading Level: 3.1. Further Search Topics: Group 2, Baseball-Fiction, Friendship-Fiction, Prejudice-Fiction, Sex Role-Fiction, Women-Fiction.

WOODCHUCKS

McNulty, Faith. Woodchuck; illus by Joan Sandin. Har-Row 64 pp.

There's a great deal of information in this little book. It describes a woodchuck's physical appearance, its habits and behavior, and its life cycle. The treatment is very direct and very honest (two of four young woodchucks are killed before the first year is over).

Only an overly repetitive, slightly condescending beginning, and the reader format hamper the book's usefulness beyond grade four. A Science-I-Can-Read-Book.

Interest Level: 1-4. Reading Level: 3.1. Further Search Topics: Nature Study, Groundhogs, Group 2, Woodchucks.

WORKING PARENTS-FICTION

Blume, Judy. Superfudge. Dutton 1980, 166 pp.

On Fudge's first day in school his older brother Peter had to rescue him from the top of the kindergarten storage cabinets. Later in the school year Fudge's eagerness to join a school guest speaker on stage almost spelled disaster. Then when Fudge unexpectedly disappeared one day everyone, including Peter, thought he had drowned. In addition to Peter's problems with Fudge, Peter had to cope with a baby sister, moving to Princeton, New Jersey, a new job for his mother, and his father's attempts to write a book. Although the book is a sequel and is best enjoyed as such, it can be read alone. It is not as amusing or well-written as it's predecessor, *Tales of a Fourth Grade Nothing*, but will still be popular with young readers.

Interest Level: 3-6. Reading Level 3.1. Further Search Topics: Brothers and Sisters-Fiction, Moving, Household-Fiction, Infants-Fiction, Working Parents-Fiction, School Stories, Family-Fiction, Best Sellers, Humorous Fiction, Everyday Stories.

Smith, Alison. Help! There's a cat washing in here!; illus by Amy Rowen. Dutton 1981, 152 pp.

Henry Walker agreed to care for his younger brother and sister for two weeks so that his mother could spend her time preparing a portfolio of her art work in the hopes of getting a much-needed job. It was a desperate move for Henry, but it was the only way he could prevent his bossy Aunt Wilhemina from moving in to run the household. Despite Henry's best efforts, almost everything seemed to go wrong. He burned the food, couldn't keep his brother and sister from misbehaving, seemed to have poisoned his sister's friend, and was faced with making a costume in one night for a school play. The worst of it all was that his mother wasn't pleased with what she was drawing, and Henry only seemed to make her feel more discouraged and unhappy. After what appeared to be certain defeat, however, Henry's efforts were rewarded. His mother was given the job, the family proved they could take care of themselves, and all ended happily.

A light, humorous tale of a young boy's growing independence and maturation under stress and increased responsibility.

Interest Level: 4-6. Reading Level: 3.1. Further Search Topics: Brothers and Sisters-Fiction, Working Parents-Fiction, Single Parent Family-Fiction, Humorous Fiction, Family-Fiction, Challenges-Fiction, Children-Growth-Fiction.

Waldorf, Mary. Jake McGee and his feet; illus by Leonard Shortall. HM 1980, 82 pp.

His severe reading difficulties made school the worst place in the world for Jake McGee. On the day that his reading tutor became so impatient with him that she sent Jake to the principal, Jake decided that he couldn't stand school any longer and ran away. He didn't actually run away, he just let his feet finally do what they wanted. His feet were always getting Jake in trouble. They walked too slowly to get him to school on time; they wouldn't stay still once he was in school; and they were always trying to trip someone.

Jake knew that in addition to having problems with his feet he had reading problems, but no one at his old school in the country had noticed. When he and his family moved to the city everything had changed. Jake's mother was always at work or tired. Jake hadn't made any friends and so was always alone. But Jake thought the biggest of all his immediate problems was his feet. The day he ran away, Jake's feet led him to a lost baby, an eccentric old woman, and a neighbor boy, all of whom helped Jake recognize and deal with his real problem.

The book is not high literary quality. The characterization is somewhat flat and the plot is fairly predictable. However, the sentences and chapters are short, the vocabulary is manageable, and Jake's feelings will be shared by many non-readers.

Interest Level: 3-5. Reading Level: 2.2. Further Search Topics: School Stories, Moving, Household-Fiction, Runaways-Fiction, Academic Problems-Fiction, Working Parents-Fiction, Loneliness-Fiction, Feet-Fiction.

WORLD WAR II

Kluger, Ruth. The secret ship. Doubleday 1978, 136 pp.

A tense, true story about the secret transportation of hundreds of European Jews to Palestine early in World War II. The transport ship became ice-bound in a Rumanian harbor, the crew mutinied and the passengers threatened to expose their plight to the world. In complete charge of the operation was a 25-year-old woman. The book closes with a summary of the Jews' continuing fight for Israel.

The historical understanding that is necessary in order to really appreciate this excellent book make it best suited to readers no younger than sixth grade.

The paper on which this book is printed is so thin that the print shows through from one page to another and the print at the beginning and the end of the book is italicized. Both factors may distract the reader.

Interest Level: 6+ Reading Level: 3.1. Further Search Topics: World War II, Jews, Women, Sex Role, Israel, Survival, Courage.

WORLD WAR II-FICTION

Coerr, Eleanor. Sadako and the thousand paper cranes; illus by Ronand Himler. Putnam 1977, 64 pp.

This is a beautiful and very sad story of a young girl who was only two years old when the atomic bomb was dropped on Hiroshima. Ten years later she contracted leukemia and died a slow, painful death. A fast and enthusiastic runner, she had been full of life and energy before her illness. Soon after she became sick Sadako's best friend folded a paper crane for her and reminded her of an old story: If someone folded 1000 paper cranes, the gods would give that person good health again. Sadako was able to fold only 644 before she died. After her death her classmates made 356 more in order that she could be buried with all 1000 paper cranes. About three years later, a statue, erected in Peace Park in Hiroshima, was dedicated to Sadako and to a hope for world peace.

Because of the theme and its straight-forward handling, this book needs a fairly mature reader.

Interest Level: 4-6. Reading Level: 3.1. Further Search Topics: Japan-Fiction, Historical Fiction, World War II-Fiction, Death-Fiction, Illness-Fiction, War-Fiction, Running-Fiction, Origami-Fiction, Read Aloud.

WORMS-FICTION

Rockwell, Thomas. How to eat fried worms; illus by Emily McCully. Watts 1973, 116 pp.

It started more as a joke than anything else, but it escalated into a strange commitment. Alan bet Billy $50 that Billy couldn't eat a worm a day for fifteen days. Billy had always been willing to take almost any dare offered and he was stubborn enough to carry them out, but when he actually faced the first worm (an enormous night crawler), he almost backed down. He and his friend Tom had to keep repeating the word "minibike" (the prize he planned to buy with the money) and smother the worm in everything imaginable in order to eat it all. After the first worm, however, the next few were easier to face. That was when Alan and his ally Joe, began using psychological warfare and almost won. In 41 very short, grotesquely funny chapters Billy becomes the proud owner of a minibike and is the first person to become hooked on worm sandwiches.

Once this book is started, it is hard to resist its gruesome fascination. Although the print is somewhat small, and there are occasionally very difficult or babytalk words, the interest is strong enough to sustain almost all readers.

Interest Level: 3-6. Reading Level: 3.1. Further Search Topics: Humorous Fiction, Worms-Fiction, Read Aloud, Best Sellers, Challenges-Fiction, Food-Fiction, Bicycles and Bicycling-Fiction.

WRITING

Walker, Alice. Langston Hughes, American poet; illus by Don Miller. Har-Row 1974, 33 pp.

Langston Hughes is one of the world's most famous black poets. He spent most of his childhood in poverty and yet he shunned and was shunned by his wealthy father because his father disliked blacks. To Hughes the two most important things in the world were his heritage and his writing. His love of black history stemmed from the stories his grandmother told him. His love of language and writing grew out of the lonely hours he spent reading as a child. Hughes began to write poetry even before he was in high school and continued to write for many years. He wrote not only poems, but children's books, novels, plays and short stories. He wrote about and for blacks around the world. He was a proud and honest man who chose to share his pride in his race and his honesty through his writing.

This book is more of an inspirational tribute to a black hero than a fact-filled biography. That isn't to say that there are no facts included in the book. There are facts, but the book will not do as the sole source for a report about Langston Hughes. The book is, however, a good introduction to the man and his writing.

Interest Level: 3-5. Reading Level: 2.2. Further Search Topics: Biography, Blacks-Biography, Writing, Poverty, Divorce and Separation, Poetry.

WRITING-FICTION

Conford, Ellen. The revenge of the incredible Dr. Rancid and his youthful assistant, Jeffrey. Little 1980, 119 pp.

There were two people Jeff hated and feared: Dewey Belasco, the sixth grade bully and Lana McCabe, Dewey's female counterpart. Only in his imagination could Jeff stand up to them. In the stories Jeff wrote in a notebook, he and his friend Dr. Rancid were superheroes who rid the world of such scum as Lana and Dewey. In real life, Jeff ran from bullies rather than face them; even if it meant that an eight-year-old boy and a girl Jeff's age were left to stand up to Dewey by themselves. Although the way Jeff took care of an injured child soon had most everyone thinking of Jeff as a hero, he saw that, too, as an indication of his failings at first. Finally, something inside Jeff snapped and he answered Dewey back when Dewey insulted him. Before long Jeff found himself flat on his back with a bloody nose and so many pains he couldn't count them. But, he had finally faced Dewey and showed Dewey that he was no longer afraid. Jeff felt good.

Similar to *The 18th Emergency* but a higher reading level. The notebook stories will appeal to fans of superheroes, but because they are stories within a story, they may also cause difficulties. Spacing between lines is somewhat narrow.

Interest Level: 5-6. Reading Level: 4.2. Further Search Topics: Courage-Fiction, Bullies-Fiction, Writing-Fiction, School Stories, Superheroes-Fiction, Humorous Fiction.

Giff, Patricia Reilly. Have you seen Hyacinth Macaw?; illus by Anthony Kramer. Delacorte 1981, 135 pp.

Abby Jones was trying very hard to be a detective, but it was difficult without any mysteries to solve. So to keep in practice, Abby filled a memo book with her notes about anything that seemed at all unusual. At the same time, Abby kept in touch with two local police detectives who gave her hints about detective work. Because of her police friends and her observations, Abby found herself involved in what seemed to be four or more mysteries. Who had moved into the apartment next door and what were the screams that came from there? What was the theft that the police were worried about? Who was Hyacinth Macaw and why had she disappeared? And why was Abby's older brother Dan acting so strangely? Was he involved in the theft?

Abby and her friend Potsie ended up trailing a suspect through the New York subway system, breaking into the next-door apartment, suspecting Abby's brother of the theft, capturing an unusual bird, releasing the bird into a pet shop and recapturing it, before they realized that all the mysteries were linked together. Hyacinth Macaw was a valuable bird stolen from Justine's Junktique Shop. The daughter of Abby's landland had taken the bird and placed it in the empty apartment next to Abby's, so that she could paint the bird's portrait. The picture was to be entered in Justine's Junktique contest. Dan and his friend Holly Monk had been secretly constructing a Purple Pigeon Purifier to enter in the contest. They needed the prize money to repair a window they had accidentally broken. By the time the mysteries were all sorted out, Dan and Holly had won a special prize; Kiki, the portrait painter, had not only been forgiven, but had also been awarded first prize; and Abby had received the reward for finding and returning the bird.

The action in this mystery is both abundant and humorous enough to make the book enjoyable to many readers. There are also some problems that need to be noted. Some readers may find the action too swift and the characters too numerous to be easily followed. Abby's memo notes are sometimes written without vowels and are almost always in incomplete sentences. The reader who is highly motivated or has help from another person will still be able to enjoy the story; however, for the others another choice may be more appropriate.

Interest Level: 4-6. Reading Level: 3.1. Further Search Topics: Mystery and Detective Stories, Humorous Fiction, Writing-Fiction, Detectives-Fiction, Birds-Fiction.

Lowry, Lois. Anastasia again! HM 1981, 145 pp.

This is a sequel that is as funny and well-written as its predecessor. Because its plot involves less common experiences, this book may not enjoy quite the wide-spread success of *Anastasia Krupnik*. However, among those readers who liked their first meeting with Anastasia, this book will find many fans.

Anastasia's parents astounded her when they announced that the family was going to move from their Cambridge, Massachusetts apartment to a house in the suburbs. She didn't like the idea of leaving the apartment, but she *hated* the idea of the suburbs. The only thing that made the move bearable was the house itself. Anastasia had said she would move only if they could find a house with a tower—and they had. After she got over the shock of moving, Anastasia began to enjoy her new home. She met a neighborhood boy who became a special friend, she tried to help her cranky elderly neighbor Mrs. Stein make friends, and she even wrote a short mystery book.

Anastasia is as spunky and original as before. She is a bit precocious, but her precocity is nothing compared to that of her brother. At two-and-a-half years old, he speaks as well as many adults. As we mentioned above, the book will be most appealing to readers who want second helpings of Anastasia's adventures. The print is slightly smaller here than in the first title.

Interest Level: 4-6. Reading Level: 2.2. Further Search Topics: Moving, Household-Fiction, City Life-Fiction, Suburbia-Fiction, Humorous Fiction, Aging-Fiction, Writing-Fiction, Family-Fiction, Everyday Stories.

MacLachlan, Patricia. Arthur, for the very first time; illus by Lloyd Bloom. Har-Row 1980, 117 pp.

A beautifully written, sensitive yet humorous story of a boy's maturation and growing awareness of the world around him. When Arthur's unhappiness at home is made more intense by the advent of a new baby, he is sent to spend the summer with his older aunt and uncle. Their eccentricities and those of their friends are at first only material for Arthur to write about in his journal. But as the summer progresses he not only learns from them, but also grows from an observer of life to a participant. His final step is helping a large and beloved pig bear her litter in a driving rain storm aided only by his independent, totally untamed young friend Moira.

The print is somewhat small, but spacing between lines is generous.

Interest Level: 4-6. Reading Level: 4.2. Further Search Topics: Read Aloud, Children-Growth-Fiction, Humorous Fiction, Friendship-Fiction, Vacation-Fiction, Relatives-Fiction, Infants-Fiction, Individualists-Fiction, Writing-Fiction, Loners-Fiction, Group 2.

APPENDIXES

BASAL READING SERIES USED IN COMPILING BIBLIOGRAPHY

American Book Reading Program
Johnson, Marjorie Seddon et al.
copyright: Litton Educational
Publishing, International
1977

American Book Company
135 West 50th Street
New York, NY 10020

Basic Reading System
Evertts, Eldonaa
1977

Holt, Rinehart and Winston, Inc.
383 Madison Avenue
New York, NY 10017

Basics in Reading Program
Aaron, Ira E. et al.
1978

Scott, Foresman and Company
1900 East Lake Avenue
Glenview, IL 60025

Bookmark Reading Program
Early, Margaret et al.
1979

Harcourt Brace Jovanovich, Inc.
757 Third Avenue
New York, NY 10017

Ginn 720 Program
Clymer, Theodore
1976

Ginn and Company
191 Spring Street
Lexington, MA 02173

Houghton Mifflin Reading Series
Durr, William K.
1976

Houghton Mifflin Company
2 Park Street
Boston, MA 02107

Keys to Reading
1975

The Economy Company
1901 North Walnut
P.O. Box 25308
Oklahoma City, OK 73125

Laidlaw Reading Program
Eller, William
1976

Laidlaw Brothers
Thatcher & Madison Streets
River Forest, IL 60305

New Macmillan Reading Program Series R
Boultinghouse, Craig
1975

Macmillan Publishing Company, Inc.
866 Third Avenue
New York, NY 10022

Pathfinder
Ruddell, Robert B. et al.
1978

Allyn and Bacon, Inc.
470 Atlantic Avenue
Boston, MA 02210

Reading Basics Plus
Amato, Dolores R.
1976

Harper and Row Publishers, Inc.
10 East 53rd Street
New York, NY 10022

Reading Caravan
Witty, Paul et al.
1968

D.C. Heath Company
125 Spring Street
Lexington, MA 02173

Reading Metro Series
Jones, Daisy Marvel
1976

Glencoe Publishing Co., Inc.
c/o Macmillan Publishing Company, Inc.
866 Third Avenue
New York, NY 10022

PUBLISHERS OF HIGH/LO MATERIALS

Addison-Wesley Publishing Co.
Reading, MA 01867

Arcade Books, Inc.
P.O. Box 1193
Champaign, IL 61820

Avon Books
959 Eighth Avenue
New York, NY 10019

Benefic Press
10300 West Roosevelt Road
Westchester, IL 60153

Bowmar/Noble Publishers, Inc.
4563 Colorado Blvd.
Los Angeles, CA 90039

Children's Book Company
P.O. Box 113
Mankato, MN 56001
(an affiliate of Creative Education)

Children's Press
1224 West Van Buren Street
Chicago, IL 60607

Creative Education
123 South Broad Street
Mankato, MN 56001

Crestwood House, Inc.
P.O. Box 3427
Mankato, MN 56001
(an affiliate of Creative Education)

Crowell Junior Books
10 East 53rd Street
New York, NY 10022

Dodd, Mead and Company, Inc.
79 Madison Avenue
New York, NY 10016

Doubleday and Company, Inc.
245 Park Avenue
New York, NY 10017

EMC Corporation
180 East Sixth Street
Saint Paul, MN 55101

Fearon-Pitman Publishers, Inc.
6 Davis Drive
Belmont, CA 94002

Garrard Publishing Company
Champaign, IL 61820

Grossett and Dunlop, Inc.
51 Madison Avenue
New York, NY 10019

Harcourt Brace Jovanovich, Inc.
757 Third Avenue
New York, NY 10017

Harvey House
20 Waterside Plaza
New York, NY 10010

Holiday House, Inc.
18 East 53rd Street
New York, NY 10022

Lerner Publications Company
241 First Avenue North
Minneapolis, MN 55401

Lothrop, Lee and Shepard Company
105 Madison Avenue
New York, NY 10016

Julian Messner
1230 Avenue of the Americas
New York, NY 10020
(a division of Simon and Schuster)

New Readers Press
Box 131
Syracuse, NY 13210

Putnam and Sons
390 Murray Hill Parkway
East Rutherford, NJ 07073

G.P. Putnam's Sons
200 Madison Avenue
New York, NY 10016

Raintree Children's Books
205 West Highland Avenue
Milwaukee, WI 53202

Ray Rourke Publishing Company
P.O. Box 868
Windermere, FL 32811
(an affiliate of Creative Education)

Scholastic Magazines, Inc.
50 West 44th Street
New York, NY 10036

Special Service Supply
Box 705
Huntington, NY 11725

Troll Associates
320 Route 17
Mahwah, NJ 07430

Franklin Watts, Inc.
730 Fifth Avenue
New York, NY 10019

The Westminster Press
906 Witherspoon Building
Philadelphia, PA 19107

Albert Whitman and Company
560 West Lake Street
Chicago, IL 60606

Xerox Education Publications
245 Long Hill Road
Middletown, CT 06457